Environmental Law and Policy

Environmental Law and Policy

Peter S. Menell
Acting Professor of Law
University of California at Berkeley
School of Law

Richard B. Stewart
Professor of Law
New York University School of Law

Little, Brown and Company
Boston   New York   Toronto   London

MV-NY

Published simultaneously in Canada
by Little, Brown & Company (Canada) Limited

Printed in the United States of America

For Dylan and Noah
P.S.M.

For William, Paul, Elizabeth, and Emily
R.B.S.

Summary of Contents

Contents

2

Analytic Frameworks for Environmental Law and Policy   23

4

Statutory Approaches to Air Pollution   229

Appendix to Chapter 4

5

Statutory Approaches to Water Pollution   447

6

Regulation of Hazardous Waste Disposal   559

7

Administrative Law and Representation
of Environmental Interests 777

8

The National Environmental Policy Act   897

9

Protection of Ecosystems and Natural Resources   1027

Preface

The field of environmental law and policy has changed dramatically over the past 25 years. The first generation of highly aspirational environmental laws established clear goals, but as with any ambitious new program faced daunting implementation hurdles. Neither the crude policy tools selected nor the rudimentary institutions given responsibility for implementing these laws were capable of achieving the ambitious statutory objectives. New social concerns — an oil shortage, recession — soon distracted national attention, threatening the resolve of regulators and fragmenting the constituency for environmental mandates. The practice of environmental law in these early years focused significantly on generating public support for environmental protection, building the bureaucratic infrastructure needed to regulate the environmental impacts of a complex industrial economy, and creating a system of administrative law to control these bureaucracies.

Since the 1970s, the field of environmental law and policy has focused increasingly on the practical dimensions of developing sound regulatory programs and experimenting with alternative policy tools to achieve legislative objectives without exacerbating other social concerns. In addition to mastery of the relevant statutes, regulations, common law doctrines, administrative law principles, and decisional law, environmental lawyers today increasingly require a sophisticated understanding of public policy analysis; the interaction of law, economics, science, and policy; the normative foundations of environmental protection; and the political and bureaucratic dimensions of environmental law and policy. Environmental lawyers must be able to solve problems, not merely spot issues. In order to be effective, environmental lawyers must be sensitive to the broader social, economic, and political realities that underlie environmental law.

Our book aims to provide students with the analytical skills, substantive knowledge, and practical judgment needed to participate in and contribute to this field as it evolves. It is as much concerned with understanding the broader structure of environmental law and policy as it is with the important building blocks of statutes, regulations, and decisions. The early chapters develop analytical tools for studying environmental law and policy. The central part of the book explores the major regulatory regimes for addressing environmental pollution. For each major medium — air, water, and soils/groundwater — we set out the basic regulatory structure and its historical development. We then select several topics in each area to explore in detail, emphasizing the skills needed to practice environmental law. The next part of the book examines the distinctive administrative and procedural aspects of environmental law and policy, analyzing key administrative law doctrines and the National Environmental Policy Act. The final chapter contains case studies of the protection of ecosystems. Most of the materials will have continuing relevance even as statutes and regulations change. Given our interests in basic institutional reform, the book has a decidedly prospective focus.

Throughout we have sought to use a functional approach to present material in the book. The practice of environmental law is heavily problem-oriented. Therefore, we use problems throughout the book that reflect both the challenges of practicing environmental law and the issues on the cutting edge of the law and of institutional design.

This project has taken many years to reach fruition and we are indebted to numerous people along the way for their advice, encouragement, and assistance in its evolution. More than two decades ago, Jim Krier saw the wisdom of integrating environmental law and policy as a means of teaching this field. We have built upon Jim's basic approach, which is more essential than ever to the understanding of this field. We also owe special thanks to Lee Breckenridge, without whom we could not have created the rich case study that elucidates the Comprehensive Environmental Response, Compensation, and Liability Act (Superfund). Bernie Black, John Dwyer, Jeff Gordon, Gillian Hadfield, Kathleen Johnson, Steve Leifer, Marcia Preston, Joe Sax, Steve Salop, and Buzz Thompson provided helpful comments and suggestions on earlier drafts. David Elbaum, Michael Naughton, Simon Steel, and Evan van Hook made important contributions to parts of the text. We are grateful to the many research assistants who helped with various tasks during the preparation of this volume: Michael Alcamo, Raj Aji, Jennifer Blackman, Steven Geary, John Gilroy, Dan Karnovsky, Peggy Kelsey, Simon Kisch, Jane Leamy, Gary Marchant, Mike Moran, Kerry Rodgers, Elizabeth Willes, and Mike Zoeller. We also wish to thank Leonor Clelo, Michele Co, Shirl David-Wynn, and Barbara Ortiz for providing tireless secretarial assistance. Last but not least, we are grateful to the highly professional staff at Little, Brown and Company's law book division.

Peter S. Menell
Richard B. Stewart

May 1994

Acknowledgments

The authors gratefully acknowledge permission to quote from the following works.

ABA Model Code of Professional Responsibility, Canons 5 and 7. Copies of this publication are available from Order Fulfillment, American Bar Association, 750 North Lake Shore Drive, Chicago, IL 60611. Reprinted by permission of the American Bar Association.

Baumol, W., & W. Oates, Economics, Environmental Policy, and the Quality of Life 212-214 (1979).

Baxter, W., People or Penguins: The Case for Optimal Pollution (1974).

Been, Locally Undesirable Land Uses in Minority Neighborhoods, 103 Yale L. J. 1383 (1994). Reprinted by permission of The Yale Law Journal Company and Fred B. Rothman & Company from *The Yale Law Journal*, Vol. *103*, pp. *1383-1422*.

Calabresi & Melamed, Property Rules, Liability Rules, and Inalienability: One View of the Cathedral, 85 Harv. L. Rev. 1089 (1972). Copyright © 1972 by the Harvard Law Review Associaton.

Caldwell, L., NEPA Revisited: A Call for a Constitutional Amendment, The Environmental Forum, Nov./Dec. 1989, 18.

Church, W., R. Nakamura & P. Cooper, What Works? Alternative Strategies for Superfund Cleanups (September 1991).

Dales, J., Pollution, Property and Prices 93-97 (1968).

Dasmann, R., Environmental Conservation 63-97 (3d ed. 1972). Copyright © 1972 by author. Reprinted by permission of John Wiley & Sons, Inc.

DeMuth & Ginsburg, White House Review of Agency Rulemaking, 99 Harv. L. Rev. 1075, 1076-1082 (1986). Copyright © 1986 by the Harvard Law Review Association. Reprinted by permission.

Devall, The Deep Ecology Movement, 20 Nat. Res. J. 299 (1980).

Dwyer, The Pathology of Symbolic Legislation, 17 Ecol. L.Q. 233 (1990).

Eskridge, Politics Without Romance: Implications of Public Choice Theory for Statutory Interpretation, 74 Va. L. Rev. 275 (1988).

Fortuna, R., & D. Lennett, Hazardous Waste Regulation: The New Era (1987).

Frieseman & Culhane, Social Impacts, Politics, and the Environmental Impact Process, 16 Nat. Res. J. 339, 339-340 (1976).

Gaba, Solid Waste and Recycled Materials under RCRA: Separating Chaff from Wheat, 16 Ecol. L.Q. 623, 623-624 (1989).

Gogol, D., Enforcement, Economics, and the Law: The Development of Economic Law Enforcement by the Connecticut Department of Environmental Protection (1976).

Haigh, Harrison & Nichols, Benefit-Cost Analysis of Environmental Regulation: Case Studies of Hazardous Air Pollutants, 8 Harvard Envtl. L. Rev. 395 (1984). Copyright © (1984) by the President and Fellows of Harvard College.

Hoppe, A License to Steal, San Francisco Chronicle, Feb. 8, 1971. Copyright © Chronicle Publishing Company, reprinted by permission of the author.

Huffman, Trusting the Public Interest to Judges: A Comment on the Public Trust Writings of Professors Sax, Wilkinson, Dunning, and Johnson, 63 Denver Univ. L. Rev. 565 (1986).

In Major Coastal Water Study: National experts urge fundamental departure from tech-based regulations. Inside EPA's Water Policy Report, Vol. 11, Num. 9, pp. 4-5 (April 28, 1993).

Landy, M., & M. Hague, The Coalition for Waste: Private Interests and Superfund, in Environmental Politics: Public Costs, Private Rewards (M. Greve & F. Smith eds. 1992).

Latin, Good Science, Bad Regulation, and Toxic Risk Assessment, 5 Yale J. Reg. 89 (1988).

Leopold, A., A Sand County Almanac (1949). Copyright © 1949 by Aldo Leopold. Reprinted with permission of Oxford University Press.

Liroff, R., Reforming Air Pollution Regulation: The Toil and Trouble of EPA's Bubble (1986). Reprinted with the permission of the World Wildlife Fund.

Lis, J., & K. Chilton, Clean Water — Murky Policy (Wash. Univ. Center for the Study of American Business 1992). Copyright © 1992 Center for the Study of American Business. Reprinted with permission.

Melnick, Pollution Deadlines and the Coalition for Failure, 75 Public Interest 123 (1984).

Menell, The Limitations of Legal Institutions for Addressing Environmental Risks, 5 J. Econ. Perspectives 93 (1991).

Miller, J., Citizen Suits: Private Enforcement of Federal Pollution Control Laws 10-13 (1987). Copyright © 1987 by Jeffrey Miller. Reprinted by permission of John Wiley & Sons, Inc.

Mohai & Bryant, Environmental Injustice: Weighing Race and Class as Factors in the Distribution of Environmental Hazards, 63 U. Colo. L. Rev. 921 (1992).

Morrison, The National Forest Management Act and Below Cost Timber Sales: Determining the Economic Suitability of Land for Timber Production, 17 Envtl. L. 507 (1987).

Olson, The Quiet Shift of Power: Office of Management & Budget Supervision of Environmental Protection Agency Rulemaking Under Executive Order 12,291, 4 Va. J. Nat. Res. L. 1 (1984).

O'Toole, R., Reforming the Forest Service 20-24 (1988). Granted with permission from Reforming the Forest Service. Randal O'Toole, © by the author 1988. Published by Island Press, Washington, D.C., and Covelo, California.

Passmore, J., Man's Responsibility for Nature 78-80, 87-88 (1974).

Pederson, Turning the Tide on Water Quality, 15 Ecol. L.Q. 69 (1988).

Project '88 — Round II, Incentives for Action: Designing Market-Based Environmental Strategies (sponsored by Senators Timothy Wirth and John Heinz, Robert N. Stavins, Project Director, May 1991).

"The Public Lands of the United States," in Land Use Controls in the United States (E. Moss ed. 1977). From Land Use Controls in the United States by National Resources Defense Council. Copyright © 1975 by National Resources Defense Council, Inc., by permission of Doubleday, a division of Bantam Doubleday Dell Publishing Groups Inc.

Roberts, Who Should Pay? EPA J. 38-39 (July/August 1991).

Sax, The Claim for Retention of the Public Lands, in Rethinking the Federal Lands 125 (S. Brubaker ed. 1984).

Sax, Mountains Without Handrails: Recreation Policy for the Federal Lands, Law Quadrangle Notes, University of Michigan Law School, Vol. 23, No. 1, Fall 1978, 14-17.

Sax, The (Unhappy) Truth About NEPA, 26 Okla. L. Rev. 239 (1973).

C. Schultze et al., Setting National Priorities: The 1973 Budget (1972).

Singer, P., Animal Liberation (1975). From Peter Singer, *Animal Liberation,* 2nd edition, New York Review of Books / Random House, New York, 1990. © Peter Singer, 1975, 1990.

Smith, The Endangered Species Act and Biological Conservation, 57 U.S.C.L. Rev. 361 (1984). Reprinted with permission of the *Southern California Law Review.*

Spurr, Clearcutting on National Forests, 21 Nat. Res. J. 223 (1981).

Stewart, Regulation in a Liberal State: The Role of Non-Commodity Values, 92 Yale L.J. 1537 (1983). Reprinted by permission of The Yale Law Journal Company and Fred B. Rothman & Company from *The Yale Law Journal,* Vol. *92,* pp. *1937-1590.*

Stroup & Baden, Natural Resources: Bureaucratic Myths and Environ-
    mental Management (1983). Reprinted by permission of Pacific
    Institute for Public Policy, San Francisco, CA.
Taylor, P., Respect for Nature 44-53 (1986). Taylor, Paul. Respect for
    Nature. Copyright © 1986 by the author. Reprinted by permission
    of Princeton University Press.
Turner, The Legal Eagles, Amicus J. (Winter 1988) 25-28, 30.
Wolfram, Modern Legal Ethics (1986).

Special Notice

We have selectively omitted citations and footnotes from cases without the use of ellipses or other indications. All footnotes are numbered consecutively within each chapter. Hence, footnotes in cases do not correspond to actual footnote numbers in the published reports.

Environmental Law and Policy

1

The "Problem" of Environmental Degradation

The materials in this chapter explore some of the many distinct considerations that lie within the label, the "problem" of environmental degradation. Problems of environmental degradation are unusually complex and often interrelated. Understanding the complexities and relationships, and the issues they pose, provides the underpinnings for the main task of the rest of the book: to consider how political institutions and the legal system can most effectively respond to conflicting demands placed upon environmental resources. Part A begins our inquiry with a broad historical perspective on our species' influence on the natural environment and an overview of the serious environmental problems confronting us today. Part B explores various normative perspectives on addressing environmental degradation.

A. NATURE AND EFFECTS OF ENVIRONMENTAL DEGRADATION

R. DASMANN, ENVIRONMENTAL CONSERVATION

(3d ed. 1972) 63-97

THE HUMAN RECORD ON THE EARTH

How long the species *Homo sapiens* has been active on this planet is in some doubt. It is fairly certain that the million years included in

1

the Pleistocene or glacial epoch encompass all truly human activity. Humankind has carried out much of its physical and social evolution during a geological epoch unusual in the history of the earth. The glacial ages stand out as turbulent exceptions to the calm and stability that has prevailed during most of geological time. They were periods of unusual climate, unusual physiography, and abnormal instability of the earth's crust. During most of the eras of geology, the surface of the earth was characterized by continents of low relief, widespread inland seas, and by relatively uniform and mild climates. The diversity of ecosystems present today and the consequent diversity of living organisms were not present. The significance of ice-age geography to human evolution was undoubtedly great. Its implications have yet to be explored. It is difficult, however, to think of human history against a background of low-lying continents and uniform climate. It is equally difficult to envision the future of humankind in such a world.

For most of the story of humankind we have little record — a few fossils here and there. Written history goes back only a few thousand years. What we call civilization, highly developed cultures that built cities and left remains in stone or brickwork, goes back about 6000 years. Before that we have various evidences in the ruins of old villages, in the cave dwellings, camp sites, and shell mounds in which human bones and implements were mixed with the remains of plant and animal associates. From such records, through comparison with the ways of existing human cultures, we can build up a theoretical picture of the past and begin to trace the probable interactions of humans with their environment. . . .

FIRE IN THE OLD STONE AGE

It is somewhat unrealistic to consider humankind without considering also its tools, equipment, and techniques. Humans have always had the combination of hands, limbs, and eyes that would permit them to use tools, and a brain that would permit them to attempt to supplement their limited physical powers. From the earliest sites where human remains have been found, tools of one kind or another have been recovered. Associated with the remains of the prehuman ancestors of *Homo sapiens* also have been tools and evidence of the use of fire. With fire as an aid and a few simple stones and sticks to help in digging, chopping, and scraping, humans could expand their occupancy beyond the area that their bodily equipment alone would permit them to occupy.

Because of recent emphasis on forest conservation, many think of fire as an enemy to be guarded against. The role of fire as a destroyer has been emphasized to the point where we forget its usefulness. For primitive humans, fire meant keeping warm. It was a way of rendering otherwise unpalatable food into a tasty form. It could be used as an aid to hunting, as it is still used by primitive peoples in many lands. With fire game animals could be driven into traps or over cliffs, or the smaller forms could be caught in it, partly burned, and thus added to the larder. With the use of fire for hunting must have come the realization that fire modifies vegetation and creates successional types more favorable for human foraging than the original climax. Thus the Indians learned that fire in the brush fields created areas of sprouting brush on which deer preferred to feed and where they could be readily stalked and killed. Fire starting in grassland could sweep into the forest, causing replacement of trees by shrubs which might yield berries or nuts useful for food. In the forest also, fire used at proper seasons and intervals could replace dense woods by grassy openings, creating that interspersion of woodland and glade which humans today still seem to prefer.

It is difficult to know the full extent to which primitive humans used fire. More and more evidence has accumulated, however, to indicate that preagricultural humans, along with their farming successors, have had major effects on their environment through burning, both deliberate and accidental. Certain major vegetation types are now considered to be fire types and thus most probably human-created types. The tropical savanna, of which the African big game country is typical, is believed to be largely a product of repeated burning, which opened up monsoon and thorn forest and pushed back the edges of the rain forests. The process of creating savanna from forest still goes on in the tropics. The chaparral of mediterranean climates is thought to be a fire type, which would tend toward evergreen forest in the absence of burning. Some believe that most of the world's grasslands are products of human use of fire. Thus, it is widely accepted that certain major grassland areas were maintained by repeated burning. The former prairie peninsula which pushed eastward from Iowa to Illinois in an otherwise forested region is an example.

The probability that humans from early times have been modifying environments with fire gives cause for thought when one seeks "natural" areas. The American scene when European humans first arrived was one shaped by the activities of the Indians over tens of thousands of years. In the absence of all human interference, desirable vegetation of so-called natural types may sometimes disappear.

ENVIRONMENTAL LIMITS AND PRIMITIVE HUMANS

Even with the aid of fire and simple stone tools, primitive humans were limited in their spread by the availability of habitat suited to their needs. Humans in a primitive state were not adapted to a nomadic life and were therefore restricted to a limited "home range" within areas of suitable habitat. In such an area they would be dependent on the productivity of limited sources of food. Good growth years when wild plants put out abundant fruit and seed would allow a tribe to thrive and increase. Poor years when wild crops failed would bring famine. The limits set by the environment would be enforced strictly. If a tribe grew in numbers beyond what the local food supply could support, the excess must either emigrate or perish. For hundreds of thousands of years, therefore, the numbers of humans were balanced against limited wild food resources, which could at best support only a sparse population.

Each new idea, each tool or cultural trait that was developed by humans would make new resources available. With improved stone axes, tall shrubs and small trees could be chopped down, and larger trees girdled and killed. With improved digging tools roots and tubers could be obtained more readily, and burrowing rodents perhaps captured. But ideas and changes came slowly, and for long periods it appears that little progress was made. During the time when the glaciers were making their last southward advance, ten to twenty thousand years ago, the rate of progress began to accelerate, and it has continued to pick up speed through the present time.

During the latter part of the Paleolithic period (around 10,000 B.C.) humans became highly skilled at hunting and developed effective spear-throwing devices and other weapons, which enabled them to obtain food from the great herds of big game that were then present. Humans moved northward to the very edges of the ice sheets in their hunting pursuits and out into the grassland areas of the world. Before or during this time they extended their area to include all of the continents of the earth. Early human records in North America are of people who had attained a high degree of hunting skill. The efficient hunting techniques opened up a new food resource for human exploitation and undoubtedly permitted a marked increase in their numbers.

Following the great expansion of the hunting cultures came a period known as the Mesolithic. The ice sheets were by then retreating northward, and forests were advancing in their wake. For unknown reasons there were marked declines in the numbers of big game animals, and many species became extinct. Humans concentrated less on hunting and in its place put more emphasis on fishing and on more efficient gathering, preparation, and storage of wild plant foods. More permanent village sites developed on lake and sea shores where food resources were most abundant. In these places, with the relatively stable food supply provided by their fisheries, humans acquired the leisure for thought and experimentation that made possible their greatest cultural advance, the development of agriculture.

The effects of the food-gathering and hunting stages of human culture on the environment can only be surmised. It seems likely that major changes in vegetation took place through the use of fire. Perhaps also humans hastened the extinction of some animal species by persistent hunting; however, the major cause of extinctions must be related to more general environmental changes. In all, the early influence of humans on the earth can be regarded as benign. Although far-reaching changes may have occurred, they were in the direction of making the earth a more suitable home for humans. Destructive changes that reduce basic resources and injure the capacity of the earth to provide for humans were to come with later cultural developments. For Paleolithic humans, conservation problems did not exist, except the difficult one of preserving themselves in a vast and often hostile and dangerous world. Nevertheless humans through their use of fire had left their old position as mere animal members of a biotic community and had become . . . an organism that dominates a community and modifies the conditions of life for all other organisms within.

DOMESTICATION AND THE RISE OF WESTERN CIVILIZATION

Perhaps the most important change in the history of humankind came with the domestication of plants and animals and the rise of the agricultural way of life. Some group of Mesolithic fisherfolk and food gatherers made the initial discoveries and opened a new period in human history. This period, because it was also associated with new and improved types of stone tools, is known as the Neolithic, or New Stone Age. Domestication of plants was perhaps a gradual development. Humans' normal interest in food would lead to the focusing of their attention on the plants which seemed best to provide it. Slowly humans must have learned the techniques of favoring the natural reproduction of plants through fire or clearing. Eventually they acquired the idea of carrying plants with them, preparing the ground, and planting them. It would seem a small change to make at the time, but its results affected the entire world. Through domestication humans learned to channel the energy and nutrients of an ecosystem in directions of their own choosing to produce their needs. . . .

When the Neolithic farmers began to settle in the river basins, a new way of life became possible. Here on deeper, richer soils, high crop yields could be obtained and the surpluses stored. These surpluses took away the threat of starvation and permitted time and leisure. Fewer people working on the richer soils could produce enough for all, so that some people could devote their attention to more specialized tasks. New agricultural tools were invented, and techniques of mastering the floodwaters that rose each year in the river basins were improved. With more efficient agricultural tools and the new techniques of irrigation farming, still greater yields could be produced. With water available throughout the year, more than one crop could be obtained from the land in each year. Greater yields meant more leisure and more time for specialization. Villages grew to towns and towns to cities. A new development called civilization appeared.

The cities became the homes of specialized workers freed from the necessity of tending to the land. They brought the opportunity for the farmer to trade surplus crops for the tools or pleasures that the city could offer. With the cities also came in time a central government, temples and palaces, armies, census takers, tax collectors, and other agencies of the state. On the land itself this resulted in a reorganization that was to have far-reaching effects. Initially it started as a funneling of surpluses into the city to be exchanged for the products of the city. But as the power of the city grew, as armies were formed and new lands conquered, there came increasing regimentation of the peasants to provide for the support of the new agencies. Large areas were reduced to the status of agricultural colonies, which sent crops, timber, and livestock to the imperial centers. The old balance, characteristic of the village way of life, between people and resources was destroyed as increasing demands were made on the farms to provide for city populations, who had no contact with the land or realization of its needs. Emphasis on the farms changed from varied subsistence crops to specialized crops raised for sale and export and eventually to monoculture, the production of one kind of crop year after year on the same land. In return the farmers received a variety of materials that they could not have produced on their farms. More important, however, the cities offered one thing that the old village way of life could not offer — security. Cities brought armies to defend the lands against the sudden sweep of barbarian invaders, slaves to improve and maintain irrigation works which protected against drought and flood, and temples where the priests could intercede with stronger gods than the village could offer for protection of the lands and the people. Thus, for security and a degree of material enrichment, the old independent village way of life was sacrificed to the new organization of civilization.

CIVILIZATION AND LAND FAILURE

It has long been a matter of surprise and concern to travelers in the homelands of western civilization that so many of the great cities and centers of ancient times are now desolate ruins located in desert lands incapable of providing for more than a few impoverished herdspeople. . . .

The Nile River and the Tigris-Euphrates rivers provide a contrast which throws light on the question of land deterioration in the region where western civilization began. The agricultural lands of Egypt, irrigated by the floodwaters of the Nile, have been farmed for at least 6000 years and yet remain productive. Egypt is still a densely populated center of civilization. By comparison the lands of Mesopotamia now support only a fraction of their former population. Yet these lands were the first home of civilization and, since Sumerian times, have supported a series of great empires. A look at the headwaters of the two river systems provides part of the answer to the differences between these regions. The headwaters of the Nile lie in the swamps of Uganda and the high mountains of Ethiopia. Until recent times these headwaters were remote from the mainstream of Western history. Native populations and livestock numbers were kept low by the pressure of an adverse environment. The Nile has had its annual flood throughout history, fed by the monsoon rains from the Indian Ocean. It has carried a load of silt and humus which, when deposited each year on the farming lands of Egypt, had added to their fertility. However, until recent times the silt load of the Nile has been relatively light and manageable.

The headwaters of the Tigris and the Euphrates lie in the highlands of Armenia, in areas that in the past have supported high populations of people and higher numbers of sheep and goats. They have been in the path of wave after wave of migrations of nomads from the plains of Asia. They have been subjected, therefore, to all of the pressures that hillside farming and overgrazing by livestock can bring to bear. They have been deforested to provide timbers for the growing cities or to provide new grazing land for flocks and herds. The erosion that has resulted has caused an ever-increasing silt load to be carried by the Tigris and Euphrates. In Sumerian times the indications are that the silt load was manageable. Subsequent empires have had an increasingly difficult task in controlling it. Armies of laborers and slaves have been kept busy keeping the irrigation canals free of silt. The silt has filled in the Persian Gulf to a distance of 180 miles out from where the rivers emptied in Sumerian times. As long as strong empires centered in the lands between the two rivers, the canals were kept open. The final breakdown came with the Mongol and Tartar invasions in the thirteenth and fourteenth centuries A.D. These nomadic horsemen from Asia were interested in destroying permanently the powerful Arab states which had opposed them. They destroyed the irrigation canals and killed or carried off the inhabitants of the region. Until recently, the task of coping with silt and rebuilding the canal system was too much for the peoples who remained in the area. The silt-laden flood waters carried soil from the highlands to the sea.

In the country of Lebanon is other evidence of what has happened to these lands. Here the Phoenicians founded their maritime empire and built the greatest navy of their day from the timber that grew on their mountains. On these mountains grew the famous cedars of Lebanon that helped to shape the Egyptian cities and were used in the temple of Solomon. Cutting of the timber started the trouble. Regeneration of the forest was prevented when the cleared lands were heavily grazed by goats and sheep. Only in a few protected spots do cedar groves remain, and forests of any kind are no longer extensive. Many formerly forested hills are now incredibly barren and almost devoid of soil. From their appearance it would be thought that the climate was now too dry to support trees. Yet, where soil remains, in the vicinity of the ancient groves, the cedars continue to reproduce and grow. . . .

WESTERN EUROPE AND AGRICULTURAL STABILITY

When the first Neolithic farming peoples were becoming established in western Europe, they brought with them the cereal-grain culture of western Asia and the domestic livestock associated with it. In Europe, however, they encountered a far different environment from that of the homeland of seed-crop agriculture. Europe was largely covered with dense, broad-leaved forest, except for clearings made by its earlier inhabitants and some naturally open areas. The climate was humid with rainfall moderately high and well distributed throughout the year. The soils were of the deciduous-forest variety, initially fertile and easy to work. The combination of soils, climate, and vegetation produced a durable environmental complex, much less subject to damage than those of the drier regions.

The usual pattern of primitive agriculture was followed in Europe. Forests were cleared, the plant debris burned, and seeds sown in the ash-enriched soil. Initially, land clearing and abandonment probably went on at a nearly equal rate, with the abandoned clearings serving for a time as grazing land. Gradually, as populations grew a more stable pattern of agriculture emerged on the better soils. With forest vegetation predominant and no extensive areas of hill range to invite flocks and herdspeople, there was initially little opportunity for the development of pastoralism apart from agriculture. Thus from early times livestock were kept close to the farm lands, and the growing of feed for the stock became as important a part of farming as the growing of food for humans. The presence of livestock close to the farm meant the regular addition of manure to the soil, and with this the organic content of the soil was replenished. On lands regularly pastured a grazing-resistant group of plant species developed that was able to support a high degree of livestock pressure without soil damage. As farming progressed northward in cooler regions, the wheat and barley adapted to the cooler climate. These were as often raised for hay crops as for grain.

Agriculture changed little in Europe until Roman times. With Roman conquest or influence many of the farming practices developed by the higher cultures of the Mediterranean region spread to the croplands of western Europe. They proved better adapted to the new area than to their lands of origin.

While agricultural practices were developing, the heavy forests served as a barrier against too rapid extension of farming lands. As time passed and more efficient means of clearing forest land were discovered, a relatively sophisticated and conservative type of agriculture was applied to the new land. Crop rotation, alternative cereal grain, root or leaf crop, clover or grass pasture on the same area in successive years, was widely practiced and served to maintain the soil. There developed also the practices of using plant and animal manures and of liming to reduce acidity, and other fertilizing practices that helped to maintain soil nutrients. With time came the rise of a well-established European peasantry, deeply attached to the land and attentive to its needs. The result was an unusual pattern in world land-use history. Not only was erosion and loss of soil fertility widely prevented, but to a large extent the land was actually improved through use. A stable agriculture, adapted to soil and climate, was achieved.

THE INDUSTRIAL REVOLUTION

With the industrial revolution came the spread of European power and influence throughout the world. Western Europe became a great industrial center, importing raw materials from other lands. The great increase in European population that followed was not, therefore, supported entirely by the products of European soils. Had this been necessary it is doubtful that the land could have been so well maintained. . . .

With the rise of the industrial civilization came the greatest dangers. Equipped with the harnessed power of rivers, coal, petroleum, and the atom, armed with machines capable of doing the work of an army of men and horses, industrialized society is able to shape any environment into a landscape of its own choosing and channel its materials into an industrial network which can create a high degree of security and material enrichment. But, with these new powers and techniques has disappeared the opportunity for long periods of adjustment to nature through small errors, small failures, and new beginnings.

The settlement of the Americas and the other new lands was part of the new industrial achievement. American raw materials and crops went first to feed the growing industrial machine in Europe. Later, industry centered in America, and demands for raw material intensified. Throughout the world spread western influence, civilization, technology, and agricultural ways. With this spread there returned an old conservation problem, not serious since the Old Stone Age, the problem of conserving the human species itself. Unique human cultures and the peoples that formed them disappeared or were incorporated by the engulfing flow of western industrial civilization.

QUESTIONS

1. What constitutes environmental degradation? If it is merely an undesirable human alteration of the natural state, then what is a natural state? What alterations are undesirable?

2. Many environmentalists speak of maintaining the "balance in nature": Nature knows best and therefore any intervention by humans is wrong. Implicit in this perspective is the notion, supported by some early ecological research, of a natural equilibrium within and among ecosystems. Recent studies, however, have led many ecologists to abandon the concept of a natural equilibrium. These studies suggest that nature is in a continuing state of disturbance and fluctuation. Change and turmoil, rather than constancy and balance, more accurately describe nature. In the words of one plant ecologist, the "balance of nature" concept "makes nice poetry, but it's not great science." Stevens, New Eye on Nature: The Real Constant is Eternal Turmoil, N.Y. Times, July 31, 1990, at B5. What are the implications of this alternative view of nature for conservation and resource management?

Consider the case of fishery management in the Adirondack Mountains, where there is heated debate over whether "rough" fish like suckers, shiners, and chubs, should be killed in some ponds to make way for trout. A New York state policy aims to "perpetuate natural aquatic ecosystems." One group argues that rough fish are part of the natural condition of the ponds and therefore should be preserved. Another group argues that some rough fish are descendants of baitfish introduced by humans and that they have crowded out trout that flourished earlier. Which of these conditions is "the" natural state? Or is the natural state the way the Adirondacks were when the Europeans first arrived? Or when the Indians first arrived? Or, for that matter, the way they were in the millenia when the region was buried under an ice-age glacier? Or in the succession of different ecosystems that followed?

3. Is it meaningful to think about what is natural without regard to humans? Is *Homo sapiens* just another species that forms the natural setting? On what basis or bases is our species different from the other species that constitute the global ecosystem?

4. Assuming that we can know what a natural state is (or that we merely want to avoid further degradation), would we want to foster (or

preserve) such a natural state (or the status quo)? Why? What role should humans play in averting "natural" disasters?

5. What is the relationship between the environment and economic development? Is economic development inexorably linked to environmental degradation or can the two be harmonized?

INDUSTRIALIZED SOCIETY AND NATURE'S THRESHOLDS[1]

Since the dawn of the industrial revolution, human demands placed upon the Earth's resources have increased dramatically. Global population has grown from one billion in the mid-nineteenth century to over five billion today. Although technological advancements have improved the carrying capacity of the Earth, many of these technologies have also placed added demands on the Earth's limited resources, thereby bringing us closer to nature's thresholds.

The remainder of this section provides introductory descriptions of the major problems of environmental degradation that we face today. Because this book focuses primarily upon environmental law and policy in the United States, the descriptions below emphasize U.S. environmental problems. But as the descriptions make clear, many environmental problems are international and global in nature.

Air Pollution and Long-Range Atmospheric Problems

From the early uses of fire, the burning of fossil fuels has been an important means by which humans have improved their living standards. The industrial revolution brought the discovery of new uses for fossil fuels as well as other materials. An unintended result of the burning of fossil fuels and other industrial processes, however, has been the release of gases and particles into the air. A number of such gases — including sulfur oxides, carbon monoxide, nitrogen oxides, and hydrocarbons — and particulate matter are responsible for serious health problems. Sulfur oxides, for example, aggravate respiratory diseases. Carbon monoxide, which has been demonstrated to bond with hemoglobin in blood, impairs mental functions, inhibits fetal development, and aggravates cardiovascular diseases. Lead impairs bone growth and

---

1. Much of the following material is adapted from: Brown, L., et al., State of the World 1987 7, 12-15, 17 (1987) and The Conservation Foundation, State of the Environment: A View Toward the Nineties xl-xlv, 81-87, 101-106, 452-453.

interferes with the nervous, circulatory, and renal systems. In addition to causing adverse health effects, air pollutants are also responsible for damage to plants, marine life, buildings, and monuments.

Although once viewed as a more or less localized environmental problem, recent studies have shown that air pollutants are carried great distances in the upper atmosphere. For example, roughly half of the toxic chemicals found in the Chesapeake Bay are the result of deposition from air pollution. As a result, fishing, a way of life for many along the Chesapeake, has become a more complicated venture. No longer can it be assumed that the fruits of a day's labor are fit for human consumption.

Another example of pollution settling is acid deposition, commonly referred to as acid rain. Acid deposition results from the emission of sulfur and nitrogen oxides, their transformation in the atmosphere into sulfates and nitrates, and their ultimate deposition onto the earth. Acid deposition has had an impact on the forests and aquatic ecosystems of the world as well as on the physical structures, such as buildings and treasured monuments.

New light was shed on thresholds of acidification when scientists at the Freshwater Institute in Manitoba, Canada, reported their findings from purposefully acidifying a small lake in northwestern Ontario. Over an eight-year period, they lowered the lake's acidity level (pH) from 6.8 to 5.0 and documented how the ecosystem changed along the way. At pH 5.9, for example, the population of one shrimp species declined dramatically, fathead minnows failed to reproduce, and one species of crustacean disappeared altogether. When the pH fell below 5.4, no species of fish was able to reproduce. The lakes and streams in Scandinavia and eastern North America are believed to have acidified in such a way. Many more remain vulnerable as acid deposition persists.

The threat of the eventual loss of the Earth's protective ozone layer and the potential for a destructive rise in atmospheric temperatures have prompted global concern about the future of the environment as it now exists. In 1974, scientists initially theorized that human-made chlorofluorocarbons (CFCs) [2] are destroying the earth's protective layer of stratospheric ozone. The theory was later confirmed by studies of the thinning of the ozone layer and appearance of a hole over Antarctica. Although ozone, the major component of smog, is undesirable near the earth's surface, its presence in the stratosphere serves to reduce the amount of ultraviolet radiation reaching the Earth's surface. It thereby protects humans from skin cancer and other

---

2. CFCs served as the propellant in many aerosol products, the cooling fluid in many refrigerators and air conditioners, industrial solvents, and in the production of synthetic foams. International agreements adopted in the late 1980s call for the phase-out of the use of these gases.

harmful health effects and enhances agricultural and marine productivity.

Later in the 1970s, scientists paid increasing attention to "the greenhouse effect," the idea that rising levels of carbon dioxide in the atmosphere, attributable to burning of fossil fuels,[3] as well as releases of other gases might raise atmospheric temperatures well beyond their natural levels. Agriculture, a highly climate-dependent sector, would face numerous adjustments. The existing patterns of world crop production evolved in response to particular climatic regimes that have been more or less stable over the last few centuries. Global climate change would bring not only higher temperatures, but also changes in rainfall patterns. As a result, areas that do not now need irrigation and drainage systems might require them to sustain crop production. Water supplies could diminish in some regions, forcing farmers to take land out of irrigated production. Altogether, investments totaling hundreds of billions of dollars could be needed in the agricultural sector to maintain global food security. Global climate change also threatens to raise sea level, which would cause devastating effects on many coastal regions.

Scientists cannot yet be certain that increases in the temperature of the atmosphere are outside the natural variability of the earth's climate. Since these issues are global in scope, they have prompted and will continue to generate international interest.

Surface Water and Groundwater Pollution

The water resources of the earth — the oceans, lakes, rivers, wetlands, and groundwater springs — form a complex hydrologic cycle. As with the air, humans have since the earliest recorded times discharged wastes into surface waters and, through seepage and runoff, groundwater. Among the prominent sources of water pollution today are discharges from industrial sources, municipal wastewater treatment plants, and runoff from agricultural fields, urban streets, timbered land, and construction sites. The disposal of solid wastes is also an important cause of water pollution. The principal concern with regard to water pollution has been the contamination of drinking water supplies. Water pollution can also cause contamination and loss of marine life, disruptions in larger ecosystems, and the destruction of recreational areas.

The threat to water resources from disposal of industrial waste is graphically illustrated through the experience of New York's Niagara

---

3. Since the mid-nineteenth century, carbon dioxide emissions from fossil fuels have risen from less than 100 million tons annually to 5.5 billion tons today.

Frontier. This area, long known as the scenic site of a world-class water-fall, has gained a second reputation. It is now a symbol of waste management methods that did not work. The spectacular falls that drew tourists to the 37-mile Niagara River flowing from Lake Erie to Lake Ontario have also attracted steel, petrochemical, and chemical industries looking for cheap power. Until the early 1940s, Hooker Electrochemical Company dumped its chemical wastes, some of them highly toxic, into an abandoned hydroelectric waterway known as the Love Canal. In 1953, Hooker bulldozed over the landfill and sold it to the Niagara Falls Board of Education for $1. The deed specifically released Hooker from liability for any harm that might result from releases of chemicals. The Board of Education promptly built an elementary school and playground on the site. Residential homes were built nearby. Although no dumping has occurred in the immediate vicinity of Love Canal since the 1940s, residents have suffered serious health problems, including miscarriages, birth defects, and liver disease, many years later. In 1978, heavy rains accumulated in the canal, causing a toxic stew to flood basements and accumulate on the surface. Health officials declared an emergency and evacuated the area. Residents attributed their health problems to these toxics, although subsequent epidemiological studies have failed to establish a statistically significant causal connection. Nonetheless, these events forcefully brought the legacy of toxic dump sites to the attention of the nation.

Natural Resources, Wildlife, and Biodiversity

The country's wildlife refuges and national parklands are increasingly threatened by energy, mining, logging, and commercial development within and outside their borders. These activities not only diminish the visual and recreational amenities that parks and refuges provide to many millions of visitors each year, but also threaten the very survival of wildlife and undermine other natural and cultural resources these parks and refuges were established, at least in part, to protect. It often comes as a shock even to frequent visitors to the national parks to learn that some of the wildlife they are accustomed to seeing may soon no longer be there as development in adjacent areas closes off vital habitat. Some major species, including the gray wolf and the mountain sheep, are likely to disappear from such parks as Yellowstone and Zion. Over the next century or two, Yosemite may lose between 8 and 15 of the 20 mammalian species that exist there now; Bryce Canyon may lose all of its current mammalian species. Climate change could wreak further havoc on parkland wildlife as changes in vegetation, temperature, and water availability alter habitat, as surrounding development closes off potential escape routes.

Outside the United States, the threat to genetic diversity is even more urgent as a result of rapid deforestation in critical areas of the Earth. The lush tropical forests of the equatorial regions, which support 40 percent of the Earth's estimated 5 million species, have been dramatically reduced in the past few decades. It is estimated that Latin American tropical forests will be reduced to only about half of their original extent by the end of the century. Continuation of deforestation also threatens to exacerbate the greenhouse effect by reducing the earth's capacity to convert carbon dioxide to oxygen, thereby increasing the concentration of carbon dioxide in the atmosphere.

As we near the end of the twentieth century, we are entering uncharted territory in the environmental experience of our species. Localized changes in natural systems are now being overlaid with global shifts, some of which are irreversible. Everyday human activities — such as driving automobiles, generating electricity, producing food, and disposing of wastes — are collectively causing changes of epic proportions within a matter of decades.

B.   PERSPECTIVES ON ENVIRONMENTAL POLICY

1.   AN ECOLOGICAL PERSPECTIVE

A. LEOPOLD, A SAND COUNTY ALMANAC

(1949)

THE ETHICAL SEQUENCE

. . . An ethic, ecologically, is a limitation on freedom of action in the struggle for existence. An ethic, philosophically, is a differentiation of social from anti-social conduct. These are two definitions of one thing. The thing has its origin in the tendency of interdependent individuals or groups to evolve modes of co-operation. The ecologist calls these symbioses. Politics and economics are advanced symbioses in which the original free-for-all competition has been replaced, in part, by co-operative mechanisms with an ethical content.

The complexity of co-operative mechanisms has increased with population density, and with the efficiency of tools. It was simpler, for example, to define the anti-social uses of sticks and stones in the days of the mastodons than of bullets and billboards in the age of motors.

The first ethics dealt with the relation between individuals; the Mosaic Decalogue is an example. Later accretions dealt with the relation between the individual and society. The Golden Rule tries to integrate the individual to society; democracy to integrate social organization to the individual.

There is as yet no ethic dealing with man's relation to land and to the animals and plants which grow upon it. Land, like Odysseus' slave-girls, is still property. The land-relation is still strictly economic, entailing privileges but not obligations.

The extension of ethics to this third element in human environment is, if I read the evidence correctly, an evolutionary possibility and an ecological necessity. It is the third step in a sequence. The first two have already been taken. Individual thinkers since the days of Ezekiel and Isaiah have asserted that the despoliation of land is not only inexpedient but wrong. Society, however, has not yet affirmed their belief. I regard the present conservation movement as the embryo of such an affirmation.

An ethic may be regarded as a mode of guidance for meeting ecological situations so new or intricate, or involving such deferred reactions, that the path of social expediency is not discernible to the average individual. Animal instincts are modes of guidance for the individual in meeting such situations. Ethics are possibly a kind of community instinct in-the-making.

THE COMMUNITY CONCEPT

All ethics so far evolved rest upon a single premise: that the individual is a member of a community of interdependent parts. His instincts prompt him to compete for his place in the community, but his ethics prompt him also to co-operate (perhaps in order that there may be a place to compete for).

The land ethic simply enlarges the boundaries of the community to include soils, waters, plants, and animals, or collectively: the land.

This sounds simple: do we not already sing our love for the obligation to the land of the free and the home of the brave? Yes, but just what and whom do we love? Certainly not the soil, which we are sending helter-skelter downriver. Certainly not the waters, which we assume have no function except to turn turbines, float barges, and carry off sewage. Certainly not the plants, of which we exterminate whole communities without batting an eye. Certainly not the animals, of which we have already extirpated many of the largest and most beautiful species. A land ethic of course cannot prevent the alteration, management, and use of these "resources," but it does affirm their right to continued existence, and, at least in spots, their continued existence in a natural state.

In short, a land ethic changes the role of *Homo sapiens* from conqueror of the land-community to plain member and citizen of it. It implies respect for his fellow-members, and also respect for the community as such.

In human history, we have learned (I hope) that the conqueror role is eventually self-defeating. Why? Because it is implicit in such a role that the conqueror knows, *ex cathedra,* just what makes the community clock tick, and just what and who is valuable, and what and who is worthless, in community life. It always turns out that he knows neither, and this is why his conquests eventually defeat themselves.

In the biotic community, a parallel situation exists. Abraham knew exactly what the land was for: it was to drip milk and honey into Abraham's mouth. At the present moment, the assurance with which we regard this assumption is inverse to the degree of our education.

The ordinary citizen today assumes that science knows what makes the community clock tick; the scientist is equally sure that he does not. He knows that the biotic mechanism is so complex that its workings may never be fully understood.

THE LAND PYRAMID

An ethic to supplement and guide the economic relation to land presupposes the existence of some mental image of land as a biotic mechanism. We can be ethical only in relation to something we can see, feel, understand, love, or otherwise have faith in.

The image commonly employed in conservation education is "the balance of nature." For reasons too lengthy to detail here, this figure of speech fails to describe accurately what little we know about the land mechanism. A much truer image is the one employed in ecology: the biotic pyramid. I shall first sketch the pyramid as a symbol of land, and later develop some of its implications in terms of land-use.

Plants absorb energy from the sun. This energy flows through a circuit called the biota, which may be represented by a pyramid consisting of layers. The bottom layer is the soil. A plant layer rests on the soil, an insect layer on the plants, a bird and rodent layer on the insects, and so on up through various animal groups to the apex layer, which consists of the larger carnivores.

The species of a layer are alike not in where they came from, or in what they look like, but rather in what they eat. Each successive layer depends on those below it for food and often for other services, and each in turn furnishes food and services to those above. Proceeding upward, each successive layer decreases in numerical abundance. Thus, for every carnivore there are hundreds of his prey, thousands of their prey, millions of insects, uncountable plants. The pyramidal form of the system reflects this numerical progression from apex to base. Man shares an intermediate layer with the bears, raccoons, and squirrels which eat both meat and vegetables.

The lines of dependency for food and other services are called food chains. Thus soil-oak-deer-Indian is a chain that has now been largely converted to soil-corn-cow-farmer. Each species, including ourselves, is a link in many chains. The deer eats a hundred plants other than oak, and the cow a hundred plants other than corn. Both, then are links in a hundred chains. The pyramid is a tangle of chains so complex as to seem disorderly, yet the stability of the system proves it to be a highly organized structure. Its functioning depends on the cooperation and competition of its diverse parts.

In the beginning, the pyramid of life was low and squat; the food chains short and simple. Evolution has added layer after layer, link after link. Man is one of thousands of accretions to the height and complexity of the pyramid. Science has given us many doubts, but it has given us at least one certainty: the trend of evolution is to elaborate and diversify the biota.

Land, then, is not merely soil; it is a fountain of energy flowing through a circuit of soils, plants, and animals. Food chains are the living channels which conduct energy upward; death and decay return it to the soil. The circuit is not closed; some energy is dissipated in decay, some is added by absorption from the air, some is stored in soils, peats, and long-lived forests; but it is a sustained circuit, like a slowly augmented revolving fund of life. There is always a net loss by downhill wash, but this is normally small and offset by the decay of rocks. It is deposited in the ocean and, in the course of geological time, raised to form new lands and new pyramids.

The velocity and character of the upward flow of energy depend on the complex structure of the plant and animal community, much as the upward flow of sap in a tree depends on its complex cellular organization. Without this complexity, normal circulation would presumably not occur. Structure means the characteristic numbers, as well as the characteristic kinds and functions, of the component species. This interdependence between the complex structure of the land and its smooth functioning as an energy unit is one of its basic attributes.

When a change occurs in one part of the circuit, many other parts must adjust themselves to it. Change does not necessarily obstruct or divert the flow of energy; evolution is a long series of self-induced changes, the net result of which has been to elaborate the flow mechanism and to lengthen the circuit. Evolutionary changes, however, are usually slow and local. Man's invention of tools has enabled him to make changes of unprecedented violence, rapidity, and scope. . . .

The combined evidence of history and ecology seems to support one general deduction: the less violent the man-made changes, the greater the probability of successful readjustment in the pyramid. . . .

. . . A thing is right when it tends to preserve the integrity, stability, and beauty of the biotic community. It is wrong when it tends otherwise. . . .

2.   AN ECONOMIC PERSPECTIVE

BAXTER, PEOPLE OR PENGUINS: THE CASE FOR OPTIMAL POLLUTION*

(1974)

. . . Recently scientists have informed us that use of DDT in food production is causing damage to the penguin population. For the present purposes let us accept that assertion as an indisputable scientific fact. The scientific fact is often asserted as if the correct implication — that we must stop agricultural use of DDT — followed from the mere statement of the fact of penguin damage. But plainly it does not follow if my criteria [based upon a utilitarian framework] are employed.

My criteria are oriented to people, not penguins. Damage to penguins, or sugar pines, or geological marvels is, without more, simply irrelevant. One must go further, by my criteria, and say: Penguins are important because people enjoy seeing them walk about rocks; and furthermore, the well-being of people would be less impaired by halting use of DDT than by giving up penguins. In short, my observations about environmental problems will be people-oriented, as are my criteria. I have no interest in preserving penguins for their own sake.

It may be said by the way of objection to this position, that it is very selfish of people to act as if each person represented one unit of importance and nothing else was of any importance. It is undeniably selfish. Nevertheless I think it is the only tenable starting place for analysis for several reasons. First, no other position corresponds to the way most people really think and act — i.e., corresponds to reality.

Second, this attitude does not portend any massive destruction of nonhuman flora and fauna, for people depend on them in many obvious ways, and they will be preserved because and to the degree that humans do depend on them.

Third, what is good for humans is, in many respects, good for penguins and pine trees — clean air for example. So that humans are, in these respects, surrogates for plant and animal life.

Fourth, I do not know how we could administer any other system. Our decisions are either private or collective. Insofar as Mr. Jones is free to act privately, he may give such preferences as he wishes to other forms of life: he may feed birds in winter and do with less himself, and he may even decline to resist an advancing polar bear on the ground

that the bear's appetite is more important than those portions of himself that the bear may choose to eat. In short my basic premise does
not rule out private altruism to competing life-forms. It does rule out,
however, Mr. Jones' inclination to feed Mr. Smith to the bear, however
hungry the bear, however despicable Mr. Smith.

Insofar as we act collectively on the other hand, only humans can
be afforded an opportunity to participate in the collective decisions.
Penguins cannot vote now and are unlikely subjects for the franchise —
pine trees more unlikely still. Again each individual is free to cast his
vote so as to benefit sugar pines if that is his inclination. But many of
the more extreme assertions that one hears from some conservationists
amount to tacit assertions that they are specially appointed representatives of sugar pines, and hence that their preferences should be
weighted more heavily than the preferences of other humans who do
not enjoy equal rapport with "nature." The simplistic assertion that agricultural use of DDT must stop at once because it is harmful to penguins is of that type.

Fifth, if polar bears or pine trees or penguins, like men, are to be
regarded as ends rather than means, if they are to count in our calculus
of social organization, someone must tell me how much each one
counts, and someone must tell me how these life-forms are to be permitted to express their preferences, for I do not know either answer. If
the answer is that certain people are to hold their proxies then I want
to know how those proxy-holders are to be selected: self-appointment
does not seem workable to me.

Sixth, and by way of summary of all the foregoing, let me point
out that the set of environmental issues under discussion — although
they raise very complex technical questions of how to achieve any objective — ultimately raise a normative question: what *ought* we to do. Questions of *ought* are unique to the human mind and world — they are
meaningless as applied to a nonhuman situation.

I reject the proposition that we *ought* to respect the "balance of
nature" or to "preserve the environment" unless the reason for doing
so, express or implied, is the benefit of man.

I reject the idea that there is a "right" or "morally correct" state of
nature to which we should return. The word "nature" has no normative
connotation. Was it "right" or "wrong" for the earth's crust to heave in
contortion and create mountains and seas? Was it "right" for the first
amphibian to crawl up out of the primordial ooze? Was it "wrong" for
plants to reproduce themselves and alter the atmospheric composition
in favor of oxygen? For animals to alter the atmosphere in favor of
carbon dioxide both by breathing oxygen and eating plants? No answers can be given to these questions because they are meaningless
questions.

All this may seem obvious to the point of being tedious, but much of the present controversy over environment and pollution rests on tacit normative assumptions about just such nonnormative phenomena: that it is "wrong" to impair penguins with DDT, but not to slaughter cattle for prime rib roasts. That it is wrong to kill stands of sugar pines with industrial fumes, but not to cut sugar pines and build housing for the poor. Every man is entitled to his own preferred definition of Walden Pond, but there is no definition that has any moral superiority over another, except by reference to the selfish needs of the human race.

From the fact that there is no normative definition of the natural state, it follows that there is no normative definition of clean air or pure water — hence no definition of polluted air — or of pollution — except by reference to the needs of man. The "right" composition of the atmosphere is one which has some dust in it and some lead in it and some hydrogen sulfide in it just those amounts that attend a sensibly organized society thoughtfully and knowledgeably pursuing the greatest possible satisfaction for its human members.

The first and most fundamental step toward solution of our environmental problems is a clear recognition that our objective is not pure air or water but rather some optimal state of pollution. That step immediately suggests the question: How do we define and attain the level of pollution that will yield the maximum possible amount of human satisfaction?

Low levels of pollution contribute to human satisfaction but so do food and shelter and education and music. To attain ever lower levels of pollution, we must pay the cost of having less of these other things. . . .

DISCUSSION PROBLEMS

How would Leopold and Baxter address the following environmental problems? How should a policymaker approach the resolution of these problems? In what ways does your approach agree with and differ from Leopold's and Baxter's perspectives? What assumptions underlie your analysis? Would your analysis provide a coherent framework for the range of environmental problems discussed in our section "Industrialized Society and Nature's Thresholds"?

1. *Acid Deposition:* Utilities in midwestern states operate coal-fired power plants emitting sulfur oxides and nitrogen oxides, which result in increased deposition (rain, snow, and dust) acidity over much of the Northeast United States and eastern Canada, contributing (to an extent hotly disputed) to reduced crop and tree growth, loss of fish and other fresh water life, corrosion of statues, structures, and monuments, and possible leaching of minerals from soils and plumbing that could con-

taminate groundwater drinking supplies. The high costs of regulating emissions would significantly injure the competitiveness of heavy industries operating in the Midwest, result in a significant rise in unemployment, and raise consumer prices.

2. *Grand Canyon:* Rafting through the Grand Canyon on the Colorado River has become an extremely popular recreational activity. The number of rafters has gone from 200 in 1955 to 120,000 in 1992. Rafters must have a permit from the Grand Canyon Park Service. About 80 percent of the permits go to commercial rafting enterprises, the other 20 percent to groups of individuals. No limits have been placed on the number of permits issued. On many days, especially during the May-September period, the river is clogged with rafts. Litter and sanitation have become problems. The mass of overnight campers is a threat to the sensitive ecosystem of the Canyon floor. As Superintendent of the Grand Canyon National Park, how would you address these concerns? By how much should access be curtailed? How would you deal with the problem of excess demand? What alternatives are available for limiting access to the river? Which approach do you favor?

2

Analytic Frameworks for Environmental Law and Policy

In order to address the myriad environmental problems confronting our society and planet —whether in international fora, the halls of legislatures, regulatory proceedings, or the courts —it is essential to have the ability to analyze the social, moral, economic, and political implications of alternative policies. This chapter focuses on the design and use of analytic frameworks for understanding and evaluating environmental problems and how the legal/regulatory system might respond to them.

There is a variety of approaches for analyzing most social problems, and environmental degradation is no exception. Environmental problems can be viewed within the larger context of allocating society's scarce resources so as to achieve some preferred allocation of all resources. Alternatively, environmental policy can be designed primarily so as to improve the distribution of society's resources, either presently or across generations. Other analytic perspectives assess environmental policy by reference to other moral principles, such as the reciprocity of risks within society or maintaining balance within nature. This chapter explores the broad range of perspectives for analyzing environmental policies.

The chapter begins with the Supreme Court's opinion in *Industrial Union Department, AFL-CIO v. American Petroleum Institute* (the *Benzene* case), which illustrates many of the analytical issues encountered in the study of environmental law and policy. Part B begins the systematic examination of analytical frameworks. For a variety of pedagogical reasons, it starts with a detailed description of the economic framework. In view of the limitedness of society's resources available to address the broad array of social problems, the economic perspective provides important insights into the design of policies to address many environmental problems. For example, air pollution cannot be addressed without devoting substantial societal resources to the task, such as in the form of pollution abatement equipment, development of new technologies, construction of mass transportation systems; these same resources, however, might be deployed to remedy other pressing social problems such as poverty (which often has environmental aspects) or other more direct environmental problems. Thus, an economic perspective, which seeks to maximize some measure of social welfare by balancing competing uses of resources, has obvious relevance to the policy analysis.

Moreover, even if you do not agree with the economic criterion for deciding the objectives of social policy, the economic framework might nonetheless be useful in devising regulatory and enforcement strategies to achieve other objectives, however derived. Furthermore, whether or not you find the economic approach consonant with your own system of values, there can be little question that economic analysis has become an important part of environmental decisionmaking. Many regulatory statutes mandate the use of economic analysis in environmental decisionmaking. A 1981 Executive Order requires executive branch agencies, to the extent permitted by statute, to base regulations on economic analysis. Therefore, lawyers and policymakers must be familiar with economic analysis if they are to participate effectively in the environmental, regulatory, and legal fora. In view of the complexity of economic analysis, we feel that it is essential to provide a detailed description of the critical assumptions underlying economic analysis and the structure of the economic framework.

The chapter introduces other analytic frameworks by way of critique and alternatives to the economic framework. It should be emphasized at the outset, however, that the purpose of presenting the economic framework first and in somewhat greater detail than the other frameworks is *not* to convince you that it is the ideal framework for environmental decisionmaking. We strongly believe that each individual must come to her or his own conclusions regarding the appropriate way of resolving environmental problems. Our goals in this chapter are to enable you to understand the economic framework on its own terms, to develop your ability to apply the framework, and to enable you to evaluate it critically along with other important analytic frameworks. At the end of the chapter we raise the question of whether it is possible to develop a single, consistent analytic framework for environmental law and policy. Even if you conclude that it is not, we are firmly convinced that the effort to do so is indispensable to developing a mastery of environmental law and policy.

A. AN INTRODUCTORY EXPLORATION

INDUSTRIAL UNION DEPARTMENT, AFL-CIO v. AMERICAN PETROLEUM INSTITUTE

448 U.S. 607 (1980)

Mr. Justice STEVENS announced the judgment of the Court and delivered an opinion in which The Chief Justice and Mr. Justice STEWART join and in Parts I, II, III-A, III-B, III-C, and III-E of which Mr. Justice POWELL joined.

The Occupational Safety and Health Act of 1970 (Act), 84 Stat. 1590, 29 U.S.C. §651 et seq., was enacted for the purpose of ensuring safe and healthful working conditions for every working man and woman in the Nation. This litigation concerns a standard promulgated by the Secretary of Labor to regulate occupational exposure to benzene, a substance which has been shown to cause cancer at high exposure levels. The principal question is whether such a showing is a sufficient basis for a standard that places the most stringent limitation on exposure to benzene that is technologically and economically possible.

The Act delegates broad authority to the Secretary to promulgate different kinds of standards. The basic definition of an "occupational safety and health standard" is found in §3(8), which provides:

> The term "occupational safety and health standard" means a standard which requires conditions, or the adoption or use of one or more practices, means, methods, operations, or processes, reasonably necessary or appropriate to provide safe or healthful employment and places of employment. 84 Stat. 1591, 29 U. S. C. §652 (8).

Where toxic materials or harmful physical agents are concerned, a standard must also comply with §6(b)(5), which provides:

> The Secretary, in promulgating standards dealing with toxic materials or harmful physical agents under this subsection, shall set the standard which most adequately assures, to the extent feasible, on the basis of the best available evidence, that no employee will suffer material impairment of health or functional capacity even if such employee has regu-

lar exposure to the hazard dealt with by such standard for the period of his working life.. . . 84 Stat. 1594, 29 U. S. C. §655(b)(5).

Wherever the toxic material to be regulated is a carcinogen, the Secretary has taken the position that no safe exposure level can be determined and that §6(b)(5) requires him to set an exposure limit at the lowest technologically feasible level that will not impair the viability of the industries regulated. In this case, after having determined that there is a causal connection between benzene and leukemia (a cancer of the white blood cells), the Secretary set an exposure limit on airborne concentrations of benzene of one part benzene per million parts of air (1 ppm), regulated dermal and eye contact with solutions containing benzene, and imposed complex monitoring and medical testing requirements on employers whose workplaces contain 0.5 ppm or more of benzene. . . .

I

Benzene is a familiar and important commodity. It is a colorless, aromatic liquid that evaporates rapidly under ordinary atmospheric conditions. Approximately 11 billion pounds of benzene were produced in the United States in 1976. Ninety-four percent of that total was produced by the petroleum and petrochemical industries, with the remainder produced by the steel industry as a byproduct of coking operations. Benzene is used in manufacturing a variety of products in motor fuels (which may contain as much as 2 percent benzene), solvents, detergents, pesticides, and other organic chemicals.

The entire population of the United States is exposed to small quantities of benzene, ranging from a few parts per billion to 0.5 ppm, in the ambient air. Over one million workers are subject to additional low-level exposures as a consequence of their employment. The majority of these employees work in gasoline service stations, benzene production (petroleum refineries and coking operations), chemical processing, benzene transportation, rubber manufacturing, and laboratory operations.

Benzene is a toxic substance.. . . Exposure to high concentrations produces an almost immediate effect on the central nervous system. Inhalation of concentrations of 20,000 ppm can be fatal within minutes; exposures in the range of 250 to 500 ppm can cause vertigo, nausea, and other symptoms of mild poisoning. Persistent exposures at levels above 25-40 ppm may lead to blood deficiencies and diseases of the blood-forming organs, including aplastic anemia, which is generally fatal.

[As authorized by the Act, the Secretary in 1971 adopted as the federal standard the American National Standards Institute "consensus standard" for occupational exposure to benzene of 10 ppm averaged over an eight-hour period. On the basis of developing research, the National Institute for Occupational Safety and Health (NIOSH), OSHA's research arm, concluded, in reliance upon epidemiological studies correlating exposure levels of 150-600 ppm over extended periods and increased cancer incidence that benzene caused leukemia. Although the studies failed to establish dose-response relations that would predict cancer incidence at lower exposure levels, NIOSH recommended that the exposure limit be set as low as possible.]

[OSHA proposed a "permanent" standard of 1 ppm. It] did not ask for comments as to whether or not benzene presented a significant health risk at exposures of 10 ppm or less. Rather, it asked for comments as to whether 1 ppm was the minimum feasible exposure limit.. . . As OSHA's Deputy Director of Health Standards, Grover Wrenn, testified at the hearing, this formulation of the issue to be considered by the Agency was consistent with OSHA's general policy with respect to carcinogens. Whenever a carcinogen is involved, OSHA will presume that no safe level of exposure exists in the absence of clear proof establishing such a level and will accordingly set the exposure limit at the lowest level feasible. . . .

The permanent standard is expressly inapplicable to the storage, transportation, distribution, sale, or use of gasoline or other fuels subsequent to discharge from bulk terminals. This exception is particularly significant in light of the fact that over 795,000 gas station employees, who are exposed to an average of 102,700 gallons of gasoline (containing up to 2 percent benzene) annually, are thus excluded from the protection of the standard.

As presently formulated, the benzene standard is an expensive way of providing some additional protection for a relatively small number of employees. According to OSHA's figures, the standard will require capital investments in engineering controls of approximately $266 million, first-year operating costs (for monitoring, medical testing, employee training and respirators) of $187 million to $205 million and recurring annual costs of approximately $34 million. The figures outlined in OSHA's explanation of the costs of compliance to various industries indicate that only 35,000 employees would gain any benefit from the regulation in terms of a reduction in their exposure to benzene. Over two-thirds of these workers (24,450) are employed in the rubber-manufacturing industry. Compliance costs in that industry are estimated to be rather low with no capital costs and initial operating expenses estimated at only $34 million ($1,390 per employee); recurring annual costs would also be rather low, totaling less than $1 million. By contrast, the segment of the petroleum refining industry that produces benzene would be required to incur $24 million in capital costs and $600,000 in first-year operating expenses to provide additional protection for 300 workers ($82,000 per employee) while the petrochemical industry would be required to incur $20.9 million in capital costs and $1 million in initial operating expenses for the benefit of 552 employees ($39,675 per employee).

Although OSHA did not quantify the benefits to each category of worker in terms of decreased exposure to benzene, it appears from the economic impact study done at OSHA's direction that those benefits may be relatively small. Thus, although the current exposure limit is 10 ppm, the actual exposures outlined in that study are often considerably lower, for example, for the period 1970-1975 the petro-chemical industry reported that, out of a total of 496 employees exposed to benzene, only 53 were exposed to levels between 1 and 5 ppm and only 7 (all at the same plant) were exposed to between 5 and 10 ppm.

II . . .

Any discussion of the 1 ppm exposure limit must, of course, begin with the Agency's rationale for imposing that limit. The written explanation of the standard fills 184 pages of the printed appendix. Much of it is devoted to a discussion of the voluminous evidence of the adverse effects of exposure to benzene at levels of concentration well above 10 ppm. This discussion demonstrates that there is ample justification for regulating occupational exposure to benzene and that the prior limit of 10 ppm, with a ceiling of 25 ppm (or a peak of 50 ppm) was reasonable. It does not, however, provide direct support for the Agency's conclusion that the limit should be reduced from 10 ppm to 1 ppm.

The evidence in the administrative record of adverse effects of benzene exposure at 10 ppm is sketchy at best. OSHA noted that there was "no dispute" that certain nonmalignant blood disorders, evidenced by a reduction in the level of red or white cells or platelets in the blood, could result from exposures of 25-40 ppm. It then stated that several studies had indicated that relatively slight changes in normal blood values could result from exposures below 25 ppm and perhaps below 10 ppm or less. Rather, it stated that because of the lack of data concerning the linkage between low-level exposures and blood abnormalities, it was impossible to construct a dose-response curve at this time. . . .

With respect to leukemia, evidence of an increased risk (i.e., a risk greater than that borne by the general population) due to benzene exposures at or below 10 ppm was even sketchier. [T]here was only one study that provided any evidence of such an increased risk. That study, conducted by the Dow Chemical Co., uncovered three leukemia deaths, versus 0.2 expected deaths, out of a population of 594 workers; it appeared that the three workers had never been exposed to more than 2 to 9 ppm of benzene. The authors of the study, however, concluded that it could not be viewed as proof of a relationship between low-level benzene exposure and leukemia because all three workers had probably been occupationally exposed to a number of other potentially carcinogenic chemicals at other points in their careers and because no leukemia deaths had been exposed to much higher levels of benzene. . . .

In the end OSHA's rationale for lowering the permissible exposure limit to 1 ppm was based, not on any finding that leukemia has ever been caused by exposure to 10 ppm of benzene and that it will *not* be caused by exposure to 1 ppm, but rather on a series of assumptions indicating that some leukemias might result from exposure to 10 ppm and that the number of cases might be reduced by reducing the exposure level to 1 ppm. In reaching that result, the Agency first unequivocally concluded that benzene is a human carcinogen. Second, it concluded that industry had failed to prove that there is a safe threshold level of exposure to benzene below which no excess leukemia cases would occur. In reaching this conclusion OSHA rejected industry contentions that certain epidemiological studies indicating no excess risk of leukemia among workers exposed at levels below 10 ppm were sufficient to establish that the threshold level of safe exposure was at or about 10 ppm. It also rejected an industry witness' testimony that a dose-response curve could be constructed on the basis of the reported epidemiological studies and that this curve indicated that reducing the permissible exposure limit from 10 to 1 ppm would prevent at most one leukemia and one other cancer death every six years.

Third, the Agency applied its standard policy with respect to carcinogens, concluding that, in the absence of definitive proof of a safe level, it must be assumed *any* level above zero presents *some* increased risk of cancer. . . .

Fourth, the Agency reiterated its view of the Act, stating that it was required by §6(b)(5) to set the standard either at the level that has been demonstrated to be safe or at the lowest level feasible, whichever is higher. Because of benzene's importance to the economy, no one has ever suggested that it would be feasible to eliminate its use entirely, or to try to limit exposures to the small amounts that are omnipresent. Rather the Agency selected 1 ppm as a workable exposure level and then determined that compliance with that level was technologically feasible and that "the economic impact of . . . [compliance] will not be such as to threaten the financial welfare of the affected firms or the general economy."

Finally [OSHA concluded] that some benefits were likely to result from reducing the exposure limit from 10 ppm to 1 ppm. This conclusion was based, again, not on evidence, but rather on the assumption that the risk of leukemia will decrease as exposure levels decrease. Although the Agency had found it impossible to construct a dose-response curve that would predict with any accuracy the number of leukemias that could be expected to result from exposures at 10 ppm, at 1 ppm, or at any intermediate level, it nevertheless "determined that the benefits of the proposed standard are likely to be appreciable."

It is noteworthy that at no point in its lengthy explanation did the Agency quote or even cite §3(8) of the Act. It made no finding that any of the provisions of the new standard were "reasonably necessary or appropriate to provide safe or healthful employment and places of employment." . . .

III

Our resolution of the issues in these cases turns, to a large extent, on the meaning of and the relationship between §3(8), which defines a health and safety standard as a standard that is "reasonably necessary and appropriate to provide safe or healthful employment," and §6(b)(5), which directs the Secretary in promulgating a health and safety standard for toxic materials to "set the standard which most adequately assures, to the extent feasible, on the basis of the best available evidence, that no employee will suffer material impairment of health or functional capacity. . . . "

In the Government's view, §3(8)'s definition of the term "standard" has no legal significance or at best merely requires that a standard not be totally irrational. It takes the position that §6(b)(5) is controlling and that it requires OSHA to promulgate a standard that either gives an absolute assurance of safety for each and every worker or reduces exposures to the lowest level feasible. The Government interprets "feasible" as meaning technologically achievable at a cost that would not impair the viability of the industries subject to the regulation. The respondent industry representatives, on the other hand, argue that the Court of Appeals was correct in holding that the "reasonably necessary and appropriate" language of §3(8), along with the feasibility requirement of §6(b)(5), requires the Agency to quantify both the costs and the benefits of a proposed rule and to conclude that they are roughly commensurate.

In our view, it is not necessary to decide whether either the Government or industry is entirely correct. For we think it is clear that §3(8) does apply to all permanent standards promulgated under the Act and that it requires the Secretary, before issuing any standard, to determine that it is reasonably necessary and appropriate to remedy a significant risk of material health impairment. Only after the Secretary has made the threshold determination that such a risk exists with respect to a toxic substance, would it be necessary to decide whether §6(b)(5) requires him to select the most protective standard he can consistent with economic and technological feasibility, or whether, as respondents argue, the benefits of the regulation must be commensurate with the costs of its implementation. Because the Secretary did not make the required threshold finding in these cases, we have no occasion to determine whether costs must be weighed against benefits in an appropriate case.

A

[W]e think it is clear that the statute was not designed to require employers to provide absolutely risk-free workplaces whenever it is technologically feasible to do so, so long as the cost is not great enough to destroy an entire industry. Rather, both the language and structure of the Act, as well as its legislative history, indicate that it was intended to require the elimination, as far as feasible, of significant risks of harm.

B

By empowering the Secretary to promulgate standards that are "reasonably necessary or appropriate to provide safe or healthful employment and places of employment," the Act implies that, before promulgating any standard, the Secretary must make a finding that the workplaces in question are not safe. But "safe" is not the equivalent of "risk-free." There are many activities that we engage in every day — such as driving a car or even breathing city air — that entail some risk of accident or material health impairment; nevertheless, few people would consider these activities "unsafe." Similarly, a workplace can hardly be considered "unsafe" unless it threatens the workers with a significant risk of harm.

Therefore, before he can promulgate *any* permanent health or safety standard, the Secretary is required to make a threshold finding that a place of employment is unsafe — in the sense that significant risks are present and can be eliminated or lessened by a change in practices. . . .

In the absence of a clear mandate in the Act, it is unreasonable to assume that Congress intended to give the Secretary the unprecedented power over American industry that would result from the Government's view of §§3(8) and 6(b)(5), coupled with OSHA's cancer policy. Expert testimony that a substance is probably a human carcinogen — either because it has caused cancer in animals or because individuals have contracted cancer following extremely high exposures — would justify the conclusion that the substance poses some risk of serious harm no matter how minute the exposure and no matter how many experts testified that they regarded the risk as insignificant. The conclusion would in turn justify pervasive regulation limited only by the constraint of feasibility. In light of the fact that there are literally thousands of substances used in the workplace that have been identified as carcinogens or suspect carcinogens, the Government's theory would give OSHA power to impose enormous costs that might produce little, if any, discernible benefit.

If the Government was correct in arguing that neither §3(8) nor §6(b)(5) requires that the risk from toxic substance be quantified sufficiently to enable the Secretary to characterize it as significant in an understandable way, the statute would make such a "sweeping delegation of legislative power" that it might be unconstitutional under the Court's reasoning in Schechter Poultry Corp. v. United States, 295 U.S. 495, 539, 55 S. Ct. 837, 847, 79 L. Ed. 1570, and Panama Refining Co. v. Ryan, 293 U.S. 388, 55 S. Ct. 241, 79 L. Ed. 446. A construction of the statute that avoids this kind of open-ended grant should certainly be favored.

C

The legislative history also supports the conclusion that Congress was concerned, not with absolute safety, but with the elimination of significant harm. The examples of industrial hazards referred to in the Committee hearings and debates all involved situations in which the risk was unquestionably significant. For example, the Senate Committee on Labor and Public Welfare noted that byssinosis, a disabling lung disease caused by breathing cotton dust, affected as many as 30 percent of the workers in carding or spinning rooms in some American cotton mills and that as many as 100,000 active or retired workers were then suffering from the disease. . . .

Moreover, Congress specifically amended §6(b)(5) to make it perfectly clear that it does not require the Secretary to promulgate standards that would assure an absolutely risk-free workplace. Section 6(b)(5) of the initial Committee bill provided that

> [t]he Secretary, in promulgating standards under this subsection, shall set the standard which most adequately and feasibly assures, on the basis of the best available evidence, that no employee will suffer *any* impairment of health or functional capacity, or diminished life expectancy even if such employee has regular exposure to the hazard dealt with by such standard for the period of his working life. (Emphasis supplied.)

On the floor of the Senate, Senator Dominick questioned the wisdom of this provision, stating:

> How in the world are we ever going to live up to that? What are we going to do about a place in Florida where mosquitoes are getting at the employee — perish the thought that there may be mosquitoes in Florida? But there are black flies in Minnesota and Wisconsin. Are we going to say that if employees get bitten by those for the rest of their lives they will not have been done any harm at all? Probably they will not be, but do we know?

He then offered an amendment deleting the entire subsection. After discussions with the sponsors of the Committee bill, Senator Dominick revised his amendment. Instead of deleting the first sentence of §6(b)(5) entirely, his new amendment limited the application of that subsection to toxic materials and harmful physical agents and changed "any" impairment of health to "material" impairment. In discussing this change, Senator Dominick noted that the Committee's bill read as if a standard had to "assure that, no matter what anybody was doing, the standard would protect him [for] the rest of his life against any foreseeable hazard." Such an "unrealistic standard," he stated, had not been intended by the sponsors of the bill. . . .

D

Given the conclusion that the Act empowers the Secretary to promulgate health and safety standards only where a significant risk of harm exists, the critical issue becomes how to define and allocate the burden of proving the significance of the risk in a case such as this, where scientific knowledge is imperfect and the precise quantification of risks is therefore impossible. The Agency's position is that there is substantial evidence in the record to support its conclusion that there is no absolutely safe level for a carcinogen and that, therefore, the burden is properly on industry to prove, apparently beyond a shadow of a doubt, that there is a safe level for benzene exposure. The Agency argues that, because of the uncertainties in this area, any other approach would render it helpless, forcing it to wait for the leukemia deaths that it believes are likely to occur before taking any regulatory action.

We disagree. As we read the statute, the burden was on the Agency to show, on the basis of substantial evidence, that it is at least more likely than not that long-term exposure to 10 ppm of benzene presents a significant risk of material health impairment. Ordinarily, it is the proponent of a rule or order who has the burden of proof in administrative proceedings. See 5 U.S.C.A. §556(d). In some cases involving toxic substances, Congress has shifted the burden of proving that a particular substance is safe onto the party opposing the proposed rule.[1] The fact that Congress did not follow this course in enacting OSHA indicates that it intended the Agency to bear the normal burden of establishing the need for a proposed standard.

In this case OSHA did not even attempt to carry its burden of proof. The closest it came to making a finding that benzene presented a significant risk of harm in the workplace was its statement that the benefits to be derived from lowering the permissible exposure level from 10 to 1 ppm were "likely" to be "appreciable." The Court of Appeals held that this finding was not supported by substantial evidence. Of greater importance, even if it were supported by substantial evidence, such a finding would not be sufficient to satisfy the Agency's obligations under the Act.

The inadequacy of the Agency's findings can perhaps be illustrated best by its rejection of industry testimony that a dose-response curve can be formulated on the basis of current epidemiological evidence and that, even under the most conservative extrapolation theory, current exposure levels would cause at most two deaths out of a population of about 30,000 workers every six years. In rejecting this testimony, OSHA made the following statement:

> In the face of the record evidence of numerous actual deaths attributable to benzene-induced leukemia and other fatal blood diseases, OSHA is unwilling to rely on the hypothesis that at most two cancers every six years would be prevented by the proposed standard. By way of example, the Infante study disclosed seven excess leukemia deaths in a population of about 600 people over a 25-year period. While the Infante study involved higher exposures than those currently encountered, the incidence rates found by Infante, together with the numerous other cases reported in the literature of benzene leukemia and other fatal blood disease, makes it difficult for OSHA to rely on the [witness'] hypothesis to assure that statutorily mandated protection for employees. In any event, due to the fact that there is no safe level of exposure to benzene and that it is impossible to precisely quantify the anticipated benefits, OSHA must select the level of exposure which is most protective of exposed employees.

---

1. See *Environmental Defense Fund, Inc. v. EPA*, 179 U.S. App. D.C. 43, 49, 57-63, 548 F.2d 998, 1004, 1012-1018 (1977), *cert. denied*, 431 U.S. 925, 97 S. Ct. 2199, 53 L. Ed. 2d 239, where the court rejected the argument that the EPA has the burden of proving that a pesticide is unsafe in order to suspend its registration under the Federal Insecticide, Fungicide, and Rodenticide Act. The court noted that Congress had deliberately shifted the ordinary burden of proof under the APA, requiring manufacturers to establish the continued safety of their products.

There are three possible interpretations of OSHA's stated reason for rejecting the witness' testimony: (1) OSHA considered it probable that a greater number of lives would be saved by lowering the standard from 10 ppm; (2) OSHA thought that saving two lives every six years in a work force of 30,000 persons is a significant savings that makes it reasonable and appropriate to adopt a new standard; or (3) even if the small number is not significant and even if the savings may be even smaller, the Agency nevertheless believed it had a statutory duty to select the level of exposure that is most protective of the exposed employees if it is economically and technologically feasible to do so. Even if the Secretary did not intend to rely entirely on this third theory, his construction of the statute would make it proper for him to do so. Moreover, he made no express findings of fact that would support his 1 ppm standard on any less drastic theory. Under these circumstances, we can hardly agree with the Government that OSHA discharged its duty under the Act.

Contrary to the Government's contentions, imposing a burden on the Agency of demonstrating a significant risk of harm will not strip it of its ability to regulate carcinogens, nor will it require the Agency to wait for deaths to occur before taking any action. First, the requirement that a "significant" risk be identified is not a mathematical straitjacket. It is the Agency's responsibility to determine, in the first instance, what it considers to be a "significant" risk. Some risks are plainly acceptable and others are plainly unacceptable. If, for example, the odds are one in a billion that a person will die from cancer by taking a drink of chlorinated water, the risk clearly could not be considered significant. On the other hand, if the odds are one in a thousand that regular inhalation of gasoline vapors that are two percent benzene will be fatal, a reasonable person might well consider the risk significant and take appropriate steps to decrease or eliminate it. Although the Agency has no duty to calculate the exact probability of harm, it does have an obligation to find that a significant risk is present before it can characterize a place of employment as "unsafe."[2]

Second, OSHA is not required to support its finding that a signifi-

---

2. In his dissenting opinion, Mr. Justice Marshall states that "when the question involves determination of the acceptable level of risk, the ultimate decision must necessarily be based on considerations of policy as well as empirically verifiable facts. Factual determinations can at most define the risk in some statistical way; the judgment whether that risk is tolerable cannot be based solely on a resolution of the facts." We agree. Thus, while the Agency must support its finding that a certain level of risk exists by substantial evidence, we recognize that its determination that a particular level of risk is "significant" will be based largely on policy considerations. At this point we have no need to reach the issue of what level of scrutiny a reviewing court should apply to the latter type of determination.

cant risk exists with anything approaching scientific certainty. Although
the Agency's findings must be supported by substantial evidence, 29
U.S.C.A. §655(f), §6(b)(5) specifically allows the Secretary to regulate
on the basis of the "best available evidence." As several courts of appeals
have held, this provision requires a reviewing court to give OSHA some
leeway where its findings must be made on the frontiers of scientific
knowledge. Thus, so long as they are supported by a body of reputable
scientific thought, the Agency is free to use conservative assumptions in
interpreting the data with respect to carcinogens, risking error on the
side of over-protection rather than under-protection.[3]

Finally, the record in this case and OSHA's own rulings on other
carcinogens indicate that there are a number of ways in which the
Agency can make a rational judgment about the relative significance of
the risks associated with exposure to a particular carcinogen. . . .[4]

E

Because our review of this case has involved a more detailed examination of the record than is customary, it must be emphasized that we
have neither made any factual determinations of our own, nor have we
rejected any factual findings made by the Secretary. . . .

In this case the record makes it perfectly clear that the Secretary
relied squarely on a special policy for carcinogens that imposed the
burden on industry of proving the existence of a safe level of exposure,
thereby avoiding the Secretary's threshold responsibility of establishing
the need for more stringent standards. In so interpreting his statutory
authority, the Secretary exceeded his power.

---

3. Mr. Justice Marshall states that, under our approach, the agency must
either wait for deaths to occur or must "deceive the public" by making a basically meaningless determination of significance based on totally inadequate
evidence. Mr. Justice Marshall's view, however, rests on the erroneous premise
that the only reason OSHA did not attempt to quantify benefits in this case was
because it could not do so in any reasonable manner. As the discussion of the
Agency's rejection of an industry attempt at formulating a dose-response curve
demonstrates, however, the Agency's rejection of methods such as dose-response curves was based at least in part on its view that nothing less than absolute safety would suffice.

4. For example, in the coke oven emissions standard, OSHA had calculated that 21,000 exposed coke oven workers had an annual excess mortality of
over 200 and that the proposed standard might well eliminate the risk entirely.

In other proceedings, the Agency has had a good deal of data from animal experiments on which it could base a conclusion on the significance of
this risk. For example, the record on the vinyl chloride standard indicated that
a significant number of animals had developed tumors of the liver, lung and
skin when they were exposed to 50 ppm of vinyl chloride over a period of 11
months. One hundred out of 200 animals died during that period.

IV

[The Court remanded a standard governing skin contact with benzene, for similar reasons.]

The judgment of the Court of Appeals remanding the petition for review to the Secretary for further proceedings is affirmed.

It is so ordered.

Mr. Chief Justice BURGER, concurring.

These cases press upon the Court difficult unanswered questions on the frontiers of science and medicine. The statute and legislative history give ambiguous signals as to how the Secretary is directed to operate in this area. The opinion by Mr. Justice Stevens takes on a difficult task to decode the message of the statute as to guidelines for administrative action. . . .

The Congress is the ultimate regulator and the narrow function of the courts is to discern the meaning of the statute and the implementing regulations with the objective of ensuring that in promulgating health and safety standards the Secretary "has given reasoned consideration to each of the pertinent factors" and has complied with statutory commands. Our holding that the Secretary must retrace his steps with greater care and consideration is not to be taken in derogation of the scope of legitimate agency discretion. When the facts and arguments have been presented and duly considered, the Secretary must make a policy judgment as to whether a specific risk of health impairment is significant in terms of the policy objectives of the statute. When he acts in this capacity, pursuant to the legislative authority delegated by Congress, he exercises the prerogatives of the legislature — to focus on only one aspect of a larger problem, or to promulgate regulations that, to some, may appear as imprudent policy or inefficient allocation of resources. The judicial function does not extend to substantive revision of regulatory policy. That function lies elsewhere — in Congressional and Executive oversight or amendatory legislation; although to be sure the boundaries are often ill defined and indistinct.

Nevertheless, when discharging his duties under the statute, the Secretary is well admonished to remember that a heavy responsibility burdens his authority. Inherent in this statutory scheme is authority to refrain from regulation of insignificant or de minimis risks. . . . When the administrative record reveals only scant or minimal risk of material health impairment, responsible administration calls for avoidance of extravagant, comprehensive regulation. Perfect safety is a chimera; regulation must not strangle human activity in the search for the impossible.

Mr. Justice POWELL, concurring in part and concurring in the judgment.

. . . I . . . agree with the plurality that the regulation is invalid to the extent it rests upon the assumption that exposure to known carcinogens always should be reduced to a level proved to be safe or, if no such level is found, to the lowest level that the affected industry can achieve with available technology.

[Justice Powell found, however, that OSHA had not relied solely on its ascription that no safe threshold exposure for a carcinogen exists, but had also claimed that the 1 ppm standard adopted was reasonably necessary to deal with a significant health risk. The Justice concluded that the record failed to establish "substantial evidence" for such a finding.]

. . . But even if one assumes that OSHA properly met this burden . . . I conclude that the statute also requires the agency to determine that the economic effects of its standard bear a reasonable relationship to the expected benefits. An occupational health standard is neither "reasonably necessary" nor "feasible," as required by statute, if it calls for expenditures wholly disproportionate to the expected health and safety benefits.

OSHA contends that §6(b)(5) not only permits but actually requires it to promulgate standards that reduce health risks without regard to economic effects, unless those effects would cause widespread dislocation throughout an entire industry. Under the threshold test adopted by the plurality today, this authority will exist only with respect to "significant" risks. But the plurality does not reject OSHA's claim that it must reduce such risks without considering economic consequences less serious than massive dislocation. In my view, that claim is untenable.

Although one might wish that Congress had spoken with greater clarity, the legislative history and purposes of the statute do not support OSHA's interpretation of the Act. It is simply unreasonable to believe that Congress intended OSHA to pursue the desirable goal of risk-free workplaces to the extent that the economic viability of particular industries — or significant segments thereof — is threatened. . . . [Such a policy] would impair the ability of American industries to compete effectively with foreign businesses and to provide employment for American workers.[5]

_____

5. Congress has assigned OSHA an extremely difficult and complex task, and the guidance afforded OSHA is considerably less than clear. The Agency's primary responsibility, reflected in its title, is to minimize health and safety risks in the workplace. Yet the economic health of our highly industrialized society requires a high rate of employment and an adequate response to increasingly vigorous foreign competition. There can be little doubt that Congress intended OSHA to balance reasonably the societal interest in health and safety with the often conflicting goal of maintaining a strong national economy.

I therefore would not lightly assume that Congress intended OSHA to require reduction of health risks found to be significant *whenever* it also finds that the affected industries can bear the costs. Perhaps more significantly, however, OSHA's interpretation of §6(b)(5) would force it to regulate in a manner inconsistent with the important health and safety purposes of the legislation we construe today. Thousands of toxic substances present risks that fairly could be characterized as "significant." . . . Even if OSHA succeeded in selecting the gravest risks for earliest regulation, a standard-setting process that ignored economic considerations would result in a serious misallocation of resources and a lower effective level of safety than could be achieved under standards set with reference to the comparative benefits available at a lower cost. I would not attribute such an irrational intention to Congress.

In this case, OSHA did find that the "substantial costs" of the benzene regulations are justified. . . . But the record before us contains neither adequate documentation of this conclusion, nor any evidence that OSHA weighed the relevant considerations. . . .

Mr. Justice REHNQUIST, concurring in the judgment.

In considering the[] alternative interpretations . . . [of the statute], my colleagues manifest a good deal of uncertainty, and ultimately divide over whether the Secretary produced sufficient evidence that the proposed standard for benzene will result in any appreciable benefits at all. This uncertainty, I would suggest, is eminently justified, since I believe that this case presents the Court with what has to be one of the most difficult issues that could confront a decision-maker: whether the statistical possibility of future deaths should ever be disregarded in light of the economic costs of preventing those deaths. I would also suggest that the widely varying positions advanced in the briefs of the parties and in the opinions of Mr. Justice Stevens, The Chief Justice, Mr. Justice Powell, and Mr. Justice Marshall demonstrate, perhaps better than any other fact, that Congress, the governmental body best suited and most obligated to make the choice confronting us in this case, has improperly delegated that choice to the Secretary of Labor and, derivatively, to this Court. . . .

If we are ever to reshoulder the burden of ensuring that Congress itself make the critical policy decisions, [this is] surely the case[] in which to do it. It is difficult to imagine a more obvious example of Congress simply avoiding a choice which was both fundamental for purposes of the statute and yet politically so divisive that the necessary decision or compromise was difficult, if not impossible, to hammer out in the legislative forge. Far from detracting from the substantive authority of Congress, a declaration that the first sentence of §6(b)(5) of the OSHA constitutes an invalid delegation to the Secretary of Labor would preserve the authority of Congress. If Congress wishes to legislate in an area which it has not previously sought to enter, it will in today's political world undoubtedly run into opposition no matter how the legislation is formulated. But that is the very essence of legislative authority under our system. It is the hard choices, and not the filling in of the blanks, which must be made by the elected representatives of the people. When fundamental policy decisions underlying important legislation about to be enacted are to be made, the buck stops with Congress and the President insofar as he exercises his constitutional role in the legislative process.

I would invalidate the first sentence of §6(b)(5) of the Occupational Safety and Health Act of 1970 as it applies to any toxic substance or harmful physical agent for which a safe level, that is a level at which "no employee will suffer material impairment of health or functional capacity even if such employee has regular exposure to [that hazard] for the period of his working life" is, according to the Secretary, unknown or otherwise "infeasible." Absent further congressional action, the Secretary would then have to choose, when acting pursuant to §6(b)(5), between setting a safe standard or setting no standard at all.[6] Accordingly, for the reasons stated above, I concur in the judgment of the Court affirming the judgement of the Court of Appeals.

Mr. Justice MARSHALL, with whom Mr. Justice BRENNAN, Mr. Justice WHITE, and Mr. Justice BLACKMUN join, dissenting.

In cases of statutory construction, this court's authority is limited. If the statutory language and legislative intent are plain, the judicial inquiry is at an end. Under our jurisprudence, it is presumed that ill-considered or unwise legislation will be corrected through the democratic process; a court is not permitted to distort a statute's meaning in order to make it conform with the Justices' own views of sound social policy. See *TVA v. Hill.*

Today's decision flagrantly disregards these restrictions on judicial authority. The plurality ignores the plain meaning of the Occupational Safety and Health Act of 1970 in order to bring the authority of the Secretary of Labor in line with the plurality's own views of proper regulatory policy. The unfortunate consequence is that the Federal Government's efforts to protect American workers from cancer and other crippling diseases may be substantially impaired.

---

6. This ruling would not have any effect upon standards governing toxic substances or harmful physical agents for which safe levels are feasible, upon extant standards promulgated as "national consensus standards" under §6(a), nor upon the Secretary's authority to promulgate "emergency temporary standards" under §6(c).

. . . In this case the Secretary of Labor found, on the basis of substantial evidence, that (1) exposure to benzene creates a risk of cancer, chromosomal damage, and a variety of nonmalignant but potentially fatal blood disorder, even at the level of 1 ppm; (2) no safe level of exposure has been shown; (3) benefits in the form of saved lives would be derived from the permanent standard; (4) the number of lives that would be saved could turn out to be either substantial or relatively small; (5) under the present state of scientific knowledge, it is impossible to calculate even in a rough way the number of lives that would be saved, at least without making assumptions that would appear absurd to much of the medical community; and (6) the standard would not materially harm the financial condition of the covered industries. The court does not set aside any of these findings. Thus, it could not be plainer that the Secretary's decision was fully in accord with his statutory mandate "most adequately [to] assure . . . that no employee will suffer material impairment of health or functional capacity. . . ."

The plurality's conclusion to the contrary is based on its interpretation of [§3(8)], which defines an occupational safety and health standard as one "which requires conditions . . . reasonably necessary or appropriate to provide safe or healthful employment. . . ." According to the plurality, a standard is not "reasonably necessary or appropriate" unless the Secretary is able to show that it is "at least more likely than not" that the risk he seeks to regulate is a "significant" one. Nothing in the statute's language or legislative history, however, indicates that the "reasonably necessary or appropriate" language should be given this meaning. Indeed, both demonstrate that the plurality's standard bears no connection with the acts or intentions of Congress and is based only on the plurality's solicitude for the welfare of regulated industries. And the plurality uses this standard to evaluate not the agency's decision in this case, but a strawman of its own creation.

Unlike the plurality, I do not purport to know whether the actions taken by Congress and its delegates to ensure occupational safety represent sound or unsound regulatory policy. The critical problem in cases like the one at bar is scientific uncertainty. While science has determined that exposure to benzene at levels above 1 ppm creates a definite risk of health impairment, the magnitude of the risk cannot be quantified at the present time. The risk at issue has hardly been shown to be insignificant; indeed, future research may reveal that the risk is in fact considerable. But the existing evidence may frequently be inadequate to enable the Secretary to make the threshold finding of "significance" that the Court requires today. If so, the consequence of the plurality's approach would be to subject American workers to a continuing risk of cancer and other fatal diseases, and to render the Federal Government powerless to take protective action on their behalf. Such an approach would place the burden of medical uncertainty squarely on the shoulders of the American worker, the intended beneficiary of the Occupational Safety and Health Act. . . .

The plurality's discussion of the record in this case is both extraordinarily arrogant and extraordinarily unfair. It is arrogant because the plurality presumes to make its own factual findings with respect to a variety of disputed issues relating to carcinogen regulation. It should not be necessary to remind the Members of this Court that they were not appointed to undertake independent review of adequately supported scientific findings made by a technically expert agency. And the plurality's discussion is unfair because its characterization of the Secretary's report bears practically no resemblance to what the Secretary actually did in this case. Contrary to the plurality's suggestion, the Secretary did not rely blindly on some draconian carcinogen "policy." If he had, it would have been sufficient for him to have observed that benzene is a carcinogen, a proposition that respondents do not dispute. Instead, the Secretary gathered over 50 volumes of exhibits and testimony and offered a detailed and evenhanded discussion of the relationship between exposure to benzene at all recorded exposure levels and chromosomal damage, aplastic anemia, and leukemia. In that discussion he evaluated, and took seriously, respondents' evidence of a safe exposure level. . . .

In recent years there has been increasing recognition that the products of technological development may have harmful effects whose incidence and severity cannot be predicted with certainty. The responsibility to regulate such products has fallen to administrative agencies. Their task is not an enviable one. Frequently no clear causal link can be established between the regulated substance and the harm to be averted. Risks of harm are often uncertain, but inaction has considerable costs of its own. The agency must decide whether to take regulatory action against possibly substantial risks or to wait until more definitive information becomes available — a judgment which by its very nature cannot be based solely on determinations of fact.

Those delegations, in turn, have been made on the understanding that judicial review would be available to ensure that the agency's determinations are supported by substantial evidence and that its actions do not exceed the limits set by Congress. In the Occupational Safety and Health Act, Congress expressed confidence that the courts would carry out this important responsibility. But in this case the plurality has far exceeded its authority. The plurality's "threshold finding" requirement is nowhere to be found in the Act and is antithetical to its basic purposes. "The fundamental policy questions appropriately resolved in Congress . . . are *not* subject to re-examination in the federal courts under the guise of judicial review of agency action." *Vermont Yankee Nuclear Power Corp. v. NRDC.* Surely this is no less true of the decision to ensure safety for the American worker than the decision to proceed with nuclear power.

Because the approach taken by the plurality is so plainly irreconcilable with the Court's proper institutional role, I am certain that it will not stand the test of time. In all likelihood, today's decision will come to be regarded as an extreme reaction to a regulatory scheme that, as the Members of the plurality perceived it, imposed an unduly harsh burden on regulated industries. But as the Constitution "does not enact Mr. Herbert Spencer's Social Statics," *Lochner v. New York,* 198 U.S. 45, 25 S. Ct. 539, 49 L. Ed. 937 (1905) (Holmes, J., dissenting), so the responsibility to scrutinize federal administrative action does not authorize this Court to strike its own balance between the costs and benefits of occupational safety standards. I am confident that the approach taken by the plurality today, like that in *Lochner* itself, will eventually be abandoned, and that the representative branches of government will once again be allowed to determine the level of safety and health protection to be accorded to the American worker.

QUESTIONS

1. What are the justifications for regulating potentially hazardous materials in general? What about in the workplace? Is the need for environmental regulation greater or less in the workplace than in other contexts? On what factors does your analysis turn? Of what relevance are market forces?

2. How would you characterize Congress's framework for regulating workers' exposure to toxic materials in the workplace? Does it strike you as a good framework? What other approaches might Congress have used? How would you compare these frameworks? Of what relevance is the enormous uncertainty regarding the health and ecosystem effects of many substances?

3. Should Congress delegate broad or narrow discretionary authority to agencies responsible for regulating environmental hazards? What factors are likely to influence the scope of delegated authority? What are the advantages and disadvantages of broad regulatory authority? Of narrow authority?

4. What are the purposes of judicial review of environmental standard setting? What scope of review is reflected in each of the opinions in the *Benzene* case? How does the enormous scientific uncertainty regarding the effects of benzene affect your analysis? In this regard, contrast the opinions of Justice Stevens and Justice Marshall. What is the proper scope of judicial review of workplace safety and health regulations?

B. ALLOCATION OF SCARCE RESOURCES: AN ECONOMIC PERSPECTIVE[7]

1. THE PROBLEM OF SCARCITY AND THE MARKET SYSTEM

a. *The Problem of Scarcity*

The economist views scarcity as the central problem of human existence. Human beings have desires or preferences for many things: a comfortable home, a pleasant environment, travel, leisure, culture, and the like.[8] They can call on resources — natural resources like land, minerals, sunlight, rainfall; accumulated capital in the form of factories, schools, inventory, and knowledge; and labor — to satisfy these desires. The central problem arises because the resources available are inadequate to satisfy *all* human desires or preferences. From the viewpoint of the individual, the problem is to deploy the resources at his or her command — either directly, or indirectly by exchange through barter or the medium of money — in order to maximize individual well-being or "utility." From the viewpoint of society as a whole, the problem is similarly one of using scarce resources to maximize the aggregate well-being of all of the individuals in the society.[9] Our concern will be to examine the problem of scarcity from the societal viewpoint.

Economic models generally assume that the relevant desires and preferences in a society are individual ones, and further that there is no generally acceptable way to compare directly the well-being particular individuals derive from satisfying their preferences. For example, it is assumed to be impossible to quantify the degree to which a governmental transfer of resources from B to A would increase A's preference-satisfaction or utility and then compare that increase with the corresponding decrease in B's preference-satisfaction or utility. As developed further below, these assumptions create serious problems for

---

7. Although the materials in sections B and C of this chapter are designed to provide students possessing little or no economics training with the necessary background to handle the materials addressed in the remainder of the book, students without formal training in economics might find it useful to consult an introductory economics textbook, such as P. Samuelson & W. Nordhaus, Economics (12th ed. 1985), for a more in-depth survey of the concepts developed in this chapter.

8. The assumption that persons have a fixed set of preferences or desires determined by forces outside the scope of economic analysis is fundamental and raises questions that we will explore later.

9. The economic framework derives from the work of the utilitarian philosopher Jeremy Bentham (1748-1832) who believed that the ultimate goal of society should be the greatest happiness of the greatest number.

those concerned with how a society could use its collective resources to increase aggregate welfare. The assumptions exclude the possibility that society as a whole has a set of preferences or a "utility function," as well as the possibility of adding up the satisfactions of various individuals in order to discover the allocation of resources that would maximize the total amount of satisfaction or utility in the society. (The assumptions that preferences are individual and incommensurable may reflect the individualistic orientation of economists and their preference for free market exchange as an institution for resolving the problem of scarcity.) Although the traditional economic framework does not permit us to describe a social utility function separately from the preference rankings of the individual members of the society, the market system, as we will see below, in effect aggregates individual members' of society "willingness to pay," forming a market demand curve which reflects the collective "willingness to pay" of the society as a whole.

b. Criteria for Evaluating Allocations of Resources

Given the foregoing, how do we go about allocating resources in ways that maximize the satisfaction of preferences? The problem can be illustrated by a simple example of a hypothetical society with resources that can be used to produce only two commodities: apples and bread (or alternatively, guns and butter or clean air and beer cans). Figure 2.1 illustrates the various quantities of apples and bread that could be produced in this hypothetical society with the existing (and fixed) resource base of land, labor, and capital (i.e, machines such as plows, mills, and ovens). The total number of apples that might be

FIGURE 2.1
The Production Possibility Frontier

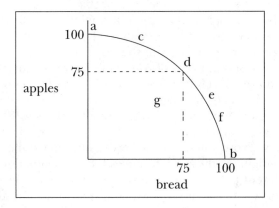

produced is indicated on the vertical axis, and the total number of loaves of bread on the horizontal axis. The curve ab, which also passes through points c, d, e, and f, represents the maximum amount of apples and bread that can be produced in various combinations of land, labor, and capital. Economists refer to this as the production possibility frontier. Thus if it were decided to devote all of the society's resources to producing apples (point a), 100 apples could be produced, and similarly for loaves of bread (point b). At point d, 75 apples and 75 loaves of bread can be produced. The graph assumes that as the society increasingly concentrates on producing a single commodity (such as apples), the cost of such additional production, measured in terms of units of the other commodity foregone, becomes increasingly larger. This illustrates the principle of diminishing returns, derived from the fact that as society devotes more and more resources to production of a given good, the additional amount of the good that can be produced with an extra unit of the resource usually (but not always) diminishes. Here, for example, some of the land in the society might be more suitable for orchards. As more and more of the total land in the society is devoted to production of a single crop, the yield from additional units of decreasingly suitable land decreases. The tradeoff between apples and bread also illustrates the concept of *opportunity cost.* The cost to the society of devoting additional resources to bread production is the loss of the opportunity to produce other commodities (here apples) with those resources, and vice versa.

In what proportion should the society produce apples and bread, assuming it is capable of producing at any point along the curve ab? If the society as a whole had a given set of preferences for apples versus loaves of bread (assume it liked them equally), the answer would be easy to determine: point d. As we have already seen, however, this possibility is excluded by the assumption that the only relevant preferences are those of individuals. Assuming (in order to simplify the analysis at this point) that the total production is to be divided equally among all the members of society, the society's problem of apples versus bread could also be easily solved if every individual had exactly the same preferences as between the two commodities. For example, if everyone preferred to consume equal units of the two commodities, point d would represent the optimum proportion from the viewpoint of society as a whole. But there is rarely if ever such an identity of tastes or preferences among all individuals. In terms of our example, some individuals will prefer to consume more bread than apples, others will have the contrary preferences, and some will want to consume equal units of the two commodities. (Note that traditional economic analysis has said nothing about the origin of these preferences.) In this situation, the choice among different proportions of production will have important distributional consequences, even if we continue to assume that the total production is divided pro rata among all members of the society. A decision to produce at point c will favor apple lovers. A decision to produce at point f will similarly favor bread lovers. Because the economist is unable to compare or aggregate the preference-satisfactions or utilities derived by various individuals from various mixes of production, she cannot judge which mix of apples and bread society should produce.[10] In the view of economic theory, these distributional issues must be resolved by reference to other considerations such as equity and justice.

c. The Theoretical Criterion of Pareto-Superiority

Despite its agnosticism regarding distributional issues, economic analysis does provide a partial ranking of the desirability of allocations of resources. According to the criterion of Pareto-superiority,[11] a reallocation of resources is preferred if some persons are made better off and no person is worse off. Assume, for example, that society is initially producing at point g. Point g is inside the production possibility frontier because for some reason resources are being deployed less efficiently than they might. If the society deployed its resources more efficiently it could move to point d and produce more apples and more bread; assuming pro rata distribution of the increased production, everyone in the society would be better off, and therefore point d is clearly preferable to point g. Point d is Pareto-superior to point g. The economist would also argue that it would be clearly preferable for society to move from point g to point e, for this would result in increased production of bread while keeping apple production constant. Even if we assume that some apple lovers would not care to consume their share of increased bread production, they would be no worse off, and other members of the society would be better off.[12] Which, if any, of

---

10. At first glance, it might appear that the appropriate solution would be to produce at point d, thus treating apple lovers and bread lovers equally. But this ignores the possibility that members of one group may be more intense in their preferences than members of the other. It also ignores the fact that production at point d will leave persons who prefer equal amounts of each commodity better off than either apple lovers or bread lovers.

11. The terminology is derived from Wilfred Pareto (1848-1923), a distinguished Italian economist who first articulated this analysis. For a good introductory discussion pitched to those with legal training, see B. Ackerman, Economic Foundations of Property Law xi-xiv (1975).

12. Note, however, that the apple lovers might be envious of the good fortune of the bread lovers. Should such envy lead us to conclude that apple lovers are made worse off by the change? In addition (relaxing for a moment the assumption that the preference satisfactions of various individuals cannot be compared at all), increased bread production and consumption would re-

the moves from point g to points a, c, f, and b would be Pareto-superior? What information do you need to answer this question?

Given the considerable number of individuals and commodities likely to be affected by resource decisions and the indirect effects of such decisions in the real world, changes that will make some people better off without making anybody worse off are undoubtedly quite rare. Even if they were more numerous, the criterion of Pareto-superiority would not always indicate which of several possible moves is preferable in economic terms. For example, the Pareto-superiority criterion would tell us that either point d or point e is preferable to point g, but would provide no economic basis for choosing between them. All points for which there is no move which will make someone better off and no one else worse off are defined as "Pareto-optimal." Moreover, the circumstance that one point, such as d, is Pareto-superior to another, such as g, does not necessarily establish that it is socially optimal to move from g to d, for there may exist a third alternative, such as point a, that would be strongly preferred by some individuals (here, apple lovers), even though a move from the status quo to that alternative would not be a Pareto-superior move. More generally, a society might reasonably choose to make some people better off while making others worse off because it thought the gains to the former in some sense outweighed or otherwise justified the latter's losses. Finally, the criterion of Pareto-superiority does not allow us to consider that some individuals' existing preferences may be foolish or unwise, or the impact of alternative resource allocations on the future development of individual preferences.

Because of the incompleteness of the Pareto criterion, economists have proposed alternative criteria for evaluating allocations of resources, although these alternatives raise other problems. Under the Kaldor-Hicks criterion, a change in the allocation of resources is preferred if it makes at least one person better off and the gainer(s) could compensate the loser(s) so that no one would be made worse off. Under the criterion, compensation need not actually be paid so that the transaction costs of compensating losers are not considered in applying the Kaldor-Hicks criterion. This criterion provides a more complete ranking than the Pareto criterion but, because compensation need not be paid, does not ensure that no one will be made worse off.

Within the context of this utilitarian philosophical perspective, two critical questions arise: (1) which Pareto-optimal allocation of re-

---

sult in bread lovers being relatively more satisfied overall than apple lovers. Is this inequality in satisfactions a justification for opposing the change? For discussion of these and related issues, see J. Rawls, A Theory of Justice §§13, 41, 48 (1971). For criticism of Rawls' position, see R. Nozick, Anarchy, State and Utopia 160-174, 232-275 (1974).

sources should be chosen; and (2) how should society be structured in order to achieve this allocation of resources. There exist a variety of systems of social organization for allocating resources. At one extreme is a system of central planning, in which a decisionmaking body (or possibly a single dictator) decides all resource allocation questions for the society. In theory, a benevolent social planner could order production choices and allocate outputs in order to achieve a desirable allocation of resources. To achieve this goal, however, the social planner must have extensive knowledge about available resources, production technologies, and individuals' preference orderings. For this reason, economists tend to be highly skeptical of central planning as an allocation mechanism.

At the other extreme is the market system, in which resources are initially allocated to the members of the society and each member is free to bargain with others, thereby using prices as a means of allocating resources. The role of government in a market system is to distribute the available resources through property endowments and to enforce bargains between the members of society. Economists have discovered that under certain conditions the market system has desirable properties with regard to the achievement of a desirable allocation of resources. It is for this reason that it is important to understand these basic properties of the market system and the conditions under which they apply (and break down).

d.   The Market System and Perfect Competition

The operation of the market system is well known to members of capitalistic societies. The government's principal role in such a society is to protect property rights and to enforce contracts. Each member of the society is both a seller of resources — his or her labor, capital, and natural resources — and a purchaser of commodities — both goods and services. Members of the society reflect their preferences for various commodities through their purchasing decisions. Producers of commodities typically respond to the price signals of the marketplace by allocating resources in such a way as to maximize their profits.

Figure 2.2 illustrates the process by which equilibrium is achieved in the market for apples. The x-axis measures the quantity of apples; the y-axis measures dollars, by which we mean nothing more than a common unit of exchange which facilitates trading. In order to derive the market demand curve (D), we can think of each of the individual members of the society participating in an auction for apples. As the auctioneer calls out hypothetical prices, such as 1 cent per apple, 2 cents per apple, 3 cents per apple, and so forth, individuals respond with their "demand," the amount of apples that they wish to purchase

FIGURE 2.2

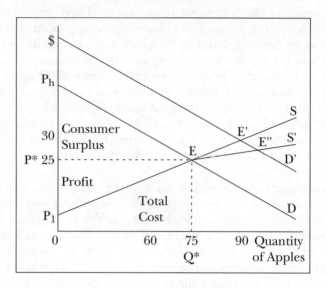

at that price (given their wealth and holding constant the price of other goods (such as bread) and their income). For each individual, therefore, we can trace an individual demand curve, the relationship between price and the quantity of apples demanded by that particular person. The market demand curve (D) is simply the sum of all individual demand curves. Thus, the market demand curve represents the amount that consumers (collectively) are willing to pay (in dollars) for apples given their initial endowment of wealth and assuming that the prices of other goods (such as bread) and their income is held constant. The area under the demand curve at each quantity represents the dollar value of the total willingness to pay for that quantity of apples. In the hypothetical market depicted in Figure 2.2, at a price of 30 cents per apple, consumers demand a total of 60 apples; at a price of 25 cents per apple, consumers demand 75 apples. The downward slope of the demand curve comports with the intuition that as the price of a good falls, consumers will demand more of it.

The market supply curve (S) can be derived in a similar manner. Instead of consumers participating in an auction to buy apples, think of all of the apple producers in the society participating in an auction to sell apples. As the auctioneer calls out hypothetical prices, each producer responds with his or her "supply," the amount of apples that he or she wishes to sell at the stated price (holding constant their cost of land, labor, and capital). It is assumed that producers choose their inputs (land, labor, and capital) and quantity supplied so as to maximize their profits. Given this assumption, each producer's supply curve will

simply be his or her cost of producing an additional apple, what economists call "marginal cost" (the cost of the marginal or last apple).[13] The
market supply curve (S) is simply the sum of all individual producer
supply curves. Thus, the market supply curve represents the amount of
apples that producers (collectively) are willing to supply given their
costs of production. In the hypothetical market depicted in Figure 2.2,
at a price of 30 cents per apple, producers offer a total of 90 apples; at
a price of 25 cents per apple, producers offer 75 apples. The upward
slope of the supply curve reflects the principle of diminishing returns
discussed above. The area under the supply curve at each quantity represents the dollar value of the total cost for that quantity of apples.

Equilibrium in the market for apples is achieved when the market
clears, that is, at the point (price-quantity combination) where supply
equals demand. In Figure 2.2, this occurs at point E, at a price of 25
cents and a total of 75 apples demanded and supplied. Notice that at
prices above 25 cents, more apples will be supplied than demanded.
This will lead apple producers to cut their price so as not to have extra
apples rotting on the shelf. The prices will be bid down until supply
equals demand at 25 cents. Similarly, if the price is initially less than 25
cents, the consumers who most value an additional apple will offer a
higher price. This process will continue until a price of 25 cents is
achieved and supply equals demand.

Under the assumptions of "perfect competition" (to be explained
shortly), we can decompose the market equilibrium into measures of
consumers' welfare, producers' profits (revenue over cost), and society's resource cost. As noted above, the area under the demand curve
up to the quantity demanded represents the dollar value of the consumers' willingness to pay for that amount of apples. Thus, at the equilibrium quantity of 75 apples, the collective willingness to pay is the area
OP_hEQ^*; but of this amount, they have to pay 25 cents per apple (which
is represented by the rectangle OP^*EQ^*). The difference between consumers' willingness to pay and what they actually have to pay is the area
of the triangle P^*P_hE. Economists refer to this amount as "consumer
surplus." Producers receive in revenue the full amount that the consumers pay (the rectangle OP^*EQ^*). However, they bear resources costs
(that is, payments for land, labor, and capital) equal to the area under
their supply curve up to the equilibrium quantity (the area OP_lEQ^*).
Thus, their net profit (total revenue less total cost) is the area of the
triangle P_lP^*E. What is the net cost to society of providing consumers
with 75 apples? Under the assumptions of our analysis, the social re-

---

13. This description of the supply curve is somewhat simplified. More
precisely, the individual supply curve is only that portion of the marginal cost
curve above the producer's "break-even" point, the point below which the producer's short run operating losses exceed its fixed costs of operating.

source cost is the same as the private resource cost (the cost of land, labor, and capital — represented by the area OP_1EQ^*).

We can also readily see that society's net surplus — consumer surplus plus producer profit — is maximized at the equilibrium E. At any production level above 75 apples (Q^*), the cost of the additional apples (reflected by the supply curve) exceeds what consumers are willing to pay for the additional apples (reflected by the demand curve). At any production level less than 75 apples, consumers are willing to pay more for additional apples than the cost of production. Thus, only at point E is the net surplus (consumers' willingness to pay less resource cost) maximized. Economists refer to such an allocation of resources as efficient.

An important feature of the market paradigm is that as prices of other goods (such as bread) and consumer income vary over time, the allocation of resources automatically adjusts accordingly. For example, if the cost of producing bread rises for a reason unrelated to the resource costs of producing apples (e.g., if an insect that thrives on wheat but not apples proliferates), the demand curve for apples will shift outward (to D') because at each price, consumers will demand more apples than they did previously as a result of the relatively higher cost of bread.[14] In effect, given the higher price of bread, consumers will substitute some apples for bread.[15] To satisfy this increased demand, apple producers will, in the short run, bid up the price of labor (the most flexible of the three inputs). The price of apples will rise because of the scarcity (to E'). This will create high profits (relative to the bread industry) in the apple industry. Over the longer run, existing apple suppliers and new suppliers attracted by high profits will seek to expand apple production. Landowners will convert from wheat fields to apple orchards and millers and bakers (particularly those with less skill in wheat milling and breadmaking or greater abilities in apple production) will take up apple labor until the cost of producing apples rises (because of the use of less suitable land or less skilled labor) and the price of apples declines (because of the increased supply) sufficiently to wipe out the temporary relatively high profits in the apple industry created by the increased demand for apples. These forces will, over the longer run, shift the market supply curve to S'. A new equilibrium (E'') is achieved in which prices reflect the members' of society trade-off between apples and bread (given the initial endowments of resources).

Formalization of this interaction has enabled economists to dem-

---

14. What will be the effect of the insect on the production possibility frontier?

15. There will also be an "income" effect reflecting the fact that consumers will now have less "real" income to spend on all goods as a result of the higher price of bread.

onstrate the two basic theorems of welfare economics: (1) optimizing behavior on the part of individuals and firms under conditions of "perfect competition" leads to a Pareto-optimal allocation of resources and (2) any Pareto-optimal allocation of resources can be achieved through a suitable initial allocation of endowments and the operation of the market system.[16] These results hold, however, only if the following exacting conditions of "perfect competition" are met: (1) consumers and producers have access to all relevant information about the commodities and markets; (2) all commodities (including resources) are traded; (3) there are large numbers of buyers and sellers in each market; and (4) there are no external costs or benefits associated with the production or consumption of commodities, that is, producers bear the full cost of producing their commodities and consumers realize the full benefits of the commodities that they purchase.

Even a cursory study of actual markets, however, indicates that the conditions of perfect competition are not universally met. Many markets are characterized by one or only a few sellers or buyers. Of particular relevance to environmental policy, many important resources — such as clean air and water — are not traded in markets and the costs of air and water pollution often are not included in the prices of goods whose production generate such pollution; even if they were, there is some question about whether their value can be priced in the same way as apples and bread. In addition, consumers often lack adequate information to make wise purchasing decisions. It is the belief of mainstream economists, nonetheless, that the beneficial attributes of the market system can be achieved through government policies designed to correct market failures. Such policies are discussed in detail below.

In theory, the allocation of resources generated by market processes could be accomplished by central government regulation if the government could somehow ascertain everyone's preferences and then order resources around to produce the correct amounts of the appropriate goods. It is argued, however, that such an alternative is cumbersome and expensive. At best, government bureaucrats would be likely to make wrong guesses about consumer preferences; at worst, they would impose their own preferences on others. Moreover, the incentives of government officials to utilize resources efficiently are far weaker than those of entrepreneurs motivated by profit and thus sensitive to the price signals of the market system.

---

16. Although these propositions were not formally proved in a general model until the middle of this century by Kenneth Arrow and Gerard Debreu, at least the first proposition bears resemblance to Adam Smith's claim in The Wealth of Nations (1776) that the unfettered market system will guide self-interested individuals "as if by an invisible hand" to do what is best not only for themselves but for society as a whole.

For these reasons, most economists believe that the market system is the best institutional structure for achieving a Pareto-optimal allocation. With little more than a basic legal system that protects private property and enforces contractual agreements (that is, bilateral trades) and government intervention closely tailored to correcting market failures, the decentralized activities of individual members of the society lead to an allocation of resources for which no person can be made better off without making someone else worse off.

It must be emphasized, however, that the market system does not provide an answer to the question of which Pareto-optimal allocation of resources should be chosen by the society. It is the premise of the progressive capitalist economies that such questions are decided politically and implemented through social welfare policies that are designed to achieve a fair initial distribution of endowments or a fair redistribution of outputs.

2.   MARKET FAILURE: COLLECTIVE GOODS AND EXTERNALITIES

As it happens, the market exchange price system commonly fails to take account of "collective goods" or "public goods" — commodities that cannot be supplied to a given individual without at the same time enabling large numbers of other individuals to enjoy them simply because it is impracticable to exclude those other individuals from such enjoyment. Markets for such commodities violate the fourth condition noted above for perfect competition — that there are no external costs or benefits associated with the production or consumption of commodities. Examples of collective goods include national defense, lighthouses, local highways, and the court system. (Can you see why such commodities are collective goods?)

The nonexcludability that distinguishes collective goods often results in their being ignored in the market exchange price system. Any given consumer seeking to maximize his or her own satisfaction would not normally be willing to pay a price that would cover all of the costs of a collective good (such as a local highway system) because most of the benefits would accrue to other consumers who could not feasibly be excluded from enjoying them. Moreover, *from the viewpoint of any given consumer* it is rational to pay nothing for a collective good, on the supposition that others will pay for it; because of the nonexcludability characteristic, our consumer could then enjoy the collective good for free. But if every individual consumer reasons in this way, no one will pay anything for the good and it will not be supplied. Economists refer to this as the free-rider problem.

incentive to produce collective goods; the inability to exclude consumers from enjoying the goods precludes the possibility of exacting payment to cover the costs of production. Thus collective goods are seldom supplied by market processes.[17] (However, under favorable circumstances, collective goods may be produced as the by-product of market processes. For example, if a cheap technology were available to extract sulfur from the sulfur dioxide in power plant and smelter stack gases, firms motivated by the opportunity to extract and sell sulfur at a profit would at the same time provide the surrounding community with the collective good of cleaner and healthier air. But even in this case the amount of clean air provided is likely to be less than members of the community would be willing to pay for. Moreover, in most instances, such favorable technology and price incentives are missing.)

The thrust of the foregoing discussion is that a market system will in many instances fail to provide adequate incentives for firms to undertake socially desirable activities that generate external, collective good benefits. In particular, activities are desirable when their marginal value to society (the value of collective goods produced plus the market price obtained by any marketable commodities produced) exceeds the marginal cost of societal resources devoted to their production (measured in terms of foregone opportunities to produce other goods with those resources), but will not be undertaken when the return (if any) to a firm on the marketable commodities alone is insufficient to cover the firm's payments for resources.

It may be apparent to you from the materials in Chapter 1 and the foregoing discussion that many forms of environmental quality have the character of collective goods. Take, for example, clean air in a large urban area. While a source of air pollution (such as a factory or automobile owner) could reduce air pollution by installing control equipment or other steps, the benefits would accrue to everyone in the air basin; the source would be unable to exclude given individuals from enjoying the cleaner air in order to exact payments to cover the costs of control. Any given individual would not be willing to pay the source to control emissions because the benefits would accrue largely to others, reasoning that if others undertake to "purchase" cleaner air he or she could enjoy the resulting benefits without contributing anything.

The problem of achieving clean air can usefully be seen as resulting from the inability of the free market system to force producers of pollution to bear the full social cost of their activities. Without some mechanism for imposing the cost of pollution upon those who produce it, suppliers of goods whose production generates pollution as a by-product bear only the cost of land, labor, and capital, and not the envi-

---

17. See M. Olson, The Logic of Collective Action (1967) for a detailed discussion of this analysis as applied in various contexts.

FIGURE 2.3

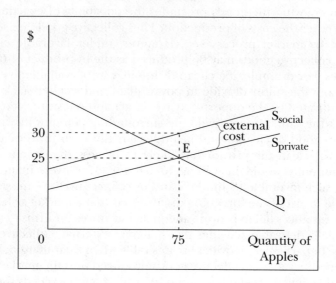

ronmental damage their production process causes. (Economists refer to such external costs, that is, costs not included in the market price, as *negative externalities*.) As a result, producers will generate an excessive amount of pollution; that is, consumers of air and water would be willing to pay more to avoid such pollution than the cost of avoidance.[18]

We can illustrate the problem of a negative externality by modifying our hypothetical market for apples. Assume that the machines used in processing apples emit one unit of "smox," an unhealthy air pollutant, for each apple produced. Assume further that the social cost of each unit of smox, in terms of breathing discomfort, is 5 cents based on consumers' willingness to pay to avoid the discomfort.[19] Would producers or consumers take the air pollution into consideration in their selling and buying decisions? Given our assumption that producers base their supply decisions solely upon the costs of land, labor, and capital, producers will behave in exactly the same manner as they did when no smox was emitted. Although consumers will bear the discomfort of breathing the polluted air, they will not change their buying behavior because the added pollution from the production of their apple(s) is spread throughout the air; therefore their purchase deci-

---

18. By contrast, collective goods produce positive externalities (nonpurchasers benefit from their production) and therefore are underproduced because the producer cannot recover the marginal social benefit of their efforts.

19. This assumes, of course, that health effects can be valued in monetary terms. We will return to this assumption in our discussion of cost-benefit analysis, infra pp. 85-86.

sions will not affect in any appreciable way the amount of pollution that they suffer. Figure 2.3 illustrates the resulting divergence between the private and social cost of apple production. S represents the market supply curve of producers. It reflects the "private" cost of producing apples, that is, the cost borne by private producers. The social cost curve (S′) reflects the full social cost of producing apples — the private costs of land, labor, and capital plus the external cost of air pollution. The difference between the private and social cost curves is the external cost (in our example, 5 cents per apple). Since producers and consumers of apples will make their decisions on the basis of the S and D curves, the equilibrium of the private market will be the same as in Figure 2.2 — a price of 25 cents and 75 apples supplied. This equilibrium is inefficient because the full social cost of the last apple sold (30 cents) exceeds the amount that consumers are willing to pay (25 cents); thus, we have market failure. What is the efficient level of apple production in light of the air pollution problem? How can society solve this market failure?

3. BARGAINING SOLUTIONS TO COLLECTIVE GOODS/EXTERNALITY PROBLEMS: THE COASE THEOREM

In a seminal article, The Problem of Social Cost, 3 J. L. & Econ. 1 (1960), Professor Ronald Coase suggested that the collective goods and externality problems would solve themselves (at least in terms of efficiency) if it were costless for people to bargain. Coase showed that regardless of whether polluters initially have the right to pollute (as they effectively do in our apple example above) or victims have the right to be free from pollution, an efficient allocation of resources will obtain if transaction costs — the costs of negotiating (broadly defined) — are zero. The allocation of rights affects only the distribution of resources, not the efficiency of resource allocation. This proposition has come to be known as the Coase Theorem.

a. Zero Transaction Costs Model

The Coase Theorem can be demonstrated by a variation on our apple/air pollution problem. Assume for our present purposes that there is only one apple producing firm and that it is located in a rural area. The net profit of the apple operation is $500 per year. (To simplify the analysis, we will assume that this amount is the full social surplus from apple production, that is, that there is no consumer surplus.)

earlier example, the apple processing equipment merely emits soot, the only adverse effect of which is to soil the clothing of the farmer when it is hung outside to dry. The soot does not cause any health or other adverse welfare effects. Over the course of a year, the total damage to the farmer from the soot emissions is $100 in soiled clothing.

In addition to halting operations of the apple processing facility, there are two other ways of eliminating the damage to the farmer: (1) by installing a screen on the apple processing equipment at a cost of $450 per year; and (2) by installing a clothes dryer in the farmer's house at a cost of $75. What then is the efficient allocation of resources? If no pollution control measure is taken, then the net surplus of the society (the apple producer and the farmer) is $500 in apple profits less $100 in damages to the farmer or $400. If the screen is installed on the apple processor, then the net surplus is $500 less $450 (for the abatement equipment) or $50. If the dryer is installed in the farmer's house, then the net surplus is $500 less $75 (for the dryer) or $425. Therefore, the efficient allocation of resources is to install the dryer in the farmer's house.

Coase asked whether the ultimate allocation of resources will depend on who — the apple producer or the farmer — has the effective entitlement[20] to the air. Let's first assume, as we did in our earlier externality example, that the apple producer effectively has the right to pollute. What allocation of resources would obtain? Since the apple producer is free to pollute, the onus is on the farmer to decide how to deal with the pollution. The farmer has four options: (1) to do nothing and bear the $100 in soot damage; (2) to install the dryer for $75 and avoid all harm; (3) offer the apple producer to pay at least the full cost of the screen of $450; and (4) offer the apple producer an amount at least equal to its profits ($500) to shut down for the year. Clearly the least costly option for the farmer is to install the clothes dryer, which is the efficient outcome.

Let's now assume that the farmer has the legally and costlessly enforceable right to be free from pollution. What allocation of resources would obtain? Since the farmer can now enjoin the apple producer from emitting soot or recover damages for soot damage, the onus is now on the apple producer to deal with the pollution. The apple producer has three options: (1) do nothing, thereby subjecting itself to either at best a damage action for $100 or at worst an injunctive action closing down the production operation causing a loss of $500 in profit; (2) install the screen on the processing equipment costing $450; or (3) offer to install the dryer in the farmer's house, costing only $75. The apple producer will choose the dryer option. As above, the efficient

---

20. By effective entitlement, we mean a legal right and a feasible means of enforcing that right.

allocation obtains, thus showing that regardless of who has the entitle-ment, an efficient allocation of resources will result so long as it is cost-less for the parties to bargain.[21]

The fact that efficiency obtains under any system of legal rights (when transaction costs are zero and parties are permitted to bargain) does not mean that the distribution of wealth is the same. Obviously, the farmer has higher net wealth if she receives the entitlement to clean air; and the apple producer is better off if it possesses the entitlement.[22] But in either case, an efficient allocation of resources results.

Why didn't this externality result in an inefficient allocation of resources (like our earlier example)? What the Coase Theorem shows is that when there are no transaction costs, a market will be created comprised of the persons who gain and lose from the externality. Rec-ognizing their potential mutual advantage from achieving an efficient allocation of resources, they will write a contract that brings about effi-cient resource use and shares the benefits of this improvement in social welfare according to the parties' respective bargaining power.

So why worry about externalities if the Coase Theorem operates? It is important to remember that the Coase Theorem is premised upon the assumption that transactions are costless. The world in which the Coase Theorem operates is analogous to the frictionless vacuum of the theoretical physicist. In the real world, of course, there is friction and the cost of negotiating a settlement is not zero. In order to appreciate more fully Coase's insight, therefore, it is important to understand what

---

21. It is important to recognize that costless bargaining means that the parties will reach agreement whenever there are gains from trade. Under op-tion (3), the apple producer gains as much as $450 (by avoiding the installation of pollution abatement equipment on its factory) if the farmer installs the dryer at a cost of $75. The Coase analysis under the zero transactions cost assumption implies that a transfer of at least $75 and as much as $450 will occur because it is in the interests of both parties. The exact level of the trans-fer within this range, however, will depend on the relative bargaining power and ability of the parties. As is discussed below, at pp. 60-63, negotiation costs and opportunism problems, which the Coase analysis considers to be transac-tion costs, could vitiate a mutually beneficial trade.

22. The means by which entitlements are enforced — either by injunc-tive remedies or damages — can significantly affect the bargaining dynamic. If the farmer's entitlement to be free from pollution is enforceable by injunctive relief, then she can demand up to the full cost to the apple producer of avoiding pollution — i.e., $450 for installing pollution abatement equip-ment — because a court would otherwise close down the factory (costing the apple producer $500). By contrast, if the farmer's entitlement is only en-forceable by a damage remedy, then the most she will be able to recover in court is $100 in damages (or only $75 if the court applies a mitigation require-ment). Hence, the apple producer would be willing to pay no more than this amount to settle the dispute. Costly litigation, however, could further alter this bargaining dynamic. See Menell, A Note of Private versus Social Incentives to Sue in a Costly Legal System, 12 J. Legal Studies 41 (1983).

is meant by the concept of "transaction costs" and the implications of transaction costs for resource allocation.

b.   Positive Transaction Costs Model

There are many factors that inhibit the efficient resolution of collective goods and externality problems in the real world. It is useful to think of four distinct types of transaction cost problems preventing or at least inhibiting efficient bargained resolutions of such problems: (1) negotiation and litigation costs; (2) free-rider problems; (3) hold-out problems; and (4) opportunism problems. *Negotiation and litigation costs* consist of the time and effort associated with hammering out an agreement and enforcing it. Even if the farmer and apple producer are willing to resolve their dispute through bargaining, the costs of drawing up a contract that specifies all possible contingencies — such as gathering the information about what to bargain about, deciding who owns the dryer, deciding who is responsible for repairing it should it break — and enforcing the agreement should one party default — such as hiring lawyers, court costs — might outweigh the benefits of an agreement.

We already encountered the second class of transaction costs, those associated with the *free-rider problem,* in our discussion of collective goods in the previous section. To illustrate how the free-rider problem arises, we need to modify our apple/air pollution example. Assume that 40 farmers reside near the apple production facility rather than one. If everything else about the problem remains the same (and now each farmer faces $100 in damages if soot is emitted), then it is clear that the efficient allocation of resources is for the filter to be installed.[23] Will this result obtain if the farmers initially have the right to clean air? If litigation costs are low, then each farmer can credibly threaten to sue if the apple producer does not prevent the soot emissions. Therefore, the apple producer will voluntarily install the filter so as to avoid being closed down by an injunctive action or having to compensate the farmers for $4000 in damages. If litigation is costly (and the costs of litigation are borne by each litigant regardless of the outcome), however, each farmer might prefer to install a dryer individually (at a cost of $75) rather than bear the full cost of litigation. Alternatively, the farm-

---

23. If no abatement action is taken, then society suffers $4000 in damages per year ($100 per farmer times 40 farmers). If each farmer installs a clothes dryer, then society incurs $3,000 in abatement costs ($75 per farmer times 40 farmers). If the apple production facility shuts down, then society loses $500 per year in profit. And if the smoke abatement equipment is installed, society incurs $450 per year in abatement cost. Therefore, the efficient allocation of resources is to install the filter.

ers might try to organize so as to share the costs of litigation. But this is where the free-rider problem might arise. If each farmer makes the private calculation of the costs and benefits of participating in the consortium, she will realize that she receives the benefits of the lawsuit whether or not she participates. And since litigation is costly, she might decide not to participate in the lawsuit. If each farmer reaches this conclusion (and is motivated solely by economic self-interest), no lawsuit will occur.

What outcome obtains if we initially give the apple producer the right to pollute? The farmers will bear the burden of dealing with the pollution problem. After they do the social surplus calculations, they will realize that the best outcome will be for them to chip in to pay for a filter for the apple production facility. As we noted above, however, each will also realize that she will enjoy the full benefits from installation of the filter even if she does not contribute to the cost of providing it. If each farmer comes to this same conclusion, then no consortium will form to negotiate with the apple producer for the purpose of having the filter installed. Therefore, the free-rider problem again frustrates the achievement of an efficient allocation of resources. Although in theory the free-rider problem can occur in any bargaining situation in which more than one party has a common interest, the free-rider problem is most likely to occur when there are large numbers of heterogeneous parties who must get together in order to obtain the benefits of cooperation.

A related impediment to negotiation is the *hold-out problem*. To illustrate this form of transaction costs, we need to modify our apple/ air pollution example again. Assume that there are five farmers residing near the apple producer. As before, each farmer will suffer $100 in damages per year if no abatement measures are taken. The efficient allocation of resources is now for each of the farmers to install a clothes dryer. (Can you see why?) Will this result obtain if the farmers initially have the right to clean air? If transaction costs were zero, then the apple producer would arrange to install a clothes dryer in each of the farmer's houses at a cost to the apple producer of $375. In a more complicated world, however, the following bargaining dynamic might occur. The apple producer negotiates with farmer #1 and arranges to pay him $75 per year to cover the cost of a clothes dryer. Farmer #2 realizes that the apple producer would probably be willing to pay even more to avoid being sued. Through savvy negotiation, she arranges for a payment of $95 per year. Farmer #3, hearing of the payments to his neighbors, holds out for $98. The apple producer, realizing the potential for extortion, might decide that it is less costly simply to install the filter and forgo bargaining with the greedy farmers. Thus, the potential for hold-outs can also lead to an inefficient allocation of resources.

The fourth type of transaction cost results from *opportunism* on the part of the parties. Opportunism occurs when a party attempts to extract a higher price for his entitlement by threatening behavior that would reduce his bargaining adversary's wealth, thus raising the adversary's willingness to buy the entitlement to avoid such a threat. We can illustrate this problem by going back to the original example of one apple producer and one farmer. As we saw in the world with zero transaction costs, if the farmer has the right to clean air, then the apple producer will offer to pay the cost of a clothes dryer and the efficient allocation of resources is achieved. Assume now that the farmer refuses to install a clothes dryer if the apple producer pays only $75; furthermore, the farmer threatens to hang out five times as much laundry as before unless the apple producer pays the farmer $500. Although this threat is clearly inefficient, the farmer might carry it out nonetheless in order to establish her credibility to extort a good settlement in future years. On the other hand, the apple producer might install the filter so as to establish its credibility in future negotiations. The net result of such behavior, however, is clearly inefficient for society.

As this discussion indicates, transaction costs can frustrate the achievement of an efficient allocation of resources in a variety of ways. As we will see throughout this book, this is particularly true in the environmental context. This does not mean, however, that Coase's analysis is unhelpful in addressing these more complex problems. Even in situations in which transaction costs are significant, the Coase Theorem provides a useful insight into how to allocate entitlements so as to achieve an efficient allocation of resources: Entitlements should be allocated to the party or parties that would have bargained for them in the absence of transaction costs. Thus, in our apple/air pollution example in which there were 40 farmers, society is most likely to achieve the efficient allocation of resources by giving the entitlement to the farmers (although this may depend on the costs of enforcing the entitlement).[24] In our example with five farmers, society is most likely to achieve an efficient allocation of resources by awarding the entitlement to the apple producer. As a first approximation, the legal system should adopt a liability rule that imposes the damage upon the party that can most inexpensively avoid the harm. Therefore, in the case of 5 farmers, the entitlement should be allocated to the apple producer since the farmers can most inexpensively avoid the social cost. In the case of 40 farmers, however, it is more efficient to allocate the entitlement to the farmers because the apple producer can least expensively avoid the social cost. This is commonly referred to as the "least cost avoider" principle. See infra pp. 172-188. In practice, however, determining which party is the least cost avoider is often difficult (and hence costly). Fur-

---

24. This problem could be remedied by enabling farmers to recover their litigation costs in legal actions to enforce their entitlement.

thermore, this method of allocating entitlements may ignore important considerations such as distributional and moral bases for assigning entitlements. Nonetheless, the Coase analysis in the presence of transaction costs poses the correct question for those wishing to achieve efficient resource allocation through the definition of entitlements.

A second important implication of Coase's analysis is that externalities are, at least from an efficiency standpoint, *reciprocal* in nature. Policy analysts have traditionally viewed our externality example as one in which the apple producer inflicts harm on the farmers and the question to be decided is how should society restrain the apple producer? Coase's analysis shows, however, that the harm is reciprocal. The reciprocal nature of the harm arises from the potential interference between apple production and clothes drying. By avoiding the harm to the farmers, we "harm" (that is, impose costs upon) the apple producer (and, in effect, the apple producer's customers). Coase's analysis reveals that from an efficiency standpoint, the real social policy question is should the apple producer be allowed to harm the farmers or should the farmers be allowed to harm the apple producer? As Coase noted, "[t]he problem is to avoid the more serious harm." In a world in which transactions are costless, society avoids the more serious harm no matter how initial entitlements are allocated. When transactions are costly, however, an analysis of transaction costs will enable social decisionmakers to determine how to allocate entitlements so as to avoid the more serious harm.

The following problem will test your understanding of and ability to apply the analytical tools developed in this section.

PROBLEM: THE COASE THEOREM AND WATER POLLUTION

Two businesses are operating along a river — a fishery and a widget factory. The fishery can earn a profit of $1,200,000 if the river is unpolluted.[25] The widget factory, however, wishes to discharge some of its waste materials into the river. If it can freely do this, the factory can earn $1,000,000 in profit from the sale of widgets; the pollution, however, will cause the fishery to shut down. On the other hand, if the factory must halt all discharge, it will not be able to produce any widgets and therefore must shut down. In addition to these two options (that is, the fishery shutting down and the factory shutting down), the factory could also install pollution abatement equipment. If the factory installs primary treatment (cost of $125,000), discharge will be reduced by

---

25. To simplify the problem, assume that there is only one time period and no external costs other than those explicitly addressed. We will relax these assumptions later in the chapter.

TABLE 2.1

Resource allocations	Pollution level (tons)	Control costs	Fish loss (value)	Net profit* Fishery	Factory
A. fishery shuts down	60	0	1,200,000	0	1,000,000
B. primary treatment	30	125,000	720,000	480,000	875,000
C. primary + secondary	10	600,000	200,000	1m	400,000
D. factory shuts down	0	1,000,000	0	1,200,000	0

* It is assumed that the Factory bears the cost of pollution abatement equipment.

half to 30 tons. If the factory installs primary and secondary treatment (total cost of $600,000), discharge will be reduced to 10 tons. Table 2.1 describes the effects of these options on the profits of the factory and the fishery.

QUESTIONS

Assume transaction costs are zero.

1. What is the efficient allocation of resources? That is, what resource allocation (A-D) should be chosen to maximize the total value produced by the society?

2. What is the ultimate allocation of resources if the Factory is entitled to pollute?

3. What is the ultimate allocation of resources if the Fishery is entitled to be free from pollution?

4. What outcome would obtain if the Fishery could relocate to an equally good, pollution-free port for $500,000?

Relax the assumption about transaction costs.

5. What result obtains if instead of a single fishery, there are 100 independent fisherfolk who use the bay (each earns a profit of $12,000 in the absence of any pollution), it is costly for them to reach agreements, and the factory has the right to discharge 60 tons annually?

6. Same facts as in question 5 except that the fisheries have the right to be free from pollution. What result would obtain?

NOTES AND QUESTIONS

1. Does it matter whether environmental problems are viewed as collective goods or negative externalities? From the perspective of the

Coase analysis, pollution problems would seem to be collective goods (or, more appropriately, collective bads). The analysis focuses upon avoiding the worst harm. We do not favor either polluters or receptors (victims) as a class. By contrast, under more traditional externality analysis, see A.C. Pigou, The Economics of Welfare (1932), pollution problems are viewed as externality problems which should be solved by imposing the social costs on the polluter. Is one of these ways of characterizing the problem more appropriate from an economic standpoint? From the perspective of other moral frameworks?

2.   Does the assignment of entitlements affect the long-run allocation of resources? In our apple / air pollution example, will assignment of the entitlement to use the air resource to the apple producer favor long-run apple production more than assignment of the entitlement to the farmers will? See Demsetz, When Does the Rule of Liability Matter?, 1 J. Legal Studies 13 (1972).

3.   Even in a world of zero or low transaction costs, doesn't the assignment of entitlements affect the ultimate allocation of resources to the extent that peoples' wealth affects their willingness to pay? But does this phenomenon make the allocation of resources less "efficient"? Does this mean that entitlements should (must) be assigned with income distribution in mind?

In a related vein, doesn't the assignment of entitlements affect the valuation of resources by the parties? Substantial empirical evidence indicates a significant divergence between consumer's willingness to pay for natural resources and their willingness to accept compensation for such resources. This phenomenon, often referred to as the endowment effect, suggests that the utility people derive from the use of resources depends upon their perception of the allocation of entitlements. One survey found that hunters were willing to pay an average of $247 to preserve a wetland hunting area but would require more than four times that amount to give up an entitlement to the same area. See J. Hammaker & D. Brown, Jr., Waterfowl and Wetlands: Toward Bioeconomic Analysis (1974); see generally, Menell, Institutional Fantasylands: From Scientific Management to Free Market Environmentalism, 15 Harv. J. L. & Pub. Pol. 489, 496-97 (1992); Sunstein, Endogenous Preferences, Environmental Law, 22 J. Legal Studies 217(1993).

What are the implications of the endowment effect for our apple/air pollution example? If the entitlement to the air resource is initially assigned to the apple producer, then the farmers' decision about whether to acquire the entitlement turns on how much they are *willing to pay*. But if they have the entitlement initially, then the ultimate allocation of the resource will turn on how much the farmers will demand for the entitlement, that is, how much they are *willing to be paid*. What if the farmers' willingness to pay is not the same as their willingness to be paid? What does this mean for efficiency? What does it mean for the Coase Theorem?

4. Does Coase's analysis — which relies upon bargaining to reassign entitlements to the highest bidder — in effect encourage bribery and extortion? Is there any other way to allocate resources efficiently in a complex society?

5. The Coase Theorem suggests that collective goods / externality problems might well be solved through private means. In fact, we do see such efforts in many contexts. Isn't the environmental movement based in part on this notion? For example, the Nature Conservancy was formed in 1950 for the purpose of conserving the natural environment. As of 1981, the Nature Conservancy had preserved almost two million acres of forests, marshes, and other important and sensitive ecosystems entirely through voluntary contributions. These reserves have been donated to appropriate government agencies or maintained by the Nature Conservancy. Does this effort suggest that the collective goods / externality problem is not significant with regard to nature conservation? Alternatively, might some contributions to the Nature Conservancy be motivated by private gain?[26] What types of communities are most likely to be able to resolve externality problems through negotiation? Can you think of any other social institutions that have traditionally addressed the free-rider problems? See Ellickson, Order Without Law (1992); Rose, The Comedy of the Commons: Custom, Commerce, and Inherently Public Property, 53 U. Chi. L. Rev. 711 (1986).

6. Is there any way that legal rules can be designed to overcome transaction cost problems? Consider the following situation. Alpha Corporation owns and operates a cement factory in a scenic rural river valley. Over the past few years, the factory has gradually expanded its operations and now employs 200 people from a nearby town. During this same period, many people from Metropolis, a large city located 80 miles away, have purchased property in the valley and built summer cottages. The air pollution from the cement factory has so reduced visibility on some days that local residents can no longer see the beautiful nearby mountain peaks. The air pollution substantially interferes with the residents' use and enjoyment of their cottages. On the other hand, pollution abatement equipment for the factory would be quite costly and might cause the plant to shut down. In view of the Coase analysis, how should a common law court resolve a nuisance dispute brought by the neighbors against the factory in the absence of transac-

---

26. Contributions of assets afford high income individuals charitable deductions equal to the appreciated value of the donations without having to realize any capital gains. Changes in the tax laws in the 1980s, however, significantly reduced this tax benefit.

tion costs? How should the court resolve this dispute in the presence of transaction costs? To whom should the court give the entitlement? How should the legal system permit this entitlement to be enforced? By an injunction? Damages? Both?

4.   POTENTIAL GOVERNMENTAL RESPONSES TO COLLECTIVE GOODS/EXTERNALITY PROBLEMS

As the preceding discussion indicates, neither the traditional market nor private bargaining can be relied upon to address adequately all collective goods / externality problems. Thus, government has an important role to play in the allocation of resources within an economic framework. This section describes the various alternative ways in which government might seek to address market failures and the potential problems of such governmental intervention.

As our discussion of the Coase analysis suggested, government might *assign legal entitlements* relating to collective goods and design the legal rules governing the enforcement of such entitlements in such a way as to enable producers of collective goods to exclude nonpaying consumers from all or part of the benefits associated with such goods, in effect changing them wholly or partially from collective goods into goods that will command a positive price in market exchange. By this means, government can create an incentive for firms to supply collective goods. The patent and copyright systems are examples of the partial transformation of a collective good — intellectual work — into a good possessing the property of excludability. If a person who creates an invention, writing, work of art, or other creation capable of being reproduced without her consent could not bring a legal action to prevent unauthorized duplication, such creations would become collective goods, resulting in inadequate incentives for their production. Copyright and patent laws empower the creator to enjoin duplication of her creation without consent. The producer can then exact a payment for her consent, and the prospect of such payments will provide an incentive for creation.[27] (But the fact that the right to exclude is limited in

---

27. As we saw in our discussion of the Coase analysis, the fact that a good is collective does not necessarily mean that it will not be produced. First, a collective good may be produced as a by-product or external benefit of activities undertaken in response to market exchange incentives. Radio and television broadcasts are a collective good from the consumer's perspective but are nonetheless produced because broadcasters can exclude advertisers from the benefit of having their messages carried. Sometimes the satisfaction derived by an individual from the production of a collective good may be sufficient to ensure its production even though others cannot be excluded from consuming it. Many scholarly works would be created and made publicly available even

time and extent, and the requirement that the creation be published, thus adding to the general stock of knowledge, ensures that the creation remains in some respects a collective good.)

All of the commodities distributed through market exchange — automobiles and legal services just as much as novels and patented inventions — are creations of the legal system. For it is the rules of property, contract, and tort (backed up by civil remedies and criminal law) that enable a person to exclude others from appropriating his or her property or person. Without these pervasive rules of exclusion, all goods would become free for the taking and market exchange would not occur.[28] This raises the question of what legal rules with respect to excludability we ought to have. The economist's answer is that legal rules should be constructed in accordance with the criterion of economic efficiency — we should choose those rules that will maximize the economic efficiency of production of goods in society as measured by willingness to pay. On this view, legal rules are simply another factor of production (along with natural resources, labor, and capital) whose purpose is the purely instrumental one of maximizing output.[29]

In theory, traditional property rights could be redefined to encourage greater production of collective environmental goods such as clean air. For example, firms supplying clean air could in principle be given the legal right to enjoin others from enjoying the benefits of clean air and then sell the contractual right to such enjoyment for a money payment. However, the physical characteristics of the atmosphere and of many other environmental amenities make this compli-

---

without copyright protection, but probably few popular novels and musical recordings. The government's creation through the patent and copyright of a right of creators to exclude others and exact payment can be seen, from the viewpoint of society as a whole, as a subsidy to such creators, and there is a question whether such a subsidy is justified in terms of the added creativity it will stimulate. See Breyer, The Uneasy Case for Copyright, 84 Harv. L. Rev. 281 (1970).

28. This of course was Hobbes' state of nature, see T. Hobbes, The Leviathan, standing in sharp contrast to that of Locke, where customary norms of excludability are generally observed, see J. Locke, Two Treatises of Civil Government bk. II, ch. 5.

Because a developed system of market exchange is dependent upon and structured by judicially enforced rules of property, contract, and tort, the existence of such a market system already represents one form of government "intervention" through the creation of a judicial system. Accordingly, the failure of the "market" to produce sufficient amounts of collective goods may be viewed as ultimately attributable to inappropriate judge-made legal rules or to the limitations of a system of court litigation in providing adequate and appropriate incentives for private actors.

29. This view of the legal system and some of its implications are developed at greater length in R. Posner, Economic Analysis of Law (4th ed. 1992).

cated.[30] Moreover, as developed in Chapter 3, there are serious limitations on the ability of a system of court litigation to provide adequate and appropriate incentives for dealing with many environmental problems.

Alternatively, viewing the problem from the perspective of avoiding externalities, the government could protect victims of external harms. The focus of policy would be upon creating strong legal remedies and effective enforcement mechanisms.

A second basic approach to "market failure" is for the government to *subsidize* private activities that produce collective goods as a by-product or to pay firms directly to supply the goods in question. In the case of clean air, for example, the government could subsidize the installation of technology for removing sulfur from stack gases or simply pay emission sources for each increment of improved air quality resulting from pollution control. The costs of subsidizing or supplying the collective good in question can then be recouped through governmental exaction of compulsory payments through the tax system, short-circuiting the transaction costs involved in voluntary bargaining among individuals over the amount of their respective contributions. Examples of this general approach include the use of federal tax incentives for installation of pollution controls by industrial firms and the federal government program of capital grants to municipalities for installing sewage treatment facilities.[31]

Alternatively, the government can impose *financial penalties,* such as fines or taxes, on firms that cause negative externalities. For example, a financial incentive to provide clean air can be imposed through governmental exaction of a fee based on pollutant emissions. In the apple/air pollution example depicted in Figure 2.3, a fine equal to the cost of the externality (5 cents per unit of smox or, since one unit of smox is produced for each apple, 5 cents per apple) would shift the private supply curve out to the social supply curve, thereby achieving an efficient allocation of resources. In effect, the fine "internalizes" the externality — apple producers now bear the full social cost of their ac-

---

30. However, there are instances where the legal system recognizes the right to exclude others from enjoying environmental amenities. In Great Britain, the right of riparian owners to fish in streams is closely protected by law; these rights are then sold to third parties at a high price. This property system has provided important incentives for the preservation of these recreation resources. See Dales, The Property Interface, in The Economics of the Environment (R. Dorfman & N. Dorfman eds. 2d ed. 1977).

31. The supply of collective goods might also be undertaken directly by the government. For example, a government authority might install in-stream reaeration devices to improve the oxygen quality of polluted streams. However, this alternative is not essentially different from the government's paying a private firm to undertake such activity.

tivities: the costs of land, labor, capital, *and* air pollution. Under this approach, the cost of reducing pollution is imposed directly on the firms producing it and, ultimately, their consumers.

A fourth means by which government can provide collective goods and control externalities is through *command and control regulation*. By this we mean that the government can exercise its coercive powers to command firms to supply collective goods or to limit their production of pollution. As we will see, the government often requires firms to install pollution abatement devices.

A fifth approach is *government ownership and management* of collective goods. For special historical and geographical reasons, the United States government owns and administers approximately one-third of the nation's land. This system was established during the Progressive era (1880-1915), when the previous practice of selling or giving away federal lands was halted in favor of government retention and management in order to protect a variety of preservation and conservation values. Government ownership and management can also be used to reduce negative externalities. As noted above, municipalities are responsible for sewage treatment in many parts of the United States.[32]

Basic Problems in Governmental Intervention

Many forms of governmental activity can be viewed as devices for correcting the failure of a system of voluntary agreement among private actors to supply goods that are not purely private in character. In this view, government represents a pact among individuals to adhere to a set of authoritative procedures (for example, court litigation or electoral representation based on a system of majority vote) for determining which collective goods should be supplied and how the costs of supplying them should be distributed, thus avoiding the costs and obstacles in attempting to reach a separate agreement for each collective good.[33]

However, governmental intervention to deal with the failure of the market raises four basic sets of problems. The first is deciding what jurisdiction — local, state, national, international, global — should be responsible for addressing particular collective goods and externality problems. The second is determining which collective goods should be

---

32. There are other ways in which the government can address market failures. Consider, for example, government dissemination of information on the benefits of clean air and moral exhortation for firms to supply it voluntarily. How efficacious would this alternative be? In what circumstances might information dissemination be effective in reducing adverse impacts upon the environment?

33. See J. Buchanan & G. Tullock, The Calculus of Consent (1962).

produced and in what quantities, or the magnitude of externalities and the extent to which they should be priced or otherwise curtailed. The third is choosing among the various forms of government intervention (redefining legal rules, subsidies, financial penalties, and direct governmental ownership and management of resources) to secure an optimal supply of collective goods or an optimal level of the externality. A pervasive difficulty endemic to all of these problems is designing political institutions to serve the public interest as efficaciously as possible.

Political jurisdictions overlap, and any single jurisdiction is rarely coextensive with a particular collective goods or externality problem. The proper jurisdiction for addressing such problems depends on a complex set of factors, including the political responsiveness of the governing bodies, the resources and effectiveness in deploying such resources of the different governing bodies, and the extent of the particular market failure. For example, if the jurisdiction responsible for resolving a particular collective goods/externality problem is too large, then the political actors within that jurisdiction will be less sensitive to the interests of the persons most strongly affected. Thus, jurisdiction over neighborhood parks is perhaps better left with localities than national governments. If the jurisdiction is too small, however, the collective goods/externality problem is replicated: each jurisdiction may free-ride on the others. Thus, military defense is best addressed at the national level (or perhaps better yet, the international level) rather than the local level. As you study the various environmental problems throughout this book, it will be important to think about the proper jurisdiction for resolving particular problems. What is the optimal jurisdiction for traditional forms of air pollution? What about acid deposition? climate change?

The problem of determining the amount and mix of collective goods to be provided through governmental intervention raises the familiar problem of scarce resources in a new guise. What proportion of society's total resources should be allocated to the production of collective goods such as environmental quality and how should such goods be allocated? The criterion of economic efficiency remains the same: Resources should be allocated to maximize the total value of resources, measured by the willingness of consumers to pay for various commodities. There are, however, serious difficulties in applying this criterion to collective goods. For the reasons we have just seen, private market exchange fails because of transaction costs to measure the willingness of individuals to pay for collective goods.

In the absence of market exchange price signals, how do we measure willingness to pay? One alternative is to ask people hypothetical questions about what they would pay for a good. Such answers, however, may be a quite imperfect reflection of the amounts individuals would actually pay for various collective goods.[34] Another alternative is to assess individuals' willingness to pay for a collective good by reference to their willingness to pay for similar goods that are traded on exchange markets and have a price. For example, one might attempt to estimate individuals' willingness to pay for a police force by looking to the prices commanded by private security services. But often collective goods have no close counterparts distributed through market exchange. Finally, one could measure willingness to pay for various collective goods by a system of voting, either directly or through a system of elected representatives. However, the results of any such political process may not bear any close relation to willingness to pay, in large part because the costs of supplying collective goods are distributed through the tax system, losses generated by changed property rules, or regulatory requirements or financial penalties that induce firms to provide cleaner air without compensation. Under any of these approaches, the resulting distribution of burdens often fails to match the distribution of benefits. In a pluralistic political process, the supply of collective goods may in large part be determined by the efforts of various factions to obtain goods from which they will benefit disproportionately in relation to their share of the burdens. For these various reasons, decisions to supply public goods may often fail to reflect individuals' willingness to pay for such goods, resulting in an inefficient allocation of resources.

The same criterion of economic efficiency can be applied to the third basic problem with governmental intervention to deal with collective good problems — the choice among alternative forms of intervention. Government intervention is never costless; at a minimum, resources must be devoted to establishing and operating courts or administrative agencies to carry out the intervention. Centralized decisionmaking about resource use inherently involves enormous information-gathering and information-processing costs. Moreover, various forms of intervention will be more or less effective in providing suitable incentives for efficient resource allocation without untoward side effects. Consider in this respect why government has generally not attempted to supply clean air by outright payments to firms to reduce pollution, even though payment for the production of collective goods is commonly used in many other contexts, such as military weapons or police services. Might considerations of efficiency explain the reluctance to pay firms for cleaner air? Or does such reluctance reflect distri-

---

34. If individuals believe that they will be assessed for the costs of providing a collective good in proportion to their stated willingness to pay for such a good, they will have an incentive to understate their true willingness to pay. On the other hand, if they believe that the costs will be disproportionately borne by others they may tend to overstate their true willingness to pay.

butional concerns or other "equity" considerations? As we shall see, a variety of factors other than economic efficiency are highly relevant to the choice of what collective goods to produce in which amounts, and to the selection of governmental tools to achieve that production.

Even if these problems could be solved in theory, there remains the pervasive and fundamental problem of whether political institutions are capable of solving them in practice. As we will see throughout the materials in this book, many of the impediments to addressing environmental problems are as much a problem of governmental failure — the shortcomings of political institutions — as they are of market failure. And in some cases, governmental failure is the principal or sole source of the misallocation of resources.

Governmental failure, like market failure, can be traced to limited (and costly) information and inadequate or otherwise distorted incentives faced by decisionmakers. In the case of political failure, the relevant decisionmakers are public officials. Though elected or appointed to serve the "public interest," they may purposefully or subconsciously serve their self-interest, for instance, by seeking to expand their authority, their agencies' budget, or their post-government employment opportunities. Furthermore, public officials are subject to strong external forces seeking to influence their decisions. As in the interaction of the private market, those private economic interests that have the most to gain from favorable legislation or agency action are likely to invest heavily to affect the outcome of political processes. On the other hand, those groups with less concentrated stakes in the outcome of political decisions or that are more widely distributed among the electorate may face difficult free-rider problems in organizing an effective lobbying campaign. As a result of the relative influences of different groups within the society upon the political actors, the political process may be systematically distorted.

Over the past three decades, political economists have formalized these interactions within a framework referred to as public choice theory. The following excerpt sets out the essence of this approach to the problem of political failure. It should be kept in mind as you study these materials that public choice theory is not necessarily (and for many, is emphatically not) a normative theory of the political process. Rather it is an attempt to explain (and predict) the dynamics and outcomes of the political process. As with the economic models applied to traditional markets, the assumptions underlying public choice theory necessarily oversimplify real-world processes. Nonetheless, the analysis that flows from these assumptions provides important insights into the political process and perform reasonably well in explaining the outcomes of the legislative process in many, although by no means all, environmental contexts. As with the preceding materials, you should scrutinize the underlying assumptions carefully as you proceed through the materials that follow. In later chapters, we will address not only market failures but also political failures affecting the allocation of environmental resources.

ESKRIDGE, POLITICS WITHOUT ROMANCE: IMPLICATIONS OF PUBLIC CHOICE THEORY FOR STATUTORY INTERPRETATION

74 Va. L. Rev. 275 (1988)

I.   PUBLIC CHOICE THEORY AS A MADISONIAN NIGHTMARE

James Madison's essays on "factions" and the desirability of representative government in The Federalist have been the starting point for much American political theory. Self-interested factions are inevitable, and Madison believed that government must be structured to minimize their influence. Although Madison believed in self-government by "the great body of the people," he opposed direct democracy because he feared that factions would dominate and displace "the permanent and aggregate interests of the community." Decision by direct vote of the people might reflect nothing more than temporary majorities, formed out of inflamed passions or transient coalitions. Madison argued that a better way to effectuate "[t]he regulation of these various and interfering interests" was representative government. [T]he public voice, pronounced by the representatives of the people, will be more consonant to the public good than if pronounced by the people themselves, convened for the purpose."

Madison believed that structural features of the legislature would prevent the representatives themselves from being dominated by factions. As a large republic, the United States would have many representatives, each having a broad constituency. This would protect many representatives against being captured by any one faction. More important protections, moreover, would come from bicameralism and the executive veto. Bicameralism would not only provide a double review of proposed legislation, but also would assure two distinct perspectives.[35] The House of Representatives, with members from smaller districts and subject to electoral scrutiny every two years, would have an

---

35. The Federalist No. 51 (J. Madison). "In republican government," noted Madison, "the legislative authority necessarily predominates. The remedy for this inconveniency is to divide the legislature into different branches; and to render them, by different modes of election and different principles of action, as little connected with each other as the nature of their common functions and their common dependence on the society will admit." Id. at 322 (C. Rossiter ed. 1961).

"immediate dependence on, and an intimate sympathy with, the people." The Senate, whose members were originally elected by state legislatures for six-year terms, would have greater leisure to acquaint themselves with the issues and discuss them deliberatively. Finally, the President's veto power would give the official with the largest constituency the power to block factional legislation even if it got through both chambers of Congress.

The genius of Madison's thought lay in its reconciliation of our potentially antipodal desires for both legitimate majoritarian government and rational public-seeking government. The former was assured by vesting policymaking authority in the popularly elected legislature. The latter was abetted by a constitutional framework assuring deliberative lawmaking and checking factional domination. Madison's ideas have had a continuing influence in American political thought. After World War II, the prevailing political theory was an optimistic pluralism tied to Madison's ideas.[36] Although the pluralists of the 1950s accepted interest group domination of government, they were optimistic that the role of interest groups would not result in mere shifting, temporary majorities. Groups, it was hoped, would emerge on all sides of each issue and the protective procedures of lawmaking (bicameralism, the veto, committee review) would ensure rational accommodation of interest group needs.

A. THE ARBITRARINESS OF MAJORITY RULE

One branch of public choice theory examines legislation and voting as a game in which rational behavior by the game players yields unhappy results for the group as a whole. Consider a three-person legislature that does nothing but allocate tax money to build roads, with one project being voted on each year. Legislator A wants a new road for her district (Decision 1). Legislator B wants to repair a road in his district and invest the surplus funds (Decision 2) or, failing that, to build A's road, which will pass through B's district. Legislator C, whose district has good roads, wants to invest all the money (Decision 3). What will the legislature do with the money, under majority voting rules?

The answer is indeterminate, for the three decisions form a "majority cycle." A pairwise vote on Decision 1 versus Decision 2 would yield Decision 2 (B and C in the majority). A vote on Decision 2 versus Decision 3 would yield Decision 3 (A and C in the majority). Yet a vote on

---

36. Professor Theodore Lowi calls this "interest-group liberalism." T. Lowi, The End of Liberalism 51 (2d ed. 1979). Examples of optimistic pluralists are W. Binkley & M. Moos, A Grammar of American Politics (1949); R. Dahl, A Preface to Democratic Theory (1956); D. Truman, The Governmental Process (1951). All of these political philosophers start with Madison, and Dahl's book is an extended analysis of Madisonian theory.

Decision 3 (the winner in 2 versus 3) against Decision 1 (the loser in 1 versus 2) would yield Decision 1 (A and B in the majority)! In other words, depending on the order of pairwise voting, any of the decisions can be adopted. Professors Duncan Black and Kenneth Arrow argued that majority cycling is the typical phenomenon when complex choices must be made. Majority cycling suggests, at least, that results achieved under "democratic" voting rules are arbitrary. The mere fact that Decision 1 is adopted may mean nothing more than that Legislator A controls the agenda (e.g., holds the chair during the proceedings).

It gets worse. Expand the hypothetical to consider the potential social loss from majority voting, as Professors James Buchanan and Gordon Tullock did in their classic work The Calculus of Consent. Assume that Legislator A controls the agenda, so that Decision 1 is the last to pair up, winning against Decision 3. In addition, assume that the social benefit of Decision 1 is 100 (55 percent of which accrues to District A and 45 percent to District B) and that the social benefit of Decision 3 is 120 (shared equally by the three Districts). Obviously, from the collective point of view, the best decision is Decision 3 (no projects this year), yet a coalition of A and B will vote for Decision 1. This is not only unfair to C (which gets no benefit even though it pays taxes), but is collectively wasteful as well (to the tune of 20).[37]

A significant game theory lesson from the Buchanan and Tullock study is the importance of symmetrical costs and benefits. In simple voting games, there is a strong tendency toward social waste when benefits and costs are asymmetrical — as when a political decision concentrates costs on a minority (C in my hypothetical) in order to give more widely distributed benefits (to A and B). Such waste is less likely when costs and benefits are symmetrical — as when the political decision distributes both benefits and costs broadly across the population or concentrates benefits and costs very narrowly.

B.   THE DYSFUNCTIONAL INTEREST GROUP MARKET
FOR LEGISLATION

Subsequent public choice scholarship has broadened the lessons of game theory by analyzing the dynamics of interest group govern-

---

37. As Buchanan and Tullock note, the dynamics of this can be changed by allowing side payments (logrolling). To avoid being closed out entirely, C can offer B up to 40 to persuade B to change its vote to Decision 3. This is an important caveat to the horrible results described in the text, but Buchanan and Tullock also demonstrate that even with side payments, winning coalitions will often form for decisions in which the total collective gains will be less than total expenditures (or the potential gains of another decision). See J. Buchanan & G. Tullock, supra note 33, at 155-157.

ment. Public choice theorists typically treat legislation as an economic transaction in which interest groups form the demand side, and legislators form the supply side.[38] On the whole, this branch of public choice theory demonstrates that the market for legislation is a badly functioning one. That is, the market systematically yields too few laws that provide "public goods" (i.e., laws that contribute to the overall efficiency of society by providing a collective benefit that would probably not arise from individuals acting separately). And it systematically yields too many laws that are "rent-seeking" (i.e., laws that distribute resources to a designated group without any contribution to society's overall efficiency).

The demand for legislation is determined by the incidence and activity of interest groups. The optimistic pluralists believed that interest groups would form in response to true disturbances in the social environment and, hence, normally would press legitimate grievances and would bring a variety of socioeconomic perspectives into the subsequent political debates. Public choice theory suggests, however, that interest groups form more selectively and, therefore, that the demand for legislation is highly biased.

Professor Mancur Olson's "logic of collective action" helps to explain why interest groups form so selectively. He argues that interest group formation involves a classic "free rider problem." Legislation is a "nonexcludable" public good that will benefit all members of the affected group even if they do not contribute to its enactment. Because group members will have incentives to free ride (i.e., collect the benefit without contributing to the effort), not enough members will contribute, and the public good will not be provided. The free rider problem is most acute for large groups in which individual stakes will usually be very small, for there the tendency to rely on others to carry the ball will be quite substantial. The problem is less acute for small groups, especially where the potential gain for each beneficiary is larger, because in those groups there is more opportunity for the members to work out a collective deal, and free riders can more easily be monitored and perhaps excluded from the law's benefits. This is most likely if the small

---

38. Some scholars, however, analyze the transaction as one in which one interest group obtains benefits at the expense of other groups or society as a whole; legislators are treated as brokers or agents who effectuate the transfer. E.g., R. McCormick & R. Tollison, Politicians, Legislation and the Economy (1981). The more common analysis, and the one employed here, treats legislation as a sale by legislators to interest groups.

Important sources for the analysis in this Part are M. Hayes, Lobbyists and Legislators (1981); M. Olson, The Logic of Collective Action (1965); J. Q. Wilson, Political Organizations (1973); Salisbury, An Exchange Theory of Interest Groups, 13 Midwest J. Pol. Sci. 1 (1969).

group enjoys consensus about its goals, for consensus substantially reduces the transaction costs of group formation.

The free rider problem means that social and economic difficulties will not always stimulate group formation, especially for large, diffuse groups like consumers and taxpayers, and that (in contrast) small, elite groups might more easily organize, though for no other reason than to raid the public fisc. These conclusions are, however, expressed in probabilities only. Olson recognized that large groups could form if there were selective benefits for their members (e.g., the information sharing and cooperative economic action that farm organizations offer their members), or if members were coerced to join (e.g., professional associations). Additionally, subsequent public choice scholarship has demonstrated that large groups will sometimes be fueled by shared ideological interests, well-recognized threats, and historical factors. Nonetheless, Olson's main point, that different groups will enjoy highly variant abilities to overcome the free rider problem, has received some empirical support and is widely accepted in the public choice literature.

Formal organization of an interest group is important if that group is to wield substantial influence in the political arena. Groups that are formally organized and willing to spend money to obtain or block legislation will tend to monopolize the attention of legislators, at the expense of groups that are not organized. The latter will not only fail to press their point of view, but will also be subject to manipulation: they may not recognize the harms they will suffer from proposed legislation and, even if informed, may be falsely reassured by symbolic action. Notably, however, unorganized interests may still have an impact if their preferences are strong and commonly held, for public opinion itself works as an important constraint on legislative action.

In a very rough way, one may plot probable demand for legislation by looking at the incidence of costs and benefits. Costs associated with legislation may be broadly distributed, as through a general tax increase or a rule applicable to the whole population, or narrowly concentrated, such as through a user fee or a license charge. Similarly, legislation may offer benefits that are broadly distributed, such as roads or other public goods, or concentrated, such as a subsidy or monopoly grant to a specific group. Under Olson's theory, one would expect concentrated benefits and, especially, concentrated costs to stimulate more interest group formation, because the smaller and more focused groups will normally be better able to surmount the free rider problem. Conversely, distributed costs or benefits will presumably not tend to produce as much organizational activity.

The supply of legislation depends on the responses of legislators to these demand patterns. Optimistic pluralists paid little attention to the incentive structures of elected representatives and generally just assumed that the representatives' policy choices represented some kind of amalgam of constituency preferences and reasonable judgment. Public choice theorists, however, suggest that representatives' supply of legislation is driven by a desire to avoid controversy and, hence, is skewed toward nondecision and rent-seeking.

Public choice theory argues that legislative behavior is driven by one central goal — the legislator's desire to be reelected. A legislator seeking reelection faces the "dilemma of ungrateful electorate": the good things a legislator does for an interest group are forgotten more easily than the bad things are forgiven. To avoid this dilemma, a legislator will typically try to avoid or finesse "conflictual" demand patterns. On the one hand, the legislator will seek out "consensual" demand patterns — issues on which her constituency is not divided. Thus, a legislator will spend a great deal of time doing "casework" (no one is hurt by this and constituents for whom favors are done are obviously happy) and "pork barreling" (from which the district received tangible goodies, paid for out of general revenues). At the same time, the legislator will try to avoid taking hard positions on those issues that divide her constituents. But on those issues around which important and organized groups have formed, the legislator will try to help the groups, though in ways that will — she hopes — escape the notice of the legislator's other constituents. On the other hand, when a legislator cannot avoid conflictual demand patterns, she will try to satisfy all the relevant interest groups through a compromise statute acceptable to all concerned. If this cannot be accomplished, the legislator's next-best strategy will be to support an ambiguous law, with details to be filled in later by courts or agencies. In that way, the legislator will be able to assure each group that it won, and then will be able to blame a court or agency if subsequent developments belie that assurance.

One can predict what sort of legislative output is likely, again, based on the incidence of costs and benefits. Legislation — whether symbolic or substantive — is unlikely where there is little organized demand (distributed benefits), or where demand is met by strong opposition (because of concentrated costs). And if such legislation is enacted, because demand is so weak, the legislation will generally not subsequently be updated to reflect changed circumstances. In situations of consensual demand patterns (primarily concentrated benefit, distributed cost measures), legislators will tend to distribute benefits to organized groups, or to grant those groups self-regulatory authority. In conflictual demand situations (concentrated cost measures), legislators will often seek to delegate regulation of the group to an agency. If the legislation distributes benefits at the expense of a concentrated group, the cost payers will tend, over time, to organize themselves effectively to influence the agency. This phenomenon, together with natural bu-

TABLE [2.2]
An Interest Group Model of Legislation

Distributed benefit/
distributed cost

Usually little interest group formation on issue. Unless there is
strong consensus on issue,
likely legislative action is no bill
or symbolic action. If law is enacted, the legislature will generally fail to monitor the
legislation's performance effectively, or to update it.

Distributed benefit/
concentrated cost

Opposition groups tend to be
stronger than support ones. Conflictual demand pattern: no bill or
delegation to agency regulation. If
the latter, agency tends to become
"captured" over time by interests
of the regulated group.

Concentrated benefit/
distributed cost

Often strong interest group activity supporting action. Consensual demand pattern if public is
ill-informed: Distribution of
benefits to organized inter-
est(s) or self-regulation for the
organized interest. Classic rent-
seeking legislation.

Concentrated benefit/
concentrated cost

Interest groups will tend to form on
both sides of issue. Conflictual demand pattern: no bill or delegation to agency regulation where
the organized interests can continue their clash.

reaucratic forces, results in what is often called "agency capture." (If
the legislation concentrates both benefits and costs, the agency will become a battleground for the competing interests.) Table [2.2] above
summarizes the demand and supply patterns for legislation.

NOTES AND QUESTIONS

In view of the pervasiveness of environmental collective goods and
externality problems in modern society and the high transaction costs
associated with resolving them, do you think that the capitalist form
of social organization is well-suited to allocating resources? Might not
socialism be better-suited? Consider in this regard the experience of
the former Soviet Union. Although the Soviet Union's economy was
not driven by "private profit," data from the past few decades indicate
that the government had placed a premium on economic growth at the
expense of environmental amenities. Since plant managers were often
evaluated on the basis of manufacturing output, adverse environmental
effects were often ignored. In many cases, this led to greater environ-

mental degradation than in the West. In addition to such catastrophes as the nuclear accident at Chernobyl and the extensive pollution of the Aral Sea, many of the densely populated areas of the former Soviet Union and Eastern Europe suffer from severe air and water pollution. Therefore, although centrally planned systems may avoid some of the disincentives created by the private-cost/social-cost dichotomy in capitalist systems, central planning may introduce other adverse incentives. Marshall Goldman, an expert on environmental policy in the former Soviet Union, concludes that "[i]f the study of environmental disruption in the Soviet Union demonstrates anything, it shows that not private enterprise but industrialization is the primary cause of environmental disruption. This suggests that state ownership of all the productive resources is no cure-all." Goldman, The Convergence of Environmental Disruption, in Ecology and Economics: Controlling Pollution in the 1970's 2 (M. Goldman ed. 1972); see also Goldman, Economics of Environmental and Renewable Resources in Socialist Systems, Part 1: Russia, in Handbook of Natural Resource and Energy Economics 725-746 (A. Kneese & J. Sweeney eds., 1985); M. Goldman, The Spoils of Progress: Environmental Pollution in the Soviet Union (1972). Does the Soviet experience preclude the possibility that some other socialist state could be more environmentally sound? Cf. S. Tsuru, Economics of Environmental and Renewable Resources in Socialist Systems, Part 2: China, in Handbook of Natural Resource and Energy Economics 746-749 (A. Kneese & J. Sweeney eds. 1985).

C. COST-BENEFIT ANALYSIS

As the previous section explained, from the perspective of the utilitarian framework underlying economic analysis, the market often provides too little of collective goods and too much of negative externalities. But how do we know what is "too little" and what is "too much"? And how should government determine the best policies to remedy these failings of the market? This section describes an important and widely used tool for considering these questions: cost-benefit analysis.

Cost-benefit analysis is of more than just theoretical importance to the study of environmental law and policy. In many instances, the law requires that cost-benefit analysis be used in environmental decisionmaking. For example, the Federal Power Act and the National Environmental Policy Act require the Federal Energy Regulatory Commission to consider all costs and benefits in deciding whether to license hydroelectric projects. Under Executive Order 12,291, 46 Fed. Reg. 13193 (1981), all executive branch regulatory agencies must conduct extensive cost-benefit analyses for major regulatory decisions and, to the extent permitted by statute, promulgate the most cost-effective policy to achieve a particular regulatory objective.

In theory, cost-benefit analysis provides an objective and rigorous framework for evaluating public policy choices. As you will see throughout our study of its applications, however, cost-benefit analysis is prone to a high degree of subjectivity in practice. Because of this and because of the normative assumptions that underlie cost-benefit analysis, the application of cost-benefit analysis to many environmental problems is controversial. In order to prepare you to participate in this debate, this section provides a concise description of how cost-benefit analysis is performed.[39] We postpone discussion of the theoretical and practical limitations of cost-benefit analysis until Part D of this chapter and numerous encounters with applications of cost-benefit analysis later in this book in connection with court cases, statutes, and other legal materials.

The first section describes the basic accounting system of cost-benefit analysis in a model in which all costs are incurred and all benefits realized with complete certainty in one period. We then discuss the evaluation of projects and policies in a model in which streams of costs and benefits occur over multiple time periods. The third section discusses the implementation of cost-benefit analysis in the presence of uncertainty about the magnitude and timing of costs and benefits. The last section distinguishes cost-benefit analysis from cost-effectiveness analysis, a related public policy tool.

1.   BASIC ANALYTICS

From the economist's perspective, the role for government policy is to ensure that the maximum net social surplus — the difference between consumers' willingness to pay and total social cost — is attained for all goods (and services) valued by members of the society. Where the requirements of perfect competition are met, the market mechanism itself will achieve the maximum net social surplus. In markets in which some benefits or costs are not captured in markets prices, the market mechanism will not achieve the maximum net social surplus. The government must intervene to overcome distortions in the market or, where no market has formed, to allocate resources directly.

Cost-benefit analysis seeks to measure directly the impact of alter-

39. For more detailed and advanced treatments of cost-benefit analysis, the interested reader might wish to consult: D. Pearce & C. Nash, The Social Appraisal of Projects; A Text in Cost-Benefit Analysis (1981); R. Tresch, Public Finance: A Normative Theory chapters 23-28 (1981); E. Stokey & R. Zeckhauser, A Primer for Policy Analysis (1978); E. Mishan, Cost-Benefit Analysis (1976); H. Raiffa Decision Analysis (1968).

native projects and policies on consumers' willingness to pay for goods (benefits) and the total social costs (costs) of providing such goods. The process for conducting cost-benefit analysis is straightforward: [40]

    (1)   Identify all relevant policy alternatives (including no action);

    (2)   Determine all impacts of the alternatives;

    (3)   Calculate values for all of the impacts (favorable impacts are considered benefits; unfavorable impacts are considered costs); and

    (4)   Calculate the net benefits (total benefits less total costs) for each alternative.

In view of the economic objective of maximizing net social surplus, the decision criterion for choosing public policies and projects is simple: select the alternative that produces the highest net benefit. (Does this criterion always lead to Pareto-superior allocations of resources? Kaldor-Hicks efficiency?)

To illustrate cost-benefit analysis, consider again the water pollution problem discussed earlier at pp. 63-64. Assume for our present purposes that the factory possesses the entitlement to pollute and that transaction costs prevent the fishery from bargaining to an efficient allocation of resources under this assignment of the entitlement. Consequently, the government seeks to consider alternative policies to achieve the maximum social surplus in the markets affected. Table 2.3 shows the cost-benefit analysis for the four available policy options. Applying the suggested decision criterion, it is clear that a policy of requiring primary and secondary treatment maximizes the net benefits.

It is important to realize that we have greatly simplified the water pollution problem for illustrative purposes. In particular, we consid-

TABLE 2.3

Policy options	Benefits (from production)		Costs (pollution abatement equipment)	Net benefits
	Fishery	Factory		
A. do nothing	0	1,000,000	0	1,000,000
B. require primary treatment	480,000	1,000,000	125,000	1,355,000
C. require primary and secondary treatment	1,000,000	1,000,000	600,000	1,400,000
D. prohibit discharge	1,200,000	0	0	1,200,000

40. See E. Stokey & R. Zeckhauser, A Primer for Policy Analysis 136 (1978).

ered only a limited set of policy options and assumed that the only relevant impacts are on the fishery and the factory and that such impacts are easily quantifiable. More realistically, water pollution policies and environmental policies generally have a broad range of impacts that must all be assessed in a careful cost-benefit analysis.

We discuss below the range of impacts that often arise in cost-benefit analysis of policies and projects affecting the environment and the principal methods for quantifying these impacts. It is important to keep in mind that within the utilitarian framework of cost-benefit analysis, we are concerned solely with the value of resources to humans. While the value of natural resources to humans can encompass a broad range of active and passive uses — from recreation to existence value — the framework nonetheless is inherently anthropocentric, a fact which might seem anomalous to many concerned with the environment. In order to enable you to focus more directly upon the economic perspective, we postpone discussion of the appropriateness of this perspective until later in this chapter.

a.   Direct Policy and Project Costs

Direct costs of environmental policies and projects comprise the resources that must be expended to implement the policy or build the project. For the water pollution problem above, these are the costs of purchasing and installing primary and secondary treatment equipment and the costs of operating it (labor, treatment chemicals, waste disposal fees, and replacement equipment). For a hydroelectric project, as an example, the direct resource costs include the costs of construction (land acquisition, materials, equipment, and labor), operation, and maintenance. In general, these resources should be valued according to their best alternative use, or *opportunity cost.* The opportunity costs of many resources are accurately reflected in market prices and wage rates. In the case of some unique resources, however, like the land for the hydroelectric plant, the opportunity cost is not necessarily current market value. If the government has an alternative use for the land that would produce net social surplus above the current market value, then the opportunity cost is the net social surplus. Notwithstanding this important caveat, direct project costs do not typically present difficult valuation problems.[41]

---

41. Valuation problems do arise, however, if the policy or project has such large effects as to alter relative prices and/or wages.

b.   Commercial Impacts

As the water pollution problem above illustrates, environmental policies can have effects on markets for goods and services. In many cases, these effects can be measured directly by reference to market prices for the goods and services in the economy, which reflect marginal social resource cost. A more careful valuation of these impacts can be derived from the demand and supply curves for the goods and services at issue. The analyst attempts to measure the loss or gain in consumer surplus and producer profits. While this is easy to conceptualize in theory, it is often difficult in practice to estimate the demand and supply curves. Economists have developed a number of empirical techniques for estimating these curves.

c.   Health Effects

Among the more important benefits of environmental policies are health improvement and reduction in health care costs and mortality. As with other resources, the appropriate economic measure of the value of life and limb is willingness to pay. As might be expected, however, asking people how much they would be willing to pay to avoid injury or death is not a very reliable valuation technique. Consequently, economists have had to develop indirect methods for placing a value on health impairment and life. The most widely accepted method is to draw inferences about valuation from peoples' actual behavior in the face of health risks.[42] Many studies estimate willingness to pay for life and limb from data on wage differentials received by workers in jobs featuring different occupational risks. Complex statistical techniques separate out the portions of the wage attributable to other variables such as education and experience. Similar techniques use data on choices regarding residential location and use of safety devices (such as smoke alarms and seat belts) to assess the extent to which individuals are willing to pay to reduce the risk of injury or death. Though some

---

42. In the 1950s and 1960s, the dominant methodology for valuing human life sought to measure a person's contribution to national income. In a path-breaking article, Thomas Schelling cogently criticized this approach and framed the analysis in terms of statistical lives: "What is it worth to reduce the probability of death — the statistical frequency of death — within some identifiable group of people none of whom expects to die except eventually?" T. Schelling, The Life You Save May Be Your Own, in Problems in Public Expenditure Analysis 127 (S. Chase ed. 1968). This insight led analysts to look to preferences individuals reveal through their behavior.

estimates of the value of life are as high as several million dollars, most estimates are between half a million and five million dollars.

d.   Recreational, Ecosystem, and Aesthetic Impacts

Pollution and public projects disrupting use of natural resources (such as hydroelectric projects that inundate scenic valleys and interrupt river flows) cause significant losses of welfare. Because the uses that these phenomena disrupt — such as clean air and wild and scenic rivers — are often collective goods, there are not available market prices that accurately reflect the social value of these uses. Economists have developed a variety of techniques for measuring peoples' willingness to pay for clean air, recreational opportunities, and other such amenities.

By a method similar to those used in valuing life, economists measure pollution costs by studying variations in property values in different areas featuring different air qualities (using statistical techniques to separate out the effects of other factors such as neighborhood attributes, social services, and transportation services).

A variety of methods are used to value recreational opportunities. The contingent valuation method (CVM) relies upon surveys of natural resource users to determine how much they would be willing to pay for changes in recreational opportunities at a particular park. See generally R. Cummings, D. Brookshire & W. Schulze, Valuing Environmental Goods: An Assessment of the Contingent Valuation Method (1986). Responses to surveys, however, are often unreliable because respondents are not required to spend any of their own money to back up their responses and hence may strategically overstate their true "willingness to pay" in order to influence survey results. An alternative technique for valuing recreational amenities is to estimate the demand curve for recreation at a particular site using the travel cost method (TCM). The TCM constructs the demand curve on the basis of the travel costs that people are willing to incur to enjoy a particular site. A third method, called hedonic pricing, attempts to place a value on each of the attributes of the public resource — pure air, scenic vistas, etc. — by reference to premia people pay for these attributes in market transactions (such as differences in land values).

Ecosystem effects of public policies and projects, such as wildlife, vegetation, and soil erosion impacts, should also be evaluated. Because of the anthropocentric focus of cost-benefit analysis, however, these effects would only be valued to the extent people are willing to pay for them. Thus, these effects are captured by analysis of recreational demand and aesthetic preferences, the likelihood of and losses from floods or other adverse land, water, and air quality effects, demand for products derived from wildlife and vegetation (such as drugs derived from certain species), and human concern for archeological and historical impacts.

e.   Option and Existence Values

Because of the uncertainty regarding and irreversibility of some environmental impacts, members of the society may be willing to pay to reduce the risks of serious environmental damage. See Arrow & Fisher, Environmental Preservation, Uncertainty, and Irreversibility, 88 Quarterly J. Econ. 312 (1974); P. Dasgupta, The Control of Resources (1982). (We discuss the concept of risk aversion in more detail below). Option value is defined as the maximum amount (above use value) that an individual would be willing to pay for an option to ensure access to an environmental amenity at some future date. In addition to current and potential use values, individuals may be willing to pay for the preservation of a resource that they have no intent or even wish to use. This might reflect their pleasure from the fact that other people have or future generations will have access to the resource if it is preserved. (Can you think of any indications of the importance of existence value in our society?)

Option value and existence value are extremely difficult to measure. The contingent valuation method can be used. Another method has been to try to determine a proportional relationship between use and nonuse values.

Notwithstanding the important advances in techniques for valuing costs and benefits of policies and projects affecting the environment, it should be evident that there remain difficult problems with valuing many environmental impacts. Environmental projects and policies often have many orders of effects. For example, the direct or first-order effect of a policy or project on an ecosystem — such as the construction costs of a bridge to an island — may over time spawn numerous second-order effects — such as widespread development of the island — possibly as large or larger than the first-order effect. A careful cost-benefit analysis should measure all of these effects, but given the limitations of the analyst's imagination and our knowledge of science, the analysis may prove inadequate. Even if all of the pathways are identified, there are serious limitations on our ability to quantify intangible effects such as aesthetic and existence value.

2.   COST-BENEFIT ANALYSIS WITH MULTIPLE PERIODS: THE CONCEPT OF PRESENT VALUE

Most public policies and projects generate streams of costs and benefits over many years. In order to evaluate such undertakings, we need a method for relating streams of net benefits across time periods. The concept of present value collapses streams of costs and benefits for alternative policies into one metric that can be directly compared across policies.

As an illustration of this concept, we will modify the water pollution problem to reflect the flow of profits and pollution control expenditures over time. To simplify the analysis, we will consider an eight-year time horizon. Under the policy of no controls, the factory will earn a profit of $125,000 per year; the fishery zero. If the government requires the factory to install primary treatment, the factory must make an initial capital outlay of $85,000 and annual maintenance expenses of $5000. The factory, therefore, has a net profit of $35,000 in the first year and $120,000 in subsequent years. The fishery earns $60,000 per year. If the government requires the factory to install primary and secondary treatment, the factory must spend $520,000 in the first year on capital equipment and $10,000 per year on maintenance. This will cause the factory to incur a net loss of $405,000 in the first year; it will earn a profit of $115,000 in subsequent years. The fishery will earn $125,000 per year with this technology in place. If the government prohibits the discharge, the factory will have to close down, enabling the fishery to earn $150,000 per year. This stream of net benefits for these policies is summarized in Table 2.4.

Which policy should be selected? If we were simply to add up the streams of net benefits, Policy C would be preferable. But is a dollar in net benefits received today worth the same as a dollar received in 1, 5, 20, or even 100 years? It seems not. If you received a dollar today and invested it in a savings account offering 5 percent annual interest, it would be worth $1.05 next year, $1.28 in 5 years, $2.65 in 20 years, and $131.50 in 100 years. This reflects the fact that money invested

TABLE 2.4
($ thousands)

Policy	1	2	3	4	5	6	7	8	Total
A. No Controls	125	125	125	125	125	125	125	125	1,000
B. Primary Treatment	95	180	180	180	180	180	180	180	1,355
C. Primary + Secondary	−280	240	240	240	240	240	240	240	1,400
D. Ban Discharge	150	150	150	150	150	150	150	150	1,200

in productive ventures increases in value over time. The interest rate represents the rate at which investments will increase in value.

In evaluating public policies, we must also take into account the productiveness of resources over time. This time value is a part of the opportunity cost of the project. Resources not expended today may be worth more tommorrow.

Cost-benefit analysis compares projects producing different net benefit streams by determining what amount of money invested today at an appropriate discount rate would generate the particular net benefit streams under consideration. This *present value* can then be compared across policies to determine which policy is the most valuable. This section first discusses how streams of net benefits are translated into a present value. It then discusses some theoretical issues regarding the choice of the discount rate used in performing the present value calculation.

a.   The Calculation of Present Value

Assume for our present purposes that the appropriate discount rate is 5 percent. To simplify our discussion, assume that the policy we wish to evaluate will generate $1 per year in year 0 (the current period) through year n, and nothing thereafter. Our objective is to answer the following questions: What amount of money invested today would produce this stream of net benefits? Obviously, any net benefit realized in the current period is the same as an investment today, that is, the present value of $1 received in the current period is $1.

Continuing to the first period, what amount of money invested today will produce $1 a year from now? We denote the amount invested today as PV_1. With a 5 percent discount rate, we know that:

$$PV_1(1+.05) = \$1$$

In words, PV_1 is an amount invested today that will grow by a factor of 1 plus the discount rate (.05) so as to equal $1 a year from now. Dividing, we see that:

$$PV_1 = \$1/(1+.05) = 95.24 \text{ cents}$$

Thus an investment of 95.24 cents today will produce $1 a year from now. Hence the present value of $1 received in year 1 is 95.24 cents. This process can be iterated to determine the present value of a stream of $1 receipts. The net present value (NPV) of a stream of $1 per year for n years is:

$$NPV = \$1 + \$1/(1.05) + \$1/(1.05)^2 + \ldots + \$1/(1.05)^n$$

This same basic discounting formula applies if instead of receiving $1 per year, society were to receive any amount of net benefits (NB_i) per year. Thus, the net present value of a stream of net benefits of NB_0 in year 0, NB_1 in year 1, NB_2 in year 2, through NB_n in year n discounted at a rate d is:

$$NPV[NB_0, NB_1, NB_2, \ldots NB_n] = NB_0 + NB_1/(1+d) + NB_2/(1+d)^2 + \ldots + NB_n/(1+d)^n$$

We are now prepared to compare the streams of net benefits generated by the water pollution policies described in Table 2.4. Table 2.5 applies our net present value formula to this policy decision using a 5 percent discount rate. Applying our decision criterion of choosing the project that produces the highest net benefit, the society would prefer only to require primary treatment.

TABLE 2.5
($ thousands)

		1	2	3	4	5	6	7	8	NPV
A.	future value	125	125	125	125	125	125	125	125	
	present value	125	113	108	103	98	93	89	85	814
B.	future value	95	180	180	180	180	180	180	180	
	present value	95	163	155	148	141	134	128	122	1,086
C.	future value	−280	240	240	240	240	240	240	240	
	present value	−280	218	207	197	188	179	171	162	1,042
D.	future value	150	150	150	150	150	150	150	150	
	present value	150	136	130	123	117	112	107	102	977

b.   The Discount Rate

Thus far, we have assumed that 5 percent is the appropriate discount rate for evaluating the power projects. What if we had used another discount rate? At discount rates below 3 percent, primary and secondary treatment is preferred. At discount rates between 3 percent and 52 percent, primary treatment is preferred. And at discount rates above 52 percent, banning discharge is preferred. This is because at higher discount rates, net benefit streams in the near term are significantly more important than net benefits received far in the future. The future is less important. Since the pollution control policies have high start-up costs with higher net benefits coming in the future, they are less attractive vis-à-vis banning discharges when the discount rate is sufficiently high.

As this example highlights, net present value calculations can be highly sensitive to the discount rate. Thus, our decision about which policy to undertake depends on what discount rate we use. If we choose too low a discount rate, we will be biased toward projects featuring higher net benefits far in the future. We also risk undertaking too many projects. If we choose too high a discount rate, we will overly favor projects with lower initial investments and quicker payback periods. We also unduly discourage projects.

Two critical questions arise: (1) which discount rate should be chosen for evaluating private projects, and (2) whether society should use a different discount rate for evaluating public projects and policies from what we use for private projects. With regard to the first question, economists agree that the discount rate that should be used in deciding on private projects — for instance, whether to build a new factory — is the rate of return that the private entity could earn on alternative investments of equal risk. Thus, the discount rate should be the opportunity cost of capital for the private entity.

When we turn to the question of what discount rate to apply to public projects and policies, we do not find a similar consensus among economists. Two views are most prominent. One view relies principally upon the fact that public investments have the effect of displacing resources — land, labor, and capital — that would otherwise be used for private consumption or investments. Therefore, according to this view, the appropriate discount rate for public projects is the rate of return generally available in the private sector, see A. Harberger, Project Evaluation: Collected Papers (1974); see also R. Mikesell, The Rate of Discount for Evaluating Public Projects (1977), which is typically estimated as the long-term interest rate on government bonds. The other view holds that the discount rate should reflect society's rate of time preference, which is based on the rate at which society trades off consumption today for consumption in the future. See Arrow, Discounting and Public Investment Criteria, in Water Resources Research (A. Kneese & S. Smith eds. 1966). This debate is ably summarized and assessed in R. Tresch, Public Finance: A Normative Theory 486-507 (1981).

Prior to the 1970s, the federal government did not have any consistent policy regarding what discount rate to use for public projects.[43]

---

43. A congressional hearing in 1969 brought out the fact that agencies were using discount rates as low as 0 percent and as high as 20 percent in evaluating projects. See Proxmire, PPB, the Agencies and the Congress, in The Analysis and Evaluation of Public Expenditures: The PPB System xiii (U.S. Cong., Joint Economic Committee, Subcommittee on Economy in Government) (1969).

In the 1970s, the Office of Management and Budget issued a circular requiring, with some exceptions, all government agencies to use a discount rate of 10 percent in their cost-benefit analyses. While this uniform rate helps to make decisionmaking across government agencies consistent, it is not clear that the 10 percent rate is appropriate for all government projects. Many economists and legal scholars today believe that the government should use a discount rate in the 1-2 percent range for evaluating projects and policies with intergenerational effects. See Farber & Hemersbaugh, The Shadow of the Future: Discount Rates, Later Generations, and the Environment, 46 Vand. L. Rev. 267 (1993). As we saw above, assumptions about the discount rate can be extremely important, especially when considering long range environmental projects and policies such as those to address climate change, lower atmosphere air pollution (such as mass transportation planning), and natural resource planning (such as hydroelectric plants). Thus, we will confront this important methodological issue throughout the study of environmental law and policy.

3.   COST-BENEFIT ANALYSIS AND UNCERTAINTY: THE CONCEPT OF EXPECTED VALUE

Thus far our analysis has proceeded upon the assumption that all net benefit streams are known with certainty. Predictions of the future, however, are rarely perfect, especially when policies and projects depend upon inherently random factors (such as weather) and incompletely understood scientific, technological, and economic factors, as is often the case in the environmental field. The treatment of uncertainty and risk will be particularly important when dealing with the regulation of toxic materials. Thus, we need to develop a way of addressing uncertainty within our cost-benefit framework.

To illustrate the treatment of uncertainty in cost-benefit analysis, we will modify our water pollution problem to take into consideration the risk that dry weather conditions can exacerbate the effects of effluents on fish populations. Scientists predict that the presence of 30 tons of pollutants in the estuary during a severe rare drought (1 in 10 probability) will reduce the fish population dramatically — resulting in a 50 percent reduction in net fishery profits.[44] A moderate drought (3 in 10 probability) will reduce fishery profits by 10 percent. In the presence of 10 tons of pollutants, a severe drought will reduce fishery profits by 20 percent; a moderate drought will not affect the fishery. How do we incorporate this uncertainty into the cost-benefit analysis?

---

44. To focus attention on the role of uncertainty, we will assume that all costs and benefits occur in one period. The data for this scenario is contained in Table 2.1.

The problem raised by uncertainty is similar to the problem raised by the receipt of net benefits over time. In order to compare policies subject to different types of uncertainty, we need to use a common metric that reflects the risks affecting the range of policies or projects under consideration. In the context of the receipt of net benefits over time, we were able to compute a net present value by discounting the stream of net benefits by an appropriate discount rate. In the context of uncertain policies or projects, we can compute the "expected value" of the policy or project, which represents the best estimate of the value of the project in light of our estimates of the probabilities of the possible outcomes and the values of such outcomes.

This section first describes how to construct a decision-flow diagram — an extremely useful framework for analyzing decisionmaking under uncertainty — and how to calculate the total expected value for each project from this diagram. It then discusses the role of risk aversion in the evaluation of public projects. The final section describes risk-benefit analysis, a specialized technique of cost-benefit analysis used for evaluating policies for the regulation of environmental risks.

a. Constructing a Decision-Flow Diagram (Decision Tree)

The first difficulty in deciding among the water pollution policies is how to represent the choices conceptually. The decision-flow diagram[45] or decision tree provides a useful construct for seeing the logical structure of decision problem. Decision trees have four elements:

(1) *decision nodes*, which indicate all possible courses of action to the policymaker (represented by a box);
(2) *chance nodes*, which indicate the uncertain events and all possible outcomes (represented by a circle);
(3) *probabilities*, which describe the likelihood of each possible outcome; and
(4) *payoffs*, the net present value of the particular outcomes.

Diagram 2.1 shows the decision tree for the water pollution policies. The flow of the diagram is from left to right. The decision node at the far left (represented by a box) indicates that there are four choices

---

45. This framework is developed in much more detail in H. Raiffa, Decision Analysis (1968); see also E. Stokey & R. Zeckhauser, supra note 39, at 201-254.

DIAGRAM 2.1
Evaluation of Water Pollution Policy Options Decision Tree
(thousands of dollars)

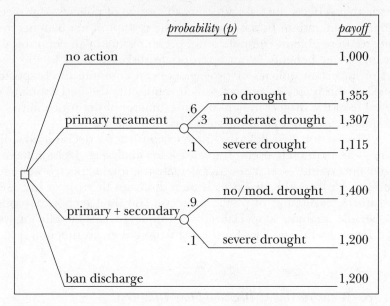

open to the decisionmaker: no action, primary treatment, primary and secondary treatment, and ban discharge. The no action and ban discharge options are completely certain;[46] their payoffs are represented at the right. The treatment policies, however, have uncertain payoffs. The chance nodes (represented by circles) show the possible outcomes for each of these policies and the probabilities of each outcome. Note that the sum of the probabilities for each chance node must equal 1. At the far right of the diagram are the net social benefits of the particular outcomes.

From this diagram, we can calculate the total expected value of each project. Before we do this, however, we need to explain what an expected value represents. As an illustration, consider a game in which a six-sided die (with 1 through 6 dots on the respective sides) is thrown and the player is awarded $1 for each dot that appears on the top of the die when it comes to rest. Assume also that each side of the die has equal probability of coming up. What is the best estimate of how much the player will win in one play of this game? With probability 1/6, the

---

46. We assume that droughts interact with pollution to cause fish kills. In the absence of pollution, there is no effect on the fishery.

DIAGRAM 2.2
Evaluation of Water Pollution Policy Options Decision Tree
(thousands of dollars)

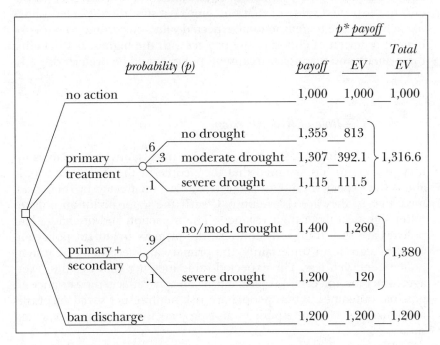

		probability (p)		payoff	p* payoff EV	Total EV
no action				1,000	1,000	1,000
		no drought		1,355	813	
primary treatment	.6 .3	moderate drought		1,307	392.1	1,316.6
	.1	severe drought		1,115	111.5	
primary + secondary	.9	no/mod. drought		1,400	1,260	1,380
	.1	severe drought		1,200	120	
ban discharge				1,200	1,200	1,200

die will land with 1 dot facing upward and the player will win $1. Therefore, the expected value of the outcome 1 dot is 1/6th of $1 or $1/6. Similarly, the expected value of the outcome 2 dots is 1/6th of $2 or $2/6. Likewise, the expected values of outcomes 3 dots, 4 dots, 5 dots, and 6 dots are $3/6, $4/6, $5/6, and $6/6 respectively. The total expected value of the game is simply the sum of the expected values of the possible outcomes.[47] Therefore, the total expected value for the game is $(1+2+3+4+5+6)/6 or $21/6 or $3.5.

Similarly, we can calculate the expected values for each outcome of each policy on the decision tree. Diagram 2.2 illustrates this calculation. Since the no action and ban discharge policies have no uncer-

---

47. In general, the total expected value of set of possible outcomes occurring with probabilities p_1 through p_n and having expected values EV_1 through EV_n is:

$$\sum_{i=1}^{n} p_i{}^*EV_i = p_1{}^*EV_1 + p_2{}^*EV_2 + \ldots + p_n EV_n$$

tainty, we merely multiply their net present values by 1 to obtain their expected values. For the treatment policies, we multiply the payoff for each outcome by the probability of that outcome's occurrence to obtain the expected value of that outcome. We sum the expected values of each outcome to get the total expected value. According to our cost-benefit criterion of choosing the project with the highest net benefits, the primary and secondary treatment policy would be preferred.[48]

b.   *The Role of Risk Aversion*

In evaluating decisionmaking under uncertainty, our analysis up until this point has assumed that the people in the society care only about the expected value of projects and are unaffected by their riskiness, that is, they are risk neutral. Clearly the water pollution policies differ significantly in their riskiness. The no action and discharge ban policies are sure things. By contrast, the primary treatment policy engenders significant uncertainty, the primary and secondary treatment policy somewhat less. The expected value measure captures the "average" outcome for each project, but in no way reflects the variance of possible outcomes. When people are risk neutral, net social surplus is maximized by choosing policies and projects that maximize expected value.

We know, however, that most people are risk averse. By this we mean that as between one policy offering a risky (that is, high variance) although high expected return and another project offering a certain although slightly lower return, most people would prefer the latter. For example, many people would prefer a sure benefit of $950 to a lottery featuring a 50 percent chance of winning $2000 and a 50 percent chance of winning nothing. If someone were indifferent between the sure thing ($950) and the lottery (expected value of $1000), the $50 premium (in expectation) that they were willing give up to avoid the risk inherent in the lottery is a measure of their risk aversion. This risk premium represents what the person in question is willing to pay to avoid the risk of the lottery.

The riskiness of public policies and projects can be thought of

---

48. In our problem, we avoided the problem of discounting over time by using estimates of the net present value of net benefit streams. In most decision problems, however, policy analysts must confront both the uncertainty and timing of net benefit streams in the decision process. This involves constructing a much more complicated decision tree that breaks down uncertainty regarding net benefits by time periods. For an illustration of this process, see E. Stokey & R. Zeckhauser, supra note 39, at 213-216.

in a similar way. Economists have developed complex techniques for measuring risk premia and incorporating them into decision analysis. See E. Stokey & R. Zeckhauser, supra note 39, at 216-219, 237-254. The typical ways in which policy analysts incorporate risk into cost-benefit analysis are by calculating risk premia for each project and adding them to the other costs of the project and, for projects producing streams of net benefits over time, by adjusting the discount rate used in evaluating particular projects to reflect the social valuation of the riskiness of such projects. In this context, the applicable discount rate has two components: (1) the riskless cost of capital or the social rate of time preference, and (2) the risk premium.

Under a fairly general set of circumstances, however, Arrow and Lind have shown that the government should not incorporate a risk premium into public policy decisions. Their theorem states that if the net benefits of a proposed government project are distributed independently of national income and spread over a sufficiently large population, then the social value of the project is best measured by its total expected value, without any adjustment for risk. The proof of this result turns on the fact that the risk premium that society in the aggregate would be willing to pay goes to zero as the effects of the projects are spread over a larger and larger number of people.[49] This theorem has obvious and important implications for the role of risk in public policy analysis. It is important to keep in mind, however, that the conditions on which the theorem is based do not hold in many important policy contexts. In particular, where the government policy may have large effects on the entire economy or significant concentrated effects on a small subset of the population, then the risk preferences of the affected people should be considered in policymaking. (What types of environmental policies might fall into these categories?)

c.   Risk-Benefit Analysis (Risk Management)

Many substances and activities that we are exposed to in our industrialized society — including pesticides, drugs, foods, cosmetics, and industrial chemicals — pose serious health risks. Consider the following risks that increase the chance of death by 1 in a million:[50] smoking 1.4 cigarettes (death caused by cancer or heart disease); drinking half a liter of wine (cirrhosis of the liver); spending 1 hour in a coal mine

---

49. For a detailed exposition of the proof, see R. Tresch, supra note 39, at 509-511.
50. Source: R. Wilson (1972), quoted in C. Hohenemser & J. Kasperson, Risk in the Technological Society 192 (1982).

(black lung disease); living 2 days in Boston (air pollution); travelling 50 miles by car (accident); drinking Miami water for 1 year (cancer caused by chloroform); eating 100 charcoal broiled steaks (cancer caused by benzopyrene); risk of accident from living within 5 miles of a nuclear reactor for 50 years (cancer caused by radiation). Moreover, many of the risks of life are highly uncertain.

Risk-benefit analysis, a branch of cost-benefit analysis, has been developed to enable public decisionmakers to evaluate policies systematically so as to reduce environmental risks. This policy tool can be used to consider what substances should be permitted in the environment and how best (in a utilitarian framework) to regulate such substances. This method of analysis is quite similar to traditional cost-benefit analysis, but because of its particular relevance to many areas of environmental law and policy and its specialized character, it is worthwhile to describe the basic elements of risk-benefit analysis in some detail here.[51]

Risk-benefit analysis asks the following question: What is the best policy for regulating a particular health risk? The answer, within our utilitarian framework, is the policy that results in the highest net benefits. Thus, risk-benefit analysis is simply an application of cost-benefit analysis. The costs of policies to reduce risk are similar to the types of costs that we have considered thus far: higher production costs due to pollution abatement equipment and workplace safety programs, losses in consumer welfare and producer profits because of product bans. The specialized aspect of risk-benefit analysis is the methodology for calculating the benefits — such as lower mortality — of risk reduction. Quantification of the benefits of risk reduction policies is complicated by the high degree of uncertainty surrounding the exposure level and effects of many substances and the difficulty of valuing health risks.

There are four stages in the quantification of the benefits of risk reduction policies: (1) emissions assessment, (2) exposure assessment, (3) dose-response assessment, and (4) valuation. In the first stage, researchers measure the amount of the substance in question in the environment and the extent to which different policies reduce this amount. The second stage measures the exposure level of humans to the substance under the various policies under consideration. The third stage measures the health risk per unit of exposure. This is typically the most difficult stage in risk assessment, requiring scientists to extrapolate from a wide variety of studies, including studies of abnormal patterns of diseases in humans (case clusters), studies of similarities in chemical

---

51. It should be emphasized that the applicability of risk-benefit analysis to environmental problems, like cost-benefit analysis generally, is controversial. Our purpose in this section is solely to describe how risk-benefit analysis is performed. We will delve into the controversies it has spawned later in this chapter and in various discussions of substantive law and policy throughout the book.

structure of substances that might identify carcinogens (structural toxicology), studies of bacteria and cultured mammalian cells to identify mutagenic effects, variable dosage animal experiments (animal bioassays), and statistical studies of disease incidence in humans (epidemiological studies).

Using the exposure levels of the various policies under consideration from the second stage and the health risk per unit of exposure from the third stage, the final stage quantifies the benefits of each policy by multiplying the exposure level (e.g., number of people exposed) times the health risk per unit exposed (e.g., 1 in 100,000 develop a fatal form of cancer) and the valuation of the adverse health effect(s) (e.g., value of a human life). The net benefits of each policy can then be calculated (benefits less costs) and the best policy chosen (taking into consideration risk preferences of the people affected if appropriate).

PROBLEMS

The EPA is considering policies to regulate X, a potentially dangerous by-product emitted by a number of important industries. Although studies of X are not conclusive, the following are the best estimates of its exposure and health effects. Currently, 1,000,000 persons — employees of and persons residing in close proximity to X-generating factories — are exposed to X in dosages that could cause health effects. On the basis of a variety of tests, scientists agree that X causes either: (A) 1 cancer in 100,000 over the lifetime of persons exposed, or (B) 1 cancer in 10,000 over the lifetime of persons exposed. Furthermore, they believe that hypothesis (A) is twice as likely as hypothesis (B), that is, the probability that hypothesis (A) is correct is 2/3 and the probability that hypothesis (B) is correct is 1/3.

The three policies under consideration are (1) an outright ban on X, which would result in $100 million in lost consumer surplus and producer profits (net present value), (2) a requirement that industries emitting X install pollution control technologies that would reduce the population exposed to X by 90 percent at a cost of $20 million (net present value), and (3) no action (status quo).

You have been asked to perform a risk-benefit analysis of the three policy options. First construct a decision tree. Then calculate the total expected values for each policy option. Assuming that the exposed population is risk neutral and that the valuation of human life used by EPA in these circumstances (and adjusted for the time of death, that is, present value) is $500,000, which policy should be chosen?

Which policy should be chosen if each member of the exposed population would be willing to pay a risk premium (above and beyond the expected value) of $100 to avoid being exposed to this risk of dying of cancer?

d.   The Implications of Cognitive Psychology

Over the past several decades, cognitive psychologists have studied the decision processes that humans actually use in making decisions. These studies have revealed that rather than making "rational" decisions using all relevant information, people tend to rely upon a limited number of heuristic principles in order to simplify their decisionmaking process. These heuristics, while often accurate proxies, sometimes lead to severe and systematic divergences from the economic model of behavior. See generally Kahneman, Slovic & Tversky (eds.), Judgment Under Uncertainty: Heuristics and Biases (1982). According to the availability heuristic, for example, people tend to overestimate the occurrence of events that are easy to imagine or recall. Thus, memorable disaster films, such as *Jaws* and *The China Syndrome,* can have a disproportionate impact on perceptions of the risks of shark attacks and nuclear meltdowns by lay people. More generally, disproportionate and biased news coverage of low probability hazards may increase their imaginability and memorability and hence their perceived riskiness. For example, the initial public reaction to recombinant DNA research may have been more affected by unsubstantiated speculation about "attack of the killer tomato" scenarios than by responsible scientific evidence indicating the risks to be relatively remote and minor. See Slovic, Fischoff & Lichtenstein, Facts versus Fears: Understanding Perceived Risk, in Kahneman, Slovic & Tversky, supra. Consequently, individuals systematically misperceive many environmental risks.

Does this imply that regulation of environmental risks should be left in the hands of "expert" decisionmakers using state-of-the-art risk assessment techniques? Might not "experts" be subject to biases? Consider the nuclear accident at Three Mile Island, in which operator error was a significant factor. Might scientific experts be overconfident about the abilities of technology while overlooking the limitations of the humans controlling the technology, especially when dealing with the frontiers of scientific knowledge?

What other biases might "expert" decisionmakers bring to the task of risk assessment? Risk assessment tends, in practice, to focus upon one or a few measurable characteristics such as deaths per year. Lay people, by contrast, see risk as a multi-dimensional concept, relating to the voluntariness of exposure, irreversibility, scientific uncertainty, the "dreadedness" of the consequences, among others factors. Does this suggest that governmental cost-benefit analysis should reflect all of the systematic individual biases identified by cognitive psychology studies? If not, what aspects of lay judgment should be incorporated into policymaking? See Gillette & Krier, Risks, Courts, and Agencies, 138 Univ. Penn. L. Rev. 1027, 1071-1074 (1990). How might risk assessment be enriched to take into account the multi-dimensional nature of environmental risks? Cf. Zeckhauser, Measuring Risks and Benefits of Food Safety Decisions, 38 Vand. L. Rev. 539, 559-560 (1985).

4. COST-BENEFIT ANALYSIS AND COST-EFFECTIVENESS ANALYSIS DISTINGUISHED

A related public policy tool is *cost-effectiveness analysis*. As highlighted above, cost-benefit analysis derives directly from the utilitarian framework. It presumes that the public policy goal is to maximize the net social surplus and proceeds to calculate the costs and benefits of alternative policies. The preferred policy yields the highest net social surplus.

Policymakers, however, often choose the goal(s) of public policy on the basis of concerns other than economic efficiency. For example, many environmental statutes seek to achieve lofty environmental quality goals, whether or not they are "efficient." Others specify quantitative environmental quality improvements and leave details of policy design and implementation to EPA. The 1990 Clean Air Act Amendments, for example, call for a specific quantitative reduction in sulfur oxide emissions by particular dates. As another notable departure from a purely economic objective, the Endangered Species Act calls for the protection of threatened and endangered species regardless of perceived benefits to humans. Even though the goal is established by means other than cost-benefit analysis, society should be concerned with acheiving that goal in the most efficient manner. Cost-effectiveness analysis looks for the policy option that achieves the policy goal(s) at lowest social cost. Like cost-benefit analysis, cost-effectiveness analysis first identifies all relevant policy alternatives. It then determines the net social cost of using each alternative to achieve the independently specified policy goal(s). Cost-effectiveness analysis is often used to highlight the inefficiency with which particular policy instruments achieve policy objectives.

D. THE LIMITATIONS OF ECONOMIC ANALYSIS AND THE PURSUIT OF SOCIAL GOALS OTHER THAN EFFICIENT RESOURCE ALLOCATION

This section examines the limitations of and alternatives to economic analysis of resource allocation. You should critically assess the relevance and importance of the various objections to the use of economic analysis. These objections will be important to your assessment of the particular legal and policy materials in the chapters that follow and will inevitably raise questions about whether it is possible to develop a framework for analyzing environmental law and policy that is on the one hand coherent and internally consistent and on the other hand responsive to the richness and diversity of considerations and values evoked by environmental problems. This section also presents alternative frameworks for environmental decisionmaking. You should scrutinize their desirability and tractability as approaches to making environmental decisions.

1. DISTORTIONS IN THE IMPLEMENTATION OF ECONOMIC ANALYSIS

While the basic methodology of economic analysis can be stated in a scientific manner, applied economics has elements of an art that requires discretionary judgments to be made in modelling the problem to be analyzed, defining and measuring the relevant variables, and dealing with the complications of second, third, and fourth order spillovers and feedback effects generated by alternative policy choices. These difficulties are exacerbated by the difficult ethical factors that are characteristic of environmental policy choices.

While many government policy decisions must be made under conditions of uncertainty, such uncertainty is often particularly acute in environmental issues. At the extreme, we do not know what effect a given activity might have on the environment. More typically, a given activity, such as use of pesticides, burning of high sulfur coal, or the generation of nuclear energy (and disposal of nuclear waste), will pose a risk of harm to the health of ecosystems and of humans, but the nature and magnitude of that risk remains shrouded in uncertainty. Uncertainties also abound in determining abatement and avoidance costs, particularly in the face of technological change.

Special difficulties are also presented in assigning a money value to reducing health risks, providing environmental amenities, and avoiding environmental degradation: such difficulties include the fact that such collective goods lack close market analogies; individuals are often quite poorly informed concerning environmental risks and are rarely called upon to value them; furthermore individuals' attitudes towards risk in the face of great uncertainty vary. Because of these complications and indeterminacies, economic analysis rarely points to a single superior choice of legal rules or governmental policies. More frequently, there are respectable economic arguments for a number of alternatives.

At best, decisionmakers attempting to utilize economic analysis for environmental decisionmaking will be left with a considerable residuum of discretionary choice, exercised on the basis of intuition, political pressure, or whatever. At worst, economic apparatus will be utilized to rationalize decisions or to advocate positions reached on other grounds.

Case Study of the Use of Cost-Benefit Analysis in Regulating Asbestos

Consider the following dispute over the relevance and application of cost-benefit analysis to EPA regulation of asbestos.

EXECUTIVE OFFICE OF THE PRESIDENT
Office of Management and Budget
Washington, D.C. 20503

March 27, 1985

Mr. A. James Barnes, Esq.
Acting Deputy Administrator
Environmental Protection Agency
401 M Street, SW
Washington, D.C. 20460

Dear Jim,

By your memorandum of March 8, you initiated a review of the legal and policy considerations bearing on the use of Section 9 of the Toxic Substances Control Act of 1976, 15 U.S.C. 2601 et seq. (TSCA). I am sending for your consideration this summary of our views on certain of the issues raised by Section 9 in general, and on the application of Section 9 to asbestos in particular. . . .

OSHA and EPA Rules

On February 13, 1984, the Occupational Safety and Health Administration (OSHA) submitted to OMB for review under Executive Order 12291 a draft proposed rule that would have tightened its exposure standard for asbestos from 2 fibers per cc to 0.5 f/cc. During its review, OMB concluded that an even tighter standard of about 0.2 f/cc appeared to yield greater net benefits. Accordingly, OSHA published an NPRM [Notice of Proposed Rulemaking] on April 10, 1984, that requested comments on both of these alternative standards.

On June 15, 1984, EPA submitted for review a draft proposed rule that would have banned four uses of asbestos beginning in 1985, citing essentially the same workplace risks that OSHA was responding to. EPA submitted a second draft proposed rule on August 15 that would have banned a fifth use of asbestos immediately, and would have banned *all* uses of asbestos by 1995.

Costs and Benefits of EPA Rules

In support of its draft rules, EPA submitted a Regulatory Impact Analysis (RIA) in March, which it updated in October. Subsequently, we asked the agency to supplement its analysis of the two rules, and to disaggregate the costs, benefits, and cost-effectiveness associated with each of thirty-odd use categories it had identified. Both TSCA and Executive Order 12291 require a balancing of costs and benefits in making regulatory decisions. From the data that EPA provided, it was apparent that the ten-year ban of all asbestos products did not meet this test. Summary measures of costs and benefits appear below. . . .

COSTS AND BENEFITS OF PROPOSED ASBESTOS BANS
(assuming no OSHA action)
(millions of 1983 dollars, net present value in 1985)

Action	Costs	Benefits	Net benefits
Five-product ban	$547	$701	$154
Ten-year total ban	$2,408	$235	-$2,173

. . .

(The numbers in this table are derived from EPA's most recent estimates. The monetized benefits use a value-per-cancer-case-avoided of $1 million. As required by EPA's guidance for Regulatory Impact Analyses, both costs and benefits are discounted to 1985 . . . at 4 percent . . .)

Taking OSHA into Account

The estimates above do not take account of the fact that OSHA already is acting to reduce workplace risks associated with asbestos. Accordingly, OMB asked EPA to reestimate the benefits of its ban proposals assuming an OSHA standard of 0.2 f/cc.

COSTS AND BENEFITS OF PROPOSED ASBESTOS BANS
(OSHA Standard at 0.2 f/cc)
(millions of 1983 dollars, NPV in 1985)

Action	Costs	Benefits	Net benefits
Five-product ban	$547	$110	-$437
Ten-year total ban	$2,408	$89	-$2,319

. . .

The ten-year total ban of asbestos failed the benefit-costs balancing test by an overwhelming margin. The five-product ban also failed the test in the aggregate (and would even if the OSHA standard were 0.5 f/cc), but this did not hold true for each of the five individual products or use categories. At an OSHA standard of 0.2, for example, banning cloth had costs of $11 million and benefits of $29 million, for a positive net benefit of $18 million. In other words, it appears to be cost-effective to ban certain uses of asbestos, but not others.

Disaggregation by Use: Costs, Benefits, and Risks

The disaggregation of the costs and benefits for each use of asbestos is essential: only by considering the uses individually can a ban be justified. Furthermore, TSCA requires EPA to consider uses individually, including "the benefits of such substance or mixture for various uses and the availability of substitutes for such uses" (Section 6(c)(1)(C)). The draft rules would have banned some uses for which EPA had identified no risk at all, some uses where the risk was quite clearly not "unreasonable," and other uses for which the agency had identified no adequate substitutes.

EPA also failed to include in its analysis the possible risk associated with asbestos substitutes. Asbestiform fibers commonly are used as substitutes for asbestos and, according to a recent report to EPA by the National Academy of Sciences, also may cause cancer. Other risks, potentially quite serious, could arise if asbestos substitutes turn out to be less effective than asbestos in some critical applications. EPA provided no data, for example, to demonstrate that banning asbestos in automobile brakes will not cause an increase in automobile accidents. In a recent letter to EPA, Stephen Margolis of the Centers for Disease Control noted:

> Motor vehicles are the leading cause of death from injury. They are the leading causes of loss of life from age 1 to 44 and the leading cause of loss of preretirement years of life in the United States. Even a small amount of erratic brake performance could easily outweigh the potential morbidity and mortality saved by reducing ambient air asbestos by .23 to 1.3 percent. Much of this decrease could be gained by adequate work practices during mechanical servicing of brakes.
>
> A reduction in ambient air asbestos levels should be encouraged, but the elimination of asbestos in brake pads as a means of accomplishing this goal should be strongly weighed against the safety performance of alternatives. . . .

Our recommendations are that EPA: . . .

- Refine its own analysis to include estimates of the risk posed by asbestos substitutes in certain uses; . . .
- Based on its expanded analysis, consider action under TSCA to ban individual uses of asbestos for which the residual risk, taking account of the risk of substitutes, is unreasonable.

Sincerely,

Robert P. Bedell
Deputy Administrator
Office of Information and
    Regulatory Affairs

SUBCOMMITTEE ON OVERSIGHT & INVESTIGATIONS, COMMITTEE ON ENERGY & COMMERCE, U.S. HOUSE OF REPRESENTATIVES, EPA'S ASBESTOS REGULATIONS: REPORT ON A CASE STUDY ON OMB INTERFERENCE IN AGENCY RULEMAKING

69-86 (Oct. 1985) . . .

C.   OMB'S INTERPRETATION OF SECTION 6 OF THE TOXIC SUBSTANCES CONTROL ACT IS INCONSISTENT WITH THE STATUTE AND ITS LEGISLATIVE HISTORY

1.   INTRODUCTION

Officials of OMB's Office of Information and Regulatory Affairs (OIRA) have cautioned EPA against issuing its proposed ban of five asbestos products and its asbestos phasedown proposal under section 6 of TSCA on economic as well as legal grounds. One of OIRA's central objections is that the monetized costs exceed the monetized benefits of the proposed regulatory actions. OMB officials attempted to support this objection by calling on the cost-benefit "balancing" requirements of the Toxic Substances Control Act. In so doing, these officials have sought to imply that section 6 of TSCA, the statutory authority underlying the promulgation of EPA's asbestos rules, mandates EPA to place a dollar value on human life and to use "formal cost-benefit analysis" as a determinative criterion for decisionmaking. However, the Subcommittee concludes that OMB's interpretation of section 6 of TSCA is contrary to both the statutory language and its legislative history. . . .

3.   THE AUTHORS OF TSCA DID NOT ADOPT FORMAL COST-BENEFIT ANALYSIS IN SECTION 6 OF THE ACT

The authors of TSCA rejected "formal cost-benefit analysis" because they recognized the inherent limitations of applying such analysis in environmental decisionmaking. Rather, they adopted an approach which more closely approximates "informal cost-benefit analysis." Under such an approach, the comparison of alternative actions is not limited to costs and benefits quantifiable in dollars, and the analysis is relied upon as a foundation for organized decisionmaking rather than a final determinative calculation.

The plain language of TSCA reveals an informal "reasonableness" approach to cost-benefit analysis rather than a formalized, numerical approach. Under section 6(a) of the Act, the threshold for regulatory action to ban or limit the use of a chemical is a finding of "unreasonable risk" by the EPA Administrator. This threshold test is supplemented by a requirement in section 6(c) that the Administrator "consider" costs and benefits in promulgating any rules under section 6(a) of the Act. . . .

This generalized consideration of costs and benefits required by section 6 is very different from the formalized, numerical, cost-benefit decision rule advocated by OMB officials. If Congress had intended EPA to translate all costs and benefits into dollar terms and to issue regulations only if the monetary benefits exceeded the monetary costs, it would have clearly evidenced this intent. It simply did not do so. In fact, the legislative history of section 6(c) indicates that Congress rejected the imposition of a requirement for detailed economic impact statements. Moreover, the authors of TSCA expressed a strong aversion to assigning a dollar value to the various health benefits of proposed regulatory action, such as avoiding premature death, and they rejected the use of quantitative measurements of net benefits as a determinative factor in decisionmaking. A finding of "unreasonable risk" was not expected to be based on a mathematical calculation but was expected to involve considerable flexibility and expert judgment by the EPA Administrator. . . .

D.   THE ECONOMIC INTERPRETATIONS ADVOCATED BY OMB DURING ITS REVIEW OF EPA'S DRAFT ASBESTOS RULES WOULD RESTRICT SUBSTANTIALLY THE AGENCY'S ABILITY TO REGULATE TOXIC CHEMICALS

1.   INTRODUCTION

Notwithstanding Congressional rejection of formal cost-benefit analysis as a determinative criterion under section 6 of TSCA, OMB has utilized such analysis to oppose the promulgation of EPA's proposed asbestos ban and phasedown rules. Moreover, many of the key assumptions utilized by OMB in this analysis represent a dramatic departure from EPA's past practices.

As Congressman Ron Wyden has stated, OMB's approach is simply a "blueprint for non-action" by manipulating the assumptions in EPA's efforts to control "a demonstrated human carcinogen" which "poses widespread and very serious health risks." Moreover, if EPA were to adopt OMB's economic interpretations in the asbestos case, the Agency would establish a precedent which would weaken severely its ability to protect the American public from cancer-causing chemicals.

2.   OMB'S MANIPULATION OF ESTIMATES OF HEALTH BENEFITS

The Office of Management and Budget employed a variety of devices to reduce dramatically the benefits projected to accrue from EPA's proposed asbestos ban and phasedown rules. OMB skewed the results of its cost-benefit analysis by assigning an arbitrary value to human life, by discounting that human life value, and by excluding consideration of certain health benefits. In so doing, OMB was able to gain valuable, but flawed, ammunition to support its assertion that EPA's proposed asbestos rules failed the so-called "benefit-cost balancing test."

a.   Placing a Dollar Value on Human Life

In the spring of 1985, OMB officials indicated that their estimates of the projected benefits of EPA's draft asbestos rules were premised on "a value-per-cancer-case-avoided of $1 million." Thus, in this case, OMB officials took the significant step of assigning a specific dollar value to saving a human life.

It is noteworthy that the asbestos case is not the first time that

OMB officials have advocated the extremely low value of $1 million per life saved in a regulatory proceeding. . . .

Clearly, OMB's attempt to place a monetary value on human life raises fundamental moral questions. In addition, this approach underscores one of the inherent flaws of formal cost-benefit analysis — "applying dollar values to items that lack a market price." Valuation is not a problem for typical consumer goods, such as automobiles or home appliances, which are "bought and sold in the marketplace regularly." However, goods not regularly traded, such as premature death or severe injury from toxic chemicals, "cannot be measured in common terms (such as dollars) that are agreeable to all concerned parties." As a Committee of the National Academy of Sciences concluded in 1975:

> Different individuals place different values on things such as human life, aesthetics, or national security. Thus, an analysis that assigns a quantitative value to one or more of these factors is necessarily subjective and, to some degree, arbitrary. . . . The outcome of the decision will depend on the value that the decision maker places on human life.

b.   Discounting of Human Lives

Another pivotal theory applied by OMB in the asbestos case is the concept of "discounting human lives saved." OMB asserted that there should be such a discounting, to factor in the 30 to 40 year latency period for asbestos-related cancer. The application of this theory reduced the benefits projected to accrue from the proposed asbestos rules substantially below the figure of $1 million per life saved.

At the 10 percent discount rate currently required by OMB's written guidance for preparing Regulatory Impact Analyses, "a life saved 40 years from now is worth roughly only one/forty-fifth as much as a life saved this year" or $22,094.93. This analysis was presented by OMB as a potential alternative in the asbestos case.

In a March 27, 1985 letter to EPA's Deputy Administrator, "OMB suggested that a discount rate as low as 4 percent might be appropriate" in the asbestos case "because the costs of banning asbestos largely take the form of reduced consumer surplus" rather than "capital expenditures." Under this scenario, avoidance of a cancer case 40 years from now translates to a present value of approximately $208,000.

According to OMB's Robert Bedell, the rationale for applying a discount rate to costs and benefits is to put costs and benefits that arise at different times on the same footing. This approach rests on the assumption that future costs and benefits should be valued less than costs and benefits which occur immediately. "OMB has asserted that benefits must be discounted over the cancer latency period to reflect the fact that exposed individuals incur no loss until they contract cancer (in 30-40 years)." Thus, OMB's thesis is that it is worth substantially more to save a life now than a life thirty to forty years from now and that any cost-benefit calculations should reflect this conclusion.

However, OMB's discounting approach would severely undermine EPA's ability to regulate chemical carcinogens and mutagens. According to EPA officials, this approach would represent a major departure from prior EPA practice. EPA's Office of Toxic Substances never has used discounting over the latency period of a chronic hazard. Although some EPA programs have discounted benefits in the past, they have typically discounted these benefits "from the time when exposure to a hazardous substance has been avoided" rather than from the time of onset of the disease, as suggested by OMB. In a case like asbestos, with a long time lag between exposure to a hazardous substance and the onset of disease, the results of these different analytical approaches vary substantially.

Documents provided to the Subcommittee reveal that EPA officials expressed serious concern that the discounting approach advocated by OMB "has the effect of greatly diminishing the projected benefits" of the Agency's proposed asbestos rules. Moreover, Don Clay, Director of EPA's Office of Toxic Substances, testified that if OMB's discounting proposal were adopted as a general public policy, it is unlikely that EPA could regulate any cancer-causing substance with a long latency period.

Even among economists, there is considerable dispute about the discounting of health and environmental benefits. According to a major article on cost-benefit analysis in the Harvard Environmental Law Review, "no consensus exists for determining the proper discount rate and a wide range of rates have been used and proposed." Some policy analysts have argued that it is inappropriate to discount benefits at all because "the 'benefit' of removing a person now from risk of future damage, which is irreversible, inevitable, and non-arrestable once the risk exposure occurs, can be considered to be a *present* benefit."

Other commentators have underscored the ethical nature of this problem. For example, Michael S. Baram stated the following in Ecology Law Quarterly in 1980:

> [F]ocusing on the search for the societally acceptable number for discounting the future clouds the larger issue: whether using these economic principles in contemporary decisionmaking adequately ensures the desirable quality of life and health for future generations. Ultimately, the discount rate issue is an ethical problem that transcends economic and legal perspectives.

EPA officials have expressed similar concerns about the concept of discounting of human life. At the Subcommittee's hearing on April

16, the Director of EPA's Office of Toxic Substances testified that he personally opposed the discounting of lives in the asbestos case on ethical grounds. Similarly, James Barnes testified at a Senate hearing on his nomination as EPA's Deputy Administrator on April 17, 1985, that:

> I have a great deal of ethical difficulty with a concept of applying a discount factor to human life. The lives of my three children are worth every bit as much to me 10 years from now as they are now. I personally reject that notion. I have talked to [EPA Administrator] Lee Thomas about it; I know that it is not one that finds favor with him.

Given the substantial controversy surrounding the issue of discounting over the latency period of cancer-causing substances, EPA officials urged OMB that this matter should be debated in full public view and not decided behind closed doors during the course of OMB's review of EPA's asbestos rules. However, according to an internal EPA document obtained by the Subcommittee, "OMB rejected this option as a means for obtaining agreement on the asbestos rulemakings." OMB's secretive approach is particularly shocking in view of the fact that a high-level OMB official has called the issue of discounting "a significant regulatory issue for the next 10 years."

The Subcommittee finds that OMB's attempt to obtain EPA's acquiescence, behind closed doors, in its approach to discounting is simply an outrage. We recommend that the Agency reject the use of discounting over the latency period of diseases caused by chronic hazards. Instead, EPA's regulatory impact analyses should indicate the distribution over time of any projected benefit from reductions in mortality and morbidity expected to accrue from a proposed regulation. In this way, the real benefits of regulatory action will not be hidden from view by a flawed and arbitrary means of measurement.

c.   "Regulatory Shell Games"

OMB officials have also strongly implied that estimates of projected benefits from EPA's asbestos rules must take account of the pending proposal of OSHA to reduce workplace exposure levels to asbestos. OMB has referred specifically to OSHA's pending proposal to lower permissible asbestos exposure limits to either 0.2 fibers or 0.5 fibers per cubic centimeter of air as an eight-hour time-weighted average. OMB officials requested EPA "to reestimate the benefits of its ban proposals assuming an OSHA standard of 0.2 f/cc, and they have stated that the "benefits of [the] EPA proposal are drastically reduced when [the] effects of [the] OSHA rulemaking are incorporated."

Clearly, estimates of benefits expected to accrue from EPA's asbestos rulemaking should take into account actual reductions in workplace exposure attributable to OSHA regulation. However, it appears that OMB may be seeking to overstate the actual effect of OSHA's proposed actions in this case.

OSHA's asbestos rulemaking marks a major shift in occupational health policy because the proposed rule would allow respirators, rather than engineering and work practice controls, as the primary means to reduce exposure from the current 2 fibers per cubic centimeter limit to the new permissible exposure limit (PEL) of either 0.2 or 0.5 fibers per cubic centimeter. This approach would represent a departure from the principle that reliance should not be placed on respirators as a means of reducing exposures to toxic substances except where feasible engineering and work practice controls cannot succeed in attaining the applicable PEL. As stated in the preamble to OSHA's carcinogen policy:

> Respirators are relied on only as a means of last resort because they simply do not provide a comprehensive and reliable method of employee protection, are uncomfortable and may themselves create safety and health hazards.

In view of this change in policy, OSHA's proposed asbestos rule has been strongly criticized on the grounds that "respirators simply cannot be relied upon to provide protection even remotely equivalent to that of engineering and work practice controls." A recent report of the U.S. Office of Technology Assessment has emphasized that the protection afforded by personal protective equipment, such as respirators, is "unequal, highly variable, and substantially lower than that predicted from laboratory measurements."

Thus, it appears that OMB is seeking to have EPA substantially reduce the projected benefits of its asbestos regulations on the grounds that OSHA will be reducing asbestos exposure levels to 0.2 or 0.5 fibers per cubic centimeter. Yet, at the same time, OMB has "forced OSHA to allow greater reliance on respirators," thereby creating a high risk that the 0.2 or 0.5 standard will not be achieved in full.

d. *Disregarding Unquantified Benefits*

OMB's cost-benefit analysis is also flawed because it expressly limited consideration to "those costs and benefits which have been quantified" by EPA. Yet, the preambles to EPA's proposed asbestos ban and phasedown rules specifically noted that the Agency's estimates of cancer deaths avoided by the proposed regulations may be low because many key factors were difficult to quantify. For example, EPA emphasized that most of its risk estimates did not include deaths from consumer and non-occupational exposures to asbestos since data are either unavailable or very uncertain. However, the Agency indicated that it "believes that many people in these categories are at risk."

The preambles also stress that "EPA did not attempt to quantify reductions of cases of asbestosis and cancers other than mesothelioma and lung cancer." Yet, the Agency noted that:

> These diseases are likely to add 10 to 20 percent more deaths to the total. OSHA estimates that at an exposure of 0.5 f/ml over a working career of 45 years, 12 workers per 1,000 will develop asbestosis (48 FR 51086; November 4, 1983) . . . . In addition, in a major study of insulation workers exposed to asbestos, about 10 percent of all excess deaths were attributed to cancers other than lung cancer and mesothelioma.

In addition, EPA's estimates of cancer cases avoided by regulatory action are "based only on exposures resulting from manufacture of asbestos products through the year 2000." However, "[w]ithout regulatory action, manufacture of asbestos products may continue beyond that date."

3.   USE OF FORMAL COST-BENEFIT ANALYSIS AS A DECISION RULE

The deficiencies in OMB's benefits analysis in the asbestos case are compounded by OMB's attempt to impose formal cost-benefit analysis as the central criterion for decisionmaking in this case. The use of formal cost-benefit analysis as such a decision rule has been rejected by the authors of TSCA, by this Subcommittee, by many prominent scholars, and by the Environmental Protection Agency itself.

For example, Peter A. Schuck, Professor of Law at Yale University, has stated:

> No knowledgeable defender of such analysis (cost-benefit analysis) would argue that it should be anything more than a tool to inform choice. Anybody who suggests that it should be plugged in mechanically to generate a result that a decision maker must accept is either misinformed or a fool. . . . I know no regulators who are not well aware of all these imperfections; nor do I know any regulators who view cost-benefit analysis as anything more than a *sometimes useful, but almost never decisive,* tool. . . .

NOTES AND QUESTIONS

1. In terms of standard cost-benefit analysis, are OMB's assumptions and suggestions defensible?

2. As the House Subcommittee Report emphasizes, one of the most problematic aspects of cost-benefit analysis is the valuation of the health effects of risks, especially the valuation and discounting of a human life. It is often said that each human life is priceless. Should society therefore ban all substances and activities that are suspected of causing non-natural deaths? Should such a ban extend to substances like the polio vaccine which saves many lives but in extremely rare cases causes severe adverse reactions and death? If not, should society ban all those substances that cause more deaths than they save? What about substances that prevent many debilitating injuries but cause the rare death? What about substances that substantially improve the quality of life for many people but occasionally cause death? Should society ban automobiles? If society shouldn't attempt to quantify all effects of policy options — including loss of life and limb — and make decisions that consider all costs and benefits, then how should it make policy decisions? If society should put a value on life, then what value should be chosen?

3. The House Subcommittee is extremely critical of OMB's discounting technique. It seems to prefer EPA's practice of discounting from the time of exposure to a cancer-causing agent rather than from the time of onset of cancer. Which approach is more sound. The Subcommittee also questions OMB's choice of discount rate. What discount rate should be used? See generally Farber & Hemmersbaugh, The Shadow of the Future: Discount Rates, Later Generations, and the Environment, 46 Vand. L. Rev. 267 (1993).

4. As discussed earlier, see supra at p. 48, cost-benefit analysis uses the Kaldor-Hicks criterion for comparing policy options. What concerns does the application of this criterion raise for the analysis of policies to regulate asbestos use? How might these concerns be addressed in policy formation?

5. Do you agree with the "regulatory shell game" criticism? How should the overlap of EPA and OSHA regulatory authority be analyzed? What about the problem that workers might not utilize respirators?

6. The House Subcommittee Report criticizes OMB's cost-benefit analysis for failing to consider important effects, such as deaths from consumer and non-occupational exposures to asbestos (for which data were unavailable or very uncertain). How should a careful cost-benefit analysis take such factors into account? How would the House Subcommittee likely respond to such an effort?

A further problem arises when quantifying effects that are known but difficult to assess. For example, it has been asserted that the process of quantification tends to "dwarf soft variables" — such as aesthetic amenities or the sense of well-being engendered by an environmentally healthy society — that lack ready market analogues. See Tribe, Technology Assessment and the Fourth Discontinuity: The Limits of Instrumental Rationality, 46 S. Cal. L. Rev. 617, 630-631 (1973). Thus, cost-benefit analysis can create a systematic bias disfavoring policies to improve environmental quality because the benefits of environmental protection are most likely to be intangible or otherwise "soft" while the costs of regulation are typically tangible and readily quantifiable. Furthermore, because of its characteristic focus on relatively short-term, incremental resource allocation decisions, economic analysis may overlook the cumulative impact of such decisions in causing basic structural shifts in living patterns. Can economic analysis be adjusted to deal with these problems?

Consider the Department of Interior's explanation for its guidelines for assessing the damage to marine mammals resulting from oil spills and releases of hazardous substances:

> . . . Despite qualitative evidence of concern for marine mammals, establishing a quantitative measure of the value of individuals of various species is no simple task. Most of the social value of marine mammals is composed of non-consumptive use value (e.g., whale watching) and existence or option value. The fact that legislation forbids or severely restricts most commercial uses of marine mammals indicates that our society values the existence and non-consumptive uses of marine mammals more than the commercial uses. Very little information is available on the value of non-consumptive use and nonuse benefits of marine mammals, in part because of the difficulties in measuring these values.
>
> Although there is a potential for injury to all species of marine mammals, most species are unlikely to be injured by all but the most serious spills. Whales, dolphins, and most seals, for example, appear to be resistant to injury due to contact with oil (National Research Council, 1985). Further, since mammals get oxygen directly from the air, rather than from sea water as fish do, they do not readily accumulate the substance from the water. On the other hand, dependence on air tends to enhance the possibility of contact with floating substances, such as oil. . . .
>
> While the evidence is still inconclusive, the only species likely to be highly impacted from the relatively small spills of concern to this study are those which would ingest the substance while preening. Hence the only marine mammals which are assumed to be killed are . . . sea otters and fur seals. . . .
>
> Fur seals are subject to commercial harvest, with the allowable harvest depending upon the size of the population. Thus, a decrease in the population of fur seals will likely lead to a reduction in the allowable harvest, and not a reduction in the unharvested population. Thus, the value per seal pelt of $15 (National Advisory Committee on Oceans and Atmosphere, 1985) will be used as the measure of the monetary damage per fur seal lost.

U.S. Department of Interior, Measuring Damages to Coastal and Marine Natural Resources V-35 – V-37 (Vol. I, Jan. 1987). Are these guidelines consistent with broadly framed economic analysis? What are the shortcomings? How would you remedy these shortcomings? With these corrections, would cost-benefit analysis be a useful tool for making decisions that have impacts upon the well-being of marine mammals?

7. It is often suggested that the purportedly objective framework of cost-benefit analysis is prone to manipulation to serve the interests of the entity performing the analysis.[52] See for example, Baram, Cost-Benefit Analysis: An Inadequate Basis for Health, Safety, and Environmental Decisionmaking, 8 Ecol. L. Quarterly 473, 489-490 (1980); Nager, Bureaucrats and the Cost-Benefit Chameleon, Regulation 37 (Sept./Oct. 1982); Wildavsky, The Political Economy of Efficiency: Cost-Benefit Analysis, Systems Analysis and Program Budgeting, 26 Pub. Adm. Rev. 292 (1966). Do you agree with the House Subcommittee's conclusion that OMB has manipulated the estimates in order to reach a particular result? What numbers should OMB have used?

EPA eventually adopted a staged ban on the use of asbestos. Its decision was subsequently overturned and remanded in the following decision. As you study this case, assess the quality of the court's analysis and its capacity to review economic analysis by regulatory agencies.

CORROSION PROOF FITTINGS v. U.S. ENVIRONMENTAL PROTECTION AGENCY

947 F.2d 1201 (5th Cir. 1991)

JERRY E. SMITH, Circuit Judge:
The Environmental Protection Agency (EPA) issued a final rule under section 6 of the Toxic Substances Control Act (TSCA) to prohibit the future manufacture, importation, processing, and distribution of asbestos in almost all products. Petitioners claim that the EPA's rulemaking procedure was flawed and that the rule was not promulgated on the basis of substantial evidence. . . . Because the EPA failed to muster substantial evidence to support its rule, we remand this matter to the EPA for further consideration in light of this opinion.

---

52. For example, in the early to mid-1970s, policy analysts at the National Academy of Sciences and General Motors Research Laboratories conducted extensive cost-benefit analyses of the Automotive Emissions Control Program, reaching contrary conclusions. *Compare* Coordinating Committee on Air Quality Studies, National Academy of Sciences, Air Quality and Automotive Emissions Control, The Costs and Benefits of Automotive Emissions Control vol. 4 (serial no. 19-24, GPO, 1974), *with* R. Schwing, B. Southworth, C. von Busek & C. Jackson, Benefit-Cost Analysis of Automotive Emission Reductions 7 J. Envtl. Econ. & Mgmt. 44 (1980) (based on study completed in 1976).

I.   FACTS AND PROCEDURAL HISTORY

Asbestos is a naturally occurring fibrous material that resists fire and most solvents. Its major uses include heat-resistant insulators, cements, building materials, fireproof gloves and clothing, and motor vehicle brake linings. Asbestos is a toxic material, and occupational exposure to asbestos dust can result in mesothelioma, asbestosis, and lung cancer.

The EPA began these proceedings in 1979. . . .

An EPA-appointed panel reviewed over one hundred studies of asbestos and conducted several public meetings. Based upon its studies and the public comments, the EPA concluded that asbestos is a potential carcinogen at all levels of exposure, regardless of the type of asbestos or the size of the fiber. The EPA concluded in 1986 that exposure to asbestos "poses an unreasonable risk to human health" and thus proposed at least four regulatory options for prohibiting or restricting the use of asbestos, including a mixed ban and phase-out of asbestos over ten years; a two-stage ban of asbestos, depending upon product usage; a three-stage ban on all asbestos products leading to a total ban in ten years; and labeling of all products containing asbestos.

Over the next two years, the EPA updated its data, received further comments, and allowed cross-examination on the updated documents. In 1989, the EPA issued a final rule prohibiting the manufacture, importation, processing, and distribution in commerce of most asbestos-containing products. Finding that asbestos constituted an unreasonable risk to health and the environment, the EPA promulgated a staged ban of most commercial uses of asbestos. The EPA estimates that this rule will save either 202 or 148 lives, depending upon whether the benefits are discounted, at a cost of approximately $450-800 million, depending upon the price of substitutes.

The rule is to take effect in three stages, depending upon the EPA's assessment of how toxic each substance is and how soon adequate substitutes will be available.[53]

---

53. The main products covered by each ban stage are as follows:

(1)   Stage 1: August 27, 1990: ban on asbestos-containing floor materials, clothing, roofing felt, corrugated and flat sheet materials, pipeline wrap, and new asbestos uses;

(2)   Stage 2: August 25, 1993: ban on asbestos-containing "friction products" and certain automotive products or uses;

(3)   Stage 3: August 26, 1996: ban on other asbestos-containing automotive products or uses, asbestos-containing building materials including non-roof and roof coatings, and asbestos cement shingles.

See 54 Fed. Reg. at 29,461-462.

IV.   THE LANGUAGE OF TSCA

A.   STANDARD OF REVIEW

Our inquiry into the legitimacy of the EPA rulemaking begins with a discussion of the standard of review governing this case. EPA's phase-out ban of most commercial uses of asbestos is a TSCA §6(a) rulemaking. TSCA provides that a reviewing court "shall hold unlawful and set aside" a final rule promulgated under s 6(a) "if the court finds that the rule is not supported by substantial evidence in the rulemaking record . . . taken as a whole." 15 U.S.C. §2618(c)(1)(B)(i). . . .

B.   EPA's BURDEN UNDER TSCA

TSCA provides, in pertinent part, as follows:

> [§2650](a) Scope of regulation. — If the Administrator finds that there is a *reasonable basis* to conclude that the manufacture, processing, distribution in commerce, use, or disposal of a chemical substance or mixture, or that any combination of such activities, presents or will present an *unreasonable risk of injury* to health or the environment, the Administrator shall by rule apply one or more of the following requirements to such substance or mixture to the extent necessary *to protect adequately* against such risk using the *least burdensome* requirements.

Id. (emphasis added). As the highlighted language shows, Congress did not enact TSCA as a zero-risk statute. The EPA, rather, was required to consider both alternatives to a ban and the costs of any proposed actions and to "carry out this chapter in a reasonable and prudent manner [after considering] the environmental, economic, and social impact of any action." 15 U.S.C. §2601(c).

1.   *Least Burdensome and Reasonable*

TSCA requires that the EPA use the least burdensome regulation to achieve its goal of minimum reasonable risk. This statutory requirement can create problems in evaluating just what is a "reasonable risk." Congress's rejection of a no-risk policy, however, also means that in certain cases, the least burdensome yet still adequate solution may entail somewhat more risk than would other, known regulations that are far more burdensome on the industry and the economy. The very language of TSCA requires that the EPA, once it has determined what an acceptable level of non-zero risk is, choose the least burdensome method of reaching that level.

In this case, the EPA banned, for all practical purposes, all present and future uses of asbestos — a position the petitioners characterize as the "death penalty alternative," as this is the most burdensome of all possible alternatives listed as open to the EPA under TSCA. TSCA not only provides the EPA with a list of alternative actions, but also provides those alternatives in order of how burdensome they are. The regulations thus provide for EPA regulation ranging from labeling the least toxic chemicals to limiting the total amount of chemicals an industry may use. Total bans head the list as the most burdensome regulatory option.

By choosing the harshest remedy given to it under TSCA, the EPA assigned to itself the toughest burden in satisfying TSCA's requirement that its alternative be the least burdensome of all those offered to it. Since, both by definition and by the terms of TSCA, the complete ban of manufacturing is the most burdensome alternative — for even stringent regulation at least allows a manufacturer the chance to invest and meet the new, higher standard — the EPA's regulation cannot stand if there is any other regulation that would achieve an acceptable level of risk as mandated by TSCA. . . .

The EPA considered, and rejected, such options as labeling asbestos products, thereby warning users and workers involved in the manufacture of asbestos-containing products of the chemical's dangers, and stricter workplace rules. EPA also rejected controlled use of asbestos in the workplace and deferral to other government agencies charged with worker and consumer exposure to industrial and product hazards, such as OSHA, the CPSC, and the MSHA. The EPA determined that deferral to these other agencies was inappropriate because no one other authority could address all the risks posed "throughout the life cycle" by asbestos, and any action by one or more of the other agencies still would leave an unacceptable residual risk.

Much of the EPA's analysis is correct, and the EPA's basic decision to use TSCA as a comprehensive statute designed to fight a multi-industry problem was a proper one that we uphold today on review. What concerns us, however, is the manner in which the EPA conducted some of its analysis. TSCA requires the EPA to consider, along with the effects of toxic substances on human health and the environment, "the benefits of such substance[s] or mixture[s] for various uses and the availability of substitutes for such uses," as well as "the reasonably ascertainable economic consequences of the rule, after consideration for the effect on the national economy, small business, technological innovation, the environment, and public health." Id. §2605(c)(1)(C-D).

The EPA presented two comparisons in the record: a world with no further regulation under TSCA, and a world in which no manufacture of asbestos takes place. The EPA rejected calculating how many lives a less burdensome regulation would save, and at what cost. Furthermore the EPA, when calculating the benefits of its ban, explicitly refused to compare it to an improved workplace in which currently available control technology is utilized. See 54 Fed. Reg. at 29,474. This decision artificially inflated the purported benefits of the rule by using a baseline comparison substantially lower than what currently available technology could yield.

Under TSCA, the EPA was required to evaluate, rather than ignore, less burdensome regulatory alternatives. TSCA imposes a least-to-most-burdensome hierarchy. In order to impose a regulation at the top of the hierarchy — a total ban of asbestos — the EPA must show not only that its proposed action reduces the risk of the product to an adequate level, but also that the actions Congress identified as less burdensome also would not do the job. The failure of the EPA to do this constitutes a failure to meet its burden of showing that its actions not only reduce the risk but do so in the Congressionally-mandated *least burdensome* fashion. . . .

2.   The EPA's Calculations

Furthermore, we are concerned about some of the methodology employed by the EPA in making various of the calculations that it did perform. In order to aid the EPA's reconsideration of this and other cases, we present our concerns here.

First, we note that there was some dispute in the record regarding the appropriateness of discounting the perceived benefits of the EPA's rule. In choosing between the calculated costs and benefits, the EPA presented variations in which it discounted only the costs, and counter-variations in which it discounted both the costs and the benefits, measured in both monetary and human injury terms. As between these two variations, we choose to evaluate the EPA's work using its discounted benefits calculations.

Although various commentators dispute whether it ever is appropriate to discount benefits when they are measured in human lives, we note that it would skew the results to discount only costs without according similar treatment to the benefits side of the equation. Adopting the position of the commentators who advocate not discounting benefits would force the EPA similarly not to calculate costs in present discounted real terms, making comparisons difficult. Furthermore, in evaluating situations in which different options incur costs at varying time intervals, the EPA would not be able to take into account that soon-to-be-incurred costs are more harmful than postponable costs. Because the EPA must discount costs to perform its evaluations properly, the EPA also should discount benefits to preserve an apples-to-apples comparison, even if this entails discounting benefits of a non-monetary nature. See What Price Posterity?, The Economist, March 23, 1991, at 73 (explaining use of discount rates for non-monetary goods).

When the EPA does discount costs or benefits, however, it cannot choose an unreasonable time upon which to base its discount calculation. Instead of using the time of injury as the appropriate time from which to discount, as one might expect, the EPA instead used the time of exposure.

The difficulties inherent in the EPA's approach can be illustrated by an example. Suppose two workers will be exposed to asbestos in 1995, with worker X subjected to a tiny amount of asbestos that will have no adverse health effects, and worker Y exposed to massive amounts of asbestos that quickly will lead to an asbestos-related disease. Under the EPA's approach, which takes into account only the time of exposure rather than the time at which any injury manifests itself, both examples would be treated the same. The EPA's approach implicitly assumes that the day on which the risk of injury occurs is the same day the injury actually occurs. Such an approach might be proper when the exposure and injury are one and the same, such as when a person is exposed to an immediately fatal poison, but is inappropriate for discounting toxins in which exposure often is followed by a substantial lag time before manifestation of injuries.[54]

Of more concern to us is the failure of the EPA to compute the costs and benefits of its proposed rule past the year 2000, and its double-counting of the costs of asbestos use. In performing its calculus, the EPA only included the number of lives saved over the next thirteen years, and counted any additional lives saved as simply "unquantified benefits." 54 Fed. Reg. at 29,486. The EPA and intervenors now seek to use these unquantified lives saved to justify calculations as to which the benefits seem far outweighed by the astronomical costs. For example, the EPA plans to save about three lives with its ban of asbestos pipe, at a cost of $128-227 million (i.e., approximately $43-76 million per life saved). Although the EPA admits that the price tag is high, it claims that the lives saved past the year 2000 justify the price. See generally id. at 29,473 (explaining use of unquantified benefits).

Such calculations not only lessen the value of the EPA's cost analy-

---

54. We also note that the EPA chose to use a real discount rate of 3 percent. Because historically the real rate of interest has tended to vary between 2 percent and 4 percent, this figure was not inaccurate. The EPA also did not err by calculating that the price of substitute goods is likely to decline at a rate of 1 percent per year, resulting from economies of scale and increasing manufacturing prowess. Because the EPA properly limited the scope of these declines in its models so that the cost of substitutes would not decline so far as to make the price of the substitutes less than the cost of the asbestos they were forced to replace, this was not an unreasonable real rate of price decline to adopt.

sis, but also make any meaningful judicial review impossible. While TSCA contemplates a useful place for unquantified benefits beyond the EPA's calculation, unquantified benefits never were intended as a trump card allowing the EPA to justify any cost calculus, no matter how high.

The concept of unquantified benefits, rather, is intended to allow the EPA to provide a rightful place for any remaining benefits that are impossible to quantify after the EPA's best attempt, but which still are of some concern. But the allowance for unquantified costs is not intended to allow the EPA to perform its calculations over an arbitrarily short period so as to preserve a large unquantified portion.

Unquantified benefits can, at times, permissibly tip the balance in close cases. They cannot, however, be used to effect a wholesale shift on the balance beam. Such a use makes a mockery of the requirements of TSCA that the EPA weigh the costs of its actions before it chooses the least burdensome alternative.[55]

We do not today determine what an appropriate period for the EPA's calculations would be, as this is a matter better left for agency discretion. See Motor Vehicle Mfrs. Assn., 463 U.S. at 53, 103 S. Ct. at 2872. We do note, however, that the choice of a thirteen-year period is so short as to make the unquantified period so unreasonably large that any EPA reliance upon it must be displaced.

Under the EPA's calculations, a twenty-year-old worker entering employment today still would be at risk from workplace dangers for more than thirty years after the EPA's analysis period had ended. The true benefits of regulating asbestos under such calculations remain unknown. The EPA cannot choose to leave these benefits high and then use the high unknown benefits as a major factor justifying EPA action.

We also note that the EPA appears to place too great a reliance

---

55. We thus reject the arguments made by the Natural Resources Defense Council, Inc., and the Environmental Defense Fund, Inc., that the EPA's decision can be justified because the EPA "relied on many serious risks that were understated or not quantified in the final rule," presented figures in which the "benefits are calculated only for a limited time period," and undercounted the risks to the general population from low-level asbestos exposure. In addition, the intervenors argue that the EPA rejected using upper estimates, see 54 Fed. Reg. at 29,473, and that this court now should use the rejected limits as evidence to support the EPA. They thus would have us reject the upper limit concerns when they are not needed, but use them if necessary.

We agree that these all are valid concerns that the EPA legitimately should take into account when considering regulatory action. What we disagree with, however, is the manner in which the EPA incorporated these concerns. By not using such concerns in its quantitative analysis, even where doing so was not difficult, and reserving them as additional factors to buttress the ban, the EPA improperly transformed permissible considerations into determinative factors.

upon the concept of population exposure. While a high population exposure certainly is a factor that the EPA must consider in making its calculations, the agency cannot count such problems more than once. For example, in the case of asbestos brake products, the EPA used factors such as risk and exposure to calculate the probable harm of the brakes, and then used, as an additional reason to ban the products, the fact that the exposure levels were high. Considering that calculations of the probable harm level, when reduced to basics, simply are a calculation of population risk multiplied by population exposure, the EPA's redundant use of population exposure to justify its actions cannot stand.

3. Reasonable Basis

In addition to showing that its regulation is the least burdensome one necessary to protect the environment adequately, the EPA also must show that it has a reasonable basis for the regulation. 15 U.S.C. §2605(a). To some extent, our inquiry in this area mirrors that used above, for many of the methodological problems we have noted also indicate that the EPA did not have a reasonable basis. We here take the opportunity to highlight some areas of additional concern.

Most problematical to us is the EPA's ban of products for which no substitutes presently are available. In these cases, the EPA bears a tough burden indeed to show that under TSCA a ban is the least burdensome alternative, as TSCA explicitly instructs the EPA to consider "the benefits of such substance or mixture for various uses and the availability of substitutes for such uses." Id. §2605(c)(1)(C). These words are particularly appropriate where the EPA actually has decided to ban a product, rather than simply restrict its use, for it is in these cases that the lack of an adequate substitute is most troubling under TSCA.

As the EPA itself states, "[w]hen no information is available for a product indicating that cost-effective substitutes exist, the estimated cost of a product ban is very high." 54 Fed. Reg. at 29,468. Because of this, the EPA did not ban certain uses of asbestos, such as its use in rocket engines and battery separators. The EPA, however, in several other instances, ignores its own arguments and attempts to justify its ban by stating that the ban itself will cause the development of low-cost, adequate substitute products.

As a general matter, we agree with the EPA that a product ban can lead to great innovation, and it is true that an agency under TSCA, as under other regulatory statutes, "is empowered to issue safety standards which require improvements in existing technology or which require the development of new technology." Chrysler Corp. v. Department of

Transp., 472 F.2d 659, 673 (6th Cir. 1972). As even the EPA acknowledges, however, when no adequate substitutes currently exist, the EPA cannot fail to consider this lack when formulating its own guidelines. Under TSCA, therefore, the EPA must present a stronger case to justify the ban, as opposed to regulation, of products with no substitutes.

We note that the EPA does provide a waiver provision for industries where the hoped-for substitutes fail to materialize in time. See 54 Fed. Reg. at 29,464. Under this provision, if no adequate substitutes develop, the EPA temporarily may extend the planned phase-out.

The EPA uses this provision to argue that it can ban any product, regardless of whether it has an adequate substitute, because inventive companies soon will develop good substitutes. The EPA contends that if they do not, the waiver provision will allow the continued use of asbestos in these areas, just as if the ban had not occurred at all.

The EPA errs, however, in asserting that the waiver provision will allow a continuation of the status quo in those cases in which no substitutes materialize. By its own terms, the exemption shifts the burden onto the waiver proponent to convince the EPA that the waiver is justified. See id. As even the EPA acknowledges, the waiver only "may be granted by [the] EPA in very limited circumstances." Id. at 29,460.

The EPA thus cannot use the waiver provision to lessen its burden when justifying banning products without existing substitutes. While TSCA gives the EPA the power to ban such products, the EPA must bear its heavier burden of justifying its total ban in the face of inadequate substitutes. Thus, the agency cannot use its waiver provision to argue that the ban of products with no substitutes should be treated the same as the ban of those for which adequate substitutes are available now.

We also are concerned with the EPA's evaluation of substitutes even in those instances in which the record shows that they are available. The EPA explicitly rejects considering the harm that may flow from the increased use of products designed to substitute for asbestos, even where the probable substitutes themselves are known carcinogens. Id. at 29,481-83. The EPA justifies this by stating that it has "more concern about the continued use and exposure to asbestos than it has for the future replacement of asbestos in the products subject to this rule with other fibrous substitutes." Id. at 29,481. The agency thus concludes that any "[r]egulatory decisions about asbestos which poses well-recognized, serious risks should not be delayed until the risk of all replacement materials are fully quantified." Id. at 29,483.

This presents two problems. First, TSCA instructs the EPA to consider the relative merits of its ban, as compared to the economic effects of its actions. The EPA cannot make this calculation if it fails to consider the effects that alternate substitutes will pose after a ban.

Second, the EPA cannot say with any assurance that its regulation will increase workplace safety when it refuses to evaluate the harm that will result from the increased use of substitute products. While the EPA may be correct in its conclusion that the alternate materials pose less risk than asbestos, we cannot say with any more assurance than that flowing from an educated guess that this conclusion is true.

Considering that many of the substitutes that the EPA itself concedes will be used in the place of asbestos have known carcinogenic effects, the EPA not only cannot assure this court that it has taken the least burdensome alternative, but cannot even prove that its regulations will increase workplace safety. Eager to douse the dangers of asbestos, the agency inadvertently actually may increase the risk of injury Americans face. The EPA's explicit failure to consider the toxicity of likely substitutes thus deprives its order of a reasonable basis. Cf. American Petroleum Inst. v. OSHA, 581 F.2d 493, 504 (5th Cir.1978) (An agency is required to "regulate on the basis of knowledge rather than the unknown."). . . .

4. Unreasonable Risk of Injury

The final requirement the EPA must satisfy before engaging in any TSCA rulemaking is that it only take steps designed to prevent "unreasonable" risks. In evaluating what is "unreasonable," the EPA is required to consider the costs of any proposed actions and to "carry out this chapter in a reasonable and prudent manner [after considering] the environmental, economic, and social impact of any action." 15 U.S.C. §2601(c).

As the District of Columbia Circuit stated when evaluating similar language governing the Federal Hazardous Substances Act, "[t]he requirement that the risk be 'unreasonable' necessarily involves a balancing test like that familiar in tort law: The regulation may issue if the severity of the injury that may result from the product, factored by the likelihood of the injury, offsets the harm the regulation itself imposes upon manufacturers and consumers." Forester v. CPSC, 559 F.2d 774, 789 (D.C. Cir. 1977). We have quoted this language approvingly when evaluating other statutes using similar language. See, e.g., Aqua Slide, 569 F.2d at 839.

That the EPA must balance the costs of its regulations against their benefits further is reinforced by the requirement that it seek the least burdensome regulation. While Congress did not dictate that the EPA engage in an exhaustive, full-scale cost-benefit analysis, it did require the EPA to consider both sides of the regulatory equation, and it rejected the notion that the EPA should pursue the reduction of workplace risk at any cost. See American Textile Mfrs. Inst., 452 U.S. at 510 n.30, 101 S. Ct. at 2491 n.30 ("unreasonable risk" statutes require "a generalized balancing of costs and benefits" (citing Aqua Slide, 569 F.2d at 839))). Thus, "Congress also plainly intended the EPA to consider the economic impact of any actions taken by it under . . . TSCA." Chemical Mfrs. Assn., 899 F.2d at 348.

Even taking all of the EPA's figures as true, and evaluating them in the light most favorable to the agency's decision (non-discounted benefits, discounted costs, analogous exposure estimates included), the agency's analysis results in figures as high as $74 million per life saved. For example, the EPA states that its ban of asbestos pipe will save three lives over the next thirteen years, at a cost of $128-227 million ($43-76 million per life saved), depending upon the price of substitutes; that its ban of asbestos shingles will cost $23-34 million to save 0.32 statistical lives ($72-106 million per life saved); that its ban of asbestos coatings will cost $46-181 million to save 3.33 lives ($14-54 million per life saved); and that its ban of asbestos paper products will save 0.60 lives at a cost of $4-5 million ($7-8 million per life saved). See 54 Fed. Reg. at 29,484-85. Were the analogous exposure estimates not included, the cancer risks from substitutes such as ductile iron pipe factored in, and the benefits of the ban appropriately discounted from the time of the manifestation of an injury rather than the time of exposure, the costs would shift even more sharply against the EPA's position.

While we do not sit as a regulatory agency that must make the difficult decision as to what an appropriate expenditure is to prevent someone from incurring the risk of an asbestos-related death, we do note that the EPA, in its zeal to ban any and all asbestos products, basically ignored the cost side of the TSCA equation. The EPA would have this court believe that Congress, when it enacted its requirement that the EPA consider the economic impacts of its regulations, thought that spending $200-300 million to save approximately seven lives (approximately $30-40 million per life) over thirteen years is reasonable.

As we stated in the OSHA context, until an agency "can provide substantial evidence that the benefits to be achieved by [a regulation] bear a reasonable relationship to the costs imposed by the reduction, it cannot show that the standard is reasonably necessary to provide safe or healthful workplaces." *American Petroleum Inst.*, 581 F.2d at 504. Although the OSHA statute differs in major respects from TSCA, the statute does require substantial evidence to support the EPA's contentions that its regulations both have a reasonable basis and are the least burdensome means to a reasonably safe workplace.

The EPA's willingness to argue that spending $23.7 million to save less than one-third of a life reveals that its economic review of its regulations, as required by TSCA, was meaningless. As the petitioners' brief and our review of EPA caselaw reveals, such high costs are rarely, if ever, used to support a safety regulation. If we were to allow such cavalier treatment of the EPA's duty to consider the economic effects of its decisions, we would have to excise entire sections and phrases from the language of TSCA. Because we are judges, not surgeons, we decline to do so. . . .

NOTES AND QUESTIONS

1. Evaluate each stage of the court's analysis. How would you defend EPA's rationale for the asbestos regulation? What factors do you believe were most important in EPA's decision?

2. Did economic analysis play a useful or a counterproductive role in the public policy and legal debate over asbestos? Should TSCA rely so heavily upon a balancing of risks and benefits that inevitably invites the application of economic analysis? Would TSCA be improved by using a regulatory threshold based solely on the protection of public health? How would that approach be implemented in this case?

3. Do the limitations and potential distortions of economic analysis indicate that we should abandon its use entirely in environmental decisionmaking? On the contrary, do they not indicate a need for more economic analysis of higher quality and richer content? Yet this last prescription is not without its own difficulties. Can the evaluative factors considered be enlarged without seriously eroding the analytic power of economics? Moreover, how do we assure that governmental decision makers will do better economic analysis?

2. DISTRIBUTIONAL CONSIDERATIONS

Economic analysis is not typically concerned with distributional considerations because there is no economic criterion for "correct" wealth distribution and because "there is no objective basis for balancing . . . distributive benefits against allocative costs." Posner, Taxation by Regulation, 2 Bell J. Econ. & Mgmt. 22, 44 (1971). Often it is simply assumed that the initial distribution of income is optimal and that any changes in distribution occasioned by the attainment of economic efficiency will be costlessly corrected by other means, such as transfer payments authorized by the legislature, or that, given a series of administrative decisions, such changes will tend to cancel out.

These assumptions may be highly unrealistic. The initial distribution of income may be far from "optimal," and reform of the tax structure in response to changes in actual distribution or changes in views about fair distribution often comes slowly and in gross. It cannot be assumed that changes in the initial distribution resulting from particular administrative, legislative, or judicial decisions will inevitably cancel out or be corrected by legislative action. Quite apart from limitations in governmental resources, a centralized system for redressing the cumulative distributional effects of many individual administrative decisions might prove unworkable because such effects are often interstitial and not easily quantified. Furthermore, redistribution through regulatory policy might alter the incentive structure that the particular regulations seek to create.

Mohai & Bryant, Environmental Injustice: Weighing Race and Class as Factors in the Distribution of Environmental Hazards

63 U. Colo. L. Rev. 921 (1992)

A prevailing assumption in this country has been that pollution is a problem faced equally by everyone in society. However, that assumption has become increasingly challenged as greater attention has been given by the media, social scientists, legal scholars, and policy makers to the issues of environmental injustice.

A major event which helped to focus national attention on issues of environmental injustice occurred in 1982 when state officials decided to locate a poly-chlorinated biphenyl (PCB) landfill near a predominantly black community in Warren County, North Carolina. Protests very similar to those of the civil rights movement of the 1960s resulted. More than 500 people were arrested including Congressman Walter E. Fauntroy who subsequently requested an investigation by the U.S. General Accounting Office (GAO) of the socioeconomic and racial composition of the communities surrounding the four major hazardous waste landfills in the South. The GAO study (1983) found that 3 of the 4 major hazardous waste landfills were located in communities that were predominantly black and living disproportionately below the poverty line. The findings of the GAO report, plus the earlier Warren County events, prompted the United Church of Christ's Commission for Racial Justice, also a participant in the 1982 protests, to conduct a nationwide study of the distribution of hazardous waste sites to determine whether there was a national pattern of disproportionate location of commercial hazardous waste facilities in minority communities similar to that seen in the South. The Commission found that there indeed was such a pattern. Specifically, the United Church of Christ study found that the proportion of minorities residing in communities that have a commercial hazardous waste facility is about double the proportion of minorities in communities without such facilities. Where two or more such facilities are located, the proportion of residents who are minorities is more than triple. In addition, using multivariate statistical techniques, this study found that race is the single best predictor of where commercial hazardous waste facilities are located, even when other socioeconomic characteristics of communities, such as average household income and average value of homes, are taken into account.

The United Church of Christ report concluded that it is "virtually impossible" that the nation's commercial hazardous waste facilities are distributed disproportionately in minority communities merely by chance; therefore in all likelihood underlying factors related to race play a role in the location of these facilities. These factors include inter alia: (1) the availability of cheap land, often located in minority communities and neighborhoods; (2) the lack of local opposition to the facility, often resulting from minorities' lack of organization and political resources as well as their need for jobs; and (3) the lack of mobility of minorities resulting from poverty and housing discrimination that traps them in neighborhoods where hazardous waste facilities are located. The United Church of Christ report noted that these mechanisms and resulting inequitable outcomes represent institutionalized forms of racism. When the report was released Dr. Benjamin F. Chavis, Jr., termed the racial biases in the location of commercial hazardous waste facilities as "environmental racism."

The striking findings of the United Church of Christ study prompted us to investigate whether other studies exist that have used systematic data to examine the social distribution of pollution, and whether the evidence from all the studies, taken together, demonstrates a consistent pattern of environmental injustice based on socioeconomic and racial factors. As part of this effort, we conducted our own study to examine inequities in the distribution of commercial hazardous waste facilities in the Detroit metropolitan area. In order to uncover more information and focus greater attention on this issue, we also convened the Michigan Conference on Race and the Incidence of Environmental Hazards at the University of Michigan's School of Natural Resources in January 1990. At the conference scholars from around the country working on this issue presented their latest findings and discussed their ideas. An important event at the Michigan Conference was the decision to request a meeting between EPA Administrator William Reilly and a representative group of Conference participants in order to bring environmental injustice to the attention of the EPA. Administrator Reilly responded positively and a meeting was held on September 13, 1990. The contacts and ensuing discussions led Administrator Reilly to form an internal agency workgroup to investigate the problem of environmental injustice and to begin drafting a policy statement on this issue. Similar events and subsequent debates concerning the EPA's efforts — including its draft report on Environmental Equity released in January 1992 — sparked considerable public dialogue about the issues of environmental injustice.

A question often raised about inequities in the distribution of environmental hazards is whether observed racial biases are simply a function of poverty. That is, is it not poverty, rather than race per se, that affects the distribution of environmental hazards? And are minorities disproportionately impacted simply because they are disproportionately poor? Classical economic theory would predict that poverty plays a role on several levels. Because of limited income and wealth, the poor do not have the financial means to buy their way out of polluted neighborhoods and into more environmentally desirable ones. Also, land values tend to be cheaper in poor neighborhoods and are thus attractive to polluting industries seeking to reduce the cost of doing business. However, race also plays a role. Housing discrimination, along with low income, further restricts the mobility of minorities. In addition, because noxious sites are unwanted (the "Not in My Back Yard" or "NIMBY" syndrome), and because industries tend to take the path of least resistance, communities with little political clout are often targeted for such facilities. Communities where hazardous waste sites are located tend to be communities in which residents are unaware of the policy decisions affecting them, residents are unorganized and lack resources for taking political action; such resources include time, money, contacts, knowledge of the political system, and others. In addition, minority communities are at a disadvantage not only in terms of the availability of resources, but also because they are underrepresented on governing bodies when location decisions are made. Underrepresentation translates into limited access to policy makers as well as lack of advocates for minority interests.

Taken together, these factors suggest that race has an additional impact on the distribution of environmental hazards; an impact which is independent of income. Thus, another objective of our investigation was to assess the relative influence of race and income on the distribution of pollution. We did so by examining the results of empirical studies which have analyzed the distribution of environmental hazards by both race and income. We also assessed the relative importance of the relationship of income and race in the distribution of commercial hazardous waste facilities in our Detroit area study.

A.   ENVIRONMENTAL INJUSTICE: WEIGHING RACE AND CLASS FACTORS

Table 1 summarizes key information from 16 studies (including our Detroit area study) which provide systematic information about the social distribution of environmental hazards. A number of interesting and important facts emerge from an examination of this Table. First, an inspection of the publication dates of these studies reveals that infor-

TABLE 1

Studies Providing Systematic Empirical Evidence Regarding the Burden of Environmental Hazards by Income and Race

Study	Hazard	Focus of study	Distribution inequitable by income?	Distribution inequitable by race?	Income or race more important?
CEQ (1971)	Air Pollution	Urban Area	Yes	NA	NA[a]
Freeman (1972)	Air Pollution	Urban Areas	Yes	Yes	Race
Harrison (1975)	Air Pollution	Urban Areas	Yes	NA	NA
		Nation	No	NA	NA
Kruvant (1975)	Air Pollution	Urban Area	Yes	Yes	Income
Zupan (1975)	Air Pollution	Urban Area	Yes	NA	NA
Burch (1976)	Air Pollution	Urban Area	Yes	No	Income
Berry et al. (1977)	Air Pollution	Urban Areas	Yes	Yes	NA
	Solid Waste	Urban Areas	Yes	Yes	NA
	Noise	Urban Areas	Yes	Yes	NA
	Pesticide Poisoning	Urban Areas	Yes	Yes	NA
	Rat Bite Risk	Urban Areas	Yes	Yes	NA
Handy (1977)	Air Pollution	Urban Area	Yes	NA	NA
Asch & Seneca (1978)	Air Pollution	Urban Areas	Yes	Yes	Income
Gianessi et al. (1979)	Air Pollution	Nation	No	Yes	Race
Bullard (1983)	Solid Waste	Urban Area	NA	Yes	NA
U.S. GAO (1983)	Hazardous Waste	Southern Region	Yes	Yes	NA
United Church of Christ (1987)	Hazardous Waste	Nation	Yes	Yes	Race
Gelobter (1987; 1992)	Air Pollution	Urban Areas	Yes	Yes	Race
		Nation	No	Yes	Race
Mohai & Bryant (1992)	Hazardous Waste	Urban Area	Yes	Yes	Race
West et al. (1992)	Toxic Fish Contamination	State	No	Yes	Race

[a] Not Applicable

Note: This table is adapted from Paul Mohai & Bunyan Bryant, Environmental Racism: Reviewing the Evidence, in Race and the Incidence of Environmental Hazards: A Time for Discourse 166 (Bunyan Bryant & Paul Mohai eds., 1992).

mation about environmental inequities has been available for some time. Rather than being a recent discovery, documentation of environmental injustices stretches back two decades. In fact, information about inequities in the distribution of environmental hazards was first published in 1971 in the annual report of the Council on Environmental Quality. This was only one year after the U.S. Environmental Protection

Agency was created, two years after the National Environmental Policy Act was passed, and one year after the first Earth Day was held — an event viewed by many as a major turning point in public awareness about environmental issues. Evidently, it has taken some time for public awareness to catch up to the issues of environmental injustice.

It is also worth noting that most of the studies that have been conducted in this period have focused on the distribution of air pollution. Clearly, systematic studies of the social distribution of other types of environmental hazards, such as water pollution, pesticide exposure, asbestos exposure, and other hazards are needed. Also worth noting is that these studies vary considerably in terms of their scope — i.e., some studies focused on single urban areas, such as Washington, D.C., or Houston, others focused on a collection of urban areas, while still others have been national in scope. This observation is important in that it reveals that the pattern of findings is not simply an artifact of the samples used. Regardless of the scope of the analyses (or methodologies employed), the findings point to a consistent pattern. It is clear from examining the results in Table 1 that regardless of the environmental hazard and regardless of the scope of the study, in nearly every case the distribution of pollution has been found to be inequitable by income. And with only one exception, the distribution of pollution has been found to be inequitable by race. Where the distribution of pollution has been analyzed by both income and race (and where it is possible to weigh the relative importance of each), in most cases (six out of nine) race has been found to be more strongly related to the incidence of pollution than income. Noteworthy also is the fact that all three studies which have been national in scope and which have provided both income and race information have found race to be more importantly related to the distribution of environmental hazards than income.

Taken together, the findings from these sixteen studies indicate clear and unequivocal class and racial biases in the distribution of environmental hazards. And, important to the debate about whether the racial biases are primarily a function of poverty, the results also appear to support the argument that race has an additional effect on the distribution of environmental hazards independent of class. Indeed, the racial biases found in these studies have tended to be greater than class biases.

BEEN, LOCALLY UNDESIRABLE LAND USES
IN MINORITY NEIGHBORHOODS:
DISPROPORTIONATE SITING OR
MARKET DYNAMICS?

103 Yale L.J. 1383 (1994)

The environmental justice movement contends that people of color and the poor are exposed to greater environmental risks than are whites and wealthier individuals. The movement charges that this disparity is due in part to racism and classism in the siting of environmental risks, the promulgation of environmental laws and regulations, the enforcement of environmental laws, and the attention given to the cleanup of polluted areas. To support the first charge — that the siting of waste dumps, polluting factories, and other locally undesirable land uses (LULUs) has been racist and classist — advocates for environmental justice have cited more than a dozen studies analyzing the relationship between neighborhoods' socioeconomic characteristics and the number of LULUs they host. The studies demonstrate that those neighborhoods in which LULUs are located have, on average, a higher percentage of racial minorities and are poorer than non-host communities.

That research does not, however, establish that the host communities were disproportionately minority or poor at the time the sites were selected. Most of the studies compare the *current* socioeconomic characteristics of communities that host various LULUs to those of communities that do not host such LULUs. This approach leaves open the possibility that the sites for LULUs were chosen fairly, but that subsequent events produced the current disproportion in the distribution of LULUs. In other words, the research fails to prove environmental justice advocates' claim that the disproportionate burden poor and minority communities now bear in hosting LULUs is the result of racism and classism in the *siting process* itself.

In addition, the research fails to explore an alternative or additional explanation for the proven correlation between the current demographics of communities and the likelihood that they host LULUs. Regardless of whether the LULUs originally were sited fairly, it could well be that neighborhoods surrounding LULUs became poorer and became home to a greater percentage of people of color over the years following the sitings. Such factors as poverty, housing discrimination, and the location of jobs, transportation, and other public services may have led the poor and racial minorities to "come to the nuisance" — to move to neighborhoods that host LULUs — because those neighborhoods offered the cheapest available housing. Despite the plausibility of that scenario, none of the existing research on environmental justice has examined how the siting of undesirable land uses has subsequently affected the socioeconomic characteristics of host communities. Because the research fails to prove that the siting process causes any of the disproportionate burden the poor and minorities now bear, and because the research has ignored the possibility that market dynamics may have played some role in the distribution of that burden, policymakers now have no way of knowing whether the siting process is "broke" and needs fixing. Nor can they know whether even an ideal siting system that ensured a perfectly fair distribution of LULUs would result in any long-term benefit to the poor or to people of color.

This Article begins to address both of these gaps in the research. Part I of this Article explains how market dynamics may affect the demographics of the communities hosting LULUs. It then demonstrates why an empirical understanding of the role market dynamics play in the distribution is necessary both to focus discussion about the fairness of the existing distribution of LULUs and to fashion an effective remedy for any unfairness in that distribution.

Part II surveys the existing research and explains why it is insufficient to determine whether the siting process placed LULUs in neighborhoods that were disproportionately minority or poor at the time the facility was opened, whether the siting of the facility subsequently drove host neighborhoods to become home to a large percentage of people of color or the poor than other communities, or whether both of these phenomena contributed to the current distribution of LULUs.

Part III undertakes empirical research to study the roles that initial siting decisions and market dynamics play in the distribution of LULUs. The research extends two of the studies most often cited as proof of environmental racism — the General Accounting Office's Siting of Hazardous Waste Landfills and Their Correlation with Racial and Economic Status of Surrounding Communities and Robert Bullard's Solid Waste Sites and the Black Houston Community — by analyzing data about the demographic characteristics of host neighborhoods in those studies at the time the siting decisions were made, then tracing demographic changes in the neighborhoods after the siting.

The larger of the two extended studies indicates that market dynamics may play a significant role in creating the disparity between the racial composition of host communities and that of non-host communities. In that sample, LULUs initially were sited somewhat disproportionately in poor communities and communities of color. After the sitings, the levels of poverty and percentages of African-Americans in the host neighborhoods increased, and the property values in these neighborhoods declined. Accordingly, the study suggests that while siting decisions do disproportionately affect minorities and the poor, market dynamics also play a very significant role in creating the uneven distribution of the burdens LULUs impose. Even if siting processes can be improved, therefore, market forces are likely to create a pattern in which LULUs become surrounded by people of color or the poor, and consequently come to impose a disproportionate burden upon those groups. The smaller study, on the other hand, finds a correlation between neighborhood demographics and initial siting decisions, but finds no evidence that market dynamics are leading the poor or people of color to "come to the nuisance."

NOTES AND QUESTIONS

1. How should the problem of disproportionate burden of environmental impacts be characterized? Is it best seen as an environmental problem? A civil rights problem? A poverty problem? Is the disproportionate siting of hazardous waste facilities of greater or lesser concern than the disproportionate availability of public and private services — for instance, education, health care services, police protection, proximity of highways, availability and quality of parks — in poorer and minority communities? Should the policy response be different?

2. Do the disproportionate siting studies indicate that health risks from waste facilities are serious?

3. How should hazardous waste facilities be sited so as to address distributional concerns? Consider the following state approaches:

- *Super Review:* A developer chooses a prospective site and applies for a permit with the state environmental review agency. This agency conducts an environmental impact assessment and evaluates whether the proposal satisfies the state's environmental criteria. The proposal is then presented to a special administrative body appointed to consider the concerns of the neighboring community.
- *Site Designation:* A state agency develops an inventory of possible sites on the basis of a broad range of criteria and with the input of local governmental offices. Review boards typically include diverse public and private interests selected from many regions of the state.
- *Local Control:* Each local government entity can create land use regulations that could block the siting of a facility. The state hazardous waste management plan cannot preempt such regulations.
- *Compensated Siting:* A developer proposes a facility to a state review board, which conducts an analysis of environmental impacts, the need for the facility, and the developer's performance record and financial strength. Upon receiving approval from this board, the affected community and the developer negotiate

a siting agreement which includes compensation for the social costs of the facility. If negotiations fail, an arbitrator establishes the terms for siting.

What are the advantages of these approaches? Disadvantages?

4. In February 1994, President Clinton issued Executive Order 12898, which seeks to promote environmental justice in minority and low-income communities. The order calls upon all federal agencies, to the extent practicable and permitted by law, to incorporate environmental justice within their mission "by identifying and addressing, as appropriate, disproportionately high and adverse human health or environmental effects of its programs, policies and activities on minority populations and low-income populations." The order establishes an Interagency Working Group on Environmental Justice to guide, coordinate, and advise federal agencies in carrying out this mandate. The order also calls for the collection of data on the distribution of environmental effects. The Executive Order expressly disavows the creation of any substantive or procedural rights, including a right to judicial review. Does this initiative appear to be a sound approach to addressing environmental justice concerns? What are its strengths? Limitations?

5. Professor Been's preliminary analysis suggests quite plausibly that both market dynamics and disproportionate siting influence the distribution of environmental burdens. What does this suggest for the efficacy of alternative policies to address distributional impacts of environmental policy? What direction should policy take?

6. We have focused thus far on the distributional consequences of hazardous waste facility siting and pollution policy. What are the distributional implications of other areas of environmental policy such as national park management, natural resource extraction (timber, fossil fuel, grazing) on public lands, and species preservation?

7. Do environmental organizations adequately represent the full range of interests affected by environmental policy? Should such organizations reach out to underrepresented people or should they focus upon a discrete set of issues of particular importance to their members, such as natural resource preservation? Given the limited resources that environmental organizations can devote to environmental protection, should preservation of the Alaskan National Wildlife Refuge (ANWR) have higher or lower priority than environmental justice concerns?

8. Where economic efficiency and distributional equity conflict, what should a legislator, administrator, or judge deciding on an issue of environmental law or policy do? Should she moderate the pursuit of efficiency in order to give some weight to considerations of distributional equity? If so, how much weight should be given to distributional equity? Should decisionmakers take at face value the low preferences for environmental quality expressed by poor people? Does the imposi-

tion of higher environmental quality than the poor would choose reflect at best parentalism, at worst sacrifice by the poor for the wealthy and educated? Would it not be cruel to encourage preferences for high environmental quality by persons who cannot afford to indulge such tastes?

How would this weighing process be complicated if we introduce other equity concerns, such as racial disparities, preservation of expectations, or avoidance of undue regional disparities, into the analysis?

9. Although the methodology is complicated and significantly subjective, it is possible to incorporate distributional considerations into cost-benefit analysis. See R. Tresch, Public Finance: A Normative Theory 541-555 (1981); see also Christiansen & Tietenberg, Distributional and Macroeconomic Aspects of Environmental Policy, in 1 Handbook of Natural Resource and Energy Economics 345 (A. Kneese & J. Sweeney eds. 1985). Should regulatory policies or projects be designed, at least in part, to achieve distributional goals? Or should the tax system and transfer programs (such as welfare, Medicaid, unemployment compensation, and Social Security) be the exclusive policies for effecting redistribution? Should this choice depend on the relative "efficiency" of these means for effecting desired redistribution? In what areas of environmental law and policy might it be "cost-effective" (relative to using the tax and transfer system) to address distributional concerns directly? In what areas is it likely to be most difficult and costly?

3. JUSTICE AMONG GENERATIONS

Many environmental problems require that costs or sacrifices be incurred today in order to prevent risks of harm occurring in the future or to preserve environmental amenities for future enjoyment. These problems raise the question of how we should balance present costs against future benefits. Where the harms to be avoided or advantages to be preserved are quite long run in nature, the problem involves the sacrifices to be incurred by one generation for the sake of its successors.

As described in Part C, the economist's approach to the allocation of resources across generations is based on the concept of discounting. The discount rate, reflecting either the private opportunity cost of resources or the social rate of time preference, implicitly establishes a trade off between current and future generations. If the discount rate is low, future periods, and hence future generations, weigh heavily in the cost-benefit balance; if the discount rate is high, society implicitly places a low value on the availability of depletable resources to future generations (or believes that discoveries of resources will rise over time).

Isn't any decision rule that treats future generations as less "important" than the current generation inherently inequitable? Does this mean that no discount rate at all should be applied in measuring future environmental costs and benefits? Note that this type of reasoning might require us to make any sacrifice that could yield a greater benefit to some future generation, no matter how remote. On the other hand, with a 5 percent discount rate, one loss of life today would be valued the same as 1730 lives in 200 years and over 3 billion lives in 450 years. See Liroff, Cost-Benefit Analysis in Federal Environmental Programs, in Cost-Benefit Analysis and Environmental Regulations: Politics, Ethics, and Methods 35, 44 (D. Swartzman, R. Liroff & K. Croke eds. 1982). Isn't there also a problem in knowing the preferences of future generations? Is it reasonable to assume that they have the same preferences as our generation?

John Rawls attempts to deal with the problem of intergenerational equity in his magisterial A Theory of Justice 284-293 (1971). Rawls argues that there is an obligation for each generation to save for its successors in order to accumulate the material basis for a society of "just institutions" — very roughly, a society in which all citizens can enjoy a full measure of equal civil liberties, have sufficient advantageous opportunities to develop their respective abilities, and are not divided by significant disparities in wealth or other advantages. Rawls does not envisage this situation as one of great wealth and supposes that after it is achieved economic growth will reach a "steady-state" in which successive generations need only replace the capital which they consume. Until a society of just institutions is achieved, however, each generation must accumulate additional capital for its successors.

The problem for Rawls is to define the source and extent of this obligation. He suggests that just institutions would be those chosen by reflective individuals behind a hypothetical "veil of ignorance" in which they were ignorant of their own status in society and would accordingly select societal arrangements on a wholly disinterested basis. In the case of intergenerational savings, Rawls supposes that individuals behind a hypothetical veil of ignorance, not knowing in which generation they would live, would agree upon a "just savings schedule" defining the appropriate sacrifice of each generation for the next until just institutions were attained. The immediate source of obligation for any one generation to save for the future lies in the just savings schedule, adopted under disinterested conditions, defining the extent of each generation's duty to provide an accumulation for its successor. But as Rawls suggests, id. at 289, the just savings principle might develop into an expression of human solidarity in which the "life of a people is conceived as a scheme of cooperation spread out in historical time."

How useful is this conception, reproduced here in bare outline, in dealing with the problem of intergenerational sacrifice? In his account Rawls does not specifically consider ecological issues or population growth. Can these issues be accommodated within the general framework of his analysis? Consider the following excerpt.

J. PASSMORE, MAN'S RESPONSIBILITY FOR NATURE

78-80, 87-88 (1974)

[E]ven if men are inevitably perturbed by the reflection that in some remote epoch their race will be extinct, their perturbation does not, of itself, generate any sort of responsibility towards a posterity whose fate they may lament but cannot prevent. The case is no doubt rather different when what is involved is the long-term exhaustion of resources rather than what James had in mind — the "running down of the Universe." For men can, in principle, so act as to delay that exhaustion whereas they cannot delay the earth's cosmological destruction. But if all that can be predicted — the hypothesis I have for the moment adopted — is a very long-term exhaustion of resources, no *immediate* action on our part seems to be called for. Anything we can do would, over millions of years, be infinitesimal in its effects; not even by reducing our consumption of petrol to a thimbleful apiece could we ensure the availability of a similar quantity to our remotest descendants.[56]

Should we, then, move to the opposite extreme and leave the future to look after itself, concentrating all our efforts on making the best we can of today? Then it would not matter whether the scientists are right or wrong in predicting an early exhaustion of resources. For the future would be none of our business. This, according to Matthew (6:34), is what Jesus taught: "Take therefore no thought for the morrow; for the morrow shall take thought for the things of itself. Sufficient unto the day is the evil thereof." Nor is it by any means a preposterous attitude. We are confronted, in the present, by evils of every kind: in some of the developing countries by precisely the starvation, the illiteracy, the abysmal housing, the filth and disease which we fear for posterity; in many of our own cities by urban decay, impoverished schools,

---

56. To draw attention to the long-term problem, furthermore, can have effects the reverse of what conservationists would hope for; I have heard an economist argue that since the human race is in any case destined to extinction, it is absurd to pay any attention to the needs of our more immediate posterity. *Compare* R. D. Laing (L'Express 29 July 1973).

rising tides of crime and violence. It might well seem odd that the conservationist — and this is an argument not uncommonly directed against him — is so confident that he knows how to save posterity when he cannot even save his own contemporaries. Over a large part of the globe, too, the "needs of posterity" are already being used to justify not only tyranny but a conspicuous failure to meet the needs of the present. One can easily be led to the conclusion that it would be better to let the morrow look after itself and to concentrate, as more than sufficient, upon the evils of our own time.

The view that men ought to concern themselves about the fate of posterity as such — as distinct from the fate of their children, their reputation, their property — is a peculiarly Western one, characteristic, even then, only of the last two centuries. It arises out of a uniquely modern view about the nature of the world, man's place in it, and man's capacities. A Stoic confronting our present situation might well believe that we were nearing the end of a cycle, that there would shortly be a vast conflagration after which everything would begin again. Within such a cycle, men could help to make the world a better place, but they could not possibly, on the Stoic view, arrest its cyclical course. For theological reasons, Augustine rejected the cyclical conception of history; Christians, he was confident, are saved or damned for eternity, not only for a particular cycle of existence. It was he who introduced into Western thought the idea of "the future of mankind." . . .

Men are now being called upon, entirely without help, to save the future. The future, it is presumed, lies entirely in their hands; tomorrow *cannot* take thought of itself; it is they, now, who have to save tomorrow, without any help either from Providence or from History. No previous generation has thought of itself as being confronted by so Herculean a task.

[Here Passmore discusses D. Meadows et al., The Limits to Growth (1972), a provocative study that predicted widespread ecological disaster within a generation unless significant changes in policy were taken, and questions whether its prescriptions can be implemented "without social and political disruption, including the risk of civil and nuclear war." He then considers Rawls' approach.]

Each generation, Rawls is suggesting, should decide what it ought to save for posterity by answering in particular terms a general question: what is it reasonable for a society to expect, at the stage of development it has reached, from its predecessor? If it then acts upon the answer at which it arrives, each generation will be better off than its predecessor but no generation will be called upon to make an exceptional sacrifice. This is as far as we can go, I should agree, if our relationship with succeeding generations is to be governed by the principle of justice. The consequence is that each generation is concerned, when it is considering what sacrifices it should make, only with the next succeeding generation, not with some remote posterity. And this, as contrasted with classical utilitarianism, presents it with an easier set of calculations to make, difficult although they still are.

But although this means that, up to a point, each generation is in a unique position, unique in respect both to exactly what it inherits and exactly what it has a duty to hand on, it does not allow for the position of a generation which is unique in a quite different sense: it cannot calculate what it should do for posterity by reflecting on what its predecessors did for it. The sacrifice required of such a generation may be heroic, and Rawls' theory is based on the concept of justice, fairness, equal shares; it leaves no room for the heroic sacrifice. Yet if the conservationists are right it is precisely such a heroic sacrifice we are now called upon to make, a sacrifice far beyond anything our ancestors had to make. And this transforms the situation.

Now, in fact, men quite often do make heroic sacrifices. They make them out of love. It is as lovers that they make sacrifices for the future more extensive than any a Benthamite calculus would admit to be rational. When men act for the sake of a future they will not live to see, it is for the most part out of love for persons, places and forms of activity, a cherishing of them, nothing more grandiose. It is indeed self-contradictory to say: "I love him or her or that place or that institution or that activity, but I don't care what happens to it after my death." To love is, amongst other things, to care about the future of what we love. (Of course, the word "love" is used in many different ways. I have in mind the sense in which to love is to cherish. I can "love ice-cream" without caring about what happens to it after I die.) This is most obvious when we love our [spouse], our children, our grand-children. But it is also true in the case of our more impersonal loves: our love for places, institutions and forms of activity. To love philosophy — to philosophize with joy — is to care about its future as a form of activity: to maintain that what happens to it after our death is of no consequence would be a clear indication that our "love of philosophy" is nothing more than a form of self-love. The tourist who writes his name on a tree or rock-face in a "beloved beauty spot" makes it only too clear what *he* loves. To love a place is to wish it to survive unspoiled. . . .

Love, no doubt, extends only for a limited distance in time. Men do not love their grand-children's grand-children. They cannot love what they do not know. But in loving their grand-children — a love which already carries them a not inconsiderable distance into the future — they hope that those grand-children, too, will have grand-children to love. They are *concerned,* to that degree, about their grand-children's grand-children. "For myself," writes Macfarlane Burnet, "I want to spare my grand-children from chaos and to hope that they will live to see *their* grand-children getting ready to bring a stable ecosystem into being."

NOTES AND QUESTIONS

1. Does Passmore provide a superior framework for defining the obligations of the current generation to sacrifice for the future? How in a democracy is it possible to undertake such sacrifices on a collective basis, particularly where the long term risks of environmental degradation are uncertain and turn on technical questions? See W. Ophuls, Ecology and the Politics of Scarcity (1977).

It has been suggested that principles of justice and ecology imply that each generation receives a "natural and cultural legacy from previous generations and holds it in trust for future generations." Weiss, The Planetary Trust: Conservation and Intergenerational Equity, 11 Ecol. L.Q. 495 (1985). According to this view, natural resources should be managed in much the way charitable trusts are administered under Anglo-American law, that is, in accordance with principles of preservation of trust assets, prohibition against waste, efficient investment of assets, and diversification of risk. Is this a useful model for natural resource decisionmaking? In what ways is this approach similar to and different from the economist's approach of managing resources to maximize their net expected present value? Cf. Williams, Running Out: The Problem of Exhaustible Resources, 7 J. Legal Studies 165 (1978).

2. As a result of economic development, scientific and technological advancements, and the opening of national and international markets, the standard of living, longevity, and many other measures of the quality of life have improved for most citizens in the United States (relative to previous generations). Furthermore, the rate of discovery of natural resources as well as technological improvements in the efficiency of use of such resources have kept pace with depletion of many resources. If these trends continue, as technological optimists predict, won't future generations be better off than the current generation? If so, in view of the many serious social problems plaguing our generation, should we be particularly concerned about providing for future generations? With regard to what environmental problems might sacrifices today be most important for the well-being of future generations? In what ways are the traditional indicators of quality of life (such as the standard of living and longevity) inadequate measures of individual and societal well-being? Cf. P. Samuelson & W. Nordhaus, Economics 117-119 (12th ed. 1985).

4.   THE PREFERENCE SHAPING FUNCTION

Economic analysis normally assumes that choices among alternatives are to be made by reference to the population's existing preferences for goods and services. These preferences are normally assumed to be fixed;[57] however, our present choices among goods and services will affect our future preferences because tastes and values are shaped by experience.[58] Preference-shaping effects are often minimal in private consumption choices, but they may be significant for governmental decisions because of the large absolute amount of resources that may be affected, their pervasive long-term character, and the fact that the process of choice is collective rather than individual. These characteristics, together with the efforts of affected agency and client interests to maintain and expand programs once initiated, often invest governmental programs with a self-generating, self-fulfilling dynamic.

These dynamic characteristics pose serious problems for proposals that agency policies be selected through economic analysis. Uncertainty is created as to whether the choices should be based on existing preferences or on the alternative sets of future preferences that would be generated by other policies that might be chosen. Because policy choice may affect preferences, administrators must at least address the question of whether policy choices should be based on individuals' actual preferences at any given time or whether such preferences should be discounted, in order to give weight either to the preferences individuals might develop if they were well informed, or to normative judgments that certain preferences should be encouraged or discouraged.

It is far from obvious that government policies should in principle be addressed solely to "consumers'" existing preferences. Congress in practice — and often in disregard of the advice of proponents of the economic allocation model — frequently adopts policies, such as making transfer payments in kind (food stamps, housing) rather than in cash, that seem implicitly to reject the criterion of maximizing the satisfaction of existing preferences. Whether these policies reflect a conclusion that existing choices will be made in ignorance or the more "paternalistic" position that the collectivity can dictate the use of transfer payments as it sees fit, they suggest that Congress would not regard allocational efficiency as an invariably correct or appropriate principle of policy choice. Moreover, putting congressional judgments to one

---

57. This assumption is defended in Becker & Stigler, "De Gustibus Non Est Disputandum," 67 Am. Econ. Rev. 76 (1977).

58. Particularly where preferences with a major ideological component are involved, as in the environmental field, rapid changes in preferences may result from dissemination of information and political debate.

Moreover, to the extent that individuals are given the opportunity to enjoy environmental amenities, they may come to value these amenities more than if they had never been exposed to them. By the same token, poor persons might legitimately contend that those who have never experienced poverty underrate the importance of industrial development in lieu of enhanced environmental quality.

side, it is hardly self-evident that only existing preferences should "count." Economic analysis cannot ultimately resolve the question of which preferences to encourage or discourage, ignore or implement; but issues of just this sort are at the heart of many governmental choices.

STEWART, REGULATION IN A LIBERAL STATE: THE ROLE OF NON-COMMODITY VALUES

92 Yale L.J. 1537, 1567-1568 (1983)

[L]iberalism has often been caricatured as a myopic social and political creed that celebrates subjectivity, egoism, and commodity values. The elements of truth in that attack stirred concern among nineteenth-century liberals, most notably John Stuart Mill. In *On Liberty*, Mill argued for limits on social and governmental authority in order to liberate individuals from society's homogenizing tendencies. But many of Mill's other writings reflect the conviction that a purely private conception of liberty could impoverish individual experience and capacity for self-realization. These concerns have been revived by contemporary scholars who criticize liberal conceptions of law and society and the law and economics movement. There is today fresh interest in developing a more "ample liberalism" that recognizes the need to develop in individuals a critical capability with respect to their preferences.

Such a capability is central to a Pelagian conception of liberalism that affirms the supreme value of individual self-determination, for without such a critical capacity one can hardly be said to choose one's own ends. This conception of liberalism also requires a substantial diversity in the conceptions of the good accessible to individuals. Such diversity depends upon heterogeneous social, intellectual, and physical environments. Voluntarism also implies opportunity for participation in the collective determination of social and physical environments that shape both the ends available to individuals and the means to realize them. These considerations suggest the following principles as elements of a more ample conception of liberalism that would have important implications for regulatory jurisprudence:

Aspiration — The social and physical environment should, consistent with liberal principles, equip and encourage individuals to examine critically their existing conceptions of the good. It should also provide opportunities for individuals to develop and pursue those conceptions which, on reflection, appear to them more worthy and fulfilling. We may term this the value of aspiration.

Diversity — A diversity of economic, cultural, and physical environments should be fostered. A homogenous society will not provide a setting in which an individual can readily discover and test divergent conceptions of the good as part of the process of reflective self-development that the principle of aspiration implies. This diversity can in some respects be promoted by limiting the power of government or dictate or shape individual preferences, but it may in other respects require collective action. Education is one example; environmental regulation is another.

Mutuality — The foundation of a liberal society is respect by each individual of every other's right to pursue his own conception of the good. But respect also implies concern for the adequacy of others' opportunities to pursue their conception of the good. Prima facie, each citizen should be afforded the material and other ingredients of such opportunities in order to advance the liberal ideal of society as a joint enterprise for pursuit of different forms of excellence. This goal may require that citizens be provided not only a minimum income or housing, but also access to non-commodity opportunities that may be created by regulation.

Civic virtue — Liberalism should invite individuals to take an active role in the direction of collective affairs through participation in voluntary associations and political activity. Such participation can nurture the sentiment of mutuality and diversify individuals' conceptions of the good to include associational and communal goals.

The decentralized, associational character of American liberalism did much to promote these four non-commodity values. Decentralization, combined with geographical, economic, ethnic, and culturalvariety, generated substantial diversity. Civic virtue was promoted by conditions favoring participation in voluntary associations and a variety of local governmental bodies. Mutuality and aspiration were fostered by church groups, farmers' cooperatives, and workers' associations. Because these values are . . . disregarded by the principle of commodity-based wealth-maximization, we may appropriately term them non-commodity values.

In excluding non-commodity values, wealth-maximization ignores the intimate and inevitable interdependencies involved in collective choices. It also ignores the powerful effects that such choices exert on individual preferences when they determine basic features of the physical and social environment. By denying that non-commodity values are an appropriate ground of individual and social choices, wealth maximization denies important and relevant conceptions of the good. Wealth maximization is not — contrary to initial appearances — consistent with liberal principles. It is instead a form of tyranny that would impose on individuals a partial, sectarian conception of the good. Liberal principles demand that regulation cultivate non-commodity values.

NOTES AND QUESTIONS

1. The "preference shaping" problem is not limited to cases where existing, well defined preferences will be altered by policies or experiences that we choose to pursue. In many instances of policy choice involving collective goods or negative externalities, most individuals have no well defined preferences because they have no past experience in evaluating such goods or bads, which by their very nature are not the subject of individual choice or exchange. How much would you pay to avoid a one in a billion chance of a nuclear power accident in the city where you live? How much would you pay to maintain the Alaska wilderness in its natural state? In such circumstances, government decisions about environmental policy are more likely to shape rather than mirror the preferences of citizens regarding environmental quality. The very realization by citizens that environmental quality is a matter of social choice, and the process of governmental decision about those choices, may themselves have an important preference-shaping effect.

2. Does the preference-shaping problem involve us in the hopeless circularity of preferring whatever we choose? Or is it possible to choose what future preferences we wish to have? Is there a "correct" or "best" set of preferences? If not, does it follow that a democratic society should not concern itself at all with the impact of collective "public good" resource allocation decisions on individual preferences? See R. Dworkin, Taking Rights Seriously 272-278 (1977).

3. How could policymakers apply Stewart's "more ample liberalism"? Can cost-benefit analysis be adjusted to take into consideration notions of aspiration, diversity, mutuality, and civic virtue? Or must we abandon cost-benefit analysis? Should environmental policies explicitly favor diversity? Or should policymakers forthrightly conclude that certain experiences and values, such as enjoyment of wilderness, are worthier than others, such as driving high-powered automobiles, and take action accordingly?

4. Use of economic analysis may influence preferences in another way. Steven Kelman argues that "microeconomics-influenced policy analysts . . . seek to influence people's preferences: (1) away from caring about preferences (which is a preference itself); (2) away from caring about equity issues in the design in public policies; (3) towards ascribing greater weight to efficiency goals in public policy decisions; (4) towards a sympathy for self-interest as a motivation for human behavior; and (5) by favoring market exchanges, towards increased calculativeness and decreased value imputed to various nonpriced things." S. Kelman, What Price Incentives? 153-154 (1981). Has Kelman confused the normative and positive roles of economics? Or are they inextricably intertwined? If the decisionmaking criteria inevitably influence soci-

ety's values, then what values should such criteria seek to instill? What decisionmaking criteria would instill these values?

5.   RIGHTS-BASED THEORIES FOR PROTECTING NATURE AND "NATURALIST" ETHICS

Thus far, the discussion has largely conceived of legal rules as instruments, in the sense that their purpose and justification is framed in terms of securing a goal or end such as economic efficiency, a just distribution of income, the pursuit of liberal values, or some combination thereof. Moreover, each of these perspectives has been anthropocentric. Alternatively, legal rules may, and often have been, conceived as expressing or embodying fundamental principles of justice or right that are accepted without reference to the achievement of some external goal. Such principles can recognize values in nature apart from impacts upon humans.

A variety of rights-based theories and "naturalist" ethics have been offered to guide human actions affecting the environment. The "conservation" ethic — propounded by Gifford Pinchot, the first Chief of the U.S. Forest Service, in the early twentieth century — extends utilitarian ideas to recognize the anthropocentric value of wise and efficient resource management. Pinchot sought to improve nature's bounty over the longterm by using appropriate timber harvesting methods, planting seedlings, and controlling nature's processes.

The preservationist ethic, dating back to the writings of Henry David Thoreau in the mid-nineteenth century, took root in American culture with the writings and activism of John Muir, who led the fight to establish Yosemite National Park in 1890 and founded the Sierra Club. Muir saw nature as a sanctuary for the human spirit, and hence his ethic was based upon a religious and aesthetic foundation. Although quite different from Pinchot's utilitarianism, Muir's preservationism was also anthropocentric.

The philosophical bases for protecting nature have been further explored and greatly expanded since the time of John Muir and Gifford Pinchot. This section excerpts two of the more prominent modern theories: animal liberation and biocentrism. Building upon a tradition of early animal right theorists, Peter Singer has articulated a moral theory recognizing the rights of all sentient beings. Aldo Leopold's *A Sand County Almanac*, excerpted in Chapter 1, has been an influential source for ecological-based systems of ethics. These theories view natural communities holistically rather than as groups of individual members or species.

P. Singer, Animal Liberation

(1975)

> All Animals Are Equal . . .
> or why the ethical principle on which human
> equality rests requires us to extend equal
> consideration to animals too

"Animal Liberation" may sound more like a parody of other liberation movements than a serious objective. The idea of "The Rights of Animals" actually was once used to parody the case for women's rights. When Mary Wollstonecraft, a forerunner of today's feminists, published her Vindication of the Rights of Woman in 1792, her views were widely regarded as absurd, and before long an anonymous publication appeared entitled A Vindication of the Rights of Brutes. The author of this satirical work (now known to have been Thomas Taylor, a distinguished Cambridge philosopher) tried to refute Mary Wollstonecraft's arguments by showing that they could be carried one stage further. If the argument for equality was sound when applied to women, why should it not be applied to dogs, cats, and horses? The reasoning seemed to hold for these "brutes" too; yet to hold that brutes had rights was manifestly absurd. Therefore the reasoning by which this conclusion had been reached must be unsound, and if unsound when applied to brutes, it must also be unsound when applied to women, since the very same arguments had been used in each case.

In order to explain the basis of the case for the equality of animals, it will be helpful to start with an examination of the case for the equality of women. Let us assume that we wish to defend the case for women's rights against the attack by Thomas Taylor. How should we reply?

One way in which we might reply is by saying that the case for equality between men and women cannot validly be extended to non-human animals. Women have a right to vote, for instance, because they are just as capable of making rational decisions about the future as men are; dogs, on the other hand, are incapable of understanding the significance of voting, so they cannot have the right to vote. There are many other obvious ways in which men and women resemble each other closely, while humans and animals differ greatly. So, it might be said, men and women are similar beings and should have similar rights, while humans and nonhumans are different and should not have equal rights.

The reasoning behind this reply to Taylor's analogy is correct up to a point, but it does not go far enough. There are obviously important differences between humans and other animals, and these differences must give rise to some differences in the rights that each have. Recognizing this evident fact, however, is no barrier to the case for extending the basic principle of equality to nonhuman animals. The differences that exist between men and women are equally undeniable, and the supporters of Women's Liberation are aware that these differences may give rise to different rights. Many feminists hold that women have the right to an abortion on request. It does not follow that since these same feminists are campaigning for equality between men and women they must support the right of men to have abortions too. Since a man cannot have an abortion, it is meaningless to talk of his right to have one. Since dogs can't vote, it is meaningless to talk of their right to vote. There is no reason why either Women's Liberation or Animal Liberation should get involved in such nonsense. The extension of the basic principle of equality from one group to another does not imply that we must treat both groups in exactly the same way, or grant exactly the same rights to both groups. Whether we should do so will depend on the nature of the members of the two groups. The basic principle of equality does not require equal or identical treatment; it requires equal consideration. Equal consideration for different beings may lead to different treatment and different rights.

So there is a different way of replying to Taylor's attempt to parody the case for women's rights, a way that does not deny the obvious differences between human beings and nonhumans but goes more deeply into the question of equality and concludes by finding nothing absurd in the idea that the basic principle of equality applies to so-called brutes. At this point such a conclusion may appear odd; but if we examine more deeply the basis on which our opposition to discrimination on grounds of race or sex ultimately rests, we will see that we would be on shaky ground if we were to demand equality for blacks, women, and other groups of oppressed humans while denying equal consideration to nonhumans. To make this clear we need to see, first, exactly why racism and sexism are wrong. When we say that all human beings, whatever their race, creed, or sex, are equal, what is it that we are asserting? Those who wish to defend hierarchical, inegalitarian societies have often pointed out that by whatever test we choose it simply is not true that all humans are equal. Like it or not we must face the fact that humans come in different shapes and sizes; they come with different moral capacities, different intellectual abilities, different amounts of benevolent feeling and sensitivity to the needs of others, different abilities to communicate effectively, and different capacities to experience pleasure and pain. In short, if the demand for equality were based on the actual equality of all human beings, we would have to stop demanding equality.

There is a second important reason why we ought not to base our opposition to racism and sexism on any kind of factual equality, even the limited kind that asserts that variations in capacities and abilities are spread evenly among the different races and between the sexes; we can have no absolute guarantee that these capacities and abilities really are distributed evenly, without regard to race or sex, among human beings. So far as actual abilities are concerned there do seem to be certain measurable differences both among races and between sexes. These differences do not, of course, appear in every case, but only when averages are taken. More important still, we do not yet know how many of these differences are really due to the different genetic endowments of the different races and sexes, and how many are due to poor schools, poor housing, and other factors that are the result of past and continuing discrimination. Perhaps all of the important differences will eventually prove to be environmental rather than genetic. Anyone opposed to racism and sexism will certainly hope that this will be so, for it will make the task of ending discrimination a lot easier; nevertheless, it would be dangerous to rest the case against racism and sexism on the belief that all significant differences are environmental in origin. The opponent of, say, racism who takes this line will be unable to avoid conceding that if differences in ability did after all prove to have some genetic connection with race, racism would in some way be defensible.

Fortunately, there is no need to pin the case for equality to one particular outcome of a scientific investigation. The appropriate response to those who claim to have found evidence of genetically based differences in ability among the races or between the sexes is not to stick to the belief that the genetic explanation must be wrong, whatever evidence to the contrary may turn up; instead we should make it quite clear that the claim to equality does not depend on intelligence, moral capacity, physical strength, or similar matters of fact. Equality is a moral idea, not an assertion of fact. There is no logically compelling reason for assuming that a factual difference in ability between two people justifies any difference in the amount of consideration we give to their needs and interests. The principle of the equality of human beings is not a description of an alleged actual equality among humans; it is a prescription of how we should treat human beings. . . .

In misguided attempts to refute the arguments [for Animal Liberation], some philosophers have gone to much trouble developing arguments to show that animals do not have rights. They have claimed that to have rights a being must be autonomous, or must be a member of a community, or must have the ability to respect the rights of others, or must possess a sense of justice. These claims are irrelevant to the case for Animal Liberation.

If a being suffers there can be no moral justification for refusing to take that suffering into consideration. No matter what the nature of the being, the principle of equality requires that its suffering be counted equally with the like suffering — insofar as rough comparisons can be made — of any other being. If a being is not capable of suffering, or of experiencing enjoyment or happiness, there is nothing to be taken into account. So the limit of sentience (using the term as a convenient if not strictly accurate shorthand for the capacity to suffer and/or experience enjoyment) is the only defensible boundary of concern for the interests of others. To mark this boundary by some other characteristic like intelligence or rationality would be to mark it in an arbitrary manner. Why not choose some other characteristic, like skin color?

Racists violate the principle of equality by giving greater weight to the interests of members of their own race when there is a clash between their interests and the interests of those of another race. Sexists violate the principle of equality by favoring the interests of their own sex. Similarly, speciesists allow the interests of their own species to override the greater interests of members of other species. The pattern is identical in each case.

[The remainder of the book consists of shocking accounts of human treatment of animals and explication of Singer's philosophy.]

P. TAYLOR, *RESPECT FOR NATURE*

44-53 (1986)

When one conceives of oneself, one's relation to other living things, and the whole set of natural ecosystems on our planet in terms of [a biocentric outlook], one identifies oneself as a member of the Earth's Community of Life. This does not entail a denial of one's personhood. Rather, it is a way of understanding one's true self to include one's biological nature as well as one's personhood. From the perspective of [this] biocentric outlook, one sees one's membership in the Earth's Community of Life as providing a common bond with all the different species of animals and plants that have evolved over the ages. One becomes aware that, like all other living things on our planet, one's very existence depends on the fundamental soundness and integrity of the biological system of nature. When one looks at this domain of life in its totality, one sees it to be a complex and unified web of interdependent parts.

The biocentric outlook on nature also includes a certain way of perceiving and understanding each individual organism. Each is seen to be a teleological (goal-oriented) center of life, pursuing its own good in its own unique way. This, of course, does not mean that they all seek their good as a conscious end or purpose, the realization of which is their intended aim. Consciousness may not be present at all, and even when it is present the organism need not be thought of as intentionally taking steps to achieve goals it sets for itself. Rather, a living thing is conceived as a unified system of organized activity the constant tendency of which is to preserve its existence by protecting and promoting its well-being.

Finally, to view the place of humans in the natural world from the perspective of the biocentric outlook is to reject the idea of human superiority over other living things. Humans are not thought of as carrying on a higher grade of existence when compared with the so-called "lower" orders of life. The biocentric outlook precludes a hierarchical view of nature. To accept that outlook and view the living world in its terms is to commit oneself to the principle of species-impartiality. No bias in favor of some over others is acceptable. This impartiality applies to the human species just as it does to nonhuman species. . . .

Now, for a moral agent to be disposed to give equal consideration to all wild living things and to judge the good of each to be worthy of being preserved and protected as an end in itself and for the sake of the being whose good it is means that every wild living thing is seen to be the appropriate object of the attitude of respect. Given the acceptance of the biocentric outlook, the attitude of respect will be adopted as the only suitable or morally fitting attitude to have toward the Earth's creatures. One who takes the attitude of respect toward the individual organisms, species-populations, and biotic communities of the Earth's natural ecosystems regards those entities and groups of entities as possessing inherent worth in the sense that *their value or worth does not depend on their being valued for their usefulness in furthering human ends* (or the ends of any other species). When such an attitude is adopted as one's ultimate moral attitude, I shall speak of that person as having *respect for nature*. . . .

The ecological relationships among organisms and between organisms and the environment in healthy ecosystems are matters of biological fact. It is the task of the science of ecology to discover and explain those relationships. But the ethical question, "How *should* human culture fit into the order of nature?" is not a question of biological fact. It is a question that confronts humans as moral agents, not as biological organisms, since it asks which way of relating ourselves to nature, among the various alternatives open to our choice, is the ethically right one to adopt. . . .

One further point is to be noted in connection with this distinction between our animal status and our moral status. . . . I shall contend in this book that, from a certain perspective, the preservation of the human species may not be a good. I will argue that, once we are willing to view the natural world from a standpoint that is not anthropocentric, the desirability of human life is a claim that needs rational substantiation. It cannot just be assumed without question. Indeed, to assume it without question is already to commit oneself to an anthropocentric point of view concerning the natural world and the place of humans in it, and this is to beg some of the most fundamental issues of environmental ethics. As long as we keep clearly in mind the difference between humans as animals and humans as moral agents, we will recognize that although as animals we *want* to survive and reproduce, as moral agents we can ask ourselves whether we ought to survive and reproduce. Our biological needs and wants do not . . . present us with final, conclusive, logically unchallengeable reasons for deciding one way rather than another. It is not inconsistent for a human to believe in all sincerity that the world would be a better place if there were no humans in it. Whether such a judgment, though consistent, is rationally acceptable is a question that must wait until the foundations of an adequate theory of environmental ethics are thoroughly examined.

DEVALL, THE DEEP ECOLOGY MOVEMENT

20 Natural Resources J. 299 (1980)

There are two great streams of environmentalism in the latter half of the twentieth century. One stream is reformist, attempting to control some of the worst of the air and water pollution and inefficient land use practices in industrialized nations and to save a few of the remaining pieces of wildlands as "designated wilderness areas." The other stream supports many of the reformist goals but is revolutionary, seeking a new metaphysics, epistemology, cosmology, and environmental ethics of person/planet. This paper is an intellectual archeology of the second of these streams of environmentalism, which I will call deep ecology. . . .

SOURCES OF DEEP ECOLOGY

What I call deep ecology in this paper is premised on a gestalt of person-in-nature. The person is not above or outside of nature. The person is part of creation on-going. The person cares for and about nature, shows reverence towards and respect for nonhuman nature, loves and lives with nonhuman nature, is a person in the "earth household" and "lets being be," lets nonhuman nature follow separate evolutionary destinies. Deep ecology unlike reform environmentalism, is not just a pragmatic, short-term social movement with a goal like stopping nuclear power or cleaning up the waterways. Deep ecology first attempts to question and present alternatives to conventional ways of thinking in the modern West. Deep ecology understands that some of the "solutions" of reform environmentalism are counter-productive. Deep ecology seeks transformation of values and social organization.

[Devall traces the roots of the deep ecology movement: the critique of the dominant Judeo-Christian view of man *versus* nature; the influx of Eastern spiritual traditions, most importantly Zen Buddhism;

the re-evaluation of Native American culture, highlighting ways of living in harmony with nature; the minority tradition of Western religious and philosophic thought, including Spinoza, Jeffers, Muir, Leopold, Naess, Heidegger, and Whitehead; the scientific discipline of ecology; and the naturalist artistic tradition of Ansel Adams and others.]

THEMES OF DEEP ECOLOGY

[M]any thinkers are questioning some of the premises of the dominant social paradigm of the modern societies. They are attempting to extend on an appropriate metaphysics, epistemology, and ethics for what I call an "ecological consciousness." Some of these writers are very supportive of reformist environmental social movements, but they feel reform while necessary is not sufficient. They suggest a new paradigm is required and a new utopian vision of "right livelihood" and the "good society." Utopia stimulates our thinking concerning alternatives to present society. Some persons, such as Aldo Leopold, have suggested that we begin our thinking on utopia not with a statement of "human nature" or "needs of humans" but by trying to "think like a mountain." This profound extending, "thinking like a mountain," is part and parcel of the phenomenology of ecological consciousness. Deep ecology begins with Unity rather than dualism which has been the dominant theme of Western philosophy. . . .

Any attempt to create artificially a "new ecological ethics" or a "new ontology of man's place in nature" out of the diverse strands of thought which make up the deep ecology movement is likely to be forced and futile. However, by explicating some of the major themes embodied in and presupposed by the intellectual movement I am calling deep ecology, some groundwork can be laid for further discussion and clarification. Following the general outline of perennial philosophy, the order of the following statements summarizing deep ecology's basic principles are metaphysical-religious, psychological-epistemological, ethical, and social-economic-political. These concerns of deep ecology encompass most of reformist environmentalism's concerns but subsume them in its fundamental critique of the dominant paradigm.

According to deep ecology:

(1) A new cosmic/ecological metaphysics which stresses the identity (I/thou) of humans with non-human nature is a necessary condition for a viable approach to building an eco-philosophy. [T]he wholeness and integrity of person/planet together with the principle of what Arne Naess calls "biological equalitarianism" are the most important ideas. Man is an integral part of nature, not over or apart from nature. Man is a "plain citizen" of the biosphere, not its conqueror or manager. There should be a "democracy of all God's creatures" according to St. Francis; or as Spinoza said, "man is a temporary and

dependent mode of the whole of God/Nature." Man flows with the system of nature rather than attempting to control all of the rest of nature. The hand of man lies lightly on the land. Man does not perfect nature, nor is man's primary duty to make nature more efficient.

(2) An objective approach to nature is required. This approach is found, for example, in Spinoza and in the works of Spinoza's twentieth century disciple, Robinson Jeffers. Jeffers describes his orientation as a philosophy of "inhumanism" to draw a sharp and shocking contrast with the subjective anthropocentrism of the prevailing humanistic philosophy, art, and culture of the twentieth century West.

(3) A new psychology is needed to integrate the metaphysics in the mind field of post-industrial society. A major paradigm shift results from psychological changes of perception. The new paradigm requires rejection of subject/object, man/nature dualism and will require a pervasive awareness of total intermingling of the planet earth. Psychotherapy seen as adjustment to ego-oriented society is replaced by a new ideal of psychotherapy as spiritual development. The new metaphysics and psychology leads logically to a posture of biospheric egalitarianism and liberation in the sense of autonomy, psychological/emotional freedom of the individual, spiritual development for Homo sapiens, and the right of other species to pursue their own evolutionary destinies.

(4) There is an objective basis for environmentalism, but objective science in the new paradigm is different from the narrow, analytic conception of the scientific method currently popular. Based on "ancient wisdom" science should be both objective and participatory without modern science's subject/object dualism. The main value of science is seen in its ancient perspective as contemplation of the cosmos and the enhancement of understanding of self and creation.

(5) There is wisdom in the stability of natural processes unchanged by human intervention. Massive human-induced disruptions of ecosystems will be unethical and harmful to men. Design for human settlement should be with nature, not against nature.

(6) The quality of human existence and human welfare should not be measured only by quantity of products. Technology is returned to its ancient place as an appropriate tool for human welfare, not an end in itself.

(7) Optimal human carrying capacity should be determined for the planet as a biosphere and for specific islands, valleys, and continents. A drastic reduction of the rate of growth of population of Homo sapiens through humane birth control programs is required.

(8) Treating the symptoms of man/nature conflict, such as air or water pollution, may divert attention from more important issues and thus be counter-productive to "solving" the problems. Economics must be subordinate to ecological-ethical criteria. Economics is to be treated as a small sub-branch of ecology and will assume a rightfully minor role in the new paradigm.

(9) A new philosophical anthropology will draw on data of hunting/gathering societies for principles of healthy, ecologically viable societies. Industrial society is not the end toward which all societies should aim or try to aim. Therefore, the notion of "reinhabiting the land" with hunting-gathering, and gardening as a goal and standard for post-industrial society should be seriously considered.

(10) Diversity is inherently desirable both culturally and as a principle of health and stability of ecosystems.

(11) There should be a rapid movement toward "soft" energy paths and "appropriate technology" and toward lifestyles which will result in a drastic decrease in per capita energy consumption in advanced industrial societies while increasing appropriate energy in decentralized villages in so-called "third world" nations. Deep ecologists are committed to rapid movement to a "steady-state" or "conservor society" both from ethical principles of harmonious integration of humans with nature and from appreciation of ecological realities. Integration of sophisticated, elegant, unobtrusive, ecologically sound, appropriate technology with greatly scaled down, diversified, organic, labor-intensive agriculture, hunting, and gathering is another goal.

(12) Education should have as its goal encouraging the spiritual . . . and personhood development of the members of a community, not just training them in occupations appropriate for oligarchic bureaucracies and for consumerism in advanced industrial societies.

(13) More leisure as contemplation in art, dance, music, and physical skills will return play to its place as the nursery of individual fulfillment and cultural achievement.

(14) Local autonomy and decentralization of power is preferred over centralized political control through oligarchic bureaucracies. Even if bureaucratic modes of organization are more "efficient," other modes of organization for small scale human communities are more "effective" in terms of the principles of deep ecology.

(15) In the interim, before the steady-state economy and radically changed social structure are instituted, vast areas of the planet biospheres will be zoned "off limits" to further industrial exploitation and large-scale human settlements these should be protected by defensive groups of people. One ecologist has called such groups a "world wilderness police."

COMPETING POLITICAL SOLUTIONS TO THE CONTINUING ENVIRONMENTAL CRISIS

Major theorists in both reformist environmentalism and deep ecology are of the opinion that the environmental crisis is continuing and becoming more severe. Reformist environmentalists continue to argue, however, that the problems can be solved within the dominant social paradigm. For example, they advocate redefining some private property rights and responsibilities. Reformers advocate passing more laws to regulate polluters or provide incentives to "clean up the mess." Some reformers seek to extend the ideal of legal rights to the natural environment, broadening common-law precedents to include a legal recognition of every person's right to a habitable environment. Some reformist writers argue that incremental changes in laws and social institutions is the most that can be done at the present point in developing our political traditions to include some idea of environmental quality. . . .

Theorists of deep ecology argue that the best of reform environmentalism can be incorporated into deep ecology. However, just changing laws to control air and water pollution, or providing procedures for safety of nuclear reactors, or setting aside small areas of land as "designated wilderness areas" is not enough. Indeed, in treating the symptoms of the malaise some of these actions may be counter-productive. At best they are temporary, limited stop-gap measures attempting to handle the problem of the environment within the values of the dominant social paradigm.

Although deep ecology requires fundamental change, the movement does not have a full articulated political-economic program, and many theorists would consider such a program to be sterile and inappropriate at this time. Instead, most deep ecologists have limited themselves to critiques of the dominant social paradigm and to suggesting alternative visions of man-in-nature without specifying how these visions may be realized. This is the case with Gary Snyder's "Four Changes," which was written at the beginning of the "environmental decade" of the 1970s and remains one of the most cognant [sic] political statements of deep ecology.

At the end of the 1970s, writers such as Theodore Roszak and Raymond Dasmann were making specific recommendations for changes in lifestyles. Both Roszak and Dasmann prefer small-scale communities. Roszak suggests revival of the "household economy." He links the search for "personhood" with the development of ecological consciousness. Dasmann elaborates on the process of "reinhabiting" landscapes which have been exploited and degraded by previous generations of humans. He wants a decentralized, small-scale, caring community. . . .

NOTES AND QUESTIONS

1. In order to be operational, a rights-based ethic must provide a basis for resolving the inevitable conflicts of rights in society. Consider the following conflict. In countries ravaged by malaria, DDT can save thousands of lives by eradicating the mosquitos that carry the disease.

Yet the bioaccumulation of DDT in birds consuming mosquitos poisons the birds and can threaten entire species. Are the rights of birds less important than those of humans? How many birds must die before society should reduce the use of DDT? How many humans must die before society should let a bird species become extinct? Do we, in the end, have to balance rights of birds against rights of humans? Is this very different from cost-benefit analysis?

2. Another way of conceiving a rights-based ethic for protecting nature would be to recognize human rights to a clean environment. Should each individual in society be guaranteed a minimally healthy environment, regardless of considerations of efficiency? The notion of a right to a healthy environment is intuitively appealing. Clearly, knowingly exposing individuals to a deadly pollutant would be wrong no matter how efficient such a policy might be. It is not unduly difficult to extrapolate from this example a general right of each person to a minimum level of environmental quality which could be viewed as one solution to the problem of income distribution in the environmental context. But the difficulties in applying and giving content to such a notion are formidable. Surely the fact that an activity poses *some* risk of environmental harm to health is not sufficient grounds for prohibiting it. How risky must such activities be before they are prohibited? How much in the way of environmental quality ought to be provided to everyone? Can these questions be answered without resort to a calculus of costs and benefits? If not, doesn't the need to resort to economic analysis to define the minimum right undercut the grounds for insisting upon such a minimum when to do so would be wildly inefficient?

3. Singer's ethical domain extends beyond anthropocentrism to a "zoocentric sentientism," but it accepts the basic assumptions of conventional ethics and human perception of the natural world. Should these assumptions carry over to "natural" ethics? Do the ecological-based ethics succeed in transcending conventional ethics? Can humans fully divorce ethics from anthropocentrism and human perception? Can humans seriously "think like a mountain"?

4. Devall describes a rough blueprint for implementing biocentrism. Is it self-evident that a major paradigm shift is desirable? needed? Can persons raised and taught to think within the dominant paradigm fully appreciate these questions?

5. Should deep ecologists content themselves with a critique of the dominant paradigm without offering a well articulated and feasible "political-economic program"? What might be gained from the critique? Are the 15 "principles" of deep ecology noted by Devall internally consistent? Beyond suggestions to move toward a "decentralized, small-scale, caring community," how can deep ecology be made operational on local, regional, and global levels?

6. In his last novel, *Island*, published in 1961, Aldous Huxley describes an ecologically stable, self-sustaining utopian society. The island

community developed free from industrialization and colonization (but is now threatened as the outside world seeks to exploit the island's natural resources). The islanders, guided by Buddhist teachings, have learned to live as part of nature as they seek spiritual fulfillment. They have "not the faintest desire to land on the backside of the moon. Only the modest ambition to live as fully human beings in harmony with the rest of life on this island at this latitude on this planet." From early in life, members of the community are taught the basics of ecology:

> Confronted by [examples of ecological damage], it's easy for the child to see the need for conservation and then to go from conservation to morality — easy for him or her to go from the Golden Rule in relation to plants and animals and the earth that supports them to the Golden Rule in relation to human beings. . . . The morality to which a child goes on from the facts of ecology and the parables of erosion is a universal ethic. . . . "Do as you would be done by" applies to our dealings with all kinds of life in every part of the world. We shall be permitted to live on this planet only for so long as we treat all nature with compassion and intelligence. . . . [Id. at . . .]

What insights can you glean from Huxley's vision for finding the path to an ecologically stable and spiritually fullfilling future? Are our existing political, religious, and cultural institutions capable of enabling the collective choices necessary to follow this path?

7. Deep ecologists have suggested that global population should be stabilized at some small fraction of current population — the figures range between 100 million and 1 billion. Can deep ecology be made operational without sacrificing what are perceived to be (at least within the dominant paradigm) other important social values? If not, and if the transition to the new ethic does not occur instantaneously, then what are the implications of paradigm shift for political stability? What political institutions and systems are best able to make the transition? What role will/should reform environmentalism play in the transition? Can incremental change achieve a major paradigm shift?

8. The deep ecology movement has attracted criticism from all quadrants of the political universe. See e.g., Sale, Deep Ecology and Its Critics, The Nation 670 (May 14, 1988). How would Baxter, supra p. 19, respond to the "naturalist" ethics? How do you respond?

6. PROCESS VALUES

Our legal and political culture places as much or more importance on *how* decisions are made as contrasted with the substantive content of *what* decisions are made. This emphasis on process values in part reflects inability to agree on substantive goals and repugnance at dictation of social policies by a central elite or dominant faction. It may also reflect a view that participation in the process of governmental decision is itself a good.

The economic analysis of government intervention to correct "market failure" appears unable to accommodate process values. Decision is a function of a centralized decisionmaker's measurement of alternative outcomes. See Tribe, Policy Science: Analysis or Ideology? 2 Phil. & Pub. Aff. 66, 83 (1972). No direct participation in the process of decision by those affected is required; indeed, the political tug and pull arising from participation might well threaten the impartiality and rationality of the decisional process. Increased resort to economic analysis as the master key to social choice might thus run directly counter to the growing criticism of government decisionmaking as remote, impersonal, and unresponsive to the concerns of the governed. On the other hand, economic analysis might merely channel participation into particular modes — such as revelation of costs and benefits and input on how to alter decision criteria to take a broader set of factors into account. The National Environmental Policy Act, the focus of Chapter 8, provides a rich testing ground for analyzing the role of process values in environmental decisionmaking.

Alternatively, the notion of process values may be seen as simply one more factor or goal to be weighted with others — efficiency, distributional equity, moral principles, duties to nature — in devising sound rules and institutions. But it can also be regarded as the dominant value. If different individuals and groups in the society are unable to agree upon the appropriate goals or principles of environmental policy, or if they are able to agree upon several goals or principles that conflict but are unable to agree on how those conflicts are to be resolved, are we not remitted to the necessity of some process for reconciling competing views? Rawls, A Theory of Justice (1971) is a grand set of variations on this theme. But it is also one of direct relevance to lawyers, concerned as they are with procedure and decisional institutions. On the other hand, is it possible to decide what procedures are fair and appropriate without reference to substantive goals? Is it the case that undue emphasis on "due process" in a society such as ours inevitably leads to short-run incremental adjustments and precludes the basic structural changes and bold policy initiatives that may be needed to deal with long-run ecological problems? These issues raise two basic, related questions that you should consider as you progress through the rest of these materials. First, to what extent is it possible to develop a coherent and consistent analytic framework for deciding questions of environmental policy that would give due weight to each of the rich variety of social goals or considerations that we have identified? Second, what sort of institutions should we develop to make environmental decisions that will necessarily involve choice among such considerations?

3

The Role of the Common Law in Addressing Environmental Degradation

An attorney intimately familiar with the citizen lawsuit as a means for improving private and public decisions bearing on environmental quality has said, "A court of equity is the only place to take effective action against polluters. Only in a courtroom can a scientist present his evidence, free from harassment by politicians. And only in a courtroom can bureaucratic hogwash be tested in the crucible of cross-examination." Comments of Victor J. Yannacone, Jr., formerly counsel for the Environmental Defense Fund, quoted in Bengelsdorf, . . . That Breathing by the People Shall Not Perish From the Smog, Los Angeles Times, August 14, 1969, at 7. Yet, not a week after this remark was reported, a Los Angeles County Superior Court judge dismissed a massive pollution class action filed on behalf of residents of Los Angeles County against 291 corporations allegedly responsible for smog in the Los Angeles Basin. "It is an impossible job for any court to try to abate smog in Los Angeles County," the judge is quoted as saying. "The problem is much too complex for a court to solve." Los Angeles Times, August 21, 1969, Pt. 1, p. 32, commenting on *Diamond v. General Motors Corp.*, No. 947429 (Los Angeles, Cal. Super. Ct.), *dismissed,* Aug. 20, 1969, *aff'd,* 20 Cal. App. 3d 374, 97 Cal. Rptr. 639 (1971).

The materials in this chapter provide an introductory look at the role of the courts as a "front line" agency in responding to environmental degradation through the development of common law rules governing litigation by private citizens against private pollution sources. Surely the courts — through the medium of the citizen suit seeking damages and injunctive relief — cannot be the sole means of regulating environmental quality,[1] but just as surely they have some role to play. We explore that role in this chapter. In each case, the emphasis is on gauging the effectiveness of citizen suits and the courts as means for improving decisions bearing on the quality of the environment. What are their strengths? What are their weaknesses? What modifications might enhance their usefulness? As a transition to the materials on administrative regulation that pervade the remainder of the book, the final section of this chapter focuses upon the efficacy of the common law and judicial process in dealing with modern, industrial environmental degradation.

A.   TRADITIONAL COMMON LAW DOCTRINES

This section summarizes the principal common law doctrines governing environmental pollution. The history of these doctrines is filled with complexities and obscurities, much of the explanation of which is beyond our present purpose. Rather, our purpose is to provide a basic background that will enable you to analyze the doctrines, to propose and assess reforms, and to understand the limitations of the common law system as a means of addressing modern, industrial environmental degradation.[2]

Our discussion below divides the common law into doctrines governing invasions of personal interests (personal injury actions) and doctrines governing invasions of property interests (trespass and nuisance). Under all of these traditional common law doctrines, the plaintiff must bring an action within the applicable statute of limitations and establish a firm causal link between the conduct of defendant and actual or imminent damage to the plaintiff's interest. Statutes of limitations present

---

1. Civil and criminal enforcement suits brought by public officials against pollution sources will be considered in Chapters 4, 5, and 6, which deal with legislative and administrative regulation of environmental degradation. Chapters 7 and 8 consider suits by private citizens to obtain judicial review of administrative action (or inaction) by government officials.

2. Those interested in a richer description of the origins, evolution, and details of the common law doctrines might wish to consult: Rodgers, Environmental Law: Air and Water §§2.1-2.20 (2d ed. 1986); Developments in the Law — Toxic Waste Litigation, 99 Harv. L. Rev. 1458, 1602-1631 (1986); W. Prosser & W. Keeton, Prosser and Keeton on Torts (5th ed. 1984).

particular problems where harms do not manifest until many years after exposure, as can occur with toxic pollutants. See Developments in the Law — Toxic Waste Litigation, 99 Harv. L. Rev. 1458, 1605-1610 (1986). The causation requirement can be particularly problematic in many environmental contexts as well because of the difficulty of showing (1) that the plaintiff or her land was (or is likely to be) exposed to a pollutant that emanated from the defendant's activities, and (2) that the plaintiff's actual or threatened adverse health condition or the actual or threatened damage to her land was caused by exposure to the defendant's pollutant as opposed to other natural or human causes. Id. at 1617-1630. The causation requirement can seriously restrict the availability of remedies for risks of future harm or for harms with multiple potential causes.

1.   INVASIONS OF PERSONAL INTERESTS

Many pollutants can cause serious personal injuries and therefore doctrines governing relief for invasions of personal interests regulate some forms of environmental degradation. In most circumstances, the common law doctrine of negligence governs relief for personal injuries. The doctrine of strict liability, however, may apply to cases involving personal injuries resulting from polluting activities.

Negligence. A negligence cause of action has four elements:

(1)   a legal duty requiring the actor to conform to a certain standard of conduct for the protection of others against an unreasonable risk,

(2)   a breach of that duty,

(3)   a reasonably close causal connection between the conduct and the resulting injury, and

(4)   an actual injury.

Prosser & Keeton on Torts §30. Judge Learned Hand's statement of the negligence standard of conduct in *United States v. Carroll Towing Co.,* 159 F.2d 169, 173 (2d Cir. 1947), is frequently cited:

Since there are occasions when every vessel will break away from her moorings, and, since, if she does, she becomes a menace to those about her, the owner's duty, as in other similar situations, to provide against resulting injuries is a function of three variables: (1) The probability that she will break away; (2) the gravity of the resulting injury, if she does; (3) the burden of adequate precautions [to avoid the injury]. Possibly it serves to bring this notion into relief to state it in algebraic terms: if the probability be called P; the injury L; and the burden B; liability depends upon whether B is less than L multiplied by P; i.e., whether B [is less than] PL.

Though straightforward in principle, this test can be especially difficult to apply in environmental cases because neither plaintiffs nor courts typically have the resources or ability to assess B, P, and L in particular concrete situations. See Developments in the Law — Toxic Waste Litigation, 99 Harv. L. Rev. 1458, 1612-1613 (1986).

   Strict Liability. The doctrine of strict liability is also available in certain circumstances to remedy personal injuries. This doctrine can be traced to the case of *Rylands v. Fletcher,* 3 H.L. 330 (1868). The *Rylands* rule imposes liability for any damages caused by "a thing or activity unduly dangerous and inappropriate to the place where it is maintained, in the light of the character of that place and its surroundings." The Restatement (Second) of Torts, §519, recognizes strict liability for damages resulting from "abnormally dangerous activities." In determining whether an activity is abnormally dangerous, the following factors are to be considered:

   (a)   whether the activity involves a high degree of risk of some harm to the person, land or chattels of others;
   (b)   whether the gravity of the harm which may result from it is likely to be great;
   (c)   whether the risk cannot be eliminated by the exercise of reasonable care;
   (d)   whether the activity is not a matter of common usage;
   (e)   whether the activity is inappropriate to the place where it is carried on; and
   (f)   the value of the activity to the community.

Id. §520. One of the comments to this section states that these factors "are all to be considered, and are all of importance. Any one of them is not necessarily sufficient of itself in a particular case, and ordinarily several of them will be required for strict liability." Id.[3]

2.   INVASIONS OF PROPERTY INTERESTS

   The common law doctrines of trespass and nuisance provide remedies for invasions of property interests. The distinction between trespass and nuisance grew out of the now-abandoned procedural forms of action: The action of trespass alleged a direct physical invasion of the

---

   3. An alternative basis of liability without fault is found in the principles of liability for defective products. See Restatement (Second) of Torts §402A.

plaintiff's land, such as the casting of water or stones onto the land; the action of case (from which nuisance is derived) alleged an indirect invasion, such as where the defendant built a spout which caused water to seep onto the plaintiff's land. The modern distinction between these actions is that trespass is an invasion of the plaintiff's interest in the exclusive possession of her land, and nuisance is an interference with the plaintiff's use and enjoyment of her land. As we shall see, however, even this distinction may not be of much significance in the pollution context.

Trespass. Under the common law rules of trespass, strict liability (that is, without fault) is imposed for intentional physical invasions of a person's interest in the exclusive possession of land.[4] Restatement (Second) of Torts §158. A physical invasion includes an intrusion by the defendant personally or through some other person or object which the defendant has caused to be deposited on the plaintiff's land. Thus impairment of one's view by the release of smoke from an adjacent property would not constitute a trespass. Suppose, however, that the smoke or other air pollutants drifted over the property line and settled on the neighbor's land? Would this constitute a trespass, even though the air pollution did not consist of visible particles? In *Martin v. Reynolds Metals Co.*, 221 Ore. 86, 342 P.2d 790 (1959), *cert. denied*, 362 U.S. 918 (1960), the court held that it did, rejecting the defendant's arguments that air pollution (fluoride particles that were not visible) did not represent the sort of "breaking and entering" needed to establish trespass and that the invasion was not actionable as trespass because it was "consequential" (a result of weather variables) rather than "direct." The court reasoned as follows:

> The view recognizing a trespassory invasion where there is no "thing" which can be seen with the naked eye undoubtedly runs counter to the definition of trespass expressed in some quarters. . . . It is quite possible that in an earlier day when science had not yet peered into the molecular and atomic world of small particles, the courts could not fit an invasion through unseen physical instrumentalities into the requirement that a trespass can result only from a *direct* invasion. But in this atomic age even the uneducated know the great and awful force contained in the atom and what it can do to a man's property if it is released. In fact, the now famous equation $E = mc^2$ has taught us that mass and energy are equivalents and that our concept of "things" must be reframed. If these observations on science in relation to the law of trespass should appear

---

4. In the case of unintentional invasions, which is treated in essentially the same way as accidental invasions of the person, see Prosser & Keeton on Torts, supra at 69-70, liability is imposed only if harm results and the defendant's conduct was negligent, reckless, or abnormally dangerous. Restatement (Second) of Torts §§157-166.

theoretical and unreal in the abstract, they become very practical and real to the possessor of land when the unseen force cracks the foundation of his house. The force is just as real if it is chemical in nature and must be awakened by the intervention of another agency before it does harm.

If, then, we must look to the character of the instrumentality which is used in making an intrusion upon another's land we prefer to emphasize the object's energy or force rather than its size. Viewed in this way we may define trespass as any intrusion which invades the possessor's protected interest in exclusive possession, whether that intrusion is by visible or invisible pieces of matter or by energy which can be measured only by the mathematical language of the physicist.

We are of the opinion therefore, that the intrusion of the fluoride particulates in the present case constituted a trespass.

Accord, Fairview Farms, Inc. v. Reynolds Metals Co., 176 F. Supp. 178 (D. Ore. 1959). Although finding that air pollution can constitute a trespass, the court nonetheless applied a nuisance-type balancing test in determining liability.

Private Nuisance. A widely adopted definition of a private nuisance is a substantial invasion of another's use and enjoyment of land that is either (1) "intentional and unreasonable"; or (2) "unintentional and otherwise actionable under the rules controlling liability for negligent or reckless conduct, or for abnormally dangerous conditions or activities." Restatement (Second) of Torts §822. Ownership of a property interest in land is thus a prerequisite to maintenance of a private nuisance action. The requirement of a "substantial" invasion[5] has been inappropriately utilized to deny recovery for nontrivial forms of environmental degradation, such as aesthetic impairment, that do not result in tangible physical changes in land or easily measured economic harm.

The type of conduct that gives rise to liability has traditionally turned on whether the conduct is "intentional" or "unintentional." Intentional conduct is that which is undertaken for the purpose of causing the harm in question or which is substantially certain to cause such harm. It is actionable if it is "unreasonable." Conduct is said to be unreasonable if the "gravity of the harm" to the plaintiff outweighs the "utility of the defendant's conduct." Restatement (Second) of Torts §826(a). The Restatement §827 states that the following factors should be considered in determining the "gravity of harm":

(a) the extent of the harm involved,
(b) the character of the harm involved,

---

5. This requirement distinguishes private nuisance from trespass, which makes *any* physical invasion of one's interest in exclusive possession of land actionable, even a trivial invasion.

    (c) the social value which the law attaches to the type of use or
       enjoyment invaded;
    (d) the suitability of the particular use or enjoyment invaded to
       the character of the locality;
    (e) the burden on the person harmed of avoiding the harm.

The Restatement §828 similarly lists various factors to be considered in
assessing the utility of defendants' conduct:

    (a) the social value which the law attaches to the primary purpose
       of the conduct;
    (b) the suitability of the conduct to the character of the locality;
    (c) whether it is impracticable to prevent or avoid the invasion, if
       the activity is maintained;
    (d) whether it is impracticable to maintain the activity it if is re-
       quired to bear the cost of compensating for the invasion.

    Even if the utility of the defendant's conduct outweighs the gravity
of the harm, the conduct is deemed "unreasonable" nonetheless if the
harm caused "is serious and the financial burden of compensating for
this and similar harm to others would not make the continuation of the
conduct not feasible." Restatement (Second) of Torts §826(b). Thus,
in an action for damages, activities that are socially beneficial (according to the test of §826(a)) but cause serious harm are "unreasonable" unless compensation is infeasible.
    Unintentional conduct is actionable if it is negligent or reckless,
or if it is actionable under the emerging principles of liability without
fault or strict liability applicable to "abnormally dangerous conditions
or activities." The doctrine of negligence, discussed below under invasions of personal interests, requires a defendant to conform to a
standard of conduct that protects others from unreasonable risks; reasonableness turns on a balancing of the probability and gravity of the
risk against the social utility of the conduct generating it. As discussed
earlier, strict liability principles trace back to *Rylands v. Fletcher*, 3 H.L.
330 (1868), which recognized liability without fault for the escape
of large quantities of water stored in a reservoir on defendant's
land.
    Public Nuisance. A public nuisance is "an unreasonable interfer-
ence with a right common to the public." Restatement (Second) of
Torts §821B. Traditionally, this principle of civil liability embraced an
eclectic miscellany of actions that disturbed the welfare of a broad segment of the community; many such actions also constituted common
law crimes. Examples include obstruction of a public highway, maintenance of houses of prostitution, and public obscenity, as well as pollution. The Restatement, §821B(2), has attempted to distill the principles
which should determine what constitutes a public nuisance:

Circumstances that sustain a holding that an interference with a public right is unreasonable include the following:

(a) Whether the conduct involves the kind of interference with the public health, the public safety, the public peace, the public ccmfort or the public convenience,

(b) whether the conduct is proscribed by a statute, ordinance or administrative regulation, or

(c) whether the conduct is of a continuing nature or has produced a permanent or long-lasting effect, and, as the actor knows or has reason to know, has a significant effect upon the public right.

The most important obstacle to utilizing public nuisance doctrine as an effective litigation remedy against environmental degradation has been a standing doctrine that restricts the class of persons who could maintain a suit for public nuisance. Historically, public nuisance actions could be maintained only by public officials unless a private plaintiff could establish individual injury that was different in kind (not merely in degree) from the rest of the community. The rationale for this restriction is suggested in 4 W. Blackstone, Commentaries *167: "[I]t would be unreasonable to multiply suits by giving every man a separate right of action for what damnifies him in common only with the rest of his fellow subjects." See generally Rothstein, Private Actions for Public Nuisance — The Standing Problem, 76 W. Va. L. Rev. 453 (1976).

Sometimes (but not always) if a plaintiff could show injury to an interest in land, "special damage" was found on the common law principle that land is unique. Conduct may accordingly constitute a public and a private nuisance simultaneously. Where no interest in land was involved, however, standing was frequently denied on the rationale that plaintiff's injury was no different in kind from that suffered by other members of the public. See Bryson & Macbeth, Public Nuisance, The Restatement (Second) of Torts, and Environmental Law, 2 Ecol. L.Q. 241, 250-252, 255 (1972). The Restatement has adopted a more liberalized test of standing in actions to *enjoin* or *abate* a public nuisance,[6] extending it to persons having "standing to sue as a representative of the general public or as a member of a class action." Restatement (Second) of Torts §821C(2)(c). This language reflects an awareness that public officials may not always have the resources or incentive to bring public nuisance actions and that it is desirable to permit private plain-

---

6. The traditional standing requirement has been retained for damage actions. Restatement (Second) of Torts §821C(1).

tiffs to bring actions to vindicate the rights of some defined class or the public as a whole.

B. ANALYSIS OF COMMON LAW DOCTRINES

1. AN ANALYTIC FRAMEWORK FOR COMMON LAW DOCTRINES

CALABRESI & MELAMED, PROPERTY RULES, LIABILITY RULES, AND INALIENABILITY: ONE VIEW OF THE CATHEDRAL

85 Harv. L. Rev. 1089 (1972)

. . . The first issue which must be faced by any legal system is one we call the problem of "entitlement." Whenever a state is presented with the conflicting interests of two or more people, or two or more groups of people, it must decide which side to favor. Absent such a decision, access to goods, services, and life itself will be decided on the basis of "might makes right" — whoever is stronger or shrewder will win. Hence the fundamental thing that law does is to decide which of the conflicting parties will be entitled to prevail. The entitlement to make noise versus the entitlement to have silence, the entitlement to pollute versus the entitlement to breathe clean air, the entitlement to have children versus the entitlement to forbid them — these are the first order of legal decisions. . . .

The state not only has to decide whom to entitle, but it must also simultaneously make a series of equally difficult second order decisions. These decisions go to the manner in which entitlements are protected and to whether an individual is allowed to sell or trade the entitlement. In any given dispute, for example, the state must decide not only which side wins but also the kind of protection to grant. It is with the latter decisions, decisions which shape the subsequent relationship between the winner and loser, that this article is primarily concerned. We shall consider three types of entitlements — entitlements protected by property rules, entitlements protected by liability rules, and inalienable entitlements. The categories are not, of course, absolutely distinct; but the categorization is useful since it reveals some of the reasons which lead us to protect certain entitlements in certain ways.

An entitlement is protected by a property rule to the extent that someone who wishes to remove the entitlement from its holder must buy it from him in a voluntary transaction in which the value of the entitlement is agreed upon by the seller. It is the form of entitlement which gives rise to the least amount of state intervention: once the original entitlement is decided upon, the state does not try to decide its value.[7] It lets each of the parties say how much the entitlement is worth to him, and gives the seller a veto if the buyer does not offer enough. Property rules involve a collective decision as to who is to be given an initial entitlement but not as to the value of the entitlement.

Whenever someone may destroy the initial entitlement if he is willing to pay an objectively determined value for it, an entitlement is protected by a liability rule. This value may be what it is thought the original holder of the entitlement would have sold it for. But the holder's complaint that he would have demanded more will not avail him once the objectively determined value is set. Obviously, liability rules involve an additional stage of intervention; not only are entitlements protected, but their transfer or destruction is allowed on the basis of a value determined by some organ of the state rather than by the parties themselves.

An entitlement is inalienable to the extent that its transfer is not permitted between a willing buyer and a willing seller. The state intervenes not only to determine who is initially entitled and to determine the compensation that must be paid if the entitlement is taken or destroyed, but also to forbid its sale under some or all circumstances. Inalienability rules are thus quite different from property and liability rules. Unlike those rules, rules of inalienability not only "protect" the entitlement; they may also be viewed as limiting or regulating the grant of the entitlement itself.

It should be clear that most entitlements to most goods are mixed. Taney's house may be protected by a property rule in situations where Marshall wishes to purchase it, by a liability rule where the government decides to take it by eminent domain, and by a rule of inalienability in situations where Taney is drunk or incompetent. This article will explore two primary questions: (1) In what circumstances should we grant a particular entitlement? and (2) In what circumstances should we decide to protect that entitlement by using a property, liability, or inalienability rule?

---

7. A property rule requires less state intervention only in the sense that intervention is needed to decide upon and enforce the initial entitlement but not for the separate problem of determining the value of the entitlement. Thus, if a particular property entitlement is especially difficult to enforce — for example, the right to personal security in urban areas — the actual amount of state intervention can be very high and could, perhaps, exceed that needed for some entitlements protected by easily administered liability rules.

II.   THE SETTING OF ENTITLEMENTS

What are the reasons for deciding to entitle people to pollute or to entitle people to forbid pollution, to have children freely or to limit procreation, to own property or to share property? They can be grouped under three headings: economic efficiency, distributional preferences, and other justice considerations.

A.   ECONOMIC EFFICIENCY

. . . Economic efficiency asks that we choose the set of entitlements which would lead to that allocation of resources which could not be improved in the sense that a further change would not so improve the condition of those who gained by it that they could compensate those who lost from it and still be better off than before. . . . To give two examples, economic efficiency asks for that combination of entitlements to engage in risky activities and to be free from harm from risky activities which will most likely lead to the lowest sum of accident costs and of costs of avoiding accidents. It asks for that form of property, private or communal, which leads to the highest product for the effort of producing.

[The authors summarize Coase's result that economic efficiency will obtain if transactions are costless.]

Such a result would not mean, however, that the *same* allocation of resources would exist regardless of the initial set of entitlements. Taney's willingness to pay for the right to make noise may depend on how rich he is; Marshall's willingness to pay for silence may depend on his wealth. In a society which entitles Taney to make noise and which forces Marshall to buy silence from Taney, Taney is wealthier and Marshall poorer than each would be in a society which had the converse set of entitlements. Depending on how Marshall's desire for silence and Taney's for noise vary with their wealth, an entitlement to noise will result in negotiations which will lead to a different quantum of noise than would an entitlement to silence. This variation in the quantity of noise and silence can be viewed as no more than an instance of the well accepted proposition that what is . . . economically efficient . . . varies with the starting distribution of wealth. . . .

All this suggests why distributions of wealth may affect a society's choice of entitlements. It does not suggest why *economic efficiency* should affect the choice, if we assume an absence of any transaction costs. But no one makes an assumption of no transaction costs in practice. Like the physicist's assumption of no friction or Say's law in macro-economics, the assumption of no transaction costs may be a useful starting point, a device which helps us see how, as different elements which may be termed transaction costs become important, the goal of economic efficiency starts to prefer one allocation of entitlements over another.

Since one of us has written at length on how in the presence of various types of transaction costs a society would go about deciding on a set of entitlements in the field of accident law,[8] it is enough to say here: (1) that economic efficiency standing alone would dictate that set of entitlements which favors knowledgeable choices between social benefits and the social costs of obtaining them, and between social costs and the social costs of avoiding them; (2) that this implies, in the absence of certainty as to whether a benefit is worth its costs to society, that the cost should be put on the party or activity best located to make such a cost-benefit analysis; (3) that in particular contexts like accidents or pollution this suggests putting costs on the party or activity which can most cheaply avoid them; (4) that in the absence of certainty as to who that party or activity is, the costs should be put on the party or activity which can with the lowest transaction costs act in the market to correct an error in entitlements by inducing the party who can avoid social costs most cheaply to do so; and (5) that since we are in an area where by hypothesis markets do not work perfectly — there are transaction costs — a decision will often have to be made on whether market transactions or collective fiat is most likely to bring us closer to the [economically efficient] result the "perfect" market would reach. . . .

B.   DISTRIBUTIONAL GOALS

There are, we would suggest, at least two types of distributional concerns which may affect the choice of entitlements. These involve distribution of wealth itself and distribution of certain specific goods, which have sometimes been called merit goods.

All societies have wealth distribution preferences. They are, nonetheless, harder to talk about than are efficiency goals. . . . Distributional preferences, on the other hand, cannot usefully be discussed in a single conceptual framework. There are some fairly broadly accepted preferences — caste preferences in one society, more rather than less equality in another society. There are also preferences which are linked to dynamic efficiency concepts — producers ought to be rewarded since they will cause everyone to be better off in the end. Finally, there are a myriad of highly individualized preferences as to who should be richer and who poorer which need not have anything to do with either equality or efficiency — silence lovers should be richer than noise lovers because they are worthier. . . .

---

8. [G. Calabresi, The Costs of Accidents (1970).]

III.   RULES FOR PROTECTING AND REGULATING
ENTITLEMENTS

Whenever society chooses an initial entitlement, it must also determine whether to protect the entitlement by property rules, by liability rules, or by rules of inalienability. In our framework, much of what
is generally called private property can be viewed as an entitlement
which is protected by a property rule. No one can take the entitlement
to private property from the holder unless the holder sells it willingly
and at the price at which he subjectively values the property. Yet a nuisance with sufficient public utility to avoid injunction has, in effect, the
right to take property with compensation. In such a circumstance the
entitlement to the property is protected only by what we call a liability
rule: an external, objective standard of value is used to facilitate the
transfer of the entitlement from the holder to the nuisance. Finally, in
some instances we will not allow the sale of the property at all, that is,
we will occasionally make the entitlement inalienable.

This section will consider the circumstances in which society will
employ these three rules to solve situations of conflict. Because the
property rule and the liability rule are closely related and depend for
their application on the shortcomings of each other, we treat them
together. We discuss inalienability separately.

A.   PROPERTY AND LIABILITY RULES

Why cannot a society simply decide on the basis of the already
mentioned criteria who should receive any given entitlement, and then
let its transfer occur only through a voluntary negotiation? Why, in
other words, cannot society limit itself to the property rule? To do this
it would need only to protect and enforce the initial entitlements from
all attacks, perhaps through criminal sanctions, and to enforce voluntary contracts for their transfer. Why do we need liability rules at all?

In terms of economic efficiency the reason is easy enough to see.
Often the cost of establishing the value of an initial entitlement by negotiation is so great that even though a transfer of the entitlement
would benefit all concerned, such a transfer will not occur. If a collective determination of the value were available instead, the beneficial
transfer would quickly come about.

Eminent domain is a good example. A park where Guidacres, a
tract of land owned by 1000 owners in 1000 parcels, now sits would, let
us assume, benefit a neighboring town enough so that the 100,000 citizens of the town would each be willing to pay an average of $100 to
have it. The park is . . . desirable [from an economic perspective] if
the owners of the tracts of land in Guidacres actually value their entitle-

ments at less than $10,000,000 or an average of $10,000 a tract. Let us assume that in fact the parcels are all the same and all the owners value them at $8000. On this assumption, the park is, in economic efficiency terms, desirable — in values foregone it costs $8,000,000 and is worth $10,000,000 to the buyers. And yet it may well not be established. If enough of the owners hold-out for more than $10,000 in order to get a share of the $2,000,000 that they guess the buyers are willing to pay over the value which the sellers in actuality attach, the price demanded will be more than $10,000,000 and no park will result. The sellers have an incentive to hide their true valuation and the market will not succeed in establishing it.

An equally valid example could be made on the buying side. Suppose the sellers of Guidacres have agreed to a sales price of $8,000,000 (they are all relatives and at a family banquet decided that trying to hold-out would leave them all losers). It does not follow that the buyers can raise that much even though each of 100,000 citizens *in fact* values the park at $100. Some citizens may try to free-load and say the park is only worth $50 or even nothing to them, hoping that enough others will admit to a higher desire and make up the $8,000,000 price. Again there is no reason to believe that a market, a decentralized system of valuing, will cause people to express their true valuations and hence yield results which all would *in fact* agree are desirable.

Whenever this is the case an argument can readily be made for moving from a property rule to a liability rule. If society can remove from the market the valuation of each tract of land, decide the value collectively, and impose it, then the holdout problem is gone. Similarly, if society can value collectively each individual citizen's desire to have a park and charge him a "benefits" tax based upon it, the freeloader problem is gone. If the sum of the taxes is greater than the sum of the compensation awards, the park will result.

Of course, one can conceive of situations where it might be cheap to exclude all the freeloaders from the park, or to ration the park's use in accordance with original willingness to pay. In such cases the incentive to free-load might be eliminated. But such exclusions, even if possible, are usually not cheap. And the same may be the case for market methods which might avoid the holdout problem on the seller side.

Moreover, even if holdout and freeloader problems can be met feasibly by the market, an argument may remain for employing a liability rule. Assume that in our hypothetical, freeloaders can be excluded at the cost of $1,000,000 and that all owners of tracts in Guidacres can be convinced, by the use of $500,000 worth of advertising and cocktail parties, that a sale will only occur if they reveal their true land valuations. Since $8,000,000 plus $1,500,000 is less than $10,000,000, the park will be established. But if collective valuation of the tracts and of the benefits of the prospective park would have cost less than

$1,500,000, it would have been inefficient to establish the park through the market — a market which was not worth having would have been paid for.

Of course, the problems with liability rules are equally real. We cannot be at all sure that landowner Taney is lying or holding out when he says his land is worth $12,000 to him. The fact that several neighbors sold identical tracts for $10,000 does not help us very much; Taney may be sentimentally attached to his land. As a result, eminent domain may grossly undervalue what Taney would actually sell for, even if it sought to give him his true valuation of his tract. In practice, it is so hard to determine Taney's true valuation that eminent domain simply gives him what the land is worth "objectively," in the full knowledge that this may result in over or under compensation. The same is true on the buyer side. "Benefits" taxes rarely attempt, let alone succeed, in gauging the individual citizen's relative desire for the alleged benefit. They are justified because, even if they do not accurately measure each individual's desire for the benefit, the market alternative seems worse. For example, fifty different households may place different values on a new sidewalk that is to abut all the properties. Nevertheless, because it is too difficult, even if possible, to gauge each household's valuation, we usually tax each household an equal amount.

The example of eminent domain is simply one of numerous instances in which society uses liability rules. Accidents is another. . . .

We should also recognize that efficiency is not the sole ground for employing liability rules rather than property rules. Just as the initial entitlement is often decided upon for distributional reasons, so too the choice of a liability rule is often made because it facilitates a combination of efficiency and distributive results which would be difficult to achieve under a property rule. . . .

NOTES AND QUESTIONS ON THE OBJECTIVES OF ENVIRONMENTAL LITIGATION

1. Just as legal rules can be evaluated in terms of efficiency and distribution of income, so they can be evaluated in terms of other societal objectives such as their contribution to an adequate resource inheritance of future generations. Judicial pursuit of this goal would raise some of the same institutional issues we have already discussed: Should we consider the impact of judicial decisions on intergenerational equity on a case-by-case basis, or should we seek to promote a more equitable distribution by relying on rules of more general applicability? More fundamentally, should judges concern themselves at all with the impact of their decisions on the distribution of wealth in any given society or

between generations? Given the widespread lack of agreement as to what principles of income distribution are just or equitable, should judges simply maximize efficiency (the size of the social pie) and leave to the legislature questions of distribution (the slicing of the pie)?

Rights-oriented theorists suggest a quite different approach to legal rules, which views them not as instruments for realizing some general social goal, such as efficiency or income equality, but as expressions of moral principles for the just resolution of particular disputes. See e.g., Fletcher, Fairness and Utility in Tort Theory, 85 Harv. L. Rev. 537 (1972). The basic concept of corrective justice first seeks to define respective rights and duties that persons owe to one another by reference to basic moral principles. When one person violates another's rights, the law requires her to pay him compensation to undo the violation and restore the pre-existing moral equilibrium insofar as the payment or damages can make the victim whole. Along these lines, the law can be seen as protecting basic human rights to health and use and enjoyment of one's home. See W. Rodgers, Environmental Law: Air and Water §2.1 at 30-31 (1986). Certainly the language of many common law decisions is framed in terms of endeavoring to do justice between the litigants before the court, rather than utilizing their dispute as an occasion for laying down rules aimed at promoting economically efficient conduct by others or achieving some preferred overall income pattern. Isn't justice between the parties in any event at least one of the objectives of adjudication even if it is not the sole objective?

The naturalist philosophers question whether an anthropocentric framework can ever adequately address the resource allocation issues of a holistic community. But does private litigation, by its very nature as a means to resolve disputes between people (including legal persons such as corporations), in effect reify the anthropocentric view? Should courts develop rules that permit nature to be represented in judicial proceedings? See Stone, Should Trees Have Standing? — Toward Legal Rights for Natural Objects, 45 S. Cal. L. Rev. 450 (1970); see also supra, pp. 147-159. Would this be enough? What other changes in the procedural and substantive doctrines of private litigation would be necessary to address adequately the concerns of the naturalist philosophers?

The various alternative conceptions of the purpose or function of legal rules create the potential for conflict; for example, efficiency may dictate the adoption of legal rules that are highly regressive in their distributional impact or that offend received principles of just dispute resolution. How frequently will such conflicts occur? Is it likely in a stable society that efficiency considerations, notions of distributional equity, and principles of adjudicatory fairness will be seriously inconsistent in a large number of cases? Is ours a stable society? Where serious conflicts do occur, how should courts deal with them?

2. It has been suggested that private litigation serves as a means of focusing attention and arousing public concern over environmental

problems that are not being adequately dealt with by regulatory controls or other governmental measures. A leading environmental litigator has stated:

> Every piece of enlightened social legislation that has come down in the past 50 or 60 years has been preceded by a history of litigation in which lawyers around the country have focused forcibly the attention of the legislature on the inadequacies of existing legislation.

Cahn, Environmentalists Blaze Legal Trail to Preserve Nature, Christian Science Monitor, Oct. 2, 1969, at 3.

Litigation can function to gather together hard evidence about previously unknown or poorly understood problems, pinpoint shortcomings in present laws, suggest the shape and direction of new laws, uncover administrative abuses, and create leverage for change. Moreover, publicity generated by a lawsuit can serve as an incentive for private firms to take steps to avoid environmental degradation.

Some observers, however, are leery about the judicial process being put to these ends. At an environmental conference in 1970, Professor Joseph Sax stated that "We have been using the lawsuit as a device to teach people that they can demand environmental controls and get them." According to a report of the conference,

> Professor Sax's educational tactic did not meet with complete favor at the table, particularly among the economists. Professor Breton remarked that he thought it wise to differentiate between the situations "where in one case the pollution is serious enough to arouse the public, and where in another we have to 'educate public opinion.'" He then warned "We should be careful not to engage in calling something education which, when other people try to sell us soap, we call advertising. . . ."

Shapiro, Our Far-Flung Correspondents, E.D. [Environmental Disruption], The New Yorker, May 23, 1970, at 93, 102. Putting this concern aside, do you think that the judicial process is a reliable means for generating information bearing on broad public policy decisions?

2. WHO SHOULD GET THE ENTITLEMENT?

WASCHAK V. MOFFAT

379 Pa. 441, 109 A.2d 310 (1954)

ALLEN M. STEARNE, Justice. The appeal is from a judgment of the Superior Court refusing to enter judgment *non obstante veredicto* for defendants in an action in trespass and affirming the judgment of the Court of Common Pleas of Lackawanna County in favor of plaintiffs.

Gas or fumes from culm banks, the refuse of a coal breaker, damaged the paint on plaintiffs' dwelling. In this action for damages the applicable legal principles are technical and controversial. Considerable confusion appears in the many cases. The field is that of *liability without fault for escape of substances from land.*

Plaintiffs are owners of a dwelling in the Borough of Taylor which is in the center of Pennsylvania's anthracite coal lands. An action in trespass was instituted against two partners, operators of a coal breaker in that Borough. Without fault on the part of defendants, gas known as *hydrogen sulfide* was emitted from two of defendants' culm banks. This caused discoloration of the white paint (with lead base) which had been used in painting plaintiffs' dwelling. The painted surface became dark or black. The sole proven damage was the cost of restoring the surface with a white paint, having a titanium and zinc base, which will not discolor. There was no other injury either to the building or occupants. The verdict was for $1,250.

While the verdict is in a relatively modest amount, the principles of law involved, and their application, are extremely important and far reaching. Twenty-five other cases are at issue awaiting the decision in this case. The impact of this decision will affect the entire coal interests — anthracite and bituminous — as well as other industries. Application of appropriate legal principles is of vital concern to coal miners and to other labor.

The pivotal facts are undisputed. To mine anthracite coal, either by deep or strip mining, requires processing in a coal breaker before marketing. Usable coal, broken to various sizes, must first be separated from its by-products of minerals, rock, etc. The by-products are deposited in piles known as culm banks, portions of which may be reclaimed, while other parts are presently regarded as waste. The mining and processing in the present case are conceded to have been conducted by defendants without fault. Fires frequently appear in the culm banks long after the accumulation. Defendants neither committed any negligent act nor omitted any known method to prevent combustion, fires or the emission of gases. In addition to *hydrogen sulfide* two other gases, *carbon monoxide* and *sulfur dioxide* were shown to have also been emitted, but it is not contended that either of these two gases affected the paint in question. *Hydrogen sulfide* was conceded to have been the gas which caused the damage. The emission of this gas is not ordinarily found in the operation of coal mining and processing. *Defendants did not know and had no reason to anticipate the emission of this gas and the results which might follow.* Of the five culm banks only two of them, the Washington Street bank and the settling basin were shown to have emitted *hydrogen sulfide.*

In the court below the case was tried on the theory of *absolute liability* for the maintenance of a nuisance. The jury was instructed that it should determine, as a *matter of fact,* whether or not what the defendants did and the conditions resulting therefrom constituted a "reasonable and natural use" of defendants' land. . . .

[The court then discussed potential rules for liability without fault for an invasion of private interests in land, rejecting, in the circumstances of this case, the rule of *Rylands v. Fletcher*, 3 H.L. 330 (1868), and also declined to follow a somewhat vaguely defined "Absolute Nuisance Doctrine."] . . .

The Rule of the Restatement [of Torts] which unquestionably is accurate and most comprehensive, is as follows:

SECTION 822. GENERAL RULE

The actor is liable in an action for damages for a nontrespassory invasion of another's interest in the private use and enjoyment of land if,
     (a)   the other has property rights and privileges in respect to the use or enjoyment interfered with; and
     (b)   the invasion is substantial; and
     (c)   the actor's conduct is a legal cause of the invasion; and
     (d)   the invasion is either
          (i)   intentional and unreasonable; or
          (ii)   unintentional and otherwise actionable under the rules governing liability for negligent, reckless or ultrahazardous conduct.

This rule we adopt. . . .

Prior to the year 1934 the Glen Alden Coal Company, owners, had ceased to mine coal in this area. The colliery in question was idle, the breaker was dismantled and minors [*sic*] in Taylor Borough were out of work. A committee of citizens of the Borough called upon the Glen Alden Coal Company requesting that the mines be reopened in order to aid the citizens. The Glen Alden Company agreed to this and leased coal lands comprising a continuous area of coal veins running from Taylor to Dickson City. When the defendants, in 1934, first began to operate the breaker a large culm bank close to the breaker was in existence and was then burning. In 1937 a new culm bank was started because of the fire in the old one and a conveyor was used to carry the culm to the new location. This was the Main Street bank and was used from 1937 to 1944. A new bank was then started known as the Washington Street bank, which was used from 1944 until October 1948. This bank was the same distance from the breaker as the Main Street bank, but in the opposite direction. In 1948 defendants commenced the construction of a settling basin in compliance with the State law concerning pollution of streams. During the construction the State inspectors approved. In 1949, six months after the Washington Street culm bank was discontinued, fire was discovered and defendants ceased using this breaker material for the settling basin. In the spring of 1949 walls in the settling basin ignited.

It is significant that plaintiffs purchased their home on June 23, 1948. It was close to the breaker, near the Washington Street bank.

Of the various gases emitted from the five culm banks, *hydrogen sulfide* was the gas which caused the damage. The record shows that this was emitted only from the Washington Street bank and the settling basin and from no others. Defendants did not know, and had no reason to be aware, that this particular gas would be so emitted and would have the effect upon the painted house. The record shows that the defendants were guilty of no negligence and used every known means to prevent damage or injury to adjoining properties.

Even if the reasonableness of the defendants' use of their property had been the *sole* consideration, there could be no recovery here. . . .

The dwelling in question had been formerly used by a mine inspector who doubtless desired to be close to the breaker. When plaintiffs purchased the dwelling they were fully aware of the surrounding situation.

In *Versailles Borough v. McKeesport Coal & Coke Co.*, 83 Pittsb. Leg. J. 379, Mr. Justice Musmanno, when a county judge, accurately encompassed the problem when he said:

> The plaintiffs are subject to an annoyance. This we accept, but it is an annoyance they have freely assumed. Because they desired and needed a residential proximity to their places of employment, they chose to found their abode here. It is not for them to repine; and it is probable that upon reflection they will, in spite of the annoyance which they suffer, still conclude that, after all, one's bread is more important than landscape or clear skies.
>
> Without smoke, Pittsburgh would have remained a very pretty *village*." . . .

In applying the rule of the Restatement, Torts, Sec. 822(d), it is evident the invasion of plaintiffs' land was clearly *not intentional*. And even if it were, for the reasons above stated, it was not unreasonable. On the contrary, since the emission of gases was not caused by any act of defendants and arose merely from the normal and customary use of their land without negligence, recklessness or ultrahazardous conduct, it was wholly *unintentional*, and no liability may therefore be imposed upon defendants.

The judgment is reversed and is here entered in favor of defendants *non obstante veredicto*. . . .

MUSMANNO, Justice (dissenting).

The plaintiffs in this case, Joseph J. Waschak and Agnes Waschak, brother and sister, own a modest home in Taylor, Pennsylvania, a town of 7,000 inhabitants in the anthracite region of the northeastern part of the State. . . .

   In 1948 the plaintiffs painted their house with a white paint. Some time later the paint began to turn to a light colored brown, then it changed to a grayish tint, once it burst into a silvery sheen, and then, as if this were its last dying gasp, the house suddenly assumed a blackish cast, the blackness deepened and intensified until now it is a "scorched black." The plaintiffs attribute this chameleon performance of their house to the hydrogen sulfide emanating from the defendants' culm deposits in the town — all in residential areas. The hydrogen sulfide, according to the plaintiffs, not only assaults the paint of the house but it snipes at the silverware, bath tub fixtures and the bronze handles of the doors, forcing them, respectively, into black, yellowish-brown and "tarnished-looking" tints. . . .

   The jury by their verdict decided that the defendants did not make a reasonable, lawful and natural use of their land. Reading the record in the case, I am satisfied that the jury was amply justified in their conclusion and I see no warrant for disturbing that verdict. When a property owner so uses his land that it injures his neighbor's the burden is on him to show that he did use his land naturally, reasonably and legally. The defendants in this case failed to meet the burden put on them by the law. . . .

   The evidence here does not show any *necessity* on the part of the defendants to locate the culm banks in the very midst of the residential areas of Taylor. . . .

   . . . The poisonous gases lifting from the defendants' culm banks were destructive of property, detrimental to health and disruptive of the social life of the town.

   There was evidence that the poisonous hydrogen sulfide was of such intensity that the inhabitants compelled to breathe it suffered from headaches, throat irritation, inability to sleep, coughing, light-headedness, nausea and stomach ailments. These grave effects of the escaping gas reached such proportions that the citizens of Taylor held protest meetings and demanded that the municipal authorities take positive action to curb the gaseous invasion.

   Did the release of the gases from the defendants' culm banks constitute under the law a nuisance? Nearly every witness testifying for the plaintiff as to the nature of the gas rising from the culm banks declared that it had the odor of rotten eggs.

   Several of the witnesses testified that because of the rotten egg smell which entered their parlors and sitting rooms, it was difficult to entertain visitors. This statement could well qualify as the prize understatement of the case.

   It must always be kept in mind that these culm banks were not mole hills. The Main Street dump measured 1,100 feet in length, 650 feet in width and 40 feet in height. If these dimensions were applied to a ship, one can visualize the size of the vessel and what would be the state of its odoriferousness if it was loaded stem to stern with rotten eggs. And that is only one of the dumps. There is another dump at Washington Street and, consequently, another ship of rotten eggs. Its dimensions are 800 feet by 750 feet by 50 feet. A third dump measures 500 feet by 500 feet by 40 feet. Then the defendants constructed a silt dam with the same rotten-egg-smelling materials.

I do not think that there can be any doubt that the constant smell of rotten eggs constitutes a nuisance. If such a condition is not recognized by the law, then the law is the only body that does not so recognize it.

Although the defendants sought to belittle the testimony adduced by the plaintiffs with regard to the intolerable conditions in Taylor caused by the defendants' gaseous banks, it is interesting to note that defendant Robert Y. Moffatt found it convenient and desirable to live outside the Borough of Taylor and, in all the years that he has been operating the coal business which is the subject of this litigation, he never found it profitable to spend a single night in Taylor. Even so, neither he nor his partner can successfully argue that they were unaware of the deleterious fumes rising from the coal refuse which they distributed through the town. . . .

Whether the facts in the case at bar constitute an actionable nuisance is not a question of law. It is one of fact for a jury to determine. . . .

There is a golden rule in law as well as in morals and it reads: "Sic utere tuo ut alienum non laedas." The defendants oppose this maxim with the one that every person has the right to a lawful, reasonable and natural use of his land. But it is entirely possible and in fact desirable that these two maxims live together in peace and harmony. The plaintiffs in this case do not question that the defendants have the right to mine coal and process it, but is it a natural and reasonable use of land to deposit poisonous refuse in residential areas when it can be deposited elsewhere? Certainly the defendants may lawfully operate a breaker in Taylor, and whatever noises, dust and commotion result from the breaker operation are inconveniences which the plaintiff and other Taylor inhabitants must accept as part of the life of a mining community. But the disposition of the poisonous refuse of a mining operation does not fall within the definition of lawful and normal use of land. . . .

The majority states that the "emission of offensive odors, noises, fumes, violations, etc., must be weighed against the utility of the operation." In this respect, the Majority Opinion does me the honor of quoting from an Opinion I wrote when I was a member of the distinguished Court of Common Pleas of Allegheny County. *Versailles Borough v. McKeesport Coal & Coke Co.*, 83 Pittsb. Leg. J. 379. That was an equity case where the plaintiffs sought an injunction against the defendant coal company for maintaining a burning gob pile which emitted smoke. The coal mine was located in the very heart of an industrialized area which contained factories, mills, garbage dumps, incinerators and railroads, all producing their own individualized smoke and vapors so that it could not be said that the discomforts of the inhabitants were due exclusively to the operation of the coal mine. Furthermore, after hearings lasting one month I found that the operation of the mine in no way jeopardized the health of the inhabitants:

> Of course, if the continued operation of this mine were a serious menace to the health or lives of those who reside in its vicinity, there would be another question before us, but there is no evidence in this case to warrant the assumption that the health of anyone is being imperiled.

In the instant case the exact contrary is true. The health of the town of Taylor *is* being imperiled. And then also, as well stated by the lower Court in the present litigation, "Many factors may lead a chancellor to grant or deny injunctive relief which are not properly involved in an action brought to recompense one for injury to his land. . . . A denial of relief by a court of equity is not always precedent for denying redress by way of damages."

Even so, there is a vast difference between smoke which beclouds the skies and gas which is so strong that it peels the paint from houses. I did say in the *Versailles* case, "One's bread is more important than landscape or clear skies." But in the preservation of human life, even bread is preceded by water, and even water must give way to breathable air. Experimentation and observation reveal that one can live as long as 60 or 70 days without food; one can keep the lamp of life burning 3 or 4 days without water, but the wick is snuffed out in a minute or two in the absence of breathable air. For decades Pittsburgh was known as the "Smoky City" and without that smoke in its early days Pittsburgh indeed would have remained a "pretty village." But with scientific progress in the development of smoke-consuming devices, added to the use of smokeless fuel, Pittsburgh's skies have cleared, its progress has been phenomenal and the bread of its workers is whiter, cleaner, and sweeter. . . .

Even if the rights of the plaintiffs were to be considered by Restatement Rules they would still be entitled to recover under the proposition that the defendants were so well informed of the probable harmful effects of their operation that their actions could only be regarded as an intentional invasion of the rights of the plaintiff. Section 825 of the Restatement of Torts declares:

> An invasion of another's interest in the use and enjoyment of land is intentional when the actor

    (a)   acts for the purpose of causing it; or
    (b)   knows that it is resulting or is substantially certain to result
from his conduct.

The record amply proves that the defendants were at least "substantially certain" that their burning culm deposits would invade the plaintiffs' interest in the use and enjoyment of their land.

If there were no other way of disposing of the coal refuse, a different question might have been presented here, but the defendants produced no evidence that they could not have deposited the debris in places removed from the residential districts in Taylor. Certainly, many of the strip-mining craters which uglify the countryside in the areas close to Taylor could have been utilized by the defendants. They chose, however, to use the residential sections of Taylor because it was cheaper to pile the culm there than to haul it away into less populous territory.

This was certainly an unreasonable and selfish act in no way indispensably associated with the operation of the breaker. It brought greater profits to the defendants but at the expense of the health and the comfort of the other landowners in the town who are also entitled to the pursuit of happiness. . . .

It is because of the many fluctuating factors in the cases themselves that the decisions do not seem to be uniform. In point of juridical history, however, they do follow a pattern of wisdom and justice. No one will deny that the defendants are entitled to earn profits in the operation of their breaker, but is it reasonable that they shall so conduct that business as to poison the very lifestream of existence? Is it not reasonable to suppose that if hydrogen sulfide emanating from culm banks can strip paint from wood and steel that it will also deleteriously affect the delicate membranes of the throat and lungs?

The defendants have made much of a case of *Pennsylvania Coal Company v. Sanderson,* 113 Pa. 126, 6 A. 453, 459, where this Court did say that: "To encourage the development of the great natural resources of a country trifling inconveniences to particular persons must sometimes give way to the necessities of a great community." But here we are not dealing with trifling inconveniences. We are dealing with a situation where in effect an inhabitant of Taylor, Pennsylvania, awakens each morning with a basket of rotten eggs on his doorstep, and then, on his way to work finds that some of those eggs have been put into his pocket. No matter how often he may remove them, an invisible hand replaces them. This can scarcely be placed in the category of "trifling inconveniences."

The decision of the Superior Court in this case is logical, fair and in keeping with the philosophy and the pragmatics of the law. It does no violence to the precedents. It applies them in the light of the facts so clearly established in the 600 printed pages of testimony.

I would affirm the decision of the Superior Court.

NOTES AND QUESTIONS

1. Would this case come out differently under the Restatement (Second) of Torts?

2. *The Definition of "Fault" as Negligence or Unreasonableness.* As we have seen, nuisance law makes intentional invasions actionable if unreasonable, and unintentional invasions actionable if negligent (or reckless or abnormally dangerous).[9] Both unreasonableness and negligence are defined by weighing the harm caused by defendant's conduct with that conduct's social utility. This approach suggests that "fault" could be defined in economic terms: A polluter acts unreasonably or is negligent whenever the marginal damages caused by pollution exceed the marginal costs of controlling pollution. From an economic viewpoint, the polluter is at "fault" in such cases because a greater measure of control would reduce the total social costs associated with use of the air resource and increase economic efficiency. From a moral viewpoint, the polluter is at "fault" because it is inflicting damage on others that is greater than the social benefits justifying the polluter's activity.

This analysis suggests that in order to determine whether a defendant's conduct is negligent or unreasonable, a court must ascertain the damages caused by pollution and the costs to the defendant of eliminating it, and then determine whether the former exceeds the latter. The award of damages in such cases should provide an incentive for defendant to modify its conduct and impose greater controls on pollution up to the point where the costs of additional controls just equals the damage avoided. Do you see why the damage award should have this effect?

If this analysis is accepted, what basis is there in *Waschak* for concluding that the defendant was without fault?

3. *The Case for Liability Without Fault.* If negligence or unreasonableness consists in a defendant's failure to control pollution to the point where its marginal control costs begin to exceed the marginal

---

9. Should the analysis differ depending on whether defendant's conduct is "intentional" and the standard is "unreasonableness" or on whether it is "unintentional" and the standard is "negligence"? Pollution is rarely, if ever, undertaken for the purpose of harming those who suffer from it. The damage is "intentional" if the polluter knows that it is substantially certain to occur as a result of its conduct. But shouldn't a polluter be under a duty to find out whether its pollution will cause damage? If so, aren't almost all instances of pollution "intentional"? Or does the fact that a polluter affirmatively "knows" of the damage it is causing introduce an additional element of blame that should lead us to impose liability more readily?

How useful are the concepts of "intention" and "knowledge" in the context of pollution, which normally results from ongoing activities and, in many cases, the polluter is a corporation? How do the majority and dissenting opinions in *Waschak* deal with these issues?

benefits of such control, strict liability or liability without fault goes beyond a negligence standard by imposing damage liability in cases where a polluting defendant is operating at or beyond that point but is nonetheless causing some residual damage to others. In such circumstances, it is inefficient for the defendant to alter its pollution control level because the social benefits from defendant's activity equal or exceed the social costs associated with it. Moreover, the award of damages will provide no incentive for defendant to change its level of control (at least in the short run), because the amount of damages it must pay will be less than the costs to defendant of controls to reduce the damage. Why in these circumstances might we wish to impose liability in the form of damages? Five possible reasons follow; you may wish to consider others:

Reflecting pollution costs in product prices: the activity level issue. If strict liability is not imposed for the damages caused by the polluting activity, these damages will not be reflected in the price of commodities produced by such activity. As a result, commodities whose production generates pollution will be underpriced relative to commodities whose production causes no pollution, resulting in resource misallocation. If the price of pollution-creating commodities reflected all of the social costs involved in their production, consumers would purchase fewer of such commodities, production would be reduced, and so would pollution. Thus, strict liability may be necessary to achieve global efficiency. Strict liability is in essence a system of cost internalization which places a financial penalty on pollution equal to its external cost. Compare the discussion on pp. 69-70.[10]

Dynamic incentives for "technology-forcing." As we have seen, damage liability will not cause a polluter to change its present behavior if it is operating at or beyond the efficient level of control, given current control technology. The prospect of repeated damage payments, however, will give the polluter an incentive to develop (or purchase from others) environmentally superior technologies that permit a greater level of pollution control at lower cost.

Loss spreading. The award of damages can operate to spread the harm done to pollution victims among all of the consumers of a polluting enterprise's products. Where the harm to the victims is acute, this loss spreading may be economically efficient. As the widespread purchase of insurance suggests, people are often willing to suffer a known but small economic harm in order to avoid the possibility of suffering a much larger harm. By imposing liability on enterprises creating envi-

---

10. But recall Coase's insight about the reciprocal nature of externalities. In assuming that it is the polluter who is imposing damage on victims and that the polluter therefore has a responsibility to make good the damage, are we not begging an important question?

ronmental harms, including liability for harms resulting even after care is taken, strict liability spreads losses widely because enterprises can purchase liability insurance or self-insure, thereby passing the costs of insurance onto their customers. Consider, however, that this system of loss spreading involves substantial administrative costs — the costs of both tort litigation and liability insurance claims processing — that may offset or exceed the economic gains of risk-spreading. Moreover, in the case of some forms of pollution damage, the loss is already spread among very large numbers of people. To what extent can a negligence rule anticipating state of the art precautions accomplish the goals of the tort system? Cf. *The T. J. Hooper*, 60 F.2d 737 (2d Cir. 1937). What about the alternative of potential victims purchasing insurance against loss?[11]

Moral rights to a healthy environment and just compensation. In addition to promoting economic efficiency for the various reasons already discussed, strict liability might be required by principles of moral rights and just compensation that are quite independent of economic efficiency. A system of strict liability, enforced by injunctive relief, protects individuals from exposure to unhealthy living conditions. Even if society were willing to permit a polluter to continue activity that causes harm to others when the total benefits exceed the total costs associated with that activity, doesn't justice require that the polluter and, ultimately, consumers of the polluters' products, devote a share of these benefits to compensate others for the costs inflicted on them? See Epstein, Nuisance Law, Corrective Justice, and Its Utilitarian Constraints, 8 J. Legal Studies 49 (1979); Epstein, A Theory of Strict Liability, 2 J. Legal Studies 151 (1973).

Easing the judicial burden. If damage liability were imposed only in cases of "fault," substantial resources would have to be invested by litigants and courts in order to determine whether or not "fault" exists in a given case. (On the economists' definition of "fault," we would have to weigh both the marginal damages caused by pollution and the marginal costs of pollution control to determine whether the defendant's degree of pollution falls short of the efficient level of control.) Imposition of damage liability without fault avoids the transaction costs in determining "fault." The court can simply award damages in all cases where the defendant's action caused the harm. If defendant is at fault (operating below the efficient control point), it will modify its conduct

---

11. What obstacles would you foresee in this alternative? One potential obstacle to private insurance might be the lack of resources available to many potential victims. The imposition of enterprise liability might not avoid this problem, however, because it adds to the cost of the product, a cost ultimately borne (at least in part) by consumers. If the product is one purchased by the poor, may not enterprise liability represent a form of compulsory insurance which the poor might not voluntarily adopt? Might such a scheme nonetheless be justified?

and reduce its emissions. If defendant is not at fault (operating at or above the efficient control points), it will simply pay damages. And over the longer run, the pollution source may modify its behavior for the various reasons already discussed.

4. *The Case Against Liability Without Fault.* The foregoing analysis suggests a number of seemingly persuasive grounds for imposing damage liability for pollution, and perhaps other forms of environmental degradation, in all cases without regard to "fault." What arguments could be mounted against such a course? We examine four such arguments here:

Plaintiff can more cheaply reduce pollution damages. A person suffering pollution may be able to avoid its adverse consequences at lower cost than the pollution source can control its emissions. In our discussion of the Coase analysis in the presence of transaction cost, supra at p. 62, we saw that entitlements should be allocated to the party that can most inexpensively avoid the harm, that is, the "least cost avoider" principle. If the plaintiff can more cheaply reduce pollution damage, then requiring the defendant, either under the rubric of strict liability or "fault,"[12] to compensate the plaintiff for the full amount of unavoided damage could reduce or destroy the plaintiff's incentive to take avoidance measures that are socially desirable.[13] Does it follow that the plaintiff, in order to recover, must prove she *cannot* reduce damages more cheaply, or should the burden on that issue be placed on the defendant? Consider the nature of the information needed to resolve the questions of who can more cheaply reduce damages, the access of the parties to that information, their ability to bear the costs involved, and the dynamic incentives for the future of assigning the burden on one party or the other.[14]

Even if the plaintiff clearly can reduce damages more cheaply,

---

12. If the plaintiff can more cheaply avoid the cost, the defendant is not at "fault" from an economic viewpoint, and arguably not from other moral viewpoints either.

13. Does it make any difference whether plaintiff knows or should have known that she could have taken measures to avoid the damage at less cost than abatement of the pollution? Consider also whether a court should take into account the damages suffered by third parties (as well as their potential for avoiding damage) in weighing the costs of abatement and avoidance in a given case.

14. Two burdens of proof are involved: the burden of producing evidence on an issue sufficient to take the issue to the fact trier, and the burden of persuading the trier that a given state of facts was more probable than not. The assessment of the relevant factors and the assignment of these respective burdens could well differ across cases.

Consider also the possibility of correction of judicial error by the market. Which burden assignment would maximize the chances that decisions in given cases that resulted in economic inefficiency would be corrected by private negotiation?

should she be denied any remedy? In *Waschak* some of the damage suffered by the plaintiff might have been avoided by use of pollution-resistant paint. Should the defendant have been required to compensate the plaintiff for the additional costs of utilizing such paint? Cf. Restatement (Second) of Torts §463 (contributory negligence defined as conduct by plaintiff "which falls below the standard to which he should conform for his own protection"); §481 (plaintiff's contributory negligence does not bar recovery where infliction of harm by defendant was "intentional"); §918 (plaintiff is not entitled to recover for harm she could have avoided by "reasonable effort or expenditure" after injury has occurred); §919 (person whose legally protected interests have been threatened or harmed by tortious conduct of another entitled to recover for expenditures reasonably made or harm suffered in a "reasonable effort" to avoid or reduce harm).

External benefits from polluting activity. Activities giving rise to pollution and other forms of external costs may also give rise to external benefits to the local community, such as providing employment when there is slack in the economy. Imposition of damage liability may cause a pollution source to shut down or reduce its level of activity. If there were no external benefits associated with such activity, shutdown in the face of damage liability would ordinarily be desirable. Where external benefits are created by the activity, however, a shutdown might not be socially desirable. Ideally, the activity should be required to bear its external costs, while those enjoying external benefits from the activity should be required to make a contribution equal to those benefits in order to permit the polluting activity to continue in business. Courts have traditionally not attempted to make such benefits assessments. But why shouldn't the courts assess external benefits in the same way as they impose external costs? Are such benefits inherently more difficult to measure than external costs as pollution damage (remembering that to an economist, the damage caused by pollution is measured by the willingness to pay of those adversely affected)? Is assessment of external costs facilitated because those who suffer such costs voluntarily come into court as plaintiffs seeking redress? Does benefits assessment too closely resemble taxation for a court to undertake it without legislative authorization? For discussion of these and related issues, see Calabresi & Melamed, Property Rules, Liability Rules and Inalienability: One View of the Cathedral, 85 Harv. L. Rev. 1089, 1116-1123 (1972).

Given the difficulties of requiring contributions from those enjoying external benefits, a court might well conclude that it is preferable (as a "second best" solution) to permit a polluting activity to continue rather than to suffer the loss of external benefits that might be triggered by imposing damage liability and forcing a shutdown of that activity. Various nineteenth-century doctrines limiting the damage liability of transportation and industrial developments that contributed importantly to economic growth might be explained on this ground. See generally M. Horwitz, The Transformation of American Law 63-108 (1977). Does this analysis justify the result in *Waschak?* How should the burdens of proof on the relevant issues be allocated?

Moral objections to liability without fault. The development in the nineteenth century of "fault" as a basis for liability was historically viewed as a product of moral enlightenment, the imposition of liability without regard to fault being viewed as barbarous and unjust. Could imposition of liability without fault for pollution damage be viewed as unjust? Consider also Fletcher's suggestion, Fairness and Utility in Tort Theory, 85 Harv. L. Rev. 537 (1972), that liability is justified only if the norm of reciprocity is violated. According to Fletcher's paradigm, defendants should be held liable for "disproportionate, excessive risk[s] of harm, relative to the victim's risk-creating activity. For example, a pilot or an airplane owner subjects those beneath the path of flight to nonreciprocal risks of harm. Conversely, cases of nonliability are those of reciprocal risks, namely those in which the victim and the defendant subject each other to roughly the same degree of risk. For example, two airplanes flying in the same vicinity subject each other to reciprocal risks of midair collision." Does Fletcher's analysis suggest that it would be unjust to permit one of two adjacent polluting factories to recover against the other for pollution damage?

Moral objections to strict polluter liability may be strongest if, as discussed below, plaintiff "came to the nuisance." In *Waschak,* the plaintiffs purchased their residence with full notice that it was subject to industrial pollution. Should this bar their recovery, either in a system requiring proof of "fault" or one based on strict liability? The defense of "coming to the nuisance" is simply a variation of the principle of assumption of risk.

What justifications might there be for a "coming to the nuisance" defense? Is it needed to prevent windfall recoveries to plaintiffs on the supposition that the prices paid by plaintiffs for their property had already been discounted to reflect pollution damage? Or does this rationale beg the question? If property owners had a right to recover for pollution damage, would there have been a discounting of the property price? [15]

---

15. Is the "coming to the nuisance" doctrine further justified in order to prevent economically inefficient patterns of land use? Physical separation of polluters and those suffering from pollution is a potential alternative to technological controls. If would-be plaintiffs are free to locate in the vicinity of a pollution source and recover full damages, won't potential incentives for efficient land use patterns be undercut? On the other hand, will denial of damage recovery provide an effective incentive for location elsewhere? Consider the income status of many of the people who locate in heavily polluted industrial areas. Even if the "coming to the nuisance" doctrine were justified by consider-

The transaction costs of imposing strict liability. The imposition of damage liability without regard to fault would involve substantial costs for courts and litigants. The resources that might be saved by abandoning the effort to determine whether "fault" existed might be swamped by the influx of greater numbers of cases. Moreover, the resources saved by abandoning the requirement of fault may be relatively modest. Causation and damages must be shown; in environmental cases, causation is often an important issue involving extensive evidentiary submissions. Also, to the extent we depart from a flat rule of liability without fault and permit, for example, a defense that plaintiff can more cheaply reduce pollution damage, the transaction cost advantages of abandoning "fault" as determinative of liability are further reduced.

Of perhaps greater importance is the social cost of insurance under alternative liability regimes. Under a system that places liability on the polluter, pollution-related injuries are insured by the polluter, either directly or through third-party liability insurance. Under a system imposing liability upon the victim, injuries are either borne directly by the victim or insured through first-party health, disability, and life insurance. The direct and administrative costs of third-party insurance are estimated to be higher than that for first-party insurance coverage for the same set of injuries. See Priest, The Current Insurance Crisis and Modern Tort Law, 96 Yale L.J. 1521, 1550-1561 (1987). First-party insurance, to the extent that it does not classify insureds into sufficiently narrow risk pools and monitoring victim conduct is costly, dulls victims' incentives to take preventive care. See Hanson and Logue, The

---

ations of economic efficiency, would its adoption be contrary to fair income distribution or justice between the parties?

Does "coming to the nuisance" justify the decision in *Waschak* on efficiency grounds? *Compare* Bryson & Macbeth, Public Nuisance, the Restatement (Second) of Torts, and Environmental Law, 2 Ecology L.Q. 241, 266-271 (1972) (suggesting that some cases where the "coming to nuisance" notion is used to deny recovery are really justified on a "homogenous community" principle governing cases where all members of the community participate in activities (such as using fossil fuel for home heating) that pose reciprocal burdens, or benefit from a central activity (such as pollution by an industrial plant that provides a town's economic livelihood) that spreads reciprocal costs (such as pollution) on everyone in the community. In these situations, external costs may be roughly matched or offset by benefits. The transaction costs involved in shifting damage may be largely wasted motion, and may not be justified by cost spreading considerations.)

Once plaintiffs have already moved into an area and are unlikely to relocate, isn't denial of relief likely to yield an inefficient outcome? Should the government intervene to pay for pollution control? See Ellickson, Alternatives to Zoning: Covenants, Nuisance Rules and Fines as Land Use Controls, 40 U. Chi. L. Rev. 681, 760 (1973). Does this analysis suggest an appropriate judicial strategy for developing and applying damage liability doctrine in pollution cases?

First-Party Insurance Externality: An Economic Justification for Enterprise Liability, 76 Cornell L. Rev. 129, 131-132 (1990). What about the fact that some members of our society cannot afford or otherwise lack access to insurance?

5. How does the foregoing analysis aid your assessment of *Waschak*? Is *Waschak* a strong case for the imposition of liability without fault? Why? Why not?

6. *An Emerging Trend Toward Strict Liability.* In part pushed by legal scholars seeking to assure that nuisance law is capable of addressing pollution problems, there has been a discernible and growing trend toward the application, implicit and explicit, of strict liability in cases involving releases of toxic pollutants. The adoption of Restatement (Second) of Torts §826(b) by the American Law Institute is one clear indication of this trend. See W. Rodgers, Environmental Law: Air and Water §2.4 (1986). In addition, some state courts have adopted a rule of strict liability for harm caused by escaping substances, *State v. Ventron*, 463 A.2d 893 (N.J. Sup. Ct. 1983), and a number of state legislatures have so provided by statute; see, e.g., Minn. Stat. §115B.045 subd. 1.

Is strict liability for environmental degradation capable of addressing the major environmental problems facing society? Consider the problems of urban air pollution, acid deposition, groundwater contamination, oil spills, and climate change.

3.   HOW SHOULD THE ENTITLEMENT BE ENFORCED?

The traditional "black letter" common law doctrines relating to air pollution, summarized above, with a few exceptions, do not distinguish between damages and injunctive relief in defining plaintiffs' right to prevail. However, in practice, as we shall see, courts differentiate between the two forms of relief, and sometimes award damages while declining to grant injunctive relief. While this difference may simply reflect the traditional discretion exercised by courts in awarding equitable relief, it also suggests the value of systematically distinguishing the two forms of relief in framing substantive rules of environmental law.

In studying the cases that follow, you should consider how the choice between injunctive and damage relief (property and liability rules) might affect the economically efficient use of environmental resources. Recall the discussion of the Coase Theorem (and particularly the implications of transaction costs) as well as the insights of Calabresi & Melamed's framework. In the frequent case of one or a few polluters and many victims, what would be the likely impact of a rule awarding victims damages for pollution injuries? What about awarding any victim an injunction against any emissions?

To the extent that you believe legal rules respecting environmental resource use are or should be based on considerations other than economic efficiency, would it still be valuable to distinguish alternative forms of relief? For example, if environmental entitlements were grounded on moral principles, might it be appropriate to protect some such entitlements by property rules, and others by liability rules? What role, if any, is there for rules of inalienability?

BOOMER V. ATLANTIC CEMENT CO.

26 N.Y.2d 219, 257 N.E.2d 870, 309 N.Y.2d 312 (1970)

BERGAN, J. Defendant operates a large cement plant near Albany. These are actions for injunction and damages by neighboring land owners alleging injury to property from dirt, smoke and vibration emanating from the plant. A nuisance has been found after trial, temporary damages have been allowed; but an injunction has been denied.

The public concern with air pollution arising from many sources in industry and in transportation is currently accorded ever wider recognition accompanied by a growing sense of responsibility in State and Federal Governments to control it. Cement plants are obvious sources of air pollution in the neighborhoods where they operate.

But there is now before the court private litigation in which individual property owners have sought specific relief from a single plant operation. The threshold question raised by the division of view on this appeal is whether the court should resolve the litigation between the parties now before it as equitably as seems possible; or whether, seeking promotion of the general public welfare, it should channel private litigation into broad public objectives.

A court performs its essential function when it decides the rights of parties before it. Its decision of private controversies may sometimes greatly affect public issues. Large questions of law are often resolved by the manner in which private litigation is decided. But this is normally an incident to the court's main function to settle controversy. It is a rare exercise of judicial power to use a decision in private litigation as a purposeful mechanism to achieve direct public objectives greatly beyond the rights and interests before the court.

Effective control of air pollution is a problem presently far from solution even with the full public financial powers of government. In large measure adequate technical procedures are yet to be developed and some that appear possible may be economically impracticable.

It seems apparent that the amelioration of air pollution will depend on technical research in great depth; on a carefully balanced consideration of the economic impact of close regulation; and of the actual effect on public health. It is likely to require massive public expenditure and to demand more than any local community can accomplish and to depend on regional and interstate controls.

A court should not try to do this on its own as a by-product of private litigation and it seems manifested that the judicial establishment is neither equipped in the limited nature of any judgment it can pronounce nor prepared to lay down and implement an effective policy for the elimination of air pollution. This is an area beyond the circumference of one private lawsuit. It is a direct responsibility for government and should not thus be undertaken as an incident to solving a dispute between property owners and a single cement plant — one of many — in the Hudson River valley.

The cement making operations of defendant have been found by the court at Special Term to have damaged the nearby properties of plaintiffs in these two actions. That court, as it has been noted, accordingly found defendant maintained a nuisance and this has been affirmed at the Appellate Division. The total damage to plaintiffs' properties is, however, relatively small in comparison with the value of defendant's operation and with the consequences of the injunction which plaintiffs seek.

The ground for the denial of injunction, notwithstanding the finding both that there is a nuisance and that plaintiffs have been damaged substantially, is the large disparity in economic consequences of the nuisance and of the injunction. This theory cannot, however, be sustained without overruling a doctrine which has been consistently reaffirmed in several leading cases in this court and which has never been disavowed here, namely that where a nuisance has been found and where there has been any substantial damage shown by the party complaining an injunction will be granted.

The rule in New York has been that such a nuisance will be enjoined although marked disparity be shown in economic consequence between the effect of the injunction and the effect of the nuisance.

The problem of disparity in economic consequence was sharply in focus in *Whalen v. Union Bag & Paper Co.* (208 N.Y. 1). A pulp mill entailing an investment of more than a million dollars polluted a stream in which plaintiff, who owned a farm, was "a lower riparian owner." The economic loss to plaintiff from this pollution was small. This court, reversing the Appellate Division, reinstated the injunction granted by the Special Term against the argument of the mill owner that in view of "the slight advantage to plaintiff and the great loss that will be inflicted on defendant" an injunction should not be granted (p. 2). "Such a balancing of injuries cannot be justified by the circumstances of this case," Judge Werner noted (p. 4). He continued: "Although the damage to the plaintiff may be slight as compared with the defendant's expense of abating the condition, that is not a good reason for refusing an injunction." (p. 5).

Thus the unconditional injunction granted at Special Term was reinstated. The rule laid down in that case, then, is that whenever the damage resulting from a nuisance is found not "unsubstantial," viz, $100 a year, injunction would follow. This states a rule that had been followed in this court with marked consistency (*McCarty v. Natural Carbonic Gas Co.*, 189 N.Y. 40; *Strobel v. Kerr Salt Co.*, 164 N.Y. 303; *Campbell v. Seaman*, 63 N.Y. 568). . . . Thus if, within *Whalen v. Union Bag & Paper Co.* (supra) which authoritatively states the rule in New York, the damage to plaintiffs in these present cases from defendant's cement plant is "not unsubstantial," an injunction should follow.

Although the court at Special Term and the Appellate Division held that injunction should be denied, it was found that plaintiffs had been damaged in various specific amounts up to the time of the trial and damages to the respective plaintiffs were awarded for those amounts. The effect of this was, injunction having been denied, plaintiffs could maintain successive actions at law for damages thereafter as further damage was incurred.

The court at Special Term also found the amount of permanent damage attributable to each plaintiff, for the guidance of the parties in the event both sides stipulated to the payment and acceptance of such permanent damage as a settlement of all the controversies among the parties. The total of permanent damages to all plaintiffs thus found was $185,000. This basis of adjustments has not resulted in any stipulation by the parties.

This result at Special Term and at the Appellate Division is a departure from a rule that has become settled; but to follow that rule literally in these cases would be to close down the plant at once. This court is fully agreed to avoid that immediately drastic remedy; the difference in view is how best to avoid it.[16]

One alternative is to grant the injunction but postpone its effect to a specified future date to give opportunity for technical advances to permit defendant to eliminate the nuisance; another is to grant the injunction conditioned on the payment of permanent damages to plaintiffs which would compensate them for the total economic loss to their property present and future caused by defendant's operations. For reasons which will be developed the court chooses the latter alternative.

If the injunction were to be granted unless within a short period — e.g., 18 months — the nuisance be abated by improved meth-

---

16. Respondent's investment in the plant is in excess of $45,000,000. There are over 300 people employed there.

ods, there would be no assurance that any significant technical improvement would occur.

The parties could settle this private litigation at any time if defendant paid enough money and the imminent threat of closing the plant would build up the pressure on defendant. If there were no improved techniques found, there would inevitably be applications to the court at Special Term for extensions of time to perform on showing of good faith efforts to find such techniques.

Moreover, techniques to eliminate dust and other annoying by-products of cement making are unlikely to be developed by any research the defendant can undertake within any short period, but will depend on the total resources of the cement industry Nationwide and throughout the world. The problem is universal wherever cement is made.

For obvious reasons the rate of the research is beyond control of defendant. If at the end of 18 months the whole industry has not found a technical solution a court would be hard put to close down this one cement plant if due regard be given to equitable principles.

On the other hand, to grant the injunction unless defendant pays plaintiffs such permanent damages as may be fixed by the court seems to do justice between the contending parties. All of the attributions of economic loss to the properties on which plaintiffs' complaints are based will have been redressed.

The nuisance complained of by these plaintiffs may have other public or private consequences, but these particular parties are the only ones who have sought remedies and the judgment proposed will fully redress them. The limitation of relief granted is a limitation only within the four corners of these actions and does not foreclose public health or other public agencies from seeking proper relief in a proper court.

It seems reasonable to think that the risk of being required to pay permanent damages to injured property owners by cement plant owners would itself be a reasonable effective spur to research for improved techniques to minimize nuisance.

The power of the court to condition on equitable grounds the continuance of an injunction on the payment of permanent damages seems undoubted. . . .

JASEN, J. (dissenting). I agree with the majority that a reversal is required here, but I do not subscribe to the newly enunciated doctrine of assessment of permanent damages, in lieu of an injunction, where substantial property rights have been impaired by the creation of a nuisance.

It has long been the rule in this State, as the majority acknowledges, that a nuisance which results in substantial continuing damage to neighbors must be enjoined. (*Whalen v. Union Bag & Paper Co.*, 208 N.Y. 1; *Campbell v. Seaman*, 63 N.Y. 568; see also, *Kennedy v. Moog Servocontrols*, 21 N.Y.2d 966.) To now change the rule to permit the cement company to continue polluting the air indefinitely upon the payment of permanent damages is, in my opinion, compounding the magnitude of a very serious problem in our State and Nation today.

In recognition of this problem, the Legislature of this State has enacted the Air Pollution Control Act (Public Health Law, §§1264-1299-m) declaring that it is the State policy to require the use of all available and reasonable methods to prevent and control air pollution (Public Health Law, §1275. . . . We have [here] a nuisance which not only is damaging to the plaintiffs, but also is decidedly harmful to the general public. . . .

I see grave dangers in overruling our long-established rule of granting an injunction where a nuisance results in substantial continuing damage. In permitting the injunction to become inoperative upon the payment of permanent damages, the majority is, in effect, licensing a continuing wrong. It is the same as saying [to] the cement company, you may continue to do harm to your neighbors so long as you pay a fee for it. Furthermore, once such permanent damages are assessed and paid, the incentive to alleviate the wrong would be eliminated, thereby continuing air pollution of an area without abatement.

It is true that some courts have sanctioned the remedy here proposed by the majority in a number of cases, but none of the authorities relied upon by the majority are analogous to the situation before us. In those cases, the courts, in denying an injunction and awarding money damages, grounded their decision on a showing that the use to which the property was intended to be put was primarily for the public benefit. Here, on the other hand, it is clearly established that the cement company is creating a continuing air pollution nuisance primarily for its own private interest with no public benefit. . . .

I would enjoin the defendant cement company from continuing the discharge of dust particles upon its neighbors' properties unless, within 18 months, the cement company abated this nuisance.

It is not my intention to cause the removal of the cement plant from the Albany area, but to recognize the urgency of the problem stemming from this stationary source of air pollution, and to allow the company a specified period of time to develop a means to alleviate this nuisance.

I am aware that the trial court found that the most modern dust control devices available have been installed in defendant's plant, but, I submit, this does not mean that *better* and more effective dust control devices could not be developed within the time allowed to abate the pollution. . . .

NOTES AND QUESTIONS

1. *The Inadequacy of Liability Rules and the Need for Injunctive Relief.* Why shouldn't defendant's enterprise simply be charged with the damages it causes? If it can pay damages and still stay in business (with or without increased pollution control measures), this is a sound indication from the market that the benefits derived from the enterprise exceed its costs and justify its existence. If the enterprise cannot pay the damages and stay in business, the costs associated with it exceed the benefits, and an award of damages is tantamount to an injunction. What arguments might be made against this position? See Calabresi, Some Thoughts on Risk Distribution and the Law of Torts, 70 Yale L.J. 499, 534-535 (1961); Polinsky, Resolving Nuisance Disputes: The Simple Economics of Injunctive and Damage Remedies, 32 Stan. L. Rev. 1075 (1980); Farber, Reassessing *Boomer:* Justice, Efficiency, and Nuisance Law 7 in Property Law and Legal Education: Essays in Honor of John E. Cribbet (P. Hay & M. Hoeflich eds. 1988).

Is injunctive relief needed to avoid the costs of repeated lawsuits to recover for future damages as they accrue? Why can't this difficulty be resolved by awarding permanent damages, as in *Boomer?* Will permanent damage awards deprive defendants of any incentive to modify their behavior to cause less pollution damage in the future? Could the terms of a permanent damage award be modified to restore this incentive?

What are the effects of the *Boomer* decision on incentives for industrial siting? What about incentives for negotiating in advance to acquire pollution easements? See Goldberg, Relational Exchange, Contract Law, and the *Boomer* Problem, in Readings in the Economics of Contract Law (V. Goldberg ed. 1989).

Might damage awards be inadequate because they fail to include all of the adverse effects of environmental degradation? For example, how could damage awards deal with an uncertain risk of future health damage from current pollution exposure? Is a damage remedy appropriate for harms with a large psychic component or those that inflict an individually small amount of damage on many individuals? How, if at all, are these difficulties ameliorated in the context of injunctive relief?

The dissent argues that the use of a liability rule is tantamount to "licensing" pollution. Should this argument be determinative? Does it comport with the principles underlying nuisance law generally?

2. *The Right to an Absolute Injunction.* Should plaintiff automatically be entitled to an injunction prohibiting any discharges by a polluter? Would not a rule limiting relief to damages empower a polluter to "take" plaintiff's property or health without plaintiff's consent upon payment of compensation in an amount determined by third parties (judge and jury), which plaintiff might find wholly inadequate? Should

courts distinguish between pollution that adversely affects health as opposed to pollution injuring only property? Normal property rules preclude condemnation of one person's property by another on payment of "just compensation"; a property owner can ordinarily dispose or retain property on whatever terms she pleases. See *Edwards v. Allvorez Mining Co.*, 38 Mich. 48 (1878) ("No man holds the comfort of his home for sale, and no man is willing to accept in lieu of it an award of damages"). The exception to this rule is where the legislature explicitly vests eminent domain powers in private agencies, such as utility companies, on a finding that the exercise of such a power will serve a public purpose. In addition, not every government-authorized modification of existing property rights constitutes a "taking." See Chapter 9.

Does this line of reasoning simply beg the question? Might not defendant with equal logic argue that the award of an injunction amounts to a "taking" of defendant's property by plaintiff (and an uncompensated taking at that)?

Consider also the practical implications of automatically granting a prohibitory injunction. Wouldn't automatic grant of a prohibitory injunction lead to unjust enrichment by plaintiff, who could extort settlement payments from defendant in an amount far exceeding plaintiff's damage? Moreover, where many potential plaintiffs are involved, doesn't the possibility that each one could obtain a prohibitory injunction threaten serious resource misallocation? Why? For a thorough analysis of these issues, see Polinsky, Resolving Nuisance Disputes: The Simple Economics of Injunctive and Damage Remedies, 32 Stan. L. Rev. 1075 (1980).

3. *Judicial Balancing of the Equities.* Courts today rarely grant prohibitory injunctions on the simple theory that the plaintiff is entitled to prohibit an invasion of his property rights. Instead, courts will normally "balance the equities" in order to determine whether a damage award is inadequate or otherwise inappropriate. If it decides that injunctive relief is appropriate, it will further "balance the equities" in order to determine the appropriate form of injunctive relief; among the possibilities are an absolute prohibition, land use accommodations, technological requirements (such as installation of best technology to abate pollution); and operational controls (such as limitations on level or hours of operation). See W. Rodgers, Environmental Law: Air and Water §2.13 (1986). For example, the dissenting judge in *Boomer* would have given defendant an 18-month "variance" to install superior controls.

How well equipped are courts to gather information on and assess the various factors involved in framing an injunction that will achieve the socially optimal result? Even if economic efficiency were the sole objective, what factors would a court have to consider in a case like *Boomer* in order to frame a decree that would provide an economically efficient solution? Shouldn't the court also consider the effects of the form of relief on the community at large? The court in *Boomer* seemed to believe it was not "channel[ing] private litigation into broad public objectives." Do you agree?

4. *Injunctions as a Spur to Technological Change.* We have already seen that the award of damages without regard to fault might provide an incentive for the development of environmentally superior technologies. How might a court use injunctive relief to promote technology forcing? What is the likely success of severe measures like those contemplated by the *Boomer* dissent? Should the court instead require defendant to undertake a specified program of research and development? Where a court awards injunctive relief that does not require a complete cessation of emissions, should it require defendant to pay, periodically, damages equal to the harm caused by its remaining emissions?

5. *Problem:* OK Ranch has operated a large cattle feedlot since the 1950s at its present location. At the time the cattle ranch was established, the neighboring area was rural with other cattle ranches in the vicinity. In the early 1960s, Smith Development Company acquired three large ranches in the neighboring area for the purpose of developing a retirement community. Smith built a golf course and began offering condominiums in the community. The first units were more than three miles from OK Ranch. The retirement community gradually expanded until newer units were within half a mile of the ranch. The stench of OK Ranch, despite the use of good feedlot management, often made it uncomfortable if not unhealthy for residents to enjoy the outdoor living that attracted them to the community. Smith Development Company sues to enjoin operation of OK Ranch. How should this case be resolved? Who should get the entitlement? How should it be enforced? What if the residents were to sue as individuals? See *Spur Industries, Inc. v. Del E. Webb Development Co.*, 494 P.2d 700 (Ariz. S. Ct. 1972).

VILLAGE OF WILSONVILLE V. SCA SERVICES, INC.

86 Ill.2d 1, 426 N.E.2d 824 (Ill. 1981)

[The plaintiffs, village of Wilsonville and other government bodies, filed suit alleging that defendant's hazardous-chemical landfill in Wilsonville constituted a public nuisance. Plaintiffs sought to enjoin further operation of the landfill and to require the defendant to remove all toxic waste buried at the site as well as all contaminated soil.

The 130-acre landfill site, surrounded by farmland and the village and situated above an abandoned coal mine, received an operational permit from the Illinois Environmental Protection Agency (IEPA) in

September 1976 and began accepting toxic wastes soon thereafter. Up until the first day of trial (June 7, 1977), each shipment to the site was accompanied by a supplemental permit issued by the IEPA. Much of the waste, including PCBs, cyanide, asbestos, mercury, and arsenic, was highly toxic to humans. The site operators disposed of the waste, 95 percent of which was contained in 55-gallon steel drums and the remainder in double-walled paper bags, in clay-lined trenches that measured 15-foot deep, 50-foot wide, and 250 to 350-foot long.

During the 104-day trial, nearby residents and numerous scientific experts presented testimony about the past and possible future effects of the landfill. Neighbors of the site complained of dust, odors, and spills of chemical waste that caused burning eyes, running noses, headaches, nausea, and shortness of breath and interfered with the recreational use of their yards. The defendants presented evidence attributing the odors to local practices of burning refuse and dumping sewage in a nearby creek. The major long-term threat posed by the site was from contamination of surface and groundwater. The surface and groundwater drainage was away from the village and toward farmland. Although the village purchased much of its water from a neighboring city, 73 private wells were in operation, at least one of which was used for drinking water. Nearby springs were used to water livestock. The groundwater flowing beneath the site is separated from the trenches by 10 to 15 feet of dense matter. Permeability studies indicated that the general permeability of the site slightly exceeded the IEPA's suggested standard for hazardous waste landfills (which was issued after the licensing of the site). Plaintiffs' experts testified that subsidence of the coal mine was likely to occur approximately 40 years after the mine was closed, thereby substantially raising the possibility of migration of the toxic materials. Defendant's experts testified that subsidence would not be deep and could be repaired by engineering techniques. Another of plaintiffs' experts opined that chemical explosions releasing poisonous gases might occur at the site.

The trial court concluded that there existed a substantial danger of contamination of groundwater and neighboring land and explosions from chemical interactions. It granted an injunction closing the site, requiring the defendant to remove all toxic wastes buried at the site and to restore the site. The judgment was affirmed by the intermediate state appellate court. The defendant appealed.]

The defendant [contends] that the courts below were in error when they failed to require a showing of a substantial risk of certain and extreme future harm before enjoining operation of the defendant's site. We deem it necessary to explain that a *prospective* nuisance is a fit candidate for injunctive relief. Prosser states: "Both public and private nuisances require some substantial interference with the interest involved. Since nuisance is a common subject of equity jurisdiction,

the damage against which an injunction is asked is often merely threatened or potential; but even in such cases, there must be at least a threat
of substantial invasion of the plaintiff's interests." (Prosser, Torts etc.
87, at 577 (4th ed. 1971). The defendant does not dispute this proposition; it does, however, argue that the trial court did not follow the
proper standard for determining when a prospective nuisance may be
enjoined. The defendant argues that the proper standard to be used is
that an injunction is proper only if there is a "dangerous probability"
that the threatened or potential injury will occur. (See Restatement
(Second) of Torts sec. 933(1), at 561, comment b (1979).) The defendant further argues that the appellate court looked only at the potential
consequences of not enjoining the operation of the site as a nuisance
and not at the likelihood of whether harm would occur. The defendant
assigns error on this basis.

In this case there can be no doubt that it is highly probable that
the chemical-waste-disposal site will bring about a substantial injury.
Without again reviewing the extensive evidence adduced at trial, we
think it is sufficiently clear that it is highly probable that the instant
site will constitute a public nuisance if, through either an explosive
interaction, migration, subsidence, or the "bathtub effect," the highly
toxic chemical wastes deposited at the site escape and contaminate the
air, water, or ground around the site. That such an event will occur was
positively attested to by several expert witnesses. A court does not have
to wait for it to happen before it can enjoin such a result. Additionally,
the fact is that the condition of a nuisance is already present at the site
due to the location of the site and the manner in which it has been
operated. Thus, it is only the damage which is prospective. Under these
circumstances, if a court can prevent any damage from occurring, it
should do so. . . .

We agree with the defendant's statement of law, but not with its
urged application to the facts of this case. Again, Professor Prosser has
offered a concise commentary. He has stated that "[o]ne distinguishing
feature of equitable relief is that it may be granted upon the threat of
harm which has not yet occurred. The defendant may be restrained
from entering upon an activity where it is highly probable that it will
lead to a nuisance, although if the possibility is merely uncertain or
contingent he may be left to his remedy after the nuisance has occurred." (Prosser, Torts sec. 90, at 603 (4th ed. 1971). This view is in
accord with Illinois law. . . .

RYAN, Justice concurring:
While I agree with both the result reached by the majority and
the reasoning employed supporting the opinion, I wish to add a brief
comment. In response to the defendant's argument that the trial court
failed to apply the proper standard for determining when a prospective
nuisance may be enjoined, the majority concluded that the court had

in fact applied the correct rule. . . . I am concerned that [this rule] may be an unnecessarily narrow view of the test for enjoining prospective tortious conduct in general. Any injunction is, by its very nature, the product of a court's balancing of competing interests, with a result equitably obtained. Prosser, in discussing the law of nuisance, quoted by the majority, states:

> [I]f the possibility [of harm] is merely uncertain or contingent [the plaintiff] may be left to his remedy after the nuisance has occurred. Prosser, Torts sec. 90, at 603 (4th ed. 1971).

Prosser thus recognizes that there are cases in which the possibility of inflicting harm is slight and where the plaintiff may be left to his remedy at law. However, I believe that there are situations where the harm that is potential is so devastating that equity should afford relief even though the possibility of the harmful result occurring is uncertain or contingent. The Restatement's position applicable to preventative injunctive relief in general is that "[t]he more serious the impending harm, the less justification there is for taking the chances that are involved in pronouncing the harm too remote." (Restatement (Second) of Torts sec. 933, at 561, comment b (1979).) If the harm that may result is severe, a lesser possibility of it occurring should be required to support injunctive relief. Conversely, if the potential harm is less severe, a greater possibility that it will happen should be required. Also, in the balancing of competing interests, a court may find a situation where the potential harm is such that a plaintiff will be left to his remedy at law if the possibility of it occurring is slight. This balancing test allows the court to consider a wider range of factors and avoids the anomalous result possible under the more restrictive alternative where a person engaged in an ultrahazardous activity with potentially catastrophic results would be allowed to continue until he has driven an entire community to the brink of certain disaster. A court of equity need not wait so long to provide relief.

Although the "dangerous probability" test has certainly been met in this case, I would be willing to enjoin the activity on a showing of probability of occurrences substantially less than that which the facts presented to this court reveal, due to the extremely hazardous nature of the chemicals being dumped and the potentially catastrophic results.

NOTES AND QUESTIONS

1. Is the outcome in this case consistent with Calabresi and Melamed's framework? How is this case different from *Boomer*?

2. How serious were the effects of the environmental contamination in this case? How can the risks most effectively be addressed? How

about assuring a safe drinking water supply to the community by replacing groundwater wells with water from uncontaminated reservoirs and containment and quarantine of the site? Shouldn't the court consider the environmental and health risks of removing the contaminated soil and treating it or disposing of it elsewhere?

3. The decision in *Village of Wilsonville* turns critically upon how the court assesses the uncertainty about future effects. Which opinion — majority or concurrence — comports better with the economist's approach to decisionmaking under uncertainty? Is either opinion consistent with a rights-based approach? In view of the court's limited ability to assess scientific uncertainties, should it err on the side of safety?

4. Suppose that *Village of Wilsonville* was a private nuisance case brought by the neighboring farmers and that the court issued the same injunction. Suppose further that the farmers were willing to agree not to enforce the injunction if the defendant paid them $1 million. Should the court approve this settlement? What are the strongest arguments in favor? against?

C.   THE EFFICACY OF THE COMMON LAW IN ADDRESSING ENVIRONMENTAL DEGRADATION: THE EXAMPLE OF *RESERVE MINING*

The *Reserve Mining* litigation highlights the problems courts face in deciding environmental disputes. How should a court evaluate the risks created by an industrial process when they cannot be quantified with any scientific accuracy? What level of scientific uncertainty will satisfy a legal burden of proof on such issues as causation and damages? What remedy should be afforded with respect to an ongoing industrial operation employing large numbers of people which poses uncertain health risks to the local area? The *Reserve Mining* litigation is an early example of courts confronting these complex issues, attempting to balance the conflicting commitments of society to industrial development and public health. The opinions provide an important analytical framework and show the limitations of the judiciary in making policy decisions when assessing technology and its risks.[17]

_____

17. The *Reserve Mining* litigation was maintained by both public and private plaintiffs. It is included in these materials on private litigation because it illustrates obstacles to recovery that would likely be even more acute in the case of an action maintained by a private party alone.

In 1947, the Reserve Mining Company, a jointly owned subsidiary of Armco and Republic Steel, proposed to build a mine and processing plant for the exploitation of the vast amount of taconite, a low-grade form of iron ore, in Silver Bay, Minnesota. In 1955, Reserve opened its plant, in which the taconite was purified by crushing it and removing the iron ore using large magnets. The state, which welcomed the employment provided by the plant, gave Reserve a permit to dump the tailings from its benefication process into Lake Superior. These tailings contained the mineral cummingtonite-grunerite. It was thought that the tailings would settle at the bottom of the lake. The tailings were discharged into Lake Superior at a rate of 67,000 tons per day.

The plant represented a capital investment of over $350 million, employed 3,300 employees, and produced 12 percent of the iron ore in the United States. The operation was profitable, but in 1969, concern began to grow over the pollution of Lake Superior caused by the tailings. In February 1972, the United States, the States of Minnesota, Wisconsin and Michigan, and various environmental groups filed suit against Reserve on federal and state law claims of pollution and nuisance. When it began, the case focused exclusively on the water pollution and ecological damage to Lake Superior. However, in June 1973, the focus of the dispute shifted to the public health dangers created by the tailings and the emissions from the processing plant. The plaintiffs claimed that Reserve was discharging asbestos-like fibers into the environment, polluting the air and the public water supply.

The health risk claims raised many difficult scientific questions, which could not be resolved conclusively, given the state of medical knowledge. The parties disputed the chemical characterization of the cummingtonite-grunerite fibers and their medical effects. Amosite asbestos was and is a known carcinogen. When inhaled in occupational settings with relatively high exposure levels, it can cause various forms of cancer and asbestosis. The plaintiffs claimed that the cummingtonite-grunerite in the processed taconite tailings was similar or identical in shape and form and similar in chemistry to amosite asbestos. This correlation was sharply disputed by Reserve. It was also difficult to accurately measure the concentration of the asbestos-like fibers in the air and water and thus the level of the public's exposure. Finally, there was uncertainty over whether ingestion of asbestos or asbestos-like fibers could cause cancer, or whether the particles had to be inhaled in order to be dangerous.

Judge Miles Lord presided over the trial. According to Professor Farber,

[p]erhaps the best way of capturing Judge Lord's local reputation is to say that by comparison William O. Douglas was considered a hair-splitting legalist. In the view of many lawyers, Judge Lord was on the bench

to do justice; he did not allow anything to stand in the way — whether it was Congress, appellate courts, or the evidence in a case. This righteous attitude — which produced the nickname, "Miles the Lord" — led him into continual conflicts with the U.S. Court of Appeals for the Eighth Circuit, in *Reserve Mining* as well as later cases. Nevertheless, until he lost his temper late in the proceedings, Judge Lord's writings in *Reserve Mining* gave every impression of being thorough and well considered.

Farber, Risk Regulation in Perspective: *Reserve Mining* Revisited, 21 Envtl. L. 1321, 1326-1327 (footnote omitted).

To help evaluate the conflicting scientific evidence, the trial court appointed experts to act as independent technical advisers and impartial witnesses. The trial lasted 139 days, during which over 100 witnesses were examined, over 1600 exhibits were introduced, and over 18,000 pages of transcript were recorded. The court determined that it could not wait for science to answer all of the questions conclusively. It found that there were substantial health risks associated with the Silver Bay facility and held that Reserve Mining was in violation of state and federal pollution and nuisance laws. By the end of the trial, Judge Lord had become impatient with Reserve, as seen in his initial memorandum opinion and order:

> Defendants have the economic and engineering capability to carry out an on land disposal system that satisfies the health and environmental considerations raised. For reasons unknown to this Court they have chosen not to implement such a plan. In essence they have decided to continue exposing thousands daily to a substantial health risk in order to maintain the current profitability of the present operation and delay the capital outlay (with its concomitant [sic] profit) needed to institute modifications. The Court has no other alternative but to order an immediate halt to the discharge which threatens the lives of thousands. In that defendants have no plan to make the necessary modifications, there is no reason to delay any further the issuance of the injunction.
>
> Up until the time of writing this opinion the Court has sought to exhaust every possibility in an effort to find a solution that would alleviate the health threat without a disruption of operations at Silver Bay. Faced with the defendants' intransigence, even in the light of the public health problem, the Court must order an immediate curtailment of the discharge.

United States v. Reserve Mining Co., 380 F. Supp. 11, 20-21 (D. Minn. 1974).

Reserve appealed and a panel of the Eighth Circuit issued a temporary stay of the injunction pending a full appeal of the order. The panel then considered whether to make that stay permanent pending an appeal of the merits of the District Court's opinion.

RESERVE MINING CO. V. UNITED STATES

498 F.2d 1073 (8th Cir. 1974)

BRIGHT, Circuit Judge.

A   THE SUBSTANCE OF THE CONTROVERSY

Although there is no dispute that significant amounts of waste tailings are discharged into the water and dust is discharged into the air by Reserve, the parties vigorously contest the precise nature of the discharge, its biological effects, and, particularly with respect to the waters of Lake Superior, its ultimate destination. Plaintiffs contend that the mineral cummingtonite-grunerite, which Reserve admits to be a major component of its taconite wastes and a member of the mineral family known as amphiboles, is substantially identical in morphology (or shape and form) and similar in chemistry to amosite asbestos, a fibrous mineral which has been found, in certain occupational settings, to be carcinogenic. The plaintiffs further argue that the mineral fibers discharged represent a serious health threat, since they are present in the air of Silver Bay and surrounding communities and, by way of dispersion throughout Lake Superior, in the drinking water of Duluth and other communities drawing water from the lake.

Reserve has maintained the litigation that its cummingtonite-grunerite does not have a fibrous form and is otherwise distinguishable from amosite asbestos. There was testimony as to the comparisons of mineralogy between Reserve's cummingtonite-grunerite and amosite asbestos, based on electron microscope analysis of morphology, x-ray diffraction analysis of crystal structure, and laboratory analysis of chemical composition. As for the dispersion through Lake Superior, there was considerable testimony as to whether Reserve was the sole source of cummingtonite-grunerite in the lake and whether the presence of the mineral could thus be used as a "tracer" for Reserve's discharge. Reserve further claimed that the tailings largely settled to the bottom of the lake in the "great trough" area within close range of the plant.

The district court found, as plaintiffs contended, that Reserve discharged particles identical to and similar to amosite asbestos, and that the particles discharged into Lake Superior were dispersed widely.

In considering whether our temporary stay of that injunction should remain in effect, we note the usual formulation of the applicable standards to be met by the party seeking a stay under Fed. R. Civ. P. 62 and Fed. R. App. P. 8: (1) a strong showing that he is likely to succeed on the merits of the appeal; (2) a showing that, unless a stay is granted, he will suffer irreparable injury; (3) a showing that no substantial harm will come to other interested parties; and (4) a showing that a stay will do no harm to the public interest. See, e.g., *Long v. Robinson*, 432 F.2d 977, 979 (4th Cir. 1970).

The first element goes to the sensible administration of justice: a stay should not ordinarily be granted if the court determines that the injunction will ultimately take effect in any event. The other three elements, while distinguishable in some contexts, dissolve into a single equitable judgment: balancing the health and environmental demands of society at large against the economic well-being of those parties and local communities immediately affected. Of course, foremost considerations must be given to any demonstrable danger to the public health. . . .

. . . Given the concededly enormous economic impact that an immediate plant closure would have upon Reserve, given the personal impact on its approximately 3,000 employees and their families, and given the social and economic impact upon the communities in which the employees live, we think that our preliminary resolution of the health hazard question should control our action as to whether to grant or deny a stay.

HEALTH ISSUE

A.   TESTIMONY BEFORE THE DISTRICT COURT

We have reviewed the testimony on the health issue, giving careful and particular attention and weight, as we should at this interim stage of review, to the testimony of the impartial court witnesses and that of plaintiffs' chief medical witness, Dr. Irving Selikoff, Director of the Environmental Sciences Laboratory of Mt. Sinai School of Medicine. While not called upon at this stage to reach any final conclusion, our review suggests that this evidence does not support a finding of substantial danger and that, indeed, the testimony indicates that such of finding should not be made. In this regard, we conclude that Reserve appears likely to succeed on the merits of its appeal on the health issue. We proceed now to trace the outlines of the testimony supporting this view.

1.   *Two Key Unknowns*

The theory by which plaintiffs argue that the discharges present a substantial danger is founded largely upon epidemiological studies of asbestos workers occupationally exposed to and inhaling high levels of asbestos dust. A study by Dr. Selikoff of workers at a New Jersey asbestos manufacturing plant demonstrated that occupational exposure to amosite asbestos poses a hazard of increased incidence of asbestosis and various forms of cancer. Similar studies in other occupational contexts leave no doubt that asbestos, at sufficiently high dosages, is injurious to health. However, in order to draw the conclusion that environmental exposure to Reserve's discharges presents a health threat in the instant case, it must be shown either that the circumstances of exposure are at least comparable to those in occupational settings, or, alternatively, that the occupational studies establish certain principles of asbestos-disease pathology which may be applied to predicting the occurrence of such disease in altered circumstances.

Initially, it must be observed that environmental exposure from Reserve's discharges into air and water is simply not comparable to that typical of occupational settings. The occupational studies involve direct exposure to and inhalation of asbestos dust in high concentrations and in confined spaces. This pattern of exposure cannot be equated with the discharge into the outside air of relatively low levels of asbestos fibers. . . . .

Nor can the occupational pattern of exposure be equated with the exposure resulting from the ingestion of fibers via the Duluth drinking water. This fact was confirmed by a tissue study, discussed in detail later in this opinion, in which the tissues of recently deceased Duluth residents were examined for asbestos fibers. . . . . [The study failed to disclose the presence of significant amounts of such fibers.] Thus, it cannot be said that either the discharge into the water or the discharge into the air results in circumstances of exposure comparable to those in an occupational context.

If this is true, no conclusions about health hazards in occupational settings may be utilized in the present situation except on the ground that certain principles of asbestos-disease pathology may be extrapolated from relevant medical knowledge and applied in altered circumstances. The principal altered circumstance is the lower level of exposure. In order to make a prediction, based on the occupational studies, as to the likelihood of disease at lower levels of exposure, at least two key findings must be made. First, an attempt must be made to determine, with some precision, what that lower level of exposure is. Second, that lower level of exposure must be applied to the known pathology of asbestos-induced disease, i.e., it must be determined whether the level of exposure is safe or unsafe.

Unfortunately, the testimony of Dr. Arnold Brown[18] indicates that neither of these key determinations can be made. Dr. Brown testified that, with respect to both air and water, the level of fibers is not readily susceptible of measurement. This results from the relatively imprecise state of counting techniques and the wide margin of error which neces-

---

18. Dr. Brown, a research pathologist associated with the Mayo Clinic of Rochester, Minnesota, served the court both in the capacity of a technical advisor and that of an impartial witness.

sarily result, and is reflected in the widely divergent sample counts received by the court. . . . [The court then cited relevant testimony by Dr. Brown.] This testimony indicates that little more can be said about the level of fibers present in air or water other than that some fibers are present.

Even assuming that one could avoid imprecision and uncertainty in measuring the number of fibers at low levels, there remains vast uncertainty as to the medical consequences of low levels of exposure to asbestos fibers. In order to predict the likelihood and magnitude of disease resulting from exposure, one must have some idea of the relevant threshold value and dose-response relationships.[19] Although there seems to be agreement that threshold values and dose-response relationships are observable with respect to cancer generally, the particular values and relationships associated with asbestos-induced cancer appear to be unknown.

2. The Tissue Study

This study was prompted by an almost complete lack of knowledge with respect to the human ingestion of asbestos fibers, since previous experiments had dealt largely with the effects of fiber inhalation, where interaction by asbestos with the respiratory tract was established. [If ingested fibers] do not interact with the tissues but simply are eliminated by the body as wastes, presumably no disease will result. Accordingly, the court-appointed experts formulated a "protocol" or study plan designed to test whether people who drink Lake Superior waters accumulate asbestos-like fibers in body tissues from taconite.

This protocol involved analysis by electron microscope of the tissues of recently deceased Duluth residents who had ingested Duluth water for at least 15 years, that is, since the beginning of operations by Reserve. As a "control" check on results, samples were taken from the residents of Houston, Texas, where the water is free of asbestos fibers. . . .

Those results, as explained to the court by one of its own experts, Dr. Pooley,[20] indicated that the tissues of Duluth residents were virtu-

---

19. A threshold value is that level of exposure below which no adverse health effects occur, while the dose-response relationship quantifies the association between disease-producing levels of exposure and the incidence of disease.

20. Dr. Frederick D. Pooley is a world renowned scientist from Cardiff, Wales, Great Britain, and an expert in the field of identifying physical and chemical properties of asbestos and asbestos-like fibers. Dr. Selikoff, plaintiffs' expert, described Dr. Pooley as the "one man who has competence and knowledge in this matter," i.e., the scientific examination of tissue for the presence of asbestos or asbestos-like fibers.

ally free of any fibers which could be attributed to the Reserve discharge.[21] . . .

Plaintiffs, however, sought subsequently to discount the significance of these tissue studies. First, the argument was made and was accepted by the district court, that the specimens of tissue from body organs surveyed were too minute, and thus fibers that were present may have been overlooked. . . . [The court countered this criticism by citing previous testimony by plaintiffs' expert, Dr. Selikoff, that the tissue study was soundly designed.]

Although, based on our review of the testimony, we agree with Dr. Brown's statement that the ingestion of asbestos fibers cannot be exonerated as a hazard, we feel that, on any fair reading of the circumstances of the protocol, the results of the tissue study must weigh heavily against the assessment of any demonstrated hazard to health. We think it is clear that the tissue study raises a major obstacle to the proof that ingestion of Duluth water is hazardous. . . .

B.   EVALUATION OF TESTIMONY . . .

Considering all of the above, we think one conclusion is evident: although Reserve's discharges represent a possible medical danger, they have not in this case been proven to amount to a health hazard. The discharges may or may not result in detrimental health effects, but, for the present, that is simply unknown. The relevant legal question is thus, what manner of judicial cognizance may be taken on the unknown.

We do not think that a bare risk of the unknown can amount to proof in this case. Plaintiffs have failed to prove that a demonstrable health hazard exists. This failure, we hasten to add, is not reflective of any weakness which it is within their power to cure, but rather, given the current state of medical and scientific knowledge, plaintiffs' case is based only on medical hypothesis and is simply beyond proof.

We believe that Judge Lord carried his analysis one step beyond the evidence. Since testimony clearly established that an assessment of the risk was made impossible by the absence of medical knowledge, Judge Lord apparently took the position that all uncertainties should be resolved in favor of health safety. Since the appropriate threshold level for safe toleration of fibers was unknown, the district court tipped the balance in favor of attempting to protect against the unknown and

---

21. Several aspects of Dr. Pooley's testimony regarding the tissue study should be noted. The few fibers which were found were not, in the main, "closely associated" with the tissue specimens, indicating that contamination was a likely source of the fibers. No "asbestos bodies," indicative of long-term residence of the fibers in the tissues, were found. Finally, there was no indication of occupational exposure characterized by very large numbers of fibers.

simply assumed that Reserve's discharge presents a health hazard. In doing so, he disregarded the tissue studies of his own experts which provided direct evidence to the contrary. If we are correct in our conclusion that evidence does not exist in the record on which to find Reserve's discharges to be unsafe, the district court's determination to resolve all doubts in favor of health safety represents a legislative policy judgment, not a judicial one. See *Industrial Union Department, AFL-CIO, et al. v. Hodgson,* No. 72-1713, 499 F.2d 467, at 474 (D.C. Cir., filed April 15, 1974). As Judge McGowan stated in *Industrial Union Department, AFL-CIO,* with regard to legislative resolution of a similar issue:

> [S]ome of the questions involved in the promulgation of these standards are on the frontiers of scientific knowledge, and consequently as to them insufficient data is presently available to make a fully informed factual determination. Decision making must in that circumstance depend to a greater extent upon policy judgments and less upon purely factual analysis. [Id. at 474.]

We emphasize that our evaluation rests not on any view that the discharge exposes North Shore residents to no risk, but rather on the view that, given the evidence, no substantial danger has been, or could be proven. . . . Although we are sympathetic to the uncertainties facing the residents of the North Shore, we are a court of law, governed by rules of proof, and unknowns may not be substituted for proof of a demonstrable hazard to the public health.

. . . [We] are satisfied that the circumstances call for a stay conditioned upon assurances that there will be a speedy termination of Reserve's discharges into Lake Superior and control of its emission into the air.

The controversy between Reserve and governmental agencies over alleged pollution of Lake Superior has existed for more than five years. In retrospect, it must now be painfully clear to all who participated in the original decision to permit the discharge of tailings into Lake Superior, that such a decision amounted to a monumental environmental mistake. The actors in that decision, 25 years ago, included leading citizens and governmental officials of Minnesota as well as officials of Reserve, Armco, and Republic Steel. That decision obviously was made in good faith to create jobs, to provide other economic opportunities in an economically depressed area of northern Minnesota, and to utilize the almost unlimited supply of hitherto unusable, low-grade, taconite ore found in that area. To us there are neither heroes nor villains among the present participants in this lawsuit, nor among their predecessors in government, business, and society who were once allies in encouraging and creating a taconite industry in northern Minnesota. Nevertheless, the pollution of Lake Superior must cease as quickly as feasible under the circumstances.

Accordingly, our stay of the injunction will be conditioned upon Reserve taking prompt steps to abate its discharges into air and water. We invited Reserve to advise this court concerning plans for the on-land disposal of its tailings and the significant control of its air emissions. Reserve's counsel stated that the company envisioned a three and one-half year to five year "turn-around" time, but added that investigation continues in an effort to reduce further the time for achieving abatement.

Our stay of the injunction rests upon the good faith preparation and implementation of an acceptable plan.[22]

[The stay was conditioned upon expeditious presentations and consideration of a plan for dealing with Reserve's air emissions and tailings. Plaintiffs' subsequent application to the Supreme Court to vacate this stay was denied, 418 U.S. 911, 419 U.S. 802 (1974), Justice Douglas dissenting. However, four other justices stated that the denial was without prejudice to plaintiffs' renewal of their application if the Court of Appeals failed to dispose of the controversy on the merits by January 31, 1975.]

The Eighth Circuit, sitting en banc, later heard a full appeal on the merits of the trial judge's determinations:

RESERVE MINING CO. V. ENVIRONMENTAL PROTECTION AGENCY

514 F.2d 492 (8th Cir. 1975) (en banc)

[The court reviewed in considerable detail the history of the litigation and the evidence respecting the possible health effects of air pollution from the plant. With respect to air pollution, the court concludes as follows:]

We think it significant that Dr. Brown, an impartial witness whose court-appointed task was to address the health issue in its entirety,

---

22. We note that the trial court has characterized Reserve's approach to abatement as one of "intransigence" and seems to have considered this as a factor in closing down the plant. See Judge Lord's Memorandum of April 20, 1974, at 12. In his supplementary memorandum, Judge Lord commented critically on Reserve's failure in this litigation to present the trial court with a reasonable proposal for on-land disposal of its taconite tailings and control of its air emissions and noted that Reserve continued to produce unrealistic proposals despite his admonition last February that the Government had made a prima facie case . . . We expect that the parties will cooperate in achieving a plan acceptable to all concerned.

joined with plaintiffs' witnesses in viewing as reasonable the hypothesis that Reserve's discharges present a threat to public health. . . . [Doctor Brown stated:]

> Based on the scientific evidence, I would be unable to predict that the number of fibers in the air of Silver Bay, as seen on four days in October, that I would be unable to predict that cancer would be found in Silver Bay.
>
> Now, going beyond that, it seems to me that speaking now in general terms, where it has been shown that a known human carcinogen, sir, and I make that distinction and I shall make it again, I suspect, a human carcinogen is in the air of any community, and if it could be lowered I would say, as a physician that, yes, it should be lowered. And if it could be taken out of the air completely, I would be even more happy.
>
> But the presence of a known, human carcinogen, sir, is in my view cause for concern, and if there are means of removing that human carcinogen from the environment, that should then be done.

He explained further:

> As a physician, I take the view that I cannot consider, with equanimity, the fact that a known human carcinogen is in the environment. If I knew more about that human carcinogen, if I knew what a safe level was in the air, if I knew what a safe level was in the water then I could draw some firm conclusions and advise you in precise terms. That information is not available to me and I submit sir, it's not available to anyone else. And that until that information is developed in a scientific way, using techniques that would be acceptable to the medical community, until that time has arrived, then I take only the view that I have expressed.
>
> But with asbestos, . . . we're dealing with a different situation, we're dealing with a material which is known to cause cancer not only in animals, but in humans.

[The court then reviewed the evidence on health risks and water pollution, concluding as follows:]

These concepts of potential harm, whether they be assessed as "probabilities and consequences" or "risk and harm," necessarily must apply in a determination of whether any relief should be given in cases of this kind in which proof with certainty is impossible. . . .

In assessing probabilities in this case, it cannot be said that the probability of harm is more likely than not. Moreover, the level of probability does not readily convert into a prediction of consequences. On this record it cannot be forecast that the rates of cancer will increase from drinking Lake Superior water or breathing Silver Bay air. The best that can be said is that the existence of this asbestos contaminant in air and water gives rise to a reasonable medical concern for the public health. The public's exposure to asbestos fibers in air and water creates some health risk. Such a contaminant should be removed.

. . . [T]he existence of this risk to the public justifies an injunction decree requiring abatement of the health hazard on reasonable terms as a precautionary and preventive measure to protect the public health.

[The court then found that Reserve's air emissions violated certain Minnesota air pollution control regulations, and were, accordingly, an enjoinable nuisance under Minnesota law. Reserve's discharges into Lake Superior were found to violate Minnesota's water quality standards; the federal Refuse Act, 33 U.S.C. §407 (1970), forbidding discharges into navigable waters without a permit; and the federal Water Pollution Control Act, which prohibited certain discharges "endangering the health or welfare of persons." The court held that the existence of an "acceptable but unproved medical theory" that Reserve's discharges were carcinogenic sufficed to satisfy the "endangering" provision.]

REMEDY

As we have demonstrated, Reserve's air and water discharges pose a danger to the public health and justify judicial action of a preventive nature.

In fashioning relief in a case such as this involving a possibility of future harm, a court should strike a proper balance between the benefits conferred and the hazards created by Reserve's facility. In its pleadings Reserve directs our attention to the benefits arising from its operations. . . .

[The court recited the revenues, employment, and ore production attributable to Reserve's operation.]

With respect to the water, [the] probabilities [of harm] must be deemed low for they do not rest on a history of past health harm attributable to ingestion but on a medical theory implicating the ingestion of asbestos fibers as a causative factor in increasing the rates of gastrointestinal cancer among asbestos workers. With respect to air, the assessment of the risk of harm rests on a higher degree of proof, a correlation between inhalation of asbestos dust and subsequent illness. But here, too, the hazard cannot be measured in terms of predictability, but the assessment must be made without direct proof. But, the hazard in both the air and water can be measured in only the most general terms as a concern for the public health resting upon a reasonable medical theory. Serious consequences could result if the hypothesis on which it is based should ultimately prove true.

A court is not powerless to act in these circumstances. But an immediate injunction cannot be justified in striking a balance between unpredictable health effects and the clearly predictable social and economic consequences that would follow the plant closing.

In addition to the health risk posed by Reserve's discharges, the district court premised its immediate termination of the discharges upon Reserve's persistent refusal to implement a reasonable alternative plan for on-land disposal of tailings. . . .

During these appeal proceedings, Reserve had indicated its willingness to deposit its tailings on land and to properly filter its air emissions. At oral argument, Reserve advised us of a willingness to spend 243 million dollars in plant alterations and construction to halt its pollution of air and water. Reserve's offer to continue operations and proceed to construction of land disposal facilities for its tailings, if permitted to do so by the State of Minnesota, when viewed in conjunction with the uncertain quality of the health risk created by Reserve's discharges, weighs heavily against a ruling which closes Reserve's plant immediately.

Indeed, the intervening union argues, with some persuasiveness, that ill health effects resulting from the prolonged unemployment of the head of the family on a closing of the Reserve facility may be more certain than the harm from drinking Lake Superior water or breathing Silver Bay air. . . .

We believe that on this record the district court abused its discretion by immediately closing this major industrial plant. In this case, the risk of harm to the public is potential, not imminent or certain, and Reserve says it earnestly seeks a practical way to abate the pollution. A remedy should be fashioned which will serve the ultimate public weal by ensuring clean air, clean water, and continued jobs in an industry vital to the nation's welfare.

Reserve must be given a reasonable opportunity and a reasonable time to construct facilities to accomplish an abatement of its pollution of air and water and the health risk created thereby. . . .

We cannot ignore, however, the potential for harm in Reserve's discharges. This potential imparts a degree of urgency to this case that would otherwise be absent from an environmental suit in which ecological pollution alone were proved. Thus, any authorization of Reserve to continue operations during conversion of its facilities to abate the pollution must be circumscribed by realistic time limitations. Accordingly, we direct that the injunction order be modified as follows.

A. THE DISCHARGE INTO WATER

Reserve shall be given a reasonable time to stop discharging its wastes into Lake Superior. A reasonable time includes the time necessary for Minnesota to act on Reserve's present application to dispose of its tailings at Milepost 7 (Lax Lake site) . . . or, to come to agreement on some other site acceptable to both Reserve and the state. Assuming agreement and designation of an appropriate land disposal site, Reserve is entitled to a reasonable turn-around time to construct the necessary facilities and accomplish a changeover in the means of disposing of its taconite wastes.

We cannot now precisely measure this time. Minnesota must assume the obligation of acting with great expedition in ruling on Reserve's pending application or otherwise determining that it shall, or that it shall not, afford a site acceptable to Reserve. We suggest, but do not determine, that with expedited procedures a final administrative decision should be reached within one year after a final appellate decision in this case.

Upon receiving a permit from the State of Minnesota, Reserve must utilize every reasonable effort to expedite the construction of new facilities. If the parties cannot agree on the duration of a reasonable turn-around time, either party may apply to the district court for a timetable which can be incorporated in the injunction decree, subject to our review.

Should Minnesota and Reserve be unable to agree on an on-land disposal site within this reasonable time period, Reserve, Armco and Republic Steel must be given a reasonable period of time thereafter to phase out the Silver Bay facility. In the interests of delineating the rights of the parties to the fullest extent possible, this additional period of time is set at one year after Minnesota's final administrative determination that it will offer Reserve no site acceptable to Reserve for onland disposal of tailings.

If at any time during negotiations between Reserve and Minnesota for a disposal site, the United States reasonably believes that Minnesota or Reserve is not proceeding with expedition [to] facilitate Reserve's termination of its water discharge, it may apply to the district court for any additional relief necessary to protect its interests. . . .

B.   AIR EMISSIONS

Pending final action by Minnesota on the present permit application, Reserve must promptly take all steps necessary to comply with Minnesota law applicable to its air emissions, as outlined in this opinion. . . .

We wish to make it clear that we view the air emission as presenting a hazard of greater significance than the water discharge. Accordingly, pending a determination of whether Reserve will be allowed to construct an on-land disposal site or will close its operations, Reserve must immediately proceed with the planning and implementation of such emission controls as may be reasonably and practically effectuated under the circumstances.

Subsequent Developments in Reserve Mining

Judge Lord disagreed with the Eighth Circuit's rulings and tried to avoid its implications. The day after the en banc appeals court announced its decision, he held a hearing at which all of the parties were called together. When the Eighth Circuit learned of this and read the transcript, it amended its opinion with a special "order on remand." The court called the trial court's proceedings "irregular" and held that because it had not yet formally issued a mandate returning the case to the district level "all . . . actions taken by the trial judge at these proceedings [were] a complete nullity." The Eighth Circuit "deem[ed] it necessary to advise the trial judge and counsel for all parties, including intervenors, that they must respect the letter and spirit of [its] opinion." The order made clear that Judge Lord's behavior was inappropriate. 514 F.2d at 540-541.

Judge Lord continued to defy the Eighth Circuit's orders. In a series of hearings in November 1975, the trial court discussed the health evidence bearing on the location of the proposed on-land disposal facility and the logistics of supplying pure drinking water to the city of Duluth and other nearby communities. The health evidence hearings were held for the "educational" benefit of the state officials whom the court had requested to attend. Judge Lord ordered Reserve to pay $100,000 to Duluth to finance the water supply costs. Reserve appealed to the Eighth Circuit seeking a writ of mandamus vacating this order and enjoining further interference by the trial court with the Minnesota administrative proceedings. According to the Eighth Circuit,

[a]lthough Judge Lord states that this proceeding was within his jurisdiction to develop new health evidence, it is obvious that the court below acted in defiance of this court's previous mandate, and that Judge Lord continues to attempt to influence the state administrative process concerning the feasibility and location of the on-land disposal site. . . . Disregard of this court's mandate by a lawyer would be contemptuous; it can hardly be excused when the reckless action emanates from a judicial officer. It is one thing for a district judge to disagree on a legal basis with a judgment of this court. It is quite another to openly challenge the court's ruling and attempt to discredit the integrity of the judgment in the eyes of the public.

Reserve Mining Co. v. Lord, 529 F.2d 181, 186-187 (8th Cir. 1976).

In discussing the $100,000 payment order, the Eighth Circuit found that Reserve had not been given notice of a motion to assess damages against it at the hearings and did not have an opportunity to be heard or cross-examine any witnesses. In fact, Judge Lord said at one of the hearings that he had "dispensed with the usual adversary proceeding" because he did not want to waste any more time on what he believed were "misrepresentations by Reserve." The court of appeals concluded that Judge Lord had become greatly biased against Reserve and had "shed the robe of the judge . . . to assum[e] the mantle of the advocate." 529 F.2d at 185. Because of its "obvious impropriety," the order was dissolved and a refund of the $100,000 payment was directed. 529 F.2d at 189 n.8.

The Eighth Circuit determined that "the record disclose[d] a deliberate denial of due process to the parties, a gross bias exhibited against defendant Reserve Mining Company, and an intentional violation [of] the mandate of [the appellate] court," and sua sponte ordered that Judge Lord be recused from further participation in the proceedings. It remanded the case to the Chief Judge of the District of Minnesota for reassignment. 529 F.2d at 188-189. Chief Judge Devitt assigned the case to himself.

The court of appeals also ordered the Army Corps of Engineers to continue "filtration, supervision of filtering units and supply of bottled water until construction of permanent facilities ha[d] been completed." On remand, Chief Judge Devitt held that Reserve was liable for the costs of the United States in filtering and supplying water. After finding liability, the court noted its hope that Reserve "would be a responsible company and recognize [its legal liability]." The exact amount of money owed was left to the parties for agreement, with the possibility of a court determination if no accord could be reached. *United States v. Reserve Mining Co.*, 408 F. Supp. 1212, 1219 (D. Minn. 1976).

Meanwhile, the Minnesota agencies were trying to decide whether and where to allow Reserve to build its on-land disposal facility. Reserve chose a place called Milepost 7, located near the Silver Bay plant. However, the state preferred a site called Milepost 20. The Department of Natural Resources (DNR) and the Minnesota Pollution Control Agency (PCA) appointed a hearing officer to investigate Reserve's Milepost 7 plans and make recommendations as to whether the permit should be granted. After nine months of hearings and deliberations, during which 160 witnesses testified, 1000 exhibits were admitted, and 18,000 pages of transcript were recorded, he recommended that the state deny the Milepost 7 permit request and encourage an application for the Milepost 20 location. While at first the PCA Board rejected these findings, it later reversed itself and joined the DNR in approving them. In

July 1976, the hearing officer's recommendations were adopted by the agencies without any further hearings. Reserve, however, refused to accept the Milepost 20 site and appealed the administrative decision to the state district court, which formed a special three-judge panel to decide the dispute.

As Reserve litigated these issues in the state system, the plaintiffs re-filed in the federal court several motions that had never been adjudicated. *United States v. Reserve Mining Co.,* 412 F. Supp. 705 (D. Minn. 1976). First, they sought an order imposing penalties on Reserve for violations of Minnesota pollution laws and regulations. Chief Judge Devitt decided that while a penalty assessment was not authorized for the violations claimed by Minnesota, it was appropriate for noncompliance with the original permits issued by the state in 1947. The court imposed a penalty of $2500 for each day between May 20, 1973, when the penalty statute was enacted and April 20, 1974, the date of Judge Lord's injunction, totaling $837,500. 412 F. Supp. at 707-710.

Second, the plaintiffs requested a sanction assessing a penalty against Reserve for violating certain court rules and orders regarding discovery. The court determined that "Reserve's bad faith in the conduct of the defense of this lawsuit and its failure to truthfully and fully comply with discovery requests and court orders justify sanctions by way of imposition of a portion of plaintiffs' litigation expenses on defendants." 412 F. Supp. at 707. Reserve was ordered to pay $200,000 to the plaintiffs. 412 F. Supp. at 713.

Third, Chief Judge Devitt held that Reserve was liable for the reasonable expenses incurred by the City of Duluth in maintaining a supply of pure drinking water for its residents. 412 F. Supp. at 713. The court concluded that it had resolved all of the issues remaining within its jurisdiction. All that was left for decision was the choice of a site for the on-land disposal facility. Chief Judge Devitt expressed his hope that this problem would be resolved quickly, bringing an end to the long dispute, "so that Minnesota and its people [could] return to a normal and productive society with the environment preserved and public health protected." 412 F. Supp. at 714.

However, no such agreement was forthcoming. The plaintiffs therefore filed a motion in federal court for an order imposing a deadline for stopping Reserve's discharges into Lake Superior. *United States v. Reserve Mining Co.,* 417 F. Supp. 789 (D. Minn. 1976). The court decided that it had the authority to do so. "Now, after almost 16 months of study, discussion, negotiation, debate, extensive hearings and official actions by state agencies, no agreement has been reached: Reserve still demands Milepost 7 which Minnesota will not permit, and Minnesota offers Milepost 20 which Reserve does not want." Chief Judge Devitt ordered that Reserve terminate all discharges into Lake Superior by

July 7, 1977, one year from the date of his decision. 417 F. Supp. at 790-791.

Reserve appealed all of these orders by the district court, except the one imposing the costs of providing the City of Duluth with clean water, but the Eighth Circuit affirmed the trial court's rulings. The court of appeals noted, though, that if the parties resolved the dispute either through a settlement or litigation, they could request a modification of the termination order. *United States v. Reserve Mining Co.*, 543 F.2d 1210, 1212 (8th Cir. 1976).

In January 1977, the three-judge state district court panel overturned the agency decision. The state appealed to the Minnesota Supreme Court, which affirmed the lower court's ruling. *Reserve Mining Co. v. Herbst*, 256 N.W.2d 808 (Minn. 1977). The hearing officer had determined that while the dam proposed for Milepost 7 would be safe, Milepost 20 would still be a prudent alternative. Milepost 20 was in a more isolated location and therefore, in the unlikely instance of a dam break, the consequences would be less severe. The Supreme Court disagreed with this analysis, holding that the correct standard was not absolute safety, but only reasonable safety. "There was no substantial evidence to support a finding that the location of the dam at Mile Post 7 presented a significant threat to public health or safety, and no such finding was made." Therefore, the denial of a permit for Milepost 7 was incorrect insofar as it was based on the hearing officer's decision regarding the safety of the required dam. 256 N.W.2d at 828-830.

The court next addressed the holding that alternative sites to Milepost 7 would have less adverse effects on the surrounding land, water, and natural resources. It particularly disputed the finding that land-use principles supported Milepost 20. Milepost 7 was located near the Silver Bay processing plant. On the other hand, Milepost 20 was sixteen miles away. Therefore, the court believed that Reserve's choice would only be an extension of an existing site, while the state's recommended location would create a new industrial area. In addition, Milepost 20 was located within the Superior National Forest, a protected wilderness zone. Thus, "the selection of Mile Post 20 [did] violence to the principle of consolidated land uses." 256 N.W.2d at 830-833.

In evaluating the effects that each proposed disposal site would have on the surrounding air quality, the Supreme Court made two observations. The state agencies had determined that since some carcinogenic fibers would be released into the air around either site, it would be prudent to locate the facility farther from the main population centers. However, substituting target communities was not the proper way of handling the potential health threat. If a material health threat was found to exist at either site, the correct alternative was to reduce the emissions or to shut down the facility. Second, the court noted the pervasive uncertainties in the determinations regarding air quality.

The number of fibers that would be released from each site, as well as their health effects, could only be roughly estimated, with large margins of error. Therefore, the court held that the hearing officer's conclusion that the Milepost 20 site was preferable because it would have less impact on the surrounding air quality was "unsupported by the evidence." 256 N.W.2d at 833-841.

Finally, the Supreme Court considered the relative availability of the two sites. As noted above, Milepost 20 was located in the Superior National Forest. It was questionable whether Reserve could receive the necessary approvals to use the site. Even if it could, there certainly would be long delays as the various federal agencies gave their approval to all of the intermediate steps. On the other hand, the land on which the Milepost 7 facility was planned was owned by the State of Minnesota, Reserve, and private parties. The Supreme Court determined that because it would be easier to obtain the Milepost 7 land, the discharges into Lake Superior could be terminated earlier if this site were chosen, without a shut-down of the Silver Bay plant. Milepost 20 was therefore not a "feasible and prudent" alternative as required by state law. 256 N.W.2d at 841-843. Thus, the Supreme Court affirmed the lower court and held that the state must issue Reserve a permit for construction of the Milepost 7 on-land disposal facility.

With this ruling by the Minnesota Supreme Court, Reserve returned to the federal court and moved for a modification of the order terminating the discharges on July 7, 1977. Chief Judge Devitt agreed and issued a stay of his original order until April 15, 1980, by which time all taconite discharges must cease. *United States v. Reserve Mining Co.*, 431 F. Supp. 1248, 1249 (D. Minn. 1977).

Reserve now had the permits to build the facility at its preferred site. Still, the litigation continued. When the PCA granted the permits, as ordered by the Supreme Court, Reserve disputed certain conditions restricting the level of fibers in the surrounding air and water that would constitute a violation as well as the definition of the fibers to be counted. Again, the administrative decision was appealed to a three-judge panel of the state district court. This lower court reversed the agency and rewrote sections of the permits as requested by Reserve. The Supreme Court, however, reversed the district panel and reinstated the original conditions for the permits. *Reserve Mining Co. v. Minnesota Pollution Control Agency*, 267 N.W.2d 720 (Minn. 1978).

The PCA permit had set the acceptable level of fibers in the air as that "ordinarily found in a control city such as St. Paul." Reserve requested, and the trial court had added, a section which defined non-compliance as the creation of a fiber count "in excess of a medically significant level." The Supreme Court noted that the Eighth Circuit, which still had jurisdiction over the pollution dispute, had itself created the control city standard. This test, the court believed, still applied and could only be modified by the federal panel.

The Supreme Court concluded with dictum expressing its opinion of the entire dispute and its hope that this would be the last appeal:

> Although it is our duty to resolve disputes which arise between the competing interests of commerce and the general public, we think it appropriate to observe that neither the interests of clients nor the administration of justice is served by protracted litigation of this kind. Courts are ill-equipped to deal with technical engineering problems. It is now the responsibility of Reserve, an industry important to the people of Minnesota, and of PCA, an agency charged with protecting the environment, to make mutual concessions and exercise restraint to reach an accord and end this controversy.

267 N.W.2d at 727.

Finally, in March 1980, after nearly eleven years of dispute, Reserve stopped discharging its taconite tailings into Lake Superior. The land disposal facility at Milepost 7 had increased in cost to 370 million dollars.

The difficulties of the American steel industry in the 1980s took their toll on Reserve's operations. Professor Farber reported that:

> the issue of waste disposal soon became rather academic for Reserve. In June 1982, the company temporarily shut down, blaming deterioration in the steel industry. It reopened six months later, but then closed for another six months. The company never did regain its financial footing. In 1986, LTV, which had replaced Republic as a co-owner of Reserve, filed for bankruptcy under Chapter 11 and withdrew from the partnership. Shortly thereafter, Armco announced it was closing Reserve's operations. By August 1988, the Armco subsidiary running Reserve had also filed under Chapter 11. At last report, Reserve had been sold for fifty-two million dollars to a firm called Cyprus Minerals Co., which had resumed operations on a greatly reduced scale.

Farber, 21 Environmental Law 1321, 1336 (footnotes omitted).

Cyprus Minerals renamed its new subsidiary Cyprus Northshore Mining Corp. As the purchase was being completed all the permits were transferred, allowing use of the air quality equipment and the Milepost 7 disposal facility. Cyprus Northshore has also had its troubles with the Reserve plant. It was forced to close for three months in June 1992 to reduce inventory, although the plant is currently operating.

Professor Farber concluded,

> [g]iven a choice between land disposal and doing nothing, the *Reserve Mining* court was clearly correct to opt for land disposal, . . . but there is some reason to believe that land disposal was not really necessary. By

1977, a water filtration system had been installed in Duluth which removed 99.9% of the asbestos fibers. This reduces the risk by a factor of one thousand, thereby decreasing the expected number of deaths to one every 600 years (1.5 deaths per year divided by a thousand). Whatever a "significant risk" may be, certainly that level does not qualify. . . .

Perhaps, however, the prompt conversion to land disposal can be justified by the possibility of ecological damage to the Lake. That was the initial issue in the case, which was never tried because of what appeared to be a more urgent concern about public health. Ultimately, the sheer symbolic outrage of dumping sixty-seven thousand tons of waste daily in a pristine lake may have been enough to justify a switch to land disposal. Therefore, in retrospect, if land disposal is to be justified, the justification should not rest too heavily on a concern about drinking water, for that concern may have been fully addressed by filtration.

However, since water filtration apparently was not proposed to the court of appeals, it would be unfair to blame the court for overlooking filtration as an alternative to land disposal. Given the options which the court of appeals did have available, it made the right choice. . . .

Farber, 21 Environmental Law 1321, 1355-1357 (footnotes omitted).

NOTES AND QUESTIONS

1. The *Reserve Mining* litigation should serve to remind you of the importance of evaluating the potential adverse affects of new industrial technologies before they are introduced. How well equipped is the common law to perform this task? *Reserve Mining* involved technology assessment in remedying the problems that appeared after the plant was built. Do you feel that the *Reserve Mining* courts did a good job of technology assessment? What factors should they have considered? Do you think that these factors were adequately considered?

2. The extensive medical and scientific evidence in *Reserve Mining* raises questions about the proper standard for assessing such information in a legal proceeding. Should scientific standards of proof be applied in legal decisionmaking? A related question concerns the scope of scientific expertise. Does Dr. Brown's testimony venture beyond his scientific expertise? What significance should such testimony be accorded by the court?

3. The *Reserve Mining* decision should also remind you of the pervasive uncertainty present in many environmental controversies. How does the panel opinion deal with the problem of uncertainty? Does the court require proof that adverse health effects have already occurred as a prerequisite to granting relief? Is this a sound policy where (partic-

ularly in the case of carcinogens) adverse health effects are long term in nature, so that symptoms may not appear until many years after the basic damage has been done?

While the court of appeals' en banc decision did not sustain the district court's immediate closure of the Silver Bay plant, does it adopt a significantly different framework for assessing uncertain environmental risks from that utilized in the panel decision staying the district court's order? Does the en banc opinion provide workable and sound guidelines for risk assessment in future controversies? Would its approach be unduly restrictive as applied to new industrial processes, whose prohibition would not involve shutdown of a pre-existing facility?

4. *Reserve Mining* illustrates the pervasive importance of burden of proof rules (the burden of coming forward with evidence on an issue and the ultimate persuasion burden on that issue) in the face of the uncertainties characteristic of many environmental problems. Consider the following from Krier, Environmental Litigation and the Burden of Proof, in Law and the Environment 105, 107 (M. Baldwin & J. Page eds. 1970):

. . . [B]urden of proof rules at present have an inevitable bias against protection of the environment and preservation of natural resources. This is the case for the following reasons. Essentially two classes of demands can be made on such resources as air, land, water, wildlife and so on: (1) demands which consume or deteriorate those resources (water pollution, the slaughter of wildlife, the harvesting of forests) (2) demands which do not consume or deteriorate them (swimming, bird-watching, hiking and camping). In a world without laws, those who wish to use resources for consumptive or deteriorating ends will *always* prevail over those who wish to use them for nonconsumptive or nondeteriorating ends. This is simply because consuming users, by exercising their demands, can foreclose nonconsuming users from exercising theirs, while the contrary cannot hold true. In short, the polluter's use can stop the swimmer from using and enjoying a lake, but the swimmer's use cannot stop the polluter from polluting the lake.

Of course, we live in a system with laws, but it is a loaded system. And it is loaded precisely because of the point I have just made. For even in a world with rules against resource consumption (against, for example, pollution), the leverage inherent in resource consumers means that they can continue their conduct until sued. In short, they will almost inevitably be *defendants*, and those whose uses preserve rather than deteriorate will ineluctably be *plaintiffs*. And it is of the simple facts of our present system that (for a host of reasons) plaintiffs most generally carry the major burden of proving most of the basic issues in a lawsuit. The result is striking: Even with a system of substantive rules *against* resource consumption, our present rules ensure that in cases of doubt about any facet of those rules, resource consumption will prevail. . . .

5. Should polluters bear the burden of establishing that their activities will *not* result in harm to human health or the natural environment? Who is better equipped to develop information in order to resolve uncertainties concerning the potential adverse effects of such activities: victims or polluters? What would be the consequences of enjoining any activity with uncertain but potentially adverse environmental effects pending resolution of the uncertainty? See Burdens of Proof in Environment Litigation, Hearing Before the Environment Subcommittee of the Senate Commerce Committee, 93d Cong., 2d Sess. (1974) (Ser. No. 93-126); *Environmental Defense Fund v. EPA*, 548 F.2d 998 (D.C. Cir. 1977) (burden of persuasion on the issue of safety in hearing to suspend certification of pesticide placed on manufacturer).

Alternatively, courts might prohibit only those activities that threaten a *significant* risk of harm. But how are courts to decide how "significant" or large the risk must be (defined both in terms of the probability of harm and its magnitude) in order for relief to be afforded? Would such an approach license the judges to interfere with private property on the basis of ad hoc, subjective judgments not subject to political accountability? Are the "policy judgments" involved in assessing risk in the face of uncertainty any different from the "policy judgments" involved in the other court decisions we have reviewed?

6. Compare the results reached by the courts in *Reserve Mining* and *Village of Wilsonville* and that reached by OSHA in the *Benzene* case, supra, p. 25. How do they differ? To the extent that they do, what explains the difference?

7. What does *Reserve Mining* suggest about the ability of courts to address modern problems of environmental degradation? What alternative institutions in society could be called upon? How would these institutions perform in addressing complex environmental problems?

PROBLEMS ON THE COMPARATIVE ADVANTAGES AND INHERENT LIMITATIONS OF THE COMMON LAW AS A MEANS OF ADDRESSING ENVIRONMENTAL DEGRADATION

For each of the factual settings described below, answer the following sets of questions:

(a) Under traditional common law doctrines, what actions would be viable? Who would bring suit? Who would prevail? What remedies would be awarded? Will these actions result in a satisfactory allocation of resources?

(b) What reforms of the substantive doctrine defining plaintiff's right to recovery would you recommend? What reforms of judicial process rules would you recommend?

(c)   What would be the best social regulatory system — common law (as reformed) or administrative — for addressing the resource allocation problems?

1. A factory in the town of Brownville emits a steady stream of non-toxic black smoke. Homes in the vicinity of the factory gradually turn a dingy color.

2. Air quality in the Los Diablos metropolitan area has steadily declined over the past decades, largely because of the growing use of motor vehicles. Last year, air quality was so unhealthy during 100 days that state officials advised against running and other outdoor activities. Persons with respiratory ailments are unable to go outside on these days without suffering severe breathing discomfort.

3. Factories in the State of Industria emit high levels of sulfur dioxide and other pollutants associated with "acid rain" through tall smoke stacks. Forests in downstream states have thinned in recent years. Lakes and rivers in downstream states have become more acidic. Scientists suspect that higher acidity levels have resulted in some loss of marine life.

4. Hundreds of factories are located along the banks of the Monahoga River. As a result of discharges from the factories, this once pristine river is no longer safe for drinking, swimming, or fishing.

5. Chemville has been a major chemical manufacturing center for decades. It was recently discovered that the incidence of birth defects in the town is much higher than the national average. The town's main water reservoir and wells on numerous landowners' property are fed by groundwater. The town recently detected various carcinogens in the town's water supplies.

6. A growing majority of scientists believe that emissions of carbon dioxide, chlorofluorocarbons, methane, and other gases are contributing to warming of the atmosphere. Among the effects predicted are significant rises in temperature, more severe weather patterns, changes in rainfall, evaporation, and soil moisture, and rising sea level.

4

Statutory Approaches
to Air Pollution

It should be clear from the materials covered thus far that effective pollution control is impossible without some form of government intervention and that intervention through the judicial system alone is not enough. The courts suffer severe shortcomings with respect to inquiry initiation, comprehensive oversight, continuing administration, and fiscal powers. Legislative action appears to be necessary if significant improvements in environmental quality are to be realized. Recognition of this point, however, only marks the beginning of further inquiries for those concerned with the form and function of political and legal institutions. Legislative actions can take many forms. Debates about the relative merits of each will be at the center of debate over environmental protection policy far into the future, and some grasp of issues central to these debates is crucial to an understanding of how the legal system can most effectively cope with environmental problems, and, indeed, with other social ills.

A. INTRODUCTION

1. AIR POLLUTION: NATURE, EFFECTS, CAUSES, AND CONTROL TECHNOLOGIES[1]

Before we can undertake the analysis of statutory approaches to air pollution, it is important to understand the scientific and technical dimensions of the problem. In the absence of pollutants, the Earth's air consists principally of nitrogen (78 percent) and oxygen (21 percent). Air pollution consists of the many gases and particles that are emitted by natural and man-made sources. Like many environmental problems, the nature and effects of air pollution are scientifically complex, and the causes are deeply intertwined with the functioning of our economy. Although we have learned much about air pollution over the past few decades, there remains significant uncertainty about many aspects of the science of air pollution.

Following the dawn of the industrial revolution, "smoke" pollution in urban, industrial areas gradually increased. The principal sources of such smoke were coal-burning furnaces and industrial processes. Smoke pollution reached new levels of intensity in eastern and midwestern cities in the 1940s and 1950s. In October 1948 in Donora, Pennsylvania, for example, the combination of high emissions and a severe temperature inversion caused 43 percent of the town's 10,000 inhabitants to fall ill and killed 20 people. Similar "killer fogs" have been recorded as early as 1930 in Belgium (6000 ill; 60 dead) and during various times in the 1950s in London, England.

Since these episodes, substantial research efforts have been conducted to understand the relationships between the various constituents of air pollution and human health. Chart 4.1 presents a concise description of the sources and effects of the most pervasive types of local or regional air pollution. We later briefly discuss problems that involve the global atmosphere — stratospheric ozone depletion and potential global climate change resulting from emissions of carbon dioxide and other greenhouse gases.

Particulate matter (PM), or total suspended particulates (TSP), includes solid or liquid particles of a wide variety of sizes — ranging from visible particles such as soot and smoke to those that can only be seen with the use of a powerful microscope. Recent scientific studies indicate that fine particulates, rather than larger particles, are the principal source of health risks. Modern filtering and scrubbing technologies are

---

1. The discussion that follows is drawn from the following sources: Council on Environmental Quality, Environmental Quality annual reports (1970-1985); U.S. EPA, Air Quality Criteria for Particulate Matter and Sulfur Oxides (1982).

CHART 4.1

Typology of Major Local and Regional Air Pollutants

Pollutant	Sources	Health and other effects
particulate matter (TSP)	industrial processes (50%); coal-fired utilities (19%); motor vehicles (11%); coal-fired boilers (6%)	exacerbate asthma and other respiratory or cardiovascular symptoms; soil and injure buildings; impair visibility; interfere with plant growth
sulfur oxides (SO)	coal-fired utilities (60%); industrial processes (15%)	aggravates respiratory diseases; irritates eyes and respiratory tract; contributes to acid deposition
carbon monoxide (CO)	motor vehicles (85%); industrial processes (7%)	bonds strongly with hemoglobin in the blood; impairs mental functions; inhibits fetal development; aggravates cardiovascular disease
nitrogen oxides (NO)	motor vehicles (40%); coal-fired utilities (22%); natural gas-fired boilers (15%)	precursor to formation of photochemical oxidants
hydrocarbons (HC)	industrial processes (50%); motor vehicles (39%)	contributes to cancer; precursor to formation of photochemical oxidants
ozone (O₃) as index of photochemical oxidant or smog	HC and NO emissions	contributes to acid deposition, aggravates respiratory and cardiovascular illnesses, impairs visibility, injures rubber, textiles, and paints, and causes plants to drop their leaves and fruit prematurely
lead	leaded gasoline; lead smelting and processing; manufacture of lead products; combustion of coal and refuse; certain pesticides	accumulates in body organs; impairs bone growth; interferes with nervous, circulatory, and renal systems

231

able to substantially reduce emissions of particulate matter, although there is developing concern about pervasive health effects from particulate matter that continues to be emitted.

Sulfur oxides (SO) are the class of acrid, corrosive, and poisonous gases produced when fossil fuels containing sulfur are burned or metal-bearing ores containing sulfur are smelted.[2] Emissions of sulfur oxides can be prevented by using fuels containing low sulfur content or technologies — such as fluidized beds — to remove sulfur from coal prior to burning. In addition, scrubbing technology — in which flue gases are scrubbed with lime to remove sulfur emissions — can be used to reduce emissions of sulfur oxides.

Carbon monoxide (CO) is a colorless, odorless, poisonous gas that is produced by the incomplete burning of carbon in fuels. Since carbon monoxide is slightly lighter than air, it dissipates relatively quickly in rural environments. In densely populated urban areas with heavy automobile use, however, carbon monoxide tends to accumulate in city streets. Emissions of carbon monoxide from internal combustion engines can be significantly reduced by ensuring complete combustion of gasoline. This is accomplished by automobile engine modifications designed to ensure an adequate supply of oxygen during combustion. Such modifications include proper tuning, exhaust gas recirculation, and redesign of the combustion chamber. Carbon monoxide emissions are also reduced by the use of catalytic converters and thermal devices that control automobile exhaust gases, and by changes in fuel composition.

Hydrocarbons (HC), like carbon monoxide, are the result of incomplete combustion of fuels and other carbon-containing substances. Control of these gases from automobiles using internal combustion engines — changes in engine design, fuels, and use of catalysts and thermal devices on exhausts — is accomplished in the same ways as control of carbon monoxide. Control of hydrocarbons from stationary sources, including refineries, chemical plants, and facilities using solvents and coatings, is more difficult and may require process changes. Hydrocarbons, as explained below, can react with other pollutants to create ozone-type smog. The more reactive hydrocarbons are sometimes called volatile organic compounds (VOCs), reactive organic compounds (ROCs), reactive hydrocarbons (RHCs), or non-methanol organic gases (NMOG).

Nitrogen oxides (NO) are produced when fuel is burned at very high temperatures, as occurs most typically in stationary combustion plants and automobiles. During high temperature combustion, nitrogen, which is ordinarily inert, combines with oxygen and tends to stay

---

2. The effects of sulfur oxides and particulate matter are described in detail in the Appendix to this chapter.

combined ("fixed") if cooled quickly. The control of nitrogen oxides from stationary sources can be accomplished by careful adjustment of flame and stack gas temperatures and scrubbing flue gases with caustic substances or urea. Control of nitrogen oxides from automobiles is more difficult because reducing the temperature of combustion will tend to increase the amount of carbon monoxide and hydrocarbons produced. Some reduction of nitrogen oxide emissions is achieved by catalytic control of automobile exhaust gases.

Lead appears in the air as an oxide aerosol or dust principally as a result of emissions of automobiles using leaded gasoline. In the early 1930s, automotive engineers discovered that adding small quantities of lead to gasoline significantly reduced the problem of engine knock. Lead emissions also result from lead smelting and processing, the manufacturing of lead products, and the use of pesticides containing lead. Lead emissions have been substantially reduced by the use of unleaded gasoline. Lead emissions from industrial processes can be reduced by cleaning stack gases.

Interactions among pollutants. Under the influence of sunlight, nitrogen oxides combine with gaseous hydrocarbons to form a complex variety of *photochemical oxidants.* These oxidants, together with solid and liquid particles in the air, make up what is commonly known as smog. The principal form of photochemical oxidant is *ozone* (O_3), an unstable, toxic form of oxygen, whose concentrations are used as an index of smog. A related chemical reaction, involving sulfur oxides, nitrogen oxides, ozone, and sunlight, is responsible for the formation of sulfates and nitrates which fall to the ground as *acid deposition,* in either wet (acid rain or snow) or dry form. Acid deposition is associated with a wide range of adverse environmental effects including the acidification of lakes and rivers, resulting in harm to marine life, denuding of forests, and deterioration of monuments and buildings.

Toxic hazardous air pollutants. In addition to the pervasive air pollutants discussed above, there are a number of less widespread though more potently toxic pollutants emitted in particular industrial processes. Examples of such pollutants are mercury, emitted from smelters and sewage sludge incinerators and associated with central nervous system disorders; asbestos, emitted from asbestos mills, manufacturing processes, and renovation and demolition of buildings containing asbestos insulation, and associated with cancer; benzene, emitted from maleic anhydride plants used in the plastics industry and during the transfer of gasoline and other refined oil products and associated with leukemia; coke oven emissions, associated with cancer; and many others. During the 1970s, regulatory attention focused almost exclusively on the widespread "conventional" pollutants described above. Since the early 1980s, toxic pollutants have received increasing attention.

Geographic incidence of effects. As the discussion above suggests, the health risks from air pollution are greatest in densely populated and industrial areas. Not all of the effects of air pollution, however, are confined to urban and industrial areas. As a result of the transport of air pollutants, exacerbated by the use of tall stacks, the effects of air pollution are felt far from the point of emission. Acid deposition often occurs far from the source. In addition, visibility in remote wilderness areas is reduced by distant air pollution emissions.

Global Atmospheric Problems. Finally, attention has recently focused on global atmospheric problems. Chlorofluorocarbons (CFCs), hydro-chlorofluorocarbons (HCFCs) and other ozone-depleting chemicals are used in refrigeration systems, solvents, and certain agricultural and other products. They have been found to deplete the ozone layer at the stratospheric level of the atmosphere (as opposed to lower atmosphere smog-type ozone), which allows increased ultraviolet radiation to reach the Earth's surface, causing increases in skin cancer and other adverse health effects. Increased emissions of greenhouse gases (GHGs) as a result of human activity threaten increases in the atmosphere's overall temperature and other forms of climate change. The most important GHG is carbon dioxide (CO_2), but methane, nitrous oxides, CFCs and HCFCs, nitrogen oxides, hydrocarbons, and carbon monoxide are also significant. Deforestation and the destruction of blue-green algae in the oceans also contribute to increases in GHGs by destroying vegetation that stores CO_2 ("sinks").

2. DESIGNING A REGULATORY REGIME FOR AIR POLLUTION: THE ARRAY OF REGULATORY TOOLS

Emissions of air pollution by private entities are a classic externality and hence will not be adequately controlled by market forces. Free-rider problems prevent those exposed to air pollution from effectively organizing to resolve air pollution complaints privately. Consequently, some form of government intervention is needed in order to control emissions of air pollution below the level that maximizes the profits of pollution sources.

From an economic perspective, government intervention must alter the incentives of private entities to pollute. The three traditional techniques are (1) command and control regulation, (2) pollution charges, and (3) emission control subsidies. Command and control regulation consists of direct requirements on production methods or outputs. For example, the government could dictate the inputs (e.g., low sulfur coal), the production processes (e.g., installation of scrubbers), or the outputs (e.g., 20 percent reduction in emissions). Pollution charges impose a fee upon each unit of pollution. The fees can vary according to the level and location of the emissions. The subsidy approach pays polluters for their efforts at reducing emissions. Examples include the construction of pollution treatment facilities by the government and direct payments or tax breaks to pollution sources for installation of pollution control equipments.

If government regulators were to have full information about production technologies and costless means of enforcing policies, all three systems of regulation could achieve the same pollution reduction goal. In practice, however, the policies differ dramatically in terms of the information required by the regulators, incentives for developing better pollution control technologies, enforcement mechanisms, and costs to the public fisc and the private sector, among other factors. The challenge of policy analysis is in defining environmental protection objectives and tailoring the regulatory instruments to achieve these objectives most effectively.

In this and succeeding chapters, we will be looking more closely at these three general ways of implementing environmental policy. But these three categories by no means exhaust the possible alternatives. We have already examined the possibility of judicial redefinition of property rights. Consider other alternatives. One such alternative that will be examined in considerable detail below is the creation of a limited number of rights to pollute that can be freely traded, by purchase and sale, among sources. This approach limits the total amount of pollution, but allows market forces to decide how much each source controls its emissions and provides a market incentive for each source to reduce its emissions further.

As another example, might government dissemination of information on the extent and impact of pollution affect private behavior? Los Angeles County has a "Smog Alert" system that advises the public when pollution reaches levels dangerous to health and requests the public to postpone or curtail the use of automobiles. Consumers could be informed about the extent of air pollution associated with products that they buy. On the federal level, the Securities and Exchange Commission has, as result of litigation, been required to insist on disclosure by corporations subject to its jurisdiction of the extent of their compliance with environmental regulations. In addition, mandatory disclosure by companies of toxic materials stored on site has encouraged reductions and substitution of less toxic materials in production processes. As these examples suggest, government dissemination of information may involve a more or less explicit attempt at moral suasion to induce individuals to act in more socially desirable ways. How effective or appropriate is such a technique? Would individuals tend not to buy products whose manufacturer contributed heavily to environmental degradation if individuals had information about such effects? Suppose the "information" were conveyed to consumers by a "pollution excise tax" rather than governmental publication?

Conflicts over environmental resource use might be resolved or assuaged by government-sponsored mediation, conciliation, and arbitration. Mediation and conciliation have been utilized with considerable success in dealing with pollution problems in Japan. See K. Fujikura, J. Gresser & A. Morishima, Environmental Law in Japan (1981). The growing dissatisfaction in the United States with administrative regulation and court litigation as methods of conflict resolution may presage greater interest in techniques like mediation and conciliation. But query: How is it possible to conduct negotiation and reach binding agreements between pollution sources and scattered, unorganized receptors? Moreover, what incentive would sources have to reach agreement in the absence of regulation, liability, or other legal tools to induce changes in behavior?

Alternatively, the government might itself take direct measures to control environmental degradation or reduce its adverse effects. For example, the government could impose emission controls on pollution sources owned by the government. It could utilize its purchasing power to stimulate demand for environmentally superior technologies by, for example, purchasing low-polluting automobiles. Alternatively, it could refuse to purchase any supplies from manufacturers who did not control their own pollution. Or it might intervene to improve or preserve environmental quality by constructing reaeration devices in polluted rivers or precluding development on public lands.

Various types of policy tools can also be combined in mixed strategies. For example, it is possible to combine regulatory controls and pollution charges by requiring all sources to meet a given level of control while imposing a fee based on the extent of remaining emissions. A system of transferable pollution rights — under which permits to emit a given amount of pollutant would be traded among polluters for a price determined by market forces — would also combine characteristics of the regulatory and pollution charge approaches.

Moreover, within each approach there are various techniques of implementation. For example, there are two basic strategies of direct regulation: case-by-case screening and standards. Under case-by-case screening, which usually involves some form of licensing system, particular products or projects must receive administrative approval before they may be sold or undertaken. Typically, approval is granted or denied pursuant to some general criterion such as "unreasonable risk." This system of screening is used, for example, to decide which pesticides may be marketed and whether and where strip mining, highway construction, dams, and other development activities may be undertaken. Standards establish a specific rule of conduct governing all members of a category of products or processes. For example, regulatory standards specify the maximum amounts of air pollutants that may be emitted by new automobiles, or maximum pollutant levels in water dis-

charges from industrial plants, or the requirements that must be followed in handling, transporting, treating, and disposing toxic wastes.

Moreover, standards can either specify particular measures that
must be taken to prevent environmental degradation — such as installation of incinerators in apartment buildings or catalytic converters on
cars — or they can provide a given level of performance that must be
achieved — for example, a factory may be required to limit emissions
to x tons daily with the choice among alternative control measures left
to the factory. This distinction between *specification* standards and *performance* standards is fundamental. Other things being equal, it would be
desirable to utilize performance standards, since they leave individual
pollution sources freedom to select methods of pollution reduction
that are cheapest and most appropriate in their particular circumstances. But performance standards are often difficult to administer
because in many instances reliable and inexpensive technology to monitor emissions is not available. Accordingly, specification standards,
such as installation of designated control equipment or use of low-sul-
fur fuel, are often utilized in order to ease problems of monitoring and
enforcement. However, specification standards also require an enforcement agency to employ engineers to review abatement proposals and
inspectors to ensure that abatement measures are being utilized. Determination of the relative merits of performance versus specification standards often involves assessment of a complex set of factors that vary
depending upon the environmental problem in question. Another fundamental distinction in environmental regulatory strategy is that
between environmental quality or ambient standards, and technology-
based standards. Under the former approach, standards are set limiting
the maximum permissible level of pollution in a given environmental
medium: air, water, soil, groundwater. These environmental quality or
ambient standards are established in order to prevent or reduce adverse effects on health in the environment. Regulatory controls must
then be imposed on pollution sources to ensure that total releases of
pollution are limited to the extent necessary to achieve the environmental quality or ambient standards.

Technology-based standards are established directly for categories
of products or processes, based on the levels of emissions control that
can be achieved by technology that is available at a cost judged to be
"reasonable." Such standards may consist of specification standards that
mandate use of given technology or performance standards that require a given level of pollution control, based on what can be achieved
by a given technology, but allow sources the flexibility to achieve that
level by means other than that technology, if they can.

Environmental quality standards have the virtue of focussing on
the ultimate goal — a healthy and clean environment — and setting
controls to achieve that goal. Controls based on available technology

may either be inadequate to achieve that goal, or they may be more stringent than necessary to achieve it, resulting in regulatory overkill. On the other hand, it may be very difficult to determine the appropriate environmental quality standard, given scientific uncertainty about the effects of different levels of pollution and the potential need to give more consideration to the costs and feasibility of achieving such standards. Consider the *Benzene and Asbestos* cases, supra, pp. 25, 116. It may also be difficult administratively to determine what levels of control from particular sources is necessary and appropriate in order to achieve the environmental quality standard. As we shall see, most pollution control statutes rely on a combination of technology-based standards and environmental quality standards.

Finally, the sanctions for violation of regulatory controls can include criminal sanctions, court injunctions, or civil penalties imposed either by courts or administrative agencies, or liability for injury or loss.

A similar variety of implementing strategies and sanctions can be used in conjunction with policy tools other than traditional command and control regulation. Each of these approaches and the various techniques for implementing them must be assessed in light of the differing goals and objectives of environmental policy that we have already explored. These alternatives may vary widely in economic efficiency. Consideration must also be given to distributional considerations and issues of moral principle. A subsidy to business firms to cut down on pollution, for example, might strike many people as repugnant. A subsidy to the drivers of old cars (which are heavy polluters) to encourage them to drive new cars, on the other hand, might strike many people as good policy if they believe that most old cars are owned by poor people. Some environmentalists have opposed proposals for pollution charges or tradeable permits on moral grounds, claiming that they involve a "license to pollute." (Doesn't command and control regulation also involve a "license to pollute"?)

These examples are only illustrative of relevant policy objectives and possible conflicts among them. In addition, the potential range of available approaches and techniques is conditioned by prevailing political, administrative, and legal cultural norms, which may closely restrict the options that are practically available at any given time. The changes in our understanding of and reaction to environmental problems over time, as well as uncertainties over the ultimate impact of any given approach, suggest that a heavy premium should be placed on flexibility in environmental policies — the capacity to respond to changed conditions, knowledge, or preferences — and on experimentation with alternative approaches in order to expand and test our institutional repertoire.

Despite the wealth of potential alternative forms of government intervention, far and away the most popular response by American governments to problems of pollution — and, indeed to all environmental problems — has been direct, "command and control" regulation. Tax subsidies and other positive fiscal incentives have seen more limited use. Pollution taxes or fees have been almost totally ignored. Tradeable permits and market-based information strategies, such as "ecolabelling" have attracted growing interest in recent years.

It is worth speculating about why such a clear and strong tradition of pollution control through regulation, as opposed to other means of governmental intervention, has developed. If the tradition acts at times as a barrier to more effective approaches, understanding its roots could be important to attaining worthwhile change. Some observers have suggested that the history of air pollution control in the United States illustrates the "catastrophe theory of planning" — the direct and immediate response by government to dramatic incidents, such as the disastrous Donora air pollution episode, the igniting of the Monongahela River in late 1969, and the discovery of a vast chemical waste dump beneath the town of Love Canal. Such a theory may expose the roots of the regulatory tradition. Governmental response to crisis is often typified by quick (and, therefore, generally crude) measures aimed at preconceived "wrongdoers" such as industrial polluters. It is designed to punish those wrongdoers, prohibit the offending behavior, and placate intense public concern. The goal is immediate relief (the long term is a remote consideration) and clear results. The prohibitions and penalties of the regulatory program best suit all of these ends. As time passes and experience is gained, it may become clear that an existing program, conceived out of crisis, is unsatisfactory, and that more systemic measures are necessary. But the path of least resistance — and, usually of least expense to the government in the short run, a matter of importance to politicians — is to improve the old, rather than to abandon it for an entirely new approach to government intervention. It may be, as well, that the roots of the regulatory tradition lie in the fact that most people, including most public decisionmakers, do not understand either the ways in which social and economic systems function to produce pollution problems or the sophisticated market-based programs of control offered by theoreticians and experts. Or it may be that command and control regulation is the most effective approach, particularly when real-world problems of implementation and administration are taken into account.

As this and subsequent chapters highlight, the escalating cost of environmental protection — now in excess of $120 billion annually in the United States — and the growing recognition of the failures of crisis-oriented regulatory approaches has created opportunities for considering new approaches to environmental problems. In particular, interest in and implementation of incentive-based instruments such as emissions trading has grown dramatically in recent years. The coming decade will undoubtedly see expansion of these initiatives as well as rapid learning about the implementation challenges of these regulatory techniques. The combination of legal and policy analysis in this book is designed to enable you to evaluate these developments and to contribute to the evolution of this dynamic field.

Before turning to the complex interplay of factors in the choice of regulatory tools to address air pollution in the American economy, it is instructive to think about some of these issues in a simpler, more certain world. The following problem illustrates the challenges of controlling air pollution in a relatively simple context:

A PRELIMINARY EVALUATION OF REGULATORY POLICIES: REGULATING AIR QUALITY IN MALAMBIA

In the democratic, federal republic of Malambia, the electorate has become outraged over the steadily growing air pollution problem. Although various Malambian states have air pollution laws in place, it is felt that a national solution is needed.

Three years ago, the national government commissioned studies of the causes of air pollution and options for reducing emissions. The studies found that two industries, the gadget industry and the widget industry, each comprised of one firm having one plant, are responsible for substantially all of the undesirable emissions. (Each industry employs 30 percent of the Malambia labor force; the costs of retraining workers are very high.) Currently, the gadget industry emits 200 tons of smox, a deleterious air pollutant, per day; the widget industry emits 100 tons of smox per day. Because both industries use tall stacks and generally windy conditions prevail in Malambia, air quality is uniform, regardless of where and in what quantities smox is emitted. Population density in Malambia is also uniform.

Health studies show that the risk of serious disease caused by smox is significant above a daily output of 220 tons per day; health risks are publicly acceptable below this level.

Economic and technological feasibility studies show that the gadget industry could reduce smox emissions by 25 percent through the introduction of "A" scrubbing technology (at a cost of $100,000 per day). The gadget industry could further reduce emissions another 25 percent (down to 100 tons per day) by introducing the "B" fluidized bed process for pretreating its raw materials (at a cost of an additional $500,000 per day). Use of the "C" scrubbing process in the widget industry would reduce smox emissions by 60 percent (at a cost of $30,000 per day). The "D" pretreatment process would reduce smox emissions from the widget industry by another 30 percent (down to 10 tons per day; at a cost of an additional $25,000 per day). Although implementation of any of these technologies would not significantly affect the level of unemployment, the costs of these control measures would be borne directly by workers in these industries.

Control technology	Industry	% Reduction	Cost
A	gadget	25	$100,000
B	gadget	25	$500,000
C	widget	60	$30,000
D	widget	30	$25,000

    (a)   How should Malambia meet its goal of healthful air quality? What would be the results of a rule mandating proportional emission reductions have to require? What would be the least cost method of achieving the goal? What are the equity and efficiency implications of these alternatives?

    (b)   How would the following factors affect your analysis?
- (i) uncertainty about health effects
- (ii) uncertainty about technological and economic feasibility of control technologies
- (iii) numerous heterogeneous firms in either/both industries
- (iv) varying air quality across regions
- (v) varying population density
- (vi) mobility of citizens
- (vii) hundreds of industries
- (viii) sensitivity of level of employment to control costs
- (ix) automobile pollution
- (x) international competition
- (xi) economic growth
- (xii) costly enforcement
- (xiii) interjurisdictional pollution

3. THE EVOLUTION OF AIR POLLUTION REGULATION

a. Federal Air Pollution Control Legislation Prior to 1970

Legislative and administrative control of air pollution was long the preserve of municipalities, counties, and states. Beginning in the last decades of the nineteenth century, municipalities adopted a variety of regulatory measures, from general prohibitions against the discharge of "dense smoke" to prohibitions on the use of high sulfur coal. During the twentieth century the states assumed a gradually increasing regulatory role. In some instances state and local regulation was successful, particularly in reducing concentrations of particulate matter. The clean-up of Pittsburgh, the "Smokey City," through regulatory controls after World War II is a case in point. But in many other instances, pollution both from stationary sources and motor vehicles continued to increase. The 1950s and 1960s witnessed a steadily developing concern on the part of scientists, government officials, and the public generally with air pollution. For historical review and discussion, see S. Edelman, The Law of Air Pollution Control (1970); Laitos, Legal Institutions and Pollution, Some Intersections Between Law and History, 15 Nat. Resources J. 423 (1975); Kennedy & Porter, Air Pollution: Its Control & Abatement, 8 Vand. L. Rev. 854 (1955); McQuillan, Abatement of the Smoke Nuisance in Large Cities, 46 Cent. L.J. 147 (1898).

In 1955, the federal government entered the field with enactment of the Air Pollution Control Act of 1955, ch. 360, 69 Stat. 322 (1955). It was intended simply "to provide research and technical assistance relating to air pollution control," a major purpose being to determine the causes and effects of air pollution. The Act authorized the Secretary of the Department of Health, Education and Welfare ("HEW") (presently the Department of Health and Human Services ("HHS")) to recommend, support, and undertake research programs for air pollution control. It declared that air pollution control responsibility rested primarily with the states. (This declaration has appeared in or attended the passage of all the federal air pollution legislation enacted since 1955, but with a steady enlargement of the federal government's role).

The Motor Vehicle Act of 1960, Pub. L. No. 86-493, 74 Stat. 162 (1960), specifically authorized federal research into the effects of air pollution from motor vehicles and methods for controlling such pollution.

The federal regulatory effort began in 1963 with passage of the Clean Air Act, Pub. L. No. 88-206, 77 Stat. 392 (1963). The Act authorized the Secretary of HEW to investigate interstate air pollution problems and to recommend action, although such recommendations were only advisory. In the case of serious threats to public health, the Secretary could recommend that the Attorney General undertake enforcement action but only after cumbersome procedures, including convening relevant state and local pollution control agencies to address the threat, were followed. By 1970, fewer than a dozen conferences had been held and only a single enforcement action had been brought. See J. Esposito, Vanishing Air 118-151 (1970); U.S. Council on Environmental Quality, Environmental Quality, First Annual Report 86 (1970). Perhaps of greater long term consequence, the 1963 Act provided for the collection of scientific data on the effects of air pollution and the development of air quality criteria.

In 1965, the federal control effort was extended to new motor vehicles. The 1965 Motor Vehicle Air Pollution Control Act, Pub. L. No. 89-272, 79 Stat. 992 (1965), authorized the Secretary of HEW to prescribe "standards applicable to any class or classes of new motor vehicles or new motor vehicle engines. . . ." While there was no express proscription of state controls on new motor vehicle emissions, the legislative history of the statute stressed the desirability of uniformity in regulating new motor vehicles because of fear over the potentially disruptive effect on manufacturers of varying state standards. See Currie, Motor Vehicle Air Pollution: State Authority and Federal Pre-emption, 68 Mich. L. Rev. 1083 (1970).

The first comprehensive federal scheme of air pollution control was the 1967 Air Quality Act, Pub. L. No. 90-148, 81 Stat. 485. The 1967 Amendments strengthened the federal policy role by specifying an orderly procedure for adoption and achievement by the states of ambient air quality standards. First, HEW was directed to designate broad "atmospheric regions" of the nation in which meteorology, topology, and other factors influencing air pollution concentrations were relatively homogeneous. Second, HEW was required to designate air quality regions based upon "jurisdictional boundaries, urban-industrial concentrations, and other factors including atmospheric areas necessary to provide adequate implementation of air quality standards." Clean Air Act, §107(a)(2). The basic principle was to designate areas in which air pollution could be regulated through an integrated set of controls. Regions might include portions of two or more states as well as a state or a portion thereof. Third, states were required to adopt ambient air quality standards for the various air quality regions, defining permissible concentrations of pollutants in the atmosphere. These standards were required to be based upon HEW criteria documents (describing the adverse effects of various concentrations of air pollutants) and HEW documents describing pollution control techniques; the standards were subject to HEW approval. If a state failed to promulgate adequate standards, HEW was authorized to establish such standards after a process of consultation and public hearing. Fourth, states were required to adopt, subject to HEW approval, implementation plans to achieve the ambient standards by imposing sufficient limitations on sources of air pollution within each region to ensure that the permissible atmospheric concentrations of pollutants were not exceeded. However, it was unclear whether HEW had power to promulgate itself an implementation plan for a region if a state's plan was inadequate. See Martin & Symington, A Guide to the Air Quality Act of 1967, 33 L. & Contemp. Prob. 239, 260-261 (1968). Moreover, the sole federal authority to enforce limitations on pollution sources was the cumbersome conference procedure carried over from the 1963 Act. In addition, the federal controls on new motor vehicles were made expressly preemptive of state controls. See Currie, supra.

The Air Quality Act of 1967 reflected widespread belief that state and local efforts to control air pollution were inadequate and that a much stronger federal role was required. See Comment, A History of Federal Air Pollution Control, 30 Ohio St. L.J. 516, 529 (1969). The Act in practice, however, proved quite ineffective in achieving rapid and pervasive control of air pollution.

In part, this ineffectiveness reflected the Act's emphasis on air quality control regions based upon meteorological and geographical factors. States and political subdivisions objected to HEW designation of regions cutting across established jurisdictional lines, causing substantial delays in the designation process. When regions were established that did not conform to established political jurisdictions, it proved difficult to obtain agreement by the different states or political subdivisions on standards or implementation plans. In an effort to foster interstate cooperation, the Act authorized 100 percent federal funding for Regional Commissions voluntarily established by the states in an interstate air quality control region, but no such Commissions were formed.

Another shortcoming of the 1967 Act in achieving rapid control of air pollution consisted of the delays involved in accomplishing the elaborate steps specified by the Act. Delays were involved at the federal level in designating regions and issuing criteria documents and documents on control techniques. Delays were also involved at the state level in adopting standards and implementation plans; despite a 15-month deadline in the Act for accomplishing these steps, many states lacked the information, personnel, or political will to meet the deadline. As a result, by the spring of 1970, not one state had adopted a full-scale set of standards and implementation plans. Finally, the cumbersome conference procedures for federal enforcement provided scant assurance that any implementation plans would actually be carried out. For more detailed analysis and criticism of the 1967 Act, see J. Esposito, Vanishing Air (1970); Martin & Symington, A Guide to the Air Quality Act of 1967, 33 L. & Contemp. Prob. 239 (1968).

b.   Federalism Issues in Air Pollution Control Policy

Before turning to the 1970 Amendments to the Clean Air Act, which made major changes in an effort to deal with the perceived shortcomings of pre-existing federal legislation, it is worthwhile to reflect upon the possible reasons for the general structure of the 1967 Act and its allocation of responsibility between federal and state governments.

On one view, the Act could be interpreted on the premise that environmental policy decisions should basically be made by the states, who have a legitimate interest in independence to decide upon the appropriate balance between environmental quality and other uses of economic resources. In this view, the federal role is properly confined to directing state attention to air pollution problems; providing states with technical data that the federal government can generate more cheaply on a centralized basis (as opposed to the duplicative tasks involved in 50 states each developing such data); and dealing with interstate "spillovers."

On the other hand, the Act might be read on the premise that air pollution is a national concern, even where it does not cross state lines. On this view, the substantial role accorded the states in the 1967 Amendments might be explained on several alternative grounds. First, it might reflect the inevitable shortcomings of excessive centralization in a large, geographically and economically diverse nation. A national policy of adequate air quality, in the context of local variations in geography, meteorology and industrial development, and the large number of sources to be controlled, might best be accomplished by according states considerable leeway in framing standards and control measures, subject to overall federal supervision and direction. Rigorous dictation of detailed air pollution control requirements by the national government would involve costly and time-consuming centralization of information, could threaten excessive rigidities and uniformities, and might prove unenforceable without state and local cooperation. Alternatively, one might believe that national pollution controls and national enforcement measures were the only effective way to ensure cleaner air because the states cannot be relied upon to take vigorous measures to deal with environmental degradation. On this view, the 1967 Act would have to be explained as a political compromise. Given the natural opposition by industry and some state officials to a forceful and predominant federal role in air pollution policy and the difficulties in changing the political status quo through legislation, a halfway measure emerged. As a third alternative, one might believe that a substantial state role in implementing a national policy of cleaner air was preferable to detailed federal intervention, *provided* that there was adequate incentive for the states to take vigorous and effective measures. The 1967 Act might provide such an incentive by threatening more sweeping federal intervention if states failed promptly to carry out the federal policy of improving air quality; there is evidence that in some states the Act did have such an incentive effect.

Which of these possible explanations most persuasively explains the structure of the 1967 Air Quality Act?

The issues raised in the above discussion of the 1967 Act are basic to any development of environmental controls and incentives in a federal system. They determine the appropriate extent and form of national dictation of environmental policies. They also raise constitutional questions of the extent to which the federal government can force states and local governments to implement national environmental measures.

At this point, you should develop your own preliminary views on these issues of federalism in the context of environmental policy.

To what extent is environmental quality an appropriate concern of the federal government? Given our traditions in favor of decentralized decisionmaking, there must be substantial, affirmative justification for intervention by the federal government in an area of domestic policy. Consider the following five possible justifications for a strong federal role. One possible justification is the existence of substantial environmental spillovers from one state to another. The originating state is likely to treat the adverse effects on the receiving state as an "external cost," and give inadequate regard to the welfare of the latter state. Moreover, exertion of national power to resolve interstate conflicts was a basic reason for creation of the federal government. In the materials that follow, you should examine the extent to which federal environmental legislation is designed to deal with interstate spillovers, and how effective it has been in addressing them. Suppose, moreover, that the effects of pollution are confined to the state generating them. What special reason is there for federal intervention in order, for example, to force California to have cleaner air than it wishes? Why isn't California competent to trade off the costs and benefits of intrastate pollution control? Indeed, aren't California officials far more competent than federal officials to make such tradeoffs because they are closer to California citizens and more responsive to their preferences for environmental quality?

A second possible justification for federal legislation is that states might seek to attract industry by adopting less stringent and therefore less costly environmental regulation. If each state follows this strategy, or fears that others will and adopts laxer regulations in order to prevent flight of its industry, a form of "commons" or "prisoners' dilemma" problem might arise in which each state adopts laxer standards than it would independently prefer. If so, federal legislation to establish a minimum level of controls might be justified in order to secure for states the environmental quality that they prefer. Is this scenario persuasive? How significant are environmental compliance expenditures in competitiveness and locational decisions? See Revesz, Rehabilitating Interstate Competition: Rethinking the "Race to the Bottom" Rationale for Federal Environmental Regulation, 67 N.Y.U.L. Rev. 1210 (1992); Stewart, Environmental Regulation and International Competitiveness, 102 Yale L.J. 2039 (1993).

A third potential justification for federal legislation arises with respect to regulation of products but not regulation of industrial processes. State environmental regulation could be used as a protectionist means of favoring local producers. For example, a compulsory bottle recycling law would favor in-state producers who would enjoy greater scale economies and lower transportation costs in complying with it, compared to out-of-state producers. The Supreme Court has used the commerce clause to strike down state regulation that discriminates against or imposes excessive burdens on interstate commerce. It has, however, shown considerable deference to state environmental regulation despite adverse effects on out-of-state producers. See, e.g., *Minnesota v. Clover Leaf Creamery Co.,* 449 U.S. 456 (1981) (upholding Minnesota law banning non-recyclable plastic milk containers but not paperboard containers despite evidence that the measure was designed to protect Minnesota's paperboard industry). Moreover, otherwise legitimate but conflicting state product requirements could create a regulatory crazy-quilt that limits many of the advantages of a common market. The federal government might therefore set a uniform standard to govern the common market.

A fourth potential justification for federal legislation is that state regulation is unduly lax because industry, developers, and unions might be systematically "overrepresented" in state decisionmaking and environmental interests systematically "underrepresented." Why might this be so? If it were so, would federal intervention be justified to "correct" this disparity? Is there a stronger case for federal intervention where serious adverse health effects or irreversible environmental degradation is threatened? For discussion of these and related issues, see Stewart, Pyramids of Sacrifice? Federalism Problems in State Implementation of National Environmental Policies, 86 Yale L.J. 1196 (1977).

A final justification for federal regulation is the notion that environmental quality is a fundamental right that should be federally guaranteed on a uniform basis for all citizens. Citizens exposed to higher levels of pollution in states with lower standards could be analogized to victims of discrimination. This "rights rhetoric" reflects in part the social and practical roots of the environmental movement in the civil rights movement. Can environmental quality properly be considered a right akin to basic civil liberties? Early efforts by environmental advocates to persuade the courts to recognize a constitutional right to environmental quality were wholly unsuccessful. See, e.g., *Tanner v. Armco Steel Corp.,* 340 F. Supp. 532 (S.D. Tex. 1972); Krier, The Environment, the Constitution, and the Coupling Fallacy, Univ of Mich., Law Quadrangle Notes, No. 3 (1988).

To the extent that national direction of environmental policy is appropriate, to what extent should the federal government rely upon state and local governments to implement national policies? On the one hand are the dangers of overcentralization, with accompanying

disregard of important local variations and circumstances; the limited
extent of federal enforcement resources and Congress's reluctance to
create a national police force; and the interrelation of pollution control
measures and land use planning, traffic control, and other subjects of
state and local control. On the other hand, state and local governments
may lack the capability or political incentive to take effective implementation measures. How should one decide which aspects of policy formulation and enforcement should be delegated to state and local
governments? Should the selection vary depending on the type of environmental measures in question — regulation, fees, subsidies, or alternative measures?

You should consider these federalism issues in evaluating the
Clean Air Act, and also the Clean Water Act, addressed in Chapter 5,
and hazardous waste regulation, addressed in Chapter 6.

c.   Overview of the Clean Air Act Amendments of 1970

The 1970 Clean Air Amendments created the basic structure of
the Clean Air Act, currently codified at 42 U.S.C. §§7401-7671q. The
1970 Amendments represent a remarkable effort on the part of the
Congress to constrain the administrative discretion of the executive.
Congress's determination in the Amendments to mandate administrative action along legislatively predetermined lines in part reflected profound dissatisfaction with the lack of tangible achievements in federal
air pollution control programs over the previous decade. Despite successive grants of additional powers to the federal government and an
increasing degree of public concern over air pollution, most air pollution indices showed a continuing increase in emissions and a decline
in ambient air quality. This trend was in part attributed to the weakness
of state governmental units responsible for pollution control policy and
their vulnerability to "blackmail" by industrial and labor interests. Federal legislators concluded that a broader measure of national authority
to determine and ensure enforcement of air pollution control measures was accordingly required, particularly in the case of stationary
source emissions, where the responsibility for control under the 1967
Air Quality Act rested with the states, and the federal government's
powers to revise inadequate standards or ensure effective enforcement
were quite limited.

In addition, many members of Congress viewed the National Air
Pollution Control Administration (NAPCA) of the Department of
Health, Education, and Welfare (the agency responsible for federal air
pollution control programs) as lacking in zeal, particularly in its discharge of the large discretionary authority that it enjoyed under prior
legislation to regulate emissions from new automobiles. Oriented to-

ward research and engineering, NAPCA appeared to many to be following rather than forcing the auto manufacturers' adoption of automotive emission control technologies. The need for measures that would stiffen the bureaucratic spine and assure more rigorous controls seemed obvious.

This diagnosis of undue laxity on the part of NAPCA was, in the case of Democratic members of Congress, reinforced by partisan political considerations. It was, after all, a Republican administration headed by President Nixon that could now be blamed for such ineffectiveness. A Democratic Congress's enactment of detailed statutory directives mandating that the executive achieve sweeping improvements in air quality on a short timetable seemed, in these circumstances, a most astute political move. If the Nixon Administration failed to carry out such a mandate, it could be faulted for "selling out" to industry in a time of growing environmental concern. Even if the Nixon Administration did succeed in making a reasonable show of enforcement, the Democratic Congress could claim a fair measure of the credit. Such considerations were also consonant with the presidential ambitions of Senator Edmund Muskie, the chief architect of the Clean Air Amendments that were eventually enacted into law.

The legislators' perception of administrative laxity and the need for corrective measures matched a more general sense of growing disillusionment with administrative agencies that was developing not only among "reform" figures (such as Ralph Nader) but also legal commentators and judges. The notion that agencies were habitually "captured" by or otherwise unduly deferential to the interests which they were charged with regulating was achieving widespread currency.[3]

While Congress was determined, for the various reasons just outlined, to press for straightforward action to improve air quality, the complex nature of air pollution problems and associated administrative and political considerations resulted in a complicated statute.

Environmental Quality-Based Approach. The bedrock of the Clean Air Amendments is provision for geographically uniform federal ambient standards of air quality in lieu of the near-exclusive reliance on state-set air quality standards in prior legislation. The 1970 Amendments required the Administrator of the new federal Environmental Protection Agency (to which NAPCA's functions had been transferred in 1970 by President Nixon's executive reorganization) to establish nationally uniform primary and secondary ambient air quality standards for widespread air pollutants for which criteria documents (describing such pollutants' adverse effects) had been issued under Section 108 of the Act. Under Section 109 of the Act, primary standards must specify

---

3. See generally Stewart, The Reformation of American Administrative Law, 88 Harv. L. Rev. 1667 (1975).

permissible pollution concentrations "requisite to protect the public health" while "allowing an adequate margin of safety." Secondary standards were required to protect against "welfare" effects of pollution, such as impairment of visibility and damage to plant life and materials. In the case of those pollutants for which criteria documents had already been issued by the federal government — particulate matter, sulfur oxides, nitrogen oxides, photochemical oxidants, hydrocarbons, and carbon monoxide — EPA was required to promulgate ambient standards within 120 days of the Amendment's enactment.[4]

Section 110 of the Act establishes a system of state implementation plans (SIPs) to achieve the federal standards. Following adoption by EPA of ambient standards, the states are required to devise, within nine months, implementation plans to limit emissions within each air quality region[5] in order to ensure attainment and maintenance of the federal standards. The Amendments direct the Administrator, within four months from the date of their submission, to approve such plans if they will ensure attainment of the primary standards within three years and the secondary standards within a "reasonable time." If state plans are inadequate, the Administrator is required to promulgate a plan for the state that will achieve the federal standards within the applicable time deadlines. The Amendments authorize the Administrator to grant limited extensions of the deadlines for achieving the primary ambient standards if a state shows that it is not feasible to meet the statutory timetables. The resulting statutory timetable mandated achievement of the federal primary ambient standards by 1975 (if the principal extensions authorized by the Act were fully granted, the deadline would be 1977). You should at this point review carefully the provisions of Section 110, particularly the required ingredients of state implementation plans (SIPs) set forth in Section 110(a)(2).

While states are thus required to implement federal ambient standards, Section 116 provides that, except as provided in Sections 209, 211(c)(4) and 233 (preempting state controls on new motor vehicle emissions, fuel additives, and aircraft emissions), nothing in the Clean Air Act shall preclude the right of any state or political subdivision

---

4. Under Section 108 of the Act, as amended, the EPA is required to issue additional criteria documents for pollutants that, in the judgment of the Administrator, have an adverse effect on public health or welfare, and result from numerous or diverse mobile or stationary sources. Following the issuance of additional criteria documents, the Administrator is required by Section 109 of the Act to adopt, within 90 days, ambient standards for the pollutants in question.

5. In order to speed the process of designating air quality control regions, Section 107 of the amended Act provided that EPA must within 90 days designate any additional air quality control regions deemed necessary for achievement of the federal ambient standards, and that any areas of a state not designated as a region shall constitute an air quality control region.

thereof to adopt or enforce any "emission standard or limitation" or any "requirement respecting control or abatement of pollution" more stringent than those established by federal law.

Technology-Based Approach. In addition to the basic system of uniform federal ambient standards to be achieved through state emission controls, the 1970 Amendments provided for three sets of nationally uniform federal emission limitations to be established by the EPA Administrator.

First, Section 111 of the Act provides for nationally uniform federal emission limitations for new stationary sources of air pollution, requiring "the application of the best system of emissions reduction which (taking into account the cost of achieving such reductions) the Administrator determines has been adequately demonstrated." These geographically uniform controls on all new sources reduce the advantages that "clean" states would otherwise enjoy in attracting industrial development and population at the expense of the heavily-polluted and heavily-unionized northeastern and midwestern states.[6] Moreover, it was expected that the federal emission limitations for new sources would be quite stringent, effectively preventing deterioration of air quality in "clean" regions whose ambient concentrations were well below the federal standards.

Second, Section 112 of the Act authorizes nationally uniform emission limitations for "hazardous air pollutants" that "may cause, or contribute to, an increase in mortality, or an increase in serious, irreversible, or incapacitating reversible illness," but are not covered by Section 109 ambient standards and Section 110 SIPs. Here the Congress contemplated controls on relatively isolated, highly dangerous toxic pollutants that should be prohibited entirely or restricted to the extent necessary to protect the public health.

The third set of federal emission limitations in the Clean Air Amendments applies to new motor vehicles. Uniform federal controls on emissions from new motor vehicles had been authorized by Congress in 1965 in terms that afforded broad discretion to the executive branch as to the level and timing of controls. Section 202 of the amended Act drastically curtailed the Administrator's discretion by requiring that a 90 percent reduction in existing automotive pollutant levels be achieved by 1975-1976, with limited provision for a one-year

---

6. However, "clean" states still enjoyed an advantage under the Act in accommodating new development; even though new stationary sources must meet the same federal emission limitations regardless of where they are located, states whose current ambient levels are substantially below the federal standards could accommodate new growth without violating those standards, whereas states whose emissions are currently in excess of the federal ambient standards could not accommodate such growth without further reducing emissions from existing sources in order to make room for new sources.

administrative extension of the time deadlines. These drastic constraints were justified by Senator Muskie on the ground that they were assertedly required in order to achieve federal primary ambient standards for automotive pollutants within the statutory timetable for ambient standards. While conceding that there was no assurance that automobile manufacturers could devise and install the technology required for 90 percent reductions, Senator Muskie was optimistic that the deadlines would force the development of the necessary control technology. See 116 Cong. Rec. 32902, 32905-32906, 42382 (1970). Violation of the federal emission limitations was made subject to a civil penalty of not more than $10,000 for each noncomplying vehicle distributed or sold.

While not explicit, the provisions of Section 202 of the Act appear to contemplate that federal emission limitations on new automobiles should be geographically uniform. Section 209 of the Act continues the 1967 preemption of state standards "relating to the control of emissions from new motor vehicles or new motor vehicle engines," but authorizes EPA to waive this preemption with respect to California. The California congressional delegation successfully argued that the severe smog problem in Los Angeles and some other urban areas in California justified a separate California standard. See Currie, Motor Vehicle Air Pollution: State Authority and Federal Pre-emption, 68 Mich. L. Rev. 1083 (1970).

Enforcement. Congress' record in policing administrative implementation of federal control programs suggested that congressional oversight would not assure implementation of Congress' directives. In addition, the history of both state and federal regulation of pollution documented an enforcement effort that was patchy and protracted. While this history might have suggested to Congress that it consider alternatives to regulatory controls — such as emission fees — that would substantially undercut the incentive of polluters to interpose debilitating procedural delays, Congress instead sought to make the regulatory approach more stringent and effective.

Section 113 of the Act provided for greatly strengthened federal enforcement authority, going far beyond the cumbersome conference abatement procedure provided in prior law. The EPA Administrator was authorized to issue an administrative order or seek an injunction in federal district court mandating compliance with federal emission limitations for new sources of hazardous pollutants; and to similarly enforce provisions of state implementation plans after 30 days' notice by the Administrator to the noncomplying source and to relevant state officials. If the Administrator finds, after 30 days' notice to a state, that it has systematically failed to enforce its plan, the Administrator may assume enforcement of the entire plan. Knowing violations of administrative enforcement orders or of federal emission limitations are subject to criminal penalties of up to $25,000 per day of violation ($50,000 in the case of a second offense) and imprisonment. Section 205 of the Act authorizes a civil penalty of $10,000 per vehicle for sale or distribution of motor vehicles in violation of federal pollution controls for new motor vehicles. Section 303 of the Act continues the Administrator's emergency power to seek injunctive relief in federal district court against air pollution presenting "an imminent and substantial endangerment to the health of persons." To buttress administrative enforcement of the Act, Congress in Section 304 of the Act also authorized "citizen suits" both against the EPA Administration and private sources of pollution. This provision is discussed in greater detail infra at pp. 547–549.

d. Overview of the Clean Air Act Amendments of 1977

As might have been anticipated in view of the ambitious goals of the 1970 Act, the national ambient air quality standards were not achieved within the 1975-1977 deadlines. The 1977 Amendments to the Clean Air Act retained the overall structure of the 1970 Act while making detailed revisions to its substantive provisions. Passed in the midst of the Arab oil embargo and economic recession, the environmental fervor that accompanied the passage of the 1970 Act had receded somewhat and the 1977 Amendments reflected a compromise of industrial, union, and environmental interests.

One important reason for the 1977 Amendments was that the 1970 Act required achievement of ambient air standards everywhere in the nation no later than 1977, an impossible task in many heavily polluted urban areas, particularly those afflicted with smog produced by emissions from both stationary sources and mobile sources such as automobiles, trucks, and buses. The Amendments extended the deadline for non-attainment areas until 1982, with allowance for further extensions until 1987. It also imposed strict pollution control and preconstruction review procedures on major new sources of pollution in nonattainment areas and required the adoption of "reasonably available control technology" (RACT) by existing sources in these areas, which were also authorized to adopt California's more stringent standards for new automobile emissions. In the case of those areas of the nation that already had air cleaner than that required by the ambient standards, Congress, building on EPA regulations, imposed limits on additional pollution and special controls on new sources in order to prevent significant deterioration of existing air quality. The Act also postponed the deadlines established in 1970 for achieving motor vehicle emission reductions and eased control burdens on coal-burning power plants and certain other industrial facilities.

e.   *Overview of the Clean Air Act Amendments of 1990*

In the years following 1977, EPA struggled to implement the Act's complex provisions. Deadlines for regulatory action and for attainment of standards were routinely missed. The Act proved ineffective in dealing with emerging new problems, such as toxic air pollutants and acid deposition. Following years of political stalemate, Congress, spurred by proposals by the Bush Administration, in 1990 enacted detailed, complex amendments running to hundreds of pages. As in 1977, Congress did not fundamentally change the pre-existing structure, but simply added ambitious new provisions on top of it.

Title I of the 1990 amendments dealt with the problem of continuing failures to meet NAAQS attainment deadlines by classifying regions by the extent to which their existing pollution levels exceed the standards for ozone, carbon monoxide, and PM-10 (particulate matter smaller than 10 microns). The greater the excedance, the more time regions are given to reach attainment. In the case of ozone, for example, Los Angeles is given until the year 2010. But the more severely polluted areas are also subject to stricter control requirements. In the case of ozone, for example, these requirements include mandatory annual reductions in emissions of NO and VOCs (volatile organic compounds — the more volatile hydrocarbons), the precursor pollutants that interact in the atmosphere to form ozone; installation of retrofit RACT controls on existing stationary sources; development of alternative fuels and very low emission vehicle fleets; and, if necessary, transportation controls. Sanctions, including cut-offs of federal highway funds and imposition of yet more restrictive controls, are imposed on states that fail to achieve reductions on schedule.

Title II deals with automotive air pollution. The Amendments require ambitious further reductions in emissions from new vehicles and for the first time specifically deal with fuels as elements in pollution control strategy by requiring development of reformulated, low-emitting fuels and of vehicles operating on "clean fuels" such as natural gas or methanol.

Title III deals with the problem of toxic air pollutants. Unlike the Section 109 "criteria" pollutants for which NAAQS are established, toxic pollutants are emitted by a relatively small number of sources in smaller quantities, but the pollutants in question can be potent carcinogens or otherwise threaten serious health risks. The 1970 amendments dealt with toxic pollutants through Section 112, which apparently required source emission limitations based solely on health effects. EPA's efforts to implement this provision were, for reasons explained below, a failure. Congress in 1990 amended Section 112 to mandate the use of technology-based emissions controls on a specific list of 189 toxic air pollutants in accordance with schedules and deadlines set forth in the statute.

The 1970 Act had also proven ineffective in dealing with acid deposition; indeed, in some respects it made the acid deposition problem worse. Acid deposition involves sulfur and nitrogen compounds formed by the interaction of SO_2 and NO emissions with other elements in the atmosphere. These compounds fall to earth in precipitation or in dry form. They result in acidification of lakes and streams and pose a risk to trees, soils, and human health. In order to avoid local violations of ambient air quality standards, utilities and others sources began in the early 1970s to build tall stacks and take other steps to disperse SO_2 and NO_x concentrations widely. These measures (which EPA and Congress later addressed with regulations and statutory provisions that effectively eliminated the regulatory advantages of building tall stacks) reduced local ambient concentrations but promoted the formation of sulfur and nitrogen compounds which fell to earth as acid deposition hundred of miles sway. The largest emitters were in the midwest; the principal recipients were the northeast states and Canada. This regional struggle, among others, stymied efforts to address the problem by legislation.

In Title IV of the 1990 amendments Congress adopted the Bush Administration's proposal to reduce total loadings of sulfur emissions by approximately 50 percent over a 10-year period by requiring utilities to make phased reductions in emissions. However, those sources that reduce their emissions faster than required by the schedule (as well as non-utility sources that reduce emissions below the level otherwise required) can sell their excess reductions to other utilities who found the scheduled reductions more difficult or costly to achieve. The effect is to create a national market in pollution rights, which is expected to substantially reduce the costs of achieving the 50 percent emission reduction. The Title IV sulfur provisions thus incorporate two important innovations in regulatory policy: First, basing control strategy on limiting total emission loadings of a pollutant throughout a broad area as opposed to ambient standards limiting pollution concentrations anywhere or technology-based controls on sources; second, use of marketable permits to achieve compliance flexibility as compared to mandatory, source-specific controls. Title IV also provides for new, technology-based limitations on emissions of NO from existing and new utility sources.

Title V provides for a federal system of operating permits for major pollution sources. Modeled on the Clean Water Act, it requires each major stationary source to obtain a state-issued permit incorporating all of the control and other requirements mandated by federal law. Sources must pay permit fees to EPA or state permitting authorities of not less than $25 per ton annually, up to a maximum of 4000 tons. This measure was designed to simplify compliance and enforcement by incorporating all requirements for a source in one document. Previously, for example, some requirements might be found only in a state's SIP. However, SIPs continue to exist, and ensuring consistency between the permit, the SIP, and EPA's evolving views of what federal law requires will not be an easy task. Also, air pollution may be discharged from many different units and points within a facility, unlike water pollution discharges, which commonly are discharged through one or a few outfalls. A requirement to obtain multiple permits for each of many air pollution discharge points could hamper a firm's flexibility in responding to shifting market conditions and production variables.

Title VII of the Amendments strengthens the enforcement provisions of the Act. EPA is given authority to issue administrative penalty orders of up to $25,000 per day of violations, and EPA inspectors may issue "field citations" for minor violations with penalties of up to $5000 per day of violation. "Knowing" violations of most regulatory requirements (including not only permit and emission limitation requirements but also record-keeping and reporting requirements) are made criminal felonies. The Amendments also create a misdemeanor of "negligent endangerment" for the negligent release of any hazardous air pollutant (whether or not subject to regulatory controls) that results in imminent endangerment of another person, and a similar felony of "knowing endangerment."

The Amendments also added a new Title VI to the Act, Sections 501-507. These provisions require the phase out of chlorofluorocarbons (CFCs), HCFCs, and other chemicals that deplete the stratospheric ozone layer, ban non-essential products containing such substances, require labelling of products manufactured with such substances, and regulate their substitutes. These provisions implement U.S. commitments to international agreements — the Vienna Convention and the Montreal Protocol — for phase out of substances that deplete stratospheric ozone. This international effort is sharply reducing emissions of ozone, depleting chemicals. The buildup of these chemicals in the atmosphere is expected to stop by the end of the century, at which point the ozone layer will begin a new recovery.[7]

Implementing the 1990 Amendments will be an immensely complicated task, requiring dozens of EPA rulemaking proceedings on controversial issues. While the Amendments were adopted with bipartisan acclaim, some economists have suggested that the costs imposed by many of the new provisions will be far greater than the benefits. At

---

7. Stevens, Ozone-Depleting Chemicals Building Up at Slower Pace, N.Y. Times, Aug. 26, 1993, at A1.

the same time, most economists believe that more flexible and better targeted approaches could achieve comparable benefits of the present scheme at a fraction of the cost. See Portney, Policy Watch: Economics and the Clean Air Act, 4 J. Econ. Perspectives 173, 179-180 (1990).

B.   ENVIRONMENTAL QUALITY-BASED APPROACHES: THE NATIONAL AMBIENT AIR QUALITY STANDARDS AND THEIR IMPLEMENTATION

The 1970 Amendments sought to speed the regulatory process by requiring that EPA promulgate within 90 days National Ambient Air Quality Standards (NAAQSs) for the six pollutants for which air quality criteria had already been issued: particulate matter, sulfur oxides, carbon monoxide, nitrogen oxides, hydrocarbons, and photochemical oxidants (ozone). The first section below will take you through the challenging process of setting NAAQSs.

Recognizing the gaps in scientific knowledge about air pollution, the 1970 Amendments required the Environmental Protection Agency to periodically review evidence on other potential pollutants and to promulgate regulations as justified by scientific evidence of adverse human health or welfare effects. Section 2 discusses the legal standard for listing new air pollutants.

The 1970 Amendments retained a significant role for the states in regulating air pollution. State governments, subject to federal approval, must translate NAAQSs establishing permissible concentrations into enforceable limitations on the discharge of pollutants from sources within their jurisdiction. Section 3 discusses this process.

1.   SETTING NATIONAL AMBIENT AIR QUALITY STANDARDS

a.   The National Ambient Air Quality Standards for Sulfur Oxides

PROBLEM IN REGULATORY DECISIONMAKING

You have just been appointed Administrator of the U.S. Environmental Protection Agency. Section 109 of the Act requires that you review and revise national ambient standards every five years. You have just received a revision of the criteria documents for sulfur oxides (contained in the Appendix to this chapter).

National Ambient Air Quality Standards prescribe a maximum concentration of a pollutant in the air at ground levels that is not to be exceeded anyplace. The standard may be expressed, for example, in terms of a maximum annual average, maximum 24-hour average, maximum hourly average, maximum instantaneous concentration, or a combination of the above.[8] For each pollutant, the Administrator must promulgate a primary standard to protect health and a secondary standard to protect "welfare."[9] Recall that the primary standards must be achieved within relatively short statutory deadlines. Section 109 of the Act contains the following directions for establishing primary and secondary national ambient standards:

> (b)(1) National primary ambient air quality standards, prescribed under subsection (a) of this section shall be ambient air quality standards the attainment and maintenance of which in the judgment of the Administrator, based on such criteria and allowing an adequate margin of safety, are requisite to protect the public health. Such primary standards may be revised in the same manner as promulgated.
>
> (2) Any national secondary ambient air quality standard prescribed under subsection (a) of this section shall specify a level of air quality the attainment and maintenance of which in the judgment of the Administrator, based on such criteria, is requisite to protect the public welfare from any known or anticipated adverse effects associated with the presence of such air pollutant in the ambient air. Such secondary standards may be revised in the same manner as promulgated.

In establishing ambient air quality standards for sulfur oxides, you should refer to excerpts from the criteria document for sulfur oxides reproduced in the Appendix to this chapter. You should establish annual and 24-hour primary and secondary standards, and any additional standards you deem appropriate. Keep in mind that your choices are subject to judicial review.

---

8. Average concentrations are normally expressed in parts per million (for example, if in a sample of air the ratio of sulfur dioxide (by volume) to air (by volume) was 2:1,000,000, the sample would contain 2 parts per million (ppm) of sulfur dioxide), or in micrograms of the pollutant per cubic meter of air ($\mu g/m^3$). For purposes of this problem, use the $\mu g/m^3$ measure. (Parts per million can be converted into $\mu g/m^3$ by multiplying by 2600 (at the reference temperature of 25°C used by EPA, 40 C.R.F. §50.3)).)

9. Effects on "welfare" are defined by the Act, Section 302(h), as including, but not limited to, "effects on soil, water, crops, vegetation, man-made materials, animals, wild life, weather, visibility and climate, damage to and deterioration of property, and hazards to transportation, as well as effects on economic values and on personal comfort and well-being."

Primary Standards:

Annual: _____ $\mu g/m^3$
24-hour: _____ $\mu g/m^3$
Other: _____ $\mu g/m^3$ per _____
                                    (specify relevant time period)

Secondary Standards:

Annual: _____ $\mu g/m^3$
24-hour: _____ $\mu g/m^3$
Other: _____ $\mu g/m^3$ per _____
                                    (specify relevant time period)

NOTES AND QUESTIONS

1. What reasons would you give for the standards you chose?

2. Should ambient standards be set for sulfur dioxide alone, or should they be set for *combinations* of sulfur dioxide and other pollutants, such as particulate matter? Would the statute permit the use of such a standard? What difficulties would you foresee in implementing such a standard?

3. What factors may be considered under the Act in setting the primary and secondary ambient standards? What additional factors might be relevant? How do the standard-setting provisions in the Clean Air Act resemble or differ from the OSHA provisions in the *Benzene* case, supra, p. 25, or the TSCA provisions in the *Asbestos* case, p. 116, supra? Consider in particular the following:

   (a)   Does the statute permit the Administrator in setting primary standards to take into account the cost of achieving them? Secondary standards? If not, why not? What is the possible relevance of the fact that unemployed persons and their families tend to have greater health problems?

   (b)   If protecting the public health is the sole consideration in setting the primary standards, does that imply that the standards should be set at zero? How should the burden of uncertainty be allocated? For discussion of these issues in a related context, see Blank, The Delaney Clause, Technical Naivete and Scientific Advocacy in the Formulation of Public Health Policies, 62 Calif. L. Rev. 1084 (1974).

   (c)   Must health standards be set to protect the most susceptible individuals in the country? The report on the Senate version of the 1970 Amendments indicated that standards should be set to "protect the health of any group of the population," including those suffering from emphysema. See S. Rep. No. 91-1196, 91st Cong., 2d Sess. 10 (1970).

(d) Must secondary standards be set to prevent *any* adverse effects on "welfare"? Since control costs would have an adverse effect on welfare, shouldn't they be considered in order to ensure that the net overall effect of standards on welfare is positive?

(e) Is it entirely clear that the standards should be the same everywhere in the nation? Why might it be appropriate to have geographical variations in standards?

4. What other available information besides that contained in the criteria document would you want to consider in setting standards? Would you like to know more about how the criteria document was prepared? John Esposito, in his book Vanishing Air 280-387 (1970) (a study produced by Ralph Nader's Center for the Study of Responsive Law) recounts the efforts of the coal industry (coal combustion in power generation is a major source of SO) and certain senators (notably Senator Jennings Randolph of West Virginia) to attack the conclusions in draft versions of the document and to have them eliminated or qualified. Why might government regulatory officials have wished to overemphasize the significance of statistical correlations and downplay possible limitations in data? See Blank, supra. Compare Brookhaven Scientists Apply Caution to Reports of Coal Conversion Deaths, 8 BNA Envir. Rep. Current Develops. 450 (1977), describing government-sponsored research concluding that 21,000 persons die prematurely each year because of fossil-fuel combustion east of the Mississippi River and that a massive switch to coal for electric power generation could increase premature deaths annually by 14,000. Under sharp questioning from Senator Jennings Randolph of West Virginia, who speculated that the conclusions had been "leaked" by nuclear power advocates, the scientists conducting the research asserted that there were "large" and "great" uncertainties involved, and that the actual number of premature deaths could range from 0 to 50,000.

5. Is there a scientifically "correct" method of establishing environmental quality standards? Ordinarily, there is no clear threshold separating "safe" and "harmless" pollution levels from "unsafe" or "harmful" levels; instead, there are in many cases gradations of potential adverse effects whose precise nature and magnitude is clouded in uncertainty. Do the SO critical documents indicate the existence of thresholds for adverse health and environmental effects from SO exposure, or is the dose-response relation continuous?

Even if risk assessment concludes that thresholds exist, there is still the risk management question of social choice as to whether resources should be devoted to avoiding such thresholds and the resulting adverse effects. On the other hand, if there are no thresholds, must the standards be set at zero? If not, how should they be set?

6. Choices among alternative environmental quality standards represent decisions about resource allocation. On the face of it, wouldn't the statutory requirements for setting SO_2 ambient standards appear completely irrational to the economist? She would certainly maintain that standards should be based on an assessment of the costs and benefits of various control measures; more specifically, standards should be set at the point where the marginal benefit (in terms of reduced mortality, illness, materials damage, etc.) from somewhat more stringent standards just equals the marginal costs to society of achieving those standards. Is this an appropriate approach to standard setting? What data would it require? Is such data available? How would we ensure that agencies perform good cost-benefit analyses? Are the problems of performing good cost-benefit analyses any greater than those of practicing good science?

7. Does the preceding discussion persuade you that economic analysis does not represent a very useful approach to setting environmental quality standards? If so, and if science can't tell us the "correct" standard, what alternative criteria for choosing standards would you offer? If there is no single set of correct standard-setting criteria, don't we have to put our faith in a process of decision that is assumed to fairly represent and consider the various values and considerations at stake? Does this suggest that environmental quality standards should be fixed by the legislature? By administrative agencies? By courts?

8. A related institutional issue concerns the geographic pattern of air quality standards and the choice of the political unit to determine such standards. In view of the geographic diversity of population patterns, meterological conditions, resource bases, and control costs, economic analysis would favor (subject to transaction cost constraints) non-uniform ambient standards reflecting geographical variations in the costs and benefits of pollution control. See Krier, Commentary: The Irrational National Air Quality Standards: Macro- and Micro-Mistakes, 22 U.C.L.A.L. Rev. 323 (1974). A related argument for nonuniform controls is that people want "separate facilities" — areas of high development where they are willing to tolerate moderate pollution concentrations on the one hand and areas that are undeveloped and virtually pollution free on the other. See J. H. Dales, Pollution, Property and Prices 88-93 (1968). On the other hand, given the ubiquitous inevitability of human exposure to the atmosphere, might society wish to assure a basic level of healthy air quality everywhere in the nation? The Senate Report on the 1970 Clean Air Amendments asserted that "protection

of health is a national priority," and that standards must accordingly "protect the health of persons regardless of where such persons reside." S. Rep. No. 91-1196, 91st Cong., 2d Sess. 10, 11 (1970).

Even if you are persuaded that the health-related primary standards should be geographically uniform, what about the generally more stringent secondary standards designed to protect against "welfare" losses such as damage to materials and vegetation, impairment of visibility, and other aesthetic losses? Should air quality be as high in Los Angeles as in the Colorado wilderness (or as low in the wilderness as in Los Angeles)? *See* Stewart, Regulation in a Liberal State: The Role of Non-Commodity Values, supra p. 144.

Does Section 116 of the Clean Air Act adequately serve the various interests in environmental diversity by permitting states to adopt ambient standards more stringent than the federal standards? Note that the only potential for diversity afforded by Section 116 is the opportunity for air quality *higher* than that required by the federal standards. It may be worth asking why the law recognizes that states have a legitimate interest in setting higher standards (say to protect health at the price of economic growth), but not a legitimate interest in setting lower standards (say to achieve growth at the price of health). Would it be unreasonable for an economically depressed state to wish to set very low standards (or none at all) in order to attract industry?[10] It might be argued that a system of national standards would make no sense at all if states could set either higher or lower standards. But does this follow? Might not such a system significantly alter the balance of power between polluting and antipolluting interests in a state?

Perhaps these questions suggest that primary and secondary standards should not be uniform, but that they should be established by the federal government because it is best equipped to assess the interdependent needs of the entire nation with respect to air quality, and also most able to avoid parochialism, interstate conflict, and pressures from polluter interests.[11] Geographically variable national standards

---

10. Perhaps the masked rationale for the provision as enacted is that a higher standard in one state will not adversely affect affairs in a neighboring state, while a lower standard would. But is the first half of this statement so clearly correct? It might be erroneous in that a higher standard in State A, for example, could lower the economic well-being of State B. State A may have features unique to it and very attractive to industry (such as a harbor). Industrial location in State A might well result in a spill-over of the benefits to State B — increased employment, growth of firms manufacturing supplies for the industries in State A, and so forth. Stringent standards in State A might cause enterprises within it to look elsewhere for suitable locations. State B would suffer as a result.

11. The Nixon Administration argued that a chief advantage of "uniform nationwide air quality standards" is that they provide "an opportunity to take into account factors that transcend the boundaries of any single state. States

would in theory be responsive to substantial regional variations in the costs of improving air quality and could also secure important national interests in environmental diversity that might be ill-served by relying upon the states to preserve areas of exceptionally high environmental quality.

What *disadvantages* would there be in a system of nonuniform federal ambient standards? What political obstacles would such a scheme encounter? What administrative problems would it create?

Many considerations, then, appear to call for national administration of air quality standards; other considerations (largely of political and administrative feasibility) seem to suggest that such standards should be uniform. Do uniform minimum national air quality standards represent the best balance of competing considerations? For general discussion of the criteria for geographical allocation of environmental policy decisions, see Zerbe, Optimal Environmental Jurisdictions, 4 Ecology L.Q. 193 (1974).

b.   *Judicial Review of Ambient Standards*

In *NRDC v. Train,* 411 F. Supp. 864 (S.D.N.Y. 1976), discussed further below, the court held that the EPA Administrator was statutorily required to promulgate ambient air quality standards for lead, stating that inadequate scientific knowledge was not a sufficient basis for declining to set a NAAQS. A scientific battle ensued over the setting of the standard, requiring several revisions of the lead criteria document on which the standard would be based. In December 1977, EPA finally issued a proposed ambient lead standard of 1.6 micrograms per cubic meter, monthly average. Further controversy postponed final adoption of the proposed standard until February 1979. 44 Fed. Reg. 10,128 (1979). The principal scientific basis of the standard was the prevention of elevated levels of lead in the blood of young children. Excessive lead blood levels can create a risk of brain damage and other adverse health effects. Humans ingest lead from food and other sources, and carry appreciable levels of lead in their blood. Among the matters in controversy were the level of blood lead that should be considered "safe," the pathways by which airborne lead might be absorbed in the body, and the relative contribution of airborne and other sources of lead. An in-

---

cannot be expected to evaluate the total environmental impact of air pollutants, or take it into account in standard setting." Hearings Before the Subcomm. on Air and Water Pollution of the Senate Comm. on Public Works, 91st Cong., 2d Sess., Pt. I, at 134 (1970) (remarks of Robert W. Finch, then Secretary of Health, Education and Welfare). Would not this advantage be preserved even in the case of geographically *variable* national standards?

dustry group challenge to these regulations resulted in the following decision:

LEAD INDUSTRIES ASSOCIATION V. ENVIRONMENTAL PROTECTION AGENCY

647 F.2d 1130 (D.C. Cir. 1980), **cert. denied,** *449 U.S. 1042 (1980)*

J. SKELLY WRIGHT, Chief Judge:
. . . Congress left the formulation of the specific standards to EPA's Administrator. This task presents complex questions of science, law, and social policy under the Act. The record is lengthy — approximately 10,000 pages — and it is highly technical. The Administrator's task required both "a legislative policy determination and an adjudicative resolution of disputed facts." *Mobil Oil Corp. v. FPC,* 483 F.2d 1238, 1257 (D.C. Cir. 1973).

These are conceptually distinct types of decisions, and it is important that we keep this in mind in reviewing the Administrator's decisions. . . . Where factual determinations were necessary the Administrator often had to make decisions in the face of conflicting evidence. . . . In reviewing these conclusions we can examine the record to ascertain whether there is substantial evidence in the record when considered as a whole which supports the Administrator's determinations. . . . [T]he information available may be insufficient to permit fully informed factual determinations. In such instances the Administrator's decisions necessarily had to rest largely on policy judgments. Policy choices of this sort "are not susceptible to the same type of verification or refutation by reference to the record as are [other] factual questions." . . . While we will indeed scrutinize such judgments carefully, we must adopt a different mode of judicial review. . . .

[Petitioners were the Lead Industries Association (LIA), and St. Joe Minerals Corp. (St. Joe).]

The petitioners' first claim is that the Administrator exceeded his authority under the statute by promulgating a primary air quality standard for lead which is more stringent than is necessary to protect the public health because it is designed to protect the public against "subclinical" effects which are not harmful to health. According to petitioners, Congress only authorized the Administrator to set primary air quality standards that are aimed at protecting the public against health effects which are known to be *clearly harmful.* They argue that Congress so limited the Administrator's authority because it was concerned that excessively stringent air quality standards could cause massive economic dislocation.

In developing this argument St. Joe contends that EPA erred by refusing to consider the issues of economic and technological feasibility in setting the air quality standards for lead. St. Joe's claim that the Administrator should have considered these issues is based on the statutory provision directing him to allow an "adequate margin of safety" in setting primary air quality standards. In St. Joe's view, the Administrator must consider the economic impact of the proposed standard on industry and the technological feasibility of compliance by emission sources in determining the appropriate allowance for a margin of safety. St. Joe argues that the Administrator abused his discretion by refusing to consider these factors in determining the appropriate margin of safety for the lead standards, and maintains that the lead air quality standards will have a disastrous economic impact on industrial sources of lead emissions.

This argument is totally without merit. . . .

Where Congress intended the Administrator to be concerned about economic and technological feasibility, it expressly so provided. For example, Section 111 of the Act, 42 U.S.C. §7411, directs the Administrator to consider economic and technological feasibility in establishing standards of performance for new stationary sources of air pollution based on the best available control technology. . . . In contrast, Section 109(b) speaks only of protecting the public health and welfare. . . .

. . . [I]f there is a problem with the economic or technological feasibility of the lead standards, St. Joe, or any other party affected by the standards, must take its case to Congress, the only institution with the authority to remedy the problem.

It may well be that underlying St. Joe's argument is its feeling that Congress could not or should not have intended this result, and that this court should supply relief by grafting a requirement of economic or technological feasibility onto the statute. [The court rejected this contention.]

For its part, LIA maintains that its claim that the Administrator exceeded the bounds of his statutory authority does not depend on the supposition that he is required, or even permitted, to consider economic and technological feasibility in setting air quality standards. LIA contends that, instead, its argument is based on the fact that Congress itself was concerned about the question of the economic feasibility of compliance with air quality standards, a concern which was reflected in the statute it enacted. According to LIA, Congress was mindful of the possibility that air quality standards which are too stringent could cause severe economic dislocation. For this reason it only granted the Administrator authority to adopt air quality standards which are "designed to protect the public from adverse health effects that are clearly harmful[.]" LIA finds support for its interpretation of congressional intent in various portions of the legislative history of the Act. For example, it notes that the Senate Report on the 1970 legislation states that EPA "would be required to set a national *minimum* standard of air quality," S. Rep. No. 91-1196, at 10 (emphasis added), and that Senator Muskie pointed out during the floor debates that "air quality standards which will protect the public must be set as *minimum standards*". . . . 1 Legis. Hist., at 125 (emphasis added). LIA then argues that the Administrator based the lead air quality standards on protecting children from "subclinical" effects of lead exposure which have not been shown to be harmful to health. . . .

Section 109(b) does not specify precisely what Congress had in mind when it directed the Administrator to prescribe air quality standards that are "requisite to protect the public health." The legislative history of the Act does, however, provide some guidance. The Senate Report explains that the goal of the air quality standards must be to ensure that the public is protected from "adverse health effects." S. Rep. No. 91-1196, at 10. And the report is particularly careful to note that especially sensitive persons such as asthmatics and emphysematics are included within the group that must be protected. It is on the interpretation of the phrase "adverse health effects" that the disagreement between LIA and EPA about the limits of the Administrator's statutory authority appears to be based. . . .

We agree that LIA's interpretation of the statute is at odds with Congress' directives to the Administrator. As a preliminary matter, though it denies this, LIA does at times seem to be arguing, along with St. Joe, that the Administrator should have considered economic and technological feasibility in setting the standards, a claim that must be rejected for reasons we have already stated. Be that as it may, it is not immediately clear why LIA expects this court to impose limits on the Administrator's authority which, so far as we can tell, Congress did not. The Senate Report explains that the Administrator is to set standards which ensure that there is "an absence of adverse effects." The Administrator maintains that the lead standards are designed to do just that, a claim we will examine in due course. But LIA would require a further showing — that the effects on which the standards were based are *clearly* harmful or *clearly* adverse. We cannot, however, find the source of this further restriction that LIA would impose on the Administrator's authority. It may be that it reflects LIA's view that the Administrator must show that there is a "medical consensus that [the effects on which the standards were based] are harmful. . . ." If so, LIA is seriously mistaken. This court has previously noted that some uncertainty about the health effects of air pollution is inevitable. And we pointed out that "[a]waiting certainty will often allow for only reactive, not preventive regulat[ory action.]" *Ethyl Corp. v. EPA*, . . . 541 F.2d at 25. Congress apparently shares this view; it specifically directed the Administrator to allow an adequate margin of safety to protect against effects which have not yet been uncovered by research and effects whose medical significance is a matter of disagreement. . . .

HEALTH BASIS FOR THE LEAD STANDARDS

LIA does not question a number of the steps in the Administrator's analysis. It does not disagree with his selection of children between the ages of one and five years as the target population, or the decision to set a standard that would keep 99.5 percent of the children below the maximum safe individual blood lead level. In addition, LIA does not challenge the Administrator's suggestion that the standards should be based on an assumption that non-air sources contribute 12 ug Pb/dl to blood lead levels. LIA does, however, challenge other key elements in the Administrator's analysis.

A.   MAXIMUM SAFE INDIVIDUAL BLOOD LEAD LEVEL

LIA attacks the Administrator's determination that 30 ug Pb/dl should be considered the maximum safe individual blood lead level for children, maintaining that there is no evidence in the record indicating that children suffer any health effects that can be considered adverse at this blood lead level. [The court then discussed the record in detail.]

Our conclusion that there is ample support for the Administrator's determination that EP [a body chemical whose presence indicates possible impairment of hemoglobin synthesis] elevation at 30 ug Pb/dl is the first adverse health effect that children experience as a result of lead exposure is, of course, sufficient to sustain his selection of 30 ug Pb/dl as the maximum safe individual blood lead level. Given this, we cannot say that his further determination that a maximum safe individual blood lead level of 30 ug Pb/dl would in addition provide protection against the more serious adverse health effects of lead exposure was irrational.

To be sure, the Administrator's conclusions were not unchallenged; both LIA and the Administrator are able to point to an impressive array of experts supporting each of their respective positions. However, disagreement among the experts is inevitable when the issues involved are at the "very frontiers of scientific knowledge," and such disagreement does not preclude us from finding that the Administrator's decisions are adequately supported by the evidence in the record. It may be that LIA expects this court to conclude that LIA's experts are right, and the experts whose testimony supports the Administrator are wrong. If so, LIA has seriously misconceived our role as a reviewing court. . . .

B.   MARGIN OF SAFETY

Both LIA and St. Joe argue that the Administrator erred by including multiple allowances for margins of safety in his calculation of the lead standards. Petitioners note that the statute directs the Administrator to allow an "adequate margin of safety" in setting primary air quality standards, and they maintain that as a matter of statutory construction the Administrator may not interpret "margin" of safety to mean "margins" of safety. In petitioners' view, the Administrator in fact did just this insofar as he made allowances for margins of safety at several points in his analysis. They argue that margin of safety allowances were reflected in the choice of the maximum safe individual blood lead level for children, in the decision to place 99.5 percent of the target population group below that blood lead level, in the selection of an air-lead/blood-lead ratio at 1:2, and in the Administrator's estimate of the contribution to blood lead levels that should be attributed to non-air sources. The net result of these multiple allowances for margins of safety, petitioners contend, was a standard far more stringent than is necessary to protect the public health. St. Joe suggests that EPA should have adopted an approach which required decisions on:

(1)   The maximum level of lead in air which is protective of health; i.e., a threshold beyond which the public health is not protected; and

(2)   An adequate margin of safety by which the level which is protective of health must be reduced. . . .

We agree with the Administrator that nothing in the statutory scheme or the legislative history requires him to adopt the margin of safety approach suggested by St. Joe. Adding the margin of safety at the end of the analysis is one approach, but it is not the only possible method. Indeed, the Administrator considered this approach but decided against it because of complications raised by the multiple sources of lead exposure. . . .

We also agree with the Administrator's suggestion that petitioners have ignored the distinction between scientific judgments based on the available evidence and allowances for margins of safety. In every instance in which the Administrator's judgment on a particular issue differed from petitioners' they attribute his decision to an allowance for a margin of safety. To be sure, there is no bright line that divides these two types of decisions, but they are nonetheless conceptually distinct. . . .

[The court rejected a variety of additional substantive and procedural objections to EPA's decision, and upheld the new lead standard in full.]

NOTES AND QUESTIONS

1. Would the standards for sulfur oxides that you adopted pass muster under the standard of review applied in *Lead Industries?*

2. In *Lead Industries,* industry directed much of its fire to EPA's conclusions regarding the relation between air-lead and blood-lead levels. The court disavowed both responsibility and authority for judging the merits of competing expert views. How can this be avoided in a review of whether agency action is arbitrary or capricious? Does it follow that as long as an administrator can produce a shred of expert testimony to support his or her findings, those findings will be upheld by a court? Is the approach taken by the court in *Lead Industries* consistent with the *Benzene* and *Asbestos* decisions, supra, pp. 25, 116?

3. In *Hercules, Inc. v. EPA*, 598 F.2d 91 (D.C. Cir. 1978), upon which the *Lead Industries* court relied, industry representatives challenged regulations under the Clean Water Act limiting discharges of toxaphene and endrin, two toxic chemicals, in effluent discharges. The court, in explaining its standards of review, stated that rulemaking based on findings at "the frontiers of scientific knowledge" would be entitled to deference because they rest "to a greater extent on policy judgments." Id. at 106. What does this mean? Should an administrative decision be subject to lesser scrutiny because it is characterized as a policy judgment? Which is a court better equipped to review and evaluate, an agency's resolution of technical issues or its policy judgments? Is it possible in principle to distinguish risk assessment (the quantification of risk) and risk management (decision about whether and how to reduce risk)? In practice?

4. Decisions on regulatory risks must confront two opposing types of errors. On the one hand, decisionmakers may decide that a risk is serious and commit substantial societal resources to reducing it, only to find out later that the risk was far less serious than originally thought. This is the problem of false positives. On the other hand, decisionmakers may decide that a risk is not serious enough to regulate, only to find out later that the risk was in fact serious and that serious harms have been caused as a result of the failure to regulate. This is the problem of false negatives. In general, should we be more concerned about false positives or false negatives? Some have urged recognition of a "prevention principle " under which steps should always be taken to eliminate

or reduce potential but unproven risks of significant environmental or
health harm. Is this a sensible rule of thumb? Should the probability as
well as the magnitude of potential harm be taken into account? The
costs of prevention? The presence of other, better-established risks?
The costs of gathering more information?

5. The fact that an agency decision may turn on highly technical
issues does not necessarily lead to the conclusion that the decision
should be left to "experts." Judge Oakes, for one, has argued that one
of the advantages of judicial review of the reasonableness of such decisions is that agencies are forced to present their decisions in terms
lay people can understand. See Oakes, Substantive Judicial Review in
Environmental Law, 7 Envtl. L. Rep. 50029 (1977). Why is it important
for lay people to be able to understand the reasons for agency action?
What governmental interests are served by a public informed on the
basis for government decisionmaking? See generally Morgan, The Constitutional Right to Know Why, 17 Harv. C.R.-C.L.L. Rev. 297 (1982).

2. LISTING OF AIR POLLUTANTS

Congress recognized in 1970 that scientific information was not
adequate to identify all air pollutants that pose a threat to human
health and welfare. Therefore, in Section 108 of the Clean Air Act
Amendments, Congress established a process whereby EPA would periodically review and update the list of air pollutants for which NAAQSs
were required.

NRDC v. TRAIN

411 F. Supp. 864 (S.D.N.Y. 1976)

STEWART, District Judge:
Natural Resources Defense Council ("NRDC") and other named
plaintiffs bring this action against the Environmental Protection
Agency ("EPA") and its administrator Russell Train for failure to list
lead as a pollutant under §108 of the Clean Air Act of 1970. . . .
     . . . Section 108 provides that the Administrator shall publish,
and from time to time revise, a list including each air pollutant

(A) which in his judgment has an adverse effect on public
health or welfare;
(B) the presence of which in the ambient air results from numerous or diverse mobile or stationary sources; and
(C) for which . . . he plans to issue air quality criteria under
this section.

Plaintiffs contend that the statutory language, legislative history and purpose, as well as current administrative interpretation of the 1970 Clean Air Act, all militate in favor of finding that the Administrator's function to list pollutants under §108 is mandatory, once it is determined by the Administrator that a pollutant "has an adverse effect on public health and welfare" and comes from the requisite numerous or diverse sources. Defendants concede in this action that lead comes from the requisite sources and that the Administrator has found lead to have the required "adverse effect." Defendants argue, however, that the language of §108(a)(1)(C) "for which . . . [the Administrator] plans to issue air quality criteria" is a separate and third criterion to be met before §108 requires placing a pollutant on the list. This construction of §108(a) leaves the initial decision to list a pollutant within the sole discretion of the Administrator. Defendants contend such discretion is required because the Administrator must choose between alternative remedies provided in various sections of the Act and that any decisions to utilize the remedies provided by §§108-110 "involves complex considerations." . . .

Congress, in passing the Clean Air Act of 1970, was concerned with the delays and inefficiencies incurred in implementing the 1963 and 1967 air pollution acts. . . . Thus, in the language of the 1970 Act, Congress attempts to achieve cleaner air by specifying procedures and timetables to be followed, all of which are reflective of Congress' determination "to speed up, expand, and intensify the war against air pollution in the United States." H.R. Rep. 91-1146, 91st Cong., 2d Sess. 5 (1970), U.S. Code Cong. & Admin. News, p. 5356. . . .

We think the reasonable reading of the disputed language in §108 is that the Administrator must include on the initial list to be issued 30 days after December 31, 1970, all those pollutants "for which air quality criteria had not been issued before [that date]" but which pollutants he has already found in his judgment to have an adverse effect on public health or welfare and to have come from the requisite sources. The Senate Committee Report supports our reading of the language. The Report states that §108 requires the initial list to "include all those pollution agents which have, or can be expected to have, an adverse effect on health and welfare and which are emitted from widely distributed mobile and stationary sources, and all those for which air quality criteria are planned." S. Rep. No. 91-1196, 91st Cong., 2d Sess. 54 (1970). It is to the initial list alone that the phrase "but for which he plans to issue air quality criteria" is directed; the phrase cannot mean that the Administrator need not list pollutants which meet the two requisites clearly set forth in the section. Again, that construction would comport with neither the clear legislative intent to have strict mandatory health procedures in effect by mid-1976 nor the language of the Act itself. While the Administrator is provided with much discretion to make the threshold determination of whether a pollutant has "an adverse effect on health," after that decision is made, and after it is determined that a pollutant comes from the necessary sources, there is no discretion provided by the statute not to list the pollutant. We think that Congress intended to trigger the elaborate procedures of §§108-110 whenever the above two factors were found to exist. . . .

Finally, we turn to an additional argument of defendants that the Administrator needs discretion not to list lead under §108 because the data which would be necessary to support an ambient air standard for lead is arguably lacking. . . . We do not think that the potential lack of data would have been an appropriate consideration prior to listing a pollutant under §108 in any event. Under the statutory scheme, the listing of a pollutant is no more than a threshold to the remedial provisions. . . . The statute appears to assume that, for each pollutant which must be listed, criteria and a national standard can be established. A twelve month period is provided for that purpose. However, Congress cannot require the impossible. It may be that a pollutant exists which meets the listing requirements of §108 but for which no criteria or national standard is possible. That issue is not before this court. . . .

NOTES AND QUESTIONS

1. In the 1977 Amendments to the Clean Air Act, Congress changed §108(a)(1)(A) to provide that criteria be issued for pollutants contributing to air pollution "which may reasonably be anticipated to endanger public health or welfare." How does this change the threshold for listing? Does it affect the setting of standards under §109?

2. Section 109(c) of the Act, added by the 1977 Amendments, requires the EPA Administrator to undertake every five years a "thorough review" of existing criteria and standards and "make" such revisions in such criteria and standards and promulgate such new standards as may be appropriate in accordance with [§§108 and 109(b)]. The section also provides that an independent scientific review committee is to assist in such review.

In recent years proposals have been made to adopt more restrictive standards for SO, based on studies of experts on exercising asthmatics, and photochemical oxidants, but the Administrator has declined to do so. Currently, there is much concern about the health effects of particulates; more recent studies have suggested that the concentrations permitted under existing standards might be responsible for up to 50,000 premature deaths annually from lung, cardiovascular, and other diseases. However, Professor James H. Ware, Dean of Academic Affairs at the Harvard School of Public Health, recently testified before Congress that at least five more years of research would be needed to understand the health effects of particulate matter at current concentrations. Even then it would be difficult to establish a threshold to serve as a basis for standard setting; current studies indicate adverse effects across a wide range of concentrations. Professor Ware stated that it will therefore be "difficult if not impossible to establish a standard that clearly protects human health with an adequate margin of safety and is supported scientifically." Particulate matter is emitted from diesel buses and trucks, industrial and electric utility power plants, woodburning, mining, and construction activities. A restrictive standard on traditional industrial sources could paralyze economic activity. He noted that much particulate emissions from widespread sources, such as woodburning and construction activity, have not traditionally been subject to regulation, and stated that EPA's tendency to target controls on industrial emissions "dissipates precious resources on measures that will have relatively little air quality benefit." Clean Air Report, August 12, 1993, pp. 7-8.

Suppose that the Administrator decides to tighten the ambient air quality standard for particulate matter. Is this decision subject to judicial review? If so, under what standard of review? That applied by the court in *Lead Industries? NRDC v. Train?* A different standard?

3. What if EPA were to determine that a widespread pollutant endangered public health or welfare and was not amenable to the NAAQS strategy of the Clean Air Act, but could be controlled adequately through other regulatory strategies? Consider, for example, deposition of various acid sulfur and nitrogen particles formed by atmospheric interactions of SO emissions and NO emissions. Isn't EPA the most knowledgeable institution for designing air pollution regulatory policy? Why would Congress try to commit EPA to the NAAQS approach for all widespread air pollutants? Listing a pollutant under section 108 triggers an elaborate and protracted process of setting ambient standards under section 109 and then revising SIPs under §110, identifying the various emission sources, determining the reductions necessary to achieve the ambient standards, and devising and implementing source controls in order to achieve the necessary reductions. EPA had argued that this elaborate process would be counterproductive in the case of lead, because a combination of controls on lead in gasoline under section 202[12] and technology-based stationary source emission limitations under section 111 would reduce lead pollution more quickly and effectively. Nonetheless, the district court's decision was affirmed in *NRDC v. Train*, 545 F.2d 320, 328 (2d Cir. 1976), holding that EPA does not have discretion to list only those pollutants for which it thinks the NAAQSs-SIP process is the appropriate regulatory

---

12. During the 1980s EPA by regulation eliminated almost all lead additives in gasoline.

policy. "Congress sought to eliminate, not perpetuate, opportunity for administrative foot-dragging." Id. How might a requirement of using the NAAQS approach affect EPA's incentives for listing new pollutants? How should responsibility be allocated among legislative, administrative, and judicial institutions for regulating air pollution?

PROBLEM: LISTING OF GREENHOUSE GASES

You have just been hired by the Clean Air Coalition (CAC), a consortium of leading national environmental organizations. CAC is considering strategies to force the United States to take aggressive action to reduce greenhouse gas emissions so as to forestall human-induced climate change. Greenhouse gases (GHGs) — principally CO_2, methane, the CFCs, nitrous oxides, and low-level ozone and its precursors, HC and NO — are emitted by a great variety of industrial and agricultural services including fossil fuel combustion, deforestation, fertilizer use, rice growing, and cattle farming. When they mix in the middle atmosphere — miles above the earth's surface — they trap reradiation of solar energy from the Earth, creating a warming effect. The increases in GHGs from human activities are predicted to cause increases in global temperature and other changes in global climate, although no statistically significant correlation between increases in GHGs and global temperature trends has yet been established. The extent and rapidity of warming is fiercely debated. There are major uncertainties created by limitations in climate change models, atmospheric interactions among gases, and the effects of the oceans. Chlorofluorocarbons are already being phased out, so the major concern is other greenhouse gases such as carbon dioxide and methane.

- Is EPA required under §108 to list carbon dioxide and methane?
- From the perspective of the CAC, what are the advantages and disadvantages of using the NAAQS approach to address the threat of global climate change?
- Return to the questions following *NRDC v. Train*. Does this problem alter your answers to those questions?

3. STATE IMPLEMENTATION PLANS

The overriding requirement of the Clean Air Act, sections 109-110, is achievement of the federal ambient standards within specified deadlines. As *Lead Industries* makes clear, the section 109 ambient standards are supposedly established without regard to the costs or technological feasibility of achieving them. In areas where concentrations of pollutants exceed ambient standards, achievement of those standards may require section 110 state implementation plan (SIP) controls on existing sources that are not technologically or economically feasible.[13] In contrast to the section 111 New Source Performance Standard (NSPS) approach, basing controls on technological and economic feasibility, sections 109 and 110 utilize the pressure of deadlines to meet health-based standards in order to force adoption and development of control technology.

The steps involved in creating a SIP to achieve ambient standards in areas where they are presently exceeded are (1) determining the extent to which ambient standards are presently exceeded; (2) determining the existing level of emissions from sources in the regions; (3) calculating the degree of reduction in existing emissions that would be required to reduce ambient concentrations to the levels permitted by the ambient standards; and (4) allocating the necessary reductions in emissions among existing sources.

Each of these stages in the SIP design process involves controversial issues that have spawned litigation. Data on existing concentrations are often sparse. The determination of emissions reductions necessary to achieve ambient standards involves technical debate about appropriate diffusion modelling, which also bears on the geographical allocation of emission reduction burdens among various sources. See, e.g., *NRDC v. EPA*, 478 F.2d 875 (1st Cir. 1973); *Texas v. EPA*, 499 F.2d 289 (5th Cir. 1974). In *Cleveland Electric Illuminating Co. v. EPA*, 572 F.2d 1150 (6th Cir. 1978), the court considered 23 petitions by 32 companies and an intervention by the State of Ohio challenging EPA's Real-Time Air-Quality-Simulation Model (RAM) and the procedures by which it was produced. EPA used the RAM to produce a federal implementation plan for Ohio following the state's failure to adopt an adequate SIP. Under a straight rollback model, the ratio between the maximum ambient concentration permitted by NAAQS and the maximum concentration in areas of violation is calculated. All sources must then reduce new emissions by that proportion. When violations are not widespread but occur in only one or a few parts of a region, this model may result in overcontrol because some sources' existing emissions are not contributing to the violation. The RAM model used diffusion modelling to predict how emissions from sources or groups of sources would affect ambient concentrations, used the model to pinpoint responsibility for NAAQS violations on particular sources or groups of

---

13. Unless existing sources are sufficiently controlled to make ambient air quality somewhat better than required by the ambient standards, there would appear to be no possibility for construction of new sources, because emissions from such sources (even if they meet rigorous New Source Performance Standards, Section 111) would create an increase in ambient concentrations in excess of that permitted by the statutory scheme.

sources, and target reduction requirements on such sources. The sources thus targeted for control attacked the validity of the model, which attempted to take account of 1000 major sources and 2000 "area" groups of sources in Ohio. Despite the fact that the RAM model's predictions of ambient concentrations often varied significantly from actual measured concentrations, the court upheld EPA's reliance on the model. A further complication is presented by the fact that the correlation between ambient concentrations of some gases and emissions is not linear. For instance, a 50 percent reduction in emissions may reduce ambient concentrations by less or more than 50 percent, depending on interactions with other emissions, weather patterns, and so forth. Transboundary movements of pollutants between regions create still further complications. This is true, for example, of photochemical oxidant and its precursors, NO_x and HC.

The allocation of abatement burdens will also involve social and economic judgments that the Act leaves to the discretion of the states in the first instance. Frequently a SIP (as drafted by a state or revised by EPA) will impose controls on a given source that the source regards as (a) unduly burdensome in proportion to limitations imposed on others or (b) technologically or economically infeasible. If the SIP is state-drafted, then either type of claim may be presented to state environmental authorities and pursued in the state courts. But can either type of claim afford grounds for relief by EPA or the federal courts? This substantive question, which arises out of the mixed federal-state character of the scheme, is related to procedural issues of timing. Section 307 of the Clean Air Act requires that petitions for federal court review of EPA's approval or promulgation of a SIP must be filed within 30 days of EPA's action "or after such date if such petition is based solely on grounds arising after such 30th day." This provision creates a dilemma for sources wishing to challenge a SIP provision as infeasible or unduly burdensome. If a challenge is brought within the 30-day period, the date for actual compliance with the SIP's limitation lies several years in the future; this time horizon (with the attendant possibility that new control technologies may become available or that economic conditions will change) makes it difficult for the source to establish compelling claims of hardship. On the other hand, should a source defer its hardship claim until a later date (perhaps in defense of a government action to enforce SIP emission limitations), it runs the risk of a ruling that the grounds of its hardship claim were foreseeable at the time of the SIP's approval, and that the claim is therefore barred by the 30-day provision in Section 307. See *Getty Oil Co. (Eastern Operations) v. Ruckelshaus*, 467 F.2d 349 (3d Cir. 1972), *cert. denied*, 409 U.S. 1125 (1973). This procedural requirement, which was copied from similar provisions in wartime price control statutes, was calculated to prevent long, drawn-out challenges to SIP implementation and (perhaps) to

diminish their chance of success. For discussion of this and related issues, see Luneberg & Roselle, Judicial Review Under the Clean Air
Amendments of 1970, 15 B.C. Ind. & Com. L. Rev. 667 (1974).

The following Supreme Court decision resolved some of these
questions about the scope of potential escapes from the technology-
forcing logic of the ambient standards and their implementation.

UNION ELECTRIC COMPANY V. ENVIRONMENTAL PROTECTION AGENCY

427 U.S. 246 (1976)

Mr. Justice MARSHALL delivered the opinion of the Court.

[In accordance with the requirements of the Clean Air Act, Missouri adopted a SIP for the Metropolitan St. Louis Region imposing
controls on SO_2 emissions. The SIP was approved by EPA. It required
reductions in SO_2 emissions from three of Union's coal-fired electric
power plants. Union did not seek review of EPA's approval of the SIP
within 30 days, as provided under §307(b)(1). Instead it obtained variances from Missouri, which later expired. It then sought review of
EPA's approval of the SIP, contending that it was invalid for two reasons: First, the reductions required of Union were not technologically
or economically feasible; if enforced, Union would be required to shut
down its plants and curtail electric service. Second, federal ambient
standards could be met through controls less stringent than those contained in the SIP. The Court rejected both contentions.]

The Administrator's position is that he had no power whatsoever
to reject a state implementation plan on the ground that it is economically or technologically infeasible. . . . After surveying the relevant
provisions of the Clean Air Act Amendments of 1970 and their legislative history, we agree that Congress intended claims of economic and
technological infeasibility to be wholly foreign to the Administrator's
consideration of a state implementation plan.

. . . [T]he 1970 Amendments to the Clean Air Act were a drastic
remedy to what was perceived as a serious and otherwise uncheckable
problem of air pollution. The Amendments place the primary responsibility for formulating pollution control strategies on the States, but
nonetheless subject the States to strict minimum compliance requirements. These requirements are of a "technology-forcing character,"
Train v. NRDC, 421 U.S., at 91, and are expressly designed to force
regulated sources to develop pollution control devices that might at the
time appear to be economically or technologically infeasible.

This approach is apparent on the face of §110 (a)(2). The provision sets out eight criteria that an implementation plan must satisfy,

and provides that if these criteria are met and if the plan was adopted after reasonable notice and hearing, the Administrator "shall approve" the proposed state plan. The mandatory "shall" makes it quite clear that the Administrator is not to be concerned with factors other than those specified. . . . [N]one of the eight factors appears to permit consideration of technological or economic infeasibility. . . .

Section 110(a)(2)(A)'s three-year deadline for achieving primary air quality standards is central to the Amendments' regulatory scheme and, as both the language and the legislative history of the requirement make clear, it leaves no room for claims of technological or economic infeasibility. . . .

. . . As Senator Muskie, manager of the Senate bill, explained to his chamber:

> The first responsibility of Congress is not the making of technological or economic judgments — or even to be limited by what is or appears to be technologically or economically feasible. Our responsibility is to establish what the public interest requires to protect the health of persons. This may mean that people and industries will be asked to do what seems to be impossible at the present time. 116 Cong. Rec. 32901-32902 (1970).

See also id., at 32919 (remarks of Sen. Cooper); 33115 (remarks of Sen. Prouty). This position reflected that of the Senate committee:

> In the Committee discussions, considerable concern was expressed regarding the use of the concept of technical feasibility as the basis of ambient air standards. The Committee determined that (1) the health of the people is more important than the question of whether the early achievement of ambient air quality standards protective of health is technically feasible; and (2) the growth of pollution loads in many areas even with application of available technology, would still be deleterious to public health.
>
> Therefore, the Committee determined that existing sources of pollutants either should meet the standard of the law or be closed down. . . ."
> S. Rep. No. 1196, 91st Cong., 2d Sess., 2-3 (1970).

[The Court then addressed Union's second contention: that EPA lacks authority to approve a SIP that imposes infeasible controls when such controls are not necessary to meet the federal ambient standards.]

Section 116 of the Clean Air Act, as added, 84 Stat. 1689, 42 U.S.C. 1857d-1, provides that the States may adopt emission standards stricter than the national standards. *Amici* argue that such standards must be adopted and enforced independently of the EPA-approved state implementation plan. This construction of §§110 and 116, however, would not only require the Administrator to expend considerable time and energy determining whether a state plan was precisely tailored to meet the federal standards; but would simultaneously require States desiring stricter standards to enact and enforce two sets of emission standards, one federally approved plan and one stricter state plan. We find no basis in the Amendments for visiting such wasteful burdens upon the States and the Administrator, and so we reject the argument of *amici*.

We read the "as may be necessary" requirement of §110(a)(2)(B) to demand only that the implementation plan submitted by the State meet the "minimum conditions" of the Amendments. . . . Beyond that, if a State makes the legislative determination that it desires a particular air quality by a certain date and that it is willing to force technology to attain it — or lose a certain industry if attainment is not possible — such a determination is fully consistent with the structure and purpose of the Amendments, and §110(a)(2)(B) provides no basis for the EPA Administrator to object to the determination on the ground of infeasibility. . . .

Perhaps the most important forum for consideration of claims of economic and technological infeasibility is before the state agency formulating the implementation plan. So long as the national standards are met, the State may select whatever mix of control devices it desires, . . . and industries with particular economic or technological problems may seek special treatment in the plan itself. . . . Moreover, if the industry is not exempted from, or accommodated by, the original plan, it may obtain a variance, as petitioner did in this case; and the variance, if granted after notice and a hearing, may be submitted to the EPA as a revision of the plan, §110(a)(3)(A). . . . Lastly, an industry denied an exemption from the implementation plan, or denied a subsequent variance, may be able to take its claims of economic or technological infeasibility to the state courts. . . .

Even if the State does not intervene on behalf of an emission source, technological and economic factors may be considered in at least one other circumstance. When a source is found to be in violation of the state implementation plan, the Administrator may, after a conference with the operator, issue a compliance order rather than seek civil or criminal enforcement. Such an order must specify a "reasonable" time for compliance with the relevant standard, taking into account the seriousness of the violation and "any good faith efforts to comply with applicable requirements." §113(a)(4) of the Clean Air Act, as added. . . . Claims of technological or economic infeasibility, the Administrator agrees, are relevant to fashioning an appropriate compliance order under §113(a)(4). Brief for Respondent 36 n.34.[14]

---

14. . . . Some courts have suggested that in criminal or civil enforcement proceedings the violator may in certain circumstances raise a defense of economic or technological infeasibility. See *Buckeye Power, Inc. v. EPA*, 481 F.2d 162, 173 (6th Cir. 1973); *Indiana & Michigan Electric Co. v. EPA*, 509 F.2d 839, 847 (7th Cir. 1975). We do not address this question here.

Mr. Justice POWELL, with whom The Chief Justice joins, concurring.

I join the opinion of the Court because the statutory scheme and the legislative history, thoroughly described in the Court's opinion, demonstrate irrefutably that Congress did not intend to permit the Administrator of the Environmental Protection Agency to reject a proposed state implementation plan on the grounds of economic or technological infeasibility.

Environmental concerns, long neglected, merit high priority, and Congress properly has made protection of the public health its paramount consideration. . . . But the shutdown of an urban area's electrical service could have an even more serious impact on the health of the public than that created by a decline in ambient air quality. The result apparently required by this legislation in its present form could sacrifice the well-being of a large metropolitan area through the imposition of inflexible demands that may be technologically impossible to meet and indeed may no longer even be necessary to the attainment of the goal of clean air.

I believe that Congress, if fully aware of this draconian possibility, would strike a different balance.

NOTES AND QUESTIONS

1. Does the operation of §110 change your view as to what pollutants should be listed under §108? What standards should be set under §109?

2. Was Union Electric's petition for review of EPA's approval of the SIP timely? See §307(b)(1) of the Act.

3. While the Court was confident that the technological infeasibility of SIP requirements is not a valid basis for challenging EPA approval of an SIP, several courts of appeals had previously concluded otherwise. See, e.g., *Buckeye Power Inc. v. EPA*, 481 F.2d 162 (6th Cir. 1973). Does the *Union Electric* rationale rule out infeasibility as a federal defense to enforcement of a particular emission limitation contained in a SIP? See *Friends of the Earth v. Potomac Electric Power Co.*, 419 F. Supp. 528 (D.D.C. 1976). Is the reasoning of the *Boomer* case, supra, p. 193, of any relevance in this context? If infeasibility were successfully asserted as a defense to enforcement of a given limitation, the SIP would presumably have to be redrawn to impose additional controls on other sources of the same pollutant, in order to ensure that total emissions would not increase and result in a violation of the ambient standards.

Suppose that in a given region there are five sources of SO_2 — A, B, C, D, E — with daily SO_2 emissions of 100, 50, 30, 10 and 10 tons respectively. Sources B and D are newer and have extensive pollution abatement equipment. Source A provides many jobs in the area, but is teetering on the edge of bankruptcy. The relevant state adopts a SIP halving emissions from each source. What are the implications of permitting source A to defend against an enforcement action on the ground that it is not technologically or economically feasible for it to reduce its emissions to 50 tons per day? Should the other potentially affected sources be permitted to intervene in the enforcement proceeding to contest the defending source's claim of infeasibility?

On the other hand, if the sole route for challenging SIP provisions is a proceeding to review the EPA's approval or promulgation of the SIP itself, the 30-day time limit in §307(b)(1) may make it difficult for a source to establish the infeasibility of controls that will only be enforced at some point in the future. See generally, Currie, Judicial Review Under Federal Pollution Laws, 62 Iowa L. Rev. 1221, 1254-1260 (1977).

Note that *Union Electric* arose in the context of an EPA review of a state SIP. When EPA issues a federal implementation plan for a region because of the state's failure to prepare an adequate SIP, courts have sometimes required EPA to consider technological feasibility in setting the control requirements for a particular facility. See, e.g., *Bunker Hill Co. v. EPA*, 572 F.2d 1286 (9th Cir. 1977).

4. Is the decisionmaking process for allocating and, if necessary, adjusting the emissions reductions required by §§109 and 110 well crafted to achieve the NAAQSs expeditiously and cost effectively? Is it likely that controls requiring a shutdown of a city's principal source of power would ever be enforced? What should be done when the "technology forcing" logic of the Act has not achieved its intended result and it is not technologically feasible for an important source, such as a power plant, to meet SIP requirements? You should review the various provisions for extensions of the statutory deadlines for achieving the primary federal standards contained in §§110(f) and (g). Note that §110(f) requires considerable foresight by state governors, while §110(g) includes a number of stringent conditions and limitations. However, *Train v. NRDC*, 421 U.S. 60 (1975), read the Act to authorize the grant by states of variances under SIPs without compliance with the statutory requirements for EPA approval of deadline extensions in cases where the variance would not affect achievement of the statutory deadlines. The decision effectively establishes a category of minor variances, not involving postponement of achievement of ambient standards, and a category of major variances that do involve postponement and are subject to stringent substantive limitations and procedural safeguards. See W. Rodgers, Environmental Law §3.6 (1986). Do these opportunities for extensions and variances deal adequately with the problem of

infeasibility? What alternative approaches might Congress have used to achieve the NAAQSs more quickly and effectively? What are the drawbacks to these approaches?

5. The effect of requiring electric utility generating plants to meet SIP requirements for SO_2 within the statutory time deadlines has been to force widespread adoption of a "scrubber," or flue gas desulphurization (FGD), control technology that is costly and produces considerable quantities of sludge that creates waste disposal problems. Basic process changes, such as fluidized bed combustion, that would reduce the generation of SO_2 emissions, were still a long way from commercial application at the time that SIPs were first being implemented. How do these considerations affect your assessment of the deadline strategy in the Act? What alternative regulatory approaches would avoid large investments in capital equipment that might become obsolete with advances in technology?

6. When a single source, such as a copper smelter or fossil-fuel electric generating plant is the dominant source of emissions in a given region, may a SIP use "intermittent controls" to achieve NAAQSs? Intermittent controls consist of temporary operational curtailments or fuel switching during seasons or days when adverse weather conditions would otherwise result in violation of ambient standards. During more favorable weather conditions, the plant operates at full capacity without controls. *Kennecott Copper Corp. v. Train,* 526 F.2d 1149 (9th Cir. 1975), *cert. denied,* 425 U.S. 935 (1976), upheld an EPA interpretation requiring continuous emission controls; only if such controls were economically infeasible would intermittent controls be used. As the costs and burdens of compliance with the national standards for ozone have escalated sharply in recent years, there has been renewed interest in seasonal fuel switching and other forms of intermittent controls that secure greater emissions reductions when weather conditions would otherwise result in ambient violations. What are the justifications for requiring continuous emission controls on days or for seasons when they are not necessary to ensure achievement of the ambient standards? Is such a requirement consistent with the logic of §§109 and 110?

7. *Epilogue.* As *Union Electric* indicates, the dovetailing of federal-state responsibilities in SIP preparation, revision, and enforcement creates dilemmas for pollution sources that have applied to state authorities for a variance but are nonetheless subject to federal enforcement action until a valid variance is granted. Is the allocation of decisionmaking authority established by the Act sensible?[15] Consider the following.

---

15. For general discussion of state/federal issues in enforcement and the granting of variances under the Act, see Currie, Federal Air Quality Standards and Their Implementation, 1976 Am. B. Found. Res. J. 365, 380-390, 398-407.

After the Supreme Court's *Union Electric* decision, the EPA Regional Administrator wrote to the chairman of the Missouri Air Quality Commission, following up on the Supreme Court's suggestion that the state was the proper forum for consideration of claims of technological and economic infeasibility. EPA advised that it would have no objection to the relaxation of the SO_2 controls in the challenged SIP, provided that the SIP would still provide for attainment of the NAAQS. On Union Electric's petition, the Commission agreed to consider variances for two of the three Union Electric plants in violation of the SIP, but failed to act. When EPA indicated that it would begin enforcement proceedings without waiting for the decision of the Missouri Commission on the company's variance requests, Union Electric sued to enjoin EPA from enforcing the SIP. The district court granted the requested injunction under its general equitable powers to prevent irreparable harm to the utility, holding that procedural due process required EPA to await completion of the variance proceeding. While the district court's judgment was on appeal to the Eighth Circuit, the Missouri Commission granted the requested variances to Union Electric.

The court of appeals, in *Union Electric Co. v. EPA,* 593 F.2d 299 (8th Cir.), *cert. denied,* 444 U.S. 839 (1979), reversed the injunction. Although reserving the question of whether technological or economic infeasibility could be a defense to enforcement, it held that federal enforcement could not be delayed because a variance request was pending before a state board. But this ruling had no real impact on Union Electric; since the required variances had since been granted, no shutdown resulted.

In *General Motors v. United States,* 496 U.S. 530 (1990), the Massachusetts SIP, as approved by EPA, required a GM automotive plant to reduce its VOC emissions from its painting operations to a specified level by the end of 1985. In September 1984, GM sought from Massachusetts a postponement of the 1985 deadline to give it more time to install additional controls on its existing painting lines. In June 1985, GM sought an extension until 1987 in order to install an entirely new painting process. At the end of 1985, Massachusetts approved the extension and submitted it to EPA as a SIP amendment, one day before the compliance deadline in the original SIP. In 1987, when the SIP amendment was still pending before it, EPA instituted an action for civil penalties against GM for failing to achieve the reductions by the 1985 deadline as required by the original SIP. GM defended on the grounds (1) that EPA was required to approve the proposed SIP revisions within 4 months (the time required by §110(a)(3) for EPA approval of initial SIP submissions) or a reasonable time, and that EPA had failed to do so, and (2) that EPA should therefore be barred from assessing penalties for violations of a SIP occurring after the time EPA should have acted on a SIP revision that would have eliminated the violation. The Supreme Court rejected these contentions, finding that the 4-month deadline in §110(a)(3) for EPA action on initial SIP submissions did not apply to SIP revisions, and that no other provision in the Act required EPA to act on SIP revisions within a given time period. It did find that EPA was subject to the general provision in the federal Administrative Procedure Act, 5 U.S.C. §555(b), requiring agencies to conclude matters "within a reasonable time." Without deciding whether the delay in this case violated this APA requirement — a claim not raised by GM — the Court concluded that even if EPA had violated the APA, nothing in the Clean Air Act barred EPA from enforcing the original SIP. The enforcement provisions of §113(b)(2) authorize EPA enforcement of the requirements of an "applicable implementation plan." Until the SIP revision was approved by EPA, the original SIP remained the applicable implementation plan, and was therefore enforceable, notwithstanding even unreasonable delay by EPA. GM's remedy was an APA action to compel agency action unreasonably delayed, or an application to the sanctioning court pursuant to §113(b) of the Clean Air Act to reduce otherwise applicable civil penalties on the ground that EPA's delay had prejudiced GM.

For analysis of the decision and the split among the circuits that led up to it, see Comment, *General Motors v. United States:* A Boon to Clean Air Act Enforcement, 20 Env. L. Rep. 10471 (1990). Congress considered the issue presented in *GM* in the 1990 Amendments, but failed to agree on a legislative resolution.

C.   TECHNOLOGY-BASED APPROACHES

The 1970 Clean Air Amendments were designed by Congress to have major "technology-forcing" incentives. See Bonine, The Evolution of "Technology Forcing" in the Clean Air Act, 6 Envtl. Rep. (BNA) Monograph No. 21 (1975). "Technology forcing" can be understood in several senses. Control technology may already be in use or readily available for use in a given industry; if so, the objective of governmental policy may simply be to provide adequate incentives for polluters to expend the monies necessary to install the technology. Alternatively, control technology may not be presently available for use in a given industry, and it is necessary to adapt technology currently in use in another industry. These two situations involve diffusion of existing technology. Finally, it may be necessary to engage in research and development in order to create a wholly new technology. This situation involves technological innovation. You should consider whether the incentives that will be effective in stimulating innovation are likely to be of the same type that will be appropriate in the case where appropriate technology is already in use in a given industry or is readily available. Moreover, the nature of "technology forcing" is further clouded by considerable elasticity in the determination of whether technology is "available." The notion of available technology normally implies certain assumptions about operational reliability and cost. For example, is a process for "scrubbing" NO from electric utility stack gases "available" when the process works well in the laboratory or in a small-scale pilot plant, but there are unresolved questions concerning its reliability in full-scale commercial operation? Is technology "available" when it could be installed and could operate reliably from an engineering viewpoint but would cost very large amounts of money?

Consider also questions of economic efficiency in the rate of investment in control technology over time. With the growth of knowledge, we can expect with the passage of time to develop environmentally superior technologies at lower cost. Moreover, the rate of such development can normally to some greater or lesser extent be accelerated by research and development undertaken through direct government expenditure or governmental incentives for such expenditure by private firms. This development means that it may not always be desirable to insist upon utilization of the best technology presently available to meet environmental quality objectives, particularly where such utilization would involve substantial capital investment in large-scale installations, such as stack-gas "scrubbers." If superior technology, such as a change in basic combustion techniques that would generate less pollution, may be available in the future, it may be preferable to postpone control measures rather than utilize scarce capital to install inferior technology now.[16] Of course postponement of control measures will mean that pollution must be suffered in the meantime. If the harms caused by such pollution are serious and irreversible, then it will probably be appropriate to insist upon use of whatever control technology is now available to prevent such harm.

It is against this analytical backdrop that you should examine the materials that follow, which deal with the implementation of two different approaches to "technology forcing" in the Clean Air Act. First we consider the implementation of nationally uniform emission limitations for new stationary sources based upon the criterion of available technology. Next we review the implementation of the 1970 Amendments' requirement of a 90 percent reduction of emissions from new

---

16. Installation of current technology at high capital cost not only raises the possibility of either having to make additional expenditures in the future or foregoing the use of superior future technologies; it may also reduce the incentives and resources available for developing superior technologies in the future.

light-duty motor vehicles. You should consider carefully the various advantages and disadvantages of these alternative approaches to technology forcing. Can problems of environmental degradation be resolved
by technological changes alone without basic alterations in established
living patterns? If so, how might such basic alterations be achieved?
Does the Clean Air Act rely too heavily on technological innovation to
solve environmental problems? For a general review of these and related questions, see Kramer, Economics, Technology and the Clean Air
Amendments of 1970: The First Six Years, 6 Ecology L.Q. 161 (1976).

1.   NEW SOURCE PERFORMANCE STANDARDS

NATIONAL LIME ASSOCIATION V.
ENVIRONMENTAL PROTECTION AGENCY

627 F.2d 416 (D.C. Cir. 1980)

WALD, Circuit Judge:

The National Lime Association (NLA), representing ninety percent of this country's commercial producers of lime and lime hydrate
(the industry), challenges the new source performance standards
(NSPS) for lime manufacturing plants issued by the Environmental
Protection Agency (EPA, Administrator or Agency) under §111 of the
Clean Air Act (the Act). . . . The standards limit the mass of particulate that may be emitted in the exhaust gas from all lime-hydrating
and from certain lime-manufacturing facilities and limit the permitted
visibility of exhaust gas emissions from some facilities manufacturing
lime. We find inadequate support in the administrative record for
the standards promulgated and therefore remand to the Administrator. . . .

EMISSIONS CONTROL IN THE PRODUCTION
OF LIME

Rotary kilns here and abroad have employed several different
methods of emissions controls including the fabric filter baghouse, the
electrostatic precipitator (ESP), the high energy scrubber, and the
gravel bed filter. One survey showed that of eighty-five domestic rotary
kilns, twenty-four percent used a baghouse, thirty-one percent used a
high energy scrubber and eight percent used an ESP [electrostatic pre-
cipitator]. However, use of the baghouse method is increasing because
this method requires less energy and does not itself create additional
problems of pollution control.

EPA has identified baghouses, ESPs and scrubbers as "best systems" of emissions control for rotary lime kilns. . . .

EMISSIONS CONTROL IN THE PRODUCTION OF HYDRATED LIME

Hydration emissions have been shown to be most effectively controlled by wet scrubbers and they are the *only* system of emission reduction considered by EPA for lime hydrators. . . .

The issue presented here is primarily one of the adequacy of EPA's test data on which the industry standards are based. NLA disagrees with EPA's conclusion that the standards are achievable under the "best technological system of continuous emission reduction which . . . the Administrator determines has been adequately demonstrated." Specifically, NLA claims that the test data underlying the development of the standards do not support the Administrator's conclusion that the promulgated emission levels are in fact "achievable" on a continuous basis. Promulgation of standards based upon inadequate proof of achievability would defy the Administrative Procedure Act's mandate against action that is "arbitrary, capricious, an abuse of discretion, or otherwise not in accordance with law." 5 U.S.C. §706 (1976). . . .

Our review has led us to conclude that the record does not support the "achievability" of the promulgated standards for the industry as a whole.[17] This conclusion is a cumulative one, resulting from our assessment of the many points raised by the industry at the administrative level and in this court; no one point made is so cogent that remand

---

17. An achievable standard need not be one already routinely achieved in the industry. . . . But, to be achievable, we think a uniform standard must be capable of being met under most adverse conditions which can reasonably be expected to recur and which are not or cannot be taken into account in determining the "costs" of compliance.

The statutory standard is one of achievability, given costs. Some aspects of "achievability" cannot be divorced from consideration of "costs." Typically one associates "costs" with the capital requirements of new technology. *See e.g. AFL-CIO v. Marshall,* 617 F.2d 636, 659 (D.C. Cir. 1979). However, certain "costs" (e.g. frequent systemic shutdown to service emissions control systems or use of feedstock of a certain size or composition in order to meet the new emissions standards) are more intimately intertwined with "achievability" than are the capital costs of new technology. In this case the lime industry attacks the standards as "unachievable." When questioned at oral argument, counsel for petitioner disclaimed any attack upon the expense of implementation stating that he attacked the achievability of the standard "on any reliably repetitive basis" "because of the very variables in the production of lime." This necessarily asserts that a standard which does not account for certain routine variations in conditions is "unachievable." We agree, where, as here, there is no evidence in the record that the "costs" of adjusting for such routine variations (assuming

would necessarily have followed on that basis alone. In the analysis that follows, common threads will be discerned in our discussions of individual points. Chief among these common threads is a concern that the Agency consider the representativeness for the industry as a whole of the tested plants on which it relies, at least where its central argument is that the standard *is* achievable because it *has* been achieved (at the tested plants). The Agency's failure to consider the representativeness — along various relevant parameters — of the data relied upon is the primary reason for our remand. The locus of administrative burdens of going forward or of persuasion may shift in the course of a rulemaking proceeding,[18] but we think an initial burden of promulgating and explaining a non-arbitrary, non-capricious rule rests with the Agency and we think that by failing to explain how the standard proposed is achievable under the range of relevant conditions which may affect the emissions to be regulated, the Agency has not satisfied this initial burden.

[The court then discussed in detail the factors that could affect the control of particulate emissions from various rotary kilns and hydrators and the consequent achievability of EPA's standards. These factors included, in the case of kilns, variations in quantity of particulate generated due to variations in feedstock, gas velocity and operation levels, and to dust generation; and variations in the controllability of particulate generated because of use of high sulfur coal for process heat, and variations in particle size. The court concluded that EPA had failed to adequately explain or justify the kiln standard in relation to such factors or deal with industry comments emphasizing their significance. It reached similar conclusions in the case of hydrators.]

Understandably, the Agency's main defense in court centers on

---

such adjustments be possible) were considered by the Agency in promulgating its standard.

The EPA has expressly built some flexibility into the enforcement end of the new source performance standards 40 C.F.R. §60.8(c) (1979) (relating to start up, shutdown, and malfunction) and is vested with a more general enforcement discretion, but the flexibility appropriate to enforcement will not render "achievable" a standard which cannot be achieved on a regular basis, either for the reasons expressly taken into account in compliance determination regulations (here startup, shutdown, and malfunction), or otherwise. Cf. *Portland Cement I* 486 F.2d at 398 n.91.

Because we remand for the development of a more adequate rationale for the promulgated standards we do not now specify the kinds of variations in conditions — not accounted for in the Agency's cost analysis — which might render a uniform standard "unachievable" or so "unachievable" as to represent an arbitrary or capricious exercise of the Administrator's discretion under the Act.

18. See generally *Int'l Harvester Co. v. Ruckelshaus*, 478 F.2d at 642-643: DeLong, Informal Rulemaking and the Integration of Law and Policy, 65 Va. L. Rev. 257, 298-301 (1979) (discussing shifting burdens of proof in informal rulemaking).

the industry's total failure to respond positively to EPA's suggestion that the industry either suggest additional test sites or submit data on the basis of which EPA might reconsider or subcategorize the standard to conform to local variations. EPA's point is a sympathetic one, but not, we think, dispositive. EPA has a statutory duty to promulgate achievable standards. This requires that they approach that task in a systematic manner that identifies relevant variables and ensures that they are taken account of in analyzing test data. EPA's own support document recognizes particle size as a variable but enigmatically does not discuss it at any length or explain its importance in emissions control. That the industry did not assist the Agency in any meaningful way by data or even by suggestions for additional testing is certainly discouraging. But we do not think that inaction — lamentable though it may be — lifted the burden from the Agency of pursuing what appears to be a relevant variable or at the least discussing in its document why it was not considered important.

In this respect, we believe that the industry's comments, concerning particle size distribution, when viewed in light of the material contained in EPA's own support statement and in light of the background documents on which it relied, met a "threshold requirement of materiality," mandating an Agency response which was not forthcoming here.

[EPA selected three existing plants as representative of the best-controlled facilities in the industry. When the test results at one of the plants showed emissions higher than the standard proposed and eventually adopted, EPA concluded that the plant did not incorporate the best technology available.]

. . . We think it incumbent upon the Agency, at least where it chooses to propose a standard on a data base as apparently limited as this one, to offer some supportable reason for its conclusion that a tested plant, chosen as likely to be well-controlled, does not represent best technology. The mere fact that its test results were unsatisfactory is not enough.

If, for unexplained reasons, one-third of the test plants initially chosen by EPA for their well-controlled systems fail to meet the standards, the conclusion is just as plausible that the standard is not achievable as that the plants chosen did not have well-controlled systems. It is up to EPA to dispel such doubts, and they have not done so here.

Of course, the fact that Plant A did not meet the proposed standard does not itself prove the standard is unachievable. However, ignoring the Plant A results merely because they were not satisfactory would suggest that the process by which the standard was promulgated was an arbitrary one. . . .

[The court also set aside, as inadequately supported in the record, an EPA requirement that the opacity of emissions from kiln plants not exceed 10 percent.]

Our requirement that the EPA consider the representativeness of the test data relied upon in the development and justification of its standard does not presage any new or more stringent standard of judicial review. The rigorousness of the review in which this court has engaged in previous NSPS decisions — known to some as the "hard look" standard — has already been [established]. . . .

NOTES AND QUESTIONS

1. *National Lime Association* suggests some of the difficulties faced by EPA in establishing New Source Performance Standards (NSPS) for given source categories. The difficulties are analytic, empirical, administrative, and legal. On the analytic side, what is the criterion for determining whether a "system of emission reduction" has been "adequately demonstrated," and what weight should be given to the cost of achieving control in defining a standard? Both of these questions are further complicated by the question of how many categories of NSPS should be established. For example, would all metal smelters be governed by a single NSPS, or should there be separate NSPSs for copper, lead, zinc, and aluminum smelters? What considerations would be relevant in answering this question?

From the empirical, administrative, and legal view, the problem lies in assembling the relevant information to determine the availability of technology and its costs in order to establish a NSPS and defend it in court against criticisms by industry, which will normally have better access than the agency to information about control technology and its application to that industry in terms of performance, reliability, and cost. In *National Lime Association,* EPA attempted to justify its standard by reference to technology already in use and was unsuccessful. Does a requirement that standards be based upon extensive test data bias standards toward the industry norm? Should the EPA instead have attempted to justify its standard on the basis of technology not presently in use that could be made available for new plants? What difficulties might such an approach involve?

2. Do the statutory provisions for NSPSs for new stationary sources provide an incentive for an industry, such as the lime industry, to develop superior control technologies? On the contrary, do they not impose a substantial *disincentive* for such development, since it will result in industry being required to install control equipment that it would not be required to install otherwise? What if control equipment is manufactured by firms in a specialized pollution control industry?

3. The Clean Air Act imposes substantially more stringent controls on new than on many existing sources. Furthermore, formal administrative procedures and court review work to the advantage of existing sources (by postponing ultimate compliance) and to the disad-

vantage of new sources (by postponing their completion date). Moreover, the policy of requiring control to the extent that technology is available and the source can "afford" it without shutting down results in the imposition of tighter controls on more profitable plants and industries. What justifications might there be for imposing more stringent standards on new and profitable plants and industries? What are the implications of these policies for productivity growth and the international competitiveness of U.S. industry? How might regulatory policies be modified to avoid unduly discouraging new investment? See generally Huber, The Old-New Division in Risk Regulation, 69 Va. L. Rev. 1025 (1983); Stewart, Regulation, Innovation, and Administrative Law: A Conceptual Framework, 69 Calif. L. Rev. 1256 (1981).

4. Economists have criticized EPA's implementation of the NSPSs for not only imposing excessive burdens on new as compared to existing sources, but for failing to achieve a cost-effective allocation of control burdens among different industries emitting the same pollutant. EPA sets NSPSs for each industry or industry subgroup separately, without much if any attention as to whether the cost of achieving required reductions for a given pollutant for industry A are in line with the costs of achieving the required reduction for the same pollutant in industries B, C, and so forth. As a result, the cost of achieving required reductions varies widely among industries. For example, industry A may have to spend $2000/ton for reductions of NO to meet its NSPS, while industry B may only have to spend $500/ton. It would be much cheaper to achieve the same overall level of NO reductions to shift some of the regulatory burden from A to B, to the point where their marginal costs of achieving NSPS for NO is the same. Why might it not be feasible to accomplish this result in a system of centralized command and control regulation? In *Portland Cement Assn. v. Ruckleshaus*, 486 F.2d 375 (D.C. Cir. 1973), *cert. denied*, 417 U.S. 921 (1974), Judge Leventhal rejected the portland cement industry's claim that EPA was required by §111 to consider the relative regulatory costs imposed on different industries by different NSPSs for the same pollutant; the industry had claimed that the costs of meeting the particulate NSPS for portland cement plants was far higher than the costs of meeting the particulate NSPS for electric utilities.

The problem of large variations in marginal compliance costs for different sources also arises in the SIP context. For example, SIP emission limitations for HC for source A may require A to spend $8000/ton to comply, while the limitations imposed on source B may require only $2000/ton to comply. Society could significantly reduce the cost of controlling HC emissions by shifting more of the abatement burden to B, to the point where the marginal costs of control at A and B were the same. Economic studies indicate that if pollution control burdens were redistributed in a cost-effective manner, the cost of pollution control, which today exceeds $100 billion annually, could be reduced 50 percent or more. See Ackerman & Stewart, Reforming Environmental Law: The Democratic Case for Economic Incentives for Pollution Control, 13 Colum. J. Envtl. L. 171 (1988). Equalizing marginal control costs would secure the goal of *cost effectiveness* — achieving a given societal goal with the lowest total expenditure of resources. Cost effectiveness says nothing about *how* such a goal should be set; it might, for example, be set by reference to health effects without considering costs. It is therefore distinct from cost-benefit analysis, which would set goals by the use of economic criteria. See supra p. 101. Why might it be difficult in practice under the existing regulatory system to allocate pollution control burdens so as to equalize marginal control costs among all sources, stationary and mobile, of a given pollutant?

5. What is a "new" source? As enacted in 1970, §111(a)(2) provides that new source performance standards apply to "any stationary source, the construction or modification of which is commenced after" the promulgation or proposal of regulations establishing an NSPS. In the case of brand new sources, there has in the past been some controversy over when construction "commenced." Today, the more pressing and controversial issue is determining when an existing source has been "modified" for purposes of §111. The issue is quite important because existing sources are generally subject only to controls imposed by applicable SIPs, which are in most cases substantially less stringent than the federal NSPSs. Existing sources that are "modified" are also subject to the special control and permitting requirements imposed on new sources by the non-attainment and prevention of significant deterioration provisions of the Act, described below. Consider the following problem:

PROBLEM: INTERPRETATION OF "MODIFICATION" UNDER §111

The Act, §111(a)(4) defines "modification" as:

> any physical change in, or change in the method of operation of, a stationary source which increases the amount of any air pollutant emitted by such source or which results in the emission of any air pollutant not previously emitted.

EPA regulations provide that the following, by themselves, shall not be considered a "modification":

> (1) Maintenance, repair and replacement which the Administrator determines to be routine for a source category . . .

      (2)   An increase in production rate . . . if that increase can be accomplished without a capital expenditure . . .

      (3)   An increase in the hours of operation. . . .

In addition, EPA regulations provide that, for purposes of determining whether a source change "increases the amount" of a pollutant, one should determine whether the change increases the source's *total daily emissions*. However, most new source performance standards, like most SIP requirements, are expressed in terms of emission rates, rather than total emissions over a given period of time. For example, emission standards for coal burning power plants are expressed in terms of maximum permissible pounds of emissions per million BTUs of heat input. The use of maximum emissions rates in standards in large part reflects administrative considerations; it is much easier to set and enforce emission rates limitations than to police total emissions over a given time period. Moreover, emission rate limitations may better ensure that total emissions at any given time will not result in ambient concentrations in excess of the national ambient air quality standards.

    XYZ Electric's Metropolis generating plant was built in 1940. When built, its expected useful life was 50 years. It contains three generating units, each with a design capacity of 80 megawatts. The units were historically operated at full capacity for 10 to 12 hours a day. At full capacity operation, each unit produced 10 tons of SO_2 hourly. However, deterioration in the units' components required the utility during the 1984-1987 period to reduce operating capacity to 60 megawatts, 6-8 hours daily, generating 7.5 tons of SO_2 hourly. In 1987, XYZ began what its internal memoranda describe as a "life extension" project for the facility, replacing various deteriorated components. The cost of these renovations amounted to $100 million, or about 35 percent of the cost of constructing a brand new facility with the same capacity (exclusive of pollution control costs). Pollution control costs for a "scrubber" that removes sulfur from stack gases would amount to $60 million for the existing facilities and $40 million for a new facility (the difference reflecting the additional cost of retrofitting an old plant). The project took three years; each unit in turn was shut down for an entire year while work was done on it. Since the renovation, XYZ has operated the units at full capacity (80 megawatts) 10 to 12 hours a day. Are the renovated units "modified" sources for purposes of §111? What arguments will EPA make? XYZ? What of the possibility that XYZ might, if it chose, retire the older facilities and operate the Metropolis plant for more than 12 hours a day? If EPA determines that the plant is "modified for purposes of, §111" how should a court rule on XYZ's petition for review?

NOTE ON THE REGULATION OF COAL-FIRED
POWER PLANTS

The original NSPS for coal-fired power plants (promulgated in 1971) limited emissions of SO_2 to 1.2 pounds of SO_2 for every MBTU (million British thermal units) of heat energy generated by the plant. A typical 500 megawatt coal plant burns about 200 tons of coal per hour, representing 5000 MBTU. The original standard gave sources flexibility to meet the required limitation on emissions in a variety of ways, including flue gas desulphurization ("scrubbing"), use of low sulfur coal, coal washing (removal of sulfur from coal before combustion), or a combination of these techniques.

In 1977, Congress amended §111(a) to provide that emission limitations should "reflect the degree of emission limitation and the percentage reduction achievable through application of the best technological system of continuous emission reduction which . . . the Administrator determines has been adequately demonstrated." The term "technological system of continuous emission reduction" is defined to mean a "technological process for production or operation by any source which is inherently low-polluting or non-polluting" or "a technological system for continuous reduction of the pollution generated before such pollution is emitted into the ambient air, including precombustion cleaning or treatment of fuels."

These provisions reflected congressional concern that the prior type of standard would favor low sulfur western coal in competition with high sulfur eastern coal, since it allowed a source to comply by employing low sulfur coal rather than installing expensive scrubbers to reduce emissions generated by high sulfur coal. Despite the fact that western coal has a transportation cost disadvantage compared to eastern coal for burning at midwestern and eastern plants, the eastern coal industry feared that the incentive created by regulation and the costs of scrubbers would lead to a loss of markets. They accordingly favored a requirement that all coal plants be required to scrub emissions, regardless of the sulfur content of coal. They formed an unlikely alliance with some environmental groups, who also favored universal scrubbing in order to further reduce emissions from western coal-fired plants (who would use low sulfur western coal in any event) so as to enhance visibility in national parks in the West and to reduce demand for low sulfur coal and accompanying strip-mining of scenic western areas.[19]

---

19. The provisions that ultimately emerged do not explicitly require universal scrubbing, although a House Report claimed that they do. As the D.C. Circuit concluded in its decision upholding the ultimate standards promulgated by EPA, *Sierra Club v. Costle*, 657 F.2d 298 (D.C. Cir. 1981), it is not clear that the statute prohibits the use of low sulfur coal as a means of compliance.

Following the 1977 Amendments, EPA initially proposed an NSPS standard that continued to limit emission to the atmosphere to a maximum of 1.2 lbs SO_2 per MBTU, but also required a 90 percent reduction of the potential uncontrolled SO_2 emissions from the coal burned. Since this 90 percent reduction could only be achieved by scrubbing, the standard would require universal scrubbing. Careful analysis within the EPA revealed that this policy would severely limit use of low sulfur coal and was extremely costly, as much as $4.1 billion per year by 1995 according to one internal EPA estimate. Last minute political pressures by eastern coal interests (spearheaded by Senate Majority Leader Robert Byrd of West Virginia) and environmentalists produced a compromise. EPA modified the final standard to include a variable percentage reduction option: If emissions to the atmosphere are less than .60 lbs/MBTU, potential uncontrolled emissions need only be reduced by 70 percent. If emissions to the atmosphere are between .60 and 1.2 lbs/MBTU, the percentage reduction required varies between 70 and 90 percent on a sliding scale. This option would allow greater use of low sulfur fuel than the original proposal. While scrubbing would still generally be required, in conjunction with low sulfur fuel, to achieve even 70 percent reduction of uncontrolled emissions, scrubbing to 70 percent sulfur removal is appreciably cheaper than 90 percent removal. In addition, the 70 percent provision could encourage development of a new, potentially cheaper "dry scrubbing" process.

Two careful researchers have reached the following conclusion regarding the outcome of the legislative and regulatory processes described above:

> Congress' well-intentioned effort in 1970 to improve environmental quality through an improved administrative process has led, in 1979, to an extraordinary agency decision that will cost the public tens of billions of dollars to achieve environmental goals that could be achieved more cheaply, more quickly, and more surely by other means. Indeed, the agency action is so inept that some of the nation's most populous areas will enjoy a *worse* environment than would have resulted if the new policy had never been put into effect.

B. Ackerman & W. Hassler, Clean Coal/Dirty Air: Or How the Clean Air Act Became a Multibillion-Dollar Bail-Out for High Sulfur Coal Producers and What Should Be Done About It (1981). The authors contend that NSPS and other regulatory controls should consist of

---

Although the standard must be set by reference to the level of emissions achievable by scrubbing or other technologies, the Act arguably permits that standard — defined in terms of a maximum SO_2 emissions rate — to be met by any available means, including use of low sulfur coal.

performance standards that limit emissions to the atmosphere but leave sources free to use any means they wish (including low sulfur fuel) in order to comply, because this approach will minimize costs and maximize technological opportunities. However, as pointed out in the *Sierra Club v. Costle* opinion, 657 F.2d at 316-317 n.38, no party to the litigation urged this position or challenged EPA's requirement of reduction of uncontrolled emissions. Ackerman and Hassler also condemn EPA for giving too much weight to eastern coal interests and adopting a short-sighted "technical fix" mentality that fails to set priorities and ignores problems such as the need to reduce emissions from existing coal-fired plants and resulting pollution problems other than SO_2. These criticisms were challenged by two EPA employees involved in the decision; see Smith & Randle, Comment on Beyond the New Deal 90 Yale L.J. 1398 (1981). Ackerman and Hassler make a rebuttal in Beyond the New Deal: Reply, 90 Yale L.J. 1412 (1981). The debate, while technical in many respects, is well worth a full review.

2. EMISSION LIMITATIONS ON NEW AUTOMOBILES

PROBLEM: THE AUTOMOTIVE DEADLINE EXTENSION

You are the Administrator of the Environmental Protection Agency and must decide whether to grant requests by the automobile manufacturers for extension of certain statutory deadlines for reduction of pollutant emissions from automobiles imposed by the 1970 Clean Air Amendments.

The 1970 Amendments to the Act, §202, required the Administrator to promulgate standards to ensure that carbon monoxide (CO) and hydrocarbon (HC) emissions from model year 1975 and later automobiles were reduced at least 90 percent from 1970 model year emission levels. The section also required a similar 90 percent reduction in emissions of nitrogen oxides (NOx) by model year 1976. Any time after January 1, 1972, a manufacturer may file with the Administrator an application requesting suspension, for one year only, of the 1975 model year deadlines for CO and HC, and any time after January 1, 1973 may file a similar application for a one year suspension of the 1976 deadline for NO.[20] Within 60 days after receipt of an application for suspension and after public hearings, the Administrator must grant or refuse the application. The Administrator "shall grant the suspension only if he determines":

---

20. You should disregard for purposes of this problem the amendments to §202 that have occurred since 1972.

(i)   that such suspension is "essential to the public interest or the public health and welfare of the United States," and

(ii)   "all good faith efforts have been made" to meet the standards established by the Amendments, and

(iii)   the applicant has "established that effective control technology, processes, operating methods, or other alternatives are not available or have not been available for a sufficient period of time to achieve compliance prior to the effective date of such standards," and

(iv)   the studies of emission control technology by the National Academy of Sciences (which the Amendments require) and "other information available" to the Administrator "has not indicated that technology, processes, or other alternatives are available to meet such standards."

The Administrator's grant or denial of a suspension application is subject to court review in the District of Columbia Circuit Court of Appeals. If the Administrator grants a suspension, she or he is required to issue interim standards that "shall reflect the greatest degree of emission control which is achievable by application of technology which the Administrator determines is available, giving appropriate consideration to the cost of applying such technology within the period of time available to manufacturers." Under §§203 and 205 of the Act, distribution or sale of new automobiles not conforming to §202 emission control requirements subjects a manufacturer to a civil penalty of up to $10,000 for each car produced.

A brief review of the background of the 1970 Amendments will be useful. Recall that the federal government first became involved in establishing emission controls for automobiles through the passage of the Motor Vehicle Air Pollution Control Act of 1965. The Act authorized the Secretary of HEW to establish emission standards for automobiles "giving appropriate consideration to technological feasibility and economic costs." Regulations were issued for the reduction of CO and HC emissions. Rather modest adjustments to the existing internal combustion engine (ICE) achieved substantial reductions of HC and CO emissions by 1970. HEW planned gradually to tighten the restrictions on HC and CO, and also to introduce restrictions on emissions of NO, with the development of available control technology.

The following table shows the level of emissions of the principal auto pollutants (in terms of grams emitted per mile of operation) before the institution of federal controls, the emissions required under the federal standards effective for model year 1970, and the levels required to be met by 1975-1976 under the 1970 Amendment:

	HC	CO	NOx
Uncontrolled	8.7	87.0	4.4
1970 Standards	4.1	34.0	4.4
1975/76 Standards (1970 Act)	.41	3.4	.44

As Senator Muskie candidly acknowledged at the time, the 90 percent reduction requirements were imposed by the 1970 Amendments even though (a) technology was not available in 1970 to meet the requirements, (b) it was not known whether such technology could be developed by 1975, and (c) it was not known whether, even if technology could be developed, what the cost would be. See 116 Cong. Reg. 32902, 32905-32906 (1970).

The available evidence as of 1972 indicates that the manufacturers will have substantial difficulties in meeting the HC and CO requirements by 1975, and that it is highly unlikely that they will be able to meet the NOx standard by 1976. Basically, the manufacturers are attempting to meet the 1975-1976 standards through adjustments to the existing ICE. Among the additional control techniques being used are lowering compression ratios, adjusting timing, utilizing a catalytic device on the exhaust (which will require elimination from gasoline of lead additives that destroy the catalytic elements), and recycling the exhaust gases. The manufacturers are hampered in developing adequate control technology because of the short time deadlines imposed by the 1970 Amendments, the need for at least two years of time before actual production in order to tool up production processes, and the need for reliability and adaptability to mass production methods in control technology. Even if control technology can be developed to meet the HC and CO requirements by the 1975 model year, the following problems must be faced:

(1)   The control devices will apparently add about $200 or more to the cost of the 1975 model car in comparison to the 1974 model car.

(2)   Fuel economy will probably be penalized 5 to 10 percent or more, which could eventually translate into aggregate increased fuel costs of a billion dollars or more.

(3)   Performance will be impaired (cars will be harder to start, and there will be pauses or hesitations in on-the-road operation, particularly in acceleration).[21]

(4)   Even if the standards can be met by prototypes subject to a

---

21. The penalties, in terms of cost, fuel economy, and performance, become progressively more severe as one moves toward the lower range of emission. E.g., it may cost twice as much to reduce emissions by 90 percent as to reduce them by 80 percent.

50,000-mile test and by vehicles on the production line, it is almost certain that 1975 vehicles in actual owner operation would be unable to meet the standards over their entire 50,000-mile useful life, for the following reasons: The control equipment will need regular maintenance as well as replacement of certain parts, such as the catalyst. Owners are unlikely to have the necessary maintenance and replacement performed, not only because of the expense, but because the control devices impair performance (indeed, there is already a thriving business among automobile mechanics in dismantling the control equipment installed on existing automobiles).[22] Effective inspection systems are unlikely to be installed in most states, in part because the technology for accurate testing has not been adequately developed for mass use, in part because of the high cost involved, and in part because such inspections would hardly prove to be politically popular. The probable lack of an effective inspection system, coupled with the provision in the Act that the manufacturer warranty provisions are applicable only when an owner has performed the required maintenance, makes it unlikely that the warranty (and associated recall) provisions will be effective. All of these factors mean that on-the-road emissions could be several times those achieved in prototype or production line tests.

(5)   Finally, there is a serious trade-off between obtaining reductions of HC and CO and securing reductions of NO. Even if the HC and CO standards could be met by 1975, they would (barring a breakthrough in developing a catalyst for NO) almost certainly preclude achievement of the NO standards in 1976 (presently it does not appear that the manufacturers can do better than 1.2-1.5 grams/mile for NO, or about 3 times the level required under the 1970 Amendments). Even if the NO standards could also be achieved, the costs in terms of performance, fuel economy, and price would be much more substantial than the costs associated with the achievement of HC and CO standards by 1975.

From a longer term view, the traditional ICE is not an attractive choice as a low polluting power source for automobiles. Alternative power choices, such as stratified charge, diesel, Wankel (rotary) ICE, the gas turbine, the Rankin cycle (steam) engine, or the electric battery

---

22. Moreover, the standards under the Act and the associated recall provisions deal with a statutorily defined "useful" life of 50,000 miles, yet half of all vehicle miles are logged by vehicles with over 50,000 miles.

are far more promising. In particular, the Rankin cycle engine or the electric battery would be likely to achieve not only a lower initial level of emissions on new vehicles, but the emissions would remain low over the life of the vehicle because the tuning and deterioration problems associated with the ICE are far less. While the big three domestic auto manufacturers have invested some research funds in the Rankin cycle, gas turbine, and electric battery alternatives, they have not seriously committed themselves to developing such alternative technologies. In large part, this is due to the traditional reliance by Detroit on the ICE. A major shift in automobile power-plant technology would require drastic retooling, disruption of supplier arrangements, and a basic change in thinking on the part of engineers and managers. The early deadlines imposed by the 1970 Act are also a substantial factor. While the Rankin cycle and possibly the battery are attractive alternatives over the longer run, it would probably require years of intensive research and development to overcome existing drawbacks (weight, costs, and operating characteristics) in these alternative technologies. Even if alternative technologies were developed, there would be substantial delays in converting existing manufacturing facilities to the production of new engine types.

All of the above is by way of background. You should assume that it is now April 1972. In January 1972, the National Academy of Sciences (which was required under the Clean Air Amendments of 1970 to make periodic reports on the availability of technology to achieve the 1975-1976 standards) issued a report which found that the technology needed to meet 1975 light duty vehicle emissions requirements was not presently available and that there was no certainty that any 1975 model year vehicles would meet the statutory requirements. The report concluded that while the current rate of progress made it possible that the larger manufacturers would be able to produce vehicles that would meet the requirements, provisions still must be made for catalyst replacement and other maintenance, for averaging emissions of production vehicles (i.e., requiring that vehicles on average achieve a 90 percent reduction as opposed to requiring 90 percent reduction from each vehicle), and for the availability of unleaded fuels that will not damage catalysts.

The report added that if enforcement of the requirements for 1975 vehicles were deferred for one year, the opportunity thus provided for further development and field testing would enable manufacturers to improve significantly the performance and reliability of vehicles equipped to meet the requirements in actual use.

In explaining the "advantage" of a one-year suspension of the requirements, the report also stated that even experimental vehicles have thus far been unable to satisfy the 1975 standards over a vehicle's 50,000-mile "useful life."

The report noted that the "developmental work still is required to further reduce emissions at low mileage and to provide the required durability. Durability testing is expensive and time-consuming: Three to four months are required for a 50,000-mile test. Each major change in the basic system configuration or operating conditions will require new durability tests on components such as the catalytic converter. Catalyst technology for automotive emissions control is relatively new. . . ."

In March 1972, the major automobile manufacturers file applications with the EPA Administrator for suspension of the 1975 deadline for HC and CO. The manufacturers make the following basic arguments:

Despite good faith efforts to meet the deadline within the limited time available, the 1975 deadline probably cannot be met. Adequate technology does not now exist, and will probably not be developed in time. Even if control technology could be developed, it would involve unacceptably large costs in terms of the price of automobiles and deterioration in fuel economy and performance. Such costs would seriously impair sales of cars during the 1975 model year. A serious drop in 1975 sales[23] would threaten the very existence of American Motors and Chrysler, cause serious economic hardship to the automobile companies, their employees, stockholders, and suppliers, and would actually retard the achievement of air quality by causing car owners to refrain from buying new cars and continuing to operate older, higher polluting vehicles. Moreover, the 1975 standards could be met only through hastily developed control technology subject to significant deterioration in the effectiveness of controls in actual on-the-road use, a factor that again might lead to impairment rather than improvement of air quality. Achievement of the HC and CO standards by 1975 would also increase the likelihood that it would be impossible to meet the NO standards by 1976. Finally, the additional reductions in emissions needed to meet the 1975 standards, while very costly, are comparatively

---

23. Apart from the impact of emission controls, it is estimated that about 10 million 1975 automobiles would be sold. Of course if all sales by one or more manufacturers were prohibited, the economic effect would be even more severe. Automobile production and associated activities account for approximately 15 percent of the GNP. Ford, for example, asserted that if it were unable to sell cars during the 1975 model year, 800,000 persons would become unemployed, 3,300 Ford dealers would be out of business, tax receipts would be reduced $5 billion, GNP would be reduced $17 billion, and Ford would suffer a drastic financial weakening "should it survive."

quite small.[24] There is no reliable evidence to show that a failure to achieve this small increment would endanger health.

A hearing is held before the EPA Administrator at which the manufacturers amplify these points. Various environmental groups appear at the hearing and make the following arguments: The manufacturers have not clearly demonstrated that it will be impossible to meet the 1975 standards. The possibility that the standards could be met only by technology that would reduce fuel economy and performance and increase price is not, under the Act, an excuse for failing to reduce pollution in accordance with the congressional mandate to protect health. The problem of on-the-road deterioration can be met through inspection programs and the warranty and recall provisions. The Act does not authorize the Administrator to take the NO 1976 deadline into account in passing on extension requests for the 1975 deadline. Most importantly, it is essential that the EPA not "cave in" to manufacturer pressures, that it maintain the congressional commitment to cleaner air, and that maximum pressure be exerted on the manufacturers to develop adequate control technology.

Last week, the Office of Science and Technology in the White House released a report on auto emission control which found that the costs of reducing new car emissions to achieve the 1975-1976 deadlines would exceed the benefits, in large part because geographically uniform 90 percent reductions would result in unnecessarily stringent controls (and high costs) in many areas of the nation that do not have serious air pollution problems. The report recommended adoption of a "two-car" strategy, under which the federal government would require a stringent level of controls on automobiles sold and utilized in heavily polluted regions, and a more relaxed level of control on automobiles in relatively clean regions. This strategy had been opposed by EPA staff as presenting "overwhelming" administrative and enforcement problems. The report also questioned "regulation . . . based upon a blind faith in technology" and asserted that the establishment of control requirements going beyond known technological state of the art was unwise.

Finally, limited evidence has begun to accumulate indicating that the catalytic mufflers that domestic manufacturers would have to utilize in order to meet the 1975 deadlines may transform sulfur residues in gasoline into highly toxic sulfur compounds which would then spew into the air.

---

24. As authorized by the Act, EPA had already adopted interim standards requiring additional controls on 1974 model year cars.

NOTES AND QUESTIONS ON POSTPONEMENT PROBLEMS

1. If you were the EPA Administrator, how would you decide the requests for extension? What factors may you consider under the statute? In particular, how do you determine whether a manufacturer has exercised "good faith"? What additional factors, if any, do you think should be considered? What additional information beyond that given in the problem would you want to have in reaching your decision? What (realistically) are your chances of obtaining such information?

2. How would your decision be complicated if you concluded:

(a)   that one manufacturer (say, General Motors), could meet the 1975 deadline but the others could not.

(b)   that a given manufacturer (say, Chrysler) had not shown "good faith" in developing control technology.

(c)   that foreign manufacturers were able to surpass the standards.

3. D. Harrison, in Who Pays for Clean Air (1975), mounts a powerful demonstration that billions of dollars would be saved if the federal government provided for stringent controls on models used in urban areas with serious pollution problems and less stringent controls on models used in other areas of the country. May the Administrator, in considering extension requests, pursue a "two-car" strategy? Would it be a workable strategy even if he could?

4. Commentators have strongly criticized the basic "technology-forcing" strategy of the Act, making the following points: The sanctions threatened in the Act — a penalty of up to $10,000 for each car sold — are not credible because their effect would be to shut down the industry. At best, manufacturers will be forced to install known control devices in order to forestall more intrusive government controls. But there is no incentive for leadership in developing fundamentally new control technologies, such as basic alternatives to the current ICE. The lack of proper incentives, plus the short time deadlines in the Act, lead to the development of "add on" devices such as catalysts and other tinkerings with the current ICE that are highly unstable in on-the-road use. Even if a 90 percent reduction in emissions from assembly line automobiles is achieved, reduction in emissions from automobiles in use will be far less. Incentives must be provided for development of new engine technologies that will reliably ensure continued emission reductions under conditions of actual use. See, e.g., H. Jacoby & J. Steinbrunner, Clearing the Air (1975); F. Grad. et al., The Automobile and the Regulation of its Impact on the Environment, 115-150, 279-324, 417-430 (1975); National Academy of Sciences, Coordinating

Committee on Air Quality Studies, Air Quality and Automobile Emission Control (Report for Senate Pub. Works Comm. 1974).

To what extent may and should the Administrator seek to meet these criticisms in the context of a postponement decision? Consider the following specific possibilities:

(a) Should the Administrator grant the requested extension, provided that the manufacturers commit themselves to development of new and more stable control technologies?

(b) Should the Administrator grant the extension and ensure the development of new and more stable control technologies by threatening stringent enforcement of the Section 207 warranty and recall provisions to ensure compliance with emission limitations by vehicles in actual use?

(c) Should the Administrator deny the extension request but seek to promote alternative technologies by seeking fines on noncomplying vehicles at levels far below the $10,000 per car authorized by Section 205 and adjusting the level of the fine to the extent of noncompliance? Under this approach, for example, a fine of $20 might be imposed for each .1 gram/mile by which a car's CO emissions exceeded the 1975 requirement of 3.4 grams/mile. Such an approach would reward those manufacturers who made the greatest progress in reducing emissions.

EPILOGUE

In 1972, EPA Administrator William Ruckelshaus denied the requests of the three major automobile companies and International Harvester for one-year suspensions of the 1975 HC and CO deadlines. The motor vehicle manufacturers challenged the Administrator's decision in the U.S. Court of Appeals for the District of Columbia Circuit. In a seminal opinion addressing the scope of judicial review of scientifically and technologically complex regulatory decisions, Judge Leventhal found procedural and substantive errors in the EPA's decision and remanded the denial for reconsideration. *International Harvester Company v. Ruckelshaus*, 478 F.2d 615 (1973).

The late 1970s and 1980s witnessed numerous administrative, judicial, and legislative battles over deadlines for achieving emission reductions. Economic troubles experienced by the American automobile industry during much of this period aided the industry in obtaining rollbacks of deadlines. Table 4.1 summarizes the history of federal new car emission limitations:

TABLE 4.1
History of Federal New Car Emission Limitations

	HC	CO	NO
Uncontrolled	8.7	87.0	4.4
1970-1971	4.1	34.0	4.4
1972	3.0	28.0	3.1
1973-1974	3.0	28.0	3.1
1975-1976 (U.S. — 49 States)	1.5	15.0	3.1
(California)	.9	9.0	2.0
1977-1979	1.5	15.0	2.0
1980	.41	7.0	2.0
1981	.41	3.4[a]	1.0[bc]
1982	.41	3.4[a]	1.0[bc]
1983	.41	3.4	1.0[c]
1984	.41	3.4	1.0[c]
1985	.41	3.4	1.0

[a] Subject to waivers, interim standards not to exceed 7.0 gpm. Waivers were granted to approximately 30% of 1981 and 1982 automobiles.

[b] Subject to waivers for small manufacturers. A waiver was granted to American Motors Co. (to 2 gpm).

[c] Subject to waivers for limited uses of innovative technologies or diesel engines, interim standards not to exceed 1.5 gpm. Waivers were granted for most diesel powered automobiles between 1981 and 1984.

NOTES AND QUESTIONS

1. By 1981, the United States had achieved the 1975 goals of 90 percent reduction for HC and CO. As early as 1974, respected technological experts were predicting that we would not achieve these goals until 1980. Should Congress have simply picked 1980 initially?

2. EPA's problems in implementing the "technology-forcing" provisions of the Act with respect to vehicle emissions are illustrated by efforts to set limitations for diesel emissions. In *NRDC v. EPA*, 655 F.2d 318 (D.C. Cir.), *cert. denied*, 454 U.S. 1017 (1981), industry and environmental groups challenged EPA emission standards for diesel-power automobiles and standard light duty trucks. NRDC agreed that EPA should have imposed a graduated standard, imposing stricter and more costly controls on vehicles that were already low polluting. The court rejected this contention pointing out that this would give a competitive advantage to higher polluting models, and finding that Congress seemed to have contemplated uniform standards. On the other hand, it upheld EPA's standards against industry claims that they were based on use of a "trap oxidizer" that was supposed to trap and burn up parti-

cles from diesel exhausts. Industry pointed out that no such trap had been proven in actual use. The court upheld the standard on the basis of EPA projections that the traps could be developed. In 1984, EPA postponed the effective date of the standard because of difficulties in producing an operational trap. Manufacturers then stopped producing diesel-powered automobiles, which provide significantly better fuel economy than gasoline-powered vehicles, blaming the emission standards.

NRDC v. Thomas, 805 F.2d 410 (D.C. Cir. 1986), considered similar issues regarding standards adopted by EPA in 1985 for NO_x and particulate emissions from trucks and other heavy duty motor vehicles, based on use of a trap oxidizer. The standards would become fully effective in 1991. NRDC claimed that standards for the entire industry should be based on the performance of the "industry leader" — the best-performing engine in the industry. NRDC relied on statutory language requiring NO_x standards to be set by reference to the "maximum degree of emission reduction which can be achieved by means reasonably expected to be available for production" during the time period to which the standards apply, and particulate standards to be set "which reflect the greatest degree of emission reduction achievable through the application of technology which the Administrator determines will be available for the model year in question." It also pointed to legislative history discussing *International Harvester* and expressing concern that standards should not be set by reference to the industry laggards. The court rejected the "industry leader" claims. It pointed to other statutory language requiring that costs, noise, fuel economy, and vehicle safety be taken into account in setting standards. It also noted that the standard applies to the entire industry. A standard set by reference to the industry leader would not ensure a proper balancing of cost, noise, fuel economy, and safety in the standard as applied to the entire industry.

On the other hand, the court rejected the industry's contentions that the standard was based on trap oxidizing technology that had not been shown to be available for heavy duty trucks. The maximum longevity of a trap oxidizer meeting EPA's standards was 50,000 miles in a test GM truck whose driving cycle was not representative of trucks in actual use. The EPA standard would require 150,000 miles of longevity under conditions of actual use. The court upheld as reasonable EPA's prediction, extrapolating from the GM test truck and other evidence, that technology would be available by 1991 to enable the industry to meet the standard.

3. EPA has also faced problems in enforcing the emissions standards once automobiles were on the road. A General Accounting Office study in 1979 estimated that 80 percent of all automobiles violated the

standards because of misadjustment, tampering, or deterioration. An EPA survey in 1981 estimated that only one-third of those vehicles surveyed had all devices working properly. 12 BNA Envir. Rep. Current Develops. 1938 (1981). The 1977 Clean Air Act Amendments addressed this problem by providing for inspection and maintenance ("I&M") measures in SIPs for regions that had failed to achieve NAAQSs (typically, the ozone standard) because of automobile emissions. In regions that are seriously out of compliance, EPA has required I&M measures requiring periodic inspection of emission from autos in use and maintenance to improve their performance if necessary. However, cars in use have not been required to meet the same level of performance as the prototypes under EPA tests. The 1990 Amendments strengthened the I&M provisions for non-attainment areas.

4. How would you evaluate the success of the federal new-car emission limitation program in forcing the development and adoption of new automotive technologies? On the one hand, the program has clearly achieved substantial reductions in new car emissions. On the other hand, the reductions achieved in on-the-road use are less impressive than those achieved in the prototype testing on which EPA has relied to determine compliance. Older cars from the early 1970s that are still in use emit up to 100 times more pollution than brand new cars. Moreover, there are today over 90 air quality control regions in the nation that have failed to achieve compliance with primary ambient standards for one or more automotive pollutants.

There is considerable disagreement about the cost of new-car emissions control. A study by the Brookings Institution estimates that the cost has been approximately $1600 per vehicle. R. Crandall, et. al., Regulating the Automobile (1986). EPA claims that the cost has been $460 per vehicle. The principal sources for difference are (1) The Brookings study concludes that the emission controls cost $400 in lost fuel economy; EPA argues that there has been no fuel economy loss, particularly since precise control of the air/fuel ratio should enhance fuel economy; (2) The Brookings study estimates that emission controls raise maintenance costs by $177 per vehicle; EPA argues that there has been no increase in maintenance cost since cars with modern emission controls require less frequent adjustment; and (3) The Brookings Study estimates that the use of unleaded fuel, which is needed to avoid poisoning the emission control systems, costs $370; EPA suggests that this cost is offset by maintenance savings, since unleaded fuel extends spark plug life, oil change intervals, and exhaust system life.[25]

---

25. EPA also argues that the cost of unleaded gasoline is more properly attributed to the lead control program, which required the virtual elimination of lead in gasoline in order to protect public health.

5. The 1990 Amendments required further reductions in emissions from new vehicles and for the first time focused on automotive fuels as an important element in emission control strategies. Pre-existing controls reduced emissions per mile from new automobiles by over 95 percent compared to pre-1970 emissions. But the gains from these reductions have to a considerable extent been offset by large increases in automobile use and vehicle miles travelled, particularly in metropolitan areas. Congress responded to this problem by further restricting emissions from new cars and imposing for the first time controls on fuels designed to reduce emissions. Also, it imposed new requirements on states to adopt I&M plans, restrict gas station emissions, and impose transportation control measures to restrict automobile use. The last set of requirements, however, are the least vigorous and specific.

The Amendments adopt a two-phase schedule of emissions reductions from new automobiles and light duty trucks. In Phase I, the Amendments require a 35 percent reduction in hydrocarbon emissions (from .41 gpm to .25 gpm) and a 60 percent reduction in NO (from 1.0 gpm to .4 gpm) [26] A phase-in schedule provides that 40 percent of each manufacturer's sales volume must achieve these reductions by model year 1994, 80 percent by 1995, and 100 percent thereafter. Manufacturer warranties on exhaust gas catalytic converters and electronic diagnostic systems are extended to 8 years or 80,000 miles. The Amendments also establish presumptive Phase II standards for new cars after 2003 that call for a further 50 percent reduction in hydrocarbons (to .125 gpm), NO (.2 gpm) and CO (1.7 gpm) unless EPA determines that there is no need for further reductions in order to meet NAAQSs, or that such reductions will not be cost-effective (taking into account other means of achieving attainment), or that the technology to achieve such reductions is not available. There are also provisions requiring vehicles in use to achieve specified emission levels — .32 for HC, 3.4 for CO, and .4 for NO — throughout a "useful life" of 5 years or 50,000 miles. If a substantial number of vehicles of a particular manufacturer's model fail to achieve these standards although properly maintained and used, EPA may initiate recall or other measures requiring the manufacturer to remedy the non-compliance. There are also provisions requiring emissions reductions from busses and light and heavy duty trucks and dealing with evaporative (as opposed to exhaust) emissions from vehicles and the potential for vehicle-based ("on board") systems for control of emissions from vehicle refueling operations.

---

26. These requirements must be achieved by certified testing prototypes over 50,000 miles. Somewhat less stringent standards — .31 HC and .6 NO — must be achieved over 100,000 miles.

The 1990 Amendments also require EPA to promulgate regulations requiring use of reformulated gasoline by all vehicles during the high ozone season in the eight worst ozone non-attainment regions.[27] The regulations would reduce the emission of volatile organic compounds (VOCs) by requiring, for example, increased oxygen content and reduced benzene content in gasoline. VOC emissions must be reduced at least 15 percent by 1995, and 20 percent by 2000. The regulations must also minimize the generation of air toxics. Other, less severely polluted ozone non-attainment regions can opt in and require use of reformulated gasoline if they wish. The provisions establish a system of tradeable credits whereby refiners who produce gasoline whose performance exceeds the requirements of the regulation earn credits that can be sold to those whose gasoline falls short of the requirements, thereby enabling the latter to sell their product. There are also provisions requiring EPA regulation of the oxygen content of gasoline in the 41 CO non-attainment areas, and EPA regulation of gasoline fuel volatility. The Amendments also require detergent additives to prevent accumulation of deposits in engines or fuel supply systems and prohibit all use of lead or lead additives in gasoline.

The 1990 Amendments also add §§241-250 to the Act, aimed at developing new technologies for very low-emitting "clean fuel vehicles" that use alternative clean fuels such as methanol, reformulated gasoline, natural gas, liquified petroleum gas, hydrogen, or electricity. Clean fuel vehicles must meet the following clean fuel vehicle standards:[28] HC (defined as non-methanol organic gases or NMOG): .125 gpm; CO: 3.4 gpm; NO: .4 gpm. The HC emission level required is 50 percent lower than the level required of ordinary cars. In order to spur the development of clean fuel vehicle technologies, the Amendments provide for a California pilot program requiring production and sale within California to fleet owners and others of 150,000 clean fuel vehicles in model years 1996, 1997, and 1998, and 300,000 vehicles in each model year thereafter. Serious, severe, and extreme ozone non-attainment regions must by 1994 submit SIP revisions applying the clean fuel vehicle standards to fleet vehicles unless EPA determines that other equivalent measures to deal with vehicle source emissions have been adopted. The fleet vehicles covered by this requirement include 10 or more vehicles under common ownership or control that are or can be centrally fuelled: taxis, vehicles owned by federal, state, and local governments or companies, and so forth. The fleet vehicle requirements are phased in: 30 percent of fleet vehicles must meet them in

_____

27. Baltimore, Chicago, Houston, Milwaukee, New York, Philadelphia, San Diego, and Los Angeles.
28. Prototype testing vehicles must meet these standards for 50,000 miles.

model year 1998, 50 percent in 1999, and 70 percent in 2000. In model year 2001, Phase II fleet vehicle provisions will require all fleet vehicles to achieve a further reduction in NMOG emissions to .1 gpm.

6. Recall that under §§209 and 177 of the Act federal emission standards for new vehicles preempt more stringent state standards, except that California may adopt (subject to limited review by EPA) more stringent standards, and states with non-attainment regions may adopt standards identical to California's. California in recent years has adopted standards requiring all new cars to meet by 1995 the new federal standards that become fully effective only in 1996: .25 gpm HC, 3.4 gpm CO, and .4 NO. In addition, by 1998, 2 percent of new cars must have zero emissions. New York has already adopted the tougher California standards, and over a dozen additional states are considering their adoption. Automakers claim that the tougher standards are not needed outside of California, and will add $500-$1000 to the price of a new car.[29]

7. Which is the best of the Clean Air Act's techniques for technology forcing: emission limitations based on available technology (§111); limitations based on deadlines and health standards (§§109-110, §112); limitations based on deadlines with repeated extensions when technology proves unavailable (§202)? Do the provisions in the 1990 Amendments establishing federal requirements for fleet vehicles and a California pilot program for clean fuel vehicles represent a more promising approach? Or is it enough simply to allow California, and other non-attainment states that wish to adopt California standards, the flexibility to adopt standards more stringent than those imposed nationally? Does the Act have a consistent or coherent approach to "technology forcing"? Are there alternative approaches or types of incentives that would prove superior in stimulating development of environmentally superior technologies? For discussion, see LaPierre, Technology-Forcing and Federal Environmental Protection Statutes, 62 Iowa L. Rev. 771 (1977).

---

29. The Second Circuit recently rejected the motor vehicle manufacturers' challenge pursuant to the preemption provisions of §§177 and 209 of the Act, to New York's adoption of California's Low Emission Vehicle standards for emissions without also adopting California's clean fuels program, and its adoption of California's Zero Emission Vehicle quotas. *Motor Vehicle Manufacturers Assn., Inc. v. New York Department of Environmental Conservation,* 17 F.3d 521 (2d Cir. 1994).

D. REGULATION OF HAZARDOUS AIR POLLUTANTS

In addition to commanding EPA to set NAAQSs for criteria pollutants such as sulfur oxides, the Clean Air Act requires EPA to regulate emissions of "hazardous" air pollutants. CAA §112. The regulatory approach for hazardous air pollutants has differed substantially from that pursued for the criteria pollutants. The focus in 1970s was on the widespread criteria pollutants. While there is continuing concern over sources of the criteria pollutants, notably ozone and its precursor gases, NO_x and HC, attention during the 80s and 90s has shifted toward "toxic" pollutants. Specific toxic pollutants are generally emitted by a relatively small number of sources and their effects are generally localized. What considerations justify treating hazardous air pollutants differently from criteria pollutants? What are the implications for regulatory design and the allocation of responsibility between Congress and EPA? Should states have a greater or lesser role in regulating these different sets of pollutants? How does the political economy of hazardous pollutant regulation differ from the dynamics we have seen in the context of criteria pollutants?

The evolution of the regulatory approach for hazardous air pollutants has been among the most tortured of any environmental regulatory program. Before turning to this experience, it is worthwhile focusing upon the regulatory design problems posed by hazardous pollutants. Regulation of toxic materials arises in a number of areas, including water pollution, toxic substances in commercial products, food and drug regulation, pesticides, workplace safety, and hazardous waste disposal and clean-up. Although each of these areas has distinctive considerations, they share some important elements. The potential harm from exposure is grave. Great uncertainty often exists about the extent and likelihood of harm. There is often no threshold below which exposure is completely safe. The social benefits of the production processes that emit these pollutants and the costs of emission control can be highly variable.

The first subsection explores the broader dimensions of hazardous risk regulation. The second and third subsections focus upon the complex evolution of hazardous air pollution regulation.

1.   REGULATORY DESIGN ISSUES

PROBLEM: STANDARD SETTING FOR HAZARDOUS POLLUTANTS

EPA is considering whether to regulate three carcinogenic substances (a, b, c), each emitted by a different single industrial source. The best (but by no means perfect) scientific estimates of the risks and costs of control for these substances are:

	Substances		
	a	*b*	*c*
persons exposed (per year)	5,000,000	500,000	1,000
cancer risk (per year)	.000001	.00001	.001
expected deaths (per year)	5	5	1
average control cost (per year)	$20,000,000	$5,000,000 (partial shutdown)	$20,000,000
cost per life saved	$4,000,000	$1,000,000	$20,000,000

The a and c sources can absorb the control costs and remain in business. The b source, however, would have to partially shut down in order to meet best available technology (BAT) requirements, thus causing severe unemployment in the vicinity of the plant (the $5 million control cost for b includes economic costs of dislocation and unemployment associated with the partial shutdown).

(a)   Assume that EPA, because of limited resources, can issue regulations to control only two of these hazards during the coming year (and since new hazards may appear on next year's agenda, the hazard that is not regulated this year may not be regulated next year). Which hazard(s), if any, would you choose?

(b)   Now assume that EPA has resources available to regulate all three substances. Which would you regulate?

NOTES AND QUESTIONS

1. What are the justifications for national emission standards in the context of regulating hazardous pollutants? Are the justifications for national standards stronger or weaker in this context than with regard to criteria pollutants?

2. Should cost-benefit analysis be used in setting standards for hazardous air pollutants? Consider the following articles:

HAIGH, HARRISON & NICHOLS, BENEFIT-COST
ANALYSIS OF ENVIRONMENTAL REGULATION:
CASE STUDIES OF HAZARDOUS AIR POLLUTANTS

8 Harv. Envtl. L. Rev. 395, 396-397, 404-415, 429-430 (1984)

This article evaluates alternative methods of integrating benefit-cost considerations into the regulation of toxic substances. The use of benefit-cost considerations in this context is highly controversial and widely debated. The debate, however, has incorporated little or no reference to specific decisions made by environmental policy makers. Proponents of benefit-cost analysis point to the general virtues of explicit evaluation of benefits and costs. Critics, on the other hand, stress the philosophical difficulties involved in making judgments about life and death or the practical difficulty of estimating the costs and benefits of control. These broad debates do not consider what is at stake in particular circumstances and, indeed, whether those who assess the scientific evidence very differently might find much common ground in actual regulatory decisions. . . .

This article focuses on the ideas that benefit-cost analysis can yield widely accepted policy recommendations despite large uncertainties in many parameter estimates. Critics caricature benefit-cost analysis as a mindless toting up of costs and benefits, but benefit-cost principles are more properly viewed as framework for exploring opportunities to increase health and other benefits or reduce unnecessary costs. The crucial concept is *marginalism.* Given an existing regulation, benefit-cost analysis identifies marginal changes that increase benefits more than costs, or decrease costs more than benefits.

Critics argue that the data on benefits and costs of regulatory alternatives are simply too uncertain to use risk assessment or benefit-cost results in policymaking. In some cases, however, all plausible estimates of the parameters lead to the same policy recommendation. Thus, the results in such cases remain robust with respect to uncertainty.

II. THE CASE STUDIES

A. STEPS IN ESTIMATING BENEFITS

These studies estimate the benefits of pollution control standards by tracing the links from emissions to exposure to risk. The purposes of the analysis are either to estimate the dollar value that affected parties place on the reduced risk or to use the risk estimates to calculate the implicit cost per statistical life saved. The steps used, presented schematically in Figure 1, apply in assessing the benefits of controlling virtually any dangerous pollutant. The following discussion provides a general overview of the calculations associated with each step in the context of regulating airborne carcinogens.

FIGURE 1

Steps in Estimating Benefits

Emissions ———→ Exposure ———→ Risk ———→ Dollar Valuation

The change in emissions due to regulation is the most straightforward of the calculations that produce benefit estimates. For each plant, the EPA estimates the emissions with and without controls in place. The difference between these two estimates equals the emissions reduction attributable to the regulation imposed.

Emissions reduction estimates are converted into more meaningful estimates of exposure reductions by calculating an "exposure factor" for individual plants.[30] The exposure factor indicates the amount of exposure caused by a unit of emissions from a particular source. Both the dispersion pattern of emissions and the population pattern in the area surrounding the plant contribute to calculating this factor.

In many cases, EPA estimates emissions dispersion using a "model plant." For a given level of emissions, the dispersion model uses meteorological data to generate estimates of average annual pollutant concentrations at various distances from the source. The estimated concentrations are then combined with plant-specific population data to estimate total exposure levels for a given level of emissions.

Exposure levels are expressed in terms of "$\mu g/m^3$-person-years," which is simply the average annual concentration (in micrograms per cubic meter) multiplied by the number of people exposed and the period of exposure.[31] This summary measure of exposure provides sufficient information to predict total risk under certain conditions. Dividing the exposure level by the total level of emissions gives the exposure factor, expressed in terms of $\mu g/m^3$-person-years per kilogram emitted.

Reduced exposure is translated into reduced risk using the unit risk factor for the particular pollutant. A unit risk factor represents the risk of cancer posed by exposure to one unit of a substance — measured as the risk of cancer per $\mu g/m^3$-person-year. . . .

---

30. If a plant with an exposure factor of 0.6 $\mu g/m^3$-person-years/kg reduces its emissions by 1 million kilograms, for example, exposure falls by $0.6(1,000,000) = 600,000$ $\mu g/m^3$-person-years.

31. Thus, for example, 1000 people exposed, on average, to 10 $\mu g/m^3$ for one year generate 10,000 $\mu g/m^3$-person-years of exposure, as do 10,000 people exposed to 1 $\mu g/m^3$.

Over the past decade or two, a substantial literature has accumulated on the issue of valuing reductions in risks to life. Economists agree that the appropriate criterion is "willingness to pay." The principle is a simple one: an individual values each benefit just as much as the amount he would be willing to pay to secure it.

Inferences drawn from actual behavior provide the best estimates of willingness to pay. Many studies have estimated willingness to pay for reduced risks to life based on the wage premiums associated with occupational risks. Bailey has reviewed several empirical studies, adjusting them for consistency. His estimate covers a range of $170,000 to $715,000 per life saved, with an intermediate estimate of $360,000 in 1978 dollars, or approximately $500,000 in 1982 dollars. Other studies, however, have estimated much higher wage premiums for occupational risks, with the highest estimates in excess of $5 million per life saved in 1982 dollars. Thus, the published estimates from wage studies range from several hundred thousand dollars to several million dollars per statistical life saved.

Many of the calculations in this article forgo the final step of placing a dollar value on lives saved and presenting a single net benefit result. However, estimates of the reductions in lives saved and the implicit cost per statistical life saved are presented. These results are then compared with reasonable estimates of the value of this risk reduction to determine if the regulation is likely to pass a benefit-cost test.

B. THE CASE STUDIES

Benzene, coke oven emissions, and acrylonitrile are all high-priority section 112 pollutants. . . . Although the following case studies use a common underlying methodology to estimate the benefits of controls for all three pollutants, the empirical details of the methodology vary considerably with each pollutant. . . .

1. Maleic Anhydride (Benzene) Case Study

Maleic anhydride plants emit benzene, a major industrial chemical used in making nylon, plastics, insecticides and polyurethane foams. A 1977 study by the National Institute of Occupational Safety and Health showed an abnormally high incidence of leukemia in workers exposed to benzene while employed at two plants in the rubber industry. Following this study, the EPA listed benzene under section 112.

In April 1980, almost three years after listing benzene, EPA proposed an emission standard for maleic anhydride plants that use benzene as a feedstock. The [best available technology] BAT standard called for an emissions reduction of roughly ninety-seven percent from uncontrolled levels. A majority of the plants, however, already had installed controls of ninety percent or better, probably in response to state regulations directed at hydrocarbons or the hope that the benzene recovered would pay for the controls. As a result, the proposed BAT standard was expected to reduce full-capacity emissions by less than ninety percent, from 5.6 million kilograms per year to just under 0.5 million kilograms per year.

The costs of implementing the proposed standard were estimated at $2.6 million per year in 1982 dollars. These costs are quite affordable to the maleic anhydride industry, whose total sales grossed $142 million in 1979. The cost estimates are meaningless in isolation, however; they can be judged appropriately only in relation to the benefits they secure. As estimated, the proposed regulations would have reduced exposure by 3.6 million $\mu g/m^3$-person-years and saved 0.4 lives annually.

2. Coke Oven Emissions Case Study

Coke, produced by distilling coal in ovens, is essential to the production of iron and steel. In 1978, U.S. plants produced approximately 44 billion kilograms of coke. Epidemiological studies of coke-oven workers show that emissions from the coking process increased the risks of lung, trachea, bronchus, kidney, and prostate cancers. Although the toxic elements include gases and respirable particulate matter, most attention has focused on the polycyclic organic matter (POM) contained in coal tar particulates.

Coke oven emissions are released from numerous fugitive sources, including leaks and imperfections in the ovens. Charging emissions occur when coal is added to the ovens at the beginning of the coking process. Door leaks are the result of imperfect fits between the ovens and the doors through which the finished coke is later removed. Finally, imperfect seals on the lids and offtakes on the tops of the ovens create topside leaks.

If the EPA listed coke oven emissions under section 112, the Agency would probably specify standards similar to the following as BAT: twelve percent of doors visibly leaking; three percent of lids visibly leaking and six percent of offtake systems visibly leaking; and sixteen seconds of visible emissions for each charging. EPA estimates suggest that only thirty-seven of the fifty-four identified coke plants would have to increase control efforts to meet these standards (and some of those plants already meet one or two of the three potential BAT standards). EPA estimates annual control costs for those plants at $24.5 million.

Plant-specific emission estimates indicate that coke oven emissions would fall by 289,000 kg/year and exposure would fall by approximately 819,000 $\mu g/m^3$-person-years if the above BAT standards were imposed. Coke oven emissions are very potent carcinogens; this relatively slight reduction in exposure would save an estimated 10.6 lives each year.

3. Acrylonitrile Case Study

Acrylonitrile is an important industrial feedstock, employed primarily in the production of chemicals used to make a wide range of common products including rugs, clothing, plastic pipes, and automobile hoses. Almost a billion kilograms of acrylonitrile were produced in 1981. Extensive evidence indicating acrylonitrile's carcinogenicity exists. Specifically, epidemiological studies have associated acrylonitrile with respiratory cancers.

While EPA has neither listed acrylonitrile nor proposed specific regulations, EPA contractors have identified available control options that could reduce emissions by at least ninety-five percent from uncontrolled levels. All thirty existing plants, however, already have implemented some type of controls. Thus, potential BAT standards would only cut annual emissions from 3.6 million kilograms to 0.5 million kilograms, a reduction of slightly less than eighty-seven percent. Uniform controls would create an estimated annual expense of almost $29 million in 1982 dollars. Reduced exposure to acrylonitrile, just over 450,000 $\mu g/m^3$-person-years, would avoid only one case of cancer every five years (0.2 lives per year).

C. ANALYSIS OF THE BEST AVAILABLE TECHNOLOGY STANDARDS

Table 1 summarizes the results of the BAT standards analyzed. Controls on coke oven emissions produce much greater health benefits than do controls on the emissions of benzene or acrylonitrile. BAT controls on coke ovens would result in almost eleven fewer cases of cancer each year, compared to reductions of 0.4 cancer death for maleic anhydride benzene controls and 0.2 cancer deaths for acrylonitrile standards.

The final line of Table 1 presents the most relevant figure in measuring the cost-effectiveness of the three control standards — the value placed on saving a life that is necessary to justify incurring control costs. To justify acrylonitrile controls on benefit-cost grounds, the value of a statistical life would have to be at least $144 million, an implausible figure from virtually any perspective. The cost-effectiveness figure for benzene, $6.5 million, also is larger than the range of plausible esti-

TABLE 1
Benefits and Costs of BAT Standards

Annual Costs and Benefits	Benzene[a]	Coke Ovens	Acrylonitrile
Control Cost ($1000)	2,577	24,511	28,988
Number of Plants	8	37	31
Reduced Emissions (1000 kg)	5,059	289	3,112
Reduced Exposure			
($1000 \mu g/m^3$-person-yrs) [b]	3,646	819	455
Lives Saved[c]	.4	10.6	.2
Cost-Effectiveness			
Emissions ($/kg)	.51	84.8	9.3
Exposure ($/$\mu g/m^3$-yr)	.71	29.9	63.7
Lives saved ($1 million/life)	6.5	2.3	144

a. Estimates are based upon the 1980 proposed standard for maleic anhydride plants.

b. Exposure reductions are calculated by aggregating the concentrations changes for people at different distances from each plant. For example, if 1000 people have their exposure reduced by 10 micrograms per cubic meter ($\mu g/m^3$) in a given year, exposure would be reduced by 10,000 $\mu g/m^3$-person-years.

c. Lives saved are calculated by multiplying the exposure reduction by a unit risk factor that measures the increased probability of contracting cancer as a result of exposure to 1 $\mu g/m^3$ for one year. For example, if the exposure is reduced by 100,000 $\mu g/m^3$-per-year for a carcinogen that increases the risk of cancer by 1.5 at 10^{-4} for each $\mu g/m^3$-per-year, a total of 15 statistical lives would be saved. (Note: this article assumes that all cancer cases result in premature death.)

mates. Controls on coke oven emissions are the most attractive of the three BAT options. To justify the coke oven emissions standards on benefit-cost grounds, the value of a life saved must be equal to or greater than $2.3 million. That value does fall within the range of the published benefit estimates. Nevertheless, all three BAT options would fail a conventional benefit-cost test based upon a value of $1 million per life saved.

D.   ANALYSIS OF ALTERNATE STANDARDS

Benefit-cost criteria assist policymakers in evaluating regulatory alternatives beyond uniform BAT standards as well. This section analyzes two alternatives for each pollutant: (1) a relaxed uniform standard; and (2) a set of differential standards that would be more stringent for plants located in more densely populated areas than for plants that cause less exposure.

Choosing the appropriate degree of control is a common issue in

TABLE 3
Benefits for Alternative Strategies

Percentage of BAT Results	Benzene[a]	Coke Ovens	Acrylonitrile
Relaxed Uniform Standard[b]			
Benefits	94	80	62
Costs	57	61	29
Differential Standard[c]			
Benefits	96	81	60
Costs	37	33	18
Cost per Life Saved (in $1 million)			
Relaxed Uniform[b]	3.9	1.8	64.2
Differential[c]	2.5	.93	42.1
Net Benefits ($ million/year)			
BAT	−2.2	−13.9	−28.8
Relaxed uniform	−1.1	−6.4	−8.0
Differential	−.6	.5	−4.9

a. Estimates are based upon data available to EPA when the standard was proposed.
   b. Defined as:
      maleic anhydride: 90 percent
      coke ovens: doors open
      acrylonitrile: AN monomer and nitrile elastomer plants
   c. Defined as:
      maleic anhydride: 97 percent control for plants with exposure factors greater than .6
      coke ovens: doors and topside for plants with factors greater than 2.0
      acrylonitrile: BAT controls for AN monomer and nitrile elastomer plants with exposure factors greater than .2

pollution regulation. Controls should be tightened as long as the marginal benefits exceed the marginal costs. Negative net benefits at one control level do not imply that regulation is undesirable at all levels, because a less stringent alternative may provide positive net benefits.

Pollution control regulations can also be targeted to specific firms. The EPA and other regulatory agencies typically develop regulations for broad source categories. Section 112 is typical; the BAT standards apply to all plants within the source category. This approach ignores the fact that plants located in high density areas affect many more people and produce much greater exposure reduction for the same amount of emission control.

Table 3 summarizes the application of these alternate regulatory strategies to the three pollutants. Alternatives that target controls on the high-exposure plants are referred to as "differential standards."

Both the relaxed standards and the differential standards reduce costs much more than they reduce benefits. The cost-per-life-saved estimates, however, are still quite high. In fact, the only alternative that yields positive net benefits at a value per life saved of $1 million is differential standards for coke oven emissions. The other alternatives result in net losses ranging from $0.6 million for differential standards for maleic anhydride plants to $28.8 million for the BAT standards for acrylonitrile plants.

F.   SUMMARY

Huge uncertainties pervade estimates of the benefits of regulating airborne carcinogens. As a result, the figures presented in Part II must be viewed with a strong dose of skepticism; they may well be in error by orders of magnitude. These uncertainties, however, do not alter the major conclusions of the case studies.

The clearest conclusions emerge for the four source categories emitting acrylonitrile. The cost-effectiveness ratios for emission controls were ten or more times higher than the plausible range of values for risk reduction. Nothing in this section has suggested that benefit estimates err by that margin.

The calculations for benzene emitted from maleic anhydride plants gave a substantially narrower result, although the estimated cost per life saved was still in excess of $6 million. Several factors suggest that an accurate estimate of the expected cost-effectiveness ratio would be substantially higher. They include: (1) the general issue of the appropriate dose-response model; (2) evidence that the CAG overestimated the linear model's risk factor; and (3) a significant rise in the cost per life saved when the estimates are adjusted for less than full capacity operation.

The most ambiguous results arise in the case of coke ovens, although a BAT standard for charring emissions almost certainly would fail a benefit-cost test. Whether the uniform door and topside standards generate positive expected net benefits remains in doubt. Two issues raised in Part III, however, weigh against those standards: (1) the likelihood that the pure linear model overestimates the expected risk; and (2) the evidence suggesting that a value on risk reduction much in excess of $1 million per life saved cannot be justified. In fact, it is unclear whether even differential standards limited to high-exposure coke plants would yield positive net benefits. Such standards, however, unquestionably represent an alternative superior to uniform BAT standards.

LATIN, GOOD SCIENCE, BAD REGULATION, AND TOXIC RISK ASSESSMENT

5 Yale J. Reg. 89 (1988)

Regulation of toxic substances is an extremely complex, uncertain, and controversial enterprise. The regulatory process is customarily divided into two discrete functions: risk assessment ostensibly is a scientific activity that develops estimates of health hazards at varying exposure levels, while risk management is a political activity that balances competing interests and values to determine whether identified toxic risks should be considered unacceptable or tolerable. This sharp distinction between the scientific and social policy dimensions of toxic regulation is embodied in the Environmental Protection Agency's (EPA's) guidelines for estimating carcinogenic hazards, which provide that risk assessment must "use the most scientifically appropriate interpretation" and should "be carried out independently from considerations of the consequences of regulatory action." The requirement for adoption of the "most scientifically appropriate interpretation" reflects EPA's current priority on attaining "good science" in risk-assessment proceedings. In other words, EPA and other federal agencies now stress the need for scientifically credible risk assessment and presume that their analyses should be grounded exclusively on the best available scientific theories and data even if the resulting predictions do not achieve the degree of reliability ordinarily required for valid scientific conclusions.

This Article challenges the conventional view that scientific perspectives should dominate the risk-assessment process. To paraphrase Talleyrand, risk assessment is too important and too uncertain to be left exclusively to the risk-assessors. I contend instead that social policy considerations must play as prominent a role in the choice of risk estimates as in the ultimate determination of which predicted risks should be deemed unacceptable. . . .

Inadequate scientific knowledge and inadequate data usually prevent derivation of risk estimates based on reliable science. Toxic risk assessment suffers from fundamental uncertainties about causal mechanisms for cancer and other hazards, extrapolative relationships between high-dose and low-dose responses and between animal test data and human risks, latent effects and latency periods, special sensitivities in exposed subpopulations, synergistic or co-carcinogenic effects of various substances, past and present exposure levels, dispersion patterns for contaminants, and virtually every other area of required knowledge. These uncertainties generally preclude reliable assessments of relevant effects, and there is no scientific consensus on how they should be resolved. For example, conflicting risk estimates submitted in Food and

Drug Administration (FDA) proceedings on saccharine varied by more than a millionfold, and predictions of the hazards posed by TCE, a drinking-water contaminant, varied by many millions. One discussion of TCE regulation noted that the "estimates provide a range of uncertainty equivalent to not knowing whether one has enough money to buy a cup of coffee or pay off the national debt."

Under current regulatory practices, Agency scientists produce risk assessments that seldom approach the level of reliability normally expected of scientific findings; indeed, many estimates are little more than educated guesses. Yet, the choice among competing estimates — a prediction of only a minuscule hazard or one a million times greater — can determine whether toxic exposures are characterized as "acceptable" or "unacceptable" irrespective of any values in the risk-management process. Absent a scientific consensus on which risk-assessment principles should be applied, I contend that an agency's choice among competing risk estimates should not be exclusively a result of provisional scientific judgments. If substantial uncertainty exists about the extent of toxic hazards and the possible benefits from risk reductions, social consequences and political values must play an integral role in determining which speculative risk estimates are adopted.

There is an inherent tension between the disciplinary norms of good science and good regulation. Unlike in pure scientific research, where the proper response to uncertainty is reservation of judgment pending the development of adequate data and testable hypotheses, the risk-assessment process cannot be suspended without significant social consequences. A finding that a vital issue is currently indeterminate would be entirely consistent with the practice of good science, but "no decision" on a possible toxic hazard inescapably is a decision that promotes interests which benefit from the regulatory status quo. Risk assessment is not driven by the pursuit of knowledge for its own sake, the explicit goal of science, but by the need to decide whether potentially severe health hazards should be allowed to continue or whether high control costs should be imposed with potentially severe economic consequences. Thus, scientists in regulatory proceedings are expected to produce "answers" in a timely manner even if their predictions are highly speculative. Any reluctance to relax the standards of proof and certainty generally required of valid science may introduce a bias in favor of regulatory inaction.

The illusion that risk assessment is a purely scientific activity reduces the visibility and political accountability of policy judgments that often guide regulatory decisions on toxic hazards. A comparison of conflicting risk-assessment principles adopted by agencies under different administrations shows that regulators frequently do consider policy criteria when they select specific risk estimates. Federal agencies have recently employed controversial risk-assessment assumptions to justify inaction on some hazardous substances. Regulators have also attempted to make determinations based on "good science" without considering the implications of this approach for decisionmaking costs, regulatory delays, and opportunities for obstructive or strategic behavior by affected parties. Risk assessors often respond to scientific uncertainties by adopting conservative safety-oriented positions on some important issues while they use best-current-scientific-guess, middle-of-the-range, methodological-convenience, or least-cost treatments on other material issues. EPA and other agencies have never explained the scientific or policy rationales underlying these inconsistent treatments of uncertainty, and risk managers may not recognize that substantial inconsistency exists. In light of these diverse risk assessment practices, I contend that regulatory policy judgments as well as scientific judgments must be applied coherently, explained forthrightly, and tested actively through public debate. . . .

NOTES AND QUESTIONS

1. What critical assumptions underlie the Haigh, Harrison, and Nichols approach? What does this approach assume about the shape of the dose-response relationship for hazardous air pollutants? Are these assumptions sensible?

2. Latin notes that risk assessors often respond to the uncertainties of their task by adopting conservative safety-oriented assumptions about toxic effects. Is this a sensible approach to incorporating uncertainty into the risk assessment process?

Uncertainty enters each stage of risk assessment and conservative estimating techniques are often used at each level. At the emissions stage, EPA commonly assumes that plants operate at full capacity, although that is rarely the case. In estimating exposure, EPA often assumes that exposed individuals are born, live, and die at the point of maximum pollution concentration, ignoring the mobility of people in their daily lives and over their life cycles, as well as the opportunities for averting behavior. The greatest uncertainties lie in translating exposure estimates into risk estimates. Epidemiologic studies seek to correlate differences in population exposure to a toxic air pollutant with differences in levels of illness or death. Such studies, however, require good data, are costly, and face difficulties in sorting out the many potential causes of illness or death. Therefore, scientists resort to high dosage experiments using highly susceptible animal subjects to identify cause and effect relationships, which must then be extrapolated to humans subject to much lower exposures for a much longer period. Other assumptions — such as the use of the upper-bound estimate of low-dose risks, the assumption that a substance producing benign tumors in animals might produce malignant ones in humans — further ensure the conservativeness of risk assessments.

This process of compounding conservative assumptions has been sharply critized by economists on policy grounds. See Nichols & Zeckhauser, The Perils of Prudence: How Conservative Risk Assessments Distort Regulation, 10 Regulation 13 (Nov./Dec. 1986). As an example, a risk estimate that is a multiple of five independent factors where each factor is conservatively estimated at twice its expected value will be 32 times greater than the expected risk. Does this suggest that risk assessors should focus solely upon expected value risk estimates? Should regulators make their best estimate of risk without using conservative assumptions, and then apply a "margin of safety" factor at the end of the calculus? Would this increase the transparency and accountability of regulatory decisions? See *Lead Industries,* supra. What is the relevance of the trade-off between regulatory false positives and false negatives? See Page, A Generic View of Toxic Chemicals and Similar Risks, 7 Ecology L.Q. 207 (1978).

3. In view of the limitations of risk assessment noted above, Professor Dwyer argues that the use of risk assessment for setting environmental policy should be minimized and that technology-based standards should serve as the dominant mode of regulatory standard setting, at least until better risk information is developed. In his view, risk assessment should be used to augment technology-based standards by screening out trivial risks (that is, those not needing regulation) and identifying significant residual risks deserving stricter regulation. See, e.g., Dwyer, Limits of Environmental Risk Assessment, 116 Journal of Energy Engineering 231 (Dec. 1990). Does this approach strike a reasonable balance of the competing considerations? What advantages and disadvantages do you see?

4. The risk assessment framework ignores the distribution of toxic risks in our society, yet it is apparent that this distribution varies geographically and demographically. Should equity concerns enter into toxics policy? How should they be defined? How might such concerns be incorporated into risk policy? See Hornstein, Reclaiming Environmental Law: A Normative Critique of Comparative Risk Analysis, 92 Colum. L. Rev. 562 (1992); Doniger, The Gospel of Risk Management: Should We Be Converted? 14 Envtl. L. Rep. 10222 (June 1984). How should equity be defined? Should regulation be set so as to reduce the risk to the most exposed individual to a given level, even though there are only a few exposed individuals and the costs of control are very high, as in the case of the few individuals who live near radioactive uranium ore processing wastes in remote areas of the West? Or should we allocate resources in order to maximize reduction of total health risks, which would dictate that more should be spent to reduce emis-

sions to which many people are exposed? Should race and class play a role in regulatory decisions?

5. To what extent should lay perceptions of risks affect regulatory policy? Data on disease and death rates indicate that Americans' life expectancy is longer than ever before. Life expectancy at birth in 1986 was 74.8 years, up 4 years since 1970. This drop was due largely to reductions in deaths due to heart disease and strokes. Cancer deaths rose slightly. Two-thirds of cancer deaths, however are attributable to smoking, diet, and alcohol. By contrast, the best scientific evidence attributes less than 8 percent of cancer deaths to carcinogens in the workplace, environmental pollution, food additives, and industrial products combined. Cancers attributable to general environmental exposures are estimated at around 2 percent of all cancers. Doll & Peto, The Causes of Cancer: Quantitative Estimates of Avoidable Risks of Cancer in the United States Today, 66 J. Natl. Cancer Inst. 1191 (1981). Yet surveys indicate that Americans believe that environmental risks are greater than ever before. How should risk policy respond to these perceptions? Does this data indicate that the environmental regulatory effort to reduce health risks should be refocused? Consider that around 450,000 Americans die of cancer each year. Two percent of 450,000 is a significant number. Still, are we targeting resources on the best means of cancer prevention? Given the incompleteness of our scientific understanding of carcinogenesis, especially interactive effects, the difficulty of measuring the effects of low dosage toxics, and the political determinants of the research that is conducted, should we rely exclusively or even significantly upon the "best" scientific evidence in devising toxics regulatory policy?

6. The interaction of lay misperceptions of environmental risks and the political economy of regulatory decisionmaking can lead to some perverse regulatory priorities. In 1989, EPA promulgated emission limitations for industrial sources of benzene, an air pollutant believed to cause leukemia. Industrial sources were required to reduce emissions of benzene to levels where someone living right next to an emitting plant 24 hours a day for 70 years would have a 1 in 10,000 lifetime risk of benzene-induced leukemia. The regulations will impose up-front capital costs of approximately $1 billion, plus substantial ongoing operating costs. EPA conservatively estimates that these regulations will save two lives per year. Environmentalists objected to the standard as too lenient, arguing that a 1 in 1 million maximum individual risk would be a better basis for regulation. See Hershey, U.S. Adopts Limits on the Use of Benzene, N.Y. Times, Sept. 1, 1989, at A1, col. 5.

By contrast, EPA has estimated that radon, a decay product of uranium in soils whose radioactive byproducts can be inhaled and cause cancer, causes between 5000 and 20,000 lung cancers annually and that as many as one million homes have dangerous radon levels. See Jackowitz, Radon's Radioactive Ramifications: How Federal and State Governments Should Address the Problem, 13 B.C. Envtl. Att. L. Rev. 329 (1988). EPA estimates that living in a house with an average level of radon (1 picocurie per liter of air) creates an estimated lifetime lung cancer risk of between 1 in 300 and 1 in 75. U.S. EPA, A Citizen's Guide to Radon 10 (1986).[32] EPA lacks authority, however, to regulate home construction and ventilation practices. Congress in 1988 passed the Indoor Radon Abatement Act which provides modest funds, $3 million per year over three years, to assist EPA and the states in developing programs to promote public awareness of indoor radon risks.[33] Can you justify the priorities reflected in our benzene and radon policies?

7. In order to avoid such perverse results in risk reduction policy, EPA has been developing a framework for prioritizing risk regulation based upon risk management principles. This approach cuts across areas of environmental regulation and attempts to systematize the Agency's environmental improvement efforts. In 1987, EPA published Unfinished Business: A Comparative Assessment of Environmental Problems, which contains a staff ranking of environmental problems. The scientists listed ranked indoor air pollution, global climate change, and chemical discharges into estuaries and coastal waters high on the list, while assigning relatively low rankings to clean-up of toxic waste dumps, underground storage tanks, and municipal waste sites, areas receiving much of EPA's resources. The report concluded that "E.P.A.'s priorities appear more closely aligned with public opinion than with our estimated risks." Is the answer more extensive and forceful use of risk analysis and risk management techniques to render regulatory priorities? Who should be responsible for ordering priorities? Congress? EPA? The White House? The courts? Recall the debate over asbestos regulation, supra, p. 116. See generally Hornstein, Reclaiming Environmental Law: A Normative Critique of Comparative Risk Analysis, 92 Colum. L. Rev. 562 (1992).

---

32. Like other toxics issues, the magnitude of the problem and the type and degree of government intervention are controversial. See generally S. Krimsky and A. Plough, Environmental Hazards: Communicating Risks as a Social Process 130-179 (1988).

33. Homeowner efforts to address radon problems further highlight the irrationality of lay risk perceptions. A recent study of 14,000 homeowners who had tested the radon levels in their homes and discovered levels of at least 4 picocuries per liter of air or higher — indicating a lifetime lung cancer risk of at least 1 in 75 — found that only 18 percent had taken remedial action 18 months later. The typical remedy for radon problems is better ventilation, which costs only about $500 to $1,000 per home. Consumer Reports, Radon: The Problem No One Wants to Face, 623 (Oct. 1989). It should be noted that most homeowners have not even tested the radon levels in their homes.

2. THE EVOLUTION OF REGULATORY POLICY FOR HAZARDOUS AIR POLLUTANTS

The tortured evolution of regulatory policy for hazardous air pollutants illustrates well the interaction of regulatory design, institutional choice, delegation of decisionmaking authority within government, the limitations of judicial review, and the political economy of environmental regulation. This section surveys this history, while the next analyzes the 1990 Amendments to §112. It culminates with a series of problems exploring the requirements and efficacy of the current regulatory approach.

Federal regulation of hazardous air pollutants was first introduced in the Clean Air Act Amendments of 1970. Fueled by growing public awareness of environmental problems, political competition between Senator Muskie and President Nixon to claim the environmental mantle produced a highly aspirational statute. Section 112 of the Act epitomized the outcome of this process. It stated simply that EPA shall set emission limitations for hazardous air pollutants "at that level which . . . provides an ample margin of safety to protect the public health." The statute did not provide that either technological or economic factors were to be taken into account in adopting emission limitations.

DWYER, THE PATHOLOGY OF SYMBOLIC LEGISLATION

17 Ecology L.Q. 233 (1990).

II. AGENCY RESISTANCE TO SYMBOLIC LEGISLATION . . .

A. REGULATION AND LITIGATION UNDER SECTION 112

As the potential impact of section 112 became clear, EPA gradually developed a two-fold strategy to deal with the "ample margin of safety" criterion. First, the Agency effectively rewrote section 112 by construing it to permit consideration of economic and technological factors in issuing emission standards. Second, EPA developed a cumbersome decisionmaking process for listing pollutants and adopting emission standards, thereby forcing substantial delays. This second tactic reflects EPA's tendency to "study" a problem interminably when faced with a difficult regulatory choice or an ambiguous or unpalatable statutory mandate.

1. Regulation Between 1970 and 1977: Tentative Reliance on Economic Factors

From the enactment of section 112 in 1970 until the 1977 amendments, EPA adopted emission standards for only four chemicals. Almost immediately after passage of the 1970 Act, the Agency listed three chemicals (asbestos, mercury, and beryllium) as hazardous air pollutants, the first step in the regulatory process. Eight months later, EPA issued proposed emission standards, but did not adopt final standards until nearly sixteen months after that, and then only in response to a court order. In 1975, EPA listed a fourth chemical, vinyl chloride, with proposed emission standards. The final rule was promulgated in late 1976.

At first, EPA half-heartedly denied that it took economic considerations into account. There is, however, ample evidence that the opposite was true. For example, the final standards for beryllium and mercury are virtually identical to the proposed standards that EPA concededly based on economic considerations. . . .

EPA was more forthright about its use of economic factors in the proposed and final emission standards for vinyl chloride. . . .

2. Rewriting Section 112: The Development of Best Available Technology Standards

By the time EPA adopted the final vinyl chloride regulations in 1976, it had issued the first of a series of guidelines for regulating suspected carcinogens, a category that includes many hazardous air pollutants. An explicit premise of these guidelines was that, for many hazardous air pollutants, it would not be possible to eliminate risk "without unacceptable social and economic consequences." These guidelines formed the basis of EPA's evolving regulatory policy under section 112. The "ample margin of safety" criterion [in Section 112] would be read to permit consideration of costs and technological feasibility in setting emission standards. . . .

. . . The Agency assumed that in the absence of contrary evidence carcinogens do not have a threshold level; every level of exposure presents some non-zero risk that exposed humans will develop cancer. Thus, construing section 112 strictly would require a zero-emission standard to provide an "ample margin of safety." This standard, EPA felt, would

> produce massive social dislocations, given the pervasiveness of at least minimal levels of carcinogenic emissions in key American industries. Since few such industries could soon operate in compliance with zero-

emission standards, closure would be the only legal alternative. Among the important activities affected would be the generation of electricity from either coal-burning or nuclear energy; the manufacturing of steel; the mining, smelting, or refining of virtually any mineral (e.g. copper, iron, lead, zinc, and limestone); the manufacture of synthetic organic chemicals; and the refining, storage, or dispensing of any petroleum product.

EPA's position was that the legislative history did not indicate that Congress intended such drastic results and that the "ample margin of safety" language in section 112 permitted "some residual risk." Although EPA insisted that it would rely primarily on evidence of health risks in setting emission standards, the Agency acknowledged that it would also weigh "social and economic factors," such as

the benefits of the activity or substance producing risk, the distribution of the benefits versus the distribution of the risks; the availability and possible environmental risks of substitutes for that substance or activity; and the cost of reducing the risk further.

Based on this view of the statutory policy, EPA proposed that existing sources of hazardous air pollutants be required to use the "best available technology" to control emissions from source categories presenting significant risks to public health. . . .

3. Paralysis by Analysis: The Development of Elaborate Internal Review Procedures

Rewriting section 112 was not EPA's only implementation strategy. During the late 1970s and early 1980s, EPA also developed an extensive internal review process that delayed, and indeed almost eliminated, the adoption of emission standards. Although EPA had listed and issued proposed emission standards for asbestos, mercury, and beryllium within a year of the enactment of the Clean Air Act in 1970, by the early 1980s, EPA took as long as four years to decide whether to list a chemical and several additional years to issue proposed regulations. . . .

Several critics correctly view EPA's extensive analysis and review process under section 112 as a means to avoid or delay issuing standards under a provision that the Agency finds irrational. This view comports closely with EPA's own explanation for the delay. During a 1983 congressional oversight hearing, EPA Administrator Ruckelshaus stated, "Where the [statutory] mandates are unclear or appear to suggest unfeasible programs, they tend to slow down, to 'study the problem,' as the saying goes." . . .

4.   Regulation Between 1977 and 1987: Increasing Judicial and Congressional Pressure

Given the lengthy internal review process, it is not surprising that EPA made few regulatory decisions for hazardous air pollutants during the late 1970s and early 1980s.

[Dwyer describes efforts by Congress to pressure EPA, through oversight hearings and proposed legislation, to regulate more chemicals under section 112.]

EPA's continued inaction under section 112 stemmed in part from its growing doubts that strict controls of many hazardous air pollutants would reduce health risks significantly. By the mid-1980s, EPA found itself in the unenviable position of implementing a statute that it believed served a limited public health purpose at potentially great social and economic costs. As Administrator Ruckelshaus testified, benefits from section 112 controls were "relatively low," and "standards that eliminate more than one cancer case per year are more the exception than the rule." The result was that while EPA began to make substantial progress in evaluating potential hazardous air pollutants, its record for actually regulating such pollutants under section 112 failed to improve.[34]

5.   NRDC v. EPA: The Demise of BAT Standards

Until 1985, environmental groups used judicial review mainly to force EPA to issue standards for listed hazardous pollutants. Only one suit challenged the adequacy of EPA's standards, and that case, which settled, did not involve the BAT policy. . . .

In 1985, NRDC sued EPA, arguing that the Agency impermissibly

---

34. The following table shows the lengthy delays that have occurred between listing chemicals as hazardous, issuing proposed standards, and issuing final standards.

Chemicals	Listing	Proposed Standard	Final Standard
beryllium	[3/31/71]	[12/7/71]	[4/6/73]
asbestos	[3/31/71]	[12/7/71]	[4/6/73]
mercury	3/31/71	12/7/71	4/6/73
vinyl chloride (revisions)	12/24/75	6/2/77	9/30/86
benzene	6/8/77	4/18/80 - 1/5/81	6/6/84
radionuclides	12/27/79	4/6/83	2/6/85
arsenic	6/5/80	7/20/83	8/4/86
coke emissions	9/18/84	4/23/87	———

had relied on nonhealth factors in setting emission standards for vinyl chloride. The group's position that the "ample margin of safety" language required EPA to set zero-emission standards for nonthreshold pollutants not only struck at the heart of the BAT policy, but advocated the most extreme view possible of section 112.

The Agency maintained that section 112 did not require a zero-emissions standard because Congress could not have intended to require standards that would impose staggering economic and social costs. EPA reasoned that since the statute did not require risk-free standards, it had authority to adopt emission standards under the BAT policy. Attempting to reach a middle ground, the court of appeals construed section 112 as requiring EPA to regulate only "significant" or "unacceptable risks."[35] The court rejected NRDC's position that EPA could never consider costs and technological feasibility in setting emission standards, but, in a significant reversal of EPA policy, it strictly limited EPA's use of these factors in setting emission standards.

The court acknowledged that EPA's interpretation of a statute deserves great deference when the Agency's technical expertise guides its interpretation, particularly where the substantive area involves unresolved scientific issues. The court concluded, however, that in applying the BAT formulation to set the vinyl chloride emission standard, the EPA Administrator had failed to exercise discretion in determining an "acceptable risk to health," and had "simply substituted technological feasibility for health as the primary consideration."

Because section 112 makes protection of health the primary consideration, the court held that EPA must first "make an initial determination of what is 'safe,' . . . based exclusively upon the Administrator's determination of the risk to health at a particular emission level." Emphasizing that it did not equate "safe" with "risk-free" or even free from uncertainty, the court stated that EPA must set an emission standard that results in "acceptable" risk to health without considering costs or technological feasibility. "Once safety is assured," EPA may reduce the emission standard further to provide an ample margin of safety. In this second step, EPA may take into account the limitations of scientific knowledge in measuring risks, as well as costs and technological feasibility.

The decision was an important victory for environmental groups. By requiring EPA to determine a "safe" level of exposure without considering costs and feasibility, the court vindicated the symbolic value of legislation that places the protection of health above all other considerations. It also effectively forced EPA's policymaking underground.

---

35. *NRDC v. USEPA*, 824 F.2d 1146 (D.C. Cir. 1987) (en banc).

6. *Regulation is a Vacuum: Setting Health-Based Emission*
   Standards

EPA had two options. Pursuant to the Vinyl Chloride decision, it could adopt standards to ensure a "safe" level of exposure that did not consider costs or feasibility. This approach risked closure of major industries but might have forced Congress to reconsider the substantive criteria in section 112. Alternatively, EPA could devise a strategy, consistent with the letter but not the spirit of the court's construction of section 112, allowing it to weigh nonhealth-related factors in setting standards. EPA apparently chose the second option and has attempted to rewrite section 112 silently in an effort to avoid judicial review. . . .

NOTES AND QUESTIONS

1. Why might Congress enact such an infeasible regulatory program? How could it remain in its original form for such a long time?

2. The Congress seems to have been under the impression that hazardous air pollutants were not dangerous below some threshold. As EPA discovered, however, any emissions of carcinogens and many other hazardous air pollutants present risks. Should a statute that is premised upon a critical mistaken fact be interpreted literally? How would a contract that is based upon a material erroneous fact or the completion of an impossible task be interpreted? Should it matter that Congress wished to believe that thresholds existed, whether or not they did?

3. Following the Vinyl Chloride decision, EPA developed a two-stage framework for managing hazardous air pollutants. See 54 Fed. Reg. 38044 (1989). For the first stage of analysis, defining the concept of "acceptable risk" to human health, EPA concluded the maximum acceptable individual risk — that is, the cancer risk to a person living near the pollution source and exposed to the maximum concentration of the pollutant for 24 hours per day over 70 years — was less than 1 in 10,000 chances. For the second stage, establishing an "ample margin of safety," EPA sought to ensure that the individual lifetime risk of contracting cancer from the pollutant was less than 1 in 1 million for 99 percent of all persons living within 50 kilometers of all emission sources. See Marchant, "Acceptable" Risk for Hazardous Air Pollutants, 13 Harv. Envtl L. Rev. 535 (1989).

4. Were environmentalists well served by pressuring EPA to adhere to the letter of the law?

3. The 1990 Amendments to Section 112

The overhaul of §112 was among the most dramatic changes in the 1990 Amendments. Whereas the original section was but a few paragraphs, the new provisions (Title III) cover 122 pages of the 700-plus page legislation. This one title is longer than the entire Clean Air Act Amendments of 1977.

At this point, it is worthwhile to work through the provisions of §112. In view of the complexity of the provisions, it will be helpful to develop an outline of the key provisions. The new §112 establishes a list of 189 toxic air pollutants that must be regulated through maximum available control technology (MACT) standards issued by EPA in accordance with a statutory timetable. EPA may add or delete listed pollutants. Controls are to be established for "major sources," defined as those that emit or have the potential to emit 10 tons or more per year of any listed substance, or 25 tons or more of any combination of listed substances, and for "area sources" emitting smaller amounts. MACT standards are applicable immediately to new sources; existing sources have 3 years to comply, with a potential one-year extension. EPA must study and report to Congress on any substantial health risks that may remain after application of MACT controls, and adopt health-based controls on sources posing any such risks. EPA is also instructed to devise a national urban toxics strategy to reduce health risks associated with air toxics emissions in urban areas by 75 percent. EPA is directed to identify 100 hazardous pollutants that could cause serious health harms in the event of accidental release and to promulgate accident prevention regulations. The Amendments also establish an independent Chemical Safety and Hazard Investigation Board to investigate accidents and make recommendations. Owners and operators of facilities with such hazardous chemicals are under a duty, backed up by liability, to operate safely and make engineering analyses of their facilities to identify hazards. Finally EPA must issue new or revised NSPSs for municipal, commercial, and industrial incinerators. For further discussion see Comment, The 1990 Clean Air Act Amendments: Section 112 Comes of Age, 59 U. Cin. L. Rev. 1253 (1991).

The following questions will hone your understanding of the provisions:

- What is the standard for adding a pollutant to the list?
- What sources of hazardous air pollutants must be regulated? May EPA regulate other sources? What sources may not be regulated?
- What emission standards must be established? To what extent can economic and technological feasibility enter into the determination of standards?

- Do the 1990 Amendments retain a health-based standard? What is it? When and under what circumstances does it become effective?
- How quickly must EPA promulgate emission standards? What are the consequences of failing to meet these deadlines?
- What decisions by EPA are subject to judicial review? When may petitioners challenge these decisions?
- What actions may sources take to delay application of government emission limitations?
- X Corporation's plant currently emits (on an annual basis) 60 tons of vinyl chloride, 80 tons of hexane, 30 tons of heptachlor, and 20 tons of chlorinated dioxins. It can reduce these emissions by 54, 76, 28, and 16 tons, respectively, within the next year. Assuming that emission standards for these pollutants will not have been proposed within this period, how would these emission reductions affect X Corporation's regulatory requirements under Section 112?

NOTES AND QUESTIONS

1. What approach(es) to regulatory design are reflected in the 1990 Amendments to §112? To what extent do these provisions respond to the problems that arose in implementing the original hazardous air pollutant provisions? To what extent do the 1990 Amendments to §112 codify EPA's original approach to interpreting the original hazardous air pollutant provisions? Its approach following the 1987 Vinyl Chloride decision? Does §112(f)(2) merely delay implementation of the original §112 requirements? What are the key differences in approach?

2. Based upon your analysis of regulatory design issues in paragraph 1, do you feel that the new regulatory scheme addresses the environmental problems posed by air toxics effectively? What are its advantages? Disadvantages? Do the new approaches properly prioritize risk regulation? Do they deal more effectively with the political and economic considerations involved in toxics regulation? Are the new provisions likely to spur innovation in reducing emissions of hazardous air pollutants? Will they substantially improve human health and welfare? Will the costs be commensurate with the benefits? What alternative approaches might be preferable?

3. Note that §112(i)(5) provides for an early reduction program. Sources that reduce their total toxics emission by 90 percent prior to proposal of technology-based standards for particular toxic pollutants are excused from compliance with such standards for a period of six years after their promulgation. EPA is to develop an index to weight

the toxicity of various toxic pollutants in order to calculate the average 90 percent reduction figure. This early reduction alternative can be viewed as an innovative form of "environmental contracting" in which a facility agrees to achieve a large and rapid overall reduction in total pollutant loadings in exchange for compliance with burdensome pollutant-by-pollutant regulatory requirements. The flexibility afforded by a facility-wide approach can provide significant cost savings and opportunities for innovation, which in turn allow for greater overall pollution reductions. In the Netherlands and some other European nations, this approach takes the form of an actual written contract between a facility or an industry and regulatory authorities specifying an overall, facility-wide reduction in total pollution loadings in lieu of otherwise applicable regulatory requirements. In some cases, contracts are written to cover total residuals in all media — air, water, and wastes — and provide for cross-media as well as cross-pollutant indexing. See Stewart, Environmental Regulation and International Competitiveness, 102 Yale L.J. 2039, 2090-2093 (1993). Is such an approach desirable in the U.S. regulatory context? Feasible? How would compliance with contract terms be monitored and enforced?

4. How would Haigh, Harrison, and Nichols evaluate the new §112? A respected environmental economist estimated the benefits from the program, based on a value of $3 million per statistical life saved, at between 0 and $4 billion annually. He estimated costs at between $6 and $10 billion annually. See Portney, Policy Watch: Economics and the Clean Air Act, 4 J. Econ. Perspectives 173 (1990).

E.   PROBLEMS OF GROWTH AND NON-ATTAINMENT

The Clean Air Act Amendments of 1970 were primarily aimed at controlling air pollution in the large urban and industrial areas of the United States in which the health risks of air pollution were most acute. The 1970 Amendments did not address the important question of what should be done about the 80 percent of the nation's area which already enjoyed air cleaner than that required by the National Ambient Air Quality Standards. Should air quality in these areas — which included scenic national parks — be allowed to deteriorate to the nationally uniform standards established by the NAAQSs? Or did Congress intend that pollution in such areas be subject to additional limitations? The first set of materials in this section address the problems of growth in these regions, where air quality is equal to or better than that required by NAAQSs. The second set of materials deals with the thorny problem of what to do with those "non-attainment" regions which did not achieve the NAAQSs within the 1975-1976 statutory deadlines. Should construction of any new sources in these regions be prohibited? Would such a prohibition simply prolong the effective life of old, poorly controlled sources? What policies and tools should be used to balance achievement of air pollution goals and economic growth in non-attainment regions?

1. ATTAINMENT REGIONS: THE EVOLUTION OF PSD CONTROLS

SIERRA CLUB V. RUCKELSHAUS

344 F. Supp. 253 (D.D.C. 1972), aff'd by an equally divided Court, 412 U.S. 541 (1973)

JOHN H. PRATT, District Judge.

Initially, this matter came before the Court on plaintiffs' motion for temporary restraining order wherein they sought to enjoin the Administrator of the Environmental Protection Agency from approving certain portions of state air pollution plans — implementing the national primary and secondary standards — which had been submitted to the Administrator pursuant to Section 110 of the Clean Air Act of 1970. . . .

The Administrator, in recent testimony before Congress, indicated that he had declined to require state implementation plans to provide against significant deterioration of the existing clean areas — i.e., areas with levels of pollution lower than the secondary standard — because he believed that he lacked the power to act otherwise. . . .

Previously, the Administrator had promulgated a regulation permitting states to submit plans which would allow clean air areas to be degraded, so long as the plans were merely "adequate to prevent such ambient pollution levels from exceeding such secondary standard." 40 C.F.R. §51.12(b) (1972).

Plaintiffs claim that the Administrator's interpretation of the extent of his authority is clearly erroneous and that his declination to assert his authority, evidenced in his remarks before Congress and his promulgation of a regulation that is contrary to the Clean Air Act, amounts to a failure to perform a nondiscretionary act or duty.

[The Court held that it accordingly had jurisdiction under Section 304 of the Act, authorizing "citizen suits" against the EPA Administrator to require performance of nondiscretionary duties imposed on him by the Act, to hear plaintiffs' claim, and that plaintiffs therefore need not await the Administrator's approval of SIPs and then seek review of such approval in a court of appeals pursuant to Section 307.]

In discussing the merits of the present action — i.e., the extent of the Administrator's authority and the validity of the questioned regulation — we turn to the stated purpose of the Clean Air Act of 1970, the available legislative history of the Act and its predecessor, and the administrative interpretation of the Act.

PURPOSE OF THE ACT

In Section 101(b) of the Clean Air Act, Congress states four basic purposes of the Act, the first of which is

> To protect and enhance the quality of the Nation's air resources so as to promote the public health and welfare and the productive capacity of its population.

On its face, this language would appear to declare Congress' intent to improve the quality of the nation's air and to prevent deterioration of that air quality, no matter how presently pure that quality in some sections of the country happens to be.

LEGISLATIVE HISTORY

The "protect and enhance" language of the Clean Air Act of 1970 stems directly from the predecessor Air Quality Act of 1967, 81 Stat. 485. The Senate Report underlying the 1967 Act makes it clear that all areas of the country were to come under the protection of the Act. S. Rep. No. 403, 90th Cong., 1st Sess. 2-3 (1967).

The administrative guidelines promulgated by the National Air Pollution Control Administration (NAPCA) of the Department of Health, Education and Welfare (HEW), which at that time had the responsibility of carrying out the directives of the Air Quality Act of 1967, point up the significance of the "protect and enhance" language as follows:

> [A]n explicit purpose of the Act is "to *protect* and *enhance* the quality of the Nation's air resources" (emphasis added). Air Quality standards which, even if fully implemented would result in significant deterioration of air quality in any substantial portion of an air quality region clearly would conflict with this expressed purpose of the law. . . .

Turning now to the legislative history of the 1970 Act, we note at the outset that both Secretary Finch and Under Secretary Veneman of

HEW testified before Congress that neither the 1967 nor the proposed Act would permit the quality of air to be degraded. . . .

More important, of course, is the language of the Senate Report accompanying the bill which became the Clean Air Act of 1970. The Senate Report, in pertinent part, states:

> In areas where current air pollution levels are already equal to or better than the air quality goals, the Secretary shall not approve any implementation plan which does not provide, to the maximum extent practicable, for the continued maintenance of such ambient air quality. S. Rep. No. 1196, 91st Cong., 2d Sess., at 2 (1970). . . .

ADMINISTRATIVE INTERPRETATION

As we noted under our discussion of the legislative history of the 1967 Act, the 1969 guidelines promulgated by HEW's NAPCA emphasized that significant deterioration of air quality in any region would subvert the "protect and enhance" language of the 1967 Act. We also pointed out that Secretary Finch and Under Secretary Veneman applied this same administrative interpretation to the very same language found in the proposed 1970 Act.

On the other hand, the present Administrator, in remarks made in January and February 1972 before certain House and Senate Subcommittees, has taken the position that the 1970 Act allows degradation of clean air areas. Several Congressional leaders voiced their strong disagreement with the Administrator's interpretation. . . .

The Administrator's interpretation of the 1970 Act, as disclosed in his current regulations, appears to be self-contradictory. On the one hand, 40 C.F.R. §50.2(c) (1970) provides:

> The promulgation of national primary and secondary air quality standards shall not be considered in any manner to allow significant deterioration of existing air quality in any portion of any State.

Yet, in 40 C.F.R. § 51.12(b), he states:

> In any region where measured or estimated ambient levels of a pollutant are below the levels specified by an applicable secondary standard, the State implementation plan shall set forth a control strategy which shall be adequate to prevent such ambient pollution levels from exceeding such secondary standard.

The former regulation appears to reflect a policy of nondegradation of clean air but the latter mirrors the Administrator's doubts as to his authority to impose such a policy upon the states in their implementation plans. In our view, these regulations are irreconcilable and they demonstrate the weakness of the Administrator's position in this case.

INITIAL CONCLUSIONS

Having considered the stated purpose of the Clean Air Act of 1970, the legislative history of the Act and its predecessor, and the past and present administrative interpretation of the Acts, it is our judgment that the Clean Air Act of 1970 is based in important part on a policy of nondegradation of existing clean air and that 40 C.F.R. §51.12(b), in permitting the states to submit plans which allow pollution levels of clean air to rise to the secondary standard level of pollution, is contrary to the legislative policy of the Act and is, therefore, invalid. Accordingly, we hold that plaintiffs have made out a claim for relief.

[The court granted a preliminary injunction against the EPA Administrator's approval of state plans permitting significant deterioration of existing air quality.]

NOTES AND QUESTIONS

1. What is the rationale for a federal nondegradation policy? Is it justified by considerations of economic efficiency (giving full scope for diversity in tastes and the possible efficiencies in "separate facilities," see supra pp. 261–263)? Is it justified by other considerations, such as principles of environmental diversity designed to foster a variety of preferences and attitudes towards the natural environment and associated industrial and social development? Might we find constitutional resonance with the theme of environmental diversity in the First Amendment and the federal structure of the Constitution which, prior to the era of pervasive industrialization, was calculated to promote social and cultural diversity? Might PSD policies be justified as a means of postponing exploitation of the pollution increment otherwise permitted by the federal ambient standards in order to protect the standards themselves against revision in the face of continued pressures for economic growth?

2. Under §116 of the Act, states with air cleaner than that required by the federal standards are free to insist upon maintenance of their existing air quality. Why might they be reluctant to do so? Is the court's decision inconsistent with the spirit of §116?

3. How do the possible justifications for a nondegradation policy bear upon the soundness of the courts' construction of the Act? If "clean" states would really benefit from a nondegradation policy, would

we not expect to see an explicit nondegradation requirement in the statute? On the other hand, if a nondegradation requirement would entail sacrifices on the part of "clean" states for the benefit of the nation as a whole, shouldn't we require explicitness in the statute? Wouldn't a requirement of explicitness at least enhance the possibility that "clean" states would be compensated for the burdens thrust upon them?

In light of these considerations, how persuasive is the courts' interpretation of the statute? Is the "protect and enhance" language of the preamble anything more than hortatory? Also, of what relevance is the administrative practice prior to the 1970 Amendments and the testimony by administration officials based on that practice? Under the pre-1970 law, states set ambient standards and devised corresponding implementation plans, subject to federal approval. See supra, pp. 242-244. In these quite potentially fluid circumstances, involving geographically varying standards with no firm guiding principles, existing air quality might serve as a useful and appropriate benchmark. But of what relevance is prior air quality under the 1970 Amendments, which firmly establish uniformity in federal ambient standards as the basic foundation of the entire system? Consider also the Senate Report relied upon in the initial *Sierra Club* decision, supra. Wasn't §111, imposing NSPS requirements on new or modified stationary sources, the means chosen by Congress to deal with the threat of degradation of air quality in "clean" areas? Congress could have easily enacted a specific nondegradation policy. Why didn't it? What explains the legislative history relied upon by the court?

4. Do the constitutional overtones in a principle of environmental diversity support venturesome statutory construction by judges of a sort that would not be justified under normal practices? As a result of the *Sierra Club* decisions, Congress was, as we shall see, required to confront an issue of great significance for the future that might otherwise have been submerged, resulting in relatively unrestricted development. Is this sufficient justification for the courts' decisions? On the other hand, is it equitable for the courts to force "clean" states to preserve existing air quality for the sake of national policies? Consider that the burden of economic nondevelopment in such states will be borne primarily by the poor, while the benefits may accrue, to a disproportionate extent, to the wealthy who can afford to travel to pristine areas or are educated to derive vicarious enjoyment from their preservation. Consider also the inability of the courts to mandate redistribution of wealth from the gainers from its decision to the losers.

For discussion of these issues, see Stewart, The Development of Administrative and Quasi-Constitutional Law in Judicial Review of Environmental Decisionmaking: Lessons from the Clean Air Act, 62 Iowa L. Rev. 714 (1977). Other regulatory measures to preserve pristine environments are considered in Robinson, Wilderness: The Last Frontier,

59 Minn. L. Rev. 1 (1974). For a valuable review of nondegradation policies in federal pollution control, see Hines, A Decade of Nondegradation Policy in Congress and the Courts: The Erratic Pursuit of Clean Air and Clean Water, 62 Iowa L. Rev. 643 (1977).

In December 1974, the EPA promulgated nonsignificant deterioration (NSD) regulations establishing allowable increments in pollution concentrations over existing levels for designated areas. Congress codified and revised these regulations in the 1977 Amendments to the Clean Air Act. The new provisions, referred to as Prevention of Significant Deterioration (PSD) and Visibility Protection, are contained in §§160-169A of the Act. You should carefully review these provisions before turning to the notes and questions that follow.

NOTES AND QUESTIONS

1. In addition to preserving and enhancing air quality in scenic federal lands of national importance, the Act seeks to regulate deterioration of air quality in other moderately polluted areas where air quality is presently better than required under the federal ambient standards. What legitimate federal interest is there in regulating deterioration in the latter areas? Why shouldn't Clayton, Missouri, or Tallahassee, Florida, be permitted to develop economically (and degrade its air quality) to the same extent as areas that are presently industrialized (and dirty), so long as the area complies with federal ambient standards?

Conceivably there is a national interest in containing or reducing total emissions of pollutants, even if they do not cause local ambient violations, because such pollutants are transported over long distances and may contribute to pollution damage elsewhere, or because it is deemed prudent to limit total atmospheric loadings of pollutants in view of scientific uncertainty about the effects of pollution. Can Congress' PSD provisions be justified as a means for limiting total atmospheric loadings? Is it equitable in its treatment of less-developed areas?

2. Professor Peter Pashigian suggests that the underlying political motivation for PSD policy might not be as lofty as the ideals of environmental diversity and aspiration suggested earlier.

> Environmental policy has fostered a curious set of multiple standards. On the one hand, minimum national standards are supposed to be met in all air control regions. On the other hand, areas with air quality superior to these minimum standards are required to control economic development and prevent air quality from deteriorating beyond a prescribed amount, even if the resulting air quality is still superior to the minimum

standard. Environmental policy has given a stamp of approval for industrial-urban locations to merely achieve the minimum standards while imposing higher than minimum standards on areas with superior air quality.

Why these implicit multiple standards become an integral part of environmental policy is the central focus of this paper. The major premise advanced and tested is that PSD policy was developed to attenuate the locational competition between developed and less developed regions and between urban and rural areas. The votes cast in the House on PSD policy are examined and show opposition to PSD policy comes from the South, the West, and the rural locations, areas with higher growth rates and with generally superior air quality. PSD policy is opposed in these areas because it places limits on growth. The strongest supporters of PSD policy are northern urban areas, many of whom have lower air quality and are not directly affected by PSD policy. It is argued that federal PSD policy raised the cost of factor mobility [e.g., industrial investment and labor] and thereby allowed northern locations with lower air quality to improve local air quality without as large a loss of factors to areas with superior air quality.

Pashigian, Environmental Regulation: Whose Self-Interests Are Being Protected? 23 Economic Inquiry 551, 552-553 (1985).

As this excerpt highlights, PSD policy turns fundamentally on the scope of the jurisdiction making the policy determination. If decided regionally or locally, there would be less pressure for preserving pristine areas. The elected representatives of less developed states and regions appear to favor the potential for development. Decided nationally, however, PSD is heavily determined by the votes of people who do not live in the areas most directly affected. There are a variety of factors driving this tension. Pashigian highlights one. Another factor concerns the way in which people in different regions use, enjoy, and envision the lands in question. Many Westerners see the land and resources of the West as their means of economic survival and path to economic prosperity, while many (often affluent) Easterners see unique unspoiled terrain that must be preserved. This tension dates back to the days of Teddy Roosevelt, whose greatest legacy is the creation of the vast system of national forests, parks, and wildlife refuges throughout the West. Roosevelt, a New York City native, spent many summers in the West and devoted much of his political career to its protection. This tradition continues today, with much of the most protective legislation drafted and supported by Easterners whose main contact with the West comes through vacation trips. See Timothy Egan, As Easterners Try to Save West, Westerners Blanch, N.Y. Times, Aug. 29, 1993, at A1. What is the appropriate jurisdiction for deciding the level of protection for rural, unique, and unspoiled lands? What arguments can you make in favor of national jurisdiction? Local jurisdiction? As you ponder these questions, think about the forces that have shaped the make-up of the populations in the West, the forces that shape the political representation of these areas, and the interests of future generations. Do you think that Westerners today applaud or regret the resource protection policies developed during the Roosevelt era?

3. How effective are Congress' PSD provisions likely to be in preventing deterioration of air quality in relatively clean areas? Outside of mandatory designation of certain federal lands, the statute basically relies upon procedural requirements, including notice, public hearings, and approval by a majority of affected residents, to check redesignation of relatively clean areas as Class III, in which substantial increments of emissions are permitted. Will these requirements impose significant checks on the pressures for economic development? In fact, there have been few if any redesignations of Class II areas to Class III.

4. You should review carefully the permitting procedures required for new sources in PSD areas. What "major" sources are subject to permitting requirements? How is it determined whether emissions from a new source will result in violation of the PSD requirements? How does the Act deal with the problem of increased emissions from small stationary sources or additional vehicles that are not subject to the permitting requirements for large new stationary sources but whose emissions, combined with those of major sources that are subject to permitting, might exceed the PSD increments? Suppose haze and decreased visibility in one state is the result of emissions from an upwind state. To what extent can the downwind state force controls on upwind sources? See *State of Vermont v. Thomas*, 850 F.2d 99 (2d Cir. 1988).

5. Note that the PSD provisions require emission limitations based on "best available control technology" by major new or modified stationary sources in PSD areas, and "best available retrofit technology" for existing stationary sources in federal Class I areas with outstanding visibility. An example of the latter is the retrofit of SO_2 and particulate controls on the Navaho Power Plant in Arizona in order to protect visibility around the Grand Canyon. Is the imposition of these special case by case emission limitations logically consistent with the §§109 and 110 ambient standard approach to emission limitations and the §111 NSPS approach for new sources, or do they render the Act an incoherent patchwork of regulatory philosophies? Do these new provisions provide appropriate incentives for the development of environmentally superior technologies?

6. How should the requirement that new sources in PSD areas install "best available control technology" (BACT) to limit emissions be defined in particular circumstances? Should states or EPA have the lead role in setting BACT? In 1980, EPA issued a rule on the subject, 45 Fed. Reg. 52676, whose very general terms gave broad discretion to states to

determine BACT in particular cases. The only specific limitation on state discretion was that BACT limitations could not be less stringent than NSPS limitations established pursuant to §111 for the pollutants in question.

On December 1, 1987, J. Craig Porter, Assistant EPA Administrator for Air and Radiation, wrote a memorandum to EPA Regional Administrators entitled "Improving New Source Review Implementation." It stated that BACT for a source should presumptively be set equal to the lowest emission rate technologically achievable for a source of the type in question. The burden fell to the source to demonstrate that this degree of control was not technologically or economically feasible in its particular circumstances. This policy is called "top-down" BACT. The memorandum was not published in the Federal Register, and there was no notice or opportunity for public comment prior to its issuance. Subsequent EPA decisions reviewing state SIPs applied the provisions of this memorandum.

Many industries, particularly the paper industry, opposed the new policy. They objected to its content and the manner in which it was issued. In July 1989, the American Paper Institute sued EPA claiming that such a major change required a formal rulemaking process including public comment. EPA agreed to reconsider the new approach in a July 1991 settlement. See 56 Fed. Reg. 34202 (July 26, 1991).

The Bush Administration favored a return to the original policy and pushed EPA to propose a new rule. EPA drafted such a rule, which was sent to the Office of Management and Budget for review in October 1992. This proposed rule would have effectively overruled the 1987 memo and reaffirmed the approach taken in 1980. Many environmentalists and staff members at EPA opposed this new rule, challenging it as an unwarranted departure from settled policy. They claimed that, without the constraints of top-down BACT, the states would be too susceptible to political pressure from industry adequately to protect their air quality. In addition, they argued that the top-down approach created national uniformity and prevented competition between states.

As the 1992 presidential election approached, the issue was temporarily shelved. EPA announced that there were too many new Clean Air Act regulations that needed to be issued first. Finally, in a January 1993 memo, then-EPA administrator William Reilly wrote that the top-down policy did not have to be changed, effectively killing any revision. However, he also stated that EPA should convene a regulatory negotiation to discuss new source review and BACT policies. See 58 Fed. Reg. 11602 (Feb. 26, 1993).

The top-down BACT history is a nice story in bureaucratic politics. The original Carter Administration rule left discretion to the states, perhaps because of the inability of EPA Headquarters to fashion a more precise standard. During the Reagan Administration, which was committed to eliminating overly stringent regulation, an EPA official tightened regulation through an intra-agency memorandum that did not go through the notice and comment rulemaking process and was not subject to White House review. When the Bush Administration proposed a return to the Carter rule, it was denounced by environmentalists for reversing settled policy. EPA dragged out reconsideration of top-down BACT until it was too late in the Administration to make a change.

What about the merits of top-down BACT? Why shouldn't the states, which must accommodate new growth within the limits imposed by PSD increments, have broad discretion to determine how far beyond NSPS a particular new source should be required to go by way of controls?

2.   NON-ATTAINMENT REGIONS

While attempting to respond to the problem of growth in areas with air quality better than required by ambient standards, EPA in the mid-1970s was also wrestling with the failure to achieve ambient standards in many areas with pollutant concentrations higher than permitted by federal law and with continued pressure for new industrial and commercial development in such areas. As of 1977, over half of the nation's air quality regions were not in compliance with primary ambient standards for one or more pollutants, despite maximum invocation of extensions of the statutory deadlines for meeting such standards.

The 1977 Amendments to the Clean Air Act further postponed the deadlines for attainment of the NAAQSs to 1982, with extension to 1987 for automobile-type pollutants (photochemical oxidant, CO, NO_x). Do these extensions demonstrate that the 1970 Amendments were unwise in requiring nationally uniform health-based standards to be achieved within short time deadlines?

The non-attainment provisions of the 1977 Act were contained in Part D to Title I of the Act, comprising Sections 171 to 178. While, as explained below, these provisions were significantly modified by the 1990 Amendments, some of the essential features of the 1977 non-attainment provisions persist:

- States must revise SIPs to ensure attainment and maintenance of NAAQs by the applicable statutory deadlines; EPA must review such plans, and either approve them or remand to the state for necessary revisions. If the state fails to develop an adequate plan, EPA is to promulgate a federal implementation plan for the state. See §172.
- Non-attainment SIPs must provide for implementation of "all reasonably available control measures as expeditiously as practi-

cable," including at a minimum reductions from emissions from existing sources as may be obtained through the adoption of "reasonably available control technology" (RACT). See §172(c)(1). EPA has issued control technology guidance documents (CTGs) defining RACT levels of control for categories of existing sources.

- Non-attainment SIPs must require "reasonable further progress" (RFP) in reducing emissions in order to achieve and maintain NAAQSs attainment. See §172(c)(2). How is RFP defined?
- Major new or modified sources are subject to special preconstruction review and permitting requirements. See §173. These include emissions reduction to the "lowest achievable emissions rate" (LAER) and an "offset" requirement that emissions from a new or modified major source be more than offset by reductions from existing sources. What is a "major new or modified" source? How is LAER defined and how does it compare to the NSPS limitations for new sources under §111 and the BACT limitations for new or modified major emitting facilities under the PSD provisions of §165? How is the amount of offset determined, and how are offset requirements enforced? How close, geographically, must be the new source and the sources from which offsetting reductions are obtained? Suppose the offsetting reductions would have occurred regardless of Clean Air Act regulations, for example, as a result of a plant shutdown due to economic factors; are they still creditable as offsets?[36]
- States with non-attainment requirements may adopt the California emissions standards for new motor vehicles sold or used within the state in lieu of the otherwise applicable federal standards. See §177.

Substantial progress has been made since 1970 in achieving compliance with the NAAQs for SO_2 and particulate matter. Achievement of the NAAQs for photochemical oxidant has been extremely difficult. As Figure 4.1 illustrates, many of the most densely populated regions in the country were not in compliance with these standards by 1984, and most of these failed to meet the 1987 deadlines established by the 1977 Act.

These areas have high levels of NO_x and HC emissions from automobiles, and from stationary sources as well. In addition, automobile emissions of CO have led to serious non-attainment problems in a significant number of regions. In most areas, attainment of both the standards for photochemical oxidant (measured as ozone) and CO would require appreciable limitations on automobile use through inspection

---

36. For discussion of the last two questions, see *Citizens Against the Refinery's Effects v. EPA*, 643 F.2d 183 (4th Cir. 1981).

FIGURE 4.1

Monitored Sites Violating Ambient Standards for Ozone, 1983–84

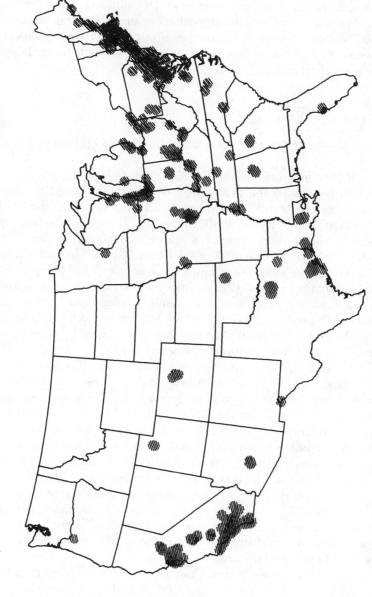

Source: U.S. Environmental Protection Agency, Region IX.

and maintenance (I&M) programs to limit emissions per vehicle and by transportation control measures to limit automobile vehicle miles travelled. States have sought to avoid such publicly unpopular measures by focussing on stationary sources of HC and NO, by optimistic SIP assumptions about emissions reduction progress, and by adopting "soft" transportation control measures in order to avoid political controversy. EPA often approved such SIPs, generating legal challenges by environmental groups such as the following:

DELANEY V. EPA

898 F.2d 687 (9th Cir. 1990), cert. denied, *498 U.S.98 (1990)*

[Maricopa and Pima Counties, Arizona, failed to attain the NAAQS for CO by the initial 1982 deadline established by the 1977 Amendments and also failed to qualify for an extension of the deadline. Arizona submitted a revised SIP which EPA disapproved as inadequate. Local residents then brought a citizen suit action in district court against EPA pursuant to §304 of the Clean Air Act. The Court required EPA, by August 1988, to promulgate, pursuant to §110(c), a federal implementation plan (FIP) for Arizona adequate to achieve the CO standards, unless Arizona earlier submitted an adequate plan. Arizona submitted a further revised SIP, which EPA approved before the August 1988 deadline. The local residents sought review of EPA's approval of the SIP in the Court of Appeals pursuant to §307.]

Because the Clean Air Act amendments of 1977 made the 1982 compliance deadline absolute, the amendments did not specify an additional deadline for non-attainment areas that failed to obtain revised implementation plan approval and national ambient air quality standard compliance by the 1982 deadline. In this circumstance, the EPA adopted the policy that it should evaluate the adequacy of the Maricopa and Pima county plans based on whether they provide for attainment by three years from the date it approved those plans, August 10, 1991. Petitioners contend that the EPA's policy is arbitrary and capricious. Now that the 1977 amendments' deadline for compliance has passed, petitioners assert, Pima and Maricopa Counties must attain the carbon monoxide ambient air quality standard as soon as possible utilizing every available control measure.

The EPA contends that Congress expressed no clear intent on the attainment deadline that the EPA should apply in evaluating the Maricopa and Pima county plans because the 1977 amendments did not specify a deadline for nonattainment areas that failed to obtain revised state implementation plan approval and national ambient air quality standard compliance by the 1982 deadline. The EPA argues that this amounts to a "statutory gap."

. . . The EPA contends that Congress knew some states should not attain by the 1982 deadline and did not intend that states implement draconian measures.

Although we recognize the EPA's predicament, we cannot accept the EPA's position. . . . When Congress has explicitly set an absolute deadline, congressional intent is clear. It is a semantic game to claim that once a state fails to meet an absolute deadline, a statutory gap is created because Congress has not provided a back-up deadline for its explicitly absolute deadline. . . . We believe that the only reasonable interpretation of the 1977 amendments is that if the 1982 deadline that Congress specified is not met, the national ambient air quality standards must be attained as soon as possible with every available control measure. . . .

The plans that the EPA approved for Maricopa and Pima Counties are similar. Both require that:

(1)   gas stations sell only high oxygen content fuel during winter months (when carbon monoxide levels are highest);
(2)   large employers reduce the amount of single car commuting by their employees;
(3)   automobiles be tested for emission levels while under load as well as while idling.

Petitioners point out that neither the Maricopa plan nor the Pima plan adopts most of the forty-five measures recommended in a study of Maricopa County conducted by the Maricopa Association of Governments, a regional planning organization. Similarly, neither plan adopts most of the twelve measures recommended by Cambridge Systematics, a group that conducted an EPA-sponsored study of Maricopa County. The excluded measures include major expansion of mass transit, imposition of parking controls, significant use of bus and carpool lanes, reductions in bus fares, restrictions on truck travel during peak periods, application of the Maricopa and Pima county oxygenated fuel program and automobile emission testing program to the entire state, elimination of waivers to the automobile emission testing program, and adoption of year-round daylight savings time. The Maricopa Association of Governments noted that immediate implementation of all the measures it identified could have produced attainment within one year.

Petitioners contend that it was arbitrary and capricious for the EPA to approve the plans without more control measures. The EPA contends that it properly approved the Maricopa and Pima plans with just the three control measures that they contain, because additional control measures "could not be demonstrated to further accelerate the projected attainment date."

The EPA has, however, arbitrarily shifted from Arizona the burden of demonstrating that control measures would not accelerate the projected attainment date. An EPA guidance document explicitly provides that each of the eighteen measures listed in 42 U.S.C. Section 7408 is presumed reasonably available; a state can reject one of these measures only by showing that the measure would not advance attainment, would cause substantial widespread and long-term adverse impact, or would take too long to implement.

Neither the Maricopa plan nor the Pima plan contains serious commitment to many of the measures listed in section 7408, including: (1) limiting portions of roads to common carriers; (2) improving transit systems with major changes in existing facilities; (3) controlling on-street parking; (4) establishing autofree zones; (5) instituting road user fees that discourage single occupant automobile trips; or (6) retrofitting older vehicles with emission control devices. . . . Yet Arizona has made no claim that any of the control measures that section 7408 or the Maricopa Association of Governments identified is impracticable or unreasonable in either Maricopa County or Pima County.

We, therefore, conclude that the EPA arbitrarily and capriciously found that the Maricopa and Pima plans provide for sufficient control measures.

[The court also held that EPA had arbitrarily disregarded its published guidance document stating that SIPs must contain contingency measures requiring additional steps to reduce emissions in the event that the SIP, when implemented, fails to achieve the emissions reductions that it projects.] We direct the EPA to disapprove the [Maricopa and Pima County] plans and to promulgate federal implementation plans consistent with this opinion within six months. . . .

NOTES AND QUESTIONS

1. Were the emissions control measures that Arizona failed to adopt "draconian"?

2. The court says that the 1977 Amendments compel the following conclusion: "[I]f the 1982 deadline . . . is not met, the national ambient air quality standards must be attained as soon as possible with every available control measure. . . ." Is the court correct? If so, shouldn't the court have required a plan that would immediately curtail vehicle use, by gasoline rationing or similar means, to the extent necessary to meet the standards? The court estimated that the measures which it discussed would take a year to implement following adoption of a FIP.

3. While the court's decision was viewed by some as extreme, it was handed down eight years after the 1982 deadline had passed, and

EPA still had to write a plan and see that it was implemented. Does this show that Congress' reliance on deadlines and "action forcing" litigation is a failure? What alternatives might be considered?

MELNICK, POLLUTION DEADLINES AND THE COALITION FOR FAILURE

75 Pub. Interest 123, 123 (1984)

At first the activity on the floor of the House of Representatives seemed ordinary enough. Representative Henry Waxman (D-California), chairman of the subcommittee with jurisdiction over the Clean Air Act, and one of Congress's staunchest supporters of rigorous environmental regulation, was engaged in yet another battle with his formidable committee chairman, Representative John Dingell (D-Michigan), known to some as "Tailpipe Johnny" for his annual efforts to relax auto emission standards. But this time something had gone awry. Waxman was endorsing an appropriation bill rider that would prevent the Environmental Protection Agency (EPA) from imposing a construction ban on states failing to meet the Clean Air Act's 1982 deadline for attaining health-based air quality standards. He and his allies railed against former EPA Administrator Anne Gorsuch Burford's threat to impose such a ban in the 213 counties throughout the nation that exceeded those standards, calling her action "heavy-handed" and advising her successor to be more "flexible" in accommodating states that make "good faith" efforts to comply with the act. Dingell — who in 1982 led an effort to weaken the entire Clean Air Act — opposed Waxman's rider, warning, "[I]f you vote for this amendment, you are voting for dirty air." No wonder one House member announced that she was "astounded at this debate" of June 2, 1983, and another admitted to being "totally confused."

The paradox of Clean Air Act opponents asking for rigorous enforcement, and supporters calling for administrative flexibility, becomes all the more striking when one considers the history of the act. Ever since its passage in 1970, the Clean Air Act has been billed as an "action forcing" statute. In place of vague commands to regulate in the "public interest" or to establish "reasonable" or "feasible" requirements, one finds in the act explicit, often numerical standards coupled with strict time limits. The requirement that auto makers reduce new car emissions by 90 percent within five years was the most visible element of this regulatory strategy. Such clear standards, environmental advocates have maintained, protect Congress's prerogative to set public policy, prevent agency "capture" or mismanagement, and allow citizens to seek relief in court whenever administrators fail to do their job. If ever an agency was in need of supervision it was the EPA under Administrator Gorsuch. Not only were the political executives appointed by President Reagan hostile to many of the statutes they were charged with carrying out; they were also frequently incompetent and, in at least one case, even dishonest. This hardly seemed to be the year for environmental advocates to put their trust in administrative discretion.

These unexpected positions, however, become understandable once one examines the immediate political context. The 97th Congress had witnessed a long and acrimonious battle over the revision of the Clean Air Act. Considering the act far too restrictive, the Reagan administration and many sectors of the business community sought to revise it as soon as possible. Environmental groups and congressional sponsors of the legislation of 1970 and 1977, in contrast, remained satisfied with the basic structure of the act and opposed any set of amendments that failed to tackle such growing problems as acid rain and airborne carcinogens. By the end of 1982, weeks of committee hearings and markups had produced only stalemate. Administrator Gorsuch saw that an announcement of the construction ban was a convenient way of forcing Congress to open the act to amendment. . . .

Even before the appropriations rider became law, Gorsuch's replacement, William Ruckelshaus, announced that he opposed rapid, wholesale application of the construction ban. If this solved the immediate difficulties of the environmental advocates, it only highlighted their long-standing problem. Congress and the EPA once again showed that they would not stand behind the standards and deadlines previously announced with great seriousness. Every major participant now knows that loopholes will always appear in the nick of time, thus obviating the need to impose sanctions in areas that fail to meet air quality standards. . . . [Experience] shows that "action forcing" regulatory statutes seldom work as planned, and also shows why many Congressmen refuse to acknowledge this failure.

A DECADE OF DELAY

In 1970, agency officials advised Senator Edmund Muskie (D-Maine), the chief sponsor of the act, that most areas of the country could probably meet health-based air quality standards by 1980. Muskie, trying to show that he cared more about the environment than did his chief political rival, Richard Nixon, cut in half the time allotted for reaching the goal. This political one-upmanship was later dubbed "technology forcing." But it did not "force" the development of pollution control technology nearly enough. By 1975, almost every metropolitan area in the country was still violating one or more standards. As this first deadline passed, Senator Muskie, who had previously berated the EPA for allowing polluters' compliance schedules to extend past the statutory deadline, suddenly urged administrators to find "flexibility" in the act. Just as Waxman did not want to open the act to amendment in 1983, Muskie and his allies did not want to expose the act to a full-scale congressional debate while the country was in the 1975 recession and while the "energy crisis" was the leading topic of political discussion. The EPA temporized until Congress passed the 1977 amendments.

The 1977 amendments extended the deadlines to 1982 for most areas, and to 1987 for areas with especially serious "mobile source" pollution problems. The amendments also contained provisions to ensure that the deadlines would not slip a second time. The EPA received authority to impose large fines on recalcitrant polluters. At the same time, the amendments prohibited the EPA from using enforcement discretion to create de facto extensions. Only depriving administrators of such flexibility, the authors of this legislation indicated, would convince industry and the states that this time the federal government meant business. The most powerful expression of Congress's no-nonsense approach was the automatic ban on construction of new facilities in states failing to implement plans that "provide for attainment of national primary ambient air quality standards not later than December 31, 1982."

Sponsors of the 1977 amendments expected to make "mid-course corrections" as 1982 approached. However, as early as 1979 the EPA was already "conditionally" approving state plans that failed to meet all the requirements of the 1977 amendments. These conditional approvals were designed both to lift the construction ban and to relieve the EPA of its responsibility to promulgate fully adequate plans. (The EPA's single prior attempt to write an implementation plan by itself had proven disastrous.) It was no secret that many of the plans approved by the EPA could not possibly produce attainment of the standards by 1982. . . . EPA Assistant Administrator David Hawkins, formerly an attorney for the Natural Resources Defense Council and subsequently chief lobbyist for the National Clean Air Coalition, had convinced the environmentalists that the massive imposition of sanctions would have "disastrous effects," and he hoped the sanctions would become a "historical footnote." Thus, environmental groups played along with the game and agreed not to challenge the EPA's strategy in court — that is, until they decided that the Reagan administration was being too lenient. A chief characteristic of "action forcing" statutes is that they allow private litigants and the courts to decide which actions to "force."

Nevertheless, the EPA did make significant progress in reducing air pollution under the 1977 amendments, and the use of sanctions was a key element of this effort. By imposing civil penalties on some polluters, the federal government spurred many of the country's largest and most recalcitrant polluters to reduce their emissions. Moreover, the EPA announced that it would cut off certain federal funds and ban new construction in states that failed to adopt the automobile "inspection and maintenance" programs required by the 1977 amendments. It showed it was serious about inspection and maintenance by applying these sanctions in two states (California and Kentucky) that failed to meet the EPA halfway.

It is quite clear that the EPA's threats do become credible and produce results when the agency demands that states and polluters take selective actions (installing scrubbers or instituting auto inspection and maintenance programs) that Congress has clearly endorsed and thus will most likely stand behind. Conversely, neither threats nor cajoling work when regulators make open-ended demands that states do absolutely everything and anything necessary to attain national standards, or insist on the use of expensive or disruptive controls not clearly supported by Congress. The reality of pollution control is that regulators and polluters bargain over what controls are "reasonably available," with each side keeping in mind the extent of its political support. If application of these "reasonably available" controls fails to result in attainment of national standards by statutory deadlines, then Congress either provides new deadlines (as it did for the steel industry in special legislation passed in 1982) or it lets the deadlines quietly slip by.

SHIFTING JUSTIFICATIONS

If deadlines for "forcing" the attainment of air quality standards have had nine lives, it is largely because their advocates have been quicker than cats in jumping from one justification to another. As each rationale has collapsed under the weight of experience, another has risen to take its place. The deadline has become a hollow symbol in search of a tenable underpinning.

The sponsors of the 1970 act originally claimed that deadlines were justified by the urgency of protecting public health. "The health of people," the 1970 Senate report declared, "is more important than the question of whether early achievement of ambient air quality standards protective of health is technically feasible." The first blow to this argument was the recognition that primary standards do not constitute "thresholds," that is, points at which adverse health effects begin and end. . . .

This does not mean, however, that the rapid attainment of primary standards is always unimportant or unreasonable. . . . The difficulty is that the costs and benefits of meeting the deadlines vary tremendously, not just from pollutant to pollutant, but from area to area.

Consider the case of ozone, commonly known as smog. In revising its ozone standard in 1979, EPA relied predominantly on a study showing that when six healthy adults exercised heavily (the equivalent of running six miles in an hour) while exposed to ozone levels of 0.15 parts per million (ppm), several of them experienced such discomfort as headaches and chest tightness. Adding a 20 percent "margin of safety," EPA set the standard of 0.12 ppm. It is not unusual for Los Angeles to experience ozone concentrations of almost four times this level, and attaining the standards there would require massive industrial closures and restrictions on auto use. Few doubt that such controls would cause misery far exceeding that caused by air pollution. Clearly urgency cannot be divorced from consideration of the widely varying cost, feasibility, and benefit of attaining primary standards.

As the urgency argument lost force, deadline advocates switched their focus. In the words of Henry Waxman (who, representing, Los Angeles, admits that shutting down the city is not an environmental necessity), "The purpose of deadlines is simple: to force the development of better technologies to control air pollution." By stimulating innovation, so the argument goes, deadlines make the previously infeasible become feasible and thus reduce the cost of pollution control. One problem, of course, is that deadlines can stimulate technological innovation only if they are believable. Time after time Congress has backed down, not just on deadlines for attaining air quality standards, but on deadlines for meeting new car emission standards as well. Congress has cried wolf too often. The future of "technology forcing" lies not in further use of phony deadlines, but in those pollution control strategies that make emission rights scarce and valuable.

CONGRESS AS POLICY MAKER

The final rationale for deadlines is more sophisticated and more overtly political, but ultimately unconvincing. This argument concedes that deadlines must be adjusted and that such adjustments undercut technology forcing, but it stresses that political choices about the pace of pollution control should be made by Congress rather than by faceless bureaucrats negotiating with polluters in back rooms. . . . What these advocates of legislative specificity generally ignore . . . is the institutional capacity of Congress.

To use air quality deadlines to exercise real control over the pace of pollution reduction, Congress must first set deadlines that are realistic, striking a rough balance between expected environmental benefits and the costs Congressmen are willing to impose on their constituents. Since the extent of pollution, and thus the cost of cleanup, varies from area to area, Congress must take the second step of setting different deadlines for different parts of the country. And since it is hard to know in advance the cost or even the benefits of control, it will always be necessary to take the third step of revising deadlines on a regular basis. . . .

It is hardly surprising that Congress has never — neither in 1975 nor in 1982 — lived up to its responsibility to revise outmoded deadlines. . . . The many steps in the legislative process afford any of a number of actors an opportunity to block or delay action. While in 1975 it was Senator Muskie who dragged his feet, in 1976 his chief senatorial opponent, Jake Garn (R-Utah) was able to kill Muskie's bill with an end-of-the-session filibuster. In 1982 Representative Dingell suspended the House committee's work on his bill after losing several close votes; in 1983 Representative Waxman was the one advocating caution.

While it is always good fun to ridicule the glacial speed with which Congress proceeds, the legislative branch's proclivity for slow, painstaking deliberations is one of its chief virtues. Its many veto points allow large numbers of interests to be heard and in some way accommodated. . . . "Action forcing" seldom works on Congress. And when it does, it threatens to rob that body of its most cherished institutional advantages.

The American constitution makes coalition building in Congress difficult in order to guard against the danger of faction, both minority and majority. It also places the "energy" necessary for "good administration," as the Federalist puts it, in the executive branch. The energetic branch can respond to new circumstances in ways that the deliberative branch cannot. The history of air pollution control shows that the real adjustment of deadlines comes in negotiation among state and federal administrators and polluters. . . .

Setting unattainable deadlines has several advantages for Congressmen. They can take credit for establishing ambitious environmental goals, criticize administrators for failing to meet them (a move which is especially attractive when the president belongs to the other party), and even condemn the poor bureaucrats for threatening to impose "unreasonable" sanctions. These advantages for individual Congressmen, though, do not make the choice made by Congress as a whole any less illusory. In this case institutional capacity is destiny.

THE SYMBOLS OF ENVIRONMENTALISM

The most curious aspect of the politics of deadlines is not that most Congressmen vote for them, or even that business and the states make little effort to eliminate them (having learned not to pay any attention), but that leading environmental advocates, both in public interest groups and in Congress, cling to them so tenaciously. It is possible that environmentalists still believe that deadlines will in some way help the EPA to reduce the emissions of a few polluters. Perhaps federal regulators can convince some states and businesses that the deadlines have teeth: GM may have learned the game by now, but perhaps the local paper mill has not; if California cannot be pushed around, maybe New Hampshire can. Of course, the small — and decreasing — payoff from this game must be balanced not only against its unfairness, but also against the required expenditure of administrative time and credibility. Not surprisingly, many air pollution control officials argue that retaining deadlines can actually impede environmental protection.

Not to be overlooked is the fact that litigation plays a major role in the strategy of environmental groups and that unmet deadlines make for easy courtroom victories. For example, when the National Resources Defense Council (NRDC) decided that the Reagan administration's EPA had let Illinois get away with too much, it filed suit to compel the EPA to enforce on a selective basis provisions of the law that the NRDC itself conceded should not be applied across the board. Such suits give private litigants, such as the NRDC, an enviable opportunity to amend policy set by public administrators. Environmental groups, though, are politically savvy, and recognize that they must watch out for political backlash. . . .

Speculation about the incremental advantages of deadlines for environmental groups should not distract us from the obvious: The value of deadlines is primarily symbolic. But what do they symbolize? Most immediately, environmentalist fear that dropping deadlines will indicate that their movement is in retreat. . . .

The leaders of the environmental movement refuse to make this trade, because for them the symbolism of deadlines goes deeper than concern over their political reputation. Deadlines — or, perhaps more accurately, the ghost of deadlines passed — constitute a reminder of how much remains to be done. In a very real sense deadlines are made to be broken. Each time we fail to meet a deadline we are reminded that more effort is needed, that our environment is not yet clean. Deadlines are a time for soul searching and rededication. Although deadlines do not directly advance the process of cleaning up the environment, abolishing them, as the National Commission's dissenters said, "would legitimize the perpetual failure to provide healthful air quality." While we can tolerate this failure for years — perhaps forever — we should never deem it "legitimate."

Thus deadlines are, to put it bluntly, a symbol of government failure. Another deadline missed, another right violated, another promise unfulfilled. Perpetual failure to meet deadlines gives those advocating more pollution control a key rhetorical advantage. Why is the government still refusing to do what is right? How can it condone this miserable situation? How long must we tolerate dirty air?

One can answer those questions with another (albeit less rhetorically powerful) question: Why is it "illegitimate" for Los Angeles to continue its present level of activity and to accept a peak ozone concentration of (to be optimistic) 0.20 ppm, not just for ten years but forever? The health risk associated with this level of pollution is quite small compared either with the other risks of urban life or with the benefits of prosperity. What many people like about that city — its climate, its size, its sprawling freeway system — is precisely what makes its smog so bad. . . .

THE SUCCESS NO ONE ADMITS

What is often overlooked is that, by many standards, the federal government's effort to reduce air pollution has been a remarkable success. While GNP has grown and the price of clean fuels has skyrocketed, air quality has improved in almost all major cities. Between 1974 and 1978 the number of "unhealthy days" (as determined by the Council on Environmental Quality) dropped 18 percent, "very unhealthy days" by 35 percent, and "hazardous days" by 55 percent. Think what would be said if similar gains were discovered in welfare or crime statistics. To be sure, serious problems such as acid rain remain. And regulation has produced serious inefficiencies and inequities, especially by protecting existing sources and discouraging the construction of new ones. Moreover, these gains have frequently come not because the Clean Air Act is "fundamentally sound" (as environmentalists claim) but despite the fact that it is fundamentally flawed (as most air pollution control professionals readily admit). But when one discards the arbitrary standards proclaimed in the act, it is hard to conclude that government has indeed failed again.

. . . Cynicism in private can be comic. But the spread of public cynicism can be tragic. Just as surely as pollution is harmful to public health, our Byzantine strategies for protecting the environment have become hazardous to the public spirit. In some policy areas, perhaps, our symbols are laudable but our practices are disappointing. In pollution control, however, our symbols are more in need of reform than our practices.

The Non-Attainment Provisions of the 1990 Clean Act Amendments

The 1990 Amendments adopted a somewhat new approach to

dealing with non-attainment. Instead of imposing uniform compliance deadlines for all regions of the nation, as the 1970 and 1977 Amendments did, Congress in 1990 adopted different timetables and graduated requirements for different regions, depending on the extent to which new existing pollution levels exceed NAAQSs for the most serious non-attainment pollutants: ozone, CO, and PM10. See §§181-190.

In the case of ozone, for example, the 1990 Amendments establish six different non-attainment classifications, based on the extent to which regions' ozone concentrations exceed the one-hour NAAQSs standard for ozone of .12 ppm, with six corresponding attainment dates.

Classification	Concentrations	Existing Ozone Deadline	Number of Attainment Regions (examples)
Marginal	.121 - .138	1993	36 Albany, NY; Toledo, OH; Paducah, KY
Moderate	.138 - .160	1996	36 St. Louis, MS; Phoenix, AZ; Miami, FL
Serious	.160 - .180	1999	16 Atlanta, GA; Boston, MA; El Paso, TX
Severe I	.180 - .190	2005	5 Milwaukee, WI; Phila, PA; San Diego, CA
Severe II	.190 - .280	2007	3 New York, NY; Chicago, IL; Houston, TX
Extreme	.280 and above	2010	1 Los Angeles, CA

There are similar schedules for CO and PM10 (particulate matter 10 microns or less in size) non-attainment areas.

There are special SIP requirements for these non-attainment areas, geared to the extent of non-compliance. In the case of ozone, for example, "marginal" areas must within three years submit a comprehensive inventory of NO_x and VOC (the more volatile hydrocarbons that interact with NO_x to form photochemical oxidant) emissions, updated every three years. SIPs must be revised within two years to conform to new EPA guidelines for existing vehicle emission inspection and maintenance (I&M) requirements, and new or revised EPA guidelines requiring adoption of reasonably available control technology (RACT) by existing sources. New stationary sources of VOCs must achieve a 1.1 ton offset reduction from existing sources for each ton of new emissions.

"Moderate" areas must within 3 years modify their SIPs to adopt an updated I & M program even if there were no previous programs for the area. RACT controls for major stationary sources of VOCs must be implemented by 1995. VOC offsets for new sources are 1.15:1. With some exceptions, advanced Stage II vehicle refuelling systems must be installed by gasoline stations in order to reduce VOC emissions further. In addition, the general requirement of "reasonable further progress" towards attainment contained in the 1977 Amendments is given specific, operational meaning. The region's SIP must adopt specific annual reduction requirements for VOCs and NO sufficient to ensure by 1996 a 15 percent reduction from 1990 levels of each pollutant.

"Serious" areas must adopt all of the above requirements and in addition adopt SIP provisions requiring the following:

- Improved monitoring of the ozone and ozone precursor concentrations, and NO and VOC emissions.
- An expanded definition of "major sources" subject to permitting and LAER requirements to include sources that emit or have the potential to emit 50 tons or more of VOCs annually, or even less when aggregated with other, small net increases from the same source. This reduction of the otherwise applicable threshold — 100 tons/year — significantly expands the number of sources subject to regulation.
- A VOC offset ratio for new sources of 1.2/1 (a 1.3/1 offset will allow certain small sources to avoid LAER).
- Enhanced I&M requirements to reduce VOC and NO emissions from in-use vehicles.
- Adoption of a clean fuel fleet vehicle program for fleet vehicles unless EPA determines that the SIP contains adequate, equivalent measures to reduce VOC and NO.

In addition such areas are subject to emission reductions "milestones." In addition to achieving a 15 percent reduction in 1990 NO and VOC emissions by 1996, serious regions must thereafter achieve an average 3 percent additional reduction each year; regulators can relax the 3 percent requirement on a showing that it is not feasible to achieve it in light of available technology.

In addition to all of the above, "severe" areas must adopt mandatory transportation control plans to limit vehicle miles travelled; adopt (with certain exceptions) a VOC offset requirement of 1.3:1; in the case of failure to achieve required emissions reduction milestones, impose penalty fees on sources that fail to reduce VOCs by 80 percent, and adopt a clean fuel vehicle program. The regulatory threshold for stationary sources is reduced to 25 tons/year.

The one "extreme" area (Los Angeles) must in addition to all of the above control a source or contiguous group of sources that emit or have the potential to emit 10 tons of VOCs annually; adopt a 1.5:1 VOC offset; adopt a clean fuel vehicle program not limited to fleet vehicles; and institute traffic control measures to reduce use of high-polluting vehicles during peak periods.

If a marginal, moderate, or serious area fails to meet its statutory attainment deadline, it is reclassified automatically to the next highest category, and must submit SIP revisions satisfying the requirements for that category. Failure by severe or extreme areas to meet deadlines subjects them to additional control requirements and potential sanctions. In 1996 and every three years thereafter, "serious" or "severe" areas that fail to achieve the "reasonable further progress" milestone reductions in ozone concentrations required in the Act will be reclassified to the next higher category ("severe" and "extreme" respectively). In lieu of reclassification they may elect to either adopt SIP controls which EPA determines will bring the region into compliance with its milestones or adopt a system of economic incentives, including emission fees, transferrable pollution permits, and incentives to reduce vehicle use, that will achieve compliance with the next milestone.

If a state fails to adopt or implement any of the requirements described above, EPA may, in addition to bringing an action requiring it to do so, either cut off federal highway funds or establish a 2:1 offset requirement for new sources. See §179.

These measures will operate in conjunction with the provisions in the 1990 Amendments amending Title II of the Act to reduce further emissions from new motor vehicles, and require use of reformulated gasoline in the more highly polluted regions. See supra, p. 309.

Perhaps the most notable changes in the 1990 Amendments are the use of a classification system based on the degree of non-attainment; the use of strict numerical criteria — 15 percent VOC reduction by 1996 and 3 percent annually thereafter — to define "reasonable further progress"; the extension of regulatory controls to smaller stationary sources in more polluted areas; and mandatory clean vehicle and clean fuel measures.

The Act contains similar although less complex provisions for CO, PM, SO_2, and lead non-attainment regions. §§186-193.

In addition, Congress modified §176 to provide that federal agencies shall not "engage in, support in any way or provide financial assistance or license, permit or approve any activity which does not conform 'to a SIP.' " "Conformity" to a SIP means:

> (A) conformity to an implementation plan's purpose of eliminat-
> ing or reducing the severity and number of violations of the national
> ambient air quality standards and achieving expeditious attainment of
> such standards; and
> (B) that such activities will not —
>> (i) cause or contribute to any new violation of any standard in
> any area;
>> (ii) increase the frequency or severity of any existing violation
> of any standard in any area; or
>> (iii) delay timely attainment of any standard or any required
> interim emission reductions or other milestones in any area.

Section 176 also contains special provisions to ensure that federal transportation funds are spent consistently with measures to ensure attainment.

NOTES AND QUESTIONS

Are the non-attainment provisions of the 1990 Amendments an
improvement over those of the 1977 amendments? If so, why didn't
Congress adopt such an approach earlier? Does the 1990 legislation
meet Melnick's criticism of deadlines? Will the 1990 Amendments prevent *Delaney* problems, see p. 348, from arising in the future? To what
extent do the 1990 Amendments simply require and make politically
more palatable a regulatory strategy that is fundamentally flawed? The
essential problem in meeting the non-attainment provisions of the 1990
amendments is that emissions from large stationary sources have already been strictly regulated, particularly in the case of VOCs. In many
cases, additional reductions will be very costly. There are greater opportunities for reductions from small stationary sources that have not been
regulated or regulated extensively and from cars and trucks through
transportation control plans. But these alternatives involve serious administrative and political problems.

For example, efforts to reduce emissions from vehicles in use have
been dogged by administrative and political difficulties. Inspection and
Maintenance Programs to ensure that automobile emission control systems are properly maintained may be able to achieve a further 10 percent reduction in VOC emissions, at substantial cost (thousands of
dollars per ton). Employer car pooling and mass transit programs can
also make modest contributions. But direct efforts to reduce driving by
regulatory restrictions or pricing systems have been much more contro-

versial. In the early 1970s, environmental groups instituted litigation challenging the adequacy of SIP mobile source provisions and pushed for limitations on driving, high taxes or regulatory restrictions on parking, and strict regulation of "indirect sources" such as shopping centers that would generate increased automobile traffic. These efforts produced a sharp political reaction, including congressional amendments to the Clean Air Act prohibiting EPA from imposing parking surcharges and indirect source controls. Land use and zoning controls to reduce automobile use have proved even more controversial. How, if at all, do the 1990 Amendments address these problems?

NON-ATTAINMENT PROBLEM

Pease Air Force Base is located in the Portsmouth-Dover-Rochester New Hampshire / Maine interstate air quality control region, which currently has peak ozone concentrations of .165 ppm (the NAAQS for ozone is .12 ppm). Pursuant to congressional legislation, the Defense Department in 1988 decided to close Pease and transfer it to the Pease Redevelopment Authority, an agency of the state of New Hampshire, for use as an industrial park and a cargo/general aviation/commuter aviation facility. At peak operation in 1988, aircraft and motor vehicle operations at Pease AFB emitted 105,000 tons of VOC annually and 50,000 tons of NO_x. By 1990 the base was shut down entirely. The Defense Department, pursuant to the National Environmental Policy Act,[37] prepared an environmental impact statement on the conversion, which called for a 20-year development project, resulting eventually in VOC emissions of 150,000 tons annually, and NO_x emissions of 60,000 tons. Most of these emissions would be attributable to automobile traffic that would be generated by the new facility; the balance would come from aircraft operations and light industry. Following enactment of the 1990 Amendments and litigation threats from environmental groups and a nearby town concerned about aviation noise, Defense, the Redevelopment Authority, and the New Hampshire Departments of Environmental Conservation and Transportation entered into an agreement providing for a limited "Phase I" development through 1994, limiting annual emissions to 90,000 tons of VOC and 40,000 tons of NO. The agreement provides for limits on development of the industrial park and aircraft operations and a commitment by New Hampshire to build a new interchange at the interstate highway closest to Pease that will reduce congestion of traffic to the facility and in doing so ensure that pollution concentrations in the immediate vicinity will

---

37. Discussed in Chapter 8.

be somewhat less than current levels. The agreement provides that any operations or further development of Pease shall be subject to any conditions that may be imposed in the revised SIP for the region, which, pursuant to the 1990 Amendments, is due to be submitted at the end of 1993 following completion of a more comprehensive inventory of VOC and NO emissions. Defense certifies that the redevelopment plan conforms to the current New Hampshire SIP, adopted in 1986, which provides for an average 10 percent reduction in emissions from existing sources over a six-year period through RACT requirements on existing sources, and the imposition of the Clean Air Act's LAER, offset, and other permitting requirements on major new stationary sources.

(1)   What legal challenges to the Pease redevelopment might be made at the present time by local environmental groups or the nearby town?

(2)   Suppose that redevelopment of Pease goes forward and that the region also fails to achieve the applicable emission reduction milestones contained in the 1986 SIP or the 1990 Amendments. What sanctions and other problems will the region face in that event? What steps should New Hampshire take to minimize the risk of sanctions or other threats to its plans to regain the economic momentum that it enjoyed in the 1970-1980 period?

(3)   What light does this problem shed on the logic and likely success of the 1990 Amendments?

NOTE ON TRANSITIONAL PROBLEMS

After the 1990 Amendments were passed, EPA took the position that they governed the Arizona non-attainment problem and that accordingly it did not have to carry out *Delaney*'s mandate. Is EPA right? If so, has Arizona been rewarded for foot-dragging? This is an example of a transitional problem created by the 1990 Amendments. Transitional problems are by their very nature temporary. But because Congress amends the environmental laws with some frequency, in part because they are very detailed and therefore become rapidly obsolescent due to changes in information and circumstances, transitional problems are always with us. The following decision represents a judicial effort to deal with significant transitional problems not addressed by Congress. The case also illustrates the mind-boggling technical complexity created by the elaborate and detailed legal/regulatory system created by the Clean Air Act.

CITIZENS FOR A BETTER ENVIRONMENT v. WILSON

775 F. Supp. 1291 (N.D. Cal. 1991)

THELTON E. HENDERSON, Chief Judge.

BACKGROUND

The 1982 Bay Area Air Quality Plan ("1982 Plan"), which represents the plan for achieving minimum federal air quality standards in the Bay Area, required MTC [Metropolitan Transportation Commission] to implement a contingency plan in the event the Bay Area was not making Reasonable Further Progress ("RFP") toward attaining the National Ambient Air Quality Standards ("NAAQS") for carbon monoxide and ozone. On September 19, 1989, we found that (1) RFP had not been made for ozone or carbon monoxide in the Bay Area, and (2) that MTC had nevertheless failed to implement the contingency plan for the transportation sector. See *Citizens for a Better Environment v. Deukmejian*, 731 F. Supp. 1448 (N.D. Cal. 1990) ("CBE I").

Accordingly, we ordered MTC to implement the contingency plan for the transportation sector, which contains two components. Id. at 1461. The second component, which is at issue here, required MTC to adopt, within six months, sufficient additional transportation control measures ("TCMs") to bring the region "back within the RFP line." Id. 1982 Plan at H-2. In response, MTC passed Resolution 2131 on February 28, 1990, adopting 16 additional TCMs.

These 16 additional TCMs (referred to by the parties as the "2131 TCMs" after the Resolution number) included, among other things, preservation of ferry services added after the October 1989 earthquake, fare coordination between BART [Bay Area Rapid Transit] and buses, expanding participation in Caltrans' Fuel Efficient Traffic Signal Management Program, and a request that the state legislature raise the Bay Bridge toll to two dollars. MTC estimated that these 16 measures would reduce hydrocarbon (or VOC — volatile organic compound) emissions, which are a precursor to ozone, by 3.83 tons per day ("tpd") by 1996. The measures were also estimated to reduce carbon monoxide emissions by 74.1 tpd by 1996. . . .

Plaintiffs contend that the adoption of the above 16 measures did not fulfil MTC's obligation under the contingency plan because they will not achieve sufficient reductions to put the San Francisco Bay Area back on the "RFP line" *as defined in the 1982 Plan.* Accordingly, they urge us to find MTC in contempt of our September 19, 1989, ruling requiring MTC to adopt sufficient TCMs to bring the region back within the RFP line; alternatively, they seek a summary judgment that MTC is in continuing violation of the contingency plan.

MTC does not dispute its obligation, under the 1982 Plans' contingency plan, to adopt sufficient additional TCMs to put the Bay Area back on the RFP line. However, it contends that to determine whether the region is currently making reasonable further progress (and therefore "on the RFP line"), we must look to the new reduction schedules set forth in the recent 1990 amendments to the Clean Air Act ("1990 amendments"), rather than the RFP benchmarks committed to in the 1982 Plan. . . .

MTC also contends that, in any event, the record demonstrates that RFP has been satisfied for the Bay Area for both ozone and carbon monoxide whether RFP is measured by the terms of the 1982 Plan or the 1990 amendments. . . .

DISCUSSION

[The court first considered MTC's claim that RFP should be measured by reference to the 1990 Amendments.] The 1982 Plan (the SIP for the Bay Area) contains RFP benchmarks for ozone and carbon monoxide based on data available at the time the Plan was prepared. Thus, for example, with respect to ozone, the 1982 Plan committed to an "RFP line" that required reducing hydrocarbon emissions by 85 tpd and achieving a 430 tpd hydrocarbon emissions level in the Bay Area by 1987, the then applicable statutory deadline. . . .

Unfortunately, most areas, including the Bay Area, failed to achieve NAAQS by 1987. In response, Congress amended the Clean Air Act in 1990 to require that most SIPs, including the 1982 Plan, be revised over the next two to three years to provide for strategies that will result in attainment of NAAQS by the new statutory deadlines. . . . For the Bay Area, which has been designated a "moderate" non-attainment area, NAAQS for ozone must be achieved by 1996; NAAQS for carbon monoxide must be achieved by 1995.

Congress also added some additional teeth to the RFP requirement, hoping to avoid a repetition of its experience with the 1977 amendments, which generated disappointingly little compliance with the statutory deadline. Previously, RFP referred only to such annual incremental reductions that were sufficient in the judgment of the Administrator to allow for attainment by the statutory deadline; under the

1990 amendments it refers to such annual incremental reductions in emissions "as are required by this part." . . .

The phrase "as are required by this part" refers to specific reduction schedules that must be incorporated into the new, revised SIPs. In moderate non-attainment areas, for example, the revised SIPs must demonstrate that hydrocarbon emissions will be reduced 15 percent by November 15, 1996 from the base year of 1990 (accounting for any growth) pursuant to section 182(b), 42 U.S.C. §7511a(b)(1)(A)(i). Similarly, the revised SIPs must demonstrate the carbon monoxide (CO) levels will decline 23.73 percent in the Bay Area from current levels by December 31, 1995, beginning from base year 1989. Section 187(a)(7), 42 U.S.C. §7512a(a)(7), and April 5, 1991 Order at 4.[38]

. . . The question is, do the RFP commitments in the 1982 Plan remain enforceable during this interim period, or are obligations relating to RFP now governed solely by reference to the 1990 amendments.

Congress neglected to address this precise issue, either by statute or through legislative history, thus creating some ambiguity and uncertainty, and there is no apparent case authority; thus, we turn to the statutory scheme and Congress' overall purposes to resolve this question. . . .

. . . [T]he 1990 amendments include two strongly worded savings clauses, one of which is pertinent here:

> *Any provision* of any applicable implementation plan that was approved or promulgated by the Administrator [of EPA] pursuant to this section as in effect before November 15, 1990 *shall remain in effect* as part of such applicable implementation plan, except to the extent that a revision to such provision is approved or promulgated by the Administrator pursuant to this chapter.

Section 110(n), 42 U.S.C. §7410(n)(1) (emph. added). This unconditional and sweeping savings clause — which saves "any provision" of "any SIP" until the SIP is formally revised — makes it "crystal clear" that Congress intended to hold agencies to their existing SIP obligations pending approval of new SIPs.

This, however, does not end the matter. The RFP commitments in the 1982 Plan were designed with the then applicable 1987 statutory

---

38. The 23.73 percent CO figure is determined by the percentage by which the "design value" for the Bay Area exceeds the NAAQS standard for CO. The design value is the second highest reading of carbon monoxide emissions in the Bay Area in the year 1989. The 15 percent hydrocarbon figure applies to areas, such as the Bay Area, that have been designated "moderate" non-attainment areas. This percentage reduction should achieve NAAQS for ozone because the ozone design value for the Bay Areas is 14.3 percent above NAAQS for ozone.

deadline in mind. Thus, for example, the 1982 Plan contains a visual RFP graph for hydrocarbons that begins in 1979 and ends in 1987. MTC contends that because the 1982 Plan did not project RFP beyond 1987, the RFP commitments in the Plan only "existed" through 1987, leaving the Bay area without any enforceable or definable RFP commitments until Congress amended the Clean Air Act in 1990 to include new reduction schedules and attainment deadlines. . . .

We disagree that the RFP commitments in the 1982 Plan suddenly ceased to exist on January 1, 1988. Congress was clear that SIPs remain in force until a new SIP is approved regardless of whether the statutory deadline has passed. There is no basis or authority for singling out a central component of the SIP — the RFP commitments — and determining those provisions and commitments vanish simply because the statutory deadline passes.

MTC also argues that, even assuming RFP commitments exist to be saved, we should nonetheless construe the section 110(n) savings clause to except RFP commitments. Otherwise, MTC argues, there will be a conflict between MTC's obligations to satisfy the RFP benchmarks in the 1982 Plan and its obligations to demonstrate that the reductions required by the 1990 amendments will be satisfied by 1995 and 1996. We can avoid such a conflict, MTC urges, if we simply view the RFP commitments in the 1982 Plan as ending . . . and the "new" reduction schedules set forth in the 1990 amendments as applying from now henceforth.

While this argument has superficial appeal, we conclude that MTC has set up a false conflict. If Congress intended to keep existing SIPs fully enforceable, absent substitution of a new SIP, there is no "conflict" in requiring MTC to abide by the 1982 Plan, including the RFP commitments contained therein, while the 1982 Plan undergoes the lengthy revision process, even though this may involve some additional obligation or effort on MTC's part.

Indeed, construing the savings clause to except RFP commitments from its scope, as MTC urges, would create a gap in SIP enforceability that we do not believe Congress intended, and is contrary to the overall statutory scheme. . . . [M]aintaining SIP enforceability pending the SIP revision process is a cornerstone of the statutory scheme. Yet MTC's approach arguably leaves states without RFP commitments during this lengthy interim period.

Finally, holding agencies to their existing RFP requirements is most consistent with the overall purpose of the Act, which is "to protect and enhance the quality of the Nation's air resources so as to promote the public health and welfare and the productive capacity of its population." 42 U.S.C. §7401. The Act's requirements with respect to SIPs emphasize that this purpose — healthy air — is to be attained "as expeditiously as practicable," but, in any event, *no later than* the attainment deadlines. 42 U.S.C., §§7502(a)(2)(A), 7512(a) (emph. added). Although MTC focuses on Congress' extension of the deadlines, the legislative history underscores that Congress regarded them as outside limits. . . .

In sum, we conclude that Congress intended to hold agencies to RFP commitments contained in existing SIPs, pending formal SIP revision. . . .

[The Court next considered plaintiffs' motion for contempt for MTC's violation of its September 19, 1989 Order, and for summary judgment that MTC's failure to adopt more stringent TCM violated the applicable provisions of the 1982 SIP. The Court refused to impose contempt sanctions, finding that its previous order had failed to specify sufficiently precisely what measures were necessary to comply with the 1982 SIP.]

To obtain a summary judgment, plaintiffs must demonstrate that there are no genuine disputes of fact, and that they are entitled to judgment as a matter of law. Fed. R. Civ. P. 56. . . .

1. OZONE

(a) RFP Benchmarks under the 1982 Plan for Ozone

The 1982 Plan's initial strategy for achieving NAAQS for ozone was to reduce hydrocarbon emissions from stationary sources (e.g. factories and household products) and from vehicles through the Inspection and Maintenance Program ("I&M Program"), commonly known as the "smog check program." TCMs contribute relatively little to ozone reduction (the original ten TCMs in the 1982 Plan contributed a 1.8 tpd hydrocarbon emission reduction). 1987 RFP Report. Thus, the 1982 Plan did not even consider hydrocarbon emission reductions from TCMs in making its attainment demonstration.

In *CBE II* [746 F. Supp 976] (enforcing the contingency plan for stationary sources), we held that the 1982 Plan measured RFP for ozone by two different benchmarks: (a) the residual "emissions levels" and (b) the "emission reductions." The former denotes the level of hydrocarbons in the air, while the latter concerns the amount of reductions in hydrocarbon emissions that are achieved from various control measures that are adopted. The 1982 Plan committed to achieving an hydrocarbon emissions level of 430 tpd and reductions totalling 85 tpd by 1987. Thus, RFP, as defined by the 1982 Plan, is satisfied at this post-1987 juncture, if defendants have satisfied both the 430 tpd hydrocarbon emissions level commitment and the 85 tpd emission reduction commitment.

(b)   Achievement of RFP for ozone under the 1982 Plan

[Plaintiff argues] that recent data compiled by MTC and other agencies (referred to as the "updated data"), demonstrates that the Bay Area is substantially out of compliance with the hydrocarbon emission levels committed to in the 1982 Plan — at least with respect to the transportation sector. In particular, plaintiffs point to MTC's 1991 estimated inventory for mobile sources for regional hydrocarbons, which is 199 tpd, and thus well over the 143 tpd the 1982 Plan committed to achieve, with respect to the transportation sector, by 1987. . . . .

It is true that the updated data from the 1987 inventories indicates a higher emissions level that those committed to by the 1982 Plan. However, the updated data rests on a different set of assumptions and different methodology than that which was used to develop the RFP line in the 1982 Plan. Thus, as explained below, we agree with MTC that comparing the 1982 Plan RFP requirements to the updated data would improperly "mix apples with oranges."

The 1982 Plan committed to a 430 tpd emissions level for hydrocarbons based on 1979 inventory data, whereas the new data which will be used to develop the revised SIP will be based on 1987 inventory data. The 1979 and 1987 inventories are based on different types and categories of ROG (reactive organic gases) sources, and the methodologies used to calculate ROG emissions from specific types of sources vary. For example, the 1987 inventory will include data on various source categories that were not included in the 1979 inventory; also the travel models utilized have changed.

Moreover, the 430 tpd limit only has relevance in relation to the 1982 Plan's projection (based on the 1979 inventory data and models and assumptions in use at the time), that hydrocarbon levels would be 515 tpd in 1987 absent 1982 Plan controls. This is because the 1982 Plan arrived at the 430 tpd figure by determining the percentage reduction in emissions necessary to achieve NAAQS for ozone, based on the design value for the Bay Area, and then subtracting this percentage from the projected 515 tpd "uncontrolled" emissions level. Thus, the 430 tpd emissions level only has meaning insofar as the critical assumption — that uncontrolled levels would be 515 tpd — remains constant. As such, it would be inappropriate to compare the RFP benchmarks generated by the 1982 Plan on a ton for ton basis to the projections generated by the 1987 inventory data, since that data will provide an entirely new set of projections concerning pre-control levels. For example, the new data could indicate that pre-control levels are 1000 tpd; however, if the design value indicates that the Bay Area exceeds NAAQS for ozone by 15 percent, then the relevant RFP benchmark would be 850 tpd, not 430 tpd.

Accordingly, we conclude that plaintiffs can not demonstrate liability by reliance on the updated data which is based on new assumptions, models and inventories. Rather, if we are to measure RFP by the terms of the 1982 Plan, we must also stay true to the assumptions and methodology of the 1982 Plan in order to preserve internal consistency. . . . We agree with MTC that the approach taken in Miller's Decl., Exh. F, reflects an analysis most consistent with the assumptions and methodology of the 1982 Plan, particularly in that it continues the 1982 Plan's assumptions regarding uncontrolled emissions.

As MTC points out, Miller's Exh. F indicates that RFP for ozone will be achieved by year end 1991, even without reliance on *any* hydrocarbon reductions from contingency TCMs. Specifically, Exh. F projects that by year end 1991, hydrocarbon emissions levels would be 529 tpd by the end of 1991 (99 tpd over the 430 tpd emissions level), but that hydrocarbon emission reductions of 99.1 tpd would be achieved by year end 1991, resulting in an emissions level of 429.9 tpd.

However, Miller assumed that hydrocarbon emission reductions from the I & M Program would be 30.5 tpd in 1991. As discussed in more detail infra, this figure no longer warrants reliance in light of the findings of a more recent 1991 study (not available at the time Miller prepared his June 25, 1990 declaration), which indicates that the I & M Program will only achieve approximately 18 percent hydrocarbon reductions by 1992, instead of the formerly anticipated 25 percent. . . .

Although the new study raises questions regarding whether RFP has been made for ozone, the record does not demonstrate that RFP has not been made. The majority of the hydrocarbon emission reductions stem from stationary source control measures. However, Miller's Decl., Exh. F, which projects 63.9 tpd reductions from varying stationary source control measures for 1991, is over one year old [data are not available to update these figures]. For example, Exh. F indicates that reductions from aerosol paint control measures may be greater than stated if a total ban is imposed, noting that a hearing was set for June 20, 1990. Thus, the current record is inadequate to demonstrate that RFP has not been satisfied for ozone.

[The court then discussed CO issues.] Viewed together, the above data describes a regional RFP line for CO for the transportation sector which descends from a 1934 tpd CO emissions level in 1979 to a 1541 tpd CO emissions level in 1987. Thus, plaintiffs argue "regional RFP" for CO would be satisfied, under the 1982 Plan, if there is a transportation sector CO emissions level of 1541 tpd and a reduction in CO emissions of 393 tpd.

[The court discussed at length various modelling analyses and empirical studies since 1982.]

As discussed earlier, the 1982 Plan set the desired regional emissions level for CO at 1541 tpd for the transportation sectors. Plaintiffs argue that the 1541 tpd standard is not satisfied because MTC's projections [were] based on the 1987 inventory data, and updated models show that the estimated inventory for mobile sources for 1991 is 1623 tons per day (resulting in an 82 tpd shortfall), and the 16 additional TCMs MTC adopted only make up a portion of the difference. . . . As explained above, however, we conclude that this is not an appropriate manner of establishing liability.

On the other hand, an analysis based on the assumptions of the 1982 Plan does yield a shortfall. The 1982 Plan assumes that the carbon monoxide emissions level would be 1892.3 tpd in 1990. We credit the I & M Program with 278.9 tpd. Adding an additional 16-20 tpd for the original TCMs and 41.8 tpd for the 2131 TCMs [so named because of the number of the resolution adopting them], leaves a shortfall of 10.6 to 14.6 tpd.

As we are persuaded that the contingency 2131 TCMs adopted by MTC, while providing significant progress, are not sufficient to put the Bay Area back on the RFP line, as defined in the 1982 Plan for carbon monoxide, a remedy is appropriate. However, models and projections are by their nature inexact, and we are not convinced that it is appropriate or necessary at this juncture to impose a precise "ton per day" reduction requirement.

In the process of adopting the 2131 TCMs, MTC developed a comprehensive list of potential TCMs that includes dozens of possibilities. Brittle Decl. at ¶5, and Exh. A. While MTC refined this list down to sixteen TCMs, id. at ¶7, and implicitly argues that no other TCMs are possible, the record does not persuade us that adoption of additional TCMs would not be feasible. Satisfaction of this Court's September 19, 1989 remedial order — that MTC fully implement the transportation contingency plan — rests with MTC. We therefore place the burden on MTC to either identify additional feasible TCMs (including authorized or funded "stalled" 2131 TCMs) or demonstrate why such additional TCMs are infeasible. No court, of course, will require impracticable measures or measures that cause a substantially disproportionate hardship for the air quality benefits accrued, regardless of the ton per day shortfall. On the other hand, infeasibility means more than inconvenience, unpopularity, or moderate burdens. We choose this pragmatic approach believing that it is in keeping with both the spirit of the Clean Air Act and the constraints imposed by practical realities.

NOTES AND QUESTIONS

1. Compare the *CBE* decision with Judge Newman's opinion in *Coalition Against Columbus Circle v. New York*, 967 F.2d 764 (2d Cir. 1992). A proposed redevelopment project at Columbus Circle agreed to chan-

nel $338 million to New York City's transit system in return for the city's approval of the project. Local citizen groups, neighbors, and businesses filed a "citizen suit" to block the project.

The City has for many years experienced local CO levels in violation of the federal ambient CO standards. Its 1984 SIP, still in effect at the time of the litigation, provided that if an environmental review of a development project "identifies a violation or exceedence of the carbon monoxide standard, then the City commits to assure that mitigating measures will be implemented by the project sponsor or the City, so as to provide for attainment of the standard by December 31, 1987, and maintenance of it thereafter." By the time of this litigation, the only CO violation in New York was at East 59th Street between Madison and Fifth Avenues. The proposed redevelopment project, on West 59th Street several blocks west of the "hot spot," would attract increased traffic, resulting in some increases in local CO emissions, including emissions at the East 59th Street "hot spot." However, these increases would not result in any material increase in the CO standard violation at the hot spot. Modelling projected that the project would increase CO concentrations at the "hot spot" from 12.9 ppm to 13.3 ppm (the CO NAAQS is 9 ppm), but under EPA rules for rounding off integers, this change would not be legally cognizable.

The district court found that the City's efforts to eliminate its CO violation were inadequate, and therefore that it could not approve any new project that would increase CO emissions in the vicinity. It therefore enjoined construction of the project. The court of appeals reversed. It first found that Congress in the 1990 amendments had extended the overall deadlines for compliance by non-attainment regions; hence the City's commitment to achieve the CO-standard by 1987 had been postponed. The court found that the savings clause in §110(n)(1) of the Act, relied upon in the *CBE* decision, preserving "[a]ny provision of any applicable implementation plan" included New York's 1984 SIP commitment. This commitment, however, was not to undertake some specific measure, which could be enforceable immediately. Instead, it was a general undertaking to take unspecified measures to achieve the CO standard by the applicable attainment date, which had now been postponed by virtue of the 1990 amendments. Hence, the City was not in violation of the 1984 SIP.

2. The court in *CBE* notes that the non-attainment provisions adopted by the 1977 Amendments were not effective. Why then, does it require enforcement of 1982 SIP provisions that are a relic of this failed regime? Does *Coalition Against Columbus Center* effectively penalize states that adopted "honest" specific and adequate SIPs, and reward those whose SIPs are inadequate? Can the savings clause be read so as to avoid this result?

3. Do *CBE* and *Coalition Against Columbus Center* support or under-

F. INCENTIVE-BASED APPROACHES

The foregoing materials have highlighted numerous problems that have arisen in the efforts to control air pollution. The existing system of regulating air pollution is primarily based on a best available technology (BAT) approach. If an industrial process or product generates some nontrivial risk, the responsible plant or industry must install whatever technology is available to reduce or eliminate this risk, so long as the costs of doing so will not cause a shutdown of the plant or industry. BAT requirements are largely determined through federal regulations, which tend to be uniform for a given category of sources. The use of the BAT principles is explicit in the NSPS, BACT, and LAER requirements applicable to new stationary sources, and in the control requirements for new automobiles, which have been relaxed or tightened in response to the degree of control that can be achieved in the near term by available technology. The national ambient air quality standards are supposed in theory to be met regardless of the availability and cost of technology. But in practice the degree of control required of existing sources is based on EPA and state determinations of reasonably available control technology (RACT) for categories of industrial sources. As Melnick points out, when technology has not been available at a reasonable cost to permit achievement of NAAQs in accordance with statutory deadlines, the deadlines have been tacitly ignored, and eventually postponed by Congress.

The BAT strategy was embraced by Congress and administrators in the early 1970s in order to impose immediate, readily enforceable federal controls on a relatively few widespread pollutants, while avoiding widespread industrial shutdowns. This approach is premised on government regulators' being able to perform three tasks reasonably effectively: (1) to evaluate technological means of reducing air pollution; (2) to dictate appropriate regulatory requirements to pollution sources; and (3) to monitor and enforce regulatory requirements. The experience of the 1970s and 1980s has demonstrated some serious practical limitations of this approach:[39]

1. Uniform BAT requirements waste tens of billions of dollars annually by ignoring variations among plants and industries in the cost of reducing pollution and by ignoring geographic variation in pollution effects. A more cost-effective strategy of risk reduction could free enormous amounts of resources for additional pollution reduction or other purposes.

2. BAT controls, and the litigation they provoke tend to impose

---

39. This discussion is adapted from Ackerman & Stewart, Reforming Environmental Law, 37 Stan. L. Rev. 1333 (1985).

disproportionate penalties on new products and processes. A BAT strategy typically imposes far more stringent controls on new sources because there is no risk of shutdown. Also, new plants and products must run the gauntlet of lengthy regulatory and legal proceedings to win approval; the resulting uncertainty and delay discourage new investment. By contrast, existing sources can use the delays and costs of the legal process to burden regulators and postpone or "water down" compliance. BAT strategies also impose disproportionate burdens on more productive and profitable industries because these industries can "afford" more stringent controls. This "soak the rich" approach penalizes growth and international competitiveness.

3. BAT controls can ensure that established control technologies are installed. They do not, however, ensure that they are maintained and operated properly. Moreover, BAT controls do not provide strong incentives for the development of new, environmentally superior strategies, and may actually discourage their development. Such innovations are essential for maintaining long-term economic growth without simultaneously increasing pollution and other forms of environmental degradation.

4. BAT involves the centralized determination of complex scientific, engineering, and economic issues regarding the feasibility of controls of a variety of pollutants from many hundreds of pollution categories. Such determinations impose massive information-gathering burdens on administrators and provide a fertile ground for complex litigation in the form of massive adversary rulemaking proceedings and protracted judicial review. Given the high costs of regulatory compliance and the potential gains from litigation brought to defeat or delay regulatory requirements, it is often more cost-effective for industry to "invest" in such litigation rather than to comply. Moreover, this system tends to create a "democracy deficit" because important public policy decisions are made through a myriad of decisions in an archaic bureaucratic-regulatory process accessible only to Washington "insiders."

5. A BAT strategy is inconsistent with intelligent priority setting. Simply regulating to the hilt whatever pollutants happen to get on the regulatory agenda may preclude an agency from dealing adequately with more serious problems that come to scientific attention later. BAT also tends to reinforce regulatory inertia. Foreseeing that "all or nothing" regulation of a given substance under BAT will involve large administrative and compliance costs, and recognizing that resources are limited, agencies often seek to limit sharply the number of substances on the agenda for regulatory action.

These criticisms reflect the results of the available empirical studies. Of twelve studies of the costs of regulating various air pollutants, seven indicated that traditional command and control regulation were more than 400 percent more expensive than the least-cost solution;

four revealed that they were about 75 percent more expensive; one suggested a modest cost-overrun of 7 percent. Even if a reformed system could cut costs by "only" one-third, it could save more than $14 billion a year on air pollution control expenditures alone.[40] Annual expenditures to comply with federal pollution control laws were estimated by EPA at $115 billion in 1990, rising to $185 billion by 2000.[41]

At around the time that the Clean Air Act was substantially overhauled in 1970, many economists and some environmentalists had advocated the use of incentive-based approaches to control air pollution. As in other areas of overuse of a common resource — for example, parking on public streets — economists advocated the imposition of fees upon polluting activities — the equivalent of parking meters. The Coalition to Tax Pollution, a Washington-based environmental organization, proposed that a charge be imposed on emissions of sulfur oxides. For a variety of reasons that will be explored below, such proposals were not adopted.

Growing recognition of the failings of command and control strategies and the costs of regulation have refocused attention on economic incentive approaches. Incentive-based approaches have gradually worked their way into the EPA's regulatory strategy for controlling air pollution. Moreover, Congress, as explained below, has endorsed a broad experiment with these techniques as a means for addressing acid deposition. Further applications of these approaches are emerging in state and local air pollution programs. In addition, as we will see in subsequent chapters, incentive-based approaches are being introduced into many other areas of environmental protection. See Project 88: Harnessing Market Forces To Protect Our Environment (1988); Project 88, Round II: (1990) .

This section begins with a general overview of economic incentive approaches for pollution problems. It also discusses the philosophical and practical objections that have been raised against the use of these regulatory instruments. Subsequent sections describe the principal applications of these instruments, including the emissions trading programs under the Clean Air Act, the acid deposition program established by the 1990 Amendments, the expanded use of incentive-based approaches in Los Angeles and elsewhere, and the potential use of these instruments to address global climate change.

Since experience with incentive-based approaches is limited, you should be sensitive to the substantial gap between the theoretical argu-

---

40. See Portney, Air Pollution Policy, in Public Policies for Environmental Protection 27, 65 (P. Portney (ed.) 1990) (reporting projected cumulative expenditures on air pollution control for 1979-1988 at $427.71 billion).

41. U.S. EPA, Environmental Investments, The Cost of A Clean Environment (1990).

ments for these approaches and the complexity of the real world. As you work through these materials, try to develop a critical understanding of the promise and limitations of these instruments, as compared to those of traditional regulation. Since the ultimate objective is improving our regulatory system, keep the following questions in mind: Will economic incentive systems perform better than command and control regulation in practice? What factors contribute to their effectiveness? What factors detract?

1.   AN OVERVIEW OF ECONOMIC INCENTIVE SYSTEMS

a.   Emission Fees

C. SCHULTZE, ET AL. SETTING NATIONAL PRIORITIES: THE 1973 BUDGET

368-373 (1972)

Many economists, joined recently by a coalition of conservation groups, have urged that economic incentives be given a major role in controlling pollution through imposition of "effluent charges" (or taxes) on each unit of pollution by industry into the air or water. This would provide business firms with an incentive to reduce pollution in order to lower their tax burden. . . .

. . . Cutting back pollution by, say 90 percent, would be relatively inexpensive to some industries but very costly in others. . . .

What is needed, therefore, is a variable standard that would concentrate the reduction in pollution where the costs of reduction are least. . . . Each firm should reduce pollution to the point where the cost of removing an additional unit is the same as that for every other firm. . . .

[A] tax could be levied on each unit of each kind of pollutant discharged into the air or water. Faced with these taxes or "effluent charges," each firm would find it in its own interest to reduce pollution by an amount related to the cost of reduction and through the use of the least-cost means of doing so. It would compare the cost of paying the effluent charge with the cost of cleaning up pollution, and would choose to remove pollution up to the point where the additional cost of removal was greater than the effluent charge. The larger the effluent charge, the greater the percentage of pollutants a firm would find it advantageous to remove. Firms with low costs of control would remove a larger percentage than would firms with high costs — precisely the situation needed to achieve a least-cost approach to reducing pollution for the economy as a whole. The kinds of products whose manufacture generate a lot of pollution would become more expensive and would carry higher prices than those that generated less, and consumers would be induced to buy more of the latter.

The effluent charge approach has another advantage. In the case of regulations that require the removal of a specific percentage of pollutants, once a firm has achieved that point, it has no incentive to cut pollution further. Indeed it has a positive incentive not to do so, since the additional reduction is costly and lowers profits. With effluent charges, however, firms are taxed for every unit of pollution they have not removed. They would have a continuing incentive to devote research and engineering talent toward finding less costly ways of achieving still further reductions. . . .

NOTES AND QUESTIONS

As Schultze explains, under a fee system, a pollution source that can reduce pollution more cheaply will eliminate relatively more pollution, and pay relatively less in taxes on its remaining emissions, than a source with higher control costs, which will reduce emissions less and pay correspondingly more in taxes. More technically, each will control emissions up to the point that the marginal cost of eliminating an additional ton of pollution (which tends to rise with additional increments of control) just equals the tax per ton of pollutant. Do you see why? Since all sources pay the same tax, it follows that their marginal control costs will be the same. This identity ensures that society is achieving the aggregate reductions obtained in the most economically efficient, least-cost manner. If sources' marginal control costs differed, society could save money by shifting more of the abatement burden to those sources with lower marginal control costs.

1. An important premise of Schultze's argument is that pollution control costs vary widely across different sources. As Chart 4.2 shows, this is indeed the case. Why can't traditional regulatory controls be adjusted in order to achieve a least-cost allocation of the abatement burden?

2. Emission fees have other advantages beyond those mentioned by Schultze. They eliminate regulatory bias against new plants and products by treating emissions from new and old sources the same. They also greatly simplify the administrative tasks needed to implement a control program and limit the issues that might give rise to litigation. Rather than deciding BAT for hundreds or thousands of different sources through complex rulemaking proceedings, the government sets a fee that is uniform for all sources of a given pollutant and collects the amount due from each. A pollution fee will mean the products produced by more highly polluting processes will cost more to produce

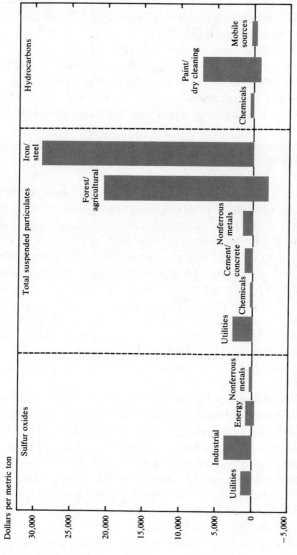

CHART 4.2

Ranges in Incremental Control Costs for Existing and New-Source Standards in Various Industries

Source: R. Crandall, Controlling Industrial Pollution (1983).

379

and will therefore carry a higher price to consumers than products
manufactured by less polluting processes. Consumers will therefore
have an incentive, via the price system, to switch their purchases in
favor of the latter products. The sales of high pollution products will
fall, and pollution will therefore diminish as well. Finally, a fee determination — whether by Congress or an administrative agency — is a far
more publicly visible decision than a host of "BAT" decisions, a factor
that promotes political accountability.

3. *Problem:* Refer back to the Malambia problem on pp. 240-241.
Because of the inefficiency of proportional emission reductions, Malambia decides to try an emission fee system. The government imposes
a fee of $1000 per ton on smox emitted on both industries. How much
pollution will each industry produce? Is this result efficient? Is it equitable?

4. Emission fees give rise to a number of implementation problems. Consider the following:

- *Valuation.* As previous material on the valuation of the benefits
  of environmental improvement have highlighted, it is extremely difficult to assign dollar figures to the social cost of pollution. Yet in order for emission fees to be efficient, they must
  use "correct" dollar values. Alternatively, the government could
  set the desired level of emissions and use a fee system to induce
  sources to reduce aggregate emissions to the desired level determined by other means. For example, the goal could be set by
  legislative or administrative regulation, as under §109 of the
  Clean Air Act. But how would the government know how to set
  the fee that would alleviate the desired level of emissions?
  How would the fee system deal with inflation and industrial
  growth?
- *Non-Linearity of Environmental Damages.* The environmental damage of many pollutants varies according to the concentration
  and location of emissions. For example, the first few units of a
  pollutant such as sulfur oxides may cause little or no damage;
  addition units may reduce visibility; still further pollution, may
  create "toxic hot spots," causing health damage. Consequently,
  an efficient emission fee system should have variable fees reflecting the actual relationship between emissions and environmental damages in each area.
- *Monitoring.* Emission fees require a reliable monitoring system.
  Monitoring of emissions is complicated by the technical difficulty and costs involved in measuring gas emissions, the administrative costs of monitoring systems, the ubiquity of sources,
  and potential for evasion.
- *Polluter Incentives.* Economic incentive systems assume that regu-

lated entities will behave rationally. Yet many polluters, such as public utilities or government facilities, may not be fully subject or responsive to the discipline of the market.

To what extent are these problems greater in the context of emission fees than for command and control regulation? For a provocative critique of economic incentive systems, see Latin, Ideal Versus Real Regulatory Efficiency: Implementation of Uniform Standards and "Fine-Tuning" Regulatory Reforms, 37 Stan. L. Rev. 1267 (1985), and the response by Ackerman & Stewart, Reforming Environmental Law, 37 Stan. L. Rev. 1333 (1985).

   5. Economic incentive approaches to address environmental problems have been assailed on a variety of normative grounds. A common attack on effluent fees has been that they amount to the government selling "licenses to pollute." Professor Steven Kelman has articulated four concerns about the use of charges in environmental policy:

- they make "a social statement of indifference towards the motives of polluters in reducing pollution";
- they fail to make "a statement stigmatizing polluting behavior";
- they bring "environmental quality into a system of markets and prices of which it previously has not been a part"; and
- they frequently produce "a situation where wealthier people choose to pay the charge and continue behaving as before, while poorer people, to avoid the charge, are the ones to change their behavior."

S. Kelman, What Price Incentives? Economists and the Environment 27-28 (1981). Do you find these criticisms persuasive? How would an economist respond to these arguments? Does command and control regulation avoid these criticisms? To what extent do Kelman's arguments turn on perceptions? Could these perceptions be addressed through other government policy instruments? Would it be a good idea to replace legal prohibitions on racial discrimination with a discrimination tax? If not, is pollution different?

   6. Are there other moral objections to fee systems? Consider the following colloquy:

   SCENE: The new Federal Licensing Bureau. A bored clerk is approached by a middle-age applicant who looks nervous.

Applicant: I'd like to apply for a license to emit sulphur oxides. I have this small backyard smelter and . . .
Clerk: Okay. That'll be $10,000.
Applicant: Did you say $10,000? That's exorbitant!

Clerk: Look Mac, sulphur oxides aggravate lung diseases, dissolve nylon stockings, peel paint and create killer fogs. The right to do all that doesn't come cheap.

Applicant: I'm sorry, I didn't realize . . .

Clerk: Remember, it's high fees that reduce damage to health and property. Now if you want something cheap I can let you have a license good for tossing three beer cans and a sandwich wrapper out your car window. That's only ten bucks.

Applicant: Littering? I don't know, there doesn't seem to be much profit in it.

Clerk: Ah, you're looking for a profit? Confidentially, I think our best buy is a Mugging License. It entitles you to hit three old ladies over the head in the park of your choice and snatch their purses. Most guys come out ahead on this one.

Applicant (surprised):   Hitting old ladies over the head? That sounds anti-social somehow.

Clerk (shrugging):   It's no different than a license to poison people's lungs. And it's only $100.

Applicant (indignant):   That's highway robbery!

Clerk: Nope. Highway Robbery is $200. But it's a non-renewable, non-transferable, one-shot deal.

Applicant: I hate to risk that kind of money.

Clerk: Tell you what. Get a group of your friends together and take out a License to Riot. You can burn and loot five stores in the ghetto of your choice. The fee's relatively low because it's part of our Urban Renewal Program.

Applicant (shaking his head):   It seems like these days people are getting away with murder.

Clerk: Not unless they got 50,000 bucks, buddy. Remember, we got to keep the charges sufficiently high to encourage control of everyone's criminal instincts.

Applicant (appalled):   What kind of concept is that? It just means the rich can get away with crimes like poisoning people's lungs that the poor can't afford to commit.

Clerk (yawning):   So what else is new? Next.

Hoppe, A License to Steal, San Francisco Chronicle, Feb. 8, 1971.

7. Perhaps the greatest impediment to the adoption of effluent fees has been politics. Despite some early flirtation with effluent fees, most environmental organizations have pursued a command and control regulatory agenda that relies heavily on litigation and has relatively little regard for economic efficiency and flexibility. They have tended to emphasize the normative arguments against market-based in policy instruments. Industry, not surprisingly, has been disinclined to support

new taxes. Even though effluent fees promise more cost-effective regulatory controls, industry has discovered that the existing command and control system can work to its advantage in resisting regulation. Litigation can be used to water down and delay compliance. Moreover, under the existing system, once a firm complies with the applicable BAT regulation, pollution is free. Especially for older plants, there are distinct advantages to the status quo. Regulatory agencies have also been generally opposed to effluent fees. Command and control regulation is better understood by the lawyers, engineers, and other technically-oriented personnel who have tended to dominate federal and state environmental regulatory offices. Also, an effluent fee approach would threaten the established regulatory bureaucracy. Effluent fees also raise problems of congressional and bureaucratic "turf." Would an effluent fee system fall under the jurisdiction of the tax committees in Congress or the environmental committees? Would it be administered by the EPA or the Treasury Department?

More recently, the political tide seems to be shifting somewhat on the use of effluent fees to address environmental problems. See Passell, Cheapest Protection of Nature May Lie in Taxes, Not Laws, N.Y. Times, Nov. 24, 1992, at C1. Persistent government budget deficits have stirred interest in the revenue raising potential of effluent fees. Many municipalities have adopted curbside fees for trash removal. See Menell, Beyond the Throwaway Society: An Incentive Approach to Regulating Municipal Solid Waste, 17 Ecology L.Q. 655 (1990). The European Community is seriously considering a tax on energy, based in part on the carbon content of fuels, to reduce CO_2 emissions in order to deal with potential global climate change. President Clinton's energy tax proposal, offered in his original deficit-reduction plan, was justified in part on environmental grounds.

Nonetheless, there still remain substantial political impediments to widespread adoption of effluent fees. The European Community, fearing adverse impacts on its industries' competitiveness, will not implement its proposed energy tax unless Japan and the United States impose equivalent economic burdens on CO_2 emitters. Congress dramatically scaled back President Clinton's proposed energy tax. It is unlikely that established industries will welcome the imposition of fees on activities that have been subject only to affordable technological controls. One means of attempting to counter this opposition is through offsetting tax reductions that lead to a revenue-neutral result. For example, California has recently enacted a revenue-neutral change in its sales tax on new automobiles that imposes higher taxes on cars that have low gas mileage and lower or no taxes on those that are fuel efficient. See Levenson and Gordon, Drive+: Promoting Cleaner and More Fuel Efficient Motor Vehicles Through a Self-Financing System of State Sales Tax Incentives, 9 J. Pol. Anal. & Mgmt. 409 (1990). Tradeable permits offer another way around the major political impediments to effluent fees:

b.   Tradeable Permits

J. DALES, POLLUTION, PROPERTY AND PRICES

93-97 (1968)

[Professor Dales focuses upon the problem of water pollution but the basic model he outlines could be adopted as a means to control most air pollution problems. Dale envisages a Water Quality Board that would address water pollution.]

Let us try to set up a "market" in "pollution rights." The Board starts the process by creating a certain number of Pollution Rights, each Right giving whoever buys it the right to discharge one equivalent ton of wastes into natural waters during the current year. Suppose that the current level of pollution is roughly satisfactory. On this assumption, if half a million tons of wastes are currently being dumped into the water system, the Board would issue half a million Rights. All waste dischargers would then be required to buy whatever number of Rights they need; if a factory dumps 1000 tons of waste per year it will have to buy 1000 Rights. To put the market into operation, let us say that the Board decides to withhold 5 percent of the Rights in order to allow for the growth of production and population during the first year, and therefore offers 475,000 Rights for sale. Since the demand is for 500,000, the Rights will immediately command some positive price — say, 10 cents each.

Even at 10 cents per Right some firms will find it profitable to treat their raw wastes before they discharge them, or to dispose of them in some way other than discharging them into the water. They will thereby reduce the number of Rights they are compelled to buy, and, when the price has risen enough to reduce the demand by 25,000 Rights, the market will be in equilibrium. As time goes on, we would expect the growth of population and industry to result in an increase in the demand for Rights, and since the number of Rights issued by the Board cannot be increased the price of the Rights will move upward. As it does so, the incentive for waste dischargers to treat, or reduce, their wastes, so that they reduce the number of Rights they must buy, increases.

Once the market is in full operation, individual holders will buy and sell Rights on their own initiative. . . . Firms that go out of business during the year, or that experience a slump in production, or that bring new waste disposal practices into operation, will have Rights to sell; new firms, or those that find that their production is exceeding their expectations, will appear as buyers in the market. Similarly for municipalities; those that build new or better sewage treatment plants will be sellers of Rights, while those that experience growth in their populations and do nothing to reduce their wastes will be buyers. All of these buyers and sellers, through their bids and offers, will establish the price of the Rights. The price will no doubt display minor fluctuations from time to time, like other prices; but it will probably show an upward trend over time. That makes sense; if economic growth (which causes pollution) is to continue, and yet pollution is to be checked, the cost of disposing of wastes must rise — and this increasing cost is registered in the rising price of Pollution Rights. . . .

Anyone, of course, should be allowed to buy Pollution Rights, even if they do not use them. Conservation groups might well want to buy up some Rights merely in order to prevent their being used. In this way at least part of the guerilla warfare between conservationists and polluters could be transferred into a civilized "war with dollars"; both groups would, I think, learn something in the process. Pure speculators should also be able to buy Rights in the expectation of being able to sell them later at a higher price — and also to sell them short if they think the price will go down in the future. Speculation is a risky business for the speculators, but it does help to "make a good market" and if enough speculators can be found to play the Rights market they will help to even out temporary price fluctuations and thus help the Board stabilize the market. . . .

How would the Government use the money that the [Board] took in by selling pollution rights? In any way the government sees fit. Let us say it goes to consolidated revenues. There is no problem in disposing of money!

Once in operation, the Pollution Rights market will, by establishing a price for Rights, relieve the Board of any necessity to set the proper price by trial-and-error methods. The market will also automatically solve the problem of new-comers. As population and factories grow, the price of Rights will automatically rise, and existing polluters will find it profitable to reduce their own wastes in order to sell some of their existing Rights at a profit or in order to avoid buying so many of them next year; reduced demand by existing holders will release a supply for new buyers.

NOTES AND QUESTIONS

1. *Problem:* Refer back to the Malambia problem on pp. 240-241. Because of the inefficiency of proportional emission reductions, Ma-

lambia opts for a tradeable permit system. Each permit allows the holder to emit one ton of smox per day. The government auctions off 220 of these permits. What will be the outcome of the auction? Is this result efficient? Equitable?

2. The system of transferable pollution permits, which can be viewed as a revised system of property rights in environmental resources, has two important advantages, in principle, over both regulatory and emission fee approaches.

First, it can achieve a desired degree of pollution control, and do so at least cost. Like the regulatory approach it will, if enforced, ensure that the desired level of emissions is not exceeded. Like the effluent fee approach, control will be achieved at least cost because the transferable feature of the permits establishes an effective price for each unit of pollution emitted, leading to an appropriately greater degree of emission control by those sources that can do so most cheaply.

A second basic advantage is that a transferable permit system can assure that the desired level of emissions will be maintained in the face of industrial growth and price inflation without the necessity of further governmental action. Why is this an advantage? What steps must the government take to cope with growth and/or inflation under a regulatory or fee approach?

3. Tradeable permits hold an additional significant advantage over effluent fees: political viability. Although Dales' scheme calls for an initial auction of permits, the scheme would also work if permits were granted to existing sources in proportion to the emissions which are currently allowed to emit under existing regulations. In this way, the political losers would be compensated for changes in the regulatory regime. If the market functions smoothly, the more efficient producers will be able to bid the most for permits. Will the long-run equilibrium be the same under this permit allocation scheme as a government auction? How should tradeable permits be allocated?

4. Would a tradable permit system enable pollution to concentrate in the same location, potentially creating toxic hot spots? (Note that this is a potential problem under an effluent fee approach as well.) Will this be a serious problem, practically speaking? Does it depend on the type of pollutant? Some have suggested that in order to deal with this problem the value of permits could vary depending on the extent of the pollution problem in different zones. For example, more permits would be required in order to emit a ton of a pollutant in a relatively more polluted area than in a less polluted area. In essence, the government would designate "exchange rates" between zones. What problems might this create? Does this solution undercut the feasibility or the claimed advantages of a transferable permit system? How can the problem of geographical concentration of pollution sources be dealt with under a fee system? A regulatory system?

5. Is a transferrable permit system biased against improvements in environmental quality? Note Dales' suggestion that it would be possible for environmental groups or the government to achieve improvements in environmental quality under a transferable permit system by entering the market, purchasing, and retiring pollution permits. How likely a possibility is this? On the other hand, if the government unilaterally reduces the amount of pollution permitted under existing permits, will it not be open to a charge of unconstitutional "taking" of property without just compensation? Would not a limited life for permits, say 5 years, alleviate this problem, enabling the government to reduce the number of permits periodically? What problems might such an approach produce? What about a system that provides that permit rights will be depreciated on a fixed schedule, say, 10 percent per year, so that a permit to emit 100 tons this year will entitle the holder to emit only 90 tons next year?

6. The efficiency and incentive advantages of a transferrable permit system depend on the existence of a well-functioning market for permits (note that this is not true for effluent fees). What are the obstacles to the development of such a market? What can the government do to reduce those obstacles? A market is more likely to work if there are many sources. This suggests that the permit scheme should cover a broad geographic area. Would this exacerbate the "hot spot" problem? For what type of pollutants is a tradeable permit system best suited?

2.   ACCOMMODATING GROWTH: THE EMISSIONS TRADING PROGRAM

The non-attainment regulatory program and, to a lesser extent, the PSD program both represent a threat to new industrial and commercial development that has air pollution associated with it. Should new stationary sources be permitted in areas that have not achieved the ambient standards or are subject to strict PSD limitations on additional pollution? To permit additional sources of pollution in such regions threatens the basic purpose of the regulatory programs. On the other hand, to prohibit substantially all new industrial development in most regions of the nation would create severe economic disruption and overwhelming political opposition. Moreover, new sources can be designed to be less polluting and achieve greater emissions reductions at less cost than existing sources. In essence, a regulatory technique was needed that would enable greater economic output with the same or less pollution. Traditional command and control regulation was not well suited to meet this challenge. It is not surprising, therefore, that this was one of the first areas in which EPA experimented with incentive-based approaches.

This problem initially arose when the original 1975-1976 deadlines for achieving the national primary standards expired. The original 1970 Act had no provisions telling EPA what to do with new sources being built in non-attainment areas. In order to resolve its dilemma, EPA by administrative regulation adopted an "offset" policy allowing new sources to be built in non-attainment areas, provided that more than compensatory reductions were obtained by SIP regulation or otherwise from existing sources. Congress subsequently endorsed this offset strategy in the 1977 Amendments. EPA subsequently, by administrative regulation, expanded the offset principle for use in other contexts.

a.   Understanding the Basics of Emission Trading Policy

R. Liroff, Reforming Air Pollution Regulation: The Toil and Trouble of EPA's Bubble

(1986)

A BRIEF OVERVIEW OF TRADING PROPOSALS

Emissions trading proposals come in many different forms. These have emerged, one by one, in response to special circumstances of diverse programs established by the Clean Air Act. . . .

BUBBLES

EPA's bubble policy[42] derives its name from the placing of an imaginary bubble over emission points of pollutants. The level of emissions allowed from the one opening in the imaginary bubble is the sum of the emissions that would result from placing traditional controls on individual points under the bubble. The company operating the points is then free to adjust the level of control among the individual points so it can reach that sum at least cost.[43] It has the opportunity to control most the points that are the cheapest to clean up and to control least those that are the most expensive. As the company reduces discharges

---

42. The "bubble policy" for existing sources once was a discrete statement of EPA policy, but it was later merged into an "emissions trading policy statement" that included principles for bubbles, netting, offsets, and banking.

43. Only emissions of the same pollutant can be traded. For example, increases in sulfur dioxide can be traded only for decreases in sulfur dioxide

more than is required at some points, it earns ERCs [emission reduction credits] that can be applied against other points where controls will be less stringent. The company's savings can be substantial. For example, if using methods traditionally dictated by regulators to reduce total emissions at a facility from 100 tons to 60 tons would cost a company $5 million, the company might be able to achieve the same reductions in emissions by using an alternative approach that cost only $3.5 million (Figure 1.1).

In theory, the bubble's flexibility provides a powerful incentive for companies to develop new, less costly means of pollution control or to find the least expensive mixes of readily available control technologies and production changes. Presumably, plant managers know their plants more intimately than do regulators and thus have better senses of where novel abatement opportunities lie.

[The "bubble" concept thus allows managers the feasibility to reallocate the controls otherwise required on emissions from different outlets within a plant, in order to achieve the same overall level of emissions at less cost. EPA has also extended the bubble concept to enable two different sources in a SIP region to trade pollution control requirements. Source A may increase its emissions of a given pollutant if, by agreement with A, Source B reduces its emissions an equivalent amount.]

NETTING

Among the most demanding administrative and technological requirements of the Clean Air Act are those triggered by increased emissions from modified points in sources. However, a company can avoid or reduce these requirements when it compensates for those increases by reducing emissions from other points within that source and thereby earning ERCs. Because this trading approach causes the net emissions from the entire source to stay at the same level as they were before the modifications, it is commonly known as netting. For example, if modification of one point in a source would increase that point's emissions by 100 tons per year, and such an increase normally would require a control technology that removed 98 percent of the emissions at that point, the company might be able to avoid installing the control technology — and to save some money — by reducing emissions by 100 tons at another point within the source. [Alternatively, the source might reduce emissions by something less than 98 tons at the new point

---

and not for decreases in particulate matter or nitrogen dioxide. Moreover, the ambient impact of these changes—their impact on concentrations of the pollutant in the air—must be equivalent.

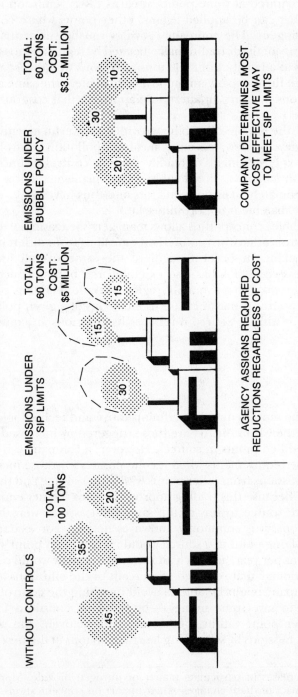

FIGURE 1.1
EPA's Bubble Policy for Existing Sources

WITHOUT CONTROLS

TOTAL: 100 TONS

45   35   20

EMISSIONS UNDER SIP LIMITS

TOTAL: 60 TONS
COST: $5 MILLION

30   15   15

AGENCY ASSIGNS REQUIRED REDUCTIONS REGARDLESS OF COST

EMISSIONS UNDER BUBBLE POLICY

TOTAL: 60 TONS
COST: $3.5 MILLION

20   30   10

COMPANY DETERMINES MOST COST EFFECTIVE WAY TO MEET SIP LIMITS

Adapted from U.S. Environmental Protection Agency, *Controlled Trading: How to Reduce the Cost of Air Pollution Control* (Washington D.C.: U.S. Environmental Protection Agency, 1981), p. 5.

390

and reduce emissions at existing points sufficiently to make up 100 tons.][44]

Netting and the bubble are conceptually similar, in that increased controls at one point are traded for decreased controls at another. However, the bubble initially was developed to ease the obligations of companies to reduce emissions from existing sources. Netting, in contrast, was intended to reduce the administrative and pollution reduction obligations of sources [that were "modified" and thus subject to special new source review and emissions control requirements].

OFFSETS

In [non-attainment] regions, current policies allow industries to construct new or modified major sources of pollution if they offset those sources' emissions by reducing emissions from existing sources by even greater amounts (Figure 1.2). In other words, industries can construct those sources if they can generate ERCs from their own existing sources or acquire ERCs that other dischargers of pollutants have earned for reductions they have made in the area.

This offset policy differs from netting in several respects. First, it applies to both new and modified sources, not solely to modified sources. Second, it was developed originally for areas whose air is dirtier than ambient standards, whereas netting operates in areas both cleaner and dirtier than the ambient standards. Third, netting merely requires existing emissions to be reduced by amounts equal to new emissions, whereas the offset policy requires existing emissions to be lowered by an amount greater than the new emissions added.

BANKING

The transfer of ERCs from one discharger of pollution to another is facilitated by another major component of EPA's emissions trading policy, banking, which allows ERCs to be recorded in a central administrative ledger for future use in the same area. The ledger usually is maintained by state or local air pollution control officials. If a company that has earned ERCs chooses, its credits can be purchased or leased by another discharger of the same pollutant for use in a bubble or offset transaction. By giving geographically proximate industries ready access

---

44. [Ed. Note: When a source nets out new emissions with reductions from existing emissions, it is no longer a "modified" source and is thus not subject to the new source review procedures under PSD and non-attainment regulations.]

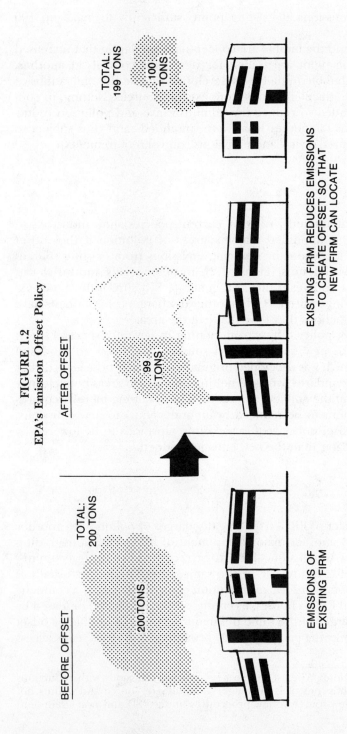

FIGURE 1.2
EPA's Emission Offset Policy

BEFORE OFFSET

TOTAL:
200 TONS

200 TONS

EMISSIONS OF
EXISTING FIRM

AFTER OFFSET

99
TONS

TOTAL:
199 TONS

100
TONS

EXISTING FIRM REDUCES EMISSIONS
TO CREATE OFFSET SO THAT
NEW FIRM CAN LOCATE

Adapted from U.S. Environmental Protection Agency, *Controlled Trading: How to Reduce the Cost of Air Pollution Control* (Washington D.C.: U.S. Environmental Protection Agency, 1981), p. 5.

to confirmed credits so that the companies do not have to search widely for them, ERC banks may facilitate emissions trading. The banks may also encourage companies to reduce their own emissions, since they may believe that the credits they could earn would be more readily marketable than would be the case without a bank.

NOTES AND QUESTIONS

1. What are the policy arguments for and against trading in the following contexts? Do they differ among the contexts?

- *NSPS.* Trading within a "source" (netting) allows new or modified units within the source to escape full NSPS control requirements, provided offsetting emissions reductions are obtained elsewhere in the same plant.
- *PSD.* Trading within a "source" (netting) allows new or modified units to escape full best available control technology (BACT) controls and special PSD monitoring and review requirements, provided offsetting emissions reductions are obtained.
- *NA (Non-attainment).* Trading within a source (netting) allows new units to escape full lowest achievable emission rate (LAER) controls and other §173 requirements provided offsetting emissions are obtained. Trading between different sources (offsets) allows a new source to enter a non-attainment region. (Note that even though the new source must obtain more than offseting reductions from existing sources through government regulatory changes or market agreements between sources, the new source is subject to pre-construction review and special control requirements including LAER.)
- *SIP control reallocations.* Trading within or among existing sources (bubble) allows emission reduction requirements to be reallocated.

2. EPA has sought to articulate a consistent set of principles governing the various emission trading systems in an Emission Trading Policy Statement, 51 Fed. Reg. 43,814 (1986), and proposed regulations for Economic Incentive Programs, 58 Fed. Reg. 11110 (1993).

3. Trading programs have been hampered by "regulatory overhang"; sources are constrained by the need to obtain regulatory approval and other regulatory restrictions. Netting has been the most widespread form of trading; transaction and regulatory costs are minimized because trading occurs within the same plant. Intra-plant bubbling has also been widely used. Bubbling between plants and market

offset trades have been much less frequent. Nonetheless, thousands of trades have occurred, resulting in cost savings of a billion dollars or more. On the other hand, environmentalists have been worried about "paper trades," where credits have been earned as a result of actual emissions at a facility being less than those permitted by regulation, or credits have been earned as a result of plant shutdown or operating curtailments that probably would have occurred in any event. To the extent that these are serious problems, how can they be addressed? For a review of trading programs, see R. Liroff, Reforming Air Pollution Regulation: The Toil and Trouble of EPA's Bubble (1986); Hahn & Hester, Where Did All the Markets Go? An Analysis of EPA's Emissions Trading Programs, 16 Yale J. Reg. 109 (1989); Dudek & Palmisano, Emissions Trading: Why is This Thoroughbred Hobbled? 13 Colum J. Envtl. L. 217 (1988); Dwyer, The Use of Market Incentives in Controlling Air Pollution: California's Marketable Permits Program, 20 Ecology L.Q. 103 (1993).

b. Legality of the Emissions Trading Programs

CHEVRON U.S.A. INC. v. NATURAL RESOURCES DEFENSE COUNCIL ET AL.

467 U.S. 837, 839 (1984)

Justice STEVENS delivered the opinion of the Court.

In the Clean Air Act Amendments of 1977, Pub. L. 95-95, 91 Stat. 685, Congress enacted certain requirements applicable to States that had not achieved the national air quality standards. . . . The amended Clean Air Act required these "nonattainment" States to establish a permit program regulating "new or modified major stationary sources" of air pollution. Generally, a permit may not be issued for a new or modified major stationary source unless several stringent conditions are met. The EPA regulation promulgated to implement this permit requirement allows a State to adopt a plantwide definition of the term "stationary source." Under this definition, an existing plant that contains several pollution-emitting devices may install or modify one piece of equipment without meeting the permit conditions if the alteration will not increase the total emissions from the plant. The question presented by these cases is whether EPA's decision to allow States to treat all of the pollution-emitting devices within the same industrial grouping as though they were encased within a single "bubble" is based on a reasonable construction of the statutory term "stationary source."

I

The EPA regulations containing the plantwide definition of the term stationary source were promulgated on October 14, 1981. 46 Fed. Reg. 50766. Respondents filed a timely petition for review in the United States Court of Appeals for the District of Columbia Circuit pursuant to 42 U.S.C. §7607(b)(1). The Court of Appeals set aside the regulations. *National Resources Defense Council, Inc. v. Gorsuch,* . . . 685 F.2d 718 (1982).

The court observed that the relevant part of the amended Clean Air Act "does not explicitly define what Congress envisioned as a 'stationary source,' to which the permit program . . . should apply," and further stated that the precise issue was not "squarely addressed in the legislative history." Id., at 273, 685 F.2d, at 723. In light of its conclusion that the legislative history bearing on the question was "at best contradictory," it reasoned that "the purposes of the non-attainment program should guide our decision here." Id., at 276, n.39, 685 F.2d, at 726, n.39. Based on two of its precedents concerning the applicability of the bubble concept to certain Clean Air Act programs, the court stated that the bubble concept was "mandatory" in programs designed merely to maintain existing air quality [PSD programs], but held that it was "inappropriate" in programs enacted to improve air quality. Id., at 276, 685 F.2d, at 726. Since the purpose of the permit program — its *"raison d'etre,"* in the court's view — was to improve air quality, [non-attainment programs] the court held that the bubble concept was inapplicable in these cases under its prior precedents. Ibid. It therefore set aside the regulations embodying the bubble concept as contrary to law. We granted certiorari to review that judgment . . . , and we now reverse.

The basic legal error of the Court of Appeals was to adopt a static judicial definition of the term "stationary source" when it had decided that Congress itself had not commanded that definition. Respondents do not defend the legal reasoning of the Court of Appeals. Nevertheless, since this Court reviews judgments, not opinions, we must determine whether the Court of Appeals' legal error resulted in an erroneous judgment on the validity of the regulations.

II

When a court reviews an agency's construction of the statute which it administers, it is confronted with two questions. First, always, is the question whether Congress has directly spoken to the precise question at issue. If the intent of Congress is clear, that is the end of the matter; for the court, as well as the agency, must give effect to the unambiguously expressed intent of Congress.[45] If, however, the court determines Congress has not directly addressed the precise question at issue, the court does not simply impose its own construction on the statute, as would be necessary in the absence of an administrative interpretation. Rather, if the statute is silent or ambiguous with respect to the specific issue, the question for the court is whether the agency's answer is based on a permissible construction of the statute.

"The power of an administrative agency to administer a congressionally created . . . program necessarily requires the formulation of policy and the making of rules to fill any gap left, implicitly or explicitly, by Congress." *Morton v. Ruiz,* 415 U.S. 199, 231 (1974). If Congress has explicitly left a gap for the agency to fill, there is an express delegation of authority to the agency to elucidate a specific provision of the statute by regulation. Such legislative regulations are given controlling weight unless they are arbitrary, capricious, or manifestly contrary to the statute. Sometimes the legislative delegation to an agency on a particular question is implicit rather than explicit. In such a case, a court may not substitute its own construction of a statutory provision for a reasonable interpretation made by the administrator of an agency.

We have long recognized that considerable weight should be accorded to an executive department's construction of a statutory scheme it is entrusted to administer, and the principle of deference to administrative interpretations

> has been consistently followed by this Court whenever decision as to the meaning or reach of a statute has involved reconciling conflicting policies, and a full understanding of the force of the statutory policy in the given situation has depended upon more than ordinary knowledge respecting the matters subjected to agency regulations. . . .
>   . . . If this choice represents a reasonable accommodation of conflicting policies that were committed to the agency's care by the statute, we should not disturb it unless it appears from the statute or its legislative history that the accommodation is not one that Congress would have sanctioned. *United States v. Shimer,* 367 U.S. 374, 382, 383 (1961). . . .

In light of these well-settled principles it is clear that the Court of Appeals misconceived the nature of its role in reviewing the regulations at issue. Once it determined, after its own examination of the legislation, that Congress did not actually have an intent regarding the applicability of the bubble concept to the permit program, the question before it was not whether in its view the concept is "inappropriate" in the general context of a program designed to improve air quality, but

---

45. The Judiciary is the final authority on issues of statutory construction and must reject administrative constructions which are contrary to clear congressional intent. . . .

whether the Administrator's view that it is appropriate in the context of this particular program is a reasonable one. Based on the examination of the legislation and its history which follows, we agree with the Court of Appeals that Congress did not have a specific intention on the applicability of the bubble concept in these cases, and conclude that the EPA's use of that concept here is a reasonable policy choice for the agency to make.

III . . .

Section 111(a) defined the terms that are to be used in setting and enforcing standards of performance for new stationary sources. It provided:

> For purposes of this section:
>
> (3) The term "stationary source" means any building, structure, facility, or installation which emits or may emit any air pollutant. 84 Stat. 1683.

In the 1970 Amendments that definition was not only applicable to the NSPS program required by §111, but also was made applicable to a requirement of §110 that each state implementation plan contain a procedure for reviewing the location of any proposed new source and preventing its construction if it would preclude the attainment or maintenance of national air quality standards.

In due course, the EPA promulgated NAAQS's, approved SIP's, and adopted detailed regulations governing NSPS's for various categories of equipment. In one of its programs, the EPA used a plantwide definition of the term "stationary source." In 1974, it issued NSPS's for the nonferrous smelting industry that provided that the standards would not apply to the modification of major smelting units if their increased emissions were offset by reductions in other portions of the same plant.[46]

NONATTAINMENT

The 1970 legislation provided for the attainment of primary NAAQS's by 1975. In many areas of the country, particularly the most

---

46. The Court of Appeals ultimately held that this plantwide approach was prohibited by the 1970 Act, see *ASARCO Inc.*, 188 U.S. App. D.C., at 83-84, 578 F.2d, at 325-327. This decision was rendered after enactment of the 1977 Amendments, and hence the standard [the plant-wide definition of "source" in the smelter NSPS] was in effect when Congress enacted the 1977 Amendments.

industrialized States, the statutory goals were not attained. In 1976, the 94th Congress was confronted with this fundamental problem, as well as many others respecting pollution control. As always in this area, the legislative struggle was basically between interests seeking strict schemes to reduce pollution rapidly to eliminate its social costs and interests advancing the economic concern that strict schemes would retard industrial development with attendant social costs. The 94th Congress, confronting these competing interests, was unable to agree on what response was in the public interest: legislative proposals to deal with nonattainment failed to command the necessary consensus.

In light of this situation, the EPA published an Emissions Offset Interpretative Ruling in December 1976, see 41 Fed. Reg. 55524, to "fill the gap," as respondents put it, until Congress acted. [This ruling provided that a new source could locate in a non-attainment area only if it achieved the "lowest achievable emissions rate" and offset its emissions by more than compensating reductions from existing sources.] The 1976 Ruling did not, however, explicitly adopt or reject the "bubble concept."

IV

The Clean Air Act Amendments of 1977 are a lengthy, detailed, technical, complex, and comprehensive response to a major social issue. A small portion of the statute — 91 Stat. 745-751 (Part D of Title I of the amended Act, 42 U.S.C. §§7501-7508) — expressly deals with nonattainment areas. The focal point of this controversy is one phrase in that portion of the Amendments. . . .

Most significantly for our purposes, the statute provided that each plan shall

"(6) require permits for the construction and operation of new or modified major stationary sources in accordance with section 173. . . ." Id., at 747 . . .

The 1977 Amendments contain no specific reference to the "bubble concept." Nor do they contain a specific definition of the term "stationary source," though they did not disturb the definition of "stationary source" contained in §111(a)(3), applicable by the terms of the Act to the NSPS program. Section 302(j), however, defines the term "major stationary source" as follows:

(j) Except as otherwise expressly provided, the terms 'major stationary source' and 'major emitting facility' mean any stationary facility or source of air pollutants which directly emits, or has the potential to emit, one hundred tons per year or more of any air pollutant (including any major emitting facility or source of fugitive emissions of any such pollutant, as determined by rule by the Administrator). 91 Stat. 770.

V

The legislative history of the portion of the 1977 Amendments dealing with nonattainment areas does not contain any specific comment on the "bubble concept" or the question whether a plantwide definition of a stationary source is permissible under the permit program. It does, however, plainly disclose that in the permit program Congress sought to accommodate the conflict between the economic interest in permitting capital improvements to continue and the environmental interest in improving air quality. Indeed, the House Committee Report identified the economic interest as one of the "two main purposes" of this section of the bill. It stated:

> Section 117 of the bill, adopted during full committee markup establishes new provisions eventually enacted as part of the non-attainment provisions added by the 1977 Amendments. These provisions have two main purposes: (1) to allow reasonable economic growth to continue in an area while making reasonable further progress to assure attainment of the standards by a fixed date; and (2) to allow States greater flexibility for the former purpose than EPA's present interpretative regulations afford.
>
> The new provision allows States with nonattainment areas to pursue one of two options. First, the State may proceed under EPA's present "tradeoff" or "offset" ruling. The Administrator is authorized, moreover, to modify or amend that ruling in accordance with the intent and purposes of this section.
>
> The State's second option would be to revise its implementation plan in accordance with this new provision. H.R. Rep. No.95-294, p.211 (1977).

[The Court discussed the Senate legislative history, finding that it failed to address the definition of "source."]
Senator Muskie made the following remarks:

> I should note that the test for determining whether a new or modified source is subject to the EPA interpretative regulation [the Offset Ruling] — and to the permit requirements of the revised implementation plans under the conference bill — is whether the source will emit a pollutant into an area which is exceeding a national ambient air quality standard for that pollutant — or precursor. Thus, a new source is still subject to such requirements as "lowest achievable emission rate" even if it is constructed as a replacement for an older facility resulting in a net reduction from previous emission levels.

A source — including an existing facility ordered to convert to coal — is subject to all the nonattainment requirements as a modified source if it makes any physical change which increases the amount of any air pollutant for which the standards in the area are exceeded. 123 Cong. Rec. 26847 (1977).

VI

As previously noted, prior to the 1977 Amendments, the EPA had adhered to a plantwide definition of the term "source" under a NSPS program. After adoption of the 1977 Amendments, proposals for a plantwide definition were considered in at least three formal proceedings. [The Court then reviewed the EPA's rulemaking proceedings regarding the definition of source, which proposed different definitions at different times in the proceedings.]

In August 1980, however, the EPA adopted a regulation that, in essence, applied the basic reasoning of the Court of Appeals in these cases. The EPA took particular note of the two then-recent Court of Appeals decisions, which had created the bright-line rule that the "bubble concept" should be employed in a program designed to maintain air quality but not in one designed to enhance air quality. Relying heavily on those cases, EPA adopted a dual definition of "source" for nonattainment areas that required a permit whenever a change in either the entire plant, or one of its components, would result in a significant increase in emissions even if the increase was completely offset by reductions elsewhere in the plant. The EPA expressed the opinion that this interpretation was "more consistent with congressional intent" than the plantwide definition because it "would bring in more sources or modifications for review," 45 Fed. Reg. 52697 (1980), but its primary legal analysis was predicated on the two Court of Appeals decisions.

In 1981 a new administration took office and initiated a "Government-wide reexamination of regulatory burdens and complexities." 46 Fed. Reg. 16281. In the context of that review, the EPA reevaluated the various arguments that had been advanced in connection with the proper definition of the term "source" and concluded that the term should be given the same definition in both nonattainment areas and PSD areas.

In explaining its conclusion, the EPA first noted that the definitional issue was not squarely addressed in either the statute or its legislative history and therefore that the issue involved an agency "judgment as how to best carry out the Act." Ibid. It then set forth several reasons for concluding that the plantwide definition was more appropriate. It pointed out that the dual definition "can act as a disincentive to new investment and modernization by discouraging modifications to existing facilities" and "can actually retard progress in air pollution control by discouraging replacement of older, dirtier processes or pieces of equipment with new, cleaner ones." Ibid. Moreover, the new definition "would simplify EPA's rules by using the same definition of 'source' for PSD, nonattainment new source review and the construction moratorium. This reduces confusion and inconsistency." Ibid. Finally, the agency explained that additional requirements that remained in place would accomplish the fundamental purposes of achieving attainment with NAAQS's as expeditiously as possible. . . .

VII

In this Court respondents expressly reject the basic rationale of the Court of Appeals' decision. That court viewed the statutory definition of the term "source" as sufficiently flexible to cover either a plantwide definition, a narrower definition covering each unit within a plant, or a dual definition that could apply to both the entire "bubble" and its components. It interpreted the policies of the statute, however, to mandate the plantwide definition in programs designed to maintain clean air and to forbid it in programs designed to improve air quality. Respondents place a fundamentally different construction on the statute. They contend that the text of the Act requires the EPA to use a dual definition — if either a component of a plant, or the plant as a whole, emits over 100 tons of pollutant, it is a major stationary source. They thus contend that the EPA rules adopted in 1980, insofar as they apply to the maintenance of the quality of clean air, as well as the 1981 rules which apply to nonattainment areas, violate the statute.

STATUTORY LANGUAGE

The definition of the term "stationary source" in §111(a)(3) refers to "any building, structure, facility, or installation" which emits air pollution. See supra. . . . at 846. This definition is applicable only to the NSPS program by the express terms of the statute; the text of the statute does not make this definition applicable to the [non-attainment] permit program. Petitioners therefore maintain that there is no statutory language even relevant to ascertaining the meaning of stationary source in the [non-attainment] permit program aside from §302(j), which defines the term "major stationary source." See supra. . . . We disagree with petitioners on this point.

The definition in §302(j) tells us what the word "major" means — a source must emit at least 100 tons of pollution to qualify — but it sheds virtually no light on the meaning of the term "stationary source."

It does equate a source with a facility — a "major emitting facility" and a "major stationary source" are synonymous under §302(j). The ordinary meaning of the term "facility" is some collection of integrated elements which has been designed and constructed to achieve some purpose. Moreover, it is certainly no affront to common English usage to take a reference to a major facility or a major source to connote an entire plant as opposed to its constituent parts. Basically, however, the language of §302(j) simply does not compel any given interpretation of the term "source."

Respondents recognize that, and hence point to §111(a)(3). Although the definition in that section is not literally applicable to the permit program, it sheds as much light on the meaning of the word "source" as anything in the statute. As respondents point out, use of the words "building, structure, facility, or installation," as the definition of source, could be read to impose the permit conditions on an individual building that is a part of a plant. A "word may have a character of its own not to be submerged by its association." *Russell Motor Car Co. v. United States,* 261 U.S. 514, 519 (1923). On the other hand, the meaning of a word must be ascertained in the context of achieving particular objectives, and the words associated with it may indicate that the true meaning of the series is to convey a common idea. The language may reasonably be interpreted to impose the requirement on any discrete, but integrated, operation which pollutes. This gives meaning to all of the terms — a single building, not part of a larger operation, would be covered if it emits more than 100 tons of pollution, as would any facility, structure, or installation. Indeed, the language itself implies a "bubble concept" of sorts: each enumerated item would seem to be treated as if it were encased in a bubble. While respondents insist that each of these terms must be given a discrete meaning, they also argue that §111(a)(3) defines "source" as a facility, among other items.

We are not persuaded that parsing of general terms in the text of the statute will reveal an actual intent of Congress. We know full well that this language is not dispositive; the terms are overlapping and the language is not precisely directed to the question of the applicability of a given term in the context of a larger operation. To the extent any congressional "intent" can be discerned from this language, it would appear that the listing of overlapping, illustrative terms was intended to enlarge, rather than to confine, the scope of the agency's power to regulate particular sources in order to effectuate the policies of the Act.

LEGISLATIVE HISTORY

In addition, respondents argue that the legislative history and policies of the Act foreclose the plantwide definition, and that the EPA's interpretation is not entitled to deference because it represents a sharp break with prior interpretations of the Act.

Based on our examination of the legislative history, we agree with the Court of Appeals that it is unilluminating. The general remarks pointed to by respondents "were obviously not made with this narrow issue in mind and they cannot be said to demonstrate a Congressional desire. . . ." *Jewell Ridge Coal Corp. v. Mine Workers,* 325 U.S. 161, 168-169 (1945). Respondent's argument based on the legislative history relies heavily on Senator Muskie's observation that a new source is subject to the LAER requirement. But the full statement is ambiguous and like the text of §173 itself, this comment does not tell us what a new source is, much less that it is to have an inflexible definition. We find that the legislative history as a whole is silent on the precise issue before us. It is, however, consistent with the view that the EPA should have broad discretion in implementing the policies of the 1977 Amendments.

More importantly, that history plainly identifies the policy concerns that motivated the enactment; the plantwide definition is fully consistent with one of those concerns — the allowance of reasonable economic growth — and, whether or not we believe it most effectively implements the other, we must recognize that the EPA has advanced a reasonable explanation for its conclusion that the regulations serve the environmental objectives as well. . . . Indeed, its reasoning is supported by the public record developed in the rulemaking process, as well as by certain private studies.

Our review of the EPA's varying interpretations of the word "source" — both before and after the 1977 Amendments — convinces us that the agency primarily responsible for administering this important legislation has consistently interpreted it flexibly — not in a sterile textual vacuum, but in the context of implementing policy decisions in a technical and complex arena. The fact that the agency has from time to time changed its interpretation of the term "source" does not, as respondents argue, lead us to conclude that no deference should be accorded the agency's interpretation of the statute. An initial agency interpretation is not instantly carved in stone. On the contrary, the agency, to engage in informed rulemaking, must consider varying interpretations and the wisdom of its policy on a continuing basis. Moreover, the fact that the agency has adopted different definitions in different contexts adds force to the argument that the definition itself is flexible, particularly since Congress has never indicated any disapproval of a flexible reading of the statute.

Significantly, it was not the agency in 1980, but rather the Court of Appeals that read the statute inflexibly to command a plantwide definition for programs designed to maintain clean air and to forbid such a definition for programs designed to improve air quality. The distinction the court drew may well be a sensible one, but our labored review of the problem has surely disclosed that it is not a distinction that Congress ever articulated itself, or one that the EPA found in the statute before the courts began to review the legislative work product. . . .

POLICY

The arguments over policy that are advanced in the parties' briefs create the impression that respondents are now waging in a judicial forum a specific policy battle which they ultimately lost in the agency and in the 32 jurisdictions opting for the "bubble concept,"[47] but one which was never waged in the Congress. Such policy arguments are more properly addressed to legislators or administrators, not to judges.

In these cases the Administrator's interpretation represents a reasonable accommodation of manifestly competing interests and is entitled to deference: the regulatory scheme is technical and complex, the agency considered the matter in a detailed and reasoned fashion, and the decision involves reconciling conflicting policies. Congress intended to accommodate both interests, but did not do so itself on the level of specificity presented by these cases. Perhaps that body consciously desired the Administrator to strike that balance at this level, thinking that those with great expertise and charged with responsibility for administering the provision would be in a better position to do so; perhaps it simply did not consider the question at this level; and perhaps Congress was unable to forge a coalition on either side of the question, and those on each side decided to take their chances with the scheme devised by the agency. For judicial purposes, it matters not which of these things occurred.

Judges are not experts in the field, and are not part of either political branch of the Government. Courts must, in some cases, reconcile competing political interests, but not on the basis of the judges' personal policy preferences. In contrast, an agency to which Congress has delegated policymaking responsibilities may, within the limits of that delegation, properly rely upon the incumbent administration's views of wise policy to inform its judgments. While agencies are not directly accountable to the people, the Chief Executive is, and it is entirely appropriate for this political branch of the Government to make such policy choices — resolving the competing interests which Congress itself either inadvertently did not resolve, or intentionally left to be resolved by the agency charged with the administration of the statute in light of everyday realities.

---

47. *[Ed Note:* The EPA regulation at issue allowed but did not require states to use a plantwide definition of "source."]

When a challenge to an agency construction of a statutory provision, fairly conceptualized, really centers on the wisdom of the agency's policy, rather than whether it is a reasonable choice within a gap left open by Congress, the challenge must fail. In such a case, federal judges — who have no constituency — have a duty to respect legitimate policy choices made by those who do. The responsibilities for assessing the wisdom of such policy choices and resolving the struggle between competing views of the public interest are not judicial ones: "Our Constitution vests such responsibilities in the political branches." *TVA v. Hill*, 437 U.S. 153, 195 (1978).

We hold that the EPA's definition of the term "source" is a permissible construction of the statute which seeks to accommodate progress in reducing air pollution with economic growth. "The Regulations which the Administrator has adopted provide what the agency could allowably view as . . . [an] effective reconciliation of these twofold ends. . . ." *United States v. Shimer*, 367 U.S., at 383.

The judgment of the Court of Appeals is reversed.

NOTES AND QUESTIONS

Chevron is a landmark decision on the scope of judicial review of agency decisions and the allocation of responsibility between courts and agencies in interpreting and implementing statutes. We will examine this aspect of the decision more fully in Chapter 7. But you should consider the following questions at this time:

1. Does the Court give any satisfactory reason for its conclusion that the failure of Congress to resolve an issue in a statute must be taken as a decision by Congress that the issue should be resolved by the administrative agency responsible for implementing the statute, rather than by the courts? Is the Court's approach in *Chevron* consistent with the plurality opinion in *Benzene*, supra p. 25?

2. What are the policy arguments in favor of a plantwide definition of "source"? Against? Which is more consistent with the basic purpose and structure of the Act's provisions dealing with new sources and non-attainment areas?

3. Could EPA validly adopt a rule stating that two or more geographically separate plants in a region that agreed on a joint control strategy would be deemed a single source? Would it make a difference if the plants were 100 yards apart from each other? One mile? 200 miles?

3.   ACID DEPOSITION

As previously discussed, see supra, pp. 248-250, the initial focus of regulation under the 1970 Amendments on local concentrations of SO_2 and NO_x ignored the atmospheric transformation, interstate transportation, and eventual deposition of acidic sulfur and nitrogen compounds that acidify lakes and streams and reduce visibility. They also pose potential risks to trees and other vegetation, soils, and human health, but the extent of any such risks have not been demonstrated or quantified. See Kulp, Acid Rain: Causes, Effects, and Control, Regulation, Winter 1990, at 41. Indeed, control measures such as tall stacks aimed at local SO_2 concentrations exacerbated the problem of long-distance acid deposition pollution. Environmental groups in the late 1970s and early 1980s considered a variety of legal initiatives to attack the acid deposition problem:

1. Common law damage or injunction actions. For example, a New Hampshire farmer suffering crop or timber injury might bring an action for damages or an injunction against midwestern utilities emitting large amounts of sulfur from uncontrolled power plants that nonetheless met local SIP requirements ensuring compliance with ambient standards for SO_2 in the vicinity of the plant.

2. Litigation under §115 of the Act, based on a 1979 letter from EPA Administrator Costle to Secretary of State Muskie concluding, on the basis of evidence showing that SO_2 and NO_x emissions in the United States were causing acid deposition in Canada, and vice-versa, that "acid deposition is endangering public welfare in the U.S. and Canada and . . . U.S. and Canadian sources contribute to the problem not only in the country where they are located but also in the neighboring country."

3. Litigation action under §§110(a)(2)(D) and 126 to require upwind, midwestern states to control pollution sources in order to prevent acid deposition in New England.

4. Adoption by New Hampshire, under §116, of a stringent acid deposition standard, which would then be used to force controls against upwind states under §§110(a)(2)(D) and 126.

5. Litigation under §§108 and 109 to require EPA to adopt a NAAQS for acid deposition.

What problems do you see in these approaches? Congressional action to address the problem was stalled for many years by scientific uncertainty and controversy regarding the extent of environmental and health risks attributable to acid deposition, which can lower pH in lakes, killing plant and fish life; injure trees and other forms of vegetation; corrode buildings; and pose a health risk. But the exact extent of these risks was and still is hotly debated. Acid deposition has, for example, been widely blamed for deterioration and loss of forests in the

Northeast, but the relative contribution of acid deposition compared to other forms of pollution, such as ozone, is still unclear. The most recent scientific evidence suggests that acid deposition is a substantial but not alarming environmental problem.[48]

Electric utilities, which are the principal sources of SO_2 emissions and the dominant stationary source of NO emissions, emphasized these scientific uncertainties in resisting legislation. Coal producing interests, particularly in Illinois, Kentucky, Ohio, Pennsylvania, West Virginia, and other states with high sulfur coal deposits also opposed legislation. These opponents had powerful political allies in Congress, including Representative John Dingell of Michigan, Chairman of the House Commerce Committee, and former Senate Majority Leader Robert Byrd of West Virginia. The political situation was exacerbated by regional conflicts. The principal sources of SO_2 emissions in the United States are in the midwest, Appalachia, and south central states; most of the deposition occurs in the Northeast. The problem is less severe in the West, but emissions in California can reduce visibility in scenic regions to the east and also threaten high alpine lakes in the Rockies. United States sources cause acid deposition in Canada, while emissions from some

---

48. Compare the following assessments:

"Preliminary results of the decade-long National Acid Precipitation Assessment Program ("NAPAP") state that precipitation is the dominant cause of acidity in 75 percent of the acidified lakes and 50 percent of the acidified streams in this country. Five percent of Northeastern lakes are acidic, including 11 percent in the Adirondacks. In the Northeast, a 30-percent reduction in sulfur dioxide emissions would yield a 50-percent recovery of acidified lakes in 50 years. Continued sulfur dioxide emissions at current levels would turn twenty percent of the lakes in the Blue Ridge Mountain region acidic, but would not change the number of acidified lakes in the Northeast." Note, The Clean Air Act Amendments of 1990 and the Use of Market Forces to Control Sulfur Dioxide Emissions, 28 Harv. J. Legis. 235, 245 (1991).

Five major conclusions about forest health and air quality in the United States and Canada are drawn from the available scientific information: (1) The vast majority of forests in the United States and Canada are *not* affected by decline. (2) There is experimental evidence that acidic deposition and associated pollutants can alter the resistance of red spruce to winter injury; through this mechanism, acidic deposition may have contributed to dieback and mortality of red spruce at high elevations in the northern Appalachians. (3) Natural stresses are important factors contributing to recent declines of sugar maples. (4) Natural stresses are important factors contributing to growth reductions in natural pine stands in the Southeast. (5) Ozone is an important factor in a decline of pines in southern California and is the pollutant of greatest concern with respect to possible regional scale impacts on North American forests.

Joseph Barnard, Changes in Forest Health and Productivity NAPAP Summary Compendium Document ch. 16 (1990).

Canadian sources end up in the United States. Areas with high economic growth wish to ensure that any program designed to deal with acid deposition will allow them to expand their electricity production.

After years of political deadlock, Congress in the 1990 Amendments adopted an entirely new pollution control strategy to deal with acid deposition. This strategy had initially been proposed by the Bush administration, with the input of the Environmental Defense Fund, one of the national environmental groups. Title IV of the Amendments adds §§410-416 to the Act. They require a 10 million ton reduction in SO_2 emissions (an approximate 50 percent reduction from existing levels) and a 2 million ton reduction in NO_x emissions by electric utilities within 10 years. The NO reduction program, set forth in §407, relies on technology-based standards to force retrofit of controls on existing utility boilers. The sulfur emissions provisions, however, rely on a new system of transferrable pollution allowances to reduce total national loadings of sulfur.

The foundation of the sulfur program is a system of SO_2 emissions allowances. Each allowance enables the holder to emit one ton of SO2 in a particular year, or a subsequent year. The allowances may be freely bought and sold anywhere in the continental United States. Each utility unit must hold allowances equal to its emissions. If its emissions exceed its allowances, the utility is subject to an automatic penalty of $2000/ton, a price which is substantially above the expected marginal cost of controlling emissions. In addition, a unit whose emissions exceed its allowances must reduce its emissions below its allowances in the following year in an amount needed to offset the excess emissions during the previous year.

EPA is to issue allowances to units as part of a two-phase emissions reduction program. In Phase I, 110 existing high-polluting electric utility generating units specifically listed in the statute are subject to annual SO_2 emission limits based on the average quantity of fossil fuel consumed by the plant during 1985-1987: 2.5 lbs SO_2 for each million BTUs of fuel input. EPA will issue to each Phase I unit allowances equal to the emissions allowed under this formula. The units must either achieve these limitations by 1995 or obtain, by purchase or otherwise, extra allowances from other units equal to its excess emissions. The Act also allows the owner or operator of a Phase I unit to reassign the SO_2 reduction requirements for that unit to another unit or units under its control. Phase I is designed to achieve a 3.5 million ton reduction in SO_2 and governs until 2000.

The Act provides that Phase I units that adopt control technologies to reduce their existing emissions by 90 percent or more (which would require use of "scrubbers" to reduce emissions from high sulfur coal) can postpone the Phase I compliance deadline from 1995 to 1997, or receive special bonus allowances for reductions below 1.2 lb/million BTUs during 1995-1997. Also, EPA must maintain a reserve of 300,000 bonus allowances for Phase I units that employ renewable energy technologies such as solar, geothermal, biomass, or wind sources. In addition, there is a special allocation of 200,000 extra annual allowances during 1995-1999 for units located in Illinois, Indiana, and Ohio, and a modest extra allowance for small diesel refiners.

Phase II, which becomes operative in 2000, is designed to achieve an additional 6.5 million tons/SO_2 reduction. It applies to all generating units (other than very small units) and establishes, for most units, emission limitations equal to 1.2 pounds/million BTUs fuel input, based on their fuel use during 1985-1987. Allowances equal to the emissions established by the formula will be issued to units by EPA. By the year 2000, Phase II units must limit their emissions to this amount or purchase extra allowances from other units to cover excess emissions. The Act provides for a four-year extension of the year 2000 deadline for Phase II compliance for those utilities that repower their units with certain innovative lower-emitting coal combustion technologies. There are also provisions for special bonus allowances for plants in "high growth" states (Florida); plants in Illinois, Indiana, Ohio, Georgia, Alabama, Missouri, Pennsylvania, West Virginia, Kentucky or Tennessee; certain municipal power plants; certain relatively clean existing plants with low capacity utilization; plants in certain states that were required to convert from oil to coal during 1980-1985; and plants in certain states that have already achieved emissions reductions below .8 lbs/million BTUs. The Act also provides for a permanent cap on utility SO_2 emissions of 8.9 million pounds.

The Amendments make no provision for EPA to issue allowances to new sources. Such sources must obtain allowances from existing sources. Plants that begin operation after 1990 but before 2000 will in most cases receive allowances based on an emission rate of only .3 lbs/million BTUs and 65 percent capacity operation.

Because allowances can be bought and sold, units that reduce their emissions below the required level can sell their excess allowances to others, so long as they retain sufficient allowances to cover their remaining emissions. Sources that find it more difficult and costly to achieve the Phase I and Phase II limitations may buy extra allowances from others to cover their excess emissions. A unit need not ever actually achieve the 2.5 lbs/million BTU Phase I or 1.2 lbs/million BTU Phase II limitations; the law merely requires that it have allowances equal to its emissions. Existing units receive for free an initial allocation of allowances from EPA, based on the emissions set forth in the allocation formula, but must obtain any additional allowances from other units who reduce emissions below that required by these standards. Thus, the Act does not ensure that any particular unit will achieve any particular level of control. Because the market for allowance trading is national, the Act merely ensures that total national loadings of SO_2 from utilities will be reduced over time to 8.9 million tons.

The Act allows units total flexibility in deciding how to reduce emissions and how much to reduce emissions. Sources can, for example, seek to reduce pollution by installing scrubbers or lower-pollution combustion technologies such as fluidized bed processes. They may switch to cleaner fuels, such as oil, natural gas, or low sulfur or washed coal. They may reallocate capacity utilization from high-polluting to low-polluting units. They can shut down existing units and build new, less-polluting facilities including (in theory) nuclear plants. They may adopt renewable energy technologies. Or they may seek to reduce emissions by lowering consumption of energy through demand management techniques such as energy pricing schemes to reduce peak demand or assisting customers, through interest-free loans and information services, to adopt conservation measures such as insulation, low flow shower heads, energy-efficient lighting technologies, and so on. Indiana Public Service Co., for example, is committed to an aggressive program to reduce demand, electricity generation, and therefore pollution not only of SO_2, but also NO_x and CO_2. Such programs represent a radical change of thinking from utilities' traditional self-conception as generating ever-expanding amounts of electricity, to a new vision of utilities as total energy service and management enterprises dedicated to reducing energy use when it is cost-effective to do so. The flexibility afforded by the 1990 Amendments and the opportunity to earn profits by reducing emissions and freeing up allowances for sale are expected to reduce the cost of achieving the 10 million ton reduction in SO_2 emissions from $5 billion a year to $4 billion or less.

SO_2 is emitted not only by utilities but also by industrial sources that burn fossil fuels for process heat, etc. Utilities account for about 80 percent of SO_2 emissions, industrial sources the balance. Industrial sources are not subject to the sulfur limitations established by Title IV of the 1990 Amendments, although they, like utility units, may of course be subject to SIP limitations based on the NAAQs for SO_2. Under the 1990 Amendments, industrial sources may participate as sellers in the allowances market if they reduce their existing SO_2 emissions below the levels required by law. For example, if XYZ Steel currently complies with SIP requirements that limit its emissions from an industrial boiler to 100,000 tons annually, but later reduces its emissions to 80,000 tons, it could sell its excess emission reduction credits — 20,000 tons — to a utility, which could use these credits as allowances to cover excess or new emissions.[49]

_____

49. Earlier versions of the Amendments would have established a system of tradeable allowances for NO_x emissions, and allowed interpollutant trading of SO_2 and NO allowances. Congress eventually decided to impose traditional command and control limitations on NO emissions. Section 403(c) of the Act, however, directs EPA to study the possibility of NO/SO_2 trading.

Allowances are issued for each year. However, units can trade allowances for future years, although they cannot actually use an allowance until the year for which it is issued. Thus Unit A can agree today with B to sell it some of A's allowances for the year 2001. In addition, the Act appears to contemplate "banking" of allowances. For example, if A doesn't use all of its 1998 allowances, it can save or "bank" the unused allowances for its own use in later years or sell the unused allowance to others for their future use.

EPA must establish a central accounting system to keep track of allowance transfers. Sources must install continuous emissions monitoring systems to monitor SO_2 emissions and report the results to EPA.

A basic concern with the allowance system is whether a well-functioning market in allowances will develop. This concern is especially acute on the part of new sources, which must obtain their allowances from existing units. Many electric utilities are owned by multi-state holding companies. There is worry that these utility systems will horde allowances, reallocating them internally as need arises, but not offering them for outside sale. Such a pattern would, for example, shut out newly-emergent independent power producers. Economists, however, believe that outside sales will be made if substantial profits can be made by doing so. Another worry stems for the fact that utilities are subject to state public utility regulation. State public utility commissions might refuse to allow a utility to sell allowances for use outside the state, reasoning that any extra allowances should be reserved to accommodate future growth within the state. If a well-functioning market exists, future allowances should be available. But regulators' skepticism about the development of such a market could prove a self-fulling prophecy. In addition, if state regulators require that all of the profits from allowance sales be passed through to electricity consumers, the incentive of utilities to find innovative, cost-effective ways to reduce emissions will be undercut.

The Act seeks to ensure a "market maker" role for EPA by requiring it to withhold 2.8 percent of the allowances that existing utility units would otherwise receive and place them in reserves for direct sale or auction. EPA is required to offer 50,000 allowances per year for sale at $1500 per ton (adjusted for inflation) beginning in 2000. Half of these sales would be for use in the year of sale (spot sales) and half for use in future years (advance sales). During 1993-1999, there would be advance sales only, in the amount of 25,000 allowances annually. Allowances would be offered first to independent power producers that had been unable to purchase allowances on the open market. The sale proceeds would be distributed pro rata to the utility units whose allowances had been withheld to make up the reserve.

In addition, the Act requires EPA, beginning in 1993, to auction to the public 150,000 allowances annually during Phase I and 250,000 allowances annually during Phase II. Part of the allowances auctioned would be for current use, and a portion for future use. Proceeds would again be paid pro rata to existing utility units. In addition, any existing holder of allowances can submit them to EPA for sale at auction. In addition, EPA will have a reserve of 530,000 allowances to distribute from 2000 to 2009.

There have been a number of trades in allowance futures thus far. For example, TVA sold allowances to an Ohio utility. In 1993, Long Island Lighting Company agreed to sell sulfur reduction credits to Amax Energy Inc., which sells coal and natural gas to midwest utilities. Amax wants to use the credits to sell them along with coal or natural gas to its utility customers, who could use the credits to cover the resulting emissions. New York, however, has sought to block the transaction on the ground that it would produce increased acid deposition in New York. The Environmental Defense Fund has intervened in defense of the trade, arguing that a transaction-by-transaction review of environmental effects will prevent creation of a viable market, and that in the long run the local environmental effects of trades should balance out. See Wald, Lilco's Emissions Sale Spurs Acid Rain Concerns, N.Y. Times, March 18, 1993, at B1. The Chicago Board of Trade has petitioned EPA for permission to set up a futures market in SO_2 allowances. Such a market would provide utilities assurance that they could obtain from the market allowances to cover future growth. Meanwhile, a number of brokerage firms specializing in sulfur emissions trading have successfully negotiated private, off-exchange sales. See Taylor, CBOT Plan for Pollution-Rights Market is Encountering Plenty of Competition, Wall St. J., August 24, 1992, at C1.

NOTES AND QUESTIONS

1. Are SO_2 emissions from utilities the most promising target for launching a full scale trading system? What advantages are there in using utility SO_2 emissions to develop a trading system? What disadvantages? What other environmental problems might be considered as candidates for a trading program?

2. Why did Congress adopt a trading system for dealing with SO_2 emissions rather than an SO_2 tax or fee?[50] Why did Congress in effect

---

50. Senator Byrd of West Virginia favored a cost-sharing program based on a nation-wide sulfur emission tax; the proceeds would be allocated to "dirty" plants to underwrite the costs of control. He and others also pushed strongly for federal funding of retirement benefits for miners of high sulfur coal, who might lose their jobs because of the sulfur-reduction program. Should the government provide compensation for workers who lose jobs because of environmental controls?

give existing sources allowances without charge, but not give such allow-ances to new sources?

3. How and to what extent did the adoption of a tradeable allow-ances strategy help to soften the economic and political conflicts that had prevented legislation in the past? Why were allowances based on historical fuel use multiplied times a uniform emissions factor, rather than on historical emissions of SO_2? What explains the various post-ponement and bonus provisions in Phase I and Phase II? Why were such provisions necessary, given the regulatory "level playing field" cre-ated by the allowance system, which gives sources the flexibility to use whatever means they wish to reduce emissions, including the option of buying allowances if emission reductions prove too difficult or costly?

4. Suppose that future scientific evidence shows that the harm caused by acid deposition is (a) much greater than previously thought or (b) much less than previously thought. To what extent does the use of tradeable allowances limit (legally, practically, politically) the government's ability to change regulatory policy in light of these new facts, as compared to use of a traditional command and control regula-tory system? In this connection, what is the significance of the following provision in §403(f): "[An] allowance is not a property right. Nothing in this title or in any other provision of law shall be construed to limit the authority of the United States to terminate or limit such authoriza-tion."

5. Does a nationwide allowance trading program create a danger of "hot spots"? It is logically possible that most of the emissions reduc-tions required by the Act might be achieved by sources in a few areas (such as the West and the eastern seaboard) leaving other areas far less controlled (such as the midwest). EPA studies project that reductions will be roughly proportionate to existing emissions in each region, al-though this outcome is not legally or otherwise guaranteed. Does this feature of a tradeable permit system argue against its use for dealing with other types of environmental problems?

6. What further steps might Congress have taken to ensure a well-functioning market in SO_2 allowances? See Van Dyke, Emissions Trad-ing to Reduce Acid Deposition, 100 Yale L.J. 2707 (1991); Bartels, Marron & Lipsky, Clean Air, Clear Market: Making Emissions Trading Work: The Role of a Computer-Assisted Auction, 131 Pub. Util. Fort-nightly, June 15, 1993, at 14.

7. How should state public utility regulatory commissions treat costs and revenues incurred by utilities in connection with the allow-ance system? Should the costs of buying allowances be passed on to a utility's customers in the form of higher rates, or should those costs be borne by the utility and its shareholders? What about revenues earned from the sale of allowances?

8. The allowance trading program will lower the costs of reducing

SO$_2$ emissions by 10 million pounds from $5 billion to $4 billion or less annually. But is the program's goal sensible, even at a reduced price? Adoption of more cost-effective means of achieving an environmental protection goal does not obviate the problem of deciding what that goal ought to be. Paul Portney of Resources for the Future, a well-respected researcher, points to evidence from the 10-year National Acid Precipitation Assessment Project that the extent of lake and stream acidification is much less than previously thought, that the extent to which power plant emissions are responsible for acidification is unclear, that acid deposition has not demonstrated adverse effects on agriculture, and that its effects on forests are limited to mountain tops in the northeast. Reducing SO$_2$ and NO$_x$ will reduce visibility impairment and reduce potential but unknown human health risks. The estimated compliance costs of the program for liabilities he estimates at $4 billion. Because of major uncertainties regarding benefits, Portney estimates benefits at between $2 and 9 billion annually. By contrast, Portney estimates the annual benefits of the VOC reduction requirements in the 1990 amendments (federal motor vehicle emission controls, reformulated fuels, and non-attainment provisions), designed to reduce urban smog, at between $4 and 12 billion annually, while the annual costs would be between $19 and 22 billion. Portney, Policy Watch: Economics and the Clean Air Act, 4 J. Econ. Perspectives 173 (1990).

9. Given the adoption of a program designed to reduce SO$_2$ emissions by 50 percent, is there any need to retain the existing features of the Act dealing with SO$_2$, including the SO$_2$ NAAQS, implementing SIP provisions, NSPS, BACT, and LAER for SO$_2$, and PSD SO$_2$ increment limits? To what extent will retention of these command and control regulatory requirements, along with the ability of states to impose even more stringent restrictions, undercut the flexibility needed to make the SO$_2$ allowance trading program an efficient, cost-effective incentive system?

10. For additional analysis and evaluations of the sulfur trading program, see Johnson, A Market Without Rights: Sulfur Dioxide Emissions Trading, Regulation (Fall 1991) 24 (emphasizing the weak character of the property interests created by the allowance system and emphasizing the impediments to trading); Recent Developments, The Clean Air Act Amendments of 1990 and the Use of Market Forces to Control Sulfur Dioxide Emissions, 28 Harv. J. Legis. 235 (1991); Dennis, Smoke for Sale: Paradoxes and Problems of the Emissions Trading Program of the Clean Air Act Amendments of 1990, 40 U.C.L.A.L. Rev. 1101 (1993).

4.   OZONE PRECURSOR TRADING

Ozone non-attainment has become the most serious compliance problem under the Clean Air Act. Accordingly, Congress in 1990 enacted a detailed set of new regulatory requirements to address this problem. There is a developing view that new, market-based approaches may be necessary to deal with ozone noncompliance in the most severely polluted regions.

The RECLAIM Program. The South Coast Air Quality Management District in California, which encompasses greater Los Angeles, has concluded that the traditional command and control regulatory system has reached its limits, and is developing a marketable permits program for stationary sources of SO_2 and NO_x called Regional Clean Air Incentive Market or "RECLAIM." The initial markets will include about 400 sources of NO_x and several thousand sources of VOCs. Each covered facility is subject to a cap on facility-wide emissions, aggregated under the "bubble" principle. The emissions cap for each facility will then be reduced annually, by percentages geared to compliance with the "reasonable further progress" requirements for non-attainment areas established by the 1990 Amendments. Sources may, however, freely trade emission rights with each other. At present, there will be separate markets for NO_x and VOCs, although the possibility of interpollutant trading is being studied. Trading areas are zoned to avoid creation of hot spots as a result of emissions bunching. There is an elaborate system of monitoring requirements to ensure current tracking of emissions. Small facilities such as dry cleaners, restaurants, and gas stations would continue to be regulated by traditional means, but their inclusion in the trading system is being studied. New sources would have to buy emission rights from existing sources.

It is estimated that the trading system will reduce compliance costs by hundreds of millions of dollars annually and save thousands of jobs that would otherwise be lost. The District and many environmental groups support the plan because it is likely to be more successful in promoting attainment than traditional regulation. Industry supports the plan because it allows them the freedom to contract with smaller sources, where control costs are often substantially lower. The large sources can provide the necessary capital, which the small sources often lack, to finance their reductions, and obtain in return emission credits. The District would face political and administrative difficulties in racheting down small-source emissions through regulatory controls.

The RECLAIM program was approved in November 1993 by the South Coast Air Quality Management District and will be implemented beginning in 1994. There are many complex and controversial issues involved in the implementing details. One of the most controversial is establishing the "baseline" for determining the initial allocation of credits.

If the RECLAIM program proves successful as applied to stationary sources, could it be extended to include motor vehicle emissions? How might this extension be accomplished? What problems would be encountered? A limited form of trading between stationary and mobile sources has already been adopted by the District. Unocal Corporation, in cooperation with the District, developed a South Coast Recycled Auto Project (SCRAP) which purchased over 8000 pre-1971 cars (which emit 100 times more VOCs than new cars) for $700 each. Unocal received partial credit toward its control requirements for the estimated 6400 tons of VOC, CO and NOx emissions reductions obtained. The estimated cost per ton of VOC reductions under the SCRAP program was $7000/ton. Additional VOC controls from stationary sources in Los Angeles cost $20,000/ton and up.

Despite the superior efficiencies promised by the RECLAIM scheme, one must again ask whether the goal of achieving the federal 0.12 24-hour ozone standard in Los Angeles is worthwhile, even under a more cost-effective system of implementation? A careful analysis by Krupnick & Portney, Controlling Urban Act Pollution: A Benefit-Cost Assessment, 252 Science 522 (April 26, 1991) estimated the benefits of such compliance as at most $4 billion annually, with costs of $13 billion annually.

Northeast Trading. States in the northeastern United States are considering the development of an interstate trading system to combat the regional ozone problem. Congress in the 1990 Amendments recognized the need for a regional approach by creating an ozone transport region comprising the New England states, New York, New Jersey, Pennsylvania, Delaware, Maryland, and the D.C. metropolitan area. Clean Air Act §184(a). An interstate commission, composed of representatives of the participating states and EPA, is to develop an attainment plan for the region. The New England states plus New York have also established a separate regional planning authority known as NESCAUM. Other provisions of the Act dealing with the interstate aspects of ozone non-attainment include §§176A, 182(j), and 184.

Both regional bodies are considering development of interstate trading programs for ozone precursors. Initial interest has focussed on NO from stationary sources, but stationary source VOC and VOC/NO trading are also being studied, and there is some discussion of eventually including mobile sources in a trading system. While some of the participating states, such as Massachusetts, are developing intrastate trading systems, the development of an interstate market is being hampered by differences in state rules and legal and political controversies. It is obviously far more difficult to develop a common trading market in a region that includes many states than it is in a local area, such as

Los Angeles, located entirely within one state. For example, should trading be limited to emissions offsets for new sources, or should it extend to all emissions? Should states be able to restrict sales of credits generated within the state to sources outside the state and if so on what terms? Could a state, for example, impose a greater than 1:1 trading ratio for out of state sales? How should credits generated by plant shut-downs or operating curtailments be treated? Should banking be al-lowed, and if so, on what terms? How should an interstate registry of credits and trades be developed? What restrictions does the Clean Air Act place on interstate trading? Can the state in which a credit is gener-ated trade with sources in an upwind state? A downwind state? Can a credit generated in an attainment region be traded with a non-attain-ment region? What about trades among non-attainment regions falling in different non-compliance categories?

The parochial interests of states and a regulatory approach that scrutinizes each trade to ensure that it does not reduce existing air quality anywhere in the region could severely restrict the development of a trading market. Does EPA have authority to issue uniform federal rules for interstate trading? Should it, or Congress, authorize un-restricted trading throughout the Ozone Transport Region?

Note that Congress' creation of the Ozone Transport Region rep-resents a return to the airshed appropriate to regulating strategy that was initiated in the 1960s but abandoned in 1970. Does experience indicate that the abandonment of the airshed approach was a mistake?

5.   OTHER EXAMPLES OF MARKET INCENTIVES FOR AIR POLLUTION CONTROL[51]

a.   The Lead Phase-Down

Lead is a toxic substance, as explained in the *Lead Industries* deci-sion, supra, p. 264. In 1982, under §211 of the Clean Air Act, the EPA issued regulations reducing the allowable lead content of gasoline. The agency simultaneously authorized trading, within and among refiners, of the remaining allowed content of lead in their gasoline. Leaded gas-oline producers and importers could transfer, through purchase and sale, lead content credits freely among themselves, but their credits expired quarterly if unused. In 1985, the EPA further lowered the lead

---

51. This section summarizes the discussion in D. Dudek, R. Stewart & J. Wiener, Environmental Policy for Eastern Europe: Technology-Based versus Market-Based Approaches, 17 Colum. J. Envtl. L. 1 (1992), which discusses additional examples of market-based approaches for dealing with pollution, toxic waste, and natural resource management.

content limits. To provide leaded gasoline producers and importers with additional flexibility in complying with the new limits, the agency issued regulations permitting producers and importers whose gasoline in 1985 contained less lead per gallon than the applicable standard to "bank" lead content credits in order to avoid the expiration of their credits and apply them to future requirements. These banked credits could also be sold to others.

Banking and trading were active and resulted in cost savings on the order of hundreds of millions of dollars over the few years of the program. The program allowed sources flexibility in meeting the phase-out requirements. Thus flexibility was especially important in the cases of small refiners, who faced greater difficulties in converting their refineries to be able to maintain octane levels in the gasoline produced without using lead additives. This flexibility was politically important, because it allowed the government to reduce residual lead levels further than it could have under a less flexible command and control approach. Firms were not required to apply to the EPA for permission to enter into trades; they simply reported their trades to the government as part of their regularly required reports of the lead content in their gasoline. The program successfully reduced the lead content in gasoline by 90 percent.

b. Chlorofluorocarbon Reduction

Both trading and taxes are now tools in the effort to phase out chlorofluorocarbons (CFCs) in order to protect the stratospheric ozone layer. To implement the 1987 Montreal Protocol (and its 1990 update, the London Adjustments and Amendments) and the national legislation following from it, the EPA has issued regulations requiring a phase-out of CFC production and consumption by the year 2000 and implementing the phase-out by issuing depreciating allowances to each producer and importer of CFCs. CFC producers, importers, and other interested parties may trade these allowances. The EPA is able to monitor production and imports of CFCs and to keep track of allowance trades. Producers are aware of potential buyers and sellers and can trade allowances freely. In addition to issuing CFC allowances, the United States has imposed a tax on CFC production and importation.

c. Climate Change

If nations or the international community decide to take action to address potential climate change, the use of market-based incentives could be extremely helpful in implementing policy. Numerous sources emit a multitude of greenhouse gases (GHGs) in every sector of the economy, including energy, agriculture, and transportation, while "sinks" such as forests and oceans absorb these gases. The widely varying costs of control across gases, sectors, and nations as well as the global dispersion of the emissions make market mechanisms especially attractive in this context.

Options for addressing GHG emissions include tradeable allowances and fees. Either of these mechanisms could be employed domestically or internationally, although the considerations may differ in each context. To the extent feasible, an allowance or fee should be comprehensive, including all GHGs (carbon dioxide, methane, nitrous oxide, CFCs, and hydrochlorofluorocarbons, and precursor gases) and all sinks or reservoirs of GHGs, such as forests. An index could be devised to express, in terms of carbon dioxide equivalence, the relative contribution of each gas to global climate change. The tax or allowance could then be expressed in carbon dioxide equivalents, allowing nations or sources the flexibility to achieve requirements by reducing whatever GHG or expanding whatever sink was cheapest and most feasible for each nation or source.

Under tradeable allowances, GHG emitters would receive allowances and be free to trade them. Because the cost of limiting GHG emissions is likely to vary considerably among emitters, market-based allocation of compliance burdens could achieve significant cost savings and promote innovation. Trading is a particularly appropriate tool for addressing GHG emissions because, unlike toxic air and water pollutants, GHG emissions mix globally in the atmosphere. Moreover, the spatial distribution of their emissions sources is essentially irrelevant — they do not pose the problem of local toxic "hot spots" that some pollutants do.

International trading could begin informally in cooperative arrangements among nations. For example, one nation could provide another nation with technology and investment to reduce emissions or with assistance in reforestation and receive in return a part of the resultant GHG reduction as a credit against its own emission reduction obligations. Regional or group "bubbles" could be authorized to foster regional trading. The 1992 framework Convention on Climate Change adopted in Rio authorizes "joint implementation" of any GHG emission limitations that may eventually be adopted by international agreement. This provision could allow trading of GHG limitation obligations among nations. Ultimately, an international market in allowances traded among private actors could develop. Either informal or formalized trading would facilitate the transfer of resources and technology, on a decentralized market basis, to developing nations and the Soviet Union and Eastern European nations to assist them toward a low-GHG pattern of economic development. See R. Stewart & J. Wiener, The

Comprehensive Approach to Climate Change Police: Issues of Design and Practicality, 9 Ariz. J. Intl. & Comp. L. 83 (1992).

6.   ENVIRONMENTAL CONTRACTING

Environmental contracting is another means of overcoming the dysfunctions of command and control regulation. It involves a negotiated agreement between government authorities and industry on comprehensive targets and timetables for reductions of pollution or other risks in lieu of unilaterally imposed, piecemeal regulatory requirements for specific types of pollution from particular sources or process units. Environmental contracting is emerging as an important new development in Europe, and its more informal equivalent has been used for a number of years in Japan and elsewhere. Such contracts may be negotiated with an entire industry or on a facility by facility basis.

The Netherlands has recently begun to use formal environmental contracts on an industry-wide basis as a means of achieving the ambitious pollution reductions goals contained in its National Environmental Policy Plan. This plan sets comprehensive, multi-media national targets for pollution reduction and environmental improvement over the next 20 years, with interim benchmarks.[52] Each industry is allocated a designated share of the required reductions and improvements. The responsible government authorities and a number of industry groups, such as the basic metals industry, have signed or are currently negotiating contracts in which the industry agrees to achieve the overall targets assigned to it. In return, the government agrees to substitute the contractual arrangements for the pollutant by pollutant regulations otherwise applicable and to restrict changes in requirements during the period of the contract, which can run for 10 to 15 years. The program's purpose is to give industry flexibility to achieve overall reductions in a more cost-effective fashion and to provide it with relative certainty regarding requirements over an extended period of time in exchange for greater reductions than would otherwise be required or achieved under traditional regulation.[53] If industry facilities fail to meet their commitments, they face penalties and reinstatement of the traditional

---

52. See Jyt A. Peters, Voluntary Agreements Between Government and Industry: The Basic Metal Covenant as an Example, in Environmental Contracts and Covenants: New Instruments for a Realistic Environmental Policy? (J. van Dunne, ed., 1993) 19 (hereinafter Environmental Contracts).

53. The contracts are regarded as instruments of private law. There is controversy in the Netherlands over the government's authority to substitute such arrangements for otherwise applicable regulatory requirements. See P.J.J. van Buuren, Environmental Covenants: Possibilities and Impossibilities, An Administrative Lawyer's View, in Environmental Contracts 49.

regulatory system. Similar agreements are being negotiated in Germany, Belgium, and Denmark.

The United States has had limited experience with the contractual approach. In 1991, EPA Administrator Reilly initiated the 33/50 program under which industry would voluntarily agree to significant overall reductions of toxic pollutants.[54] Congress adopted an ambitious program of technology-based controls for 191 specified toxic pollutants in §112 of the Clean Air Act, but §112(h) also authorizes an alternative "early reduction" program. See pp. 334–335 supra. Industries that achieve a 90 percent reduction in toxic pollutants before the EPA promulgates regulations imposing technology-based toxics controls are exempt from compliance with the new regulations for five years after they come into effect. Through this provision, the government is essentially offering a unilateral contract, promising sources flexibility and assurance against future modification of requirements for a limited time. In exchange, the government receives substantial reductions earlier than it could through the cumbersome system of command and control regulation, which requires years of rulemaking proceedings and other steps to implement new controls.

The EPA has also experimented with negotiating comprehensive agreements on a facility by facility basis.[55] A joint study by Amoco and EPA of Amoco's Yorktown, Virginia, refinery found that a comprehensive plantwide, multi-media approach (including residuals in air, water, and on land) would better achieve the goal of reducing overall releases of chemicals from the site than does the existing piecemeal command and control system.[56] It would do so by identifying all sources of releases (some of which are not regulated under current law); taking cross-media effects into account (a piecemeal focus on air pollution may simply take residuals from air discharges and put them into the water); and allowing Amoco the flexibility to evaluate all available control options for all sources within the plant and implement the most cost-effective combination. For example, the study found that airborne hydrocarbons could be controlled at roughly the same level as required by current regulations but at only 25 percent of the cost, if reductions were targeted at the emissions sources selectively. The study concluded,

---

54. U.S. Environmental Protection Agency, Office of Pollution Prevention and Toxics, EPA's 33/50 Program, Second Progress Report (1992) 102. The implicit quid pro quo was that the EPA, and perhaps Congress, would moderate the push for detailed controls on toxic pollutants or at least give the participating industries some form of credit for the reductions achieved.

55. See David Stamps, Making a Case for Facility-Wide Compliance, Envtl. Info. Digest, Oct. 1992, at 6-9.

56. See Amoco-U.S. E.P.A. Pollution Prevention Project, Yorktown, Virginia: Executive Summary 15-18 (December 1991, revised May 1992) (on file with author); Stamps, supra.

however, that the piecemeal deadlines imposed by existing statutes and regulations do not allow sufficient time to plan and implement such an integrated approach. Accordingly, the project was abandoned. The study observes that the "command and control, end of pipe treatment" approach used in the United States over the past 20 years is not well suited to current environmental policy needs.

In order to expand the use of environmental contracting in the United States, significant changes in existing environmental legislation would be required. As the major federal environmental statutes have been amended over the past 15 years, they have grown progressively more prescriptive and detailed, establishing highly specific mandatory requirements and recipes for EPA regulation, and tight deadlines for implementation. The broad principles of standing established by federal administrative law and the "citizen suit" provisions in federal environmental statutes enable environmental groups or the pollution control authority to bring suit to force the EPA and regulated industry to comply with these requirements and deadlines. As a result, even if the EPA believed that a negotiated alternative to existing regulatory requirements would be beneficial, both it and the regulated industry could, and in many cases would be, sued for deviating from the letter of the law.

QUESTIONS

Is environmental contracting a desirable alternative to traditional regulation? What problems do you see in implementing the contracting idea? What solutions would there be if the industry failed to honor the contract? What if Congress or EPA decided that new information required greater and earlier reductions of pollution than provided in a contract. Should the signatories to the contract include parties other than the federal government and the industry? What changes would be required in current law to enable experimental use of the contracting approach?

7.   INFORMATION STRATEGIES

Another alternative to traditional regulation is reliance on dissemination of information. Some information strategies are market-based. Consumers concerned about environmental issues may well prefer products that are less polluting or are made by less polluting processes, even if such products cost somewhat more. Advertisers are beginning to respond to this demand, advertising products as "recycled," "recyclable," "biodegradable," or "environment-friendly." State Attorneys General, the EPA, and the Federal Trade Commission are increasingly concerned about false and misleading environmental claims. Enforcement actions have been brought against firms advertising plastic bags and disposable diapers as "recyclable" or "biodegradable" where the bags can only be recycled at special recycling centers that do not exist in the communities where the product is sold, and the diapers are biodegradable only if exposed to sun light and open air for an extended period, whereas they are typically disposed of in covered landfills. Even where a claim is not false or misleading, it may be too vague or general to be informative. But to provide consumers with detailed data and analysis on the environmental attributes of products would overwhelm them with information that they would not read.

One potential solution to this problem is an "ecolabeling" system under which products would be evaluated in terms of their environmental performance. Those with superior performance would be allowed to carry a standardized label or logo of environmental quality. The European Community is beginning to implement an ecolabel scheme, and the idea is under discussion in the United States. The implementation of an ecolabel system, however, involves many difficulties. What attributes should be considered? Ideally one should do a total "life cycle" analysis of a product, looking at the environmental effects associated with the acquisition of raw materials, manufacture, consumption, and recycling and disposal. A full life cycle analysis is, however, a complex and costly undertaking. Also, how should different environmental effects be weighted? How does one compare, for example, the greater air pollution associated with the manufacture of product A with the greater landfill requirements associated with the disposal of product B? Also, the result of the analysis may vary in different locations. The environmental effects of cloth versus disposable diapers, for example, vary depending on such factors as the transportation, energy costs, and water use, which are associated with recycling cloth diapers, and the landfill costs associated with disposable diapers. Finally, who decides ecolabel awards? A private organization? Will it be neutral and objective? The federal government? Will it be subject to political pressures? Would its decisions have to be made through elaborate rulemaking proceedings, subject to judicial review? Would it be preferable to impose taxes on all of the adverse environmental effects associated with a product and provide the consumer with information in the form of higher prices on products with greater adverse effects?[57] What about

_____

57. Another potential market-based information strategy is to provide investors with information about the environmental performance of companies. The SEC requires public disclosure of environmental liabilities, but only if they are material in financial terms. Several mutual funds have been developed, offering investments in environmentally responsible or "green" companies; they don't have a large share of mutual fund investments.

noncompliance labeling? See generally Menell, Eco-Information Policy: A Comparative Institutional Perspective (forthcoming).

Public disclosure of a company's environmental performance may also generate public pressures on the company to change its ways. Here the relevant "market" is not the consumer market for goods and services but the "market" of public relations and politics. The Clean Air Act, like the other federal environmental laws, requires detailed reporting to the government by facilities of monitoring data on their compliance with permit or other regulatory requirements. This information is used by environmental groups in citizen suit actions to force compliance and is also occasionally used in public relations campaigns against violators. The most striking impact of regulatory disclosure requirements was that of the Emergency Planning and Community-Right-To-Know Act of 1986, which provides for state programs of emergency response planning for facilities that have designated toxic chemicals on the site in amounts exceeding designated thresholds. Facilities must also prepare and file with public authorities a toxic chemical release form that provides information on the amounts of toxic chemicals present at the facility and the amounts released to the environment through different waste streams (air, water, and so forth). The resulting public disclosure of large toxic releases at sites, particularly in the form of air pollution emissions, stirred strong public and political reaction in the localities where the facilities were sited. Because of EPA's difficulties and delays in implementing §112 of the Clean Air Act, many of the toxic air emissions had not been subject to effective regulation. The public reaction triggered by EPCRA reporting, however, led many facilities to control their air emissions, cut back on the use of toxic chemicals, and take other pollution prevention measures.

In the past few years, Congress and EPA have pushed voluntary and cooperative pollution prevention efforts. Congress passed the Pollution Prevention Act of 1990, which establishes within EPA a source reduction program and information clearinghouse on pollution prevention. In addition, as we have seen, §112 of the Clean Air Act creates significant incentives for early reduction of hazardous air pollution emission. EPA has developed a number of programs that help businesses to identify alternative technologies that save money and reduce adverse impacts on the environment. Under EPA's Green Lights Program, EPA conducts audits of lighting utilization for companies agreeing to install cost-effective lighting systems. EPA's Energy Star Computers Program awards a special logo to computer manufacturers that build approved energy saving devices into their systems. EPA's Green Buildings Program promotes increased efficiency in heating, ventilation, and air conditioning in commercial buildings. What incentives does business have to participate in such programs? Should participants be "rewarded" by fewer inspections or lighter sanctions for regulatory violations? What other "carrots" might the government offer to encourage participation? Might such programs provide a basis for environmental contracts between government and firms, displacing otherwise applicable regulations? What explains the apparent large number of opportunities for businesses to reduce environmental impacts in ways that will save them money by promoting resource efficiency? Why haven't companies already implemented these steps?

APPENDIX TO CHAPTER 4

EXCERPTS FROM AIR QUALITY CRITERIA FOR PARTICULATE MATTER AND SULFUR OXIDES

(1969, 1982, and 1988)

[The following are excerpts from the air quality criteria documents for sulfur oxides and particulate matter. The introductory three paragraphs and the conclusion (which contains findings regarding the welfare effects of SO_2) are from the original 1969 criteria document issued by the Department of Health, Education and Welfare. The other excerpts dealing with health effects are from updates to the criteria documents for SO_2 and particulate matter issued by EPA in 1982 and 1988.]

These documents present criteria of air quality in terms of the effects empirically obtained and published for various concentrations of one family of pollutants, the sulfur oxides, their acids and acid salts, and particulate matter. These effects do not, for the most part, derive solely from the presence of sulfur oxides in the atmosphere. They are the effects that have been observed when various concentrations of sulfur oxides, along with other pollutants, have been present in the atmosphere. Many of these effects are produced by a combination of sulfur oxides pollution and undifferentiated particulate matter; the contributions of each class are difficult to distinguish. Moreover, laboratory studies have shown that a combination of sulfur oxides and particulates may produce an effect that is greater than the sum of the effects caused by these pollutant classes individually. Because of the interactions between pollutants, and the reactions of pollutants with oxygen and with water in the atmosphere, and because of the influence of sunlight and temperature on these reactions, the criteria for sulfur oxides cannot be presented as exact expressions of cause and effect that have been replicated from laboratory to laboratory. . . .

Particulate matter [PM] and sulfur oxides are emitted into the atmosphere from a number of sources, both natural and manmade. Natural source emissions include terrestrial dust, sea spray, biogenic emanations, volcanic emissions, and emissions from wildfires. The predominant manmade sources are stationary point sources, industrial and nonindustrial fugitive sources, and transportation sources. Manmade sulfur oxides arise mainly from the combustion of fuels. Solid and liquid fossil fuels contain sulfur, usually in the form of inorganic sulfides or sulfur-containing organic compounds. . . .

Sulfur dioxide is a non-flammable, non-explosive colorless gas that most people can taste at concentrations from 0.3 ppm to 1 ppm (about 0.9 $\mu g/m^3$ to 3 $\mu g/m^3$) in air. At concentrations above 3 ppm (about 8.6 μg/m^3), the gas has a pungent, irritating odor. In the atmosphere, sulfur dioxide is partly converted to sulfur trioxide or to sulfuric acid and its salts by photochemical or catalytic processes. . . .

HEALTH EFFECTS
EPIDEMIOLOGIC STUDIES: SUMMARY AND CONCLUSIONS (1982)

[Epidemiologic studies attempt to determine the cause of adverse health effects by correlating death and disease statistics of large populations with statistics on the environmental hazards to which those populations have been exposed. Such a study correlates variations over time in death (mortality) or disease (morbidity) with the variations over time in a given population's exposure, or variations in mortality and morbidity across geographically different populations with different exposure levels.]

Epidemiologic studies do not have the precision of laboratory studies, but they have the advantage of being carried out under ambient air conditions. In most epidemiologic studies, indices of air pollution level are obtained by measuring selected pollutants, most commonly particulates and sulfur compounds. To use these same studies to establish criteria for individual pollutants is justified by the experimental data on interaction of pollutants. However, in reviewing the results of epidemiologic investigations it should always be remembered that the specific pollutant under discussion is being used as an index of pollution not as a physicochemical entity.

In general, the epidemiological studies reviewed here provide strong evidence for induction by marked elevations of atmospheric levels of PM and SO$_2$ of severe health effects, such as mortality and respiratory disease, in certain populations at special risk. Populations at special risk for such effects appear to include, mainly, the elderly and adults with chronic preexisting cardiac or respiratory diseases (e.g., bronchitis). Increased respiratory tract illnesses and more transient effects, e.g., decrements in pulmonary function, also appear to be associated for children with lower chronic exposures to SO$_2$ and PM.

Health Effects Associated with Acute Exposures to Particulate Matter and Sulfur Oxides

[I]t is widely accepted that increases in mortality occur when either SO$_2$ or PM (as BS) levels increase beyond 24-hour levels of 1000 μg/m^3. Such increased mortality, mainly in the elderly or chronically ill, might logically be attributed in part to even brief exposures to very high short-term peak (hourly) levels in the pollutants, which at times increased to several thousand $\mu g/m^3$ during certain major pollution episodes. However, none of the available epidemiological data have been collected or analyzed in a manner so as to either credibly substantiate or refute this possibility. Much more clearly established are marked increases in mortality and morbidity being associated with prolonged episodic elevations of PM and SO_2 which average out to daily levels of 1000 $\mu g/m^3$, especially in the presence of high humidity (fog) conditions, but which include continuous exposures to high pollutant (PM and SO_2) concentrations for several days without intermittent relief or return to near normal levels at points between short-term pollution peaks. Thus, although 24-hour concentrations of PM and $SO_2 \geq$ 1000 $\mu g/m^3$ can be stated as levels at which mortality has notably increased, great care must be exercised in generalizing these observations in attempting to predict likely effects associated with comparable elevations at other times and locations. In particular, the prolonged or continuous nature of the high pollutant exposures and other interacting factors present, e.g., high humidity levels, must be taken into account as additional important determinants of mortality increases observed so far during major air pollution episodes; and marked increases in mortality should not be expected to occur regularly as a function of short-term peak excursions of 24-hour PM or SO_2 levels above 1000 $\mu g/m^3$. Consistent with this are numerous examples in the epidemiological literature evaluated above where no detectable increases in mortality were found to occur on various scattered days when PM and/or SO_2 levels reached comparably high ($\geq$ 1000 $\mu g/m^3$) 24-hour levels as on other days (or sets of successive days) when mortality was clearly increased.

Even more difficult to establish are to what extent smaller but significant increases in mortality and morbidity are associated with nonepisodic 24-hour average exposures to SO_2 and/or levels below 1000 $\mu g/m^3$. Concisely summarized in Table 14-7 are findings from several key studies reviewed above which appear to demonstrate with a reasonably high degree of certainty mortality and morbidity effects associated with acute exposures (24 hrs) to these pollutants. The first two studies cited, by Martin and Bradley (1960) and Martin (1964), deal with a relatively small body of data from London in the late 1950s. No clear "threshold" levels were revealed by their analyses regarding SO_2 or BS levels at which significantly increased mortality began to occur. However, based on their findings, and reanalyses of the Martin and Bradley data by Ware et al. (1981), mortality in the elderly and chronically ill was clearly elevated in association with exposure to ambient air containing simultaneous SO_2 and BS levels above 1000 $\mu g/m^3$; and some indications exist from these analyses that slight increases in mortality may have been associated with nonepisodic BS and PM levels in the range of 500-1000 $\mu g/m^3$ (with greatest certainty demonstrated for levels in excess of 750 $\mu g/m^3$). Much less certainty is attached to suggestions of mortality increases at lower levels. . . . Still the Mazumdar et al. (1981) and certain other analyses (Appendix 14F) of 1958-59 to 1971-72 London winter mortality data are strongly indicative of small, but significant increases in mortality occurring at BS levels below 500 $\mu g/m^3$ and, possibly, as low as 150 to 200 $\mu g/m^3$.

Only very limited data exist by which to attempt to delineate any specific physical and chemical properties of PM associated with the observed increases in mortality. . . . Neither can the relative contributions of SO_2 or PM be clearly separated based on these study results nor can possible interactive effects with increases in humidity (fog) be completely ruled out. . . .

Similar analysis of the Lawther morbidity studies listed in Table 14-7 suggests that acute exposure to elevated 24-hour PM levels in the range of 250-500 $\mu g/m^3$ (BS) in association with 24-hour SO_2 levels of 500-600 $\mu g/m^3$ were most clearly associated with the induction of respiratory disease symptoms among large (>1000) populations of chronically ill London bronchitis patients. A smaller population (≈ 80) of selected, highly sensitive London bronchitic patients appeared to be affected at somewhat lower BS and SO_2 levels, but specific exposure-effect levels could not be determined on the basis of the reported data. Again, however, little can be said in terms of specifying physical or chemical properties of PM associated with these observed morbidity effects beyond the comments noted above in relation to Martin's studies on mortality.

HEALTH EFFECTS ASSOCIATED WITH CHRONIC EXPOSURES TO PM AND SO_2

In regard to chronic exposure effects of SO_2 and particulate matter, the best pertinent epidemiological health studies are summarized in Table 14-8. The studies by Ferris et al. (1973, 1976) suggest that lung function decrements may occur in adults at TSP [total suspended particulates] levels in excess of 180 $\mu g/m_3$ in the presence of relatively low estimated SO_2 levels, whereas no effects were observed by the same investigators at TSP levels below 130 $\mu g/m^3$. Other studies listed in Table 14-8 suggest that significant respiratory effects occur in children in association with long-term (annual average) PM levels in the approximate range of 230-301 $\mu g/m^3$ (BS) in association with SO_2 levels of 181-275 $\mu g/m^3$.

No specific particulate matter chemical species can clearly be implicated as causal agents associated with the effects observed in the studies listed in Table 14-8. . . .

TABLE 14-7

Summary of Quantitative Conclusions from Epidemiological Studies Relating Health Effects to Acute Exposure to Ambient Air Limits of SO₂ and pH

Type of Study	Effects Observed	24-hr average pollutant level ($\mu g/m^3$)		Reference
		BS	SO₂	
Mortality	Clear increases in daily total mortality or excess mortality above 1 15-day moving average among the elderly and persons with preexisting respiratory or cardiac disease during the London winter of 1958-59	≥1000	≥1000	Martin and Bradley (1960), Martin (1964)
	Analogous increases in daily mortality in London during 1958-59 to 1971-72 winters	500-1000	500-1000	
	Some indications of likely increases in daily total mortality during the 1958-59 London winter, with greatest certainty (95% confidence) of increases occurring at BS and SO₂ levels above 750 $\mu g/m^3$	500-1000	500-1000	
	Analogous indications of increased mortality during 1958-59 to 1971-72 London winters, again with greatest certainty at BS and SO₂ levels above 750 $\mu g/m^3$ but indications of small increases at BS levels <500 $\mu g/m^3$ and possibly as low as 150-200 $\mu g/m^3$			
Morbidity	Worsening of health status among a group of chronic bronchitis patients in London during winters from 1955 to 1960	≥250-500*	≥500-600	Lawther (1958); Lawther et al. (1970)
	No detectable effects in most bronchitis, but positive associations between worsening of health status among a selected group of highly sensitive chronic bronchitis patients and London BS and SO₂ levels during 1967-68 winter	<250*	<500	Lawther et al. (1970)

*Note that the 250-500 $\mu g/m^3$ BS levels stated here may represent somewhat higher pH concentrations than those actually associated with the observed effects reported by Lawther (1970). This is due to the estimates of pH mass (in $\mu g/m^3$ BS) used by Lawther being based on the D.S.I.R. calibration curve found by Waller (1964) to approximate closely a site-specific calibration curve developed by Waller in central London in 1956, but yielding somewhat higher mass estimates than another site-specific calibration developed by Waller, a short distance away, in 1963. However, the precise relationship between estimated BS mass values based on the D.S.I.R. curve versus the 1963 Waller curve cannot be clearly determined due to several factors, including the nonlinearity of the two curves and their convergence at low BS reflectance values.

TABLE 14-8
Summary of Quantitative Conclusions from Epidemiological Studies Relating Health Effects to Chronic Exposure to Ambient Air Levels of SO$_2$ and pH

Type of study	Effects observed	Annual ave. pollutant levels ($\mu g/m^3$) particulate matter			Reference
		BS	TSP	SO$_2$	
Cross-sectional (4 areas)	Likely increased frequency of lower respiratory symptoms and decreased lung function in children in Sheffield, England	230-301*	—	161-175	Lunn et al. (1967)
Longitudinal and cross-sectional	Apparent improvement in lung function of adults in association with decreased pH pollution in Berlin, N.H.	—	160	**	Ferris et al. (1973, 1976)
Longitudinal and cross-sectional	Apparent lack of effects and symptoms, and no apparent decrease in lung function in adults in Berlin, N.H.		80-131	**	Ferris et al. (1973, 1976)

* Note that 85 levels stated here in $\mu g/m^3$ must be viewed as only crude estimates of the approximate pH (BS) mass levels associated with the observed health effects, given ambiguities regarding the use or nonuse of site-specific calibrations in Sheffield to derive the reported BS levels in $\mu g/m^3$.

** Note that sulfation rate methods indicated low atmospheric sulfur levels in Berlin, N.H. during the time of these studies. Cross estimation of SO$_2$ levels from that data suggest that <25-50 $\mu g/m^3$ SO$_2$ levels were generally present in Berlin, N.H. and did not likely contribute to observed health effects.

CONTROLLED HUMAN STUDIES: SUMMARY AND
CONCLUSIONS

Unlike community epidemiological studies that investigate health
responses of large population cohorts under highly variable ambient
exposure conditions, controlled human exposure (clinical) studies typically evaluate much smaller numbers of subjects but under much better defined and carefully controlled exposure conditions. In the latter
type of studies, exposures to either single pollutants or combinations
of pollutants are usually carried out in environmentally controlled
chambers in which relative humidity, temperature, and pollutant concentrations are designed to approximate representative ambient air exposure conditions, especially those thought to be associated with the
induction of acute effects.

Generally inherent in the design of controlled human exposure
studies carried out in the United States are limitations on the range or
types of pollutant exposures and types of subjects studied so as to assure
(as approved by human rights and medical ethics committees) that the
experimental exposures to the pollutants being tested per se will not
lead to serious morbidity, irreversible illness, or death. Consequently,
the types of pulmonary responses typically assessed in controlled exposure studies are typically "transient" and "reversible." . . .

In general, the population groups at special risk to air pollution
include the young, the elderly, and individuals predisposed by some
particular disease, including asthma, bronchitis, cystic fibrosis, emphysema, and cardiovascular disease. In the normal population, there are
also nondiseased but hypersensitive individuals. . . .

Sulfur Dioxide Effects

Sulfur dioxide has been found to affect a variety of physiological
functions. These include sensory processes [and] subjective perceptions of irritative or painful SO_2 effects. . . .

Of much more concern are cardiovascular or respiratory effects
found to be associated with exposure to SO_2. For healthy subjects at
rest, in general, such effects have not been consistently observed except
at exposure levels above 5 ppm (13.1 $\mu g/m^3$). These include, for example, observations by Frank et al. (1962) of marked pulmonary flow resistance increases (mean = 39% at 5 ppm (13.1 $\mu g/m^3$)) and consistent
observations by numerous other investigators . . . of increased airway
resistance or other bronchoconstrictive effects with exposures of
healthy adult subjects to SO_2 levels of 5 ppm (13.1 $\mu g/m^3$) or
higher. . . .

Probably of more crucial importance are the findings of several investigators suggesting potentiation [making more potent] of SO_2 airway effects in normal subjects as the result of increased oral inhalation of SO_2, due either to forced mouth breathing or increased exercise levels or both. . . . These studies suggest possible bronchoconstriction effects in healthy adults with oral breathing of 1.0 to 2.5 ppm (2.6 to 6.6 $\mu g/m^3$) SO_2, raising the possibility of such effects being seen at similar concentrations in healthy adults exercising at sufficient workloads to induce a shift to oronasal breathing.

[Studies of the effects of exercise on healthy adults exposed to various concentrations of SO_2 are discussed.] The weight of available evidence, therefore, appears to indicate that induction of pulmonary mechanical function effects may occur at ≥ 1 to 3 ppm (2.6 to 7.9 $\mu g/m^3$) SO_2 in exercising healthy adults but not at ≤ 0.50 ppm (1.31 $\mu g/m^3$) SO_2 even with exercise or forced oral breathing. . . .

A clearer picture of probable enhanced susceptibility or special risk for SO_2-pulmonary function effects appears to be emerging now in regard to asthmatic subjects. . . .

The Sheppard et al. (1980, 1981) results appear to demonstrate that some asthmatic subjects may be approximately an order of magnitude more sensitive to SO_2 exposure than normal, nonsensitive healthy adults. That is, whereas nonsensitive healthy adults display increased bronchoconstriction at 5 to 10 ppm while at rest and at levels possibly as low as 1 ppm with oral or oronasal breathing, clinically defined mild asthmatics appear to be sensitive, as a group, down to 0.25 ppm SO_2 and the most sensitive (as individuals) possibly down to 0.1 ppm under moderate exercise (Ve $\approx$ 30 liters/minute) conditions. Most importantly, with brief 10 minute exposures to SO_2 concentrations encountered in U.S. cities (0.1 to 0.5 ppm), Sheppard et al. (1981) demonstrated that moderate exercise increased the bronchoconstriction produced by SO_2 in subjects with mild asthma. . . .

The health significance of pulmonary function changes and associated symptomatic effects demonstrated to occur in response to SO_2 by the above human exposure studies is an important issue for present air quality criteria development purposes. In contrast to the sensory effects of SO_2 earlier described as probably being of little health significance, much more concern is generally accorded to the potential health effects of pulmonary function changes (such as increased bronchoconstriction) and associated symptomatic effects (such as coughing, wheezing and dyspnea or shortness of breath) observed with human exposures to SO_2, especially in sensitive population groups such as asthmatics. . . .

Particulate matter, especially hygroscopic salts, have been shown to be potentially important in enhancing the pulmonary function effects of SO_2 exposure. Airway resistance increased more after combined exposure to SO_2 and sodium chloride in several studies, although others have failed to demonstrate the same effect. This difference in response to the SO_2-NaCl aerosol mixtures may be due principally to the relative humidity at the time of the exposure. McJilton et al. (1976) have demonstrated in guinea pigs that changes in pulmonary mechanical function were seen only when the mixture (SO_2/NaCl) was administered at high relative humidity (r.h. $> 80\%$). The effect is ascribed to absorption of the highly soluble SO_2 into the droplet before inhalation, whereas at a r.h. $< 40\%$ the aerosol was a crystal. . . .

In contrast to the apparent enhancement of SO_2-induced pulmonary airway effects by combined exposure with certain particulate matter aerosols, there is less evidence that supports the hypothesis that synergistic interactions between SO_2 and other gaseous pollutants, such as O_3 or NO_2, produce greater-than-additive effects of each individually on pulmonary mechanical functions. . . .

Sulfuric Acid and Sulfate Effects

In addition to SO_2 being absorbed by hygroscopic particles, whereby its effects may be potentiated, sulfur dioxide is also transformed into sulfur trioxide during transport and (in combination with moisture) sulfuric acid is formed. The latter may exist as a sulfuric acid droplet or can be converted to sulfates in the presence of ammonia, which is found in the ambient air and in expired human breath.

Respiratory effects from exposure to sulfuric acid mist (0.35 to 0.5 $\mu g/m^3$) have been reported to include increased respiratory rate and decreased maximal inspiratory and expiratory flowrates and tidal volume (Amdur et al., 1952). However, several other studies of pulmonary function in nonsensitive healthy, adult subjects (Newhouse et al., 1978; Sacker et al., 1978; Kleinman et al., 1978; Avol et al., 1979; Leikauf et al., 1981; Kerr et al., 1981; Horvath et al., 1981) indicated that pulmonary mechanical function was little affected when subjects were exposed at 0.1 to 1.0 $\mu g/m^3$ sulfuric acid for 10 to 120 minutes. . . .

In studies with asthmatic subjects, no changes in airway function have been demonstrated after exposure to sulfuric acid and sulfate salts at concentrations less than 1000 $\mu g/m^3$. However, at higher concentrations (1000 $\mu g/m^3$), reduction in specific airway conductance (SG_{aw}) and forced expiratory volume ($FEV_{1.0}$) have been observed after sulfuric acid (H_2SO_4) and ammonium bisulfate (NH_4HSO_4) exposures as reported by Utell et al. (1981). No studies, on the other hand, have as yet evaluated the effects of sulfuric acid or other published sulfate salt aerosols on nasal or tracheobronchial mucus clearance functions.

REVIEW OF THE NATIONAL AMBIENT AIR QUALITY STANDARDS FOR SULFUR OXIDES: UPDATED ASSESSMENT OF SCIENTIFIC AND TECHNICAL INFORMATION ADDENDUM TO THE 1982 OAQPS (1988)

EXECUTIVE SUMMARY

This paper evaluates and interprets the updated scientific and technical information that the EPA staff believes is most relevant to the review of primary (health) national ambient air quality standards (NAAQS) for sulfur oxides and represents an update of the 1982 sulfur oxides staff paper. . . .

Because much of the recently available health effects information on SO_2 is related to short-term exposures, the staff paid particular attention to updating information on short-term peak concentrations. The staff found that:

(1) Maximum 5 minute to hourly SO_2 concentrations are found near major point sources. The newer information tends to support earlier conclusions that near such sources, the 5 to 10 minute peak SO_2 concentration is likely to be within a factor of 1.4 to 2.4 times the hourly average. Maximum peak to mean ratios can be higher.

(2) Short duration peaks (less than 30 seconds to 2 minutes) in excess of 0.5 ppm appear likely to occur near numerous smaller sources of SO_2. None of the recently published assessments of the health effects of SO_2 has addressed exposures of such limited duration. Due to limitations of the monitoring instruments, it is not presently possible to assess the extent to which such peaks may be occurring in particular urban locations.

UPDATED ASSESSMENT OF THE PRIMARY STANDARDS

The updated staff assessment of key controlled human studies of peak (minutes to an hour) SO_2 exposures is summarized in Table 1. Both recently published studies and those assessed in the 1982 staff paper are included. The major effects observed in these studies are increases in airway resistance and decreases in other functional measures indicative of significant bronchoconstriction in sensitive asthmatic or atopic subjects. At 0.4 ppm SO_2, changes in functional measures are accompanied by mild increases in perceptible symptoms such as wheezing, chest tightness, and coughing. At higher concentrations, ef-

TABLE 1
Updated Staff Assessment of Key Controlled Human Studies

SO_2 concentration on (5-60 minutes)	Observed Effects[1]	Comments/Implications
1-2 ppm	Substantial changes in 8 of 12 subjects ($\triangle$ SRaw 100-600%) exposed to 2 ppm. At 1 ppm, functional changes ($\triangle$ SRaw 170-200%), symptoms in free breathing asthmatics at moderate exercise.[2]	Effects range from moderate to incapacitating for some individuals. At 2 ppm, 80% of mild asthmatics could experience at least a doubling of SRaw. Some might not tolerate exposure at moderate exercise. Approximately 80% at 1 ppm could experience at least a doubling of SRaw.[3] Some asthmatic mouth breathers have significant bronchoconstriction at 2 ppm even at light activity.
0.6-0.75 ppm	Functional changes ($\triangle$ SRaw 120-260%), symptoms in free breathing asthmatics at light-moderate exercise.[4]	Effects indicative of clinical significance; on average, changes were mild to moderate although severe for some individuals; 25-50% of mild, freebreathing asthmatics at moderate exercise could experience at least a doubling of airway resistance.[3]
0.5 ppm	Significant functional changes ($\triangle$ SRaw 50-100%), symptoms in free breathing asthmatics at moderate, but not at light exercise.[5] At heavy exercise, $\triangle$ SRaw 220-240%.[6]	On average, mild responses at moderate or higher exercise, symptoms possibly of clinical significance; severe responses for some individuals. About 20-25% could experience at least a doubling in airway resistance.
0.4 ppm	Functional changes ($\triangle$ SRaw 70%), symptoms in free breathing asthmatics at moderate-heavy exercise.[7]	Lowest level of clinically significant response for some free breathers. Approximately 10% of mild, free breathing asthmatics could experience a doubling in airway resistance.[3]

0.1-0.3 ppm	No effects in free breathing asthmatics at light exercise. Slight but not significant functional changes in free-breathing subjects at moderate-heavy exercise (0.25 ppm),[6] but not at lower levels.[7]	Significant effects unlikely at moderate exercise. Effects of SO_2 indistinguishable at heavy exercise. Possibility of more significant responses in small percentage of sensitive asthmatics at 0.28 ppm.[3]

[1] Specific Airway Resistance (SRaw) is the lung function measure most often reported in SO_2 studies. Unless otherwise noted, ($\triangle$ SRaw_%) reflects group mean increase over clean air control at rest. Light, moderate, heavy exercise refers to ventilation rates approximating $\leq$ 35 L/min, 40-45 L/min, and $\geq$ 50 L/min, respectively. Effects reflect results from range of moderate temperature/humidity conditions (i.e., 7-26°C, 36-90% RH). Studies at 0.5-0.6 ppm indicate that exercise-induced bronchoconstriction associated with cold and/or dry air exacerbates response to SO_2 while warm, humid air mitigates asthmatic responses relative to moderate conditions.

[2] Schacter et al. (1984); Roger et al. (1985); Horstman et al. (1986).

[3] Horstman et al. (1986).

[4] Mackney et al. (1984); Schacter et al. (1984); Linn et al. (1983 a.b. 1984 a.b.c. 1985 a).

[5] Kirpatrick et al. (1982); Linn et al. (1984b); Roger et al. (1985); Schacter et al. (1984).

[6] Sethel et al. (1983a,b: 1985).

[7] Linn et al. (1983b, 1984a).

fects are more pronounced and the fraction of asthmatic subjects who respond increase, with clearer indications of clinically or physiologically significant effects at 0.6-0.75 ppm and above.

Given practical considerations related to monitoring, modeling, data manipulation and storage, and implementation, the staff previously recommended consideration of a 1-hour averaging time to protect against the responses to short-term peak (5-10 minute) SO_2 exposures observed in the controlled human studies. Based on this updated staff assessment, the range of potential 1-hour levels of interest is revised from 0.25 to 0.75 ppm to 0.2 to 0.5 ppm (525 to 1300 $\mu g/m^3$). The lower bound represents a 1-hour level for which the maximum 5 to 10 minute peak exposures are unlikely to exceed 0.4 ppm, which is the lowest level where potentially significant responses in free (oronasal) breathing asthmatics have been reported in the criteria document addendum. The upper bound of the range represents a 1-hour level for which 5 to 10 minute peak concentrations are unlikely to exceed 1 ppm, a concentration at which the risk of significant functional and symptomatic responses in exposed sensitive asthmatics and atopics appears high. In evaluating these laboratory data in the context of decision making on possible 1-hour standards, the following considerations

TABLE 2
Updated Staff Assessment of Short-Term Epidemiological Studies

Measured SO_2 - $\mu g/m^3$ (ppm) - 24 hour mean

Effects/ study	Daily mortality in London[1]	Aggravation of bronchitis[2]	Small, reversible declines in children's lung function[3]	Combined effects levels
Effects Likely	500-1000 (0.19-0.38)	500-600 (0.19-0.23)	—	500 (0.19)
Effects Possible	—	500 (0.19)	250-450 (0.10-0.18)	250 (0.10)
No Effects Observed	—	—	100-200 (0.04-0.08)	<200 (0.80)

[1] Deviations in daily mortality during London winters (1958-1972). Early winters dominated by high smoke and SO_2, principally from coal combustion emissions, and with frequent fogs (Martin and Bradley, 1960; Ware et al., 1981; Mazumdar et al., 1981, 1982; Schwartz and Marcus, 1986).

[2] Examination of symptoms reported by bronchitics in London. Studies conducted from the mid-1950s to the early 1970s (Lawther et al., 1970).

[3] Studies of children in Steubenville (1978-80) and in the Netherlands (1985-86) before, during, and after pollution episodes characterized by high particle and SO_2 levels (Dockery et al., 1982; Dassen et al., 1986).

are important: (a) the significance of the observed or anticipated responses to health, (b) the relative effect of SO_2 compared to normal day to day variations in asthmatics from exercise and other stimuli, (c) the low probability of exposures of exercising asthmatics to peak levels, and (d) five to ten minute peak exposures may be a factor of two greater than hourly averages.

Independent of frequency of exposure considerations, the upper bound of the range contains little or no margin of safety for exposed sensitive individuals. The limited geographical areas likely to be affected and low frequency of peak exposures to active asthmatics if the standard is met add to the margin of safety. The widespread use of medication among asthmatics that prevents or rapidly relieves bronchoconstrictive effects due to natural and commonly encountered stimuli (e.g., exercise, cold air) further adds to the margin of safety. The data do not suggest other groups that are more sensitive than asthmatics to single peak exposures, but qualitative data suggest repeated peaks might produce effects of concern in other sensitive individuals. Potential interactions of SO_2 and O_3 have not been investigated in asthmatics. The qualitative data, potential pollution interactions, and other considerations listed above should be considered in determining the need for evaluating the margin of safety provided by alternative 1-hour standards.

EFFECTS ON VEGETATION: SUMMARY

. . . There are several possible plant responses to SO_2 and related sulfur compounds: (1) fertilizer effects appearing as increased growth and yields; (2) no detectable response; (3) injury manifested as growth and yield reductions, without visible symptom expressions on foliage or with very mild foliar symptoms that would be difficult to perceive as being induced by air pollution without the presence of a control set of plants grown in pollution-free conditions; (4) injury exhibited as chronic or acute symptoms on foliage with or without associated reduction in growth and yield; and (5) death of plants and plant communities.

A number of species of plants are sensitive to low concentrations of SO_2. Some of these plants may serve as bioindicators in the vicinity of major sources of SO_2. Even these sensitive species may be asymptomatic, however, depending on the environmental conditions before, during, and after SO_2 exposure. Various species of lichens appear to be among the most sensitive plants. . . .

The amount of sulfur accumulated from the atmosphere by leaf tissues is influenced by the amount of sulfur in the soil relative to the sulfur requirement of the plant. After low-level exposure to SO_2, plants grown in sulfur-deficient soils have exhibited increased productivity. . . .

Each plant is a different individual genetically, and therefore its genetic susceptibility and the influence of the environment at the time of exposure must be considered for each plant and each pollutant. The data presented in this chapter exemplify the fact that each plant is a separate entity, and, because of the variation in response shown by the different plant species and different cultivars of the same species, making generalizations is difficult. With this in mind, this chapter concludes that in arid regions, some species of vegetation would probably not show visible signs of SO_2 injury even at concentrations as high as 11 ppm for 2 hours. On the other hand, in many nonarid regions where environmental conditions such as high temperature, high humidity, and abundant sunlight enhance plant responsiveness to SO_2 exposure, many species of sensitive and intermediately responsive vegetation would likely, from time to time, show visible injury when exposed to peak (5 minutes), 1-hour, and 3-hour SO_2 concentrations in the range of 2600-5200 $\mu g/m^3$ (1-2 ppm), 1300-5200 $\mu g/m^3$ (0.5-2 ppm), and 790-2100 $\mu g/m^3$ (0.3-0.8 ppm) respectively.

In general, the studies cited in this chapter indicate that regardless of the type of exposure and the plant species or variety, there is a critical SO_2 concentration and a critical time period after which plant injury will occur. . . .

EFFECTS ON VISIBILITY AND CLIMATE: SUMMARY

Traditionally, visibility has been defined in terms of distance from an object that is necessary to produce a minimum detectable contrast between that object and its background. Although visibility is often defined by this "visual range," it includes not only being able to see or not see a target, but also seeing targets at shorter distances and appreciating the details of the target, including its colors. Visibility impairment can manifest itself in two ways: (1) as a layer of haze (or a plume), which is visible because it has a visual discontinuity between itself and its background, or (2) as a uniform haze which reduces atmospheric clarity. The type and degree of impairment are determined by the distribution, concentrations, and characteristics of atmospheric particles and gases, which scatter and absorb light traveling through the atmosphere. Scattering and absorption determine light extinction.

On a regional scale, the extinction of light is generally dominated by particle scattering. In urban areas, absorption by particles becomes important and occasionally dominant. Extinction by particles is usually dominated by particles of diameter 0.1 to 2 μm (fine particles). Extinction due to scattering is closely proportional to the fine-particle mass concentration, with extension/fine mass concentration ratios in the range of about 3 m^2/g for relative humidities below 50-70 percent.

Studies performed over the last decade have shown that visibility is a sensitive parameter perceived by the public to indicate polluted air. Loss in the aesthetic value of natural vistas has been ascribed to aerosols of fine PM. A number of studies have been conducted to determine the economic benefit associated with good or improved visibility. The results of these studies, including both contingent and actual market approaches, show that the value people place on visibility is substantial. Although the circumstances of studies differ, the results are broadly consistent, providing evidence that estimation procedures are valid. And, finally, hazards to ground and air transportation have been associated with greatly reduced visibility caused by high concentration of fine PM.

Although the effects on ground transportation from incidents of reduced visibility owing to air pollution are not well documented, they are probably minimal. On the other hand, the effects on aircraft operations are both well documented and significant. Historical records from the National Weather Service indicate that of occasions of visibility of 3 miles (5 km) or less about half occur in the absence of fog, precipitation, or blowing material such as sand or dust. At such low visibility, noninstrument-rated pilots or planes are grounded and commercial air traffic operations at major airports may be significantly reduced.

Pollutants released to the atmosphere alter the environment in ways other than visibility reduction. They may lead to slow and subtle changes in the nature of the atmosphere and, possibly, in climate. For example, a fraction of the solar radiation may be absorbed by aerosols, further reducing the amount of radiation reaching the earth's surface and, at the same time, heating the aerosol layer itself. On a hazy day, the direct solar radiation may be reduced to about one-half of that on a clear day, but most of the energy reappears as diffuse skylight. There is, however, an overall loss of up to about 10 to 20 percent of the radiation reaching the surface. . . .

The attenuation of solar radiation from scattering and absorption by particles in the atmosphere is probably an important factor in climatic change on all scales. But solar radiation and aerosol levels measured at stations remote from pollutant sources have not, as yet, displayed any trend that can be related to human causes.

Cloud- and precipitation-forming processes may be divided into two broad classes: macrophysical and microphysical processes. Macrophysical processes involve the rise and descent of air masses and the amount of water vapor available for condensation. Atmospheric aerosols, primarily those that are strongly hygroscopic, influence the microphysics of cloud formation. The incorporation of particles into rain and fog droplets can change the characteristics of precipitation by changing its chemical composition. The complex interactions of cloud- and precipitation-formation processes, however, obscure the specific role of manmade aerosols. Accordingly, climatic effects cannot be related quantitatively to pollutant emissions.

EFFECTS ON MATERIALS: SUMMARY

The nature and extent of damage to materials by SO_x and PM have been investigated by field and laboratory studies. Both physical and economic damage functions have been developed for specific damage/effect parameters associated with exposure to these pollutants. To date, only a few of these functions are relatively reliable in determining damage, while none has been generally accepted for estimating costs.

The best documented and most significant damage from SO_x and PM is the acceleration of metal corrosion and the erosion of paint. Erosion of building materials and stone due to SO_x is also established, but the importance of SO_x relative to other agents is not clear. Although evidence of damage to fibers (cotton and nylon), paper, leather and electrical components has been reported, reliable damage estimates have not.

Relatively accurate physical damage functions have been calculated for the effects of SO_2 on the corrosion of galvanized steel. Determination of variables such as time of wetness and surface configuration affect the applicability of the functions. Similar, but less accurate, functions have also been developed for estimating erosion rates of oil-based paints from exposure to SO_2. The large-scale replacement of oil-based paint by much more SO_2-resistant latex paint, however, makes these estimates obsolete. The least reliable of the "significant" damage functions are those for soiling from PM. The poorly understood deposition rates and poorly characterized chemical and physical properties related to reflectance make general application of the functions difficult, if not impossible.

The limitations of these and other physical damage functions hinder accurate estimates of total material damage and soiling. Coupled with these limitations is the lack of material exposure estimates. These problems presently preclude complete and accurate estimates of the costs of damage based on a physical damage function approach. Studies based on this approach estimated materials damage in 1970 attributable to SO_x as ranging from \$0.6 to 1.2 billion, in 1970 dollars. Estimates of soiling costs due to PM were based principally on other approaches and ranged up to \$99 billion. Best estimates of economic loss in 1970 attributable to SO_2 and TSP, in 1978 dollars, are \$0.9 billion in materials damage and \$2 billion in soiling, respectively. Improvements in SO_2 and TSP have resulted in estimated annual benefits of \$0.4 for SO_2 and \$0.2 to \$0.7 billion for TSP. These estimates are crude, but can serve to represent the direction and magnitude of changes in benefits associated with improvement in air quality. Approaches to cost estimation with data requirements different from those necessary for the physical damage function approach have been attempted. Whether these approaches yield results adequate for decisionmaking purposes is not clear at present.

ACIDIC DEPOSITION: SUMMARY

Occurrences of acid precipitation (rain and snow) in many regions of the United States, Canada, and Scandinavia have been implicated in the disappearance of fish, other animals, and plant life in ponds, lakes, and streams. In addition, acidic precipitation appears to possess the potential for impoverishing sensitive soils, degrading natural areas, injuring forests, and damaging stone monuments and buildings.

Sulfur and nitrogen oxides, emitted through the combustion of fossil fuels, have been implicated as the chief contributors to the acidification of precipitation. The fate of sulfur and nitrogen oxides, as well as other pollutants emitted into the atmosphere, depends on their dispersion, transport, transformation, and deposition. Emissions from automobiles occur at ground level, those from electric power generators from smoke stacks 300 meters (1000 feet) or more in height. Transport and transformation of the sulfur and nitrogen oxides are in part associated with the height at which they are emitted. The greater the height, the greater the likelihood of a longer residence time in the atmosphere and a greater opportunity for the chemical transformation of the oxides to sulfates, nitrates or other compounds. Ozone and other photochemical oxidants are believed to be involved in the chemical transformations. Because of long range transport, acidic precipitation in a particular state or region can be the result of emissions from sources in states or regions hundreds of miles away rather than local sources. To date the complex nature of the chemical transformation processes has not made possible the demonstration of a direct cause-and-effect relationship between emissions of sulfur and nitrogen oxides and the acidity of precipitation.

Natural emissions of sulfur and nitrogen compounds are also involved in the formation of acidic precipitations; however, in industrialized groups anthropogenic emissions exceed natural emissions.

Precipitation is arbitrarily defined as being acidic if its pH is less than 5.6. Currently the acidity of precipitation in the Northeastern United States, the region most severely impacted, ranges from pH 3.0 to 5.0. Precipitation episodes with a pH as low as 3.0 have been reported for other regions of the United States. The pH of precipitation can vary from event to event, from season to season and from geographical area to geographical area. . . .

Sensitivity of a lake to acidification depends on the acidity of both wet and dry deposition, the soil system of the drainage basin, canopy effects of ground cover and the composition of the watershed bedrock.

An extremely close mutual relationship exists between the chemistries of the environment and of living organisms. There is a continuing exchange of nutrients and of energy. The two are closely intertwined responses. There is no action without a reaction. . . .

The capacity of organisms to withstand injury from weather extremes, pesticides, acidic deposition, or polluted air follows the principle of limiting factors. Limiting factors are . . . factors which, when scarce or overabundant, limit the growth, reproduction and/or distribution of an organism. The increasing acidity of water in lakes and streams appears to be such a factor. Significant changes that have occurred in aquatic ecosystems with increasing acidity include the following:

(1)   Fish populations are reduced or eliminated.
(2)   Bacterial decomposition is reduced and fungi may dominate saprotrophic communities. Organic debris accumulates rapidly, tying up nutrients, and limiting nutrients mineralization and cycling.
(3)   Species diversity and total numbers of species of aquatic plants and animals are reduced. Acid-tolerant species dominate.
(4)   Phytoplankton productivity may be reduced due to changes in nutrient cycling and nutrient limitations.
(5)   Biomass and total productivity of benthic macrophytes and algae may increase due partially to increased lake transparency.
(6)   Numbers and biomass of herbivorous invertebrates decline. Tolerant invertebrate species, e.g., air-breathing bugs (water-boatmen, back-swimmers, water striders) may become abundant primarily due to reduced fish predation.
(7)   Changes in community structure occur at all trophic levels.

Studies indicate that pH levels between 6.0 and 5.0 inhibit reproduction of many species of aquatic organisms. Fish populations become seriously affected at a pH lower than 5.0.

Disappearance of fish from lakes and streams follows two general patterns. One results from sudden short-term shifts in pH, the other arises from a long-term decrease in the pH of the water. A major injection of acids and other soluble substances occurs when polluted snow melts during warm periods in winter or early spring. Fish kills are a dramatic consequence of such episodic injections.

Long-term increases in acidity interfere with reproduction and spawning, producing a decrease in population density and a shift in size and age of population to one consisting primarily of larger and older fish. Effects on yield often are not recognizable until the population is close to extinction; this is particularly true for late-maturing species with long lives. Even relatively small increases (5 to 50 percent) in mortality of fish eggs and fry can decrease yield and bring about extinction. . . .

Acidic precipitation may indirectly influence terrestrial plant productivity by altering the supply and availability of soil nutrients. Acidification increases leaching of plant nutrients (such as calcium, magnesium, potassium, iron, and manganese), increases the rate of weathering of most minerals, and also makes phosphorus less available to plants. Acidification also decreases the rate of many soil microbiological processes such as nitrogen fixation by *Rhizobium* bacteria on legumes and by the free-living *Azotobacter,* mineralization of nitrogen from forest litter, nitrification of ammonium compounds, and overall decay rates of forest floor litter. . . .

Erosion of stone monuments and buildings and corrosion of metals can result from acidic precipitation. Because sulfur compounds are a dominant component of acidic precipitation and are deposited during dry deposition also, the effects resulting from the two processes cannot be distinguished. In addition, the deposition of sulfur compounds on stone surfaces provides a medium for microbial growth that can result in deterioration.

U.S. Department of Health, Education, and Welfare, Public Health Service, Quality Criteria for Sulfur Oxides (1969)

Conclusion

The conclusions which follow are derived from a careful evaluation by the National Air Pollution Control Administration of the foreign and American studies cited in previous chapters of this document. They represent the Administration's best judgment of the effects that may occur when various levels of pollution are reached in the atmosphere. The data from which the conclusions were derived, and qualifications which should be considered in using the data, are identified by chapter reference in each case. . . .

2. *Effects on Visibility*

At a concentration of *285 $\mu g/m^3$* (0.10 ppm) of sulfur dioxide, with comparable concentration of particulate matter and relative humidity of 50 percent, *visibility may be reduced* to about five miles.

3. *Effects on Material*

At a mean sulfur dioxide level of *345 $\mu g/m^3$* (0.12 ppm), accompanied by high particulate levels, the *corrosion rate* for steel panels may be increased by 50 percent.

4. *Effects on Vegetation*

(a)   At a concentration of about *85 $\mu g/m^3$* (0.03 ppm) of sulfur dioxide (annual mean), *chronic plant injury* and *excessive leaf drop may occur.*

(b)   After exposure to about *860 $\mu g/m^3$* (0.3 ppm) of sulfur dioxide for 8 hours, some species of trees and shrubs show *injury*. (American data; see Chapter 5, Section C.)

(c)   At concentrations of about *145 µg/m³* to *715 µg/m³* (0.05 ppm to 0.25 ppm), sulfur dioxide may react synergistically with either ozone or nitrogen dioxide in short-term exposures (e.g., 4 hours) to produce *moderate to severe injury* to sensitive plants.

5

Statutory Approaches to Water Pollution

The United States has developed a complex regulatory regime to improve and protect water quality throughout the nation over the past two decades. This chapter builds upon your understanding of at least equally complex regulatory approaches described in Chapter 4 by setting forth the regulatory regime governing water quality and inviting you to evaluate it. As you study the materials in this chapter, compare the approaches used to protect water quality to the approaches used to protect air quality. To what extent are the regulatory regimes similar? What might explain or justify the differences?

A. INTRODUCTION

1. WATER POLLUTION: NATURE, CAUSES, EFFECTS[1]

Water pollution comprises a broad range of effluents and conditions, many of which are introduced by humans but also some attributable to natural processes. Chart 5.1 summarizes the effects and sources of the major water pollutants.

Biological Oxygen Demand (BOD). An important measure of water

---

1. This section draws upon The Conservation Foundation, State of the Environment: A View Towards the Nineties, 87-106 (1987).

CHART 5.1
Major Water Pollutants

Pollutants	Effects	Sources	
		Point	*Non-Point*
Biochemical Oxygen Demand (BOD)	reduces fish and other aquatic life, which depend on dissolved oxygen to survive	POTWs; industrial facilities; sewer overflows	agricultural runoff; urban run-off; septic systems; landfills; silvicultural runoff
Bacteria—esp. human and animal wastes	Most forms are harmless, but some present serious risk of disease to humans. Exposure vectors: swimming, consumption of shellfish	POTWs; sewer overflows	agricultural runoff; urban run-off; septic systems
Nutrients — esp. phosphates and nitrogen	stimulates algal blooms and accelerates eutrophication of water bodies	POTWs; sewer overflows	agricultural runoff (fertilizer); urban runoff; septic systems; silviculture
Suspended Solids — esp. soil sediment	causes brown, turbid waters which impair recreational uses of waters and harm aquatic wildlife		agricultural runoff (soil erosion); construction runoff; silviculture
Total Dissolved Solids (TDS) — salts	harm aquatic organisms and impair recreational uses of waters	sewer overflows	agricultural runoff; urban run-off; mining runoff
Toxics	risks to humans and aquatic life — Exposure vectors: direct contact; contamination of drinking water; consumption of fish	POTWs; industrial facilities; sewer overflows	agricultural (pesticides); urban runoff; construction; mining; septic systems; landfills; silviculture
Thermal	reduces dissolved oxygen; direct thermal effects	power plants; indus. facilities	

quality is the level of dissolved oxygen. Dissolved oxygen, usually present in clean waters at levels of 5 ppm (parts per million) or more, is necessary for fish and other aquatic life to survive. The decomposition of organic pollutants, such as those in municipal sewage, and chemicals, such as those in industrial wastes, depletes oxygen levels. Temperature can also change the amount of dissolved oxygen by affecting the solubility of oxygen. Biological oxygen demand (BOD) measures the oxygen-depleting capacity of a substance discharged into water.

Bacteria. Bacteria from human and animal wastes can pose significant public health risks to humans from infection and disease. Humans come in contact with these bacteria through drinking water, swimming, and consumption of shellfish from contaminated waters. Prior to the advent of public sanitation systems, bacterial infection through drinking water posed particularly grave threats to human populations. In many developing countries, such risks are among the most serious health concerns.

Nutrients. Nutrients, such as phosphorus and nitrogen, can stimulate algal blooms and growth of nuisance water plants, accelerate eutrophication (the aging of lakes and reservoirs), and cause problems with oxygen depletion as the plants die and decompose. Nutrients can over enrich water bodies, allowing algal blooms. Such blooms block light from reaching submerged aquatic vegetation, thereby killing off valuable nursery habitat for fish and shellfish. The primary sources of nutrients are fertilizer runoff from croplands and urban lawns, runoff from feedlots, and discharges from municipal waste water treatment plants.

Suspended Solids. Brown, turbid water caused by suspended solids, such as soil sediment and other particles, can significantly reduce beneficial uses of water by people and can harm aquatic wildlife. These particles also can carry nutrients, pesticides, bacteria, and other harmful substances. Many rivers have always carried high sediment loads because of natural erosion occurring in their watersheds. But erosion from cropland, construction sites, range land, and forest land has elevated sediment to a major water pollutant.

Total Dissolved Solids (TDS). Dissolved solids are inorganic salts and other substances from natural and human sources after they have dissolved in water. Most commonly these dissolved substances are measured together as total dissolved solids. TDS harm aquatic organisms and impair recreational uses of waters.

Toxics. Toxic substances, including metals, come from industrial facilities, mining operations, pesticide use, acidic deposition, construction activities, among others. These substances are hazardous to humans and aquatic life.

Thermal. Many power plants and some industrial facilities use river waters to cool equipment in their production process. Although these cooling uses of the water do not introduce contaminants, the return of the water into the river, at higher temperature, may accelerate the biological and chemical processes of decomposition, utilizing more oxygen and promoting algal blooms, and reduce the river's capacity to retain dissolved oxygen, harming fish and aquatic life.

NATIONAL WATER COMMISSION, WATER POLICIES FOR THE FUTURE

69-71 (1973)

. . . One view of pollution is expressed in the Federal Water Pollution Control Act Amendments of 1972, which defines "pollution" as "man-made or man-induced alteration of the chemical, physical, biological, and radiological integrity of water." [§502(19).] Thus, natural water quality appears to be regarded as a norm from which any deviation constitutes pollution. This is not a good standard on which to base the definition of pollution. In some places water is naturally toxic, naturally hot, naturally turbid, naturally radioactive, or naturally acid or alkaline. Some lakes are naturally choked with algae, and the eutrophication of lakes is a natural process in their aging. Oil seeps in large quantity occur in nature. Heavy sediment loads occur naturally in many flowing streams. Man-induced changes due to discharges of specific chemicals can actually improve the usefulness of water, for example, where wastes which contain lime neutralize the excess natural acidity of streams, or where nutrients are needed to support aquatic life. . . .

Tolerance of foreign materials in water varies greatly among different water uses. The ranking of purposes for which water is used in terms of the quality levels required in natural watercourses might be represented as follows: (1) preservation of the natural environment, as in the "wild river" program; (2) water contact sports, such as swimming and waterskiing; (3) use as a source of a potable domestic water supply; (4) preservation of aquatic life; (5) noncontact recreational uses, such as boating; (6) agricultural use, such as irrigation and livestock watering; (7) industrial use; (8) navigation; (9) disposal and transport of wastes. Only use (1) requires natural water quality. In all other cases water quality different from that which would exist in nature will adequately support the desired uses. In fact, natural water itself often is unfit to satisfy important uses. . . .

2. CONTROL TECHNOLOGIES

As noted in Chart 5.1, water pollution sources can usefully be divided into two categories: point sources and non-point sources. This distinction is particularly important from the perspective of developing control technologies. Like most forms of air pollution, point sources of water pollution emanate from a specific outflow. Control technologies can, therefore, capture and treat the effluent before reintroducing water into the natural environment. Indeed, treatment may be much easier to accomplish in the case of water pollution, which can be channelled through a single treatment works and outfall, than air pollution, which is emitted in hot gases that are often released through many stacks, vents and valves or other "fugitive" small quantity outlets in a given plant. By contrast, non-point sources, such as agricultural runoff, cannot easily be contained and treated, making abatement all the more difficult. As with air pollution, however, pollution prevention — such as substituting less toxic materials in a production process or using natural pest control methods rather than pesticides — can address both point and non-point pollution problems at the source, rather than relying on "end of pipe" controls on pollution once it has been generated.

Municipal Sewage. Most sewage in the United States passes through publicly owned treatments works (POTWs) which treat the wastewater before releasing into the environment. State of the art POTWs utilize three levels of treatment. Primary treatment first filters large solids from the effluent and then uses settling tanks to settle out some organic solids. Secondary treatment uses aeration tanks to metabolize (by bacteria) some organic wastes, producing water, carbon dioxide, and ammonia. Settling tanks are then used to settle out bacterial sludge for reuse or treatment. Tertiary treatment uses further aeration methods and settling tanks as well as the addition of methanal to feed bacteria to consumer nitrates. An iron compound is added to convert phosphates to compounds that adhere to sludge that is settled out. Chlorine is added to water to kill bacteria before it is discharged. The cost of treatment increases substantially at each stage.

Industrial Point Sources. Industrial facilities use a variety of filtering and settling technologies like those employed by POTWs to remove contaminants from waste streams. In addition, toxic chemicals are treated through chemical neutralization and other techniques.

Non-point Sources. These diverse sources of water pollution cannot be addressed through centralized treatment technologies. Therefore, control technologies are highly source and context specific. *Agricultural runoff* can be addressed through regulation of irrigation practices, soil conservation programs, and regulation of fertilizer and pesticide use. *Urban runoff* can be controlled by routing storm drains to POTWs, installation of overflow controls, street cleaning, land use control, design standards for parking lots, restrictions on the discharge of hazardous materials, and periodic household hazardous waste collection programs. *Mining runoff* can be addressed through restrictions on mining practices. *Silviculture runoff* can be controlled by restrictions on timber harvesting and harvesting practices, tree planting programs, and soil conservation programs.

B.   OVERVIEW OF THE CLEAN WATER ACT

The basic federal legislation dealing with water pollution is the Federal Water Pollution Control Act (FWPCA), 42 U.S.C. §1251 et seq., which was shaped in its present form by extensive amendments in 1972.[2] The Act was substantially amended in 1977 and renamed the Clean Water Act (CWA). It was further amended in 1987. The Act is long and complex; this overview represents a bare outline of its basic structure.

Like the Clean Air Act, the CWA is the product of incremental legislation over a considerable period resulting in an increasingly dominant federal role. Earlier versions of the Act, tracing back to 1948, authorized federal research programs and cumbersome federal remedies to deal with interstate water pollution problems. The 1965 Amendments adopted a water use "zoning" system using ambient water quality standards. States were required to classify all waters within the state by their intended use (swimming, fishing, water supply, navigation, industrial wastes disposal); to adopt ambient water quality standards limiting pollution concentrations for each stretch of water to the extent needed to support the use for which it was zoned (such as stringent standards for swimming areas, less stringent for areas used for navigation or waste disposal); and then to adopt implementation plans to control discharges sufficiently to achieve the various ambient standards. Each of these steps was subject to federal approval; the basic structure was quite similar to the Air Quality Act of 1967.

The process of implementing this complex scheme proved time-consuming. In the late 1960s, the federal government began to utilize the Rivers and Harbors Act of 1889 — forbidding deposit of "refuse" in navigable waters without a permit from the Secretary of the Army — to require sources of water pollution to obtain federal permits with specific federally enforced discharge limitations to speed achievement of clean water goals. While this provision in the Rivers and Harbors Act (sometimes called the Refuse Act) had originally been aimed at obstructions to navigation, it was broadly interpreted by federal courts

---

2. There are a number of other federal statutes bearing on water pollution, the most important of which is the Safe Drinking Water Act of 1974, 42 U.S.C. §1401 et seq.; and the Marine Protection, Research and Sanctuaries Act of 1972 (popularly known as the Ocean Dumping Act), 33 U.S.C. §1401 et seq.

during the 1960s to prohibit almost all forms of water pollution discharges. See *United States v. Standard Oil Co.*, 384 U.S. 224 (1966).

1.   CONTROLS ON INDUSTRIAL POINT SOURCES

The 1972 amendments to the Act maintained the basic structure of state-set ambient standards and implementation plans established in 1967. On top of that structure was superimposed a system (adapted from the federal program governing the use of navigable waters under the Rivers and Harbors Act) of nationally uniform technology-based effluent limitations established by the federal EPA for major "point sources" of water pollution, with specific time deadlines for compliance. Congress' stated goals were to eliminate the discharge of pollutants into navigable waters by 1985, and by 1983 to achieve "wherever attainable, an interim goal of water quality which provides for the protection and propagation of fish, shellfish, and wildlife and provides for recreation in and on the water." CWA §101(a)(1),(2). These goals are still found in the Act, but they are long past attainment.

The NPDES Permit Requirement for Point Sources. Section 301(a),(b) of the CWA prohibits discharges from "point sources" of water pollution into "waters of the United States" without a National Pollution Discharge Elimination System (NPDES) permit issued pursuant to §402 of the Act. The permit requirement is fundamental to the CWA. Permits are to incorporate all applicable effluent limitation requirements and to serve as the reference point for compliance monitoring and enforcement.[3] Permits are issued for five years, subject to renewal. NPDES permits are only required for discharges into "waters of the United States," a term that has been expansively interpreted to go far beyond the traditional conception of navigable waters subject to federal jurisdiction.

The CWA defines a "point source" that must have an NPDES permit as "any discernible, confined and discrete conveyance, including

---

3. One important issue that has received little judicial attention is the extent of the protection afforded by a permit from the Act's otherwise applicable prohibition of any pollution discharge. Does a permit that is silent on the question cover only those pollutants specifically listed in a permit application, or does it cover other pollutants that are discharged but not specifically listed? A practical problem is presented by the cost and technical difficulty of identifying all of the pollutants in a waste stream, some of which may be present only in trace concentrations or occur rarely. EPA regulations require that applications only list these pollutants contained on an EPA list. But a pollutant not on EPA's list might be significant in particular circumstances. Can the permitting authority issue a permit that authorizes the discharge of unlisted pollutants? A permit that is specifically limited to listed pollutants?

but not limited to any pipe, ditch, channel, tunnel, conduit, well, discrete fissure, container, rolling stock, concentrated animal feeding operation, or vessel or other floating craft from which pollutants are or may be discharged." The statute specifically excludes agricultural stormwater discharges and return flows from irrigated agriculture from the definition. §502(14). A "non-point source" is any source that is not a point source. Non-point sources include diffuse runoff from, for example, agricultural or forestry operations, parking lots, and industrial and commercial sites.

There has been substantial litigation over what constitutes a "point source." Early in the implementation of the Act, EPA by regulation sought to ease its administrative and political burdens by exempting from the permit difficult-to-control point sources (such as toilets in pleasure boats) and most discharges from agricultural and silvicultural operations even though they otherwise meet the definition of a point source. These regulations were judicially invalidated, *NRDC v. Costle,* 568 F.2d 1369 (D.C. Cir. 1977), adding as many as 100,000 sources to EPA's regulatory inventory of point sources.[4] In other circumstances, courts have often deferred to EPA, both when it has adopted an expansive definition of "point source," see *United States v. Earth Sciences, Inc.,* 599 F.2d 368 (10th Cir. 1979) (pond filled with ore processing wastes that overflows into adjacent creek during heavy spring runoff is a "point source"), and when it adopts a more restrictive approach, see *National Wildlife Federation v. Gorsuch,* 693 F.2d 156 (D.C. Cir. 1982) (dams that release water from the bottom of the reservoir that is colder, less oxygenated and contains more sediment than surface waters are not "point sources"). Suppose that a laboratory worker pours contaminated human blood out of test tubes into a river. May he be prosecuted for discharging pollution without a permit?

The CWA provides that the administration of the NPDES permit program may be delegated by EPA to the states. §402(b). Today, almost three-fourths of the states administer NPDES programs.

Technology-Based Effluent Limitations for Existing Industrial Point Sources. Section 301 of the CWA, as enacted in 1972, required that all NPDES permits for existing industrial point sources include technology-based effluent (emission) limitations established in accordance with "effluent guidelines" to be issued by EPA pursuant to §304. Under §301(b)(1)(A), all industrial point sources were initially required by 1977 to meet effluent limitations requiring "application of the best practicable control technology currently available as defined by the Administrator pursuant to Section 304(b)" (BPT). Section 301(b)(2)(A)

---

4. EPA has successfully sought to deal with the increased administrative burdens resulting from this decision with the use of area permits that include many individual discharges and other economizing administrative techniques.

required that, by 1983, industrial point sources must achieve effluent limitations that "shall require application of the best available technology economically achievable for such category or class [of source], which will result in reasonable further progress toward the national goal of eliminating the discharge of all pollutants, as determined by the Administrator pursuant to Section 304(b)(2). . ." (BAT).

The statute leaves obscure the precise relation between the specific effluent limitations contemplated by §301, which specify numerical limits on pollutants discharged from particular point sources and must be incorporated in NPDES permits, and the "guidelines" issued by EPA pursuant to §304. The CWA also does not specify the extent of geographical uniformity required in the §301 effluent limitations. The Supreme Court, however, sustained the EPA's claim of authority to issue binding, nationally uniform "single number" regulations specifying the degree of water pollution control that must be achieved by every source in an EPA-defined industrial category. *E. I. DuPont de Nemours & Co. v. Train,* 430 U.S. 112 (1977), p. 466, infra. Accordingly, EPA-promulgated BPT and BAT effluent limitations must generally be met by all sources in the category to which they apply, regardless of an individual source's age, economic position, the ambient quality of the water into which it discharges, or other variables.[5]

Effluent Limitations for New Industrial Sources. Section 306 of the CWA requires that new industrial point sources of pollution utilize controls that "reflect the greatest degree of effluent reductions which the Administrator determines to be achievable through application of the best available demonstrated control technology, processes, operating methods, or other alternatives. . . ." These new source performance standards (NSPS) are generally more stringent than the BPT or BAT technology-based effluent limitations for existing sources. Under §306(d), new sources that comply with NSPS are exempt for 10 years from more stringent controls. This exemption does not, however, apply to more stringent controls based on the need to achieve state water

---

5. However, §301(c) provides for relaxation of the 1983 BAT limitations for individual sources that establish that some lesser degree of control "will represent the maximum use of technology within the economic capability of the owner or operator and . . . will represent reasonable further progress toward the elimination of the discharge of pollutants."

In addition, EPA regulations implementing the 1977 BPT limitations provided for a waiver for an individual source that can show that the factors relevant to control at that source are fundamentally different in kind from those considered by EPA in establishing industry-wide guidelines. The Supreme Court in *DuPont* sustained EPA's power to issue industry-wide limitations on the express understanding that some allowance would be made for variations in individual plants. This "fundamentally different factor" variance was subsequently codified in the Act and extended to all effluent limitations for existing sources. See infra, p. 497.

quality standards, or on technology-based controls for toxic pollutants. See *NRDC v. EPA*, 822 F.2d 104 (D.C. Cir. 1987).

Effluent Limitations For Toxic Discharges from Industrial Point Sources. The 1972 Amendments added to §307 the Act, directing the Administrator to establish effluent limitations for "toxic" pollutants based upon the "toxicity of the pollutant, its persistence, degradability," and relevant biological factors respecting the receiving environment.[6] The cost of control was not mentioned as a relevant factor. As in the case of the similar provisions in §112 of the Clean Air Act as it existed prior to the 1990 Amendments, EPA experienced enormous difficulty in implementing a system of effluent limitations that were supposed to be based on the health effects of toxic pollutants, apparently without consideration of cost; as a result, few controls on toxic pollutants were adopted.[7] NRDC brought "citizen suit" litigation against EPA, challenging its failure to initiate legal action to control toxics. A settlement of the litigation through a consent decree required EPA to promulgate technology-based effluent limitations for a large number of specific toxic substances. *NRDC v. Train*, 8 ERC 2120 (D.D.C. 1976). This consent decree — which has come to be known as the "Flannery Decree," named for the judge who decided the case — in effect mandated EPA adoption of a far-reaching new regulatory program along lines not found in the CWA. It represents a striking example of how environmental group litigation can be used to prod regulatory agencies into taking action.[8]

The 1977 Amendments. The 1977 Amendments made important changes in the system of effluent limitations for existing sources. It distinguished three categories of pollutants: toxic pollutants, "conventional" pollutants (suspended solids, fecal coliform bacteria, pH, and oxygen-demanding organic matter), and all other pollutants, termed "nonconventional" (such as waste oil).

Discharges of *conventional* pollutants were to be controlled by "best conventional pollution control technology" (BCT) by 1984. There was no provision for extensions or waivers of this requirement. BCT was understood as a level of control somewhat more stringent than BPT. The BCT provision was adopted because a National Commission on

---

6. Section 307 appears to contemplate geographically uniform effluent limitations, yet the criteria for establishing such limitations are based on the ambient effects of the pollutants subject to control. Are these two aspects of the statute consistent? Compare §112 of the Clean Air Act prior to the 1990 Amendments. See supra, p. 327.

7. See Hall, The Control of Toxic Pollutants Under the Federal Water Pollution Control Act Amendments of 1972, 63 Iowa L. Rev. 609 (1978).

8. Compare NRDC's later litigation strategy under §112 of the Clean Air Act, which in effect sought to require EPA to adopt zero emission standards. See supra, p 331.

Water Quality study had concluded that the costs of BAT control of conventional pollutants would exceed the benefits. BCT thus represents in effect a relaxation of the BAT requirements that would otherwise apply to "conventional" pollutants.

Discharges of *nonconventional* pollutants (that is, all pollutants other than conventional pollutants and toxic pollutants) remained subject to BAT. The deadline for BAT compliance, however, was postponed to July 1, 1987, with provisions for further extensions for innovative technologies. BAT limitations for nonconventional pollutants might be modified on a case by case basis on a showing of technological infeasibility or a showing that control to BAT levels was not necessary to meet applicable water quality standards.

Discharges of *toxic* pollutants were to be controlled by application of BAT by July 1, 1984, for a specific list of 129 toxic chemicals; for toxic pollutants not on the original list, but subsequently designated by EPA, the deadline was three years after adoption by EPA of limitations for such pollutants but no later than July 1, 1987, with extensions of up to three years for innovative technologies. There was no provision for waivers or variances. This provision in effect codified the technology-based approach for dealing with specific toxics that had been adopted in the Flannery Decree.

The 1987 Amendments. The 1987 Amendments made three important changes in the effluent limitations system for industrial point sources. First, the deadline for attaining conventional and toxic limitations was postponed to "no later than March 31, 1989." Where such deadlines cannot be met because of EPA delay in issuing categorical effluent limitations, EPA may issue administrative orders to specify the degree of control required of a particular source. Second, sources using "innovative production processes" or "innovative control techniques" that have the potential for attaining better effluent levels or attaining existing requirements more cheaply can obtain an additional two years to comply "if it is also determined that such innovative system has the potential for industry-wide application." §301(k). Third, a new "anti-backsliding" provision limits the ability of a source to obtain a new permit with less stringent requirements than its old permit when subsequently issued effluent limitations are less stringent than those contained in the old permit. §406(o).

2.   CONTROLS ON MUNICIPAL WASTE TREATMENT PLANTS

Under the 1972 Amendments, municipal sources of water pollution resulting from waste treatment must achieve "secondary treatment" by 1977 and by 1983 must utilize "best practicable waste treatment" technology over the life of the works. Municipal sewage treatment plants are known as publicly owned treatment works, or POTWs. Title II of the Act created a vast program of federal grants to finance 75 percent of the cost of construction of publicly owned treatment works in order to meet the federal secondary treatment requirements. For the fiscal years 1973-1975 alone some $18 billion in expenditures was directed, and a total of over $50 billion has been spent over the life of the construction grant program. The 1977 Amendments authorized postponements of up to 6 years in the original 1977 secondary treatment deadline for POTWs in cases where federal funding delays or construction difficulties delayed compliance. In 1981, Congress authorized further extensions of the deadline for secondary treatment to 1988, relaxed the definition of secondary treatment, and repealed entirely the second-stage requirement of "best practicable waste treatment technology."

In 1987, Congress provided for a phase-out of the construction grants program, and in its place provided start-up funding for a revolving $20 billion fund for low-interest loans to municipal and local governments for water pollution control programs. The funds can be used to deal with water pollution problems attributable to storm sewer systems and non-point sources as well as to publicly owned treatment works. Storm sewers that are separate from sanitary sewers can cause significant discharges of pollutants into water bodies. The 1987 CWA Amendments directs EPA to institute a phased system of controls on storm sewers. §402(p). When storm sewers are combined with sanitary sewers, as is often the case in older cities, heavy rains can result in massive flows that exceed POTW capacities, resulting in discharges of both storm runoff and untreated raw sewage into water bodies. Congress has not addressed this costly problem, although EPA is struggling to address it by administrative means.

In order to ensure that the comparatively less stringent federal effluent limitations applicable to POTWs and the federal subsidy of POTW facilities do not provide an unfair competitive advantage to those industrial sources that discharge (via municipal sewers or otherwise) into a POTW ("indirect dischargers"), §307 requires industry pretreatment of such discharges to eliminate toxics or other substances that could harm the municipal treatment process or that might not be adequately treated. In addition, indirect dischargers must assume an appropriate share of POTW waste treatment costs.[9] In 1977 Congress added §307(h)(1) to the Act, authorizing POTWs to give "credit" to indirect dischargers for the pollution in such discharges that is treated

---

9. For a comprehensive review of the pretreatment provisions and their implementation, see Gold, EPA's Pretreatment Program, 16 B.C. Envtl. Aff. L. Rev. 459 (1989).

by the POTW. Indirect dischargers can apply such credits to the BPT
or BAT effluent limitation reductions otherwise required of all sources
in a given industrial category. This removal credit provision has, predictably, given rise to litigation over the extent and terms of the credit.
See *NRDC v. EPA,* 790 F.2d 289 (3d Cir. 1986), *cert. denied,* 479 U.S.
1084 (1987), and prior litigation discussed therein.

3.   WATER QUALITY-BASED EFFLUENT LIMITATIONS

The principal emphasis in the implementation of the 1972
FWPCA Amendments has been adoption and enforcement of nationally uniform federal technology-based effluent limitations established
without regard to water quality objectives at any given location. Nonetheless, the ambient water quality standards established by the states
and approved by the federal government pursuant to the 1965 Amendments continue in force. States have the responsibility to designate the
uses — such as public water supplies, swimming, recreation, propagation of fish and wildlife, agriculture, industrial — of navigable waters
within their boundaries and to establish ambient water quality standards (called "criteria") designed to protect such uses. States must review designated water body uses and criteria every three years and
submit the criteria for EPA review. CWA §303.

As with the SIP approval process of the Clean Air Act, EPA reviews
the adequacy of proposed state criteria to protect the designated water
uses. If EPA determines that the proposed designations or criteria are
inconsistent with the applicable requirements of the Clean Water Act,
EPA must propose changes necessary to meet the requirements of the
Act. If the state fails to adopt such changes within 90 days, EPA must
promulgate criteria. CWA §303. EPA has by regulation forbidden states
from lowering water quality standards in waters of exceptional recreational or ecological significance ("Outstanding National Resource Waters") and erected a presumption against lowering standards in other
waters. 40 C.F.R. §131.12. The implementation of these nondegradation policies, however, is left largely to the states.

Under CWA §§301(b)(1)(C) and 303(d), NPDES permits must
ensure compliance with applicable state water quality standards. If the
technology-based effluent limitations incorporated in NPDES permits
are not adequate to ensure such compliance, the permits must contain
the additional limitations required. These water-quality based effluent
limitations are established through a process analogous to the SIP process for ensuring achievement of the national ambient air quality standards. If a water quality standard, expressed in terms of permissible
concentrations of a pollutant anywhere in a water body, is exceeded,
state regulators are supposed to calculate the extent of effluent reduc-

tion from point sources discharging into the water body that is needed in order to achieve the standard and then allocate the burden of achieving the necessary reductions among the responsible sources.

The requirement that NPDES permits ensure attainment of state water quality standards has assumed major significance because the federal effluent limitations will fall short of achieving ambient criteria in a large percentage of the 3100 water quality zones established by the states. These noncomplying zones are termed "water quality limited segments." In the 1987 Amendments, Congress was particularly concerned about failures to establish or meet adequate ambient standards for toxic pollutants. It required states to develop numeric water quality standards for toxics and adopt source by source individual toxic control strategies to deal with toxic "hot spot" problems that persist despite compliance with national technology-based toxic effluent limitations. §304(*l*).[10]

If the national technology-based effluent limitations are more stringent than necessary to meet ambient standards or goals at a given site, the Act generally requires that sources at that site adhere to such limitations. Critics have attacked this feature of the Act as "control for control's sake." Congress has, however, provided that in certain circumstances sources may not be required to meet technology-based limitations if they can establish that a lesser degree of control will maintain water quality. It has adopted variance provisions for thermal pollution from electric generating plants and industrial facilities (§316); discharges of nonconventional pollutants (§301(g)); deep ocean discharges by POTWs (§301(h)); and deep ocean discharges by certain industrial sources (§403).[11] Also, §302(b)(2)(B) provides for relaxation

---

10. An additional possible source of water quality-related effluent limitations is found in §302, which requires EPA to impose additional point source controls beyond the federal "best available technology" limitations if needed to contribute to the achievement or maintenance of the Act's goal of swimmable and fishable water everywhere by 1983. In establishing additional water quality-related effluent limitations under §302, however, Congress directed EPA to hold public hearings to consider the relationship of the "economic and social costs" of such limitations (including economic and social dislocations in affected communities) to the "social and economic benefits to be obtained," and also to determine whether the additional limitations can be achieved with "available technology or other alternate control strategies." If a source demonstrates that there is "no reasonable relationship" between the social costs and benefits resulting from such additional limitations, the EPA must modify them accordingly. There has, however, been no substantial implementation by EPA of §302. Why not? Why hasn't Congress taken steps to force such implementation?

11. For example, §316(a) provides an exception to technology-based standards for thermal pollution (heat discharges from utility or industrial cooling systems for steam-fired generators or boilers) if a source can carry the burden of showing that federal thermal effluent limitations are "more stringent

of controls needed to achieve state water quality standards when they exceed the economic capability of a given source.

4. NON-POINT SOURCES AND GROUNDWATER

The federal system of effluent limitations and permits is directed at point sources discharging into oceans, lakes, rivers, and streams through discharge pipes or similar discrete conveyances. However, experience has shown that today roughly one-half of water pollution problems is attributable to non-point sources, such as runoff from agricultural, mining, and forestry activities, and intrusion of salt water into the ground water of coastal areas as a result of excessive extraction of fresh groundwater supplies. Section 208 seeks to deal with non-point pollution through federal encouragement of local water quality planning by regional authorities within each state. EPA has given comparatively little attention to the non-point source problem until quite recently, and non-point sources are likely to represent a serious obstacle to achievement of state and federal water quality objectives. Environmental groups have sought to require federal and state officials to impose controls on non-point sources. See, e.g., *NRDC v. Costle*, 564 F.2d 573 (D.C. Cir. 1977). The courts have ruled, however, that Congress gave EPA discretion to address non-point pollution through a combination of research and cooperative planning rather than through federal regulatory requirements. See *Sierra Club v. Abston Constr. Co.*, 10 ERC 1416 (N.D. Ala. 1977).

Groundwater pollution raises related concerns. The Clean Water Act does not establish ambient groundwater standards or systematic controls on sources of groundwater pollution. Point sources of groundwater pollution, however, are subject to CWA effluent limitations. Moreover, §502 of the Act mandates federal control of deep-well injection of wastes into the ground, subject to a significant exception for oil and gas production.[12] Groundwater pollution is addressed in part by the Resource Conservation and Recovery Act (RCRA) and the Com-

---

than necessary to assure the protection and propagation of a balanced, indigenous population of shellfish, fish, and wildlife in and on the body of water into which the discharge is to be made."

12. EPA programs to control surface discharges of pollution may indirectly generate groundwater problems. An example is EPA's proposed funding of a massive system of collection sewers, treatment centers, and ocean discharges for domestic wastes in central and eastern Long Island; the net effect of the system would be to discharge into the ocean the groundwater utilized for domestic water supply in the area, lowering the fresh water table, generating salt water intrusion, and necessitating eventual importation from elsewhere of fresh water supplies. See Tripp, Tensions and Conflicts in Federal Pollution Control and Water Resource Policy, 14 Harv. J. Legis. 225, 251 & n.88 (1977).

prehensive Environmental Response, Clean-up, and Liability Act (CERCLA), covered in Chapter 6.

5.   ENFORCEMENT AND ADMINISTRATION

Section 309 of the CWA, paralleling the enforcement provisions in §113 of the Clean Air Act, grants EPA authority to issue administrative orders to enforce federal effluent limitations and permit requirements or to seek injunctive relief in court. It also authorizes criminal fines and imprisonment for violation of such requirements. In addition, the CWA authorizes court-imposed civil penalties of up to $10,000 per day for violations of EPA enforcement orders, federal effluent limitations, or permit requirements. EPA possesses emergency powers to enjoin pollution that presents an "imminent and substantial endangerment" to public health or welfare. §504.

The Act authorizes EPA to delegate issuance and enforcement of NPDES permits to states whose regulatory programs and procedures conform to requirements specified by EPA regulations. As noted above, approximately three-quarters of the states have received such delegations. EPA may, however, veto a permit issued by a state exercising delegated federal authority if it fails to incorporate applicable national effluent limitations, ensure achievement of applicable water quality-standards, or otherwise meet federal requirements. EPA's refusal to veto state permits is generally not itself subject to judicial review. EPA vetos, on the other hand, are subject to federal court review and have been successfully challenged on the ground that the state-issued permit did not violate federal law. See *Ford Motor Co. v. EPA*, 567 F.2d 661 (1977). EPA also retains backup enforcement authority to redress permit violations. EPA review of state permits and its specification of the requirements for delegated programs have been a continuing source of federal-state friction. Other areas of tension include federal review of state water quality standards and EPA efforts to address non-point sources of water pollution. As in the Clean Air Act, states generally retain authority to impose requirements more stringent than those required by federal law. CWA §510.

6.   WETLANDS

Section 404 of the Act authorizes the Army Corps of Engineers to issue permits allowing the discharge of dredged or fill materials into "waters of the United States." EPA has authority to review and object to permit grants. CWA §404(c). This regulatory authority has been used to control the dredging and filling of wetlands for agriculture or residential, commercial, and industrial development. There has been increasing recognition of the ecological importance of wetlands as wildlife habitat, water filters, and a protection against flooding. Efforts to deal with the rapid loss of wetlands to agricultural, commercial and residential development has, however, encountered sharp opposition from agricultural and development interests. Among the more controversial issues are what constitutes a "wetland." EPA and the Corps of Engineers jointly issued in 1989 a handbook with an expansive definition of wetlands, under which an area might qualify as a wetland if it were wet for only a few days a year, or had wetlands-type vegetation. Development interests have unsuccessfully pushed for its amendment. Another controversial issue is whether the "waters of the United States" that are subject to permit jurisdiction include isolated potholes or other wet areas that are not hydrologically connected to streams, rivers, lakes or oceans but may be used by migratory birds. *Hoffman Homes Inc. v. EPA,* 961 F.2d 1310 (7th Cir. 1992), held that such isolated waters are not covered by, and therefore are not protected by, the Act. A further controversial issue is whether denial of a permit to fill wetlands constitutes a "taking" of property for which the government must pay compensation under the Fifth or Fourteenth Amendments to the Constitution. Cf. *Lucas v. South Carolina Coastal Council,* 112 S. Ct. 2886 (1992), discussed in Chapter 9.

In 1993 the Clinton Administration announced a wetlands program policy initiative with an "interim" goal of "no-net loss" of wetlands and a long-term goal of enhancing the quantity and quality of wetlands. The proposal seeks to deal with the controversial issue of wetlands determinations in agricultural areas by giving jurisdiction over the issue to the Agriculture Department. It also reversed a Bush Administration policy that exempted conversion of wetlands in Alaska (whose wetlands cover a vast percentage of the state) so long as the total amount converted did not exceed 1 percent of all wetlands in the state. The Clinton program also proposes to establish a wetlands mitigation bank, under which development in wetlands could be permitted in certain circumstances if the permittee undertook offsetting reconversion or protection of other wetlands.

7.   DRINKING WATER

Drinking water quality is regulated under the Safe Drinking Water Act, 42 U.S.C. §§300i et seq. Requirements are applicable to "public water systems" containing at least 15 service connections or regularly serving at least 25 individuals at least 60 days per year. EPA must promulgate, for various pollutants, "maximum contaminant level goals" (MCLGs) at levels at which "no known or anticipated adverse effects in the health of persons occur and which allows an adequate margin of safety." EPA must then establish legally enforceable "maximum contamination levels" for these pollutants. MCLs are to be set as close to MCLGs as "feasible," defined as "use of the best technology, treatment techniques, and other means, which the Administrator finds are generally available, taking into consideration the costs of achievement."

8.   OIL SPILLS

Section 311 of the Act prohibits spills of oil and other hazardous substances into waters of the United States, including the exclusive economic zone, which consists of ocean waters extending 200 miles from the coast. EPA and the Coast Guard have established plans and procedures, in cooperation with affected states, for removal and cleanup of spills. Owners and operators of vessels and onshore or offshore facilities that spill oil or hazardous substances are liable, subject to very limited defenses, to the government for the costs of cleanup and for damages to publicly owned natural resources. After the 1989 Exxon Valdez spill in Prince William Sound, Alaska, Congress passed the Oil Pollution Act of 1990, strengthening the Clean Water Act's oil spill provisions by, among other matters, imposing higher limits on liability and requiring insurance or other evidence of financial responsibility by all vessels. The Act also affirmed the right of states to establish additional systems of cleanup and liability, even if inconsistent with proposed international conventions to deal with oil spills. Exxon eventually pled guilty to two criminal offenses in connection with the Exxon Valdez spill and agreed to pay the United States and Alaska $1 billion to reimburse the costs of damage assessment studies and response actions by the governments and to restore or replace the natural resources damaged by the spill. See infra, pp. 1201-1209, for further discussion of the Exxon Valdez case.

NOTES AND QUESTIONS

1. Do the Act's basic goals of "fishable, swimmable" water everywhere in the nation and "zero discharge" make any sense? Economically? Ecologically? Morally? Politically? Consider the following perspective:

> Not only is such a goal impractical, it is inherently undesirable. Since no production activity is 100 percent efficient in the engineering sense, every such activity must generate some minimal quantity of waste, and that waste must be disposed of somewhere, somehow — if not into our waters, then into the earth or atmosphere. Even human existence creates wastes

which constitute a problem of public sanitation. The fact is that zero pollution implies not only zero economic growth, but zero production and zero population!

The design of an effective environmental policy is, by its very nature, a search for the best compromise. The more resources we use to clean up the air and water, the fewer will be available to fight poverty and disease. This is the true social cost of overzealous environmental policy.

W. Baumol & W. Oates, Economics, Environmental Policy, and the Quality of Life 211-212 (1979).

Why doesn't the CWA require that point source discharge limitations be set in order to achieve the goals of making all water fishable and swimmable, on the model of SIP limitations under the Clean Air Act?

2. Effluent controls under the CWA have largely been driven by the nationally uniform technology-based limitations established by EPA for different categories of industrial point services. Does reliance on uniform technology-based controls make more sense in regulation of water pollution than air pollution? Less sense? What considerations of federalism justify or explain the approach taken in the CWA? See *supra* pp. 244-248.

3. The basic aim of CWA is to push the nation towards extremely ambitious clean water goals through a "technology-forcing" strategy of steadily more stringent national effluent limitations for all point sources. However, the technology-forcing aspect of water pollution control is different in important respects from that for air pollution controls. In many instances, workable air pollution control technology to eliminate emissions from sources such as internal combustion engine automobiles or coal-fired power plants is not available in a purely engineering sense. By contrast, engineering *is* presently available to turn all point sources discharges of water pollution into distilled drinking water, achieving the FWPCA's stated goal of zero discharge. However, the costs of installing the requisite engineering would be enormous — trillions of dollars. In the absence of controlling federal ambient standards or engineering constraints, EPA must somehow weigh the costs and benefits of different levels of control in establishing effluent limitations. However, the statute provides no clear guidance as to how the ultimate balance should be struck.

In these circumstances, one potential objective of the CWA would be to provide incentives for the development of new technologies that would reduce water pollution discharges at less cost than present technology. What incentives does the CWA provide for development of lower-cost-control technology? How successful are they likely to be? Compare the CWA in this respect to the various approaches to "technology forcing" in the Clean Air Act, pp. 244-248 supra. For discussion, see La Pierre, Technology-Forcing and Federal Environmental Statutes, 62 Iowa L. Rev. 771 (1977).

C. TECHNOLOGY-BASED APPROACHES IN THE CLEAN WATER ACT

1. EPA's AUTHORITY TO ISSUE UNIFORM CATEGORICAL EFFLUENT LIMITATIONS

E. I. DUPONT DE NEMOURS & CO. V. TRAIN

430 U.S. 112 (1977)

[Eight chemical companies challenged EPA's adoption by regulation of nationally uniform BPT, BAT, and new source effluent limitations for discharges of inorganic chemicals for various categories of chemical plants.]

Mr. Justice STEVENS delivered the opinion of the Court. . . .

EPA began [the process of promulgating effluent limitations pursuant to §301] by engaging a private contractor to prepare a Development Document. This document provided a detailed technical study of pollution control in the [chemical] industry. The study first divided the industry into categories. For each category, present levels of pollution were measured and plants with exemplary pollution control were investigated. Based on this information, other technical data, and economic studies, a determination was made of the degree of pollution control which could be achieved by the various levels of technology mandated by the statute. The study was made available to the public and circulated to interested persons. It formed the basis of "effluent limitation guideline" regulations issued by EPA after receiving public comment on proposed regulations. These regulations divide the industry into 22 subcategories. Within each subcategory, precise numerical limits are set for various pollutants. The regulations for each subcategory contain a variance clause, applicable only to the 1977 limitations.[13] . . .

---

13. [The regulations provide that in individual NPDES permit determinations for particular sources the limitations adopted in the regulations] may be made "either more or less stringent" to the extent that "factors relating to the equipment or facilities involved, the process applied, or other such factors related to such discharges are fundamentally different from the factors considered" in establishing the limitations. . . .

THE ISSUES

The broad outlines of the parties' respective theories may be stated briefly. EPA contends that §301(b) authorizes it to issue regulations establishing effluent limitations for classes of plants. The [NPDES] permits granted under §402, in EPA's view simply incorporate these across-the-board limitations, except for the limited variances allowed by the regulations themselves and by §301(c) [which authorizes EPA to grant variances from 1983 BAT limitations to a particular source and to establish a less stringent limitation for that source on a showing that the modified requirements "(1) will represent the maximum use of technology within the economic capability of the owner or operator; and (2) will result in reasonable further progress toward the elimination of the discharge of pollutants."]. The §304(b) guidelines, according to EPA, were intended to guide it in later establishing §301 effluent-limitation regulations. Because the process proved more time consuming than Congress assumed when it established this two-stage process, EPA condensed the two stages into a single regulation.

In contrast, petitioners contend that §301 is not an independent source of authority for setting effluent limitations by regulation. Instead, §301 is seen as merely a description of the effluent limitations which are set for each plant on an individual basis during the permit-issuance process. Under the industry view, the §304 guidelines serve the function of guiding the permit issuer in setting the effluent limitations [but do not mandate or authorize EPA to impose a uniform "single number" requirement on all sources in a given industry category.].

I

We think §301 itself is the key to the problem. The statutory language concerning the 1983 [BAT] limitations, in particular, leaves no doubt that these limitations are to be set by regulation. Subsection (b)(2)(A) of §301 states that by 1983 "effluent limitations for *categories and classes* of point sources" are to be achieved which will require "application of the best available technology economically achievable *for such category or class.*" (Emphasis added.) These effluent limitations are to require elimination of all discharges if "such elimination is technologically and economically achievable for a *category or class* of point sources." (Emphasis added.) This is "language difficult to reconcile with the view that individual effluent limitations are to be set when a permit is issued." *American Meat Institute v. EPA,* 526 F.2d 442, 450 (CA7 1975). The statute thus focuses expressly on the characteristics of the "category

mally, such classwide determinations would be made by regulation, not in the course of issuing a permit to one member of the class.[14]

Thus, we find that §301 unambiguously provides for the use of regulations to establish the 1983 effluent limitations. Different language is used in §301 with respect to the 1977 [BPT] limitations. Here, the statute speaks of "effluent limitations for point sources," rather than "effluent limitations for categories and classes of point sources." Nothing elsewhere in the Act, however, suggests any radical difference in the mechanism used to impose limitations for the 1977 and 1983 deadlines. . . . We conclude that the statute authorizes the 1977 limitations as well as the 1983 limitations to be set by regulation, so long as some allowance is made for variation in individual plants, as EPA has done by including a variance clause in its 1977 limitations.[15]

The legislative history supports this reading of §301. . . . The Conference Report on §301 states that "the determination of the economic impact of an effluent limitation [will be made] on the basis of classes and categories of point sources, as distinguished from a plant by plant determination." Sen. Conf. Rep. No. 92-1236, p. 121 (1972), Leg. Hist. 304. In presenting the Conference Report to the Senate, Senator Muskie, perhaps the Act's primary author, emphasized the importance of uniformity in setting §301 limitations. He explained that this goal of uniformity required that EPA focus on classes or categories of sources in formulating effluent limitations. Regarding the requirement contained in §301 that plants use the "best practicable control technology" by 1977, he stated:

> The modification of subsection 304(b)(1) is intended to clarify what is meant by the term "practicable." The balancing test between total cost and effluent reduction benefits is intended to limit the application of technology only where the additional degree of effluent reduction is wholly out of proportion to the costs of achieving such marginal level of reduction for *any class or category* of sources.

---

14. Furthermore, §301(c) provides that the 1983 limitations may be modified if the owner of a plant shows that "such modified requirements (1) will represent the maximum use of technology within the economic capability of the owner or operator; and (2) will result in reasonable further progress toward the elimination of the discharge of pollutants." This provision shows that the §301(b) limitations for 1983 are to be established prior to consideration of the characteristics of the individual plant. *American Iron & Steel Institute v. EPA,* supra, at 1037 n.15. Moreover, it shows that the term "best technology economically achievable" does not refer to any individual plant. Otherwise it would be impossible for this "economically achievable" technology to be beyond the individual owner's "economic capability."

15. We agree with the Court of Appeals . . . that consideration of whether EPA's variance provision has the proper scope would be premature.

The Conferees agreed upon this limited cost-benefit analysis in order to maintain *uniformity within a class and category* of point sources subject to effluent limitations, and to avoid imposing on the Administrator any requirement to consider the location of sources within a category or to ascertain water quality impact of effluent controls, or to determine the economic impact of controls on any individual plant in a single community.

118 Cong. Rec. 33696 (1972), Leg. Hist. 170 (emphasis added). He added that:

The Conferees intend that the factors described in section 304(b) be considered only within classes or categories of point sources and that such factors not be considered at the time of the application of an effluent limitation to an individual point source within such a category or class.

118 Cong. Rec. 33697 (1972), Leg. Hist. 172.

This legislative history supports our reading of §301 and makes it clear that the §304 guidelines are not merely aimed at guiding the discretion of permit issuers in setting limitations for individual plants.

What, then, is the function of the §304(b) guidelines? As we noted earlier, §304 requires EPA to identify the amount of effluent reduction attainable through use of the best practicable or available technology and to "specify factors to be taken into account" in determining the pollution control methods "to be applicable to point sources . . . within such categories or classes." These guidelines are to be issued "[f]or the purpose of adopting or revising effluent limitations under this Act." As we read it, §304 requires that the guidelines survey the practicable or available pollution-control technology for an industry and assess its effectiveness. The guidelines are then to describe the methodology EPA intends to use in the §301 regulations to determine the effluent limitations for particular plants. . . .

. . . The petitioner's view of the Act would place an impossible burden on EPA. It would require EPA to give individual consideration to the circumstances of each of the more than 42,000 dischargers who have applied for permits, Brief for Respondents in No. 75-978, p.30 n.22, and to issue or approve all these permits well in advance of the 1977 deadline in order to give industry time to install the necessary pollution-control equipment. We do not believe that Congress would have failed so conspicuously to provide EPA with the authority needed to achieve the statutory goals. . . .

NOTES AND QUESTIONS

1. Must the Act be read to require uniform "single number" emission limitations for categories of industrial point sources, regardless of variations in the costs of control among sources or in the extent of control required to protect the waters into which they discharge? What mandates in the Act approach this reading? Does it simply give EPA discretion to adopt such an approach? Why would Congress want to mandate uniform requirements for all sources in a given category, regardless of local water quality impacts, cost, and other relevant variables?

Would an interpretation that allowed use of §304 guidelines to establish uniform presumptive limits for source categories, while allowing departures from uniformity on a particularized showing of justification by a particular applicant under §301, represent a better accommodation of need for expedition and administrative efficiency on the one hand and flexibility on the other? Would it represent sounder reading of the Act? For a defense of uniform technology-based controls based on administrative and information-gathering problems, see Latin, Ideal versus Real Regulatory Efficiency: Implementation of Uniform Standards and "Fine Tuning" Regulatory Reforms, 37 Stan. L. Rev. 1267, 1314-1318 (1985). Would setting individually tailored limitations for 42,000 industrial point sources impose an "impossible" administrative burden?

2. As will be discussed shortly, EPA promulgation of effluent limitations involves an elaborate and time consuming rulemaking process. What if a source applies for a permit before effluent limitations have been issued for a relevant pollutant? (Recall that the CWA prohibits discharge of water pollution without a permit.) In that case, §402(a)(1) provides that permits are to be issued subject to "such conditions as the Administrator determines are necessary to carry out the provisions of this Act." In issuing such permits, EPA and states have followed a case by case approach based on "best engineering judgment," although one commentator has found that permit conditions in practice tend to represent the "best deal" that regional EPA officials think they can get in the face of limited time and other resources. See Latin, Regulatory Failure, Administrative Incentives, and the New Clean Air Act, 21 Envtl. L. 1647 (1991).

2. THE PROCESS OF FORMULATING TECHNOLOGY-BASED STANDARDS

In analyzing EPA's development of effluent limitations through rulemaking, one must first distinguish the treatment of new sources and old sources. New sources are subject to the NSPS requirements of §306, which provide for the "greatest degree of effluent reductions . . . achievable through application of the best available demonstrated control technology." This provision and its implementation through rule-making procedures establishing requirements for new sources by industrial categories is similar to the new source performance standards under §111 of the Clean Air Act. The principle of national uniformity in standards has been less controversial in the context of new sources. As is the case under the Clean Air Act, NSPSs pursuant to the CWA have spawned litigation over whether EPA has adequately demonstrated the availability of the technology on which the NSPS are based. See, e.g., *FMC Corp. v. Train,* 539 F.2d 973 (4th Cir. 1976) (overturning the NSPS for the "Plastic and Synthetics Point Source Category"). There are, however, some differences between the new source provisions of the CWA and the Clean Air Act. For example, CWA §306 does not apply to modified sources, which are covered by CWA effluent limitations for existing sources. In addition, §306 directs EPA to consider zero discharge standards for new sources.

Establishing uniform effluent limitations for existing sources presents greater difficulties because such sources display greater variation in control costs, processes, and other circumstances than is the case with new sources. The first stage effluent limitations based on "best practicable technology currently available" (BPT) are generally supposed to reflect "the average performance of the best existing plants" in an industry. *Tanners' Council of America, Inc. v. Train,* 540 F.2d 1188, 1191 (4th Cir. 1976). Standards set at such a level could pose severe hardship for some existing plants, many of them old, that perform less well and face high control costs. The second stage, "best available technology economically achievable" (BAT), is supposed to reflect, at a minimum, the control levels achieved by the best performing plant in an industry category but may reflect control technology used in another industry that can be transferred, or to technologies that are not currently in use at all but can be projected to be available by the time that the BAT deadlines (originally 1983, later postponed by Congress to 1987) are supposed to be met. Such standards could pose even more serious burdens on existing plants with poorer performance. They are applicable to nonconventional pollutants and to toxic pollutants.[16]

In issuing these effluent limitations, EPA must confront two basic sets of questions. First, is technology "available" in an engineering

---

16. Recall that "best conventional technology" limitations for "conventional pollutants" are supposed to be somewhat stricter than BPT (but in practice are frequently the same as BPT), while limitations for new sources are supposed to be stricter than BAT. Thus (in theory), the federal technology-based effluent limitations, in order of ascending stringency, are BPT, BCT, BAT, and NSPS.

sense? Can sources commercially obtain end-of-pipe or other engineering controls or processes that are reliable and will ensure that the standards will be obtained? Second, to what extent must or may the costs and environmental benefits of different levels of controls be taken into account by regulators in setting standards? We consider these two sets of issues in turn.

a.   *The Availability of Technology from an Engineering Perspective*

AMERICAN MEAT INSTITUTE v. EPA

526 F.2d 442 (7th Cir. 1975)

TONE, Circuit Judge.

The regulations before us cover the "Red Meat Processing Segment of the Meat Products Point Source Category." The common characteristic of the plants in this segment of the meat industry is that they all slaughter animals (but not poultry) and produce fresh meat, which may be sold as whole, half, or quarter carcasses, or as smaller meat cuts. Plants that produce only fresh meat are called slaughterhouses; those that also produce cured, smoked, canned, or other prepared meat products are called packinghouses. Both types of plants usually perform some by-product processing, such as rending (separation of fats and water from tissue), blood processing, and hide processing.

EPA employed North Star Research Institute to study the industrial processes used by slaughterhouse and packinghouses, the wastes generated, and the treatment technologies in use or available to these plants, and to recommend, inter alia, effluent limitations under §301(b). North Star proceeded to study relevant literature and information on the meat industry it had previously gathered for EPA. In conjunction with AMI, it prepared questionnaires which were distributed to slaughterhouses and packinghouses. From the responses to the questionnaires and information acquired from various other sources, North Star classified the plants into four subcategories and attempted to identify those in each subcategory having the most effluent control. To verify the questionnaire responses, selected plants from these groups were inspected and monitored to a very limited extent. . . .

After reviewing the North Star report, distributing copies to industry representatives, and receiving their comments, EPA revised the report and published the revision as a Draft Development Document in October 1973. The standards recommended in this document were then incorporated into proposed regulations, which the agency published the same month. . . .

After publication of the proposed regulations, EPA received further comments. On February 28, 1974, it promulgated the final regulations which are the subject of this review proceeding. [The regulations established 1977 BPT effluent guidelines and 1983 BAT effluent guidelines.] In addition, a revised version of the October 1973 Draft Development Document was published under date of February 1974 as the Final Development Document (hereinafter sometimes cited as FDD).

The regulations classify slaughterhouses and packinghouses into the following four subcategories:

(1)   simple slaughterhouses, which slaughter animals and perform a limited number, usually no more than two, of by-product processing operations;

(2)   complex slaughterhouses, which slaughter animals and perform several, usually three or more, by-product processing operations;

(3)   low-processing packinghouses, which not only slaughter animals but process meat from animals killed at that plant into cured, smoked, canned, and other prepared meat products, normally processing less than the total kill; and

(4)   high-processing packinghouses, which not only slaughter animals but process meat from both animals killed at the plant and animals killed elsewhere.

The regulations limit the discharge of "BOD5," "TSS," and ammonia, in addition to other pollutants not involved in this proceeding. Two of these terms require explanation:

BOD5. The initials "BOD" stand for "biochemical oxygen demand" and describe pollutants which, when they decompose, deplete oxygen necessary to support aquatic life. BOD5 is BOD measured over a five-day period.

TSS. The initials "TSS" stand for "total suspended solids," which are particles of organic and inorganic matter suspended in the water or floating on its surface.

The regulations permit the discharge of certain amounts of BOD5 and TSS per 1000 pounds (or per 1000 kilograms) of live weight killed ("LWK"). The 1983 ammonia standard is set in terms of milligrams of ammonia per liter of effluent (9 mg/l), which shows the concentration of ammonia in the effluent. The regulations challenged in this case are the existing source limitations for 1977 and 1983 relating to BOD5 and TSS, and those for 1983 relating to ammonia. . . .

AMI's first challenge is directed at the 1977 effluent limitations, which require application of "the best practicable control technology currently available." For guidance in interpreting that term, EPA looks to Senator Muskie's written explanation to the Senate, . . . in which he stated as follows:

> The Administrator should establish the range of "best practicable" levels based upon the average of the best existing performance by plants of various sizes, ages, and unit processes within each industrial category. In those industrial categories where present practices are uniformly inadequate, the Administrator should interpret "best practicable" to require higher levels of control than any currently in place if he determines that the technology to achieve those higher levels can be practicably applied. . . .

This, we think, is a reasonable view of the Administrator's responsibility. The "best practicable technology" will normally be defined based on the average performance of the best existing plants. If, however, the Administrator concludes that present practices in an industrial category are uniformly inadequate, he may require levels of control based on technology not presently in use in the category (or, it would seem, technology in use only by a single plant), if he determines, by applying the criteria listed in §304(b)(1)(B), that this technology can be practicably applied throughout the category. One of these criteria is the cost of applying the proposed technology in relation to the resulting effluent reduction. With these principles in mind, we turn to AMI's challenges to the 1977 standards.

It appears from EPA comments introducing the final regulation . . . that the 1977 effluent limitations are based primarily on the technology of biological treatment through a three-lagoon system. This is considered "secondary" treatment, that is, treatment which takes place after the waste water has passed through "primary" inplant treatment systems. In a three-lagoon system, waste water from the plant flows first into the anaerobic lagoon, where organic matter in the effluent is partially consumed by anaerobic bacteria (bacteria that do not require free oxygen). To increase oxygen levels in the waste water, it is then mechanically aerated in the aerated lagoon. The water then flows to the aerobic lagoon, where most of the remaining organic matter is consumed by aerobic bacteria (bacteria that do need oxygen). After being held there for a relatively long period, the waste water is discharged.

AMI's first argument, aimed at the 1977 effluent limitations for all four subcategories of plants, is that, while the proposed lagoon system qualifies as practicable, it cannot achieve the limitations on a year-round basis because of seasonal and climatic effects. Winter conditions, according to AMI, impair the efficiency of both anaerobic and aerobic lagoons, while algae growth in the summer increases BOD5 and TSS.

(1) THE EFFECT OF WINTER TEMPERATURES ON THE ANAEROBIC LAGOON

The optimum temperature for an anaerobic lagoon is approximately 90°F. Cold temperatures cause it to function less efficiently by slowing bacterial activity. The issue is the magnitude of this effect. AMI relies on an authority which says that removals are reduced to 70%. It conceded in its submittal to the agency, however, that the effect of winter temperatures on the anaerobic lagoon is small.

EPA argues that winter temperatures are counteracted by the heat of incoming waste water (80-100°F.) and by the insulating grease cover that forms over the pool. An article concerning the Wilson plant at Cherokee, Iowa, reports that the grease cover on the anaerobic pool, after taking some time to build up, insulated the effluent and maintained satisfactory temperatures. The anaerobic pond at that plant operated at a 92 percent level of efficiency in February 1970. EPA's conclusion is also supported by data on other plants supplied by the State of Iowa, which show, for example, that at one plant the anaerobic temperature on two dates in January 1972 was 77-78°F.

We conclude that there is firm record support for EPA's conclusion on the effect of cold weather on the efficiency of the anaerobic lagoon.

(2) THE EFFECT OF WINTER TEMPERATURES ON THE AEROBIC LAGOON

Like anaerobic lagoons, aerobic lagoons operate less efficiently in winter. Cold temperatures inhibit aerobic microorganisms, and ice and snow covers reduce the oxygen content of water. EPA argues that these difficulties can be ameliorated by increasing detention time, thereby giving the microorganisms more time to work, by using additional aerobic ponds, or by using submerged aerators. We agree with AMI that EPA's argument as to these countermeasures is inadequately supported by the record.

The record does suggest, however, that winter conditions do not make compliance with the 1977 standards impossible, since some plants have succeeded in complying with the BOD5 standards in winter. One such plant was the Wilson plant at Cherokee, Iowa, which maintained a 45 percent level of aerobic removal of BOD5 in February. The American Beef plant at Oakland, Iowa, also met the BOD5 limitations during the winter months, as did several other plants. AMI's argument that some of these plants should be disregarded because they did not discharge in some winter months is unsound. As counsel for EPA pointed out during oral argument, a plant which does not discharge during a given period may be continuing its operations while storing its effluent. Our examination of the record confirms that the plants in question continued operations during periods when they did not discharge. The time of release is unimportant, so long as the effluent is successfully treated before release.

(3)   THE EFFECT OF SUMMER WEATHER ON AEROBIC LAGOONS

Warm weather promotes the growth of algae. On the basis of comments in the record by industry representatives, state pollution authorities, and others about the effect of algae on aerobic lagoons, AMI argues that algae growth increases TSS and BOD5 counts. Two of these comments refer in general terms to problems at individual plants without giving detailed supporting data; another comment is heavily qualified and inconclusive; and the others are purely conclusory.

EPA states that the Illinois Beef plant at Genesco, Illinois, and the Swift plant at Glenwood, Iowa, were able to meet the standards during summer months, as was the Routh plant at Sandusky, Ohio. AMI does not respond directly to these assertions, and from our examination of the record we conclude that data from these plants fail to show the correlation between summer weather and TSS predicted by AMI.

With respect to BOD5, EPA cites data from five plants that complied with the 1977 effluent limitations during the summer. AMI does not contest the figures regarding summer performance for two of these plants (Wilson, Cherokee, and Swift, Glenwood) but argues that Illinois Beef and another plant should be disregarded. . . . Nevertheless, the ability of even two plants using the proposed technology to meet the BOD5 and TSS standards in summer demonstrates that the standards are attainable in warm weather and is sufficient to overcome AMI's weakly supported position.

In summary, we find sufficient basis in the record for the Administrator's conclusion that temperature changes do not render the 1977 effluent limitations unattainable by the 1977 technology he designated.

NOTES AND QUESTIONS

1. As *Meat Institute* indicates, much litigation regarding EPA effluent limitations revolves around technological feasibility and whether the plants selected by EPA contractors as models for establishing limitations for all plants in a given industrial category are representative of the category. These and the other issues discussed below are also staples

of litigation challenging technology-based emission limitations issued under the Clean Air Act.

2. A related issue is the extent of the flexibility that EPA may exercise in categorizing and subcategorizing industries and establishing different limitations for different groups. EPA has used this authority in order to establish less stringent limitations for economically marginal plants by, for example, creating a separate subcategory for older plants with older, higher-cost process technologies. This tactic was successfully challenged in *American Iron & Steel Institute v. EPA,* 568 F.2d 284 (3d Cir. 1977). Industry sometimes seeks further or different subcategorization of plants, often unsuccessfully. See, e.g., *Reynolds Metals Co. v. EPA,* 760 F.2d 549 (4th Cir. 1985).

3. Technology-based effluent limitations can be based on in-plant process changes as well as "end of pipe" controls. *American Petroleum Institute v. EPA,* 540 F.2d 1023 (10th Cir. 1976), *cert. denied sub nom. Exxon Corp. v. EPA,* 430 U.S. 922 (1977).

4. The circumstances under which effluent limitations can be based on interindustry transfer of technology often raise complex controversies over arcane engineering and scientific questions. See, e.g., *Kennecott v. EPA,* 780 F.2d 445 (4th Cir. 1985), *cert. denied,* 479 U.S. 814 (1986); *Reynolds Metals Co. v. EPA,* 760 F.2d 549 (4th Cir. 1985) (transferability of technology for oil and grease removal from aluminum forming and coil coating industries to can-making industry). EPA has authority to adopt effluent limitations, even though they cannot be achieved by any technology presently available. Limitations based on EPA predictions that a technology will become commercially available prior to the deadline for compliance are, however, subject to stringent judicial scrutiny. See, e.g., *Hooker Chemicals & Plastics Corp. v. Train,* 537 F.2d 620 (2d Cir. 1976).

5. Another important issue is the extent to which BPT, BCT, or BAT guidelines must make exception for "upsets" (such as temporary equipment failures) or "bypasses" (such as the need to bypass control equipment in order to do routine maintenance on it or to deal with an emergency shutdown). This issue also arises in air pollution regulation as well. Effluent limitations are generally expressed in terms of a limit on pollution concentrations in effluent or the amount of pollution discharged in relation to process inputs or other process parameters. For example, in *Meat Institute* the effluent limitations for BOD and TSS were set in terms of amounts discharged per 1000 lbs. of live weight killed, and for ammonia in terms of effluent concentrations. These limits are not to be exceeded at any time. But no control technology will operate flawlessly 100 percent of the time. In practice it may only be possible, because of upsets or bypasses, to meet effluent limitations 98 or 99 percent of the time. Must EPA make explicit provision in particular effluent limitations for upsets and bypasses by providing for some-

thing less than compliance 100 percent of the time, on the ground that effluent limitations which require the impossible are arbitrary? EPA has resisted such a requirement, arguing that sources can reduce the incidence of upsets and bypasses by better control equipment, monitoring, and maintenance; that allowing a fixed period of noncompliance in limitations would eliminate the pressure on sources to make such improvements and sanction violations not attributable to control failures; that a regulation allowing exceedences for circumstances beyond the source's control would be difficult to administer and enforce; and that EPA in practice takes genuine, unavoidable operational problems into account in enforcement decisions. Judicial response to the debate has varied. See, e.g., *FMC Corp. v. Train*, 539 F.2d 973 (4th Cir. 1976), and *American Petroleum Institute v. EPA*, 661 F.2d 340 (5th Cir. 1981) (requiring provision in effluent guidelines for upsets and bypasses); *Weyerhaeuser Co. v. Castle*, 590 F.2d 1011 (D.C. Cir. 1978); and *Corn Refiners Assn. v. Castle*, 594 F.2d 1223 (8th Cir. 1979) (refusing to require same). EPA has adopted generic regulations governing NPDES permits that provide for upset and bypass defenses to violations in certain specified circumstances. 40 C.F.R. §122.60(g), (h). For example, in the case of a bypass, the bypass must be "unavoidable to prevent loss of life, personal injury, or severe property damage." The burden is on the source to establish such a defense.

6. Challenges to EPA effluent limitation regulations may in some cases focus on the extent of risk posed by a pollutant. For example, in *EDF v. EPA*, 598 F.2d 62 (D.C. Cir. 1978), industry challenged a toxic effluent limitation for PCBs with low chlorine content (less chlorinated PCBs), on the ground that the only firm scientific evidence of adverse health and environmental effects from PCBs were based on studies and experience with more chlorinated PCBs and that there was not an adequate basis in the rulemaking record for strict controls on less chlorinated PCBs. The court found that the accumulated evidence in the record demonstrated that EPA had properly based its standard on consideration of the factors enumerated in §307(a)(2) for setting toxic limitations: "the toxicity of the pollutant, its persistence, degradability, the usual or potential presence of the affected organisms in any waters, the importance of the affected organisms and the nature and extent of the effect of the toxic pollutant on such organum." The court particularly stressed the provision in §307(a)(2) directing EPA to set a standard "with an ample margin of safety." The court stated:

> EPA, in its expert policy judgment, relied on its knowledge about a known substance to assess the danger of one about which less is known. . . . [B]y requiring EPA to set standards providing an "ample margin of safety," Congress authorized and indeed, required EPA to protect against dangers before their extent is conclusively determined.

7. Disputes also arise as to the classification of a pollutant, which determines which effluent limitations apply. For example, in *Rybachek v. EPA*, 904 F.2d 1276 (9th Cir. 1990), the placer-mining industry argued that EPA had improperly adopted BAT controls for settleable solids, claiming that they are "conventional pollutants" and thus subject to less demanding BCT standards. The court accepted EPA's argument that while the CWA states that "conventional pollutants" "includ[e]" suspended solids as conventional pollutant, §304(a), it does not classify settleable solids, which therefore must be categorized as a nonconventional pollutant under §301(b)(2)(F), and is thus subject to BAT controls. The court also noted EPA's argument that settleable solids are "a toxic pollutant indicator" and should be subject to BAT controls on that ground as well.

b. *The Role of Costs and Environmental Benefits in Setting Effluent Limitations*

W. BAUMOL & W. OATES, ECONOMICS, ENVIRONMENTAL POLICY, AND THE QUALITY OF LIFE

212-214 (1979)

In Figures 14-1 and 14-2 we depict the marginal cost (i.e., the cost of cutting back emissions by one additional unit) of reducing pollutant discharges for a typical petroleum refinery and for a beet-sugar plant. The steep upward slope of both curves indicates the rapid rise in marginal cost. The petroleum refinery, for example, can eliminate 10 percent of its emissions at a cost of less than two cents per pound. But by the time 90 percent of the emissions have been eliminated, the cost of further reductions is more than twenty-two cents per pound. The beet-sugar plant displays similar cost patterns.[17]

The important point we make here is how steeply marginal cost rises with each successive increase in pollution-control objectives. Some estimates by federal agencies of the cost of reducing water pollution in the United States are quite revealing. The analysis indicates that the total cost over a ten-year period of eliminating 85 to 90 percent of the water pollution in the United States would be on the order of $61 bil-

---

17. A second notable feature of these marginal-cost curves is how much cheaper in general it is for the beet-sugar plant to reduce emissions. This suggests that, if we are trying to clean up a river with both a beet-sugar plant and a petroleum refinery on its banks, we can do so much more inexpensively by concentrating on emissions reductions by the beet-sugar plant. . . .

FIGURE 14-1
Marginal Cost of BOD-Discharge Reduction in Petroleum Refining

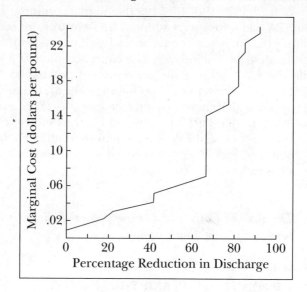

FIGURE 14-2
Marginal Cost of BOD-Discharge Reduction by a Beet-Sugar Refinery

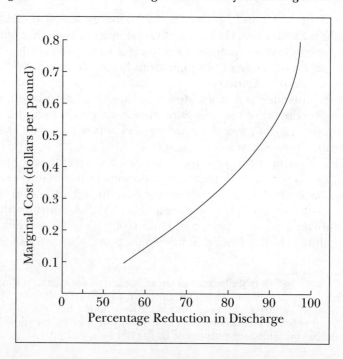

lion. To raise this to a 95 to 99 percent reduction of water pollution would involve an *additional* cost of $58 billion, bringing the total to $119 billion. Moreover, to squeeze out the last percent or two to reach total elimination of water pollution would require an additional $200 billion!

While costs of elimination of pollution rise with increasing rapidity as one approaches zero pollution levels, the gain in benefits will typically fall. That is, once concentrations of pollutants have declined sufficiently, further reductions will in many cases contribute little more to the general welfare. In fact, natural processes will often take care of low pollution levels.

RYBACHEK V. EPA

904 F.2d 1276 (9th Cir. 1990)

[Industry challenged EPA's adoption of BPT and BAT limitations for the placer-mining industry, which mines gold and other metals by installing sluice boxes in streams to filter the ore-bearing alluvial or glacial deposits in the stream bed. The lighter and smaller particles are flushed through the sluice, which retains the larger and heavier ore-bearing particles. EPA based its BPT limitations for sluice waste water on the use of settling ponds to settle out sediment (which can contain toxics) before discharge of the waste water. It based its BAT standards on use of 100 percent recycled, recirculating process water, with zero discharge of pollutants to the stream. (Query: How are the sediments to be disposed of?).]

DETERMINATION OF BPT

We turn first to petitioners' argument that the EPA erred in its determination that settling ponds are the best practicable control technology currently available (BPT) within the placer mining industry. There is no dispute that settling ponds are currently available pollution control technology; in fact, the AMA concedes that they are now used by almost all miners. Rather, petitioners contend that the EPA failed to use a "cost-benefit analysis" in determining that settling ponds were BPT for placer mining. They also argue that the EPA failed to consider costs when it set forth BPT limitations governing settleable solids for small mines.

The Clean Water Act controls when and how the EPA should require BPT. Under 33 U.S.C. §1311(b)(1)(A), the Act requires "effluent limitations for point sources . . . which shall require the application of best practicable control technology currently available [BPT]." Under this section, the EPA is to determine whether a technology is BPT; the factors it considers "should include . . . total cost of" the technology "in relation to effluent benefits to be achieved" from it, the age of equipment, engineering aspects, "non-water quality environmental impact . . . and such other factors as the Administrator deems appropriate."

From this statutory language, it is "plain that, as a general rule, the EPA is required to consider the costs and benefits of proposed technology in its inquiry to determine the BPT." *Association of Pacific Fisheries v. EPA,* 615 F.2d 794 (9th Cir. 1980). The EPA has broad discretion in weighing these competing factors. It may determine that a technology is not BPT on the basis of this cost-benefit analysis only when the costs are "wholly disproportionate" to the potential effluent-reduction benefits.

We look first to whether the EPA properly considered the costs of BPT and second to whether it properly weighed these costs against the benefits.

. . . The EPA used a model-mine analysis to estimate the costs to mines of installing settling ponds. The Agency developed several model mines to represent the typical operating and compliance costs that open-cut mines and dredges of various sizes would incur. Commenters attempted to insure that the model-mine analysis reflected actual industry conditions, and the EPA accordingly modified the analysis when it thought it appropriate during the rulemaking. The EPA then determined, for each of its model mines, the incremental costs that would be incurred to construct and operate settling ponds to retain waste water long enough to achieve a certain settleable solids level. It proceeded to conduct a detailed and complex assessment of the effect of the compliance costs on the mining industry's profits.

The EPA then properly weighed these costs against the benefits of settling ponds. Its data indicated that placer mine waste water contained high levels of solids and metals that were reduced substantially by simple settling. The upshot of the EPA's analysis was its estimation that installation of settling ponds by open-cup mines industry-wide would remove over four million pounds of solids at a cost of approximately $2.2 million — a removal cost of less than $1 per pound of solids.

We would uphold the EPA's determination of BPT.

DETERMINATION OF BAT: ANALYSIS OF COSTS

We next confront the AMA's challenge to the EPA's determination that recirculation of process waste water is the best available technology economically achievable (BAT) in the placer mining industry. By definition, BAT limitations must be both technologically available and economically achievable. We conclude that the EPA's BAT limitations were both and therefore uphold them.

The technological availability of recirculating process wastewater is not in dispute; in fact, placer mines commonly practice it. It is recirculation's economic achievability that petitioners challenge.

In determining the economic achievability of technology, the EPA must consider the "cost" of meeting BAT limitations, but need not compare such cost with the benefits of effluent reduction. The Agency measures costs on a "reasonableness standard"; it has considerable discretion in weighing the technology's costs, which are less-important factors than in setting BPT limitations.

The record demonstrates that the EPA weighed the costs that recirculation would impose on gold placer mining. . . .

WEYERHAEUSER CO. V. COSTLE

590 F.2d 1011, 1044 (D.C. Cir. 1978)

[The pulp and paper industry challenged EPA regulations establishing BPT limitations for pulp, paper, and paperboard mills.]

Petitioners also challenge EPA's manner of assessing two factors that all parties agree must be considered: cost and non-water quality environmental impacts. They contend that the Agency should have more carefully balanced costs versus the effluent reduction benefits of the regulations, and that it should have also balanced those benefits against the non-water quality environmental impacts to arrive at a "net" environmental benefit conclusion. . . .

In order to discuss petitioners' challenges, we must first identify the relevant statutory standard. Section 304(b)(1)(B) identifies the factors bearing on [BPT] in two groups. First, the factors shall

> include consideration of the total cost of application of technology in relation to the effluent reduction benefits to be achieved from such application,

and second, they

> shall also take into account the age of equipment and facilities involved, the process employed, the engineering aspects of the application of various types of control techniques, process changes, non-water quality environmental impact (including energy requirements), and such other factors as the Administrator deems appropriate[.]

The first group consists of two factors that EPA must compare: total cost versus effluent reduction benefits. We shall call these the "comparison factors." The other group is a list of many factors that EPA must "take into account": age, process, engineering aspects, process changes, environmental impacts (including energy), and any others EPA deems appropriate. We shall call these the "consideration factors." Notably, section 304(b)(2)(B), which delineates the factors relevant to setting 1983 [BAT] limitations, tracks the 1977 provision [BPT] provision before us except in one regard: in the 1983 section, all factors, including costs and benefits, are consideration factors, and no factors are separated out for comparison.

Based on our examination of the statutory language and the legislative history, we conclude that Congress mandated a particular structure and weight for the 1977 comparison factors, that is to say, a "limited" balancing test.[18] In contrast, Congress did not mandate any particular structure or weight for the many consideration factors. Rather, it left EPA with discretion to decide how to account for the consideration factors, and how much weight to give each factor. In response to these divergent congressional approaches, we conclude that, on the one hand, we should examine EPA's treatment of cost and benefit under the 1977 standard to assure that the Agency complied with Congress' "limited" balancing directive. On the other hand, our scrutiny of the Agency's treatment of the several consideration factors seeks to assure that the Agency informed itself as to their magnitude, and reached its own express and considered conclusion about their bearing. More particularly, we do not believe that EPA is required to use any specific structures such as a balancing test in assessing the consideration factors nor do we believe that EPA is required to give each consideration factor any specific weight.

[The Court upheld the challenged regulations.]

---

18. Senator Muskie described the "limited" balancing test:

The modification of subsection 304(b)(1) is intended to clarify what is meant by the term "practicable." The balancing test between total cost and effluent reduction benefits is intended to limit the application of technology only where the additional degree of effluent reduction is wholly out of proportion to the costs of achieving such marginal level of reduction for any class or category of sources.

The Conferees agreed upon this limited cost-benefit analysis in order to maintain uniformity within a class and category of point sources subject to effluent limitations, and to avoid imposing on the Administrator any requirement to consider the location of sources within a category or to ascertain water quality impact of effluent controls, or to determine the economic impact of controls on any individual plant in a single community.

APPALACHIAN POWER CO. V. TRAIN

545 F.2d 1351 (4th Cir. 1976)

[EPA issued BAT effluent limitations for the steam electric power industry dealing with heat, which is defined as a pollutant by the CWA. Steam electric power plants have traditionally used "once through" cooling systems to cool and condense steam from generator turbines; water is removed from a water body, used for cooling, and returned to the same water body at a higher temperature. The resulting thermal discharges raise the temperature of the receiving waters, which may result in injury to aquatic life. Closed cycle cooling systems recirculate water through a plant; heat picked up from the turbines is dissipated through huge cooling towers. EPA effluent limitations issued under §306 require closed cycle cooling for new steam electric power plants. The regulations challenged here would require backfit (retrofit) of closed cycle cooling by large existing plants (at least 500 megawatts generating capacity) that came on line after 1969, and by all existing plants that came on line after 1973. EPA estimated the capital costs of retrofit at $5.2 billion, the industry at $6.5 billion. Retrofit would also involve temporary reduction or shutdown of plant operation for an extended period and a permanent reduction in generating efficiency, requiring the utility to obtain replacement power at additional, perhaps substantial cost. The EPA had rejected a request by the Atomic Energy Commission (AEC) that 55 existing nuclear steam electric plants be exempted from the backfit requirements on the ground that the environmental impact statements prepared in accordance with the National Environmental Policy Act in connection with the plants' construction found that their thermal discharges would not have an adverse effect on aquatic life or that their effects were too small to justify the expense of closed cycle cooling retrofit. EPA rejected this request, invoking the unelaborated opinion of its General Counsel that "it would not be legally defensible" to grant it.]

Industry contends that EPA's [BAT] thermal backfit requirements for existing units are invalid because the agency failed to balance the overall social benefits to be derived from its regulations against their social costs. . . .

EPA, on the other hand, takes the position that the language of the Act pertaining to the [BAT] standards requires no balancing of social benefits against social costs. Moreover, the agency asserts that even if the Act were held to so require, it has, in its rulemaking, analyzed the benefits of the challenged regulations [and] found them to be worth the associated costs. It further asserts that it agrees with its environmental contractor, Energy Resources Company (ERCO), when it states that "benefits cannot be properly assessed within the present state of the Art." We disagree with EPA's (and partially with Industry's) assertions, and, accordingly, set aside and remand for further consideration. . . .

In *DuPont [v. Train]*, 541 F.2d 1018, . . . we rejected Industry's contention that benefits derived from a particular level of effluent reduction must be quantified in monetary terms, and such contention is rejected here. This reflects the simple fact that such benefits often cannot be reduced to dollars and cents. Nevertheless, EPA is under a statutory duty to determine whether, in fact, its regulations for 1983 will "result in reasonable further progress toward the national goal of eliminating the discharge of all pollutants. . . ." [CWA §301(b)(2)(A).] Accordingly, the agency must consider the benefits derived from the application of its effluent reduction requirements in relation to the associated costs in order to determine whether, in fact, the resulting progress is "economically achievable," and whether the progress is "reasonable."

EPA argues, however, that it has, in fact, assessed the benefits to be derived from its regulations. . . .

[EPA referred to a table that it had generated during the rulemaking proceedings.] According to that table, EPA calculated the incremental production costs, capital costs, fuel consumption and capacity reduction which would result from the application of closed cycle cooling at existing plants of various ages. These incremental values were then compared to the amount of heat kept out of the water by such systems. Based upon the resulting cost-effectiveness ratios, EPA concluded that the thermal control technology there analyzed resulted in more favorable effluent reduction benefits when applied to newer and larger generating units. [The table indicated that the cost per unit of heat removed was lower for large plants that came on line after 1969 and all plants that came on line after 1973 than for other existing plants.]

Industry challenges EPA's reliance upon these figures on the ground that they do not indicate whether the regulations will result in reasonable further progress toward the national goal. We agree. EPA's study merely establishes the cost-effectiveness of [retrofitting] cooling towers at individual plant sites. It in no way indicates whether, in light of the associated costs, application of such systems will result in reasonable effluent reduction levels.

In response to this, EPA cites the report of its environmental contractor, ERCO, which it claims satisfactorily analyzes the environmental benefits and risks associated with the various alternatives which were before it. The foundation of this report was apparently a random sample taken of various power companies throughout the country. Based upon this sample, the report concludes that if a generating unit uses less than 30 percent of a stream's flow, there will be no ecological danger. If as much as 70 percent of the stream flow is used more than 5 percent of the time, however, there will be a high risk of such danger. Between these two extremes, the report concludes that there is a medium risk of danger. Yet, nowhere in the report does ERCO state upon what basis it reached this conclusion. We are left to guess.

Moreover, we further note, finding it to be of some significance, that the record is replete with allusions to the effect of heat upon aquatic life; damage to eggs; different effects on adults and juveniles; the growth of algae; interrupted migration; the thresholds of aquatic communities; differences between streams, lakes and estuaries; are to mention but a few. Yet, despite agreement that the literature is full of learned papers on the subject at hand, EPA contends that the state of the art is not such that the incremental benefits of heat removal from the discharge of generating plants can be predicted. . . . [W]e consider this position with a certain degree of caution. The references are simply too numerous and are stated by too many people on both sides who are ostensibly qualified to speak. . . .

Assuming that EPA's conclusion is correct, that the state of the art is such that the incremental effects of heat are not known with any degree of certainty, the least EPA could have done would have been to articulate what the state of the art was and why, according to scientific opinion, predictions could not be made. Even assuming that it might not be possible to articulate with reasonable certainty the achievability of the benefits to be derived from a specified amount of heat removal, it seems to us that the expectancy might be stated, for if there is no expectancy of benefits to aquatic life, is the expenditure of billions of dollars justified under any standard?

At the very least, on the best information available, the ecological benefits expected from the ordered reduction should be stated, and if impossible so to do, EPA should state why. It may well be, for example, that a 90 percent reduction in thermal pollution at a cost of $5 billion is entirely reasonable even when it is shown that an 80 percent reduction would cost but $2 billion, for it is possible that the elimination of the additional 10 percent in total heat discharged would have positive environmental effects which would far outweigh the additional $3 billion in cost. By the same token, if no tangible environmental benefits will accrue by increasing the thermal reduction level from 80 percent to 90 percent, the additional expenditure of $3 billion might be considered unjustified. Thus, in choosing among alternative strategies, EPA must not only set forth the cost of achieving a particular level of heat reduction but must also state the expected environmental benefits, that is to say the effect on the environment, which will take place as a result of reduction,[19] . . .

_____

19. By tangible environmental benefits, we mean something more than BTU's of heat rejected. Certainly, to exaggerate to make the point, it could not seriously be contended that a reviewing court could say that an overall reduc-

It should be made clear, however, that our remand here is very narrow in scope since we do not disapprove the general principle of requiring installation of cooling devices on a part of the planned and existing electrical generators in the country.

Yet, while we are unable to say the EPA has not acted reasonably, neither are we able to say it has not acted "perfunctorily or arbitrarily," . . . To sustain these regulations on the present record, this court would have to trust completely EPA's conclusions. . . .

On remand, then, EPA must state the benefits especially to aquatic life, for the various alternatives considered if that can be done. If these benefits cannot be stated with any degree of certainty, EPA will state the expected benefits according to whatever scientific opinion it relies upon, fully explicating the basis, including the opinion, upon which it relies. If no expected benefits can be stated, EPA must state why they cannot be and the scientific opinion which supports that conclusion.

NOTES AND QUESTIONS

1. What is the difference between the role of control costs and environmental benefits in setting BPT and BAT standards? In the statute? The statute as construed by the courts? In logic? Consider the following statement from *Reynolds Metals Co. v. EPA,* 760 F.2d 549, 565 (4th Cir. 1985): "For BPT there must be a 'limited balancing' of costs against benefits, but as regards BAT [and] NSPS . . . no balancing is required — only that costs be considered along with the other [relevant factors]." Is this a correct statement of the law? How is it possible to "consider" a factor such as costs without weighing or balancing it against other relevant factors in making a decision? Is *Weyerhaeuser's* distinction between "consideration factors" and "comparison" factors logical? Persuasive? What does EPA have to do to show a court that it has "considered" a factor? Can EPA be challenged on the ground that it failed *adequately* to "consider" a factor?

2. Why shouldn't EPA be required to balance the incremental costs of control against incremental environmental benefits in setting any and all effluent limitation standards? And shouldn't those benefits

---

tion of, say, 10 BTU's of heat discharged into the nation's rivers at a cost of $5 billion represents a reasonable reduction level. So we see that it is only when the reduction level and the associated costs are compared with the environmental benefits to be expected that a critical evaluation of EPA's actions can be made. In this respect, §304(b)(1)(B), for example, requires "consideration of the total cost of application of technology in relation to the effluent reduction benefits" for 1977 standards. Had Congress intended merely to require a standard of the percentage of heat removal, it would have provided for a simple equation and the drafters would have done so.

be expressed not in terms of pollution removed, but of actual benefit to the environment? What difficulties would EPA encounter in performing such an analysis in establishing nationwide "single number" effluent limitations for a given industry? If environmental benefits are taken into account, must or should effluent limitations be set on a facility by facility basis?

3. What provisions of the CWA does *Appalachian Power* invoke in order to require EPA to analyze the environmental benefits of successive increments of control? Is the court's reasoning persuasive? Compare the technique used by the *Benzene* plurality to limit OSHA's discretion in setting standards, see supra, p. 25, and the *Asbestos* case reviewing EPA's ban on asbestos under TSCA, p. 116, supra.

4. On remand from *Appalachian Power,* EPA abandoned its efforts to issue new BAT limitations for thermal pollution from the steam electric power industry. Is this because the Fourth Circuit required the impossible? Or is it because EPA finally took a hard look at the costs and benefits of retrofitting closed cycle cooling, and concluded that the costs of retrofit were unwarranted? In the absence of effluent limitation guidelines, EPA and state permitting agencies have dealt with thermal pollution issues in connection with NPDES permit renewals on a case by case basis, using "best engineering judgment." To date, retrofit has been required at only a very few plants.

5. *Appalachian Power* represents an exception to the usual judicial approach to reviewing issues of cost and benefit in connection with EPA adoption of effluent limitations. The prevailing approach is illustrated by *Rybachek* and *Weyerhaeuser.* Which approach is the better? Should the CWA be amended to require more explicit cost-benefit analysis? Consider that in many instances additional control of water pollution in the United States will not provide any significant benefits to human health.

6. Suppose that EPA refuses to perform a study of incremental control costs and incremental benefits (whether expressed in terms of pollutants removed or actual environmental benefit), but industry submits its own study, which purports to show that costs are grossly disproportionate to benefits? See *BASF Wyandotte Corp. v. Costle,* 598 F.2d 637, 656-657 (1st Cir. 1979), involving an industry challenge to BPT standards.

[The court stated] that the obligation the Act imposes on EPA is only to perform a limited cost-benefit balancing to make sure that costs are not "wholly out of proportion" to the benefits achieved. A Legislative History of the Water Pollution Control Act Amendments of 1972 (1973) (statement of Senator Muskie). The Agency has considerable discretion to decide how to go about considering costs and benefits and need not "perform the elaborate task of calculating incremental balances" of mar-

ginal costs and benefits [citing *Weyerhaeuser*]. We agree with the *Weyer-haeuser* court that "when an incremental analysis has been performed by industry and submitted to EPA, it is worthy of scrutiny by the Agency."
. . . DuPont's study, indicating rapidly increasing costs for removal of incremental amounts of pollutants, certainly was "worthy of scrutiny," and we assume that EPA did not ignore it. Largely through no fault of DuPont's, however, the study tested a carbon absorption model very different from the one that formed the basis for EPA's costs estimates. Most notably, DuPont studied contact times of 22, 44 and 66 minutes whereas EPA prepared costs estimates for systems with contact times of 60, 300, 600, and 750 minutes. Generally, the longer the effluent remains in contact with the carbon, the more efficient the treatment will be. We are not prepared to say that the DuPont study demonstrates that incremental costs of EPA's model system were wholly out of proportion to incremental benefits, nor will we require EPA explicitly to respond to every study submitted by commenters.

For general discussion, see Note, Cost-Benefit Analysis and the Federal Water Pollution Control Act Amendments of 1972: A Proposal for Congressional Action, 67 Iowa L. Rev. 1057 (1982).

   7. In *Chemical Manufacturers Association v. EPA*, 870 F.2d 177 (5th Cir. 1989), CMA challenged BPT limitations for the chemical industry, claiming that they impermissibly pushed controls beyond the "knee of the curve" — the point at which marginal control costs shift and begin to rise steeply. CMA claimed that increasing the removal of pollutants from 96 to 99 percent would cost almost twice as much per pound removed as 96 percent removal. The cost per pound removed would increase from 38 cents per pound to 71 cents per pound. CMA argued that this shift demonstrated that 99 percent control was well beyond the "knee of the curve." EPA argued that the "knee of the curve" test was applicable only to BCT controls going beyond BPT. The court of appeals upheld EPA's position:

   The BCT provisions were intended to establish an intermediate level between BPT and the stricter BAT limitations for conventional pollutants by adding a cost-effectiveness test for incremental technology requirements that exceed BPT technology. Under BCT, additional limitations on conventional pollutants that are more stringent than BPT can be imposed only "to the extent that the increased cost of treatment [would] be reasonable in terms of the degree of environmental benefits."
   Thus, Congress intended that cost would occupy a different role in EPA's promulgation of BPT limitations than it would in the promulgations of BCT because of the different aims of the two standards. While Congress did not consider cost to be irrelevant to BPT, it clearly intended it to be a less significant factor than in the promulgation of BCT limitations. The relevant inquiry with respect to BPT, as indicated above, is whether the costs are "wholly disproportionate" to the benefits. . . .

In the current case, the regulation will require a 10 percent increase above current industry costs to remove 108 million additional pounds. The EPA reasonably concluded that these costs were not "wholly disproportionate" to the benefit.

870 F.2d at 205-206. Under the court's reading, what is the difference in the CWA's treatment of costs and benefits for BPT and for BCT? Is the difference sensible?

8. What consideration must EPA give to costs and environmental benefits in setting BCT limitations? As discussed in *American Paper Institute v. EPA*, 660 F.2d 954 (4th Cir. 1981), Congress in 1977 believed that BPT controls had achieved considerable success in reducing "conventional" pollutants, and that a highly ambitious second stage of BCT controls was unwarranted. It enacted §304(b)(4)(B), directing EPA to set BCT limitations by reference to the following:

Factors relating to the assessment of best conventional pollutant control technology (including measures and practices) shall include consideration of the reasonableness of the relationship between the costs of attaining a reduction in effluents and the effluent reduction benefits derived, and the comparison of the cost and level of reduction of such pollutants from the discharge from publicly owned treatment works to the cost and level of reduction of such pollutants from a class or category of industrial sources, and shall take into account the age of equipment and facilities involved, the process employed, the engineering aspects of the application of various types of control techniques, process changes, non-water quality environmental impact (including energy requirements), and such other factors as the administrator deems appropriate.

The court held that this provision requires EPA to perform two distinct analyses in setting BCT levels. First, it must examine the costs to the industry of successive increments of BCT control and balance those costs against the effluent reductions obtained. The court referred to this as an "industry cost-effectiveness test." Second, EPA must examine the incremental cost of the proposed BCT limitation for an industry and compare it with the incremental cost to POTWs of reducing conventional pollutants; the industry cost should not be appreciably greater than the POTW cost. EPA had argued that it need not analyze the costs of incremental industry pollution controls against effluent benefits; it claimed the language in the first phrase of §304(b)(4)(B) requiring "consideration of the reasonableness of the relationships between the costs of attaining a reduction in effluents and the effluent reduction benefits derived" did not require incremental cost-benefit analysis but was only a generalized requirement of "consideration" of costs and benefits; the specific comparison to be used in undertaking this consideration was POTW costs, as set forth in the second phrase of

§304(h)(4)(B). The court, over a dissent, rejected this argument as "contrary to the plain meaning of the words, " emphasizing that the two phrases in the statute were conjoined by the word "and," which, the court reasoned, makes clear that two distinct analyses are required.

In making the POTW comparison, EPA had used the costs to POTWs of using "advanced secondary treatment" (AST) techniques that would reduce conventional pollutant discharges beyond the level achieved by "secondary treatment," which generally consists of filtering out solid matters and the use of aerobic ponds to treat the remaining effluent. The industry challenged EPA's use of the higher-cost AST benchmark rather than the lower cost of secondary treatment, arguing that POTWs are not generally required to achieve more than secondary treatment and that AST techniques had not yet been developed when §304 was enacted. The court upheld EPA on this issue, finding that nothing in the statute mandated use of any particular POTW benchmark, and that EPA's choice of AST was reasonable.

9. As Baumol and Oates point out, see supra, p. 479, the incremental cost of eliminating a given amount of pollution not only tends to rise with higher levels of control, but also varies widely across industries. Ideally, effluent limitations for control of the same pollutant should be set in such a way as to equalize the marginal costs of control across all industries, thereby minimizing the resource costs to society of reducing pollution. See supra, p. 378. In practice, EPA makes no effort to calibrate inter-industry marginal control costs when setting effluent limitation for particular industries, and no court has required such an effort. Why not? Should courts require it to do so?

10. The factors that Section 304 requires EPA to consider in setting both BPT and BCT controls include "non-water quality environmental impact." §304(b)(1)(B), (4)(B). To what extent, if at all, does the obligation to "consider" such impacts constrain the exercise of EPA's discretion? In *Kennecott Copper Co. v. EPA,* 612 F.2d 1232 (10th Cir. 1979), millowners challenged EPA's BPT regulations for gold and silver cyanidization mills. They pointed out that EPA devoted only "four pages of generalized discussion" in a several hundred-page document to non-water quality impacts, and they claimed that EPA's effluent limitations would compel the use of technology that would cause water containing cyanide to seep into and contaminate groundwater, a potentially serious non-water quality impact. However, the Tenth Circuit found that EPA's brief discussion did "'take into consideration' the fact that proper design of impoundment facilities could avoid the problem," and so rejected the industry's challenge. Id. at 1246. See also *Weyerhaeuser Co. v. Costle,* 590 F.2d 1011, 1053 (D.C. Cir. 1978) (excerpted supra at p. 483) ("since Congress intended EPA's internal structure to protect the non-water quality environment, the judicial function is completed when we have assured ourselves that EPA expressly considered the probable environmental impacts of its regula-

tions"). Do you agree? Can EPA water quality regulators be relied upon to give adequate weight to non-water quality impacts? Are the courts capable of meaningful review of a comparison of different environmental impacts?

11. While the role of costs typically appears in litigation brought by industry, it is sometimes raised in litigation brought by environmental groups. For example, in *NRDC v. EPA*, 863 F.2d 1420 (9th Cir. 1988), EPA had refused to adopt BAT limitations requiring on-shore oil wells discharging process waters into coastal waters to reinject such waters into the ground, citing uncertainty about the costs of retrofitting this control technique. The court found that uncertainty over costs was not a sufficient ground for refusing to adopt the requirement. Reinjection was concededly technologically feasible, was required of new wells, and was practiced by some existing wells in California. The court found that cost is a less important factor in setting BAT standards than for BPT standards. There was, moreover, considerable, if conflicting, cost data in the record. "EPA should not delay requiring technologically feasible limitations as BAT in order to wait for more precise cost figures." Id. at 1426.

3.   VARIANCES: LIMITED FLEXIBILITY

ENVIRONMENTAL PROTECTION AGENCY V. NATIONAL CRUSHED STONE ASSN.

449 U.S. 64 (1980)

Justice WHITE delivered the opinion of the Court.

In April and July 1977, the Environmental Protection Agency (EPA), acting under the Federal Water Pollution Control Act Amendments of 1972 (Act), 33 U.S.C. §1251 et seq., promulgated [BPT] pollution discharge limitations for the coal mining industry and for that portion of the mineral mining and processing industry comprising the crushed stone, construction sand, and gravel categories. Although the Act does not expressly authorize or require variances from the 1977 [BPT] limitation, each set of regulations contained a variance provision. . . . [T]he Court of Appeals set aside the variance provision as "unduly restrictive" and remanded the provision to EPA for reconsideration.

[The EPA BPT regulations for the industries in question provided that in order to] obtain a variance from the limitations set forth in the regulations a discharger must demonstrate that the "factors relating to the equipment or facilities involved, the process applied, or other such factors relating to such discharger are fundamentally different from the factors considered in the establishment of the guidelines." Although a

greater than normal cost of implementation will be considered in acting on a request for a variance, economic ability to meet the costs will
not be considered. A variance, therefore, will not be granted on the
basis of the applicant's economic inability to meet the costs of implementing the uniform standard.

The Court of Appeals for the Fourth Circuit rejected this position
. . . the court held that:

> if [a plant] is doing all that the maximum use of technology within its
> economic capability will permit and if such use will result in reasonable
> further progress toward the elimination of the discharge of pollutants
> . . . no reason appears why [it] should not be able to secure such a
> variance should it comply with any other requirements of the variance.

We granted certiorari to resolve the conflict between the decision
below and *Weyerhaeuser Co. v. Costle,* 191 U.S. App. D.C. 309, 590 F.2d.
1011 (1978), in which the variance provision was upheld. . . .

Section 301(c) of the Act explicitly provides for modifying the
1987 [BAT][20] effluent limitations with respect to individual point
sources. A variance under 301(c) may be obtained upon a showing
"that such modified requirements (1) will represent the maximum use
of technology within the economic capability of the owner or operator;
and (2) will result in reasonable further progress toward elimination of
the discharge of pollutants." Thus, the economic ability of the individual operator to meet the costs of effluent reductions may in some circumstances justify granting a variance from the 1987 [BAT] limitations.

No such explicit variance provision exists with respect to BPT standards, but in *E. I. DuPont de Nemours v. Train,* 430 U.S. 112 (1977),
we indicated that a variance provision was a necessary aspect of BPT
limitations applicable by regulations to classes and categories of point
sources. 430 U.S. at 128, . . . The issue in this case is whether the BPT
variance provision [in the EPA regulations] must allow consideration
of the economic capability of an individual discharger to afford the
costs of the BPT limitation. For the reasons that follow, our answer is
in the negative.

II

The plain language of the statute does not support the position
taken by the Court of Appeals. Section 301(c) is limited on its face to
modifications of the 1987 BAT limitations. It says nothing about relief

20. [Ed. Note: The 1972 Amendments originally established 1983 as the
deadline for meeting BAT limitations. The 1977 Amendments extended this
deadline to 1987.]

from the 1977 BPT requirements. Nor does the language of the Act support the position that although §301(c) is not itself applicable to BPT standards, it requires that the affordability of the prescribed 1977 technology be considered in BPT variance decisions. . . .

More importantly, to allow a variance based on the maximum technology affordable by the point source, even if that technology fails to meet BPT effluent limitations, would undercut the purpose and function of BPT limitations. Rather than the 1987 requirement of the best measures economically and technologically feasible, the statutory provisions for 1977 contemplate regulations prohibiting discharges from any point source in excess of the effluent produced by the best practicable technology currently available in the industry. The Administrator was referred to the industry and to existing practices to determine BPT. . . . Necessarily, if pollution is to be diminished, limitations based on BPT must forbid the level of effluent produced by the most pollution-prone segment of the industry, that segment not measuring up to "the average of the best existing performance." So understood, the statute contemplated regulations that would require a substantial number of point sources with the poorest performances either to conform to BPT standards or to cease production. To allow a variance based on economic capability and not to require adherence to the prescribed minimum technology would permit the employment of the very practices that the Administrator had rejected in establishing the best practicable technology currently in use in the industry. . . .

. . . The regulations permit a variance where "factors relating to the equipment or facilities involved, the process applied, or such other factors relating to such discharger are fundamentally different from the factors considered in the establishment of the guidelines." If a point source can show that its situation, including its costs of compliance, is not within the range of circumstances considered by the Administrator, then it may receive a variance, whether or not the source could afford to comply with the minimum standard. In such situations, the variance is an acknowledgment that the uniform BPT limitation was set without reference to the full range of current practices, to which the Administrator was to refer. . . . A variance based on economic capability, however, would not have this character: it would allow a variance simply because the point source could not afford a compliance cost that is not fundamentally different from those the Administrator has already considered in determining BPT. It would force a displacement of calculations already performed, not because those calculations were incomplete or had unexpected effects, but only because the costs happened to fall on one particular operator, rather than on another who might be economically better off.

Because the 1977 limitations were intended to reduce the total pollution produced by an industry, requiring compliance with BPT standards necessarily imposed additional costs on the segment of the industry with the least effective technology. If the statutory goal is to be achieved, these costs must be borne or the point source eliminated. . . .

III

The Administrator's present interpretation of the language of the statute is amply supported by the legislative history, which persuades us that Congress foresaw and accepted the economic hardship, including the closing of some plants, that effluent limitations would cause; and that Congress took certain steps to alleviate this hardship, steps which did not include allowing a BPT variance based on economic capability.

In rejecting EPA's interpretation of the BPT variance provision, the Court of Appeals relied on a mistaken conception of the relation between BPT and BAT standards. The court erroneously believed that since BAT limitations are to be more stringent than BPT limitations, the variance provision for the latter must be at least as flexible as that for the former with respect to affordability. The variances permitted by §301(c) from the 1987 limitations, however, can reasonably be understood to represent a cost in decreased effluent reductions that can only be afforded once the minimal standard expressed in the BPT limitation has been reached. . . .

NOTES AND QUESTIONS

1. The controversy in *National Crushed Stone* grows out of the Supreme Court's *DuPont* decision, which upheld EPA's adoption of uniform effluent limitations, "so long as some allowance is made for variations in individual plants." See supra, p. 466. Is this proviso consistent with the reasons given by the court in *DuPont* for upholding uniform effluent limitations? With the fact that Congress provided a variance provision in §301(c) for BAT limitations, but made no similar provision for BPT limitations? If a variance system is required, why should it be defined in terms of "fundamentally different factors"? Why should it not explicitly include cost?

2. EPA subsequently by regulation extended the "fundamentally different factors" (FDF) variance it had adopted for BPT limitations to BAT and industrial POTW pretreatment limitations. The Supreme Court upheld this action against a challenge that it was invalid insofar as it applied to toxic substances. *CMA v. NRDC*, 470 U.S. 116 (1985). Section 307(*l*) had provided that EPA "may not modify any portion of

this section," which established effluent limitations for toxic pollutants. The Court in *CMA* reasoned that §307(*l*) did not prohibit FDF variances for toxics limitations, reasoning that such variances are not an exception from such limitations, but instead tailor the limitations to the particular circumstances of a source. The 1987 Amendments codified the "fundamentally different factors" standard for variances and made it applicable to BAT, BPT, and toxic effluent limitations. CWA §§301(*l*)(N). A source may obtain a variance if it is fundamentally different in respect of the factors considered by EPA in establishing limitations, and if other requirements are met. The factors include such variables as "the age of equipment and facilities involved, the process employed, the application of various types of control techniques," but "cost" is explicitly excluded, and the quality of receiving wastes is not mentioned. The level of controls imposed in connection with a variance are based on a case by case exercise of "best engineering judgment." One commentator reports that FDF variances have rarely been granted in the context of BPT limitations. Pedersen, Turning the Tide on Water Quality, 15 Ecology L.Q. 69, 86 n.81 (1988).

3. What constitutes a "fundamentally different factor" justifying an FDF variance? Suppose the effluent limitations are based on the use of holding ponds, and a source does not have and cannot obtain sufficient acreage to build holding ponds? Suppose that the source could meet the limitations, but would have to use control technologies that are far more costly than holding ponds?

Georgia-Pacific Corp. v. EPA, 671 F.2d 1235 (9th Cir. 1982), upheld EPA's position that an FDF variance should not be given to a Georgia-Pacific pulp and paper mill that was unique in its industry category because the mill included an alcohol plant that received sulfite waste from paper and pulping operations and processed some of it into alcohol and other by-products. Waste from the alcohol plant was treated together with other wastes from the plant before discharge. Georgia-Pacific argued that the inclusion of the alcohol plant justified a less stringent effluent limitation for the mill. EPA rejoined that the alcohol plant recovered some of the sulfite raw waste load (RWL) from one pulp and paper operation, resulting in a total RWL for the plant as a whole of 170 pounds of BOD per ton of paper produced, as compared to the industry average of 207 pounds. Query: On these facts, could EPA have used the FDF variance procedure to establish stricter effluent limitations for Georgia-Pacific's plant than those imposed on the rest of the industry?

4. Not surprisingly, there has been no provision for variances, whether based on cost or FDF, from effluent limitations for new sources. The FDF and cost-based variances respond to the problems of imposing nationally uniform, technology-based requirements on existing sources and therefore find no counterpart in the Clean Air Act.

5. Suppose that a plant is unable, for economic reasons, to meet a BPT requirement, but that it can establish that its existing controls are adequate to prevent any material adverse effects on water quality. Or suppose that a plant establishes that the adverse environmental consequences (caused by the chemicals and energy needed to fuel control processes and on-land disposal of waste) of BPT compliance are substantial, and the environmental benefits negligible. Does the CWA permit EPA to give such a plant a variance? Should it? Consider the following.

WEYERHAEUSER CO. V. COSTLE

590 F.2d 1011, 1041 (D.C. Cir. 1978)

[This part of the *Weyerhaeuser* opinion deals with EPA's denial of variances from national, technology-based effluent limitations based on the quality of receiving waters.]

Some of the paper mills that must meet the effluent limitations under review discharge their effluent into the Pacific Ocean. Petitioners contend that the ocean can dilute or naturally treat effluent, and that EPA must take this capacity of the ocean ("receiving water capacity") into account in a variety of ways. They urge what they term "common sense," i.e., that because the amounts of pollutant involved are small in comparison to bodies of water as vast as Puget Sound or the Pacific Ocean, they should not have to spend heavily on treatment equipment, or to increase their energy requirements and sludge levels, in order to treat wastes that the ocean could dilute or absorb.[21]

Based on the [pre-1972 regulatory] experience, Congress adopted a new approach in 1972. Under the Act, "a discharger's performance . . . measured against strict technology-based effluent limitations — specified levels of treatment — to which it must conform, rather than against limitations derived from water quality standards to which it and other polluters must collectively conform." . . .

[B]y eliminating the issue of the capacity of particular bodies

---

21. Apart from this simple "common sense" version of the argument, there is a more sophisticated economic version called the "optimal pollution" theory. This economic theory contends that there is a level or type of pollution that, while technologically capable of being controlled, is uneconomic to treat because the benefit from treatment is small and the cost of treatment is large. These economic theories are premised on a view that we have both adequate information about the effects of pollution to set an optimal test, and adequate political and administrative flexibility to keep polluters at that level once we allow any pollution to go untreated. As discussed in this section, it appears that Congress doubted these premises.

of receiving water, Congress made nationwide uniformity in effluent regulation possible. Congress considered uniformity vital to free the states from the temptation of relaxing local limitations in order to woo or keep industrial facilities. In addition, national uniformity made pollution cleanup possible without engaging in the divisive task of favoring some regions of the country over others.

More fundamentally, the new approach implemented changing views as to the relative rights of the public and of industrial polluters. Hitherto, the right of the polluter was pre-eminent, unless the damage caused by pollution could be proven. Henceforth, the right of the public to a clean environment would be pre-eminent, unless pollution treatment was impractical or unachievable. . . . [The court rejected the mills' claim for a variance based on the ability of receiving waters to absorb effluents without material environmental harm.]

NOTE AND QUESTIONS

1. Recall the discussion of national uniformity in the Clean Air Act, supra pp. 261-263, and the political economy of nondegradation policy, supra pp. 341-342. Might the motivation for national uniformity be preventing economic advantages rather than protecting water quality? Is national uniformity environmentally sound? What will be the longer run effects on industrial location? Does the Clean Water Act preclude EPA from granting a variance from federal technology-based effluent limitations in a case such as *Weyerhaeuser?* If EPA has discretion to grant such a waiver in cases like *Weyerhaeuser,* should it do so?

2. The court in *Crown Simpson Pulp Co. v. Costle,* 642 F.2d 323, *cert. denied,* 454 U.S. 1053 (1981) (9th Cir.), reached a similar result, upholding EPA's denial of a variance based on water quality impacts. Congress in 1982 enacted legislation authorizing variances from BOD and pH limitations for two paper mills in California discharging through deep ocean outfalls that had been the subject of the *Crown Simpson Pulp* litigation. See CWA §301 (m) (1). Do these provisions make sense?

3. Recall that in *Appalachian Power* (see supra, p. 485) EPA had refused the Atomic Energy Commission's recommendation that many existing nuclear generating plants be excluded from BAT regulations requiring retrofit of closed cycle cooling. AEC had relied on Environmental Impact Statements showing that the adverse effects of thermal discharges from such plants were insignificant or small. EPA rejected the proposal as "legally undefensible." Was EPA right? Why? Is it relevant that the exclusion was sought as a part of an effluent limitation rulemaking, rather than an ad hoc exception from an effluent limitation already adopted?

4. CWA §301(g), added in 1977, provides for a variance from BAT standards on a showing that the source complies with BPT requirements and applicable water quality standards, and that the variance will not result in the imposition of additional control requirements on any point or non-point source, and will "not interfere with" attainment of the CWA goal of fishable, swimmable water, and will not result in accumulations threatening health or the environment. The latter goals presumably require consideration of the need for water quality in excess of that required by current state water quality standards. How easy will it be for sources to obtain §301(g) variances?

Congress has also adopted a number of additional, more specialized variances based on water quality impacts. See supra, p. 460.

PROBLEM: EVALUATION OF A VARIANCE APPLICATION FOR INTAKE CONTROLS

CWA §316(a) provides for a case by case variance from otherwise applicable thermal effluent limitations (whether based on federally-based BPT or BAT limitations or limitations required to meet state water quality standards) on a showing by a source that such limitations are more stringent than necessary to protect a balanced, indigenous population of aquatic life in receiving waters. Section 316(b) requires EPA or state permitting agencies to require use of "best technology available" (BTA) relating to the "location, design, or capacity" of intake structures in order to "minimize adverse environmental impact" from cooling water intake systems.

ABC, a steam electric power plant built in 1971, uses a once-through cooling system that draws very large amounts of cooling water from and discharges heated water back into Esperance Bay. There is no evidence that the heated discharge water harms aquatic life populations in the Bay. The intake system kills large numbers of fish eggs, larvae, and small fish through impingement on the screens of the intake or entrainment through the plant's cooling system. Populations of adult fish in the Bay, however, have not declined since ABC began operation. Biologists who act as consultants to ABC attribute this phenomenon to the fact that many millions of fish eggs and many small fish never grow to adulthood even under natural conditions, and to the methods by which fish populations compensate for losses of individuals. For example, if some small fish are destroyed, the remaining individuals will have relatively more food from limited supplies, will be subject to less crowding and cannibalism, and therefore will be more likely to grow to adulthood than they otherwise would. More food and better habitats also spur faster growth and earlier sexual maturity, increasing the production of eggs and larvae. The biologists concede that at some point, which is difficult to predict in advance, losses of individual eggs, larvae, and small fish may become so large as to outstrip the capacity of these compensatory mechanisms to maintain adult populations. Local environmental groups demand that EPA either issue BTA regulations requiring retrofit of closed cycle cooling on all existing steam electric plants, or at least impose such requirements on ABC, whose NPDES permit is up for 5-year renewal. Closed cycle cooling would reduce water intake by 95 percent (some water still has to be taken from a water body to make up for evaporative losses from a closed-cycle cooling system), and would reduce intake losses of early life forms by the same percentage.

EPA adopts regulations requiring retrofit of closed-cycle cooling at all existing large generation plants. ABC submits documents to EPA which show that retrofit of closed-cycle cooling at ABC would cost between $1 and $2 billion. As an alternative to retrofitting its facility, ABC offers to purchase or secure easements on 15,000 acres of Bay wetlands that have been converted to agricultural or other uses, and to reconvert them to functioning wetlands. It provides studies from aquatic biologists asserting that the reconverted wetlands acreage would provide habitat and food sufficient to generate twice the number of fish eggs, larvae, and small fish destroyed by ABC's intake system. Does the CWA allow EPA to accept ABC's proposal and include the wetlands restoration program in ABC's permit renewal? If so, may EPA approve ABC's proposal? Should it? If EPA refuses, what remedies are potentially available to ABC?

NOTE ON DEADLINES AND ENFORCEMENT FLEXIBILITY

To what extent can regulators build flexibility into the effluent limitation systems by allowing individual sources to postpone or violate compliance deadlines? *Bethlehem Steel Corp. v. Train,* 544 F.2d 657 (3d Cir. 1976), considered Bethlehem's request to EPA for an extension of the 1977 statutory deadline for BPT compliance. EPA agreed that Bethlehem had proceeded in good faith but could not, despite all reasonable efforts, achieve the BPT compliance deadline. EPA nonetheless concluded that it lacked legal authority to postpone the deadline and proposed to issue an Enforcement Compliance Schedule Letter (ECSL) stating that it would not initiate enforcement proceedings if Bethlehem proceeded diligently to achieve compliance at a later date determined to be reasonable by EPA. Bethlehem's NPDES permit, however, continued to require a 1977 compliance date. This permit requirement would be enforceable against Bethlehem (including civil penalties) by environmental groups under the citizen suit provisions of §505 of the CWA. The court of appeals held that it could not require EPA formally to postpone the compliance deadline, despite the fact that it was impossible for Bethlehem to achieve it despite all good faith compliance efforts. Accord, *United States Steel Corp. v. Train,* 556 F.2d 822 (7th Cir. 1977).

Congress in the 1977 Amendments authorized extension of the BPT compliance date to 1979 if a source had acted in "good faith" to meet the 1977 deadline but had been unable to do so and had met certain other requirements. CWA §309(a)(5)(B). What is "good faith"? Does a source show "good faith" if it brings unsuccessful legal actions challenging the applicable BPT limitations? See *Monongahela Power Co. v. EPA,* 586 F.2d 318 (4th Cir. 1978). Compare the comparable problems that arose in connection with deadlines under the Clean Air Act, including the *General Motors* case, supra p. 283.

Even when deadlines or other statutory mandates are violated, EPA retains considerable enforcement discretion, including statutory authorization (added in 1977) to set compliance schedules for compliance with a "final deadline" not to exceed a time which EPA determines to be "reasonable," taking into account the seriousness of the violation and "any good faith efforts" to comply. CWA §309(a)(5)(A).

PROBLEM: WATER POLLUTION AT DAFFY SWAMP

Duck Hunters Unlimited (DHU), a nonprofit duck hunting, wildlife conservation, and ecosystem protection organization, operates the Daffy Swamp Shooting Range. DHU acquired Daffy Swamp, a 500 acre marshy area adjoining the Lazy River in 1968. Prior to that time, the land contained various industrial facilities and was significantly polluted with petroleum, metals, and chemical wastes. DHU spent approximately $800,000 in the early 1970s removing the facilities and cleaning up the area. These efforts restored the marsh to a relatively clean condition and fostered the return of waterfowl during their annual migrations. By 1975, the marsh was attracting large flocks of ducks and geese.

Since 1977, DHU has allowed its members to hunt waterfowl at Daffy Swamp. These hunters fire lead shot, which more often than not lands in the marsh.

The booming economy of the 1980s spurred the development of suburban communities in the vicinity of Daffy Swamp. The distant sounds of gunfire during hunting season bother some of the new neighbors. Moreover, local environmental groups find duck hunting to be a morally and environmentally repugnant activity. Local fisherfolk are concerned about the effect of lead contamination on fish in the Lazy River.

Neither DHU nor the Daffy Swamp Shooting Range has ever possessed a NPDES permit.

1. Has DHU or its members who have hunted at the Daffy Swamp Shooting Range violated the Clean Water Act?

2. Upon threat of suit by neighbors, local environmental groups, and fisherfolk, DHU applied for an NPDES permit. The regulatory authorities informed DHU that its permit would be governed by effluent limitations applicable to *Explosives Manufacturing Point Source Category, Subpart C — Explosives Load, Assemble, and Pack Plants Subcategory*, 40 C.F.R. §457.30-32. 32. This category, however, does not establish an effluent limit for lead. What arguments could DHU make to convince regulatory authorities that this category is inappropriate? What alternative categories should it suggest for the Daffy Swamp Shooting Range? If regulatory authorities rejected DHU's arguments for using an alternative category, what arguments could DHU make to obtain a variance?

QUESTIONS ON THE PRINCIPAL STRATEGY OF THE CWA

Note the various ways in which the CWA, as amended over time, and EPA's implementation of the Act have sought to soften the rigorous logic of uniform technology-based standards, which all existing sources are supposed to meet by certain deadlines:

- Deadlines have been postponed by statute. For example, Congress extended the BAT compliance deadline from 1983 to 1987.
- EPA enforcement policies have relaxed strict compliance with deadlines when they are unrealistic.
- EPA by regulation provided for FDF variances, an innovation subsequently endorsed and extended by Congress.
- Congress provided for cost-based variances from BAT standards.
- Congress created a new category of standards for discharges of "conventional pollutants," less rigorous than the BAT standards to which such pollutants would otherwise be subject.
- Congress created a variety of generic and more specialized variances from technology-based standards based on the effects of discharges in receiving waters.

Does this show that the technology-based approach adopted in 1972 is unsound? Or does it show that the approach is basically sound, subject to inevitable adjustments, which have been appropriately achieved by legislative and administrative processes? Has the CWA been more successful in coping with the problems created by uniform standards and compliance deadlines than the Clean Air Act?

D. CONTROL OF NON-POINT SOURCES

"Non-point source" (NPS) is not defined in the CWA. EPA has defined NPS pollution as contamination "caused by diffuse sources that are not regulated as point sources and normally associated with agricultural, silvicultural and urban runoff, runoff from construction activities, etc. . . . [N]onpoint source pollution does not result from a discharge at a specific, single location (such as a single pipe) but generally results from land runoff, precipitation, atmospheric deposition, or percolation." U.S. EPA, Office of Water Regulations and Standards, Nonpoint Source Guidance (August 1987).[22] Other sources of NPS pollution are mining activities, saltwater intrusion, and failing septic systems. The principal NPS pollutants include suspended solids, bacteria, nutrients, man-enhanced sediment, chemical fertilizers and pesticides, minerals and acids from active and abandoned mines, microbial pollutants, oil, salt and other chemicals from road maintenance, and runoff from commercial and industrial sites. Sediment from soil erosion is the major source of NPS pollution, often carrying other NPS pollutants, including plant nutrients, pesticides, and plant and animal pathogens into waterways.

NPS pollution from all sources accounts for up to 99 percent of suspended solids in water, 50 percent or more of other conventional pollutants, and up to 50 percent of water pollution by toxics.[23] NPS

---

22. Reprinted in Environmental Law Institute, Law of Environmental Protection 12-43 (S. Novick et al. (eds). 1993).

23. See Robert D. Fentress, Comment, Nonpoint Source Pollution, Groundwater, and the 1987 Water Quality Act: Section 208 Revisited?, 19 Envtl. L. 807, 813 (1989). Sediment can destroy habitat by covering areas where species spawn, or by eliminating bottom-living plant and animal species. Phosphorous and nitrogen contained in NPS runoff from agricultural sources can stimulate excessive algae and aquatic plant growth that chokes water bodies and exhausts oxygen supplies. Toxics dissolved in runoff are particularly available to aquatic biota. These toxics can enter the food chain, causing adverse effects on fish, wildlife, microorganisms, and the surrounding habitat. Bacteria, viruses, and infectious agents and disease-producing organisms from human and animal waste can enter the water supply through NPS pollution, affecting drinking water, the availability of shell fish and sport fish, and reducing the recreational potential of the receiving water bodies. In addition to the damage caused to receiving surface water bodies, runoff from NPS can leach into and pollute ground water supplies. D. Mandelker, Controlling Nonpoint Source Water Pollution: Can it be Done?, 65 Chi.-Kent L. Rev. 479 (1989).

pollution from agricultural runoff is arguably the leading source of water pollution in the United States. Agricultural runoff affects 60 percent of impaired river miles in the country, and 57 percent of our impaired lake acres. See Office of Water, US EPA, National Water Quality Inventory: 1990 Report to Congress, EPA No. 503/9-92/006, at 8, 22 (1992). Agricultural return flows from irrigation systems, which Congress specifically exempted from the statutory definition of "point source" in 1977 (see 33 U.S.C. §1362(14)), discharge significant amounts of metals and other toxics leached from crop soils.

Unlike point source (PS) pollution, which usually emanates from a distinct outflow — the end of a pipe — NPS pollution is typically ubiquitous, greatly complicating the task of regulation. NPS pollution is rarely amenable to uniform technology-based effluent limitations. Since NPS pollution is often carried by naturally occurring precipitation, owners or operators of NPSs often have little control over the amount or timing of NPS pollution discharges. In addition, the diversity of types of NPSs, from large agricultural enterprises to municipal parking lots, makes the establishment of uniform regulations difficult. Since NPS pollution enters the water supply from diffuse sources, it is difficult to attribute violations of effluent standards to any particular NPS.

Ultimately, NPS pollution must be controlled by tailoring the regulatory approach to the particular type of NPS activity or process. In many cases, this will require regulation of land-use practices that create NPSs, a subject traditionally under the jurisdiction of local governments. Agricultural runoff, for example, can be controlled by regulation of irrigation practices, soil conservation programs, and regulation of pesticide and fertilizer use. Urban runoff, by contrast, can be controlled by routing storm drains to treatment facilities, street cleaning, design standards for parking lots, and restrictions on discharge of oil, paints, and other hazardous materials in storm drains. Such approaches are often expensive and difficult to enforce. Controlling runoff from construction sites, mining operations, and silvicultural activities present comparable difficulties. In addition, powerful agricultural, mining, development, and other interests strongly oppose controls that would disrupt their activities.

Congress made its first significant effort to control NPS pollution through the passage of §208 of the CWA in 1972. Section 208 requires states to identify areas that, "as a result of urban-industrial concentrations and other factors, [have] substantial water quality control problems," and to designate a regional planning organization to develop area-wide waste treatment management (WTM) plans for the control of pollution in such areas. WTM plans must identify and establish procedures and methods to control NPS problems from urban and industrial NPSs; agriculture; silviculture; mining; salt water intrusions from groundwater extraction and irrigation; construction; and land disposal of wastes. Section 208 WTM Plans are subject to approval by the Administrator of EPA.[24]

In 1977, Congress added §208(j), containing the Rural Clean Water Program, to the CWA. This program is administered by the Department of Agriculture through the Soil Conservation Service. It authorizes grants of funds for owners and operators of rural land to install and maintain measures incorporating the "best management practices" (BMPs) for controlling NPS pollution. BMPs can be structural measures, such as sedimentation ponds, or they can be process-based measures, such as leaving field boundaries near waterways undisturbed or carefully scheduling applications of pesticides and fertilizers.

In 1987, Congress made a further attempt to address the NPS pollution problem in a new §319 of the CWA. Section 319 requires states to produce an assessment report, identifying navigable waters not expected to attain or maintain water quality standards without additional NPS control and also identifying NPSs that impair achievement of water quality standards. The report must also include a method for identifying BMPs and measures to reduce NPS pollution from the identified sources. States must also submit a management program with a detailed plan for preventing NPS pollution from flowing into the state's navigable waters. This plan must be implemented within four fiscal years from the date of its submission. The management plan must contain proposed BMPs and measures to reduce NPS pollution. States must submit both the assessment report and the management program to EPA for approval. EPA must prepare assessment reports for states that do not submit an assessment report or whose assessment reports EPA does not approve. EPA, however, is not authorized to promulgate its own management program if a state fails to submit an approvable plan. EPA, therefore, cannot force states or individuals to adopt regulatory programs to control NPS pollution. States with approved management programs are, however, eligible for EPA technical assistance and grants.

Section 319 improved upon §208 in many ways. It added the requirement that BMPs take account of impacts on groundwater. Moreover, §319 management program plans must contain scheduled annual implementation milestones, a feature not required under §208 plans. Section 319 introduced state groundwater quality protection grants of up to $150,000 per fiscal year and imposes greater monitoring and reporting requirements on states and EPA than §208. See Fentress, supra note 23, at 821-827. Yet it continues to rely on a planning approach without enforceable controls.

_____

24. CWA §208(b)(3). §208 also requires the Administrator to make grants to planning agencies to cover the reasonable costs of developing and operating a WTM planning process. Id. at (f). However, by 1980 the federal government stopped issuing grants for §208 planning. Federal agencies are also required to provide technical assistance to agencies carrying out the WTM planning process. Id. at (g)-(i).

CWA §303 requires that each state have an EPA-approved "continuing planning process" to protect all waters within the state. As a part of this process, states must determine Total Maximum Daily Loads (TMDL) for effluents from point sources for waters where effluent limitations on point sources will not achieve state water quality standards. TMDL determinations must also include NPSs discharges when BMPs are not sufficient to achieve water quality standards. The TMDL limitations from point sources must be factored into NPDES limitations for PS, but there is no similar requirement for NPSs.

None of these measures provide an adequate remedy for the problem of NPS pollution. They do not provide any means for the federal government to compel states to implement an NPS program. NPSs remain the most significant source of pollution in our nation's waterways.[25] Examples of the NPS problem were presented at a Senate hearing by William C. Baker, president of the Chesapeake Bay Foundation, who said progress in cleaning up the bay had been "glacial at best." "The oil that washes down the Chesapeake's storm drains in a year equals the *Exxon Valdez* spill," Baker told senators. He reeled off a list of other examples demonstrating what is faced in cleaning up the bay. For instance, he said, a multitude of urban sources contribute as much non-point pollution to the bay as does crop land. He also said more zinc reaches Baltimore harbor from pollution runoff than from industrial discharges. Baker warned that in the next 30 years, population in the watershed around the bay is expected to grow by 20 percent — 3 million more people. He said this will surely lead to greater non-point pollution problems without new controls. BNA Env. Rep. Current Developments, July 19, 1991.

The political and administrative difficulties inherent in regulating NPSs have caused the federal government to focus its regulatory attention on PSs. San Francisco Bay provides a relatively extreme but by no means unique example. The California State Water Resources Control Board estimates that POTWs and other PS dischargers contribute less than 3 percent of total pollutant loadings to the Bay. Even if the PSs in this region could be regulated to the point of zero discharge, this would reduce the total annual pollutant loadings of 9,600 tons by less than 310 tons.[26] The sharp difference in the regulatory treatment of point and non-point sources generates considerable political and litigation

---

25. See U.S. EPA, Office of Water, The Watershed Protection Approach: Annual Report, EPA 840-S-93-001, at 3 (1993); Office of Water and Office of Policy, Planning, and Evaluation, United States E.P.A., Incentive Analysis for Clean Water Act Reauthorization: Point Source/Nonpoint Source Trading for Nutrient Discharge Reductions i (1992).

26. California Association of Sanitation Agencies, Statement Before the Subcomm. on Water Resources and Environment of the House Comm. on Public Works and Transportation on the Reauthorization of the Clean Water Act 4-5 (April 1, 1993).

controversy over the classification of particular sources. See supra p. 454

Two proposals for addressing the NPS problem are receiving particular attention. These are the watershed protection approach, discussed infra at pp. 514-517, and point/non-point pollution trading, discussed infra at pp. 521-524.

E.   THE QUALITY-BASED APPROACH
OF THE CWA

MISSISSIPPI COMMISSION ON NATURAL RESOURCES V. COSTLE

625 F.2d 1269, 1275 (5th Cir. 1980)

[Mississippi challenged EPA's refusal to approve its water quality standards for dissolved oxygen (DO), which provided for a daily average DO standard of not less than 5.0 mg/l, but allowed a level of 4.0 mg/l daily average for low-flow days with the lowest water level that occurs for seven consecutive days in ten years.

The CWA requires EPA to develop and publish "criteria" for water quality accurately reflecting the latest scientific knowledge. §304(a). These "criteria" specify the different minimum standards of water quality that, in EPA's view, are needed to support different uses of water bodies (swimming, fishing, navigation, etc.). The uses of various water bodies are designated by the states. State water quality standards are subject to EPA review and approval. If EPA determines that a state standard does not meet the requirements of the CWA and the state fails to adopt an adequate standard, EPA may promulgate a standard for the state. CWA §303(c). EPA gave notice of the availability of *Quality Criteria for Water*, also called the Red Book, on October 26, 1973. It thereafter became EPA's policy to request a state to justify its standards whenever the state submitted for approval water quality criteria for designated uses that were less stringent than those in the Red Book. EPA notified Mississippi that it questioned the adequacy of its DO standard because it allowed water quality below the 5.0 mg/l instantaneous minimum specified in the Red Book. Mississippi refused to alter its standards to conform to those in the Red Book.

EPA proposed a standard that would prohibit DO concentrations below 5.0 mg/l daily average. In September 1978, two public hearings were held in Mississippi as part of the rulemaking process. In response to public comment, Mississippi reaffirmed a standard of 5.0 mg/l daily average 4.0 mg/l 7 days Q10. 4.0 mg/l. EPA disapproved Mississippi's standard and promulgated a 5.0 mg/l daily average standard with a 4.0 mg/l instantaneous standard.]

VI.   DISAPPROVAL OF MISSISSIPPI'S STANDARD

A.   SCOPE OF AUTHORITY

The Commission contends that EPA exceeded its statutory authority by tipping the balance of federal and state power created by Congress in the FWPCA. The Commission argues that EPA may substitute its judgment only if a state fails to act or acts irresponsibly. Furthermore, the Commission asserts that EPA misconstrues its authority as allowing disapprovals of standards that do not meet the requirements of EPA policy instead of those not meeting the requirements of the Act.

Congress did place primary authority for establishing water quality standards with the states. . . . As noted above, the legislative history reflects congressional concern that the Act not place in the hands of a federal administrator absolute power over zoning watershed areas. The varied topographies and climates in the country call for varied water quality solutions.

Despite this primary allocation of power, the states are not given unreviewable discretion to set water quality standards. All water quality standards must be submitted to the federal Administrator. The state must review its standards at least once every three years and make the results of the review available to the Administrator. EPA is given the final voice on the standard's adequacy. . . .

EPA's role is more dominant when water quality criteria are in question. Although the designation of uses and the setting of criteria are interrelated chores, the specification of a waterway as one for fishing, swimming, or public water supply is closely tied to the zoning power Congress wanted left with the states. The criteria set for a specific use are more amenable to uniformity. Congress recognized this distinction by placing with EPA the duty to develop and publish water quality criteria reflecting the latest scientific knowledge shortly after [the 1972 FWPCA's adoption] and periodically thereafter. EPA correctly points out that by leaving intact the Mississippi use designations it has acted in the manner least intrusive of state prerogatives. . . .

The statute enumerates the following requirements for water quality standards:

Such standards shall be such as to protect the public health or welfare, enhance the quality of water and serve the purposes of this chapter. Such standards shall be established taking into consideration their use and value for public water supplies, propagation of fish and wildlife, recre-

ational purposes, and agricultural, industrial, and other purposes, and
also taking into consideration their use and value for navigation.

[CWA §303(c)(2).] One purpose of the Act is

the national goal that wherever attainable, an interim goal of water quality which provides for the protection and propagation of fish, shellfish,
and wildlife and provides for recreation in and on the water be achieved
by July 1, 1983.

[CWA §101(a)(2).] The EPA Administrator did not improperly construe his authority both interpreting the [Act] as allowing him to translate these broad statutory guidelines and goals into specifics that could
be used to evaluate a state's standard. One "requirement of the Act"
is that EPA formulate these policies for water quality criteria. [CWA
§304(a)(1).] It was not unreasonable for the EPA Administrator to interpret the Act as allowing him to require states to justify standards not
in conformance with the criteria policy. . . .

B.   SUBSTANTIVE AND PROCEDURAL ASPECTS
OF THE DISAPPROVAL

The Commission asserts that EPA failed to consider all relevant
factors by excluding economic considerations in setting the DO criteria. EPA determined that while economic factors are to be considered
in designating uses, those factors are irrelevant to the scientific technical factors to be considered in setting criteria to meet those uses. . . .
We note at the outset that EPA states it did examine the economic
impact of its criteria and "concluded that a significant impact [was] not
likely to occur." Nevertheless, we are convinced that EPA's construction
is correct. Congress itself separated use and criteria and states that "the
water quality criteria for such waters [shall be] based on such uses."
[CWA §303(c)(2).] The statute requires EPA to develop criteria "reflecting the latest *scientific* knowledge." [CWA §304(a)(1)] (emphasis
added). The interpretation that criteria were based exclusively on scientific data predates the 1972 amendments. Furthermore, when Congress
wanted economics and cost to be considered, it explicitly required it.
EPA policy does permit downgrading when "substantial and widespread adverse economic and social impact" would otherwise result.
General downgrading is not possible in this case, however, because Mississippi has the same standard for all uses. Furthermore, the statute
requires that waters be at least fishable and swimmable "wherever attainable." [CWA §101(a)(2).] Mississippi's lowest use is fishable water.

EPA does allow downgrading for particular stream segments, and suggested this course to the Commission in its disapproval letter.

The Commission also argues that EPA's disapproval was a clear error of judgment. EPA has determined that most fishable waters require a DO concentration of 5.0 mg/l. It determined that the fish species in Mississippi, as throughout the South, would be adversely affected by a 4.0 mg/l average during the stressful low flow periods. EPA cited laboratory and field studies supporting its position. Its disapproval of the state standard was not arbitrary or capricious.

. . . Because EPA's disapproval of the DO standard was proper, it was within the scope of the Administrator's authority to promulgate a substitute standard. [The Court also held that the standards promulgated by EPA were not arbitrary or capricious.]

NOTES AND QUESTIONS

1. Could Mississippi rezone some of its waters, designating them for industrial use rather than for fishing, and then adopt the less stringent Red Book Standards applicable to waters zoned for industrial use?

2. May a discharger challenge EPA's approval of a state water quality standard on the ground that the standard is more stringent than necessary to secure the uses for which a water body is zoned? See *Homestake Mining Co. v. EPA,* 477 F. Supp. 1279 (D.S.D. 1979). Compare *Union Electric,* supra, p. 277.

3. What remedies does EPA have if a state fails to take effective action against point sources to achieve its water quality standards? If a state fails to take effective action against non-point sources? See generally Gaba, Federal Supervision of State Water Quality Standards Under the Clean Water Act, 36 Vand. L. Rev. 1167 (1983).

4. Congress adopted a system of national uniform technology-based effluent limitations in 1972 because it concluded that the prior strategy based on water quality standards had failed. Why then did it retain this strategy as part of the amended Act? (In part, the answer has to do with differences between the House, which tended to favor retention of the prior strategy, and the Senate, which favored a technology-based approach.) Both the CWA and the Clean Air Act rely on a combination of technology-based standards and standards based on environmental quality. What explains the differences between the combination embodied in the CWA and that in the Clean Air Act? Which is the more successful?

5. In response to growing concern over toxic pollutants, half of which are discharged by non-point sources, Congress in 1987 required adoption by states of water quality standards for toxic pollutants, speci-

fying maximum permissible concentrations of various toxic pollutants. CWA §303(c)(2)(B). Such "numeric" standards are to be contrasted with "narrative" standards adopted by some states that establish water quality standards in descriptive terms: for instance, that water quality "shall support a balanced and general population of aquatic life." States must also adopt appropriate strategies to eliminate violations of numeric standards in toxic "hot spot" water segments, although the only enforceable controls required are those directed at point sources. CWA §304(*l*). Toxic standards are developed through bioassay or biomonitoring techniques that seek to measure or simulate actual water body conditions and determine the effects of specific toxic pollutants. Recently, EPA invoked its authority under §303(c) of the Act to propose a "national toxics rule" that would impose water quality standards for toxics on a dozen states that have not adopted such standards, or adopted standards that EPA believes to be inadequate. See 57 Fed. Reg. 60848 (1992). May EPA use its §303(c) authority to adopt uniform standards for all such states, regardless of variations in local conditions and water uses? For example, EPA's toxic standards are based in part on the need to prevent bioaccumulation of toxics in fresh water fish that people eat. Should the standards be the same in regions where people eat a great deal of fresh water fish and regions where they eat little or none?

6. *Problem:* Return to the Daffy Swamp Problem on p. 502. The state in which Daffy Swamp and the Lazy River are located has water quality criteria for lead. Lead levels in the Lazy River violate these criteria. What can the state do with regard to the Daffy Swamp Shooting Range to address this lead pollution problem?

PEDERSEN, TURNING THE TIDE ON WATER QUALITY

15 Ecology L.Q. 69, 70-73 (1988)[27]

Since 1972, Congress has based the statutory framework not on water quality, but on requiring equal limits on all technically similar sources wherever they may be located. Because water quality varies with location, this broad approach is inefficient, ineffective, and quite predictably results in controls that are tighter than they need to be to preserve environmental quality or that are too lenient to make any real difference. In addition, this approach has tempted regulators and environmentalists to define successful water pollution control simply by tallying how many regulated sources have installed how much technology.

27. Mr. Pedersen is a former Associate General Counsel of the U.S. EPA.

[Pedersen notes that the Act has not led to perceptible improvements in many water bodies, and that some — such as the Chesapeake Bay — have deteriorated markedly over the past 20 years.]

Protecting an ecosystem, however, is far more challenging than legislators will acknowledge: it requires regulation to assure that minimum water standards are met. As of 1984, over half of the pollutants in the nation's water were generated by nonpoint sources such as irrigation return flows or runoff from fields and streets. Restraining these sources may call for regulation of where and how people may farm, cut trees, or construct roads and buildings. Moreover, even if the pollution input to a lake or stream could be held constant by such methods, its impact would vary with the amount of water available to dilute pollution. Thus, to protect water quality fully, the government either must adjust its demands for varying water levels or must keep water levels constant by limiting offstream uses of water.[28]

. . . If there is to be an effective federal water pollution control law, therefore, significant decisions must be made specifying the level of protection to be afforded each body of water and identifying who will make those determinations. . . .

Rather than attempt to address such philosophically and politically sensitive issues, Congress has carefully designed its water pollution statutes to avoid them. . . .

Congress could correct these flaws by changing the current statute to emphasize actual environmental standards and by requiring actual achievement of them. Although the present law still requires states to set water quality standards and to submit them to EPA for approval, it does not define those standards broadly enough or require adequate steps to attain them. Congress should mandate that all such standards include a satisfactory and enforceable attainment plan requiring EPA approval. EPA would promulgate plans if the states did not provide them.

In addition to forcing the actual attainment of water quality standards, Congress should allow states to choose acceptable quality levels for most of their waters. This discretion should not be unbounded,

---

28. In the last comprehensive survey of the nation's water budget, the U.S. Water Resources Council concluded after a quantitative survey that

[t]here is already . . . encroachment on optimum instream conditions [for wildlife] for most months throughout the West. In much of the arid West, the water supply is already depleted by more than 90 percent in many months. This means a loss of desirable aquatic life and attendant instream values. . . .

By the year 2000, given the projected offstream use, the instream conditions will worsen significantly in most basins.

however. At the very least, Congress should require full protection of water quality in national parks, wilderness areas, and other federal reserves. . . .

NOTE ON THE WATERSHED PROTECTION APPROACH TO CONTROLLING NON-POINT SOURCE POLLUTION

EPA and a variety of other interested parties have advocated shifting to a watershed protection approach (WPA) to controlling NPS pollution.[29] Rather than imposing effluent-specific and source-specific command and control regulations on pollution sources, the WPA would adopt a risk-prioritized approach to addressing the problems of complete watersheds. A watershed is "a geographic area in which water, sediments, and dissolved materials drain to a common outlet, a point on a larger stream, a lake, an underlying aquifer, an estuary, or an ocean."[30] The WPA approach would administer watersheds as complete units defined by their underlying hydrology, rather than managing individual portions of watersheds according to arbitrarily defined political boundaries. This administrative structure would include management of all waters, including surface and ground waters, and both inland and coastal waters. In addition, it would encompass management of the land from which water drains into a particular watershed. All aspects of the watershed's quality would be considered under this approach in an integrated way, including chemical water quality, physical water quality, habitat quality, and biodiversity. Issues of water quantity, including basic demand and supply, would also be included in the WPA.

The watershed protection approach involves three stages. First, appropriate watersheds are identified and mapped. Second, all of the "stakeholders" in the watershed are assembled to analyze the threats to the watershed, and to devise responses to these threats based on a risk-based analysis. These stakeholders would include state environmental, public health, agriculture, and natural resource agencies, local environmental regulatory boards and commissions, Indian tribes, representatives of the public and of environmental groups, and industry and development interests. In the third step, the selected response mechanisms are applied to the watersheds' problems. Progress towards achiev-

---

29. See e.g., United States EPA, Office of Water, The Watershed Protection Approach: Annual Report 1992, EPA 840-S-93-001 (1993); United States EPA, Office of Water, The Watershed Protection Approach: An Overview, EPA /503/9-92/002 (1991) hereinafter Overview.

30. Overview, supra, note 29, at 1.

ing water quality goals is then regularly monitored, and adjustments are made in response mechanisms as required.[31]

The WPA is likely to be an important tool for addressing water quality in the future. Implementing WPA projects will be difficult, however, until the authority of agencies to use the approach is clarified. Currently, a WPA project can involve areas of overlapping regulatory jurisdictions. In addition, it is not always clear what sources of funding can be used to support WPA projects.

Senators Baucus and Chafee have introduced a CWA reauthorization bill, the Water Pollution Prevention and Control Act of 1993, which would provide a statutory basis for the WPA.[32] Title III of this bill, entitled "Watershed Planning and Nonpoint Pollution Control," provides for comprehensive watershed management to allow for the prioritization of threats to watersheds and for the identification of the most cost-effective measures for promoting water quality. The Act would allow state governors to designate waters and associated land areas as watershed management units (WMUs), within which waters that were not meeting water or sediment quality standards would be identified. Governors of more than one state can jointly designate multi-state WMUs. Following designation, the Governor is required to designate a public or nonprofit entity to develop and implement a management plan for the WMU, which may be submitted to EPA for approval. Projects and activities included in a plan and not otherwise required by law are eligible for special funding and regulatory incentives. For example, EPA or a state may issue a permit to a PS that does not ensure attainment and maintenance of water quality standards if the receiving water is part of a WMU and the WMU plan includes enforceable requirements that provide for attainment and maintenance of water quality standards prior to the expiration for the plan. Also, states or EPA may extend NPDES permits to 10 years terms (as opposed

---

31. EPA headquarters has created a support team with representatives from all offices within the Office of Water to help EPA Regions, states, and local governments pursue the WPA. In addition, the Office of Water works with EPA's budgeting process to provide Regional Offices with the flexibility necessary to shift a portion of their resources to WPA projects. Moreover, EPA has provided states that are experimenting with the WPA more flexibility in meeting regulatory requirements, through such measures as aligning NPDES permits on uniform five-year cycles. Several states and many EPA Regions are already conducting their own experiments with the WPA strategy. EPA Region VIII, for example, has begun compiling a regional Watershed Inventory, with information on the physical characteristics, the past and present human uses, the principal activities affecting water quality, the current condition of wildlife habitat in the watershed, and the current value and condition of the ecosystem of which the watershed is part.

32. S. 1114, 84 Cong. Rec. S7243 (daily ed. June 15, 1993).

to the normal five-year term) for PSs located within WMUs with approved plans.

IN MAJOR COASTAL WATER STUDY: NATIONAL EXPERTS URGE FUNDAMENTAL DEPARTURE FROM TECH-BASED REGULATIONS. INSIDE EPA'S WATER POLICY REPORT

Vol. 11, Num. 9, pp.4-5 (April 28, 1993)

A panel of national experts in a long-awaited study is urging a fundamental departure from existing technology-based controls for coastal pollution to a new "integrated coastal management" approach. Because the proposal is consistent with numerous plans for watershed management, the study is expected to give a significant boost to that approach during Clean Water Act reauthorization debates.

The Study has greatly pleased coastal city officials who say it justifies their contention that expensive technology controls are unnecessary for certain coastal discharges. It is also prompting some officials to predict that the study's conclusions could be applied to inland waters as well.

The National Research Council's (NRC) *Managing Wastewater in Coastal Urban Areas* "offers a wide-ranging critique of existing wastewater management policy and proposed a new and fundamentally different paradigm," according to the report. The current approach mandates expensive secondary treatment technology of publicly owned treatment works. Coastal cities have sought to gain Clean Water Act waivers, arguing that their discharge pipes extend far into the ocean and can safely release effluent that has less than secondary treatment. This technology-based regime has not adequately protected coastal waters from some problems and has been "overprotective" regarding other problems, the study notes.

In examining problems with the existing system — the first "outside review" since 1975 of the 1972 Clean Water Act's policies — NRC cites seven areas where improvements can be made. For instance, in recognition that coastal systems vary widely and should not be subject to the same technology or approach, the study urges that coastal wastewater and stormwater management be "tailored to the characteristics, values, and uses of the particular receiving environment." . . .

In a key recommendation on "levels of treatment," the study recommends: "Coastal municipal wastewater treatment requirements should be established through an integrated process on the basis of environmental quality as described, for example, by water and sediment quality criteria and standards, rather than by technology-based regulations." The study notes that "chemically-enhanced primary treatment" is "nearly equivalent" to the EPA performance standards for secondary treatment. In a highly controversial EPA lawsuit against San Diego, CA, the city is seeking to avoid secondary treatment for its Point Loma treatment facility. . . .

Noting that techniques to monitor bacteria levels in coastal waters are greatly needed, the study calls upon EPA, public health agencies, and wastewater treatment agencies to develop such monitoring techniques. Lastly, the study calls for coastal water management systems to be "flexible" so they can change whenever new information is developed about environmental quality. . . .

To implement the various improvements recommended, the study proposes an "integrated coastal managements" (ICM) approach. Under this approach, standards would be developed taking account of "risk, uncertainty, and variability among regions and sites." All pollution sources would be considered, and all media — land, air, or water. Controls should achieve benefits "at least commensurate with the costs" they impose and management actions should be phased in to allow for changes in plans when dictated by new information. Moving from the existing approach to the new one "will involve risk taking and inevitably experience some setbacks," the study cautions. . . .

"The clarion call of this report is that one size does not fit all, even among coastal waters," says a local official, who believes the recommendations "may well be applicable beyond coastal waters." An NRC member, who expresses hopes that Congress will adopt the report's recommendations in CWA reauthorization, says the existing "rigid technology-based standards" have "stifled innovation" in the U.S. Europeans feel the U.S. system is "ludicrous" because, for instance, it is forcing Boston Harbor to install 50-year old technology to achieve secondary treatment. . . .

F.   INCENTIVE-BASED APPROACHES TO WATER POLLUTION

Review the materials analyzing the shortcomings of a "best available technology" (BAT) approach at pp. 374-376, supra. The problems with a BAT approach are more acute in the CWA than under the Clean Air Act because the CWA places relatively greater emphasis on use of uniform technology-based regulation. Under the Clean Water Act's BAT strategy, the EPA has adopted nationally uniform effluent limitations for some 500 different industries.

Proposal for Marketable, Fixed-Term Discharge Permits: The Jacoby-Schaumburg Plan[33]

Professor Henry D. Jacoby and Grant W. Schaumburg . . . proposed that the current allocation of discharge rights to cities and industries in a river basin, along with the effluent or treatment standards typically governing such allocations, be replaced by an administered market in fixed-term discharge permits. The market would be instituted by converting existing discharge rights with respect to BOD (and perhaps one or two additional waste parameters) into permits which could be sold to other present or prospective dischargers, or to nondischargers who wished to enter the market for speculative or conservationist purposes. Different sets of permits might be used for summer and winter conditions in order to make more efficient use of seasonably variable assimilative capacity. Demand for these waste-disposal opportunities would then determine their market prices. Overall stream quality would be improved and maintained by limits on the total number of permits outstanding at any time.

Under this plan, transfer of permits from one zone to another would be regulated by exchange rates so set by the issuing authority that trading could not cause water quality to fall below the stream standard at any point. For example, if discharges of BOD into stream-zone B are twice as harmful to a critical reach as identical discharges into zone A further upstream, then a permit might allow a polluter to discharge either 1 pound per day into zone B or 2 pounds per day into zone A. If a zone-B discharger wishes to increase his waste load by 100 pounds and a zone-A discharger can abate 200 pounds of his waste load at less cost then B would be willing to pay him for the corresponding discharge rights, A would abate accordingly and sell the necessary permits to B. New dischargers could also buy into the market in this manner.

The proposed system leads to least-cost configurations of waste control in the basin. . . .

Currently there is considerable interest in promoting trading. The Jacoby-Schaumburg plan would allow a smooth, continuous adjustment of discharge privileges while maintaining stream standards. It would provide continuing incentives to find improved methods of waste control, all at smaller administrative cost and greater economic efficiency. The major expense of the proposed permit system would be for continuous monitoring of discharges — a feature of any adequate control system.

---

33. Environmental Law Institute, Effluent Charges on Air and Water Pollution 36-38 (1973).

The proponents of this plan also deemed it superior to effluent charges because, unlike the latter, it would not only rely on indirect incentives to control stream quality. Charges may be set incorrectly if based on imperfect information concerning technological alternatives, abatement costs, or other factors influencing investment decisions, and political pressures may forestall upward adjustments. The need to adjust charges repeatedly in the light of experience or in response to economic growth would entail heavier administrative costs than the permit market here proposed.

J. LIS & K. CHILTON, CLEAN WATER — MURKY POLICY

Washington Univ. Center for the Study of American Business 1992

Effluent Fees. Effluent fees put a price on wastewater discharge. Any source of emission — including nonpoint-sources — would pay a fee on the amount of pollutant discharged. If the cost of polluting is higher than preventing or treating effluent discharge, the natural desire is to discharge less. Fees, as discussed earlier, should be set in proportion to the amount of damage the discharge's effluent creates. Existing programs thus far have not adhered to this important criterion. . . .

Germany. A cooperative association in Germany's heavily industrialized Ruhr Valley has successfully used a "polluter pays" system since 1913. Fees are based on the expected — not actual — amount and quality of the discharger's effluent. The funds generated by the charges help build and operate waste-treatment facilities in the basin.

Fees are linked to a permitting system that sets a minimum effluent standard for each discharger. Fees generate revenue for the water-quality-management program's administrative costs and government subsidies to public-treatment works. Dischargers calculate their fee by determining their expected volume of several key pollutants. A discharger receives 50 percent reduction in its fee if it stays within its prescribed effluent limit. This reduction may motivate dischargers to remain in compliance; however, fees are generally too low to provide much incentive for further action.

France. France has a system of charges similar to the German program.

The Netherlands. Since 1969, the Netherlands have administered a fee system that has encouraged discharges to avoid polluting. Effluent fees in the Netherlands are higher than those in Germany and France. Fees are based on the volume and concentration of a discharger's ef-

fluent. Actual discharge levels are used to determine fees for large dischargers while small dischargers pay a fixed fee. As with Germany and
France, revenues are used to finance water-quality improvement projects.

A 1983 study of the Netherlands' effluent fee system concluded
that charges had a measurable impact on water quality. Increases in
effluent charges were significantly correlated with declines in water-
borne pollutants.

United States. The use of effluent fees has been limited in the
United States. Federally funded public treatment works are encouraged
to charge user fees to industries and consumers that fully cover all operating and capital costs. However, user fees are small compared to a
fee level that might alter pollution behavior.

Marketable Permits. Pollution-control programs using marketable
permits (effluent-discharge permits that may be bought or sold among
polluters) have been tried in a few areas of the United States. Nonetheless, cost savings for the few tradeable-permit systems established thus
far have been much less than expected. Administrative complexities
seem to have been an important limitation.

Fox River. In 1981, Wisconsin developed a permit-trading system
to offer dischargers more flexibility to control biological oxygen demand in the Fox River. Early cost savings estimates of $7 million a year
proved to be too high.

In six years of operation, only one trade occurred. Although the
initial goal was to provide flexibility through trading, the trading process for the Fox River itself is highly restrictive. A polluter first must
prove the need to purchase additional discharge allowances. Also, the
trading process is administratively complex.

SMITH & FALZONE, FRANCE: WATER POLLUTION

BNA, Intl. Envt. Rep. Ref. file 3 (Sept. 9, 1987)

The Water Law of December 16, 1964, prescribed the way water
regulation should be carried out by dividing France into six regions
and establishing in each a River Basin Agency to help control, on a
regional level, discharges into waterways and water use in general. Representatives of elected bodies, the water users, and the public administration make up a River Basin Committee — a type of "water
parliament" for the area — which is responsible for rational management of water resources. The funding for the regional agencies comes

from a water use tax on those drawing upon the public water supply for drinking water, irrigation, or industrial use, and on those discharging pollutants into the waterways of the area. The tax is decided by the Basin Committee, and its rate is based upon the quantity of water used or pollution discharged. The pollution tax is calculated using six parameters; oxidizable matter, suspended solids, phosphorus, soluble salts, nitrogen dioxide, and toxic substances, although Environment Ministry officials have indicated plans to expand the list as additional pollution problems need to be addressed.

The six river basin agencies participate technically and financially in the fight against water pollution through five-year investment programs which take into account water management needs and the needs and possibilities of the water users. The River Basin Committees redistribute the incoming tax monies in the form of grants and low-interest loans in order to help local water users or municipalities finance pollution reduction technologies. The Environment Ministry harmonizes the action of the six agencies, and the Budget Ministry holds a veto power over water taxes it deems to be too high.

The Water Law further provides for a water "police," whose oversight and enforcement role is set out in the Decree of February 23, 1973. In principle, all direct or indirect discharges of matter generally liable to alter the quality of surface waters, ground water, or waters of the sea must receive authorization under the Water Law.

NOTE ON POINT/NON-POINT TRADING

Currently there is considerable interest by EPA and others in trading between point sources, which are subject to federal effluent controls, and non-point sources, which are not. EPA is imposing increasingly strict controls on point sources, and Congress is considering even stricter measures. A point source facing more stringent controls often discharges into the same water body as non-point sources, whose marginal control costs for a given pollutant are often far lower than that of point sources, but are generally not subject to any controls at all. Under a trading system, a point source could satisfy its increased effluent limitation requirements by paying non-point sources to reduce their discharges and obtaining a regulatory credit against its requirements in the amount of such reductions. For example, assume a point source that is already subject to 90 percent BPT controls for phosphates that is facing 98 percent BAT control requirements that will cost 10 cents/lb phosphate to meet. Neighboring farms using phosphate-based fertilizers that run off into the same water basin could reduce this runoff (by using substitutes, better fertilizer, and water management, etc.)

at 2 cents/lb. To meet its BAT requirements, the point service could pay the farmers something between 2 cents/lb and 10 cents/lb to reduce their runoff in the appropriate amount. Would such an arrangement be lawful under the current CWA?

Point/non-point trading would apply the "bubble" or "offset" approach used under the Clean Air Act to watershed management. See Esther Bartfeld, Point-Nonpoint Source Trading: Looking Beyond Potential Cost Savings, 23 Envtl. L. 43 (1993); David Letson, Point/Nonpoint Source Pollution Reduction Trading: An Interpretive Survey, 32 Nat. Res. J. 219, 221 & n.7 (1992). Such trading would not be appropriate for all areas. The waterbodies to which the strategy will be applied must be part of an identifiable watershed, or at least a sufficiently large portion of one to allow for comprehensive watershed management. There must also be a sufficient number and appropriate distribution of both PSs and controllable NPSs to provide a basis for trades. There must be a numeric water quality standard for the subject waterbodies, and there must be accurate and sufficient data on the waterbody to establish pollution baselines and track the effects of trades. In addition, the marginal cost of controls on NPSs must be significantly lower than the marginal costs of PS controls for trading to provide significant benefits.

Under most proposals, participating PSs must still meet the national technology-based effluent limitations: trading would be a means of shifting more stringent discharge limitation requirements based on ambient water quality standards, rather than a way of "trading" out of natural technology-based requirements.

Trading may be easier to develop for some types of pollutants than for others. In the case of pollutants such as biochemical oxygen demand that do not accumulate, the timing of the pollution loading as well as the total amount of discharge are important considerations in developing a trading regime. If too much BOD is dumped at one time, it may cause a fish kill, whereas the same amount spread out over a longer period of time could have no effect. Trading systems for such pollutants therefore have to take into account the time periods over which discharges occur as well as total amounts. The effects of other pollutants that do not break down rapidly and accumulate, such as phosphorus, are largely a function of total loadings without regard to the precise timing of discharges. Trading systems for such pollutants are simpler. See Letson, supra, at 226.

There are various possible ways of implementing a point/non-point trading system. The PS could contract directly with the owner of the NPS to install and maintain the BMP or, a PS owner or operator could contract with a third party to install and maintain a BMP that would provide the necessary amount of reduction in NPS pollution.

Finally, under a hybrid trading/fee approach, PSs could be required to contribute a fixed fee per unit of discharge to a publicly-administered fund which supports BMPs for NPSs within the watershed. This last approach eliminates the difficulty of finding trading partners, but provides less of a guarantee that the NPS measures will actually be carried out than if PS owners and operators are directly obligated to procure NPS pollution reductions. See Bartfeld, supra, at 88.

Many NPS loadings are less predictable both in their timing and in their concentrations than PS loadings, and NPS discharges may be more difficult to monitor than PS discharges. Some proposals deal with these problems by requiring a NPS/PS trading ratio of greater than 1:1. Also, NPS pollution tends to load most heavily during times of heavy precipitation. These are the times when stream flows are highest, however, and NPS has a relatively lesser impact on stream water quality at these times. A 1:1 trading of PS and NPS pollution, therefore, may not realistically reflect the impact of pollution on watersheds with several streams.[34]

Although a PS/NPS trading program would increase information costs, pose new administrative complexities, and operate successfully in only some circumstances, it would bring previously unregulated NPS loadings under NPDES regulatory authority and substitute enforceable obligations for relatively weak incentives for reductions provided by existing CWA NPS programs. Where trading occurs, the PS permit must be revised to allow it to release more effluents than would otherwise be allowed but also must include the BMP arrangements as enforceable obligations. Trading could also reduce the costs of control to PSs, provide financing and know-how to NPSs, and mobilize a broader range of effluent reduction approaches.

At present, there is no direct authority in the CWA for conducting PS/NPS trading. The CWA does, however, provide for the allocation of total allowable pollution loadings between PSs and NPSs, which would be an important first step in any trading program. As noted previously, states are required to establish Total Maximum Daily Loads (TMDLs) of certain pollutants for waterbodies that have not met water quality

---

34. See Bartfeld, supra, at 62. The beneficial impact of NPS BMPs on receiving waters is also altered by the exact location of the NPS. Reductions in discharges from an NPS that is set well back from any body of surface water would have a less beneficial effect on water quality than similar reductions from an NPS that is located on a water body's edge. Id. at 94-95. Also, there may be unintended consequences from BMPs that would affect the relative benefits of NPS pollution reductions. Conservation tillage, for example, which is a common approach to reducing NPS pollution through agricultural runoff, may increase pooling, thereby increasing the possibility of groundwater contamination. Id. at 97.

standards after the imposition of effluent limitations. CWA §303(d). They must also calculate the reductions in TMDLs that would be required in order to meet applicable water quality standards, and use this calculation to establish Wasteload Allocations (WLAs) for existing or future PSs, and Load Allocations (LAs) for existing or future NPSs and natural background sources of pollution. See 40 C.F.R. §§130.1.15. These determinations could provide the basis for establishing a PS/NPS trading program. EPA has urged Congress to amend the CWA to sanction or promote point/non-point trading.

Some experiments in trading have been initiated at the state level. One example is the Tar-Pamlico River Basin in North Carolina. Several POTWs discharge into the Tar and Pamlico Rivers and their tributaries. In addition, these waters are subject to large NPS loadings of nitrogen and phosphorus from local agriculture. A coalition of municipal dischargers, in cooperation with the Environmental Defense Fund, suggested a trading system as an alternative to stricter effluent limitations for new and expanding POTWs. The municipal dischargers joined together into a Basin Association, which assumes primary responsibility for achieving the desired nutrient level reductions. As an alternative to individual plant nutrient restrictions, the Association members are collectively responsible for achieving a total nutrient loading target. Within the aggregate total, members of the Association are permitted to trade discharge allocations among themselves. If the Association exceeds the aggregate total discharge level, they must offset excess discharges through payments into a NPS control fund administered by the state at a fixed rate of 56 dollars per kilogram. See Bartfeld, supra, at 86-87.

NOTES AND QUESTIONS

1. The Jacoby-Schaumburg excerpt points to one difficulty with transferable pollution permits, namely that all of the permits in a given region might be bought up and used by sources in a delimited sector of that region, leading to unduly high pollution levels in that sector. How do they propose to deal with this possibility? Does their solution undercut the feasibility or the claimed advantages of a transferable permit system? How can the problem of geographical concentration of pollution sources be dealt with under a fee system? A regulatory system? How could a trading system be designed to deal with pollutants, such as BOD, for which the timing as well as the total amount of discharges is important?

2. The EPA and the Army Corps of Engineers have issued guidelines for the use of mitigation banking in connection with wetlands development. Agricultural or commercial developers who meet other

regulatory criteria for §404 permits to develop wetlands must in addition take steps to mitigate adverse environmental effects. Such mitigation measures can include protection, through acquisition of conservation easements, of other wetlands otherwise vulnerable to development, or restoration of former wetlands that have been converted to other uses. A wetlands banking program would establish a market system of mitigation credits that developers could purchase. The credits would be based on public or private restoration or protection projects involving relatively large tracts of wetlands in ecologically valuable areas. See U.S. EPA, U.S. Department of the Army, Memorandum to the Field on Establishment and Use of Wetlands Mitigation Banks in the Clean Water Act Section 404 Regulatory Program (August 23, 1993). A trading system could reduce the costs and administrative burdens to developers of securing mitigation. It could also provide ecological benefits by avoiding piecemeal efforts and targeting mitigation resources on large areas of wetlands of high ecological value. Trading ratios could be adjusted for wetlands of different quality, and greater than 1:1 trading ratios could be established in order to reverse wetlands losses. What are the advantages and disadvantages of this approach? What lessons might it suggest for pollution control, including control in pristine or scenic areas such as natural parks?

3. Representative Gerry Studds has proposed legislation that would require a broad range of water polluters to pay fees that would be used to clean up America's waterways. H.R. 2199 (1993). H.R. 2199 would raise approximately $4 billion annually through taxes ranging from 6 cents to $63 per pound on discharges of hundreds of chemicals, based on toxicity. To address some forms of non-point pollution, the legislation would tax fertilizers and pesticides. The tax rate would be adjusted annually for inflation plus 3 percent to encourage pollution prevention. These revenues would go to a clean water trust fund. Is this a desirable innovation? How should the trust fund monies be spent?

4. Are the potential moral and political objections to trading and fees the same in the CWA context as in the context of air pollution control? Is it relevant that most water pollution in the United States does not pose a direct, significant threat to human health? Are the failures of non-point source control relevant?

5. Wouldn't a system of River Basin Commissions (which use a combination of regulation, effluent fees, transferrable permits, and publicly funded projects) similar to the French model be preferable to the present structure of the CWA? See Roberts, River Basin Authorities: A National Solution to Water Pollution, 83 Harv. L. Rev. 1527 (1970). Why hasn't Congress adopted such an approach?

G.   INTERSTATE SPILLOVERS

In an international or federal system, significant problems of jurisdictional, substantive, and remedial law arise when water or air pollution from one state (A) is deposited in a downwind or downstream state
(B). What problems might the residents of state B face in securing an
effective remedy against such pollution by a suit against the polluter in
the courts of A for injunctive relief or damages? What if the litigation
were brought in the courts of state B? In either case, which state's substantive and remedial law would apply, and how might it affect the outcome?

Illinois v. Milwaukee, 406 U.S. 91 (1972) (*Milwaukee I*), involved a
claim by Illinois for injunctive relief against Wisconsin for Milwaukee's
allegedly inadequately treated sewage discharges into Lake Michigan.
The Court held that such cases were governed by the federal common
law of interstate pollution, and could be brought in federal district
court under the federal question jurisdiction of 28 U.S.C. §1331. The
litigation had been brought as an original action in the Supreme Court,
which held that it should more appropriately proceed in the district
court. The Court was vague as to the substantive content of the federal
common law governing such actions, stating that the appropriate remedy, if any, in such a case, must be left to the sound discretion of the
court in fashioning equitable remedies.

The federal district court tried the case and issued an injunction
requiring Milwaukee to impose controls more stringent than those imposed under the technology-based effluent limitations of the 1972 Federal Water Pollution Control Act, which had been enacted in the
interim. Upon affirmance by the court of appeals, the case again
reached the Supreme Court in *Milwaukee v. Illinois*, 451 U.S. 304 (1981)
(*Milwaukee II*). This time the Court held that the federal common law
of interstate pollution that it had recognized in *Milwaukee I* had been
preempted by the federal Water Pollution Control Act, reasoning that
the Act represented a comprehensive regulatory solution to water pollution problems that had occupied the field and provided a more appropriate solution to interstate pollution problems than case by case
court litigation.

In *International Paper Co. v. Ouellette*, 479 U.S. 481 (1987), the
Court confronted a suit for damages and injunctive relief brought by
Vermont residents in Vermont state court against a pollution source
in New York whose discharges into Lake Champlain assertedly injured
plaintiffs. The Court held that an injunctive remedy was preempted by
the CWA. Construing the savings clause provisions of §§505(e) and 510,
which are too general to provide any real guidance on the issue in
question, the Court emphasized that under the CWA, EPA had the

dominant role in dealing with interstate problems, while the receiving state had only an "advisory" role. EPA, or, in a case where administration of the federal NPDES permitting program had been delegated to a state, the permitting authority in the state where the discharging source is located, must provide a receiving state notice and opportunity for hearing, and must also take its views and interests into account. The receiving state does not have the right to block a permit or insist on compliance with its water standards. Its only recourse is to apply to the EPA Administrator to disapprove the permit if he concludes that the discharge will have an undue impact on interstate waters. See §§301(a)(2), 302(b), 302(d)(2). The Court found that to use the substantive common or other law of the receiving state to impose controls on a source more stringent than required under the CWA (which would be based either on the federal technology-based effluent limitations or the water quality standards of the originating state) would be inconsistent with the "subordinated" position of receiving states in the statutory scheme. However, the Court noted that the CWA allows a state to impose controls on sources within the state that are more stringent than those required under federal law. §510. Accordingly, New York might choose to impose more stringent controls on International Paper. Therefore plaintiffs' suit might be brought under New York law, and might proceed in a Vermont court, assuming appropriate jurisdiction and choice of law.

The Court accordingly dismissed that part of plaintiffs' suit seeking injunctive relief under Vermont law. It also dismissed the part seeking compensatory damages under Vermont law. Query: Is the latter action consistent with the court's basic rationale?

To what extent does the CWA provide effective relief for a receiving state? Consider the following:

ARKANSAS v. OKLAHOMA

112 S. Ct. 1046 (1992)

[EPA issued an NPDES permit to a new municipal sewage treatment plant in Fayetteville, Arkansas, which included limitations on the amount of pollution in its effluent discharges. EPA issued the permit because Arkansas had not been delegated administration of the NPDES process. The plant discharged into a river that flowed into the Illinois River in Oklahoma. The state of Oklahoma had challenged EPA's proposed issuance of the permit on the ground that the discharge violated Oklahoma water quality standards. Those standards provide that "no degradation [of water quality] shall be allowed" in the upper Illinois River, including the portion of the River immediately downstream from the Arkansas-Oklahoma state line. This portion of the river was already in violation of Oklahoma state water quality standards. EPA first ruled that §301(b)(1)(C) of the Clean Water Act "requires an NPDES permit to impose any effluent limitations necessary to comply with applicable state water quality standards,"[35] including the standards of a downstream state. EPA also determined that in this case, the permit should be upheld if the record showed "by a preponderance of the evidence that the authorized discharges would not cause an actual *detectable* violation of Oklahoma's water quality standards," i.e., a measurable increase in pollution concentrations.

On petitions for judicial review of EPA's decision, Arkansas argued that the Clean Water Act did not require an Arkansas point source to comply with Oklahoma's water quality standards. Oklahoma challenged the EPA's determination that the Fayetteville discharge would not produce a detectable violation of the Oklahoma standards. The court of appeals did not accept either of these arguments.]

The Court [of Appeals] first ruled that the statute requires that "where a proposed source would discharge effluents that would contribute to conditions currently constituting a violation of applicable water quality standards, such [a] proposed source may not be permitted." Then the court found that the Illinois River in Oklahoma was "already degraded," that the Fayetteville effluent would reach the Illinois River in Oklahoma, and that effluent could "be expected to contribute to the ongoing deterioration of the scenic Illinois River" in Oklahoma even though it would not detectably affect the River's water quality.

[The Supreme Court declined to decide whether the CWA *requires* EPA to ensure that an EPA permit for an upstream state source will not cause any violation of water quality standards in a downstream state.] Even if the Clean Water Act itself does not require the Fayetteville discharge to comply with Oklahoma's water quality standards, the statute clearly does not limit the EPA's authority to mandate such compliance.

Since 1973, EPA regulations have provided that an NPDES permit shall not be issued "[w]hen the imposition of conditions cannot ensure compliance with the applicable water quality requirements of all affected States.[36] 40 C.F.R. §122.4(d) (1991). Those regulations — relied

---

35. Section 301(b)(1)(C) provides, in relevant part, that

there shall be achieved —

  (C) not later than July 1, 1977, any more stringent limitation, including those necessary to meet water *quality standards . . . established pursuant to any State law or regulations . . . or required to implement any applicable water quality standard established pursuant to this chapter.* 33 U.S.C. §1311 (b)(1)(C) (emphasis supplied).

36. This restriction applies whether the permit is issued by the EPA or by an approved state program. See 40 C.F.R. §123.25 (1991).

upon by the EPA in the issuance of the Fayetteville permit — constitute a reasonable exercise of the Agency's statutory authority.

Congress has vested in the Administrator broad discretion to establish conditions for NPDES permits. Section 402(a)(2) provides that for EPA-issued permits "[t]he Administrator shall prescribe conditions for such permits to assure compliance with the requirements of [§402(a)(1)] and *such other requirements as he deems appropriate.*" . . . (emphasis supplied). Similarly, Congress preserved for the Administrator broad authority to oversee state permit programs:

> No permit shall issue . . . if the Administrator . . . objects in writing to the issuance of such permit as being outside the guidelines and requirements of this chapter. [CWA §402(d)(2).]

The regulations relied on by the EPA were a perfectly reasonable exercise of the Agency's statutory discretion. The application of state water quality standards in the interstate context is wholly consistent with the Act's broad purpose, "to restore and maintain the chemical, physical, and biological integrity of the Nation's water." [CWA §101(a).] Moreover . . . §301(b)(1)(C) expressly identifies the achievement of state water quality standards as one of the Act's central objectives. The Agency's regulations conditioning NPDES permits are a well-tailored means of achieving this goal.

The Court of Appeals construed the Clean Water Act to prohibit any discharge of effluent that would reach waters already in violation of existing water quality standards. We find nothing in the Act to support this reading.

Although the Act contains several provisions directing compliance with state water quality standards, see, e.g., [§301(b)(1)(c),] the parties have pointed to nothing that mandates a complete ban on discharges into a waterway that is in violation of those standards.

The Court of Appeals also concluded that the EPA's issuance of the Fayetteville permit was arbitrary and capricious because the Agency misinterpreted Oklahoma's water quality standards. Contrary to the EPA's interpretation of the Oklahoma standards, the Court of Appeals read those standards as containing the same categorical ban on new discharges that the court had found in the Clean Water Act itself. Although we do not believe the text of the Oklahoma standards supports the court's reading (indeed, we note that Oklahoma itself had not advanced that interpretation in its briefs in the Court of Appeals), we reject it for a more fundamental reason — namely, that the Court of Appeals exceeded the legitimate scope of judicial review of an agency adjudication.

As discussed above, EPA regulations require an NPDES permit to comply with the applicable water quality requirements of all affected

States. 40 C.F.R. §122.4(d) (1991). This regulation effectively incorporates into federal law those state law standards the Agency reasonably determines to be "applicable." In such a situation, then, state water quality standards — promulgated by the States with substantial guidance from the EPA and approved by the Agency — are part of the federal law of water pollution control.

Two features of the body of law governing water pollution support this conclusion. First . . . we have long recognized that interstate water pollution is controlled by *federal* law. . . . Recognizing that the system of federally approved state standards as applied in the interstate context constitutes federal law is wholly consistent with this principle. Second, treating state standards in interstate controversies as federal law accords with the Act's purpose of authorizing the EPA to create and manage a uniform system of interstate water pollution regulation.

Because we recognize that, at least insofar as they affect the issuance of a permit in another State, Oklahoma standards have a federal character, the EPA's reasonable, consistently held interpretation of those standards is entitled to substantial deference. Cf. *Chevron U.S.A., Inc. v. Natural Resources Defense Council, Inc.*, 467 U.S. 837. [EPA] ruled that the Oklahoma standards — which require that there be "no degradation": of the upper Illinois River — would only be violated if the discharge effected an "actually detectable or measurable" change in water quality.

This interpretation of the Oklahoma standards is certainly reasonable and consistent with the purposes and principles of the Clean Water Act. As [EPA] noted, "unless there is some method for measuring compliance, there is no way to ensure compliance." . . . Moreover, this interpretation of the Oklahoma standards makes eminent sense in the interstate context: if every discharge that had some theoretical impact on a downstream State were interpreted as "degrading" the downstream waters, downstream States might wield an effective veto over upstream discharges.

The EPA's application of those standards in this case was also sound. [EPA] scrutinized the record and made explicit factual findings regarding four primary measures of water quality under the Oklahoma standards: eutrophication, aesthetics, dissolved oxygen, and metals. In each case, [EPA] found that the Fayetteville discharge would not lead to a detectable change in water quality. [It] therefore concluded that the Fayetteville discharge would not violate the Oklahoma water quality standards. Because we agree that these findings are supported by substantial evidence, we conclude that the Court of Appeals should have affirmed both the EPA's construction of the regulations and the issuance of the Fayetteville permit.

In sum, the Court of Appeals made a policy choice that it was not authorized to make. Arguably, as that court suggested, it might be wise to prohibit any discharge into the Illinois River, even if that discharge would have no adverse impact on water quality. But it was surely not arbitrary for the EPA to conclude — given the benefits to the River from the increased flow of relatively clean water and the benefits achieved in Arkansas by allowing the new plant to operate as designed — that allowing the discharge would be even wiser. It is not our role, or that of the Court of Appeals, to decide which policy choice is the better one, for it is clear that Congress has entrusted such decisions to the Environmental Protection Agency.

NOTES AND QUESTIONS

1. Does *Oklahoma* ensure downstream states the protection that was denied in *Milwaukee II* and *Ouellette?* What limits, if any, are there on EPA's authority to "interpret" a downstream state's standards so as to conclude that they would not be violated by upstream discharges? Could EPA disregard a particular downstream state standard as unreasonably stringent if it would have the effect of precluding any new discharges in the upstream state? If upstream state discharges are contributing to violations of a downstream state's standards, how should the burden of reducing discharges to achieve compliance be allocated among sources in the two states?

2. Why did Congress fail to deal more explicitly with interstate pollution issues? What measures might it have adopted to deal with the problem? How does the Clean Air Act deal with the analogous problem of interstate air pollution spillovers? See Clean Air Act §§110(a)(2)(D), 126, 115. What does this record say about the federalism justifications for national environmental regulation? See supra, pp. 244-248.

H. ENFORCEMENT

1. INTRODUCTION

No program of environmental regulation is better than its enforcement system. The best standards in the world would accomplish nothing unless they were complied with, and purely voluntary compliance cannot be expected within our social and economic institutions. The following excerpt outlines some of the compliance problems encountered in the early stages of contemporary environmental law:

D. Gogol, Enforcement, Economics, and the Law: The Development of Economic Law Enforcement by the Connecticut Department of Environmental Protection

(1976)

DEFINING THE ENFORCEMENT PROBLEM IN CONNECTICUT

. . . The major problems were (1) a few recalcitrant polluters who resisted all Department efforts demanding compliance, (2) a large number of violators who complied with the law once detected and pressured into action, but who did not meet the environmental standards voluntarily, and (3) unwieldy enforcement tools which relied heavily on costly, time-consuming litigation.

THE RECALCITRANT POLLUTERS

It is easy to overdramatize the problems of law enforcement by focusing on the most troublesome cases. Nonetheless, under existing procedures a few sources were able to avoid or greatly delay compliance with the law, even after having been found in violation of the law and notwithstanding strenuous Department efforts to force compliance. The Department's inability to deal with these cases was harmful to the environment, unfair to the competitors who complied with the law, and costly to the State in terms of resources involved in prosecution. Perhaps worst of all, the existence of publicized scofflaws created no deterrent effect which might encourage others to comply with the law voluntarily.

The number of "recalcitrants" was small, but their impact was significant. From the roughly 10,000 registered sources of air pollution in Connecticut, and of the 3,750 sources inspected in the period 1972-1974, only 323 cases involved violations serious enough to require administrative orders mandating compliance according to a certain schedule. But of these 323 cases, 42 were so recalcitrant that they accounted for 75 percent of all unjustified delays in the same period.[37]

---

37. Other units of the Department faced similar recalcitrance. The Water Compliance Unit reported average delays in compliance plans of one year; the Water Resources Division reported delays in removing illegal fill averaging nine months. These and other statistics are drawn from Profiles of Environmental Enforcement in Connecticut, a study conducted by the Connecticut Enforcement Project and now on file with the Department.

Despite constant pressure from the Department, adverse publicity in a number of cases, and the institution of suit by the Attorney-General in several others, these sources were not pressed into timely compliance. Even in the few cases where litigation proceeded beyond the complaint stage, the recalcitrant sources continued to delay by dilatory trial and settlement tactics.

The reason for such recalcitrance is not hard to find. Delay in meeting environmental standards pays off handsomely in the absence of effective sanctions. Any costs of control that are avoided by a violator are costs which are saved and which can be invested in presumably profitable ventures. Thus, for example, an asphalt batching plant which can avoid installing the equipment needed to control its particulate emissions could save approximately $2,665 per month in annualized capital costs and the costs of operating and maintenance. Moreover, even where pollution control equipment is already installed, the high operating and maintenance costs alone discourage voluntary compliance.

Facing these kinds of incentives for violation, polluting sources were not deterred by vague Department threats or even the institution of litigation. As long as the day of final compliance could be postponed, violation remained profitable. . . .

THE LACK OF VOLUNTARY COMPLIANCE

In addition to being unable to deal with troublesome cases, the Department also realized that its current enforcement efforts offered little incentive for voluntary compliance. Of the 3,750 inspections of air pollution sources conducted in the two-year period 1972-1974, the Department discovered 1,350 violations — a violation rate of over one in three. While 79 percent of these violations were promptly corrected within a few month[s'] period, the fact remained that there was no compliance until detection and Department action. Thus, although there were relatively few recalcitrant cases, the Department needed an efficient and effective way of dealing with them not only on grounds of individual enforcement, but also as a matter of general deterrence.

The problem of general deterrence was especially difficult since sources who did not comply with the law gained a significant and unfair economic advantage over competitors who obeyed the law. Where sources felt that they could get away with violations, even temporarily, they had strong economic reasons to do so. The Department soon realized that the rate of voluntary compliance depended on (1) how effectively the Department dispatched a small number of tough cases that attracted publicity, and (2) whether or not regulated sources perceived

that others in similar situations had been able to ignore the law successfully and without sanction. . . .

Despite the availability of large civil and criminal sanctions under
federal and state law, seeking remedies through the courts proved to
be clumsy, time-consuming, and inefficient. . . .

NOTES AND QUESTIONS

1. What is the solution to the problems identified by Gogol? More
resources for government enforcement agencies? Private rights of action to enable environmental groups and other private plaintiffs to enforce requirements against polluters? Changes in environmental
policies to make them seem fairer to industry? Use of market-based
incentives, such as fees or taxes or transferrable permit systems? With
the maturation of environmental regulation, more attention has been
devoted to monitoring compliance and to enforcement. In reviewing
the materials that follow, you should consider how effectively current
approaches deal with the problems noted by Gogol.

2. The growing array of environmental regulations cannot enforce themselves. Enforcement requires a substantial commitment of
investigative, administrative, and litigation resources. Recalcitrant polluters who regularly and repeatedly violate the law, as well as those who
commit violations intermittently and sometimes inadvertently, pose an
enormous problem of monitoring, detection, and enforcement. Competitive pressures and the incentives of managers to cut corners in order to meet internal corporate profit targets undermine compliance.
There are over a million industrial and commercial facilities subject to
federal environmental regulation. How should the government set its
priorities where resources for total enforcement are unavailable? The
following materials look at the more important areas of enforcement
and some of the issues surrounding them. The focus is on the federal
enforcement system, although state and local authorities also have a
major role in enforcement and face similar problems.

3. An effective program of environmental enforcement requires
government collection of information regarding compliance. Federal
and state environmental regulatory authorities have inspectors who visit
facilities, often unannounced, in order to search for violations. The
number of inspectors is, however, small in relation to the number of
sources. In view of the costs of enforcing laws, economists have suggested that the most efficient approach to enforcement is to impose
very high penalties when violations are detected, in order to make up
for the fact that many violations go undetected. See Becker, Crime and
Punishment: An Economic Approach, 76 J. Pol. Econ. 169 (1968);

Becker & Stigler, Law Enforcement, Malfeasance, and Compensation of Enforcers, 3 J. Legal Studies 1 (1974); R. Posner, Economic Analysis of Law §7.2 (4th ed. 1993). Thus, if the chance of detection is 1 in 10, fines or other sanctions should be 10 times higher than if the authorities were 100 percent successful in detecting and prosecuting violations. What problems do you see in this approach? What special difficulties might it encounter in the case of environmental violations as opposed, for example, to bank robberies?

4. The major federal environmental regulatory statutes require sources to file reports with the government that contain data that enable the government to determine compliance. For example, under the CWA, NPDES sources must file Discharge Monitoring Reports (DMRs) on the composition of their effluents. These reports can furnish the basis for enforcement actions. Much of the information forming the basis for criminal prosecutions is obtained from "whistle-blowers," disgruntled employees, or even undercover work.

2.   CIVIL ENFORCEMENT BY THE FEDERAL GOVERNMENT

Under the Clean Water Act, the EPA has three basic sets of enforcement options available in response to violations of the statute. It may issue an administrative notice of violation, assess administrative penalties, or initiate a civil enforcement action in court. Traditionally, the government enjoys broad discretion in deciding whether to bring enforcement action and what sort of action to bring. Section 309(a)(1) of the CWA provides, however, that "whenever" the Administrator finds a violation of §§301, 302, 306, 307, 308, 318, or 405 of the statute, she "shall proceed" to "notify the person in alleged violation and [the state in which the violation is present] of such finding," or "issue an order to comply," or "file a civil action" under §309(b). To what extent does this constrain the government's enforcement discretion? To the extent that it does, who can enforce those constraints, and how?

The first and simplest enforcement tool available to EPA is administrative issuance of a Notice of Violation (NOV). A NOV may produce compliance from polluters that were unaware that there was a violation, or they may be prompted to comply when they learn that the EPA is monitoring them. In the case of states that administer delegated NPDES programs, EPA may issue a NOV to the state to correct its failure to take appropriate enforcement action against a violator. If the state does not commence "appropriate enforcement action" within 30 days of EPA's issuance of a NOV, then EPA "shall" proceed with further enforcement action.

If a source does not comply with a NOV by taking corrective action, §309(g) authorizes EPA to assess administrative penalties of up to $10,000 per violation after providing public notice and a reasonable opportunity for comment. Each day of violation is a separate offense. Any person who submits comment on a proposed penalty order may petition EPA to set aside the order and provide a hearing if one has not already been held. §309(g)(4)(C). Persons against whom penalties have been assessed may seek review in federal district court. §309(g)(8).

As a final option, EPA may request that the Department of Justice initiate a civil suit against the polluter. The suit might seek one or several types of relief, including an injunction, remedial action, and civil penalties. Civil penalties can be very large. Section 309(d) provides for penalties of up to $25,000 per day for each violation. Thus a source that violates its NPDES permit over a period of months can run up potentially enormous penalties. In the typical case, however, courts do not assess the maximum possible penalty. The CWA lists five factors for the court to consider in setting penalties: the seriousness of the violation, any economic benefit resulting from the violation, any history of such violations, any good faith efforts to comply with applicable requirements, the economic impact of the penalty on the violator, as well as "such other matters as justice may require." In fiscal year 1992, the EPA referred 361 civil cases to the Justice Department, and obtained $50.7 million in judicially imposed civil penalties. EPA Enforcement Accomplishments Report, FY 1992, EPA 230-R-93-001, April 1993. All civil penalties are deposited into the general Treasury fund. (Where do monies deposited in the fund go?) As in the case of most litigation, the great majority of cases are settled. In many cases, settlements are reached before the government files a complaint in court. In such cases, the settlement is embodied in a consent decree that is filed together with the complaint in court. Consent decrees must be approved by the court and are then entered as a judgment of the court. The government generally insists on a consent decree filed in court because a violation of the decree is sanctionable as contempt of court, whereas a settlement by itself is merely a contract. By regulation, the Department gives the public 30 days notice of the filing of a consent decree and opportunity for public comment. Many other cases are settled after filing; the same consent decree procedure is followed.

In calculating administrative penalties and determining what civil penalties to seek in settlement or from the court, EPA uses a mathematical model (called the BEN model, which is based on average industry compliance methods and costs) to establish the economic gain enjoyed by the polluter as a result of the violation. The penalties sought by the government include not only the economic gain from noncompliance (as calculated by the BEN model), but an additional "gravity" component, based on the seriousness of the offense, degree of noncompliance, the degree of cooperation shown by the violator, and other factors. EPA, Policy on Civil Penalties, Feb. 16, 1984. This "preliminary deterrence amount" figure may be adjusted for other factors including the history of noncompliance, ability to pay, and the strength of the case in litigation. The EPA Clean Water Act Penalty Policy for Civil Settlement Negotiations, Feb. 11, 1986, also contemplates lower penalties if the violator agrees to undertake an acceptable "mitigation project" financed by an "environmentally beneficial expenditure" (EBE). EBEs can, for example, include projects to restore and preserve wetlands that may have been harmed by a discharge, or a pollution prevention program to reduce future discharges from the violating source below the levels legally required. Violators prefer such projects because their costs are more clearly tax deductible and they may also generate favorable local publicity.

3.   CRIMINAL PROSECUTIONS

In addition to civil remedies, the federal environmental regulatory statutes also provide for criminal sanctions. During the 1980s, the Department of Justice increased its commitment of resources to the prosecution of environmental crimes, and Congress amended many environmental regulatory statutes to make offenses formerly classified as misdemeanors into felonies. Former EPA Administrator William Reilly put it this way: "Our message about environmental law is simple. Polluters will pay. Environmental crime today is no less a crime than theft or blackmail or assault. And more and more assuredly, if you do the crime, you'll do the time." Enforcement Actions at EPA Continue to Climb in Civil, Criminal Cases, Penalty Assessments, 22 Envt. Rep. (BNA) 1832 (1991). In fiscal year 1992, the Justice Department completed prosecution of 64 criminal cases resulting in the conviction of 99 defendants, 44 of whom received jail sentences. About two-thirds of the cases involved prosecutions of corporations as defendants, and about two-thirds involved prosecutions of individuals. The overlap in these fractions is explained by the fact that a substantial number of cases involved prosecutions both against corporations and their officers or employees. State and local prosecutions of environmental crimes have also increased markedly in recent years

The Clean Water Act defines several categories of criminal violation that are classified as felonies. §309(c)(1) punishes negligent violations of permit requirements and pollution control requirements, including record-keeping violations, punishable by fines of between $5000 and $50,000 per day of violations and/or up to three years in jail, with repeat offenders facing fines of up to $100,000 per day and/

or up to six years in jail. Section 309(c)(2) punishes "knowing" violations of these same requirements with maximum penalties identical to those for negligence. Under §309(c)(4), it is a criminal violation to make "any false material statement, representation, or certification in any application, record, report, plan or document filed or required to be maintained under this chapter" or to tamper with a monitoring device. Initial violations of §(c)(4) may be punished by fines of up to $10,000, and/or two years in jail. Subsequent violations may be punished by sanctions twice as severe.

The statute also contains a "knowing endangerment" section to punish persons who "know at the time" of a violation "that [they] place[] another person in imminent danger of death or serious bodily injury." §309(c)(3). Penalties under this section are severe, providing for up to $250,000 in fines and/or up to 15 years in prison. See *U.S. v Protex Indus.*, 874 F.2d 740 (10th Cir. 1989). Finally, the CWA contains "delisting" provisions in §508(a), which prohibits the federal government from contracting for goods and services provided by a facility involved in a criminal conviction for violation of the CWA until EPA has certified that the violation has ceased.

The Resource Conservation and Recovery Act and the Clean Air Act share similar criminal provisions, including penalties for reporting and record-keeping violations. RCRA §§3008(d) & (e), CAA §113(c). Certain environmental statutes include strict liability offenses. For example, the Rivers and Harbors Act states that "[i]t shall not be lawful to throw, discharge, or deposit . . . or cause to be thrown . . . any refuse matter of any kind . . . into any navigable water [or tributary of any navigable water] of the United States," 33 USC §407. One who violates this provision "shall be guilty of a misdemeanor . . . punishable by a fine" of between $500 and $2500 and/or 30 days to one year in jail. 18 USC §411. There is no requirement that the violation be "knowing" or negligent.

Corporations can be held responsible for the actions of their officers or employees under the doctrine of respondeat superior and may be required to pay fines for violations, as well as undertake remedial measures and compensate victims. Individual corporate officers can be sentenced to prison terms for their own actions and for the acts of individuals under their supervision. As one commentator has pointed out, corporations cannot be jailed, but managers can, and "incarceration is the one cost of business you can't pass on to the consumers." See Smith, No Longer Just A Cost Of Doing Business: Criminal Liability Of Corporate Officials For Violations Of CWA And RCRA, 53 La. L. Rev. 119 (1992). The CWA defines a "person" subject to criminal sanctions to include "any responsible corporate officer." §309(c)(6). There is, however, considerable dispute about just how much knowledge and involvement a manager must have in order to be criminally liable for the actions of subordinates. Knowledge of their violations, coupled with failure to take corrective action, is probably enough. See *United States v. Dee*, 912 F.2d 741 (4th Cir. 1990). But suppose that a manager fails to detect her subordinates' violations because she fails to adequately carry out her supervisory responsibilities? Is that a "knowing" violation by the manager? Suppose she suspects violations but deliberately turns a "blind eye" to her subordinates' actions?

Another problem that arises in establishing a "knowing violation" is the extent to which the government must prove that the defendant knew at the time of the violation that his or her conduct violated the law. Generally, in criminal prosecutions the government need not prove that defendant knew of the specific statute or regulation that he is charged with violating. But consider cases brought under the Resource Conservation and Recovery Act (RCRA), which makes it a criminal offense to "knowingly" ship hazardous waste to a disposal facility that lacks a federal or state permit. Must the government show that the defendant knew that a facility to which he shipped waste lacked a permit? Must the defendant also know that shipment to an unpermitted facility is illegal? If so, what proof of knowledge is required? In *United States v. Johnson & Towers*, 741 F.2d 662 (3d Cir.), *cert. denied*, 469 U.S. 1208 (1984), the court held that the government must prove both knowledge of the permit requirement and knowledge that the company lacked a permit. The court held, however, that the jury may infer such knowledge from the fact that a defendant holds a responsible position within a corporation engaged in the production of hazardous waste and should therefore know that hazardous waste is subject to stringent regulation. Accord, *United States v. MacDonald & Watson Oil Co.*, 933 F.2d 35 (1st Cir. 1991). The court in *United States v. Hoflin*, 880 F.2d 1033 (9th Cir. 1989), *cert. denied*, 493 U.S. 1083 (1990), however, rejected the knowledge requirements of *Johnson & Towers* in a RCRA prosecution, holding that knowledge of the permit requirement and knowledge that a company lacks a permit are not elements of the offense.

It is important to recognize that not all criminal violations can or should be prosecuted. Enforcement resources are limited. Moreover, environmental regulatory requirements are voluminous, complex, and overbroad in many applications. It would be foolish and unfair to treat every violation of every requirement of every regulation and permit condition as a crime, even if the violation was "knowing." Consider a municipal sewage treatment plant which, because of unexpected engineering deficiencies, emits 5 percent more BOD than required in its permit. The violation has no discernible adverse environmental effect. The needed repairs will take substantial time. If the plant manager continues to operate the plant, will she be committing a "knowing" violation of the CWA, punishable by up to five years in jail? Should she be prosecuted if she does not immediately shut down the plant? Consider that the shutdown will cause untreated sewage to be discharged, also violating the plant's permit.

Enforcement policies must also give due consideration to the efforts of dischargers to identify, correct, and disclose violations. The goal of government enforcement policies should not be to bring as many enforcement actions as possible, but to maximize compliance. There is growing recognition of the importance of environmental compliance audits and other corporate management information systems to track and correct violations of regulatory requirements. Corporations and their managers, however, could be deterred from instituting and implementing environmental compliance systems if the government could obtain and use the company's audit information to establish "knowing" violations by senior managers and the corporation in cases where the violations disclosed by the audit had not been instantaneously corrected. On the other hand, the government obviously cannot rely solely on "voluntary" compliance. How should government decisions about prosecutions take these various factors into account?

Traditionally, government prosecutors have been extremely reluctant to adopt rules or standards to guide prosecutive decisions. They believe, often with good reason, that such decisions are highly contextual and fact-specific, and also fear that defendants could invoke asserted noncompliance with rules or standards as a defense against prosecution. Some leading administrative law and criminal law scholars, however, criticize prosecutors' failure to adopt guidelines for prosecutorial decisions. See K. Davis, Discretionary Justice (1969); Vorenberg, Decent Restraint of Prosecutorial Discretion, 94 Harv. L. Rev. 1521 (1981).

In July 1991, the Justice Department issued a memorandum titled Factors in Decisions on Criminal Prosecutions for Environmental Violations in the Context of Significant Voluntary Compliance of Disclosure Efforts By the Violator. The factors, which are designed to guide federal prosecutorial decisions, include:

(1) Whether the violator made complete and timely voluntary[38] disclosure, and in particular whether the disclosure substantially aids the government in its investigation;

(2) Whether there was full, prompt cooperation with the government after disclosure;

(3) Whether the violator has a regular, intensive, and comprehensive environmental compliance program, for example an

---

38. Disclosures are not considered voluntary if they are required by law, regulation, or permit.

environmental audit program, with sufficient resources and other measures to prevent future violations, and whether such program was adopted in good faith.

(4) Whether internal disciplinary action was taken against the responsible corporate officials and employees, and subsequent compliance efforts made.

PROBLEM: WHETHER TO EXERCISE PROSECUTORIAL DISCRETION IN ENFORCING A CWA PERMIT

The BestTech Corporation conducts a regular, comprehensive audit of its compliance with environmental requirements. An audit uncovers information that a BestTech plant's discharges violate conditions in its NPDES permit limiting discharges of four different pollutants. The violations are due to sloppy maintenance and control equipment failures. The responsible employees have also been falsifying Best-Tech's monitoring reports in order to conceal the violations from regulatory authorities. BestTech then takes corrective action on its own, but does not bring the violations to the government's attention. The cost and difficulty of correcting the violations varies considerably, and Best-Tech undertakes the easier and least costly actions first. When the government learns of the violations some months later as the result of an inspection, the company has still not achieved compliance with respect to one of the four pollutants, but states (honestly) that it planned to get to it. How should the government view BestTech's efforts? What criminal enforcement actions might the government bring? What civil remedies might it seek? What sanctions should the government seek to impose in this case? Suppose you are retained by BestTech shortly after the initial audit. What do you counsel?

Corporations and individuals convicted in environmental prosecutions, whether as a result of guilty pleas or verdicts, are sentenced under the Federal Sentencing Guidelines, 18 U.S.C.A. §3553, which are promulgated by the United States Sentencing Commission and become effective unless disapproved by Congress. The Guidelines, which became effective on November 1, 1987, were designed to reduce sentencing disparity among similarly situated defendants for similar conduct. Part Q of the guidelines applies specifically to "Offenses Involving the Environment" committed by individuals. The guidelines establish a "Base Offense" level depending on the nature of the violations, and then introduces mitigating and aggravating factors to arrive at a final sentence. For example, there is a base offense category for knowing violations of a statute, regulation, or permit condition prohibiting the release of a pollutant in excess of a specified amount. If the release contaminates the general environment, that is an aggravating factor that will increase the sentence, while cooperation with the authorities is a mitigating factor that will reduce it. The level of sanctions which the Commission adopted for environmental violations is relatively high. Most first-time offenders convicted of a knowing violation of pollution control requirements will serve some jail time. For example, in *United States v. Ellen*, 961 F.2d 462 (4th Cir.), *cert. denied*, 43 S. Ct. 217 (1992), the project manager in a property development project involving 86 acres of wooded wetlands and tidal marshes was convicted on five counts of filling wetlands without a permit, CWA §§301(a) and 309(c)(2)(A), and was sentenced to six months in prison and one year of supervised release conditioned on four months home detention and 60 hours of community service. Aggravating circumstances were involved in *United States v. Pozsgai*, 757 F. Supp. 21 (E.D. Pa. 1991), modified, 947 F.2d 938 (3d Cir. 1991), where the defendant continued to dump construction debris on 14 acres of wetlands, which he owned, without a §404 permit despite repeated warnings to stop from the Army Corps of Engineers and EPA. He was convicted and sentenced to three years in prison on 14 preguidelines counts, and concurrent 27 months on 26 counts governed by the guidelines along with five years probation, one year supervised release and a $5000 fine.[39]

Specific sentencing guidelines for environmental offenses by organizations have not yet been adopted because of controversy over the structure of the guidelines, the level of fines, and the treatment of aggravating and mitigating factors. A recent draft proposal by an advisory group to the Sentencing Commission would make an organization's failure to have a specified type of environmental auditing and compliance program a significant aggravating factor. The draft also provides that mitigating factors could not reduce the level of a fine below 50 percent of the fine level otherwise applicable. Industry has strongly attacked this scheme, arguing that criminal sentencing guidelines are not an appropriate means of regulatory corporate compliance programs, that businesses should have greater flexibility in designing compliance programs appropriate for their particular circumstances, and that adoption of such programs should be a mitigating factor. They also argue that the 50 percent cap on fine reductions is unjustified because

---

39. While the purpose of the guidelines has been to promote uniformity, one leading prosecutor of environmental crimes has argued that the flexibility given to sentencing courts in the guidelines has resulted in significant inconsistency, and that jail sentences have generally been substantially less than what the guidelines permit. Barrett, Criminal Enforcement of Environmental Laws; Sentencing Environmental Crimes under the Federal Sentencing Guidelines — a Sentencing Lottery, 22 Envtl. L. 1421 (1992).

there is no similar cap with respect to organizational violations outside the environmental area and the cap will remove desirable incentives for business to adopt strong compliance programs, make full disclosure of violations, and otherwise cooperate with the government. Query: Should environmental violations be treated more harshly than other types of corporate crime, such as tax fraud or consumer fraud?

Currently, environmental offenses by corporations are sentenced under generic guidelines for organizational violations. Sanctions can be quite large. In the settlement of the federal government's criminal and civil litigation against Exxon for the Valdez spill, Exxon paid $125 million in criminal fines and $900 million in natural resource damages.[40] Of course the consequences of the spill, at least in the short run, were dramatic and severe, but as pointed out by critics of the prosecution, the government's case rested largely on counts charging strict liability offenses by Exxon (violation of the Refuse Act and the Migratory Bird Treaty Act) and a count charging negligent violation of the Clean Water Act (discharging oil without a NPDES permit). For further discussion of the *Valdez* spill, its consequences, and government enforcement actions, see pp. 1201-1208 infra.

Even in less dramatic cases, criminal sanctions can be significant. For example, in *United States v. Ashland Oil Co.*, 765 F. Supp. 270 (W.D. Pa. 1993), Ashland was fined $2.5 million for an oil spill into the Monongahela River, which resulted from the negligent construction and maintenance of an oil storage tank that ruptured. Note that this fine was imposed solely on the basis of negligence.

Both of these cases involved large, wealthy corporations. Should they be forced to pay a larger fine for the same offense than a smaller corporation? Why bring costly criminal prosecutions against corporations at all, since corporations can't be sent to jail? Why not simply rely on suitably large civil penalties rather than criminal fines?

4. CITIZEN SUITS

Congress in §505 of the CWA provides for two types of citizen suit remedies that may be invoked by "any citizen"[41] against (a) the EPA Administrator, for failure to perform an act or duty under the Act

---

40. $100 million of the $125 million criminal fine was, however, remitted; the $100 million was paid as restitution to the United States and the State of Alaska for damages which they suffered as a result of the spills.

41. Section 505(g) defines "citizen" as "a person or persons having an interest which is or may be adversely affected." This provision relates to the requirement of standing in constitutional and administrative law, which is discussed in Chapter 7.

"which is not discretionary with the Administrator"; and (b) any polluter who is in violation of an effluent standard or limitation established under the Act, or an order issued with respect to such standard or limitation. In either case, the plaintiff must give 60 days notice prior to bringing suit. In the case of an action against EPA, the notice must be provided to it, in order to allow for corrections of the violation before suit is filed. In the case of an action against a private party assertedly in violation of regulatory requirements, for failure to meet regulatory requirements imposed by the CWA, notice must be provided to the private party to enable it to correct the violation, and to EPA or the relevant state to allow them to commence an enforcement action against the polluter. If EPA or a state has already commenced an enforcement action or commences such an action after notice, the citizen may not bring his or her own action, but may intervene in the government action as of right. Section 505(d) authorizes the court in a citizen suit action to award costs of litigation (including reasonable attorney and expert witness fees) to any prevailing or substantially prevailing party, whenever the court determines such an award is "appropriate."

The purpose of these provisions is to enlist litigation by private citizens, including environmental groups and state and local governments (who also qualify as "persons" who can bring citizen suits), to help ensure effective implementation and enforcement of the Act. At the same time, the limits and conditions on citizen suits imposed by §505 are designed to ensure needed flexibility to the government in administering the Act and to promote a degree of coordination and consistency in enforcement policies. You should carefully review those limits and conditions.

There are similar citizen suit provisions in the Clean Air Act, RCRA, and other federal environmental regulatory statutes. These provisions contain two distinct types of remedies: (1) a private right of initiation against EPA to require that it comply with the "action forcing" mandates and deadlines that Congress has included in these statutes and (2) private rights of action against private persons who violate regulatory requirements. Is there a need for both types of remedies, or should Congress have instead selected one or the other? Which type of remedy would you think more important in ensuring environmental protection? See Stewart & Sunstein, Public Program and Private Rights, 96 Harv. L. Rev. 1193 (1982).

a.   Private Rights of Initiation

SIERRA CLUB V. TRAIN

557 F.2d 485, 487-488 (5th Cir. 1977)

COLEMAN, Circuit Judge:

The Sierra Club filed a "citizen's suit" under [CWA §305] for a writ of mandamus directing Russell Train, Administrator of the Environmental Protection Agency (EPA), to enforce the Federal Water Pollution Control Act Amendments of 1972 (FWPCAA) as required by [CWA §309(a)(3)] . . . and for an injunction requiring Abston Construction Company, Inc. and Mitchell & Neely, Inc. to cease polluting Daniel Creek, and to restore it to its natural condition. . . .

The substantive issue in this case is one of statutory construction, specifically whether [§309(a)(3)] imposes a discretionary or a non-discretionary duty on the EPA Administrator to issue an order requiring compliance with the FWPCAA. In statutory terms, the question is whether or not "shall" imposes a mandatory duty. If [§309(a)(3)] imposes a mandatory duty, then the District Court's Dismissal of Train as a defendant for lack of subject matter jurisdiction was in error and must be reversed since §1365(a)(2) confers jurisdiction on district courts over suits to compel the EPA Administrator to perform a mandatory duty; however, if the duty is discretionary, the district court's dismissal was correct and should be affirmed.

The pertinent portions of FWPCAA, requiring construction, are set forth immediately following. Section 309 provides:

> (a)(3) Whenever on the basis of any information available to him the Administrator finds that any person is in violation of . . . [the Act], he shall issue an order requiring such person to comply with . . . [the Act], or he shall bring a civil action in accordance with subsection (b) of this section. . . .
>
> (b) The Administrator is authorized to commence a civil action for appropriate relief . . . for any violation for which he is authorized to issue a compliance order under subsection (a) of this section.

[Sierra Club argued that, while the authority to bring a civil action under §309(b) might be discretionary, §309(a) mandates issuance by the Administrator of a compliance order in case of violation.]

Reason would dictate that the duties prescribed by [§309(a)(3)] be found discretionary. Since the Administrator at his discretion may bring suit, concluding the Administrator's duty to issue an abatement order to be mandatory would be unreasonable. For example, if the Administrator did issue an abatement order which was not complied with and the Administrator did not commence a suit for failure to comply, the empty gesture of issuing an abatement order would not foster the [Act's] goal of pollution elimination. The citizen's alternative would be to file a suit to enforce the [Act's] effluent limitation standards, but this right exists in the absence of the issuance of a compliance order by the Administrator. The citizen possesses the same right under the FWPCAA with or without issuance of a compliance order to bring suit against and receive damages from an alleged polluter. In the quest to eliminate pollution, a compliance order by the Administrator is unnecessary. On the other hand, the issuance of orders which the Administrator does not intend to pursue in court would be an exercise in practical futility, undermining the prestige and the effectiveness of the EPA.

We hold that the duties imposed by [§309(a)(3)] on the EPA Administrator are discretionary. Since [§305(a)(2)] only grants jurisdiction over citizen suits to force the EPA Administrator to perform a *mandatory* duty imposed by the [Act], and since [§309(a)(3)] imposes a *discretionary* duty, the dismissal of Train as a defendant for lack of subject matter jurisdiction is affirmed.

NOTES AND QUESTIONS

United States v. Phelps Dodge Corp., 391 F. Supp. 1181 (D. Ariz. 1975), and *South Carolina Wildlife Federation v. Alexander,* 457 F. Supp. 118 (D.S.C. 1978), reached the opposite result, reaffirming that "shall" is mandatory, and rejecting the argument that EPA's discretion whether to initiate civil enforcement actions in court implies that it has the same discretion with respect to administrative enforcement. *Alexander* also rejected the government's argument that it has discretion whether to "find" a violation in the first place, reasoning that when "any information available" to the government clearly establishes a violation, the Administration must find a violation and thereupon initiate administrative enforcement proceedings. Why should EPA have discretion not to enforce the law against those who violate it? Is the *Train* decision justified by the fact that EPA's enforcement resources are limited? By the circumstance that regulatory requirements may, as applied to particular sources, be overinclusive and unduly burdensome? By the fact that citizens can remedy EPA's failure to bring an enforcement action by bringing their own private right of action against a polluter?

J. MILLER, CITIZEN SUITS: PRIVATE ENFORCEMENT OF FEDERAL POLLUTION CONTROL LAWS

10-13 (1987)

While the citizen suit was conceived and designed to allow private enforcement of the law against polluting violators, until recently its most celebrated uses were against EPA for its failures to implement the environmental statutes in a timely and complete manner. Suits by national environmental organizations to force EPA to promulgate water pollution effluent limitations and air quality standards for toxic pollutants, and similar actions have done much to shape implementation of the statutes.[42] [H]owever, there has been a growing recognition among the regulated community, the environmental community, and EPA of the importance and potential of citizen suit enforcement. This recognition has developed primarily from the enforcement efforts of NRDC [Natural Resources Defense Council] and a coalition of national and regional environmental organizations.

A number of factors converged to produce this effort. NRDC had long focused on what it perceived to be defects in EPA's effluent guidelines program under the Clean Water Act, particularly with respect to toxic pollutants. This focus was incomplete without assuring that the guidelines were applied correctly in permits and the permits were enforced. [M]any of the national environmental groups, including NRDC, perceived a breakdown in EPA enforcement in 1981 and 1982, particularly under the Clean Water Act, and were anxious to reverse this trend. With a seed money grant to fund a few initial citizen suit enforcement cases, NRDC hoped to produce a self sustaining effort by recovering attorneys fees and using them to fund future cases.

NRDC initially focused its attention on major industrial discharges with repeated violations of national pollutant discharge elimination system (NPDES) permits in New York and New Jersey. Using student interns under the supervision of a former EPA regional enforcement attorney, it reviewed state and federal files of the targeted discharges. It narrowed its target list on the basis of the number and apparent seriousness of the violations as indicated by review by its technical consultants. NRDC focused its attention on discharges violating effluent

---

42. For example, NRDC's suit to force EPA to promulgate effluent standards for toxic pollutants required under Clean Water Act §307, (*NRDC v. Train,* 519 F.2d 287 . . . D.C. Cir. 1975) led to a settlement under which EPA focused on toxic pollutants in developing effluent guidelines for best available technology under Clean Water Act §307 and to the amendment of Clean Water Act §307 in 1977 giving legislative approval to this shift of emphasis.

Citizen and Federal Enforcement

| | Citizen Enforcement | | Federal Enforcement | |
| | Citizen Suit Notices and Case Filings | | Referral of Cases to the Department of Justice and Case Filings | |
	All Statutes[*]	Clean Water Act[*]	All Statutes[**]	Clean Water Act[**]
1978	7/7	1/1	262/131	137/69
1979	28/23	9/8	242/184	1/81
1980	35/17	6/4	204/163	55/49
1981	23/17	6/6	116/118	36/32
1982	32/26	19/16	110/47	46/14
1983	131/70	108/62	162/199	56/77
1984[***]	93/29	87/26	167/92	63/41

[*] The figure to the left is the number of notices of intent to sue; the figure to the right is the number of suits actually filed. The disparity in 1983 and 1984 suggests that more cases are yet to be filed as a result of notices in those years. The cases not brought under the Clean Water Act are predominantly Clean Air Act and RCRA cases.

[**] The figure to the left is the number of cases referred by EPA to the Department of Justice; the figure to the right is the number of cases filed by the Department of Justice.

[***] The figures are through April 30, 1984 for private enforcement and through June 30, 1984 for government enforcement.

limitations for toxic pollutants and transferred the cases not involving toxic pollutant violations to other environmental groups. NRDC then sent notices of violation to its enforcement targets and reviewed information it received as a result. By the time it actually filed cases, it was dealing with a small percentage of the violators it initially investigated. After a successful pilot effort in New York and New Jersey, NRDC expanded the project to other areas.[43]

A cursory look at the statistics of citizen and federal enforcement confirms that citizen enforcement has grown quickly, is concentrated in Clean Water Act cases, and corresponds to a marked decline in federal enforcement from 1980 to 1982. Indeed, since 1982 private judicial enforcement has been almost as much of a regulatory presence as EPA judicial enforcement under the Clean Water Act. While a not insignificant level of private enforcement has been evident for some time, citi-

43. [Ed. Note: By 1984 NRDC had examined over 1000 discharges, issued 131 60-day notices of intent to sue, and filed 18 suits. By 1988 over 880 notices had been filed by NRDC and others since 1983. See Mann, Polluter-Financed Environmentally Beneficial Expenditures: Effective Use or Improper Abuse of Citizens' Suits Under the Clean Water Act?, 20 Envtl. L. 176 (1990). New Jersey Public Interest Research Group (NJPIRG) has also made especially vigorous use of CWA citizen enforcement suits.]

zen enforcement suits have mushroomed over the last two years, largely as a result of the NRDC effort. . . .

In the meantime, the regulated community had become concerned with the proliferation of citizen suits. Its concern was forcefully articulated in a letter from the Chemical Manufacturers Association (CMA) to EPA in June of 1984. CMA complained that citizen suits were being brought against NPDES permit violations that, for a variety of reasons, CMA did not view as appropriate for enforcement. The letter also solicited testimony of EPA witnesses in defense of the cases. It expressed concern that such cases would hamper EPA's own enforcement effort and suggested that the new wave of citizen suits would force the regulated community to be more aggressive in negotiating and contesting future NPDES permits.

NOTES AND QUESTIONS

1. What problems might be created by a dual system of public and private enforcement? What about the problems created by overly inclusive statutes and regulations? The government can deal with this problem by selective enforcement, targeting the violations that are significant and disregarding the trivial. Will private enforcers have incentives to disregard trivial violations? What if they disagree with the government about what violations are significant? How do the provisions in CWA §309 dealing with private enforcement actions seek to address these problems? The problems of coordination and consistency in enforcement policy are further complicated by the fact that in many instances states also have authority to bring enforcement actions against violations of federal requirements, producing a three-tier enforcement system: federal, state, and private.

2. Why have such a high proportion of citizen suits been brought under the CWA? Is it due to the NPDES permit system, which incorporates all of a facility's regulatory requirements in a single permit document and requires regular reporting of compliance with permit conditions to the government and the public? By contrast, under the Clean Air Act, there was until recently no single permit for a facility. Also, water pollutants are discharged from a point source in one or a few pipes, whereas air pollutants may be released from many different stacks and outlets at a given facility. To what extent will the permit requirement added by the 1990 Clean Air Act Amendments, see supra p. 255, facilitate private and public enforcement?

GWALTNEY OF SMITHFIELD, LTD. V. CHESAPEAKE BAY FOUNDATION, INC.

484 U.S. 49, 53 (1987)

Justice MARSHALL delivered the opinion of the Court.

In this case, we must decide whether §505(a) of the Clean Water Act, confers federal jurisdiction over citizen suits for wholly past violations. . .

I . . .

Between 1981 and 1984, petitioner [Gwaltney] repeatedly violated the conditions of [its] permit by exceeding effluent limitations on five of the seven pollutants covered. These violations are chronicled in the Discharge Monitoring Reports (DMRS) that the permit required petitioner to maintain. . . . The most substantial of the violations concerned the pollutants fecal coliform, chlorine, and total Kjeldahl nitrogen (TKN). Between October 27, 1981, and August 30, 1984, petitioner violated its TKN limitation 87 times, its chlorine limitation 34 times, and its fecal coliform limitation 31 times. . . . Petitioner installed new equipment to improve its chlorination system in March 1982, and its last reported chlorine violation occurred in October 1982. . . . The new chlorination system also helped to control the discharge of fecal coliform, and the last recorded fecal coliform violation occurred in February 1984. . . . Petitioner installed an upgraded wastewater treatment system in October 1983, and its last reported TKN violation occurred on May 15, 1984.

Respondents Chesapeake Bay Foundation and Natural Resources Defense Council . . . sent notice in February 1984, to Gwaltney, the Administrator of EPA, and the Virginia State Water Control Board, indicating respondents' intention to commence a citizen suit under the Act based on petitioner's violations of its permit conditions. Respondents proceeded to file this suit in June 1984, alleging that petitioner "has violated . . . [and] will continue to violate its NPDES permit."

Before the District Court reached a decision, Gwaltney moved in May 1985, for dismissal of the action for want of subject matter jurisdiction under the Act. Gwaltney argued that the language of §505(a), which permits private citizens to bring suit against any person "alleged to be in violation" of the Act, requires that a defendant be violating the Act at the time of suit. . . .

Gwaltney contended that because its last recorded violation occurred several weeks before respondents filed their complaint, the District Court lacked subject-matter jurisdiction over respondents' action. . . .

The District Court rejected Gwaltney's argument, concluding that §505 authorizes citizens to bring enforcement actions on the basis of wholly past violation. [The court of appeals affirmed.]

II

A

. . . The most natural reading of "to be in violation" is a requirement that citizen-plaintiffs allege a state of either continuous or intermittent violation, that is, a reasonable likelihood that a past polluter will continue to pollute in the future. Congress could have phrased its requirement in language that looked to the past ("to have violated"), but it did not choose this readily available option.

Respondents urge that the choice of the phrase "to be in violation," rather than phrasing more clearly directed to the past, is a "careless accident," the result of a "debatable lapse of precision." [But] Congress has demonstrated in other statutory provisions that it knows how to avoid this prospective implication by using language that explicitly targets wholly past violations.[44]

Respondents seek to counter this reasoning by observing that Congress also used the phrase "is in violation" in §309(a) of the Act, which authorizes the Administrator of EPA to issue compliance orders. . . . That language is incorporated by reference in §309(b), which authorizes the Administrator to bring civil enforcement actions. . . . Because it is little questioned that the Administrator may bring enforcement actions to recover civil penalties for wholly past violations, respondents contend, the parallel language of §309(a) and §505(a) must mean that citizens, too, may maintain such actions.

---

44. For example, the Solid Waste Disposal Act was amended in 1984 to authorize citizen suits against any "past or present" generator, transporter, owner, or operator of a treatment, storage, or disposal facility "who has contributed or who is contributing" to the "past or present" handling, storage, treatment, transportation, or disposal of certain hazardous wastes. 42 U.S.C. §6972(a)(1)(B) (1982 ed. Supp. 111). Prior to 1984, the Solid Waste Disposal Act contained language identical to that of §505(a) of the Clean Water Act, authorizing citizen suits against any person it alleged to be in violation of waste disposal permits or standards. 42 U.S.C. §6972(a)(1). Even more on point, the most recent Clean Water Act amendments permit EPA to assess administrative penalties without judicial process on any person who "has violated" the provisions of the Act. Water Quality Act of 1987, §314, Pub. L. 100-4, 101 Stat. 46.

Although this argument has some initial plausibility, it cannot withstand close scrutiny and comparison of the two statutory provisions. The Administrator's ability to seek civil penalties is not discussed in either §309(a) or §309(b); civil penalties are not mentioned until §309(d), which does not contain the "is in violation" language. . . . In contrast, §505 of the Act does not authorize civil penalties separately from injunctive relief; rather, the two forms of relief are referred to in the same subsection, even in the same sentence. [Citing §505(a).] The citizen suit provision suggests a connection between injunctive relief and civil penalties that is noticeably absent from the provision authorizing agency enforcement. A comparison of §309 and §505 thus supports rather than refutes our conclusion that citizens, unlike the Administrator, may seek civil penalties only in a suit brought to enjoin or otherwise abate an ongoing violation.

B . . .

One of the most striking indicia of the prospective orientation of the citizen suit is the pervasive use of the present tense throughout §505. A citizen suit may be brought only for violation of a permit limitation "which is in effect" under the Act. [§505(f).] Citizen-plaintiff must give notice to the alleged violator, the Administrator of EPA, and the State in which the alleged violation "occurs." §505(b)(1)(A). . . . The most telling use of the present tense is in the definition of "citizen" as "a person . . . having an interest which is or may be adversely affected" by the defendant's violations of the Act. [§505(g).] This definition makes plain what the undeviating use of the present tense strongly suggests: the harm sought to be addressed by the citizen suit lies in the present or the future, not in the past.

Any other conclusion would render incomprehensible §505's notice provision, which requires citizens to give 60 days notice of their intent to sue to the alleged violator as well as to the Administrator in the State. [§505(b)(1)(A).] If the Administrator or the State commences enforcement action within that 60 day period, the citizen suit is barred, presumably because governmental action has rendered it unnecessary. [§505(b)(1)(B).] It follows logically that the purpose of notice to the alleged violator is to give it an opportunity to bring itself into complete compliance with the Act and thus likewise render unnecessary a citizen suit. If we assume, as respondents urge, that citizen suits may target wholly past violations, the requirement of notice to the alleged violator becomes gratuitous. . . .

. . . Permitting citizen suits for wholly past violations of the Act could undermine the supplementary role envisioned for the citizen suit. This danger is best illustrated by an example. Suppose that the

Administrator identified a violator of the Act and issued a compliance order under §309(a). Suppose further that the Administrator agreed not to assess or otherwise seek civil penalties on the condition that the violator take some extreme corrective action, such as to install particularly effective but expensive machinery, that it otherwise would not be obliged to take. If citizens could file suit, months or years later, in order to seek the civil penalties that the Administrator chose to forgo, then the Administrator's discretion to enforce the Act in the public interest would be curtailed considerably.

III

Our conclusion that §505 does not permit citizen suits for wholly past violations does not necessarily dispose of this lawsuit, as both lower courts recognized. . . . The Court of Appeals acknowledged . . . that "[a] very sound argument can be made that [respondents'] allegations of continuing violations were made in good faith," 791 F.2d, at 308, n.9, but expressly declined to rule on this alternative holding. Because we agree that §505 confers jurisdiction over citizen suits when the citizen-plaintiffs make a good-faith allegation of continuous or intermittent violation, we remand the case to the Court of Appeals for further consideration.

. . . The statute does not require that a defendant "be in violation" of the Act at the commencement of suit; rather, the statute requires that a defendant be "*alleged* to be in violation." . . . We agree with the Solicitor General that "Congress's use of the phrase 'alleged to be in violation' reflects a conscious sensitivity to the practical difficulties of detecting and proving chronic episodic violations of environmental standards." Brief for United States as Amicus Curiae 18. Our acknowledgement that Congress intended a good-faith allegation to suffice for jurisdictional purposes, however, does not give litigants license to flood the courts with suits premised on baseless allegations. Rule 11 of the Federal Rules of Civil Procedure, which requires pleadings to be based on a good-faith belief, formed after reasonable inquiry, that they are "well grounded in fact," adequately protects defendants from frivolous allegations.

[The Court indicated that principles of mootness might require dismissal of a citizen suit action if it became clear that violation had permanently and totally ceased.] Mootness doctrine thus protects defendants from the maintenance of suit under the Clean Air Act based solely on violations wholly unconnected to any present or future wrongdoing, while it also protects plaintiffs from defendants who seek to evade sanction by predictable "protestations of repentance and reform."

NOTES AND QUESTIONS

1. Lurking beneath the issue of statutory construction addressed in *Gwaltney* are potential constitutional questions. Article III of the Constitution limits the jurisdiction of Article III federal courts to "cases or controversies." As we shall see in Chapter 7, the Supreme Court has construed Article III to require a plaintiff who seeks to challenge unlawful government action to show that the action has caused him "injury in fact" that would be redressed by a victory against the government. Exposure to environmental harm or a significant risk of harm is sufficient to establish injury. Does this same "injury in fact" requirement apply to a citizen suit enforcement action against a private polluter? See *Sierra Club v. SCM Corp.*, 580 F. Supp. 862 (W.D.N.Y.), *aff'd*, 747 F.2d 99 (2d Cir. 1984) (requiring showing of injury in fact). If so, does the plaintiff have to show an actual or threatened ongoing violation, redressable by injunction, that threatens harm to plaintiff? Could Congress constitutionally authorize a plaintiff to bring private actions for civil penalties for wholly past violations? Would it matter whether the past violations had threatened or continued to threaten plaintiff with harm? What if Congress awarded a bounty to private parties who successfully prosecuted wholly past violations?

Justice Marshall refers to a provision of the Solid Waste Disposal Act that authorizes citizen suits with regard to past conduct. See supra, n. 44. Is this provision consistent with the "case or controversy" requirement of Article III? Does it exceed Congress's constitutional authority?

2. Legislative proposals have been made to change the result in *Gwaltney* by amending the CWA to authorize plaintiffs to bring actions for civil penalties for entirely past violations. Putting aside the constitutional issues noted above, would such legislation be desirable as a matter of policy?

3. CWA §505(b)(1)(B) precludes an independent citizen suit if EPA or a state "has commenced and is diligently prosecuting a civil or criminal action in a court . . . to require compliance. . . ." Does this bar operate when a federal or state agency is seeking to remedy a violation through administrative proceedings, or does it apply only when an enforcement agency seeks judicial relief? What if all administrative proceedings have the essential adjudicatory processes of court proceedings and can obtain equivalent relief? See *Baughman v. Bradford Coal Co.*, 592 F.2d. 215 (3d Cir.) *cert. denied*, 441 U.S. 961 (1979) (adjudicatory administrative proceedings can be a "court" in these instances); but see *Friends of the Earth v. Consolidated Rail Corp.*, 768 F.2d. 57 (2d Cir. 1985) ("court" refers only to judicial proceedings).

4. Does *Gwaltney* prevent citizens from challenging the terms of a settlement agreement between a polluter and a state or federal govern-

ment if the settlement has caused the violations to cease and eliminated any reasonable likelihood of their recurrence? See *Atlantic States Legal Foundation v. Eastman Kodak*, 933 F.2d. 124 (2d Cir. 1991), holding that it does.

NOTE ON EBE SETTLEMENTS

Civil penalties imposed by a court, whether imposed in connection with a citizen suit or a government enforcement action, are deposited directly into the general Treasury fund. Alternatively, settlements, whether obtained in a citizen suit or a government suit, may involve so-called Environmental Beneficial Expenditures (EBEs). EBEs, as previously noted, are funds paid by defendants under a settlement agreement to be applied to a specific environmentally-related project, such as restoration of a wetlands polluted as a result of a violation. Some EBEs may not be aimed at remedying the effects of a violation. For example, they have been used to acquire conservation easements to protect ecologically valuable resources when resources have been damaged by the violation, to establish a fund to support environmental research, or to support public education. Defendants favor EBEs because they are more clearly tax deductible than civil penalties and also generate favorable publicity. Environmental plaintiffs favor EBEs because they prefer to see monies spent to support environmentally worthy projects rather than going into the general Treasury. Settlements of private enforcement actions also typically provide for payment of plaintiff's attorneys fees and other litigation costs.

As previously noted, the government sometimes includes EBEs in settlements of actions that it brings. However, the government generally insists, for reasons of deterrence, that a violator also pay a civil penalty at least equal to the economic benefit derived from the violation. It also insists that there be some nexus between the violation and the EBE, on the principle that specific relief obtained through the enforcement power should redress and prevent violations, rather than using the enforcement power as generalized leverage to extract contributions to unrelated good causes.[45] Thus, an EBE proposal to restore wetlands damaged by pollution and to preserve additional wetlands in the immediate vicinity would satisfy the nexus test. The restoration element would undo the consequences of past violations, and the preservation element would provide appropriate redress for the injury imposed on the public and the environment in the interim between the violation and the restoration. The use of EBEs to preserve an eco-

---

45. For discussion of the nexus principle, see *Local No. 93 v. Cleveland*, 478 U.S. 501 (1986).

logically important woodland located far away from the violations, however, would not satisfy the nexus test.

The Justice Department monitors citizen enforcement actions and seeks to ensure that settlements of those actions conform to the principles that the Department follows in settlements of the cases that it brings, including the payment of some civil penalties and the nexus requirement for EBEs. CWA §505(c)(3) authorizes the United States to intervene as a party in any citizen suit as a matter of right, and if not a party the Government must still be provided notice and an opportunity to comment on any proposed consent decree. Courts, however, need not necessarily accede to the government's objections. In *Sierra Club v. Electronic Controls Design Inc.,* 909 F.2d 1350 (9th Cir. 1990), the court upheld an EBE settlement provision where the Justice Department did not intervene and later objected to the settlement. The defendant agreed to make contributions to local environmental agreements, but not to pay any civil penalties.

In *NJPIRG v. Powell Duffryn Terminals,* 913 F.2d 64 (3d Cir. 1990), the district court found for plaintiffs in a citizen suit that went to trial, assessed over $3 million in civil penalties against the defendant, and then directed that the penalties be paid into a trust fund (whose trustees would be appointed by the judge) to be used "to directly impact environmental problems in New Jersey." On the intervention and objection of the United States, the court of appeals directed that the penalty assessment be paid into the Treasury. The federal government has, however, fared less well in private cases that have been settled. For example, in *NRDC and Sierra Club v. Interstate Paper Corp.,* 29 ERC (BNA) 1135 (1988), the court approved an EBE that provided funds to the Georgia Conservancy to educate schoolchildren, despite objection by the Department of Justice and acknowledgement by the court that the terms were not closely related to the violations. A citizen suit settlement does not necessarily preclude the government from bringing a subsequent statutory enforcement action. See id.[46]

The structure of incentives driving private enforcement has been the subject of extensive economic analysis. See generally R. Posner, Economic Analysis of Law (4th ed. 1993). From an economic perspective, effective citizen enforcement requires the tailoring of incentives to bring actions in accordance with the particular ends sought. Many contend that government resources alone are insufficient to reach all polluters and hence effective enforcement demands the enlistment of private attorney generals through citizen suit provisions. Critics have argued, however, that environmental citizen suit provisions, as currently drafted, have become a vehicle for furthering the objectives of an "enforcement cartel." This cartel, led by national environmental

---

46. For discussion of EBEs, see Mann, supra n.43.

groups like the NRDC and NJPIRG, have used readily available information, attorneys fee recoveries in excess of the salaries paid to the groups' lawyers, and settlements to fund agendas beyond the scope of Congressional intent which do little to reduce pollution. See Greve, The Private Enforcement of Environmental Law, 65 Tul. L. Rev. 339 (1990). Which view do you find most persuasive? Apart from lack of governmental prosecutorial resources, what other purposes might citizen suits serve within our multi-branch system of government?

6

Regulation of Hazardous Waste Disposal

With extensive regulatory systems in place to control emissions of pollutants into the air and effluents into the water, it was only a matter of time before comparable regulatory controls would be needed on land disposal of wastes. By foreclosing the traditional outlets for pollution, the air and water regulatory programs funneled more wastes into slag piles, evaporation pits, and landfills. In addition to limiting the disposal options of polluting entities, these programs led to the generation of new sludges as a byproduct of air and water control pollution technologies, which also had to be disposed somewhere other than in the air or water. Thus, unregulated land disposal of waste was the last major loophole of environmental law.

By the mid-1970s, the United States was generating approximately 250 million metric tons of hazardous wastes per year. Improper land disposal of these wastes poses a number of potentially serious human health and environmental risks. Open dumps provide a breeding ground for insects, birds, and rodents, which can transport disease to human populations. Decomposing wastes produce noxious and combustible gases that pollute the air and can accumulate and spontaneously explode. Runoff following rainstorms carries toxic materials into lakes and river systems. Of greatest significance, hazardous materials can leach into the soil, thereby threatening groundwater resources. Groundwater provides drinking water to a substantial proportion of the United States population.

Prior to the mid-1970s, there was essentially no federal regulation of hazardous waste disposal. The Solid Waste Disposal Act of 1965 provided modest funding to state and local officials for research and planning and gave the Department of Health, Education, and Welfare advisory powers with respect to local solid waste regulation. The law had little effect on the regulation of hazardous waste. Moreover, what state and local regulation existed was incomplete and often poorly enforced. As a result, approximately half of the hazardous wastes generated were dumped, typically in the form of sludges, into unlined, open pits located on the generator's property. These wastes eventually evaporated into the air or percolated into the soils, thereby threatening the groundwater system. Another 30 percent were buried in landfills, which were also subject to leaching into groundwater. Much of the remainder was burned in an uncontrolled manner.

Whereas the environmental threats posed by hazardous wastes were largely neglected prior to the mid-1970s, these problems emerged in the late 1970s and 1980s as the leading area of congressional, regulatory, and judicial attention in the environmental field. The first section of this chapter focuses upon The Resource Conservation and Recovery Act (RCRA), a broad federal regulatory program enacted in 1976 to ensure the safe passage of hazardous wastes from "cradle to grave." As ambitious as this regulatory scheme was, it became clear by the late 1970s that prospective regulation would not be sufficient to address the numerous abandoned waste dumps threatening groundwater systems throughout the nation. The second section of this chapter describes and analyzes The Comprehensive Environmental Response, Compensation, and Liability Act (CERCLA), also known as Superfund, a unique regulatory-liability framework aimed at cleaning up the plethora of abandoned hazardous waste sites. The final section explores the increasing role of common law courts, through the development of toxic tort doctrines, in addressing problems of hazardous waste disposal and environmental risks generally.

A. PROSPECTIVE REGULATION: THE RESOURCE CONSERVATION AND RECOVERY ACT

In view of Congress's traditional inclination toward command and control approaches to environmental problems, it is not surprising that Congress turned to this approach in confronting the environmental problems posed by hazardous waste disposal. The Resource Conservation and Recovery Act was the first major federal regulatory statute aimed at the problems of hazardous waste disposal. It seeks to control, in intricate detail, the entire hazardous waste stream from generation to disposal. How this regulatory system operates and whether it efficaciously addresses the human health and environmental risks of hazardous waste disposal are the principal inquiries of this section.

The Resource Conservation and Recovery Act has become perhaps the most complicated federal regulatory statute. It has led one federal circuit judge to call review of its provisions a "mind-numbing journey." *American Mining Congress v. EPA*, 824 F.2d 1177, 1189 (D.C. Cir. 1987). In order to understand how such a regulatory maze could have evolved, it is necessary to study the process by which it developed. The first section provides an overview of the regulatory system, highlighting the political factors that underlie its evolution. In view of the enormous complexity of RCRA, it will not be possible here to explore all facets of the regulatory system. After the overview, therefore, we focus upon two major regulatory battlegrounds to illustrate the structure, complexity, and limitations of the regulatory scheme: (1) the scope of the statute, as delineated by the definition of a solid waste; and (2) the land disposal regulations. The final section explores policy perspectives on RCRA.

1. OVERVIEW OF THE REGULATORY SYSTEM

As with the air and water problems that it confronted in the early 1970s, Congress faced a bewildering set of scientific, technological, and economic issues when it turned its attention to the regulation of hazardous waste disposal in the mid-1970s. The hazardous waste stream is generated by a diverse range of mining, industrial, agricultural, governmental, commercial, and household activities. Substantially every sector of the economy generates hazardous wastes. Among the factors complicating the development of an effective regulatory system for hazardous waste disposal are scientific uncertainty about risks to human health and the environment; incomplete understanding of risk pathways, especially through groundwater; the vast economic and technological complexity of the industrial processes that generate hazardous waste; and limited knowledge of technologies to recover, treat, and dispose of hazardous wastes. In the face of these uncertainties, Congress opted for the same general approach that we have seen in The Clean Air Act Amendments of 1970 and The Federal Water Pollution Control Act of 1972: bestowing broad discretionary authority upon EPA to regulate hazardous waste generation, transportation, storage, treatment, and disposal in order to protect "human health and the environment."

The Resource Conservation and Recovery Act of 1976, 42 U.S.C.

§§6901-92,[1] directed EPA to develop standards for tracking and disposing waste within 18 months. Subtitle C of the Act creates a program for federal regulation of hazardous wastes.[2] Among the myriad regulatory tasks delegated to EPA were identification of hazardous wastes; development of a record-keeping system for tracking wastes from generation to disposal ("cradle to grave"); promulgation of standards for treatment, storage, and disposal of hazardous wastes and requirements for location, design, and construction of disposal facilities; development of contingency plans for accidents; and promulgation of financial responsibility requirements for treatment, storage, and disposal facilities.

Despite this broad regulatory mandate, Congress did not initially provide EPA with adequate resources to tackle this enormous agenda. The Carter Administration EPA, while committed to implementing RCRA, quickly fell behind schedule in promulgating regulations and was unable to achieve the ambitious 18-month deadline established by the Act. A citizen suit in 1979 compelled EPA to promulgate Subtitle C regulations according to a court-determined schedule.[3] Pursuant to this direction, EPA issued major RCRA regulations in February 1980 and May 1980.

In January 1981, midway through the implementation of RCRA, the Reagan Administration took office. President Reagan had campaigned upon a platform of significant deregulation of United States industry, with environmental regulation as a prime target. Through his political appointments and executive oversight of the EPA, President Reagan brought this philosophy to the agency. During the early Reagan Administration, EPA sought to delay issuance of regulatory standards, weaken regulatory requirements, and relax enforcement of federal regulations. See Hill, An Overview of RCRA: The "Mind-Numbing" Provisions of the Most Complicated Environmental Statute, 21 Envtl. L. Rep. 10254 (May 1991); Florio, Congress as Reluctant Regulator: Hazardous Waste Policy in the 1980's, 3 Yale J. Reg. 351 (1986).

The issuance of land disposal regulations illustrates this strategy. The Carter Administration had first proposed uniform design standards for hazardous waste facilities in December 1978. In response to comments, EPA in October 1980 considered adopting a site-specific risk assessment approach, which would require EPA to evaluate the potential risks for each facility. The Reagan Administration formally proposed this rule in February 1981, allowing an eight-month comment period. It did not anticipate promulgating a final standard until the fall

---

1. Although establishing a new comprehensive framework for waste policy, RCRA technically amended the Solid Waste Disposal Act (SWDA).

2. Subtitle D creates a separate program of federal guidelines for state regulation of nonhazardous wastes.

3. *Illinois v. Costle*, 9 Envtl. L. Rep. 20243 (D.D.C. 1979).

of 1983. In November 1981, a federal district court ordered EPA to promulgate regulations for existing hazardous waste land facilities by February 1, 1982. Notwithstanding this order, EPA did not issue final standards for land disposal facilities until July 1982. The regulations did not take effect until January 1983, four and one half years after the statutory deadline.

The final regulations and their implementation further reflected the Reagan Administration's resistance to congressional intent. The final standards applied only when a facility sought a "final permit." Many facilities, however, were operating under "interim permits" and hence were allowed to continue their activities without regard to the regulations. Such facilities were not required to submit final permit applications unless EPA so requested. EPA was slow in making such requests, effectively delaying the requirements of RCRA well beyond the actual implementation date of the already late regulations.

The Reagan Administration's handling of hazardous waste policy infuriated Congress in other ways as well. In testimony before congressional committees, EPA clung to the environmental soundness of land disposal of hazardous waste, despite mounting scientific evidence questioning this technology and the increasing availability of promising alternatives including incineration, neutralization, recycling, and biological treatment. Of perhaps greater political significance, top EPA officials became involved in a scandal involving mismanagement of and political favoritism in the handling of the hazardous waste programs. This led to the resignation of one EPA Administrator and the resignation and dismissal of top hazardous waste policy personnel.

Within this atmosphere of EPA foot-dragging, political manipulation, and malfeasance, Congress began the reauthorization process for RCRA. By 1983, numerous studies of the extent of unsafe hazardous waste disposal indicated that the risks were greater than those perceived when RCRA was enacted in 1976. Yet no comprehensive federal program was in force. Moreover, it was evident that EPA could not be relied upon to implement a discretionary program. Numerous witnesses urged Congress to legislate a comprehensive hazardous waste regulatory program, subjecting disposal firms to meet stringent requirements and requiring them to obtain permits.

The Hazardous and Solid Waste Amendments of 1984 (HSWA) responded to this clamor by establishing tight regulatory deadlines for EPA to set standards. These provisions are unprecedented in their level of detail and intrusion into EPA's management practices. Unlike RCRA, the HSWA established minimum regulatory standards. Moreover, if EPA failed to implement these standards within the deadlines, citizens could sue EPA to force compliance with more stringent statutory standards. These so-called hammers were thought necessary to overcome EPA's reluctance to act and to eliminate the benefits to industry from regulatory delay. EPA's failure to regulate would result in what industry perceived as draconian regulatory requirements. Since the passage of the HSWA, hazardous waste law and policy have been driven by these ambitious regulatory standards and exacting timetables.

With this statutory background, we are prepared to summarize the key features of what has come to be considered the most complicated federal environmental regulatory program. Since we are principally concerned with hazardous waste law and policy in this chapter, our focus here will be on the Subtitle C provisions. It should also be emphasized that this brief overview cannot capture the complexity of the vast statute or the more than 500 pages of regulations in the Code of Federal Regulations implementing Subtitle C.[4]

Scope of RCRA's Subtitle C Program. The scope of Subtitle C is delimited by the waste materials that Congress has authorized EPA to regulate. RCRA applies generally to "solid waste." The more exacting Subtitle C regulations apply to "hazardous waste." Thus, in order to fall within the scope of Subtitle C, a waste must be classified as both a solid and a hazardous waste.

RCRA defines "solid waste" broadly to include "any garbage, refuse, sludge from a waste treatment plant, or air pollution control facility and other discarded material, including solid, liquid, semisolid, or contained gaseous material resulting from industrial, commercial, mining, and agricultural operations, and from community activities." SWDA §1004(27). The statutory definition excludes domestic sewage, irrigation return flows, industrial water discharges regulated under the Clean Water Act, and nuclear wastes. Despite the comprehensiveness of this definition, difficult interpretive issues have arisen, especially in the context of waste materials that are recycled. EPA faces the dilemma of encouraging legitimate recycling activities that will encourage conservation of resources and reduce hazardous waste problems while at the same time not promoting activities — such as uncontrolled burning of hazardous wastes for fuel and applying contaminated waste oils to dirt roads as a dust suppressant — that increase risks to human health and the environment. Section 2 explores these issues in detail.

RCRA defines "hazardous waste" as:

> a solid waste, or combination of solid wastes, which because of its quantity, concentration, or physical, chemical, or infectious characteristics may —
>
>> (A) cause, or significantly contribute to an increase in mortality or an increase in serious irreversible, or incapacitating reversible, illness; or

---

4. For a more extensive overview of RCRA (as amended by the HSWA) and implementing regulations, see Hill, An Overview of RCRA: The "Mind-Numbing" Provisions of the Most Complicated Environmental Statute, 21 Envtl. L. Rep. 10254 (May 1991).

(B) pose a substantial present or potential hazard to human
health or the environment when improperly treated, stored, transported, or disposed of, or otherwise managed.

SWDA §1004(5). RCRA §3001 instructs EPA to "develop and promulgate criteria for identifying the characteristics of hazardous waste, and
for listing hazardous waste . . . taking into account toxicity, persistence, and degradability in nature, potential for accumulation in tissue,
and other related factors such as flammability, corrosiveness, and other
hazardous characteristics." In accordance with this provision, EPA has
developed two approaches for identifying hazardous wastes. Under the
characteristics approach, a solid waste is considered hazardous if it possesses one or more of the following properties (as defined by regulations): (1) ignitability, (2) corrosivity, (3) reactivity, or (4) toxicity. 40
C.F.R. §261.21-.24 (1989). Under the *listing* approach, EPA designates
a solid waste as hazardous by placing it, pursuant to rulemaking procedures, on one of four special lists.[5] The criteria for listing are (1) the
waste possesses one or more of the four characteristics noted above; (2)
the waste is acutely hazardous (that is, shown to be fatal in low doses to
humans or in animal studies); or (3) the waste contains one or more
substances listed in "Appendix VII" and poses "a substantial present or
potential hazard to human health and the environment when improperly . . . managed." 40 C.F.R. §261.11(a) (1989).

The key difference between the two categories of hazardous wastes
for purposes of the regulatory system is that characteristic wastes are
considered hazardous only to the extent that they exhibit hazardous
properties whereas listed wastes, once designated as such, are considered hazardous regardless of the circumstances. This difference is of
principal significance with regard to the application the so-called mixture and derived from rules. 40 C.F.R. §261.3(a)(2), (c)(2) (1989). If
a mixture of a characteristic waste with other substances removes the
hazardous property(ies) — for example, by neutralizing its corrosivity — then the resulting mixture is not considered hazardous.[6] By contrast, a mixture containing a listed waste is deemed hazardous even if
the combined mixture does not exhibit any hazardous properties, unless the sole basis for listing the waste was that it exhibited one or more
hazardous characteristics. The "derived from" rule classifies any residue
from the treatment of a listed hazardous waste as hazardous. The "mix-

---

5. "F-listed" wastes are spent chemicals, wastes, and by-products generated by a variety of industries. "K-listed" wastes are primarily sludges and by-
products generated by a single industry. "P" and "U" wastes are off-specification
commercial chemical products and pesticides or residues when discarded or
accidentally spilled.

6. Mixing of a characteristic waste with other materials to remove its hazardous property(ies) ordinarily constitutes treatment and hence requires a
RCRA Subtitle C permit. See infra, p. 567.

ture" and "derived from" rules were struck down on procedural grounds in 1991 and are currently being reconsidered by EPA. See *Shell Oil v. EPA,* 950 F.2d 741 (D.C. Cir. 1991).

A facility possessing a listed waste may seek to avoid the RCRA Subtitle C requirements by petitioning EPA to "delist" the relevant waste or mixture. This administrative process, however, is both time consuming and expensive because EPA must adhere to notice and comment rulemaking procedures. SWDA §3001(f).

A number of wastes have been excluded by regulation or statute from Subtitle C regulation. EPA has exempted household hazardous wastes and agricultural wastes used as fertilizer. In 1980, Congress exempted five categories of "special wastes" from Subtitle C regulation pending EPA review: (1) oil and gas industry wastes; (2) mineral extraction and benefaction wastes; (3) coal combustion wastes; (4) mineral processing wastes; and (5) cement kiln wastes. These categories were thought to be large volume, relatively low-toxicity wastes. Thus far, EPA has only formally excluded the first two categories of special wastes from Subtitle C regulation, although the final three are effectively excluded until such time as EPA makes a formal determination.

"Cradle to Grave" Regulatory System. RCRA creates an elaborate system for tracking hazardous waste from the time it is generated until its ultimate disposal, hence the phrase "cradle to grave." RCRA divides the universe of entities that shepherd hazardous waste through its life cycle into three categories — (1) generators; (2) transporters; and (3) treatment, storage, and disposal (TSD) facilities.

Generators are defined as "[a]ny person, by site, whose act or process produces hazardous waste . . . or whose act first causes hazardous waste to become subject to regulation." See SWDA §3002; 40 C.F.R. Parts 261-62. Generators bear responsibility for determining whether their solid waste is hazardous. Upon making such a determination, they must obtain a hazardous waste identification number from EPA, which must be used on the manifest that follows the waste to its ultimate disposal. Failure to properly identify waste as hazardous subjects generators to liability for improper transport or disposal. Generators may not store wastes for more than 90 days without triggering stringent RCRA storage requirements. Generators must carefully package and label wastes and ship them to an authorized TSD facility. The manifest follows the shipment from transporter or intermediate storage facility to the ultimate TSD destination. Generators bear responsibility for ensuring that shipped wastes reach their ultimate TSD destination within 35 days. If a generator does not receive endorsed copies of the manifest indicating proper delivery within 45 days from the transporter and the TSD facility, it must file a report with the EPA detailing the circumstances and the generator's efforts to locate the waste. In addition, generators must biennially submit reports on waste generating activities.

RCRA also exhorts generators to minimize the generation of hazardous wastes.

Prior to 1984, the above requirements applied only to "large quantity generators," those producing or accumulating more than 1000 kilograms of hazardous waste in a calendar month, with lower cutoffs for some acutely hazardous wastes. The Hazardous and Solid Waste Amendments significantly expanded the scope of the regulatory system by requiring that "small quantity generators" (SQGs) producing or accumulating between 100 and 1000 kilograms of hazardous waste per month be included within the manifest tracking system and instructing EPA to develop standards for small quantity generators. This change in the law dramatically increased the number of generators covered by RCRA. EPA has since imposed the full set of large quantity generator requirements upon SQGs, subject to a few relaxed standards such as allowing wastes to accumulate on-site for 180 days and less onerous reporting and recordkeeping requirements.[7]

RCRA's transporter regulations largely mirror the generator requirements. SWDA §3003. Transporters carrying hazardous waste must obtain an EPA identification number. They must participate in the manifest system, maintain records, use proper containers and labeling, handle wastes properly (for instance, not mix dissimilar wastes), and file biennial reports on their hazardous waste activities. They are also subject to regulations governing the response to hazardous waste spills during transport.

Standards for Treatment, Storage, and Disposal Facilities. Of the three categories of participants in the hazardous waste stream, TSD facilities are subject to the most extensive and stringent regulation. SWDA §3004. The definition of a TSD facility encompasses entities engaged in activities to alter "the physical, chemical, or biological character or composition of any hazardous waste," "recover energy or material resources from the waste," "render such waste nonhazardous, or less hazardous, safer to transport, store, or dispose of, or amenable for recovery, amenable for storage, or reduced in volume," "hold hazardous wastes for a temporary period," or discharge, deposit, inject, dump, spill, leak, or place hazardous waste into or on any land or water so that such waste may enter the environment. 40 C.F.R. §260.10 (1989). In view of the breadth of this definition, generators and transporters must be extremely careful to avoid falling within the ambit of the TSD regulations.

In addition to participating in the manifest system and carrying

---

7. Generators producing less than 100 kilograms of hazardous waste per month remain exempt from RCRA (with some lower cutoffs for acutely hazardous waste), but must ensure that their hazardous waste is disposed on-site or at a state-authorized disposal facility.

out record-keeping and reporting obligations similar to those borne by generators and transporters, TSD facilities are subject to a series of substantive regulatory requirements over their life cycle. Prior to operation, new TSD facilities must obtain an operating permit. SWDA §3005(c).[8] TSD facilities must be designed to minimize releases of hazardous materials. They may not be located on floodplains or within 200 feet of an active earthquake fault. They must install groundwater monitoring systems to detect releases of hazardous materials and respond to any contamination exceeding groundwater protection standards.[9]

During the period of operation, TSD facilities must adhere to security measures intended to minimize hazardous releases and respond to emergencies. These measures include installing fencing and warning systems, conducting periodic inspections, training personnel to handle hazardous wastes properly and react to emergency situations, satisfying financial responsibility requirements, preparing a contingency plan, maintaining adequate emergency equipment, and entering into agreements with local authorities to address releases of hazardous materials. Query: Are financial responsibility requirements in combination with liability for leaks sufficient to ensure proper treatment, storage, and disposal of hazardous wastes?

Subtitle C actually regulates hazardous waste "beyond the grave" by imposing stringent regulations upon the closure of TSD facilities. During the closure phase, the facility must complete treatment and disposal of all wastes that are not destined for other facilities, dismantle and decontaminate equipment, and minimize the risk of future release of hazardous materials from the site. 40 C.F.R. §§264.111, 265.111 (1989). All of this work proceeds under a detailed closure plan that must be approved by EPA. 40 C.F.R. §§264.112, 265.112 (1989). RCRA regulations allow TSD facilities to "clean close" surface impoundments[10] and waste piles by removing or decontaminating all hazardous waste, equipment, structures, and contaminated soils, thereby escaping further regulation. See, e.g., 40 C.F.R. §264.228(a)(1) (1989). Surface impoundments and waste piles not achieving these requirements and other facilities are subject to a 30-year period of post-closure regulatory requirements, including groundwater monitoring and cor-

---

8. Facilities operating under interim status prior to the passage of the HSWA, those seeking permits, and certain other facilities may, subject to strict and short deadlines, operate under interim status. RCRA §3005(e).

9. Interim status facilities must implement a groundwater monitoring system within one year of obtaining their interim status but in general are subject to less stringent monitoring and remediation requirements.

10. A surface impoundment is a human-made pond, pit, or lagoon. 40 C.F.R. §260.10 (1989).

rective action, maintaining and monitoring hazardous waste disposal systems, and securing the site. 40 C.F.R. §264.117 (1989).

Requirements for Specific Hazardous Waste Treatment, Storage, and Disposal Units. In addition to the general requirements for TSD facilities, RCRA imposes minimum technological standards for particular treatment, storage, and disposal units, and limits how particular hazardous wastes may be disposed on land.

EPA has developed detailed design, operating, and closure requirements for tanks, incinerators, and industrial boilers used for storing, treating, or disposing of hazardous waste. Due to the great concern about groundwater contamination, the most stringent requirements apply to waste treatment technologies in which hazardous wastes are placed directly on the land — landfills, surface impoundments, waste piles, and land treatment units. In the Hazardous and Solid Waste Amendments of 1984, Congress expressly required that new landfills and surface impoundments contain two or more liners, a leachate collection system, and groundwater monitoring wells. SWDA §3004(o)(1). The HSWA provides limited exemptions for alternative designs and operating practices that must be at least as effective as the above requirements and monofills — impoundments containing only one kind of waste. SWDA §3004(o)(2),(3).

The land disposal restrictions are the most controversial provisions of the HSWA. SWDA §3004(d)-(g). They are often referred to as the "land ban" because of the severe hammer and tight deadlines that Congress used to spur agency action. These provisions prohibit the disposal of hazardous waste on land in five phases unless EPA establishes treatment standards "which substantially diminish the toxicity of the waste or substantially reduce the likelihood of migration of hazardous constituents from the waste so that short-term and long-term threats to human health and the environment are minimized." SWDA §3004(m)(1).[11] These land disposal restrictions apply regardless of whether facilities meet the stringent technological requirements described above. Section 3 explores EPA's implementation of these provisions.

State Programs. As in other areas of environmental law, Congress intended the hazardous waste program to be implemented as part of a federal and state partnership with the states having a major role in

_____

11. Land disposal of hazardous waste is also permitted where "it has been demonstrated to [EPA], to a reasonable degree of certainty, that there will be no migration of hazardous constituents from the disposal unit . . . for as long as the wastes remain hazardous." SWDA §3004(d)(1), (e)(1), (g)(5). This procedure is referred to as the "no mitigation" petition. In addition, EPA may, in certain carefully constrained circumstances, grant limited variances for land disposal. SWDA §3004(h)(2),(3).

implementing the program. Following the models of the air and water programs, RCRA provides for states to assume primary responsibility to implement and enforce a state hazardous waste program that acts "in lieu of" EPA's program. In order to establish such a program, a state must obtain EPA authorization by demonstrating that its program is at least as stringent as the federal program and possesses adequate resources to enforce the requirements effectively. Almost all of the states have received authorization for some or all of their Subtitle C program.

Enforcement and Clean-up of Dangerous Sites. RCRA provides a broad array of civil and criminal enforcement tools. SWDA §3008. EPA may issue administrative orders requiring compliance, revoking a facility's operating permit, or assessing a civil penalty of up to $25,000 per day of noncompliance for each requirement. EPA may also file suit in federal court seeking an injunction mandating compliance. RCRA also authorizes the government to seek criminal fines and imprisonment for knowing violation of Subtitle C requirements. RCRA also authorizes citizen suits to enforce its provisions following notice to the relevant government enforcement authority and a 60-day waiting period. SWDA §7002. Citizens may not, however, pursue an action where the government has "commenced and is diligently prosecuting" a court action seeking compliance.

RCRA also provides EPA with broad authority to abate hazardous waste conditions that "may present an imminent and substantial endangerment to health or the environment." SWDA §7003. Until 1980, this section provided the principal means by which the government could address the threats posed by leaking hazardous waste sites. As we will see in Section B, these provisions have been largely supplanted by the more expansive enforcement provisions of the Comprehensive Environmental Response, Compensation, and Liability Act of 1980.

NOTES AND QUESTIONS

1. What are the justifications for hazardous waste regulation? What are the justifications for a federal role in hazardous waste policy? What approaches are reflected in RCRA's statutory scheme? Are these approaches consistent with the justifications for hazardous waste policy?

2. Are command and control approaches more or less appropriate in hazardous waste policy than in the air and water contexts? What alternative regulatory approaches could be used? In comparison to these approaches, what are the effects of RCRA on incentives to minimize hazardous waste generation; develop better production, recovery, treatment, and disposal technologies; and dispose of hazardous waste illegally? Does RCRA encourage the production of the necessary technological and monitoring data at reasonable administrative cost?

3. The interactions between the legislative and executive branches in defining and implementing hazardous waste policy are reminiscent of the experience in regulating hazardous air pollutants under §112 of the Clean Air Act. What political factors explain the problems that have been encountered in achieving coherent and effective regulation in these areas of environmental law and policy? What do these case studies suggest about the relative power of the legislative and executive branches in determining regulatory policy? Does this allocation of power ensure that institutional capacities of the different branches will be best utilized?

4. Are legislative hammers an effective means of spurring good regulation? What are their advantages and disadvantages? In what circumstances will they be most effective? Least effective?

5. Does RCRA limit the judiciary's role to merely imposing statutory requirements when regulatory deadlines are missed? To what extent does or should the distrust of agency integrity underlying the HSWA affect judicial review of agency action?

2. DELINEATING THE SCOPE OF RCRA: WHAT WASTES ARE COVERED?

One of the principal challenges in implementing RCRA has been delineating its scope. Whether a production process uses or generates a "solid" and "hazardous" waste can significantly affect the economic viability of an enterprise. As a result, industry groups have sought through the regulatory process to narrow the scope of these terms. Not surprisingly, many environmental organizations have sought broad interpretations of these statutory terms. Defining the scope of these terms, therefore, has generated complex regulations and frequent judicial review. These materials highlight the rich interplay of complex statutory terms, the regulatory process, and judicial review.

GABA, SOLID WASTE AND RECYCLED MATERIALS UNDER RCRA: SEPARATING CHAFF FROM WHEAT

16 Ecology L.Q. 623, 623-624 (1989)

. . . Although [RCRA is] frequently characterized as regulating wastes from "cradle to grave," this expression obscures a critical aspect of the statute. RCRA is not a comprehensive statute that covers all hazardous substances. Rather, the Subtitle C regulatory system applies only to hazardous "solid wastes," and under the crucial language of the statute, its regulatory reach extends only to materials that have been "discarded." In fact, RCRA is a "deathbed to grave" statute, and one of the most difficult issues is determining when the death has occurred.

The limitation of RCRA's coverage to "solid wastes" that have been "discarded" raises difficult questions concerning the scope of the statute. Some materials that might otherwise be "discarded" as wastes may be reused in a variety of ways that have commercial value. Are these recyclable materials subject to regulation as "wastes" under RCRA? If so, how stringently should they be regulated?

These questions highlight a basic conflict that makes regulating recyclable materials particularly difficult. On the one hand, recycling and resource conservation are clear objectives of RCRA. Putting materials that would otherwise be discarded to commercial use decreases the problems associated with their final disposal. Diminishing landfill capacity and rising disposal costs increase the importance of recycling. Recycling processes, however, create many of the same environmental hazards posed by improper disposal. Indeed, some types of so-called recycling, such as burning wastes for fuel or applying waste as a dust suppressant, may be disguised forms of incineration and land disposal — means of disposal strictly regulated under RCRA. Excluding such "recycling" from regulation would create a potentially enormous and environmentally dangerous loophole in RCRA's coverage. . . .

AMERICAN MINING CONGRESS V. EPA

824 F.2d 1177 (D.C. Cir. 1987)

STARR, Circuit Judge:

These consolidated cases arise out of EPA's regulation of hazardous wastes under the Resource Conservation and Recovery Act of 1976 ("RCRA"), as amended, 42 U.S.C. §§6901-6933 (1982 & Supp. III 1985). Petitioners, trade associations representing mining and oil refining interests, challenge regulations promulgated by EPA that amend the definition of "solid waste" to establish and define the agency's authority to regulate secondary materials reused within an industry's ongoing production process. In plain English, petitioners maintain that EPA has exceeded its regulatory authority in seeking to bring materials that are not discarded or otherwise disposed of within the compass of "waste."

I

RCRA is a comprehensive environmental statute under which EPA is granted authority to regulate solid and hazardous wastes. RCRA was enacted in 1976, and amended in 1978, 1980, and 1984.

Congress' "overriding concern" in enacting RCRA was to establish the framework for a national system to insure the safe management of hazardous waste. In passing RCRA, Congress expressed concern over the "rising tide" in scrap, discarded, and waste materials. 42 U.S.C. §6901(a)(2). As the statute itself puts it, Congress was concerned with the need "to reduce the amount of waste and unsalvageable materials and to provide for proper and economical solid waste disposal practices." Id. §6901(a)(4). Congress thus crafted RCRA "to promote the protection of health and the environment and to conserve valuable material and energy resources." Id. §6902.

RCRA includes two major parts: one deals with non-hazardous solid waste management and the other with hazardous waste management. Under the latter, EPA is directed to promulgate regulations establishing a comprehensive management system. Id. §6921. EPA's authority, however, extends only to the regulation of "hazardous waste." Because "hazardous waste" is defined as a subset of "solid waste," id. §6903(5), the scope of EPA's jurisdiction is limited to those materials that constitute "solid waste." That pivotal term is defined by RCRA as

> any garbage, refuse, sludge from a waste treatment plant, water supply treatment plant, or air pollution control facility *and other discarded material,* including solid, liquid, semisolid or contained gaseous material, resulting from industrial, commercial, mining, and agricultural operations, and from community activities. . . .

42 U.S.C. §6903(27) (emphasis added). As will become evident, this case turns on the meaning of the phrase, "and other discarded material," contained in the statute's definitional provisions.

EPA's interpretation of "solid waste" has evolved over time. On May 19, 1980, EPA issued interim regulations defining "solid waste" to include a material that is "a manufacturing or mining by-product and sometimes is discarded." 45 Fed. Reg. 33,119 (1980). This definition contained two terms needing elucidation: "by-product" and "sometimes discarded." In its definition of "a manufacturing or mining by-product," EPA expressly *excluded* "an intermediate manufacturing or mining product which results from one of the steps in a manufacturing or mining process and is typically processed through the next step of the process within a short time." Id.

In 1983, the agency proposed narrowing amendments to the 1980 interim rule. 48 Fed. Reg. 14,472 (1983). The agency showed especial concern over *recycling* activities. In the preamble to the amendments, the agency observed that, in light of the interlocking statutory provisions and RCRA's legislative history, it was clear that "Congress indeed intended that materials being recycled or held for recycling can be wastes, and if hazardous, hazardous wastes." Id. at 14,473. The agency also asserted that "not only can materials destined for recycling or being recycled be solid and hazardous wastes, but the Agency clearly has the authority to regulate recycling activities as hazardous management." Id. While asserting its interest in recycling activities (and materials being held for recycling), EPA's discussion left unclear whether the agency in fact believed its jurisdiction extended to materials recycled in an industry's on-going production processes, or only to materials disposed of and recycled as part of a waste management program. In its preamble, EPA stated that "the revised definition of solid waste sets out the Agency's view of its jurisdiction over the recycling of hazardous waste. . . . Proposed section 261.6 then contains exemptions from regulations for those hazardous waste recycling activities that we do not think require regulation." Id. at 14,476. The amended regulatory description of "solid waste" itself, then, did not include materials "used or reused as effective substitutes for raw materials in processes using raw materials as principal feedstocks." Id. at 14,508. EPA explained the exclusion as follows: "[These] materials are being used essentially as raw materials and so ordinarily are not appropriate candidates for regulatory control. Moreover, when these materials are used to manufacture new products, the processes generally are normal manufacturing operations. . . . The Agency is reluctant to read the statute as regulating actual manufacturing processes." Id. at 14,488. This, then, seemed clear: EPA was drawing a line between discarding and ultimate recycling, on the one hand, and a continuous or ongoing manufacturing process with one-site "recycling," on the other. If the activity fell within the latter category, then the materials were not deemed to be "discarded."

After receiving extensive comments, EPA issued its final rule on January 4, 1985. 50 Fed. Reg. 614 (1985). Under the final rule, materials are considered "solid waste" if they are abandoned by being disposed of, burned, or incinerated; or stored, treated, or accumulated before or in lieu of those activities. In addition, certain recycling activities fall within EPA's definition. EPA determines whether a material is a RCRA solid waste when it is recycled by examining both the material or substance itself and the recycling activity involved. The final rule identifies five categories of "secondary materials" (spent materials, sludges, by-products, commercial chemical products, and scrap metal). These "secondary materials" constitute "solid waste" when they are disposed of; burned for energy recovery or used to produce a fuel; reclaimed; or accumulated speculatively. Id. at 618-19, 664.[12] Under the

---

12. Under the final rule, a "use constituting disposal" is defined as direct placement on land of wastes or products containing or derived from wastes. A material is "accumulated speculatively" if it is accumulated prior to being recycled. If the accumulator can show that the materials feasibly can be recycled, and that during a one-year calendar period the amount of material recycled or

final rule, if a material constitutes "solid waste," it is subject to RCRA regulation *unless* it is directly reused as an ingredient or as an effective substitute for a commercial product, or is returned as a raw material substitute to its original manufacturing process.[13] Id. In the jargon of the trade, the latter category is known as the "closed-loop" exception. In either case, the material must not first be "reclaimed" (processed to recover a usable product or regenerated). Id. EPA exempts these activities "because they are like ordinary usage of commercial products." Id. at 619.

II

Petitioners, American Mining Congress ("AMC") and American Petroleum Institute ("API"), challenge the scope of EPA's final rule. Relying upon the statutory definition of "solid waste," petitioners contend that EPA's authority under RCRA is limited to controlling materials that are *discarded or intended for discard.* They argue that EPA's reuse and recycle rules, as applied to inprocess secondary materials, regulate materials that have not been discarded, and therefore exceed EPA's jurisdiction.

To understand petitioners' claims, a passing familiarity with the nature of their industrial processes is required.

Petroleum. Petroleum refineries vary greatly both in respect of their products and their processes. Most of their products, however, are complex mixtures of hydrocarbons produced through a number of interdependent and sometimes repetitious processing steps. In general, the refining process starts by "distilling" crude oil into various hydrocarbon streams or "fractions." The "fractions" are then subjected to a number of processing steps. Various hydrocarbon materials derived from virtually all stages of processing are combined or blended in order to produce products such as gasoline, fuel oil, and lubricating oils. Any hydrocarbons that are not usable in a particular form or state are returned to an appropriate stage in the refining process so they can even-

---

transferred for recycling is 75% or more of the amount present at the beginning of the year, the materials are not considered solid wastes. A material is "reclaimed" if it is processed to recover a usable product, or if it is regenerated. Id.

13. Specifically, the final rule excludes materials recycled by being: "(1) [u]sed or reused as ingredients in an industrial process to make a product, *provided the materials are not being reclaimed;* or (2) [u]sed or reused as effective substitutes for commercial products; or (3) [r]eturned to the original process from which they are generated, without first being reclaimed." Id. (emphasis added). In the third category, the material must be returned to the original manufacturing process as a substitute for raw material feedstock, and the process must use raw materials as principal feedstocks.

tually be used. Likewise, the hydrocarbons and materials which escape from a refinery's production vessels are gathered and, by a complex retrieval system, returned to appropriate parts of the refining process. Under EPA's final rule, this reuse and recycling of materials is subject to regulation under RCRA.

Mining. In the mining industry, primary metals production involves the extraction of fractions of a percent of a metal from a complex mineralogical matrix (i.e., the natural material in which minerals are embedded). Extractive metallurgy proceeds incrementally. Rome was not built in a day, and all metal cannot be extracted in one fell swoop. In consequence, materials are reprocessed in order to remove as much of the pure metal as possible from the natural ore. Under EPA's final rule, this reprocessed ore and the metal derived from it constitute "solid waste." What is more, valuable metal-bearing and mineral-bearing dusts are often released in processing a particular metal. The mining facility typically recaptures, recycles, and reuses these dusts, frequently in production processes different from the one from which the dusts were originally emitted. The challenged regulations encompass this reprocessing, to the mining industry's dismay.

Against this factual backdrop, we now examine the legal issues presented by petitioners' challenge.

III

We observe at the outset of our inquiry that EPA's interpretation of the scope of its authority under RCRA has been unclear and unsteady. As previously recounted, EPA has shifted from its vague "sometimes discarded" approach of 1980 to a proposed exclusion from regulation of all materials used or reused as effective substitutes for raw materials in 1983, and finally, to a very narrow exclusion of essentially only materials processed within the meaning of the "closed-loop" exception under the final rule. We emphasize, therefore, that we are confronted with neither a consistent nor a longstanding agency interpretation. Under settled doctrine, "[a]n agency interpretation of a relevant provision which conflicts with the agency's earlier interpretation is 'entitled to considerably less deference' than a consistently held agency view." *I.N.S. v. Cardoza-Fonseca,* — U.S. — , 107 S. Ct. 1207, 1221 n.30, 94 L. Ed. 2d 434 (1987) (quoting *Watt v. Alaska,* 451 U.S. 259, 273, 101 S. Ct. 1673, 1681, 68 L. Ed. 2d 80 (1981)). See also *FEC v. Democratic Senatorial Campaign Committee,* 454 U.S. 27, 37, 102 S. Ct. 38, 44, 70 L. Ed. 2d 23 (1981); *Adamo Wrecking Co. v. United States,* 434 U.S. 275, 287 n.5, 98 S. Ct. 566, 574 n.5, 54 L. Ed. 2d 538 (1978); *Skidmore v. Swift & Co.,* 323 U.S. 134, 140, 65 S. Ct. 161, 164, 89 L. Ed. 124 (1944); *National Fuel Gas Supply Corp. v. FERC,* 811 F.2d 1563 (D.C. Cir. 1987).

A

[The court summarized the two steps of statutory interpretation enunciated in *Chevron v. NRDC*, 467 U.S. 837 (1984), supra, p. 394: (1) Has Congress directly spoken to the specific issue in question, thereby resolving the interpretative inquiry; and (2) "[I]f the statute is silent or ambiguous with respect to the specific issue, the question for the court is whether the agency's answer is based on a permissible construction of the statute," id. at 843-844.]

B

Guided by these principles, we turn to the statutory provision at issue here. Congress, it will be recalled, granted EPA power to regulate "solid waste." Congress specifically defined "solid waste" as "discarded material." EPA then defined "discarded material" to include materials destined for reuse in an industry's ongoing production processes. The challenge to EPA's jurisdictional reach is founded, again, on the proposition that in-process secondary materials are outside the bounds of EPA's lawful authority. Nothing has been discarded, the argument goes, and thus RCRA jurisdiction remains untriggered.

1

The first step in statutory interpretation is, of course, an analysis of the language itself. . . . Here, Congress defined "solid waste" as "discarded material." The ordinary, plain-English meaning of the word "discarded" is "disposed of," "thrown away" or "abandoned."[14] Encompassing materials retained for immediate reuse within the scope of "discarded material" strains, to say the least, the everyday usage of that term.

Although the "ordinary and obvious meaning of the [statutory] phrase is not to be lightly discounted," *Cardoza-Fonseca*, 107 S. Ct. at 1213, we are hesitant to attribute decisive significance to the ordinary meaning of statutory language. To be sure, our inquiry might well and wisely stop with the plain language of the statute, since it is the statute itself that Congress enacts and the President signs into law. But as the

---

14. The dictionary definition of "discard" is "to drop, dismiss, let go, or get rid of as no longer useful, valuable, or pleasurable." Webster's Third New International Dictionary, G. & C. Merriam Co. (1981). It bears noting that the term "discarded" is neither inherently difficult to define nor is so intimately tied to knowledge of the industry and the practicalities of regulation that definition requires agency expertise.

Supreme Court recently observed, the "more natural interpretation" (or plain meaning) is not necessarily determinative. . . .

In short, a complete analysis of the statutory term "discarded" calls for more than resort to the ordinary, everyday meaning of the specific language at hand. For, "the sense in which [a term] is used in a statute must be determined by reference to the purpose of the particular legislation." . . .

As we previously recounted, the broad objectives of RCRA are "to promote the protection of health and the environment and to conserve valuable material and energy resources. . . ." 42 U.S.C. §6902. But that goal is of majestic breadth, and it is difficult . . . to pour meaning into a highly specific term by resort to grand purposes. Somewhat more specifically, we have seen that RCRA was enacted in response to Congressional findings that the "rising tide of scrap, discarded, and waste materials" generated by consumers and increased industrial production had presented heavily populated urban communities with "serious financial, management, intergovernmental, and technical problems in the disposal of solid wastes." Id. §6901(a). In light of this problem, Congress determined that "[f]ederal action through financial and technical assistance and leadership in the development, demonstration, and application of new and improved methods and processes to reduce the amount of waste and unsalvageable materials and to provide for proper and economical solid waste disposal practices was necessary." Id. Also animating Congress were its findings that "disposal of solid and hazardous waste" without careful planning and management presents a danger to human health and the environment; that methods to "separate usable materials from solid waste" should be employed; and that usable energy can be produced from solid waste. Id. §6901(b), (c), (d).

The question we face, then, is whether, in light of the National Legislature's expressly stated objectives and the underlying problems that motivated it to enact RCRA in the first instance, Congress was using the term "discarded" in its ordinary sense — "disposed of" or "abandoned" — or whether Congress was using it in a much more open-ended way, so as to encompass materials no longer useful in their original capacity though destined for immediate reuse in another phase of the industry's ongoing production process.

For the following reasons, we believe the former to be the case. RCRA was enacted, as the Congressional objectives and findings make clear, in an effort to help States deal with the ever-increasing problem of solid waste disposal by encouraging the search for and use of alternatives to existing methods of disposal (including recycling) and protecting health and the environment by regulating hazardous wastes. To fulfill these purposes, it seems clear that EPA need not regulate "spent" materials that are recycled and reused in an ongoing manufacturing or industrial process.[15] These materials have not yet become part of the waste disposal problem; rather, *they are destined for beneficial reuse or recycling in a continuous process by the generating industry itself.* . . .

2

Our task in analyzing the statute also requires us to determine whether other provisions of RCRA shed light on the breadth with which Congress intended to define "discarded." As the Supreme Court reiterated a few years ago, in interpreting a statute, "[w]e do not . . . construe statutory phrases in isolation; we read statutes as a whole." *United States v. Morton,* 467 U.S. 822, 828, 104 S. Ct. 2769, 2773, 81 L. Ed. 2d 680 (1984). The structure of a statute, in short, is important in the sensitive task of divining Congress' meaning.

In its brief, EPA directed us to a number of statutory provisions, arguing that they support its expansive definition of "discarded." This turned out, however, to be a wild goose chase through the labyrinthine maze of 42 U.S.C., for as counsel for EPA commendably recognized at oral argument, those statutory provisions speak in terms of "hazardous" (or "solid") waste."[16] In consequence, EPA's various arguments based on the statute itself are, upon analysis, circular, relying upon the term "solid waste" or "hazardous waste" to extend the reach of those very terms. . . .

[Judge Mikva's dissenting opinion is omitted.]

---

15. EPA argues that a narrow reading of "discarded" would "vitiate" RCRA's remedial purpose. EPA Brief at 30-31. We cannot agree. EPA provides no explanation for this remarkable proposition, and we fail to see how not regulating in-process secondary materials in an on-going production process will subvert RCRA's waste disposal management goals. Our difficulty in discerning the stated necessity of this regulatory outreach is reinforced by the fact that the agency itself previously concluded that its regulatory authority did not extend to ongoing production processes of a manufacturer.

16. Section 6901(b)(3), for example, refers to environmentally unsound practices for the "disposal or use of solid waste." 42 U.S.C. §6901(b)(3). Subsections 6901(d)(1), (2) refer to solid waste as a potential source of energy. Section 6903(7) defines "hazardous waste management" to include, among other things, recovery of hazardous wastes. . . .

Section 6935 addresses "used oil" collected by and utilized in the "oil recycling industry." Oil recyclers typically collect discarded used oils, distill them, and sell the resulting material for use as fuel in boilers. Regulation of those activities is likewise consistent with an everyday reading of the term "discarded." It is only when EPA attempts to extend the scope of that provision to include the recycling of undiscarded oils at petroleum refineries that conflict occurs.

AMC v. EPA reviewed the following regulations (50 Fed. Reg. 614 (Jan. 4, 1985)):

REGULATIONS ON MANAGEMENT AND IDENTIFICATION OF HAZARDOUS WASTE

40 C.F.R. Parts 260, 261

PART 260 — HAZARDOUS WASTE MANAGEMENT SYSTEM: GENERAL

§260.30   *Variances from Classification as a Solid Waste*

In accordance with the standards and criteria in §260.31 and the procedures in §260.33, the Regional Administrator may determine on a case-by-case basis that the following recycled materials are not solid wastes:

(a) Materials that are accumulated speculatively without sufficient amounts being recycled (as defined by §261.1(c)(8)(B) of this Chapter);

(b) Materials that are reclaimed and then reused within the original primary production process in which they were generated;

(c) Materials that have been reclaimed but must be reclaimed further before the materials are completely recovered.

§260.31   *Standards and Criteria for Variances from Classification as a Solid Waste*

(a) The Regional Administrator may grant requests for a variance from classifying as a solid waste those materials that are accumulated speculatively without sufficient amounts being recycled if the applicant demonstrates that sufficient amounts of the material will be recycled or transferred for recycling in the following year. If a variance is granted, it is valid only for the following year, but can be renewed, on an annual basis, by filing a new application. The Regional Administrator's decision will be based on the following standards and criteria:

(1) The manner in which the material is expected to be recycled, when the material is expected to be recycled, and whether this expected disposition is likely to occur (for example, because of past practice, market factors, the nature of the material, or contractual arrangements for recycling);

(2) The reason that the applicant has accumulated the material for one or more years without recycling 75 percent of the volume accumulated at the beginning of the year;

(3) The quantity of material already accumulated and the quan-

tity expected to be generated and accumulated before the material is recycled;

(4) The extent to which the material is handled to minimize loss;

(5) Other relevant factors.

(b) The regional Administrator may grant requests for a variance from classifying as a solid waste those materials that are reclaimed and then reused as feedstock within the original primary production process in which the materials were generated if the reclamation operation is an essential part of the production process. This determination will be based on the following criteria:

(1) How economically viable the production process would be if it were to use virgin materials, rather than reclaimed materials;

(2) The prevalence of the practice on an industry-wide basis;

(3) The extent to which the material is handled before reclamation to minimize loss;

(4) The time periods between generating the material and its reclamation, and between reclamation and return to the original primary production process;

(5) The location of the reclamation operation in relation to the production process;

(6) Whether the reclaimed material is used for the purpose for which it was originally produced when it is returned to the original process, and whether it is returned to the process in substantially its original form;

(7) Whether the person who generates the material also reclaims it;

(8) Other relevant factors.

(c) The Regional Administrator may grant requests for a variance from classifying as a solid waste those materials that have been reclaimed but must be reclaimed further before recovery is completed if, and after initial reclamation, the resulting material is commodity-like (even though it is not yet a commercial product, and has to be reclaimed further). This determination will be based on the following factors;

(1) The degree of processing the material has undergone and the degree of further processing that is required;

(2) The value of the material after it has been reclaimed;

(3) The degree to which the reclaimed material is like an analogous raw material;

(4) The extent to which an end market for the reclaimed material is guaranteed;

(5) The extent to which the reclaimed material is handled to minimize loss;

(6) Other relevant factors. . . .

PART 261 — IDENTIFICATION AND LISTING OF HAZARDOUS WASTE

SUBPART A — GENERAL

§261.1   Purpose and Scope

(a) This part identifies those solid wastes which are subject to regulation as hazardous wastes under parts 262 through 265, 268, and parts 270, 271, and 124 of this chapter and which are subject to the notification requirements of section 3010 of RCRA. . . .

(b)(2) This part identifies only some of the materials which are solid wastes and hazardous wastes under sections 3007, 3013, and 7003 of RCRA. A material which is not defined as a solid waste in this part, or is not a hazardous waste identified or listed in this part, is still a solid waste and a hazardous waste for purposes of these sections if:

(i) In the case of sections 3007 and 3013, EPA has reason to believe that the material may be a solid waste within the meaning of section 1004(27) of RCRA and a hazardous waste within the meaning of section 1004(5) of RCRA; or

(ii) In the case of section 7003, the statutory elements are established.

(c) For the purposes of §§261.2 and 261.6:

(1) A "spent material" is any material that has been used and as a result of contamination can no longer serve the purpose for which it was produced without processing;

(2) "Sludge" has the same meaning used in §260.10 of this chapter;

(3) A "by-product" is a material that is not one of the primary products of a production process and is not solely or separately produced by the production process. Examples are process residues such as slags or distillation column bottoms. The term does not include a co-product that is produced for the general public's use and is ordinarily used in the form it is produced by the process.

(4) A material is "reclaimed" if it is processed to recover a usable product, or if it is regenerated. Examples are recovery of lead values from spent batteries and regeneration of spent solvents.

(5) A material is "used or reused" if it is either:

(i)   Employed as an ingredient (including use as an intermediate) in an industrial process to make a product (for example, distillation bottoms form one process used as feedstock in another process). However, a material will not satisfy this condition if distinct components of the material are recovered as separate end products (as when metals are recovered from metal-containing secondary materials); or

(ii) Employed in a particular function or application as an effective substitute for a commercial product (for example, spent pickle liquor used as phosphorous precipitant and sludge conditioner in wastewater treatment).

(6) "Scrap metal" is bits and pieces of metal parts (e.g., bars, turnings, rods, sheets, wire) or metal pieces that may be combined together with bolts or soldering (e.g., radiators, scrap automobiles, railroad box cars), which when worn or superfluous can be recycled.

(7) A material is "recycled" if it is used, reused, or reclaimed.

(8) A material is "accumulated speculatively" if it is accumulated before being recycled. A material is not accumulated speculatively, however, if the person accumulating it can show that the material is potentially recyclable and has a feasible means of being recycled; and that — during the calendar year (commencing on January 1) — the amount of material that is recycled, or transferred to a different site for recycling, equals at least 75 percent by weight or volume of the amount of that material accumulated at the beginning of the period. In calculating the percentage of turnover, the 75 percent requirement is to be applied to each material of the same type (e.g., slags from a single smelting process) that is recycled in the same way (i.e., from which the same material is recovered or that is used in the same way). Material accumulating in units that would be exempt from regulation under §261.4(c) are not to be included in making the calculation. (Materials that are already defined as solid wastes also are not to be included in making the calculation.) Materials are no longer in this category once they are removed from accumulation for recycling, however.

§261.2 Definition of Solid Waste

(a)(1) A *solid waste* is any discarded material that is not excluded by §261.4(a) or that is not excluded by variance granted under §§260.30 and 260.31.

(2) A *discarded material* is any material which is:

(i) *Abandoned,* as explained in paragraph (b) of this section; or

(ii) *Recycled,* as explained in paragraph (c) of this section; or

(iii) Considered *inherently wastelike,* as explained in paragraph (d) of this section.

(b) Materials are solid waste if they are *abandoned* by being:

(1) Disposed of; or

(2) Burned or incinerated; or

(3) Accumulated, stored, or treated (but not recycled) before or in lieu of being abandoned by being disposed of, burned, or incinerated.

(c) Materials are solid wastes if they are *recycled* — or accumulated, stored, or treated before recycling — as specified in paragraphs (c)(1) through (4) of this section.

(1) *Used in a manner constituting disposal.*

(i) Materials noted with a "*" in Column 1 of Table 1 are solid wastes when they are:

(A) Applied to or placed on the land in a manner that constitutes disposal; or

(B) Contained in products that are applied to or placed on the land (in which cases the product itself remains a solid waste).

(ii) However, commercial chemical products listed in §261.33 are not solid wastes if they are applied to the land and that is their ordinary manner of use.

(2) *Burning for energy recovery.*

(i) Materials noted with a "*" in column 2 of Table 1 are solid wastes when they are:

(A) Burned to recover energy;

(B) Used to produce a fuel;

(C) Contained in fuels (in which case the fuel itself remains a solid waste).

(ii) However, commercial chemical products listed in §261-.33 are not solid wastes if they are themselves fuels.

(3) *Reclaimed.* Materials noted with a "*" in column 3 of Table 1 are solid wastes when reclaimed.

(4) *Accumulated speculatively.* Materials noted with a "*" in column 4 of Table 1 are solid wastes when accumulated speculatively.

TABLE 1

	Use constituting disposal (§261.2(c)(1)) (1)	Energy recovery/fuel (§261.2(c)(2)) (2)	Reclamation (§261.2(c)(3)) (3)	Speculative accumulation (§261.2(c)(4)) (4)
Spent materials	(*)	(*)	(*)	(*)
Sludges (listed in 40 CFR part 261.31 or 261.32)	(*)	(*)	(*)	(*)
Sludges exhibiting a characteristic of hazardous waste	(*)	(*)		(*)
By-products (listed in 40 CFR part 261.31 or 261.32)	(*)	(*)	(*)	(*)
By-products exhibiting a characteristic of hazardous waste	(*)	(*)		(*)
Commercial chemical products listed in 40 CFR 261.33	(*)	(*)		
Scrap metal	(*)	(*)	(*)	(*)

Note: The terms "spent materials," "sludges," "by-products," and "scrap metal" are defined in §261.1.

(d) *Inherently waste-like materials.* The following materials are solid wastes when they are recycled in any manner:

(1) Hazardous Waste Nos. F020, F021 (unless used as an ingredient to make a product at the site of generation), F022, F023, F026, and F028.

(2) The administrator will use the following criteria to add wastes to that list:

(i) (A) The materials are ordinarily disposed of, burned, or incinerated; or

(B) The materials contain toxic constituents listed in Appendix VIII of Part 261 and these constituents are not ordinarily found in raw materials or products for which the materials substitute (or are found in raw materials or products in smaller concentrations) and are not used or reused during the recycling process; and

(ii) The material may pose a substantial hazard to human health and the environment when recycled.

(e) *Materials that are not solid waste when recycled.*

(1) Materials are not solid wastes when they can be shown to be recycled by being:

(i) Used or reused as ingredients in an industrial process to make a product, provided the materials are not being reclaimed; or

(ii) Used or reused as effective substitutes for commercial products; or

(iii) Returned to the original process from which they are generated, without first being reclaimed. The material must be returned as a substitute for raw material feedstock, and the process must use raw materials as principal feedstocks.

(2) The following materials are solid wastes, even if the recycling involves use, reuse, or return to the original process (described in paragraphs (e)(1)(i) through (iii) of this section):

(i) Materials used in a manner constituting disposal, or used to produce products that are applied to the land; or

(ii) Materials burned for energy recovery, used to produce a fuel, or contained in fuels; or

(iii) Materials accumulated speculatively; or

(iv) Materials listed in paragraph (d)(1) of this section. . . .

§261.4   Exclusions

(a) *Materials which are not solid wastes.* The following materials are not solid wastes for the purpose of this part:

(1)(i) Domestic sewage; and

(ii) Any mixture of domestic sewage and other wastes that passes through a sewer system to a publicly-owned treatment works for treatment. "Domestic sewage" means untreated sanitary wastes that pass through a sewer system.

(2) Industrial wastewater discharges that are point source discharges subject to regulation under section 402 of the Clean Water Act, as amended.

[*Comment:* This exclusion applies only to actual point source discharge. It does not exclude industrial wastewaters while they are being collected, stored or treated before discharge, nor does it exclude sludges that are generated by industrial wastewater treatment.]

(3) Irrigation return flows.

(4) Source, special nuclear or by-product material as defined by the Atomic Energy Act of 1954, as amended, 42 U.S.C. 2011 et seq.

(5) Materials subjected to in-situ mining techniques which are not removed from the ground as part of the extraction process.

(6) Pulping liquors (i.e., black liquor) that are reclaimed in a pulping liquor recovery furnace and then reused in the pulping process, unless it is accumulated speculatively as defined in §261:1(c) of this chapter.

(7) Spent sulfuric acid used to produce virgin sulfuric acid, unless it is accumulated speculatively as defined in §261.1(c) of this chapter.

QUESTIONS

1. How would the operations of the oil and mining industries at issue in *AMC* be treated under the above regulations? Work through all plausibly relevant provisions.

2. What precisely was EPA's 1985 definition of "solid waste"? Based upon the purposes underlying RCRA, how would you defend this interpretation? Note that approximately one-third of the environmentally damaging incidents cited by Congress as the rationale for RCRA involved the mismanagement of recyclable materials. See H.R. Rep. No. 1491, 94th Cong., Sess. 5, reprinted in 1976 U.S. Code Cong. & Admin. News at 18, 22.

3. How did the court interpret RCRA's definition of "solid waste"? Does the majority's opinion show EPA the discretion it is due under *Chevron?* In what way does the majority's opinion constrain EPA's discretion in defining "solid waste"?

4. Does the court pay adequate attention to the provisions of §§260.30 and 260.31 in rendering its decision? To what extent do these provisions address the concerns of the court?

5. Should any recyclable "wastes" be regulated under RCRA? If so, where should the line be drawn between those recyclable "wastes" that are to be regulated and those that are not?

6. Review the current version of EPA's solid waste regulations (contained in the statutory/regulatory supplement). Has EPA significantly narrowed its definition of solid waste relative to the regulations

under review in *AMC v. EPA?* How would the practices of the petroleum and mining industries be treated under these regulations? Are these regulations consistent with RCRA as interpreted by the D.C. Circuit's opinion in *AMC v. EPA?* Explain.

DISCUSSION PROBLEMS

For each of the following problems, carefully apply the relevant law — statutory provisions of RCRA, EPA's current regulations (as contained in the Statutory/Regulatory Supplement), and judicial interpretation of the statute — to determine whether the waste from the activity in question falls within RCRA's definition of solid waste.

(1) Toxic metal-containing sludges from the chemical industry go through a reclamation process that results in a soil-like solid that can be used for landfill cover materials. Are the sludges solid wastes?

(2) Toluene is used as a solvent in a manufacturing process. After use, it is absorbed in an on-site carbon absorption system. After the absorption and desorption process, the solvent is decanted from water and reused in the original process. What is the status of the toluene during the various stages of manufacturing?

(3) Non-halogenated spent solvents (heavy alcohol, ketones, hydrocarbons, and heavy residuals) from a chemical manufacturing plant are physically mixed into a product that is sold as marine fuel. Are the spent wastes solid waste?

(4) Primary metal smelters produce large volumes of wastewater. Many smelting operations use surface impoundments to collect, treat, and dispose of the wastewater. These impoundments continuously produce sludges, which precipitate from the waste water. These sludges can be later reclaimed. Are these sludges "solid waste"?

(5) An underground gasoline storage tank springs a leak and contaminates the surrounding soil. Is the gasoline a "solid waste"?

(6) The production of steel in electric furnaces results in the generation of a zinc-bearing slag. This slag is then shipped to a metal reclamation facility that reclaims the zinc in the same type of electric furnace that generated the slag. Is the zinc-bearing slag a solid waste at the point at which it is generated? Is it a solid waste at the point at which it arrives at a reclamation facility?

(7)   Refer back to the Daffy Swamp problem at p. 502. Does the lead shot constitute "solid waste"?

If you found these problems confounding, you are not alone. Commentators have called the regulations defining solid waste "the most complex environmental regulations ever written." Williams and Cannon, Rethinking the Resource Conservation and Recovery Act for the 1990s, 21 Envtl. L. Rep. 10063, 10064 (1991). Even EPA has admitted that the definition of solid waste is "difficult to understand and implement for EPA, the states, and industry. Permitting and enforcement are hampered by the complexity of those definitions." Office of Solid Waste and Emergency Response, U.S. Environmental Protection Agency, RCRA, The Nation's Hazardous Waste Management Program at a Crossroads 38 (No. 205-001) (July 1990). Comparable complexity arises in determining which solid wastes are hazardous for purposes of RCRA.

The importance of these definitional issues turns upon the difference in regulatory treatment of waste materials falling within as opposed to outside the scope of RCRA's Subtitle C regulations. Section 1 outlined the major requirements of the RCRA Subtitle C regulatory framework: the manifest system, standards for TSD facilities, and requirements for specific TSD units. The next section focuses upon one of the major motivations for seeking to avoid Subtitle C regulation — the land disposal restrictions.

3.   REGULATION OF LAND DISPOSAL OF HAZARDOUS WASTES

R. FORTUNA & D. LENNETT, HAZARDOUS WASTE REGULATION: THE NEW ERA

(1987)

LAND DISPOSAL RESTRICTIONS

EVOLUTION OF THE RESTRICTIONS

The most fundamental deficiency of the RCRA regulations prior to 1984 was the absence of any preference or priority for protective methods of hazardous waste management. With few exceptions the generator exercised complete discretion to use either a landfill or a treatment process for the same waste. This policy of neutrality existed despite EPA acknowledgments that land disposal facilities could not ensure permanent containment. To make matters worse, the myriad deficiencies in the land disposal permitting standards issued by EPA encouraged additional land disposal by failing to reflect the long-term societal costs and uncertainties associated with disposal, contributing in essence to a regulatory subsidization of land disposal. The resulting price differentials between land disposal and more permanent management options thereby encourage additional land disposal.

Fortunately, in the void left by EPA there emerged a variety of public and private sector organizations prepared to shape a national waste management policy. Concurrent with the beginning of the reauthorization process in January 1982, with the introduction of H.R. 6307, a number of major studies and state government actions collectively served to crystallize the long-felt need for change in national hazardous waste policy and regulation.

For example, a landmark study was issued by the State of California's Office of Appropriate Technology, which stated that over 75 percent of the waste generated in California should be restricted or prohibited from landfill disposal. This study led to the issuance of an Executive Order by Governor Jerry Brown, which established an explicit policy favoring treatment over land disposal, and to the enactment of a specific schedule of restrictions of a wide range of wastes. California's general restrictions and their failure to effectively cover surface impoundments and injection wells both played a key role in shaping HSWA's provisions.

Closely following the California study were reports from the U.S. Congress' Office of Technology Assessment and the National Academy of Sciences confirming the desirability of substantial reductions in the use of land disposal. These studies demonstrated that there was no shortage of methods to treat wastes by alternative technologies, and that their use was stifled by the existence of massive regulatory loopholes.

The National Academy of Sciences study concluded that there exists technology capable of dealing with every hazardous waste so as to eliminate concern for future hazards. The report went on to note that no new major and cost-effective technology exists or is likely to be developed that could be a panacea to dispose of all hazardous wastes.

Similarly, the Office of Technology Assessment report concluded that a number of pre-HSWA regulatory policies and practices may serve as disincentives for waste reduction and treatment activities, and that the available capacity for off-site management of wastes is not a barrier to shifting management away from land disposal. Lastly, the report concluded that until the private sector perceives the regulatory structure as not containing a bias in favor of land disposal technologies, investment in new treatment technology research and development and commercial development may be limited.

Juxtaposed to these technology-oriented reports was a series of studies confirming the environmental risks posed by land disposal. A key study issued in September 1982 demonstrated that four state-of-the-art land disposal facilities in the study leaked, despite utilization of the best available dual liners and leachate collection systems. SCA Chemical Services, Inc., discovered that its state-of-the-art landfill in Wilsonville, Illinois, was leaking large volumes of organic solvents, resulting in a virtually unprecedented court-ordered exhumation of the entire landfill.[17] This event was pivotal in the transformation of SCA from a landfill-oriented firm to one that strongly advocated legislative restrictions on the land disposal of a wide range of hazardous wastes. Dow Chemical Co. confirmed that in 1982 over 99 percent of their wastes were incinerated, recycled, or treated.

EPA itself issued a report in 1983 which found there were over 180,000 surface impoundments (puts, ponds, and lagoons) used for the management of wastes, over 30,000 of which were used for the management of industrial wastes. Of these industrial waste lagoons, 70 percent were operating without any liner or retention system whatsoever, and 39 percent were determined to have a high potential to contaminate groundwater. Ironically, many of these de facto groundwater discharge lagoons were and are being used for purposes of treating and discharging industrial wastewater into surface water in accordance with permits issued under the Clean Water Act. Other studies confirmed that over 30 percent of current "Superfund" sites were caused by leaking lagoons.

In late 1984, EPA also issued its most comprehensive survey of waste generation and management practices to date, which opened many eyes to the true magnitude and scope of this nation's patterns of hazardous waste generation and mismanagement. This study revealed that a mere 4 percent of the nation's hazardous waste was recycled in 1981. Only 5 percent of the nation's 250 million tons of hazardous waste was disposed of in landfills, while injection wells and lagoons accounted for 58 percent (10 billion gallons) and 38 percent of the hazardous waste managed, respectively. In addition, other surveys revealed that hazardous waste injection facilities, or deep wells so-called for their injection of wastes below the drinking water aquifer, were associated with some of the most significant uncertainties and vast areas of environmental contamination from any management method.

The growing consensus regarding the need to utilize management technologies not subject to the uncertainties of land disposal high-

---

17. [Ed. note: recall the discussion of the *Village of Wilsonville* case, supra, p. 200.]

lighted by these surveys and reports was not lost on certain segments of the hazardous waste treatment industry or the states. Firms that had invested in permanent treatment technology bore witness to the absence of demand for more protective management, and served notice of their intent to withhold further investment until the law provided greater certainty that protection would take priority over tradition.

Despite the burgeoning evidence and support for fundamental change, EPA was actively pursuing its own brand of regulatory reform. In response to an inquiry from Congressman John Lafalce (D-NY), whose Congressional District includes the Love Canal area, EPA Administrator Gorsuch stated that "Landfilling represents the lowest risk option currently available for dealing with the large quantities of hazardous wastes generated each year. . . ."

Furthermore, the Assistant Administrator for EPA's hazardous waste program, Rita Lavelle, testified before the Congress that "we believe that most wastes can be satisfactorily managed in the land and that it can be done with a reasonable margin of safety more cheaply in this manner . . . it may be that recycling or destruction is preferable from a strictly health and environmental protection standpoint, but for many wastes, the reduction in risk achieved is probably marginal and may not be worth the cost."

These and other Administration actions, while important, did not themselves drive the reauthorization process. Rather, they served to catalyze a series of Congressional investigations that revealed the true scope of the nation's hazardous waste problem, and the fundamental deficiencies in the statute itself.

STATUTORY LAND DISPOSAL RESTRICTIONS . . .

NATIONAL POLICY

For the first time, Congress established an explicit national policy which identified a hierarchy of waste management preferences beginning with waste minimization and utilizing the "best treatment, storage, and disposal techniques for each waste." Specifically HSWA states: "The Congress hereby declares it to be the national policy of the U.S. that wherever feasible, the generation of hazardous waste is to be reduced or eliminated as expeditiously as possible. Waste that is nevertheless generated should be treated, stored, or disposed of so as to minimize the present and future threat to human health and the environment."

In selecting the "best" management methods for each waste, Congress provided overall guidance in amendments to the findings and objectives sections of RCRA, Sections 1002 and 1003. Specifically, Congress made the following new findings with respect to hazardous waste:

(1)   the placement of inadequate controls will result in substantial risks to human health and the environment;

(2)   if hazardous waste management is improperly performed in the first instance it is likely to be expensive, complex, and time-consuming; and

(3)   certain classes of land disposal facilities are not capable of assuring long-term containment of certain hazardous wastes, and to avoid substantial risk to human health and the environment, reliance on land disposal should be minimized or eliminated, and land disposal, particularly land and surface impoundment, should be the least-favored method for managing hazardous wastes. . . .

Land Disposal Restrictions. One of the most fundamental and significant changes instituted by the 1984 Amendments are the statutory presumptions against the land disposal of specific hazardous wastes. Those presumptions against the land disposal of specific wastes and the high level of pre-treatment required are intended to be the primary source of public health protection, and relieve the dependence on liners and location standards to prevent environmental releases. These presumptions place the burden on EPA to justify the continued use of land disposal, rather than to justify the imposition of restrictions. Specifically, the Administrator is directed to prohibit wastes from land disposal unless he or she determines that one or more methods of land disposal of a hazardous waste is not required in order to protect human health and the environment for as long as the waste remains hazardous. In addition, in the event that the Administrator fails to issue regulations justifying the continued use of land disposal in a timely manner, the wastes are generally prohibited from land disposal. There are variations on this basic theme for certain listed wastes, injected wastes, and contaminated soils.

While the statute presumptively prohibits the land disposal of virtually all hazardous wastes (e.g., the California list uses concentration cutoffs in defining "prohibited wastes"), the presumption can be overcome by a pre-treatment that "substantially diminishes the toxicity" or substantially reduces the likelihood of migration; or by a waste-specific petition that demonstrates there will be "no migration . . . for as long as the waste remains hazardous." . . .

In determining whether the prohibition against land disposal of a hazardous waste is not required to protect human health and the environment, the Administrator is directed to apply three criteria: (1) the long-term uncertainties associated with land disposal; (2) the goal of managing wastes in an appropriate manner in the first instance; and (3) the persistence, toxicity, mobility, and propensity to bioaccumulate of such hazardous wastes and their hazardous constituents. These three criteria were intentionally selected to heavily disfavor the land disposal of many wastes. . . .

The threshold for deciding when a waste is "toxic enough" is not specified in the statute. However, the threshold for such decisions is low, relative to the provision as it was structured originally in the Senate bill. The Senate bill stated that wastes would have to be "highly toxic, highly persistent" in order to be prohibited, rather than merely toxic and persistent, but the modifier "highly" was eliminated from the final law. Thus, while HSWA obviously could not establish a quantitative mechanism for integrating these properties into a decision rule, it does provide a lower threshold for making such determinations than the original Senate version.

Waste Prohibition Schedule. By November 8, 1986, the Agency must schedule for land disposal prohibitions all RCRA listed and identified hazardous wastes that are not included on the "Dioxin and Solvents" or "California" Lists discussed below. The issuance of the schedule by itself does not prohibit any specific wastes. Rather, it specifies which of the remaining listed and identified wastes will be scheduled for determinations at one of the following three junctures: 45, 55, or 66 months after enactment. Thus, the schedule does not by itself prohibit any wastes; rather it establishes priorities for prohibition determinations of the balance of listed and identified hazardous wastes that are to be issued at a later date.

The schedule is to be based on a ranking of the listed and identified wastes, which considers their intrinsic hazard and their volumes such that decisions regarding the large-volume wastes with a high intrinsic hazard shall be scheduled first, and low-volume wastes with a lower intrinsic hazard shall be scheduled last. . . .

Dioxins and Solvents. Also on November 8, 1986, the Administrator is required to issue final regulations prohibiting from one or more methods of land disposal (except for underground injection) both dioxin-containing (F020-F023, F026, F027) and listed solvent wastes (F001-F005, plus various K, U, and P wastes), except for methods of land disposal which the Administrator determines will be protective of human health and the environment. A method of land disposal is prohibited unless the Administrator determines that the prohibition of one or more methods is not required in order to protect human health and the environment for as long as the waste remains hazardous, taking into account the three criteria discussed above. . . .

The "California" List. By July 8, 1987, the Administrator must evaluate another list of wastes and issue regulations respecting the acceptability of their continued land disposal, using the same criteria, presumptions, process, and deferrals for injection wells, and soils as required for dioxins and solvent wastes discussed above. This list is so named because it was patterned after the landfill restrictions previously imposed by the State of California. . . .

Scheduled Characteristic and Listed Waste Prohibitions. By 45, 55, and 66 months after enactment or August 8, 1988, June 8, 1989, and May 8, 1990, the Administrator must issue final regulations prohibiting those RCRA listed and characteristic wastes from one or more methods of land disposal according to the schedule described above. Decisions regarding the remaining RCRA listed and characteristic wastes are to be roughly divided into thirds, with characteristic waste determinations that are not on the California list reserved for 66-month deadline. Wastes subject to those prohibition determinations are hereafter referred to as "scheduled wastes."

The same criteria, pretreatment requirements, and petition processes are employed for these listed and characteristic waste prohibitions; however, the consequences of a failure by EPA to make the required determinations differs slightly from the approach that applies to the dioxins, solvents, and California wastes.

If by 45 months and 55 months after November 8, 1984, for those wastes respectively designated on the Schedule, the Administrator fails to issue regulatory determinations regarding the prohibitions and/or conditions (pretreatment) on land disposal, such hazardous wastes may only be disposed of into a landfill or surface impoundment if:

(1)   such impoundments and landfills fully comply with the dual liner and other containment requirements applicable to new facilities (Chapter 10); and

(2)   prior to such disposal the generator has "certified" to the Administrator that such generator has investigated the available treatment capacity and has determined that the use of such landfill or surface impoundment is the only "practical" alternative to treatment currently available to the generator.

This "minimum regulatory control" continues in effect until the Administrator issues such regulations or at the very latest until 66 months after enactment (May 8, 1990). At that time all wastes listed and identified on the Schedule, including those scheduled for prohibition at 66 months for which a determination has not been made, are prohibited from all forms of land disposal. . . .

PRETREATMENT AND THE PETITION PROCESS

The statute provides two mechanisms by which a waste can qualify for a permanent exemption from the ban.

The first is the petition process whereby an interested party may attempt to demonstrate to the Administrator, to "a reasonable degree of certainty," that there will be "no migration" of "hazardous constituents" from the disposal unit or injection zone for as long as the wastes remain hazardous. This petition process is available for all wastes otherwise subject to land disposal prohibitions (except for the restrictions on dust suppression, liquids in landfills, Class IV wells, and salt domes) for any or all methods of land disposal. . . .

The second method of "relief" from the absolute prohibitions involves applying a pretreatment process(es) to a given waste prior to its placement in a land disposal environment so as to minimize migration and both short-term and long-term threats to human health and the environment. The decision to ban a given waste from one or more methods of land disposal is separate from the decision on the nature and level of pretreatment that will be required in order to render the placement of such pretreated waste protective of health and the environment. However, subjecting a waste to the specified level of pretreatment can allow a waste to be land disposed which would have been prohibited in an untreated state. The Administrator is required to issue these pretreatment regulations simultaneous with the promulgation of regulations governing the various prohibition determinations. . . .

VARIANCES AND EXTENSIONS

The land disposal prohibitions on dioxins, solvents, the California list, and the Scheduled wastes are effective on the dates contained in the statute or on the dates of regulatory promulgation, as explained above. However, the Administrator may establish an effective date different from that which would otherwise apply to these wastes if he or she determines that adequate alternative treatment, recovery, or disposal capacity that protects human health and the environment will not be available by the dates of the respective prohibitions. The statute assumes that such capacity will be available unless the Administrator makes an affirmative finding to the contrary.

The provision, however, places limitations on the granting of capacity waivers. Nationally applicable capacity waivers established by the Administrator cannot last for more than 2 years after the effective date of the prohibition that would otherwise apply to the wastes affected by such variances. In addition, the Administrator may also grant case-by-case extensions of the effective dates for up to one year, where an applicant demonstrates that there is a binding contractual commitment to construct or otherwise provide such alternative capacity but due to circumstances beyond the control of such applicant, the necessary alternative capacity cannot reasonably be made available by the effective date(s) of the prohibitions. An individual facility extension may be granted only after opportunity for public notice and comment, consultation with appropriate State agencies, and publication of such findings. Such case-by-case extensions are renewable once for no more than one additional year, thereby resulting in a maximum extension of 2 years generally and 2 additional years on a case-by-case basis.

Where a general variance or case-by-case extension is granted during the period in which the variance or extension is in effect, the affected hazardous wastes may be disposed of in a landfill or surface impoundment only if such facilities meet the minimum technology requirements for new facilities. . . .

HAZARDOUS WASTE TREATMENT COUNCIL V. UNITED STATES ENVIRONMENTAL PROTECTION AGENCY

886 F.2d 355 (D.C. Cir. 1989), **cert. denied,** *111 S. Ct. 139 (1990)*

WALD, Chief Judge, SILBERMAN and D. H. GINSBURG, Circuit Judges. Opinion concurring in part and concurring in the result filed by Circuit Judge SILBERMAN.

Per Curiam:

In 1984, Congress amended the Resource Conservation and Recovery Act ("RCRA"), 42 U.S.C. §6921-6991 (1982 & Supp. IV 1986), to prohibit land disposal of certain hazardous solvents and wastes containing dioxins except in narrow circumstances to be defined by Environmental Protection Agency ("EPA") regulations. See Hazardous and Solid Waste Amendments, §201(a), 42 U.S.C. §6924(e) (Supp. IV 1986). In these consolidated cases, petitioners seek review of EPA's final "solvents and dioxins" rule published pursuant to Congress' 1984 mandate. We conclude that the rule under review is consistent with RCRA, but remand one aspect of the rulemaking to the agency for further explanation.

I

A.   STATUTORY SCHEME

The Hazardous and Solid Waste Amendments of 1984 ("HSWA"), Pub. L. No. 98-616, 98 Stat. 3221 (1984), inter alia, substantially strengthened EPA's control over the land disposal of hazardous wastes regulated under RCRA's "cradle to grave" statutory scheme. In preambular language to the HSWA, Congress, believing that "land disposal facilities were not capable of assuring long-term containment of certain hazardous wastes," expressed the policy that "reliance on land disposal should be minimized or eliminated." 42 U.S.C. §6901(b)(7). In order to effectuate this policy, HSWA amended section 3004 of RCRA to prohibit land disposal of hazardous waste unless the waste is "pretreated" in a manner that minimizes "short-term and long-term threats to human health and the environment," id. §6924(m), or unless EPA can determine that the waste is to be disposed of in such a fashion as to ensure that "there will be no migration of hazardous constituents from the disposal [facility]. . . ." Id. §6924(d)(1), (e)(1), & (g)(5).

As amended, RCRA requires EPA to implement the land disposal prohibition in three phases, addressing the most hazardous "listed" wastes first. See id. §6924(g).[18] In accordance with strict statutory deadlines, the Administrator is obligated to specify those methods of land disposal of each listed hazardous waste which "will be protective of human health and the environment." Id. In addition, "[simultaneously] with the promulgation of regulations . . . prohibiting . . . land disposal of a particular hazardous waste, the Administrator" is required to promulgate regulations specifying those levels or methods of treatment, if any, which substantially diminish the toxicity of the waste or substantially reduce the likelihood of migration of hazardous constituents from the waste so that short-term and long-term threats to human health and the environment are minimized. Id. §6924(m).

Respecting two categories of hazardous wastes, including the solvents and dioxins at issue here[19] Congress, however, declined to wait for phased EPA implementation of the land disposal prohibition. For these wastes, Congress imposed earlier restrictions, prohibiting land disposal after dates specified in the HSWA except in accordance with pretreatment standards or pursuant to regulations specifying "protective" methods of disposal. Id. §6924(e)(1). These prohibitions, as applied to the solvents and dioxins listed in the HSWA, were to take effect November 8, 1986. Id. . . .

---

18. EPA was given the task of dividing the wastes presently "listed" as hazardous under RCRA into thirds according to their "intrinsic hazard," 42 U.S.C. §6924(g)(2) (Supp. IV 1986). In keeping with RCRA's deadline, the resulting schedule, promulgated in 1986, see 51 Fed. Reg. 19,300 (1986), required EPA to implement the land disposal prohibition and promulgate treatment standards for each third by dates no later than 45, 55, and 66 months after enactment of the HSWA, respectively. See 42 U.S.C. §6924(g)(4). One aspect of EPA's regulations governing the "first third" of these wastes was recently upheld on review in *Chemical-Waste Management, Inc. v. EPA*, 869 F.2d 1526 et al. (D.C. Cir. March 14, 1989).

19. The other category is the so-called "California List" wastes, the rule for which is the subject of *Hazardous Waste Treatment Council v. Thomas*, 885 F.2d 918.

B.   THE RULEMAKING UNDER REVIEW

In January 1986, EPA issued a notice of proposed rule-making announcing its draft implementation of the land disposal prohibition for solvents and dioxins. See 51 Fed. Reg. 1602 (1986) (hereinafter "Proposed Rule"). Approximately ten months later, after receiving extensive public commentary on the draft blueprint, EPA published a final solvents and dioxins rule differing in some respects from its draft approach. See 51 Fed. Reg. 40,572 (1986) (hereinafter "Final Rule"). . . .

1.   Section 3004(m) Treatment Standards

In the Proposed Rule, EPA announced its tentative support for a treatment regime embodying both risk-based and technology-based standards. The technology-based standards would be founded upon what EPA determined to be the Best Demonstrated Available Technology ("BDAT"); parallel risk-based or "screening" levels were to reflect "the maximum concentration [of a hazardous constituent] below which the Agency believes there is no regulatory concern for the land disposal program and which is protective of human health and the environment." Proposed Rule at 1611. The Proposed Rule provided that these two sets of standards would be melded in the following manner:

First, if BDAT standards were more rigorous than the relevant health-screening levels, the latter would be used to "cap the reductions in toxicity and/or mobility that otherwise would result from the application of BDAT treatment[.]" Id. Thus, "treatment for treatment's sake" would be avoided. Second, if BDAT standards were less rigorous than health-screening levels, BDAT standards would govern and the screening level would be used as "a goal for future changes to the treatment standards as new and more efficient treatment technologies become available." Id. at 1612. Finally, when EPA determined that the use of BDAT would pose a greater risk to human health and the environment than land disposal, or would provide insufficient safeguards against the threats produced by land disposal, the screening level would actually become the 3004(m) treatment standard. Id.

EPA invited public comment on alternative approaches as well. The first alternative identified in the Proposed Rule (and the one ultimately selected by EPA) was based purely on the capabilities of the "best demonstrated available technology." Id. at 1613. Capping treatment levels to avoid treatment for treatment's sake, according to EPA, could be accomplished under this technology-based scheme by "the petition process":

Under this approach, if a prescribed level or method of treatment under section 3004(m) resulted in concentration levels that an owner/operator believed to be overly protective, the owner/operator could petition the Agency to allow the use of an alternative treatment level or method or no treatment at all by demonstrating that less treatment would still meet the petition standard of protecting human health and environment.

Id. at 1613. And the function served by health-screening levels of providing a default standard when the application of BDAT technology would itself pose a threat to human health and the environment could likewise be fulfilled by the petition process: "an owner operator could [] petition the Agency . . . to allow continued land disposal of the waste upon a demonstration that land disposal of the waste would not result in harm to human health and the environment." Id.

The Agency received comments supporting both approaches, but ultimately settled on the pure-technology alternative. Of particular importance to EPA's decision were the comments filed by eleven members of Congress, all of whom served as conferees on the 1984 RCRA amendments. As EPA recorded in the preamble to the Final Rule:

[these] members of Congress argued strongly that [the health screening] approach did not fulfill the intent of the law. They asserted that because of the scientific uncertainty inherent in risk-based decisions, Congress expressly directed the Agency to set treatment standards based on the capabilities of existing technology.

The Agency believes that the technology-based approach adopted in [the] final rule, although not the only approach allowable under the law, best responds to the above stated comments.

Final Rule at 40,578.

EPA also relied on passages in the legislative history supporting an approach under which owners and operators of hazardous waste facilities would be required to use " 'the best [technology] that has been demonstrated to be achievable.' " Id. (quoting 103 Cong. Rec. S9178 (daily ed. July 25, 1984) (statement of Senator Chaffee). And the agency reiterated that the chief advantage offered by the health-screening approach — avoiding "treatment for treatment's sake" — could "be better addressed through changes in other aspects of its regulatory program." Id. As an example of what parts of the program might be altered, EPA announced that it was "considering the use of its risk-based methodologies to characterize wastes as hazardous pursuant to section 3001 [of RCRA]." Id.; see 42 U.S.C. §6921 (1982 & Supp. IV 1986).[20]

---

20. Under section 3001, the Administrator is empowered to list particular wastes as hazardous, and thus within RCRA's ambit, "taking into account toxicity, persistence, [] degradability in nature, potential for accumulation in

Petitioner CMA challenges this aspect of the rule as an unreasonable construction of section 3004(m)'s mandate to ensure that "short-term and long-term threats to human health and the environment are minimized." 42 U.S.C. §6924(m) (1982 & Supp. IV 1986). In the alternative, CMA argues that EPA has failed to explain the basis — in terms of relevant human health and environmental considerations — for its BDAT regime, which allegedly requires treatment in some circumstances to levels far below the standards for human exposure under other statutes administered by EPA. Thus, CMA claims that EPA's action in promulgating a technology-based rule is arbitrary and capricious. . . .

II.   SECTION 3004(M) TREATMENT STANDARDS

CMA challenges EPA's adoption of BDAT treatment standards in preference to the approach it proposed initially primarily on the ground that the regulation is not a reasonable interpretation of the statute. CMA obliquely, and Intervenors Edison Electric and the American Petroleum Institute explicitly, argues in the alternative that the agency did not adequately explain its decision to take the course that it did. . . .

A.   THE CONSISTENCY OF EPA'S INTERPRETATION WITH RCRA

Our role in evaluating an agency's interpretation of its enabling statute is as strictly circumscribed as it is simply stated: We first examine the statute to ascertain whether it clearly forecloses the course that the agency has taken; if it is ambiguous with respect to that question, we go on to determine whether the agency's interpretation is a reasonable resolution of the ambiguity. *Chevron,* 467 U.S. at [837,] 842-45.

1.   *Chevron Step I: Is the Statute Clear?*

We repeat the mandate of §3004(m)(1): the Administrator is required to promulgate "regulations specifying those levels or methods

---

tissue, and other related factors such as flammability, corrosiveness, and other hazardous characteristics." 42 U.S.C. §6921(a) (1982). The statute provides that the Administrator "shall [] revise[] [these lists] from time to time as may be appropriate." Id. EPA's current list is set forth at 40 C.F.R. Part 261, Subparts C and D.

of treatment, if any, which substantially diminish the toxicity of the waste or substantially reduce the likelihood of migration of hazardous constituents from the waste so that short-term and long-term threats to human health and the environment are minimized." 42 U.S.C. §6924(m)(1).

CMA reads the statute as requiring EPA to determine the levels of concentration in waste at which the various solvents here at issue are "safe" and to use those "screening levels" as floors below which treatment would not be required. CMA supports its interpretation with the observation that the statute directs EPA to set standards only to the extent that "threats to human health and the environment are minimized." We are unpersuaded, however, that Congress intended to compel EPA to rely upon screening levels in preference to the levels achievable by BDAT.

The statute directs EPA to set treatment standards based upon either "levels or methods" of treatment. Such a mandate makes clear that the choice whether to use "levels" (screening levels) or "methods" (BDAT) lies within the informed discretion of the agency, as long as the result is "that short-term and long-term threats to human health and the environment are minimized." To "minimize" something is, to quote the Oxford English Dictionary, to "reduce [it] to the smallest possible amount, extent, or degree." But Congress recognized, in the very amendments here at issue, that there are "long-term uncertainties associated with land disposal," 42 U.S.C. §6924 (d)(1)(A). In the face of such uncertainties, it cannot be said that a statute that requires that threats be minimized unambiguously requires EPA to set levels at which it is conclusively presumed that no threat to health or the environment exists.

Nor are we at all persuaded by CMA's interpretation of *NRDC v. EPA*, 824 F.2d 1146, 1163 (D.C. Cir. 1987) (en banc), in which we held that EPA was not permitted to "substitute [] technological feasibility for health as the primary consideration under Section 112 [of the Clean Air Act]."[21] That provision requires the Administrator to set air pollution standards "at the level which in his judgment provides an ample margin of safety to protect the public health." 42 U.S.C. §7412(b)(1)(B). EPA had set emission standards for vinyl chloride, however, "based solely on the level attainable by the best available control technology," 824 F.2d at 1149, despite its finding that such levels would create health risks. It had neither stated that the risks it found were insignificant, nor explained how the risks it accepted were consistent with its statutory duty to provide "an ample margin of safety." Id. This court held that EPA had erred in failing to consider whether the

---

21. [Ed. Note: This case was discussed supra, p. 331.]

best available technology was sufficient to provide the statutorily mandated margin of safety. Id. at 1164-66.

Contrary to CMA's implication, however, the court did not hold, or even imply, the converse — that EPA could not require generators to use technologies that would reduce emissions to a point *below* that which would provide an "ample margin of safety." Indeed, the court noted that "Congress. . . recognized in section 112 that the determination of what is 'safe' will always be marked by scientific uncertainty and thus exhorted the Administration to set . . . standards that will provide an 'ample margin' of safety," id. at 1165; we then concluded that "[once] 'safety' is assured, the Administrator should be free to diminish as much of the statistically determined risk as possible by setting the standard at the lowest feasible level." Id.

This is not to say that EPA is free, under §3004(m), to require generators to treat their waste beyond the point at which there is no "threat" to human health or to the environment. That Congress's concern in adopting §3004(m) was with health and the environment would necessarily make it unreasonable for EPA to promulgate treatment standards wholly without regard to whether there might be a threat to man or nature. That concern is better dealt with, however, at Chevron's second step; for, having concluded that the statute does not unambiguously and in all circumstances foreclose EPA from adopting treatment levels based upon the levels achievable by BDAT, we must now explore whether the particular levels established by the regulations supply a reasonable resolution of the statutory ambiguity.

2.   *Chevron Step II: Is EPA's Interpretation Reasonable?*

The screening levels that EPA initially proposed were not those at which the wastes were thought to be entirely safe. Rather, EPA set the levels to reduce risks from the solvents to an "acceptable" level, and it explored, at great length, the manifest (and manifold) uncertainties inherent in any attempt to specify "safe" concentration levels. The agency discussed, for example, the lack of any safe level of exposure to carcinogenic solvents, 51 Fed. Reg. at 1,628; the extent to which reference dose levels (from which it derived its screening levels) understate the dangers that hazardous solvents pose to particularly sensitive members of the population, id. at 1,627; the necessarily artificial assumptions that accompany any attempt to model the migration of hazardous wastes from a disposal site, id. at 1,642-53; and the lack of dependable data on the effects that solvents have on the liners that bound disposal facilities for the purpose of ensuring that the wastes disposed in a facility stay there, id. at 1,714-15. Indeed, several parties made voluminous comments on the Proposed Rule to the effect that EPA's estimates of the various probabilities were far more problematic than even EPA recognized. See, e.g., Comments of Natural Resources Defense Council, Record at 29,000-62.

CMA suggests, despite these uncertainties, that the adoption of a BDAT treatment regime would result in treatment to "below established levels of hazard." It relies for this proposition almost entirely upon a chart in which it contrasts the BDAT levels with (1) levels EPA has defined as "Maximum Contaminant Levels" (MCLs) under the Safe Drinking Water Act; (2) EPA's proposed "Organic Toxicity Characteristics," threshold levels below which EPA will not list a waste as hazardous by reason of its having in it a particular toxin; and (3) levels at which EPA has recently granted petitions by waste generators to "delist" a particular waste, that is, to remove it from the list of wastes that are deemed hazardous. CMA points out that the BDAT standards would require treatment to levels that are, in many cases, significantly below these "established levels of hazard."

If indeed EPA had determined that wastes at any of the three levels pointed to by CMA posed no threat to human health or the environment, we would have little hesitation in concluding that it was unreasonable for EPA to mandate treatment to substantially lower levels. In fact, however, none of the levels to which CMA compares the BDAT standards purports to establish a level at which safety is assured or "threats to human health and the environment are minimized." Each is a level established for a different purpose and under a different set of statutory criteria than concern us here; each is therefore irrelevant to the inquiry we undertake today.

The drinking water levels, for example, are established under a scheme requiring EPA to set "goals" at a level at which "no known or anticipated adverse effects on the health of persons occur." 42 U.S.C. §300g-1(b)(4). EPA is then to set MCLs as close to its goals as "feasible," taking into account, among other things, treatment costs. 42 U.S.C. §§300g-1(b)(4), (5). Since SDWA goals are set only to deal with "known or anticipated" adverse health effects, a mere "threat" to human health is not enough in that context. Moreover, SDWA levels are set without reference to threats to the environment. Finally, EPA must consider costs in setting its MCLs; there is no similar limitation in §3004 of RCRA.

Similarly, in promulgating the OTC levels, EPA made clear that, "[in] establishing a scientifically justifiable approach for arriving at [OTC levels], EPA wanted to assure a *high degree of confidence* that a waste which releases toxicants at concentrations above the [OTC level] would pose a hazard *to human health*." EPA Hazardous Waste Management System; Identification and Listing of Hazardous Waste . . . , Proposed Rule, 51 Fed. Reg. 21,648, 21,649 (1986) (emphases added). Thus it is clear that wastes with toxicant levels below the OTC thresholds may still pose *"threats* to human health [or] *the environment."* Id. at 21,648 (emphases added).

Finally, CMA points to the "delisting levels" as appropriate points of comparison. The term is a bit misleading, however. EPA delists particular wastes in response to individual petitions, see, e.g., 42 U.S.C. §6921(f)(1), and it has not adopted formal, or even *de facto,* levels below which any waste will be delisted. That EPA has delisted, in particular circumstances, wastes containing concentrations of solvents higher than those called for by the BDAT standards adds nothing to CMA's argument. The treatment standards establish a generic approach, requiring that all wastes deemed to be hazardous be treated to a set level in order to minimize threats to health and to the environment. If a waste is listed as hazardous, and an individual generator wants to dispose of it without meeting the BDAT standards, it may petition to have its particular waste delisted. If the agency grants the delisting petition, only the petitioner is affected; the generally required level of treatment remains the same. Hence, there is no inconsistency between a "delisting level," accepted in particular circumstances, that permits a higher level of a particular contaminant than the BDAT level otherwise generally applicable.

In sum, EPA's catalog of the uncertainties inherent in the alternative approach using screening levels supports the reasonableness of its reliance upon BDAT instead. Accordingly, finding no merit in CMA's contention that EPA has required treatment to "below established levels of hazard," we find that EPA's interpretation of §3004(m) is reasonable. . . .

B.   WAS EPA'S EXPLANATION ADEQUATE?

The Supreme Court has made it abundantly clear that a reviewing court is not to supplement an agency's reasons for proceeding as it did, nor to paper over its plainly defective rationale: "The reviewing court should not attempt itself to make up for such deficiencies [in the agency's explanation]; we may not supply a reasoned basis for the agency's action that the agency itself has not given." *Motor Vehicles Manufacturers Ass'n v. State Farm Mut. Auto Ins. Co.,* 463 U.S. 29, 43, 77 L. Ed. 2d 443, 103 S. Ct. 2856 (1983) (citing *SEC v. Chenery Corp.,* 332 U.S. 194, 196, 91 L. Ed. 1995, 67 S. Ct. 1575 (1947)). "We will, however, 'uphold a decision of less than ideal clarity if the agency's path may reasonably be discerned.'" Id. (quoting *Bowman Transportation, Inc. v. Arkansas-Best Freight System, Inc.,* 419 U.S. 281, 286, 42 L. Ed. 2d 447, 95 S. Ct. 438 (1974)). Accordingly, in order to determine whether we can affirm EPA's action here, we must parse the language of the Final Rule to see whether it can be interpreted to make a sensible argument for the approach EPA adopted. We find that it cannot.

As we have said, EPA, in its Proposed Rule, expressed a tentative preference for an approach that combined screening levels and BDAT. It indicated that it thought either that approach or BDAT alone was consistent with the statute, and recognized that there were myriad uncertainties inherent in any attempt to model the health and environmental effects of the land disposal of hazardous wastes. It initially concluded, however, that despite those uncertainties, the better approach was to adopt the combination of screening levels and BDAT. Nevertheless, in the Final Rule, it rejected its earlier approach, and adopted a regime of treatment levels defined by BDAT alone.

In order fully to convey the inadequacy of EPA's explanation, we quote the relevant portion of the Final Rule at length:

> Although a number of comments on the proposed rule favored the first approach; that is, the use of screening levels to "cap" treatment that can be achieved under BDAT, several commenters, including eleven members of Congress, argued strongly that this approach did not fulfill the intent of the law. They asserted that because of the scientific uncertainty inherent in risk-based decisions, Congress expressly directed the Agency to set treatment standards based on the capabilities of existing technology.
>
> The Agency believes that the technology-based approach adopted in today's final rule, although not the only approach allowable under the law, best responds to the above-stated comments. Accordingly, the final rule establishes treatment standards under RCRA section 3004(m) based exclusively on levels achievable by BDAT. The Agency believes that the treatment standards will generally be protective of human health and the environment. Levels less stringent than BDAT may also be protective.
>
> The plain language of the statute does not compel the Agency to set treatment standards based exclusively on the capabilities of existing technology. . . . By calling for standards that minimize threats to human health and the environment, the statute clearly allows for the kind of risk-based standard originally proposed by the Agency. However, the plain language of the statute does not preclude a technology-based approach. This is made clear by the legislative history accompanying the introduction of the final section 3004(m) language. The legislative history provides that "[The] requisite levels of [sic] methods of treatment established by the Agency should be the best that has been demonstrated to be achievable" and that "[the] intent here is to require utilization of available technology in lieu of continued land disposal without prior treatment." (Vol. 130, Cong. Rec. 9178, (daily ed., July 25, 1984)). Thus, EPA is acting within the authority vested by the statute in selecting [sic] to promulgate a final regulation using its proposed alternative approach of setting treatment standards based on BDAT.

> The Agency believes that its major purpose in adopting the risk-based approach of the proposal (i.e., to allow different standards for relatively low-risk, low-hazard wastes) may be better addressed through changes in other aspects of its regulatory program. For example, EPA is considering the use of its risk-based methodologies to characterize wastes as hazardous pursuant to section 3001.

51 Fed. Reg. at 40,578.

To summarize: after EPA issued the Proposed Rule, some commenters, including eleven members of Congress, chastised the agency on the ground that the use of screening levels was inconsistent with the intent of the statute. They stated that because of the uncertainties involved, Congress had mandated that BDAT alone be used to set treatment standards. EPA determined that the "best [response]" to those comments was to adopt a BDAT standard. It emphasized, however, that either course was consistent with the statute (and that it was therefore not *required* to use BDAT alone). Finally, it asserted, without explanation, that its major purpose in initially proposing screening levels "may be better addressed through changes in other aspects of its regulatory program," and gave an example of one such aspect that might be changed.

This explanation is inadequate. It should go without saying that members of Congress have no power, once a statute has been passed, to alter its interpretation by post-hoc "explanations" of what it means; there may be societies where "history" belongs to those in power, but ours is not among them. In our scheme of things, we consider legislative history because it is just that: *history*. It forms the background against which Congress adopted the relevant statute. Post-enactment statements are a different matter, and they are not to be considered by an agency or by a court as legislative history. An agency has an obligation to consider the comments of legislators, of course, but on the same footing as it would those of other commenters; such comments may have, as Justice Frankfurter said in a different context, "power to persuade, if lacking power to control." *Skidmore v. Swift & Co.*, 323 U.S. 134, 140, 89 L. Ed. 124, 65 S. Ct. 161 (1944).

It is unclear whether EPA recognized this fundamental point. On the one hand, it suggested that the adoption of a BDAT-only regime "best-respond[ed]" to the comments suggesting that the statute required such a rule. On the other hand, EPA went on at some length to establish that the comments were in error, in that screening levels are permissible under the statute. EPA's "rationale," in other words, is that several members of Congress (among others) urged upon it the claim that Proposition X ("Congress mandated BDAT") requires Result A ("EPA adopts BDAT"), and that although Proposition X is inaccurate, the best response to the commenters is to adopt Result A.

Nor is anything added by EPA's bald assertion that its reason for initially preferring Result B (screening levels) "may be" better served by other changes in the statutory scheme. In its Proposed Rule, EPA had, after extensive analysis of the various alternatives, come to the opposite conclusion. It is insufficient, in that context, for EPA to proceed in a different direction simply on the basis of an unexplained and unelaborated statement that it might have been wrong when it earlier concluded otherwise.

In the entire relevant text of the Final Rule, EPA neither invokes nor discusses the uncertainties inherent in the land disposal process in support of its determination to use BDAT. EPA's only mention of the concept is in its description of the commenters' argument that, because of such uncertainties, Congress mandated BDAT — an argument that EPA rejected. While it may be that EPA intended that reference to act as an incorporation of all the uncertainties it outlined in its Proposed Rule, or all the many challenges to its assumptions that commenters submitted in response to the Proposed Rule, that intent, if indeed it exists, is so shrouded in mist that for this court to say that we could discern its outlines would be as illogical as the agency's explanation in the Final Rule itself.

Accordingly, we grant the petitions for review in this respect. . . .

NOTES AND QUESTIONS

1. Does the Hazardous Waste Treatment Council (HWTC) challenge or support the BDAT regulations? What about the Chemical Manufacturers' Association? What motivates these organizations to take the positions that they do? Are either of these organizations' interests aligned with the broader public interest in regulating hazardous waste disposal?

2. What exactly do the EPA and the court mean by "BDATs"? Must TSD facilities actually use a particular technology? Or may they achieve the level of performance reached by BDAT by means of other treatment technologies? How would they be selected?

3. In its Proposed Rule, EPA expressed support for a hybrid risk-based/technology-based approach. In what ways would this approach have been different from the rule ultimately chosen? EPA asserts that it will be able to better achieve the chief advantage of a risk-based approach through other changes in the regulatory program. What are those changes? Do you agree with EPA's assertion?

4. The CMA argues that BDAT levels inappropriately mandate control "below established levels of hazard." To illustrate this point, the CMA shows that BDAT levels are below "Maximum Contaminant Levels" EPA has established under the Safe Drinking Water Act and levels

EPA has used in granting petitions to delist wastes. How are MCLs determined under the Safe Drinking Water Act, §300g-1? What standard is applied in delisting decisions under RCRA? Is the CMA's argument convincing on policy grounds? Is the court's analysis satisfactory?

5. How would you evaluate the court's performance in reviewing EPA's regulatory choice? Does it require EPA to conscientiously confront the difficult regulatory choices raised by this litigation on remand?

6. Following the remand, EPA acknowledged that its "objective is not to require further treatment of prohibited wastes containing threshold levels of hazardous constituents at which listed wastes themselves would no longer be deemed hazardous" but nonetheless explained its selection of technology-based treatment standards over risk-based screening levels on the ground that it was "presently unable to promulgate such levels." 55 Fed. Reg. 6640, 6641 (Feb. 26, 1990). In view of the fact that EPA is able to determine such levels in its delisting and characteristics programs, the only explanation for its reliance on technology-based standards under Section 3004(m) would appear to be a shortage of resources at the agency. See Williams and Cannon, Rethinking the Resource Conservation and Recovery Act for the 1990s, 21 Envtl. L. Rep. 10063, 10066 (1991).

PROBLEM

Many treatment technologies pose significant environmental risks. For example, incineration of wastes can result in air pollution and concentrated hazardous ash. Recycling technologies can yield hazardous by-products.

(A) Suppose that available treatment technologies for a particular hazardous waste (X) pose greater risks to human health and the environment than disposing X in a triple-lined monofill with a leachate collection system. Given the current state of liner and leachate collection technology, however, it cannot be established to a reasonable degree of certainty that X will never migrate from an appropriately designed, maintained, and operated monofill. Is EPA required to choose triple-lined monofill disposal as the only permissible means of disposal for X? May EPA permit the use of triple-lined monofills for disposing of X? Cite to relevant statutory authority.

(B) Suppose instead that the best demonstrated available technology treatment for X probably achieves a slightly lower risk to human health and the environment than the use of triple-lined monofills but is an order of magnitude more expensive. May EPA take this cost factor into consideration in regulating the disposal of X?

(C) Suppose that EPA believed that recycling treatment technologies for X are likely to improve dramatically over the next decade. Although triple-lined monofills for X are currently less expensive and pose less risk to human health and the environment, it is expected that recycling will be cheaper and more efficacious within the decade. Moreover, EPA is confident that monofills can be relied upon to prevent migration of X for at least 20 years. How should EPA regulate the disposal of X? What options does EPA have under the HSWA?

(D) Does this regulatory regime make sense? What other regulatory approaches might EPA have chosen? On the basis of the following list of objectives of hazardous waste disposal policy, which approach should EPA have chosen?

- Net reduction of human health and environmental risk considering all pathways — for instance, does the approach reduce groundwater pollution at the cost of more serious and immediate risks from other pathways (such as air pollution)?
  - Incentives for illegal disposal.
  - Cost of control — Is the cost of control disproportionate to environmental benefits? Is the means chosen cost-effective?
    - Administrative costs.
  - Effects on innovation in control technologies.
  - Incentives for efficient waste minimization upstream.

(E) What factors explain Congress' choice of regulatory framework? What factors explain EPA's implementation of the regulatory scheme?

4. POLICY PERSPECTIVES ON RCRA

RCRA has had significant effects on hazardous waste management practices in the United States. The number of facilities managing hazardous wastes has dropped from more than 180,000 facilities prior to the enactment of RCRA in 1976 to less than 2000 permitted TSD facilities by 1986. Firms in the TSD industry are on average better capitalized and significantly more carefully and heavily regulated. On the other hand, the stringency of RCRA TSD regulations, difficulties in siting new waste facilities (attributable to the Not-In-My-BackYard (NIMBY) syndrome), and heightened concern about environmental liability (with the decreased availability and dramatically higher cost of liability insurance) raise questions about the adequacy of TSD capacity in the United States. These factors have significantly increased the cost of disposing hazardous waste, which creates incentives for generators to minimize their hazardous waste levels.

The Hazardous and Solid Waste Amendments of 1984, especially the "land ban" hammers, have been remarkably effective at spurring EPA to set regulatory standards within statutory deadlines. As highlighted above, EPA has opted for a technology-oriented approach for the largest and most significant task — setting treatment standards for hazardous waste. The desirability of this approach, however, remains to be seen.

Commentators have forcefully criticized RCRA's regulatory framework and EPA's implementation of the land disposal restrictions as being inconsistent in the treatment of hazards and for disregarding the relationship between environmental benefits and control costs. Consider the following excerpts:

> [B]ecause the land disposal restrictions do not take into account risk-based levels, they sometimes require wastes to be treated to levels substantially below those that would warrant delisting. Then, under the present system for listed wastes, even those treatment residues must continue to be managed as hazardous wastes (i.e., disposed of in a RCRA Subtitle C landfill) unless and until a delisting is obtained. On a policy level, little justification exists for this kind of inconsistency in the definitional system of hazardous waste management.

Williams & Cannon, Rethinking the Resource Conservation and Recovery Act for the 1990s, 21 Envtl. L. Rep. 10063, at 10069.

> [T]he system generates mind-boggling complexities for mixed streams and treatment residuals due to the linking of the mixture rule with the land ban. The chemical-specific treatment standards are based on pure waste streams. EPA's rationale has been that generators can always separate waste streams if mixing makes treatment standards unachievable. But many streams were mixed before land disposal regulations came into existence, and mixing of many waste streams is hard-wired into the manufacturing process. Moreover, separate wastewater treatment for each of a number of different process streams (50 or more in some cases) makes no sense from a process and technology standpoint. Yet, EPA applies these standards to all mixtures of waste streams as well as the residuals from treatment of any of the original waste streams.
>
> Assume, for example, that two waste streams exist. The standard for waste stream A is: chemical X = 1 part per million (ppm). The standard for waste stream B is: chemical X = 10 ppm. In setting each of these standards for chemical X, EPA uses the best demonstrated available technology on each stream. When waste streams A and B are mixed, under the waste-code carry-through principle the mixture of the two

streams must meet the most stringent standard. Therefore, the mixture would have to meet a standard of X = 1 ppm. This is clearly a problem because, if waste stream B could have been treated to one ppm, that is what the waste stream B chemical X standard would have been set at originally. It is therefore highly unlikely that the mixture of these two waste streams will meet the required treatment standard; the only way the generator can technically comply with the EPA treatment standard is never to mix the two waste streams.

Id. at 10069-10070.

EPA estimated the cost/benefit ratio of its "land ban" rules for solvents to be approximately $90 million per cancer case avoided. 51 Fed. Reg. 40,634 (1986). For another set of "land ban" rules, it estimated the ratio at about $200 million per cancer case avoided. 53 Fed. Reg. 31,207 (1988). For another, the cost was about $30 million to avoid .07 cancer cases, or over $400 million per cancer avoided. 54 Fed. Reg. 26,646 (1989). None of these estimates take account of the time at which risks are incurred. However, EPA has said that "it can be generally observed that the effect of restricting land disposal is to reduce risk in absolute terms while shifting it forward temporally." 52 Fed. Reg. 25,786 (1987). In other words, while the "land ban" rules will result in somewhat fewer cancers, they will probably be incurred earlier, as we trade the long-term dangers of land disposal for the short-term dangers of incineration and other treatment. The estimates of $90 million and greater per cancer far exceed the cut-off points generally used to determine cost-effectiveness of a federal regulation.

Pederson, The Future of Federal Solid Waste Regulation, 16 Colum. J. Envtl. L. 109, 131 n.96 (1991).

Commentators have also strongly criticized the regulatory system's underregulation of the great majority of wastes falling outside of the scope of RCRA Subtitle C program. Of the approximately 10 billion metric tons of solid waste generated per year in the United States, only about 250 million metric tons are subject to RCRA Subtitle C regulations. Much of the remainder — including mining wastes, oil exploration and production wastes, fly ash and scrubber sludge from utility boilers, and municipal solid waste — has toxicological similarities to RCRA Subtitle C wastes but has been subject to minimal regulatory controls. See Williams & Cannon, supra, at 10067-10068; Pederson, supra, at 109, 113-114, 118-120.

Risk management techniques, like those discussed in Chapters 2 and 4, have been proposed as a means for prioritizing the regulatory agenda, establishing systematic definitional thresholds for the scope of RCRA Subtitle C, and setting treatment standards. How well would this approach perform in regulating hazardous waste disposal? To what extent is it permissible within the existing statutory framework?

In recent years, EPA and other government agencies have encouraged companies to reduce the production of hazardous wastes and pollution through the dissemination of information and other voluntary devices. These efforts range from conducting and disseminating research on source reduction to small grants for demonstration projects and modest rewards and recognition for accomplishments in pollution prevention. See Pollution Prevention Act of 1990; Freeman, et al., Industrial Pollution Prevention: A Critical Review, 42 J. Air & Waste Mgmt. Assn. 618 (1992).

As in other areas of environmental law and policy, frustration with command and control techniques for regulating hazardous waste treatment and disposal have led commentators to incentive-based approaches. See Russell, Economic Incentives in the Management of Hazardous Wastes, 13 Colum. J. Envtl. L. 257 (1988); Hahn, An Evaluation of Options for Reducing Hazardous Waste, 12 Harv. Envtl. L. Rev. 201, 216 (1988). Among the instruments proposed are feedstock taxes, tradeable feedstock permits, tradeable waste generation permits, disposal taxes, disposal subsidies, and deposit-refund schemes. How would these approaches measure up in terms of the following objectives for hazardous waste disposal policy?

- Net reduction of human health and environmental risk considering all pathways,
  - Incentives for illegal disposal,
- Cost of control,
  - Administrative costs,
- Effects on innovation in control technologies,
- Incentives for efficient waste minimization upstream.

B.   CLEANUP OF DANGEROUS WASTE SITES: THE SUPERFUND PROGRAM

The dangers of unregulated land disposal of hazardous waste were graphically brought to national attention in the summer of 1978 when the spotlight of media reporting focused on the surfacing of toxic chemicals in basements and schoolyards in the community of Love Canal, New York.[22] Love Canal was an abandoned hydroelectric channel located in Niagara Falls. Between 1942 and 1953, the Hooker Chemical Company filled the canal with more than 21,000 tons of chemical wastes. In 1953, Hooker covered the waste with earth and clay and sold it to the Niagara Falls Board of Education for $1. A school and play-

---

22. For a comprehensive history of the events leading up to the Love Canal crisis, see A. Levine, Love Canal: Science, Politics, and People (1982).

ground were built upon the site. The surrounding vacant land was developed into a residential community.

In the years that followed, residents noticed foul odors after heavy rains and during humid conditions, but most attributed these odors to nearby industrial facilities. Increased precipitation in the early 1970s raised groundwater levels, causing thick, black, oily sludges to seep into basements and accumulate on the surface. In 1976, a joint U.S.-Canada commission responsible for monitoring conditions in Lake Ontario identified high levels of the insecticide Mirex in fish; these contaminants were traced to Love Canal. This finding generated public concern, leading to the initiation of groundwater and epidemiological studies. In August 1978, New York's Health Commissioner declared a public health emergency, which catapulted the Love Canal situation to national attention. The news media descended upon Love Canal, broadcasting images of a middle America community mired in a swamp of toxic waste. The Health Commissioner's report, Love Canal: Public Health Time Bomb, coined a powerful metaphor for focusing public attention upon the risks of abandoned hazardous waste sites.

Even before the Love Canal crisis propelled the problem of abandoned hazardous waste sites to national attention, EPA had already begun drafting a blueprint for expanding its authority.[23] The prolonged economic recession of the 1970s revealed the vulnerability of public support for ecological programs. Administrator Costle sought to broaden EPA's political base by emphasizing the agency's role in protecting public health. The agency would need expanded authority in order to address the problems posed by abandoned hazardous waste sites.

Within two months of Love Canal's appearance in national headlines, EPA had completed ambitious draft legislation designed to address the problems of abandoned hazardous waste sites. The basic structure of the legislation, which has been aptly characterized as "shovels first, lawyers later," was borrowed from the hazardous spills provision from the Clean Water Act (§311). The government was authorized to respond to emergencies immediately with funding from a trust fund, which was to be replenished through damages collected from responsible parties. Because of the economic recession, the trust fund would have to be initially financed through an off-budget device. EPA proposed that the seed money be raised through a fee on chemical feedstocks.

In order to dramatize the extent of the hazardous waste problem and mobilize public and congressional attention, EPA directed the regional offices to identify potentially dangerous waste sites throughout

---

23. This discussion draws on Chapter 5, Passing Superfund, in M. Landy, Roberts & Thomas, The Environmental Protection Agency: Asking the Wrong Questions (1990).

the nation. This list proved invaluable in sustaining momentum for the legislation when progress in the Congress stalled. The final version of the Comprehensive Environmental Response, Compensation, and Liability Act of 1980 (CERCLA), which emerged from Congress in the waning days of the Carter Administration, contained the key elements of EPA's initial draft. The Hazardous Substance Response Trust Fund was created from special taxes on petroleum and certain chemicals (87.5 percent of the initial fund) and general tax revenues (12.5 percent). The legislation has come to be known as Superfund.

The Superfund Amendments and Reauthorization Act of 1986 (SARA) expanded the initial Superfund from $1.6 billion to $13.6 billion ($8.5 billion authorized for 1986-1991; $5.1 billion authorized for 1991-1994) by increasing petrochemical taxes and introducing a general environmental tax on corporate income. SARA also mandated strong cleanup standards, legislated many aspects of the government's settlement policy, and authorized EPA to use a variety of incentive devices to encourage settlements.

Superfund differs substantially from the traditional standard-setting statutes that we have encountered thus far. It relies significantly upon legal institutions as a funding and cost allocation mechanism for a government cleanup program and as an incentive device for deterring hazardous conditions, identifying problem sites, and encouraging private cleanups.

In order to teach this complex and unique regulatory-liability regime — much of which lies in understanding the scope of liability and the multi-party context of enforcement policy and settlement negotiations — we will use a rich factual setting and a series of discussion questions. The first section excerpts two leading cases to illustrate the structure, principal liability provisions, and broad scope of Superfund. The next section provides a complex hypothetical Superfund case, the evaluation of which illuminates the practice and challenges of Superfund's liability regime. The following sections look at the interaction between Superfund and the Bankruptcy Code and insurance law, respectively. The fifth section builds upon the CERCLA hypothetical to highlight some of the ethical dimensions of corporate environmental advising. The sixth section discusses the remedy selection process. The seventh section examines the enforcement and settlement policy issues presented in Superfund practice. The final section evaluates the Superfund regulatory-liability regime from a policy perspective.

1.   STATUTORY FRAMEWORK

Once EPA becomes aware of a dangerous hazardous waste site, it first makes a preliminary assessment of the conditions. If an evaluation of how the site was used and what wastes were deposited indicates the potential for serious environmental harm, a site investigation is conducted. Based upon the proximity of the site to groundwater supplies and residences, the seriousness of the contamination, and other factors, the site is assigned a formal hazard ranking. Sites receiving a ranking above EPA's threshold are placed on the National Priorities List (NPL), making them eligible for Superfund monies.[24]

Superfund offers the government two principal means of responding to a release or threatened release of hazardous waste.[25] Under the emergency cleanup provisions of §104, the government may cleanup first, and seek cost recovery later under §107.[26] Section 107 casts a broad net of liability, extending to site owners and operators, waste generators, and transporters. Alternatively, §106 authorizes the government to issue administrative orders and seek injunctive remedies requiring the cleanup of actual or threatened releases. Failure to comply with such orders exposes responsible parties to fines of up to $25,000 per day.

We will be focusing much of our attention on the liability provisions of Superfund, as these are the most complex and significant provisions of the statute from a legal standpoint and quite relevant to the policy analysis. At this point, it is worthwhile carefully reviewing the liability provisions (§§106-107), as well as relevant definitions (§101). The following cases flesh out the Superfund liability regime.

STATE OF NEW YORK V. SHORE REALTY CORP.

759 F.2d 1032 (2d Cir. 1985)

OAKES, Circuit Judge:
This case involves several novel questions about the scope of the Comprehensive Environmental Response, Compensation, and Liability Act of 1980, 42 U.S.C. §§9601-9657 (1982) ("CERCLA"). . . .

---

24. EPA may also use the Superfund to undertake emergency removal actions.

25. In addition to civil liability under CERCLA, those who violate federal hazardous waste laws may be subject to serious criminal penalties. See 42 U.S.C. §6948, SWDA §3008.

26. §107 is not limited to government actions. Private persons can clean up and seek costs recovery from responsible parties.

Under CERCLA, the Superfund can finance up to 90 percent of the capital costs of remediation, which include excavation, construction of facilities or containment devices, and stabilization. States are required to pay the full costs of operations and maintenance, which include pumping and filtering operations, maintenance of facilities, and monitoring. In 1986, SARA shifted 10 percent of the capital expenditure burden onto the states. In order to finance their share as well as to address the costs of clean-up of non-NPL sites, a majority of states have established funding mechanisms. CERCLA §104(c).

On February 29, 1984, the State of New York brought suit against Shore Realty Corp. ("Shore") and Donald LeoGrande, its officer and stockholder, to clean up a hazardous waste disposal site at One Shore Road, Glenwood Landing, New York, which Shore had acquired for land development purposes. At the time of the acquisition, LeoGrande knew that hazardous waste was stored on the site and that cleanup would be expensive, though neither Shore nor LeoGrande had participated in the generation or transportation of the nearly 700,000 gallons of hazardous waste now on the premises. . . .

FACTS . . .

LeoGrande incorporated Shore solely for the purpose of purchasing the Shore Road property. All corporate decisions and actions were made, directed, and controlled by him. By contract dated July 14, 1983, Shore agreed to purchase the 3.2 acre site, a small peninsula surrounded on three sides by the waters of Hempstead Harbor and Mott Cove, for condominium development. Five large tanks in a field in the center of the site hold most of some 700,000 gallons of hazardous chemicals located there, though there are six smaller tanks both above and below ground containing hazardous waste, as well as some empty tanks, on the property. The tanks are connected by pipe to a tank truck loading rack and dockage facilities for loading by barge. Four roll-on/roll-off containers and one tank truck trailer hold additional waste. And before June 15, 1984, one of the two dilapidated masonry warehouses on the site contained over 400 drums of chemicals and contaminated solids, many of which were corroded and leaking.[27]

It is beyond dispute that the tanks and drums contain "hazardous substances" within the meaning of CERCLA. 42 U.S.C. §9601(14). The substances involved — including benzene, dichlorobenzenes, ethyl benzene, tetrachloroethylene, trichloroethylene, 1,1,1-trichloroethene, chlordane, polychlorinated biphenyls (commonly known as PCBs), and bis (2-ethylhexyl) phthalate — are toxic, in some cases carcinogenic, and dangerous by way of contact, inhalation, or ingestion. These substances are present at the site in various combinations, some of which may cause the toxic effect to be synergistic.

The purchase agreement provided that it could be voided by Shore without penalty if after conducting an environmental study

_____

27. When these drums concededly were "bursting and leaking," Shore employees asked the State to enter the site, inspect it, and take steps to mitigate the "life-threatening crisis situation." Pursuant to stipulation and order entered on June 15, 1984, Shore began removing the drums. Some may still remain at the site.

Shore had decided not to proceed. LeoGrande was fully aware that the tenants, Applied Environmental Services, Inc., and Hazardous Waste Disposal, Inc., were then operating — illegally, it may be noted — a hazardous waste storage facility on the site. Shore's environmental consultant, WTM Management Corporation ("WTM"), prepared a detailed report in July, 1983, incorporated in the record and relied on by the district court for its findings. The report concluded that over the past several decades "the facility ha[d] received little if any preventive maintenance, the tanks (above ground and below ground), pipeline, loading rack, fire extinguishing system, and warehouse have deteriorated." WTM found that there had been several spills of hazardous waste at the site, including at least one large spill in 1978. Though there had been some attempts at cleanup, the WTM testing revealed that hazardous substances, such as benzene, were still leaching into the groundwater and the waters of the bay immediately adjacent to the bulkhead abutting Hempstead Harbor. After a site visit on July 18, 1983, WTM reported firsthand on the sorry state of the facility, observing, among other things, "seepage from the bulkhead," "corrosion" on all the tanks, signs of possible leakage from some of the tanks, deterioration of the pipeline and loading rack, and fifty to one hundred fifty-five gallon drums containing contaminated earth in one of the warehouses. The report concluded that if the current tenants "close up the operation and leave the material at the site," the owners would be left with a "potential time bomb." WTM estimated that the cost of environmental cleanup and monitoring would range from $650,000 to over $1 million before development could begin. After receiving this report Shore sought a waiver from the State Department of Environmental Conservation ("DEC") of liability as landowners for the disposal of the hazardous waste stored at the site. Although the DEC denied the waiver, Shore took title on October 13, 1983, and obtained certain rights over against the tenants, whom it subsequently evicted on January 5, 1984.

Nevertheless, between October 13, 1983, and January 5, 1984, nearly 90,000 gallons of hazardous chemicals were added to the tanks. And during a state inspection on January 3, 1984, it became evident that the deteriorating and leaking drums of chemicals referred to above had also been brought onto the site. Needless to say, the tenants did not clean up the site before they left. Thus, conditions when Shore employees first entered the site were as bad as or worse than those described in the WTM report. As LeoGrande admitted by affidavit, "the various storage tanks, pipe lines and connections between these storage facilities were in a bad state of repair." While Shore claims to have made some improvements, such as sealing all the pipes and valves and continuing the cleanup of the damage from earlier spills, Shore did nothing about the hundreds of thousands of gallons of hazardous waste standing in deteriorating tanks. In addition, although a growing number of drums were leaking hazardous substances, Shore essentially ignored the problem until June, 1984. See supra note [27].

On September 19, 1984, a DEC inspector observed one of the large tanks, which held over 300,000 gallons of hazardous materials, with rusting floor plates and tank walls, a pinhole leak, and a four-foot line of corrosion along one of the weld lines. On three other tanks, flakes of corroded metal "up to the size and thickness of a dime" were visible at the floorplate level. . . . In addition, defendants do not contest that Shore employees lack the knowledge to maintain safely the quantity of hazardous chemicals on the site. And, because LeoGrande has no intention of operating a hazardous waste storage facility, Shore has not and will not apply for a permit to do so. Nor do defendants contest that the State incurred certain costs in assessing the conditions at the site and supervising the removal of the drums of hazardous waste.

CERCLA . . .

CERCLA authorizes the federal government to respond in several ways. EPA can use Superfund resources to clean up hazardous waste sites and spills. 42 U.S.C. §9611. The National Contingency Plan ("NCP"), prepared by EPA pursuant to CERCLA, id. §9605, governs cleanup efforts by "establish[ing] procedures and standards for responding to releases of hazardous substances." At the same time, EPA can sue for reimbursement of cleanup costs from any responsible parties it can locate, id. §9607, allowing the federal government to respond immediately while later trying to shift financial responsibility to others. . . . In addition, CERCLA authorizes EPA to seek an injunction in federal district court to force a responsible party to clean up any site or spill that presents an imminent and substantial danger to public health or welfare or the environment. 42 U.S.C. §9606(a). . . .

Congress intended that responsible parties be held strictly liable, even though an explicit provision for strict liability was not included in the compromise. Section 9601(32) provides that "liability" under CERCLA "shall be construed to be the standard of liability" under section 311 of the Clean Water Act, 33 U.S.C. §1321, which courts have held to be strict liability, see, e.g., *Steuart Transportation Co. v. Allied Towing Corp.*, 596 F.2d 609, 613 (4th Cir. 1979), and which Congress understood to impose such liability. . . . Strict liability under CERCLA, however, is not absolute; there are defenses for causation solely by an act of God, an act of war, or acts or omissions of a third party other than an employee or agent of the defendant or one whose act or omission occurs in connection with a contractual relationship with the defendant. 42 U.S.C. §9607(b).

DISCUSSION

A.   LIABILITY FOR RESPONSE COSTS UNDER CERCLA

We hold that the district court properly awarded the State response costs under section 9607(a)(4)(A). The State's costs in assessing the conditions of the site and supervising the removal of the drums of hazardous waste squarely fall within CERCLA's definition of response costs, even though the State is not undertaking to do the removal. See id. §§9601(23), (24), (25). . . .

1. *Covered Persons.* CERCLA holds liable four classes of persons:

(1)   the owner and operator of a vessel (otherwise subject to the jurisdiction of the United States) or a facility,[28]

(2)   any person who at the time of disposal of any hazardous substance owned or operated any facility at which such hazardous substances were disposed of,

(3)   any person who by contract, agreement, or otherwise arranged for disposal or treatment, or arranged with a transporter for transport for disposal or treatment, of hazardous substances owned or possessed by such person, by any other party or entity, at any facility owned or operated by another party or entity and containing such hazardous substances, and

(4)   any person who accepts or accepted any hazardous substances for transport to disposal or treatment facilities or sites selected by such person.

42 U.S.C. §9607(a). As noted above, section 9607 makes these persons liable, if "there is a release, or a threatened release which causes the incurrence of response costs, of a hazardous substance" from the facility, for, among other things, "all costs of removal or remedial action incurred by the United States Government or a State not inconsistent with the national contingency plan."

Shore argues that it is not covered by section 9607(a)(1) because it neither owned the site at the time of disposal nor caused the presence or the release of the hazardous waste at the facility. While section 9607(a)(1) appears to cover Shore, Shore attempts to infuse ambiguity into the statutory scheme, claiming that section 9607(a)(1) could not have been intended to include all owners, because the word "owned" in section 9607(a)(2) would be unnecessary since an owner "at the time

---

28. CERCLA defines the term "facility" broadly to include any property at which hazardous substances have come to be located. See 42 U.S.C. §9601(9).

of disposal" would necessarily be included in section 9607(a)(1). Shore claims that Congress intended that the scope of section 9607(a)(1) be no greater than that of section 9607(a)(2) and that both should be limited by the "at the time of disposal" language. By extension, Shore argues that both provisions should be interpreted as requiring a showing of causation. We agree with the State, however, that section 9607(a)(1) unequivocally imposes strict liability on the current owner of a facility from which there is a release or threat of release, without regard to causation.

Shore's claims of ambiguity are illusory; section 9607(a)'s structure is clear. Congress intended to cover different classes of persons differently. Section 9607(a)(1) applies to all current owners and operators, while section 9607(a)(2) primarily covers prior owners and operators. Moreover, section 9607(a)(2)'s scope is more limited than that of section 9607(a)(1). Prior owners and operators are liable only if they owned or operated the facility "at the time of disposal of any hazardous substance"; this limitation does not apply to current owners, like Shore. . . .

Shore's causation argument is also at odds with the structure of the statute. Interpreting section 9607(a)(1) as including a causation requirement makes superfluous the affirmative defenses provided in section 9607(b), each of which carves out from liability an exception based on causation. Without a clear congressional command otherwise, we will not construe a statute in any way that makes some of its provisions surplusage. . . .

Our interpretation draws further support from the legislative history. Congress specifically rejected including a causation requirement in section 9607(a). . . .

Furthermore, as the State points out, accepting Shore's arguments would open a huge loophole in CERCLA's coverage. It is quite clear that if the current owner of a site could avoid liability merely by having purchased the site after chemical dumping had ceased, waste sites certainly would be sold, following the cessation of dumping, to new owners who could avoid the liability otherwise required by CERCLA. Congress had well in mind that persons who dump or store hazardous waste sometimes cannot be located or may be deceased or judgment-proof. . . .

2. *Release or Threat of Release.* We reject Shore's repeated claims that it has put in dispute whether there has been a release or threat of release at the Shore Road site. The State has established that it was responding to "a release, or a threatened release" when it incurred its response costs. We hold that the leaking tanks and pipelines, the continuing leaching and seepage from the earlier spills, and the leaking drums all constitute "releases." 42 U.S.C. §9601(22). Moreover, the corroding and deteriorating tanks, Shore's lack of expertise in han-

dling hazardous waste, and even the failure to license the facility, amount to a threat of release.

In addition, Shore's suggestion that CERCLA does not impose liability for threatened releases is simply frivolous. Section 9607(a)(4)(A) imposes liability for "all costs of removal or remedial action." The definitions of "removal" and "remedial" explicitly refer to actions "taken in the event of the threat of release of hazardous substances."

3. *The NPL and Consistency with the NCP.* Shore also argues that, because the Shore Road site is not on the NPL, the State's action is inconsistent with the NCP and thus Shore cannot be found liable under section 9607(a). This argument is not frivolous. Section 9607(a)(4)(A) states that polluters are liable for response costs "not inconsistent with the national contingency plan." And section 9605, which directs EPA to outline the NCP, includes a provision that requires EPA to publish the NPL. Nevertheless, we hold that inclusion on the NPL is not a requirement for the State to recover its response costs.

The State claims that, while NPL listing may be a requirement for the use of Superfund money, it is not a requisite to liability under section 9607. See *New York v. General Electric Co.*, 592 F. Supp. 291, 303-04 (N.D.N.Y. 1984). The State relies on the reasoning of several district courts that have held that liability under section 9607 is independent of the scope of section 9611, which governs the expenditure of Superfund monies, and by extension, section 9604, which governs federal cleanup efforts. See, e.g., id.; *United States v. Northeastern Pharmaceutical & Chemical Co.*, 579 F. Supp. 823, 850-51 (W.D. Mo. 1984) ("NEPACCO"); *United States v. Wade*, 577 F. Supp. 1326, 1334-36 (E.D. Pa. 1983). These courts have reasoned that CERCLA authorizes a bifurcated approach to the problem of hazardous waste cleanup, by distinguishing between the scope of direct federal action with Superfund resources and the liability of polluters under section 9607. While implicitly accepting that Superfund monies can be spent only on sites included on the NPL, they conclude that this limitation does not apply to section 9607. And it is true that the relevant limitation on Superfund spending is that it be "consistent with" the NCP, 42 U.S.C. §9604(a), while under section 9607(a)(4)(A), liability is limited to response costs "not inconsistent with" the NCP. This analysis, however, is not so compelling as might be; the distinction between section 9604 and section 9607 blurs for two reasons. First, as we noted above, Congress envisioned section 9607 as a means of reimbursement of monies spent by government on cleanup pursuant to section 9604. The money that the federal government presumably would be spending is Superfund money. That is to say, Congress may have seen section 9607 as equal in scope to sections 9604 and 9611. Second, it is difficult to accept the State's argument that section 9607's statement "[n]otwithstanding any other provision or rule of law" supports the distinction. Shore's argument is not based on implying limitations on the scope of section 9604 into section 9607 but on an interpretation of "not inconsistent with" the NCP under section 9607 itself.

Still, we reject Shore's argument. Instead of distinguishing between the scope of section 9607 and the scope of section 9604, we hold that NPL listing is not a general requirement under the NCP. We see the NPL as a limitation on remedial, or long-term, actions — as opposed to removal, or short-term, actions — particularly federally funded remedial actions. The provisions requiring the establishment of NPL criteria and listing appear to limit their own application to remedial actions. Section 9605(8)(A) requires EPA to include in the NCP "criteria for determining priorities among releases or threatened releases . . . for the purpose of taking remedial action and, to the extent practicable taking into account the potential urgency of such action, for the purpose of taking removal action." . . .

CERCLA's legislative history also supports our conclusion. Congress did not intend listing on the NPL to be a requisite to all response actions. . . .

Moreover, limiting the scope of NPL listing as a requirement for response action is consistent with the purpose of CERCLA. The NPL is a relatively short list when compared with the huge number of hazardous waste facilities Congress sought to clean up. And it makes sense for the federal government to limit only those long-term — remedial — efforts that are federally funded. We hold that Congress intended that, while federally funded remedial efforts be focused solely on those sites on the NPL, states have more flexibility when acting on their own.

Finally, we reject Shore's argument that the State's response costs are not recoverable because the State has failed to comply with the NCP by not obtaining EPA authorization, nor making a firm commitment to provide further funding for remedial implementation nor submitting an estimate of costs. See 40 C.F.R. §300.62 (1984) (describing the states' role in joint federal-state response actions). EPA designed the regulatory scheme — the NCP — focusing on federal and joint federal-state efforts. See, e.g., id. §300.6 (defining "lead agency"). Shore apparently is arguing that EPA has ruled that the State cannot act on its own and seek liability under CERCLA. We disagree. Congress envisioned states' using their own resources for cleanup and recovering those costs from polluters under section 9607(a)(4)(A). We read section 9607(a)(4)(A)'s requirement of consistency with the NCP to mean that states cannot recover costs inconsistent with the response methods outlined in the NCP. . . .

4. *Affirmative defense.* Shore also claims that it can assert an affirmative defense under CERCLA, which provides a limited exception to liability for a release or threat of release caused solely by

an act or omission of a third party other than an employee or agent of the defendant, or than one whose act or omission occurs in connection with a contractual relationship, existing directly or indirectly, with the defendant (except where the sole contractual arrangement arises from a published tariff and acceptance for carriage by a common carrier by rail), if the defendant establishes by a preponderance of the evidence that (a) he exercised due care with respect to the hazardous substance concerned, taking into consideration the characteristics of such hazardous substance, in light of all relevant facts and circumstances, and (b) he took precautions against foreseeable acts or omissions of any such third party and the consequences that could foreseeably result from such acts or omissions.

42 U.S.C. §9607(b)(3). We disagree. Shore argues that it had nothing to do with the transportation of the hazardous substances and that it has exercised due care since taking control of the site. Who the "third part(ies)" Shore claims were responsible is difficult to fathom. It is doubtful that a prior owner could be such, especially the prior owner here, since the acts or omissions referred to in the statute are doubtless those occurring during the ownership or operation of the defendant. Similarly, many of the acts and omissions of the prior tenants/operators fall outside the scope of section 9607(b)(3), because they occurred before Shore owned the property. In addition, we find that Shore cannot rely on the affirmative defense even with respect to the tenants' conduct during the period after Shore closed on the property and when Shore evicted the tenants. Shore was aware of the nature of the tenants' activities before the closing and could readily have foreseen that they would continue to dump hazardous waste at the site. In light of this knowledge, we cannot say that the releases and threats of release resulting of these activities were "caused solely" by the tenants or that Shore "took precautions against" these "foreseeable acts or omissions." . . .

Judgment affirmed.

UNITED STATES EPA v. MONSANTO CO.

858 F.2d 160 (4th Cir. 1988)

SPROUSE, Circuit Judge:

Oscar Seidenberg and Harvey Hutchinson (the site-owners) and Allied Corporation, Monsanto Company, and EM Industries, Inc. (the generator defendants), appeal from the district court's entry of summary judgment holding them liable to the United States and the State of South Carolina (the governments) under section 107(a) of the Comprehensive Environmental Response, Compensation, and Liability Act of 1980 (CERCLA). 42 U.S.C.A. §9607(a) (West Supp. 1987). The court determined that the defendants were liable jointly and severally for $1,813,624 in response costs accrued from the partial removal of hazardous waste from a disposal facility located near Columbia, South Carolina. The court declined, however, to assess prejudgment interest against the defendants. We affirm the district court's liability holdings. . . .

I

In 1972, Seidenberg and Hutchinson leased a four-acre tract of land they owned to the Columbia Organic Chemical Company (COCC), a South Carolina chemical manufacturing corporation. The property, located along Bluff Road near Columbia, South Carolina, consisted of a small warehouse and surrounding areas. The lease was verbal, on a month-to-month basis, and according to the site-owners' deposition testimony, was executed for the sole purpose of allowing COCC to store raw materials and finished products in the warehouse. Seidenberg and Hutchinson received monthly lease payments of $200, which increased to $350 by 1980.

In the mid-1970s, COCC expanded its business to include the brokering and recycling of chemical waste generated by third parties. It used the Bluff Road site as a waste storage and disposal facility for its new operations. In 1976, COCC's principals incorporated South Carolina Recycling and Disposal Inc. (SCRDI), for the purpose of assuming COCC's waste-handling business, and the site-owners began accepting lease payments from SCRDI. SCRDI contracted with numerous off-site waste producers for the transport, recycling, and disposal of chemical and other waste. Among these producers were agencies of the federal government and South Carolina, and various private entities including the three generator defendants in this litigation. Although SCRDI operated other disposal sites, it deposited much of the waste it received at the Bluff Road facility. The waste stored at Bluff Road contained many chemical substances that federal law defines as "hazardous."

Between 1976 and 1980, SCRDI haphazardly deposited more than 7,000 fifty-five gallon drums of chemical waste on the four-acre Bluff Road site. It placed waste laden drums and containers wherever there was space, often without pallets to protect them from the damp ground. It stacked drums on top of one another without regard to the chemical compatibility of their contents. It maintained no documented safety procedures and kept no inventory of the stored chemicals. Over time many of the drums rusted, rotted, and otherwise deteriorated. Hazardous substances leaked from the decaying drums and oozed into the ground. The substances commingled with incompatible chemicals that had escaped from other containers, generating noxious fumes, fires, and explosions.

On October 26, 1977, a toxic cloud formed when chemicals leaking from rusted drums reacted with rainwater. Twelve responding firemen were hospitalized. Again, on July 24, 1979, an explosion and fire resulted when chemicals stored in glass jars leaked onto drums containing incompatible substances. SCRDI'S site manager could not identify the substances that caused the explosion, making the fire difficult to extinguish.

In 1980, the Environmental Protection Agency (EPA) inspected the Bluff Road site. Its investigation revealed that the facility was filled well beyond its capacity with chemical waste. The number of drums and the reckless manner in which they were stacked precluded access to various areas in the site. Many of the drums observed were unlabeled, or their labels had become unreadable from exposure, rendering it impossible to identify their contents. The EPA concluded that the site posed "a major fire hazard."

Later that year, the United States filed suit under section 7003 of the Resource Conservation and Recovery Act, 42 U.S.C. §6973, against SCRDI, COCC, and Oscar Seidenberg. The complaint was filed before the December 11, 1980, effective date of CERCLA, and it sought only injunctive relief. Thereafter, the State of South Carolina intervened as a plaintiff in the pending action.

In the course of discovery, the governments identified a number of waste generators, including the generator defendants in this appeal, that had contracted with SCRDI for waste disposal. The governments notified the generators that they were potentially responsible for the costs of cleanup at Bluff Road under section 107(a) of the newly-enacted CERCLA. As a result of these contacts, the governments executed individual settlement agreements with twelve of the identified off-site producers. The generator defendants, however, declined to settle.

Using funds received from the settlements, the governments contracted with Triangle Resource Industries (TRI) to conduct a partial surface cleanup at the site. The contract required RAD Services, Inc., a subsidiary of TRI, to remove 75% of the drums found there and to keep a log of the removed drums. RAD completed its partial cleanup operation in October 1982. The log it prepared documented that it had removed containers and drums bearing the labels or markings of each of the three generator defendants.

The EPA reinspected the site after the first phase of the cleanup had been completed. The inspection revealed that closed drums and containers labeled with the insignia of each of the three generator defendants remained at the site. The EPA also collected samples of surface water, soil, and sediment from the site. Laboratory tests of the samples disclosed that several hazardous substances contained in the waste the generator defendants had shipped to the site remained present at the site.

Thereafter, South Carolina completed the remaining 25% of the surface cleanup. It used federal funds from the Hazardous Substances Response Trust Fund (Superfund), 42 U.S.C. §9631, as well as state money from the South Carolina Hazardous Waste Contingency Fund, S.C. Code Ann. §44-56-160, and in-kind contribution of other state funds to match the federal contribution.

In 1982, the governments filed an amended complaint, adding the three generator defendants and site-owner Harvey Hutchinson, and including claims under section 107(a) of CERCLA against all of the nonsettling defendants. The governments alleged that the generator defendants and site-owners were jointly and severally liable under section 107(a) for the costs expended completing the surface cleanup at Bluff Road.

In response, the site-owners contended that they were innocent absentee landlords unaware of and unconnected to the waste disposal activities that took place on their land. They maintained that their lease with COCC did not allow COCC (or SCRDI) to store chemical waste on the premises, but they admitted that they became aware of waste storage in 1977 and accepted lease payments until 1980.

The generator defendants likewise denied liability for the governments' response costs. Among other defenses, they claimed that none of their specific waste materials contributed to the hazardous conditions at Bluff Road, and that retroactive imposition of CERCLA liability on them was unconstitutional. They also asserted that they could establish an affirmative defense to CERCLA liability under section 107(b)(3), 42 U.S.C. §9607(b)(3), by showing that the harm at the site was caused solely through the conduct of unrelated third parties. All parties thereafter moved for summary judgment.

After an evidentiary hearing, the district court granted the governments' summary judgment motion on CERCLA liability. The court found that all of the defendants were responsible parties under section 107(a), and that none of them had presented sufficient evidence to support an affirmative defense under section 107(b). The court further concluded that the environmental harm at Bluff Road was "indivisible," and it held all of the defendants jointly and severally liable for the governments' response costs. *United States v. South Carolina Recycling & Disposal, Inc.*, 653 F. Supp. 984 (D.S.C. 1984) (SCRDI).

As to the site-owners' liability, the court found it sufficient that they owned the Bluff Road site at the time hazardous substances were deposited there. Id. at 993 (interpreting 42 U.S.C.A. §9607(a)(2) (West Supp. 1987)). It rejected their contentions that Congress did not intend to subject "innocent" landowners to CERCLA liability. The court similarly found summary judgment appropriate against the generator defendants because it was undisputed that (1) they shipped hazardous substances to the Bluff Road facility; (2) hazardous substances "like" those present in the generator defendants' waste were found at the facility; and (3) there had been a release of hazardous substances at the site. SCRDI, 653 F. Supp. at 991-93 (interpreting 42 U.S.C.A. §9607(a)(3) (West Supp. 1987)). . . . This appeal followed. . . .

II

A.   SITE-OWNERS' LIABILITY

In light of the strict liability imposed by section 107(a), we cannot agree with the site-owners' contention that they are not within the class of owners Congress intended to hold liable. The traditional elements of tort culpability on which the site-owners rely simply are absent from the statute. The plain language of section 107(a)(2) extends liability to owners of waste facilities regardless of their degree of participation in the subsequent disposal of hazardous waste.

Under section 107(a)(2), any person who owned a facility at a time when hazardous substances were deposited there may be held liable for all costs of removal or remedial action if a release or threatened release of a hazardous substance occurs. The site-owners do not dispute their ownership of the Bluff Road facility, or the fact that releases occurred there during their period of ownership. Under these circumstances, all the prerequisites to section 107(a) liability have been satisfied.[29] See *Shore Realty*, 759 F.2d at 1043-44 (site-owner held liable under CERCLA section 107(a)(1) even though he did not contribute to the presence or cause the release of hazardous substances at the facility).[30]

The site-owners nonetheless contend that the district court's grant of summary judgment improperly denied them the opportunity to present an affirmative defense under section 107(b)(3). Section 107(b)(3) sets forth a limited affirmative defense based on the complete absence of causation. See *Shore Realty*, 759 F.2d at 1044. It requires proof that

---

29. The site-owners' relative degree of fault would, of course, be relevant in any subsequent action for contribution brought pursuant to 42 U.S.C.A. §9613(f) (West Supp. 1987). Congress, in the Superfund Amendments and Reauthorization Act of 1986, Pub. L. 99-499, §113, 100 Stat. 1613, 1647 (1986) [hereafter SARA], established a right of contribution in favor of defendants sued under CERCLA section 107(a). . . .

30. Congress, in section 101(35) of SARA, acknowledged that landowners may affirmatively avoid liability if they can prove they did not know and had no reason to know that hazardous substances were disposed of on their land at the time they acquired title or possession. 42 U.S.C.A. §9601(35) (West Supp. 1987). This explicitly drafted exception further signals Congress' intent to impose liability on landowners who cannot satisfy its express requirements.

the release or threatened release of hazardous substances and resulting damages were caused solely by "a third party other than . . . one whose act or omission occurs in connection with a contractual relationship, existing directly or indirectly, with the defendant. . . ." 42 U.S.C. §9607(b)(3). A second element of the defense requires proof that the defendant "took precautions against foreseeable acts or omissions of any such third party and the consequences that could foreseeably result from such acts or omissions." Id. We agree with the district court that under no view of the evidence could the site-owners satisfy either of these proof requirements.

First, the site-owners could not establish the absence of a direct or indirect contractual relationship necessary to maintain the affirmative defense. They concede they entered into a lease agreement with COCC. They accepted rent from COCC, and after SCRDI was incorporated, they accepted rent from SCRDI. See *United States v. Northernaire Plating Co.*, 670 F. Supp. 742, 747-48 (W.D. Mich. 1987) (owner who leased facility to disposing party could not assert affirmative defense). Second, the site-owners presented no evidence that they took precautionary action against the foreseeable conduct of COCC or SCRDI. They argued to the trial court that, although they were aware COCC was a chemical manufacturing company, they were completely ignorant of all waste disposal activities at Bluff Road before 1977. They maintained that they never inspected the site prior to that time. In our view, the statute does not sanction such willful or negligent blindness on the part of absentee owners. The district court committed no error in entering summary judgment against the site-owners.

B.   GENERATOR DEFENDANTS' LIABILITY

The generator defendants first contend that the district court misinterpreted section 107(a)(3) because it failed to read into the statute a requirement that the governments prove a nexus between the waste they sent to the site and the resulting environmental harm. They maintain that the statutory phrase "containing such hazardous substances" requires proof that the specific substances they generated and sent to the site were present at the facility at the time of release. The district court held, however, that the statute was satisfied by proof that hazardous substances "like" those contained in the generator defendants' waste were found at the site. SCRDI, 653 F. Supp. at 991-992. We agree with the district court's interpretation.

Reduced of surplus language, sections 107(a)(3) and (4) impose liability on off-site waste generators who: "arranged for disposal . . . of hazardous substances . . . at any facility . . . *containing such hazardous substances* . . . from which there is a release . . . of a hazardous substance." 42 U.S.C.A. §§9607(a)(3), (4) (West Supp. 1987) (emphasis supplied). In our view, the plain meaning of the adjective "such" in the phrase "containing such hazardous substances" is "[a]like, similar, of the like kind." Black's Law Dictionary 1284 (5th ed. 1979). As used in the statute, the phrase "such hazardous substances" denotes hazardous substances alike, similar, or of a like kind to those that were present in a generator defendant's waste or that could have been produced by the mixture of the defendant's waste with other waste present at the site. It does not mean that the plaintiff must trace the ownership of each generic chemical compound found at a site. Absent proof that a generator defendant's specific waste remained at a facility at the time of release, a showing of chemical similarity between hazardous substances is sufficient.[31]

The overall structure of CERCLA'S liability provisions also militates against the generator defendants' "proof of ownership" argument. In *Shore Realty*, the Second Circuit held with respect to site-owners that requiring proof of ownership at any time later than the time of disposal would go far toward rendering the section 107(b) defenses superfluous. Shore Realty, 759 F.2d at 1044. We agree with the court's reading of the statute and conclude that its reasoning applies equally to the generator defendants' contentions. As the statute provides — "[n]otwithstanding any other provision or rule of law" — liability under section 107(a) is "subject only to the defenses set forth" in section 107(b). 42 U.S.C.A. §9607(a) (West Supp. 1987) (emphasis added). Each of the three defenses established in section 107(b) "carves out from liability an exception based on causation." *Shore Realty*, 759 F.2d at 1044. Congress has, therefore, allocated the burden of disproving causation to the defendant who profited from the generation and inexpensive disposal of hazardous waste. We decline to interpret the statute in a way that would neutralize the force of Congress' intent.

Finally, the purpose underlying CERCLA's liability provisions counsels against the generator defendants' argument. Throughout the statute's legislative history, there appears the recurring theme of facilitating prompt action to remedy the environmental blight of unscrupulous waste disposal. In deleting causation language from section 107(a), we assume as have many other courts, that Congress knew of the synergistic and migratory capacities of leaking chemical waste, and the technological infeasibility of tracing improperly disposed waste to its source. In view of this, we will not frustrate the statute's salutary goals by en-

---

31. CERCLA plaintiffs need not perform exhaustive chemical analyses of hazardous substances found at a disposal site. See SCRDI, 653 F. Supp. at 993 n.6. They must, however, present evidence that a generator defendant's waste was shipped to a site and that hazardous substances similar to those contained in the defendant's waste remained present at the time of release. The defendant, of course, may in turn present evidence of an affirmative defense to liability.

grafting a "proof of ownership" requirement, which in practice, would be as onerous as the language Congress saw fit to delete. See *United States v. Wade*, 577 F. Supp. 1326, 1332 (E.D. Pa. 1983) ("To require a plaintiff under CERCLA to 'fingerprint' wastes is to eviscerate the statute."). . . .

III

The appellants next challenge the district court's imposition of joint and several liability for the governments' response costs.[32] The court concluded that joint and several liability was appropriate because the environmental harm at Bluff Road was "indivisible" and the appellants had "failed to meet their burden of proving otherwise." SCRDI, 653 F. Supp. at 994. We agree with its conclusion.

While CERCLA does not mandate the imposition of joint and several liability, it permits it in cases of indivisible harm. See *Shore Realty,* 759 F.2d at 1042 n.13; *United States v. ChemDyne*, 572 F. Supp. 802, 810-11 (S.D. Ohio 1983). In each case, the court must consider traditional and evolving principles of federal common law,[33] which Congress has left to the courts to supply interstitially.

Under common law rules, when two or more persons act independently to cause a single harm for which there is a reasonable basis of apportionment according to the contribution of each, each is held liable only for the portion of harm that he causes. *Edmonds v. Compagnie Generale Transatlantique*, 443 U.S. 256, 260 n.8, 99 S. Ct. 2753, 2756 n.8, 61 L. Ed. 2d 521 (1979). When such persons cause a single and indivisible harm, however, they are held liable jointly and severally for the entire harm. Id. (citing Restatement (Second) of Torts §433A (1965)). We think these principles, as reflected in the Restatement (Second) of

---

32. The site-owners limit their joint and several liability argument to the contention that it is inequitable under the circumstances of this case, i.e., their limited degree of participation in waste disposal activities at Bluff Road. As we have stated, however, such equitable factors are relevant in subsequent actions for contribution. They are not pertinent to the question of joint and several liability, which focuses principally on the divisibility among responsible parties of the harm to the environment.

33. As many courts have noted, a proposed requirement that joint and several liability be imposed in all CERCLA cases was deleted from the final version of the bill. See, e.g., *Chem-Dyne*, 572 F. Supp. at 806. "The deletion," however, "was not intended as a rejection of joint and several liability," but rather "to have the scope of liability determined under common law principles." Id. at 808. We adopt the *Chem-Dyne* court's thorough discussion of CERCLA's legislative history with respect to joint and several liability. We note that the approach taken in *Chem-Dyne* was subsequently confirmed as correct by Congress in its consideration of SARA's contribution provisions. See H.R. Rep. No. 253(I), 99th Cong. 2d Sess., 79-80 (1985), reprinted in 1986 U.S. Code Cong. & Admin. News at 2835, 2861-62.

Torts, represent the correct and uniform federal rules applicable to CERCLA cases.

Section 433A of the Restatement provides:

> (1)   Damages for harm are to be apportioned among two or more causes where
>> (a)   there are distinct harms, or
>> (b)   there is a reasonable basis for determining the contribution of each cause to a single harm.
> (2)   Damages for any other harm cannot be apportioned among two or more causes.

Restatement (Second) of Torts §433A (1965).

Placing their argument into the Restatement framework, the generator defendants concede that the environmental damage at Bluff Road constituted a "single harm," but contend that there was a reasonable basis for apportioning the harm. They observe that each of the off-site generators with whom SCRDI contracted sent a potentially identifiable volume of waste to the Bluff Road site, and they maintain that liability should have been apportioned according to the volume they deposited as compared to the total volume disposed of there by all parties. In light of the conditions at Bluff Road, we cannot accept this method as a basis for apportionment.

The generator defendants bore the burden of establishing a reasonable basis for apportioning liability among responsible parties. *Chem-Dyne,* 572 F. Supp. at 810; Restatement (Second) of Torts §433B (1965).[34] To meet this burden, the generator defendants had to establish that the environmental harm at Bluff Road was divisible among responsible parties. They presented no evidence, however, showing a relationship between waste volume, the release of hazardous substances, and the harm at the site.[35] Further, in light of the commingling

---

34. Section 433(B)(2) of the Restatement provides: Where the tortious conduct of two or more actors has combined to bring about harm to the plaintiff, and one or more of the actors seeks to limit his liability on the ground that the harm is capable of apportionment among them, the burden of proof as to the apportionment is upon each such actor. Restatement (Second) of Torts §433(B)(2) (1965).

35. At minimum, such evidence was crucial to demonstrate that a volumetric apportionment scheme was reasonable. The governments presented considerable evidence identifying numerous hazardous substances found at Bluff Road. An EPA investigator reported, for example, that in the first cleanup phase RAD Services encountered substances "in every hazard class, including explosives such as crystallized dynamite and nitroglycerine. Numerous examples were found of oxidizers, flammable and nonflammable liquids, poisons, corrosives, containerized gases, and even a small amount of radioactive material." Under these circumstances, volumetric apportionment based on the overall quantity of waste, as opposed to the quantity and quality of hazardous substances contained in the waste would have made little sense.

of hazardous substances, the district court could not have reasonably apportioned liability without some evidence disclosing the individual and interactive qualities of the substances deposited there. Common sense counsels that a million gallons of certain substances could be mixed together without significant consequences, whereas a few pints of others improperly mixed could result in disastrous consequences.[36] Under other circumstances proportionate volumes of hazardous substances may well be probative of contributory harm.[37] In this case, however, volume could not establish the effective contribution of each waste generator to the harm at the Bluff Road site.

Although we find no error in the trial court's imposition of joint and several liability, we share the appellants' concern that they not be ultimately responsible for reimbursing more than their just portion of the governments' response costs.[38] In its refusal to apportion liability, the district court likewise recognized the validity of their demand that they not be required to shoulder a disproportionate amount of the costs. It ruled, however, that making the governments whole for response costs was the primary consideration and that cost allocation was a matter "more appropriately considered in an action for contribution between responsible parties after plaintiff has been made whole." SCRDI, 653 F. Supp. at 995 & n.8. Had we sat in place of the district court, we would have ruled as it did on the apportionment issue, but may well have retained the action to dispose of the contribution questions. See 42 U.S.C.A. §9613(f) (West Supp. 1987). That procedural course, however, was committed to the trial court's discretion and we find no abuse of it. As we have stated, the defendants still have the right

---

36. We agree with the district court that evidence disclosing the relative toxicity, migratory potential, and synergistic capacity of the hazardous substances at the site would be relevant to establishing divisibility of harm.

37. Volumetric contributions provide a reasonable basis for apportioning liability only if it can be reasonably assumed, or it has been demonstrated, that independent factors had no substantial effect on the harm to the environment. Cf. Restatement (Second) of Torts §433A comment d, illustrations 4, 5 (1965).

38. The final judgment holds the defendants liable for slightly less than half of the total costs incurred in the cleanup, while it appears that the generator defendants collectively produced approximately 22% of the waste that SCRDI handled. Other evidence indicates that agencies of the federal government produced more waste than did generator defendant Monsanto, and suggests that the amounts contributed by the settling parties do not bear a strictly proportionate relationship to the total costs of cleaning the facility. We note, however, that a substantial portion of the final judgment is attributable to litigation costs. We also observe that the EPA has contributed upwards of $50,000 to the Bluff Road cleanup, and that any further claims against the EPA and other responsible government instrumentalities may be resolved in a contribution action pursuant to CERCLA section 113(f).

to sue responsible parties for contribution, and in that action they may assert both legal and equitable theories of cost allocation.[39]

IV

The generator defendants raise numerous constitutional challenges to the district court's interpretation and application of CERCLA. They contend that the imposition of "disproportionate" liability without proof of causation violated constitutional limitations on retroactive statutory application and that it converted CERCLA into a bill of attainder and an ex post facto law. They further assert, along with the site-owners, that the trial court's construction of CERCLA infringed their substantive due process rights.

The district court held that CERCLA does not create retroactive liability, but imposes a prospective obligation for the post-enactment environmental consequences of the defendants' past acts. SCRDI, 653 F. Supp. at 996. Alternatively, the court held that even if CERCLA is understood to operate retroactively, it nonetheless satisfies the dictates of due process because its liability scheme is rationally related to a valid legislative purpose. Id. at 997-98. We agree with the court's latter holding, and we find no merit to the generator defendants' bill of attainder and ex post facto arguments.

Many courts have concluded that Congress intended CERCLA's liability provisions to apply retroactively to pre-enactment disposal activities of off-site waste generators. They have held uniformly that retroactive operation survives the Supreme Court's tests for due process validity. We agree with their analyses.

In *Usery v. Turner Elkhorn Mining Co.*, 428 U.S. 1, 96 S. Ct. 2882, 49 L. Ed. 2d 752 (1976), the Supreme Court, in a different context, rejected a due process challenge to the retroactive operation of the liability provisions in the Black Lung Benefits Act of 1972. The Court stated that "a presumption of constitutionality" attaches to "legislative Acts adjusting the burdens and benefits of economic life," and that "the burden is on one complaining of a due process violation to establish that the legislature has acted in an arbitrary and irrational way." Id. at

---

39. Contrary to the generator defendants' request, it would be premature for us to interpret the effect of settlement on the rights of nonsettling parties in contribution actions under CERCLA section 113(f)(2), 42 U.S.C.A. §9613(f)(2) (West Supp. 1987). We observe, however, that the possibility this subsection precludes contribution actions against settling parties signals legislative policy to encourage settlement in CERCLA cleanup actions. At the same time, we recognize that the language of CERCLA's new contribution provisions reveals Congress' concern that the relative culpability of each responsible party be considered in determining the proportionate share of costs each must bear.

15, 96 S. Ct. at 2892. It reasoned that although the Act imposed new liability for disabilities developed prior to its enactment, its operation was "justified as a rational measure to spread the costs of the employees' disabilities to those who have profited from the fruits of their labor." Id. at 18, 96 S. Ct. at 2893.

The reasoning of *Turner Elkhorn* applies with great force to the retroactivity contentions advanced here. While the generator defendants profited from inexpensive waste disposal methods that may have been technically "legal" prior to CERCLA's enactment, it was certainly foreseeable at the time that improper disposal could cause enormous damage to the environment. CERCLA operates remedially to spread the costs of responding to improper waste disposal among all parties that played a role in creating the hazardous conditions. Where those conditions are indivisible, joint and several liability is logical, and it works to ensure complete cost recovery. We do not think these consequences are "particularly harsh and oppressive," *United States Trust Co. v. New Jersey*, 431 U.S. 1, 17 n.13, 97 S. Ct. 1505, 1515 n.13, 52 L. Ed. 2d 92 (1977) (retrospective civil liability not unconstitutional unless it is particularly harsh and oppressive), and we agree with the Eighth Circuit that retroactive application of CERCLA does not violate due process. *United States v. Northeastern Pharmaceutical & Chemical Co., Inc.*, 810 F.2d 726, 734 (8th Cir.1986), *cert. denied*, — U.S. — , 108 S. Ct. 146, 98 L. Ed. 2d 102 (1987).

Nor does the imposition of strict, joint and several liability convert CERCLA into a bill of attainder or an ex post facto law. *United States v. Conservation Chemical Co.*, 619 F. Supp. 162, 214 (W.D. Mo. 1985). The infliction of punishment, either legislatively or retrospectively, is a sine qua non of legislation that runs afoul of these constitutional prohibitions. See *Nixon v. Administrator of General Services*, 433 U.S. 425, 473-84, 97 S. Ct. 2777, 2805-11, 53 L. Ed. 2d 867 (1977) (bill of attainder analysis); *Weaver v. Graham*, 450 U.S. 24, 28-30, 101 S. Ct. 960, 963-65, 67 L. Ed. 2d 17 (1981) (ex post facto law analysis). CERCLA does not exact punishment. Rather it creates a reimbursement obligation on any person judicially determined responsible for the costs of remedying hazardous conditions at a waste disposal facility. The restitution of cleanup costs was not intended to operate, nor does it operate in fact, as a criminal penalty or a punitive deterrent. Cf. *Tull v. United States*, 481 U.S. 412, 107 S. Ct. 1831, 1838, 95 L. Ed. 2d 365 (1987) (distinguishing civil penalties under Clean Water Act from equitable remedy of restitution). Moreover, as this case amply demonstrates, Congress did not impose that obligation automatically on a legislatively defined class of persons.[40] . . .

---

40. The existence of joint and several liability in cases of indivisible harm does not transform an otherwise constitutional obligation into one that exacts

WIDENER, Circuit Judge, concurring and dissenting:

I concur in the majority opinion in all respects save its decision not to require the district court to treat the issue of allocation of costs of cleanup among the various defendants, at 172-173, and, as to that, I respectfully dissent. While it may be true that a subsequent suit for contribution may adequately apportion the damages among the defendants, I am of opinion that the district court, as a court of equity, is required to retain jurisdiction and answer that question now.

So far as I know, it is now and has been the general law without any variance that when a court of equity has jurisdiction it "will decide all matters in dispute and decree complete relief," e.g. *Alexander v. Hillman,* 296 U.S. 222, 242, 56 S. Ct. 204, 211, 80 L. Ed. 192 (1935), see Pomeroy's Equity Jurisprudence, 3rd Ed (1905) §181, 231, and that a court of equity should dispose of a case "so as to end litigation, not to foster it; to diminish suits, not to multiply them." *Payne v. Hook,* 74 U.S. (7 Wall) 425, 432, 19 L. Ed. 260, 262 (1869). . . .

I see great danger in postponing the ultimate apportioning of the damages to a later day. As an example, a small generator which deposited a few gallons of relatively innocuous waste liquid at a site is jointly and severally liable for the entire cost of cleanup under this decision. And with that I agree. If that generator were readily available and solvent, however, the government might well, and probably would, proceed against him first in collecting its judgment. The vagaries of and delays in his subsequent suit for contribution might result in needless financial disaster. I do not see this as a desired or even permissible result.

The statute involved, 42 U.S.C. 9613(f)(1), provides that "*[a]ny person* may seek contribution from any other person who is liable or potentially liable under section 9607(a) of this title during or following any civil action under section 9606 of this title or under section 9607(a) of this title." (Italics added.) Thus, the statute plainly provides that discretion with respect to contribution is not in the district court to consider relief or not as the majority opinion holds; rather, it is in the generator to seek relief, for "any person" certainly includes the generators of the waste. So, since the matter was brought before the district court, that court had no discretion but to decide the question. To repeat, the discretion is in the party to make the claim, not in the district court to defer decision. While I agree that the claims may be asserted in a separate action, if they are asserted in the main case they must be decided. . . .

---

punishment. "Where there are opportunities for contribution . . . as well as for joinder or impleader of responsible parties (Fed. R. Civ. P. Rules 14, 20 and 21), it can hardly be said that imposition of joint and several liability would be unconstitutional." *Conservation Chemical,* 619 F. Supp. at 214-15.

Not only do the statute and federal procedural law require the course I have suggested, I think that the interests of justice as well as judicial economy are best served by proceeding in that manner.

NOTES AND QUESTIONS

1. In what ways do Superfund's liability provisions go beyond the scope of responsibility under traditional tort principles? Consider the following elements:

- standard of liability
- causation
- range of parties that can be held liable
- defenses

2. Does the *Monsanto* case imply that any responsible party, no matter how insignificant its contribution to the dangerous waste site, is liable for the entire cost of cleanup? What must a de minimis party show in order to escape such crushing liability? Is this showing possible in the context of most seriously contaminated waste sites? What other options exist for allotting liability? Consider Judge Widener's dissent.

An amendment proposed by then Representative Gore would have apportioned liability according the following criteria:

   (i)   the ability of the parties to demonstrate that their contribution to a discharge, release or disposal of a hazardous waste can be distinguished;
   (ii)   the amount of the hazardous waste involved;
   (iii) the degree of toxicity of the hazardous waste involved;
   (iv)   the degree of involvement by the parties in the generation, transportation, treatment, storage, or disposal of the hazardous waste;
   (v)   the degree of care exercised by the parties with respect to the hazardous waste concerned, taking into account the characteristics of such hazardous waste; and
   (vi)   the degree of cooperation by the parties with federal, state, or local officials to prevent any harm to the public health or the environment.

126 Cong. Rec. at H9461. Although the Gore amendment only passed in the House of Representatives and hence was not incorporated into the final version of Superfund, a few courts have held that the Gore approach is consistent with congressional intent and more fair than the indiscriminate imposition of joint and several liability. See, e.g., *United*

States v. A & F Materials Co., 578 F. Supp. 1249, 1256 (1984). Is this approach more fair than the *Chem-Dyne/Monsanto* approach? Is it more workable? Is it permissible under Superfund? Might it hinder the government's ability to expedite cost recovery cases?

3. Suppose that a generator of waste ensured that its wastes were disposed only at state-licensed hazardous waste facilities. Would conclusive evidence of such efforts absolve the generator of Superfund liability? What if the state were seeking recovery of its response costs?

4. Are there any circumstances in which the owner of contaminated land is not liable for response costs? If so, what steps would a purchaser of land have to take in order to insulate itself from Superfund liability?

5. Superfund's legislative history evinces a congressional intent to impose the costs of hazardous waste cleanup upon those entities responsible for creating the public health hazard. Do the liability provisions, as interpreted by the courts, carry out this purpose?

2. UNITED STATES ENVIRONMENTAL PROTECTION AGENCY V. RETEP CHEMICAL CORPORATION: A CASE STUDY

Site History

Formation of RETEP Chemical Corporation

As oil prices began to rise rapidly in the early 1970s, James Reid, an engineer working for Amalgamated Technologies, and Steven Tepperman, Vice-President of Amalgamated Technologies in charge of corporate development, came up with an innovative idea for a new venture: a company that would convert contaminated solvents and oily wastes generated by industrial processes into chemical fractions that could be reused or burned as fuel. Amalgamated Technologies would benefit from the venture because its many divisions could use any recycled products and fuels that were not repurchased by the generators of the wastes. For example, Amalgamated Technologies' cement division could burn a wide range of waste products because of the high temperatures at which its kilns operate. Reid and Tepperman hastily drew up some revenue and cost projections for their proposed venture and presented them to the Amalgamated Technologies Board of Directors. The Board liked the idea of profiting from the mounting energy crisis and approved the project.

On the advice of tax and corporate counsel, the Amalgamated Technologies Board decided to set up the venture as a wholly owned subsidiary corporation called RETEP Chemical Corporation ("RE-TEP"). James Reid was named president of RETEP. (Mr. Reid resigned his post at Amalgamated Technologies.) The Board of Directors of RE-TEP comprised four members of Amalgamated Technologies' Board (Alexander Maxwell, President of Amalgamated Technologies; Susan Friedman, Vice President and Treasurer of Amalgamated Technologies; Steven Tepperman; and Daniel Williams, Esq., General Counsel to Amalgamated Technologies) and James Reid.

RETEP began with $1,000,000 in contributed capital. Until operations were underway, Amalgamated Technologies provided RETEP with support personnel. RETEP was also able to purchase some of its start-up equipment from Amalgamated Technologies at reduced prices.

Since Amalgamated Technologies promised RETEP a captured market for products that were not repurchased by generators, Reid was most concerned with assuring a steady supply of waste products. With the electrical and electronic machinery industry exhibiting the greatest growth and growth potential in Massachusetts, Reid decided that RE-TEP should be prepared to process the waste generated by firms in that industry. According to studies available at the time, the electrical and electronic machinery industry in Massachusetts was a large generator of solvents, second only to a related industry producing measuring, analyzing, and controlling instruments (photographic, medical and optical, and chronometers). Although it was on the decline, the textile mill products industry (dyeing and finishing) in Massachusetts also generated significant quantities of waste solvents. In addition, both the electrical machinery and measurement instrument industries, as well as the non-electrical machinery industry and the rubber industry, generated large volumes of contaminated waste oils.

Reid concluded that RETEP should have capability to recover solvents from these waste streams. This would require a large investment in distillation equipment. RETEP would also need detoxification (aqueous treatment) facilities for treating subsidiary wastes of its recycling customers.

History of the RETEP Site

In November 1973, RETEP purchased a five-acre site in Brower, Massachusetts for $500,000. This purchase was financed in part by a $300,000, 20-year mortgage from the Atlantic Security Bank. RETEP immediately assembled a pre-fabricated building to serve as an office and laboratory and installed a distilling tower, small boiler (for supplying steam for distillation), small electrical transformer, and storage tanks. RETEP also began construction of a treatment building for detoxification (containing processing tanks, pumps, and storage tanks) and an unloading dock.

In February 1974, RETEP received a hazardous waste treatment and disposal license from the Massachusetts Department of Environmental Quality Engineering (DEQE). RETEP began operations on April 1, 1974. With fuel prices high as a result of the OPEC oil embargo, RETEP had to pay between 2 and 10 cents per gallon of solvents and oily wastes. It purchased some wastes directly from generators who agreed to repurchase the recovered products from RETEP at a predetermined price. RETEP also purchased wastes from collectors who remove wastes from generators free of charge. RETEP converted these wastes to products that it could sell to Amalgamated Technologies. RETEP also treated and disposed of small quantities of aqueous wastes for a fee based on volume and content of the waste stream.

As one of a few recovery operations in the Massachusetts Bay area in the mid-1970s, RETEP had little difficulty obtaining the types of waste products it could recycle most profitably. RETEP could afford to turn away waste products containing high levels of contaminants or impurities. In June 1975, RETEP expanded its facility by leasing a five-acre tract adjoining its facility from 21st Century Realty.[41] RETEP added additional storage capacity and detoxification equipment (evaporation tanks, filtration equipment) on the new tract.

RETEP's business continued to thrive through the latter part of 1975, 1976, and most of 1977. By late 1977, however, numerous economic and regulatory changes began to alter RETEP's profitability. The continuing energy crisis led many waste generators to modify their industrial processes in order to reduce their output of contaminated wastes; many generators also installed on-site recycling equipment. Increased competition in the waste recovery business attributable to the entry of two waste reprocessing firms in eastern Massachusetts also reduced the availability of contaminated solvents and waste oils for RETEP. Moreover, RETEP faced higher charges for disposal of residual sludges at secure landfills as a result of increased state and federal regulation of disposal facilities and a growing shortage of disposal sites.

These factors increased both the price RETEP had to pay for contaminated solvents and the cost of processing wastes. Amalgamated Technologies contributed to RETEP's problems by pressuring Reid to sell Amalgamated Technologies burnable wastes at sub-market prices. As a result of this array of factors, RETEP began accepting more highly

---

41. The lease with 21st Century Realty expressly stated that "hazardous wastes may not be disposed on the leased land. The lessee may not handle waste materials on the land without a valid permit from the Department of Environmental Quality Engineering. The lessee shall be strictly liable for any contamination of the land."

contaminated solvents for recycling. These wastes yielded smaller reusable streams and higher proportions of hazardous sludges. Instead of sending these sludges immediately to landfills, RETEP began storing some of them on site for later reprocessing.

As the availability of desirable wastes continued to decline in early 1979, RETEP's utilization of its recycling capacity fell below 50 percent. Financial pressures caused RETEP to fall behind on its mortgage payments to Atlantic Security Bank and other creditors. After falling behind on three monthly payments, Atlantic Security sent RETEP a stern letter threatening to take action if payments were not forthcoming. A bank officer arranged a meeting with Jim Reid to discuss the problems at the company. The bank officer threatened to foreclose on the mortgage if RETEP did not turn its operations around immediately.

To make up for reduced revenues in its recycling operations, RETEP began accepting more aqueous wastes solely for treatment and disposal. The primary source of these wastes was fabricated metal products producers generating streams of plating waste and heavy metal sludges (from electroplating processes). Generators paid RETEP $50 to $75 per ton to dispose of their dilute aqueous waste. Since RETEP's facility was not designed to handle large quantities of aqueous waste, James Reid took a number of stopgap measures to increase the plant's capacity to treat such volumes. RETEP dug a large evaporation pit and lined it with cement. RETEP also purchased additional equipment and agents for precipitating heavy metals in solution.

RETEP initially used the evaporation pit exclusively for reduction of the water content of low toxicity wastes. As its disposal operations increased, however, RETEP began placing higher toxicity wastes in the evaporation pond. On October 8, 1980, a small fire broke out in its distillation tower. The fire caused a few barrels of flammable, toxic chemicals to explode, causing the release of a noxious cloud of chemicals. The Brower Fire Department responded to the emergency, evacuated nearby residents, and put out the fire. It discovered the dangerous conditions at the site and contacted the Department of Environmental Quality Engineering (DEQE). DEQE promptly investigated and discovered the use of the evaporation pit as well as numerous other dangerous conditions in violation of RETEP's permit (such as storage of hazardous sludges containing heavy metals, leaking storage tanks, improper labelling of waste drums). DEQE took steps to modify RETEP's license and to require RETEP to take remedial action. RETEP contested the modification of its license and an agreement for judgment was ultimately reached in February 1981, which imposed a compliance schedule on RETEP for discontinuing use of the evaporation pit, cleaning up leaked materials, installing concrete pads in drum storage areas, reducing volumes of hazardous materials, installing monitoring wells (to obtain groundwater samples for quality analysis), and filing regular reports with DEQE.

Financial conditions at RETEP rapidly deteriorated. It missed its mortgage payments with Atlantic Security Bank in April, May, and June of 1981. To protect its security, the bank foreclosed on the mortgage in July 1981. Later in that month, RETEP filed for bankruptcy. The leased property returned to the control of 21st Century Realty.

EPA was made aware of the conditions in March 1982. Emergency actions to minimize immediate threats of contamination to the local community were undertaken by federal and state agencies in the summer of 1982. EPA's preliminary assessment and site investigation took a little over three years to complete. In September 1985, the RETEP site was placed on the National Priorities List. At that time, EPA sent out Notice of Responsibility letters to all identified potentially responsible parties notifying them of their potential liability for conditions at the RETEP site. Based upon preliminary evaluation of remedial options, EPA estimates that surface and subsurface cleanup costs will likely exceed $10 million and could run as high as $50 million. Subsurface cleanup and groundwater remediation will take many years to complete.

PROBLEM: SUPERFUND LIABILITY OF RETEP ACTORS

On the basis of the statutory provisions (including defenses to and exemptions from liability), determine whether and to what extent the following actors are liable under Superfund.

1. *Owner/Operator Liability*

- *RETEP Chemical Corporation*
- *RETEP's officers and directors*
- *Amalgamated Technologies*
- *21st Century Realty*
- *Atlantic Security Bank.* Consider EPA's lender liability rule, excerpted in the statutory/regulatory supplement.

2. *Generator Liability*

- Beginning in 1974, *American Shoe,* a large shoe manufacturer in New England, began sending waste solvents to RETEP Chemical Corporation for recycling. American Shoe's generation of waste solvents declined after 1976 as its business fell off. It stopped sending waste solvents to RETEP in early 1978. Over the course of the relationship, American Shoe repurchased recycled solvents from RETEP equivalent to 90 percent of the recoverable materials sent.

- Begininng in 1976, *Infinity Semiconductor* sold its solvent wastes to Chemical Tank Lines, which in turn sold them to RETEP Chemical Corporation. Infinity Semiconductor did not have any direct dealings with RETEP.

- In 1978 and 1979, *DKL Engraving* hired C&J Sanitation to transport a large quantity of heavy metal contaminated acid wastes to RETEP Chemical Corporation.

- Over the period 1974 through 1979, *Lustre Cleaners,* a small family-owned, dry cleaning establishment, sold its waste solvents to Chemical Tank Lines, a waste collection and transportation firm. Chemical Tank Lines paid a modest amount for such wastes and earned a profit by selling the wastes to recyclers and waste-to-energy incinerators. A small portion of the Lustre Cleaners' waste solvents were sold to RETEP Chemical Corporation. Lustre Cleaners had no knowledge of where its wastes were ultimately disposed.

- In 1978, *Quicksilver Metal Finishing* contracted with a waste transporter to deliver 8 barrels of highly toxic waste sludges to the Safety Disposal facility in central Massachusetts. In order to reduce travel time, the transporter delivered the materials to RETEP Chemical Corporation instead. Identifying labels on the barrels and other records discovered at the RETEP site clearly trace the materials to Quicksilver.

- In 1974, *Roberts Electrical Supply Company* sold a small electrical transformer to RETEP Chemical Corporation for use on the site. The transformer contained PCBs, which later leaked at the RETEP site and necessitated additional cleanup costs.

- In 1974, *Redi-Trailers Inc.* sold used trailers and building materials to RETEP Chemical Corporation for use as offices and storage sheds. They contained asbestos, which later complicated the cleanup effort.

- In 1976, *ACME Disposal* sold RETEP Chemical Corporation ten used, large-capacity liquid waste storage tanks for use in RETEP's waste recovery process. Because the tanks had previously been used and contained hazardous sludge residues, RETEP obtained the tanks at a significant discount below the cost of new tanks. The tanks subsequently leaked, contaminating soils in the waste recovery area.

- From 1974 to 1979, *Chemical Supply Inc.* sold large quantities of chemicals to RETEP for use in the detoxification treatment process. These included acidic and alkaline materials used to neutralize wastes and precipitation chemicals that make heavy metal constituents insoluble, thereby causing separation from waste streams. Some of the chemicals were spilled during the treatment process and contaminated soils in the aqueous treatment area.

- From 1974 through 1978, *Chemical Arbitrage Inc.* purchased reclaimed chemicals from RETEP Chemical Corporation. Some of its drums with chemical residues were discovered on the site.
- In late 1978, the municipal solid waste collector for *Boxfield, Massachusetts,* a small town north of Boston, delivered trash from the town to the RETEP site for use as fill.
- *Susan and Ted Smith* have lived in Boxfield, Massachusetts since 1972. A sealed trash bag containing junk mail addressed to their house as well as partially filled discarded chemical household cleansers was found amidst the fill materials at the RETEP site.

3. *Transporter Liability*

- *Chemical Tank Lines* collects waste streams from small establishments — dry cleaners, service stations — and sells them to waste recyclers and waste-to-energy facilities. It takes care to ensure that its customers' waste streams do not contain highly toxic materials. During the period 1974 to 1979, it sold a modest amount of recyclable wastes to the RETEP Chemical Corporation.
- *C&J Sanitation* hauls highly toxic waste for many large New England hazardous waste generators. In 1978 and 1979, it transported large quantities of highly contaminated wastes to the RETEP Chemical Corporation.

4. *Apportionment of Liability.* In addition to the potentially responsible parties identified above, EPA's investigation of RETEP's records revealed that almost 200 generators, ranging from major Fortune 100 companies to small dry cleaning enterprises, sent wastes to the sites. EPA has rough figures indicating the types and quantities of wastes sent from most of these generators. Waste quantities per generator vary from less than one 42 gallon barrel to over 50,000 barrels. In addition, generators vary significantly in terms of how much waste was recycled and returned or sold to other entities. EPA's investigation identifies approximately 50 transporters who delivered wastes to RETEP over its years of operation. Like the generators, the transporters vary in terms of their size, waste type, waste volume, and extent of recycling. In fact, a few transporters actually hauled away more recycled solvents than they delivered in the form of contaminated wastes.

- How much is each responsible party liable for?
- Were the case to go to trial, how would liability be apportioned?

- What do you think would be a fair basis for apportioning liability for cleanup costs?
- To what extent are the various PRPs morally culpable for the environmental harms? Is the likely share of liability commensurate with moral culpability?

3.   BANKRUPTCY AND SUPERFUND

The high costs of environmental cleanup dictated by Superfund frequently push site owners and other potentially responsible parties into bankruptcy, which can have significant implications for the government's ability to expedite cleanup efforts and recover response costs.

The Bankruptcy Code offers firms facing insolvency two options: liquidation and reorganization. Under Chapter 7 of the Bankruptcy Code, the debtor's assets are sold and the proceeds distributed to creditors in order of priority of their claims: (1) secured creditors; (2) priority creditors;[42] (3) other unsecured creditors; and (4) equity holders. 11 U.S.C. §§701-66. Under Chapter 11, the firm may continue its operation under a court-approved reorganization plan which reschedules and discharges some of the firm's debts[43] to creditors. 11 U.S.C. §§1101-74. The reorganization is designed to give the debtor a "fresh start" so as to preserve the value of the operating firm for the benefit of the creditors and other interested parties.

There is significant tension between the Bankruptcy Code and Superfund: Superfund aims to cleanup environmental damage expeditiously and to impose liability for response costs on responsible parties while the bankruptcy law seeks the expeditious collection and sale of the debtor's assets and the equitable distribution of proceeds to creditors under Chapter 7 or to provide reorganized debtors a "fresh start" under Chapter 11 so as to benefit creditors and other interested parties.

---

42. Priority claims include, in the following order, administrative costs (costs of administrative services necessary to preserve the estate during the bankruptcy proceeding), employees' wages, pension plan contributions, and taxes. 11 U.S.C. §507.

43. A debt is defined as a "liability on a claim." 11 U.S.C. §101(12). A claim is defined as a:

> (A) right to payment, whether or not such right is reduced to judgment, liquidated, unliquidated, fixed, contingent, matured, unmatured, disputed, undisputed, legal, equitable, secured, or unsecured; or
> (B) right to an equitable remedy for breach of performance if such breach gives rise to a right to payment, whether or not such right to an equitable remedy is reduced to judgment, fixed, contingent, matured, unmatured, disputed, undisputed, secured or unsecured.

11 U.S.C. §101(5).

Confrontations between these bodies of law arise in the following contexts:[44]

Automatic Stay. Once a petition for bankruptcy has been filed,
claims against the debtor are automatically stayed in order to allow for
an orderly liquidation procedure designed to treat all creditors equitably. 11 U.S.C. §362(a). Creditors may not collect from the debtor without the approval of the bankruptcy court. 11 U.S.C. §362(b) contains
eleven exceptions to the automatic stay, including proceedings by a
governmental unit to enforce their "police or regulatory power," including steps to enforce injunctions or judgments, other than monetary
awards, obtained prior to the filing of the bankruptcy petition. In *Penn
Terra Ltd. v. Department of Environmental Resources,* 733 F.2d 267 (3d Cir.
1984), the court held that the police power exception "extends to permit an injunction and enforcement of an injunction, and to permit the
entry of a money judgment, but does not extend to permit enforcement
of a money judgment." Although the automatic stay precludes the execution of a money judgment, it rarely delays environmental cleanup
orders, even though compliance with such orders can require the
debtor to expend substantial resources. Some recent cases, however,
have taken a more narrow approach to this exception. In *In re Torwico
Electronics, Inc.,* 131 B.R. 561 (Bankr. D.N.J. 1991), the court held that
"obligations to clean up environmental contamination that occurred
pre-petition, and that can only be satisfied by spending money, should
generally be defined as money judgments."

The manner in which the government seeks compliance with an
environmental statute, however, can affect its ability to force a bankrupt
entity to expend resources to comply with environmental requirements. In *In re Kovacs,* 681 F.2d 454 (6th Cir. 1982), *vacated and remanded on other grounds,* 459 U.S. 1167 (1983), the court held that a
state's enforcement of the debtor's obligation to clean up industrial
water pollution was subject to the stay because the state was seeking
"what in essence amounted to a monetary judgment." Rather than directly enforcing the environmental law against the debtor, the state
had first secured appointment of a receiver to handle the affairs of
the bankrupt estate, thereby relieving the debtor of any control of the
property in question. Its action against the debtor, therefore, was found
to be an attempt to defray the response costs, which does not fall within
the exception to the stay.

Abandonment of Contaminated Properties. In order to preserve the
debtor's estate, a bankruptcy trustee can seek to abandon burdensome
properties. 11 U.S.C. §554(a). Abandonment of a contaminated prop-

---

44. For a comprehensive discussion of the resolution of environmental
claims in bankruptcy proceedings, see S. Cooke, The Law of Hazardous Waste
ch. 20 (1992).

erty would essentially relieve a site owner from liability under Superfund. In *Midlantic National Bank v. New Jersey Department of Environmental Protection*, 474 U.S. 494 (1986), the Supreme Court held that bankruptcy courts do "not have the power to authorize an abandonment without formulating conditions that will adequately protect the public's health and safety." Some lower courts have read this decision narrowly, holding that "[f]ull compliance with all environmental laws is not authorized when there is an *immediate* threat to the public health and safety and an imminent danger of death or illness." *In re FCX, Inc.*, 19 ELR 20849 (Bankr. E.D.N.C. Feb. 3, 1989). The court in *In re Peerless Plating Co.*, 70 B.R. 943 (Bankr. W.D. Mich. 1987) took a broader view, holding that a trustee may not abandon a hazardous waste site in violation of environmental laws unless: (1) the environmental law is "so onerous as to interfere with the bankruptcy itself"; (2) the environmental law "is not reasonably designed to protect the public health or safety from identified hazards"; or (3) "the violation caused by the abandonment would merely be speculative or indeterminate."

Priority of Response Cost Liabilities and Remediation Responsibilities. In a Chapter 7 liquidation, the debtor's assets are distributed according to the priority hierarchy described above. Secured creditors have priority with regard to security interests in and mortgages on the debtor's property. Priority creditors have priorities on the unencumbered assets of the debtor. If environmental cleanup obligations are characterized as general unsecured claims, there will typically be few or no funds available after priority creditors are paid for remediation or cost recovery. If they are considered administrative expenses of preserving the estate during the bankruptcy proceedings, however, they come at the top of the priority creditor class, see supra note 42. Courts have held that response costs for post-petition remedial action qualify as administrative expenses to the extent that they remedy ongoing effects of a release of hazardous substances. *In re Chateaugay Corp.*, 944 F.2d at 1009-1010; see also *In re Peerless Plating Co.*, 70 B.R. at 948-949. These costs have been limited, however, to remediation of conditions that pose an imminent and identifiable harm to the environment and public health. *In re National Gypsum Co.*, 139 B.R. at 413.

Dischargeability of Response Cost Liabilities and Remediation Responsibilities. Demands for response costs incurred prior to the filing of a bankruptcy petition clearly fall within the Bankruptcy Code's definition of a claim and hence are dischargeable in a Chapter 11 reorganization.[45] Moreover, in *In re Chateaugay Corp.*, 944 F.2d 997 (2d Cir. 1991), the Second Circuit held that unincurred CERCLA response costs for pre-petition conduct resulting in release or threatened release of haz-

---

45. Only individuals, and not corporations, may discharge debts in Chapter 7 liquidations. 11 U.S.C. §727(a)(1).

ardous substances are contingent "claims" within the broad meaning of that term in the Bankruptcy Code[46] and hence dischargeable as well.[47] The bankruptcy court in *In re National Gypsum Co.*, 139 B.R. 397 (Bankr. N.D. Tex. 1992), interpreted the term "claims" more narrowly, holding that only future response and natural resource damage costs based on pre-petition conduct that can be "fairly contemplated" by the parties at the time of the bankruptcy are dischargeable claims within the meaning of the Bankruptcy Code. Moreover, a reorganized corporation would still be subject to §106 administrative orders or injunctive relief to address contamination on any properties that they own.

With regard to environmental remediation injunctions, the court in *In re Chateaugay Corp.* ruled that a cleanup order that "accomplishes the dual objectives of removing accumulated wastes and stopping or ameliorating ongoing pollution emanating from such wastes is not a dischargeable claim," 944 F.2d at 1008; but orders to clean up a site that impose obligations distinct from any obligation to stop or ameliorate ongoing pollution are dischargeable claims within the meaning of the Code. The court emphasized, however, that most environmental injunctions will "fall on the non-'claim' side of the line."

PROBLEM: IMPLICATIONS OF RETEP'S BANKRUPTCY FOR THE CLEANUP PROCESS AND COST RECOVERY

Apply the above overview of bankruptcy law to the RETEP case:

- What actions might RETEP Chemical Corporation, its equity holders, and its nongovernmental creditors take to recover the greatest portion of available assets from the estate and minimize those applied to cleanup efforts?
  - Analyze the choice of a Chapter 7 or Chapter 11 filing. Which is most advantageous to RETEP's equity holders? To secured creditors? To the government?
  - To what extent will the automatic stay limit compliance with environmental remediation requirements?
  - Will RETEP's trustee in bankruptcy be allowed to abandon the RETEP site?
  - To what extent will response costs incurred after the filing of the bankruptcy petition be considered administrative expenses of the estate?

---

46. See note 43.

47. The court noted that reaching a contrary result — i.e., concluding that unincurred CERCLA response costs were not "claims" — would preclude the government from receiving even partial recovery against a dissolving corporation in a Chapter 7 liquidation.

- To what extent are response costs — either past costs already incurred or future, as yet unincurred, costs — at the RETEP site dischargeable in bankruptcy?
- What other actions might RETEP and its creditors take in the bankruptcy process to minimize the resources going to address environmental contamination?

- How should the government structure its enforcement actions so as to hold RETEP Chemical Corporation responsible for remediating the contamination at the site?
- Patriot Plating Company sent approximately 20 barrels of hazardous waste to RETEP Chemical Corporation. In addition, it had sent modest amounts of hazardous waste to two other sites that were subsequently placed on the National Priority List. Although Patriot's business is well-managed and profitable, the potential liability for response costs at these sites along with the high legal costs have pushed Patriot into bankruptcy. In light of the Bankruptcy Code and Superfund, how should the government pursue Patriot Plating Company?

DISCUSSION QUESTIONS

Should environmental concerns receive special priority in the resolution of a debtor's estate? Judge Newman, in *In re Chateaugay Corp.*, 944 F.2d at 1002, discussed the relationship between the Bankruptcy Code and Superfund as follows:

[T]o whatever extent the Code and CERCLA point in different directions, we do not face in this context a conflict between two statutes, each designed to focus on a discrete problem, which happen to conflict in their application to a specific set of facts. Cf. *SCM Corp. v. Xerox Corp.*, 463 F. Supp. 983 (D. Conn. 1978) (discussing need to harmonize antitrust and patent laws). Here, we encounter a bankruptcy statute that is intended to override many provisions of law that would apply in the absence of bankruptcy — especially laws otherwise providing creditors suing promptly with full payment of their claims. Of course, the comprehensive nature of the bankruptcy statute does not relieve us of the obligation to construe its terms, nor may we resolve all issues of statutory construction in favor of the "fresh start" objective, regardless of the terms Congress has chosen to express its will. Our point is the more limited one that in construing the Code, we need not be swayed by arguments advanced by EPA that a narrow reading of the Code will better serve the environmental interests Congress wished to promote in enacting CERCLA. If the Code, fairly construed, creates limits on the extent of environmental cleanup efforts, the remedy is for Congress to make exceptions to the Code to achieve other objectives that Congress chooses to reach, rather than for courts to restrict the meaning of across-the-board legislation like the bankruptcy law in order to promote objectives evident in more focused statutes.

Do you agree with this structure for statutory interpretation? Should Congress amend the Bankruptcy Code in order to elevate the priority of environmental cleanup claims? Can you think of any circumstances in which allowing the objectives of the Bankruptcy Code to control will enhance the government's ability to clean up and recover response costs for a contaminated waste site?

If you think that Congress should elevate environmental claims in bankruptcy resolutions, what priority should such claims receive?[48] What would the effect of such a change be on credit markets?[49]

4. INSURANCE COVERAGE OF SUPERFUND LIABILITIES

Who actually pays for the costs of environmental remediation, natural resource damages, and the costs of resolving liability disputes is determined not only by Superfund's liability regime, but also the interpretation of insurance contracts held by potentially responsible parties. Superfund's unprecedented imposition of retroactive liability for environmental contamination has generated a flood of insurance litigation to determine who bears ultimate responsibility for the costs of cleaning up environmental contamination.

Insurance law is a hybrid of common law, contract law, and state insurance regulation. Most disputes over insurance coverage of hazardous waste cleanup focus on the interpretation of commercial insurance policies. In general, the plain meaning of insurance contracts governs

---

48. A number of states have enacted "superlien" statutes which elevate the priority of environmental cleanup claims. See S. Cooke, The Law of Hazardous Waste §20.01[2][b] (1992).

49. As originally enacted in 1983, §13 of the Massachusetts Oil and Hazardous Release Prevention and Response Act elevated the state's claim for response costs (plus 12 percent interest per year) above all prior or subsequent creditors with regard to any of the debtor's property. The mortgage industry responded quickly. The Federal Home Loan Mortgage Corporation suspended purchases of condominium and apartment mortgages and threatened to stop buying mortgages on single-family residences. The legislature promptly amended the statute to limit the superlien to the contaminated property. With regard to "clean" properties of the debtor, the state's lien comes after previously recorded interests and does not attach to property acquired after the state's lien attaches. See Mass. Gen. Laws Ann. ch. 21E, §13 (amended 1983); Koelbel, The Impact of State "Superlien" Statutes on Real Estate Transactions, 5 Va. J. Nat. Res. 296 (1986).

their interpretation. Where ambiguities are found, the maxim *contra proferentem* directs courts to interpret ambiguities against the drafter. Since the common law of contracts and insurance regulation vary across states, however, the potential exists for variation in interpretation.

Most commercial insurance involved in hazardous waste cleanup disputes are standard form agreements.[50] This section reviews the three types of insurance policies commonly involved in hazardous waste litigation:[51] (1) the Comprehensive General Liability policy; (2) the Environmental Impairment Liability (EIL) policy; and (3) commercial property insurance.

The Comprehensive General Liability (CGL) Policy. Because of Superfund's wide net of liability, the interpretation of the CGL policy has emerged as a major issue in the ultimate resolution of many Superfund cases. The CGL policy was first standardized in 1941 and has been revised frequently. Since 1966, the standard CGL policy has stated that the insurance company "will pay on behalf of the insured all sums which the insured shall become legally obligated to pay as damages because of (A) bodily injury or (B) property damage to which this insurance applies, caused by an occurrence. . . ." As we discuss below, there have been important changes in the provisions of these policies in response to changes in liability regimes, most importantly the creation of Superfund. Because of Superfund's retroactive application, much of the extensive Superfund insurance litigation involves policies that were not written with this type of liability regime in mind. Hence, Superfund has led to significant coverage disputes, particularly in the following areas:

Duty to Defend. CGL insurers have the right and duty to defend "suits" against the insured. Since the costs of resolving Superfund disputes begin immediately after a governmental agency sends a Notice of Responsibility to a potentially responsible party, often long before the filing of a formal lawsuit, the question arises as to when the insurer's duty to defend begins. The majority of courts have held that a Notice of Responsibility does trigger the duty to defend because failure to participate in the administrative process can often result in fines for failure to cooperate in the cleanup process and greater potential liability. See, e.g., *Hazen Paper Co. v. United States Fidelity & Guaranty Co.*, 555 N.E.2d 576, 581 (Mass. 1990); but see *Detrex Chemical Industry v. Employers Insur-*

---

50. Most of the standardization of insurance policies has occurred through coordination practices of the insurance industry. These practices have a limited exemption from the antitrust laws; see McCarran-Ferguson Act, 15 U.S.C. §§1011-1015. In addition, state insurance law regulates particular policy provisions.

51. For a comprehensive treatment of insurance issues raised by CERCLA, see K. Abraham, Environmental Liability Insurance Law (1991); Cooke, The Law of Hazardous Waste ch. 19 (1992).

ance of Wausau, 746 F. Supp. 1310 (N.D. Ohio 1990). The insurer is obligated to defend any claim that could possibly fall within the scope of the policy coverage.

Interpretation of "Damages." CGL policies generally require insurers "to pay on behalf of the Insured all sums which the Insured shall become legally obligated to pay *as damages* because of . . . property damage." If the term "damages" is interpreted to limit coverage to legal remedies, then recovery of response costs, which are regarded as equitable relief, will be barred. A few courts have held that this language is an unambiguous term of art in the insurance field, which limits recovery to legal remedies, thereby precluding coverage of Superfund response costs. See, e.g., *Continental Insurance Companies v. Northeastern Pharmaceutical and Chemical Co.,* 842 F.2d 977 (8th Cir. 1988), *cert. denied,* 488 U.S. 821 (1988). A majority of courts, however, have held that the term is open to interpretation. In states applying a "plain meaning" interpretation of insurance terms, courts have found that a layperson would include both equitable and legal relief in the definition of damages. *New Castle County v. Hartford Accident and Indemnity Co.,* 673 F. Supp. 1359 (D. Del. 1987) (interpreting Delaware law); see also *Hazen Paper Co. v. United States Fidelity and Guaranty Co.,* 555 N.E.2d 576, 582-583 (Mass. 1990). The fact that insurance law is state specific has led to substantial variation in the interpretation of insurance terms. The complexity of insurance coverage for Superfund response costs has even led to conflicts in interpretation within the same state.

Definition of an Occurrence. Liability insurance policies contain either a claims-made or occurrence trigger for coverage. Claims-made policies cover liability for claims actually made during the policy period. By contrast, occurrence-based policies provide coverage for liability arising out of injury or damage occurring during the period in which the policy is in force, regardless of when the lawsuit alleging liability is brought. CGL policies have an occurrence trigger. The 1973 standard form CGL policy defined an "occurrence" as:

> an accident, including continuous or repeated exposure to conditions which results in bodily injury or property damage neither expected nor intended from the standpoint of the insured.

Because of Superfund's retroactive application, the scope of insurance coverage for environmental cleanup depends critically upon how the occurrence trigger is interpreted.

Since companies may have had numerous insurance policies over the period during which hazardous wastes may have leaked, it is necessary to determine when policy coverage is triggered, that is, when an "occurrence" occurs. Analogizing to asbestos cases in which medical experts testified that exposure to airborne asbestos fibers results in immediate lung damage, some courts have held that property damage is triggered when "exposure" occurs, for instance, dumping of wastes on the ground. See, e.g., *Sandoz Inc. v. Employer's Liability Assurance Corp.*, 554 F. Supp. 257 (D. N.J. 1983). A few courts have held that the policy is triggered when bodily injury or property damage "manifest" or is discovered. See, e.g., *Allstate Insurance Co. v. Quinn Construction Co.*, 713 F. Supp. 35 (D. Mass. 1989). The "continuous trigger" approach holds that bodily injury or property damage occurs over the entire period between exposure and manifestation on the theory that damage continues as wastes migrate over time. See, e.g., *New Castle County v. Continental Casualty Co.*, 725 F. Supp. (D. Del. 1989) *aff'd*, 933 F.2d 1162 (3d Cir. 1991). A fourth test used by some courts rejects the above *per se* approaches and seeks to identify on a case by case basis when the "injury in fact" actually occurred. This approach is reasonably workable when there is a single initial harm, such as the disposal of wastes in one area which progressively causes harm. Only the policy in effect at the time of the disposal would be triggered. The "injury in fact" approach becomes problematic, however, when multiple harms cumulatively contribute to a hazardous waste problem. See K. Abraham, supra note 51, at 99-101.

The determination of which policies are triggered does not completely resolve the allocation of insurer responsibility. See K. Abraham, supra note 51, at 106-128. Since CGL policies typically limit the recovery per occurrence, it is necessary to determine the number of occurrences during each policy period. Further questions arise in allocating coverage among the triggered policies.

Pollution Exclusion Clause. Prior to 1973, the standard form CGL did not limit coverage for environmental pollution. The 1973 revision introduced the following exclusion:

> This insurance does not apply:
>   (f) to bodily injury or property damage arising out of the discharge, dispersal, release or escape of smoke, vapors, soot, fumes, acids, alkalis, toxic chemicals, liquids or gases, waste materials or other irritants, contaminants or pollutants into or upon the land, the atmosphere or any water course or body of water; but this exclusion does not apply if such discharge, dispersal, release or escape is sudden and accidental.

While the first clause of this provision seems to exclude coverage for Superfund-type damages, the latter introduces substantial confusion regarding the extent of this exclusion. Since the meaning of "sudden and accidental" is not specifically defined in the policy, there has been extensive litigation of this term in many of the states since the mid-1970s.

In the late 1970s and early 1980s, most courts construed "sudden and accidental" broadly, extending coverage for releases of pollutants that were unintended and unexpected. In 1986, the North Carolina Supreme Court broke from this pattern of interpretation, holding that a release must be instantaneous in order to fall within the "sudden and accidental" exception to the pollution exclusion clause. *Waste Management of Carolinas v. Peerless Insurance Co.*, 340 S.E.2d 374 (1986). Many courts since have interpreted the "sudden and accidental" exception to require temporal — for instance, release occurs within a relatively short time period, as opposed to slow leaking — and unexpected elements, thereby narrowing the scope of coverage. See, e.g., *Lumbermens Mutual Casualty Co. v. Belleville Industries, Inc.*, 555 N.E.2d 569 (Mass. 1990). Yet, a review of the case law reveals dozens of cases on each side of this issue.

In response to the judicial confusion regarding the interpretation of the pollution exclusion clause, the standard form CGL was modified in 1986 by removing the "sudden and accidental" exception and expressly excluding coverage for any "loss, cost, or expense arising out of any governmental direction or request that [the insured] monitor, clean up, remove, treat, detoxify or neutralize pollutants." The 1986 "absolute pollution exclusion clause" does not, however, eliminate coverage for personal injury, pollution caused by finished products, and fires, explosions, or other occurrences caused by a release of pollutants.

The "Owned-Property" Exclusion. In order to exclude coverage under the CGL policy for losses within the scope of commercial property insurance, the CGL standard form policy bars property damage to property owned, occupied, rented, or used by the insured or in the care, custody or control of the insured. The majority of courts have interpreted this exclusion narrowly in the hazardous waste cleanup context, extending coverage where the insured is required to prevent or mitigate pollution on its own property that is causing or threatens to cause damage to third parties, including the public at large. See *Allstate Insurance Co. v. Quinn Construction Co.*, 713 F. Supp. 35 (D. Mass 1989).

The Environmental Impairment Liability (EIL) Policy. In the late 1970s, insurers began offering the Environmental Impairment Liability (EIL) policy to limit their exposure to the burgeoning environmental cleanup liabilities while affording protection to insureds facing specific environmental exposures. Although many insurers modified the model EIL policy, policies issued typically included coverage for third-party claims and governmental cleanup obligations caused by "the emission, discharge, dispersal, disposal, seepage, release or escape of any liquid, solid, gaseous or thermal irritant, contaminant or pollutant into or upon land, the atmosphere or any watercourse or body of water."

EIL policies cover claims made during the policy period and hence avoid the problem of unending prospective liability associated with occurrence-based policies. A triggering problem can still arise, however, in determining the date on which a pollution incident occurs.

EIL insurers have refused coverage when there is reason to believe that the pollution began prior to the effective date of the policy ("retroactive date"), thereby causing litigation over the "time of occurrence" similar to that plaguing CGL coverage.

The EIL policy has proven to be an incomplete and risky insurance device. Because of its "claims-made" feature, the EIL policy provides no prospective coverage for environmental liabilities. An insurer may refuse to renew a policy for an insured who faces significant liability for environmental problems. More generally, because of the uncertainties surrounding environmental liability, insurers have dramatically curtailed EIL underwriting, thereby leaving insureds without coverage for damages that occurred but had not yet manifested in claims during their EIL policy period. Those insurers willing to write EIL policies today carefully evaluate the insured's site and operations. Policies typically have low policy limits and high premiums.

Commercial Property Insurance. Commercial property insurance protects against physical loss or damage to the insured's covered properties, including costs of debris removal. "Named perils" policies cover those losses attributable to specified risks.[52] "All risks" policies insure against all risks not expressly excluded. Coverage is triggered by direct loss of covered property during the policy period.

Numerous obstacles limit the coverage of environmental cleanup costs under commercial property policies. Unlike CGL and EIL policies, commercial property insurance does not provide coverage for liability. Nonetheless, commercial property insurance may cover the costs of Superfund cleanups to the extent that the contamination falls within the property damage coverages of the policy, such as fire or other covered perils. A second potential impediment to insurance for environmental contamination concerns the scope of covered property. The property expressly covered by commercial property insurance policies include buildings, structures, machinery, equipment, and business or personal property of the insured. Courts have reached conflicting conclusions with regard to whether land and groundwater are covered by commercial property policies.

In response to Superfund liability, standard "named perils" commercial property insurance policies issued after 1986 expressly exclude coverage for land and water. They also expressly exclude from debris removal coverage the removal of pollutants and environmental restoration of land or water. "All risks" policies typically limit pollution cleanup and removal coverage to sudden and accidental releases and specify aggregate limits of $10,000 or less per policy period.

---

52. The 1985 standard form commercial property insurance policy covered fire, smoke, lightning, explosion, wind, civil commotion, vandalism, malicious mischief, sprinkler leakage, sinkhole collapse, volcanic action, breakage of glass, falling objects, weight of snow, ice or sleet, and water damage.

PROBLEM: SCOPE OF INSURANCE COVERAGE FOR RETEP RESPONSE COSTS

Analyze the scope of coverage of the following insurance policies. What insurance disputes are likely to arise? How would insurance coverage disputes be resolved? To what extent is this allocation of responsibility equitable?

(1) RETEP Chemical Corporation carried the following types of insurance during its years of operation:

- Between November 1973 and December 1978, RETEP carried a standard form CGL policy issued by Massachusetts Casualty Insurance, that is, the 1973 CGL policy described above. The policy provided for up to $200,000 per occurrence, with an aggregate limit for any policy period of $600,000.
- Beginning in January 1979 until the time of its bankruptcy, RETEP carried a standard form CGL policy issued by the Hartford Group Insurance Company. The policy provided for up to $250,000 per occurrence, with an aggregate limit of $750,000.
- Between November 1973 up until its bankruptcy, RETEP carried a standard form commercial property insurance policy issued by Massachusetts Casualty Insurance. The "named perils" policy covered loss due to fire, smoke, lightning, explosion, wind, civil commotion, vandalism, malicious mischief, sprinkler leakage, sinkhole collapse, volcanic action, breakage of glass, falling objects, weight of snow, ice or sleet, and water damage. The policy provided for up to $150,000 per occurrence up to an aggregate limit for any policy period of $450,000.

2. A&D Automotive carried the following types of insurance:

- Between January 1, 1973 and the RETEP bankruptcy, A&D Automotive carried a standard form CGL policy issued by U.S. Casualty Insurance Group, that is, the 1973 CGL policy described above. The policy provided for up to $100,000 per occurrence, with an aggregate limit for any policy period of $300,000.
- From January 1, 1979, through December 31, 1980, A&D Automotive carried a standard form EIL policy from U.S. Casualty Insurance Group. It provided up to $80,000 per occurrence, with an aggregate limit for each policy period of $160,000.
- From January 1, 1981 through December 31, 1986, A&D Automotive carried a standard form EIL policy from National Insurance Underwriters. It provided up to $30,000 per occurrence, with an aggregate limit of $90,000.

DISCUSSION QUESTIONS

1. Based upon principles of contract interpretation, how should the 1973 standard form CGL policy be interpreted with regard to the following clauses?

- coverage of Superfund response costs "as damages"
- the occurrence trigger — which theory best comports with the policy language and intent of the parties? Exposure, manifestation, continuous trigger, injury-in-fact?
- pollution exclusion clause
- owned property exclusion

2. Are the curtailments in insurance coverage and availability — the 1986 modifications to the CGL and commercial property policies and the strict requirements and lower limits for EIL coverage — a beneficial or detrimental development for encouraging businesses to improve their environmental performance? economic performance?

5.   ETHICAL RESPONSIBILITIES IN CORPORATE LEGAL ADVISING ON ENVIRONMENTAL RISKS

PROBLEM: ADVISING AMALGAMATED TECHNOLOGIES ON THE RETEP VENTURE

Imagine yourself a lawyer at Amalgamated Technologies' outside firm in the early 1970s. Dan Williams, AT's general counsel, called you last week to get your advice on how AT should structure its proposed solvent and waste recovery project. He noted that AT's Board of Directors would like to structure the new venture in a way that will generate the greatest amount of profit. Moreover, because of some liability problems in other divisions of the corporation, the Board would like to explore ways to limit potential liabilities.

You promptly asked the tax and corporate departments of your firm to analyze the legal consequences of alternative ways of structuring the venture. The tax department's memorandum concludes that there would be modest, although not substantial, tax advantages to setting up the project as a wholly owned subsidiary. The corporate department's legal analysis identifies potential liability as the major "corporate" factor affecting the structure of the project. Under prevailing doctrines of piercing the corporate veil in Massachusetts (as of the early 1970s), the legal department is confident that AT could effectively limit its exposure to liability by setting up the project as a wholly owned subsidiary and taking steps to ensure that AT and its subsidiary take care to respect their corporate separateness, for instance, by transacting all business at arms length, not intermingling funds. In any case, the corporate people are of the view that it would be prudent to use this form of corporate structure.

You are scheduled to advise the Board of Directors tomorrow on the proposed project. Having advised AT and other corporations in the past on the use of subsidiary corporations and seen some unsuccessful subsidiaries milked dry by their parents (leaving creditors with worthless claims), you are concerned that AT might not be sensitive to the full social impact of its corporate decisionmaking, especially with regard to the management of hazardous materials.

- What is the "morally" ethical thing to advise?
- Based upon the following excerpts from the ABA Model Code of Professional Responsibility and Wolfram's treatise on legal ethics, what is the "legally" ethical scope of advice? That is, what range of advice is proper under the Code?
  - What would you advise?
  - Must you advise AT to use a wholly owned subsidiary?

- What are the implications of Superfund and similar state legislation for lawyers advising clients about activities that are legal but pose serious environmental risks?
- How would you present your opinion? What action, if any, would you take if the AT Board of Directors rejects your advice?

AMERICAN BAR ASSOCIATION, MODEL CODE OF PROFESSIONAL RESPONSIBILITY

(1981)

CANON 5[53]

A Lawyer Should Exercise Independent Professional Judgment on Behalf of a Client.

---

53. The Canons are statements of axiomatic norms, expressing in general terms the standards of professional conduct expected of lawyers in their relationships with the public, with the legal system, and with the legal profession. They embody the general concepts from which the Ethical Considerations and the Disciplinary Rules are derived.

ETHICAL CONSIDERATIONS[54]

EC 5-1 The professional judgment of a lawyer should be exercised, within the bounds of the law, solely for the benefit of his client and free of compromising influences and loyalties. Neither his personal interests, the interests of other clients, nor the desires of third persons should be permitted to dilute his loyalty to his client.

CANON 7

A Lawyer Should Represent a Client Zealously Within the Bounds of the Law.

ETHICAL CONSIDERATIONS

EC 7-1 The duty of a lawyer, both to his client and to the legal system, is to represent his client zealously within the bounds of the law, which includes Disciplinary Rules and enforceable professional regulations. The professional responsibility of a lawyer derives from his membership in a profession which has the duty of assisting members of the public to secure and protect available legal rights and benefits. In our government of laws and not of men, each member of our society is entitled to have his conduct judged and regulated in accordance with the law; to seek any lawful objective through legally permissible means; and to present for adjudication any lawful claim, issue, or defense.

EC 7-2 The bounds of the law in a given case are often difficult to ascertain. The language of legislative enactments and judicial opinions may be uncertain as applied to varying factual situations. The limits and specific meaning of apparently relevant law may be made doubtful by changing or developing constitutional interpretations, inadequately expressed statutes or judicial opinions, and changing public and judicial attitudes. Certainty of law ranges from well-settled rules through areas of conflicting authority to areas without precedent.

EC 7-3 Where the bounds of law are uncertain, the action of a lawyer may depend on whether he is serving as advocate or adviser. A lawyer may serve simultaneously as both advocate and adviser, but the two roles are essentially different. In asserting a position on behalf of his client, an advocate for the most part deals with past conduct and must take the facts as he finds them. By contrast, a lawyer serving as

---

54. The Ethical Considerations are aspirational in character and represent the objectives toward which every member of the profession should strive. They constitute a body of principles upon which the lawyer can rely for guidance in many specific situations.

adviser primarily assists his client in determining the course of future conduct and relationships. While serving as advocate, a lawyer should resolve in favor of his client doubts as to the bounds of the law. In serving a client as adviser, a lawyer in appropriate circumstances should give his professional opinion as to what the ultimate decisions of the courts would likely be as to the applicable law. . . .

EC 7-8 A lawyer should exert his best efforts to insure that decisions of his client are made only after the client has been informed of relevant considerations. A lawyer ought to initiate this decision-making process if the client does not do so. Advice of a lawyer to his client need not be confined to purely legal considerations. A lawyer should advise his client of the possible effect of each legal alternative. A lawyer should bring to bear upon this decision-making process the fullness of his experience as well as his objective viewpoint. In assisting his client to reach a proper decision, it is often desirable for a lawyer to point out those factors which may lead to a decision that is morally just as well as legally permissible. He may emphasize the possibility of harsh consequences that might result from assertion of legally permissible positions. In the final analysis, however, the lawyer should always remember that the decision whether to forego legally available objectives or methods because of non-legal factors is ultimately for the client and not for himself. In the event that the client in a non-adjudicatory matter insists upon a course of conduct that is contrary to the judgment and advice of the lawyer but not prohibited by Disciplinary Rules, the lawyer may withdraw from the employment.

EC 7-9 In the exercise of his professional judgment on those decisions which are for his determination in the handling of a legal matter, a lawyer should always act in a manner consistent with the best interests of his client. However, when an action in the best interest of his client seems to him to be unjust, he may ask his client for permission to forego such action.

WOLFRAM, MODERN LEGAL ETHICS*

(1986)

§5.6.2   STANDARDS OF LAWYER LIABILITY
FOR MALPRACTICE

GENERAL OUTLINE OF THE LEGAL MALPRACTICE TORT

The legal malpractice tort that is recognized in all American jurisdictions begins as a special application of the reasonable person standard for conduct liability. Lawyers may also occasionally be found liable to clients under such theories as fraud or breach of contract, but the tort theory is by far the most important theory of recovery. Malpractice law requires that a lawyer exercise in behalf of clients the care, skill, and diligence that is commonly exercised by lawyers practicing in similar situations. If a lawyer fails to exercise the level of care that is commonly observed by other professionals, the lawyer can be required to compensate the injured client for all financial harm that has been proximately caused by the negligent omission or commission. Legal malpractice law can thus be regarded as a special application to lawyers of the general fourfold negligence formula of duty, breach of duty, proximate causation, and damages. . . .

Nature of the Standard of Care

In general, courts have elaborated lawyers' malpractice duties through the common-law process of deciding cases on the basis of the concrete facts of particular situations. Generalizations are rightly suspect, although the following general guide from the 1954 decision in *Hodges v. Carter* has been frequently cited as a general measure of lawyer competence and diligence in both litigation and non-litigation situations:

> Ordinarily when an attorney engages in the practice of the law and contracts to prosecute an action in behalf of his client, he impliedly represents that (1) he possesses the requisite degree of learning, skill, and ability necessary to the practice of his profession and which others similarly situated ordinarily possess; (2) he will exert his best judgment in the prosecution of the litigation entrusted to him; and (3) he will exercise reasonable and ordinary care and diligence in the use of his skill and in the application of his knowledge to his client's cause.

The definition of the applicable standard of care has largely been a process of comparing the defendant's performance with the parallel performance of other lawyers in similar situations. Occasionally courts will impose absolute standards. If it were shown that most practitioners, and thus the practitioner of ordinary competence, acted unreasonably, no court should permit that to serve as the standard for malpractice. . . .

Mere Errors of Judgment — Lawyer Due Care in the Face of Uncertainty

A common expression in opinions denying that a lawyer's representation amounted to malpractice is that a lawyer is not liable for mere errors of judgment if the lawyer acted in the "good faith" belief that the lawyer's advice and other assistance was in the best interest of the client. . . .

Forecasting the probable outcome of litigation that may stretch years into the future or stating how a court will decide an unsettled issue of law are the kinds of uncertainties with which a lawyer is often forced to work. But the presence of uncertainty should not create an immunity from malpractice liability. Clients reasonably expect that the lawyer's training and skill makes the lawyer a valuable source of information about probable outcomes in the legal system. . . .

Preventing the Risk of Uncertainty by Planning

A final point about legal uncertainty is that it can often be avoided by commonly employed and less risky alternative arrangements. While the mysteries of the rule against perpetuities confound the finest minds, there is rarely good reason for a client's transmission of property to fall afoul of the rule so long as a proper savings clause is drafted into the dispositive document. Similarly, while the differences between a special and a general appearance may be legally doubtful, a plaintiff's lawyer who debates the point with an objecting defendant instead of serving the defendant with new and indisputably valid process within the statute of limitations, and thus removing the basis for the objection, commits malpractice. In a planning setting, a lawyer should employ an approach whose legal efficaciousness is doubtful and unsettled only after thorough research and full consultation with a client about the risks involved and possible alternative courses of action that involve materially less risk.

6. THE REMEDY SELECTION PROCESS

Even after liability issues have been resolved, there are substantial legal and technical questions surrounding the selection of a remedy. In fact, much of the practice of CERCLA revolves around the remedy selection process. To a significant extent, this process determines the quality and cost of cleanup. Hence it is of critical importance to the efficacy of the Superfund program.

The remedy selection process is governed by the National Oil and Hazardous Substances Pollution Contingency Plan, referred to as the National Contingency Plan or NCP, which was initially prepared pursuant to §311 of the Clean Water Act and expanded by CERCLA to address all releases of hazardous substances. Following the enactment of CERCLA in 1980, EPA developed a multi-stage process for selecting a remedy for NPL sites. In the Superfund Amendments and Reauthorization Act of 1986, Congress added §121 to CERCLA, which codifies elements of the remedy selection process, mandates cleanup standards, and adds some new requirements. Section 121 states that remedial actions "shall attain a degree of cleanup . . . which assures protection of human health and the environment" and creates a strong presumption that permanent remedies be selected. In essence, Congress has required EPA to clean up contaminated properties, including heavily polluted industrial areas, to the levels of all environmental statutes. In view of the great uncertainties surrounding hydrogeology and the lack of proven technologies to remediate groundwater, these requirements present daunting challenges to EPA. Figure 1 provides a schematic overview of the current remedy selection process.

During the scoping stage, the agency assembles existing site data and begins identifying the *applicable* or *relevant and appropriate* requirements (ARARs) — including federal, state, or local health-based and other environmental standards and requirements that restrict activities that can be undertaken at the site (for instance, floodplains or wetlands) — that the cleanup must attain or otherwise adhere to. A requirement is *applicable* to the release or remedial action if it "specifically addresses a hazardous substance, pollutant, contaminant, remedial action, location, or other circumstance found at a CERCLA site." 40 C.F.R. §300.400(g)(1) (1992). If the agency determines that a requirement is not applicable to a specific release, the requirement may nonetheless be *relevant and appropriate*.

The following comparisons shall be made, where pertinent, to determine relevance and appropriateness:

(i)   The purpose of the requirement and the purpose of the CERCLA action;

(ii) The medium regulated or affected by the requirement and the medium contaminated or affected at the CERCLA site;

(iii) The substances regulated by the requirement and the substances found at the CERCLA site;

(iv) The actions or activities regulated by the requirement and the remedial action contemplated at the CERCLA site;

(v)   Any variances, waivers, or exemptions of the requirement and their availability for the circumstances at the CERCLA site;

(vi) The type of place regulated and the type of place affected by the release or CERCLA action;

(vii) The type and size of structure or facility regulated and the type and size of structure or facility affected by the release or contemplated by the CERCLA action;

(viii) Any consideration of use or potential use of affected resources in the requirement and the use or potential use of the affected resource at the CERCLA site.

FIGURE 1
Proposed Remedy Selection Process Under Reauthorization

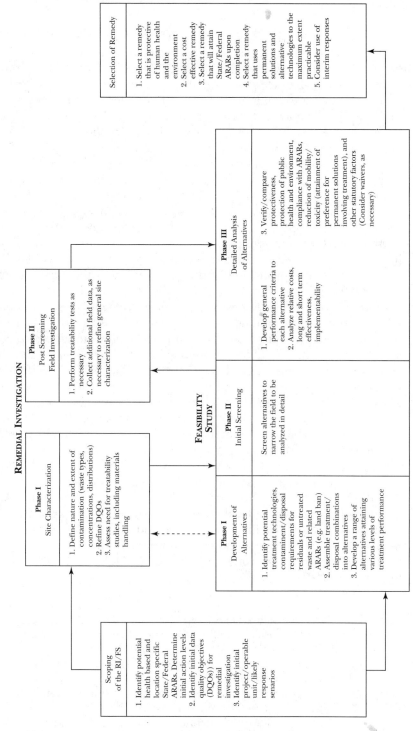

SOURCE: U.S. EPA, Memorandum: Interim Guidance on Superfund Selection of Remedy (Dec. 24, 1986).

40 C.F.R. §300.400 (g)(2) (1992). In addition to ARARs, the agency may identify other advisories, criteria, or guidance *to be considered* (TBC) for a particular release. 40 C.F.R. §300.400(g)(3) (1992). "Only those state standards that are promulgated, are identified by the state in a timely manner, and are more stringent than federal requirements may be applicable or relevant and appropriate. . . . [T]he term *promulgated* means that the standards are of general applicability and are legally enforceable." 40 C.F.R. §300.400(g)(4) (1992).

During the remedial investigation (RI), the agency collects and analyzes data about site and waste characteristics, hazards, and routes of exposure for the purpose of evaluating remedial alternatives. During the feasibility study (FS), which takes place concurrently with the RI, the agency develops and evaluates potential remedial alternatives. Following the RI/FS, the agency selects a remedy according to the following hierarchy of criteria. The proposed remedy must satisfy two *threshold criteria:* (A) overall protection of human health and the environment, and (B) compliance with ARARs. The EPA then weighs five *balancing criteria:* (C) long-term effectiveness and permanence; (D) reduction of toxicity, mobility, or volume through treatment; (E) short-term effectiveness; (F) implementability; and (G) cost. Finally, the agency considers the following *modifying criteria:* (H) state acceptance and (I) community acceptance. 40 C.F.R. §300.430(f)(1) (1992). EPA then releases the proposed remedy for public comment, after which the agency issues a final remedy in a "record of decision" (ROD).

The critical legal issue throughout this process is the determination of ARARs. The cleanup of a contaminated site potentially invokes dozens of federal, state, and local environmental and land use requirements. A groundwater treatment alternative, for example, could plausibly invoke provisions of the Safe Drinking Water Act, the Clean Water Act, the Clean Air Act, the Resource Conservation and Recovery Act, not to mention state and local environmental and land use provisions. Sorting out the applicability or relevance and appropriateness of these provisions is quite complex and extends well beyond the scope of CERCLA. The regulations provide for waiver of an ARAR under the following circumstances:

(1)   The alternative is an interim measure and will become part of a measure and will become part of a total remedial action that will attain the ARAR;

(2)   Compliance with the requirement will result in greater risk to human health and the environment than other alternatives;

(3)   Compliance with the requirements is technically impracticable from an engineering perspective;

(4)   The alternative will attain a standard of performance that is equivalent to that required under the otherwise applicable

standard, requirement, or limitation through use of another
method or approach;

(5)   With respect to a state requirement, the state has not consistently applied, or demonstrated the intention to consistently
apply, the promulgated requirement in similar circumstances
at other remedial actions within the state; or

(6)   For Fund-financed response actions only, an alternative that
attains the ARAR will not provide a balance between the need
for protection of human health and the environment at the
site and the availability of Fund monies to respond to other
sites that may present a threat to human health and the environment.

40 C.F.R. §300.430(f)(1)(ii)(C) (1992).

Lawyers involved in the remedy selection process must be aware
of a broad array of legal and regulatory materials. As noted above,
§§104 and 121 provide the general structure for the remedy selection
process. By contrast to the liability provisions of CERCLA, however,
where much of the relevant authority is found in the statute and case
law interpreting these provisions,[55] much of the relevant authority governing the remedy selection process is found in the Code of Federal
Regulations (Part 300 — National Oil and Hazardous Substances Pollution Contingency Plan) and numerous guidance documents and manu-
als issued by the agency. These latter materials are critical to a full
understanding of the remedy selection process. For example, although
the regulatory criteria for granting waivers appear relatively flexible —
see, e.g., §400.430(f)(1)(C)(3) & (6) — guidance documents interpret
these criteria strictly. For example, the waiver criterion in subsection
(6) may only be applied with regard to cleanups exceeding $60 million;
it has only been granted once in the history of the program.

The following action is one of the few cases addressing the remedy
selection process and the scope of ARARs.

UNITED STATES v. AKZO COATINGS OF AMERICA, INC.

949 F.2d 1409 (6th Cir. 1991)

ENGEL, Senior Circuit Judge.

This is an appeal by the State of Michigan from the entry of a
consent decree between the United States Environmental Protection
Agency ("EPA") and twelve defendants pursuant to the Comprehensive

---

55. As we saw earlier, in some areas, such as municipal and lender liability, EPA has issued guidance documents that clarify the law and EPA's enforcement policy.

Environmental Response, Compensation, and Liability Act of 1980
("CERCLA"), as amended by the Superfund Amendments and Reauthorization Act of 1986 ("SARA"), 42 U.S.C. §9601 et seq. The consent
decree would require the defendants, or potentially responsible parties
("PRPs"), to engage in remedial work to clean up a hazardous waste
site in Rose Township, Oakland County, Michigan ("Rose Site"). The
proposed remedial plan at the Rose Site calls for the excavation and
incineration of surface soils contaminated with polychlorinated biphenyls ("PCBs"), lead, arsenic and other toxic materials and the flushing
of the subsurface soils contaminated with a variety of volatile and semi-
volatile organic compounds.

The state challenges the legality of the remedial action, and seeks
to prevent entry of the consent decree. The Natural Resources Defense
Council, the Environmental Defense Fund and the Sierra Club have
filed a brief as amici curiae supportive of the state's position. The majority of the state's and amici's objections to the decree focus on the
effectiveness of soil flushing at the Rose Site, where layers of clay are
interspersed among beds of sand and silt. The PRPs cross appeal the
district court's determination that the decree must comply with Michigan's groundwater anti-degradation law.

I. STATUTORY OVERVIEW . . .

The federal legislative scheme and its history are persuasive that
Congress did not intend to leave the cleanup under CERCLA solely in
the hands of the federal government. CERCLA, as amended by SARA,
provides a substantial and meaningful role for the individual states in
the selection and development of remedial actions to be taken within
their jurisdictions. In this case for example, pursuant to 42 U.S.C.
§9621(f) the State of Michigan had a reasonable opportunity to comment on the RI/FS, the RAP proposed in the amended ROD, and other
technical data related to the implementation of the proposed remedy.
The state was also entitled to and did participate in the settlement negotiations that led to the decree at issue. Id. Further, CERCLA is designed
to accommodate more stringent "applicable or relevant and appropriate requirements" ("ARARs"), i.e., environmental standards of the
state in which a site is located. 42 U.S.C. §9621(d). Once a consent
decree is proposed by EPA, see id. §9622(a), the state can challenge it
if EPA has proposed implementation of a remedy for which the federal
agency has waived a valid and more stringent state requirement. Id.
§9621(d)(4), (f)(2)(B). The state may also enforce a decree to the
extent the remedial action fails to comply with any state environmental
requirements which have not been waived by EPA. Id. §9621(e).

If no PRPs can be located, or if they are insolvent, a state or political subdivision may enter into a contract or cooperative agreement with EPA, whereby both may take action on a cost-sharing basis. 42 U.S.C. §9604(c), (d). A state may also sue PRPs for remedial and removal costs if such efforts are consistent with the National Contingency Plan (NCP). Id. §9607(a)(4)(A). However, assuming it is not the "lead" agency, the state is limited in its ability to require alternative relief if and when a consent decree is entered into between PRPs and EPA. See id. §9621(f).

II.   FACTS

The Rose Site consists of about 110 acres on which liquid and solid industrial wastes were illegally dumped in the late 1960s. In 1979, the Michigan Toxic Substance and Control Commission declared a toxic substance emergency at the Site, and 5,000 drums of toxic waste were immediately removed. Investigation disclosed that the drums contained, among other chemical compounds, PCBs, phthalates, organic solvents, oil and grease, phenols and heavy metals. In 1983, the Rose Site was placed on the NPL.

All sites placed on the NPL must undergo a Remedial Investigation and Feasibility Study ("RI/FS") to determine the extent of contamination and possible remedies. 42 U.S.C. §9620(e)(1). Under a cooperative agreement with EPA, the Michigan Department of Natural Resources ("MDNR") began the RI/FS evaluation of the Rose Site in 1984. That study, completed in June of 1987, showed two primary areas of contamination: (1) an area which is less than one acre in size but contains groundwater contaminated by vinyl chloride and surface soils having elevated levels of arsenic; and (2) twelve acres in the southwest corner of the Site that contain surface soils contaminated with PCBs, lead, arsenic and other toxic metals; subsurface soils contaminated with a variety of volatile organic compounds ("VOCs") and semi-volatile organic compounds ("SVOCs"); and groundwater contaminated with PCBs, metals, VOCs and SVOCs.

A.   THE RI/FS AND THE ORIGINAL ROD

After a detailed screening of possible remedies, the 1987 RI/FS recommended excavation and on-site thermal destruction to remedy the soil contamination,[56] plus ground water treatment to cleanse the water under the Rose Site. Soil flushing, a method by which the contam-

---

56. This involves, almost literally, a baking of the soil using electrically-powered rods.

inated soil is flushed with water and the resulting flushate is treated to designated cleanup levels and reinjected into the soil, was found to be ineffective at this Site due to the variable permeability of the Rose Site soils. RI/FS, Exh. 3.1a, Table 9-1, at 146.

Pursuant to section 117(a) of CERCLA, 42 U.S.C. §9617(a), which requires that the public be given a reasonable opportunity to comment on a proposed cleanup, EPA published a notice of the remedy and held a public meeting near the Site. In September 1987, EPA issued a Record of Decision ("ROD"), setting forth its proposed remedy as recommended in the RI/FS. The State of Michigan concurred in the ROD, which required, among other steps:

(1) Excavation of approximately 50,000 cubic yards of contaminated soil, incineration of the excavated soils that were contaminated with PCBs, VOCs and SVOCs, and proper treatment and disposal of the resulting incinerated ash; and

(2) Extraction and on-site treatment of contaminated ground water with diversion to adjacent marshlands or an alternate location.

The 1987 ROD issued by EPA included a detailed explanation of the reasons for selecting the proposed remedy, and included specific findings that the remedy satisfied the requirements of CERCLA, complied with federal and state ARARs, and was cost effective. Soil flushing, though not adopted in the 1987 ROD, was not ruled out completely. The ROD listed eight criteria EPA would consider before substituting soil flushing for thermal incineration: economies of scale, community acceptance, cleanup time, land regulations, reliability of soil flushing, implementability, complete site remediation, and cost effectiveness.

B. THE PROPOSED CONSENT DECREE

In June of 1987, shortly before issuance of the original ROD, EPA began settlement negotiations with the PRPs. The State of Michigan participated in these discussions. In the course of the negotiations, EPA was persuaded that the soil flushing method might be a viable, less costly alternative to the incineration of the VOC/SVOC contaminated soil, and could still result in a cleanup that would comply with all federal and state ARARs.

In August of 1988, EPA and the twelve PRPs who are defendants in this action signed the consent decree which included a soil flushing remedy for the site. While under the original plan 50,000 cubic yards of contaminated soil were to be incinerated, the consent decree calls for incineration of only half that amount, augmented by soil flushing for the remaining 25,000 cubic yards. In economic terms this is represented as effecting savings of roughly $12 million. To offset the danger that this process might be insufficient, the decree requires the PRPs to prove, both in a laboratory and at the Rose Site, that soil flushing is capable of meeting Phase I water target cleanup levels ("TCLs") for the subsurface soils contaminated with VOCs and SVOCs within ten years after implementation of the system. Absent such proof, the PRPs would be required to fund and implement an alternate, permanent remedy designed to meet Phase I TCLs. Under the proposed consent decree, EPA is required to review the remedial action at the site at least every five years, and is permitted to seek further response action from the defendants if EPA determines that supplemental remedies are necessary. . . .

. . . In consideration of the work to be performed and the payments to be made by the settling defendants, the United States agrees in the proposed consent decree not to sue them, with some exceptions, for claims available under sections 106 and 107 of CERCLA and other federal and state environmental laws which are based on facts about the Site and its contamination known to EPA at the time of the entry of the decree. The covenant does contain reopening provisions which would allow EPA to seek further injunctive relief or cost recovery if conditions unknown until after entry of the decree reveal that the remedial action is not protective of human health and the environment. See Consent Decree XVII.

C.   PROCEEDINGS IN THE DISTRICT COURT AND THE AMENDED ROD

In September of 1988, EPA filed the proposed consent decree with the U.S. District Court for the Eastern District of Michigan pursuant to 42 U.S.C. §9622(d)(1)(A). As required by 42 U.S.C. §9622(d)(2) and 28 C.F.R. §50.7, notice of the proposed consent decree was published in the Federal Register on September 26, 1988. At the same time, EPA published a three page document entitled Proposed Settlement Plan — Explanation of Significant Differences ("ESD"). The ESD was published to comply with section 9617(c), which requires EPA to explain why a settlement or consent decree to which the agency agrees differs in any significant respect from the final plan or ROD previously issued for a particular site. In this case the ESD explained the basis for the decision to allow defendants to try soil flushing at the Rose Site in conjunction with incineration, when the 1987 ROD had called for soil incineration only.

As required by 42 U.S.C. §9617(a), EPA provided a period for public comment on the proposed changes to the ROD. EPA received written comments from the Michigan Department of Natural Resources and the Michigan Toxic Substances Control Commission, two congressmen, two private environmental organizations (the Environmental Defense Fund and the Michigan Environmental Council), several residents of Rose Township, and the settling defendants. Only the comments from the settling defendants expressed support for the terms of the consent decree.

Those who objected to soil flushing were concerned that it was not a well-demonstrated technology, especially in Michigan's cold weather climate; that flushing may take as long as fifteen years to clean up the site as opposed to two years for incineration; that monitoring of soil flushing's effectiveness is extremely difficult, and that flushing may violate Michigan's groundwater anti-degradation laws.[57] There were also concerns that the consent decree did not adequately define defendants' obligations in the event soil flushing failed to achieve established cleanup levels within the required time frame.

The settling defendants asserted that the proposed consent decree would protect human health and the environment, and included a study by the Gradient Corporation, an environmental consulting firm, which estimated that approximately 12,325 pounds of organic chemicals would be removed by the soil incineration method and that approximately 12,234 pounds of organic chemicals would be removed by the soil flushing method. The study added that the two amounts would be even closer in volume than this, because an additional amount of soil that was not to be incinerated under the original remedy would be subjected to soil flushing under the consent decree.

On January 18, 1989, after considering the comments received, EPA issued an amended ROD for the Rose Site. The amended ROD formally adopts soil flushing as a remedy for VOC and SVOC-contaminated subsurface soils, but only if pilot testing proves that flushing is as protective as thermal destruction. In adopting the remedy it originally ruled out, EPA reasons that (1) the excavation of PCB contaminated soils will remove most of the unflushable contaminants; (2) the geology of the contaminated area may not be as complex as initially thought; and (3) pilot testing has not yet been performed to rule out soil flushing. EPA, in the amended ROD, further asserts that (1) if Phase II target cleanup levels are achieved, flushing will have done as well as incineration was required to do under the original ROD, and will have brought the Site into compliance with all federal and state ARARs; (2) flushing is more cost effective than incineration; (3) assuming the groundwater treatment system uses granular activated carbon to cap-

---

57. M.C.L.A. §323.1, et seq., (Michigan Water Resources Commission Act ("WRCA")) and Mich. Admin. Code R. 323.2201, et seq., (the "Part 22 Groundwater Regulations") are collectively referred to as Michigan's anti-degradation law.

ture the contaminants, soil flushing will satisfy CERCLA's preference for remedies utilizing permanent and innovative treatments; and (4) soil flushing will reduce toxicity, mobility, and the volume of contaminants to the same extent as thermal destruction.

The State of Michigan filed a complaint with the district court and moved to intervene in the action between EPA and the settling defendants on February 14, 1989, pursuant to 42 U.S.C. §9621(f)(2)(B). This provision allows a state to challenge a proposed consent decree which allegedly fails to meet the state's environmental protection standards. On May 4, 1989, the U.S. District Court held that Michigan could intervene in order to challenge entry of the consent decree. . . .

On July 18, 1989, one day after oral argument, the district court granted EPA's motion for entry of the consent decree. . . .

In its opinion, the district court held that Michigan's groundwater anti-degradation law does represent an ARAR for purposes of CERCLA, but found that the consent decree embodying a soil flushing remedy did not violate the state ARAR. The court found that Michigan's concerns about the complex geology of the Site had been adequately addressed by EPA, and observed that soil flushing had been used, with state approval, at other Michigan sites. The district court concluded that, on the administrative record, EPA's decision to enter into the consent decree was not arbitrary or capricious, and was reasonable, fair and not contrary to relevant federal and state laws. In addition, the district court held that CERCLA's provisions allowing EPA to settle claims for remedial action with the PRPs preempted the State of Michigan from imposing additional remedial action requirements on defendants under Michigan's Water Resources Commission Act, M.C.L.A. §323.6; Michigan's Environmental Protection Act, M.C.L.A. §691.1201 et seq.; and the common law of public nuisance.

III.   ISSUES ON APPEAL

The State of Michigan now appeals the entry of the consent decree, and the district court's finding that CERCLA preempts some of the state's environmental remedies against these defendants. The PRPs cross-appeal the district court's finding that Michigan's anti-degradation law is an ARAR. . . .

V.   WHETHER THE CONSENT DECREE IS ARBITRARY AND CAPRICIOUS

The State of Michigan first argues, along with amici curiae, that EPA's decision to modify its ROD and consent decree to include soil flushing as a remedy for the Rose Site was arbitrary and capricious because the record does not support EPA's conclusion that the Site is conducive to soil flushing. Under the arbitrary and capricious standard, a lower court's discretionary action "cannot be set aside by a reviewing court unless it has a definite and firm conviction that the court below committed a clear error of judgment in the conclusion it reached upon the weighing of the relevant factors." *McBee v. Bomar,* 296 F.2d 235, 237 (6th Cir. 1961). Cf. *Motor Vehicle Manufacturers Ass'n v. State Farm Mutual,* 463 U.S. 29, 43, 103 S. Ct. 2856, 2866, 77 L. Ed. 2d 443 (1983) (In articulating the arbitrary and capricious standard, the Supreme Court stated that it would "uphold a decision of less than ideal clarity if the agency's path may reasonably be discerned.").

The 1987 RI/FS and ROD identified soil flushing as not applicable at the site for the following reasons:

a.   The soils are marginally suitable for this technology because of variable permeabilities;

b.   The soils contain both soluble and insoluble chemicals — flushing is only reliable for soluble chemicals and would have to be used with another technology to remove the entire source;

c.   Pilot testing would have to be performed before such a remedy is implemented; and

d.   Flushing is not well demonstrated, especially in cold weather environments like that of Michigan.

For the reasons that follow, we believe that the concerns noted in the RI/FS have all been adequately addressed by EPA in the ESD it published when it filed the decree with the district court. See generally Exh. 3.18, Explanation of Significant Differences.

As evidenced by its placement at the top of EPA's concerns in 1987, there is no question that EPA originally considered the soil conditions at the Rose Site to be the prime deterrent to the use of soil flushing. However, after the RI/FS was performed and after more soil samples were taken, EPA found that the soils to be flushed were not as complex as once thought. . . .

. . . It must be emphasized, however, that the Remedial Action Plan ("RAP") annexed to the consent decree expressly requires that the settling defendants demonstrate to EPA, both in a laboratory and on-site, that soil flushing will work *before* it is implemented. The required demonstration includes additional field tests to further define the permeability of the soils.

Based on our thorough review of the scientific evidence in the record, we do not find EPA's decision to experiment with soil flushing at the Rose Site to be arbitrary or without foundation. . . .

VII.   WHETHER THE PROPOSED DECREE COMPLIES WITH THE LAW

In their challenges to the legality of the decree and the district court's judgment, the parties raise five significant issues. Defendants argue that the district court erred in its ruling that Michigan's anti-degradation law is an applicable or relevant and appropriate environmental requirement ("ARAR"). The State of Michigan, on the other hand, questions whether the decree's remedial action will attain potential state ARARs. Next, the state argues that soil flushing by definition violates Michigan's anti-degradation law, allegedly a state ARAR. . . .

A.   WHETHER MICHIGAN'S ANTI-DEGRADATION LAW IS AN ARAR

The State of Michigan and amici curiae contend that the proposed remedy is not in accordance with the law because it does not meet the state's ARARs. Under CERCLA, the remedial action selected must comply with identified state ARARs that are more stringent than applicable federal standards unless the ARARs are waived. The relevant provision provides in part:

> With respect to any hazardous substance, pollutant or contaminant that will remain onsite, if (i) any standard, requirement, criteria, or limitation under any Federal environmental law, . . . or (ii) any promulgated standard, requirement, criteria, or limitation under a State environmental . . . law that is more stringent than any Federal standard, . . . is legally applicable to the hazardous substance or pollutant or contaminant concerned or is relevant and appropriate under the circumstances, . . . the remedial action selected . . . shall require, at the completion of the remedial action, a level or standard of control for such hazardous substance or pollutant or contaminant which at least attains such legally applicable or relevant and appropriate standard, requirement, criteria, or limitation.

42 U.S.C. §9621(d)(2)(A). Before deciding whether the decree must comply with such laws, we need to determine whether there are any state ARARs applicable to the Rose Site.

The district court found that the Michigan Water Resources Commission Act ("WRCA"), and its corresponding agency rules, Mich. Admin. Code R. 323.2201 (1980), et seq., ("Part 22 Rules") satisfy each of the criteria for ARARs to which a proposed remedy must comply under section 9621(d). Section 6(a) of the WRCA provides, in part:

> It shall be unlawful for any persons directly or indirectly to discharge into the waters of the state any substance *which is or may become injurious* to the

public health, safety, or welfare; or which is or may become injurious to domestic, commercial, industrial, agricultural, recreational or other uses which are being or may be made of such waters. . . .

M.C.L.A. §323.6(a) (emphasis added). The corresponding agency rules, the Part 22 Rules, provide for the nondegradation of groundwater in usable aquifers. Mich. Admin. Code R. 323.2205 (1980). Defendants challenge the district court's conclusion that said Michigan law and rules, collectively referred to as Michigan's anti-degradation law, qualify as a state ARAR.[58]

Under 42 U.S.C. §9621(d), supra, a state environmental requirement or standard constitutes a state ARAR to which the remedy must comply if it is (1) properly promulgated, (2) more stringent than federal standards, (3) legally applicable or relevant and appropriate, and (4) timely identified.

1.   Whether Michigan's Anti-Degradation Law is Properly Promulgated

To be considered an ARAR, the anti-degradation law must be "promulgated." 42 U.S.C. §9621(d)(2)(A)(ii). According to EPA, "promulgated" as used in section 9621 refers to "laws imposed by state legislative bodies and regulations developed by state agencies that are of general applicability and are legally enforceable." EPA, Superfund Program; Interim Guidance on Compliance with Applicable or Relevant and Appropriate Requirements; Notice of Guidance, 52 Fed. Reg. 32495, 32498 (Aug. 27, 1987) [hereinafter Interim Guidance]. See also Preamble, National Oil and Hazardous Substances Pollution Contingency Plan, 55 Fed. Reg. 8666, 8841 (Mar. 8, 1990) (codified at 40 C.F.R. §300.400(g)(4)) [hereinafter NCP, Final Rule]. EPA evidently desired to differentiate "advisories, guidance, or other non-binding policies, as well as standards that are not of general application," Interim Guidance, 52 Fed. Reg. at 32498, from laws or rules promulgated by state legislatures or agencies that are imposed on all citizens of a partic-

---

58. There are several kinds of applicable or relevant and appropriate environmental requirements (ARARs).

ARARs may be chemical-specific (e.g., an established level for a specific chemical in groundwater), action-specific (e.g., a land disposal restriction for RCRA hazardous wastes), or location-specific (e.g., a restriction on actions that adversely affect wetlands). Thus, the concept is much broader than that of a specific cleanup level for a site.

Starfield, The 1990 Nat'l Contingency Plan — More Detail and More Structure, But Still a Balancing Act, 20 Envtl. L. Rep. 10222, 10230 (June 1990).

ular state, which is the case with Michigan's anti-degradation law since it was enacted by the Michigan legislature, and the accompanying administrative rules were properly developed by the Michigan Water Resources Commission. *Akzo Coatings,* 719 F. Supp. at 583.

While defendants concede that Michigan's anti-degradation law has general applicability, they contend that it was not properly promulgated because its vagueness and lack of a quantifiable standard render it legally unenforceable.[59] A standard is not constitutionally vague if it is drafted "with sufficient definiteness that ordinary people can understand what conduct is prohibited and in a manner that does not encourage arbitrary and discriminatory enforcement." *Kolender v. Lawson,* 461 U.S. 352, 357, 103 S. Ct. 1855, 1858, 75 L. Ed. 2d 903 (1983). As noted above, the WRCA does not permit anyone "directly or indirectly to discharge into the waters of the state any substance which is or may become injurious to the public health, safety, or welfare; or . . . to domestic, commercial, industrial, agricultural, recreational or other uses. . . ." We believe such a standard is "sufficiently specific to provide a fair warning that certain kinds of conduct are prohibited." *Colten v. Kentucky,* 407 U.S. 104, 110, 92 S. Ct. 1953, 1957, 32 L. Ed. 2d 584 (1972).

To be sure, when the WRCA was enacted in 1929 the Michigan legislature may have intended "injurious" to mean concentrations of contaminants measurable only in parts per thousand rather than parts per billion or per trillion, as we are capable of measuring today. However, any legislature desiring to prohibit "immoral conduct," for example, faces the same dilemma because the standard of what constitutes acceptable conduct changes over time. Cf. *Fowler v. Board of Educ.,* 819 F.2d 657, 664-65 (6th Cir. 1987) (due to the need to govern wide ranges of conduct, various courts including the Supreme Court have rejected vagueness challenges to laws prohibiting federal or state employees from engaging in "misconduct," "immorality," or "conduct unbecoming").

Moreover, section 323.5 of the WRCA expressly requires the Water Resources Commission to "establish pollution standards for lakes,

---

59. According to EPA, in order for potential state ARARs to be "legally enforceable" they "must be issued in accordance with state procedural laws or standards and contain specific enforcement provisions or be otherwise enforceable under state law." NCP, Final Rule, 55 Fed. Reg. at 8746. Defendants do not, and could not, contend that Michigan's anti-degradation law lacks specific enforcement provisions under state law. Section 6(c) of the WRCA, as drafted at the time of the consent decree, states that a violation of section 6(a) "may be abated according to law in an action brought by the Attorney General in a court of competent jurisdiction." M.C.L.A. §323.6(c). Moreover, section 10 of the WRCA provides for both civil remedies and criminal sanctions for violations of the WRCA or its accompanying administrative rules. M.C.L.A. §323.10.

rivers, streams, and other waters of the state. . . ." As we find is the case with section 323.6 of the WRCA, the Part 22 Rules which prohibit "degradations" of "groundwaters in any usable aquifer which would deteriorate the local background groundwater quality," Mich. Admin. Code R. §§323.2202(g), 323.2205, are neither vague nor unenforceable. Likewise, the fact that a "degradation" of groundwaters may occur only when it is "determined by the commission to be a deterioration in terms of magnitude of the change and importance of the parameters describing groundwater quality," id. §323.2202(g), does not render Michigan's anti-degradation law constitutionally infirm. The "background water quality," measured by a hydrogeological study as required under the Part 22 Rules, provides a standard beyond which would-be polluters may not pollute. According to EPA, "[g]eneral State goals that are duly promulgated (such as a non-degradation law) *have the same weight as explicit numerical standards,* although the former have to be interpreted in terms of a site and therefore may allow more flexibility in approach." Interim Guidance, 52 Fed. Reg. at 32,498 (emphasis added).

Defendants emphasize that EPA, in its proposed rules, requires "general state goals" to be implemented by means of "specific requirements," which Michigan's current implementing regulations fail to do, as they only prohibit "degradations" of the "local background groundwater quality." However, as evidenced by its proposed rules *as a whole,* EPA is not limiting the validity of general state goals solely to those which are implemented via specific numerical standards promulgated in corresponding agency rules. Rather, the type of standard provided is one of several factors courts should consider in deciding whether a state goal is an ARAR. EPA's proposed rules state:

> General State goals that are contained in a promulgated statute and implemented via specific requirements found in the statute or in other promulgated regulations are potential ARARs. For example, a State anti-degradation statute which prohibits degradation of surface waters below specific levels of quality *or* in ways that *preclude certain uses of that water* would be a potential ARAR. *Where such promulgated goals are general in scope,* e.g., a general prohibition against discharges to surface waters of "toxic materials in toxic amounts," *compliance must be interpreted within the context of implementing regulations, the specific circumstances of the site, and the remedial alternatives being considered.*

EPA, National Oil and Hazardous Substances Pollution Contingency Plan; Proposed Rule, 53 Fed. Reg. 51394, 51,438 (Dec. 21, 1988) [hereinafter Proposed Rule] (emphasis added). EPA's final revisions are even clearer: "Even if a state has not promulgated implementing regulations, a general goal can be an ARAR if it meets the eligibility criteria for state ARARs. However, EPA would have considerable latitude in determining how to comply with the goal in the absence of implementing regulations." NCP, Final Rule, 55 Fed. Reg. at 8746. Hence, EPA's own publications recognize that general requirements containing no specific numerical standards, or any implementing regulations at all for that matter, can be enforceable ARARs.

We are unable to find any legally binding case law supporting defendants' contention that Michigan's anti-degradation law is unenforceably vague. . . .

2.   Whether Michigan's Anti-Degradation Law is More Stringent than Federal Standards

Section 9621(d)(2)(A)(ii) also requires that for state standards to apply to a remedial action plan, they must be "more stringent than any Federal standard, requirement, criteria or limitation. . . ." The district court summarily concluded that

> [a]lthough it is difficult to compare a federal statute containing specific requirements with a state agency rule that contains a broad prohibition, this Court finds that the broad prohibition is more stringent than the federal statute setting minimal standards. Accordingly, Michigan's anti-degradation law also complies with this aspect of 42 U.S.C. §9621(d).

Akzo Coatings, 719 F. Supp. at 584. The district court, however, is not left without authority for its conclusion. In its proposed revision of the NCP, EPA stated: "Where no Federal ARAR exists for a chemical, location, or action, but a State ARAR does exist, or where a state ARAR is broader in scope than the Federal ARAR, the State ARAR is considered more stringent." Proposed Rule, 53 Fed. Reg. at 51435. Senator Mitchell, one of the principal authors of section 9621, similarly explained during the debate on SARA that a "more stringent" state requirement within the meaning of section 9621(d)(2)(A) "includes *any* State requirement where there is no comparable Federal requirement." 132 Cong. Rec. S. 14,915 (Oct. 3, 1986) (emphasis added).

We find that no comparable federal statute or rule identified by the parties broadly regulates direct or indirect discharges of any injurious or potentially injurious substance into groundwater resources as does section 6(a) of the WRCA. The WRCA is not directly comparable to the federal Safe Drinking Water Act ("SDWA"), 42 U.S.C. §300g-1(a)(2) because it is broader in coverage and, depending on the site, as or more demanding in terms of cleanup requirements than the SDWA. We believe, therefore, that the WRCA is more stringent than the SDWA.

With regard to coverage, the provisions of the SDWA apply only to a limited number of substances while the WRCA applies to "any substance which is or may become injurious to the public health," M.C.L.A. §323.6(a). Second, the SDWA applies only to public drinking water supply systems serving a certain minimum number of customers, 42 U.S.C. §§300(f)-(g)(4), while the WRCA applies to any waters of the state, whether private or public, including groundwaters. M.C.L.A. §323.6(a).

Likewise, we find that the WRCA's cleanup requirements implemented by means of that Act's accompanying regulations are equally or in some cases more demanding, and thus not less stringent, than the federal maximum contaminant levels ("MCLs") under the SDWA. The Part 22 Rules prohibit degradation of groundwater "from local background groundwater quality." Mich. Admin. Code R. 323.2205(1). . . .

In many instances, especially when dealing with synthetic compounds which do not naturally occur in groundwater, the Part 22 Rules will be more stringent than the SDWA. For example, the SDWA would limit the vinyl chloride concentration, which at the Rose Site is 140 parts per billion ("ppb") at several monitoring wells, to only 2 ppb. 40 C.F.R. §141.61 (1989). However, with no influence by discharges, the background concentration of vinyl chloride in the groundwaters of the Rose Site should be at or near zero. If the state commission determined the difference between the SDWA and the WRCA standards to be substantial enough, the level of cleanup required would therefore be higher under the Part 22 Rules as compared to the federal standard for vinyl chloride and other synthetic compounds. . . . Accordingly, even if we focus on the Rose Site alone, as EPA seems to require with general state goals, see Interim Guidance, 52 Fed. Reg. at 32498, we find that the WRCA and the Part 22 rules are more stringent than federal standards under the SDWA.

3. Whether Michigan's Anti-Degradation Law is Legally Applicable to the Rose Site or Relevant and Appropriate to the Remedial Action Selected

The third requirement under section 9621(d) is that the potential ARARs be "legally applicable to the hazardous substance or pollutant or contaminant concerned or [] relevant and appropriate under the circumstances of the release or remedial action selected. . . ." To determine whether this requirement is satisfied, we must re-examine the scope of Michigan's anti-degradation law. Section 6(a) of the WRCA prohibits persons from discharging, "directly or indirectly," certain substances into the groundwaters. The Part 22 Rules define "discharges" to be "the addition of materials to ground waters from any facility or operation which acts as a discrete or diffuse source. . . ." Mich. Admin. Code R. 323.2202(j).

The record in this case clearly establishes an ongoing, indirect discharge of injurious substances from the soil into the groundwater at the Site caused by the natural infiltration of water through contaminated soils, which in turn results in the leaching of contaminants. The RI/FS (Exh. 3.1a, at 20), the 1987 ROD (Exh. 3.1c, at 11), the 1987 Responsiveness Summary (Exh. 3.1c, at 17-18), and the amended ROD (Exh. 3.22a, at 3) all reflect that soils contaminated with toxic chemicals on site will, unless remediated, act as a "continual source of groundwater degradation." Exh. 3.22a, Rod Amendment, at 3. The record also establishes that the nature and distribution of these contaminants is such that they are or may become "injurious to the public health, safety or welfare . . . or [to] uses which are being made or may be made of such waters. . . ." M.C.L.A. §323.6(a). . . .

We thus agree with the district court that "because soil flushing diffusely discharges toxicants from the soil into the ground water, the anti-degradation rules are legally applicable to the clean up of the Rose Township site" and to soil flushing in particular. . . .

Even if Michigan's anti-degradation law were not applicable to this site, its consideration would certainly be "relevant and appropriate." Among possible factors to be considered, the environmental media ("groundwater"), the type of substance ("injurious") and the objective of the potential ARAR ("protecting aquifers from actual or potential degradation''), are all "relevant" in this case because they pertain to the conditions of the Rose Site. Moreover, considering the aforementioned factors, the use of Michigan's anti-degradation law is well-suited to the site at issue and therefore "appropriate" in this case. See Proposed Rule, 53 Fed. Reg. at 51,436; 40 C.F.R. §300.400(g)(2) (1990).

Accordingly, we conclude that Michigan's anti-degradation law is properly promulgated, more stringent than the federal standard, legally applicable or relevant and appropriate, as well as timely identified (the latter factor not having been argued on appeal), and therefore constitutes an ARAR within the meaning of 42 U.S.C. §9621(d)(2). The fact that Michigan's anti-degradation law is an ARAR, however, does not resolve the question of whether the decree must comply with that ARAR. A decree must comply with all federal and state ARARs *unless* EPA "waives" an ARAR and the state either does not challenge the waiver or the waiver is upheld in court against the state challenge. See 42 U.S.C. §9621(d)(4), (f)(2).

B. WHETHER THE DECREE'S REMEDIAL ACTION WILL ATTAIN THE CLEANUP REQUIREMENTS OF MICHIGAN'S ANTI-DEGRADATION LAW

The briefs and district court opinion generate considerable confusion on the issues of whether the decree's remedial action will attain the cleanup requirements of Michigan's anti-degradation law and if not, whether EPA actually and properly "waived" that ARAR. While the district court found that the state had not designated any portions of the record that establish EPA had failed to consider Michigan's anti-degradation law to be an ARAR, *Akzo Coatings*, 719 F. Supp. at 586 n.6, several references in the government's brief and in its correspondence during negotiations with defendants suggest that, as with the Aviex Site, it never considered the WRCA and Part 22 Rules to be an ARAR. In any event, the State of Michigan does not, and cannot at this point, allege that cleanup standards at the completion of the remedial action will fall below the ARARs. The state consented to the 1987 ROD and agreed that all ARARs would be met by the accompanying RAP. The 1987 ROD contains the same TCLs as the amended ROD, so the state has implicitly agreed that the amended ROD and consent decree's TCLs satisfy all ARARs, including Michigan's groundwater regulations. Instead, the state's argument that the consent decree does not attain ARARs only consists of criticisms of the selected methodology; i.e., soil flushing will fail to attain the decree's TCLs and thus the ARARs for the Rose Site.

The state argues that EPA has a duty to determine, prior to submitting the decree to the court, whether soil flushing would attain ARARs. In contrast, defendants argue and the district court agreed that based on section 9621(d)(2), "whether the Consent Decree complies with the state ARAR is to be measured 'at the completion of the remed[ial action.]' " *Akzo Coatings*, 719 F. Supp. at 586 (quoting 42 U.S.C. §9621(d)(2)(A)). As evidenced by its title, however, section 9621(d)(2)(A)'s purpose refers to the "degree of cleanup" required under CERCLA, which is naturally measured at the completion of the remedial action. That provision does not address the issue of whether EPA has a duty to initially ascertain that the chosen remedy will in fact achieve ARARs.

EPA's own regulations indicate that the agency has some obligation to evaluate proposed remedial actions in terms of whether they will attain ARARs *before* implementation. Once the initial screening is done, "[A]lternatives shall be assessed to determine whether they attain [ARARs]." 40 C.F.R. §300.430(e)(9)(iii)(B) (1990). "The ROD shall describe the following statutory requirements as they relate to the scope and objectives of the action: . . . The [ARARs] . . . that the remedy *will* attain." 40 C.F.R. §300.430(f)(5)(ii)(B) (1990) (emphasis added). . . .

Our review of the various CERCLA provisions dealing with ARARs also supports the state's argument that EPA must determine prior to implementation whether a remedy will meet designated ARARs for a particular site. . . .

In this case it is clear EPA never conclusively determined during negotiations that soil flushing would attain the relevant ARAR at the completion of the remedy:

Had EPA made such a determination, it never would have required a laboratory test or required the implementation of an alternate permanent remedy if the defendants cannot satisfy EPA that soil flushing will work at the Rose Site. All EPA determined was that soil flushing may be a viable remedy at the site and determined to give the defendants a chance to demonstrate whether it will work.

Brief for the United States, at 32 n.38. Section 9621(d)(4) requires that EPA make specific findings and publish them when it invokes a waiver, the latter requirement clearly not having been complied with in this case. We nevertheless hold that EPA has waived the ARARs for soil flushing based on the finding that "the remedial action selected is only part of a *total* remedial action that will attain such level or standard of control when completed." 42 U.S.C. §9621(d)(4)(A) (emphasis added). See Exh. 3.22a, Rod Amendment, at 4 (In reference to the effectiveness of soil flushing, the amended ROD stated: "*provided* appropriate target cleanup levels are met, all ARARs as in the ROD, would be attained.") (emphasis added). In other words, EPA recognized that if soil flushing did not in fact attain the ARARs the defendants would have to carry out an alternative remedy to comply with them. Accordingly, the district court correctly allowed the state to intervene under section 9621(f), prior to entry of the consent decree, to challenge the waiver of Michigan's anti-degradation law.

Under section 9621, a state may intervene in an action before entry of the consent decree and challenge the waiver of an ARAR, and if the waiver is not supported by *substantial evidence*, the court is required to conform the remedial action to that ARAR. 42 U.S.C. §9621(f)(2)(B). In this case, as we find that EPA implicitly waived all ARARs for soil flushing on the basis that the decree as a whole would attain them, the state must show by substantial evidence that EPA's waiver is unlawful.

We do not believe that the state has met its evidentiary burden in this respect. . . .

. . . [W]e find that there is substantial evidence in the record to support and justify EPA's conclusion that the remedial action *as a whole* will attain the ARARs for the Rose Site. Should soil flushing fail, defendants must propose an alternate remedy that will attain all TCL's embodied in the decree and be as protective to human health and the environment as excavation and incineration.

Again, we emphasize that EPA cannot and is under no legal obligation to determine with absolute certainty whether a proposed remedial action will attain ARARs. If the decree is binding on the parties, requires attainment of all ARARs, and provides sufficient safeguards for careful implementation of proposed remedies which include proven technologies that either have been or are being used at similar sites or which are subject to testing under specified performance conditions, then it will be difficult for a court which lacks scientific expertise to find that the state has proven by substantial evidence that the remedial action at a particular site will not attain ARARs. The record contains evidence indicating that both soil flushing and incineration have been successfully used to remedy hazardous sites to pre-determined cleanup levels. Moreover, the state in this case may always come back to court at the completion of the remedial action and persuade us that the Phase I and/or Phase II TCLs have not been achieved. See 42 U.S.C. §9621(e). We agree with the district court that the state has failed to present enough evidence to persuade us that the remedial action as a whole will not attain ARARs at its completion. . . .

IX.   CONCLUSION

In summary, it is necessary to make some additional comments regarding the scope of our review. We have meticulously pored over the voluminous record and examined, in detail, all of the arguments made on appeal. Cf. *Ethyl Corp.,* supra, 541 F.2d at 36 ("The more technical the case, the more intensive must be the court's efforts to understand the evidence . . . [to] properly perform its appellate function."). We believe the consent decree adequately takes into account all of CERCLA's requirements.

In particular, we do not find that the adoption of soil flushing as a remedy for the Rose Site subsurface soils is an arbitrary and capricious choice. EPA's reversal of its original opinion on the effectiveness of soil flushing has been adequately explained. . . . Allowing defendants to test soil flushing under EPA's supervision and pursuant to an established timetable is both fair and reasonable, especially given the fact that both EPA and the State of Michigan regard soil flushing as a cost-effective, proven technology.

We have found Michigan's anti-degradation law to be an ARAR. Nevertheless we conclude that EPA implicitly waived that ARAR, and that the state has not met its burden to show, by substantial evidence, that the waiver was unjustified. In essence, we agree with the district court that the remedial action as a whole can attain all federal and state ARARs. . . .

WELLFORD, Senior Circuit Judge, concurring: . . .

I disagree with the conclusion reached in part VIIA that Michigan's anti-degradation law is an ARAR under 42 U.S.C. §9621(d)(2)(A). To be legally enforceable and avoid a vagueness challenge, state ARARs must be specific and definite so "that ordinary people can understand what conduct is prohibited." *Kolendar v. Lawson,* 461 U.S. 352, 357 (1983); see also *Colten v. Kentucky,* 407 U.S. 104 (1972). The majority concedes that Michigan's current implementing regulations to its WRCA fail to provide "specific requirements" since they merely forbid " 'degradations' of the 'local background groundwater quality.' " Michigan's policies with regard to soil flushing are inconsistent, and I would find these laws to be unenforceable, vague and insufficient to be classified as ARARs. See *Kelley v. United States,* 618 F. Supp. 1103 (W.D. Mich. 1985).

I agree with the rationale and result reached in part VIIA-1 and 2 that Michigan's laws, which are more stringent than federal standards, were properly promulgated despite my conclusion that they are not ARARs. I disagree, however, with the majority's conclusion that Michigan's anti-degradation law, under CERCLA or SARA, is legally applicable as an ARAR to the Rose Site or relevant and appropriate to the remedial action selected in the consent decree. . . .

QUESTIONS

1. In view of the high cost of meeting the anti-degradation law, why is Michigan so keen to impose these restrictions?

2. Evaluate the court's scrutiny of EPA's decision to allow soil flushing. What standard of review did the court apply? Do you think that the standard applied was appropriate for this type of decision?

3. Do you agree with the majority's decision that the Michigan anti-degradation law is applicable and/or relevant and appropriate?

4. Do you agree with the court's determination that EPA had in fact waived the anti-degradation ARAR? Does the court's analysis imply that EPA implicitly waives all ARARs that might not be attained if the "remedial action selected is only part of a *total* remedial action that will attain such level or standard of control when completed"?

5. Is it feasible for EPA to determine prior to implementation whether a remedy will meet designated ARARs? Should EPA waive ARARs whenever it cannot determine at the time of remedy selection that the remedy will attain the requirement? What incentive would such a

waiver provide for those implementing a remedy to make extraordinary efforts, develop new technologies, or incorporate improved technologies as they become available?

ARAR PROBLEM

In selecting a remedy for the RETEP site, the EPA adopted, inter alia, as ARARs the following requirements. What challenges could be brought against these ARARs? How should these decisions be defended?

1. *State Water Resources Control Board, Resolution No. 68-16.* In October 1968, the State Water Resources Control Board adopted the following resolution:

> (1)   Whenever the existing quality of water is better than the quality established in policies as of the date on which such policies become effective, such existing high quality will be maintained until it has been demonstrated to the State that any change will be consistent with the maximum benefit to the people of the State, will not unreasonably affect present and anticipated beneficial use of such water and will not result in water quality less than that prescribed in the policies.
>
> (2)   Any activity which produces or may produce a waste or increased volume or concentration of waste and which discharges or proposes to discharge to existing high quality waters will be required to meet waste discharge requirements which will result in the best practicable treatment or control of the discharge necessary to assure that (a) a pollution or nuisance will not occur and (b) the highest water quality consistent with the maximum benefit to the people of the State will be maintained.

At the time that this resolution was adopted, the State Water Resources Board did not consider itself subject to the State Administrative Procedure Act. The resolution was not available for public comment. The State has enforced this resolution in many circumstances. The State has interpreted this anti-degradation standard to require cleanup of hazardous wastes flowing into a neighboring river to zero detection levels. EPA has interpreted the resolution less stringently.

2. *RCRA Subtitle C Regulations — Cleanup of TCE (a listed waste — F001).* Tests from the RETEP site indicate the presence of TCE, a listed hazardous waste when used in degreasing. Records do not indicate whether these residues were attributable to degreasing activities on the site. Records indicate that some of these materials might have been used for degreasing at a few of the generators' facilities. It is also possi-

ble that TCE was used in degreasing at the RETEP facility, although records are inconclusive.

   3. *RCRA Subtitle C Regulations — Cleanup of TCE (a listed waste — F001) in Groundwater and Soils.* Tests from the RETEP site indicate the presence of TCE in groundwater and soils.

   4. *RCRA Post-Closure Regulations.* EPA seeks to have the RETEP site cleaned up in accordance with RCRA's post-closure requirements. The RETEP site was never issued a RCRA permit.

DISCUSSION QUESTIONS

   In view of the high cost of remediation and the large number of sites in need of work, do CERCLA's clean-up standards sensibly address the cleanup tasks? What other cleanup standards could be used? What would be the advantages and drawbacks of these approaches?

7.   SUPERFUND ENFORCEMENT POLICY AND THE SETTLEMENT PROCESS

   At the time CERCLA was enacted, Congress expected that the broad and clear liability regime would encourage quick and efficacious settlement agreements, obviating the need for complex and costly litigation and speeding the cleanup of dangerous waste sites. The legislation, however, offered EPA little guidance in structuring the settlement process. EPA encountered tremendous difficulty in developing and implementing a settlement policy.

   EPA's approach to settlement policy went through three phases during the first five years of the Superfund program. See generally Developments in the Law — Toxic Waste Litigation, 99 Harv. L. Rev. 1458, 1505 (1986). EPA's initial attempt to implement the Superfund emphasized the role of settlements. EPA approached each site on a case by case basis. The lack of clear settlement standards hindered negotiations as PRPs maneuvered for more favorable terms. The unguided discretion of negotiators not only frustrated legitimate settlement efforts, but also lent itself to abuse by EPA personnel. Some of the early settlements were attacked as "sweetheart deals" for industry. In 1983, allegations that the Superfund program was being manipulated for political and personal gain led to the resignation or firing of more than 15 EPA officials, including Administrator Burford and Assistant Administrator Lavelle. William Ruckelshaus was brought back to head the agency and salvage its reputation.

In the second phase of Superfund implementation, Administrator Ruckelshaus shifted the strategy toward aggressive enforcement and the use of litigation rather than settlement. EPA's 1983 policy emphasized government-conducted, Superfund-financed cleanups. The agency did not prohibit settlements, but significantly discouraged them by adhering to rigid, unpublished criteria. This approach helped to restore EPA's credibility, but led to the criticism that the agency unduly discouraged beneficial negotiated cleanup agreements.

In late 1984, EPA embarked on an intermediate approach to settlement policy. It released the Interim CERCLA Settlement Policy, which set out procedures and substantive criteria for settlement negotiations.[60] In order to encourage private party cleanup proposals and to facilitate negotiations, the Settlement Policy institutionalized an agency practice to notify PRPs of their potential liability, the identity of other PRPs, and available data on quantities and nature of wastes at the site (by PRP) at the earliest feasible time. With regard to substantive criteria, the Settlement Policy set out an objective of complete cleanup by private parties or 100 percent cost recovery of government expenditures, but recognized limited flexibility to consider lesser settlements. As further incentives to settlement negotiations, the Settlement Policy authorized contribution protection and releases from future government liability for settling parties when specific criteria could be met.

Even before the interim settlement policy was issued, Congress had begun the reauthorization process for Superfund. Because of the slow progress in resolving Superfund cases, a major focus of the reauthorization process was settlement policy. To an unprecedented degree, the Superfund Amendments and Reauthorization Act of 1986 legislated a settlement policy. With regard to settlement procedures, Congress largely codified EPA's Interim CERCLA Settlement Policy of notifying PRPs early in the process and furnishing available information, although it left the use of these procedures to the discretion of the agency. §122(e). To further encourage settlement, Congress imposed a moratorium on government cleanup actions for 120 days following the notification of PRPs. In addition, EPA may not commence a remedial investigation and feasibility study until 90 days have passed. As an aid to allocating costs, SARA authorizes EPA to issue nonbinding allocations of responsibility (NBARs). §122(e)(3).

SARA also guides the substantive content of Superfund settlement agreements. Section 122(b) expressly authorizes "mixed funding,"

---

60. The Interim CERCLA Settlement Policy is contained in the Statutory/Regulatory Supplement. Although it was never issued as a final rule, it is still relied upon as a clear working statement of EPA's approach for structuring negotiations and evaluating settlements. While the 1986 SARA provisions supersede conflicting requirements of the Interim CERCLA Settlement Policy, the interim policy remains a useful description of EPA's settlement policy.

whereby the government agrees to pay for part of the cost of cleanup of an NPL site conducted by PRPs. To assist the many minor parties who bear the draconian threat of joint and several liability and incur disproportionate legal costs, Section 122(g)(1) directs EPA to promptly reach settlements with de minimis parties where practicable and in the public interest. Section 122(f) authorizes the granting of covenants not to sue subject to specified conditions and reopener clauses. Section 113(f) provides PRPs who settle with protection against contribution actions by nonsettlors for matters addressed in the settlement; it also authorizes settling parties to seek contribution from nonsettlors.

EPA has issued additional guidance documents further delineating its settlement policy. The Statutory/Regulatory Supplement contains EPA's guidance dealing with de minimis settlements and contribution protection as well as its model consent decree.

In order to cover the challenging terrain of enforcement and settlement policy, this section begins with a series of problems that will hone your understanding of SARA's settlement provisions. It then turns to the *Cannons* case, which illustrates the court's role in reviewing a consent decree. This is followed by a report analyzing the success and pitfalls of different government enforcement strategies. The section ends with a problem evaluating enforcement options for the *RETEP* case.

PROBLEMS: DEVISING ENFORCEMENT STRATEGY IN THE SHADOW OF SARA'S SETTLEMENT PROVISIONS

After carefully studying SARA's settlement provisions (§§122 and 113(f)), analyze the following problems from the perspective of a government lawyer:

1. Marginal Corporation operates a widget manufacturing operation on its three-acre tract of land. Because of improper waste management practices by Marginal and now-defunct predecessor corporations, the property has become contaminated with hazardous substances. EPA has performed a preliminary assessment and site investigation of the site and is presently determining whether the site should be added to the National Priorities List. It is clear that substantial source control work and groundwater remediation will have to be conducted.

Marginal does not appear to have enough assets to satisfy the claims of its secured creditors, and thus is considering declaring bankruptcy under Chapter 7 of the bankruptcy code. Its one hope is to sell the business to Gekko Corporation, which has stated its intention to continue the widget manufacturing operation with current employees. Gekko is hesitant to purchase the property for fear of assuming liability for extensive cleanup costs.

Gekko and Marginal have come to EPA and the State with the following proposition. Gekko will purchase the property if EPA and the State agree to release the company for all current and future liability for cleanup. Such release would take effect on the date of sale. In return, Gekko would agree to pay into the Superfund the sum of $4 million, with an additional $1 million going to the State. Furthermore, for each of the next five years that the widget manufacturing operation remains in business, the Superfund would receive an additional $100,000.

Gekko points out that the arrangement has several advantages to the governments. Without a release from liability, Gekko would not purchase the property, and the governments would receive very little, if any, private defrayal of cleanup costs. Marginal would cease to exist, rather than continuing to generate income which could then be applied to response costs. The amounts mentioned in the proposal would also greatly offset any windfall that would accrue to Gekko through the purchase of contaminated property at reduced rates with the possibility of subsequent resale following cleanup by EPA. Finally, Gekko points out that Marginal is in an area of depressed employment, and thus the local government should favor facilitating the continued operation of this tax-paying employer.

- What are the ethical, legal, and policy objections to Gekko's proposal?
- Are there any limitations on the type of document that can be used to embody the agreement?

2. There are ten companies who each contributed approximately 10 percent by volume of hazardous waste to the XYZ site. After protracted negotiations, 8 of the companies have agreed to pay 90 percent of the cleanup costs. They would like the United States to agree not to settle with the remaining two parties for the balance of outstanding cleanup costs, since the settlors would like free rein to sue the nonsettlors for contribution. Without such language, they will refuse to settle.

- Should the government agree to such language?
- What alternative language could the Government offer to assuage their concerns?
- If the Government does settle with the remaining two parties, are there any arguments the original settlors could make to pierce the veil of contribution protection afforded to settlors under CERCLA?

3. One hundred parties have been identified as generators of waste sent to the XYZ site. Ten of the parties contributed very small

amounts of waste relative to others, and thus seek a de minimis settlement from EPA. The major parties, however, would like the opportunity to reach a settlement with the de minimis parties before negotiations between the de minimis parties and EPA commence.

- Should the Government refrain from negotiating a settlement with the de minimis parties until the majors have attempted to work out a deal with them?
- If a de minimis / majors settlement is reached and soon thereafter the majors settle with the U.S., can the U.S. provide a covenant-not-to-sue and contribution protection to the de minimis parties?
- Does it matter whether the U.S. is informed of the terms of the de minimis / majors settlement?

United States v. Cannons Engineering Corp.

899 F.2d 79 (1st Cir. 1990)

Selya, Circuit Judge.

"Superfund" sites are those which require priority remedial attention because of the presence, or suspected presence, of a dangerous accumulation of hazardous wastes. Expenditures to clean up such sites are specially authorized pursuant to 42 U.S.C. §9611 (1987). After the federal government, through the United States Environmental Protection Agency (EPA), identified four such sites in Bridgewater, Massachusetts, Plymouth, Massachusetts, Londonderry, New Hampshire, and Nashua, New Hampshire (collectively, the Sites), the EPA undertook an intensive investigation to locate potentially responsible parties (PRPs). In the course of this investigation, the agency created a de minimis classification (DMC), putting in this category persons or firms whose discerned contribution to pollution of the Sites was minimal both in the amount and toxicity of the hazardous wastes involved. See 42 U.S.C. §9622(g) (1987). The agency staked out the DMC on the basis of volumetric shares, grouping within it entities identifiable as generators of less than one percent of the waste sent to the Sites. To arrive at a PRP's volumetric share, the agency, using estimates, constituted a ratio between the volume of wastes that the PRP sent to the Sites and the total amount of wastes sent there.

The EPA sent notices of possible liability to some 671 PRPs, including generators and nongenerators. Administrative settlements were thereafter achieved with 300 generators (all de minimis PRPs). In short order, the United States and the two host states, Massachusetts and New Hampshire, brought suits in the United States District Court for the District of Massachusetts against 84 of the PRPs who had rejected, or were ineligible for, the administrative settlement. The suits sought recovery of previously incurred cleanup costs and declarations of liability for future remediation under the Comprehensive Environmental Response, Compensation and Liability Act (CERCLA), 42 U.S.C. §§9601-9675 (1987). The actions were consolidated.

With its complaint, the United States filed two proposed consent decrees. The first (the MP [major parties] decree) embodied a contemplated settlement with 47 major PRPs, that is, responsible parties who were ineligible for membership in the DMC. This assemblage included certain generators whose volumetric shares exceeded the 1% cutoff point and certain nongenerators (like the owners of the Sites and hazardous waste transporters). The second consent decree (the DMC decree) embodied a contemplated settlement with 12 de minimis PRPs who had eschewed participation in the administrative settlement. As required by statute, notice of the decrees' proposed entry was published in the Federal Register. 53 Fed. Reg. 29,959 (Aug. 9, 1988). No comments were received.

The government thereupon moved to enter the decrees. Seven non-settling defendants objected.[61] After considering written submissions and hearing arguments of counsel, the district court approved both consent decrees and dismissed all cross-claims against the settling defendants. *United States v. Cannons Engineering Corp.*, 720 F. Supp. 1027, 1052-53 (D. Mass. 1989). The court proceeded to certify the decrees as final under Fed. R. Civ. P. 54(b). Id. These appeals followed.

I

We approach our task mindful that, on appeal, a district court's approval of a consent decree in CERCLA litigation is encased in a double layer of swaddling. In the first place, it is the policy of the law to encourage settlements. See, e.g., *Donovan v. Robbins*, 752 F.2d 1170, 1177 (7th Cir. 1985); *City of New York v. Exxon Corp.*, 697 F. Supp. 677, 692 (S.D.N.Y. 1988). That policy has particular force where, as here, a government actor committed to the protection of the public interest has pulled the laboring oar in constructing the proposed settlement. See *F.T.C. v. Standard Financial Management Corp.*, 830 F.2d 404, 408

---

61. The objectors, all de minimis PRPs, included the six appellants, Olin Hunt Specialty Chemicals, Inc., Cyn Oil Corp., Beggs & Cobb Corp., Scott Brass, Inc., Kingston-Warren Corp., and Crown Roll Leaf, Inc. (Crown). Although all of them raise slightly different combinations of points, their positions are sufficiently alike that, by and large, except in Crown's case, we refrain from identifying particular arguments with particular appellants.

(1st Cir. 1987) (discussing need for judicial deference "to the agency's determination that the settlement is appropriate"); *S.E.C. v. Randolph*, 736 F.2d 525, 529 (9th Cir. 1984) (similar). While "the true measure of the deference due depends on the persuasive power of the agency's proposal and rationale, given whatever practical considerations may impinge and the full panoply of the attendant circumstances," *Standard Financial*, 830 F.2d at 408, the district court must refrain from second-guessing the Executive Branch.

Respect for the agency's role is heightened in a situation where the cards have been dealt face up and a crew of sophisticated players, with sharply conflicting interests, sit at the table. That so many affected parties, themselves knowledgeable and represented by experienced lawyers, have hammered out an agreement at arm's length and advocate its embodiment in a judicial decree, itself deserves weight in the ensuing balance. See *Exxon*, 697 F. Supp. at 692. The relevant standard, after all, is not whether the settlement is one which the court itself might have fashioned, or considers as ideal, but whether the proposed decree is fair, reasonable, and faithful to the objectives of the governing statute. . . .

The second layer of swaddling derives from the nature of appellate review. Because approval of a consent decree is committed to the trial court's informed discretion, . . . the court of appeals should be reluctant to disturb a reasoned exercise of that discretion. In this context, the test for abuse of discretion is itself a fairly deferential one. . . .

II . . .

Originally, the EPA extended an open offer to all de minimis PRPs, including five of the six appellants, proposing an administrative settlement based on 160% of each PRP's volumetric share of the total projected response cost, that is, the price of remedial actions, past and anticipated. See id. at 1030 n. 1. The settlement figure included a 60% premium to cover unexpected costs and/or unforeseen conditions. Settling PRPs paid their shares in cash and were released outright from all liability. They were also exempted from suits for contribution, see 42 U.S.C. §9622(g)(5) (1987).

Following consummation of the administrative settlement, plaintiffs entered into negotiations with the remaining PRPs. These negotiations resulted in the proposed MP decree (accepted by 47 "major" defendants) and the DMC decree. The terms of the former have been memorialized in the opinion below, 720 F. Supp. at 1034, and do not bear repeating. The latter was modelled upon the administrative settlement, but featured an increased premium: rather than allowing de minimis PRPs to cash out at a 160% level, an eligible generator could resolve its liability only by agreeing to pay 260% of its volumetric share of the total projected response cost. The EPA justified the incremental 100% premium as being in the nature of delay damages. . . .

III . . .

Our starting point is well defined. The Superfund Amendments and Reauthorization Act of 1986 (SARA), P.L. 99-499, §101 et seq., 100 Stat. 1613, authorized a variety of types of settlements which the EPA may utilize in CERCLA actions, including consent decrees providing for PRPs to contribute to cleanup costs and/or to undertake response activities themselves. See 42 U.S.C. §9622 (1987). SARA's legislative history makes pellucid that, when such consent decrees are forged, the trial court's review function is only to "satisfy itself that the settlement is reasonable, fair, and consistent with the purposes that CERCLA is intended to serve." H.R. Rep. No. 253, Pt. 3, 99th Cong., 1st Sess. 19 (1985), reprinted in 1986 U.S. Code Cong. & Admin. News 3038, 3042. Reasonableness, fairness, and fidelity to the statute are, therefore, the horses which district judges must ride. . . .

A. PROCEDURAL FAIRNESS

We agree with the district court that fairness in the CERCLA settlement context has both procedural and substantive components. *Cannons,* 720 F. Supp. at 1039-40. To measure procedural fairness, a court should ordinarily look to the negotiation process and attempt to gauge its candor, openness, and bargaining balance. . . .

In this instance, the district court found the proposed decrees to possess the requisite procedural integrity, *Cannons,* 720 F. Supp. at 1040-41, and appellants have produced no persuasive reason to alter this finding. It is clear the district court believed that the government conducted negotiations forthrightly and in good faith, and the record is replete with indications to that effect. Most of appellants' contrary intimations are vapid and merit summary rejection. But their flagship argument — that the procedural integrity of the settlement was ruptured because appellants were neither allowed to join the MP decree nor informed in advance that they would be excluded — requires comment.

Appellants claim that they were relatively close to the 1% cutoff point, and were thus arbitrarily excluded from the major party settlement, avails them naught. Congress intended to give the EPA broad discretion to structure classes of PRPs for settlement purposes. We can-in separating minor and major players in this instance, that is, in determining that generators who had sent less than 1% of the volume of hazardous waste to the Sites would comprise the DMC and those generators who were responsible for a greater percentage would be treated as major PRPs. While the dividing line was only one of many which the agency could have selected, it was well within the universe of plausibility. . . .

Nor can we say that appellants were entitled to more advance warning of the EPA's negotiating strategy than they received. At the time de minimis PRPs were initially invited to participate in the administrative settlement, the EPA, by letter, informed all of them, including appellants, that:

> The government is anxious to achieve a high degree of participation in this de minimis settlement. Accordingly, the terms contained in this settlement offer are the most favorable terms that the government intends to make available to parties eligible for de minimis settlement in this case.

Cannons, 720 F. Supp. at 1033. Appellants knew, early on, that they were within the DMC and could spurn the EPA's proposal only at the risk of paying more at a later time. Although appellants may have assumed that they could ride on the coattails of the major parties and join whatever MP decree emerged — the government had, on other occasions, allowed such cafeteria-style settlements — the agency was neither asked for, nor did it give, any such assurance in this instance. As a matter of law, we do not believe that Congress meant to handcuff government negotiators in CERCLA cases by insisting that the EPA allow polluters to pick and choose which settlements they might prefer to join. And as a matter of equity, we think that if appellants were misled at all, it was by their own wishful thinking. . . .

B.   SUBSTANTIVE FAIRNESS

Substantive fairness introduces into the equation concepts of corrective justice and accountability: a party should bear the cost of the harm for which it is legally responsible. See generally Developments in the Law — Toxic Waste Litigation, 99 Harv. L. Rev. 1458, 1477 (1986). The logic behind these concepts dictates that settlement terms must be based upon, and roughly correlated with, some acceptable measure of comparative fault, apportioning liability among the settling parties according to rational (if necessarily imprecise) estimates of how much harm each PRP has done. Cf. *Rohm & Haas,* 721 F. Supp. at 685 (the most important aspect of judicial review is relationship of settlement figure to proportion of settlor's waste); *Cannons,* 720 F. Supp. at 1043 (charging more than proportionate liability must be justified in some way, as by unexpected costs or unknown conditions); *Kelley,* 717 F. Supp. at 517 (approving settlement because it was unlikely that settlor's comparative fault was less than percentage of cleanup costs it agreed to pay); *United States v. Conservation Chemical Co.,* 628 F. Supp. 391, 401 (W.D. Mo. 1985) (liability apportionment should be made on basis of comparative fault).

Even accepting substantive fairness as linked to comparative fault, an important issue still remains as to how comparative fault is to be measured. There is no universally correct approach. It appears very clear to us that what constitutes the best measure of comparative fault at a particular Superfund site under particular factual circumstances should be left largely to the EPA's expertise. Whatever formula or scheme EPA advances for measuring comparative fault and allocating liability should be upheld so long as the agency supplies a plausible explanation for it, welding some reasonable linkage between the factors it includes in its formula or scheme and the proportionate shares of the settling PRPs. . . .

Not only must the EPA be given leeway to construct the barometer of comparative fault, but the agency must also be accorded flexibility to diverge from an apportionment formula in order to address special factors not conducive to regimented treatment. While the list of possible variables is virtually limitless, two frequently encountered reasons warranting departure from strict formulaic comparability are the uncertainty of future events and the timing of particular settlement decisions. Common sense suggests that a PRP's assumption of open-ended risks may merit a discount on comparative fault, while obtaining a complete release from uncertain future liability may call for a premium. . . . By the same token, the need to encourage (and suitably reward) early, cost-effective settlements and to account inter alia for anticipated savings in transaction costs inuring from celeritous settlement. . . . Because we are confident that Congress intended EPA to have considerable flexibility in negotiating and structuring settlements, we think reviewing courts should permit the agency to depart from rigid adherence to formulae wherever the agency proffers a reasonable good-faith justification for departure.

We also believe that a district court should give the EPA's expertise the benefit of the doubt when weighing substantive fairness — particularly when the agency, and hence the court, has been confronted by ambiguous, incomplete, or inscrutable information. In settlement negotiations, particularly in the early phases of environmental litigation, precise data relevant to determining the total extent of harm caused and the role of each PRP is often unavailable. . . . Yet, it would disserve a principal end of the statute — achievement of prompt settlement and a concomitant head start on response activities — to leave matters in limbo until more precise information was amassed. As long as the data the EPA uses to apportion liability for purposes of a consent decree falls along the broad spectrum of plausible approximations, judicial intrusion is unwarranted — regardless of whether the court would have opted to employ the same data in the same way. . . .

In this instance, we agree with the court below that the consent decrees pass muster from a standpoint of substantive fairness. They adhere generally to principles of comparative fault according to a volumetric standard, determining the liability of each PRP according to volumetric contribution. And, to the extent they deviate from this formulaic approach, they do so on the basis of adequate justification. In particular, the premiums charged to de minimis PRPs in the administrative settlement, and the increased premium charged in the DMC decree, seem well warranted.

The argument that the EPA should have used relative toxicity as a determinant of proportionate liability for response costs, instead of a strictly volumetric ranking, is a stalking horse. Having selected a reasonable method of weighing comparative fault, the agency need not show that it is the best, or even the fairest, of all conceivable methods. The choice of the yardstick to be used for allocating liability must be left primarily to the expert discretion of the EPA, particularly when the PRPs involved are numerous and the situation is complex. . . .

Appellants' next asseveration — that the decrees favor major party PRPs over their less culpable counterparts — is a gross distortion. While the DMC and MP decrees differ to some extent in application of the volumetric share formula, requiring lower initial contributions under the latter, the good-faith justification for this divergence is readily apparent. In return for the premium paid, de minimis PRPs can cash out, thus obtaining two important benefits: reduced transaction costs and absolute finality with respect to the monetization of their overall liability. . . . The major PRPs, on the other hand, retain an open-ended risk anent their liability at three of the Sites, see *Cannons*, 720 F. Supp. at 1042, making any comparison of proportionate contributions a dubious proposition. At the very least, assumption of this unquantifiable future liability under the MP decree warranted some discount — and the tradeoff crafted by the government's negotiators seems reasonable. Indeed, the acceptance of the first and second DMC settlement offers by so many of the de minimis PRPs is itself an indication of substantive fairness toward the class to which appellants belong. See Seymour, 554 F. Supp. at 1339. On this record, the district court did not misuse its discretion in ruling that the decrees sufficiently tracked the parties' comparative fault.

The last point which merits discussion under this rubric involves the fact that the agency upped the ante as the game continued, that is, the premium assessed as part of the administrative settlement was increased substantially for purposes of the later DMC decree. Like the district court, we see no unfairness in this approach. For one thing, litigation is expensive — and having called the tune by their refusal to subscribe to the administrative settlement, we think it not unfair that appellants, thereafter, would have to pay the piper. For another thing, rewarding PRPs who settle sooner rather than later is completely consonant with CERCLA's makeup.

Although appellants berate escalating settlement offers as discriminating among similarly situated PRPs, we think that the government's use of such a technique is fair and serves to promote the explicit statutory goal of expediting remedial measures for hazardous waste sites. See 42 U.S.C. §9622(a) (1987); see also Cannons, 720 F. Supp. at 1037 (emphasizing congressional interest in expedited cleanups). . . . We believe that the EPA is entitled to make use of a series of escalating settlement proposals in a CERCLA case and that, as the district court ruled, the serial settlements employed in this instance were substantively fair.

C. REASONABLENESS

In the usual environmental litigation, the evaluation of a consent decree's reasonableness will be a multifaceted exercise. We comment briefly upon three such facets. The first is obvious: the decree's likely efficaciousness as a vehicle for cleansing the environment is of cardinal importance. . . . Except in cases which involve only recoupment of cleanup costs already spent, the reasonableness of the consent decree, for this purpose, will be basically a question of technical adequacy, primarily concerned with the probable effectiveness of proposed remedial responses.

A second important facet of reasonableness will depend upon whether the settlement satisfactorily compensates the public for the actual (and anticipated) costs of remedial and response measures. Like the question of technical adequacy, this aspect of the problem can be enormously complex. The actual cost of remedial measures is frequently uncertain at the time a consent decree is proposed. Thus, although the settlement's bottom line may be definite, the proportion of settlement dollars to total needed dollars is often debatable. Once again, the agency cannot realistically be held to a standard of mathematical precision. If the figures relied upon derive in a sensible way from a plausible interpretation of the record, the court should normally defer to the agency's expertise.

A third integer in the reasonableness equation relates to the relative strength of the parties' litigating positions. If the government's case is strong and solid, it should typically be expected to drive a harder bargain. On the other hand, if the case is less than robust, or the outcome problematic, a reasonable settlement will ordinarily mirror such factors. In a nutshell, the reasonableness of a proposed settlement must take into account foreseeable risks of loss. . . . The same variable, we suggest, has a further dimension: even if the government's case is sturdy, it may take time and money to collect damages or to implement private remedial measures through litigatory success. To the extent that time is of essence or that transaction costs loom large, a settlement which nets less than full recovery of cleanup costs is nonetheless reasonable. . . . The reality is that, all too often, litigation is a cost-ineffective alternative which can squander valuable resources, public as well as private.

In this case, the district court found the consent decrees to be reasonable. . . . We agree. Appellants have not seriously questioned the technological efficacy of the cleanup measures to be implemented at the Sites. Insofar as they contend that the settlements are not designed to assure adequate compensation to the public for harms caused — at times, they seem to argue that the settlements overcompensate — they are whistling past the graveyard. The risks of trial and the desirability for expedition seem to have been blended into the mix. Given the totality of the record-reflected circumstances, the lower court's finding of reasonableness strikes us as irreproachable.

D.   FIDELITY TO THE STATUTE

Of necessity, consideration of the extent to which consent decrees are consistent with Congress' discerned intent involves matters implicating fairness and reasonableness. The three broad approval criteria were not meant to be mutually exclusive and cannot be viewed in majestic isolation. Recognizing the inevitable imbrication, we turn to the final criterion. We have recently described the two major policy concerns underlying CERCLA:

> First, Congress intended that the federal government be immediately given the tools necessary for a prompt and effective response to the problems of national magnitude resulting from hazardous waste disposal. Second, Congress intended that those responsible for problems caused by the disposal of chemical poisons bear the costs and responsibility for remedying the harmful conditions they created.

Dedham Water Co. v. Cumberland Farms Dairy, Inc., 805 F.2d 1074, 1081 (1st Cir. 1986) (quoting *United States v. Reilly Tar & Chemical Corp.*, 546

F. Supp. 1100, 1112 (D. Minn. 1982)). The district court thought that these concerns were addressed, and assuaged, by the proposed settlements. So do we.

It is crystal clear that the broad settlement authority conferred upon the EPA must be exercised with deference to the statute's overarching principles: accountability, the desirability of an unsullied environment, and promptness of response activities. The bases appear to have been touched in this instance. Appellants concede that the government made a due and diligent search to uncover the identity of PRPs; the classification of perpetrators and the use of a modified volumetric share formula appear reasonably related to assuring accountability; the settlements will unarguably promote early completion of cleanup activities; and the technical efficacy of the selected remedial measures is not in issue. On this basis, the consent decrees seem fully consistent with CERCLA.

One can, of course, conjure up ways in which particular consent decrees, while seemingly fair and reasonable, might nevertheless contravene the aims of the statute. Rather than attempting to catalogue a virtually endless list of possibilities, we address, in terms of what we discern to be the congressional will, certain points raised by the appellants.

1. *De Minimis Settlements.* In the SARA Amendments, Congress gave the EPA authority to settle with a de minimis PRP so long as (i) the agreement involved only a "minor portion" of the total response costs, and (ii) the toxicity and amount of substances contributed by the PRP were "minimal in comparison to the other hazardous substances at the facility." 42 U.S.C. §9622(g)(1) (1987). The two determinative criteria are not further defined. Appellants, for a variety of reasons, question the boundaries fixed for the DMC class in this instance, contending that drawing lines so sharply, and adhering to those lines so blindly, thwarts CERCLA's legitimate goals.

We have already dealt with the burden of this argument, see supra Parts III(A), (B), and need not linger at this juncture. It suffices to say that, had Congress meant the agency to employ a purely mechanical taxonomy, it would have so provided. We believe that Congress intended quite the opposite; the EPA was to have substantial discretion to interpret the statutory terms in light of both its expertise and its negotiating strategy in a given case. Therefore, in attempting to gauge a consent decree's consistency with the statute, courts must give a wide berth to the agency's choice of eligibility criteria. In this case, the criteria selected fell well within the ambit of Executive discretion.

2. *Disproportionate Liability.* In the SARA Amendments, Congress explicitly created a statutory framework that left nonsettlors at risk of bearing a disproportionate amount of liability. The statute immunizes

settling parties from liability for contribution and provides that only the amount of the settlement — not the pro rata share attributable to the settling party — shall be subtracted from the liability of the nonsettlors.[62] This can prove to be a substantial benefit to settling PRPs — and a corresponding detriment to their more recalcitrant counterparts.

Although such immunity creates a palpable risk of disproportionate liability, that is not to say that the device is forbidden. To the exact contrary, Congress has made its will explicit and the courts must defer. See Exxon, 677 F. Supp. at 694 ("To the extent that the non-settling parties are disadvantaged in any concrete way by the applicability of [42 U.S.C. §9613(f)(2)] to the overall settlement, their dispute is with Congress."). . . . Disproportionate liability, a technique which promotes early settlements and deters litigation for litigation's sake, is an integral part of the statutory plan.

In a related vein, appellants assail the district court's dismissal of their cross-claims for contribution as against all settling PRPs. They contend, in essence, that the district court failed to appreciate that they would potentially bear a greater proportional liability than will be shouldered by any of the settling parties. They claim this result to be both unfair and inconsistent with the statutory plan.

As originally enacted, CERCLA did not expressly provide for a right of contribution among parties found jointly and severally liable for response costs. When CERCLA was amended by SARA in 1986, Congress created an express right of contribution among parties found liable for response costs. See 42 U.S.C. §9613(f)(1) (1987). Congress specifically provided that contribution actions could not be maintained against settlors. See 42 U.S.C. §9613(f)(2) (1987). This provision was designed to encourage settlements and provide PRPs a measure of finality in return for their willingness to settle. See H.R. Rep. No. 99-253, Part I, 90th Cong., 1st Sess. 80 (1985), reprinted in 1986 U.S. Code Cong. & Admin. News 2835, 2862. Congress plainly intended non-settlors to have no contribution rights against settlors regarding matters addressed in settlement. Thus, the cross-claims were properly dismissed; Congress purposed that all who choose not to settle confront the same sticky wicket of which appellants complain.

---

62. The statute provides:

A person who has resolved its liability to the United States or a State in an administrative or judicially approved settlement shall not be liable for claims for contribution regarding matters addressed in the settlement. Such settlement does not discharge any of the other potentially liable persons unless its terms so provide, but it reduces the potential liability of the others by the amount of the settlement.

42 U.S.C. §9613(f)(2) (1987).

The statute, of course, not only bars contribution claims against settling parties, but also provides that, while a settlement will not discharge other PRPs, "it reduces the potential liability of the others by the amount of settlement." 42 U.S.C. §9613(f)(2) (1987). The law's plain language admits of no construction other than a dollar-for-dollar reduction of the aggregate liability. . . .

3. *Indemnity.* On a similar note, appellants bemoan the dismissal of their cross-claims for indemnity against the settling PRPs. We are unmoved. Although CERCLA is silent regarding indemnification, we refuse to read into the statute a right to indemnification that would eviscerate §9613(f)(2) and allow non-settlors to make an end run around the statutory scheme. . . .

4. *Notice.* The appellants also contend that the government's negotiating strategy must be an open book. We disagree. Congress did not send the EPA into the toxic waste ring with one arm tied behind its collective back. Although the EPA may not mislead any of the parties, discriminate unfairly, or engage in deceptive practices, neither must the agency spoon feed PRPs. In the CERCLA context, the government is under no obligation to telegraph its settlement offers, divulge its negotiating strategy in advance, or surrender the normal prerogatives of strategic flexibility which any negotiator cherishes. In short, contrary to the objectors' thesis, the EPA need not tell de minimis PRPs in advance whether they will, or will not, be eligible to join ensuing major party settlements.

5. *Exclusions from Settlements.* The CERCLA statutes do not require the agency to open all settlement offers to all PRPs; and we refuse to insert such a requirement into the law by judicial fiat. Under the SARA Amendments, the right to draw fine lines, and to structure the order and pace of settlement negotiations to suit, is an agency prerogative. After all, "divide and conquer" has been a recognized negotiating tactic since the days of the Roman Empire, and in the absence of a congressional directive, we cannot deny the EPA use of so conventional a tool. So long as it operates in good faith, the EPA is at liberty to negotiate and settle with whomever it chooses.

6. *Crown.* Appellant Crown raises an argument unique to it. The facts are these. In 1986 and thereafter Crown failed to comply with EPA's requests for information and documents concerning the amount and nature of the waste it had sent to the Sites. The information requests were authorized by statute, see 42 U.S.C. §§6927, 9604(e) (1987), and all PRPs were on notice that compliance therewith was a condition precedent to participation in any class settlement. Crown nonetheless disdained compliance. Eventually, the government had to file suit to obtain the information.

Crown argues that it was unfairly subjected to a double penalty because withholding the information resulted both in its exclusion from the settlements and in the imposition of bad-faith penalties. We see nothing amiss. EPA's authority to enforce §3007 of the Resource Conservation and Recovery Act, 42 U.S.C. §6927 (1987), and CERCLA §104(e), 42 U.S.C. §9604(e) (1987), is completely independent of its authority to settle Superfund cases. Conditioning settlement eligibility on a PRP's compliance with an outstanding information request was a perfectly reasonable approach, especially since the data Crown refused to supply was the data necessary to verify the nature and amount of the wastes sent to the Sites, and thus provide a foundation for settlement.

We draw this phase of our inquiry to a close. The district court held unequivocally that "the proposed Consent Decrees are consistent with the Constitution and CERCLA." Appellants have offered no convincing reason why this ruling should be set aside.

IV

Appellants complain that the district court erred in failing to hold an evidentiary hearing on the suitability of the consent decrees. They are wrong.

We review a district court's declination to convene an evidentiary hearing on a confirmation motion only for abuse of discretion. . . . That being so, it rests with the proponent of an evidentiary hearing to persuade the court that one is desirable and to offer reasons warranting it. . . .

In general, we believe that evidentiary hearings are not required under CERCLA when a court is merely deciding whether monetary settlements comprise fair and reasonable vehicles for disposition of Superfund claims. . . . As in other cases, the test for granting a hearing "should be substantive: given the nature and circumstances of the case, did the parties have a fair opportunity to present relevant facts and arguments to the court, and to counter the opponent's submissions?" *Aoude v. Mobil Oil Corp.*, 862 F.2d 890, 894 (1st Cir. 1988) *(Aoude I)*. In this case, that inquiry must be answered in the affirmative. There was no showing of any substantial need for an evidentiary hearing. The issues were fully argued and compendiously briefed. We have been advised of no particular matter which, fairly viewed, necessitated live testimony. The district court's determination that no evidentiary hearing was required fell well within the realm of the court's discretion. . . .

Affirmed.

W. Church, R. Nakamura & P. Cooper, What Works? Alternative Strategies for Superfund Cleanups

(September 1991)

EXECUTIVE SUMMARY . . .

Since government funds are inadequate to bear the full costs of a national cleanup program, and since most Superfund sites involve Potentially Responsible Parties (PRPs) who are statutorily liable for cleanup costs, EPA's main task at most sites is determining how to get others to pay the cleanup bill. Congress and the courts have provided EPA with an unusually rich assortment of legal means for getting PRPs to assume these responsibilities. We examine the strategies used at actual sites in order to assess which best fulfill the multiple (and sometimes conflicting) objectives of the Superfund program: an effective and speedy cleanup, at minimum governmental expense, with minimal transaction costs for all parties.

Over the decade-long life of Superfund, and across geographic regions, EPA has made different uses of the tools provided it by the authorizing statutes. In practice, the agency has assembled the tools into three broad packages or approaches intended to produce PRP compliance via alternative paths. In order to avoid the ambiguity and conceptual baggage that accompanies such terms as "enforcement," "fund lead" or "settlement," we have labeled these three approaches Prosecution, Accommodation, and Public Works. All three of these implementation strategies are predicated on the assumption that the liability provisions in the statutes — together with the judicially appended doctrine of strict, joint and several liability — can and should be used to make the responsible parties pay for cleanups.

The *Prosecution* approach emphasizes coercion and relies on the government's superior legal position to force PRPs to assume their full responsibilities. The central task of government in this strategy is to put PRPs into a position where they capitulate to all government demands. Prosecution stresses the use of unilateral orders, non-negotiable demands, and litigation to compel compliance.

The *Accommodation* strategy stresses the mutual, rather than conflicting, interests of EPA and PRPs in site cleanup. Here the strategy is to structure negotiations so that both the government and PRPs can gain by agreement, and minimize the time and transaction costs required. The statutory tools emphasized in Accommodation are provisions for mixed funding, for negotiation moratoria and the use of alternative dispute resolution, and for government help in allocating cleanup costs among groups of PRPs.

Finally, in the *Public Works* approach, the government elects to clean up sites itself, and then (if possible) send PRPs the bill through subsequent cost recovery actions. The statutory tools utilized here are the emergency removal provisions, the authority to proceed with governmentally financed cleanups in the face of absent or uncooperative PRPs, and the use of cost recovery actions.

Our conclusions are based on an analysis of six Superfund cleanups. The sites were chosen to examine the efficacy of the Prosecution, Accommodation, and Public Works approaches in both small, relatively simple cleanups, and at large, complex sites. These case studies are described in detail in the central chapters of the report. They constitute a rich (and, so far as we can ascertain, unique) source of information on how the Superfund program operates "on the ground," at a level far removed from the grand policy pronouncements and recommendations of experts that characterize much of the national debate over Superfund.

Based on a close examination of these six cleanups in three EPA regions, we have come to the following conclusions:

- *Implementation strategies vary in their applicability to particular sites. Thus, the question of which strategy to use is less a matter of "What works?" than "What works best in which circumstances?"* Each of the strategies we have identified makes a set of assumptions regarding the hierarchy of agency goals, the strategic environment at a Superfund site, and the likely behavior of relevant participants. Yet these factors can all be expected to vary from site to site. We conclude that decisions about implementation strategy should be based on conscious choice on a site-by-site basis, rather than on established routines or the current approach being espoused by EPA headquarters. Making such site-specific decisions requires EPA to encourage use of a range of mechanisms at the regional level, where the tendency has heretofore been toward specialization in particular approaches.
- *At a basic level, all strategies "work" in the sense of eventually bringing about some form of cleanup. None, however, deliver on all the goals of the program.* Prosecution is most successful at minimizing government costs and risks, but is often slow in achieving resolution of key issues and frequently involves high transaction costs. Accommodation can reduce transaction costs, but at the price of higher government outlays in effort, money, and risk. Public Works is speedy at getting remediation underway, but is limited in what can be accomplished at a site and often bogs down in cost recovery. Thus each strategy buys success in one dimension at the expense of vulnerability to criticism on the others.
- *For simple sites, any of the three strategies can prove effective. For com-*

plex sites, none are wholly successful, and the tradeoffs indicated above are all the more dramatic. At simple sites the limited stakes for individual PRPs seldom justify the substantial transaction costs that inevitably follow contested proceedings, particularly in light of the unfavorable legal position of the PRPs at most Superfund sites. This loss-cutting mentality is much less in evidence when the stakes are higher, at large, complex sites.

- *A policy of demanding that PRPs absorb all costs associated with cleaning up a site — engineering, construction, administration, and all future risks — is unrealistic in light of Superfund's strategic environment.* The goal of no-cost cleanups for the government is based on extrapolating from the legal doctrine of strict, joint and several liability — in which PRPs can be held individually responsible for all cleanup costs, regardless of fault or proportional contribution of waste to a site — to an evaluative standard which regards this allocation of cleanup burdens as the only acceptable outcome. In all our case studies the government eventually assumed some of the costs of cleanup. These costs were sometimes paid indirectly, through the government's forgiving a portion of its past administrative expenses, or assuming some future risks (such as the uncertainty against non-settlers). In other cases, the government directly assumed a share of the cleanup costs. We observed this tendency toward less than 100 percent settlements even when the government adopted a Prosecution strategy, seeking full payment of all costs by PRPs. In these cases, the tendency of federal judges to push the government and PRPs into settlement negotiations rather than [going] quickly to a trial on the liability issues, and to exert pressure on both sides to compromise, produced outcomes in which the government settled for less than full assumption of costs and risks by the settling PRPs. The critical question in these cases is whether the compromise outcomes finally accepted could have been obtained earlier in the process, with fewer transaction costs for all parties, had the government adopted from the outset a more flexible and realistic negotiating position.

- *Finally, whichever strategy is employed, we believe that EPA should develop internal structures to coordinate and rationalize what often appears to be an idiosyncratic, crisis-driven system of implementation.* Superfund cases inevitably involve large numbers of federal, state, and local government actors and a myriad of private parties, all of whom come to the process with different preferences and priorities. There emerges from this milieu a significant problem arising out of what policy analysts call "the complexity of joint action." The requirements of achieving settlement are

often at odds with the desire of each participant to achieve particularistic goals. Since all of the implementation strategies require a degree of consistency and concerted action by the
government, we suggest that EPA develop the organizational
capacity to take greater control over the process of internalizing
more of the transaction costs currently split among government
agencies, and between the government and the PRPs. Further,
we suggest that EPA develop more effective procedures for ensuring institutional memory at individual Superfund sites, and
the capacity to deal with site negotiations as on-going enterprises that do not shift with changes in governmental personnel.

PROBLEM: DEVELOPING AN ENFORCEMENT STRATEGY IN U.S. EPA v. RETEP CHEMICAL CORP., ET AL.

1. Were the government to pursue an abatement action strategy
under §106, which party(ies) should it bring an enforcement action
against? What is your rationale for this approach? What are the implications for obtaining expeditious cleanup? What other ramifications do
you foresee — for instance, how might the target(s) respond to this
approach?

2. Were the government to cleanup the site from the trust fund
under §104 and later seek cost recovery from potentially responsible
parties under §107, which party(ies) should the government pursue?
Suppose the government targeted one or a few clearly liable "deep
pockets" — for example, some Fortune 100 generators — irrespective
of their actual contribution to the RETEP site? What ramifications do
you foresee — for instance, how might the target(s) respond to this
approach?

The ABA Model Code of Professional Responsibility states that
"[A] government lawyer in a civil action or administrative proceeding
has the responsibility to seek justice and to develop a full and fair record, and he should not use his position or the economic power of
the government to harass parties to bring about unjust settlements or
results." Ethical Consideration 7-14 (1981). Does this ethical consideration limit a government's lawyer use of a "deep pockets" strategy in
Superfund cost recovery actions?

Consider the following other aspects of developing a government
settlement strategy:

- What incentives should the government utilize in resolving this
  case?
- Should the government issue NBARs? If so, sketch how you

would allocate responsibility among the major groups of
PRPs — site owners/operators, generators, and transporters —
and within these groups.

- Should de minimis settlements be offered? If so, to whom and
  on what basis?
- Should the government be willing to enter into a mixed funding agreement?

3. How should the government proceed in responding to the conditions at the RETEP site — a prosecution strategy, an accommodation
strategy, or a public works approach? What are the advantages and disadvantages with each approach?

PROBLEM: ETHICAL RESPONSIBILITIES IN JOINT
REPRESENTATION OF RETEP PRPs

Following initial emergency removal actions by the government,
EPA sent notice of responsibility letters to 120 parties. (The involvement of parties at the RETEP site is described in Sections 2 and 3,
supra.) The threat of joint and several liability for tens of millions of
dollars in response costs spurred these parties to seek legal counsel.

Brower's modest-sized legal community was inundated with inquiries. Although most of the larger PRPs retained their principal law
firms in Boston and New York, many of the middle-sized and smaller
firms based in Brower had little or no prior representation in environmental matters. Despite the dearth of experienced Superfund lawyers
in Brower, many of these firms did not feel that they could afford
higher priced legal counsel from Boston.

You are an attorney at Erskine and Fisher, one of the larger firms
in Brower with 25 attorneys, with some experience in Superfund matters. Erskine and Fisher successfully represented American Shoe on
some unrelated business matters and hence American Shoe quickly retained your services to handle its representation in the RETEP matter.
Erskine and Fisher has also received inquiries from Infinity Semiconductor, DKL Engraving, Lustre Cleaners, and Patriot Plating Company.
Because of financial difficulties, DKL Engraving, Lustre Cleaners, and
Patriot Plating Company are concerned with keeping legal fees to a
minimum.

There would be significant economies of scale — legal research,
discovery, attending meetings — in representing multiple parties in the
RETEP cleanup matter. This would save your clients money and enable
you to develop substantial expertise in Superfund law. In addition, it
would enable you and your firm to expand your reputation in this growing area of legal practice.

The ABA Model Code of Professional Responsibility prohibits an attorney from representation that would adversely affect the lawyer's "independent personal judgment," or that would involve the lawyer "representing differing interests." DR 5-105(A). "Differing interests" "include every interest that will adversely affect either the judgment or the loyalty of a lawyer to a client, whether it be a conflicting, inconsistent, diverse or other interest." The Model Code does permit multiple representation "if it is obvious that [the lawyer] can adequately represent the interest of each and if each consents to the representation after full disclosure." DR 5-105(C).

Similarly, the Model Rules of Professional Conduct prohibit a lawyer from representing "a client if the representation of that client would be directly adverse to another client, unless: (a) the lawyer reasonably believes the representation will not adversely affect the relationship with the other client; and (b) each client consents after consultation." Rule 1.7(a). Comment 4 (Loyalty to Client) states:

> A possible conflict does not itself preclude the representation. The critical questions are whether the conflict will eventuate, and if it does, whether it will materially interfere with the lawyer's independent professional judgment in considering alternatives or foreclose courses of action that reasonably should be pursued on behalf of the client. Consideration should be given to whether the client wishes to accommodate the other interest involved.

Comment 4 (Loyalty to Client). The standard for evaluating the attorney's judgment is objective: whether a disinterested lawyer would recommend that a client not accept representation because of the conflict. Comment 7 (Consultation and Consent).

QUESTIONS

1. Based upon the Model Code and the Model Rules, evaluate the legality and propriety of representing Infinity Semiconductor, DKL Engraving, Lustre Cleaners, and/or Patriot Plating Company in addition to American Shoe in negotiations with the government over the cleanup of the RETEP site. What disclosures must you make if you decide to represent more than one party? What disclosures should you make if you decide to represent more than one party? Are the Model Code and Model Rules consistent?

2. Suppose that negotiations break down and the government sues all PRPs to recover cleanup costs. How does this affect the legality and propriety of representing Infinity Semiconductor, DKL Engraving, Lustre Cleaners, and/or Patriot Plating Company in addition to Ameri-

can Shoe. What disclosures must you make if you decide to represent any parties other than American Shoe in the litigation? What disclosures should you make if you decide to represent more than one party? Suppose that all parties would like to retain you after full disclosure of potential conflicts of interest because of your experience and in order to reduce attorney fees. Can you still represent them? What problems might arise down the road? Should you refuse to represent any or all of the parties?

NOTES AND QUESTIONS

1. In most Superfund cases involving many parties, the PRPs agree to use a steering committee consisting of representatives of major sub-groups of PRPs having similar interests (such as large low toxicity generators, de minimis generators, transporters) to manage the negotiations. This approach enables PRPs to share expenses of technical consultants, avoid the difficulty of negotiating among dozens of parties simultaneously, and develop and present a unified negotiating position in settlement meetings with the government. PRPs typically negotiate complex agreements governing the role of the steering committee. In what ways is this arrangement more or less questionable than representation of multiple PRPs by common counsel? Are the ethical concerns in the RETEP problem above more or less problematic if a steering committee structure is utilized? See generally Litell, Consent and Disclosure in Superfund Negotiations: Identifying and Avoiding Conflicts of Interest Arising From Multiple Client Representation, 17 Harv. Envtl. L. Rev. 225 (1993).

2. Should the Department of Justice be disqualified from representing both the EPA and the U.S. Army regarding the cleanup of a contaminated military facility? See *Colorado v. U.S. Department of the Army,* 707 F. Supp. 1562 (D. Colo. 1989).

8.   POLICY PERSPECTIVES ON SUPERFUND

MENELL, THE LIMITATIONS OF LEGAL INSTITUTIONS FOR ADDRESSING ENVIRONMENTAL RISKS

5 J. Econ. Perspectives 93 (1991)

Deterring environmental degradation and compensating victims of environmental harms are among the most important and difficult problems facing modern industrial societies. The choice of regulatory institutions to control environmental risks — whether courts, administrative agencies, markets or some combination — significantly determines the achievement of these objectives. For a variety of historical and political reasons, the United States relies heavily upon courts, through traditional decentralized adjudication, to assign responsibility for environmental harms. The common law tort system remains, with the exception of job-related injuries, a principal means of compensating victims of environmental pollution. In addition, the federal Superfund legislation uses the court system to assign liability for the clean-up of dangerous hazardous waste sites. . . .

B.   THE INSTITUTIONAL LIMITATIONS OF SUPERFUND LITIGATION

Although Congress removed many of the doctrinal impediments to recovery for environmental risks in designing CERCLA's liability regime, the limitations of legal institutions nonetheless inhibit the effort to expeditiously clean-up unsafe waste sites while significantly raising social cost. The problems of CERCLA's liability regime are reflected in the incentive structure of Superfund litigation.

Most Superfund sites involve many potentially responsible parties (PRPs), often more than one hundred. The cost of clean-up ranges from a few to well over one hundred million dollars, with the average currently around twenty-five million dollars. The prospect of strict and joint and several liability for these costs encourages most parties to devote substantial resources to a legal strategy.

In cases in which there are just a few PRPs, the fear of liability may encourage the parties to cooperate with the government in choosing a remedy and funding clean-up. Even in these cases, however, the moral indignation of PRPs — many of whom complied fully with the law, sent their wastes to sites licensed by the state environmental agency, and had no knowledge of the unsafe disposal practices — holds up settlement negotiations.

In the more common case involving many PRPs, however, the difficulty of coordinating numerous parties with conflicting interests often precludes agreement on a remediation and cost allocation plan. The government, therefore, must resort to the Superfund to remedy the site and then seek recovery from PRPs. Even though the Superfund provides the resources for clean-up, the liability system can delay remediation. Since EPA needs good documentation to support a later response cost action, its site investigations will be more time-consuming and expensive than if it were only concerned with remediation. Despite the statutory presumptions, causation is becoming much more difficult to establish now that EPA is moving beyond clean-up of concentrated contamination at major waste disposal sites to the remediation of diffuse groundwater contamination below large industrial areas with many firms. In these cases, EPA must devote substantial time and effort to determining the source(s) of contamination of invisible, incompletely charted aquifers, sometimes hundreds of feet below the surface. As in the toxic tort context, the limitations of science and the costs of establishing causal connections severely hamper the effort to assign legal responsibility for groundwater pollution.

Furthermore, major PRPs — those who contributed heavily to the site or who have deep pockets — have a strong incentive to use the courts and the public oversight process to prevent EPA from choosing expensive remedial measures, further adding to the delay in (and possibly, the quality of) clean-up. Consequently, in at least those cases involving many PRPs, the liability system may hinder the goal of fast and effective remedial action.

The major social costs of relying upon a liability system to fund clean-ups arise when the government sues to recover response costs. Whether or not the government goes after all PRPs in one action or targets one or a few "deep pockets," the transaction costs of the recovery action often rival the direct costs of cleaning up the site. If the government goes after all PRPs, the court must first sort out myriad procedural and legal issues — such as statute of limitations questions, the extent of discovery, the admissability of evidence, creative defenses, and the scope of liability (e.g., whether parent corporations are liable)[63] — and then allocate responsibility among the parties. As a result of the complexity of these tasks, substantially all response cost cases have settled prior to judicial allocation of responsibility. This does not mean, however, that settlement is inexpensive. The process often does not begin until extensive data about responsibility has been gathered, a particularly complex task given the poor records of most old and orphaned waste sites and the multitude of PRPs. Even after records have been compiled, the negotiations are complicated by the lack of clear standards for allocating responsibility and the difficulty of negotiating among tens, and sometimes hundreds, of lawyers.[64]

The implications of cost recovery differ little if the government

---

63. The establishment of precedents has resolved some of the legal challenges. Because of the complexity and ambiguities of CERCLA, however, many of the legal issues are still unresolved after more than a decade of litigation. Other issues are fact-specific and therefore must be decided on a case by case basis.

64. Experience in resolving these cases by the private bar, the development of better EPA settlement policies, and the use of alternative dispute resolution methods have reduced the costs of settlement negotiations. Nonetheless, the underlying adversarial nature of the process makes it difficult to reduce these transaction costs significantly. Furthermore, settlement becomes more difficult as EPA moves to cases in which causation is harder to establish.

targets just a few PRPs for litigation. These defendants typically petition the court to bring other PRPs into the case or bring later contribution actions, possibly resulting in more complex litigation.

The transaction and other social costs of CERCLA's liability regime extend beyond the initial cost recovery action. Most PRPs have multiple insurers over the lifetime of waste disposal sites. Cost recovery actions, therefore, spawn extensive secondary litigation between the PRPs and their insurers and among these insurers. In addition, the large liabilities of Superfund send some companies into bankruptcy, generating a further layer of litigation.

The extraordinary social cost of this litigation can be pieced together from a variety of sources. EPA spends approximately 12 percent of Superfund monies on enforcement, which includes litigation costs, data collection and review, and report preparation. Butler (1985)[65] estimates the total (private and governmental) transaction costs of CERCLA liability to be between 24 and 44 percent of the direct costs of clean-up. The Office of Technology Assessment (1985) estimates that the National Priority List could reach 10,000 sites, costing in excess of 100 billion dollars to remedy. With rapidly escalating remediation costs, in part attributable to stricter clean-up standards enacted in 1986, the *transaction costs* of CERCLA's clean-up effort could exceed 44 billion dollars.[66]

In addition to its transaction cost burden, CERCLA liability has contributed significantly to the liability insurance crisis. In order for insurance markets to operate efficiently, insurers must be reasonably able to estimate the probability distribution for classes of risks. CERCLA's imposition of retroactive liability has introduced enormous uncertainty into the distribution of losses for environmental risks generally. This uncertainty has been magnified by inconsistent judicial interpretations of the coverage of insurance contracts for Superfund liability. While this inconsistency should decrease over time as appellate

---

65. [J. Butler, Insurance Issues and Superfund: Hearing Before the Committee on Environment and Public Works, U.S. Senate, 99th Cong., 1st Sess., 1985, 115-37.]

66. [More recent estimates of the total cost of hazardous waste cleanup range from $150 billion to $750 billion. See Robert E. Litan, Superfund: Assessing the Program and Options for Reform (1992) (prepared for Enhancing Environmental Quality Through Economic Growth, a symposium sponsored by the American Council for Capital Formation). With regard to the magnitude of transaction costs, a Rand study of five Fortune 100 companies found that transaction costs accounted for 34 percent of PRP spending at multi-party sites and 7 percent at single-party sites. The same study found that 88 percent of spending by insurers was attributable to transaction costs. J. Acton & L. Dixon, Superfund and Transaction Costs (Rand Corp., Institute for Civil Justice, 1992). The Rand study did not include smaller PRPs who may spend a higher proportion of resources on transaction costs.]

courts resolve conflicts, substantial uncertainty still exists in many juris-dictions and across jurisdictions more than a decade after the passage of CERCLA. Similarly, the potential for joint and several liability has exacerbated the evaluation of the loss distribution by dramatically in-creasing the variance of loss for hazardous waste disposal risks. Disposal of a thimble of hazardous waste at a large disposal site exposes an entity to enormous potential liability. Furthermore, the transaction costs of CERCLA litigation — especially the multi-party battles over insurance coverage — have raised the administrative costs of liability insurance significantly.

These factors have led to dramatically higher costs of liability in-surance and substantially reduced availability of insurance as some lines of environmental insurance have dried up (Sommerfield, 1990[67] (quot-ing one senior vice president of a major insurance broker as saying "If they let you buy the [environmental risk] coverage, you don't need it")). Municipalities have had particular difficulty in obtaining insur-ance because almost all municipal solid waste landfills are potential Superfund sites. As easily identifiable, solvent parties, municipalities face enormous potential liability, even though much of what they de-posited — household refuse — has low toxicity.[68]

[W]e are left with the question of whether the CERCLA liability regime contributes to the goal of efficient deterrence of environmental degradation. As with the toxic tort system, the answer is largely nega-tive. The Resource Conservation and Recovery Act provides a compre-hensive prospective regulatory system for preventing releases of hazardous wastes in the environment. In addition, RCRA's financial responsibility and enforcement provisions are capable of handling vio-lations of these regulations and any environmental risks that arise on regulated sites. When viewed against this backdrop, CERCLA's liability provisions are little more than an extremely costly funding mechanism. To the extent that CERCLA has a significant deterrent effect, it is likely to be inefficient. The inability of generators and transporters to con-tract around joint and several liability encourages inefficient monitor-ing of waste sites (e.g., by generators or their insurers), possibly inefficient waste disposal operations as more firms bring waste disposal in-house, and inefficient activity levels — e.g., installation of "fail-safe" environmental controls — as some firms are over-deterred.

---

67. [F. Sommerfield, Going Bare, Institutional Investor, March 1990, 24, 99-102.]

68. To ease this concern, EPA, in late 1989, issued an enforcement policy stating that household hazardous waste will not be considered hazardous for the purposes of Superfund.

C.   TOWARD A MORE EFFECTIVE INSTITUTIONAL STRUCTURE

[T]he attributes of legal institutions significantly limit their usefulness in prospectively regulating the disposal of hazardous waste and retrospectively cleaning up the many dangerous abandoned waste sites. RCRA's hybrid regime of monitoring, minimum safety standards, financial responsibility requirements, and civil and criminal liability for regulatory violations and unsafe conditions is well suited to addressing the prospective regulatory concern. CERCLA's establishment of a public fund for remediating dangerous orphaned waste sites is also institutionally sound. Its extensive reliance upon a liability system for funding this clean-up effort, however, reflects a significant mismatch between a regulatory institution and a public policy problem.

CERCLA's attempt to allocate the costs of clean-up among the many generators and transporters that sent or carried hazardous waste (often legally) to a long since abandoned waste site is highly questionable as a mechanism for systematically making "polluters pay." Since proper disposal of waste does not constitute "pollution," at least not to the same degree as improper disposal, the principal polluters are the former site owners and operators. While the generators and transporters might have paid lower disposal fees as a result of poor regulation of poor waste disposal practices, the benefits of these artificially low prices were reaped long ago by purchasers of goods manufactured during the operation of the waste site and past shareholders. Although some customers and shareholders of these companies may be same, the link between those who benefitted from past pollution and current shareholders and customers is attenuated.

It seems probable that broad-based taxation systems, such as those used to establish and supplement the Superfund, provide the best institutional approach for funding the clean-up of orphaned waste sites. Although it would be administratively impossible to impose taxes directly upon those who benefitted from lower waste disposal costs, a tax system targeted to hazardous waste-related activities could achieve a comparable degree of matching as CERCLA's liability system, without the enormous transaction costs and distortions in liability insurance markets. Liability rules should be confined to cases in which there are readily identifiable responsible parties, such as those who currently own the property in question and caused or could have identified the dangerous conditions prior to acquisition and those who otherwise bear direct responsibility for the dangerous conditions, e.g., through inadequate waste disposal practices during prior ownership of the property.

ROBERTS, WHO SHOULD PAY?

EPA J. 38-39 (July/August 1991)

"Superfund is unquestionably the most effective and important environmental program on the books." That statement is not from an environmentalist or EPA official, but from a friend who has worked for years as a corporate lawyer handling transactions between businesses. He rarely contacts EPA, couldn't name an EPA contractor if you paid him, and has no real conception of the complex issues involving clean-up standards or EPA settlement policies.

So, why does this corporate lawyer have such a high regard for Superfund? In a phrase: strict joint and several liability.

Superfund is not nice to polluters. It is not a polluter bail-out program. It is not a public works program. It was designed to operate on a very simple premise: The polluter should pay, not the taxpayer. And corporate America has gotten the message.

Across the country, businesses now scrutinize their waste management activities. They spend millions of dollars to carefully manage their wastes and more importantly, to change their production practices to reduce the waste they generate in the first place.

They clean up old contamination on their property to make their businesses more attractive to potential purchasers and more dependable to financial institutions looking for reliable collateral. My corporate lawyer friend showed me a 60-page, single-spaced questionnaire prepared by his firm, to be completed by any company his clients may be interested in purchasing. An environmentalist could not have produced a more thorough audit. And all this goes on without a single EPA employee in sight.

This makes Superfund one of the least bureaucratic and most cost-effective federal environmental programs. Using Superfund liability as an incentive for environmentally sound conduct requires no new volumes to the Code of Federal Regulations, no EPA time devoted to regulatory development, and no lengthy delays in implementation.

It also gives industry the flexibility to find the least expensive measurers to reduce the threat of contamination. If that means changes in production practices, fine. If it means cleaning a leaking landfill before hazardous substances migrate into ground water, fine. With Superfund cleanups costing an average of $20 to 30 million, the business community has worked hard to find lower cost methods to reduce pollution, lower the risk of contamination, and avoid expensive clean-up costs. The business community has found that it is cheaper to avoid creating a Love Canal in the first place than to clean it up afterwards. That's good for business and good for the environment.

How does Superfund's liability standard produce this kind of behavior? Essentially, Superfund closes the legal loopholes polluters could use to avoid paying clean-up costs. First, Superfund denies polluters the "I tried my best" defense. By adopting a strict liability standard, which means that polluters must pay without regard to fault, Congress invoked a well-established legal doctrine to force polluters to pay for cleanups. . . .

Second, Superfund liability borrows another well-established legal principle by imposing liability jointly and severally among polluters. Congress recognized that many contaminated sites contained the commingled wastes of many companies and that it would be virtually impossible for EPA to prove who caused what. To avoid protracted legal fights between EPA and polluters and to speed clean-up activities, Congress allowed the imposition of liability as long as EPA could identify one or more of the responsible polluters.

Those identified by EPA have always been free to search out other responsible parties and, through legal action, compel them to pay their fair share of clean-up costs. But the time and cost of this litigation was borne by the polluters, not by taxpayers.

So why is a program that has accomplished so much with a minimum of command-and-control intervention been subjected to such criticism?

Before answering this question, it's important to identify the critics. They don't seem to be in Congress. Congress passed Superfund with its "polluter pays" liability system in 1980, continued it in 1986, and reauthorized it for another five years in 1990.

The most active, current effort to amend the liability scheme in Superfund has been in the narrow area of lender liability. But, even the most vocal advocates of change in this area have made it clear that they have no interest in abandoning Superfund's current liability system altogether.

One can only conclude that the Administration feels the same way. Presidents Carter, Reagan, and Bush have each signed Superfund legislation that enacted and preserved the Superfund liability system.

Dozens of state governments have passed "mini" Superfund statutes that have similar liability programs. It would appear that legislators on the state level feel just as strongly as the federal government about forcing the polluters to pick up the clean-up tab.

And let's not forget the American people. In one public survey after another, the public rates the management of hazardous and toxic waste as one of the nation's top environmental priorities. More importantly, a national survey conducted by the Environment Opinion Study, Inc., last year found that 70 percent of the public disapproves of the way industry and business have attempted to preserve and protect the environment. Clearly, the American people have not lessened their commitment to see the "polluter pay."

Sadly, but predictably, the critics of the Superfund liability program are the polluters themselves. They complain about high "transaction costs" and legal fees, even though no one has quantified those costs, much less compared them to taxpayer's savings under the current program.

They complain about the potential reach of joint and several liability but find it hard to present data to show real instances of unfairness.

They assert that a tax-based public works program should replace the liability program, but we hear only silence when we ask who will support a sufficient tax (i.e., the "T" word).

And they complain that Superfund's retroactive liability makes business pay for mismanagement which occurred years ago, although they don't explain why the taxpayers should pay to clean up industry's old Superfund sites.

When the dust settles on this issue, we still face the challenging task of cleaning up our soils and ground water to make them safe for our families and our children. It's a costly, time-consuming, and difficult task. And, although Superfund is hardly a perfect program, its liability system will help us clean up these sites more quickly, discourage the creation of future sites, and keep taxpayer costs to a minimum.

LANDY & HAGUE, THE COALITION FOR WASTE: PRIVATE INTERESTS AND SUPERFUND*

In Environmental Politics: Public Costs, Private Rewards
(M. Greve & F. Smith (eds.) 1992)

THE TWO PREMISES OF SUPERFUND

Superfund's policy design is based on two central premises. The first premise, "Shovels First," holds that in light of the dire and imminent risks posed by abandoned waste sites, priority will be accorded to prompt and speedy cleanup. The second premise, "Polluters Pay," states that the cleanup of Superfund sites will be paid for by the parties who polluted them. . . .

[T]he Shovels First and Polluters Pay premises combine to create perverse incentives that, in the end, hamper cleanup efforts. The most difficult conceptual and practical problem of site cleanup is the determination of "how clean is clean." The answer to this question —and, hence, the desirable extent of cleanup at a given site —cannot be determined simply on scientific grounds. In principle, one would want to

---

*Reprinted from Michael S. Greve and Fred L. Smith, Jr., (eds.), Environmental Politics: Public Costs, Private Rewards, reprinted with permission of Greenwood Publishing Group, Inc., Westport CT. Copyright © 1992 by the editors.

clean until the site can be called perfectly "safe." However, environmental health risk is relative; there is no scientifically identifiable point at which an "unsafe" site becomes "safe." No matter how much cleanup has been performed at a site, it can always be argued that more cleanup would reduce the risk even further.

If local communities were required to contribute to cleanup spending, residents would have a reason to inquire what palpable good an expensive restoration process would be likely to achieve and whether most of the benefits could not be obtained at substantially lower cost. Their answer to the question, "How clean is clean?" would be informed by their understanding of the sacrifices they have to make to obtain a given degree of cleanliness. However, under Superfund, cleanup spending is a free good for affected communities. Superfund's premises stipulate that abandoned waste sites pose severe health hazards, and that cleanup will be paid for by others. As a result, communities that have such sites have no reason to want to control cleanup spending. To the contrary: They have every reason to insist on the most extensive and expensive cleanup.

The pressure on the EPA to implement "Cadillac solutions" actually increases the risk posed by abandoned waste sites to the population as a whole. Rather than being able to spread its limited resources over many sites, thereby eliminating the genuine dangers they might pose, the agency finds itself spending more and more money at a small number of sites so as to reduce what have already become small risks to evermore infinitesimal levels.

THE ORIGIN OF SUPERFUND

Superfund has proven to be a terrible burden to the EPA. Few sites have actually been cleaned up, and the liability regime has not been able to provide the large sums expected of it. The program is widely viewed to be a failure, and the EPA is routinely blamed for this.

Most embarrassingly, the initial fears that abandoned waste sites constituted a "ticking time bomb" and a manifest threat to public health have not been borne out. The studies done at Love Canal that did indicate serious health risk were later discredited, and the much more scientifically respectable studies conducted subsequently failed to show any significant risk beyond the heightened mental health problems stemming from the hysteria engendered by the incident.[69] Studies elsewhere have been similarly inconclusive. EPA's own internal assessments of program priorities admit that the toxic waste site problem is

---

69. See M. Landy, M. Roberts & S. Thomas, The Environmental Protection Agency: Asking the Wrong Questions 167 (1990); see also Love Canal: False Alarms Caused by Botched Study, Science 212 (19 June 1991): 1404-1407.

overrated and that too much of the agency's resources are spent on it.[70]

Nonetheless, despite its clear awareness of these problems, the EPA has been unwilling to launch a major public relations and lobbying effort to revise the faulty premises that impede reform. The reasons have nothing to do with Superfund's perceived environmental benefits and everything to do with the EPA's institutional interests.

Shovels First and Polluters Pay were conceived of and championed by EPA. The agency was particularly eager to gain authority over hazardous waste cleanup because this new responsibility would aid it in its efforts to reposition itself as a public health agency. In the late 1970s, the EPA no longer wanted to be viewed as a "bugs and bunnies" outfit that only protected swamps and forests. In an era of difficult economic conditions, the EPA could no longer count on sustained public support for ecological activities that appeared to provide individual citizens with few tangible benefits. In order to secure a stable political base, the agency had to be perceived as being at the center of efforts to ward off threats to the public health, the most notable being the threat of cancer.

This shift in strategy bore fruit quickly. It enabled EPA to acquire new resources at a time of strict budgetary austerity. Whereas the overall 1979 budget for environment and natural resources increased by less than 1 percent (from \$12.1 to \$12.2 billion), EPA was able to increase its operating budget by 25 percent. One-third of this increase was earmarked for programs devoted to controlling pollutants posing a public health risk. In order to demonstrate that abandoned waste sites posed the sort of public health threats that fit the agency's mission, EPA Administrator Douglas Costle appointed a task force, headed by Deputy Administrator Barbara Blum, with instructions to use the Resource Conservation and Recovery Act (RCRA) and the Safe Drinking Water Act to bring as many cases as possible to the Justice Department. The agency also launched a nationwide effort to discover new sites. Blum ordered regional officials to produce a list of sites in their region and to rank the 10 worst — a request that inspired deep resentment among regional officials, who knew that long after the headlines had faded, they would be faced with the task of calming the fears of angry residents and local officials.

Despite this dissension in the ranks, the effort was a success. Throughout the course of the legislative debate, EPA released lists of new sites in many different locales. The agency warned that hundreds of Love Canals existed across the country. Later, when the bill appeared

---

70. U.S. EPA, Unfinished Business: A Comparative Assessment of Environmental Problems (Feb. 1987), 128-134.

to be endangered by opposition from the House Ways and Means Committee, EPA worked with favorably disposed congressional staffers to compile a list of sites in each committee member's district. Even Ronald Reagan's election in November 1980 could not stop the momentum created by the "ticking time bomb" image. . . .

IS REFORM IMPOSSIBLE?

Superfund's faulty premises block improvement of the program and provide a cloak for private gain at public expense. Environmentalists benefit from the powerful boost the law gives to community organizing efforts by instilling fear and resentment about abandoned waste sites. The hazardous waste treatment industry benefits from the law's bias in favor of "Cadillac" cleanup solutions. Lawyers and consultants benefit from the huge amount of business created by Superfund's extraordinarily complex liability scheme.

On the other hand, there is no natural constituency —other than the public at large —for reforming the statute. Although Superfund liability represents a major cost to the business sector as a whole, that sector has been handicapped in efforts to reform it because different provisions of the regime have very different impacts on different segments of the business community. Once a firm has been identified as a PRP, it is in its interest to drag as many other firms, banks, and insurers as possible into the liability net. Thus, while strict, retroactive, and joint and several liability imposes immense and unpredictable costs on the private sector as a whole, it may also, in a given circumstance, enable a particular firm to spread the pain of cleanup payments. Therefore, up to now at least, the business sector has not been able to achieve the unity required to launch a major assault on the liability regime.

The closest business has come to overcoming this fractionalization and to forging a broad coalition for reform is a proposal by the American International Group (AIG), the largest underwriter of commercial and industrial insurance in the United States, to circumscribe the liability regime as a whole and to fund site cleanup by means of a broadly based tax on business. AIG proposes that the use of liability to raise funds for Superfund be abandoned, and that cleanup be paid for instead by a fund financed by a fee on all commercial and industrial insurance premiums, with a mechanism to cover self-insured companies as well. Strict and joint and several liability would continue to apply to all current and future waste disposal to ensure that generators, transporters, and disposers would have incentives to handle waste responsibly.

Although this proposal directly challenges the Polluter Pays premise, it makes no effort to refute Shovels First. Rather, it is couched as an effort to speed the cleanup which has been unduly hampered by the delays that the efforts to recoup from PRPs inevitably impose. AIG's literature uncritically cites information from the General Accounting Office (GAO) and the Office of Technology Assessment (OTA) attesting to the broad scope and seriousness of the abandoned site problem.

This selective criticism of the law is dictated by prudence. To attack the premise of "ticking time bombs" is to invite the wrath of all those in Congress, the media, and the environmental movement who have championed the idea of a hazardous waste health crisis. By confining its reform efforts to the Polluters Pay premise, the industry hopes to avoid setting off a political avalanche that would bury its most important objective, which is to diminish its liability exposure.

By saving the billions of dollars in losses that society incurs in the effort to establish liability for old sites, the AIG proposal offers important public benefits. However, by failing to insist on a careful evaluation of the actual danger to society posed by abandoned sites in general and the specific risks posed by individual sites, the AIG scheme might actually increase society's overinvestment in toxic waste management. On the one hand, the proposed tax would not fall on individuals and thus perpetuate the misconception that cleanup is free. On the other hand, the proposed tax would eliminate the last remaining source of resistance to boundless Superfund spending. For all its inefficiency, the liability scheme at least created one constituency —the PRPs —that favored less cleanup. If the liability scheme is abolished without being replaced with a mechanism to force an assessment of costs and benefits, the political momentum will go even further in the direction of expanding the program. . . .

NOTES AND QUESTIONS

1. Menell argues that the nature of legal institutions make Superfund an extremely costly environmental program. Landy and Hague argue further that the program creates perverse incentives to inflate cleanup costs. By contrast, Roberts asserts that Superfund is "one of the least bureaucratic and most cost-effective environmental programs." Can you reconcile these positions?

2. As Landy and Hague highlight, the issue of "how clean is clean?" is critical to the efficacy of the Superfund program. Many within the EPA acknowledge that the health benefits of Superfund are small relative to other public health programs (and absolutely) and that 80 percent of the environmental benefits from cleanup can typically be accomplished with 20 percent of the cleanup expenditure — emer-

gency response and containment. In view of this cost/benefit relationship, do the cleanup standards make sense?

3. Roberts asserts that there is widespread support for Superfund, as reflected in public surveys and reauthorizations. What assumptions are implicit in this mode of analysis? Can you think of alternative explanations for the apparent public support for Superfund?

4. In addition to Superfund, RCRA requires all facilities seeking permits to undertake "corrective action" to clean up existing contamination. RCRA §3004(u). EPA also has authority to require corrective action at interim status facilities that choose to shut down rather than seek a final RCRA permit. RCRA §3008(h). EPA has interpreted its corrective action authority broadly, applying to all releases of hazardous waste from any solid waste management unit at a facility regardless of the time at which waste was placed in the unit and requiring corrective action on all contiguous property under the owner or operator's control. 50 Fed. Reg. 28,702 (1985). Thus, the cleanup of contaminated property is considerably more pervasive than efforts at Superfund sites.

5. Although more than $11 billion of federal funds have been spent on responding to dangerous hazardous waste sites, not to mention state, municipal, and private outlays, the cleanup mandated by Superfund and related state laws has barely begun. Some 1200 sites are on the NPL, a number which is expected to grow to 2000 by the end of the century and to 4000 before cleanup is eventually achieved. We have barely started to address the question of natural resource damages, an aspect of Superfund which will be discussed in Chapter 9. In addition, federally owned sites number in the thousands; many, especially military installations and sites operated by the Department of Energy, will cost much more than typical NPL sites to remedy. Beyond these cleanup problems, there are leaking underground storage tanks numbering in the hundreds of thousands and abandoned mine sites. Therefore, the policy dimensions of Superfund are of great significance.

PROBLEM: EVALUATION OF SUPERFUND REFORM PROPOSALS

Evaluate the following Superfund reform proposals along the following criteria: speed of cleanup, cost effectiveness of cleanup, efficient deterrence of environmental problems, transaction costs, transition problems, political impediments. Which proposal(s) do you favor? Is there any other proposal which you would prefer?

- *Status Quo.* The current Superfund program.
- *Eliminate Joint and Several Liability.*
- *Administrative Apportionment.* EPA is required to join all PRPs

after the discovery of a site. On the basis of the available data, an administrative law judge apportions liability according to common law principles or a statutory standard.

- *Expanded Funding for Orphan Shares.* The Superfund would be expanded to cover the shares of insolvent and recalcitrant parties.
- *Municipal Liability Cap.* Municipalities shall pay no more than 4 percent of cleanup costs.
- *Municipal Solid Waste Exemption.* Municipal solid waste shall be excluded from the definition of "hazardous substances."
- *Liability Release for All Closed Co-disposal Sites.* All sites that accepted both municipal solid waste and industrial waste and that were closed at the time of amendment would be cleaned up using the Superfund. It is estimated that this would cover approximately 250 of the current 1200 NPL sites. See K. Probst & P. Portney, Assigning Liability for Superfund Cleanups: An Analysis of Policy Options (RFF 1992).
- *Liability Release for All Sites Closed Before 1981.* It is estimated that this would cover approximately 580 of the current 1200 NPL sites. See Probst & Portney, supra.
- *Liability Release for Current NPL Sites.* This release would not apply to sites added to the NPL after Superfund is amended.
- *American International Group (AIG) Proposal.* Abolish the Superfund liability regime[71] and fund cleanup with a fee on commercial and industrial insurance premiums.
- *Cleanup Standards.* Congress provides clearer cleanup goals and requires EPA to better prioritize cleanup activities within and across sites.
- *Cleanup Standards.* Congress mandates the use of risk-benefit analysis in choosing remediation plans. This would eliminate the preference for permanence in remedy selection. In addition, EPA shall consider the future use of sites (in conjunction with deed restrictions) in selecting remedies.
- *Cleanup Standards.* Congress replaces ARARs with national numerical standards.
- *Landy and Hague Proposal.* Abolish the Superfund liability regime. Congress would establish a fixed budget each year for site cleanup as a whole, which would be allocated to states on the basis of a pre-established formula, and the states would be given discretion to apply these funds to cleanup problems.

---

71. The RCRA liability regime would remain in force.

C.   COMMON LAW APPROACHES: TOXIC TORTS

A third approach to the regulation of hazardous waste disposal, as well as air and water pollution, is the use of common law tort actions for injuries to persons and property caused by toxic chemicals or other hazardous substances or agents. Toxic tort litigation represents one of the emerging areas of environmental liability, along with Superfund liability and natural resource damages liability.[72] The law in this area grows out of products liability law and traditional tort liabilities for environmental harms. A federal statutory provision for private damage actions for toxic injuries was considered by Congress in connection with the enactment of CERCLA, but ultimately rejected.

As highlighted toward the end of Chapter 3, traditional common law doctrines are quite limited in their ability to address modern environmental problems. Consider the following traditional doctrinal impediments to recovery for the harms attributable to environmental risks:

- *Statute of Limitations.* Tort actions must be brought within the relevant statute of limitations, which is typically 3 to 6 years. Yet a plaintiff's toxic injury, such as cancer, may not manifest itself for decades. When should the limitations clock begin to run — at exposure, the manifestation of disease, or when the plaintiff discovered its cause?
- *Causation.* Traditional common law doctrines require plaintiffs to establish that their injuries were caused by the defendant's actions. While this is relatively straightforward where the defendant's automobile crashed into the plaintiff's vehicle, the causal mechanism by which environmental exposures result in illnesses, such as cancer, are often unknown or incompletely understood. Moreover, many diseases associated with toxic exposure are also associated with other risk factors, such as smoking and diet. To what extent should the traditional causation requirement be modified to reflect these circumstances?
- *Standard of Liability.* Negligence can be particularly difficult to prove, especially where a defendant's use, disposal, or release of substances were only later discovered to be hazardous. The scope of strict liability has traditionally been quite narrow, limited to "abnormally dangerous" activities. Should the scope of strict liability be expanded to encompass the broad range of environmental risks?

---

72. Natural resource damage liability is examined in Chapter 9(E).

- *Expert Testimony.* Related to problems with scientific evidence are problems with scientific experts. Judges are called upon to assess expert testimony in deciding whether it may be admitted into evidence before a jury or in connection with the disposition of motions for summary judgment. Many scientists believe that in the absence of direct evidence of the mechanism of illness, well-controlled epidemiologic studies are generally the only reliable means to establish the extent of a causal association between toxic exposures and human illnesses. But in some cases an attending physician or a consulting expert claims to be able to trace a particular plaintiff's illness to a particular exposure without epidemiologic evidence. Some researchers and physicians who are proponents of the new and controversial field of clinical ecology attack the traditional focus of medical science on establishing a causal link between a single hazardous substance and a particular illness by isolating the mechanism of disease or by statistical means involving data on many individuals. Clinical ecologists urge a holistic approach, claiming that a given individual's illness must be diagnosed on a case by case basis by reference to her particular immune system and all of the myriad factors that make up her environment and might disrupt the individual's immune system. How closely should judges scrutinize proffered expert opinion on the cause of a plaintiff's illness, particularly when the opinion is not within the scientific mainstream?
- *Remedies.* Even before diseases manifest themselves, toxic exposures can cause serious emotional distress and the need for medical monitoring. To what extent should courts recognize and provide relief for these less tangible injuries? Should an enhanced risk of injury be a sufficient basis for tort recovery?

Over the past decade, numerous courts have grappled with the difficult issues posed by environmental risks. Although the law is still evolving, important doctrinal shifts have already occurred. In order to appreciate the challenges of toxic tort litigation, the first section discusses the nature of modern environmental risks. The second section surveys the emerging case law, highlighting the ways in which courts have confronted doctrinal hurdles and developed novel doctrines. The last section discusses alternative institutional approaches for compensating victims of environmental risks.

1. THE NATURE OF ENVIRONMENTAL RISKS

In contrast to the obvious environmental problems that were the focus of regulatory attention in the early 1970s — such as dense smog and fetid waterways — many of the major environmental concerns to-day relate to barely detectable traces of substances in the air, soils, and water. Unfortunately, scientific understanding of the relationship be-tween chronic exposure to these pollutants and human health is at an early stage of development.

Because of ethical limitations on controlled human health experi-ments, scientists must rely predominantly on indirect methods to test the human toxicity of substances. The principal methods for identifying disease-causing agents are animal bioassays and epidemiological stud-ies. Animal bioassays compare the incidence of disease in a control group of animals to a group that has been exposed to a particular sub-stance. They typically use high dosages, often many thousands of times greater than environmental concentrations for relatively short periods of time, so as to keep the sample size necessary for statistical signifi-cance manageable. In order to assess the effects of environmental con-centrations, therefore, the results must be extrapolated to much lower level environmental exposures experienced by humans over a much longer period of time. Making significant assumptions about the meta-bolic similarities of humans and laboratory animals, these results are then "translated" to humans.

Epidemiological studies use statistical techniques to explain varia-tions in the disease rates of human populations. Among the complexi-ties in carrying out these studies are the often poor and incomplete data on exposure to environmental contaminants, the many factors that can cause disease, the interactive effects among these factors, and the long latency periods of many diseases, particularly cancer.

As a result of these complications, scientific understanding of the causes of disease is limited. In a few cases, specific diseases have been closely linked to a particular environmental agent. Asbestosis, a nonma-lignant scarring of the lungs linked to asbestos exposure, and mesothe-lioma, a cancer of the lining of the lungs linked almost exclusively to exposure to asbestos fibers, are among the few so-called "signature dis-eases."

Most diseases, however, have many potential causes, both environ-mental and non-environmental. The best that science can do in ex-plaining the cause of these nonsignature diseases is to determine the probabilities that they were caused by various factors. On the basis of a broad range of studies, Sir Richard Doll and Richard Peto, two noted epidemiologists, have estimated the proportions of cancer deaths in the United States attributable to various factors. Their conclusions (Table 6.1) indicate that environmental pollution is responsible for a relatively small percentage of cancer deaths in the U.S., in the range of 1 to 5 percent. Because of the difficulty of isolating interactive causes, these estimates are controversial, see Epstein & Swartz, Fallacies of Lifestyle Cancer Theories, 289 Nature 127-130 (Jan. 15, 1981), with other re-searchers reporting significantly higher percentages of cancer attribut-

TABLE 6.1
Causes of U.S. Cancer Deaths

	Percentage of all Cancer Deaths	
Factor or Class of Factors	Best Estimate	Range of Acceptable Estimates
Tobacco	30	25-40
Alcohol	3	2-4
Diet	35	10-70
Food Additives	< 1	-5[a]-2
Reproductive and Sexual Behavior	7	1-13
Occupation	4	2-8
Pollution	2	< 1-5
Industrial Products	< 1	< 1-2
Medicines and Medical Procedures	1	.5-3
Geophysical Factors	3	2-4
Infection	10?	1-?
Unknown	?	?

[a] Allowing for a possibly protective effect.
Source: R. Doll & R. Peto, The Causes of Cancer 1256 (1981).

able to environmental contaminants, see P. Barth & H. Hunt, Workers' Compensation and Work-Related Illnesses and Diseases (1980); S. Samuel, The Politics of Cancer (1979). A recent comprehensive survey of epidemiological studies by Ames, Magaw, & Gold, Ranking Possible Carcinogenic Hazards, 236 Science 271-280 (Apr. 17, 1987), suggests that the threat of cancer from various environmental exposures to pollution is substantially less than exposures to many natural sources such as peanut butter (carcinogenic risk from aflotoxins), raw mushrooms (hydrazines), and wine (ethyl alcohol). These results are also controversial. See Epstein & Swartz, Technical Comment: Carcinogenic Risk Estimation, 240 Science 1043-1045 (May 20, 1988).

2.   EMERGING TOXIC TORT CASE LAW

Traditional common law liability theories in environmental cases include trespass, nuisance, negligence, and strict liability. See supra, pp. 166-169. A trespass action may, for example, be brought in situations where hazardous materials deposited in landfills have migrated through the groundwater onto another's property. Nuisance actions may also be invoked in cases of pollution emanating from nearby properties. A negligence action may be brought to remedy personal injuries caused by toxic releases of the defendant, but plaintiffs may face difficulties in establishing that the defendant's conduct was negligent, especially where the defendant's action may not have been known to pose a significant hazard when it was undertaken. The difficulties of proving negligence have led many plaintiffs to pursue a strict liability cause of action. In addition, strict liability may be the only successful theory of recovery against generators or transporters of hazardous wastes that were later handled or disposed of negligently by someone else.

Recently, many state courts have adopted the principle of strict liability for abnormally dangerous activities in toxic tort cases involving pollution, contamination of groundwater, and exposure to hazardous wastes. Recall that this principle stems from the decision in Rylands v. Fletcher, L.R. 1 Ex. 265 (1866), *aff'd*, L.R. 34 Ex. 330 (1868), where Justice Blackburn formulated a prima facie rule of strict liability for a "person who for his own purposes brings on his lands and collects and keeps there anything likely to do mischief if it escapes," the thing escapes, and injures a neighbor's person or property. While the formulation of the principle in the Restatement of Torts §520 identifies many factors that a court is to weigh in determining whether an activity is abnormally dangerous, contemporary courts readily conclude that the use, release, or disposal of toxic substances is an abnormally dangerous activity. See, e.g., *State of New Jersey, Dept. of Environmental Protection v. Ventron Corp.*, 94 N.J. 473, 468 A.2d 150 (1983), imposing strict liability for harm caused by mercury seeping from a tract of land into a creek in a tidal estuary.[73]

Under the tort of products liability, a manufacturer or distributor is held liable to a consumer or third person injured by a product if the product has a manufacturing defect or a design defect making it unreasonably dangerous to the consumer, or if there was a failure to warn of significant hazards posed by the product. In some states manufacturers and distributors can also be held liable for breach of an expressed or implied warranty under the Uniform Commercial Code.

Generally, a statute of limitations starts to run from the time the

---

73. Another issue is defenses to strict liability. Should defendants be able to defend against strict liability in a toxic tort action by showing that they did not know and could not reasonably have known of the hazard in question? Should the answer depend on whether the plaintiff's action is based on product liability or on the various forms of liability applicable to environmental exposures? In product liability actions for personal injuries caused by asbestos exposure, defendants have attempted to escape liability on the ground that scientific knowledge at the time that the product was marketed did not establish that asbestos was hazardous in ordinary use, and that therefore they could not have warned users of hazards that were only discovered later. The New Jersey Supreme Court rejected this "state of the knowledge" defense, asserting that its recognition would frustrate the goals of risk spreading and compensation of victims. *Beshada v. Johns-Manville Products Corp.*, 90 N.J. 191, 447 A.2d 539 (1982).

cause of action accrues. Determining when the cause of action accrued is not straightforward in toxic tort litigation. The most widely followed rule today is some variant of the "discovery rule": The cause of action accrues when the plaintiff discovers or should have discovered the injury and its cause. In some states courts have adopted the discovery rule by construing existing limitations statutes; in others, the discovery rule has been specifically adopted by amending legislation. At the other extreme is the traditional rule that the statute of limitations starts to run at the time the defendant did the wrongful act. This rule is particularly harsh on plaintiffs with a latent injury, since the statute of limitations may have run even before the disease manifests itself. In between these two rules is the rule that the statute of limitation begins to run when the injury manifests itself, even if the plaintiff is not aware of it or does not know its cause.

STERLING V. VELSICOL CHEMICAL CORP.

855 F.2d 1188 (6th Cir. 1988)

FACTS

In August, 1964, the defendant, Velsicol Chemical Corporation (Velsicol), acquired 242 acres of rural land in Hardeman County, Tennessee. The defendant used the site as a landfill for by-products from the production of chlorinated hydrocarbon pesticides at its Memphis, Tennessee, chemical manufacturing facility. Before Velsicol purchased the landfill site and commenced depositing any chemicals into the ground, it neither conducted hydrogeological studies to assess the soil composition underneath the site, the water flow direction, and the location of the local water aquifer, nor drilled a monitoring well to detect and record any ongoing contamination. From October, 1964, to June, 1973, the defendant deposited a total of 300,000 55-gallon steel drums containing ultrahazardous liquid chemical waste and hundreds of fiber board cartons containing ultrahazardous dry chemical waste in the landfill.

[The chemicals leached into the groundwater and migrated off-site, contaminating wells used for drinking water by nearby residents with carbon tetrachloride and chloroform. In 1967, the United States Geological Survey studied the site, finding subsurface contamination but erroneously concluding that the contamination flowed to the east, whereas the domestic wells were to the west. In fact, the contamination flowed northwest. The State of Tennessee ordered the landfill closed in 1973. Intensive testing of groundwater was undertaken in 1978 by federal and state authorities, who advised the residents to stop using the wells. Various civil actions for damages were brought by several dozens of plaintiffs against Velsicol, who removed them to federal district court on grounds of diversity jurisdiction. On its own motion and over defendant's objection, the court consolidated the individual claims in a class action. It then tried the claims of five representative plaintiffs selected by plaintiff's counsel.]

After a bench trial of the five claims, the district court found Velsicol liable to the plaintiffs on legal theories of strict liability, common law negligence, trespass, and nuisance. The court concluded that the defendant's hazardous chemicals, which escaped from its landfill and contaminated plaintiffs' well water, were the proximate cause of the representative plaintiffs' injuries. The district court awarded the five individuals compensatory damages totaling $5,273,492.50 for their respective injuries, plus prejudgment interest dating back to July, 1965, of $8,964,973.25. All damages, except for $48,492.50 to one plaintiff for property damage claims, were awarded for personal injuries. The district court also awarded $7,500,000 in punitive damages to the class as a whole. The court deferred to individual hearings, to be held after trial, the issues of causation and injury of any other persons purporting to be members of the class entitled to share in this award. . . .

CLASS ACTION CERTIFICATION

[Velsicol challenged the district court's certification of a class action.]

The procedural device of a Rule 23(b)(3) class action was designed not solely as a means for assuring legal assistance in the vindication of small claims but, rather, to achieve the economies of time, effort, and expense. . . . However, the problem of individualization of issues often is cited as a justification for denying class action treatment in mass tort accidents. While some courts have adopted this justification in refusing to certify such accidents as class actions, numerous other courts have recognized the increasingly insistent need for a more efficient method of disposing of a large number of lawsuits arising out of a single disaster or a single course of conduct. In mass tort accidents, the factual and legal issues of a defendant's liability do not differ dramatically from one plaintiff to the next. No matter how individualized the issue of damages may be, these issues may be reserved for individual treatment with the question of liability tried as a class action. . . .

In the instant case, each class member lived in the vicinity of the landfill and allegedly suffered damages as a result of ingesting or otherwise using the contaminated water. Almost identical evidence would be required to establish the level and duration of chemical contamination, the contaminated water and the type of injuries allegedly suffered, and the defendant's liability. The single major issue distinguishing the class members is the nature and amount of damages, if any, that each sustained. To this extent, a class action in the instant case avoided duplication of judicial effort and prevented separate actions from reaching inconsistent results with similar, if not identical, facts. The district court clearly did not abuse its discretion in certifying this action as a Rule 23(b)(3) class action. However, individual members of the class still will be required to submit evidence concerning their particularized damage claims in subsequent proceedings.

PROXIMATE CAUSATION . . .

Velsicol argues that proof of the plaintiffs' exposure to its chemicals and the causal connection between that exposure, if any, and their subsequent injuries impermissibly was based upon insufficient evidence. Specifically, the defendant asserts that there was no evidence that two known carcinogens (carbon tetrachloride and chloroform) were in the plaintiffs' wells in the late 1960's and early 1970's when they allegedly were consuming the contaminated water. To overcome this lack of evidence, Velsicol contends that the plaintiffs introduced into evidence an invalid water computing model that erroneously concluded that the plaintiffs were exposed to significant levels of contaminants as early as 1970. By extrapolation, the plaintiffs' model purported to show that dramatically high concentrations of carbon tetrachloride and chloroform were in the plaintiffs' wells as early as 1970 and, therefore, that the plaintiffs had been exposed to the chemical contaminants in sufficiently high dosages for a prolonged period of time sufficient to cause their resultant injuries.

[The court rejected Velsicol's criticism of plaintiffs' modelling assumptions.]

Next, Velsicol argues there was insufficient evidence to prove causation between plaintiffs' ingestion, if any, of Velsicol's chemicals and their alleged resultant injuries. . . . On the basis of expert testimony (consisting of treating physicians, medical specialists, scientists, psychiatrists, clinical psychologists, engineers, hydrologists, and the plaintiffs themselves), numerous studies, and extensive literature, the district court concluded that Velsicol's chemicals and the duration of the plaintiffs' exposure to them were *capable* of causing the types of injuries alleged by the plaintiffs. The court also concluded that all of the five representative plaintiffs' presently ascertainable and reasonably anticipated future injuries were proximately caused by ingesting or otherwise using the contaminated water. . . .

juries, they must prove to a "reasonable medical certainty," though they need not use that specific terminology, that their ingestion of the contaminated water caused each of their particular injuries. . . . This standard implicates the qualifications of the witnesses testifying, the acceptance in the scientific community of their theories, and the degree of certainty as to their conclusions. This standard is of particular importance when dealing with injuries or diseases of a type that may inflict [sic] society at random, often with no known specific origin. [Tennessee common law requires plaintiffs to establish that their particular injuries more likely than not were caused by ingesting the contaminated water but] their proofs may be neither speculative nor conjectural. Medical testimony that ingesting the contaminated water "possibly," "may have," "might have," or "could have" caused the plaintiffs' presently ascertainable or anticipated injuries does not constitute the same level of proof as a conclusion by a reasonable medical certainty. Although it is argued that a lesser standard of proof allocates loss on a socially acceptable basis, it is the province of the state legislatures to make such changes as they have done in some areas by establishing "no-fault" or other alternate systems.

While upon review of the record in its entirety we cannot say that the district court abused its discretion in making its determination of the proximate causation between Velsicol's chemical dumping operations, the resultant contamination of the plaintiff's water supply and the capacity of the contaminated water to cause the harms alleged, we find the district court erred in attributing all of the representative plaintiffs' alleged injuries to drinking or otherwise using the contaminated water. We, therefore, address each category of the district court's damage award.[74]

COMPENSATORY DAMAGES

Velsicol argues that, even assuming proof of a proximate causation, the district court improperly awarded the five representative plaintiffs compensatory damages for their respective injuries and disabilities. The five representative plaintiffs, their exposure to Velsicol's chemicals, and their respective injuries are as follows:

Steven Sterling: Plaintiff Sterling, who was born December 25, 1922,

---

74. On appeal, Velsicol does not specifically argue that the district court erred in awarding the five representative plaintiffs damages for pain and suffering. See, e.g., *Dixie Feed & Seed Co. v. Byrd,* 52 Tenn. App. 619, 376 S.W.2d 745 (1963), *cert. denied,* Tenn. S. Ct., *cert. denied,* 379 U.S. 15, 85 S. Ct. 147, 13 L. Ed. 2d 84 (1964). Finding that the court had a proper basis for its award, therefore, we do not address this category of damages.

	Sterling	Wilbanks	Ivy	Johnson	Maness
Extent of Injury and Disability	$150,000	$150,000	$75,000	$150,000	$250,000
Increased Risk of Cancer and Immune System Impairment	$75,000	$75,000	$75,000	$150,000	$500,000
Post-Traumatic Stress Disorder	$50,000	$25,000	$50,000	$250,000	
Fear of Increased Risk of Cancer and Disease	$75,000	$100,000	$50,000	$250,000	$250,000
Physical Pain	$125,000	$250,000	$50,000	$125,000	$150,000
Emotional Suffering Impaired Quality of Life	$150,000	$75,000	$50,000	$100,000	$500,000
Real Property	$48,492.50				
Lost Wages and Earning Capacity				$250,000	$500,000
Learning Disorders					$150,000
Total	$673,492.50	$675,000	$350,000	$1,275,000	$2,300,000

dence (Sterling well) for drinking purposes until November, 1977, and for all other purposes until November, 1978. During that time, he claimed to have drunk between ten and twelve glasses of the well water each day. He observed that, beginning in 1975, the well water developed a distinct odor, a bad taste, and contained an oily substance. Sterling testified that after ingesting, and otherwise using, the well water for a prolonged period of time, he suffered from headaches, nervousness, stomach and chest pains, shortness of breath, ringing in his ears, fatigue, loss of appetite and weight, nausea, coughing, vomiting, and peripheral neuropathy. Sterling further testified that he suffered from an enlarged liver with abnormal hepatic function, and an eighty percent reduction in his kidney function. Additionally, he developed emphysema in early 1976. Sterling was a heavy smoker for over forty-five years and previously worked in a cotton mill.

[The court reviewed the personal injuries claimed by the other four representative plaintiffs. All claimed symptoms such as nausea, fatigue, headaches, dizziness, and shortness of breath. In addition, James Wilbanks claimed loss of eyesight and loss of a kidney due to cancer. Curry Ivy, who had a history of serious health problems prior to drinking the contaminated water and was a heavy smoker, claimed partial loss of eyesight, liver and kidney damage, and severe emphysema. Daniel Johnson claimed eyesight loss and liver and kidney damage. He was also totally disabled and unable to work as a result of psychological problems. James Maness, who was born in 1976, drank from the wells, as did his mother when she was pregnant. He claimed severe allergies, epilepsy, diabetes, blood discrasias, and an enlarged liver, and was borderline retarded with severe learning disabilities. In addition, Sterling owned property, adjacent to the dump site, whose groundwater was contaminated. The District Court awarded damages as appears in the table.]

A.   EXTENT OF INJURY AND DISABILITY

Velsicol asserts there was insufficient medical proof of the causal connection between ingestion of contaminated water and certain injuries.

1.   *Presently Ascertainable Injuries . . .*

Velsicol specifically avers that the plaintiffs failed to prove to a reasonable medical certainty that Wilbanks' kidney cancer, all of the plaintiffs' loss of kidney and liver functions and central nervous system injuries, and Wilbanks' and Ivy's optic atrophy and neuritis were caused by ingesting contaminated water. With respect to Wilbanks' kidney cancer, plaintiffs' testifying physician, Dr. Rhamy, stated that "based upon a reasonable medical certainty . . . it's more likely [that Wilbanks' kidney cancer] was caused by the chemicals. . . ." While Dr. Rhamy conceded that "[n]o one knows what causes cancer of the kidney," his testimony that Wilbanks' environmental exposure to carbon tetrachloride was the reasonable and probable cause for his kidney cancer constitutes sufficient medical proof. The plaintiffs' testifying physicians, Drs. Balistreri, Clark, Rhamy, and Rodricks, further testified to a reasonable medical certainty that each of the plaintiff's loss of kidney and liver functions and central nervous system disorders were caused by their exposure to the contaminated water.

However, the plaintiffs failed to prove to a reasonable medical certainty that either Wilbanks' or Ivy's optic atrophy and neuritis were caused by ingesting or otherwise using the contaminated water. While plaintiffs' own expert neuroopthamologist, Dr. Drewery, stated that Ivy's eye problems and his exposure to carbon tetrachloride were causally related and that his reduction in visual acuity and visual field were compatible with toxic exposure, Dr. Drewery, based upon his own tests, concluded that Ivy did not have optic atrophy. Indeed, no physician diagnosed Ivy as suffering from optic atrophy. Dr. Drewery's statement that he was unable to "uncover any . . . other medically probable explanation for Mr. Ivy's visual problems than chemical exposure," when considered in view of his negative diagnosis, and Dr. Rhamy's observation that Ivy had a paleness of the optic disc (which Dr. Drewery did not observe) does not constitute sufficient medical proof. Similarly, no physician diagnosed or testified to a reasonable medical certainty that Wilbanks' visual difficulties were caused by his exposure to contaminated water. . . .

2.   Increased Risk of Cancer and Other Diseases

. . . The district court awarded the five representative plaintiffs damages predicated upon their being at risk for, or susceptible to, future disease.

Where the basis for awarding damages is the potential risk of susceptibility to future disease, the predicted future disease must be medically reasonably certain to follow from the existing present injury. . . . Therefore, the mere increased risk of a future disease or condition resulting from an initial injury is not compensable. . . .

In the instant case, the district court found an increased risk for susceptibility to cancer and other diseases of only twenty-five to thirty percent. This does not constitute a reasonable medical certainty, but rather a mere possibility or speculation. Indeed, no expert witnesses ever testified during the course of trial that the five representative plaintiffs had even a probability — i.e., more than a fifty percent chance— of developing cancer and kidney or liver disease as a result of their exposure to defendant's chemicals.

For the foregoing reasons, the district court's award of compensatory damages to each of the five representative plaintiffs is remanded for recalculation to exclude that portion of the damage award attributed to increased susceptibility to cancer and other diseases.

B.   FEAR OF INCREASED RISK OF CANCER AND OTHER DISEASES

Velsicol next argues that the district court erroneously awarded the five representative plaintiffs compensatory damages or, in the alternative, excessive damages for fear of increased risk of contracting cancer and other diseases. Mental distress, which results from fear that an already existent injury will lead to the future onset of an as yet unrealized disease, constitutes an element of recovery only where such distress is either foreseeable or is a natural consequence of, or reasonably expected to flow from, the present injury. . . . To this extent, mental anguish resulting from the chance that an existing injury will lead to the materialization of a future disease may be an element of recovery even though the underlying future prospect for susceptibility to a future disease is not, in and of itself, compensable inasmuch as it is not sufficiently likely to occur. . . .

In the instant case, the plaintiffs' fear clearly constitutes a present injury. Each plaintiff produced evidence that they personally suffered from a reasonable fear of contracting cancer or some other disease in the future as a result of ingesting Velsicol's chemicals. . . .

In the instant case, the district court awarded plaintiffs damages ranging from $50,000 to $250,000. We find these awards to be excessive, particularly where plaintiffs failed to prove at trial that they have a significant increased risk of contracting cancer and other diseases. Upon a review of the opinion and the adopted findings of fact, we are unable to find any basis upon which the district court differentiated its damage awards to each plaintiff for his or her fear of increased risk of cancer and other diseases. The *Laxton* [*v. Orkin Exterminating Co.*, 639 S.W.2d 431 (Tenn. 1982),] court awarded each plaintiff $6,000 for his or her fear of increased susceptibility to cancer from consuming known carcinogens for a duration of eight months. Using *Laxton* as a guidepost, we, accordingly, vacate the district court's award and award each of the five representative plaintiffs damages based upon the duration of their exposure to the contaminated water. Plaintiff Johnson, who was exposed to the chemicals for a period of approximately two years, is awarded $18,000 versus the district court's award of $250,000; plaintiff Maness, who was exposed for approximately three years (two years during infancy and approximately one year while his mother was exposed to the chemicals during pregnancy), is awarded $27,000 versus the district court's award of $250,000; plaintiff Ivy, who was exposed for approximately four years, is awarded $36,000 versus the district court's award of $50,000; plaintiff Wilbanks, who was exposed for approximately six years, is awarded $54,000 versus the district court's award of $100,000; and plaintiff Sterling, who was exposed for approximately eight years, is awarded $72,000 versus the district court's award of $75,000.

C.   IMMUNE SYSTEM IMPAIRMENT AND LEARNING DISORDERS

. . . Velsicol specifically alleges that the court improperly admitted and relied upon testimony which purported to show Velsicol's chemicals harmed plaintiffs' immune systems because the principles upon which the experts based their conclusions were not in conformity to a generally accepted explanatory theory.

The admissibility of expert testimony is governed by Fed. R. Evid. 702 which provides:

> If scientific, technical, or other specialized knowledge will assist the trier of fact to understand the evidence or to determine a fact in issue, a witness qualified as an expert by knowledge, skill, experience, training, or education, may testify thereto in the form of an opinion or otherwise.

In accordance with Rule 702, a four-part test must be met to uphold the admission of "expert testimony": (1) a qualified expert (2) testifying on a proper subject (3) which is in conformity to a generally accepted explanatory theory (4) the probative value of which outweighs its prejudicial effect. . . . *United States v. Brown,* 557 F.2d 541 (6th Cir. 1977). . . . With respect to the third criterion, the principles upon which the scientific evidence is based must be sufficiently established to have gained wide acceptance in the field to which it belongs. As we reasoned in *United States v. Brown:*

> There are good reasons why not every ostensibly scientific technique should be recognized as the basis for expert testimony. Because of its apparent objectivity, an opinion that claims a scientific basis is apt to carry undue weight with the trier of fact. In addition, it is difficult to rebut such an opinion except by other experts or by cross-examination based on a thorough acquaintance with the underlying principles. In order to prevent deception or mistake and to allow the possibility of effective response, there must be a demonstrable, objective procedure for reaching the opinion and qualified persons who can either duplicate the result or criticize the means by which it was reached, drawing their own conclusions from the underlying facts.

557 F.2d at 556. . . . A review of the record reveals that plaintiffs failed to meet the third criterion of the test.

Plaintiffs' testifying expert immunologist, Dr. Levin, and testifying pediatrician, Dr. Crook, stated that, on the basis of clinical ecological tests, Velsicol's chemicals damaged plaintiffs' immune systems. Clinical ecology is premised on a belief that exposure to a number of factors including, but not limited to, anxiety, radiation, certain chemicals, and even some common household substances can cause dysregulation of the immune system. Treatment for immune system dysregulation consists of rigid diet and environmental control. The leading professional societies in the specialty of allergy and immunology, the American Academy of Allergy and Immunology (AAAI) and the California Medical Association (CMA), have rejected clinical ecology as an unproven methodology lacking any scientific basis in either fact or theory. While numerous other professional organizations and societies, such as the American Medical Association, the American Board of Allergy and Immunology, and the American Academy of Otolaryngic Allergy, have not discredited completely the potential usefulness of clinical ecology, few have endorsed either its scientific methodology or the results of any experiments conducted under the guise of clinical ecology. Indeed, plaintiffs' experts neither performed nor could identify any studies of the effects of carbon tetrachloride or chloroform on the immune system. In reaching their conclusions of immune system dysregulation, plaintiffs' experts neither personally examined or interviewed plaintiffs, nor performed the requisite medical tests. The experts based their opinions upon certain blood tests, which revealed a higher than normal white blood cell count, and the plaintiffs' medical histories supplied by their attorneys. Without the requisite clinical tests and a widely accepted medical basis for reaching its conclusions, plaintiffs' experts' opinions are insufficient to sustain plaintiffs' burden of proof that the contaminated water damaged their immune system.

The record reveals that plaintiff Maness was borderline retarded and suffered from a severe learning disorder. The sole evidence allegedly linking Maness' learning problems to his chemical exposure was offered by clinical ecologist, Dr. Crook. Dr. Crook testified that Maness' and his mother's ingestion of toxic chemicals "so compromised his resistance that it set him up for a variety of health problems" — in essence immune system dysregulation. Dr. Crook based his conclusions on two examinations in which he determined Maness' physical condition was normal and Maness' general medical history which was provided by his grandmother. He performed no scientific tests to determine the source of Maness' learning disorder. Despite the testimony of other physicians which attributed Maness' learning disorder to other factors, Dr. Crook dismissed the evidence reasoning that "those physicians are unaware of the role of chemical sensitivity in triggering health problems . . . I feel I have knowledge of [Maness] that they don't have." Despite his personal speculations, Dr. Crook provided no medical basis justifying his conclusion that Maness' learning disorder was caused by ingesting or otherwise using the contaminated water.

Accordingly, we reverse the district court's award of damages to all of the plaintiffs for immune system impairment and to plaintiff Maness for his learning disorder arising out of impairment to his immune system.

D. POST-TRAUMATIC STRESS DISORDER

Velsicol argues that the district court improperly awarded four of the five representative plaintiffs damages for post-traumatic stress disorder (PTSD). Both this court and the courts of Tennessee are familiar with, and have awarded compensatory damages for, PTSD. . . .

As medically defined, PTSD concerns the development of characteristic symptoms following a psychologically traumatic event generally outside the range of usual human experience. . . .

Plaintiffs' drinking or otherwise using contaminated water, even over an extended period of time, does not constitute the type of recognizable stressor identified either by professional medical organizations or courts. Examples of stressors upon which courts have based awards for PTSD include rape, assault, military combat, fires, floods, earthquakes, car and airplane crashes, torture, and even internment in concentration camps, each of which are natural or man-made disasters with immediate or extended violent consequences. . . . Whereas consumption of contaminated water may be an unnerving occurrence, it does not rise to the level of the type of psychologically traumatic event that is a universal stressor. . . .

F.   LOST WAGES AND EARNING CAPACITY

[The Court found that Johnson and Maness had failed to present sufficient evidence of the extent of their lost earnings to justify the district court's awards for this item.]

G.   DIMINUTION OF PROPERTY VALUE

Velsicol asserts that the district court erred in finding that the current value of one of the representative plaintiff's property was limited to its value as that of timberland. Velsicol asserts that . . . the fact that the plaintiff continues living on the property . . . meant the property had a higher value. . . .

The district court found that the value of all property within one mile of Velsicol's landfill, the "contaminated zone," had been rendered valueless except for $275 per acre for timber bearing potential. . . .

. . . The plaintiffs' expert witnesses, James Murdaugh (a real estate appraiser), Joseph Jones (a local bank president), and William Kail (a regional mortgage company vice-president), testified that the market value of a given piece of property is based upon a fully informed arm's-length buyer and seller and available financing to purchase the property. Murdaugh testified that the value of Sterling's property, and all property within the "contaminated zone," was rendered valueless, except for its potential timberland value. . . . Jones and Kail testified that their respective institutions would be unwilling to provide any financing for properties within one mile of the landfill site, and only limited financing to properties within three miles of the landfill, since they may be unable to recoup their investment in case of foreclosure. The fact that Sterling retained his properties is irrelevant since he would be unable to sell his property and few, if any potential buyers even could consider purchasing the property as they would have great difficulty in locating the requisite financing. We find that the district court properly valuated Sterling's property. . . .

PUNITIVE DAMAGES

[The District Court had awarded punitive damages because of Velsicol's reckless behavior in disposing of chemicals at the site and because it had unsuccessfully asserted as a defense to liability the claim that plaintiffs "came to the nuisance" and should therefore be denied recovery. The court found that this defense "is without factual basis and so outrageous as to subject the defendant to punitive damages." The court of appeals found that Velsicol's asserted legal defense was not "contrived in bad faith" and was therefore not in and of itself a permissible basis for awarding punitive damages.]

There is, however, evidence supporting the district court's determination that Velsicol violated state law in establishing, utilizing, and refusing to cease disposal operations at the landfill disposal site. It was within the district court's discretion to consider defendant's disregard of state law in making its award. Lastly, the district court need not defer its award of punitive damages prior to determining compensatory damages for the entire class of 128 individuals. So long as the court determines the defendant's liability and awards representative class members compensatory damages, the district court may in its discretion award punitive damages to the class as a whole at that time. Because the district court erred in awarding punitive damages, in part, upon the positions taken by Velsicol at trial, we remand for recomputation of punitive damages.

For the foregoing reasons, we AFFIRM IN PART, REVERSE IN PART, and REMAND for recalculation of damages.

IN RE AGENT ORANGE LITIGATION

611 F. Supp. 1223 (E.D.N.Y. 1985), aff'd on other grounds, 818 F.2d 187 (2d Cir. 1987), cert. denied, 487 U.S. 1234 (1988)

[In terms of number of parties, complexity, potential liability exposure, and political ramifications, the Agent Orange litigation presented a mass tort case of unprecedented proportions. The case involved claims by veterans of the Vietnam War from the United States,

Australia and New Zealand, and their parents, spouses and children, against some of the largest chemical corporations in the world. During the war, these companies had supplied the United States government with chemical defoliants to be used to destroy the Vietnamese jungle. This operation, originally authorized by President Kennedy, aimed to destroy the enemies' cover, crops and communication lines. Several different types of defoliants were used, but the most effective one was called Agent Orange, so named because of the colored label on its containers. This compound contained equal parts of two chemicals, 2,4-D and 2,4,5-T. Varying levels of another chemical called 2,3,7,8 tetrachlorodibenzo-p-dioxin ("dioxin") were produced in an intermediate step in the making of 2,4,5-T and remained in the final result. Dioxin has been called "perhaps the most toxic molecule ever synthesized by man." The veterans claimed that they were exposed to dioxin through the air they breathed, the water they drank, the food they ate, or through direct skin contact in Vietnam. They alleged that the dioxin was the cause of their illnesses and injuries, including various types of skin and liver disorders and cancers. Their wives and children alleged that the dioxin damaged the veterans' sperm, causing miscarriages and birth defects.

The case, which started as a single action, grew to over 600 separate actions filed by more than 15,000 named plaintiffs. These claims were eventually consolidated as a class action. The ultimate class consisted of 2.4 million veterans and their family members. In addition there were nearly 400 individual cases in which the plaintiffs had opted out of the class. At various times in the suit, from 5 to 24 chemical corporations were defendants. Plaintiffs based their actions against these companies on products liability and failure to warn claims. The defendants impleaded the United States government as a third-party defendant asserting the government contractor defense. The plaintiffs created a network of attorneys which included nearly 1500 law firms by May 1984, when the case settled. Notwithstanding the consolidation of more than 600 different lawsuits in one court, the case imposed a tremendous burden on the resources of the federal judiciary.

The case raised numerous novel and complex procedural and substantive issues. The judicial system was not certain how to handle all of the claims brought by so many people from across the United States and two foreign countries. Several difficult procedural problems, such as federal court jurisdiction, choice of law, and class action certification were raised. Substantively, tort law was stretched to its limits in recognizing the claims. The most difficult issues confronting the plaintiffs were causation and liability. The diseases which they alleged were caused by Agent Orange could have been created by many other sources. The exposure levels had been low. In addition, many of the diseases which could be caused by dioxin had long latency periods. Therefore many of the people exposed to Agent Orange might not have developed dioxin-related injuries at the time the suit was brought. Plaintiffs also faced problems in identifying the defendants responsible for their injury. The defendants had produced Agent Orange with widely varying amounts of dioxin. The army then stored the defoliant in unlabeled containers and mixed the batches of different suppliers together indiscriminately before it was sprayed. Finally, the defendants asserted a military contractor defense, asserting that they should be insulated from liability because they produced the Agent Orange in accordance with government specifications during a war.

Aside from these legal issues, the case also became a symbolic struggle for the veterans of an unpopular war who felt abused and cheated by the government and their fellow citizens. The suit brought the court into the political arena of resolving this complex dispute with many, often emotional, overtones.

The case eventually found its way onto the docket of Chief Judge Jack Weinstein in the Eastern District of New York, who has been described as "an extremely complex, unconventional man of vast imagination, Byzantine subtlety, and almost blinding brilliance, as uncomfortable with traditional formulations as any individual of genius in any field is." P. Schuck, Agent Orange on Trial: Mass Toxic Disasters in the Courts 112 (expanded ed. 1987). As soon as he took over the case, Judge Weinstein completely changed its course and focus. He quickly certified the class action, dramatically raising the stakes for the defendants. Doubting the plaintiffs' ability to prove liability yet recognizing the important public nature of the case, he structured the proceedings and exhorted the parties to settle the case. On the morning of May 7, 1983, the day trial was to begin, the parties agreed on a $180 million settlement. While $180 million was the largest tort settlement in history, when divided by the large number of potential claimants, provided each class member with a maximum of $12,700; most would receive less. All servicemembers and their biological children conceived after service were entitled to recovery, with no particularized showing of causal connection to injuries.

Following a series of hearings in which many veterans strongly opposed the agreement, Judge Weinstein approved the settlement, emphasizing the advantages of settlement for all parties and the public. *Agent Orange,* 597 F. Supp. 740. This lengthy opinion analyzed all of the major issues of the case. Weinstein began by noting the limitations of the judicial system in resolving such large and complex disputes.

> Had this court the power to rectify past wrongs — actual or perceived — it would do so. But no single litigation can lift all of the plaintiffs' burdens. The legislative and executive branches of government — state and federal — and the Veterans Administration, as well as our many private

and quasi-private medical and social agencies, are far more capable than this court of shaping the larger remedies and emotional compensation plaintiffs seek.

597 F. Supp. at 747. He also noted the opposition of class members who believed the settlement to be too low, or who wanted their day in court in order to have all of the relevant information and resolve the issue of defendants' liability one way or another. The class action was held to be a useful mechanism for handling mass tort cases. "[W]hile the class action is deemed procedural and distinct from substantive considerations for most purposes, it may become, in a case like '*Agent Orange*,' the only practicable way to secure a remedy." 597 F. Supp. at 842. He also cited the difficult problems of proving causation and the availability of the government contractor defense as factors, as well as the limited resources available to plaintiffs' counsel to wage a full scale trial. On the causation issue, he stated:

> The critical problem for the plaintiffs is to establish that the relatively small quantities of dioxin to which servicepersons were exposed in Vietnam caused their present disabilities. Here adequate proof is lacking. . . .
> In the intensive study of the Ranch Hand personnel who conducted most of the spraying and had most contact with Agent Orange, no statistically significant dermatological differences were found between these men and a control group.
> The evidence with respect to birth defects is even more tenuous. Male mediated birth defects might theoretically result from exposure of the father to Agent Orange, but no supporting data associating dioxin exposure of males with birth defects of children has been made available.
> No test, plaintiffs' experts apparently concede, is decisive in proving exposure to Agent Orange, partly because, as one expert put it, "all of us have probably been exposed to dioxin at some time." Their suggestion that combinations of symptoms "hold the most promise for determining possible exposure to dioxin," is certainly worth study, but could not now be the basis for recovery in a lawsuit, where relatively high degrees of probative force are required. . . .
> The problem of obtaining useful data on the effects of Agent Orange is particularly difficult for a number of reasons. First, the relatively young males who served in Vietnam were a highly selected, healthy group so that the expected mortality was relatively slight in their early ages and a comparison with base civilian populations is difficult. Second, there may be many confounding factors that explain diseases such as stress of combat and local natural and man-made carcinogens. Third, the cancers involved may take a long time to reveal themselves since they become important in a epidemiologic sense only in older age groups. . . .

597 F. Supp. at 782-83.

Judge Weinstein also noted that even if a statistically valid correlation between exposure to Agent Orange and illnesses could be established, the probability that any individual's illness was so caused would likely be less than 50 percent, the traditional preponderance standard for establishing causation. He also found no basis for an award of punitive damages. In conclusion, he stated:

> Even though the evidence presented to the court to date suggests that the case is without merit, many of those who testified at the Fairness Hearings indicated that they sought its prosecution not for money but for public vindication. It may be, to paraphrase Sir James George Frazer, that the litigation itself has served a useful function: like many trials, the "main object of the ceremony . . . is simply to effect a total clearance of all the ills that have been infecting a people." J. G. Frazer, The Golden Bough 666 (abridged ed. 1958).

597 F. Supp. at 857.

[The decision by Judge Weinstein which follows involves claims by several hundred plaintiffs, Vietnam veterans and their children, who elected to opt out of the class action and the class settlement and separately pursue their individual claims. Defendants, manufacturers of Agent Orange, moved for summary judgment on the ground that there was no credible evidence that exposure to dioxin was the cause of the ailments complained of by plaintiffs.]

III.   FACTS . . .

A.   EPIDEMIOLOGICAL STUDIES . . .

A number of sound epidemiological studies have been conducted on the health effects of exposure to Agent Orange. These are the only useful studies having any bearing on causation.

All the other data supplied by the parties rests on surmise and inapposite extrapolations from animal studies and industrial accidents. It is hypothesized that, predicated on this experience, adverse effects of Agent Orange on plaintiffs might at some time in the future be shown to some degree of probability. . . .

1.   Miscarriages and Birth Defects . . .

The studies to date conclude that there is as yet no epidemiological evidence that paternal exposure to Agent Orange causes birth defects and miscarriages. [Citing studies.]

[A study by the U.S. Public Health Service Center for Disease Control] concluded: "At present, *no adverse human reproductive effects have been shown to be related to exposure to phenoxy herbicides and dioxin.*" . . . (emphasis supplied).

The conclusions of the Australian study are similarly negative:

There is no evidence that Army service in Vietnam increases the risk of fathering children with anomalies diagnosed at birth. . . .

2.   Veterans' Health

Epidemiological studies addressing the effect of Agent Orange exposure on veterans' health have not furnished support for plaintiffs' claims. They have been negative or inconclusive.

The Air Force study is the most intensive examination to date of Agent Orange effects on exposed veterans. See Air Force Health Study, An Epidemiologic Investigation of Health Effects in Air Force Personnel Following Exposure to Herbicides (February 24, 1984) (Ranch Hand II Study — 1984 Report). This study utilized 1024 matched pairs of men for analysis. Id. at v. Essentially all those who had participated in the fixed wing spraying [of Agent Orange from airplanes] and who could be located were studied. The conclusion was negative. In summary,

This baseline report concludes that there is insufficient evidence to support a cause and effect relationship between herbicide exposure and adverse health in the Ranch Hand group at this time.
Id. at iii. . . .

The small Ranch Hand sample and other factors, particularly the length of time it takes for most cancers to develop, support the conclusion that more work is needed before any firm conclusion can be reached respecting morbidity. Id. at v. The authors suggest a 20-year mortality follow-up study. Id. at v., XVIII-1-3. [Judge Weinstein discussed at length other studies that reached similar conclusions.]

Plaintiffs cite a number of studies conducted on animals and industrial workers as evidence of a causal link between exposure to TCDD and the development of various hepatotoxic, hematotoxic, genotoxic, and enzymatic responses. None of these studies do more than show that there may be a causal connection between dioxin and disease. None show such a connection between plaintiffs and Agent Orange.

Plaintiffs also rely on several depositions and affidavits by experts. As indicated below, to the extent that these experts rely on available epidemiological studies, the studies supply no basis for an inference of causation. There is simply no other reliable data on which an expert can furnish reliable testimony. . . .

B.   EXPERT AFFIDAVITS

Even most of plaintiffs' experts express doubt about causation, except for some ill-defined possible "association" as compared with associations with any specific other products or natural carcinogens; none supports the conclusion that present evidence permits a scientifically acceptable conclusion that Agent Orange did cause a specific plaintiff's specific disease. See, e.g., Report of Dr. Hyman J. Zimmerman, Comments on Porphyria Cutanea Tarda & Related Matters ("[t]he relevance of [liver destruction and cancer] to man and the relevance of liver injury and PCT to exposure to DIOXIN *remains to be evaluated* by proper epidemiologic studies."). . . . Deposition of Dr. Ellen Silbergeld, at 321 ("I *think* there is *an association* [between exposure to Agent Orange and lymphoma]") [emphasis supplied]. . . .

It is significant that like Doctors Singer and Epstein, whose affidavits are described in detail below, the various experts referred to in the preceding paragraph apparently had no physical contact with individual plaintiffs. . . .

Plaintiffs offer the opinion of two experts who conclude that in the cases of the specific opt-out plaintiffs before the court, exposure to Agent Orange caused adverse health effects. One is Dr. Singer's submission. The other is Dr. Epstein's.

1.   Dr. Singer's Affidavit

Plaintiffs submitted two affidavits on causation by Dr. Barry M. Singer. Their wording is virtually identical. Dr. Singer's affidavits were accompanied by 282 "affidavits" by individual veteran plaintiffs. The latter are form statements, signed by either the plaintiff or his attorney, or both. . . .

The forms typically allege that the plaintiff "saw spraying of Agent Orange, entered defoliated areas and consumed local food and water." The forms then describe the plaintiff's diagnosed medical problems and refer to an attached "checklist" for a description of alleged Agent Orange related symptoms.

The checklists allow the individual to identify any or all of a number of symptoms which they attribute to their exposure to Agent Orange in Vietnam. In addition to general symptoms such as fatigue, space is provided in which to indicate specific skin, skeletal-muscular, gastro-intestinal, visual and behavioral disorders, as well as to identify any tumors as malignant or nonmalignant. Finally, the checklist asks for information about the individual's offspring. A perusal of the checklists reveals that plaintiffs believe they suffer most frequently from "behavioral" disorders: memory loss, increased irritability, anger and anxiety, insomnia, confusion, depression, and tremors.

The final part of the form affidavits describes the individual's medical history, and asks for a description of tobacco, alcohol, and drug use. This portion also alleges no exposure to any toxic chemical besides Agent Orange.

Dr. Singer, who is board certified in internal medicine, hematology, and oncology, reaches a number of conclusions based on his review of the numerous form affidavits with their attached checklists. He bases his opinion on his medical background, a review of the literature on the biomedical effects of Agent Orange, and an examination of the individual affidavits. He apparently did not examine any medical records or any plaintiffs. . . .

Dr. Singer notes at the outset that 2,4-D, 2,4,5-T, and 2,3,7,8-tetra-chlorodibenzo-p-dioxin ("dioxin") "are potent and toxic agents *capable of inducing* a wide variety of adverse effects both in animals and in man." Singer Aff. ¶5 (emphasis supplied). . . .

Dr. Singer also asserts that 2,4,5-T "produces liver enzyme abnormalities . . . liver swelling and centrilobular necrosis" (death of a central liver lobule, or functional unit of the liver), and that one plaintiff suffered from a bile duct microadenoma (small, usually benign tumor in the passage between the liver and gall bladder) and from fatty metamorphosis of the liver. He concludes that "these compounds *are capable of producing* marked alteration in hepatic architecture and function" and that the liver abnormalities plaintiffs allege are "*consistent with*" the known effects of polychlorinated herbicides. (Emphasis supplied.) Although Dr. Singer does not reveal the studies that he relies upon to reach this conclusion, it is clear he is not referring to [the epidemiologic] studies that analyze the effects of Agent Orange on exposed veterans. In any event, the liver disorders Dr. Singer finds in the animal and industrial studies differ substantially from those plaintiffs report they suffered. [The court summarizes similar numerous statements by Dr. Singer with respect to other diseases and symptoms suffered by the opt-out plaintiffs.]

As a review of Dr. Singer's affidavit reveals, he attributes some 37 separate diseases, disorders, and symptoms — including baldness and diarrhea — to exposure to Agent Orange. . . .

Stripped of its verbiage, Dr. Singer summarizes his overall conclusion by stating that *if* the affiants are telling the truth and *if* there is no cause for their complaints other than Agent Orange, then Agent Orange must have caused their problems. Dr. Singer states:

Assuming the truth of the affidavits submitted, and *absent any evidence of pre-existing, intervening, or superseding causes for the symptoms and diseases* complained of in these affidavits, it is my opinion to a reasonable degree of medical probability (that is, more likely than not) that the medical difficulties described by the affiants were proximately caused by exposure to Agent Orange.

(Emphasis supplied.)

. . . One need hardly be a doctor of medicine to make the statement that if X is a possible cause of Y, and if there is no other possible cause of Y, X must have caused Y. Dr. Singer's formulation avoids the problem before us: which of myriad possible causes of Y created a particular veteran's problems. . . .

2. Dr. Epstein's Affidavits

[The court described affidavits submitted by Dr. Samuel S. Epstein, and found them to be similarly deficient.]

In sum, Dr. Epstein attributes some fourteen different diseases and afflictions to exposure to Agent Orange of fifteen plaintiffs. Dr. Epstein's affidavits, even if considered timely, are insufficient to oppose the motion for summary judgment. All the diseases in the cases he relies upon are found in the general population of those who were never exposed to Agent Orange. There is no showing that the incidence of the diseases relied upon [is] greater in the Agent Orange-exposed population than in the population generally. It must be borne in mind that these are fifteen cases not taken at random but deliberately selected because of their claims from a population of 2,600,000 who served in Vietnam.

IV. LAW

A. LEGAL STANDARDS GOVERNING EXPERT OPINION . . .

1. Admissibility of Epidemiological Studies

In a mass tort case such as Agent Orange, epidemiologic studies on causation assume a role of critical importance. . . . Confronted with the reality of mass tort litigation, courts have been forced to abandon their traditional reluctance to rely upon epidemiological studies. Dore, A Commentary on the Use of Epidemiological Evidence in Demonstrating Cause-in-Fact, 7 Harv. Envtl. L. Rev. 429 (1983).

[The court found that the various epidemiologic studies of the possible effects of Agent Orange, although technically hearsay, were reliable and were admissible in evidence under Fed. Rule Evid. 803(8), recognizing an exception to the hearsay rule for trustworthy public records and reports.]

The many studies on animal exposure to Agent Orange, even plaintiffs' expert concedes, are not persuasive in this lawsuit. In a jointly-authored article, Dr. Ellen K. Silbergeld writes that "laboratory animal studies . . . are generally viewed with more suspicion than epidemiological studies, because they require making the assumption that chemicals behave similarly in different species." . . .

There is no evidence that plaintiffs were exposed to the far higher concentrations involved in both the animal and industrial exposure studies. . . . The animal studies are not helpful in the instant case because they involve different biological species. They are of so little probative force and are so potentially misleading as to be inadmissible. See Fed. R. Ev. 401-403. They cannot be an acceptable predicate for an opinion under Rule 703. . . .

2. Admissibility of Expert Opinion Under Rule 702

Rule 702 of the Federal Rules of Evidence provides for opinion testimony by experts "if scientific, technical or other specialized knowledge will assist the trier of fact to determine a fact in issue" and the witness is "qualified as an expert by knowledge, experience, training or education." The court must first determine whether the expert is sufficiently qualified in his or her field to be allowed to testify. . . .

. . . Once governed by the *Frye* test of general acceptance in the relevant scientific community, *Frye v. United States*, 293 F. 1013 (D.C. Cir. 1923), the assessment of novel testimony now involves a balancing of the relevance, reliability, and helpfulness of the evidence against the likelihood of waste of time, confusion and prejudice. [Citing decisions of federal courts.]

Courts abandoning *Frye* stress Rule 702's liberal attitude towards the admissibility of relevant expert testimony whenever it would be helpful to the trier. When either the expert's qualifications or his testimony lie at the periphery of what the scientific community considers acceptable, special care should be exercised in evaluating the reliability and probative worth of the proffered testimony under Rules 703 and 403. . . . [Cf.] Huber, Safety and the Second Best: The Hazards of Public Risk Management in the Courts, 85 Colum. L. Rev. 277, 333 (1985) ("a Ph.D. can be found to swear to almost any 'expert' proposition, no matter how false or foolish"). . . . [The court found Doctors Epstein and Singer to be qualified experts but cautioned that this determination did not guarantee the admissibility of their testimony under Rules 703 and 403.]

3. Rule 703

Rule 703 of the Federal Rules of Evidence attempts to delimit the bases upon which an expert may rely in testifying to those "reasonably relied" upon "by experts in the field." It provides:

> The facts or data in the particular case upon which an expert bases an opinion or inference may be those perceived by or made known to him at or before the hearing. If of a type reasonably relied upon by experts in the particular field in forming opinions or inferences upon the subject, the facts or data need not be admissible in evidence.

Neither Dr. Singer nor Dr. Epstein based his conclusions on observations. . . . Rather, each one relied almost wholly upon the specific anecdotal written information supplied by the plaintiffs and upon general studies and literature.

The trial court must decide whether this data is of a type reasonably relied upon by experts in the field. . . .

(i) Dr. Singer

Plaintiffs' checklists . . . submitted with Dr. Singer's affidavits are not material that experts in this field would reasonably rely upon and so must be excluded under Rule 703. . . .

Here we have statements [in the patient checklists] of problems ranging from baldness to the most serious cancers. It verges on the absurd to use [these checklists] to determine both disease and cause. While courts allow reliance on patient statements, they are based upon a personal history corroborated by medical records, a physical examination and medical tests. . . .

Plaintiffs may argue that Dr. Singer's reliance upon such checklists was necessary in light of the size of this litigation and the number of parties involved. Yet, after six years of litigation, it does not seem too much to expect plaintiff's counsel to have obtained more persuasive medical and other records. . . .

(ii) Dr. Epstein

. . . Dr. Epstein, while not a treating physician, purports to rely at least in part on medical and military records to corroborate the extent of plaintiffs' exposure and the nature of their illnesses. . . .

It is significant that no medical records of any of the nearly 300 opt-out plaintiffs have been submitted by plaintiffs [into the evidence of record]. Nor are there any affidavits or letters from any treating or examining physicians. There is nothing from any person who has even seen a plaintiff and observed any medical condition. No scrap of verification of a single plaintiff's claim is supplied by plaintiffs. . . .

To the extent Dr. Epstein has reviewed plaintiffs' medical records, he relies on them only to show that the disease complained of did not manifest itself prior to service in Vietnam. Temporal sequence is not, of course, the equivalent of causation. We must, as Dr. Epstein concedes, recognize the huge array of carcinogens and other harmful substances other than Agent Orange that people are exposed to — whether in Vietnam or in this country.

Even were we to ignore the deficiencies outlined above, it is a fatal flaw in Dr. Epstein's material, as in Dr. Singer's, that no account is taken of the relative degree of specific health problems of those exposed to Agent Orange as compared with those not exposed. All the studies to date indicate no significant differences.

. . . [T]he testimony of Doctors Singer and Epstein is insufficiently grounded in any reliable evidence. . . .

[The court found that the opinions of Doctors Epstein and Singer were not admissible because they were based on materials, not submitted into evidence, that were not reliable. It also held that the experts' opinions should be excluded under Fed. Rule Evid. 403, which requires the court to exclude relevant evidence "if its probative value is substantially outweighed by the danger of unfair prejudice, confusion of the issues, or misleading the jury."]

B.   LEGAL STANDARD GOVERNING SUMMARY JUDGMENT

The Federal Rules of Civil Procedure require that a party moving for summary judgment show "that there is no genuine issue as to any material fact and that the moving party is entitled to a judgment as a matter of law." Fed. R. Civ. P. 56(c). The initial burden rests on the moving party to demonstrate the nonexistence of a genuine issue of fact. . . . At this point, the party opposing summary judgment must point to evidence that a genuine issue as to a material fact does exist. . . .

The numerous epidemiological studies discussed supra . . . are sufficient to shift the burden to plaintiffs of showing that a material fact exists as to causation. See Rule 56(e). Plaintiffs attempted to meet their burden through expert affidavits that are wholly conclusory and unfounded in fact. . . .

In the instant case, years of discovery and tens of millions of dollars spent by the government and others on research has not yielded any competent evidence indicating a genuine issue of fact about causation. Plaintiffs have had more than enough time to develop their cases. . . .

In the *Agent Orange* litigation, it is remotely possible that a causal connection may at some time in the future be proved. As time goes on, proof of connection to Agent Orange becomes less and less likely because the aging Vietnam veterans are continuously exposed to confounding substances and morbidity rises sharply with age from many natural causes. We can say that proof has not been produced in this court sufficient to go to the jury.

NOTES AND QUESTIONS

1. Are *Sterling* and *Agent Orange* consistent in their treatment of causation issues? Even if not, can the award of damages in *Sterling* and their denial in *Agent Orange* be explained by differences in the circumstances of exposure and illness in the two cases? By differences in the nature of the expert opinion evidence offered? Does Judge Weinstein's rejection of animal studies and evaluations of medical experts and his insistence on well-controlled epidemiological studies to prove causation create an impossible burden on plantiffs in most cases?

2. If the claims of the plaintiffs in *Agent Orange* had no merit because there was no evidence of a causal link between exposure and illness, as found by Judge Weinstein in the opt-out case excerpted above, why did Judge Weinstein certify a class action in *Agent Orange* and approve a $180 million settlement of the class action?

3. *Collective Procedures for Mass Torts.* Many cases involving toxic exposures are "mass tort" situations where large numbers of individuals have been exposed to pollution, toxic wastes, or products produced by one or more defendants. In such situations, class actions could provide significant economies of scale in resolving common issues, including those relating to liability and causation. Cases such as *Agent Orange* and *Sterling,* which have certified class actions in mass toxic tort cases, probably represent the minority practice. Many courts have denied class certification in such circumstances, asserting that proof of injury and damages are inevitably individual. Moreover, causation issues may also have significant individual dimensions; the likelihood that a given individual will contract a given illness from a given exposure may depend in substantial part on her medical history, genetic inheritance, exposure to other hazards, and other factors. Finally, courts have often expressed deference to individual plaintiff's choice of counsel and venue. For an overview of the current debate over claim aggregation, see Resnik, From "Cases" to "Litigation," 1991 Duke L.J. 5. See also Rosenberg,

The Causal Connection in Mass Exposure Cases: A "Public Law" Vision of the Tort System, 97 Harv. L. Rev. 849 (1984) (questioning the claim that toxic tort litigation turns on individual determinations and arguing for systematic use of class actions in mass toxic tort cases on cost internalization and scale economy grounds).

NOTES ON VUOCOLO v. DIAMOND SHAMROCK CHEM., 573 A.2D 196 (N.J. SUPER. A.D. 1990)

In 1960 an explosion at a chemical factory released a large amount of dioxin into the environment. Although the explosion occurred in 1960, it was not until 1983 that the explosion and the dioxin release became public knowledge. In 1985, the N.J. Department of Environmental Protection (DEP) took soil samples in the area. DEP informed the plaintiff that only harmless trace amounts of dioxin were discovered in the samples, and that remedial action was not necessary. DEP did, however, conduct a street sweeping operation (25 years after the explosion) to rid the area of any contaminated dirt and dust.

In 1971 Lucy Vuocolo moved to a home less than two blocks from the plant. She was active in the neighborhood, and was frequently outside working or walking. Sometime after moving to the neighborhood, she was diagnosed as having pancreatic cancer, from which she died in 1981. Plaintiff, decedent's daughter, was unable to quantify her mother's ingestion of dioxin or even establish that she in fact ingested any amount or was even exposed. Plaintiff claimed that it was unnecessary to show causation in the traditional sense so long as she could establish that defendant put decedent at risk and decedent was ultimately injured. Plaintiff relied on expert testimony by a pathologist, who concluded that decedent died from a rare form of cancer with a male preponderance, and that decedent's exposure to dioxin may have caused or promoted the disease.

The appeals court affirmed the trial court's grant of summary judgment in favor of the defendant, noting that plaintiff's expert was unable to quantify decedent's enhanced risk due to the defendant's release of dioxin, or to conclude to a reasonable probability that defendant's release caused decedent's cancer, or even to show that the exposures substantially increased the risk of the disease. The expert's opinion was barred because it was a "net opinion" which did not provide a proper medical foundation to support the plaintiff's claim. Under the net opinion rule, expert opinion is excluded if it is based merely on unfounded speculation and unquantified possibilities.

NOTES ON COTTLE v. SUPERIOR COURT (OXNARD SHORES CO.), 5 CAL. RPTR. 2D 882 (CAL. APP. 2 DIST. 1992)

175 owners and renters of residential property located in the Oxnard Dunes housing development ("The Dunes") sued various defendants for personal injuries (physical and emotional) and property damages as a result of defendants' construction of the Dunes on a site previously used as a dumping ground for oil industry hazardous waste. The list of physical injuries in the complaint included liver damage, suppressed immune systems, increased susceptibility to leukemia, numerous forms of cancer, acquired immune deficiency syndrome, still births, headaches, dizziness, breathing problems, and skin rashes. The trial court found that the plaintiffs had established their prima facie cases for emotional injury and property damage, but issued an order excluding evidence of personal injuries. Plaintiffs sought a writ of mandamus challenging the order. The appeals court affirmed, stating that the plaintiffs must prove causation to a reasonable medical probability based on competent expert testimony, and had failed to do so. Their medical expert had opined that the exposure to these chemicals, alone and in combination, has placed the plaintiffs at significantly increased risk to develop a number of diseases, but could not link the actual current physical symptoms of the plaintiffs to the chemicals that had been dumped.

NOTES ON THE CAUSATION REQUIREMENT

Agent Orange, Vuocolo, and *Cottle* illustrate the difficulties of proving causation in fact, although *Sterling* demonstrates that plaintiffs can in some cases surmount those difficulties to the satisfaction of the trier and a reviewing court. As noted above, there are really two causation problems. The first is proving that the particular toxic substance involved is capable of causing the type of harm from which the plaintiff suffers. The second and more serious causation difficulty is that of establishing that plaintiff's exposure to a substance that is capable of causing disease in humans in fact caused the particular harm suffered by plaintiff.

The traditional standard of causation is the "preponderance of the evidence" or "but for" standard: The jury must be persuaded that it is more likely than not that the exposure to the defendant's chemicals caused the plaintiff's cancer. In many cases, this standard will not support recovery by any plaintiff even though defendant's pollution or waste has caused a significant increase in illness among an exposed population. For example, suppose that the "background" rate of a given type of cancer among a population not exposed to the hazardous substance generated by the defendant is 10 cases per 100,000. An epidemiologic study shows that the population of which plaintiff is a member has a rate of 15 cancers per 100,000, and that this elevated level of cancers is attributable to the population's exposure to defendant's hazardous substance. The first difficulty faced by a plaintiff who seeks to use this study to surmount the traditional "more probable than not" causation standard is to persuade the court to allow the epidemiologic study into evidence as probative on the causation issue. The common law traditionally insisted on particularistic proof of causation, based on a specific chain of events linking defendant's action to plaintiff's injury. The traditional paradigm of causation is "A hit B." Epidemiology, by contrast, relies on statistical generalizations based on group experience. Even if the court admits the study into evidence, plaintiff must still show that her cancer was caused by defendant. Under a more probable than not standard, none of the exposed cancer victims in the population could recover, because the study establishes only a one-third probability that any given individual's cancer was caused by exposure to the defendant's hazardous substance. Because of increasingly pervasive environmental regulation, the probability that a given cancer or other toxic injury was caused by a defendant's pollution or waste disposal is in most cases likely to be substantially less than 50 percent. Yet, despite regulation, residual risks from pollution may still cause many illnesses if the exposed population is large. Under traditional causation standards, the tort system is powerless to deal with these risks.

Two alternatives to the traditional "but for" causation standard have been adopted by some courts. One alternative is to use a more lenient "substantial factor" standard, which ascribes liability to a cause which has played an important part in the production of the harm, even though the harm might have occurred anyway as a result of independent causes. For example, the court in *Elam v. Alcolac, Inc.*, 765 S.W.2d 42 (Mo. App. 1988), *cert. denied*, 493 U.S. 817 (1989), approved use of the substantial factor standard in upholding a verdict for plaintiffs who lived near a chemical plant and claimed that the plant had caused a number of ailments. Even though "but for" causation of a particular injury from a particular chemical discharge could not be established, the court found it sufficient that the plaintiff had shown "some reasonable connection between an act or omission of the defendant and the damage that the plaintiff has suffered." The *Elam* decision is criticized in Black, Warshaw, & Hollander, *Unravelling Causation: Back to the Basics*, Toxic L. Rep., Feb. 10, 1993, at 1061. The authors chide the court for deciding, as a matter of policy, that plaintiffs in toxic tort cases do not have to meet their traditional burden without specifying what probability less than 50 percent must be established to support recovery.

Another approach to loosening the traditional causation standard is exhibited in *Allen v. United States*, 588 F. Supp. 247 (D. Utah 1984), which involved actions under the Federal Tort Claims Act to recover for cancers assertedly caused by exposure to radioactive fallout from the testing of atomic weapons during the 1940s. The district court found that the United States was negligent in not warning off-site residents of foreseeable risks of exposure to radioactive fallout. The court also ruled that if an ill plaintiff had been exposed to a hazard and provided substantial and persuasive evidence that the illness is "consistent with having been caused" by such exposure, "a fact finder *may* reasonably conclude that the hazard caused the condition absent persuasive proof to the contrary" by the defendant. 588 F. Supp. at 247 (emphasis in original). There being no jury trial under the Act, the district judge examined evidence relating to the illnesses and exposures of various representative plaintiffs, finding that some (but not others) had surmounted the threshold requirement of showing that fallout exposure was a potentially significant factor in causing their illness. The court further found that the United States had failed to carry its burden of showing that their plaintiffs' injuries had not, more probably than not, been caused by the exposure, and that their plaintiffs were accordingly entitled to recover. On the government's appeal, the court of appeals reversed on the ground that the United States had not been negligent in failing to warn.

Some commentators have suggested that courts adopt a proportionate liability approach for environmental risk cases. See, e.g., Rosenberg, The Causal Connection in Mass Exposure Cases: A "Public Law" Vision of the Tort System, 97 Harv. L. Rev. 849 (1984). Proportionate liability imposes liability on a defendant for a percentage of plaintiff's injury equal to the probability that the defendant caused it. For example, suppose that a plaintiff contracts cancer following exposure to defendant's toxic substance. Based on epidemiologic evidence, the probability that the exposure caused the cancer is 25 percent. Defendant would be liable to plaintiff for 25 percent of the damages awardable for a cancer.

The concept of proportionate liability has its roots in *Summers v. Tice*, 199 P.2d 1 (Cal. 1948). Two defendants were hunting for quail and they both fired at a bird at the same time. Birdshot from one of the shotguns struck plaintiff in the right eye, but it was impossible to determine which gun had caused the injury. The court held that the defendants were jointly and severally liable for the injury, unless one defendant was able to show that the other caused the injury.

A different approach to the problems created by causal uncertainty created by the presence of multiple defendants, each of whom might have caused plaintiff's injury, was adopted in *Sindell v. Abbott Laboratories*, 607 P.2d 924 (Cal. 1980). Plaintiff sued five pharmaceutical companies that had manufactured and sold 90 percent of DES, a drug used to prevent miscarriages during pregnancy. DES was later discovered to cause certain forms of cancer and other illness in the daughters of mothers who had taken DES. Plaintiff, a daughter who had contracted cancer, could not show which manufacturer produced the DES that her mother used. The court held that plaintiff need not identify the specific manufacturer of the drug her mother took. Each defendant was held liable for the proportion of the damages attributable to her injury represented by its market share unless it could demonstrate that it did not make the product that caused plaintiff's injury.

In *Cottle*, discussed supra, p. 753, the appellate court held that plaintiffs had failed to prove that their illnesses had been caused by exposure to toxic contaminants. A dissent argued that the trial court had sought an impossibility: evidence that exposure to particular toxic substances more probably than not caused a particular individual's illness. This level of proof is only possible with signature diseases such as asbestosis, which can be caused only by asbestos. When this traditional "cause in fact" standard cannot be satisfied, the "toxic will not bear the economic cost of the harm it is causing. As a result, industry will lack this economic incentive to reduce production and use of the toxic in the future, or to take more care with its distribution and disposal." On the other hand, full compensation awarded to every person exposed to a toxic who later develops a disease that the toxic is capable of causing will lead to an excessive imposition of liability because there will be some chance that the cancer was caused by another source. In order to address these shortcomings and to ensure that the toxic bears the economic cost of the harm that it causes, the dissent recommended a variant of market share or proportionate liability. "Under this formula defendants responsible for the toxic exposure are liable to all those who were exposed and later suffered injury — *including those who may have suffered the injury even if they had never come near the toxic substance.* (emphasis in original). But defendants are only liable for a percentage of plaintiffs' damages equal to the degree that this exposure increased plaintiffs' risk of injury. For example, assume a chemical increases the risk of cancer by 15 percent among those exposed to the toxic. All exposed to this chemical who later came down with the cancer would be entitled to recover 15 percent of their total damages from those responsible for the exposure."

Proportionate liability was endorsed by the American Law Institute Reporters' Study on Enterprise Responsibility for Personal Injury (1991): "The use of proportionate compensation based on the attributable fraction of disease would lower both the burden of proof on plaintiffs and the threshold for bringing environmental injury tort cases. . . . Proportionate compensation would avoid the pitfalls of the traditional all-or-nothing approach by overcoming the causal indeterminacy inherent in much epidemiological evidence. . . ." Id. at 371. In order to limit the expansion of litigation and attendant transaction costs that could result from unrestricted use of proportional liability, the Reporters' Study would limit its use to cases where plaintiffs could establish that the proportion of total risk attributable to a given hazard generated by defendants was at least 20 percent. Id. at 374.

Liability based on the principle of proportionate risk has not yet been endorsed by any court.

NOTES AND QUESTIONS

1. Proportionate liability has been criticized on the ground that it overcompensates those whose cancer was not caused by defendant, and undercompensates those whose cancer was caused by defendant. How would you respond to this argument? (Rosenberg argues, however, that this obligation is misplaced in a situation where individual causation is impossible to establish. From a corrective justice perspective, it is appropriate to compensate victims based on enhanced risk. From the viewpoint of incentives, the system will provide appropriate deterrence.)

2. Given the enormous uncertainties in determining the causal connection between toxic exposure and illness, what hope is there of developing, through litigation, a reliable measure of proportionate risk? Compare the market share formula adopted in *Sindell*. For additional discussion of proportionate liability, see Farber, Toxic Causation, 71 Minn. L. Rev. 1219 (1987).

3. Many toxic tort actions involve Superfund sites. Personal injury claims are brought after the government has investigated and started to clean up a site. Neighbors often also file claims for damage to their property and diminution of its value. As noted previously, Congress failed to adopt a provision that would have authorized a federal cause of action under CERCLA for personal injury. The expansive principles of liability developed under CERCLA therefore do not apply to toxic tort actions, which are governed by state tort law. Plaintiffs' counsel have, however, sought to persuade state court judges to liberalize traditional tort law requirements for recovery. What would be the implications of adopting CERCLA liability rules in the context of private tort actions for personal or property injury?

PROBLEM

Lead exposure causes serious neurological disorders, particularly among children. The elimination of leaded gasoline and the removal of lead from paints have significantly reduced the incidence of lead poisoning over the past two decades. Yet, children in inner city neigh-borhoods often have heightened blood levels due to the presence of chipping, old, lead-based paints. You have been hired by the Children's Health Organization (CHO), an advocacy group working on behalf of inner city children. Your organization would like to spearhead a visible public campaign to eliminate lead contamination in the inner cities. Your first assignment is to evaluate possible approaches.

1. The staff is currently considering bringing a class action suit on behalf of inner city children with elevated blood lead levels seeking appropriate compensatory relief. Whom should CHO sue? What relief should CHO seek? What are the impediments to this type of action? How could they be overcome?

2. The staff is also considering a massive preventive effort to strip or seal lead-based paints in inner city housing. CHO would like to im-pose the costs of this effort on the manufacturers of lead-based paints. How should the lawsuit be pitched? What are the impediments to this type of action? How could they be overcome?

3. What other common law approaches might be feasible to ad-dress this problem? What other approaches might CHO pursue? Which of the various options do you recommend?

a. Admissibility of Expert Testimony

Judge Weinstein's opinion in the *Agent Orange* opt-out case reflects considerable skepticism about expert witnesses. It asserts that, given the scientific uncertainty in the area of toxic torts, there is a strong need for robust screening by the court of expert testimony, particularly when the expert's theory is out of the mainstream of current scientific thought. See Michael D. Green, Expert Witnesses and Sufficiency of Evidence in Toxic Substances Litigation: The Legacy of Agent Orange and Bendectin Litigation, 86 Nw. U. L. Rev. 643 (1992). Judge Weinstein's approach may be contrasted with the decision of the D.C. Circuit in *Ferebee v. Chevron Chemical Co.,* 736 F.2d 1529 (D.C. Cir. 1984), upholding a jury verdict for plaintiff exposed to pesticide residues de-spite absence of either epidemiologic evidence or clear evidence from animal studies that the exposure was capable of causing the injuries in question. Ferebee, an agricultural worker, had sprayed paraquat, an herbicide, to control weeds during three summers. He contracted pulmonary fibrosis, a degenerative condition of the lung. In high concentrations, paraquat is acutely toxic; skin exposures to high concentrations can produce cystic fibrosis within days or a few weeks. There were no epidemiologic or animal tests establishing that expo-sures to the relatively low levels encountered by Ferebee causes cystic fibrosis. Although Ferebee suffered from many other health problems, his attending physicians, "eminent specialists in pulmonary medicine," testified that Ferebee's condition was due to paraquat exposure based upon their observations of him, his medical history, the acute toxicity of paraquat, and inferences from "similar" cases. The court rejected Chevron's claim that it was entitled to a directed verdict on the issue of causation and ruled that as long as "experts are willing to testify" about complex and technical issues at the frontiers of scientific knowledge, it is up to the jury to resolve conflicts in the experts' views.

A number of decisions since *Agent Orange* have also rejected defendants' claims that epidemiologic studies are required to establish causation when there is no direct proof of the mechanism of disease. See *Christophenson v. Alheed Signal Corp.*, 902 F.2d 362, 367 (5th Cir. 1990); *Werelin v. United States*, 746 F. Supp. 887, 900 (D. Minn. 1990).

In stating that more careful scrutiny is required when an expert's opinion is not generally accepted in the relevant scientific community, Judge Weinstein referred to but did not squarely rely upon the *Frye* rule. The rule, based on a 1923 criminal case, *Frye v. United States*, 293 F. 7013 (1923), states that in order to be admitted by the court, evidence must be generally accepted as reliable by the scientific community. Many thought that the *Frye* rule had died with the adoption in 1975 of the Federal Rules of Evidence. Rule 402 lists the reasons for excluding relevant evidence, but does not specifically include the circumstances that an expert's opinion is not generally accepted in the scientific community.

Daubert v. Merrell Dow Pharmaceutical Inc., 113 S. Ct. 2786 (1993), addressed the continued viability of the *Frye* test. The families of two children born with limb deformities claimed that they had been caused by the morning sickness drug Bendectin, which the children's mothers had taken while pregnant. The Ninth Circuit, following a number of other courts of appeals that had dealt with *Bendectin* litigation, upheld the district court's grant of summary judgment for defendant. The district court had found the plaintiffs' expert evidence on causation inadmissible under the "general acceptance" standard. The plaintiffs' experts relied primarily on animal studies, chemical-structure analyses that purported to show structural similarities between Bendectin and other substances known to cause cancer, and reanalyses of prior epidemiologic studies. All of the epidemiologic studies reanalyzed by plaintiff's experts had found no statistically significant correlation between Bendectin use and birth defects. The reanalyses, using novel statistical techniques to reevaluate the data, concluded that such a correlation existed.

The court of appeals in *Daubert* agreed that animal studies and chemical-structural analyses were insufficient to establish a link between Bendectin and birth defects. It held that the reanalyses of epidemiologic studies could not be relied upon because they, unlike the original epidemiologic studies, had not been published or subject to peer review. The court noted that the reanalyses had been prepared solely for purposes of litigation, and had not been published or subject to peer review, in contrast to "the massive weight of the original published studies supporting the defendant's position, all of which had undergone full scrutiny from the scientific community." The court quoted P. Huber, Galileo's Revenge: Junk Science in the Courthouse 228 (1991): "the best test of certainty we have is good science — the science of publication, replication, and verification, the science of consensus and peer review."

The Supreme Court vacated and remanded, holding that the Federal Rules of Evidence, and not *Frye*'s "general acceptance" test, provide the standard for admitting expert scientific testimony in a federal trial. The Court found nothing in the Rules or in the drafting history that indicated that "general acceptance" is a necessary precondition to admissibility. The rules allow all relevant evidence to be admissible, and make no mention of *Frye*. The Court further found that such an "austere standard" would be at odds with the Rules' basic standard that all "relevant evidence" is admissible. Rule 702, quoted supra, was held to place appropriate limits on admissibility by requiring a witness be "qualified as an expert" with respect to "scientific . . . knowledge." The testimony must be grounded in the methods of science and be based on more than unsupported speculation or belief. The trial judge has the responsibility to evaluate proffered expert testimony in order to determine whether it is scientifically valid and can be properly applied to the facts in the case at hand. The judge should consider several factors, such as whether the theory relied upon by the expert can be tested (falsifiability), whether it has been subjected to peer review and publication, the existence of standards in controlling its operation, and its acceptance within a relevant scientific community. The focus "must be solely on principles and methodology, not on the conclusions that they generate." The extent of "general acceptance" of an expert's theory or methodology within a relevant scientific community is one important factor, but it is not controlling. The Court stated that cross-examination and presentation of contrary evidence is often the appropriate means to challenge expert evidence. At the same time, the Court also emphasized the "screening" or "gatekeeping" role of the judge. The Court remanded the case to the court of appeals for "further proceedings consistent with this opinion."

Counsel and commenters have debated whether the Court's rejection of "general acceptance" as a touchstone of admissibility and its adoption of a four-factor test will result in more liberal standards or more restrictive standards of admissibility.[75] Those favoring more lib-

---

75. In *Brock v. Merrell Dow Pharmaceuticals, Inc.*, 874 F.2d 307 (5th Cir. 1989), *cert. denied*, 110 S. Ct. 1511 (1990), the court overturned a jury verdict for plaintiff in a Bendectin case, but did so not by ruling that the plaintiff's

eral admissibility of expert evidence of causation have stressed the Court's rejection of *Frye*, while their opponents have emphasized language in the Court's opinion that underscores the trial judge's "gatekeeping" responsibility in "screening" expert testimony to ensure that it is based on scientifically valid methodology before admitting it into evidence. The *Frye* "general acceptance" test depends upon the selection of the relevant scientific community. If the relevant community is defined in terms of those scientists who champion an emerging methodology — such as clinical ecology — the "general acceptance" standard may not be very restrictive.[76] Consider the potential impact of *Daubert* on the Court's rationale in *Sterling v. Velsicol,* supra at 728, upholding the exclusion of expert testimony by plaintiffs' clinical ecologists. The exclusion in *Sterling* was based on the court's application of Rule 702 as opposed to the *Frye* test, but the court relied heavily on its conclusion that clinical ecology is not widely accepted by the scientific community. The clinical ecologist experts based their opinions of plaintiffs' immune system dysregulation not on clinical medical tests, but on blood tests that revealed higher than normal white cell counts and on the medical histories supplied by plaintiffs' attorneys. The court placed considerable weight on the fact that the leading professional societies in the field of allergy and immunology have rejected clinical ecology as an unproven methodology without scientific basis in fact or theory.

NOTES AND QUESTIONS

1. Can the results, if not the rhetoric, of *Ferebee* and *Agent Orange* be reconciled on their separate facts?

2. Is it sensible to rely on the ad hoc, case by case judgment of either judges or juries to sift the competing claims of hired experts? Should judges appoint scientists as special masters or court-designated experts to help clarify and resolve the issues in dispute? How would such individuals be selected? How could it be assured that they are impartial and open-minded? What about creation of panels of experts by a body such as the National Academy of Sciences? Members of such a panel might be selected as court-appointed masters or experts, or recurring issues of scientific controversy might be referred by courts to the entire panel for an advisory opinion. Is this a good idea? Would top

---

expert testimony should have been excluded from evidence, but that plaintiff's evidence was not sufficient to sustain a verdict in her favor. How does *Daubert* affect the viability of this technique, which has been occasionally used by other judges in toxic tort cases?

76. See Judge Becker's observations on the "general acceptance" standard in *United States v. Downing,* 753 F.2d 1224 (3d Cir. 1985), which rejected *Frye* and was heavily relied upon by *Daubert*.

scientists agree to serve on such a panel? Would the panel be impartial and fair-minded? For discussion, see Brennan, Helping Courts With Toxic Torts, 51 Univ. Pitt. L. Rev. 7 (1989).

b.   Novel Remedies

Rather than simply loosening traditional causation requirements, some courts in toxic tort cases have recognized new principles of injury and remedy in order to provide relief for plaintiffs.

(i)   Emotional Distress

In *Hagerty v. L & L Marine Services, Inc.*, 788 F.2d 315 (5th Cir. 1986), plaintiff, a seaman, brought suit against his employer after he was soaked with dripolene, a toxic chemical containing benzene, toluene, and xylene. He suffered a brief period of dizziness, followed by leg cramps and stinging in his extremities. Based on these symptoms and his knowledge that dripolene is a carcinogen, plaintiff developed a fear of contracting cancer ("cancerphobia"), and sued for pain and suffering, emotional distress, and medical monitoring. Defendants contended that cancerphobia alone was not a compensable injury unless accompanied by physical manifestations. The district court agreed and granted summary judgment for defendant. The appeals court reversed: "With or without physical injury or impact, a plaintiff is entitled to recover damages for serious mental distress arising from fear of developing cancer where his fear is reasonable and causally related to the defendant's negligence. The circumstances surrounding the fear-inducing occurrence may themselves supply sufficient indicia of genuineness." The court also held that reasonable costs of medical checkups for cancer could be included in a damage award.

In *Potter v. Firestone Tire and Rubber Co.*, 274 Cal. Rptr. 885 (Cal. App. 6 Dist. 1990), Firestone deposited wastes from its manufacturing plant at a local landfill. Although Firestone gave the landfill management assurances that solvents, cleaning fluids and other toxic oils and liquids were not being deposited at the landfill, Firestone sent large amounts of these wastes to the landfill. At one point the Firestone plant engineer attempted to initiate a proper disposal program, but it was widely ignored and eventually abandoned due to its high cost. Plaintiffs, local homeowners, discovered that toxic chemicals from the landfill had contaminated their domestic water wells, and filed suit against Firestone for damages, alleging, among other matters, negligent infliction of emotional distress and intentional infliction of emotional distress. The trial court awarded compensatory damages for cancerphobia and medical monitoring, and also awarded punitive damages. On appeal, the court affirmed the awards for emotional distress and punitive damages, but reversed the medical monitoring award.

In awarding damages for emotional distress, the court of appeals rejected Firestone's argument that plaintiffs must establish a physical injury and that they must prove they are likely to develop the disease. The court then set out five criteria which must be met before recovery for fear of cancer can be allowed. "First, it is fundamental that the plaintiff prove the elements of a negligence cause of action. Thus, the plaintiff must prove (1) duty, (2) breach, (3) causation, and (4) loss or damage. . . . Second, the plaintiff must establish that the emotional distress is serious. . . . [S]erious emotional distress is such that 'a reasonable [person], normally constituted, would be unable to adequately cope with the mental stress engendered by the circumstances of the case.' . . . Third, . . . in determining whether emotional distress is serious, an objective standard should be utilized. . . . Fourth, in determining whether the circumstances are such as to cause serious emotional distress in a reasonable person, the fact finder should consider evidence regarding the likelihood that the cancer will occur." Finally, the trier of fact should consider whether the claim is genuine based on "the expert testimony, the juror's own experience, and the particular circumstances of the case."

Ayers v. Township of Jackson, 525 A.2d 287 (N.J. 1987), involved a nuisance action against the town by residents claiming damages caused from contamination of drinking water by toxic pollutants leaching from town landfill into a groundwater aquifer. Plaintiffs were awarded damages for impairment of "quality of life" due to the absence of drinking water for 20 months, and were also awarded costs of future medical monitoring. Damages for plaintiffs' emotional distress due to enhanced risk of cancer based on exposure, however, were not awarded because they were viewed as an attempt to compensate for pain and suffering, and therefore denied under the New Jersey Tort Claims Act which bars damages from a public entity for pain and suffering. The district court had awarded damages for emotional distress, totalling over $2 million, with individual awards ranging from $40 to $14,000. The New Jersey Supreme Court reversed these awards, holding that claims based on "the subjective symptoms of depression, stress, health concerns, and anxiety described by the plaintiffs and their expert witness" constituted "pain and suffering resulting from any injury" within the meaning of the New Jersey Tort Claims Act, and were therefore barred. Damages for enhanced risk of future illness due to the exposures were also denied.

(ii)   Medical Monitoring

Courts have increasingly been willing to award damages to compensate plaintiffs that have been exposed to toxics for the costs of medical monitoring in order to facilitate early detection and treatment of
cancer or other illnesses. Although *Ayers* did not approve an award of
damages for emotional distress, it was one of the first to sustain an
award of damages for medical monitoring. The New Jersey Supreme
Court stated: "[M]edical science may necessarily and properly intervene where there is a significant but unquantified risk of serious disease. . . . Compensation for reasonable and necessary medical expenses is consistent with well-accepted legal principles. . . . It is also
consistent with the important public health interest in fostering access
to medical testing for individuals whose exposure to toxic chemicals
creates an enhanced risk of disease. The value of early diagnosis and
treatment for cancer patients is well documented." The court stated
that in future cases involving recovery of medical monitoring costs involving public authority defendants, awards should be paid into a trust
fund that would reimburse plaintiffs' future monitoring expenses,
rather than paying each plaintiff immediately a lump sum equal to estimated future monitoring costs. Many other courts have upheld awards
for medical monitoring costs where plaintiffs have offered credible evidence that the nature and extent of the exposure would make monitoring medically prudent and reasonable, although they have not invoked
the trust fund concept.

In *Potter,* the court's conclusion on damages was the reverse of
Ayers. Potter awarded damages for emotional distress but disallowed
damages for medical monitoring. The court concluded that it would
depart too far from traditional tort principles to create a new cause of
action that would allow plaintiff to recover damages without a manifest
physical injury or proof of probable future disease.

(iii)   Enhanced Risk

Although courts are increasingly willing to award damages for
medical monitoring and emotional distress in cases where plaintiffs
have been exposed to hazardous substances but not yet contracted any
illness, courts are generally reluctant to award damages for the risk that
future illness may result from past exposure. For example, *Ayers* stated
that enhanced risk could potentially amount to a compensable "injury"
under the New Jersey Tort Claims Act, but that the speculative and
unquantified nature of the claim made the proof insufficient.

Our disposition of this difficult and important issue requires that we
choose between two alternatives, each having a potential for imposing

unfair and undesirable consequences on the affected interests. A holding that recognizes a cause of action for unquantified enhanced risk claims exposes the tort system, and the public it serves, to the task of litigating vast numbers of claims for compensation based on threats of injuries that may never occur. . . . On the other hand, denial of [this] cause of action may mean that some plaintiffs will be unable to obtain compensation for their injury. Despite the collateral estoppel effect of the jury's finding that the defendant's wrongful conduct caused the contamination of plaintiffs' wells, those who contract diseases in the future because of their exposure to chemicals in their well water may be unable to prove a causal relationship between such exposure and their disease.

In balancing these competing concerns, the court stated that it was constrained by the admonition in the New Jersey Tort Claims Act that courts should "exercise restraint in the acceptance of novel causes of action against public entities," and accordingly denied the claims for risk of future illness.

Two years later the New Jersey Supreme Court revisited the question without the constraint of the New Jersey Tort Claims Act in *Mauro v. Raymark Industries, Inc.,* 561 A.2d 257 (N.J. 1989), but reached the same conclusion. *Mauro* involved a claim of enhanced risk of future illness due to exposure to asbestos manufactured or supplied by defendants. Recovery was allowed for medical monitoring costs, and also for emotional distress. As for recovery for enhanced risk, the critical question was again "at what stage in the evolution of a toxic injury should tort law intercede by requiring the responsible party to pay damages?" The court noted that "[t]he long-standing rule in New Jersey is that prospective damages are not recoverable unless they are reasonably probable to occur." The court considered the policy pros and cons of this rule, and reaffirmed it, citing two factors. First, the court noted that the burden of litigating the vast number of asbestos-related claims would be much greater if these cases also "involved disposition of damage claims for the relatively unquantified enhanced risk of future diseases." Second, the court found persuasive "the availability of a future opportunity to assert such claims if and when the disease occurs, combined with the present availability of medical surveillance and emotional distress damages in appropriate cases."

In both *Ayers* and *Mauro,* Judge Handler dissented from the rulings denying recovery for enhanced risk. In *Mauro,* Judge Handler stated that he did not believe "that enhanced risk of cancer damages are any more speculative than other damage claims allowed and that they should be denied because they are not easily quantifiable." He also argued that the court's decision will allow the defendants to escape liability in many cases. "Defendants may not ever have to pay the piper. Thus, if plaintiff develops cancer at some later date, then defendants may be liable for damages only if the plaintiff can prove causation.

Proof of causation will be a very difficult burden for plaintiff since many genetic and environmental factors may affect or cause the development of cancer."

In *Werlein v. United States,* 746 F. Supp. 887 (D. Minn. 1990), the court refused to grant defendants summary judgment on plaintiff's claims for enhanced risk of future illness. The court noted that applicable Minnesota law did not recognize a cause of action for increased risk, but that "where a plaintiff has suffered a present physical injury that itself causes plaintiff to suffer an increased risk of physical harm in the future, plaintiff may recover damages for that increased risk of harm. . . . Here, defendants argue that plaintiffs have not alleged any present harm capable of causing cancer or other diseases in the future. The court disagrees. Plaintiffs' experts have testified that plaintiffs who have been exposed to contaminated air and drinking water have suffered an actual physical harm in the form of chromosomal breakage, and damage to the cardiovascular and immunal systems. These experts also have testified that the present injuries are the cause of the alleged increased future risk of disease."

NOTES AND QUESTIONS

1. Note the *Potter* court's effort to guard against large awards for fear of illness by individuals who are hypersensitive or who exaggerate the risk of illness. Adjacent property owners often successfully recover for a diminution in property value resulting from toxic releases in the neighborhood. If people have an irrationally inflated fear of risk and this fear is reflected in the diminution in property value, should the courts allow recovery for the entire diminution in market value? If not, how should the appropriate amount of damages be determined?

2. If, as *Ayers* holds, damages for "cancerphobia" and the like are a form of pain and suffering award, must plaintiffs have suffered physical injury or perhaps property damage in order to claim such damages?

3. How is enhanced risk distinguished from emotional distress? Is the latter recovery for fear of increased risk but not the risk itself? If claims for enhanced risk are unduly conjectural, what about claims for cancerphobia? If courts generally allow recovery for medical monitoring based on enhanced risk, then why not allow recovery for the risk itself? Is liability for increased risk compatible with traditional principles of corrective justice? See Schroeder, Corrective Justice and Liability for Increasing Risks, 37 U.C.L.A. L. Rev. 439 (1990); Simmons, Corrective Future and Liability for Risk Creation: A Comment, 38 U.C.L.A. L. Rev. 113 (1990), Schroeder, Corrective Justice, Liability for Risk and Tort Law, 38 U.C.L.A. L. Rev. 143 (1990).

4. Suppose a court recognizes a cause of action for the future risk of illness attributable to past exposures and plaintiff recovers for such risk. The plaintiff subsequently becomes ill. Can the plaintiff recover for the subsequent illness if he proves that it was caused by the defendant? What if the plaintiff previously recovered damages for emotional distress caused by fear of cancer? For medical monitoring?

5. *Claim Splitting.* Related to the problems in applying statutes of limitations in toxic tort cases are problems of claim splitting and preclusion. Under traditional claim preclusion, if a plaintiff sues to recover damages for an initial injury caused by defendant's conduct, the victim cannot sue again at a later date if another injury resulting from the same conduct materializes. In this traditional view, the second injury is part of the original cause of action, and the plaintiff may not split that cause of action into two suits. This rule may have harsh consequences for a plaintiff who, for example, suffers property damage as a result of contaminated groundwater, and years later develops a cancer resulting from the same contamination. See Note: Claim Preclusion in Modern Latent Disease Cases: A Proposal for Allowing Second Suits, 103 Harv. L. Rev. 1989 (1990). In *Mauro v. Raymark Industries, Inc.,* 561 A.2d 257 (N.J. 1989), the court rejected the traditional rule and allowed a plaintiff who had been exposed to hazardous substances, but had not contracted any illness to bring an action for medical monitoring, while reserving the option to sue in the future if the disease develops.

In our view, removal of the statute-of-limitations and single-controversy doctrines as a bar to the institution of suit when the disease for which plaintiff is at risk ultimately occurs enhances the quality of the remedy that tort law can provide in such cases. If the disease never occurs, presumably there will be no claim and no recovery. If it does occur, the resultant litigation will involve a tangible claim for present injury, rather than a speculative claim for future injury. Hence, juries will be better able to award damages in an amount that fairly reflects the nature and severity of the plaintiff's injury.

TOXIC TORT PROBLEM

Hometown is a city of 100,000 located in "cancer alley," a region that is heavily industrialized and also experiences significantly enhanced levels of cancer in the population. The average rate in the U.S. population of new cancers discovered annually is 10/1000. The rate in Cancer Alley is 15/1000. EPA has recently announced the results of an epidemiologic study of the risks associated with 5 large chemical plants in Cancer Alley that until quite recently, when tight regulatory controls were imposed, emitted large amounts of various toxic air pollutants that have been shown to cause cancer in test animals. The study concludes that between 30 and 60 percent of the increased incidence of cancer in residents of Cancer Alley is attributable to these air pollutants. What claims for damages may be asserted by a resident of Hometown that has recently contracted cancer? A resident that does not have cancer? How should courts dispose of such claims?

3.   ALTERNATIVE INSTITUTIONAL APPROACHES FOR COMPENSATING VICTIMS OF ENVIRONMENTAL RISKS

MENELL, THE LIMITATIONS OF LEGAL INSTITUTIONS FOR ADDRESSING ENVIRONMENTAL RISKS

5 J. Econ. Perspectives 93 (1991)

C.   INSTITUTIONAL LIMITATIONS OF THE TORT SYSTEM IN ADDRESSING ENVIRONMENTAL RISKS

. . . The common law system is characterized by its limited focus on resolving disputes between particular parties, adversarial process, generalist (and significantly independent) decisionmakers, decentralized structure, and ex post perspective. By contrast, administrative agencies tend to feature hierarchical, centralized command structures with specialist decisionmakers subject to political pressures. The ability of a regulatory institution to address a particular public policy problem depends on how well it is tailored or adaptable to the nature of the underlying regulatory problems. . . .

Although the tort system has limited flexibility along some of its dimensions, it is, in the main, poorly suited to either compensating disease victims equitably or deterring environmental risks efficiently. As a compensatory mechanism for diseases associated with environmental risks, the tort system is severely limited by its narrow focus upon disputes between litigants, generalist decisionmakers, and decentralized structure. Its emphasis on resolving disputes between particular parties requires each plaintiff to establish a reasonably clear cause and effect linkage between a defendant's conduct and the plaintiff's disease. Without this requirement, the system loses its legitimacy as a decentralized institution for meting out justice and inefficiently allocates the entire burden of disease upon sources responsible for a relatively small share of the cases. With this requirement, the common law system excludes many disease victims because science cannot provide a sufficient basis for establishing particularized causation and long latency periods prevent many victims from tracing the disease to particular environmental risks.

Even when scientific and exposure evidence can be adduced to support a plausible causal connection, the tort system is hindered by the nature of the causation inquiry. Grounded in a moral tradition of personal responsibility and administered by judges with limited scientific competence, the tort system is mired in a requirement of particularized proof of causation that was developed long before modern scientific notions of disease causation were understood: In most jurisdictions, the plaintiff must trace the *physical* chain connecting the defendant's conduct to the plaintiff's injury. While this requirement can be readily satisfied in cases involving detectable physical interactions like automobile accidents, it creates serious problems in cases involving statistical evidence such as that reflected in epidemiological studies. In one highly publicized case involving the leak of industrial solvents into municipal drinking water wells in Woburn, Massachusetts, epidemiologists estimated that the contamination explained four to six of the ten to twelve excess cases of leukemia. Under traditional legal standards, no plaintiff would be able to establish that their disease was "legally caused" by the environmental contamination despite the fact that scientific notions of cause seemed to support a conclusion that between one-third to half of the cases were attributable to the defendant's activities.

Although some courts have relaxed the requirement of particularized proof in toxic tort cases, for instance, by allowing the use of statistical evidence, there remains the problem of assessing complex and often conflicting scientific evidence. Through its adversary process, the tort system has spawned cottage industries of plaintiff and defendant expert witnesses. The tort system's generalist decisionmakers often lack the scientific competence to evaluate the qualifications of these "experts" and assess their testimony and supporting studies. Even when judges utilize special masters to assist in sorting out the complex scientific evidence, the decentralized nature of the common law system means that these same determinations will have to be made in each case that arises,[77] resulting in redundant and possibly inconsistent reso-

---

77. See, e.g., *Hardy v. Johns-Manville Sales Corp.*, 681 F.2d 334 (5th Cir. 1982) (reversing lower court for accepting the general relationship between exposure to asbestos and respiratory disease without requiring the plaintiff to adduce particularized proof). Although class actions and consolidation of cases can alleviate this problem in some contexts, the manifestation of disease is a diffuse phenomenon (with the exception of some large-scale toxic accidents like the Union Carbide disaster in Bhopal, India).

lution of generic, essentially scientific questions. Thus, the common law system is poorly structured to evaluate scientific information competently, consistently, and efficiently.

These same limitations carry over to the determination of compensation. Under traditional tort doctrine, the plaintiff is entitled to full compensation if the trier of fact concludes that it was more probable than not that the defendant caused the plaintiff's injury. In view of background risks and other potential causes of most diseases associated with pollution and the limitations of modern science, it is impossible to determine the precise cause of nonsignature diseases in individual cases. Yet courts award full compensation whenever the "more probable than not" standard is deemed satisfied, creating variability and inequity in the level of recovery: full compensation for all plaintiffs who can show that the defendants caused their injuries with greater than 50 percent likelihood and no recovery for those whose proof comes up short.

Perhaps the greatest sources of variability and inequity in the compensation of the tort system are the inconsistency of verdicts, the long delay of court proceedings, and the large share of proceeds that go to lawyers and experts. In the asbestos litigation, for example, plaintiffs received on average only 39 percent of the total paid by defendants and insurers, with the remainder going to legal fees and expenses. By contrast, 80 percent of first party insurance premiums and 62 percent of workers' compensation revenues are paid in compensation. Approximately 99 percent of the SSDI budget goes to pay claims. Moreover, these sources of compensation reach victims substantially faster than tort judgments.

Multiple layers of litigation — as a result of bankruptcy proceedings, insurance disputes, subrogation claims, and contribution actions — further contribute to the delay and overall costliness of the tort system. In addition, the tort system raises product and other costs inefficiently by supplementing first-party (individual) and social insurance with mandatory third-party insurance (such as business liability insurance), which carries with it higher administrative cost.

A variety of other factors contribute to the unevenness of recovery within the tort system. Bankruptcy of defendants leaves some victims without recourse, particularly those whose injuries manifest slowly. On the other hand, some victims are eligible for collateral sources of compensation, such as private and social insurance. On balance, therefore, the tort system is an extremely costly claims processing institution that produces highly inequitable and unsystematic levels of compensation.

The tort system's poor performance in compensating disease victims and high cost might be tolerable if it contributed significantly to other public policy goals. The institutional attributes of the tort system, however, are particularly ill-suited to the other principal public policy goal in this area — deterring environmental risks efficiently.

A regulatory regime's efficiency in deterring risky activities turns on its ability to systematically alter the incentives of those engaged in the activities to reflect the proper social tradeoff between benefits and costs. Since many risky activities actually decrease other risks in the society — for example, chlorination of tap water, which slightly increases the risk of cancer, significantly reduces the risks of pathogenic viruses and bacteria — the determination of the proper incentives for the generation of environmental risks is extremely complicated. Administrative regulation — featuring specialist decisionmakers, centralized research facilities, continual oversight of regulatory problems, and a broad array of regulatory tools — is capable of systematically assessing environmental risks, evaluating a broad range of prospective and retrospective regulatory tools, and implementing a comprehensive and flexible set of policies.[78] These interventions directly alter the incentives of private risk managers by pricing externalities, setting standards for engaging in particular activities, and proscribing certain extremely hazardous activities.

By contrast, the common law tort system is severely limited in its ability to transmit proper incentives to creators of environmental risks. As a private law institution with an ex post perspective, the tort system deters only to the extent that decisionmakers bear responsibility within their organization for their decisions (or are otherwise motivated), anticipate that private parties might be harmed, and expect that victims will bring legal actions. The long lag between environmental contamination and the onset of many diseases and the limitations of science in identifying cause inhibit the operation of this mechanism. Furthermore, given the diffused decisionmaking structure of large businesses, the time-lag between managerial decisions and eventual lawsuits, and the limited liability and insurance protection of corporations, the deterrent effect of prospective liability for environmental risks is significantly muted. In the context of accident law generally, empirical evidence of the deterrent effect of tort liability is thin. . . .

NOTES AND QUESTIONS

1. Does Menell adequately consider the general deterrent effects of contemporary toxic tort liability, which relaxes traditional limitation rules to permit plaintiffs to sue for long latency illnesses after they occur and their cause is known; imposes strict liability; relaxes traditional cau-

---

78. Having the capability to regulate effectively and actually doing it are two different things. The point here is that administrative agencies have many institutional attributes that are conducive to deterring environmental risks effectively. A complete analysis must also consider impediments to the administrative regulatory process, such as the influence of interest groups.

sation requirements; and recognizes new remedies, including recoveries for medical monitoring and emotional distress attributable to toxic exposures? Compare the incentive effects of evolving toxic tort liability with retroactive legislative adoption of sweeping cleanup liability and the administrative imposition of unprecedented, stringent new regulatory requirements.

2. Does Menell place excessive faith in the ability of regulatory systems to provide appropriate risk management incentives? Should we retain tort liability as a supplement to regulation? Or do the two systems produce uncoordinated and inappropriate incentives and excessive transactions cost?

3. If we were to abandon tort liability as a means of addressing illnesses caused by environmental exposures, two questions must be faced. First, how do we provide adequate incentives for polluters appropriately to reduce risk? Second, how would the injured be compensated for the economic and other losses incurred? See Stewart, Crisis in Tort Law?, An Institutional Perspective, 54 U. Chi. L. Rev. 184 (1987).

4. One alternative is to replace the existing tort system with a no-fault compensation system for toxic tort injuries, modelled on the systems of workers' compensation for employment-related injuries. By statute, workers' compensation has almost entirely replaced tort liability as a means of dealing with employees' claims against employers for damages for work-related injuries. The employee need not establish negligence, but only that the injurious accident arose out of or in the course of employment. In many cases this nexus requirement is unproblematic, although there are cases, such as those involving an employee who detours from his assigned driving route on personal business, that provoke litigation over coverage. Liability is limited to medical costs, a defined portion of lost wages, and scheduled damages for permanent physical disabilities such as a loss of limb. There are no awards for pain and suffering. Claims are processed administratively, at far less cost than the tort system.

Could such a system be devised for environmental injuries? How would the compensable nexus between the plaintiff's injury and a polluting defendant's conduct be defined? Would such a system simply reintroduce the problem of causation in a different institutional guise, or could such a system develop simplifying rules of thumb to avoid case by case determination of causation?

Consider in this respect the Japanese law for compensation of pollution-related health damage. Enacted in 1973, the law provided two different administrative systems of compensation. One was directed at signature-type illnesses, such as *itai-itai* disease due to cadmium exposure; compensation for such illnesses is paid by the enterprise responsible for the exposure. The other system provided compensation for illnesses, such as lung and cardiovascular disease, potentially attributable to generalized air pollution, although such diseases might be due to many other factors such as smoking. In order to recover, victims had to reside in areas with elevated levels of SO_2 (two to three times the national average), and in which there was a similar elevation of lung, cardiovascular, or similar illness among the population. Persons in the designated areas who contracted the designated illnesses were entitled to payments for medical and rehabilitation expenses, disability, and survivors' benefits and funeral expenses. Funding for benefits was provided as follows: 20 percent by a nationally uniform tax on automobile owners, 72 percent by a tax on SO_2 sources within the region, and 8 percent by a tax on SO_2 sources outside any designated region. See J. Gresser, The 1973 Japanese Law for Compensation of Pollution-Related Health Image: An Introductory Assessment, 8 L. in Japan 92 (1975). The compensation provisions for generalized air pollution were eventually repealed because of mounting costs. Does this experience suggest that it would be feasible to develop an administrative system of compensation for illnesses due to pollution and toxic wastes in the United States?

What are the political and practical limitations of no-fault administrative compensation systems? Consider the example of the Black Lung compensation program. Following a coal mine explosion and fire that killed 78 coal miners in West Virginia in 1968, Congress examined coal mine safety laws and health hazards faced by coal miners. The Federal Coal Mine Safety and Health Act of 1969 improved working conditions in the mines as well as provided health benefits for black lung disease (pneumoconiosis), a chronic irreversible chest condition caused by the inhalation of fine coal dust particles in the lungs. Payments were to be financed by an excise tax on the sale of coal. As originally administered, lung x-rays were required and claimants were also required to establish that their disease was primarily attributable to coal dust as opposed to smoking or other causes. Because of political pressure from Congress (reflecting pressures from unions and claimant groups), these requirements were dropped in 1977 causing claim payments to soar. Congress tightened eligibility requirements in 1981. Total claims paid now exceed $16 billion and are growing at a rate of $600 million per year. Coal mine interests have been successful in resisting increases in assessments to fully match the claims paid. Revenue shortfalls have been borrowed from the U.S. Treasury at zero interest. Over the life of the program, coal taxes have covered an average of 60 percent of program costs. See General Accounting Office, Black Lung Program: Further Improvements Can Be Made in Claims Adjudication (March 1990).

5. Under existing arrangements, compensation is provided not only by tort award, but also (and in greater amounts) by existing public and private systems of loss insurance: Social Security Disability Insurance, Medicaid and Medicare, employer health and disability programs, and individually-purchased loss insurance. Are these insurance

systems adequate to compensate for losses attributable to toxic torts? If not, is there any reason, from a pure risk-spreading viewpoint, to provide more generous insurance to victims of toxic exposures created by environmental pollution as opposed to those who become ill from natural causes? Why not a system of universal public insurance, funded out of tax revenues, to cover medical costs, lost wages, and other economic losses, regardless of the cause of compensation for pain and suffering?

New Zealand has adopted a universal system of public compensation for accidents, abolishing tort liability. The system is funded by assessments against automobile owners, employees, and employers, and by general tax revenues. For budgetary reasons, the program is limited to accidents and does not cover non-accidental illnesses. As applied to toxic-type illnesses, the New Zealand system would therefore have to determine whether a given claimant's illness was due to an environmental exposure or "background" causes.

6. Argue for and against the following: In most cases, the legal system is incapable of determining the cause of individual illnesses that are potentially caused by environmental exposures. The appropriate institutional solution is to abandon reliance on liability systems to manage environmental risks and provide compensation. The only way to escape the bedeviling issue of causation for environmental injuries is to rely on regulation to manage risks and to deal with compensation either through a system of universal public medical and disability insurance, or reliance on individuals to self-insure.

PROBLEM: DEVELOPING AN ADMINISTRATIVE COMPENSATION SCHEME

You were just appointed staff counsel to the Environmental Injury Compensation Commission, a Congressional study group authorized to propose an administrative system of compensation for persons injured by improperly dumped wastes. (It is assumed that most of the health injuries involved are attributable to contaminated groundwater.)

The Chairperson of the Commission is interested in developing a system that would combine some of the incentive and compensation functions of the tort law while avoiding many of the transaction costs and possible inconsistencies of the litigation process. Specifically, the Chairperson is interested in a system that would impose a "risk tax" on generators of hazardous waste likely to cause health injury, and use the proceeds to fund a system of administrative compensation for persons suffering injuries of a type caused by toxic waste releases. She asks you to consider the following questions:

1. How should the fund be financed? Should the "risk tax" be levied on

    (a)   past generators in proportion to volume and toxicity of waste deposited at sites now determined to be leaking and posing health risks;

    (b)   past generators, in proportion to volume and toxicity of all hazardous waste generated;

    (c)   current generators, in proportion to volume and toxicity of all hazardous waste generated.

2. Who should be eligible for compensation?

    (a)   all persons who contract illnesses that could have been caused by exposure to hazardous wastes;

    (b)   all persons who contract illnesses that could have been caused by exposure to hazardous wastes and who live in designated "pollution areas";

    (c)   all persons who contract illnesses that could have been caused by exposure to hazardous wastes, live in designated "pollution areas," and can show that the increased risk from toxic exposure exceeded a legislatively specified percentage (for instance, 33 percent, 50 percent) of the total risk (that is, toxic exposure risk plus background risk).

3. How much compensation should be awarded?

    (a)   full reimbursement for medical expenses and lost wages;

    (b)   reimbursement for medical expenses and lost wages, discounted by background risk (for example, if the agency determined that the background risk was 80 percent of total risk and increased risk due to toxic exposure was 20 percent, claimants would get 20 percent reimbursement).

4. Availability of alternative remedies:

    (a)   Would the administrative compensation remedy be exclusive, preempting common law remedies?

    (b)   Should claimants be given the option of electing one remedy or the other?

7

Administrative Law and Representation of Environmental Interests

As a result of legislation at both the federal and state levels providing for far-reaching regulatory controls on pollution and other forms of environmental degradation, "front line" responsibility for dealing with such degradation has in most fields passed from the courts to administrative agencies, such as the federal Environmental Protection Agency. As previous chapters have described, some of these delegations are extremely broad, reflecting the scientific complexity of many environmental problems and the inability of legislators to resolve difficult political trade-offs. In recent years, however, Congress has often legislated in greater detail, mandating very specific regulatory initiatives with exact instructions as to how they are to be carried out. See, e.g., the 1990 Amendments to §112 of the Clean Air Act, 42 U.S.C. §7412, setting forth a detailed timetable for regulating scores of hazardous air pollutants that are specifically listed by name in the statute. See supra, p. 333. In addition, there exist many other administrative agencies, such as the federal Department of Transportation or the Department of Energy, whose basic mission is not environmental protection but whose decisions have profound environmental consequences. They grant regulatory approval to private actions (such as hydro-electric projects) and provide direct or indirect funding for projects (such as highways or nuclear technologies) that cause or threaten to cause serious adverse environmental effects. Frequently such agencies, in pursuing

777

their primary missions, will disregard or downplay these adverse environmental consequences, creating a sort of "bureaucratic externality." Compare the experience with state socialism in the former Soviet Union.

Congressional and executive oversight of agency action and judicial review represent one set of potential solutions to the problem of controlling agency decisionmaking. The first section of this chapter examines the structure of federal regulatory decisionmaking, summarizing these modes of agency control. As you study these materials, think about how political and legal institutions could be reformed to make agencies more responsive to the electorate.

The remainder of the chapter presents the principal elements of judicial review of agency action. We deal here only with federal law; state administrative law and state counterparts to the National Environmental Policy Act must also be consulted by practitioners of environmental law. In examining the materials, you should bear in mind two sets of questions: First, are or should the basic standards of judicial access and review be any different in environmental controversies than in other areas of government regulation and management? Second, are or should the standards of judicial review of environmental questions differ depending on whether the agency whose action is challenged has environmental protection as its primary mission (such as the federal Environmental Protection Agency) or has other objectives as its primary mission (such as power development in the case of the Department of Energy)? In addressing these two questions, consider the implications of the fact that those groups that are directly responsible for environmental degradation or directly benefit from it are very often well-organized and endowed with considerable financial resources, whereas those who suffer the adverse effects of such degradation are often diffuse, less well organized, and face serious transaction cost obstacles to effectively pooling resources. As seen in Chapters 2 and 3, this pervasive structural feature was an important factor in the failure of free-market bargaining and exchange to deal adequately with the problem of environmental degradation and was a similarly important factor in the limitations of traditional private litigation in coping with that problem. What might be the implications of this structural feature in the context of regulation and management by administrative agencies, which often enjoy substantial discretion in setting policies that directly impinge on the economic well-being of regulated firms and other organized interests? Can the courts feasibly and appropriately serve as a fulcrum for the representation of less well organized "public" interests?

A.   THE STRUCTURE OF FEDERAL
REGULATORY DECISIONMAKING

Prior to the 1930s, the federal government operated in much, though surely not all, the way an eighth grade Civics class says that it does. Congress drafted and voted on bills. Bills that received more than majority votes by both the House of Representatives and the Senate were presented to the President. Bills the President signed became law. A Presidential veto could only be overturned by a two-thirds majority of each house of Congress. To the extent that laws were not self-executing, federal agencies and enforcement officers were delegated authority to carry out these laws. Since the scope of regulatory decisionmaking prior to the 1930s was in most instances relatively narrow, federal agencies typically did not have significant discretion in carrying out their duties.

The structure of federal regulatory decisionmaking changed markedly during the New Deal era. In order to alleviate the pervasive ills of the Great Depression, Congress enacted a wide variety of economic and social programs in the mid-1930s. Recognizing the need for flexibility and expertise in the administration of these programs, Congress created new administrative agencies with broad discretionary powers.[1] The size of the administrative state steadily increased during the 1940s and 1950s as Congress expanded these basic programs. During the 1960s and 1970s, the federal bureaucracy experienced rapid growth again as Congress responded to the call for broad environmental, health, and safety regulation, as well as civil rights and consumer protection measures.

As the previous chapters have described, the scope of delegated discretionary authority in the environmental area under many statutes is broad. See, e.g., the TSCA statute involved in the *Asbestos* case, supra, p. 116. This reflects the uncertainty surrounding the causes of environmental degradation, the health and ecosystem effects of environmental contamination, and the technological and economic feasibility of different control strategies. The degree of delegation in the environmental area also reflects, as we have witnessed in many contexts, Congressional unwillingness to make difficult political trade-offs. As we have also seen, even where Congress attempts to write quite detailed directives, as in RCRA, the resulting statutory complexity is so great that

---

1. The first of these broad delegations were successfully challenged as unconstitutional delegations of legislative powers to executive officials. See *Panama Refining Co. v. Ryan*, 293 U.S. (1935); *A.L.A. Schecter Poultry Corp. v. United States*, 295 U.S. 495 (1935). Since these decisions, however, the Supreme Court has not found any Congressional delegation to administrative agencies to be unconstitutional.

FIGURE 7-1

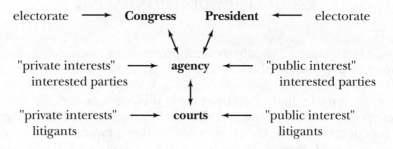

there is inevitably need to rely substantially on administrative discretion to unravel it and develop a workable regulatory program.

As a result of the expansion of the administrative state, the structure of federal regulatory decisionmaking is quite different from the model of lawmaking described in Civics lessons. Figure 7-1 illustrates a somewhat more accurate picture of the factors that influence federal regulatory decisionmaking. In most environmental legislation, Congress delegates broad powers to the Environmental Protection Agency and other administrative agencies. Such powers are not, however, carried out in a vacuum. Administrative agencies must employ decisionmaking procedures prescribed by the Administrative Procedure Act and/or the specific legislation delegating authority in promulgating regulations. Through these means, interested parties may present information to the agency. Congress, through various tools, has indirect and direct means to influence the agency's decisions. The President, both through the appointment of agency personnel and through oversight, can also influence regulatory decisions. Furthermore, parties affected by the regulatory decisions typically can seek judicial review of the agency action.

1.   CONGRESSIONAL AND EXECUTIVE OVERSIGHT OF AGENCY ACTION

As the administrative state expanded and became more complex following the New Deal, leading academics and judges argued that regulatory agencies must be made more accountable and that their activities be better coordinated. Prior to the 1970s, however, neither the executive nor legislative branch responded to this call.

In response to the wave of regulations issued by the newly created Environmental Protection Agency in 1970, the Nixon Administration established "Quality of Life" review, a process by which the Office of Management and Budget (OMB) circulated proposed and final rules among interested agencies and departments and mediated disputes among these offices. See generally Bruff, Presidential Power and Administrative Rulemaking, 88 Yale L.J. 451, 464-465 (1979). The spiralling inflation of the early 1970s led the Ford Administration to require agencies to perform inflationary impact studies. Executive Order 11821, 34 C.F.R. 203 (1974). The Carter Administration expanded executive oversight by requiring executive branch agencies to conduct more in-depth analyses of proposed rules, Executive Order 12,044, 3 C.F.R. 152 (1978), and establishing two interagency groups to review and coordinate regulatory decisionmaking: the Regulatory Analysis and Review Group (RARG) and the Regulatory Council. See generally R. Litan & W. Nordhaus, Reforming Federal Regulation 67-79 (1983).

Despite these efforts to improve the oversight of regulatory agencies, there was widespread concern during the 1980 election campaign that the regulatory agencies were "out of control." Among Ronald Reagan's top priorities during the campaign were to control and make more accountable the regulatory agencies. Within a month of taking office, President Reagan issued Executive Order 12,291, 46 Fed. Reg. 13193 (1981), requiring all executive agencies to send all proposed and final regulations to OMB for review prior to their publication in the Federal Register.[2] The order, which has had the effect of increasing the paperwork of the federal government, was, ironically, based on the Paperwork Reduction Act of 1980, 44 U.S.C. §§3501-3520, designating OMB to oversee the paperwork demands imposed by federal agencies on the private sector, as well as the Article II constitutional authority of the President as Chief Executive. Section 2 of the order requires agencies in promulgating new regulations, reviewing existing regulations, or developing legislative proposals concerning regulation, to adhere to the following requirements "to the extent permitted by law":

(a)   Administrative decisions shall be based on adequate information concerning the need for and consequences of proposed government action;

(b)   Regulatory action shall not be undertaken unless the potential benefits to society for the regulation outweigh the potential costs to society;

(c)   Regulatory objectives shall be chosen to maximize the net benefits to society;

2. The Executive Order did not apply to "independent" agencies such as the Federal Trade Commission. In addition, the following regulations are not subject to OMB review: regulations governed by the formal rulemaking requirement of the APA; regulations relating to military and foreign affairs functions; and regulations relating to agency organization, management, and personnel.

(d)   Among alternative approaches to any given regulatory objective, the alternative involving the least net cost to society shall be chosen; and

(e)   Agencies shall set regulatory priorities with the aim of maximizing the aggregate net benefits to society taking into account the condition of the particular industries affected by regulations, the condition of the national economy, and other regulatory actions contemplated for the future.

Further, the Order established a special procedure for agencies to follow whenever they are considering a "major rule." Major rule is defined as any regulation whose likely result would be: "(1) An annual effect on the economy of $100 million or more; (2) A major increase in costs or prices [for various individuals and entities]; or (3) Significant adverse effects on competition, employment, investment, productivity, innovation [or foreign trade]." §1(b)(1)-(3). The Order expressly grants OMB authority to prescribe criteria for agencies to use in order to determine whether a regulation falls within this definition. §3(b).

Agencies considering such major rules must prepare a preliminary and a final Regulatory Impact Analysis (RIA) to submit, along with all notices of proposed rulemaking and all final rules, to the Director of OMB. Each RIA is to contain descriptions of "potential costs" and "potential net benefits" of the rule, along with a description of "alternative approaches" to the rule and an explanation of why these approaches were not adopted. §3(d)(1)-(4). See the history of OMB review of EPA's asbestos rule, supra, pp. 103-116.

After receiving a preliminary RIA or a notice of proposed rulemaking without an RIA, the Director of OMB has authority under the Executive Order to direct the submitting agency to refrain from publishing either until a review has taken place. §3(f)(1). The Director may also require the agency to respond to any of his or her views and "incorporate those views and the agency's response in the rulemaking file." §3(f)(2). The Director cannot, however, alter responsibilities imposed upon the agencies by law, §3(f)(3), nor can fulfillment of the requirements of this Order prevent an agency from meeting statutory or judicially mandated deadlines. §8(a)(2).

Finally, although the Order appears to have imposed legal duties on administrative agencies as supervised by OMB, §9 states that the Order "is not intended to create any right or benefit, substantive or procedural enforceable at law by a party against the United States, its agencies, its officers, or any person" but rather is meant to "improve the internal management of the Federal government." This provision was designed to foreclose litigation by private parties challenging government actions on the ground of noncompliance with the Executive Order.

In 1985, President Reagan further expanded the executive supervision of the administrative process by requiring agencies to submit to the Director of OMB annual "draft regulatory programs," statements of their "regulatory policies, goals, and objectives for the coming year and information concerning all significant regulatory actions planned or underway, including actions taken to consider whether to initiate rule-making; requests for public comment; and the development of documents that may influence, anticipate, or could lead to the commencement of rulemaking proceedings at a later date. . . ." Executive Order 12,498, §2(a), 50 Fed. Reg. 1036 (1985). Upon receipt of an agency's draft regulatory program, the Director shall determine whether it is consistent with "the administration's policies and priorities and the draft regulatory programs submitted by other agencies," and shall consider and identify what steps, if any, are necessary to achieve such consistency. §3(a). After the reviewing process is complete, agencies are to submit a final regulatory program for that year, which will then become part of the Administration's Regulatory Program. §3(b). From this point on, if an agency chooses to take action that was not described in or is "materially different from" that described in its final regulatory program, it must advise the Director and submit the action for his review. §3(c). As was the case with Executive Order 12,291, Executive Order 12,498 states that it does not create any procedural or substantive rights or benefits. §5.

DEMUTH & GINSBURG, WHITE HOUSE REVIEW OF AGENCY RULEMAKING

99 Harv. L. Rev. 1075, 1077-1082 (1986)

I. THE EMERGENCE OF WHITE HOUSE REVIEW . . .

Our federal government did not need agency rulemaking a century ago, but could not function without it today. Beginning with the New Deal and the demise in the late 1930's of the constitutional strictures on the appropriate role of the federal government, Congress gradually extended the reach of the federal government — through regulation, subsidization, and differential taxation — into numerous areas that had previously been the domain of state governments or private markets. By the mid-1970's, the federal government's reach included the operations and prices of public utilities and common carriers; the supply of agricultural products; the terms of labor contracts and the conditions of workplaces; the design of consumer products;

the terms of importation and exportation; the provision of education, medical care, transportation, and financial services; the control of pollution, and much else.

Congress's ability to supervise these new regulatory activities did not grow proportionately, however, nor could it have. The essential inputs into the legislative process are time and information, both of which are in severely inelastic supply. The one legislative device authorized by the Constitution — the Congress — remained the cumbersome, inefficient institution the framers designed it to be. As a result, Congress increasingly delegated lawmaking authority to the executive branch, where decisionmaking is hierarchical, rather than consensual, and therefore speedier.

In the post-World War II years, the executive branch responded to the delegation of this new authority with a series of important innovations (constituting what we now call administrative law) that demonstrated its superior lawmaking versatility and encouraged further delegation. The most important of these innovations was "informal rulemaking": an agency publishes a proposed rule (say, that automobiles must be equipped with a certain kind of brake lights, or that a certain wood preservative must be taken off the market, or that hospices will be eligible for Medicare reimbursements if they meet certain operating standards); collects public comments on the proposal; and then publishes a final rule along with an explanation of the rule's rationale that takes account of the public comments. In this way, informal rulemaking combines the efficiencies of hierarchical decisionmaking with the legitimating features of legislative and judicial decisionmaking — public participation, due process, and reasoned explanation.

There is, of course, another, more conventional way to view the emergence of agency rulemaking: such rulemaking consists of "technical" decisions made by "experts" applying policies laid down in statutes, and the need for such rulemaking arises from the increasing specialization of knowledge in modern society. There is an element of truth in this story: as the extent and specialization of knowledge increases, a legislator (or a president) will be able to master less and less about more and more and of necessity will grow increasingly dependent on the advice of specialists. But the notion that rulemaking is *only* the application of expert knowledge is a constitutional fiction, employed to support a more extensive lawmaking apparatus than the Constitution provides for.

If rulemaking were just the application of neutral "expertise," there would be no occasion for notice-and-comment procedures or much of the rest of administrative law; that Congress and the courts have required such procedures shows that rulemakers possess substantial discretion to affect the distribution of society's resources. Should autos be equipped with airbags? Should Medicare pay optometrists as well as ophthalmologists for conducting post-surgical eye examinations? Should asbestos pipe be banned or cautioned against or ignored? Who should be permitted to fish for halibut off the Pacific Coast? However much expert knowledge may contribute to answering these questions, the answers (and thousands of others like them that the government provides each year) are political as well as technical and must be so as long as there are differences — in ability, income, age, preference, and so forth — among the individuals on whose behalf they are made.

Informal rulemaking solved the problem of high-volume decisionmaking in the large modern state, but it created a new problem of political control and accountability. In regulatory statutes, Congress declares itself to be in favor of safe drugs and automobiles and clean air and lakes, and opposed to cancer and poisonous drinking water. Sometimes it goes so far as to say that these verities should be pursued reasonably (the Consumer Product Safety Act) or should be achieved by a date certain (the Clean Air and Water Acts). But Congress leaves the rest to the administrative agencies, certain in the knowledge that whatever decisions they make will be subject to a cascade of informal congressional criticism (letters, press releases, and hearings) from all sides. On the only issues that count — the concrete issues such as whether asbestos products should be banned, or just how much sulfur dioxide should be permitted in the air — Congress rarely makes a formal, on-the-record decision. Congress has decided none of the questions posed in the previous paragraph, for example, yet our government has decided (or is currently deciding) all of them.

The proliferation of rulemaking authorities also created new problems of policy coordination. By the late 1970's, authority to regulate the products and byproducts of nuclear technology was haphazardly divided among the Nuclear Regulatory Commission, the Environmental Protection Agency (EPA), and the Department of Energy. Authority over the production, use, and transportation of hazardous chemicals was similarly divided among the EPA, the Food and Drug Administration (FDA), the Federal Aviation Administration (FAA), the Department of Transportation, the Occupational Safety and Health Administration (OSHA), and the Consumer Product Safety Commission. Today, the fastest growing regulatory field in Washington, regulation of recombinant-DNA research, is divided among EPA, OSHA, the National Institutes of Health, the FDA, and the Department of Agriculture.

Under these circumstances, it was inevitable that presidents would attempt to impose order on the rulemaking process. Following the wave of new health, safety, and environmental legislation in the early 1970's, executive branch agencies were issuing thousands of rules each year. For better or worse, government was allocating billions of dollars through rulemaking — subject to none of the traditional devices of public finance (taxation, authorization, appropriation, and budgeting) through which Congress and the president exert a degree of control over government spending and share responsibility for the results. However decentralized the rulemaking process may have been in practice — and however prone to manipulation by congressional committees and their staffs and by private groups — the results belonged to the president as a political matter. Just as the growth of direct federal spending led to presidential oversight of agency budgets in 1921, and just as the growth of legislation led to presidential oversight of agency positions on legislation in 1940, so the growth of regulation led to presidential oversight of the rulemaking process in the 1970's. And as long as administrative regulation remains the expansive and powerful method of governance that it is today, no president can refrain from controlling it if he wishes to advance his policies.

The considerations discussed above suggest that presidents would have strengthened their control of agency rulemaking in the 1970's even if regulatory programs had been uncontroversial or widely admired, like the Park Service and the space program. But the regulatory programs were not widely admired or uncontroversial. In the 1970's, a growing body of academic literature showed that these programs frequently yielded highly perverse results — that they raised rather than lowered prices, restrained rather than promoted competition, injured rather than improved health and safety and other aspects of consumer welfare, and pursued generally accepted goals (cleaner air and safer drugs) in quite wasteful and inefficient ways. Popular disenchantment mirrored the academic disenchantment. Presidents Ford, Carter, and Reagan all made sharp attacks on the growth of federal regulation in their campaigns for office and included "regulatory reform" among their principal domestic goals; this period was the first time since the New Deal that presidents paid much attention at all to regulatory policy.

II.   THE BENEFITS OF WHITE HOUSE REVIEW

Apart from specific statutory reforms (such as the Airline Deregulation Act of 1978), the establishment of White House review of agency rules was the most important political response to the growing popular and academic criticism of federal regulation. The characteristic failings of regulation that economists and other scholars have identified are twofold. First, regulation tends to be excessively cautious (forcing investments in risk reduction far in excess of the value that individuals place on avoiding the risks involved). Second, regulation tends to favor narrow, well-organized groups at the expense of the general public.

These failings are, at least in part, a consequence of the institutional incentives of regulators and the nature of the rulemaking process.

We all know that a government agency charged with the responsibility of defending the nation or constructing highways or promoting trade will invariably wish to spend "too much" on its goals. An agency succeeds by accomplishing the goals Congress set for it as thoroughly as possible — not by balancing its goals against other, equally worthy goals. This fact of agency life provides the justification for a countervailing administrative constraint in the form of a central budget office. Without some countervailing restraint, EPA and OSHA would "spend" — through regulations that spend society's resources but do not appear in the federal government's fiscal budget — "too much" on pollution control and workplace safety. This tendency is reinforced by the "public" participation in the rulemaking process, which as a practical matter is limited to those organized groups with the largest and most immediate stakes in the results. Although presidents and legislatures are themselves vulnerable to pressure from politically influential groups, the rulemaking process — operating in relative obscurity from public view but lavishly attended by interest groups — is even more vulnerable. A substantial number of agency rules could not survive public scrutiny and gain two legislative majorities and the signature of the president.

Centralized review of proposed regulations under a cost/benefit standard, by an office that has no program responsibilities and is accountable only to the president, is an appropriate response to the failings of regulation. It encourages policy coordination, greater political accountability, and more balanced regulatory decisions. This is not to say that cost/benefit analysis is capable of abolishing narrow political influence or that the institutional interests of a central budget office will always provide a precise counterweight to the interests of program administrators. Our claim is far weaker, though still ample to justify the review process: rulemakers should be accountable to the president before issuing their rules and should be obliged to demonstrate the costs and benefits of their rules as thoroughly as circumstances permit. Assessments of social costs and benefits force regulators to confront problems of covert redistribution and overzealous pursuit of agency goals, which experience has shown to be common in regulatory programs. OMB review subjects proposed rules to a "hard look" *before* they are issued and ensures that serious policy disagreements between a president's appointees (one with and the other without programmatic responsibilities in the area in question) will be brought to his attention.

Although the cost/benefit standard and the OMB review procedure are not necessarily related — for example, one can imagine a president elected on an "industrial policy" platform shaping regulatory policy very differently than has President Reagan — we think the standard and the review procedure will usually be complementary in practice. In any administration, the president is more likely to take a broad view of the nation's economic interest in a given rulemaking controversy than are any of his agency heads — where "broad" denotes the consideration of all of the likely benefits and costs of the rule. That the cost/benefit standard has so far recommended itself to both Democratic and Republican presidents is evidence for our position.

In addition, OMB is able to identify conflicts in the approaches adopted by different agencies with similar or related responsibilities and to coordinate their activities. The annual *Regulatory Program* is circulated in draft to give all of the regulatory agencies the opportunity to see what activity is under way at the other agencies and to express any concerns they have about coordination or conflict. It also gives the administration the opportunity to establish priorities; to move the scheduled completion times for particular rulemakings forward or back; and to coordinate related rules, such as those promulgated to implement the changes made by budget legislation or to conform with accounting or other government-wide management initiatives.

OLSON, THE QUIET SHIFT OF POWER: OFFICE OF MANAGEMENT & BUDGET SUPERVISION OF ENVIRONMENTAL PROTECTION AGENCY RULEMAKING UNDER EXECUTIVE ORDER 12,291

4 Va. J. Natural Res. L. 1, 40 (1984)

III. OMB REVIEW OF EPA RULES: SOME EMPIRICAL OBSERVATIONS

D. CASE STUDIES

In this section, . . . case studies illustrate OMB review of EPA rules under E.O. 12,291. In each case, the limited degree to which OMB's input into the rulemaking is reflected on the public record will give the reader an idea of how difficult it is to comprehend OMB's influence simply by relying on the rulemaking docket. Although the *Home Box Office v. FCC* [,567 F.2d 9 (D.C. Cir.), *cert. denied*, 434 U.S. 829 (1971),] court spoke in a slightly different context, its fear that secrecy might create "the possibility that there is here one administrative record for the public and this court and another for the [agency] and those in the know" appears to be well founded. . . .

2. New Source Performance Standards

OMB has taken great interest in EPA New Source Performance Standards (NSPS's) for new and modified stationary air pollution sources, vetoing or bottling up many NSPS's sent to it for review. In fact, OMB has "returned" at least eleven NSPS's to EPA since mid-1981. An EPA official summarized OMB review of NSPS's this way: "[A]lthough the [Clean Air] Act requires us to issue these rules, OMB doesn't like technology-based standards — they sometimes seem upset when we bring up the statute."

EPA delivered all eleven of these NSPS's well before the statutory promulgation deadline of August 7, 1982. OMB held all of them well beyond that deadline; indeed, two NSPS's were held at least ten months past the date. One rule, the stationary internal combustion NSPS, was vetoed twice during more than two years of OMB review. Though the statutory deadline has passed, OMB has made clear its intention to continue to review NSPS's currently being developed well behind EPA's required schedule. This OMB review is in direct conflict with the Executive Order.

OMB has asserted that the NSPS's are not cost effective at the levels EPA sets, and that the standards are too prescriptive and should be more flexible. As a different matter, OMB held the stationary internal combustion engine NSPS for two years, essentially because of disagreement with EPA over what constitutes a "significant" source under the Clean Air Act.

The beverage can surface coating NSPS review illustrates how OMB may act as a conduit from industry to EPA. OMB logged in the final rule from EPA in May 1982; it took well in excess of a year to be reviewed. OMB's vigorous resistance was puzzling since the rule involved "basically no net control costs" to the overall industry, although certain operators would be subject to higher control costs. EPA officials began to suspect industry influence. Their suspicions were confirmed when OMB sent to EPA a detailed six-page memorandum, complete with charts and figures, absent from the docket, criticizing the rule and "mouth[ing] verbatim the industry position." Industry lobbying of OMB on the can coating rule did indeed take place; OMB received a thick package of documents, some not in the EPA docket, and some several months after the close of the comment period.

To summarize OMB review of EPA's NSPS program: (1) OMB has extended review well beyond the statutory deadline; (2) OMB has not confined its comments solely to criteria mandated by E.O. 12,291; (3) OMB has exercised de facto veto power over some rules by holding them in "rule review limbo"; and (4) amid industry lobbying at OMB, the Office has made arguments that in some cases track industry positions verbatim.

NSPS's are issued pursuant to the Clean Air Act, which explicitly provides that all draft rules sent to OMB must be docketed prior to a rule's promulgation. OMB comments are required to be docketed as well. At the least, the Act directs that no rule may be based "in part or whole" on "any information or data which has not been placed in the docket," a command which would seem to require docketing of significant OMB comments. EPA's docketing practices appear to fall far short of the Act's mandates. At least five of the eleven NSPS dockets fail to include any reference to OMB's veto of the rule or to the accompanying written materials from OMB, and most of the dockets include absolutely no indication of OMB's extensive input into the rules.

3. *National Ambient Air Quality Standard for Particulate Matter*

The Clean Air Act charges EPA to develop health-based standards for ambient air concentrations of certain pollutants, which "in the judgment of the Administrator . . . allow . . . an adequate margin of safety . . . to protect the public health." The D.C. Circuit has emphasized the statutory command that these National Ambient Air Quality Standards (NAAQS's) are to be solely health based, and that health protection may not be compromised to reduce compliance costs.

However, soon after EPA began reconsidering its NAAQS for particulate matter, discussion between OMB and EPA ensued as to whether EPA should prepare an RIA. Ultimately, EPA agreed to hire a contractor to assess the costs and benefits of regulatory alternatives. In December 1983 EPA filed a formal draft RIA for the standards, and docketed a cost-benefit analysis of alternative standards.

Some industry representatives, particularly the American Iron and Steel Institute (AISI), favor a relaxation of the particulate matter NAAQS. The original draft of the contractor study, however, indicated that *tightening* the standard, rather than *loosening* it, would create the greatest net societal benefit. Industry attacked the contractor study when this result was revealed.

OMB also has criticized the study, objecting in detail to several of the studies upon which it relies. EPA's former Chief of Staff complained that during the NAAQS review, OMB "kept urging upon us consideration of the costs through certain types of analyses that really were not permitted . . . under the statute." Vice President Bush himself, apparently prompted by communications from Bethlehem Steel, joined OMB's effort to impress upon EPA the steel industry's concern that the standards not produce undesirable economic impacts.

The EPA docket for this rule revision contains the correspondence to and from the Vice President. There is, however, no record of communications between OMB and the steel industry, or of OMB's input into the rule.

NOTES AND QUESTIONS

1. In view of Olson's observations, do you believe that the regulatory review process improves the functioning of the regulatory agencies? Does OMB review give politically powerful interests a "second bite at the apple" and lead to undue duplication, delay, and diffusion of responsibility? Consider the example of EPA's proposed rules for asbestos, supra, p. 103. See also Howard & Benfield, Rulemaking in the Shadows: The Rise of OMB and Cost-Benefit Analysis in Environmental Decisionmaking, 16 Col. J. Envtl. L. 143 (1991); O'Brien, White House Review of Regulations Under the Clean Air Act Amendments of 1990, 8 J. Envtl. L. & Litig. 61 (1992). See generally, T. McGarity, Reinventing Rationality: Regulatory Analysis in the Federal Bureaucracy (1991).

2. Recall that the Executive Order requires that agencies "consider" RIAs only "to the extent permitted by law." This provision requires interpretation of the statute that the agency is interpreting in order to determine whether it permits the agency to consider costs and benefits. See, e.g., the *Lead Industries* case, supra, p. 264. But even if a statute does not permit an agency to consider costs and benefits, the Executive Order still requires agencies to prepare a RIA (on what rationale?). Isn't the procedural requirement that agencies prepare an analysis, subject to clearance by OMB, calculated to influence an agency's substantive decisions?

3. Would Executive Order 12,291 violate the Clean Air Act by allowing the President or the director of OMB to control, for example, the EPA Administrator's decision in an NAAQS? An NSPS? The President's Article II responsibility to ensure faithful execution of the laws must authorize the President to control to some extent the decisions of department heads or other subordinate officials. Moreover, the President has the power to discharge at will most high executive officials. Is the power to direct the decisions of such officials implicit in the power to discharge them? Does the answer depend on the type of decision in question — whether an adjudication involving individuals or adoption of a general rule? See generally Sunstein, Constitutionalism After the New Deal, 101 Harv. L. Rev. 421 (1987); Strauss, The Place of Agencies in Government: Separation of Powers and the Fourth Branch of Government, 84 Colum. L. Rev. 573, 662-667 (1984).

4. There has been remarkably little litigation involving the use by the White House of the Executive Order to control agency decisionmaking. A frequent complaint by environmental groups is that OMB uses its review power to hold up issuance of EPA regulations in-

definitely, even where a statute mandates their promulgation by a given date. In *EDF v. Thomas,* 627 F. Supp. 566 (D.D.C. 1986), the court held that OMB lacked authority to delay issuance of EPA regulations beyond the date of a statutory deadline.

NRDC v. Reilly, 969 F.2d 1147 (D.C. Cir. 1992), involved a direct challenge to the supervisory authority of the White House over agency decisionmaking. EPA had prepared rules, pursuant to §111 of the Clean Air Act, to regulate municipal waste incinerators by requiring them to separate out 25 percent of wastes prior to incineration (with a view to encouraging recycling), and prohibiting incineration of lead-acid batteries. EPA submitted a package of final rules to the Office of Management and Budget (OMB) for review pursuant to Executive Order 12,291. OMB did not approve the sections of the proposed rules covering materials separation and battery burning. EPA then appealed to the President's Council on Competitiveness (Council), headed by Vice-President Quayle. In a "Fact Sheet," the Council found the proposed rules on materials separation inconsistent with "several of the Administration's regulatory principles," including their failure to "meet the benefit/cost requirements for regulatory policy laid out in Executive Order 12291." The Fact Sheet also noted the Council's opinion that the materials separation requirement did not constitute a "performance standard" and that it violated principles of federalism. EPA subsequently abandoned the materials separation and battery burning provisions when it promulgated its final rules.

The court found EPA's explanation for the deletion of the separation requirement adequate. EPA had stated that, on further review, the air quality benefits of separation were uncertain but probably small, while the costs of the measure might be substantial. The court found that these determinations were reasonable ones, based on the evidence of record, and that EPA was therefore justified in deleting the materials separation requirement. It further stated:

> Lastly, the petitioners claim that EPA acted improperly in relying on the opinion of the Council rather than exercising its own expertise. See [*Public Citizens Health Reseach Group v. Tyson,* 746 F.2d 1479, 1505 (D. C. Cir. 1986)] ("We cannot defer when the agency simply has not exercised its expertise."). After reviewing the record, we conclude that EPA did exercise its expertise in this case. The procedural history of the rules at issue demonstrates that the Council's views were important in formulating EPA's final policy decision regarding materials separation. The fact that EPA reevaluated its conclusions in light of the Council's advice, however, does not mean that EPA failed to exercise its own expertise in promulgating the final rules.
>
> In sum, EPA's change of position on the materials separation issue was not improper. We are extremely deferential to administrative agencies in cases involving technical rulemaking decisions. . . .

Despite its continued belief that "lead acid batteries are certainly a significant course of lead in MWC emissions," 56 Fed. Reg. at 5499, EPA decided not to include a ban on the burning of lead-acid vehicle batteries in its final rules, id.; 56 Fed. Reg. at 5521. The Agency offered three reasons for its decision to omit the ban: (1) commentors questioned whether it would be possible to achieve 100 percent compliance; (2) the Resource Conservation and Recovery Act includes strict provisions against the burning of lead-acid batteries; and (3) EPA is considering a comprehensive approach to recycling lead-acid batteries under section 6 of the Toxic Substances Control Act.

The petitioners countered EPA's first rationale by suggesting that, if 100 percent compliance with a ban on burning lead-acid batteries is impossible, EPA could have adopted some lesser restriction (e.g., a 99 or 95 percent ban). EPA responded by stating that it was limited to a choice between a 100 percent ban or no ban at all. [The court rejected this claim.]

EPA's next two rationales simply recognize that the matter of lead-acid battery incineration can be addressed under other statutes. [The court of appeals found this not to be an adequate reason for EPA to abandon regulation of lead battery incineration under the Clean Air Act, and set aside this aspect of EPA's decision.]

5. During President Bush's administration, much of the oversight of controversial and important EPA rulemaking was performed by the Council on Competitiveness. This shift was prompted in part by the refusal of Senator Glenn, chair of the relevant Senate subcommittee, to confirm an administration appointee to be Associate Director of OMB for the Office of Information and Regulatory Affairs (OIRA), the official in charge of the Paperwork Reduction Act and E.O. 1229, until changes in the OMB review process were made. The Council was much criticized by environmentalists for blocking or watering down EPA rules. The Clinton Administration abolished the Council shortly after taking office and, as described below, has rewritten Executive Order 12,291. Should OMB regulatory review be abolished? If not, how should the process be modified? In prior administrations, EPA was the focus of White House regulatory review in part because of the cost of EPA regulation (estimated to reach $185 to 200 billion annually by the year 2000), but also because EPA was viewed as overly responsive to the environmental committees of the Democratic Congress. Now that the Congress and the President are of the same political party, has the need or justification for White House review of EPA rulemaking disappeared?

6. Following the implementation of Executive Order 12,291 and the surfacing of some of the questionable practices described by Olson, the Congress considered ways to "regulate" executive oversight. Among the means considered were to expressly prohibit OMB from participating in deciding what regulatory action, if any, an agency will take in any rulemaking proceeding, and to require that written com-

ments made by the Director of OMB regarding a rule under consideration by an agency be included in the rulemaking file. See, e.g., Regulatory Reform Act of 1983, H.R. 2327, 98th Cong., 1st Sess. Should such limitations be enacted? Do such limitations impermissibly constrain the authority of the Executive Branch? Could the Executive Branch circumvent such restrictions? What means, if any, would you recommend to improve the regulatory oversight process?

In response to criticisms, OMB's Office for Information and Regulatory Affairs (OIRA) has, in recent years, agreed to make available to the public draft notices of proposed rulemaking and final rules submitted for OIRA review along with copies of all related correspondence between OIRA and agency heads. These papers will become available once the agency publishes the related notices or final rules in the Federal Register. OIRA will also make available on request the agencies' "regulatory program" submissions (that is, the agencies' general plans for regulatory rules, and so forth, during the coming year) once the Administration publishes its final "Regulatory Program" in the Federal Register. OIRA makes available in its public reading room written materials, lists of meetings, and lists of communications received from or involving persons outside the government.

OIRA has further agreed to send other material to tell the agency "of all oral communication" about the agency's rules that OIRA "has with persons" from outside the government, and invite agency personnel to attend all scheduled meetings with any such persons (about the agency's rules). OIRA calls these procedures its "EPA Procedures." As of June 1989, OIRA had extended these procedures to the Departments of Labor, Housing and Urban Development, Treasury, and Transportation.

Note that these rules do not cover (and thereby keep private) (1) draft notices and rules that the agency withdraws after OMB review and never issues; (2) correspondence between OIRA desk officers and subordinate agency personnel; (3) summaries of oral communications between OIRA and the agencies. See Bruff, Presidential Management of Agency Rulemaking, 57 Geo. Wash. L. Rev. 533 (1989). Do you think OIRA's rules go far enough? Too far?

7. Olson argues that the rise of executive oversight has effected a "quiet shift" of power from the legislative and judicial branches. Congress, however, has a variety of tools for exercising control of regulatory agencies: Through its legislative powers, it can restrict the discretion of agencies; through its investigative and oversight powers, including highly publicized hearings at which agency officials are called upon to justify their decisions, Congress can monitor and influence regulatory agencies in implementing the laws; through its budgetary powers, it can place conditions on agency appropriations and "punish" agencies who disregard congressional views; through the Senate's confirmation pow-

ers, the Senate can disapprove high-level Department and agency nominations. Although Congress no longer has the one-house legislative veto, *INS v. Chadha*, 462 U.S. 919 (1983), it would seem that Congress possesses the tools to counterbalance a shift of power. What institutional impediments prevent Congress from being able to counteract systematic executive oversight? What would be the best means of enhancing congressional oversight of agencies? Is systematic legislative oversight desirable? What is the proper balance of power among the branches of government in the regulatory area? Does this depend upon whether the same political party controls the Congress and the Presidency? Consider again the example of EPA's asbestos rules, supra, p. 103.

PRESIDENT CLINTON'S REGULATORY PLANNING AND REVIEW EXECUTIVE ORDER

19 Admin. L. News (Winter 1994) 8-9

On September 30, 1993, President Clinton issued his long-awaited Executive Order to replace E.O. 12291, President Reagan's regulatory reform order. The similarities between the two orders are striking. Indeed, most of the differences merely codify practice under the Reagan order. Nevertheless, there are some material changes, and there is a substantially different tenor to the document.

Section 1 of E.O. 12866 states the Regulatory Philosophy and Principles President Clinton wishes agencies to follow. Agencies should only promulgate regulations when "necessary," and decisions as to whether and how to regulate should consider the cost and benefits of available regulatory alternatives, including the alternative of not regulating. Like the Reagan order, the Clinton order asks agencies to adopt approaches that "maximize net benefits" to society unless a law requires otherwise. [It also requires agencies to identify and aessess alternatives to direct regulation, including economic incentives. As with E.O. 12291, these principles apply "to the extent permitted by law."]

Section 3 is the definition section of the order. One potentially important change here is in the definition of "regulation." Under the Reagan order, the term was defined to include interpretive rules and statements of policy (sometimes called "non-legislative rules"), but the Clinton order [which is limited to rules or regulations "which the agency intends to have the force and effect of law"] has excluded such rules and policy statements from the definition of regulation and hence from the review function. This may create another incentive for agencies to utilize such rules instead of normal notice-and-comment rulemaking. What was defined as a "major rule" under the Reagan order is now a "significant regulatory action" [which includes rules which "may" have an annual effect on the economy of $100 million or more].

Unlike E.O. 12498, the Regulatory Plan submitted by agencies to OIRA does not purport to lock agencies into that plan, nor does OIRA play the same oversight role of these plans as it did under E.O. 12498. Rather, OIRA's function seems to be more of a clearing-house and co-ordination role. Section 4 also provides for an entity that seems to be the descendant of the Council on Competitiveness. This new entity is denominated the Regulatory Working Group, consisting of representatives of agencies with significant regulatory responsibilities, the Vice President, and presidential advisors, and chaired by the Administrator of OIRA.

Section 5 relates to existing regulations. Like Presidents Reagan and Bush before him, President Clinton is requiring agencies to review existing regulations to eliminate regulations that do not meet the philosophy and principles of regulation outline in the order. Agencies are required to create institutional review programs for periodic reviews. Again, shades of the Council on Competitiveness, the Working Group "and other interested entities" are to pursue the objectives of identifying and eliminating unnecessary existing regulations.

Section 6 contains the new rules for the centralized review of regulations. While most of E.O. 12291's review process remains, there are a number of new provisions. . . .

While E.O. 12291 required all proposed and final regulations to be sent to OIRA for review and comment before they were published in the Federal Register, E.O. 12866 does not require regulations that are not "significant regulatory actions" to be sent to OIRA at all. Agencies are to send lists of planned regulatory actions, both significant and otherwise to OIRA at specified times, and OIRA has 10 days to determine that a regulation the agency believes is not significant is significant. For those regulations that are significant, the review process seems indistinguishable from that conducted under the Reagan order for "major rules," including pre-publication submission of each proposed and final rule to OIRA for review and comment and the inclusion of a regulatory impact analysis requirement (although that term is not used) for regulations with over $100 million impact.

Under E.O. 12291, OIRA was required to complete its review within a limited period of time (never longer than 60 days). In practice, these limitations were often violated. Moreover, the order in essence allowed OIRA to toll the time periods by returning a rule to an agency for further review and comment. There was some criticism of the delay involved for several controversial rules, where some thought the review process was used for the purpose of delay. The Clinton order also imposes specified deadlines, but they are no longer than under the Reagan order (the longest period being 120 days). Moreover, under section 8 of the order, OMB can effectively toll that period by notifying the agency that OIRA is returning the rule for further consideration.

An aspect of practice under the Reagan order thought to create problems was so-called conduit communications, where persons would lobby OIRA (or the Council on Competitiveness) rather than (or in addition to) participating in the agency regulatory process. OIRA then could communicate these concerns, as if they were its own, to the agency. . . .

The order now requires that only the Administrator of OIRA (or a particular designee) can receive oral communications from persons outside the executive branch, and no meeting with outside persons can take place without inviting a representative from the affected agency. Any written communications to OIRA from outside persons must be forwarded to the affected agency. Information about these contacts and communications must be made available to the public. Moreover, the order specifies that when OIRA returns a rule to an agency for further consideration, OIRA put its reasons in writing. After the regulatory actions have been published, OIRA is to make public all documents exchanged between the agency and OIRA.

Section 7 relates to conflict resolution. The Administrator of OIRA is primarily responsible for resolving conflicts between agency heads and OIRA. When the conflict cannot be resolved by the Administrator, the President or the Vice President (if requested by the President) shall resolve it. . . .

QUESTIONS

What are the most important differences between Clinton's order and Reagan's orders? The most important similarities? Does the language matter less than how is it applied and enforced? Does Clinton's order demonstrate that the criticism of Reagan's orders were partisan, not principled?

2.   ADMINISTRATIVE LAW AND JUDICIAL REVIEW

In addition to executive and legislative oversight, the principal means of controlling agency action is through the procedural requirements imposed by administrative law and judicial review of both the procedures employed by the agency and the substantive decision reached. Through these processes, interested parties influence the outcome of the regulatory process.

The traditional model of American administrative law began to develop in the late nineteenth century, when the state and federal governments first began widespread regulation of private economic activity, particularly railroads and other public utilities. Judicial review was made available (either by statutory provision or judge-made law) to regulated firms to challenge government controls on the ground that they were not authorized by the relevant statute creating the agency in question and empowering it to act. In effect, courts policed administrative conformance to the legislative will at the behest of those resisting the coercive exercise of government power against them. In order to facilitate judicial control of administrative action, agencies were generally required to follow court-type adjudicative procedures in making decisions in particular cases: The decisions had to be based on evidence developed through trial-type adversary proceedings (including cross-examination of witnesses) and encapsulated in a printed record forming the basis for judicial review. Courts would utilize this record to determine whether the agency's findings of fact were supported by evidence; in most instances the reviewing court would not determine the facts de novo, but would defer to the agency's determinations provided they were reasonably supported in light of all the relevant evidence of record (the "substantial evidence" standard of review). Courts would also review the agency's resolution of the legal issues involved. While in theory courts would themselves decide all questions of law, in practice courts deferred to the agency's choice of law or policy so long as the agency complied, to a greater or lesser extent, with relevant statutory requirements (as construed by the court). Judicial review thus operated as a form of "transmission belt" to ensure agency conformance with the legislative will. The essential elements of the traditional model are codified in the federal Administrative Procedure Act, 5 U.S.C. §§551 et seq.

This traditional model of judicial review, which has been applied with greater and lesser degrees of rigor depending upon the prevailing political climate (the later New Deal era was, for example, one of considerable judicial deference to agencies), the particular agency involved, and the confidence reposed by individual judges in the administrative process. However, a number of developments in the last 25 years have exposed some limitations and weaknesses in the traditional model. These developments have been most notable at the federal level, and it is federal administrative law that will be the focus of this chapter.

As discussed above, a central administrative law problem is that of agency discretion resulting from broad legislative mandates creating extensive regulatory programs with little specific guidance as to which policies the agency should follow. The Federal Communications Act, §307(a), 47 U.S.C. §307(a), for example, directs the FCC to issue broadcasting licenses in the "public convenience, interest, or necessity." While recent environmental statutes, such as the Clean Air Act and

CWA, are in many instances far more detailed, they often (as we have seen) fail to provide much guidance for agency decision in many cases. Under the traditional model of administrative law, courts are limited to keeping agencies within the bounds of their statutory authority. Where agency statutes are vague, general or ambiguous, application of the traditional model leaves the agency with considerable freedom of choice. This was thought an advantage in the heyday of the New Deal during the late 1930s, when champions of the administrative process believed that social and economic problems could best be solved by giving free rein to the expert wisdom of agency officials specializing in a particular type of regulation. More recently, however, there has been considerable disillusion with the notion of "expertise" as a solvent of difficult social and economic problems. Regulatory issues are increasingly seen as involving choices among competing social and economic interests and values that cannot be resolved on technical grounds. Moreover, bureaucratic agencies making such choices are often viewed as biased in favor of certain agency missions and client interest groups. As a result, there have been increased demands on the courts to go beyond the traditional model of judicial review in order to control agency discretion in policy making.

Courts have, by and large, refused to respond to the problem of agency discretion by simply substituting their judgment for that of the agency as to social and economic policy choices. Instead, they have sought to control the agency's choices through procedural techniques. Agencies have come to rely less on case by case adjudication to make important policy decisions, and much more on rulemaking, where formal trial-type hearings are generally not required. In response, courts have developed new notice and comment procedural requirements for rulemaking. Agencies have been repeatedly directed by courts to explain their discretionary choices in great detail by reference to relevant evidence. In addition courts in some cases have narrowly construed agencies' statutory power in areas where its exercise had been especially troubling.

In order to meet criticism that agencies are biased in favor of the industries that they regulate or other client interests, courts have increasingly opened up the formal processes of agency decision and judicial review to representatives of consumer organizations, environmental groups, and other loosely organized "public" interests. The effort has been to ensure the representation of all affected interests in formal decisional processes designed to enhance agency responsiveness to all of the various constituencies with a stake in their decisions.

However, the process of transforming administrative law from the traditional model, designed to limit (by reference to statutory directives) the power of agencies to impose sanctions on regulated firms, to the new "interest representation" model has created difficulties. Procedural formalities and judicial review are expensive and time consuming. An important question is the extent to which courts will seek to control traditionally more informal means of policy making through additional procedural requirements. Excessive procedural requirements could threaten to paralyze the administrative process. Moreover, it is not clear the extent to which procedural requirements in fact produce better or more balanced agency decisions. However, if courts abandon insistence on procedural requirements, they are seemingly faced with a choice between either substituting their policy judgments for those of the agency, or largely abandoning the effort to control administrative discretion. A further consideration is whether the new approach to administration unduly diffuses decisional responsibility and impedes coordinated dispatch of public policy.

This chapter and the next, which deals with litigation under the Natural Environmental Policy Act, will explore these issues in the context of decisions by federal agencies affecting the environment. By far the greatest bulk of environmental litigation today consists of judicial review of administrative action or inaction. These two chapters cannot pretend to illustrate all of the major administrative law doctrines and issues that an environmental litigant must know. They only highlight a few of the more important matters from the viewpoint of legal importance and intellectual interest.[3]

3. THE RISE OF LEGAL ENVIRONMENTAL LAW

TURNER, THE LEGAL EAGLES

Amicus J. (Winter 1988) 25-28

Washington, D.C., in the early 1960s was in ferment. Young Jack Kennedy had been elected president and appointed an eloquent Westerner, Stewart Udall, to run the Department of the Interior. Big Ed Muskie of Maine, chairman of the Senate Public Works Committee, was the congressional Democrat most concerned with ever-worsening problems of pollution. His Republican counterpart was John Sherman Cooper of Kentucky. They were determined to stop American industry from ruining the public health and poisoning land, air, and water, but they had little to work with besides their powers of persuasion.

Accordingly, they evolved a jawboning process called the conference. Captains of the major polluting industries would be called in to

---

3. More comprehensive discussion of administrative law can be found in K. Davis & R. Pierce, Administrative Law Treatise 3d ed. 1994; B. Schwartz, Administrative Law (3d ed. 1991).

discuss ways of reducing pollution from manufacturing processes and products. The intended outcome of the conferences was an agreement on what pollution-control measures were economically and technically feasible.

These discussions produced little in the way of concrete improvements and convinced most law-makers that the country would never achieve any significant degree of pollution control without standards that required companies to go beyond economically and technically feasible control technologies toward the cleanest technology available. The decision to "drive" technology began with a system of permits issued under the Water Quality Improvement Act.

By the end of the decade, public concern over the looming environmental crisis was swelling fast. Earth Day was just around the corner.

It was against this background that the country's tiny environmental law establishment met at a conference center called Airlie House in the foothills of Virginia's Shenandoah Mountains. It was autumn 1969. Fifty people attended, some fresh out of law school and most others early practitioners of a field not even referred to as *environmental law*. The Environmental Defense Fund was by then in business, started wholly by volunteers, and was starting to use the courts to make life miserable for the pesticide industry. The Natural Resources Defense Council and the Sierra Club Legal Defense Fund were as yet little more than gleams in the eyes of a handful of idealistic young attorneys.

The conferees were full of fire and enthusiasm. They talked passionately about various legal approaches that might be used to defend the environment. Some advocated relying on the doctrine of public trust. A feature of English common law on which much of our legal system is based, the doctrine holds that the governing body has certain responsibilities to care for and protect those things held in common by all citizens. This might be extended to lakes, rivers, parks, marshes, wildlife and so forth.

Many suggested building on common law, which draws on previous decisions and opinions of the courts, rather than statutes to bolster a claim of injury. Consider a factory that discharges noxious chemicals into a creek. It is well established in common law that a person who injures another can be sued for compensation. Under common law, then, a property owner downstream from the factory could go to court seeking compensation for damage to his property and his health caused by the polluted water. Wholesale reliance on common law presumably would not have required the network of laws and agencies that now exists. The courts, on the other hand, would have been called upon to decide if avoidable injury had been inflicted by another party. If the plaintiff was victorious, his or her case could be cited and built upon by others claiming similar sorts of injury. At the time, many people believed that such an approach to environmental protection would have clogged the courts with thousands of cases and resulted in hundreds of different interpretations of similar cases. The feeling among most conferees was that common law would not provide sufficient national perspective or be comprehensive enough to improve environmental quality.

Some delegates suggested that the lawyers turn their attention to establishing a constitutional right to a healthy environment by bringing cases based on the Fourteenth Amendment to the Constitution. That amendment forbids infringement of liberty or taking of property without due process of law, the general idea being that damage inflicted on the environment by loggers, miners, polluters, or others could be headed off by suits that would argue that due process was being abused.

Others, notable among them the former New Hampshire Governor Philip Hoff and California Congressman Pete McCloskey, anticipated that the public's growing concerns about environmental quality would lead to demands for government intervention. "We are going to be deluged with environmental legislation from all quarters in the period of the next few years," Hoff told the conferees. "Conservation is going to have a very, very sharp focus in Congress in the next few years," agreed McCloskey. How right they were.

Within a few months, President Nixon had signed into law the National Environmental Policy Act (NEPA). A torrent of federal laws followed, among them: the Clean Air Act, the Clean Water Act, and the Endangered Species Act. The lawyers suddenly had a whole new arsenal of weapons. New initiatives in public trust, common law, and constitutional protections were deferred, as the lawyers delved into the statutes. And from that period on, litigation would become one of the most important tools conservationists had at their disposal.

But new laws would not be of much use without the right to bring a case to court in the first place, a right that had been denied citizens, in many instances, until the mid-sixties.

Until then, lawyers have had a very difficult time persuading courts to hear cases involving land-use disagreements, for example, since the plaintiffs could not prove — indeed, they did not claim — that a certain decision would harm them economically, the traditional requirement for what is known as "standing to sue."

Then, in the early sixties, the Consolidated Edison Company proposed to build a huge pumped storage plant on the Hudson River at Storm King Mountain near the U.S. Military Academy at West Point. The project became the premier environmental crusade in the state, but the Federal Power Commission ignored the protests and gave the project its blessing.

An organization called the Scenic Hudson Preservation Conference and three towns in the area then filed suit against the FPC. As expected, the commission asked the court to dismiss the case since the plaintiffs claimed no pecuniary interest in the project. But in a land-mark decision, the Court of Appeals for the Second Circuit ruled that Scenic Hudson should be allowed to bring suit owing to its "aesthetic, conservational, and recreational" interest in the area. The idea of a non-economic interest being sufficient to establish standing was born. The Scenic Hudson case also broke new ground by requiring that agencies consider the alternatives (including the alternative of doing nothing) and validating the conservationists' claim that scenic values should be weighted against economic values. Soon after, in a Sierra Club case brought to block a ski development at Mineral King Valley in the Sierra Nevada, the Supreme Court ruled that all the club had to do to establish standing was to allege that the interests of its members would be harmed. With some exceptions, standing has not been a serious hurdle since.

NEPA ushered in a new era of environmental awareness by requiring federal agencies to include environmental protection in all their plans and activities. And it invented the environmental impact statement, the EIS, a methodology and instrument for assessing the likely effect of projects agencies intend to build, finance, or permit. Most important, the EIS required agencies to investigate alternative ways of accomplishing the same purpose. (The alternative to building a power plant along a scenic coastline, for example, might be a program of energy conservation that would eliminate the necessity for a new facility.) NEPA also created a Council on Environmental Quality to advise the president. The center of considerable influence throughout the seventies, CEQ has withered under the Reagan administration and awaits rejuvenation.

To complete the burst of activity, Richard Nixon created the Environmental Protection Agency, which has since become the biggest bureaucracy in government outside the military. When Congress passes a pollution-control law, it is most often EPA which first must issue regulations and then enforce the law. Failure to do so can bring swift legal action, but the action may be against the government itself (as it often has been) for failing to issue regulation on time, or failing to set a proper standard, or failing to enforce its own regulations once they are in place.

Not surprisingly, attorneys, who had played supporting parts in environmental struggles up to that time, took center stage. According to some it changed everything. Rick Sutherland, co-founder of the Los Angeles-based Center for Law in the Public Interest and for the past ten years executive director of the Sierra Club Legal Defense Fund, says simply, "Litigation is the most important thing the environmental movement has done over the past fifteen years."

David Sive, who was involved in the famous Scenic Hudson case and is one of the field's pioneers is more encompassing. "In no other political and social movement has litigation played such an important and dominant role. Not even close."

John Adams, the first and so far only executive director of the Natural Resources Defense Council, echoes the sentiment, saying that "the legal victories won in the late sixties and early seventies formed the foundation on which the modern environmental movement is built."

NOTES AND QUESTIONS

1. Who do public interest environmental organizations represent? How are they funded? How do they solve the free-rider problems associated with collective goods like environmental protection?

2. What are and what should be the objectives of environmental organizations? How can environmental groups be most effective in achieving these objectives? Through participation in regulatory and other administrative proceedings? Litigation? Lobbying legislatures? Grass roots organizing and public education? Should they focus exclusively on environmental objectives, without regard to other social and economic concerns? What are the lessons of the civil rights movements for the environmental movement?

The Birth of Modern Environmental Advocacy

As highlighted in the preceding article, the *Scenic Hudson* litigation, with its innovative use of the lawsuit to hold accountable and influence public and private decisionmakers, ushered in the modern era of environmental advocacy. As you read through these materials, consider the impact of *Scenic Hudson I* on access to judicial review, procedural requirements for public agencies, and the scope of judicial review of agency decisions. *Scenic Hudson I* set important precedent for administrative law generally. At the same time, the *Scenic Hudson II* decision suggests some of the possible limitations of administrative law as a tool to promote environmental values.

SCENIC HUDSON PRESERVATION CONF. V. FPC (I)

354 F.2d 608, 619 (2d Cir. 1965)

HAYS, Circuit Judge:
[Consolidated Edison proposed to build a massive pumped storage hydroelectric project on the west side of the Hudson River at Storm

King Mountain. The project consisted of a water reservoir, a power house, and power lines. The project involved construction of a giant reservoir atop a scenic mountain on the Hudson north of New York City. During off-peak demand hours, generating facilities in the city would power pumps to raise water from the Hudson up to the reservoir. During off-peak periods, the water would be released back to the Hudson through turbines, generating electricity. The project was estimated to cost $162 million. Conservationists opposed its construction.

Consolidated Edison needed a license for the project from the Federal Power Commission (FPC) (now the Federal Energy Regulatory Commission). After elaborate hearings the FPC granted the license. The Commission noted that under the Federal Power Act, it must decide whether the project would be "best adapted to a comprehensive plan for improving or developing a waterway or waterways for the use or benefit of interstate or foreign commerce, for the improvement and utilization of water-power development, and for other beneficial public uses, including recreational purposes."]

Respondent argues that "petitioners do not have standing to obtain review" because they "make no claim of any personal economic injury resulting from the Commission's action." Section 313(b) of the Federal Power Act, . . . reads:

> (b) Any party to a proceeding under this [Act] aggrieved by an order issued by the Commission in such proceeding may obtain a review of such order in the United States Court of Appeals for any circuit wherein the licensee or public utility to which the order relates is located. . . .

. . . The Federal Power Act seeks to protect non-economic as well as economic interests. . . .

In order to insure that the Federal Power Commission will adequately protect the public interest in the aesthetic, conservational, and recreational aspects of power development, those who by their activities and conduct have exhibited a special interest in such areas, must be held to be included in the class of "aggrieved" parties under §313(b). We hold that the Federal Power Act gives petitioners a legal right to protect their special interests. . . .

Moreover, petitioners have sufficient economic interest to establish their standing. The New York-New Jersey Trail Conference, one of the two conservation groups that organized Scenic Hudson, has some seventeen miles of trailways in the area of Storm King Mountain. Portions of these trails would be inundated by the construction of the project's reservoir.

We see no justification for the Commission's fear that our determination will encourage "literally thousands" to intervene and seek review in future proceedings. . . . Our experience with public actions confirms the view that the expense and vexation of legal proceedings is not lightly undertaken.

[The Court of Appeals found that the Commission's decision had failed adequately to consider several issues, the most important of which consisted of testimony by Mr. Alexander Lurkis, a former Chief Engineer of the New York City Bureau of Gas and Electric, in which he presented "a detailed proposal for using gas turbines" as an alternative to the proposed project, a proposal that he claimed would save consumers $132 million. The record contained only a "scanty," less than ten-page discussion by Commission staff seeking to explain why the gas turbine alternative would not work. Although Mr. Lurkis did not present his plan until two months after the FPC granted the license, and four months after final oral argument, a reviewing court is statutorily authorized to require the FPC to consider "additional evidence" if it is "material" and there were "reasonable grounds for failure to adduce" it earlier.]

Especially in a case of this type, where public interest and concern is so great, the Commission's refusal to receive the Lurkis testimony, as well as proffered information on fish protection devices and underground transmission facilities, exhibits a disregard of the statute and of judicial mandates instructing the Commission to probe all feasible alternatives. . . . As Commissioner Ross said in his dissent:

> I do feel the public is entitled to know on the record that no stone has been left unturned. . . . A regulatory commission can insure continuing confidence in its decisions only when it has used its staff and its own expertise in a manner not possible for the uninformed and poorly financed public. . . . [I]t should be possible to resolve all doubts as to alternative sources. This may have been done but the record doesn't speak. . . .

The Commission has an affirmative duty to inquire into and consider all relevant facts. . . . The Commission should reexamine all questions on which we have found the record insufficient and all related matters [including danger to fish, power pooling, and the use of underground transmission wires]. The Commission's renewed proceedings must include as a basic concern the preservation of natural beauty and of national historic shrines, keeping in mind that, in our affluent society, the cost of a project is only one of several factors to be considered. The record as it comes to us fails markedly to make out a case for the Storm King project on, among other matters, costs, public convenience and necessity, and absence of reasonable alternatives. . . . [This case is] remanded for further proceedings.

SCENIC HUDSON PRESERVATION CONF. V. FPC (II)

453 F.2d 463, 468 (2d Cir.), reh'g and hearing en banc
denied by equally divided court, *453 F.2d 494, (1971)* cert.
denied, *407 U.S. 926 (1972)*

HAYS, Circuit Judge.

[This case reached the court five years after the remand by the court of appeals in *Scenic Hudson I.* In the meantime the Commission had held an additional hearing involving 100 hearing days, 675 exhibits and a record of 19,000 pages. In its new opinion] the Commission reviewed the power needs of the area served . . . and considered several possible alternatives to the Storm King project in terms of reliability, cost, air and noise pollution, and overall environmental impact. Concluding that there was no satisfactory alternative, the Commission evaluated the environmental effects of the project itself. It concluded that the scenic impact would be minimal, that no historic site would be adversely affected, that the fish would be adequately protected and the proposed park and scenic overlook would enhance recreational facilities. . . . [It found that] further undergrounding of transmission lines would result in unreliability . . . and would be too costly. [The Commission issued a license, again approving the project, but as modified to put the powerhouse entirely underground (instead of just 80 percent underground), to include fish-protection devices, to reroute certain transmission lines, and to include a park and other recreational facilities.]

Where the Commission has considered all relevant factors, and where the challenged findings, based on such full considerations are supported . . . , we will not allow our personal views as to the desirability of the result reached . . . to influence us. . . . [T]he proceedings of the Commission and its report meet the objections upon the basis of which we remanded the earlier determination . . . and . . . the evidence supporting the Commission's conclusions amply meets the statutory requirement. . . . We do not consider the five years of additional investigation which followed our remand were spent in vain. . . . [T]he Commission has reevaluated the entire project [and made some modifications]. Whether the project as it now stands represents a perfect balance of these needs is not for this court to decide. . . .

NOTES AND QUESTIONS

1. On what basis did the court grant petitioners standing to secure judicial review, and why?

2. What law gives the court the power to remand in *Scenic Hudson I?*

3. Why should the Commission not have been able to reject the gas turbine testimony on the basis of its expertise? What are the implications of the court's decision for the procedures which the Commission must follow and the content of the administrative record and of the Commission's decisions in future licensing proceedings?

4. Wasn't the remand "in vain"? After all, the Commission reached the same result. But wait: The five-year delay meant mounting costs, a deterioration in Consolidated Edison's financial position, and changing power needs, *with the consequence that the Storm King project was never built.* Can the court fairly say, then, that the litigation was not "in vain"? From whose point of view? Of course, the object is not to stop the project but to produce a better decisionmaking process. Would you say that the litigation exemplifies that better process? What are the implications of the *Scenic Hudson* litigation for the accountability of public decisionmakers, the quality of technical analysis, and the incorporation of environmental considerations in substantive decisions?

B. ACCESS TO JUDICIAL REVIEW AND PROBLEMS OF STANDING

There are a number of threshold obstacles that must be surmounted by a litigant challenging administrative action or inaction.

First is the problem of jurisdiction. Most modern regulatory statutes provide explicitly for judicial review of specified agency action in specified courts. For example, the Clean Air Act provides that "citizen suit" actions to enforce nondiscretionary agency duties against EPA are to be brought in federal district court, §304, while actions for review of other EPA actions must be brought in a court of appeals, §307.

Where statutory review provisions are absent or do not apply, a litigant may generally invoke the federal question jurisdiction of the district courts to issue declaratory judgments and to award injunctive relief against unlawful action by government officials. See 28 U.S.C. §§1331, 1361, 2201.

The Administrative Procedure Act (APA) §702 waives the sovereign immunity of the federal government in cases where the government's action is challenged as contrary to law and the plaintiff seeks injunctive or declaratory relief. These forms of specific relief, or a judicial order setting aside the agency action in question and thereby rendering it of no legal effect, are the normal remedies obtained by successful plaintiffs. These forms of relief are discussed further in Chapter 8, infra p. 1015, and 9, infra p. 1011. Money damages are not available unless a statute, such as the Federal Torts Claims Act, 60 Stat. 842 (1946) specifically provides for government liability. In addition, as discussed in Chapter 9, infra p. 1019, certain forms of government regulation and other action may be held to be a "taking" of private property. In such cases the Fifth Amendment to the Constitution requires the government to pay just compensation. The property owner must seek payment by filing an action in the United States Claims Court or, in certain cases, federal district court, pursuant to the Tucker Act.

Even where jurisdiction is otherwise available to hear a claim, review may be barred under §701(a) of the Administrative Procedure Act on the ground that statutes expressly or impliedly preclude review,[4] or on the ground that the matter challenged is committed by law to agency discretion. However, the prevailing tendency is to read these exceptions narrowly and to affirm a strong presumption in favor of review. *Abbott Laboratories v. Gardner,* 387 U.S. 136 (1967); *Citizens to Preserve Overton Park v. Volpe,* 401 U.S. 402 (1971), reproduced at pages 876-881 infra. In *Heckler v. Chaney,* 470 U.S. 821 (1985), however, the Court held that there is a presumption of nonreviewability of agency decisions declining to initiate certain enforcement actions. *Heckler* is discussed further at infra, pp. 846-848.

Even if review is not precluded altogether, there are important judge-made rules governing the *timing* of judicial review. The doctrine of ripeness limits the availability of review until the administrative process has crystallized in some specific, final decision. See *Abbott Laboratories,* supra. The doctrine of exhaustion of administrative remedies requires a litigant to utilize available administrative procedures for hearing his claim at the agency level before seeking to present that claim to a reviewing court. For discussion of these doctrines, see, L. Jaffe, Judicial Control of Administrative Action, Chapters 10 and 11 (1965).

A final limitation on access to judicial review that has attracted special prominence in the field of environmental law consists of doctrines of standing that define and limit the class of persons who are entitled to seek judicial review of administrative action. In the United States, judicial review of assertedly unlawful agency action has tradition-

---

4. An example of such preclusion is the provision in §307(b)(1) of the Clean Air Act requiring that petitions to review EPA's promulgation or approval of a SIP be brought within 30 days unless the grounds for challenge arose solely after the 30-day period. This provision should probably be read to bar not only court of appeals review under §307 after the 30-day period has run, but also access to the general jurisdiction of the federal district courts. For discussion, see Currie, Judicial Review Under the Federal Pollution Laws, 62 Iowa L. Rev. 1221, 1254-1260 (1977); *Union Electric,* supra, p. 277.

ally *not* been available to any person willing to undertake the costs of litigation. In the federal courts, a litigant must at a minimum satisfy the "case or controversy" requirement of Article III of the Constitution. But in many cases litigants must satisfy additional requirements.[5] A statute explicitly providing for judicial review of a given agency's actions may specify and limit the persons entitled to seek such review. See Federal Environmental Pesticide Control Act of 1972, 7 U.S.C. §136n(b) (review of pesticide cancellation orders by persons "adversely affected" who had participated in agency proceedings). Also, the federal courts have developed principles of standing to deal with cases where a given agency's statute provides for judicial review without specifying who may obtain it, or cases where a litigant seeks review under 28 U.S.C. §1331 or other general jurisdictional statutes vesting jurisdiction in the district courts; these statutes do not specify who may sue. These judicially developed principles of standing are based on §702 of the 1946 Administrative Procedure Act (APA), which provides that "a person suffering legal wrong because of agency action, or adversely affected or aggrieved within the meaning of a relevant statute" is entitled to judicial review thereof. This provision was itself a restatement of standing principles that had previously been developed by the federal courts in a common law fashion.

These judge-made rules of standing originally limited judicial review to persons with traditional liberty or property interests, of the sort protected by the common law, that had allegedly been infringed by government officials. If officials seized a person's property to satisfy a tax assessment or restrained his or her liberty by halting the conduct of a business, then court review would be available to test the officials' claim that their actions were duly authorized by statute. In the context of government regulation of private economic activity, this approach to standing normally limited the availability of judicial review to regulated firms subject to governmental sanctions, and excluded standing for competitors or the beneficiaries of regulatory schemes, such as consumers. See Stewart, The Reformation of American Administrative Law, 88 Harv. L. Rev. 1667, 1723-1725 (1975).

Over the past several decades, judge-made rules of standing have been liberalized at an increasingly rapid rate. Beginning in the 1960s, courts permitted additional categories of persons affected by administrative action to challenge its legality in court, including consumers, e.g., *Office of Communication of the United Church of Christ v. FCC*, 359 F.2d 994 (D.C. Cir. 1966) (viewers' standing to challenge broadcast license renewal) and environmental groups, e.g., *Scenic Hudson I*, supra. As ex-

---

5. Somewhat broader rules of standing have been developed in some state courts. See L. Jaffe, Judicial Control of Administrative Action 531-536 (1965).

emplified in the opinion in *Scenic Hudson I,* the courts' rationale for these expanded rules of standing was that the relevant substantive statute reflected an implicit purpose to protect the interests of these litigants, and that this statutorily-protected interest was a basis for standing on a par with traditional liberty and property interests. Their deeper foundations were a judicial perception of the increased reach and power of administrative agencies, a growing concern that such agencies might be unduly responsive to the interests of the regulated or otherwise afflicted with biases and "tunnel vision," and a consequent readiness to extend the right of judicial review to a wide range of affected interests in order to afford judicial scrutiny of the agencies' treatment of collective or "public" interests that might be effectively "underrepresented" in the administrative process. See Stewart, The Reformation of American Administrative Law, 88 Harv. L. Rev. 1667, 1711-1734 (1975).

The Supreme Court gave its imprimatur to broadened judge-made principles of standing in *Association of Data Processing Service Organizations v. Camp,* 397 U.S. 150 (1970), which upheld the right to judicial review of competitors challenging as contrary to relevant statutes a federal agency decision authorizing national banks to engage in the data processing business. The Court, in an opinion by Justice Douglas, held that in the absence of a given statute's intent to narrow or expand the availability of judicial review, standing in the federal courts to challenge federal government action extended to any person who (a) suffered "injury in fact" as a result of an agency's conduct and (b) was also "arguably within the zone of interests to be protected or regulated" under the substantive statute governing the agency's action. The Court said that the "injury in fact" test was constitutionally required by Article III of the Constitution, which limits the judicial power to "cases and controversies." The "arguably within the zone" test was said to be a construction of the APA, supra. These rulings had little precedent in prior standing law. Justice Douglas clearly intended that the new doctrinal framework that he offered would liberalize standing. Note that the reference to persons "arguably" "protected" as well as "regulated" by the relevant statute in his test would extend standing broadly to the beneficiaries of environmental and other regulatory programs. Developments since *Data Processing* are reflected in the materials which follow. As they indicate, environmental law cases have been at the center of debate over how broad access to the federal courts should be.

1. EVOLUTION OF STANDING DOCTRINE

SIERRA CLUB V. MORTON

405 U.S. 727, 728 (1972)

Mr. Justice STEWART delivered the opinion of the Court.

I

The Mineral King Valley is an area of great natural beauty nestled in the Sierra Nevada Mountains in Tulare County, California, adjacent to Sequoia National Park. It has been part of the Sequoia National Forest since 1926, and is designated as a national game refuge by special Act of Congress. Though once the site of extensive mining activity, Mineral King is now used almost exclusively for recreational purposes. Its relative inaccessibility and lack of development have limited the number of visitors each year, and at the same time have preserved the valley's quality as a quasi-wilderness area largely uncluttered by the products of civilization.

[The United States Forest Service, which is entrusted with the maintenance and administration of national forests, invited bids from private developers for the construction and operation of a ski resort in Mineral King that would also serve as a summer recreation area, and selected a proposal of Walt Disney Enterprises, Inc.]

The final Disney plan, approved by the Forest Service in January 1969, outlines a $35 million complex of motels, restaurants, swimming pools, parking lots, and other structures designed to accommodate 14,000 visitors daily. This complex is to be constructed on 80 acres of the valley floor under a 30-year use permit from the Forest Service. Other facilities, including ski lifts, ski trails, a cog-assisted railway, and utility installations, are to be constructed on the mountain slopes and in other parts of the valley under a revocable special-use permit. To provide access to the resort, the State of California proposes to construct a highway 20 miles in length. A section of this road would traverse Sequoia National Park, as would the proposed high-voltage power line needed to provide electricity for the resort. Both the highway and the power line require the approval of the Department of the Interior, which is entrusted with the preservation and maintenance of the national parks.

Representatives of the Sierra Club, who favor maintaining Mineral King largely in its present state, followed the progress of recreational planning for the valley with close attention and increasing dismay. They unsuccessfully sought a public hearing on the proposed development in 1965, and in subsequent correspondence with officials of the Forest Service and the Department of the Interior, they expressed the Club's objections to Disney's plan as a whole and to particular features included in it. In June 1969 the Club filed the present suit in the United States District Court for the Northern District of California, seeking a declaratory judgment that various aspects of the proposed development contravene federal laws and regulations governing the preservation of national parks, forests, and game refuges,[6] and also seeking preliminary and permanent injunctions restraining the federal officials involved from granting their approval or issuing permits in connection with the Mineral King project. The petitioner Sierra Club sued as a membership corporation with "a special interest in the conservation and the sound maintenance of the national parks, game refuges and forests of the country," and invoked the judicial review provisions of the Administrative Procedure Act, 5 U.S.C. §701 et seq.

After two days of hearings, the district court granted the requested preliminary injunction. It rejected the respondents' challenge to the Sierra Club's standing to sue, and determined that the hearing had raised questions "concerning possible excess of statutory authority, sufficiently substantial and serious to justify a preliminary injunction. . . ." The respondents appealed, and the Court of Appeals for the Ninth Circuit reversed. 433 F.2d 24. With respect to the petitioner's standing, the court noted that there was "no allegation in the complaint that members of the Sierra Club would be affected by the actions of [the respondents] other than the fact that the actions are personally displeasing or distasteful to them," id., at 33, and concluded:

> We do not believe such club concern without a showing of more direct interest can constitute standing in the legal sense sufficient to challenge the exercise of responsibilities on behalf of all the citizens by two cabinet level officials of the government acting under Congressional and Constitutional authority. Id. at 30.

---

6. As analyzed by the district court, the complaint alleged violations of law falling into four categories. First, it claimed that the special use permit for construction of the resort exceeded the maximum-acreage limitation placed upon such permits by 16 U.S.C. §197, and that issuance of a "revocable" use permit was beyond the authority of the Forest Service. Second, it challenged the proposed permit for the highway through Sequoia National Park on the grounds that the highway would not serve any of the purposes of the park, in alleged violation of 16 U.S.C. §1, and that it would destroy timber and other natural resources protected by 16 U.S.C. §§41 and 43. Third, it claimed that the Forest Service and the Department of the Interior had violated their own regulations by failing to hold adequate public hearings on the proposed project. Finally, the complaint asserted that 16 U.S.C. §45c requires specific congressional authorization of a permit for construction of a power transmission line within the limits of a national park.

Alternatively, the court of appeals held that the Sierra Club had not made an adequate showing of irreparable injury and likelihood of success on the merits to justify issuance of a preliminary injunction. The court thus vacated the injunction. The Sierra Club filed a petition for a writ of certiorari which we granted, 401 U.S. 907, to review the questions of federal law presented.

II

The first question presented is whether the Sierra Club has alleged facts that entitle it to obtain judicial review of the challenged action. . . .

The Sierra Club relies upon . . . the Administrative Procedure Act (APA), 5 U.S.C. §702, which provides:

> A person suffering legal wrong because of agency action, or adversely affected or aggrieved by agency action within the meaning of a relevant statute, is entitled to judicial review thereof.

Early decisions under this statute interpreted the language as adopting the various formulations of "legal interest" and "legal wrong" then prevailing as constitutional requirements of standing. But, in *Data Processing Service v. Camp*, 397 U.S. 150, and *Barlow v. Collins*, 397 U.S. 150, decided the same day, we held more broadly that persons had standing to obtain judicial review of federal agency action under [§702] of the APA where they had alleged that the challenged action had caused them "injury in fact," and where the alleged injury was to an interest "arguably within the zone of interest to be protected or regulated" by the statutes that the agencies were claimed to have violated.[7]

. . . [N]either *Data Processing* nor *Barlow* addressed itself to the question, which has arisen with increasing frequency in federal courts in recent years, as to what must be alleged by persons who claim injury of a noneconomic nature to interests that are widely shared. That question is presented in this case.

III

The injury alleged by the Sierra Club will be incurred entirely by reason of the change in the uses to which Mineral King will be put, and

---

7. In deciding this case we do not reach any questions concerning the meaning of the "zone of interests" test or its possible application to the facts here presented.

the attendant change in the aesthetics and ecology of the area. Thus, in referring to the road to be built through Sequoia National Park, the complaint alleged that the development "would destroy or otherwise adversely affect the scenery, natural and historic objects and wildlife of the park and would impair the enjoyment of the park for future generations." We do not question that this type of harm may amount to an "injury in fact" sufficient to lay the basis for standing under [§702] of the APA. Aesthetic and environmental well-being, like economic well-being, are important ingredients of the quality of life in our society, and the fact that particular environmental interests are shared by the many rather than the few does not make them less deserving of legal protection through judicial process. But the "injury in fact" test requires more than an injury to a cognizable interest. It requires that the party seeking review be himself among the injured.

The impact of the proposed changes in the environment of Mineral King will not fall indiscriminately upon every citizen. The alleged injury will be felt directly only by those who use Mineral King and Sequoia National Park, and for whom the aesthetic and recreational values of the area will be lessened by the highway and ski resort. The Sierra Club failed to allege that it or its members would be affected in any of their activities or pastimes by the Disney development. Nowhere in the pleadings or affidavits did the Club state that its members use Mineral King for any purpose, much less that they use it in any way that would be significantly affected by the proposed actions of the respondents.[8]

---

8. The only reference in the pleadings to the Sierra Club's interest in the dispute is contained in paragraph 3 of the complaint, which reads in its entirety as follows:

> Plaintiff Sierra Club is a non-profit corporation organized and operating under the laws of the State of California, with its principal place of business in San Francisco, California since 1892. Membership of the club is approximately 78,000 nationally, with approximately 27,000 members residing in San Francisco Bay area. For many years the Sierra Club by its activities and conduct has exhibited a special interest in the conservation and the sound maintenance of the national parks, game refuges and forests of the country, regularly serving as a responsible representative of persons similarly interested. One of the principal purposes of the Sierra Club is to protect and conserve the national resources of the Sierra Nevada Mountains. Its interests would be vitally affected by the acts hereinafter described and would be aggrieved by those acts of the defendants as hereinafter more fully appears.

In an amici curiae brief filed in this Court by the Wilderness Society and others, it is asserted that the Sierra Club has conducted regular camping trips into the Mineral King area, and that various members of the Club have used and continue to use the area for recreational purposes. These allegations were not contained in the pleadings, nor were they brought to the attention of the court of appeals. Moreover, the Sierra Club in its reply brief specifically declines to

The trend of cases arising under the APA and other statutes authorizing judicial review of federal agency action has been toward recognizing that injuries other than economic harm are sufficient to bring a person within the meaning of the statutory language, and toward discarding the notion that an injury that is widely shared is ipso facto not an injury sufficient to provide the basis for judicial review. We noted this development with approval in *Data Processing*, 397 U.S., at 154, in saying that the interest alleged to have been injured "may reflect 'aesthetic, conservational, and recreational' as well as economic values." But broadening the categories of injury that may be alleged in support of standing is a different matter from abandoning the requirement that the party seeking review must himself have suffered an injury.

Some courts have indicated a willingness to take this latter step by conferring standing upon organizations that have demonstrated "an organizational interest in the problem" of environmental or consumer protection. *Environmental Defense Fund v. Hardin*, 138 U.S. App. D.C. 391, 395, 428 F.2d 1093, 1097. It is clear that an organization whose members are injured may represent those members in a proceeding for judicial review. See, e.g., *NAACP v. Button*, 371 U.S. 415, 428. But a mere "interest in a problem," no matter how longstanding the interest and no matter how qualified the organization is in evaluating the problem, is not sufficient by itself to render the organization "adversely affected" or "aggrieved" within the meaning of the APA. The Sierra Club is a large and long-established organization, with a historic commitment to the cause of protecting our Nation's natural heritage from man's depredations. But if a "special interest" in this subject were enough to entitle the Sierra Club to commence this litigation, there would appear to be no objective basis upon which to disallow a suit by any other bona fide "special interest" organization, however small or short-lived. And if any group with a bona fide "special interest" could initiate such litigation, it is difficult to perceive why any individual citizen with the same bona fide special interest would not also be entitled to do so.

The requirement that a party seeking review must allege facts showing that he is himself adversely affected does not insulate executive action from judicial review, nor does it prevent any public interests from being protected through the judicial process. It does serve as at least a rough attempt to put the decision as to whether review will be sought in the hands of those who have a direct stake in the outcome. That goal would be undermined were we to construe the APA to autho-

rely on its individualized interest, as a basis for standing. . . . Our decision does not, of course, bar the Sierra Club from seeking in the district court to amend its complaint by a motion under Rule 15, Federal Rules of Civil Procedure.

rize judicial review at the behest of organizations or individuals who seek to do no more than vindicate their own value preferences through the judicial process.[9] The principle that the Sierra Club would have us establish in this case would do just that.

As we conclude that the court of appeals was correct in its holding that the Sierra Club lacked standing to maintain this action, we do not reach any other questions presented in the petition, and we intimate no view on the merits of the complaint. The judgment is Affirmed.

Mr. Justice Powell and Mr. Justice Rehnquist took no part in the consideration or decision of this case.

Mr. Justice BRENNAN, dissenting.

I agree that the Sierra Club has standing for the reasons stated by my Brother Blackmun in Alternative No. 2 of his dissent. . . .

Mr. Justice DOUGLAS, dissenting.

I share the views of my brother Blackmun and would reverse the judgment below.

The critical question of "standing" would be simplified and also put neatly in focus if we fashioned a federal rule that allowed environmental issues to be litigated before federal agencies or federal courts in the name of the inanimate object about to be despoiled, defaced, or invaded by roads and bulldozers and where injury is the subject of public outrage. Contemporary public concern for protecting nature's ecological equilibrium should lead to the conferral of standing upon environmental objects to sue for their own preservation. See Stone, Should Trees Have Standing? — Toward Legal Rights for Natural Objects, 45 S. Cal. L. Rev. 450 (1972). This suit would therefore be more properly labeled as *Mineral King v. Morton.*

Inanimate objects are sometimes parties in litigation. A ship has a legal personality, a fiction found useful for maritime purposes. The corporation sole — a creature of ecclesiastical law — is an acceptable adversary and large fortunes ride on its cases. The ordinary corporation

---

9. Every schoolboy may be familiar with Alexis de Tocqueville's famous observation, written in the 1830's, that "[s]carcely any political question arises in the United States that is not resolved, sooner or later, into a judicial question." I Democracy in America 280 (1945). Less familiar, however, is de Tocqueville's further observation that judicial review is effective largely because it is not available simply at the behest of a partisan faction, but is exercised only to remedy a particular, concrete injury.

"It will be seen, also, that by leaving it to private interest to censure the law, and by intimately uniting the trial of the law with the trial of an individual, legislation is protected from wanton assaults and from the daily aggressions of party spirit. The errors of the legislator are exposed only to meet a real want; and it is always a positive and appreciable fact that must serve as the basis of a prosecution." Id., at 102.

is a "person" for purposes of the adjudicatory processes, whether it represents proprietary, spiritual, aesthetic, or charitable causes.

So it should be as respects valleys, alpine meadows, rivers, lakes, estuaries, beaches, ridges, groves of trees, swampland, or even air that feels the destructive pressures of modern technology and modern life. The river, for example, is the living symbol of all the life it sustains or nourishes — fish, aquatic insects, water ouzels, otter, fisher, deer, elk, bear, and all other animals, including man, who are dependent on it or who enjoy it for its sight, its sound, or its life. The river as plaintiff speaks for the ecological unit of life that is part of it. Those people who have a meaningful relation to that body of water — whether it be a fisherman, a canoeist, a zoologist, or a logger — must be able to speak for the values which the river represents and which are threatened with destruction.

[T]he pressures on agencies for favorable action one way or the other are enormous. The suggestion that Congress can stop action which is undesirable is true in theory; yet even Congress is too remote to give meaningful direction and its machinery is too ponderous to use very often. The federal agencies of which I speak are not venal or corrupt. But they are notoriously under the control of powerful interests who manipulate them through advisory committees, or friendly working relations, or who have that natural affinity with the agency which in time develops between the regulator and the regulated. . . .

The Forest Service — one of the federal agencies behind the scheme to despoil Mineral King — has been notorious for its alignment with lumber companies, although its mandate from Congress directs it to consider the various aspects of multiple use in its supervision of the national forests.

The voice of the inanimate object, therefore, should not be stilled. That does not mean that the judiciary takes over the managerial functions from the federal agency. It merely means that before these priceless bits of Americana (such as a valley, an alpine meadow, a river, or a lake) are forever lost or are so transformed as to be reduced to the eventual rubble of our urban environment, the voice of the existing beneficiaries of these environmental wonders should be heard. . . .

Ecology reflects the land ethic; and Aldo Leopold wrote in A Sand County Almanac 204 (1949), "The land ethic simply enlarges the boundaries of the community to include soils, waters, plants, and animals, or collectively, the land."

That, as I see it, is the issue of "standing" in the present case and controversy.

Mr. Justice BLACKMUN, dissenting.

The Court's opinion is a practical one espousing and adhering to traditional notions of standing as somewhat modernized by *Data Pro-*

cessing Service v. Camp, 397 U.S. 150 (1970). . . . If this were an ordinary case, I would join the opinion and the Court's judgment and be quite content.

But this is not ordinary, run-of-the-mill litigation. The case poses — if only we choose to acknowledge and reach them — significant aspects of a wide, growing, and disturbing problem, that is, the Nation's and the world's deteriorating environment with its resulting ecological disturbances. Must our law be so rigid and our procedural concepts so inflexible that we render ourselves helpless when the existing methods and the traditional concepts do not quite fit and do not prove to be entirely adequate for new issues?

The ultimate result of the Court's decision today, I fear, and sadly so, is that the 35.3 million-dollar complex, over 10 times greater than the Forest Service's suggested minimum, will now hastily proceed to completion; that serious opposition to it will recede in discouragement; and that Mineral King, the "area of great natural beauty nestled in the Sierra Nevada Mountains," to use the Court's words, will become defaced, at least in part, and, like so many other areas, will cease to be "uncluttered by the products of civilization."

I believe this will come about because: (1) The District Court, although it accepted standing for the Sierra Club and granted preliminary injunctive relief, was reversed by the Court of Appeals, and this Court now upholds that reversal. (2) With the reversal, interim relief by the District Court is now out of the question and a permanent injunction becomes most unlikely. (3) The Sierra Club may not choose to amend its complaint or, if it does desire to do so, may not, at this late date, be granted permission. (4) The ever-present pressure to get the project under way will mount. (5) Once under way, any prospect of bringing it to a halt will grow dim. Reasons, most of them economic, for not stopping the project will have a tendency to multiply. And the irreparable harm will be largely inflicted in the earlier stages of construction and development.

Rather then pursue the course the Court has chosen to take by its affirmance of the judgment of the Court of Appeals, I would adopt one of two alternatives:

1. I would reverse that judgment and, instead, approve the judgment of the District Court which recognized standing in the Sierra Club and granted preliminary relief. I would be willing to do this on condition that the Sierra Club forthwith amend its complaint to meet the specifications the Court prescribes for standing.

2. Alternatively, I would permit an imaginative expansion of our traditional concepts of standing in order to enable an organization such as the Sierra Club, possessed, as it is, of pertinent, bona fide, and well-recognized attributes and purposes in the area of environment, to litigate environmental issues. This incursion upon tradition need not

be very extensive. Certainly, it should be no cause for alarm. It is no more progressive than was the decision in *Data Processing* itself. It need only recognize the interest of one who has a provable, sincere, dedicated, and established status. We need not fear that Pandora's box will be opened or that there will be no limit to the number of those who desire to participate in environmental litigation. The courts will exercise appropriate restraints just as they have exercised them in the past. . . .

[A]ny resident of the Mineral King area — the real "user" — is an unlikely adversary for this Disney-governmental project. He naturally will be inclined to regard the situation as one that should benefit him economically. His fishing or camping or guiding or handyman or general outdoor prowess perhaps will find an early and ready market among the visitors. But that glow of anticipation will be short-lived at best. If he is a true lover of the wilderness — as is likely, or he would not be near Mineral King in the first place — it will not be long before he yearns for the good old days when masses of people — that 14,000 influx per day — and their thus far uncontrollable waste were unknown to Mineral King.

Do we need any further indication and proof that all this means that the area will no longer be one "of great natural beauty" and one "uncluttered by the products of civilization?" Are we to be rendered helpless to consider and evaluate allegations and challenges of this kind because of procedural limitations rooted in traditional concepts of standing? I suspect that this may be the result of today's holding. . . .

The Court chooses to conclude its opinion with a footnote reference to De Tocqueville. In this environmental context I personally prefer the older and particularly pertinent observation and warning of John Donne.[10]

NOTES AND QUESTIONS

1. *Sierra Club* is often regarded as a defeat for environmental groups, but it can more plausibly be regarded as a victory. Review the court's opinion carefully in order to ascertain just what must be alleged in the way of "injury in fact" by an organization challenging environmental harm attributable to federal agency action. In how many instances will the "injury in fact" requirement block all potential litigation?

---

10. "No man is an Island, entire of itself; every man is a piece of the Continent, a part of the maine; if a Clod bee washed away by the Sea, Europe is the lesse, as well as if a Promontorie were, as well as if a Mannor of thy friends or of thine owner were; any man's death diminishes me, because I am involved in Mankinde; And therefore never send to know for whom the bell tolls; it tolls for thee." Devotions XVII.

In *Hunt v. Washington State Apple Advertising Commn.*, 432 U.S. 333 (1977), the Supreme Court set forth a three-part test for determining whether an association has standing:

(a)   the association's members would have standing to sue in their own right;
(b)   the members' interests at stake are germane to the association's purpose;
(c)   the suit is such that it does not require the participation of individual members.

The Supreme Court recently affirmed this test in *International Union v. Brock*, 477 U.S. 274 (1986). See also *Humane Society of the United States v. Hodel*, 840 F.2d 45 (D.C. Cir. 1988), discussing the germaneness requirement at length and concluding that the Humane Society, an organization dedicated to the protection of living things, had standing on behalf of its members who visited Natural Wildlife Refuges to bring suit challenging the Interior Department's action in opening refuges to hunting.

2. As footnote 8 supra (footnote 8 of the court's opinion) makes clear, the Sierra Club could easily have satisfied the "injury in fact" requirement because its members used the Mineral King Valley. Why did the Club's lawyers expressly decline to rely on this fact? How do you think Sierra Club members who used the Valley would evaluate the lawyer's tactical decision? For the subsequent history of the Mineral King controversy, see Lundmark, Mester, Cordes & Sandals, *Mineral King Goes Downhill*, 5 Ecology L.Q. 555 (1976).

3. In view of the Sierra Club's ability to satisfy "injury in fact," wasn't the Court justified in declining to expand the test for standing further than required by the case before it? Would *Sierra Club* dictate denial of standing to a domestic environmental group protesting the importation, contrary to United States statutes, of baby seals inhumanely slaughtered in remote ocean locations? Cf. *Animal Welfare Institute v. Kreps*, 561 F.2d 1002 (D.C. Cir.), *cert. denied*, 434 U.S. 1013 (1977). How could standing be established to challenge aerial killing of wolves in remote wilderness areas of Alaska? See *Defenders of Wildlife v. Andrus*, 428 F. Supp. 167 (D.D.C. 1977). How would one establish standing to protest the destruction of a cultural resource, such as a private building? Cf. *Save the Courthouse Committee v. Lynn*, 408 F. Supp. 1323 (S.D.N.Y. 1975).

4. Is it possible that some of Sierra Club's members who didn't use the Valley would suffer "injury" at the prospect of its development? May not a person derive pleasure and satisfaction from the preservation of areas of great national beauty that he or she may never visit? Consider the individuals who often contributed funds in support of litiga-

tion by environmental groups to preserve remote resources such as the Alaska National Wildlife Refuge on Alaska's North Slope, that most contributors have never visited and will never visit. Why should a dedicated environmentalist who contributes $100 to a lawsuit to stop the proposed Mineral King development be denied standing, while a hiker in the Valley would apparently be granted standing? See Sax, Standing to Sue: A Critical Review of the Mineral King Decision, 13 Nat. Resources J. 76 (1973). How would an economist deal with the standing problem?

Even if Sierra Club was properly denied standing to vindicate its own "ideological" interests or those of its members, why shouldn't it be afforded standing to represent the interests of future visitors to the Valley? Consider in this respect Justice Blackmun's suggestions as to why present users of the Valley might not adequately represent the interests of future users.

5. Why should "injury in fact" be a requirement for standing to challenge administrative action in federal court? Whatever the justification for the "injury in fact" requirement in other contexts, should it be abandoned or relaxed in environmental cases?

6. Would Justice Douglas grant standing to any self-appointed representative of a natural object? If not, what criteria would he apply? Consider the following excerpt from Stone, Should Trees Have Standing? — Toward Legal Rights for Natural Objects, 45 S. Cal. L. Rev. 450 (1972), an article relied upon by Justice Douglas:

> It is not inevitable, nor is it wise, that natural objects should have no rights to seek redress in their own behalf. It is no answer to say that streams and forests cannot have standing because streams and forests cannot speak. Corporations cannot speak either; nor can states, estates, infants, incompetents, municipalities or universities. Lawyers speak for them, as they customarily do for the ordinary citizen with legal problems. One ought, I think, to handle the legal problems of natural objects as one does the problems of legal incompetents — human beings who have become vegetable. If a human being shows signs of becoming senile and has affairs that he is de jure incompetent to manage, those concerned with his well being make such a showing to the court, and someone is designated by the court with the authority to manage the incompetent's affairs. The guardian (or "conservator" or "committee" — the terminology varies) then represents the incompetent in his legal affairs. Courts make similar appointments when a corporation has become "incompetent" — they appoint a trustee in bankruptcy or reorganization to oversee its affairs and speak for it in court when that becomes necessary.
>
> On a parity of reasoning, we should have a system in which, when a friend of a natural object perceives it to be endangered, he can apply to a court for the creation of a guardianship.

How do you assess the arguments for and against standing for natural objects? How would a guardian for nature know what is the best interest of her client? How should she know that the environment is opposed to development? Who is to say that Mineral King wouldn't like to host a ski resort? See Sagoff, On Preserving the Natural Environment, 84 Yale L.J. 205, 221-222 (1974). Are the arguments for recognizing "rights" in nature ultimately anthropocentric? Does not the ultimate justification for preserving natural objects or species lie in human satisfaction, not merely in the immediate sense of pleasure from viewing the beautiful or fanciful, but in the more extended sense of enlarging human capacities for experience and self-development, moral and aesthetic, and, ultimately, advancing human excellence? Consider, for example, the significance of nature as an inspiration and theme in the arts during the last two centuries.[11] In a world of scarcity and poverty, would recognition of rights in natural objects involve a betrayal of our obligations to our fellow human beings? Recall the arguments of Professor Baxter, supra p. 19. Are these difficulties susceptible of resolution, or as Sagoff says elsewhere in his article, supra at 223 n.48: "[Proponents of rights for natural objects] see the problem as one of 'understanding . . . mankind's place in the universe' . . . But, as Woody Allen has said, 'It's hard enough finding your way around Chinatown.'"

7. Note that the Supreme Court carefully based its decision on the "injury in fact" aspect of *Data Processing*. If Sierra Club had satisfied that requirement by alleging use of Mineral King Valley by its members, could it have also satisfied the "zone of interests" requirement of *Data Processing*?

UNITED STATES V. STUDENTS CHALLENGING REGULATORY AGENCY PROCEDURE (SCRAP)

412 U.S. 669 (1973)

SCRAP and environmental groups, brought suit in federal district court challenging the Interstate Commerce Commission's action in permitting the nation's railroads to institute a 2.5 percent across-the-board increase on railroad freight rates without filing an environmental impact statement (EIS), as assertedly required by the National Environmental Policy Act. The Commission had declined to exercise its statutory authority to suspend the proposed increase for a full seven months pending an ICC investigation of their legality. Plaintiffs' theory was that recycled goods generally incur greater transportation charges (from a

---

11. For further discussion of these issues, see Tribe, Ways Not to Think About Plastic Trees: New Foundations for Environmental Law, 83 Yale L.J. 1315 (1974): Passmore, Man's Responsibility for Nature 101-126. See also Professor Tribe's reply to Professor Sagoff, Tribe, From Environmental Foundations to Constitutional Structures: Learning from Nature's Future, 84 Yale L.J. 480 (1975).

recycling facility to the consumer and back to the recycling facility) than disposable goods (which are transported from extraction and processing locations to the consumer and then discarded), and that general increase in freight rates would therefore make recycled goods more expensive relative to disposable items, thus discouraging recycling, promoting additional virgin source extraction, and creating additional solid waste.

SCRAP alleged that it was "an unincorporated association formed by five law students . . . in September, 1971. Its primary purpose is to enhance the quality of the human environment for its members, and for all citizens. . . ." To establish standing to bring this suit, SCRAP alleged that each of it members "[u]ses the forests, rivers, streams, mountains, and other natural resources surrounding the Washington metropolitan area and at his legal residence, for camping, hiking, fishing, sightseeing, and other recreational [and] aesthetic purposes," and that these uses had been adversely affected by the increased freight rates, because of increased litter and pollution. The Court found these allegations sufficient to withstand a motion to dismiss under Rule 12(b)(6) of the Federal Rules of Civil Procedure.

The Court refused to rule plaintiff's allegations legally insufficient either on the ground that many other people would suffer similar injuries as a result of the rate increase, or because plaintiff's theory of causation was "attenuated" and might be difficult to prove as a factual matter. The Court stated:

> Of course, pleadings must be something more than an ingenious academic exercise in the conceivable. . . . And it is equally clear that the allegations must be true and capable of proof at trial. But we deal here simply with the pleadings in which the appellees alleged a specific and perceptible harm that distinguished them from other citizens who had not used the natural resources that were claimed to be affected.[12] If, as

_____

12. The Government urges us to limit standing to those who have been "significantly" affected by agency action. But, even if we could begin to define what such a test would mean, we think it fundamentally misconceived. "Injury in fact" reflects the statutory requirement that a person be "adversely affected" or "aggrieved," and it serves to distinguish a person with a direct stake in the outcome of a litigation — even though small — from a person with a mere interest in the problem. We have allowed important interests to be vindicated by plaintiffs with no more at stake in the outcome of an action than a fraction of a vote, see *Baker v. Carr,* 369 U.S. 186; a $5 fine and costs, see *McGowan v. Maryland,* 366 U.S. 420; and a $1.50 poll tax, *Harper v. Virginia Bd. of Elections,* 383 U.S. 663. While these cases were not dealing specifically with [§702] of the APA, we see no reason to adopt a more restrictive interpretation of "adversely affected" or "aggrieved." As Professor Davis has put it: "The basic idea that comes out in numerous cases is that an identifiable trifle is enough for standing to fight out a question of principle; the trifle is the basis for standing and the principle supplies the motivation." Davis, Standing: Taxpayers and Others, 35 U. Chi. L. Rev. 601. . . .

the railroads now assert, these allegations were in fact untrue, then the appellants should have moved for summary judgment on the standing issue and demonstrated to the District Court that the allegations were sham and raised no genuine issue of fact. We cannot say on these pleadings that the appellees could not prove their allegations which, if proved, would place them squarely among those persons injured in fact by the Commission's action, and entitled under the clear import of *Sierra Club* to seek review. [412 U.S. at 688-690.]

Three Justices dissented from the court's disposition of the standing question on the ground that the injuries alleged were too "remote, speculative and insubstantial in fact."

NOTES AND QUESTIONS

1. Does the Court's opinion substantially eliminate standing as an obstacle to bringing suit so far as the pleadings are concerned? How often will an environmental group desirous of challenging federal agency action be unable to muster good faith allegations that will satisfy *SCRAP*? On the other hand, doesn't the Court's position that the existence of "injury in fact" can be tested through pretrial discovery and court hearings erect substantial practical barriers to the maintenance of litigation by environmental groups? Does the Court require plaintiffs to engage in an advance trial of the case's merits in order to get into court? Is this logical or desirable?

2. Wasn't SCRAP's motivation in bringing suit essentially ideological? What point is there in insisting that SCRAP establish as an "identifiable trifle" or "injury in fact" that the ICC's action will generate additional litter in Washington, D.C., parks where it will be viewed by one of SCRAP's members? Is "injury in fact" either a necessary or sufficient condition of vigorous and effective litigation by plaintiff?[13]

NOTES ON DUKE POWER CO. V. CAROLINA ENVIRONMENTAL STUDY GROUP, 438 U.S. 59 (1978)

The Price-Anderson Act, 42 U.S.C. §2210, imposed a statutory limit of $560 million on the damages that can be recovered by private

---

13. Might the Supreme Court in SCRAP have developed a special standing rule for NEPA cases, on the ground that the EIS requirement of NEPA was specifically designed to encourage debate and dissemination of information on the environmental consequences of governmental actions, and that agency failure to prepare an EIS would therefore cause statutorily recognized "injury" to environmental groups? This issue is discussed in Chapter 8, infra p. 1005.

litigants for injuries caused by a nuclear power plant accident ($500 million of the total was guaranteed by the federal government). Residents in the vicinity of two nuclear power plants currently under construction brought a declaratory judgment action challenging the constitutionality of the Price-Anderson Act on the grounds that it violated due process by unjustifiably limiting their common law rights to obtain compensation, and offended equal protection by arbitrarily requiring those in the vicinity of a plant to bear the risks of providing nuclear power to society as a whole.

Plaintiffs claimed that, but for the insurance provided by the Price-Anderson Act, utilities and suppliers of nuclear power plant components would not build nuclear power plants because of fear of incurring enormous liabilities in the event of an accident. Accordingly, the Price-Anderson Act caused the plants in their vicinity to be built. Plaintiffs further claimed that the plants would expose them to the risk of a nuclear accident and that the plant's thermal discharges would cause a temperature rise in two lakes which they used for recreation. The Court found that the thermal pollution was sufficient "injury in fact," not addressing the risk of accident. It also held that this injury could fairly be traced to the Act. The district court had held four days of hearings, concluding, based in part on testimony before Congress by nuclear power industry officials, there was a substantial likelihood that the plants would not have been built but for the protection provided by the Price-Anderson Act. Finally, the Court rejected the government's claim that standing should be denied because there was no logical nexus between plaintiffs' due process claims and the thermal effects constituting their injury, holding that the APA §702 "zone of interests" requirement is not applicable where plaintiff claims a constitutional rather than a statutory violation by the agency. The Court then proceeded to rule against plaintiffs on the merits of their constitutional claims, concluding that the indemnity provisions of the Price-Anderson Act constituted a reasonable substitute for common law tort claims, and rejecting plaintiff's equal protection claims.

Mr. Justice Stevens, concurring in the judgment, stated:

> The string of contingencies that supposedly holds this case together is too delicate for me. We are told that but for the Price-Anderson Act there would be no financing of nuclear power plants, no development of those plants by private parties, and hence no present injury to persons such as appellees; we are then asked to remedy an alleged due process violation that may possibly occur at some uncertain time in the future, and may possibly injure the appellees in a way that has no significant connection with any present injury. It is remarkable that such a series of speculations is considered sufficient. . . .
>
> The Court's opinion will serve the national interest in removing doubts concerning the constitutionality of the Price-Anderson Act. I can-

not, therefore, criticize the statesmanship of the Court's decision to provide the country with an advisory opinion on an important subject.
Nevertheless, my view of the proper function of this Court, or of any
other federal court, in the structure of our government is more limited.
We are not statesmen; we are judges. When it is necessary to resolve a
constitutional issue in the adjudication of an actual case or controversy,
it is our duty to do so. But whenever we are persuaded by reasons of
expediency to engage in the business of giving legal advice, we chip away
a part of the foundation of our independence and our strength. [438
U.S. at 102-103.]

NOTES AND QUESTIONS

1. Suppose that *Duke Power* had denied plaintiffs' standing. Could
this not have been regarded as an environmental victory, rather than a
defeat? Should the merits of a case play any part in the decision
whether to grant standing? See Nichol, Duke Power: Anxious Imprimatur for the Nuclear Power Subsidy, 20 Santa Clara L. Rev. 381 (1980).

2. *SCRAP* and *Duke Power* have proved to be the high-water mark
for standing. The Supreme Court has since taken a somewhat more
restrictive approach to standing, primarily by tightening the requirement of "injury in fact," which it has repeatedly emphasized to be an
Article III constitutional requirement. It has developed a three part
test: (1) a plaintiff must demonstrate some concrete injury in fact; (2)
the plaintiff must show that the injury is fairly traceable to the assertedly
unlawful government action complained of; (3) the plaintiff must show
that a victory on the merits will redress the injury.

In *Simon v. Eastern Kentucky Welfare Rights Organization*, 426 U.S.
260 (1976), the Court used this test to deny standing to poor people
challenging the legality of an Internal Revenue Service ruling relaxing
the obligation of nonprofit hospitals qualifying for tax-deductible contributions to provide free health care to the poor. The plaintiffs challenged the IRS ruling as contrary to relevant provisions of the Internal
Revenue Code. They alleged that the effect of the ruling was to eliminate incentives for the hospitals in question to provide free care to
indigents and that the removal of the incentive in turn caused the denial of free care to them. The Court (in an opinion by Justice Powell)
ruled that the alleged causal connection between the IRS's ruling and
plaintiffs' injury was too speculative and attenuated to support standing
and that the complaint should be dismissed on the pleadings. See also
Allen v. Wright, 468 U.S. 737 (1984) (denying standing to the parents of
black public school students who argued that an IRS ruling extending
tax-deductible status to private schools which discriminate on the basis
of race would diminish the ability of their children to obtain public
education in integrated schools; the Court found that such injury was

not "fairly traceable" to the challenged conduct, and the prospect that the relief requested would redress the harm was "entirely speculative").

LUJAN V. DEFENDERS OF WILDLIFE

112 S. Ct. 2130, 2135 (1992)

Justice SCALIA delivered the opinion of the Court with respect to Parts #I, II, III-A, and IV, and an opinion with respect to Part III-B in which The Chief Justice, Justice White, and Justice Thomas join.

This case involves a challenge to a rule promulgated by the Secretary of the Interior interpreting §7 of the Endangered Species Act of 1973 [ESA] . . . in such fashion as to render it applicable only to actions within the United States or on the high seas. The preliminary issue, and the only one we reach, is whether the respondents here, plaintiffs below, have standing to seek judicial review of the rule.

The ESA seeks to protect species of animals against threats to their continuing existence caused by man. See generally *TVA v. Hill*, 437 U.S. 153. . . . The ESA instructs the Secretary of the Interior to promulgate by regulation a list of those species which are either endangered or threatened under enumerated criteria, and to define the critical habitat of these species. Section 7(a)(2) of the Act then provides, in pertinent part:

> Each Federal agency shall, in consultation with and with the assistance of the Secretary [of the Interior], insure that any action authorized, funded, or carried out by such agency . . . is not likely to jeopardize the continued existence of any endangered species or threatened species or result in the destruction or adverse modification of habitat of such species which is determined by the Secretary, after consultation as appropriate, with affected States, to be critical.

[Plaintiffs, environmental groups and their members, filed suit in federal district court under the citizen suit provisions in ESA §11(g), which authorize "any person" to bring suit in federal court to, among other matters, compel the Secretary to "perform any act or duty" under the Act "which is not discretionary." Plaintiffs sought a declaration that the Act applied to all actions of federal agencies outside of the United States, including those in those other nations, and enjoining the Secretary to revise the Interior Department regulations accordingly. They alleged that, as a result of Interior's regulation, other federal agencies had funded development projects in other countries without complying with the ESA, resulting in threatened loss of endangered species. The courts below had upheld plaintiffs' standing to sue and ruled in their favor on the merits.]

Respondents' claim to injury is that the lack of consultation with respect to certain funded activities abroad "increas[es] the rate of extinction of endangered and threatened species." . . . Of course, the desire to use or observe an animal species, even for purely aesthetic purposes, is undeniably a cognizable interest for purpose of standing. See, e.g., *Sierra Club v. Morton*, ... "But the 'injury in fact' test requires more than an injury to a cognizable interest. It requires that the party seeking review be himself among the injured." Id. To survive the Secretary's summary judgment motion, respondents had to submit affidavits or other evidence showing, through specific facts, not only that listed species were in fact being threatened by funded activities abroad, but also that one or more of respondents' members would thereby be "directly" affected apart from their " 'special interest' in th[e] subject." . . .

With respect to this aspect of the case, the Court of Appeals focused on the affidavits of two Defenders' members — Joyce Kelly and Amy Skilbred. Ms. Kelly stated that she traveled to Egypt in 1986 and "observed the traditional habitat of the endangered Nile crocodile there and intend[s] to do so again, and hope[s] to observe the crocodile directly," and that she "will suffer harm in fact as a result of [the] American . . . role . . . in overseeing the rehabilitation of the Aswan High Dam on the Nile . . . and [in] develop[ing] . . . Egypt's . . . Master Water Plan." App. 101. Ms. Skilbred averred that she traveled to Sri Lanka in 1981 and "observed th[e] habitat" of "endangered species such as the Asian elephant and the leopard" at what is now the site of the Mahaweli Project funded by the Agency for International Development (AID), although she "was unable to see any of the endangered species;" "this development project," she continued, "will seriously reduce endangered, threatened, and endemic species habitat including areas that I visited . . . [, which] may severely shorten the future of these species;" that threat, she concluded, harmed her because she "intend[s] to return to Sri Lanka in the future and hope[s] to be more fortunate in spotting at least the endangered elephant and leopard." Id., at 145-146. When Ms. Skilbred was asked at a subsequent deposition if and when she had any plans to return to Sri Lanka, she reiterated that "I intend to go back to Sri Lanka," but confessed that she had no current plans: "I don't know [when]. There is a civil war going on right now. I don't know. Not next year, I will say. In the future." Id., at 318.

We shall assume for the sake of argument that these affidavits contain facts showing that certain agency-funded projects threaten listed species — though that is questionable. They plainly contain no facts, however, showing how damage to the species will produce "imminent" injury to Mss. Kelly and Skilbred. That the women "had visited" the areas of the projects before the projects commenced proves nothing. . . . *Lyons*, 461 U.S. at 102. [T]he affiants' profession of an "inten[t]" to return to the places they had visited before — where they will presumably, this time, be deprived of the opportunity to observe animals of the endangered species — is simply not enough. Such "some day" intentions — without any description of concrete plans, or indeed even any specification of *when* the some day will be — do not support a finding of the "actual or imminent" injury that our cases require.

Besides relying upon the Kelly and Skilbred affidavits, respondents propose a series of novel standing theories. The first, inelegantly styled "ecosystem nexus," proposes that any person who uses *any part* of a "contiguous ecosystem" adversely affected by a funded activity has standing even if the activity is located a great distance away. This approach, as the Court of Appeals correctly observed, is inconsistent with our opinion in *National Wildlife Federation*, which held that a plaintiff claiming injury from environmental damage must use the area affected by the challenged activity and not an area roughly "in the vicinity" of it. 497 U.S., at 887-889.

To say that the Act protects ecosystems is not to say that the Act creates (if it were possible) rights of action in persons who have not been injured in fact, that is, persons who use portions of an ecosystem not perceptibly affected by the unlawful action in question.

Respondents' other theories are called, alas, the "animal nexus" approach, whereby anyone who has an interest in studying or seeing the endangered animals anywhere on the globe has standing; and the "vocational nexus" approach, under which anyone with a professional interest in such animals can sue. Under these theories, anyone who goes to see Asian elephants in the Bronx Zoo, and anyone who is a keeper of Asian elephants in the Bronx Zoo, has standing to sue because the Director of AID did not consult with the Secretary regarding the AID-funded project in Sri Lanka. This is beyond all reason.

A further impediment to redressability is the fact that the agencies generally supply only a fraction of the funding for a foreign project. AID, for example, has provided less than 10% of the funding for the Mahaweli Project. Respondents have produced nothing to indicate that the projects they have named will either be suspended, or do less harm to listed species, if that fraction is eliminated.

The Court of Appeals found that respondents had standing for an additional reason because they had suffered a "procedural injury." [The Court rejected the court of appeals' conclusion that any citizen has standing to challenge government officials' failure to observe statutorily-required procedures, such as the consultation requirements of ESA §7(a)(2). This aspect of the court's opinion is discussed in Chapter 8, infra, pp. 1007-1011.]

We hold that respondents lack standing to bring this action and that the Court of Appeals erred in denying the summary judgment motion filed by the United States.

[Justices Kennedy and Souter joined in the essential holdings of Justice Scalia's opinion, but expressed reservations about the breadth of some of its language, indicating that on different facts they might find that environmental group members had standing to complain of failure to apply the Act abroad.]

Justice STEVENS, concurring in the judgment.

In my opinion a person who has visited the critical habitat of an endangered species, has a professional interest in preserving the species and its habitat, and intends to revisit them in the future has standing to challenge agency action that threatens their destruction. Congress has found that a wide variety of endangered species of fish, wildlife, and plants are of "aesthetic, ecological, educational, historical, recreational, and scientific value to the Nation and its people." [ESA §2(a).] Given that finding, we have no license to demean the importance of the interest that particular individuals may have in observing any species or its habitat, whether those individuals are motivated by aesthetic enjoyment, an interest in professional research, or an economic interest in preservation of the species.

An injury to an individual's interest in studying or enjoying a species and its natural habitat occurs when someone (whether it be the government or a private party) takes action that harms that species and habitat.

. . . If respondents are genuinely interested in the preservation of the endangered species and intend to study or observe these animals in the future, their injury will occur as soon as the animals are destroyed. . . .

Although I believe that respondents have standing, I nevertheless concur in the judgment of reversal because I am persuaded that the Government is correct in its submission that §7(a)(2) does not apply to activities in foreign countries. As with all questions of statutory construction, the question whether a statute applies extraterritorially is one of congressional intent.

Section 7(a)(2) provides in relevant part:

> Each Federal agency shall, in consultation with and with the assistance of the Secretary [of the Interior or Commerce, as appropriate], insure that any action authorized, funded, or carried out by such agency (hereinafter in this section referred to as an 'agency action') is not likely to jeopardize the continued existence of any endangered species or threatened species or result in the destruction or adverse modification of habitat of such species which is determined by the Secretary, after consultation as appropriate with affected States, to be critical . . . .

Nothing in this text indicates that the section applies in foreign countries. The Secretary of the Interior and the Secretary of Commerce

have consistently taken the position that they need not designate critical habitat in foreign countries. . . .

Justice BLACKMUN, with whom Justice O'CONNOR joins, dissenting.

I part company with the Court in this case in two respects. First, I
believe that respondents have raised genuine issues of fact — sufficient
to survive summary judgment — both as to injury and as to redressability. Second, I question the Court's breadth of language in rejecting
standing for "procedural" injuries. . . .

[Justice Blackmun stated that in certain instances an "ecosystem,"
professional, or vocational nexus might suffice to establish standing.
He also questioned the Court's analysis of redressability.]

Were the Court to apply the proper standard for summary judgment, I believe it would conclude that the sworn affidavits and deposition testimony of Joyce Kelly and Amy Skilbred advance sufficient facts
to create a genuine issue for trial concerning whether one or both
would be imminently harmed by the Aswan and Mahaweli projects. . . .

I think a reasonable finder of fact could conclude from the information in the affidavits and deposition testimony that either Kelly or
Skilbred will soon return to the project sites thereby satisfying the "actual or imminent" injury standard. . . .

In conclusion, I cannot join the Court on what amounts to a slash-
and-burn expedition through the law of environmental standing. In my
view, "[t]he very essence of civil liberty certainly consists in the right of
every individual to claim the protection of the laws, whenever he receives an injury." *Marbury v. Madison*, 1 Cranch 137, 163, 2 L. Ed. 60
(1803).

NOTES AND QUESTIONS

1. *Lujan*'s application of the "injury in fact" test was foreshadowed
in *Lujan v. National Wildlife Federation*, 497 U.S. 871 (1990), where Justice Scalia also wrote the Court's opinion. The National Wildlife Federalism (NWF) sued the Secretary of Interior, claiming procedural and
substantive violations in Interior's implementation of the Federal Land
Policy and Management Act of 1976, 242 U.S.C. §§1701 et seq.
(FLPMA). FLPMA directed Interior to review all of the public lands
administered by it in order to determine whether various "withdrawals"
of the lands from general use by previous Interior Department administrative decisions were still appropriate. These withdrawals restricted
given tracts to limited uses, such as recreation, wilderness preservation,
and so forth. These withdrawals had accumulated over many years in
an ad hoc fashion. Congress authorized Interior to modify or terminate

any such withdrawal, if consistent with land use plans to be developed by the Secretary pursuant to FLPMA. NWF alleged that Interior was conducting a "land withdrawal review program" involving over 1500 discrete tracts, in violation of the requirements of FLPMA, the APA, and NEPA. The district court had enjoined any reclassification of any of the 1500 tracts for over two years before the Court ruled that plaintiff lacked standing. When the government challenged NWF's standing through a motion for summary judgment, it relied upon affidavits of two members, each of whom asserted that she had hiked and made visits "in the vicinity" of one tract, a small portion of which would be potentially subject to mining as a result of Interior's termination of a withdrawal. The court held that this was insufficient to establish the requisite "injury in fact" because it failed to show that the member had visited or would visit the specific area. Justice Scalia then went on to hold that NWF could not challenge the asserted "land withdrawal review program" en masse, but could only challenge legal violations with respect to particular tracts where specific action had been taken and the matter was therefore "ripe" for judicial review.

2. For an excellent analysis of *Defenders* and *NWF*, criticizing their reasoning and result but stressing their limited practical significance, see Sunstein, What's Standing after *Lujan*? Of Citizen Suits, "Injuries," and Article III, 91 Mich. L. Rev. 163 (1992). Sunstein argues that *Defenders* hinges on the characterization of the injury, and that plaintiffs should have made the following claim about statutory interpretation:

> [T]he ESA was designed to ensure not that no species would become extinct — that was not an adequate description of the injury at issue — but more precisely that endangered species would not be subject to increased threats of extinction because of federal governmental action. The injury of which the plaintiffs [should have] complained was the harm to their professional and tourist opportunities created by those increased risks.

Id. at 204. Would this satisfy the "injury in fact" requirement for standing, as interpreted by Justice Scalia?

3. The "prudential" arguably-within-the-zone-of-interests text in *Data Processing*, which was a construction of the standing provisions of the APA and could therefore be changed or eliminated by Congress, is so vague that it has rarely been used to deny standing; as a result, the Court's efforts to restrict standing have focussed on the injury-in-fact test under Article III. But there are some signs that the "zone" text may also be used to limit standing. For example, in *Air Courier Conference v. American Postal Workers Union*, 498 U.S. 517 (1991), the Court denied standing to the Postal Service Union, who challenged the Postal Service's decision to suspend its statutory monopoly of mail service in or-

der to allow private couriers to carry and deposit letters from the United States with the postal services of other nations for delivery within those nations. The statutory grant of monopoly, the Court held, was not designed to protect postal workers, but instead to protect the Postal Service against "cream skimming" competition from private couriers. Accordingly, the workers were not even arguably within the zone of interests perfected by the statute.

4. In the longer run, would unlimited standing promote sound environmental policy? Should business or development-oriented plaintiffs be empowered to use the environmental laws in order to promote their commercial interests? See, e.g., *Port of Astoria v. Hodel,* 595 F.2d 467 (9th Cir. 1979) (denying standing to port authority seeking to use NEPA to block relocation of industrial facility, holding that authority's economic interests not arguably within NEPA's protected zone); *Presidio Bridge Co. v. Secretary of State,* 486 F. Supp. 288 (W.D. Tex. 1978) (similarly denying standing to bridge operator invoking NEPA to block competing bridge). Should ideological plaintiffs be able to challenge environmental measures on the ground that they invade states' rights? See *Mountain States Legal Foundation v. Costle,* 630 F.2d 754 (10th Cir. 1980) (denying standing to Colorado legislators and citizens to challenge state's acquiescence in more stringent EPA SIP requirements).

STANDING PROBLEMS

1. The ESA §11(g) authorizes "any person" to sue the Secretary of the Interior for failure to perform a mandatory duty under the ESA. Suppose Congress amends §11(g), adding the following:

> a person who has by studying, visiting, or other means demonstrated an aesthetic, ecological, educational, historical, professional, recreational, or scientific interest in an endangered or threatened species shall be deemed to suffer a direct and particularized injury in any instance in which any person, including the United States and any other governmental instrumentality or agency, takes action that may harm or adversely affect any threatened or endangered species, or result in the destruction or adverse modification of the critical habitat of the species. A reasonable likelihood of action or a proposal to act shall be considered a sufficient threat to constitute an injury under this paragraph.

Would a U.S. zoologist writing a book on endangered species have standing to challenge a U.S. agency-financed development project in the Amazon that would destroy the habitat of several endangered species? What about a U.S. citizen who had read the book?

2. RCRA requires EPA to promulgate rules that govern the treat-

ment of hazardous wastes, such as oil residues, buried in toxic waste dumps. EPA promulgates a regulation that allows contaminated soil that contains fewer than 5 parts benzene per million to be land disposed without further treatment. Waste Reprocessing Inc., your client, believes that the standard is too lenient, and that it therefore violates that statute's mandate that EPA make land disposal facilities "safe" for the general public. Your client points out that if EPA reduced the standard to three parts per million, it could make a lot more money selling its special soil reprocessing machine that extracts and destroys certain chemical residues in soils, including benzene. Does your client have standing to make this claim in a suit against EPA?

NOTES ON CITIZEN SUIT PROVISIONS

1. As we have already seen, the citizen suit provisions in the ESA have counterparts in many other federal environmental regulatory statutes, including the Clean Air Act and the Clean Water Act. Is the provision in §304 of the Clean Air Act empowering "any person" to sue to be read literally? If so, is it constitutional? Section 505 of the Clean Water Act, which was enacted in 1972 after the decision in *Sierra Club*, authorizes suits by "any citizen," defining "citizen" to consist of "a person or persons having an interest which is or may be adversely affected." Does this language restrict standing, and if so, to what extent?

The "arguably within the zone" test was said in *Data Processing* to be a "prudential" limitation on standing created by §702 of the APA. Accordingly, Congress can presumably eliminate this limitation. But the Court has presented the "injury in fact" requirement as an Article III constitutional requirement, notwithstanding weighty scholarly opinion favoring the view that there are no constitutional inhibitions on Congress' extension of standing to seek judicial review of agencies' failure to adhere to statutory directives so long as the plaintiff in a given case litigates it with sufficient zeal to ensure an adversary process. See L. Jaffe, Judicial Review of Administrative Action 495-500 (1965). Recall that many citizen suit provisions, including those in the Clean Air Act and Clean Water Act, also authorize suits against private facilities that violate applicable regulatory requirements. Are plaintiffs in such suits subject to the same "injury in fact" requirements that apply to suits against the government?

2. Apart from constitutional issues, there are important policy issues about the desirability of mobilizing private litigants to force agency compliance with statutory deadlines and other "action forcing" provisions. Critics contend that such suits have forced EPA to take hasty and ill-considered action, required the premature enforcement of controversial measures provoking "backlash" against the environmental move-

ment, and caused EPA priorities to be unduly influenced by environmental groups. Melnick, supra, p. 35, points out that environmental groups use citizen suits selectively, to force implementation of the law in some states, or for some problems, but not others. Is this practice troubling? Defenders of the "citizen suit" principle believe that enforcement of congressionally imposed deadlines has been generally beneficial in prodding EPA to take action to protect the environment and that it is necessary to have the constant threat of privately enforced mandates to ensure adequate agency initiative in favor of environmental interests. Even if the critics are correct, isn't the appropriate solution to eliminate the statutory deadlines or permit reviewing courts to modify them, rather than to eliminate "citizen suits"? For discussion, see National Academy of Sciences-National Research Council, Committee on Environmental Decision Making, Decision Making in the Environmental Protection Agency 68-77 (1977). See generally Miller, Citizen Suits: Private Enforcement of Federal Pollution Control Laws (1987); DiMento, Citizen Environmental Litigation and the Administrative Process; Empirical Findings, Remaining Issues, and a Direction for Future Research, 1977 Duke L.J. 409.

3. The citizen suit provisions vest jurisdiction over such suits in the district courts. But citizen suits against federal agencies are limited to the enforcement of nondiscretionary duties. If plaintiffs' challenge does not involve such a duty, review must generally be sought in a court of appeals. See, e.g., Clean Air Act §307. There is often uncertainty as to which forum is proper.

EDF v. Thomas, 870 F.2d 892 (2d Cir.), *cert. denied sub nom. Alabama Power Co. v. EDF,* 493 U.S. 991 (1989), considered which court should hear a suit brought to compel EPA to issue, pursuant to §109 of the Clean Air Act, revised NAAQS for SO_x emissions in light of recent reports it had written analyzing acid deposition damage due to SO_x emissions. EPA claimed that it had not yet made any decision on whether to revise the standards and that there was nothing to review. The court held that EPA had a duty to decide, one way or another, whether to revise the standards and that review in the district court to require a decision was therefore proper. Any subsequent challenge to the substantive content of the agency's action must then be brought in the D.C. Circuit. The case was remanded for an order that EPA continue the review process it had started until a decision had been reached.

By contrast, *NRDC v. U.S. EPA,* 770 F. Supp. 1093 (E.D. Va. 1991), involved a challenge to EPA approval of Maryland's dioxin water quality standards and sought an order compelling EPA to revise national dioxin water quality standards to reflect the "latest scientific knowledge." The court granted EPA partial summary judgment on the national standard count, ruling that under the Clean Water Act the decision to revise these regulations was within the discretion of the Administrator and that therefore a citizen suit could not be maintained. The court distinguished *EDF v. Thomas* on the basis of differences between the structure and procedural requirements of the two statutes. In addition, EPA had not recently reported on the dangers of the disputed pollutant which had created an obligation to make a ruling in the Second Circuit case. See generally Currie, Judicial Review Under Federal Pollution Laws, 62 Iowa L. Rev. 1221 (1977); Chu, Judicial Review of EPA Action Under the Citizen Suit Provision, 3 Colum. J. Envir. L. 262 (1977).

4. Attempts to enforce statutory deadlines often encounter difficulties in devising an effective remedy. For example, in Air Pollution Control District of Jefferson County, Kentucky v. U.S. EPA, 739 F.2d 1071 (6th Cir. 1984), the Kentucky District petitioned EPA to restrain a power plant in Indiana from causing interstate pollution. The Clean Air Act required EPA to issue a decision on the petition within 60 days of the public hearings. A district court order issued approximately 11 months after this deadline expired, requiring EPA to act promptly on the petition; EPA did not rule until 22 months after the hearings. The plaintiff argued that EPA's delay should result in a reversal of its decision, which denied plaintiff the recovery it sought. The court of appeals ruled that failure to meet statutory and court-imposed deadlines was not grounds for reversal on the merits. One court, however, did take the unusual step of holding EPA in contempt for failing to obey its order compelling the promulgation of rules regarding radionuclide emissions. See *Sierra Club v. Ruckelshaus,* 602 F. Supp. 892 (N.D. Cal. 1984). Even here, however, EPA did not issue final regulations until 1989. Moreover, EPA then repeatedly stayed enforcement of these regulations against all licensees other than nuclear power plants. The EPA stay was finally vacated by the D.C. Circuit in 1992 as unauthorized under the Clean Air Act of 1990. *NRDC v. Reilly,* 976 F.2d 36 (D.C. Cir. 1992). Should the citizen suit provisions be written to provide for stronger sanctions against EPA? Consider that EPA's budget falls far short of its needs, given the enormous and complex character of its responsibilities under the ambitious environmental regulatory laws passed by Congress, and that the statutory deadlines are often hopelessly unrealistic.

Despite their limitations, action-forcing litigation under the citizen suit provisions has been regularly brought by environmental groups, who view citizen suits as an indispensable tool to ensure implementation of the environmental laws.

2.   ATTORNEY FEES AND INCENTIVES TO SUE

Consider again the organizational and free-rider problems involved in providing effective representation for collective interests, including in particular the interest in environmental quality. The normal remedy in litigations challenging government action that assertedly fails to protect adequately the environment is injunctive or declaratory relief, not money damages. How will such advocacy be funded? One possible answer is to create exceptions to the "American rule" that each party in litigation bears its own litigation expenses. Prevailing litigants who advance claims that assertedly serve broader public interests might be entitled to reimbursement of litigation costs from their opponents. *Alyeska Pipeline Service Company v. Wilderness Society*, 421 U.S. 240 (1975), held that federal courts lack general authority to engage in such fee-shifting, which must be specifically authorized by Congress.

The citizen suit provisions in federal environmental laws generally authorize court awards of attorney's fees. Section 304(d) of the Clean Air Act, for example, provides:

> The court, in issuing any final order in any action brought pursuant to subsection (a) of this section, may award costs of litigation (including reasonable attorney and expert witness fees) to any party, whenever the court determines such award is appropriate.

The Clean Water Act, §505(d), contains identical language. Similar provisions are found in sixteen other statutes, as well as in §307(f) of the Clean Air Act. See generally Miller, Private Enforcement of Federal Pollution Control Laws, Part III, 14 ELR 10407 (1984). Similar provisions are also found in many civil rights statutes.

Prevailing plaintiffs in citizen suit actions are routinely awarded their litigation costs. Does the "appropriate" standard allow a court to award fees to a nonprevailing party? *Sierra Club v. Gorsuch*, 672 F.2d 33, (D.C. Cir. 1982), held that it does, and awarded $91,000 in attorneys' fees to environmental groups that had unsuccessfully challenged substantive and procedural aspects of EPA's pollution control regulations for new coal-fired power plants. The court found that plaintiffs had raised important claims and contributed to the court's resolution of novel and difficult legal issues. The Supreme Court reversed in an opinion by Justice Rehnquist that held that a party claiming attorney fees must have achieved "some degree of success on the merits." It found that the "appropriate" standard was merely designed to make clear that courts could award fees to *partially* prevailing parties as well as those who prevail entirely. Given the presumption in favor of the "American rule," Congress would have to be more explicit in order to authorize awards to parties who do not prevail on any issue. *Ruckelshaus v. Sierra Club*, 463 U.S. 680 (1983). The fee award is paid by the prevailing party's opponent. In suits against federal agencies, this means that the award is paid by the federal government. Citizen suits can also be brought against private defendants for violation of regulatory requirements. When defendants in such actions prevail, they sometimes seek an award of fees against the plaintiff. Courts have held that a plaintiff who obtains some relief through a settlement may be entitled to an award. *Atlantic States Legal Foundation v. Eastman Kodak Co.,* 933 F.2d 124 (2d Cir. 1991). A prevailing defendant can be awarded attorney's fees, but there is a higher standard; it can only recover its litigation costs if the suit is "frivolous, meritless or vexatious." *National Wildlife Federation v. Consumers Power Co.,* 729 F. Supp. 62 (W.D. Mich. 1989).

After deciding whether to make a fee award, the court must then decide how much to grant. The traditional method is called the "lodestar approach," under which the court multiplies the reasonable numbers of hours needed for the case by the reasonable hourly rate. Normally, the fee rate is for the area in which the case was tried unless the party seeking the award can show that it was impossible to find adequate counsel within that region. Courts sometimes adjust the lodestar amount either up or down. For example, in *Friends of the Earth v. Eastman Kodak Co.,* 656 F. Supp. 513 (W.D.N.Y.), *aff'd,* 834 F.2d 295 (2d Cir. 1987), the court reduced the fee from the request of over $105,000 to $30,000. The court held that although the plaintiff was the prevailing party, a full award was inappropriate because the ultimate success was so small in comparison to the number of violations alleged and the amount sought in relief.

The Supreme Court has recently restricted the discretion of trial judges to increase the fee award above the lodestar. *Pennsylvania v. Delaware Valley Citizens' Council for Clean Air,* 478 U.S. 576 (1986), held that enhancing the lodestar based on "superior quality" representation was inappropriate. In *City of Burlington v. Dague,* 112 S. Ct. 2638 (1992), the Court overturned a 25 percent enhancement of the lodestar based on the contingency fee risk of the plaintiff's attorney, holding that such enhancements were not authorized by the citizen suit provisions of the Clean Water Act and RCRA.

Why has the Supreme Court been grudging in its interpretation of the attorney fee award provisions in citizen suit provisions? The fear of encouraging litigation that advances parochial rather than broad public interests? The difficulty in distinguishing the two? The lack of judicially manageable standards for subsidizing litigation? To what extent should 501(c)(3) tax deductions be available to environmental and other groups that use the proceeds for litigation against the government? See M. Breger, Halting Taxpayer Subsidy of Partisan Advocacy (1983).

The 1980 Equal Access to Justice Act (EAJA), 28 U.S.C. §2412, provides that a federal court, unless expressly prohibited by statute, shall award reasonable fees and expenses to a prevailing party (other than the United States) in any civil action brought by or against the United States "unless the court finds that the position of the United States was substantially justified or that special circumstances make an award unjust." The fees and expenses subject to award are defined statutorily to include attorney fees, but such fees are limited to $75 an hour, subject to cost of living adjustments or unusual factors. Parties eligible for awards are individuals with a net worth under $1 million, all agricultural cooperatives and tax exempt organizations, and businesses or other organizations with a net worth of less than $5 million or employing fewer than 500 people. Environmental groups have successfully used EAJA to obtain fee awards. See *EDF v. EPA,* 716 F.2d 915 (D.C. Cir. 1983).

In interpreting "substantial justification" courts have required that the government's position be stronger than one that is merely nonfrivolous. But the government may lose on the merits and still be found to have had "substantial justification" for its position. The original purpose of the Act was to prevent imposition of unreasonable regulations on small businesses that could not afford to litigate the issue. But most claimants for attorney fee awards have been individuals in controversies involving government benefits or employment. Some business firms have also used the Act, but mainly in the context of government contract disputes. A number of public interest advocacy organizations have obtained fees in connection with their efforts to force more stringent regulatory enforcement — a goal directly contrary to the purposes of this Act's principal proponents.

Provisions for award of attorney fees and court litigation expenses generally apply only to the stage of judicial review of administrative action.[14] The expenses of participating in a complex and protracted administrative proceeding, however, can exceed by many times the costs of court review. Even in the case of notice and comment rulemaking, the costs of effective participation can be high if there are large amounts of technical material that must be mastered by lawyers and expert advisers. What arrangements, if any, should be made for advancing or reimbursing such expenses out of government funds or otherwise? Note that such funding may become especially important if efforts to promote regulatory negotiation, discussed infra, are to succeed.

---

14. However, the Equal Access to Justice Act does authorize fee awards in "adversary adjudication" before agencies.

C.   RIGHTS TO INTERVENE IN AND INITIATE AGENCY PROCEEDINGS

ENVIRONMENTAL DEFENSE FUND, INC. V. RUCKELSHAUS

439 F.2d 584 (D.C. Cir. 1971)

BAZELON, Chief Judge:

This is a petition for review of an order of the Secretary of Agriculture, refusing to suspend the federal registration of the pesticide DDT or to commence the formal administrative procedures that could terminate that registration. . . .

The Federal Insecticide, Fungicide, and Rodenticide Act (FIFRA) provides that for certain purposes pesticides must be registered with the Secretary of Agriculture, and that in order to be registered a pesticide must conform to the statutory standards for product safety. "If it appears to the Administrator that a pesticide . . . causes unreasonable adverse effects on the environment, the Administrator may issue a notice" of intent to cancel the pesticide's registration. On demand "by a person adversely affected by the notice," the Administrator shall hold a hearing and also refer the matter to a scientific advisory board. FIFRA §6(b), 7 U.S.C. §136d(b). The Administrator may also summarily suspend registration when "necessary to prevent imminent hazard to the public." Such suspension halts the manufacture, sale, or use of the pesticide pending completion of the cancellation proceedings. Orders relating to suspension or cancellation are judicially reviewable in the courts of appeals at the instance of any person who will be "adversely affected."

[EDF] submitted a petition to the Secretary requesting him to issue notices of cancellation with respect to all registrations of pesticides containing DDT, and further, to suspend those registrations pending the conclusion of the administrative proceedings. They submitted extensive scientific documentation in support of their petition. The Secretary initially issued notices of cancellation with respect to some uses of DDT, and published in the Federal Register a notice announcing his intention to issue cancellation notices with respect to all other DDT uses that are not essential for the protection of human health; he invited comments on that proposal. No action was taken on the request for summary suspension. [EDF had alleged that its members would be exposed to health hazards as a result of continued DDT use. The court upheld EDF's standing. It also found reviewability despite the fact that the statute provides that the Secretary "may" institute cancellation or suspension proceedings if it appears that the pesticide does not comply with FIFRA's standards.]

On May 28, 1970, this court concluded that the Secretary's silence on the request for suspension was equivalent to a denial of that request, and that the denial was reviewable as a final order, because of its immediate impact on the parties.[15] The court remanded the case to the Secretary for a fresh determination on the question of suspension and for a statement of the reasons for his decision.

. . . If the Secretary had simply refused to issue the requested notices of cancellation, we would have no difficulty concluding that his order was a final order, ripe for review in this court in accordance with the FIFRA. Here, however, the Secretary has taken the position that investigations are still in progress, that final determinations have not yet been made concerning the uses for which cancellation notices have not yet issued. Therefore, with respect to the cancellation notices, we treat the petition as a request for relief in the nature of mandamus, to compel the Secretary to issue notices as required by statute.

The FIFRA gives this court jurisdiction to review any order granting or denying the cancellation of a pesticide registration. The Secretary could defeat that jurisdiction, however, by delaying his determination indefinitely. Petitioners contend that the Secretary's own findings with respect to DDT compel him to issue cancellation notices, and hence that his action is "unlawfully withheld or unreasonably delayed" within the meaning of the Administrative Procedure Act. In order to protect our appellate jurisdiction, this court has jurisdiction to entertain a request for relief in the form of an order directing the Secretary to act in accordance with the FIFRA.

The relevant question, therefore, is whether the FIFRA requires the Secretary to issue cancellation notices in the circumstances of this case. The statute provides that "[t]he Secretary, in accordance with the procedures specified herein, may suspend or cancel the registration of a pesticide whenever it does not appear that the [pesticide meets statutory requirements.]" That language vests discretion in the Secretary to determine whether an article is in compliance with the act, and to decide what action should be taken with respect to a nonconforming article. Nevertheless, his decisions are reviewable for abuse of discretion. For guidance in defining the limits of his discretion, we must turn to the legislative history and to the statutory scheme as a whole. [The court discussed the legislative history of FIFRA.]

---

15. *EDF v. Hardin*, 138 U.S. App. D.C. at 396-397, 428 F.2d at 1098-1099.

". . . [T]he denial of a suspension order must be reviewable as a final order where, as here, the moving papers before the court suppport the allegation that the denial subjects the public to an imminent hazard, and that any injury is irreparable."

Not only the legislative history, but also the statutory scheme itself points to the conclusion that the FIFRA requires the Secretary to issue notices and thereby initiate the administrative process [including trial-type hearings] whenever there is a substantial question about the safety of a registered pesticide. For when Congress creates a procedure that gives the public a role in deciding important questions of public policy, that procedure may not lightly be sidestepped by administrators. The cancellation decision does not turn on a scientific assessment of hazard alone. The statute leaves room to balance the benefits of a pesticide against its risks. The process is a delicate one, in which greater weight should be accorded the value of a pesticide for the control of disease, and less weight should be accorded its value for the protection of a commercial crop. The statutory scheme contemplates that these questions will be explored in the full light of a public hearing and not resolved behind the closed doors of the Secretary. There may well be countervailing factors that would justify an administrative decision, after . . . a public hearing, to continue a registration despite a substantial degree of risk, but those factors cannot justify a refusal to issue the notices that trigger the administrative process.

In this case the Secretary has made a number of findings with respect to DDT. On the basis of the available scientific evidence he has concluded that (1) DDT in large doses has produced cancer in test animals and various injuries in man, but in small doses its effect on man is unknown; (2) DDT is toxic to certain birds, bees, and fish, but there is no evidence of harm to the vast majority of species of nontarget organisms; (3) DDT has important beneficial uses in connection with disease control and protection of various crops. These and other findings led the Secretary to conclude "[t]hat the use of DDT should continue to be reduced in an orderly, practicable manner which will not deprive mankind of uses which are essential to the public health and welfare. To this end there should be continuation of the comprehensive study essentially of particular uses and evaluations of potential substitutes."

There is no reason, however, for that study to be conducted outside the procedures provided by the statute. The Secretary may, of course, conduct a reasonable preliminary investigation before taking action under the statute. . . . But when, as in this case, he reaches the conclusion that there is a substantial question about the safety of a registered item, he is obliged to initiate the statutory procedure that results in referring the matter first to a scientific advisory committee and then to a public hearing. We recognize, of course, that one important function of that procedure is to afford the registrant an opportunity to challenge the initial decision of the Secretary. But the hearing, in particular, serves other functions as well. Public hearings bring the public into the decision-making process, and create a record that facilitates judicial review. If hearings are held only after the Secretary is convinced beyond a doubt that cancellation is necessary, then they will be held too seldom and too late in the process to serve either of those functions effectively.

The Secretary's statement in this case makes it plain that he found a substantial question concerning the safety of DDT, which in his view warranted further study. Since we have concluded that is the standard for the issuance of cancellation notices under the FIFRA, the case must be remanded to the Secretary with instructions to issue notices with respect to the remaining uses of DDT, and thereby commence the administrative process.

While the Secretary recognized a substantial question concerning the safety of DDT, he concluded that the evidence did not warrant summary suspension of its registration for any purpose. . . .

The statute provides for suspension in order "to prevent an imminent hazard to the public." Congress clearly intended to protect the public from some risks by summary administrative action pending further proceedings. The administrator's problem is to determine which risks fall in that class. The Secretary has made no attempt to deal with that problem, either by issuing regulations relating to suspension, or by explaining his decision in this case. If regulations of general applicability were formulated, it would of course be possible to explain individual decisions by reference to the appropriate regulation. It may well be, however, that standards for suspension can best be developed piecemeal, as the Secretary evaluates the hazards presented by particular products. Even so, he has an obligation to articulate the criteria that he develops in making each individual decision. We cannot assume, in the absence of adequate explanation, that proper standards are implicit in every exercise of administrative discretion.

Since the Secretary has not yet provided an adequate explanation for his decision to deny interim relief in this case, it will be necessary to remand the case once more, for a fresh determination on that issue. On remand, the Secretary should consider whether the information presently available to him calls for suspension of any registrations of products containing DDT, identifying the factors relevant to that determination, and relating the evidence to those factors in a statement of the reasons for his decisions.

We stand on the threshold of a new era in the history of the long and fruitful collaboration of administrative agencies and reviewing courts. For many years, courts have treated administrative policy decisions with great deference, confining judicial attention primarily to matters of procedure. On matters of substance, the courts regularly upheld agency action, with a nod in the direction of the "substantial evidence" test, and a bow to the mysteries of administrative expertise. Courts occasionally asserted, but less often exercised, the power to set aside agency action on the ground than an impermissible factor had entered into the decision, or a crucial factor had not been considered. Gradually, however, that power has come into more frequent use, and with it, the requirement that administrators articulate the factors on which they base their decisions.

Strict adherence to that requirement is especially important now that the character of administrative litigation is changing. As a result of expanding doctrines of standing and reviewability, and new statutory causes of action, courts are increasingly asked to review administrative action that touches on fundamental personal interests in life, health, and liberty. These interests have always had a special claim to judicial protection, in comparison with the economic interests at stake in a ratemaking or licensing proceeding.

To protect these interests from administrative arbitrariness, it is necessary, but not sufficient, to insist on strict judicial scrutiny of administrative action. For judicial review alone can correct only the most egregious abuses. Judicial review must operate to ensure that the administrative process itself will confine and control the exercise of discretion. Courts should require administrative officers to articulate the standards and principles that govern their discretionary decisions in as much detail as possible. Rules and regulations should be freely formulated by administrators, and revised when necessary. Discretionary decisions should more often be supported with findings of fact and reasoned opinions. When administrators provide a framework for principled decision-making, the result will be to diminish the importance of judicial review by enhancing the integrity of the administrative process, and to improve the quality of judicial review in those cases where judicial review is sought.

Remanded for further proceedings consistent with this opinion.

ROBB, Circuit Judge (dissenting):

In my view the majority opinion substitutes the judgment of this court for the judgment of the Secretary in a matter committed to his discretion by law. . . .

NOTES AND QUESTIONS

After *EDF v. Ruckleshaus,* most courts showed some deference to agency decisions not to initiate rulemaking or enforcement action, but the degree of deference varied widely. See, e.g., *Public Citizen Health Research Group v. Auchter,* 702 F.2d 1150 (D.C. Cir. 1983) (OSHA not required to adopt "temporary emergency standard" for ethylene oxide but must initiate rulemaking to establish permanent standard); *Rockford League of Women Voters v. NRC,* 679 F.2d 1218 (7th Cir. 1982) (NRC not required to revoke construction license because of asserted safety hazards that are reviewable later at a grant of operating license; scope of judicial review "very limited" because issues are "managerial" and "technical"). In many cases the remedy afforded has been a remand to the agency for further explanation of its failure to act. See *WWHT, Inc. v. FCC*, 656 F.2d 807 (D.C. Cir. 1981), and cases there discussed.

HECKLER V. CHANEY

470 U.S. 821, 823 (1985)

Justice REHNQUIST delivered the opinion of the Court.

This case presents the question of the extent to which a decision of an administrative agency to exercise its "discretion" not to *undertake certain enforcement actions* is subject to judicial review under the Administrative Procedure Act. . . .

[State prisoners sentenced to execution by lethal injection sought judicial review of the failure of the Food and Drug Administration (FDA) to bring enforcement actions to prevent use of the drugs for lethal injection, on the ground that the drugs had not been adequately tested or approved by FDA for such use, in violation of federal statutes. The D.C. Circuit Court of Appeals held that the FDA was required to initiate enforcement actions.]

. . . For us, this case turns on the important question of the extent to which determination by the FDA *not to exercise* its enforcement authority over the use of drugs in interstate commerce may be judicially reviewed. . . .

. . . Petitioner urges that the decision of the FDA to refuse enforcement is an action "committed to agency discretion by law" under §701(a)(2) [of the APA].

Overton Park did not involve an agency's refusal to take requested enforcement action. It involved an affirmative act of approval under a statute that set clear guidelines for determining when such approval should be given. Refusals to take enforcement steps generally involve precisely the opposite situation, and in that situation we think the presumption is that judicial review is not available. This Court has recognized on several occasions over many years that an agency's decision not to prosecute or enforce, whether through civil or criminal process, is a decision generally committed to an agency's absolute discretion. . . . This recognition of the existence of discretion is attributable in no small part to the general unsuitability for judicial review of agency decisions to refuse enforcement.

The reasons for this general unsuitability are many. First, an agency decision not to enforce often involves a complicated balancing of a number of factors which are peculiarly within its expertise. Thus, the agency must not only assess whether a violation has occurred, but whether agency resources are best spent on this violation or another, whether the agency is likely to succeed if it acts, whether the particular enforcement action requested best fits the agency's overall policies, and indeed, whether the agency has enough resources to undertake the action at all. An agency generally cannot act against each technical violation of the statute it is charged with enforcing. The agency is far better equipped than the courts to deal with the many variables involved in the proper ordering of its priorities. Similar concerns animate the principles of administrative law that courts generally will defer to an agency's construction of the statute it is charged with implementing, and to the procedures it adopts for implementing that statute. See *Vermont Yankee Nuclear Power Corp. v. Natural Resources Defense Council, Inc., 435 U.S. 519, 543. . . .*

In addition to these administrative concerns, we note that when an agency refuses to act it generally does not exercise its coercive power over an individual's liberty or property rights, and thus does not infringe upon areas that courts often are called upon to protect. Similarly, when an agency *does* act to enforce, that action itself provides a focus for judicial review, inasmuch as the agency must have exercised its power in some manner. The action at least can be reviewed to determine whether the agency exceeded its statutory powers. . . .

Finally, we recognize that an agency's refusal to institute proceedings shares to some extent the characteristics of the decision of a prosecutor in the Executive Branch not to indict — a decision which has long been regarded as the special province of the Executive Branch, inasmuch as it is the Executive who is charged by the Constitution to "take Care that the Laws be faithfully executed," U.S. Const., Art. II, §2.

We of course only list the above concerns to facilitate understanding of our conclusion that an agency's decision has traditionally been "committed to agency discretion," and we believe that the Congress enacting the APA did not intend to alter that tradition. In so stating, we emphasize that the decision is only presumptively unreviewable; the presumption may be rebutted where the substantive statute has provided guidelines for the agency to follow in exercising its enforcement powers.[16] Thus, in establishing this presumption in the APA, Congress did not set agencies free to disregard legislative direction in this statu-

---

16. We do not have in this case a refusal by the agency to institute proceedings based solely on the belief that it lacks jurisdiction. Nor do we have a situation where it could justifiably be found that the agency has "consciously and expressly adopted a general policy" that is so extreme as to amount to an abdication of its statutory responsibilities. See, e.g., *Adams v. Richardson,* 156 U.S. App. D.C. 267, 480 F.2d 1159 (1973) (*en banc*). Although we express no opinion on whether such decisions would be unreviewable under §701(a)(2), we note that in those situations the statute conferring authority on the agency might indicate that such decisions were not "committed to agency discretion."

tory scheme that the agency administers. Congress may limit an agency's exercise of enforcement power if it wishes, either by setting substantive priorities, or by otherwise circumscribing an agency's power to discriminate among issues or cases it will pursue. How to determine when Congress has done so is the question left open by *Overton Park.* . . .

[The Court reviewed the Food, Drug and Cosmetic Act and found nothing to rebut the "presumption of nonreviewability." It therefore reversed the Court of Appeals' decision. Justice Marshall, concurring in the result, would have reviewed the FDA's exercise of discretion on the merits, but, exercising a deferential standard of review that he believed appropriate in such cases, would find no abuse of discretion by FDA, and therefore uphold its decision not to bring enforcement action against the drug uses in question.]

NOTES AND QUESTIONS

Does *Heckler* effectively overrule *EDF v. Ruckleshaus?* Would *Heckler*, which involved an administrative refusal to bring particular enforcement actions, create a presumption of nonreviewability of an agency's refusal to initiate rulemaking to deal with a newly discovered, nationwide environmental hazard? See Sunstein, *Reviewing Agency Inaction After Heckler v. Chaney,* 52 U. Chi. L. Rev. 653 (1985). As we have seen, Congress has effectively legislated private initiation rights by including deadlines and other mandates in EPA statutes and authorizing citizen suits to enforce them. See pp. 35, 543 supra. Is this an apt solution to the problem of administrative discretion? Is there a better one?

D.   JUDICIAL REVIEW OF AGENCY DECISIONMAKING

1.   REVIEW OF PROCEDURAL REQUIREMENTS

The federal Administrative Procedure Act (APA) provides two paradigm procedures to be followed by regulatory agencies in taking action. First, there is the trial-type hearing in cases of formal adjudication. In such cases, the agency staff and affected private parties have the right to introduce direct and rebuttal evidence through live witnesses and exercise the right of cross-examination; the agency's ultimate decision is required to be based on the evidence developed at the hearing and must ordinarily take the form of an opinion which discusses the evidence and makes relevant factual findings. See 5 U.S.C. §§554-557. Such a hearing is often required under regulatory statutes and the APA in cases of adjudication where the agency takes individual enforcement action to halt an asserted violation or impose penalties, denies or revokes a license or permit, or otherwise seeks to impose sanctions on particular party. Even where relevant statutes do not provide for a trial-type hearing in such cases, courts may find that one is required by constitutional due process.

The second basic type of procedure is "notice and comment" rulemaking. Rulemaking consists of the adoption of regulations establishing general standards of conduct for the future, in contrast with formal adjudication, which typically involves the imposition of sanctions on a specific person for past conduct or the resolution of a particular controversy between the government and a specific party. Under the notice-and-comment rulemaking procedures of the federal Administrative Procedure Act, the agency is required to give public notice of proposed regulations prior to final agency adoption. See 5 U.S.C. §553. There is no trial-type hearing.[17] Also, traditionally agency decisions in rulemaking were not "on the record," because the agency did not need not to base its decision solely on the written comments submitted but could take into account any information that it deems fit. The agency, however, upon issuing the regulations, is required to give a "concise general statement of their basis and purpose."

Informal adjudication is a third important category of decisionmaking recognized by the APA. Informal adjudication encompasses a wide variety of administrative actions that do not take the form of rules or regulations, but are instead particularized in character. Hence they are "adjudication." But they are "informal" because the relevant organic statute does not require the agency to make such decisions on the basis of a record through a trial-type hearing. Moreover, these actions do not include the coercive imposition of sanctions or restrictions on an individual, and therefore do not trigger due process claims of a right to a formal hearing. Informal adjudication is a broad residual category, encompassing virtually everything the government does other than rulemaking and formal adjudication. Examples in-

---

17. Where the relevant organic statute requires that rulemaking be performed "on the record after opportunity for agency hearing," more formal trial-type procedure must be utilized. See 5 U.S.C. §§553 (c), 556, 557. This represents another category of procedure: "formal" or "on the record" rulemaking. However, the Supreme Court has greatly restricted the applicability of formal rulemaking. These "on the record" rulemaking procedures are required only in cases where the organic statute specifically so requires. See *United States v. Florida East Coast Ry.*, 410 U.S. 224 (1973), which reiterates the traditional doctrine that constitutional due process does not require trial-type hearings in rulemaking.

clude government grants for highway construction, decisions about how to manage a particular National Forest, and grants of grazing permits to private ranchers that authorize them to graze their cattle on the public lands. The Administrative Procedure Act does not require that agencies utilize any formal procedures in such cases, and in some cases the relevant organic statute also contains no procedural requirements. As we will see below, this dearth of procedures and the resulting lack of a well-defined factual record has created problems for courts in reviewing cases of informal adjudication, many of which are of major environmental significance.

In addition, the organic statutes establishing particular administrative programs sometimes contain special procedural provisions which do not precisely track any of the APA categories. The language of these statutes often fails to make clear exactly what sort of alternative procedure — such as legislative-type "public hearings" — should be followed by the agency. For example, the various sections of the Clean Air Act demonstrate a remarkable diversity and ambiguity with respect to procedural requirements. See, e.g., §§109(A), (B); 110(a)(1); 110(a)(2); 110(b); 110(e); 110(f); 111(b)(1); 112(b)(1)(B); 202 (b)(5)(A). As a distinguished federal judge observed in a similar context, "One would almost think there had been a conscious effort never to use the same phraseology twice." *Associated Indus., Inc. v. United States Dept. of Labor*, 487 F.2d 342, 354 n.2 (2d Cir. 1973) (Friendly, J.).

The Environmental Protection Agency is charged with devising and implementing stringent new controls on a wide variety of pollution sources. Given policy decisions must strike a balance between potentially quite expensive control measures on the one hand and public health and other important environmental values on the other. In these circumstances, neither the APA model of formal adjudication nor the notice and comment rulemaking model could be regarded as wholly satisfactory.

A general requirement that EPA observe trial-type adjudicatory procedures before taking action would cripple effective implementation of pollution controls. The range of technical and economic issues involved in any given decision is often intricate and far-reaching. Polluters determined to put off the day of reckoning could utilize the machinery of trial testimony and cross-examination to spin out the agency decisional processes for months or years. See Hamilton, Procedures for the Adoption of Rules of General Applicability: The Need for Procedural Innovation in Rulemaking, 60 Cal. L. Rev. 1276 (1972). The courts have generally refused to order EPA to follow trial-type procedures unless the relevant statute plainly requires it. This practice reflects the courts' concern with the functional impact of procedural formalities and the circumstance that many of EPA's actions in implementing the Clean Air Act — adoption of ambient standards, promulgation of emission limitations, adoption or promulgation of SIPs — consist of rulemaking, which is normally not subject to trial-type hearing requirements. Many provisions in federal environmental regulatory statutes require EPA to proceed by rulemaking. See, e.g., Clean Air Act §111 (new source performance standards); Clean Water Act, §304 (effluent guidelines). Congress mandated these "wholesale" techniques of lawmaking through rulemaking because of the need for rapid implementation of the statutes' ambitious goals. Developing policy through case by case adjudication would be slow and cumbersome. The goal of uniform regulatory treatment of competing plants in the same industry was also an important factor favoring policy making through rules. See the *du Pont* decision, supra, p. 466.

However, merely requiring EPA to observe traditional notice and comment procedures might not afford sufficient procedural protection, given the importance of the decisions involved. The basic justifications for procedural formalities are to improve the quality of agency decisions by providing those with a stake in agency policy an opportunity to submit relevant evidence and argument, and to generate materials to serve as a basis for judicial review. Since notice and comment rulemaking procedures traditionally do not require the agency to base its decision on any specified set of materials and call for only a cursory explanation by the agency of its action, such procedures are unlikely to afford affected parties a significant opportunity to affect agency policy and also provide little basis for searching judicial review.

Conscious of the inadequacies of traditional notice and comment procedures but chary of the hazards in requiring trial-type hearings, the federal courts have creatively devised a new set of procedures to govern EPA and other environmental regulatory decisions involving rulemaking. This improvisation has proceeded through judge-made extensions of traditional notice and comment procedures. The first step was a requirement that EPA articulate the grounds for its action in far greater detail than had ordinarily been required in previous notice and comment rulemaking. A leading decision is the following:

KENNECOTT COPPER CORP. V. ENVIRONMENTAL PROTECTION AGENCY

462 F.2d 846, 848 (D.C. Cir. 1972)

LEVENTHAL, Circuit Judge:
[The annual secondary standard for SO_2 adopted by EPA in 1971 60 $\mu g/m^3$ annual average was challenged on the ground that there was no evidence of adverse effects on vegetation or other aspects of welfare at such a concentration.]

. . . The complaint is that there is no adequate indication of the basis of the 1971 standard of 60 micrograms per cubic meter. [The EPA had adopted the standard after notice and comment rulemaking.] It is particularly stressed that the summarizing "Resume" paragraph . . . of the 1969 Criteria refer to no effects at a level below 85 micrograms per cubic meter. While the statement of the purpose and nature of the regulations set forth the basis for the primary standards, simultaneously adopted, in some detail, as to secondary standards the Administrator said only:

> National secondary ambient or quality standards are those which, in the judgment of the Administrator, based on the air quality criteria, are requisite to protect the public welfare from any known or anticipated adverse effects associated with the presence of air pollutants in the ambient air.

In support of the EPA's annual standard of 60 micrograms per cubic meter, the Government and intervenor, National Resources Defense Council, refer to lower figures in the material in the body of the Criteria, saying that the Resume is not conclusive. In the alternative they argue that the 85 figure in the Resume supports a 60 standard, on the basis of the Administrator's judgment as to anticipated effects and a margin necessary to avoid the adverse effects noted at the 85 level.

We do not undertake to rule on these particular matters. . . .

The provision for statutory judicial review contemplates some disclosure of the basis of the agency's action. *Citizens to Preserve Overton Park v. Volpe*, 401 U.S. 402, 416, 420 (1971); *Securities and Exchange Commission v. Chenery Corp.*, 318 U.S. 80, 94 (1943). We are not to be taken as specifying that the agency must provide the same articulation as is required for orders . . . issued after evidentiary hearings. . . . We are keenly aware of the need to avoid procedural strait jackets that would seriously hinder this new agency in the discharge of the novel, sensitive and formidable, tasks entrusted to it by Congress. This concern is emphasized by the fact that in the 1970 Amendments Congress was significantly concerned with expedition and avoidance of previous cumbersome and time-consuming procedures in effect under prior law.

[The court held, however, that EPA had failed to provide an adequate explanation and justification for its 85 $\mu g/m^3$ figure and remanded the rule to EPA. Subsequently the EPA eliminated the annual secondary standard altogether for lack of evidence of adverse effects from low annual concentrations. 38 Fed. Reg. 25678 (1973). The data relied upon in the Criteria documents indicating plant damage at annual concentrations of 85 $\mu g/m^3$ SO_2, see Appendix to Chapter 4, was reexamined, and the damage was found to be attributable to high short-term SO_2 peaks far in excess of 85 $\mu g/m^3$, rather than long-term low level concentrations.]

UNITED STATES V. NOVA SCOTIA FOOD PRODUCTS CORP.

568 F.2d 240, 250 (2d Cir. 1977)

[Under the Food, Drug and Cosmetic Act, the Federal Drug Administration (FDA) conducted §553 notice and comment rulemaking proceedings to promulgate safety regulations for the smoking of fish to safeguard against botulism poisoning.]

GURFEIN, Circuit Judge. . . .

The key issues were (1) whether, in the light of the rather scant history of botulism in whitefish, that species should have been considered separately rather than included in a general regulation which failed to distinguish species from species; (2) whether the application of the proposed [time-temperature-salinity (T-T-S)] requirements to smoked whitefish made whitefish commercially unsalable; and (3) whether the agency recognized that prospect, but nevertheless decided that the public health needs should prevail even if that meant commercial death for the whitefish industry. The procedural issues were whether, in the light of these key questions, the agency procedure was inadequate because (i) it failed to disclose the scientific data and methodology upon which is relied; and (ii) because it failed utterly to address itself to the pertinent question of commercial feasibility.

[The court briefly reviewed evidence showing that botulism in hot-smoked whitefish has been extremely rare.]

Interested parties were not informed of the scientific data, or at least of a selection of such data deemed important by the agency, so that comments could be addressed to the data. Appellants argue that unless the scientific data relied upon by the agency are spread upon the public records, criticism of the methodology used or the meaning to be inferred from the data is rendered impossible.

We agree with appellants in this case, for although we recognize that an agency may resort to its own expertise outside the record in an informal rulemaking procedure, we do not believe that when the pertinent research material is readily available and the agency has no special expertise on the precise parameters involved, there is any reason to conceal the scientific data relied upon from the interested parties. Nor was an articulate effort made to connect the scientific requirements to available technology that would make commercial survival possible, though the burden of proof was on the agency. . . .

Though a reviewing court will not match submission against counter-submission to decide whether the agency was correct in its conclusion on scientific matters (unless that conclusion is arbitrary), it will consider whether the agency has taken account of all "relevant factors and whether there has been a clear error of judgment." *Overton Park*, 401 U.S. at 415.

If the failure to notify interested persons of the scientific research upon which the agency was relying actually prevented the presentation of relevant comment, the agency may be held not to have considered all "the relevant factors." . . . To suppress meaningful comment by failure to disclose the basic data relied upon is akin to rejecting comment altogether. For unless there is common ground, the comments are unlikely to be of a quality that might impress a careful agency. The inadequacy of comment in turn leads in the direction of arbitrary decision-making.

[The FDA provided only cursory responses to suggestions by the Bureau of Commercial Fisheries that regulations should be set on a species by species basis and by industry that "heating of certain types of fish to high temperatures will completely destroy the product." The FDA also failed to respond to comments by the Bureau of Commercial Fisheries that nitrite and salt as additives would make smoking at lower temperatures safer. Nor did the FDA answer claims made by the Association of Smoked Fish Processors, Inc., that the proposed regulations were not based on adequate scientific evidence concerning the variety of smoked products to be included under the regulations.]

Appellants additionally attack the "concise general statement" required by APA, 5 U.S.C. §553, as inadequate. We think that, in the circumstances, it was less than adequate. It is not in keeping with the rational process to leave vital questions, raised by comments which are of cogent materiality, completely unanswered. The agencies certainly have a good deal of discretion in expressing the basis of a rule, but the agencies do not have quite the prerogative of obscurantism reserved to legislatures. "Congress did not purport to transfer its legislative power to the unbounded discretion of the regulatory body." *FCC v. RCA Communications, Inc.*, 346 U.S. 86, 90.

The Secretary was squarely faced with the question whether it was necessary to formulate a rule with specific parameters that applied to all species of fish, and particularly whether lower temperatures with the addition of nitrite and salt would not be sufficient [to deal with the risk of botulism in whitefish]. Though this alternative was suggested by an agency of the federal government, its suggestion, though acknowledged, was never answered.

Moreover, the comment that to apply the proposed T-T-S requirements to whitefish would destroy the commercial product was neither discussed nor answered. We think that to sanction silence in the face of such vital questions would be to make the statutory requirement of a "concise general statement" less than an adequate safeguard against arbitrary decision-making.

One may recognize that even commercial infeasibility cannot stand in the way of an overwhelming public interest. Yet the administrative process should disclose, at least, whether the proposed regulation is considered to be commercially feasible, or whether other considerations prevail even if commercial infeasibility is acknowledged.

In the light of the history of smoked whitefish to which we have referred, we find no articulate balancing here sufficient to make the procedure followed less than arbitrary.

NOTE ON THE EVOLUTION OF "PAPER HEARING" AND OTHER PROCEDURAL REQUIREMENTS IN RULEMAKING

The requirement of reasoned elaboration by the agency of the grounds for its action in notice and comment rulemaking was developed further in decisions reviewing EPA postponement of automobile emissions deadlines, *International Harvester Co. v. Ruckelshaus,* supra p. 304; approval of state implementation plans, or disapproval followed by EPA promulgation of such plans, e.g., *Texas v. EPA,* 499 F.2d 289 (5th Cir. 1974); *NRDC v. EPA,* 478 F.2d 875 (1st Cir. 1973); and promulgation of emission limitations for new stationary sources, e.g., *Portland Cement Assn. v. Ruckelshaus,* 486 F.2d 375 (D.C. Cir. 1973), *cert. denied,* 417 U.S. 921 (1974). In the course of this development, not only has EPA been required to articulate in detail the reasons for its choices, but it has also been required to respond in its decision to the criticisms and contrary evidence adduced in comments by those opposing EPA's proposed action. These requirements are designed to produce more careful decisionmaking by EPA and provide the courts with a better basis for scrutinizing its policy choices.

Courts have also gone beyond traditional notice and comment procedures by effectively requiring EPA to assemble a documentary record on which its rulemaking decision is based. This development was related to the emerging principle that EPA explain in detail its action and respond to criticism. That principle requires that documentary evidence and written arguments submitted as comments to EPA by opponents be included in the materials which EPA must respond to in its decision and which a court will look to on review. See Pedersen, Formal Records and Informal Rulemaking, 85 Yale L.J. 38 (1975). In such circumstances, government lawyers eager to sustain EPA's action have not hesitated to include documents that they believe would support EPA's actions. Moveover, internal agency documents arguably contrary to EPA's decision can generally be obtained by opponents through resort to the federal Freedom of Information Act, 5 U.S.C. §552. In order to obviate the inevitable delays resulting from Freedom of Information Act litigation and in order to avoid the charge of suppressing unfavorable evidence, government lawyers customarily submit to the court unfavorable as well as favorable documentary evidence considered by the agency in the course of its decision. See Pedersen, supra. As a result, a reviewing court will normally have before it a record consisting of all of the documentary materials relevant to the agency's decision. This practice helps ensure more careful agency decisionmaking, because the agency must be prepared to defend its decision in light of all of the relevant materials. Also, when judicial review actually does occur, it will be more informed and searching, since the court will have before it all of the evidence that can be used to support or impeach the agency's action.

The requirement of detailed explanation for agency action and the accompanying development of a documentary record upon which such action must be based has, in the view of observers, stimulated considerable improvement in the quality of EPA decisionmaking. Like many new agencies, EPA was at the outset badly organized, and informal decisional processes were often chaotic. The prospect of careful judicial review based on a full documentary record led EPA (under the prod of agency lawyers) to improve its decisional processes in order to produce decisions that could be justified under detailed explanations sustainable in court on a review of all of the relevant evidence, unfavorable as well as favorable. See Pedersen, supra. In essence, what has developed is a "paper hearing," which combines the advantages of a trial-type hearing (excepting live testimony and cross-examination) while avoiding many of its drawbacks in terms of cost and delay. Some observers, however, remain highly skeptical as to the real value of such procedural requirements in improving the quality of agency decisions. See Sax, infra p. 1016. They contend that agency decisions are largely driven by political and institutional forces, that procedural requirements are largely productive of delay and higher transactions costs, and that they provide only a facade of agency rationality and responsiveness.

In contemporary notice and comment rulemaking involving important and disputed policy decisions, the responsible federal agency issues a notice of proposed rulemaking in which it sets forth a proposed rule and its supporting rationale as well as issues that the agency wishes to be addressed in the comment period. The proposed rule is typically a product of lengthy investigation and deliberation, including consultations with other interested federal government agencies and outside groups. Sometimes the agency issues an advanced notice of proposed rulemaking in which it states that it is considering issuing a proposed rule on a given subject and invites suggestions from the public. Both types of notices are published in the Federal Register. Simultaneously with a notice of proposed rulemaking, the agency establishes a file in its public records facility containing all of the agency documents (including, often, reports that it has commissioned by consultants to gather data and analyze the issue in question) relevant to the proceeding. Interested members of the public, including industry, environmental groups, and state and local governments, submit comments that typically include criticism of the agency's proposal and the factual premises and analysis underlying it. Because, under the approach initiated in *Kennecott*, supra, courts will demand that agencies respond persuasively to such criticisms and justify their responses by reference to the rulemaking record, the agency must often commission new studies and reports, which will in turn be subject to further public comment and criticism. All of the documents that are generated by the agency or outside commentators are placed in the public file. The "paper hearing" procedure evolved through judicial decisions and agency response has been codified for rulemaking under the Clean Air Act in §307(d) of the Act as amended in 1977.

Eventually the comment period and documentary record are closed. The agency then must formulate a final rule, search the relevant record, and write a justification for the rule, answering criticisms and supporting its justification by reference to the documentary record. In the case of rules defined as "significant" under Executive Order 12866, the final rule and its accompanying justification must be sent to OMB for review.[18] See supra, p. 795. OMB will often raise additional questions that must be answered before the rule is cleared. If the proposed rule survives these various hurdles, it is published in the Federal Register, along with a lengthy justification in the "Preamble" to the rule itself. This process may take anywhere from one to several years or more. Nearly 90 percent of "major" rules adopted by the EPA are challenged by at least one party, and often more, triggering review proceedings (typically in a court of appeals) that will last a year and often more. In about a third of the cases, the court of appeals finds one or more deficiencies in the rulemaking process for the EPA's decision, and remands the matter to the agency for further proceedings.

Far more controversial have been occasional court decisions which have gone beyond the requirements of detailed explanation and a "paper hearing" in rulemaking to require the EPA to grant a limited trial-type hearing on certain more or less narrowly defined issues. For example, in *International Harvester v. Ruckelshaus*, supra, p. 304, the court in remanding indicated that limited cross-examination would be an appropriate means of dealing with disputed technical issues about the performance of various automobile emission control technologies.

---

18. In the case of such rules, the notice of proposed rulemaking must also have been submitted to OMB for review.

A different question is presented where an isolated source challenges the adoption by EPA of emission limitations that apply only to that source and the regulations' validity and reasonableness assertedly turn on isolated factual issues. Here, the source claims that the proceedings are only in form rulemaking, but are functionally adjudication because they are targeted at only a single source. In *Anaconda Co. v. Ruckelshaus,* 482 F.2d 1303 (10th Cir. 1973), the court rejected Anaconda's assertion that EPA violated due process rights by refusing to provide a trial-type hearing on its claim that EPA relied on faulty monitoring data in framing emission limitations for copper smelters in the SIP promulgated by EPA for Montana. Montana had failed to submit a plan for controlling smelter emissions, and Anaconda owned the sole copper smelter in the state. The court pointed out that the Clean Air Act, §110(a)(3)(A) and (c)(1)(A), did not require a trial-type hearing in the adoption of SIPs, but only a legislative-type "public hearing." Moreover, it declined to find that due process required such a hearing, on the ground that a widespread requirement of trial-type procedures in the adoption of emission limitations would cripple implementation of the Act. Is the court's fear well-founded if trial-type hearings were limited to specific disputed factual issues, such as the reliability of monitoring data? Are "legislative" hearings and the opportunity to submit documentary evidence an adequate safeguard? In *Bunker Hill Co. v. EPA,* 572 F.2d 1286 (9th Cir. 1977), the court in remanding granted a source the right to cross-examine EPA experts concerning the technical basis of emissions limitations promulgated by EPA for that source. Similarly, in *Appalachian Power Co. v. Ruckelshaus,* 477 F.2d 495 (4th Cir. 1973), the court held that limited cross-examination must be afforded on key technical and economic issues relating to the achievability of emission limitations in a SIP at some point before they became effective.

The judicial development of "hybrid" procedures in regulatory rulemaking going beyond the basic "paper hearing" model suffered a major setback in the following Supreme Court decision:

Vermont Yankee Nuclear Power Corp. v. Natural Resources Defense Council

435 U.S. 519 (1978)

[In this decision, the Supreme Court reversed a decision by the D.C. Circuit Court of Appeals invalidating a rulemaking proceeding by the Atomic Energy Commission or AEC (whose regulatory functions with respect to radioactive hazards were in the meantime transferred as a result of legislation to the Nuclear Regulatory Commission, or NRC).

The AEC was responsible for licensing new nuclear plants. Traditional trial-type adjudicatory hearings apply in such proceedings. Opponents of nuclear power intervened in such hearings, seeking (generally with little ultimate success) to block the grant of such licenses. These opponents used their procedural rights, such as cross-examination, to the maximum extent in what many observers regarded as a tactic of delay and obstruction. The opponents of nuclear power maintained that the environmental health and safety issues that they raised were important and that formal trial-type procedures were necessary in order to probe relevant facts and overcome an overly "cozy" relation between the nuclear power industry and the Commission. In order to speed up licensing proceedings, the Commission decided to deal with certain recurring, generic issues that arose in licensing through notice and comment rulemaking. Once these issues had been resolved through rulemaking, the results could be incorporated by reference by the Commission in particular license decisions without any further hearing procedures. The Supreme Court had, in a different context, upheld this use of rulemaking to resolve generically issues that would otherwise have to be addressed through case by case adjudication and trial-type hearings. See *FPC v. Texaco, Inc.*, 377 U.S. 33 (1964). Among the recurring issues that the Commission decided to handle in this fashion was the potential hazard associated with disposal of the spent radioactive fuel used in nuclear power plants. Opponents of nuclear power have often pointed to the failure of the federal government and the nuclear industry to solve the radioactive waste disposal problem as a reason for opposing new nuclear plants. The spent fuel from nuclear plants is a tiny fraction of all high-level nuclear waste in the United States, most of which has been generated by military uses. Still, opponents of a new nuclear plant insisted that the disposal issue should be thoroughly tried in licensing proceedings. The Commission, however, decided to use rulemaking procedures to specify, in quantitative terms, the adverse environmental effects (releases of radioactivity, contamination of soil and water, and so forth) from the spent nuclear fuel generated by a new 1000 megawatt nuclear generating unit. The results of this rulemaking determination would then be factored into adjudicatory decisions to license new plants without allowing the determinations made through rulemaking to be reexamined.

There was then and at present still is no operational method for permanent disposal of high-level nuclear waste, including spent fuel. At the time of the AEC proceeding, many assumed that spent fuel would be reprocessed, allowing a substantial portion to be used again as fuel. Reprocessing, however, produces concentrated plutonium, which can be diverted to production of weapons. The Carter Administration ultimately halted United States reprocessing efforts as part of a nuclear nonproliferation strategy. Currently, the most promising method for permanent disposal of high-level wastes is burial in stable geologic formations such as salt beds or mountains. However, efforts by the Commission to develop such burial facilities have not yet succeeded, and there are unresolved scientific questions concerning the stability of such burial sites and the danger of leakage of radioactive wastes.

In the rulemaking proceedings at issue here, the Commission not only provided for submission of documents by Commission staff and interested outside parties, but also for a legislative-type public hearing at which parties could make oral statements to a Commission hearing panel. These statements, however, were not subject to cross-examination by other parties. At the hearing, Dr. Frank Pittman of the Commission staff presented a 20-page statement describing in general terms the problems in devising a secure method of storing radioactive wastes and the types of storage facilities (aboveground and underground) that might be developed. He provided some engineering details concerning a proposed temporary aboveground storage facility. Two pages of his statement were devoted to the permanent storage problem, asserting that substantial progress on underground disposition of wastes was being made and that the problem would probably be resolved in the relatively near future. The hearing panel asked a few general questions about the proposed surface storage facility. A staff background paper referred to technical publications on nuclear waste disposal issues. In their oral presentation, environmental groups strongly urged that current arrangements for nuclear waste disposal were inadequate. The Commission, relying heavily on Dr. Pittman's testimony, concluded that the environmental hazards associated with spent nuclear fuel were negligible, judging that "under normal conditions" no radioactivity would be released and that the possibility of a serious accident was "incredible." It incorporated this conclusion in a table specifying numerical values for various environmental hazards that would be posed by construction of an additional nuclear plant, including the hazards involved in disposing of spent fuel, which it found to be minimal. The table was incorporated in the final rule issued at the conclusion of the rulemaking proceedings.

Relying on the determinations made in the rule, the Commission subsequently sustained the grant of an operating license to a nuclear generating plant located in Vermont (Vermont Yankee) on the basis of these conclusions without affording any adjudicatory hearing rights on the waste disposal issue in the Vermont Yankee licensing proceeding. The D.C. Circuit Court of Appeals, in a decision by Chief Judge Bazelon, set aside the Commission's action on the ground that the rulemaking proceeding had not provided a sufficient opportunity to examine and probe the waste disposal issue, and that the license grant must therefore be set aside because it relied on the results of a faulty rulemaking proceeding. 547 F.2d 633 (D.C. Cir. 1976). The essence of the court's ruling with respect to the rulemaking proceeding is contained in the following excerpt from its opinion:

> In substantial part, the materials uncritically relied on by the Commission in promulgating this rule consist of extremely vague assurances by agency personnel that problems as yet unsolved will be solved. That is an insufficient record to sustain a rule limiting consideration of the environmental effects of nuclear waste disposal to the numerical values [selected by the Commission]. To the extent that uncertainties necessarily underlie predictions of this importance on the frontiers of science and technology, there is a concomitant necessity to confront and explore fully the depth and consequences of such uncertainties. Not only were the generalities relied on in this case not subject to rigorous probing — in any form — but when apparently substantial criticisms were brought to the Commission's attention, it simply ignored them, or brushed them aside without answer. Without a thorough exploration of the problems involved in waste disposal, including past mistakes, and a forthright assessment of the uncertainties and differences in expert opinion, this type of agency action cannot pass muster as reasoned decisionmaking.
>
> Many procedural devices for creating a genuine dialogue on these issues were available to the agency — including informal conferences between intervenors and staff, document discovery, interrogatories, technical advisory committees comprised of outside experts with differing perspectives, limited cross-examination, funding independent research by intervenors, detailed annotation of technical reports, surveys of existing literature, memoranda explaining methodology. We do not presume to intrude on the agency's province by dictating to it which, if any, of these devices it must adopt to flesh out the record. . . . Whatever techniques the Commission adopts, before it promulgates a rule limiting further consideration of waste disposal and reprocessing issues, it must in one way or another generate a record in which the factual issues are fully developed. . . .
>
> It has become commonplace among proponents of nuclear power to lament public ignorance. The public — the "guinea pigs" who will bear the consequences of either resolution of the nuclear controversy — is apprehensive. But public concern will not be quieted by proceedings like the present. . . .
>
> The Commission's action in cutting off consideration of waste disposal and reprocessing issues in licensing proceedings based on the cursory development of the facts which occurred in this proceeding was capricious and arbitrary. . . .

Judge Tamm issued an opinion concurring in the result. He agreed that the record in the rulemaking proceedings did not provide adequate data or analysis to support the Commission's conclusion that spent fuel hazards were negligible, and concluded that the Commission's decision that such hazards were insignificant was therefore "arbitrary and capricious." However, he took issue with the majority opinion's emphasis on additional procedures:

> . . . I believe the majority's insistence upon increased adversariness and procedural rigidity, uneasily combined with its non-direction toward any specific procedures, continues a distressing trend toward over-formalization of the administrative decisionmaking process which ultimately will impair its utility. . . .
>
> The appropriate remedy at this point is not to impose ad hoc procedural requirements in an attempt to raise the level of petitioners' participation, . . . but to remand for an explanation of the basis of Dr. Pittman's statements and staff conclusions with respect to the magnitude of spent fuel environmental hazards, i.e., for the documentation which the majority finds so conspicuously lacking. . . . 547 F.2d at 660-661.]

Mr. Justice REHNQUIST delivered the opinion of the Court.

In 1946, Congress enacted the Administrative Procedure Act, which as we have noted elsewhere was not only "a new, basic and comprehensive regulation of procedures in many agencies," *Wong Yang Sun v. McGrath,* 339 U.S. 33 (1950), but was also a legislative enactment which settled "long-continued and hard-fought contentions, and enacts a formula upon which opposing social and political forces have come to rest." Id., at 40. Interpreting [§553] of the Act in *United States v. Allegheny-Ludlum Steel Corp.,* 406 U.S. 742 (1972), and *United States v. Florida East Coast Ry. Co.,* 410 U.S. 224 (1973), we held that generally speaking this section of the Act established the maximum procedural requirements which Congress was willing to have the courts impose upon agencies in conducting rulemaking procedures. Agencies are free to grant additional procedural rights in the exercise of their discretion, but reviewing courts are generally not free to impose them if the agencies have not chosen to grant them. This is not to say necessarily that there are no circumstances which would ever justify a court in overturning agency action because of a failure to employ procedures beyond those required by the statute. But such circumstances, if they exist, are extremely rare.

Even apart from the Administrative Procedure Act this Court has for more than four decades emphasized that the formulation of procedures was basically to be left within the discretion of the agencies to which Congress had confided the responsibility for substantive judgments. . . .

It is in the light of this background of statutory and decisional law that we granted certiorari to review [the court of appeals' decisions] because of our concern that they had seriously misread or misapplied this statutory and decisional law cautioning reviewing courts against engrafting their own notions of proper procedures upon agencies entrusted with substantive functions by Congress. . . . We conclude that the Court of Appeals has done just that in these cases, and we therefore remand them to it for further proceedings. . . . [The Court discussed the court's decision.]

After a thorough examination of the opinion itself, we conclude that while the matter is not entirely free from doubt, the majority of the Court of Appeals struck down the rule because of the perceived inadequacies of the procedures employed in the rulemaking proceedings. The court first determined the intervenors' primary argument to be "that the decision to preclude discovery on cross-examination denied them a meaningful opportunity to participate in the proceedings as guaranteed by due process." . . . The court then went on to frame the issue for decision thusly: "Thus, we are called upon to decide whether the procedures provided by the agency were sufficient to ventilate the issues." . . . The court conceded that absent extraordinary circumstances it is improper for a reviewing court to prescribe the procedural format an agency must follow, but it likewise clearly thought it entirely appropriate to "scrutinize the record as a whole to insure that genuine opportunities to participate in a meaningful way were provided. . . ." . . . The court refrained from actually ordering the agency to follow any specific procedures, . . . but there is little doubt in our minds that the ineluctable mandate of the court's decision is that the procedures afforded during the hearings were inadequate. . . .

In prior opinions we have intimated that even in a rulemaking proceeding when an agency is making a "quasi-judicial" determination by which a very small number of persons are "exceptionally affected, in each case upon individual grounds," in some circumstances additional procedures may be required in order to afford the aggrieved individuals due process. . . . It might also be true, although we do not think the issue is presented in this case and accordingly do not decide it, that a totally unjustified departure from well settled agency procedures of long standing might require judicial correction.

But this much is absolutely clear. Absent constitutional constraints or extremely compelling circumstances "the administrative agencies 'should be free to fashion their own rules of procedure and to pursue methods of inquiry capable of permitting them to discharge their multitudinous duties' " [quoting precedent].

Respondent NRDC argues that [§553] of the Administrative Procedure Act merely establishes lower procedural bounds and that a court may routinely require more than the minimum when an agency's proposed rule addresses complex or technical factual issues or "Issues of Great Public Import." [The Court rejected this contention.] . . . In the first place, if courts continually review agency proceedings to determine whether the agency employed procedures which were, in the court's opinion, perfectly tailored to reach what the court perceives to be the "best" or "correct" result, judicial review would be totally unpredictable. And the agencies, operating under this vague injunction to employ the "best" procedures and facing the threat of reversal if they did not, would undoubtedly adopt full adjudicatory procedures in every instance.

Finally, and perhaps most importantly, this sort of review fundamentally misconceives the nature of the standard for judicial review of an agency rule. The court below uncritically assumed that additional procedures will automatically result in a more adequate record because it will give interested parties more of an opportunity to participate and contribute to the proceedings. But informal rulemaking need not be based solely on the transcript of a hearing held before an agency. Indeed, the agency need not even hold a formal hearing. See 5 U.S.C. §553(c). . . . Thus, the adequacy of the "record" in this type of proceeding is not correlated directly to the type of procedural devices employed, but rather turns on whether the agency has followed the statutory mandate of the Administrative Procedure Act or other relevant statutes. . . .

Respondent NRDC also argues that the fact that the Commission's inquiry was undertaken in the context of NEPA [the National Environmental Policy Act, see supra Chapter 8] somehow permits a court to require procedures beyond those specified in §[553] of the APA when investigating factual issues through rulemaking. The Court of Appeals was apparently also of this view, indicating that agencies may be required to "develop new procedures to accomplish the innovative task of implementing NEPA through rulemaking." . . . But we search in vain for something in NEPA which would mandate such a result. . . . Thus, it is clear NEPA cannot serve as the basis for a substantial revision of the carefully constructed procedural specifications of the APA.

In short, nothing in the APA, NEPA, the circumstances of this case, the nature of the issues being considered, past agency practice, or the statutory mandate under which the Commission operates permitted the court to review and overturn the rulemaking proceeding on the basis of the procedural devices employed (or not employed) by the Commission so long as the Commission employed at least the statutory *minima*, a matter about which there is no doubt in this case.

There remains, of course, the questions of whether the challenged rule finds sufficient justification in the administrative proceedings that it should be upheld by the reviewing court. Judge Tamm, concurring in the result reached by the majority of the Court of Appeals, thought that it did not. There are also intimations in the majority opinion which suggest that the judges who joined it likewise may have thought the administrative proceedings an insufficient basis upon which to predicate the rule in question. We accordingly remand so that the Court of Appeals may review the rule as the Administrative Procedure Act provides. We have made it abundantly clear before that when there is a contemporaneous explanation of the agency decision, the validity of that action must "stand or fall on the propriety of that finding, judged, of course, by the appropriate standard of review. If that finding is not sustainable on the administrative record made, then the Comptroller's decision must be vacated and the matter remanded to him for further consideration." *Camp v. Pitts*, 411 U.S. 138, 143 (1973). See also *SEC v. Chenery Corp.*, 318 U.S. 80 (1943). The court should engage in this kind of review and not stray beyond the judicial province to explore the procedural format or to impose upon the agency its own notion of which procedures are "best" or most likely to further some vague, undefined public good.

. . . Nuclear energy may some day be a cheap, safe source of power or it may not. But Congress has made a choice to at least try nuclear energy, establishing a reasonable review process in which courts are to play only a limited role. The fundamental policy questions appropriately resolved in Congress and in the state legislatures are *not* subject to reexamination in the federal courts under the guise of judicial review of agency action. Time may prove wrong the decision to develop nuclear energy, but it is Congress or the States within their appropriate agencies which must eventually make that judgment. In the meantime courts should perform their appointed function. . . . It is to insure a fully informed and well-considered decision, not necessarily a decision the judges of the Court of Appeals or of this Court would have reached had they been members of the decisionmaking unit of the agency. Administrative decisions should be set aside in this context, as in every other, only for substantial procedural or substantive reasons as mandated by statute, . . . not simply because the court is unhappy with the result reached. . . .

Reversed and remanded.

NOTES AND QUESTIONS

1. As the AEC waste disposal proceedings at issue in *Vermont Yankee* illustrate, agencies during the past two decades have turned increasingly to notice and comment rulemaking in order to decide major policy questions turning in part on controverted technical issues. By resorting to rulemaking, agencies have avoided the trial-type hearings required in formal adjudication. However, this shift reduces greatly procedural rights in agency decisions and may fail to generate an adequate record for judicial review. In light of these developments, has the Court in *Vermont Yankee* unwisely frozen agency procedures in the form of the 1946 APA's "notice and comment" model? Should the courts be denied a role in adjusting procedural law instead of leaving the entire

responsibility to Congress and administrators? See Stewart, Vermont Yankee and the Evolution of Administrative Procedure, 91 Harv. L. Rev. 1805 (1978); for criticism of this view, see Byse, Vermont Yankee and the Evolution of Administrative Procedure: A Somewhat Different View, id. at 1823. Or is the basic point of *Vermont Yankee* that courts lack the technical expertise and political accountability to review and supervise such matters as nuclear energy policy and should consequently be deferential to agency decisions? See Breyer, Vermont Yankee and the Court's Role in the Nuclear Energy Controversy, id. at 1833.

2. Note that the APA §553 provides for notice and comment rulemaking, but says nothing about the creation of a "record" that is to serve as the basis for judicial review. In fact, under the traditional understanding, the "legislative" notice and comment model would not produce any such record. Yet the Supreme Court seems to accept the notion of a documentary record in rulemaking and that a reviewing court may set aside a rule when it and the agency's published justification for the rule are not adequately supported by the facts and analysis in that record. Thus the Court implicitly endorses the judicially developed requirement of a "paper record" in rulemaking, but bars judicial imposition of additional procedures. Is the Court's endorsement of the principle of a "record" in notice and comment rulemaking consistent with the reasoning in its opinion?

3. After *Vermont Yankee,* what can a reviewing court do if the administrative record is insufficient to support the agency decision? The Court's opinion implies that a court, while able to remand for a deficient record, can no longer suggest what specific procedures should be employed by the agency to produce a reviewable record. The Court apparently recognized, as have commentators and agency lawyers, that even a judicial "suggestion" of what procedures might be appropriate can have the effect of a judicial order upon an administrative agency. In *Seacoast Anti-Pollution League v. Costle,* 572 F.2d 872, 880 (1st Cir. 1978), for example, the reviewing court remanded "for the limited purpose of allowing the Administrator to determine whether cross-examination would be useful" for a full and true disclosure of the factual issues concerning the impact on marine life forms of the proposed water cooling system for the Seabrook nuclear power plant. The Administrator did decide to allow cross-examination in the new hearing. See *Seacoast Anti-Pollution League v. Costle [Seacoast II].* 597 F.2d 306, 307 (1st Cir. 1979); Scalia, Vermont Yankee: The APA, the D.C. Circuit, and the Supreme Court, 1978 Sup. Ct. Rev. 345, 371-72 (1979).

4. On remand from the Supreme Court, the court of appeals concluded that the Commission's rulemaking record was insufficient to support the Commission's conclusions that the environmental hazards of spent fuel were minimal and remanded the matter to the Commis-

sion. What should the Commission do? See *Baltimore Gas & Electric Co.,* infra p. 976.

5. Legal challenges to nuclear power plant licensing proceedings have been one of the main weapons of environmental groups opposed to the continued development of nuclear power. The Court's strong language in *Vermont Yankee* can be taken as an expression of frustration at the numerous litigation proceedings and the delay in power plant construction associated with such litigation. Should the holding of *Vermont Yankee* be limited to the context of nuclear power issues? Consider the Court's similar willingness to endorse nuclear power in *Duke Power,* supra, p. 825. Why should courts be especially deferential to agency determinations in the area of nuclear power? Does this amount to judicial policymaking of the sort the Court disapproves of when exercised by lower courts?

NOTE ON OFF-THE-RECORD COMMUNICATIONS IN NOTICE AND COMMENT RULEMAKING AND SIERRA CLUB v. COSTLE

When an agency employs notice and comment rulemaking procedures to adopt standards or regulations, may persons outside the agency communicate (orally or in writing) with the agency about the matter off the record, either before or after the period for written comment has expired but before the agency's final decision? Does the answer vary depending on whether the outsider is a private person, a member of Congress, a White House official, or the President?

These questions have recently attracted lively attention. Environmental and other "public interest" advocates fear that such communications are used extensively by industry to weaken regulatory protection and present false or misleading data and argument that are not subject to rebuttal because they are not public. In some cases, particularly those that are functionally adjudicatory in character because they involve "conflicting claims to a valuable privilege," such as competing applicants for broadcast licenses, *Sangamon Valley Television Corp. v. United States,* 269 F.2d 221 (D.C. Cir. 1959), courts have held that off the record communications are prohibited by considerations of fairness. In a subsequent opinion involving rulemaking setting the terms of competition between over the air and cable television broadcasters, Judge J. Skelly Wright decried off the record communications, stressing the need of the court to be apprised of all relevant considerations and data in order to perform its reviewing function. See *Home Box Office, Inc. v. FCC,* 567 F.2d 9 (D.C. Cir.), *cert. denied,* 434 U.S. 829 (1977). On the other hand, there is fear of overformalizing the rulemaking process and recognition that informal exchange and give and take are necessary elements in the administrative process. See *Action for Children's Television v. FCC,* 564 F.2d 458 (D.C. Cir. 1977). Where the President or a White House official is involved, there are the special considerations of the President's constitutional responsibility to ensure the faithful execution of law and the potential need for coordination and central direction of the decisions of various specialized regulatory agencies. See generally Bruff, Presidential Power and Administrative Rulemaking, 88 Yale L.J. 451 (1979); Verkuil, Jawboning Administrative Agencies: *Ex Parte* Contracts by the White House, 80 Colum L. Rev. 943 (1980).

These issues were discussed by Judge Wald in *Sierra Club v. Costle.* The Environmental Defense Fund complained that extensive written and oral comments were submitted to EPA after the close of the stated period for comment on EPA's proposed NSPS for coal-fired power plants, and claimed that the standards that ultimately emerged were the result of an "ex parte blitz" by eastern coal interests.

EPA accepted all of the nearly 300 written submissions received after the comment period and placed them in the public docket of the rulemaking proceeding, but declined to reopen the comment period. The court held that this action was proper because it was consistent with the special provisions for Clean Air Act rulemaking specified in §307(d) of the Act,[19] and because no material prejudice was shown to EDF, which had time to meet these submissions with written rebuttal before EPA acted.

EDF also complained of nine off the record, post-comment-period meetings that involved high administration officials and, in two cases, Senator Byrd of West Virginia, Senate Majority Leader and a strong defender of eastern coal interests. Seven of the meetings were summarized in memoranda placed in the public docket file at EPA. The failure to prepare and docket a summary of one of the remaining meetings was found by the court to be an oversight that did not prejudice EDF. The other meeting involved the President.

The court found that §307(d) did not prohibit such off the record meetings and that *Vermont Yankee* precluded the court from imposing its own rule to that effect. It concluded, however, that oral communications containing information or other material "of central relevance" to the rulemaking should be summarized and docketed, in order to prevent circumvention of the requirement in §307 that all documents "of central relevance to the rulemaking" shall be placed in the docket as soon as possible after their availability.

The court acknowledged that this approach would necessarily

---

19. As noted by the court, these procedures, including the maintenance by EPA of a public docket of relevant documentary materials, were based in large part on the analysis and recommendation in Pedersen, Formal Records and Informal Rulemaking, 85 Yale L.J. 38 (1975).

leave substantial discretion to the EPA to determine which communications were of "central relevance" and therefore had to be docketed. It then considered whether this principle required that a summary of the meeting involving the President should be prepared and docketed:

> The court recognizes the basic need of the President and his White House staff to monitor the consistency of executive agency regulations with Administration policy. He and his White House advisers surely must be briefed fully and frequently about rules in the making, and their contributions to policymaking considered. The executive power under our Constitution, after all, is not shared — it rests exclusively with the President. . . . To ensure the President's control and supervision over the Executive Branch, the Constitution — and its judicial gloss — vests him with the powers of appointment and removal, the power to demand written opinions from executive officers, and the right to invoke executive privilege to protect consultative privacy. . . .
>
> . . . [T]he desirability of such control is demonstrable from the practical realities of administrative rulemaking. . . . Regulations such as those involved here demand a careful weighing of cost, environmental, and energy considerations. They also have broad implications for national economic policy. Our form of government simply could not function effectively or rationally if key executive policymakers were isolated from each other and from the Chief Executive. Single mission agencies do not always have the answers to complex regulatory problems. An overworked administrator exposed on a 24-hour basis to a dedicated but zealous staff needs to know the arguments and ideas of policymakers in other agencies as well as in the White House.
>
> . . . We recognize, however, that there may be instances where the docketing of conversations between the President or his staff and other Executive Branch officers or rulemakers may be necessary to ensure due process. This may be true, for example, where such conversations directly concern the outcome of adjudications or quasi-adjudicatory proceedings; there is no inherit executive power to control the rights of individuals in such settings. Docketing may also be necessary in some circumstances where a statute like this one specifically requires that essential "information or data" upon which a rule is based be docketed. But in the absence of any further Congressional requirements, we hold that it was not unlawful in this case for EPA officials not to docket a face-to-face policy session involving the President and EPA officials during the post-comment period, since EPA makes no effort to base the rule on any "information or data" arising from that meeting. Where the President himself is directly involved in oral communication with Executive Branch officials, Article II considerations — combined with the strictures of *Vermont Yankee* — require that courts tread with extraordinary caution in mandating disclosure beyond that already required by statute.
>
> Of course, it is always possible that undisclosed Presidential prodding may direct an outcome that is factually based on the record, but different from the outcome that would have obtained in the absence of

Presidential involvement. In such a case, it would be true that the political process did affect the outcome in a way the courts could not police. But we do not believe that Congress intended that the courts convert informal rulemaking into a rarified technocratic process, unaffected by political considerations or the presence of Presidential power.

The court also rejected EDF's claims that the meetings with Senator Byrd represented improper congressional pressure, distinguishing *D.C. Federation of Civic Associations v. Volpe*, 459 F.2d 1231 (D.C. Cir. 1971), *cert. denied*, 405 U.S. 1030 (1972), where the court set aside the Transportation Department's approval of a bridge across a scenic area of the Potomac River because a powerful member of Congress threatened to withhold funding for the Washington, D.C., subway system unless the bridge was built. The court noted that protection of eastern coal producers was, given the legislative background of the 1977 Amendments to §111, a statutorily legitimate consideration, unlike the subway funding in *D.C. Federation*.

In *EDF v. Blum*, 458 F. Supp. 650 (D.D.C. 1978), off the record communications from private parties led the court to set aside EPA's grant through rulemaking of permission to utilize the pesticide ferriamicide to deal with fire ants. While the court found that EDF had an opportunity to discover and rebut some of the off the record communications submitted by those favoring use of the pesticide after close of the public comment period, several such communications fell outside the "harmless error" category because they were made just before the EPA's decision and had a material impact upon it.

NOTES AND QUESTIONS

1. Judge Wald's decision in *Sierra Club v. Costle* has widely been interpreted as having broader significance beyond the specific context of White House involvement in review of rules adopted through notice and comment rulemaking under the specific procedures. It has been thought that her distinction between "hard" data and analysis, which must be placed in the rulemaking record, and "soft" political and policy arguments, which need not, also applies when private parties seek to influence the rulemaking process. Hence, private parties are not barred by the APA from informal, off the record conversation with agency officials regarding political and policy issues, although many agencies including EPA prohibit or limit such communication, especially during the period between the close of the public comment period and the promulgation of a final rule.

2. Should the President and (more important, as a practical matter) his staff have free reign to "jawbone" agency officials about pro-

posed rules, without any public disclosure of the communications? What about the danger that the White House will become a "back door conduit" for private interests seeking to block or change agency rules? What procedural safeguards should be imposed? Reconsider the materials on OMB regulatory review procedures, supra, pp. 793-795. Have these problems vanished after election of a "pro-environment" Clinton-Gore administration?

NOTE ON NEGOTIATED RULEMAKING

In response to the increasing formalization of the rulemaking process, EPA and other agencies began in the early 1980s, to experiment with negotiated rulemaking. The agency selects a facilitator to convene meetings of interested parties. They will meet with staff to propose rules, to discuss their own proposals, and to try to come up with a final, agreed upon rule, including the rule's specific language. As required by the APA, the rule must then be subject to notice and comment. The agency promises to adopt the consensus proposal, at least if subsequent notice and comment do not reveal serious flaws and the Office of Management and Budget gives its approval. The process is based on the realization that a high percentage of final rules are challenged through litigation; by using negotiated rulemaking, the agencies attempt to shorten the rulemaking process and avoid litigation by generating consensus.

The Administrative Conference of the United States has strongly recommended that agencies use negotiated rulemaking as well as recommending how they should go about doing so. See Administrative Conference Recommendations 82-4, 85-5, and its Negotiated Rulemaking Sourcebook (1990). Congress endorsed this practice with the Negotiated Rulemaking Act of 1990, 104 Stat. 4969 (1990), codified at 5 U.S.C. §§561 et seq. (Supp. VI 1992) (with technical amendments). Congress found that:

> Adversarial rulemaking deprives the affected parties and the public of the benefits of face-to-face negotiations and cooperation in developing and reaching agreement on a rule. It also deprives them of the benefits of shared information, knowledge, expertise, and technical abilities possessed by the affected parties. . . .
>
> Negotiated rulemaking can increase the acceptability and improve the substance of rules, making it less likely that the affected parties will resist enforcement or challenge such rules in court. It may also shorten the amount of time needed to issue final rules.

In the relatively few number of cases where negotiated rulemaking has been successfully used, the total time necessary for a major rule has been reduced from about three and a half years to about two and one quarter years. EPA has found that it takes about seven months to develop a proposal to the point where negotiations can begin, that negotiations take about six months, that subsequent public "comment" takes three more months, and that the analysis of the comments takes an additional ten months. Moreover, the likelihood of subsequent court challenges seems far lower than the 90 percent likelihood in the case of traditional rulemaking processes for important rules. EPA's negotiated rulemaking timetable looks like this:

3 months + 4.5 months + 6 months + 3 months + 10 months

| Initial work | Evaluation | Negotiations | Public comment | Analysis / promulgation |

Negotiated rulemaking, however, has many limitations, and even its strongest advocates recognize that it will only be successful for a small percentage of regulations. It seems to work best when each party involved has the power to influence the outcome of a pending decision, when the number of parties is fairly small, when the parties are under pressure to decide, when each party has something to gain from negotiations, when trade-offs are possible, when the issues do not easily admit of an "objective" solution, and when decisions of the group can be fairly easily implemented. It will not work well when it is difficult to find a representative who can speak for a major affected group (who authoritatively speaks for the environment?), or when the group represented finds it difficult to order its own priorities, or when a group's commitment to a particular result is based on strong principles that are resistant to compromise. And, of course, negotiation can harm the interests of those who are not present at the negotiating table.

EPA has had mixed results with negotiated rulemaking. For example, environmentalists, industry representatives, and regulators were able to agree on new rules for penalties for truck engine manufacturers whose products did not meet emission standards, restrictions on the use of pesticides in response to agricultural emergencies, and regulations on emissions from woodburning stoves. The woodburning stove regulation is a good example of the potential of the procedure. In return for more stringent requirements, industry negotiators were able to help create a uniform national policy. Without effective EPA regulations, the stove manufacturers faced the possibility of state by state variations in the pollution standards for their products. A regulatory negotiation convened to develop rules to protect farmworkers from pesticides, however, broke down before a consensus was reached when the farmworkers' representatives walked out of the conference. This

failure demonstrates one of the main difficulties with regulatory negotiation: The talks often take place in a highly politicized atmosphere
in which many of the participants are long-time adversaries. Formal
regulatory negotiations have also been convened to develop rules governing nitrogen oxide emissions and gasoline reformulations to meet
the Clean Air requirements. While proposals have developed from the
gasoline meetings, the nitrogen oxide negotiations were unsuccessful.
In June 1991, they were canceled because the participants were unwilling to make a full commitment to the proceedings. One problem mentioned was the uncertainty created by the mandatory Office of
Management and Budget review of any agreement reached. The parties
were concerned that any consensus reached could be overturned later
by OMB.

Under the Clean Air Amendments of 1990, EPA must issue over
50 major and 30 minor regulations in a relatively short period. Many of
the rules needed are too broad and will affect too many different parties for negotiations to be possible; others are candidates for consensus
solutions. Although not a formal regulatory negotiation, meetings were
held to resolve a dispute between EPA and the Navajo Generating Station, an electricity plant that was accused of discharging pollutants that
created haze over the Grand Canyon. The original proposal by EPA for
what pollution control improvements were needed called for a 70 percent reduction in emissions, measured as a monthly average. After negotiations, the parties agreed to a 90 percent reduction, measured as
an annual average. According to William Rosenberg, deputy EPA administrator for air and radiation, the change eliminated the need for
backup control equipment, resulting in 40 percent greater visibility improvement for 20 percent less investment. See Wald, U.S. Agencies Use
Negotiations To Pre-empt Lawsuits Over Rules, N.Y. Times, Sept. 23,
1991, at A-1. The agreement reached was issued as a final rule by EPA.
Certain water conservation and irrigation districts in the Grand Canyon
region later petitioned the Ninth Circuit for a review of the rule but
were denied. *Central Arizona Water Conservation District v. United States
EPA*, 990 F.2d 1531 (9th Cir. 1993). In its decision, the court noted
the "virtually unprecedented cooperation between the governmental
agency and the directly affected parties" that took place in preparing
the rule. Id. at 1545.

In addition to debating whether regulatory negotiation will in fact
produce speedier, less adversarial rulemaking, commentators disagree
over the proper role of appellate courts in reviewing rules created
through negotiation. A negotiated rule must go through the normal
notice and comment rulemaking process. Suppose that a commenter
not party to the negotiation objects to the legality or wisdom of the
negotiated rule when proposed and later seeks judicial review when the
negotiated rule is adopted as final. Should the court relax the normal

scope of review? Suppose the challenger claims that it was not afforded a full and fair opportunity to participate in the negotiations? Philip Harter has argued that after an agency has promulgated a final rule supported by all interested parties, judicial review should be very limited. See Harter, The Role of Courts in Regulatory Negotiation — A Response to Judge Wald, 11 Colum. J. Envtl. L. 51, 65 (1986). Judge Patricia Wald has questioned the wisdom of Harter's approach. She believes that courts must still look beyond consensus to determine if the agency's choice of rule is consistent with relevant statutes and reflects rational decisionmaking. See Wald, Negotiation of Environmental Disputes: A New Role for the Courts?, 10 Colum. J. Envtl. L. 1 (1985). Congress appeared to answer this debate with the following provision in the Negotiated Rulemaking Act, 5 U.S.C. §590:

> Any agency action relating to establishing, assisting, or terminating a negotiated rulemaking committee under this subchapter shall not be subject to judicial review. Nothing in this section shall bar judicial review of a rule if such review is otherwise provided by law. A rule which is the product of negotiated rulemaking and is subject to judicial review shall not be accorded any greater deference by a court than a rule which is the product of other rulemaking procedures.

For general discussion of negotiated rulemaking, see Susskind & McMahon, The Theory and Practice of Negotiated Rulemaking, 3 Yale J. Reg. 133 (1985). For discussion of the use of other alternative dispute resolution procedures in the environmental context, see L. Susskind & J. Cruikshank, Breaking the Impasse: Consensual Approaches to Resolving Public Disputes (1987); Brunet, The Costs of Environmental Alternative Dispute Resolution, 18 E.L.R. 10515, 10516 (1988); Mays, Alternative Dispute Resolution and Environmental Enforcement: A Noble Experiment or a Lost Cause?, 18 E.L.R. 10087 (1988).

PROCEDURE PROBLEM

Seagirt Electric proposes to construct a new electric generating plant that will discharge heated cooling water into the ocean. It applies to EPA for an NPDES permit for the discharges, and for a variance under §316(a) of the Clean Water Act from otherwise applicable water quality standards for heat. See supra, p. 460 n.11. The plant is bitterly opposed by Oystershell Alliance, a coalition of local environmental groups, who claim that the discharges will adversely affect populations of fish and shellfish in the receiving waters. The scientific evidence is complex and sharply disputed. The EPA Administrator decides to use the case to test new "non-adversary" approaches to regulatory decisionmaking. At the administrative hearing on the permit application, she instructs EPA staff not to take a position for or against the applicant, but to ask questions and gather information from Seagirt and Oystershell Alliance. On receipt of the hearing record, she sends it to a committee of distinguished academic marine biologists selected by her. She has a private two-hour briefing from the committee to hear the members' evaluation of the materials in the record. One month later EPA issues a decision granting the variance application and the permit. The decision discusses the evidence in the hearing record, but does not in any way refer to the committee of academics or its members' views. What claims may Oystershell Alliance assert on judicial review, and what are its chances of having EPA's decision set aside?

2. REVIEW OF SUBSTANTIVE ISSUES

The APA directs reviewing courts to "hold unlawful and set aside" agency actions and decisions that are "without observance of procedure required by law" but also "contrary to constitutional right, power, privilege, or immunity," "in excess of statutory jurisdiction, authority, or limitations, or short of statutory right," or "arbitrary, capricious, an abuse of discretion, or otherwise not in accordance with law." 5 U.S.C. §706(2)(D),(B),(C),(A). Also, where fact-finding is involved in applying law or developing policy, reviewing courts must also examine the adequacy of the evidentiary basis for the agency's factual findings; otherwise the agency would have unfettered discretion to "find" nonexistent facts and apply legal rules or policies to situations where they did not properly apply. Where agency fact-finding is made exclusively on the basis of record evidence developed at a trial-type hearing, as in formal adjudication, the APA requires reviewing courts to sustain the agency's findings if they are supported by "substantial evidence" in the record. 5 U.S.C. §706(2)(E). Under this standard, reviewing courts do not decide the facts de novo, but will sustain the agency's findings if they are among those that a reasonable trier might make on the basis of the record. The degree of deference shown by courts to administrative fact-finding is often somewhere between that afforded by reviewing courts to a jury and that afforded a trial judge in a case tried to the court. For general discussion, see L. Jaffe, Judicial Control of Administrative Action 595-623 (1965). Where there is no trial-type record, as in notice and comment rulemaking and informal adjudication, the APA apparently provides for "trial de novo by the reviewing court," 5 U.S.C. §706(2)(F), but reviewing courts have been reluctant to engage in such review. Instead, as explained below, the courts have led agencies to develop a documentary record in notice and comment rulemaking and informal adjudication, and have used the "arbitrary and capricious" standard in 5 U.S.C. §706(2)(A), which was originally designed as the standard for review of an agency's discretionary choices of law or policy, to also review the sufficiency of the documentary record to support the agency's fact finding in such cases.

Schematically, then, one can break down the task of judicial review of the substantive merits into three steps:

(1)   determination of whether the agency's fact-findings have a reasonable basis in light of the relevant evidence available to the reviewing court;

(2)   determination of whether the agency complied with and properly applied applicable statutes (and also the Constitution and the agency's own regulations);

(3)   determination of whether the agency acted reasonably in exercising whatever discretion it enjoys under the applicable statutes.

These very general principles obviously admit of great variation in their applications. Different judges at different times in different cases have shown marked variations in their willingness to find constraints on agency choice in the relevant statute or to defer to the exercise of administrative discretion or to agency fact-finding. What factors should determine the precise scope of judicial review? Can one generalize about the appropriate scope of review in environmental cases? On the one hand, the technical complexity of the scientific and economic issues involved might suggest that it was appropriate for judges, who generally are not technically trained, to give great weight to agency judgments. On the other hand, does the claim that environmental interests are entitled to special judicial protection, *EDF v. Ruckelshaus*, supra p. 841, or the fact that environmental controls are often very costly, justify especially rigorous review in environmental cases?

CITIZENS TO PRESERVE OVERTON PARK, INC. V. VOLPE

401 U.S. 402, 404 (1971)

Opinion of the Court by Mr. Justice MARSHALL, announced by Mr. Justice STEWART.

The growing public concern about the quality of our natural environment has prompted Congress in recent years to enact legislation designed to curb the accelerating destruction of our country's natural beauty. We are concerned in this case with §4(f) of the Department of Transportation Act of 1966, as amended, and §18(a) of the Federal-Aid

Highway Act of 1968. These statutes prohibit the Secretary of Transportation from authorizing the use of federal funds to finance the construction of highways through public parks if a "feasible and prudent" alternative route exists. If no such route is available, the statutes allow him to approve construction through parks only if there has been "all possible planning to minimize harm" to the park.

Petitioners, private citizens as well as local and national conservation organizations, contend that the Secretary has violated these statutes by authorizing the expenditure of federal funds for the construction of a six-lane interstate highway through a public park in Memphis, Tennessee. . . .

[Plaintiffs contended that the Secretary's approval of the park route violated the relevant statutes and that his action was also invalid for failure to make formal findings on the feasibility of alternative routes and on whether the park route reflected "all possible planning to minimize harm" to the park. These contentions were rejected by the district court, which relied on affidavits filed by the Secretary and his assistants explaining the grounds for the Secretary's action. The Department's decision had not been based on any formal hearing or record.]

A threshold question — whether petitioners are entitled to any judicial review — is easily answered. Section 701 of the Administrative Procedure Act, 5 U.S.C. §701 provides that the action of "each authority of the government of the United States," which includes the Department of Transportation, is subjected to judicial review except where there is a statutory prohibition on review or where "agency action is committed to agency discretion by law." In this case, there is no indication that congress sought to prohibit judicial review and there is most certainly no "showing of 'clear and convincing evidence' of a . . . legislative intent" to restrict access to judicial review. *Abbott Laboratories v. Gardner*, 387 U.S. 136, 141 (1967), *Brownell v. We Shung*, 353 U.S. 180, 185 (1956).

Similarly, the Secretary's decision here does not fall within the exception for action "committed to agency discretion." This is a very narrow exception. Berger, Administrative Arbitrariness and Judicial Review, 65 Col. L. Rev. 55 (1965). The legislative history of the Administrative Procedure Act indicates that it is applicable in those rare instances where "statutes are drawn in such broad terms that in a given case there is no law to apply." S. Rep. No. 752, 79th Cong., 1st Sess., 26 (1945).

Section 4(f) of the Department of Transportation Act and §138 of the Federal-Aid Highway Act are clear and specific directives. Both the Department of Transportation Act and the Federal-Aid to Highway Act provide that the Secretary "shall not approve any program or project" that requires the use of any public parkland "unless (1) there is no feasible and prudent alternative to the use of such land, and (2) such

program includes all possible planning to minimize harm to such park.
. . ." 23 U.S.C. §138 (1964 ed. Supp. V); 49 U.S.C. §1653(f) (1964 ed.
Supp. V). This language is a plain and explicit bar to the use of federal
funds for construction of highways through parks — only the most unusual situations are exempted.

Despite the clarity of the statutory language, respondents argue
that the Secretary has wide discretion. They recognize that the requirement that there be no "feasible" alternative route admits of little administrative discretion. For this exemption to apply the Secretary must find
that as a matter of sound engineering it would not be feasible to build
the highway along any other route. Respondents argue, however, that
the requirement that there be no other "prudent" route requires the
Secretary to engage in a wide-ranging balancing of competing interests.
They contend that the Secretary should weigh the detriment resulting
from the destruction of parkland against the cost of other routes, safety
considerations, and other factors, and determine on the basis of the
importance that he attaches to these other factors whether, on balance,
alternative feasible routes would be "prudent."

But no such wide-ranging endeavor was intended. It is obvious
that in most cases considerations of cost, directness of route, and community disruption will indicate that parkland should be used for highway construction whenever possible. Although it may be necessary to
transfer funds from one jurisdiction to another, there will always be a
smaller outlay required from the public purse when parkland is used
since the public already owns the land and there will be no need to pay
for right-of-way. And since people do not live or work in parks, if a
highway is built on parkland no one will have to leave his home or give
up his business. Such factors are common to substantially all highway
construction. Thus, if Congress intended these factors to be on an
equal footing with preservation of parkland there would have been no
need for the statutes.

Congress clearly did not intend that cost and disruption of the
community were to be ignored by the Secretary. But the very existence
of the statutes indicates that protection of parkland was to be given paramount importance. The few green havens that are public parks were not
to be lost unless there were truly unusual factors present in a particular
case or the cost or community disruption resulting from alternative
routes reached extraordinary magnitudes. If the statutes are to have any
meaning, the Secretary cannot approve the destruction of parkland unless he finds that alternative routes present unique problems.

Plainly, there is "law to apply" and thus the exemption for action
"committed to agency discretion" is inapplicable. But the existence of
judicial review is only the start; the standard for review must also be
determined. For that we must look to §706 of the Administrative Procedure Act, 5 U.S.C. §706 (1964 ed., Supp. V), which provides that a

"reviewing court shall . . . hold unlawful and set aside agency action, findings, and conclusions found" not to meet six separate standards. In all cases agency action must be set aside if the action was "arbitrary, capricious, an abuse of discretion, or otherwise not in accordance with law" or if the action failed to meet statutory, procedural, or constitutional requirements. 5 U.S.C. §§706 (2)(A), (B), (C), (D) (1964 ed., Supp. V). In certain narrow, specifically limited situations, the agency action is to be set aside if the action was not supported by "substantial evidence." And in other equally narrow circumstances the reviewing court is to engage in a de novo review of the action and set it aside if it was "unwarranted by the facts." 5 U.S.C. §§706(2(E), (F) (1964 ed., Supp. V).

[These alternatives were rejected by the Court, which held that the "substantial evidence" standard did not apply because the Secretary's decision was not required to be based on a trial-type hearing record, and likewise held that de novo judicial fact-finding was inappropriate.]

Even though there is no de novo review in this case and the Secretary's approval of the route of I-40 does not have ultimately to meet the substantial-evidence test, the generally applicable standards of §706 require the reviewing court to engage in a substantial inquiry. . . .

The court is first required to decide whether the Secretary acted within the scope of his authority. *Schilling v. Rogers,* 363 U.S. 666, 676-677 (1960). This determination naturally begins with a delineation of the scope of the Secretary's authority and discretion. L. Jaffe, Judicial Control of Administrative Action 359 (1965). As has been shown, Congress has specified only a small range of choices that the Secretary can make. Also involved in this initial inquiry is a determination of whether on the facts the Secretary's decision can reasonably be said to be within that range. The reviewing court must consider whether the Secretary properly construed his authority to approve the use of parkland as limited to situations where there are no feasible alternative routes or where feasible alternative routes involve uniquely difficult problems. And the reviewing court must be able to find that the Secretary could reasonably believe that in this case there are no feasible alternatives or that alternatives do involve unique problems.

Scrutiny of the facts does not end, however, with the determination that the Secretary has acted within the scope of his statutory authority. Section 706(2)(A) requires a finding that the actual choice made was not "arbitrary, capricious, an abuse of discretion, or otherwise not in accordance with law." 5 U.S.C. §706 (2)(A) (1964 ed., Supp. V). To make this finding the court must consider whether the decision was based on a consideration of the relevant factors and whether there has been a clear error of judgment. . . . Although this inquiry into the facts is to be searching and careful, the ultimate standard of review is a narrow one. The court is not empowered to substitute its judgment for that of the agency.

The final inquiry is whether the Secretary's action followed the necessary procedural requirements. Here the only procedural error alleged is the failure of the Secretary to make formal findings and state his reason for allowing the highway to be built through the park.

Undoubtedly, review of the Secretary's action is hampered by his failure to make such findings, but the absence of formal findings does not necessarily require that the case be remanded to the Secretary. Neither the Department of Transportation Act nor the Federal-Aid Highway Act requires such formal findings. Moreover, the Administrative Procedure Act requirements that there be formal findings in certain rule-making and adjudicatory proceedings do not apply to the Secretary's action here. See 5 U.S.C. §§553(a)(2), 554(a) (1964 ed., Supp. V). . . .

[The Court indicated that the "administrative record" of documents utilized by the Department in making its decision could serve as the basis for judicial review.]

That administrative record is not, however, before us. The lower courts based their review on the litigation affidavits that were presented. These affidavits were merely "post hoc" rationalizations, *Burlington Truck Lines v. United States,* 371 U.S. 156, 168-169 (1962), which have traditionally been found to be an inadequate basis for review. *Burlington Truck Lines v. United States,* supra; *SEC v. Chenery Corp.,* 318 U.S. 80, 87 (1943). And they clearly do not constitute the "whole record" compiled by the agency: the basis for review required by §706 of the Administrative Procedure Act. . . .

Thus it is necessary to remand this case to the district court for plenary review of the Secretary's decision. That review is to be based on the full administrative record that was before the Secretary at the time he made his decision. But since the bare record may not disclose the factors that were considered or the Secretary's construction of the evidence it may be necessary for the District Court to require some explanation in order to determine if the Secretary acted within the scope of his authority and if the Secretary's action was justifiable under the applicable standard.

The court may require the administrative officials who participated in the decision to give testimony explaining their action. Of course, such inquiry into the mental processes of administrative decisionmakers is usually to be avoided. *United States v. Morgan,* 313 U.S. 409, 422 (1941). And where there are administrative findings that were made at the same time as the decision, as was the case in *Morgan,* there must be a strong showing of bad faith or improper behavior before such inquiry may be made. But here there are no such formal findings and it may be that the only way there can be effective judicial review is by examining the decisionmakers themselves. See *Shaughnessy v. Accardi*, 340 U.S. 280 (1955).

The District Court is not, however, required to make such an inquiry. It may be that the Secretary can prepare formal findings . . . that will provide an adequate explanation for his action. Such an explanation will, to some extent, be a "post hoc rationalization" and thus must be viewed critically. If the District Court decides that additional explanation is necessary, that court should consider which method will prove the most expeditious so that full review may be had as soon as possible.

Reversed and remanded.

NOTES AND QUESTIONS

1. Note how the Court easily brushes aside objections to judicial review on the grounds that it is precluded by statute or that the decision is entirely within the agency's discretion. Note also how the opinion emphasizes that reviewing courts must not only determine whether the agency acted within the scope of its statutory authority, but also whether it exercised the discretion which it enjoys under the statute in a reasonable fashion. Finally, note the conclusion that reviewing courts must engage in a "substantial inquiry" even though the agency acted informally and did not base its decision on a formal trial-type record. All of these rulings are fully consonant with the developing practice in the federal courts of review of informal discretionary agency action. For vigorous advocacy of such developments, see K. Davis, Discretionary Justice (1969). But see *Heckler v. Chaney*, supra, p. 846.

2. The Court holds that the "feasible and prudent" language in the statutes sharply restrict the Secretary's authority to approve highways through parks. How persuasive is this reading of the statutes in view of the term "prudent"? The legislative history indicates that the statutory language was understood as an ambiguous compromise between highway advocates and environmentalists.[20] Is the Court's con-

---

20. See H.R. Rep. No. 1584, 90th Cong., 2d Sess. (1968); S. Rep. No. 1340, 90th Cong., 2d Sess. (1968), reprinted in 3 U.S. Code Cong. & Ad. News 3500 (1968); 114 Cong. Rec. 11914-17 (1968); Conf. Rep. No. 1799, 90th Cong., 2d Sess., reprinted in 3 U.S. Code Cong. & Ad. News 3538 (1968); 114 Cong. Rec. 23706-08, 24029, 24032-2 (1968). This legislative history is discussed in Note, The Supreme Court, 1970 Term, 85 Harv. L. Rev. 324-325 (1971).

In *Louisiana Environmental Soc., Inc. v. Coleman*, 537 F.2d 79 (5th Cir. 1976), the court set aside DOT approval of a bridge over a lake, holding that all recreational facilities were protected by the principles enunciated in *Overton*

struction nonetheless justified? Does *Overton Park* confirm that environmental interests should receive special protection from reviewing courts? If so, what justifies such protection? What form should it take, "procedural" or "substantive"?

After remand, the Secretary eventually disapproved the park route. For the subsequent history of the controversy, see 335 F. Supp. 873 (W.D. Tenn. 1972); 357 F. Supp. 846 (1973); 494 F.2d 1212 (6th Cir. 1974).

3. Note that *Overton Park* attempts to deal with the problem of generating a record for judicial review in informal rulemaking by rejecting the idea of a trial de novo by the reviewing court, which the framers of the APA apparently envisaged (see 5 U.S.C. §706(2)(F)), and giving trial courts the option of either remanding the case to the agency for development of a more adequate documentary record (based, normally, on materials that happen to have been collected in the agency's files) or seeking discovery from agency decisionmakers regarding the basis for their decision. Trial courts have generally followed the former course. After *Overton Park*, agency lawyers have taken care to ensure collection of documents in the agency's decisional files that will form an adequate receivable record in cases likely to result in litigation.

4. Note also that *Overton Park*, tracking the provisions of the APA, 5 U.S.C. §706(2)(C), (A), divides judicial review of questions of law into two steps. First, the court must determine the extent of the agency's statutory authority. This includes a determination of the extent to which a statute constrains the agency's decisional choice, and the corresponding extent to which the agency enjoys decisional discretion. Second, to the extent that the agency enjoys discretion, the court is to determine whether its exercise is "arbitrary and capricious." We next consider how courts perform these two tasks.

Park, and ruling that the ten-year delay required to construct an alternate route did not disqualify the alternate route as "feasible and prudent."

For a general analysis of the problems raised by highway routing, concluding that more extensive use of economic analysis and incentives is desirable, see Mashaw, The Legal Structure of Frustration; Alternative Strategies for Public Choice Concerning Federally-Aided Highway Construction, 122 U. Pa. L. Rev. 1 (1973). See also Note, Favoring Parks Over Highways, 57 Iowa L. Rev. 834 (1972).

MOTOR VEHICLE MANUFACTURERS ASSOCIATION v. STATE FARM MUTUAL AUTOMOBILE INSURANCE CO.

463 U.S. 29, 34 (1983)

Justice WHITE delivered the opinion of the Court.

[The National Traffic and Motor Vehicle Saftey Act provides that the Department of Transportation "shall issue" motor vehicle standards that "shall be practicable [and] shall meet the need for motor vehicle saftey."]

The regulation whose rescission is at issue bears a complex and convoluted history. Over the course of approximately 60 rulemaking notices, the requirement has been imposed, amended, rescinded, reimposed, and now rescinded again.

As originally issued by the Department of Transportation in 1967, Standard 208 simply required the installation of seatbelts in all automobiles. 32 Fed. Reg. 2415. It soon became apparent that the level of seatbelt use was too low to reduce traffic injuries to an acceptable level. The Department therefore began consideration of "passive occupant restraint systems" — devices that do not depend for their effectiveness upon any action taken by the occupant except that necessary to operate the vehicle. Two types of automatic crash protection emerged: automatic seatbelts and airbags. The automatic seatbelt is a traditional safety belt, which when fastened to the interior of the door remains attached without impeding entry or exit from the vehicle, and deploys automatically without any action on the part of the passenger. The airbag is an inflatable device concealed in the dashboard and steering column. It automatically inflates when a sensor indicates that deceleration forces from an accident have exceeded a preset minimum, then rapidly deflates to dissipate those forces. The lifesaving potential of these devices was immediately recognized, and in 1977, after substantial on-the-road experience with both devices, it was estimated by NHTSA that passive restraints could prevent approximately 12,000 deaths and over 100,000 serious injuries annually. 42 Fed. Reg. 34298.

In 1969, the Department formally proposed a standard requiring the installation of passive restraints, 34 Fed. Reg. 11148, thereby commencing a lengthy series of proceedings. In 1970, the agency revised Standard 208 to include passive protection requirements, 35 Fed. Reg. 16927, and in 1972, the agency amended the Standard to require full passive protection for all front seat occupants of vehicles manufactured after August 15, 1975. 37 Fed. Reg. 3911. In the interim, vehicles built between August 1973 and August 1975 were to carry either passive restraints or lap and shoulder belts coupled with an "ignition interlock" that would prevent starting the vehicle if the belts were not connected.

On review, the agency's decision to require passive restraints was found to be supported by "substantial evidence" and upheld. *Chrysler Corp. v. Department of Transportation,* 472 F.2d 659 (CA6 1972). [Congress subsequently repealed the interlock requirement following intense public protest.]

The effective date for mandatory passive restraint systems was extended for a year until August 31, 1976. 40 Fed. Reg. 16217 (1975); id., at 33977. But in June 1976, Secretary of Transportation William T. Coleman, Jr., initiated a new rulemaking on the issue, 41 Fed. Reg. 24070. After hearing testimony and reviewing written comments, Coleman extended the optional alternatives indefinitely and suspended the passive restraint requirement. Although he found passive restraints technologically and economically feasible, the Secretary based his decision on the expectation that there would be widespread public resistance to the new systems.

Coleman's successor as Secretary of Transportation disagreed. Within months of assuming office, Secretary Brock Adams decided that the demonstration project was unnecessary. He issued a new mandatory passive restraint regulation, known as Modified Standard 208. 42 Fed. Reg. 34,289 (1977); 49 CFR §571.208 (1978). The Modified Standard mandated the phasing in of passive restraints beginning with large cars in model year 1982 and extending to all cars by model year 1984. The two principal systems that would satisfy the Standard were airbags and passive belts; the choice of which system to install was left to the manufacturers. In *Pacific Legal Foundation v. Department of Transportation,* 193 U.S. App. D.C. 184, 593 F.2d 1338, *cert. denied,* 444 U.S. 830 (1979), the Court of Appeals upheld Modified Standard 208 as a rational, nonarbitrary regulation consistent with the agency's mandate under the Act. The Standard also survived scrutiny by Congress, which did not exercise its authority under the legislative veto provisions of the 1974 Amendments.

Over the next several years, the automobile industry geared up to comply with Modified Standard 208. . . .

In February 1981, however, Secretary of Transportation Andrew Lewis reopened the rulemaking due to changed economic circumstances and, in particular, the difficulties of the automobile industry. 46 Fed. Reg. 12,033. Two months later, the agency ordered a one-year delay in the application of the Standard to large cars, extending the deadline to September 1982, id., at 21,172, and at the same time, proposed the possible rescission of the entire Standard. Id., at 21,205. After receiving written comments and holding public hearings, NHTSA issued a final rule (Notice 25) that rescinded the passive restraint requirement contained in Modified Standard 208.

II

In a statement explaining the rescission, NHTSA maintained that it was no longer able to find, as it had in 1977, that the automatic restraint requirement would produce significant safety benefits. Notice 25, id., at 53419. This judgment reflected not a change of opinion on the effectiveness of the technology, but a change in plans by the automobile industry. In 1977, the agency had assumed that airbags would be installed in 60% of all new cars and automatic seatbelts in 40%. By 1981 it became apparent that automobile manufacturers planned to install the automatic seatbelts in approximately 99% of the new cars. For this reason, the lifesaving potential of airbags would not be realized. Moreover, it now appeared that the overwhelming majority of passive belts planned to be installed by manufacturers could be detached easily and left that way permanently. Passive belts, once detached, then required "the same type of affirmative action that is the stumbling block to obtaining high usage levels of manual belts." Id., at 53421. For this reason, the agency concluded that there was no longer a basis for reliably predicting that the Standard would lead to any significant increased usage of restraints at all.

In view of the possibly minimal safety benefits, the automatic restraint requirement no longer was reasonable or practicable in the agency's view. The requirement would require approximately $1 billion to implement and the agency did not believe it would be reasonable to impose such substantial costs on manufacturers and consumers without more adequate assurance that sufficient safety benefits would accrue. In addition, NHTSA concluded that automatic restraints might have an adverse effect on the public's view of safety regulation and, in particular, "poisoning . . . popular sentiment toward efforts to improve occupant restraint systems in the future." Id., at 53424.

State Farm Mutual Automobile Insurance Co. and the National Association of Independent Insurers filed petitions for review of NHTSA's rescission of the passive restraint Standard. The United States Court of Appeals for the District of Columbia Circuit held that the agency's rescission of the passive restraint requirement was arbitrary and capricious. 220 U.S. App. D.C. 170, 680 F.2d 206 (1982). . . .

III

Both the Act and the 1974 Amendments concerning occupant crash protection standards indicate that motor vehicle safety standards are to be promulgated under the informal rulemaking procedures of the Administrative Procedure Act. 5 U.S.C. §553. The agency's action in promulgating such standards therefore may be set aside if found to be "arbitrary, capricious, an abuse of discretion, or otherwise not in accordance with law." 5 U.S.C. §706(2)(A); *Citizens to Preserve Overton Park v. Volpe*, 401 U.S. 402, 414 (1971). . . .

IV.

The ultimate question before us is whether NHTSA's rescission of the passive restraint requirement of Standard 208 was arbitrary and capricious. We conclude, as did the Court of Appeals, that it was. We also conclude, but for somewhat different reasons, that further consideration of the issue by the agency is therefore required. We deal separately with the rescission as it applies to airbags and as it applies to seatbelts.

A

The first and most obvious reason for finding the rescission arbitrary and capricious is that NHTSA apparently gave no consideration whatever to modifying the Standard to require that airbag technology be utilized. Standard 208 sought to achieve automatic crash protection by requiring automobile manufacturers to install either of two passive restraint devices: airbags or automatic seatbelts. There was no suggestion in the long rulemaking process that led to Standard 208 that if only one of these options were feasible, no passive restraint standard should be promulgated. Indeed, the agency's original proposed Standard contemplated the installation of inflatable restraints in all cars. Automatic belts were added as a means of complying with the Standard because they were believed to be as effective as airbags in achieving the goal of occupant crash protection. 36 Fed. Reg. 12859 (1971). At this time, the passive belt approved by the agency could not be detached. Only later, at a manufacturer's behest, did the agency approve of the detachability feature — and only after assurances that the feature would not compromise the safety benefits of the restraint. Although it was then foreseen that 60% of the new cars would contain airbags and 40% would have automatic seatbelts, the ratio between the two was not significant as long as the passive belt would also assure greater passenger safety.

The agency has now determined that the detachable automatic belts will not attain anticipated safety benefits because so many individuals will detach the mechanism. Even if this conclusion were acceptable in its entirety, see infra . . . standing alone it would not justify any more than an amendment of Standard 208 to disallow compliance by means of the one technology which will not provide effective passenger protection. It does not cast doubt on the need for a passive restraint standard or upon the efficacy of airbag technology. In its most recent rulemaking, the agency again acknowledged the lifesaving potential of the airbag: "The agency has no basis at this time for changing its earlier conclusion in 1976 and 1977 that basic air bag technology is sound and has been sufficiently demonstrated to be effective in those vehicles in current use. . . . ." NHTSA Final Regulatory Impact Analysis (RIA) XI-4 (Oct. 1981), App. 264.

Given the effectiveness ascribed to airbag technology by the agency, the mandate of the Act to achieve traffic safety would suggest that the logical response to the faults of detachable seatbelts would be to require the installation of airbags. At the very least this alternative way of achieving the objectives of the Act should have been addressed and adequate reasons given for its abandonment. But the agency not only did not require compliance through airbags, it also did not even consider the possibility in its 1981 rulemaking. Not one sentence of its rulemaking statement discusses the airbags-only option. Because, as the Court of Appeals stated, "NHTSA's . . . analysis of airbags was nonexistent," 220 U.S. App. D.C., at 200, 680 F.2d, at 236, what we said in *Burlington Truck Lines, Inc. v. United States,* 371 U.S., at 167, is apropos here:

> There are no findings and no analysis here to justify the choice made, no indication of the basis on which the [agency] exercised its expert discretion. We are not prepared to and the Administrative Procedure Act will not permit us to accept such . . . practice.. . . . Expert discretion is the lifeblood of the administrative process, but "unless we make the requirements for administrative action strict and demanding, *expertise,* the strength of modern government, can become a monster which rules with no practical limits on its discretion."

New York v. United States, 342 U.S. 882, 884 (dissenting opinion) (footnote omitted).

We have frequently reiterated that an agency must cogently explain why it has exercised its discretion in a given manner, *Atchison, T. & S.F.R. Co. v. Wichita Bd. of Trade,* 412 U.S., at 806; *FTC v. Sperry & Hutchinson Co.,* 405 U.S. 233, 249 (1972); *NLRB v. Metropolitan Life Ins. Co.,* 380 U.S. 438, 443 (1965); and we reaffirm this principle again today.

The automobile industry has opted for the passive belt over the airbag, but surely it is not enough that the regulated industry has eschewed a given safety device. For nearly a decade, the automobile industry waged the regulatory equivalent of war against the airbag and lost —the inflatable restraint was proved sufficiently effective. Now the automobile industry has decided to employ a seatbelt system which will not meet the safety objectives of Standard 208. This hardly constitutes cause to revoke the Standard itself. Indeed, the Act was necessary because the industry was not sufficiently responsive to safety concerns. The Act intended that safety standards not depend on current technology and could be "technology-forcing" in the sense of inducing the development of superior safety design. *See Chrysler Corp. v. Department of Transportation,* 472 F.2d, at 672-673. If, under the statute, the agency should not defer to the industry's failure to develop safer cars, which it surely should not do, a fortiori it may not revoke a safety standard which can be satisfied by current technology simply because the industry has opted for an ineffective seatbelt design.

Although the agency did not address the mandatory airbag option and the Court of Appeals noted that "airbags seem to have none of the problems that NHTSA identified in passive seatbelts," 220 U.S. App. D.C., at 201, 680 F.2d, at 237, petitioners recite a number of difficulties that they believe would be posed by a mandatory airbag standard. These range from questions concerning the installation of airbags in small cars to that of adverse public reaction. But these are not the agency's reasons for rejecting a mandatory airbag standard. Not having discussed the possibility, the agency submitted no reasons at all. The short —and sufficient —answer to petitioners' submission is that the courts may not accept appellate counsel's post hoc rationalizations for agency action. *Burlington Truck Lines, Inc. v. United States,* 371 U.S., at 168. It is well established that an agency's action must be upheld, if at all, on the basis articulated by the agency itself. Ibid.; *SEC v. Chenery Corp.,* 332 U.S., at 196; *American Textile Mfrs. Institute, Inc. v. Donovan,* 452 U.S. 490, 539 (1981).

Petitioners also invoke our decision in *Vermont Yankee Nuclear Power Corp. v. Natural Resources Defense Council, Inc.,* 435 U.S. 519 (1978), as though it were a talisman under which any agency decision is by definition unimpeachable. Specifically, it is submitted that to require an agency to consider an airbags-only alternative is, in essence, to dictate to the agency the procedures it is to follow. Petitioners both misread *Vermont Yankee,* and misconstrue the nature of the remand that is in order. In *Vermont Yankee,* we held that a court may not impose additional procedural requirements upon an agency. We do not require today any specific procedures which NHTSA must follow. Nor do we broadly require an agency to consider all policy alternatives in reaching decision. It is true that rulemaking "cannot be found wanting simply because the agency failed to include every alternative device and thought conceivable by the mind of man . . . regardless of how uncommon or unknown that alternative may have been.. . ." Id., at 551. But the airbag is more than a policy alternative to the passive restraint Standard; it is a technological alternative within the ambit of the existing Standard. We hold only that given the judgment made in 1977 that airbags are an effective and cost-beneficial life-saving technology, the mandatory passive restraint rule may not be abandoned without any consideration whatsoever of an airbags-only requirement.

B

Although the issue is closer, we also find that the agency was too quick to dismiss the safety benefits of automatic seatbelts. NHTSA's critical finding was that, in light of the industry's plans to install readily detachable passive belts, it could not reliably predict "even a 5 percentage point increase as the minimum level of expected usage increase." 46 Fed. Reg. 53423 (1981). The Court of Appeals rejected this finding because there is "not one iota" of evidence that Modified Standard 208 will fail to increase nationwide seatbelt use by at least 13 percentage points, the level of increased usage necessary for the Standard to justify its cost. Given the lack of probative evidence, the court held that "only a well justified refusal to seek more evidence could render rescission non-arbitrary." 220 U.S. App. D.C., at 196, 680 F.2d at 232.

Petitioners object to this conclusion. In their view, "substantial uncertainty" that a regulation will accomplish its intended purpose is sufficient reason, without more, to rescind a regulation. We agree with petitioners that just as an agency reasonably may decline to issue a safety standard if it is uncertain about its efficacy, an agency may also revoke a standard on the basis of serious uncertainties if supported by the record and reasonably explained. Rescission of the passive restraint requirement would not be arbitrary and capricious simply because there was no evidence in direct support of the agency's conclusion. It is not infrequent that the available data do not settle a regulatory issue, and the agency must then exercise its judgment in moving from the facts and probabilities on the record to a policy conclusion. Recognizing that policymaking in a complex society must account for uncertainty, however, does not imply that it is sufficient for an agency to merely recite the terms "substantial uncertainty" as a justification for its actions. As previously noted, the agency must explain the evidence which is available, and must offer a "rational connection between the facts found and the choice made." *Burlington Truck Lines, Inc. v. United States,* supra, at 168. Generally, one aspect of that explanation would be a justification for rescinding the regulation before engaging in a search for further evidence.

In these cases, the agency's explanation for rescission of the passive restraint requirement is *not* sufficient to enable us to conclude that the rescission was the product of reasoned decisionmaking. To reach this conclusion, we do not upset the agency's view of the facts, but we do appreciate the limitations of this record in supporting the agency's

decision. We start with the accepted ground that if used, seatbelts unquestionably would save many thousands of crippling injuries. Unlike
recent regulatory decisions we have reviewed, *Industrial Union Dept. v.
American Petroleum Institute,* 448 U.S. 607 (1980); *American Textile Mfrs.
Institute, Inc. v. Donovan,* 452 U.S. 490 (1981), the safety benefits of
wearing seatbelts are not in doubt, and it is not challenged that were
those benefits to accrue, the monetary costs of implementing the Standard would be easily justified. We move next to the fact that there is
no direct evidence in support of the agency's finding that detachable
automatic belts cannot be predicted to yield a substantial increase in
usage. The empirical evidence on the record, consisting of surveys of
drivers of automobiles equipped with passive belts, reveals more than a
doubling of the usage rate. . . .

The agency also failed to offer any explanation why a continuous
passive belt would engender the same adverse public reaction as the
ignition interlock, and, as the Court of Appeals concluded, "every indication in the record points the other way." 220 U.S. App. D.C., at 198,
680 F.2d, at 234. We see no basis for equating the two devices: the
continuous belt, unlike the ignition interlock, does not interfere with
the operation of the vehicle. More importantly, it is the agency's responsibility, not this Court's, to explain its decision.

VI

"An agency's view of what is in the public interest may change,
either with or without a change in circumstances. But an agency changing its course must supply a reasoned analysis.. . ." *Greater Boston Television Corp. v. FCC,* 143 U.S. App. D.C. 383, 394, 444 F.2d 841, 852 (1970)
(footnote omitted), *cert. denied,* 403 U.S. 923 (1971). We do not accept
all of the reasoning of the Court of Appeals but we do conclude that
the agency has failed to supply the requisite "reasoned analysis" in this
case. Accordingly, we vacate the judgment of the Court of Appeals and
remand the cases to that court with directions to remand the matter to
the NHTSA for further consideration consistent with this opinion.

So ordered.

[Justice REHNQUIST, joined by three other justices, dissented
in part. He agreed that NHTSA's failure to consider an airbags-only
alternative was unreasonable, but would have upheld its determination
regarding non-detachable belts.]

The approach to judicial review set forth in *Overton Park* and ex-
emplified in *State Farm* requires a reviewing court to consider whether
an agency has taken a "hard look" and adequately considered alterna-

tives to its action, analyzed their implications and imparts on relevant interests, provided a reasoned justification for its decision, and responded to factual, analytic, and policy criticism by outside parties. The reviewing court carries out this inquiry by examining the agency's written decision and the support (or lack thereof) provided for its findings and reasons in the administrative record. For examples of this approach to review, see in addition to *State Farm, American Meat Institute v. EPA,* supra p. 472 (effluent limitations for meat packing plants); *Appalachian Power Co. v. Train,* supra p. 485 (retrofit of closed cycle cooling to control thermal discharges from power plants); *Kennecott Copper Corp. v. EPA,* supra p. 851 (secondary ambient air quality standard for SO_2); *National Lime Ass'n v. EPA,* supra p. 256 (NSPS for emissions from lime manufacturing plants).

CHEVRON USA V. NRDC

467 U.S. 837, 839 (1984)

Reread this decision, pp. 394-405 supra, and the questions following.

NOTES AND QUESTIONS

1. What is left of *State Farm* after *Chevron?* Cf. Garland, Deregulation and Judicial Review, 98 Harv. L. Rev. 505 (1985).

2. Do *Chevron* and *State Farm* indicate that the Court has the judicial role backwards? Does it make any sense for courts to defer to agencies on the construction of statutes, a subject on which judges likely have more expertise than courts, yet to second-guess agencies or questions of policy, as to which agencies are more expert? See Breyer, Judicial Review of Questions of Law and Policy, 38 Administrative L. Rev. 363 (1986). See also Sunstein, Law and Administration after *Chevron,* 90 Col. L. Rev. 2071 (1990).

3. The potential limits of *Chevron* deference are illustrated in *INS v. Cardoza-Fonseca,* 480 U.S. 421 (1987), reviewing a decision of the Immigration and Naturalization Service (INS) denying relief to a deportable alien who sought to remain in the United States on the ground that she would be persecuted if returned to her place of citizenship, Nicaragua. Section 243(a) of the Immigration and Nationality Act *requires* the Attorney General to grant asylum to an alien who shows that his "life or freedom . . . would be threatened" for reasons such as race, religion, nationality or political belief in his home country. In order to qualify for asylum under §243(h) an alien must show that such persecu-

tion is more probable than not. Section 208(a) of the Act grants the Attorney General *discretion* to grant asylum to an alien who shows a "well founded fear of persecution" for the same reasons. The INS had interpreted the Act to require an alien seeking discretionary relief under §208(a) to make the same showing as required for mandatory relief under §243(h): that persecution is more probable than not.

The Court, in an opinion by Justice Stevens, found that the agency's interpretation was wrong. The test for mandatory relief under §243(h), "life or freedom . . . would be threatened," connotes an objective standard. The language of §208(a), "well founded fear of persecution," focuses on the subjective belief of the alien and indicates that a lesser standard is required for discretionary relief. Justice Stevens also found this reading to be supported by the legislative history. In addition, he rejected claims that *Chevron* required deference to the interpretation of the INS:

> The question whether Congress intended the two standards to be idential is a pure question of statutory construction for the courts to decide. Employing traditional tools of statutory construction, we concluded that Congress did not intend the two standards to be identical. In *Chevron* . . . we explained:
>
>> The judiciary is the final authority on issues of statutory construction and must reject administrative constructions which are contrary to clear congressional intent. [Citing cases.] If a court, employing traditional tools of statutory construction, ascertains that Congress had an intention on the precise question at issue, that intention is the law and must be given effect.
>>
>> The narrow legal question whether the two standards are the same is, of course, quite different from the question of interpretation that arises in each case in which the agency is required to apply either or both standards to a particular set of facts. . . .

Justice Scalia concurring, found that the statutory language reflected a clear congressional intent to have different standards under §§208(a) and 243(h). Hence, under *Chevron,* no deference was due the agency because the clarity of congressional intent made it unnecessary to reach the second stage of *Chevron* analysis and inquire whether the agency's interpretation of an ambiguous statute was reasonable. He made the following criticism of the majority opinion:

> The Court also implies that courts may substitute their interpretation of a statute for that of an agency whenever they face "a pure question of statutory construction for the courts to decide," rather than a "question of interpretation [in which] the agency is required to apply [a legal standard] to a particular set of facts." No support is adduced for this proposition, which is contradicted by the case the Court purports to be

interpreting, since in *Chevron* the Court deferred to the Environmental Protection Agency's abstract interpretation of the phrase "stationary source."

Id. at 454-455.

Was the definition of "stationary source" in *Chevron* a "pure question of statutory interpretation"? On the other hand, didn't the Court's decision in *Cardozo-Fonseca* "apply [the statutory] standards to a particular set of facts"?

4. Despite *Cardozo-Fonseca,* the Court has continued to invoke *Chevron* in deferring to an agency's construction of a statute that it administers.

In *Chemical Manufacturers Assn. v. Natural Resources Defense Council,* 470 U.S. 116 (1985), discussed p. 496 supra, the EPA approved FDF variances from efficient limitations for toxic discharges variances. The Clean Water Act §301(*l*) provides that the EPA Administrator "may not modify any requirement of this section as it applies to any specific pollutant." The EPA said that this provision "prohibits only those modifications expressly permitted by other provisions of section 301, namely, those that section 301(c) and section 301(d) would allow on economic or water quality grounds." Five members of the Supreme Court upheld this interpretation, noting that they need find "only that EPA's understanding of this very 'complex statute' is a sufficiently rational one to preclude a court from substituting its judgment for that of EPA." Four members of the Court dissented. They said that "*Chevron's* deference requirement . . . was explicitly limited to cases in which congressional intent cannot be discerned through the use of traditional techniques of statutory interpretation." After examining the statute's history, they concluded that it applied, forbidding FDF variances for toxics.

Young v. Community Nutrition Institute, 476 U.S. 974 (1986), involved a provision in the Food, Drug and Cosmetic Act that "when" a "poisonous or deleterious substance" is "required in the production" of food "or cannot be . . . avoided" by good food manufacturing practice, then "the Secretary" of Health and Human Services "shall promulgate regulations limiting the quantity therein or thereon to such extent as he finds necessary for the protection of public health. . . ." The Secretary did not promulgate an appropriate regulation limiting the quantity of "aflotoxin," a concededly "deleterious" substance found on wheat. The Secretary pointed to a longstanding agency interpretation of the statute to the effect that the words "as he finds necessary . . ." modify the word "shall" (that is, the Secretary "shall, as he finds necessary for the protection of human health, promulgate. . . ."). Concluding that the statute was "ambiguous," and given *Chevron,* the Court upheld the agency's interpretation. Justice Stevens, *Chevron's* author, dissented on the ground that the statute was not ambiguous, and it could not support the agency's interpretation. He found the "intent of Congress" to be clear. He added that "to say that the statute is susceptible of two meanings, . . . is not to say that either is acceptable."

5. Does *Chevron* make a difference? Professors Peter Schuck and E. Donald Elliot found, based on a survey of judicial review cases in the lower federal courts, that the rate at which reviewing courts affirmed the agency's decision rose from 71 percent in 1984, just before *Chevron* was decided, to 81 percent in 1985, just after it was decided. They also found that the overall affirmance rate has risen substantially over the years since 1965. To the Chevron Station: An Empirical Study of Federal Administrative Law, 1990 Duke L.J. 984. On the other, Professor Thomas Merrill, in a review of Supreme Court cases, has found that the Court has invoked *Chevron* fitfully, and often failed to cite the decision at all, even though the case in question involved judicial review of agency statutory interpretation. Judicial Deference to Executive Precedent, 101 Yale L.J. 969 (1992).

6. What factors should cut for and against deference to an agency's interpretation? Did *Chevron* err in attempting to reduce the subtleties of statutory interpretation and judicial review to a formula? Consider the deference, or lack thereof, given by reviewing courts to agency interpretations of statutes in the decisions examined earlier in this book, including *American Mining Congress v. EPA,* supra p. 572 (definition of "waste" under RCRA); *Arkansas v. Oklahoma,* supra p. 527 (compliance by upstream state sources with downstream state water quality standards); *Delaney v. EPA,* supra p. 348 (deadline for SIP achievement of ambient standards); *du Pont v. Train,* supra p. 466 (nationally uniform effluent limitations under Clean Water Act); *Hazardous Waste Treatment Council v. EPA,* supra p. 596 (EPA waste treatment regulations under RCRA); *NRDC v. Train,* supra p. 270 (EPA obligation to adopt ambient standard for lead); *Sierra Club v. Ruckleshaus,* supra p. 336 (EPA obligation to prevent significant deterioration of air quality).

JUDICIAL REVIEW PROBLEM

An April 1987 Worldwatch Institute study has found that by the early 1990s half of the cities in the United States will have exhausted their landfills. In light of this concern, many municipalities are looking seriously to high temperature incineration as the best (and perhaps only) short-term solution to the mounting solid waste disposal crisis. Incineration reduces waste volume by approximately 90 percent and waste weight by 70 percent. Taking into consideration the substantial volume compression of ordinary garbage due to compaction during landfilling, the net volume reduction attributable to incineration — incinerator ash versus ordinary landfilled garbage — is approximately 21 percent. At current construction (including scrubbers), operating, and disposal costs (assuming that incinerator ash can be disposed of in ordinary landfills), the gross cost of incineration is approximately $50.83 per ton of waste in New York City. But since incineration will also generate $24.19 per ton of energy for electricity, the *net* cost of disposal via incineration comes to $26.64 per ton of waste.

Although this figure is quite high in comparison to historical solid waste disposal costs, New York City and other municipalities believe it makes incineration a viable option, though only barely so. A recent study of the composition of incinerator ash, however, reveals that it contains significant concentrations of lead and other hazardous materials. Since municipal incinerators accept waste from industrial and commercial sources, such waste often contains significant amounts of hazardous chemicals and other materials. Moreover, even ordinary household waste contains some hazardous wastes such as used batteries, cleaners and solvents, and the like. Because disposal costs for hazardous ash vastly exceed disposal costs for non-hazardous ash (as much as $280 per ton versus $33 per ton), the classification of incinerator ash (as hazardous or non-hazardous) is critical in municipalities' decision whether to proceed with incineration projects.

Consequently, pressure has mounted on EPA to promulgate regulations regarding the classification of incinerator ash. Consider the following two possible regulations that might be adopted by EPA. Were the Environmental Defense Fund to challenge these policies, what standard of judicial review would the court apply? Would the regulations be upheld by the courts?

A. Special Disposal Provisions Under Section 3004. Following notice and comment, EPA promulgates a special set of regulations for disposal of incinerator ash. Under these regulations, municipal incinerator ash containing hazardous wastes coming within §3001(b)(1) of RCRA may be disposed of in ordinary landfills (as opposed to those meeting the stringent technology-based requirements for land disposal of hazardous wastes) so long as such ash is not mixed with any other wastes, hazardous or non-hazardous. Review the provisions of RCRA §§3001, 3004, (42 APA §706, and the cases discussing standards of judicial review. Of what relevance is RCRA §3004(x)?

B. Household Waste Exemption Under Section 3001. Rather than taking the above course, EPA decides that it may better achieve its policy objectives through a generous interpretation of the household waste exclusion of §3001(i). A possible problem with using this provision is that under EPA's regulatory codification of the Hazardous and Solid Waste Amendments of 1984 (50 Fed. Reg. 28,702 (July 15, 1985)), EPA interpreted the household waste exemption as applying only to incinerators receiving exclusively household waste and/or non-hazardous wastes from commercial or industrial sources. This interpretation would not provide the certainty needed by municipalities in making decisions regarding incineration projects because some hazardous wastes received by their incinerator operators could come from small commercial sources. Since there is almost no legislative history interpreting §3001(i), EPA issues a proposed rule interpreting §3001(i)(1)(A)(ii) as not applying to hazardous waste from commercial sources generating less than 100 kilograms of hazardous waste per month. Following the comment period, EPA's policy experts determine that implementation of the proposed rule would significantly alleviate the solid waste disposal crisis without jeopardizing the goals of RCRA. Furthermore, EPA's Office of Legal Counsel finds that such a policy is consistent with the legal requirements of RCRA. Consequently, EPA issues a final rule making the aforementioned interpretation of §3001(i)(1)(A)(ii).

In addressing these questions, consider the case of an incinerator that burns only household waste that contains some hazardous constituents. Is the incinerator ash, which will also contain some hazardous constituents, subject to the strict RCRA disposal requirements applicable to land disposal of hazardous waste? How would your answer be affected if EPA adopted a regulation stating that such ash was not subject to these RCRA requirements? That such ash was subject to these RCRA requirements?

8

The National Environmental Policy Act

In addition to specific statutory and general APA requirements governing agency action, there exists an additional layer of requirements applicable to environmental decisionmaking by the federal government. These requirements are found in the National Environmental Policy Act (NEPA), enacted in 1970. Although a harbinger of the many federal environmental regulatory statutes of the 1970s, NEPA has a very different focus. Unlike these regulatory statutes, which seek to impose substantive limits on polluting activities by private entities, NEPA seeks to redirect the decisionmaking processes of federal agencies.

Why would special legislation be needed to ensure that government agencies are sensitive to environmental concerns? Because of the increasing complexity of the economy and the increased role of government, decisionmaking authority within the federal government has been delegated to a variety of agencies. Many of these agencies focus on a principal mission: building highways, expanding the electricity supply, national defense, building canals and navigation projects. Some of these agencies did not systematically assess the environmental impacts of their decisions. Even if aware of environmental effects, they tended to overemphasize the benefits of development and failed to consider whether there were alternative ways of accomplishing their missions through means less damaging to the environment. Further, there was no mechanism for addressing the interrelated effects of various agencies' activities on the environment in a coordinated, comprehensive way. Finally, some agencies were held to lack statutory authority to consider and deal with some of the adverse environmental consequences of their decisions. See, e.g., *New Hampshire v. Atomic Energy Comm'n.*, 406 F.2d 170 (1st Cir.), *cert. denied*, 395 U.S. 962 (1969) (holding that, before NEPA, the AEC could not consider nonradiological environmental impacts in deciding nuclear power plant permit applications).

The growing environmental movement of the 1960s brought attention to these failings. In 1969, Senator Henry Jackson of Washington State and Representative John Dingell of Michigan introduced bills calling for a comprehensive national environmental policy. Following vigorous debate and significant compromises, NEPA was born. By contrast to the environmental statutes we have studied thus far, NEPA is remarkably brief. Not unlike some of the provisions in these other statutes, however, NEPA is often general and vague. The bills that became NEPA did not attract widespread interest in Congress, and expectations about the legislation were low in some quarters. For example, the House Committee reported that implementing its version of NEPA would cost the federal government "approximately $1 million per year." H.R. Rep. No. 91-378, 91st Cong., 1st Sess. 11 (1969), reprinted in 1969 U.S. Code Cong. & Admin. News 2761.

At this point, you should read through NEPA's provisions. As you do, try to determine the principal features of the statutory framework and its objectives: Is NEPA predominantly procedural or substantive? What are the most important procedural requirements? What are the principal substantive requirements?

This chapter takes you through the many complicated issues involved in the interpretation of NEPA. Before turning to the detailed exploration of these issues, it is worthwhile to pause for a minute to ask how Congress might formulate and implement a comprehensive national environmental policy. What should such a policy include? What alternative institutional methods are there for defining and implementing such a policy? Note that Congress made an important decision to limit the requirements of NEPA to federal statutes and federal actions. What about the environmental effects of private industrial, commercial, and development activities? What about the environmental consequences of state and local actions?

How did Congress envision that NEPA would be enforced? Did Congress suppose that it would be self-enforcing? That it would be enforced by the President? Note that NEPA created a three-member Council on Environmental Quality (CEQ) in the Executive Office of the President to prepare an annual report on environmental conditions and trends and develop national policies to promote environmental quality. Yet the Clinton administration is dismantling CEQ in favor of a nonstatutory, more political Office of Environmental Policy in the

White House. Was it expected that NEPA be enforced by Congress itself? By public pressure on agencies? By litigation? Note that NEPA contains no provision for judicial review or enforcement. As you proceed through this chapter, do not lose sight of these larger questions. We will touch on them at various points in the chapter and return to them directly in section H.

A. IMPLEMENTATION OF NEPA

1. JUDICIAL REVIEW OF NEPA COMPLIANCE

CALVERT CLIFFS' COORDINATING COMMITTEE, INC. v. UNITED STATES ATOMIC ENERGY COMMISSION

449 F.2d 1109, 1111-1129 (D.C. Cir. 1971)

J. SKELLY WRIGHT, Circuit Judge:

These cases are only the beginning of what promises to become a flood of new litigation — litigation seeking judicial assistance in protecting our natural environment. Several recently enacted statutes attest to the commitment of the Government to control, at long last, the destructive engine of material "progress." But it remains to be seen whether the promise of this legislation will become a reality. Therein lies the judicial role. In these cases, we must for the first time interpret the broadest and perhaps most important of the recent statutes: the National Environmental Policy Act of 1969 (NEPA). We must assess claims that one of the agencies charged with its administration has failed to live up to the congressional mandate. Our duty, in short, is to see that important legislative purposes, heralded in the halls of Congress, are not lost or misdirected in the vast hallways of the federal bureaucracy.

NEPA, like so much other reform legislation of the last 40 years, is cast in terms of a general mandate and broad delegation of authority to new and old administrative agencies. It takes the major step of requiring all federal agencies to consider values of environmental preservation in their spheres of activity, and it prescribes certain procedural measures to ensure that those values are in fact fully respected. Petitioners argue that rules recently adopted by the Atomic Energy Commission to govern consideration of environmental matters fail to satisfy the rigor demanded by NEPA. The Commission, on the other hand, contends that the vagueness of the NEPA mandate and delegation leaves much room for discretion and that the rules challenged by petitioners fall well within the broad scope of the Act. We find the policies embodied in NEPA to be a good deal clearer and more demanding than does the Commission. We conclude that the Commission's procedural rules do not comply with the congressional policy. Hence we remand these cases for further rule making.

I

We begin our analysis with an examination of NEPA's structure and approach and of the Atomic Energy Commission rules which are said to conflict with the requirements of the Act. The relevant portion of NEPA is Title I, consisting of five sections. Section 101 sets forth the Act's basic substantive policy: that the federal government "use all practicable means and measures" to protect environmental values. Congress did not establish environmental protection as an exclusive goal; rather, it desired a reordering of priorities, so that environmental costs and benefits will assume their proper place along with other considerations. In Section 101(b), imposing an explicit duty on federal officials, the Act provides that "it is the continuing responsibility of the Federal Government to use all practicable means, consistent with other essential considerations of national policy," to avoid environmental degradation, preserve "historic, cultural, and natural" resources, and promote "the widest range of beneficial uses of the environment without . . . undesirable and unintended consequences."

Thus the general substantive policy of the Act is a flexible one. It leaves room for a responsible exercise of discretion and may not require particular substantive results in particular problematic instances. However, the Act also contains very important "procedural" provisions — provisions which are designed to see that all federal agencies do in fact exercise the substantive discretion given them. These provisions are not highly flexible. Indeed, they establish a strict standard of compliance.

NEPA, first of all, makes environmental protection a part of the mandate of every federal agency and department. The Atomic Energy Commission, for example, had continually asserted, prior to NEPA, that it had no statutory authority to concern itself with the adverse environmental effects of its actions. Now, however, its hands are no longer tied. It is not only permitted, but compelled, to take environmental values into account. Perhaps the greatest importance of NEPA is to require the Atomic Energy Commission and other agencies to *consider* environmental issues just as they consider other matters within their mandates. This compulsion is most plainly stated in Section 102. There, "Congress authorizes and directs that, to the fullest extent possible: (1)

the policies, regulations, and public laws of the United States shall be interpreted and administered in accordance with the policies set forth in this Act. . . ." Congress also "authorizes and directs" that "(2) all agencies of the Federal Government shall" follow certain rigorous procedures in considering environmental values. Senator Jackson, NEPA's principal sponsor, stated that "[n]o agency will [now] be able to maintain that it has no mandate or no requirement to consider the environmental consequences of its actions."

The sort of consideration of environmental values which NEPA compels is clarified in Section 102(2)(A) and (B). In general, all agencies must use a "systematic, interdisciplinary approach" to environmental planning and evaluation "in decisionmaking which may have an impact on man's environment." In order to include all possible environmental factors in the decisional equation, agencies must "identify and develop methods and procedures . . . which will insure that presently unquantified environmental amenities and values may be given appropriate consideration in decisionmaking along with economic and technical considerations." "Environmental amenities" will often be in conflict with "economic and technical considerations." To "consider" the former "along with" the latter must involve a balancing process. In some instances environmental costs may outweigh economic and technical benefits and in other instances they may not. But NEPA mandates a rather finely tuned and "systematic" balancing analysis in each instance.

To ensure that the balancing analysis is carried out and given full effect, Section 102(2)(C) requires that responsible officials of all agencies prepare a "detailed statement" covering the impact of particular actions on the environment, the environmental costs which might be avoided, and alternative measures which might alter the cost-benefit equation. The apparent purpose of the "detailed statement" is to aid in the agencies' own decision making process and to advise other agencies and the public of the environmental consequences of planned federal action. Beyond the "detailed statement," Section 102(2)[(E)] requires all agencies specifically to "study, develop, and describe appropriate alternatives to recommended courses of action in any proposal which involves unresolved conflicts concerning alternative uses of available resources." This requirement, like the "detailed statement" requirement, seeks to ensure that each agency decision maker has before him and takes into proper account all possible approaches to a particular project (including total abandonment of the project) which would alter the environmental impact and the cost-benefit balance. Only in that fashion is it likely that the most intelligent, optimally beneficial decision will ultimately be made. Moreover, by compelling a formal "detailed statement" and a description of alternatives, NEPA provides evidence that the mandated decision making process has in fact taken place and,

most importantly, allows those removed from the initial process to evaluate and balance the factors on their own.

Of course, all of these Section 102 duties are qualified by the
phrase "to the fullest extent possible." We must stress as forcefully as
possible that this language does not provide an escape hatch for foot-
dragging agencies; it does not make NEPA's procedural requirements
somehow "discretionary." Congress did not intend the Act to be such a
paper tiger. Indeed, the requirement of environmental consideration
"to the fullest extent possible" sets a high standard for the agencies, a
standard which must be rigorously enforced by the reviewing courts.

[The opinion then discussed the legislative history of NEPA.]

Thus the Section 102 duties are not inherently flexible. They must
be complied with to the fullest extent, unless there is a clear conflict of
statutory authority. Considerations of administrative difficulty, delay or
economic cost will not suffice to strip the section of its fundamental
importance.

We conclude, then, that Section 102 of NEPA mandates a particular sort of careful and informed decisionmaking process and creates
judicially enforceable duties. The reviewing courts probably cannot reverse a substantive decision on its merits, under Section 101, unless it
be shown that the actual balance of costs and benefits that was struck
was arbitrary or clearly gave insufficient weight to environmental values.
But if the decision was reached procedurally without individualized
consideration and balancing of environmental factors — conducted
fully and in good faith — it is the responsibility of the courts to reverse.
As one District Court has said of Section 102 requirements: "It is hard
to imagine a clearer or stronger mandate to the Courts."

In the cases before us now, we do not have to review a particular
decision by the Atomic Energy Commission granting a construction
permit or an operating license. Rather, we must review the Commission's recently promulgated rules which govern consideration of environmental values in all such individual decisions. The rules were
devised strictly in order to comply with the NEPA procedural requirements — but petitioners argue that they fall far short of the congressional mandate.

[The court then examined contentions by petitioners, environmental, and citizens' groups opposed to construction of a nuclear
power facility, subject to licensing approval by the AEC, that regulations
promulgated by the AEC to implement NEPA were deficient and violated the statute in four respects, which it considered in turn.]

II

[Under AEC procedures, an Atomic Safety and Licensing Board
(ASLB) independently reviews engineering and economic issues in

AEC staff recommendations to license a project even if the issuance of the license is unopposed. However, the AEC's NEPA regulations provided that a staff-prepared Environmental Impact Statement (EIS) would not be subject to Board review unless environmental issues were affirmatively raised by staff or outside parties. The AEC argued that NEPA was satisfied by the preparation of an EIS by the staff, plus its availability to the Board, without Board review.]

We believe that the Commission's crabbed interpretation of NEPA makes a mockery of the Act. What possible purpose could there be in the Section 102(2)(C) requirement (that the "detailed statement" accompany proposals through agency review processes) if "accompany" means no more than physical proximity — mandating no more than the physical act of passing certain folders and papers, unopened, to reviewing officials along with other folders and papers? What possible purpose could there be in requiring the "detailed statement" to be before hearing boards, if the boards are free to ignore entirely the contents of the statement? NEPA was meant to do more than regulate the flow of papers in the federal bureaucracy. The word "accompany" in Section 102(2)(C) must not be read so narrowly as to make the Act ludicrous. It must, rather, be read to indicate a congressional intent that environmental factors, as compiled in the "detailed statement," be *considered* through agency review processes.

. . . The Commission's hearing boards automatically consider nonenvironmental factors, even though they have been previously studied by the staff. Clearly, the review process is an appropriate stage at which to balance conflicting factors against one another. And, just as clearly, it provides an important opportunity to reject or significantly modify the staff's recommended action. Environmental factors, therefore, should not be singled out and excluded, at this stage, from the proper balance of values envisioned by NEPA. . . .[1]

III

[The court then rejected the AEC's claim that need for a period of "orderly transition" justified delaying implementation of NEPA, which was signed into law on January 1, 1971, by not applying it to projects for which hearings had been noticed prior to March 4, 1971. The court held that AEC's claimed concern with "a pressing national power crisis" was not justification for shirking its NEPA responsibilities,

---

1. In recent years, the courts have become increasingly strict in requiring that federal agencies live up to their mandates to consider the public interest. They have become increasingly impatient with agencies which attempt to avoid or dilute their statutorily imposed role as protectors of public interest values beyond the narrow concerns of industries being regulated. . . .

and observed "an unfortunate affliction of large organizations to resist new procedures and to envision massive roadblocks to their adoption."]

IV

[The regulations precluded AEC examination of environmental effects subject to regulation by other federal agencies where those agencies had certified that the project complied with such regulations.]

The sweep of NEPA is extraordinarily broad, compelling consideration of any and all types of environmental impact of federal action. However, the Atomic Energy Commission's rules specifically exclude from full consideration a wide variety of environmental issues. First, they provide that no party may raise and the Commission may not independently examine any problem of water quality — perhaps the most significant impact of nuclear power plants. Rather, the Commission indicates that it will defer totally to water quality standards devised and administered by state agencies and approved by the federal government under the Federal Water Pollution Control Act. Secondly, the rules provide for similar abdication of NEPA authority to the standards of other agencies. . . . The most the Commission will do is include a condition in all construction permits and operating licenses requiring compliance with the water quality or other standards set by such agencies. The upshot is that the NEPA procedures, viewed by the Commission as superfluous, will wither away in disuse, applied only to those environmental issues wholly unregulated by any other federal, state or regional body.

We believe the Commission's rule is in fundamental conflict with the basic purpose of the Act. NEPA mandates a case-by-case balancing judgment on the part of federal agencies. In each individual case, the particular economic and technical benefits of planned action must be assessed and then weighed against the environmental costs; alternatives must be considered which would affect the balance of values. . . . The magnitude of possible benefits and possible costs may lie anywhere on a broad spectrum. Much will depend on the particular magnitudes involved in particular cases. In some cases, the benefits will be great enough to justify a certain quantum of environmental costs; in other cases, they will not be so great and the proposed action may have to be abandoned or significantly altered so as to bring the benefits and costs into a proper balance. The point of the individualized balancing analysis is to ensure that, with possible alterations, the optimally beneficial action is finally taken.

Certification by another agency that its own environmental standards are satisfied involves an entirely different kind of judgment. Such agencies, without overall responsibility for the particular federal action in question, attend only to one aspect of the problem: the magnitude of certain environmental costs. They simply determine whether those costs exceed an allowable amount. Their certification does not mean that they found no environmental damage whatever. In fact, there may be significant environmental damage (e.g., water pollution), but not quite enough to violate applicable (e.g., water quality) standards. Certifying agencies do not attempt to weigh that damage against the opposing benefits. Thus the balancing analysis remains to be done. It may be that the environmental costs, though passing prescribed standards, are nonetheless great enough to outweigh the particular economic and technical benefits involved in the planned action. The only agency in a position to make such a judgment is the agency with overall responsibility for the proposed federal action — the agency to which NEPA is specifically directed.

The Atomic Energy Commission, abdicating entirely to other agencies' certifications, neglects the mandated balancing analysis. Concerned members of the public are thereby precluded from raising a wide range of environmental issues in order to affect particular Commission decisions. And the special purpose of NEPA is subverted.

Arguing before this court, the Commission has made much of the special environmental expertise of the agencies which set environmental standards. NEPA did not overlook this consideration. . . . [The court quoted §102(2)(C) of NEPA.] Thus the Congress was surely cognizant of federal, state and local agencies "authorized to develop and enforce environmental standards." But it provided, in Section 102(2)(C), only for full consultation. It most certainly did not authorize a total abdication to those agencies. Nor did it grant a license to disregard the main body of NEPA obligations. . . .

V

Petitioners' final attack is on the Commission's rules governing a particular set of nuclear facilities: those for which construction permits were granted without consideration of environmental issues, but for which operating licenses have yet to be issued. These facilities, still in varying stages of construction, include the one of most immediate concern to one of the petitioners: the Calvert Cliffs nuclear power plant on Chesapeake Bay in Maryland.

[The court noted that the AEC regulations provided for current preparation of an EIS for projects under construction, in advance of the application for an operating license upon completion of construction, but that the regulations precluded interim modification of the construction design or a temporary halt to construction regardless of the adverse environmental impacts disclosed by the EIS. The court held that this preclusion violated NEPA and was not justified by national energy needs.]

VI

We hold that, in the four respects detailed above, the Commission must revise its rules governing consideration of environmental issues. We do not impose a harsh burden on the Commission. For we require only an exercise of substantive discretion which will protect the environment "to the fullest extent possible." No less is required if the grand congressional purposes underlying NEPA are to become a reality.

Remanded for proceedings consistent with this opinion.

NOTES AND QUESTIONS

1. NEPA seems to reflect a congressional aspiration that federal agencies give greater weight to environmental factors and that the federal government as a whole engage in systematic planning to protect and advance environmental values. But what specific mechanism for implementing these aspirations did Congress envision? Judge Wright thinks it clear that the courts were intended to assume the principal responsibility for implementation, prophesying "a flood of new litigation." Is this clear, particularly in view of the absence from NEPA of any provisions for judicial review or enforcement?[2]

2. *Calvert Cliffs'* interpretation has powerfully shaped all of NEPA case law. Why did Judge Wright seize upon the "detailed statement" requirement of Section 102(2)(C) as the key to judicial implementation of NEPA? Are courts ill-suited or inappropriate bodies for enforcing the other sections of NEPA? Consider also Judge Wright's distinction between rigorous "procedural" duties mandated by NEPA and the Act's "general substantive policy," which he finds "flexible." Is this distinction found in the statute? Is it possible or is it desirable to differentiate "procedure" and "substance" so sharply?[3] Judge Wright

---

2. Because there is no explicit provision for judicial review in NEPA, private litigants challenging violations of the statute customarily bring suit in federal district court, invoking general federal jurisdiction (28 U.S.C. §1331) and the mandamus statute (28 U.S.C. §1361), and seeking injunctive or declaratory relief pursuant to the judicial review provisions of the APA. 5 U.S.C. §§701-706 (1988). The question of standing to challenge NEPA violations is discussed infra, p. 1010; the availability of injunctions to enforce NEPA is discussed infra, pp. 1015-1016.

3. Note that *Calvert Cliffs* arose in the context of a challenge to general AEC regulations. Might the thrust of the opinion (and, potentially, subsequent case law) have been different if the case had arisen in the context of AEC approval of a specific nuclear plant?

remarks on the resistance of bureaucracies to change, a resistance that can be expected to be quite pronounced when established agencies with goals or missions other than environmental quality are suddenly told to give greater weight to environmental factors. Is there a danger that emphasis on procedural requirements will yield only a change in the form of bureaucratic decision without altering an agency's basic policies? On the other hand, might it be argued that changing the basic procedures of agency decision is the only feasible way for courts to effect a wide-ranging change in agency policies, particularly in light of the fact that courts normally review only a small fraction of all agency decisions?

3. The court ruthlessly rejects the AEC's procedure of treating the impact statement as irrelevant in further agency review in uncontested proceedings. What does it gain by this? Can procedural formalities ever safeguard environmental interests when there is no confrontation by adversaries?[4]

4. In the original enactment of NEPA, the House and Senate passed quite different bills, and major surgery was necessary in conference to resolve them. The House measure did not include any provision like §102. Its focus had been on the founding of the Council on Environmental Quality. The Senate bill originally provided that federal agencies should make "an environmental finding" with respect to the impacts of their activities. The environmental impact statement provision was added at the instance of Professor Lynton K. Caldwell, who advised Senator Jackson regarding the legislation. Professor Caldwell testified: "I would urge that in the shaping of [national environmental] policy, it have an action-forcing, operational aspect. When we speak of policy we ought to think of a statement . . . which will compel or reinforce or assist . . . the executive agencies in particular, but going beyond this, the Nation as a whole, to take the kind of action which will protect and reinforce what I have called the life support system of this country."[5]

The conference committee deleted a Senate provision that "each person has a fundamental and inalienable right to a healthful environ-

---

4. The court also makes light of the AEC's difficulties in compliance. Yet Congress subsequently held extensive hearings on this decision's outcome, in response to warnings — strongly contested by environmentalists — that the country faced a grave power shortage if reactor licensing were halted for even a year. Noting that *Calvert Cliffs* had prolonged the already long procedural delays in nuclear licensing, Congress passed a temporary relief measure, 42 U.S.C. §2242, which did not exempt licensing from NEPA, but allowed interim operating licenses to be issued with EISs that looked only to the environmental effects of *temporary* operation — a cautious compromise. See 1972 U.S. Code Cong. & Ad. News 2355, 2358.

5. National Environmental Policy: Hearings on S. 1075, S. 237, and S. 1752 Before the Senate Comm. on Interior and Insular Affairs, 91st Cong., 1st Sess. 116 (1969) (statement of Lynton K. Caldwell, Professor of Govern-

ment." H.R. Rep. No. 91-765, 91st Cong., 1st Sess. 8 (1969), reprinted in 1969 U.S. Code Cong. & Ad. News at 2768. What might the courts have done with such a provision? The committee substituted the provision now found in NEPA §101(c) that "each person should enjoy a healthful environment." Id. at 2770. On the other hand, the conference committee deleted a House limitation that "nothing in this Act shall increase, decrease or change any responsibility or authority of any Federal official or agency created by other provision of law." Id. at 2770. Should the fact that one House of Congress was willing to warn that the Act changed nothing, and had not originally passed the §102 provisions, suggest to a court that there was something less than evangelistic fervor in Congress for sweeping new environmental requirements? Does the ambiguous provenance of NEPA suggest that the courts should decline any role in enforcing implementation of NEPA by agencies, or should enforce it only cautiously?

2. CEQ AND ITS REGULATIONS

What alternatives or complements to judicial implementation of NEPA are there? President Nixon directed CEQ to develop guidelines for the preparation of impact statements by federal agencies. President Carter by executive order delegated authority to CEQ to issue regulations governing the implementation of NEPA. E.O. 11,991, 3 C.F.R. 123 (1978). CEQ promulgated such regulations in 1978. 40 C.F.R. §§1500-1508 (1992). As a result of the President's executive order, these regulations became binding on federal agencies on July 30, 1979. The regulations have remained largely unchanged since their original adoption. They deal with, among other matters, the process for preparing EISs and their content. The regulations represent a useful synthesis of NEPA law, and courts reviewing agency actions challenged as violating NEPA accord "substantial deference" to the interpretations found in the CEQ regulations. *Andrus v. Sierra Club,* 442 U.S. 347, 358 (1979), excerpted infra, p. 936. In addition, CEQ has issued useful answers in Forty Most Asked Questions Concerning National Policy Act Regulations, 46 Fed. Reg. 18,026 (1981), as amended, 51 Fed. Reg. 15,618 (1986) (codified at 40 C.F.R. §1502 (1992).

CEQ originally served as a central repository for impact statements and monitored their preparation. However, CEQ's administrative resources were limited, and it could not begin to review in detail more than a minute fraction of the hundreds of impact statements prepared

---

ment, University of Indiana). For a review of NEPA's legislative history, see Dreyfus & Ingram, The National Environmental Policy Act: A View of Intent and Practice, 16 Nat. Resources J. 243 (1976).

every year. In 1972, Congress added §309 to the Clean Air Act, authorizing EPA to review and comment upon impact statements prepared by other agencies; EPA is to refer EISs that it finds unsatisfactory to CEQ. 42 U.S.C. §7609; see also 40 C.F.R. §1504. President Carter's reorganization plan for the Executive Office transferred CEQ's clearing-house function as an EIS repository and source of public information to EPA. See Reorg. Plan No. 1 of 1977, 42 Fed. Reg. 56,101 (1977), reprinted in 3 U.S.C. §21 app. at 371-375 (1988); see also 42 Fed. Reg. 59543 (1977). EPA also publishes notice in the Federal Register of EISs received from other agencies. However, EPA's resources are also limited, and it has other urgent regulatory priorities. Accordingly, its §309 responsibilities are only fitfully exercised.

What additional steps might be taken by a President who wanted executive agencies to give greater weight to environmental values? The difficulties of changing established bureaucratic attitudes are considerable even in the context of a given department. Suppose that the Secretary of Transportation wants greater weight given to environmental factors in highway siting but knows that the Highway Bureau places great weight on engineering and cost factors. Should the preparation of EISs be left entirely to the regional offices of the Bureau? Should they be rewritten by the Secretary's staff in Washington? What other options might the Secretary pursue? What role might Congress play in implementing NEPA?

B.   THRESHOLD ISSUES: WHEN MUST AN EIS BE FILED?

NEPA requires that "all agencies of the Federal Government shall . . . include in every recommendation or report on proposals for legislation and other major Federal actions significantly affecting the quality of the human environment" an EIS. 42 U.S.C. §4332(2)(C) (1988). This section addresses in turn (1) the requirement of a significant environmental impact, (2) the requirement of a "proposal," and (3) the requirement that the proposed action be "federal."

1. SIGNIFICANT EFFECTS ON THE QUALITY OF THE HUMAN ENVIRONMENT

HANLY V. KLEINDIENST

471 F.2d 823, 831-840 (2d Cir. 1972)

[This important decision addresses two basic issues: (1) What are the criteria for determining whether a proposed federal action is a "major" federal action "significantly affecting the quality of the human environment" within the meaning of Section 102(2)(C) of NEPA, requiring that an impact statement be filed with respect to such action? and (2) What procedures is a federal agency to follow in making its determination whether an impact statement is required?

The proposed construction by the General Services Administration (GSA) of an office building and high-rise jail (the MCC) in a densely populated area of lower Manhattan near the United States Courthouse was challenged by neighborhood residents because of failure to file an impact statement.

In an earlier opinion, *Hanly v. Mitchell,* 460 F.2d 640, *cert. denied,* 409 U.S. 990 (1972) *(Hanly I),* the court of appeals held that the environmental effects to be considered in determining the need for an impact statement were not confined to the air and water pollution and garbage which the facility might create, but extended to "noise, traffic, overburdened mass transportation systems, crime, congestion, and even availability of drugs" on the ground that they reflected the "profound influences of . . . high density urbanization [and] industrial expansion" within the meaning of §101(a) of NEPA.

On remand GSA again determined, after preparing an "environmental assessment" of the proposed project, that no impact statement was required. On appeal from the district court's denial of a preliminary injunction, the court of appeals held in *Hanly II* that the standard for judicial review of GSA's determination of whether environmental impact was "significant" was whether its decision was "arbitrary, capricious, an abuse of discretion, or otherwise not in accordance with law." Judge Mansfield's opinion then continued:]

Although the existing environment of the area which is the site of a major federal action constitutes one criterion to be considered, it must be recognized that even a slight increase in adverse conditions that form an existing environmental milieu may sometimes threaten harm that is significant. One more factory polluting air and water in an area zoned for industrial use may represent the straw that breaks the back of the environmental camel. Hence the absolute, as well as comparative, effects of a major federal action must be considered. . . .

The Assessment [record of the GSA determination] makes clear that the MCC will not produce any unusual or excessive amounts of smoke, dirt, obnoxious odors, solid waste, or other forms of pollution. The utilities required to heat and air-condition the building are readily available and the MCC is designed to incorporate energy-saving features, so that no excessive power demands are posed. The GSA further represents that the building will conform to all local codes, use and zoning, and attaches a letter from the New York City Office of Lower Manhattan Development dated August 4, 1971, indicating approval of the Annex, which includes the MCC. . . .

Appellants offer little or no evidence to contradict the detailed facts found by the GSA. For the most part their opposition is based upon a psychological distaste for having a jail located so close to residential apartments, which is understandable enough. It is doubtful whether psychological and sociological effects upon neighbors constitute the type of factors that may be considered in making such a determination since they do not lend themselves to measurement. However we need not decide that issue because these apartments were constructed within two or three blocks of another existing jail, The Manhattan House of Detention for Men, which is much larger than the proposed MCC and houses approximately 1,200 prisoners. Furthermore the area in which the MCC is located has at all times been zoned by the City of New York as a commercial district designed to provide for a wide range of uses, *specifically including "Prisons."*

Despite the GSA's scrupulous efforts the appellants do present one or two factual issues that merit further consideration and findings by the GSA. One bears on the possibility that the MCC will substantially increase the risk of crime in the immediate area, a relevant factor as to which the Assessment fails to make an outright finding despite the direction to do so in *Hanly I.* Appellants urge that the Community Treatment Program and the program for observation and study of nonresident out-patients will endanger the health and safety of the immediate area by exposing neighbors and passersby to drug addicts visiting the MCC for drug maintenance and to drug pushers and hangers-on who would inevitably frequent the vicinity of a drug maintenance center. If the MCC were to be used as a drug treatment center, the potential increase in crime might tip the scales in favor of a mandatory detailed impact statement. The Government has assured us by post-argument letter addressed to the Court that:

> Neither the anticipated nonresident presentence study program nor any program to be conducted within the Metropolitan Correction Center will include drug maintenance.

While we do not question the Government's good faith, a finding in the matter by GSA is essential, since the Assessment is ambiguous as to the scope of the non-resident out-patient observation program and makes no finding on the subject of whether the MCC will increase the risk of crime in the community. . . .

Notwithstanding the absence of statutory or administrative provisions on the subject, this Court has already held in *Hanly I* at 647 that federal agencies must "affirmatively develop a reviewable environmental record . . . even for purposes of a threshold section 102(2)(C) determination." We now go further and hold that before a preliminary or threshold determination of significance is made the responsible agency must give notice to the public of the proposed major federal action and an opportunity to submit relevant facts which might bear upon the agency's threshold decision. We do not suggest that a full-fledged formal hearing must be provided before each such determination is made, although it should be apparent that in many cases such a hearing would be advisable for reasons already indicated. The necessity for a hearing will depend greatly upon the circumstances surrounding the particular proposed action and upon the likelihood that a hearing will be more effective than other methods in developing relevant information and an understanding of the proposed action. The precise procedural steps to be adopted are better left to the agency, which should be in a better position than the court to determine whether solution of the problems faced with respect to a specific major federal action can better be achieved through a hearing or by informal acceptance of relevant data.

In view of the Assessment's failure to make findings with respect to the possible existence of a drug maintenance program at the MCC, the increased risk of crime that might result from the operation of the MCC, and the fact that appellants have challenged certain findings of fact, we remand the case for the purpose of requiring the GSA to make a further investigation of these issues, with directions to accept from appellants and other concerned citizens such further evidence as they may proffer within a reasonable period, to make supplemental findings with respect to the issues, and to redetermine whether the MCC "significantly affects the quality of the human environment.". . .

FRIENDLY, Chief Judge (dissenting):

The learned opinion of my brother Mansfield gives these plaintiffs, and environmental advocates in future cases, both too little and too much. It gives too little because it raises the floor of what constitutes "major Federal actions significantly affecting the quality of the human environment," 42 U.S.C. §4332(2)(C), higher than I believe Congress intended. It gives too much because it requires that before making a threshold determination that no impact statement is demanded, the agency must go through procedures which I think are needed only when an impact statement must be made. The upshot is that a threshold determination that a proposal does not constitute major Federal

action significantly affecting the quality of the human environment becomes a kind of mini-impact statement. The preparation of such a statement under the conditions laid down by the majority is unduly
burdensome when the action is truly minor or insignificant. On the
other hand, there is a danger that if the threshold determination is this
elaborate, it may come to replace the impact statement in the grey
area between actions which, though "major" in a monetary sense, are
obviously insignificant (such as the construction of the proposed office
building) and actions that are obviously significant (such as the construction of an atomic power plant). We would better serve the purposes of Congress by keeping the threshold low enough to insure that
impact statements are prepared for actions in this grey area and thus
to permit the determination that no statement is required to be made
quite informally in cases of true insignificance.

While I agree that determination of the meaning of "significant"
is a question of law, one must add immediately that to make this determination on the basis of the dictionary would be impossible. Although
all words may be "chameleons, which reflect the color of their environment," *C.I.R. v. National Carbide Corp.*, 167 F.2d 304, 306 (2 Cir. 1948)
(L. Hand, J.), "significant" has that quality more than most. It covers a
spectrum ranging from "not trivial" through "appreciable" to "important" and even "momentous." If the right meaning is at the lower
end of the spectrum, the construction of the MCC comes within it; *per
contra* if the meaning is at the higher end.

The scheme of the National Environmental Policy Act argues for
giving "significant" a reading which places it toward the lower end of
the spectrum. . . .

It is not readily conceivable that Congress meant to allow agencies
to avoid [NEPA's EIS requirements] by reading "significant" to mean
only "important," "momentous," or the like. One of the purposes of the
impact statement is to insure that the relevant environmental data are
before the agency and considered by it prior to the decision to commit
Federal resources to the project; the statute must not be construed so
as to allow the agency to make its decision in a doubtful case without
the relevant data or a detailed study of it. This is particularly clear because of the absence from the statute of any procedural requirement
upon an agency in making the threshold determination that an impact
statement is not demanded, although the majority has managed to con-
trive one. What Congress was trying to say was "You don't need to make
an impact statement, with the consequent expense and delay, when
there is no sensible reason for making one." I thus agree with Judge J.
Skelly Wright's view that "a statement is required whenever the action
arguably will have an adverse environmental impact," *Students Challenging Regulatory Agency Procedures (S.C.R.A.P.) v. United States*, 346 F. Supp.
189, 201 (D.D.C. 1972) (three-judge court) (emphasis in original),

. . . with the qualification, doubtless intended, that the matter must be *fairly* arguable. . . .

I thus reach the question whether, with the term so narrowed, the GSA's refusal to prepare an impact statement for the MCC can be supported. Accepting the majority's standard of review, I would think that, even with the fuller assessment here before us, the GSA could not reasonably conclude that the MCC does not entail potentially significant environmental effects. I see no ground for the majority's doubt "whether psychological and sociological effects upon neighbors constitute the type of factors that may be considered in making such a determination [of significant environmental *effect*] since they do not lend themselves to measurement." The statute speaks of "the overall welfare and development of man," [§101(a)] and makes it the responsibility of Federal agencies to "use all practicable means . . . to . . . assure for all Americans safe, healthful, productive, and aesthetically and culturally pleasing surroundings." [§101(b).] Moreover, [§102(2)(B)] directs that "presently unquantified environmental amenities and values . . . be given appropriate consideration in decision-making along with economic and technical considerations." . . .

I do not mean anything said in this opinion to imply that GSA will be unable to conclude in an impact statement that construction of the MCC is justified. Furthermore, as I have suggested in another case, "Once it is determined in any particular instance that there has been good faith compliance with those procedures [of NEPA], we seriously question whether much remains for a reviewing court." *City of New York v. United States* (II), 344 F. Supp. 929, 940 (E.D.N.Y. 1972). . . . However, as said in *City of New York v. United States* (I), 337 F. Supp. 150, 160 (E.D.N.Y. 1972):

> To permit an agency to ignore its duties under NEPA with impunity because we have serious doubts that its ultimate decision will be affected by compliance would subvert the very purpose of the Act and encourage further administrative laxity in this area.

The energies my brothers would require GSA to devote to still a third assessment designed to show that an impact statement is not needed would better be devoted to making one.

I would reverse and direct the issuance of an injunction until a reasonable period after the making of an impact statement.

Epilogue

Hanly II did not close the case. After the Supreme Court denied certiorari, 412 U.S. 908 (1973) (second time), the district court on remand denied plaintiffs' request for an injunction (third time), and the appeals court affirmed the district court, 484 F.2d 448 (2d Cir. 1973); and the Supreme Court again denied certiorari, 416 U.S. 936 (1974) (third time). Thus, the local residents lost. But would an agency be willing to repeat the GSA's course?

a. Agency Process for Determining Whether an EIS Is Required

The 1978 CEQ regulations establish procedures that federal agencies must follow in determining whether an EIS is required. Agencies must prepare Environmental Assessments (EAs), concise documents[6] providing the evidence and analysis necessary to make a threshold determination. EAs must include discussions of the proposed action's rationale, alternative actions, environmental impacts of the proposed and alternative actions, and a list of the agencies and private parties contacted. If an agency determines that its proposed action will not have a significant effect on the human environment, then it must prepare a Finding of No Significant Impact (FONSI) explaining its determination. See 40 C.F.R. §§1501.4(b), 1501.4(e), 1508.9, 1508.13 (1992).

b. When Is the Magnitude of Effects "Significant"?

How should the threshold of significance of effects needed to trigger an EIS preparation be set? Presently agencies prepare some 500 EISs and 45,000 EAs annually. An average of 90 NEPA actions are filed in court annually; about a third challenge the adequacy of EISs, the rest challenge the failure to prepare an EIS.[7] Given limited agency resources and the relative infrequency of judicial review, should the EIS

---

6. Conciseness is not always achieved in practice, especially by agencies that are eager to impress the thoroughness of their EAs on courts that may be asked to require them to prepare an EIS. In one recent case, a circuit court charged with that decision was confronted by a record containing about 1800 pages of EAs. See *City of Waltham v. United States Postal Serv.*, 11 F.3d 235, 238 (1st Cir. 1993).

7. See Council on Environmental Quality, Environmental Quality: 23rd Annual Report of the Council on Environmental Quality — 1992 (1993), at 153, 162, 169. Agencies prepared 512 EISs in 1992, 456 in 1991, and 477 in 1990. The average total for the years 1983-1992 was 502. The 45,000 figure may be an underestimate; it represents the number of EAs surveyed by the CEQ in 1992. Ninety-two NEPA complaints, including 32 challenges to the adequacy of EISs or claims that a supplemental EIS was required, were filed in 1991, and 85 in 1990; the average number for the years 1982-1991 was 90. Id. at 162, 164-165, 167.

requirement be limited to a smaller number of truly important federal actions? On the other hand, if the project is small, won't the EIS be correspondingly brief? Consider Judge Friendly's view in *Hanly II*. Should the degree of controversy over a project be an important factor in determining whether an EIS should be prepared? Why? Consider also whether it makes sense to have an EIS procedure for construction of federal buildings in New York but no such procedures for purely private construction in the same neighborhood.[8]

One question is what standard agencies should use to determine the environmental significance of a proposed action. Some circuits have stated that an EIS is required whenever a project "*may* cause a significant degradation" of the human environment. *City of Davis v. Coleman,* 521 F.2d 661, 673 (9th Cir. 1975). This approach, however, seems to have been rejected in *Marsh v. Oregon Natural Resources Council,* 490 U.S. 360, 374 (1989), excerpted infra, p. 986, stating that the test is whether proposed action "will affec[t] the quality of the human environment in a significant manner."

The determination of significance will in any event inevitably be highly context-specific. The CEQ regulations defining "significantly" list a number of factors to be considered. 40 C.F.R. §1508.27 (1992). An important issue in determining whether the effects of a project are "significant" as well as determining the type of an EIS if one is prepared is how far the secondary or indirect effects of a project must be taken into account. For example, in *City of Davis v. Coleman,* supra, the Ninth Circuit required preparation of an EIS in connection with construction of a highway interchange on the ground that the interchange would lead to significant industrial development in the immediate vicinity, even though there was uncertainty regarding the precise extent and nature of the development. We discuss the issue of secondary or indirect effects further at p. 963, infra.

What standard should a court use to review an agency's FONSI determinations that no impact statement is required because the proposed action will not significantly affect the quality of the human environment?[9] Two basic approaches emerged in the lower federal courts.

---

8. Many states, however, also have environmental assessment requirements, many of which apply to private projects that require some form of state or local permit or approval. See infra, p. 1025.

9. NEPA §102(2)(C) requires EISs for "major federal actions significantly affecting the quality of the human environment." Does the term "major" represent an independent criterion, so that a project must both be "major" in size as well as "significant" in its effects before an EIS is required? Some courts have thought so. See, e.g., *Jicarilla Apache Tribe of Indians v. Morton,* 471 F.2d 1275 (9th Cir. 1973). But most have focused on "significance" without giving "major" independent effect. If a project's environmental effects are "signifi-

One, assertedly more deferential to the agency, was to set aside its determination of no significant impact only if the court determines that the agency's action was "arbitrary and capricious." This standard is derived from the Administrative Procedure Act, 5 U.S.C. §706(2)(A) (1988). As explained in *Overton Park*, supra, p. 876, under this standard the reviewing court must consider whether the agency's decision "was based on a consideration of the relevant factors and whether there has been a clear error of judgment." 401 U.S. at 416. The ultimate standard of review is "narrow" but the court's inquiry into the agency's decision must be "searching and careful." Note that in *Hanly II*, the court purports to use the deferential "arbitrary and capricious" test for reviewing agency action — yet it reverses the agency action anyway. Did it really apply the test it claimed to?

The other, assertedly less deferential approach is for the reviewing court independently to determine whether the agency's decision not to prepare an EIS was "reasonable." For example, in *Save Our Ten Acres v. Kreger*, 472 F.2d 463 (5th Cir. 1973), a group of Army Corps of Engineers employees opposed to being relocated challenged the Corps' decision not to prepare an EIS for a new building on a downtown site. The court of appeals stated that the district court should proceed

> to examine and weigh the evidence of both the plaintiff and the agency to determine whether the agency reasonably concluded that the particular project would have no effects which would significantly degrade our environmental quality. This inquiry must not necessarily be limited to consideration of the administrative record, but supplemental affidavits, depositions and other proof concerning the environmental impact of the project may be considered if an inadequate evidentiary development before the agency can be shown. . . . If the court concludes that no environmental factor would be significantly degraded by the project, GSA's determination not to file the impact statement should be upheld. On the other hand, if the court finds that the project may cause a significant degradation of some human environmental factor . . . the court should require the filing of an impact statement. . . .

472 F.2d at 467. The court explained, "[t]he spirit of the [NEPA] would die aborning if a facile, ex parte decision that the project was minor or did not significantly affect the environment were too well shielded from impartial review." Id. at 466. See also *City of Davis v. Coleman*, 521 F.2d at 674, dismissing as "bureaucratic doubletalk" the agency's negative

---

cant" then the project is presumably a "major" one for NEPA purposes, and if its effects are not "significant" it should not be deemed "major." The CEQ regulations state: "Major reinforces but does not have a meaning independent of significantly." 40 C.F.R. §1508.18 (1992).

declaration that construction of a highway interchange would have no significant environmental effects.[10]

In *Marsh v. Oregon Natural Resources Council,* 490 U.S. 360, 377 (1989), excerpted infra p. 989, the Supreme Court eventually settled the debate among the circuits by adopting the arbitrary and capricious standard for judicial review. Is this relatively deferential standard of review appropriate when an agency's action is challenged as violating NEPA? Such an approach to review is understandable when Congress delegates to an agency, such as the Transportation Department, broad responsibility to carry out a particular mission, such as building highways. But consider that NEPA was enacted in order to redirect agencies' missions and promote greater consideration of environmental values. Given the purpose of NEPA, should courts defer to determinations by mission-oriented agencies that their actions are not subject to its requirements? On the other hand, can federal courts appropriately decide de novo what the environmental effects of any agency's action are, and whether NEPA's EIS threshold is triggered? Is there a solution to this dilemma?

c. *What Types of Effects Are Covered?*

Should the types of effects constituting an "adverse impact on the human environment" be defined so broadly as to include, as in *Hanly,* crime and drugs? Is there not a danger that such a broad definition, encompassing a host of vague and subjective factors, will unduly dilute the utility and efficacy of the EIS procedure? Consider that a broad definition of "environment" in this context may extend opportunities for NEPA challenges to litigants whose motivating concern is not ecological. For example, in *Save Our Ten Acres v. Kreger,* supra, the litigation against a new government office building was mounted by government employees who objected to being relocated there. Must the assertedly adverse social impacts of building low-income housing in a neighborhood be considered in an EIS? See *Trinity Episcopal Sch. Cor. v. Romney,* 523 F.2d 88 (2d Cir. 1975); Ackerman, Impact Statements and Low Cost Housing 46 S. Cal. L. Rev. 754 (1973).

NEPA appears to take a broad view of what constitutes the "human environment." Section 101(a) states that

---

10. For discussion, see McGarity, The Courts, the Agencies, and NEPA Threshold Issues, 55 Tex. L. Rev. 801 (1977). Later court of appeals decisions have sought to justify this less deferential approach to review by claiming that an EIS is a "procedure" required by law and that the APA, 5 U.S.C. §706(2)(D), requires reviewing courts independently to determine whether agencies have complied with procedures required by law.

it is the continuing policy of the Federal Government . . . to use all practical means and measures, including financial and technical assistance, in a manner calculated to foster and promote the general welfare, to create and maintain conditions under which man and nature can exist in productive harmony, and fulfill the *social, economic,* and other requirements of present and future generations of Americans.

(Emphasis added.) Early courts were split as to the interpretation of this language. Some courts found that significant social or economic effects alone were sufficient to mandate an EIS.[11] Others found that social or economic effects might be significant enough to require an EIS, but only when those effects were accompanied by some effects on the physical environment.[12] The majority approach, however, has been that nonphysical effects cannot by themselves mandate an EIS, but if there is a significant physical effect, nonphysical effects must also be evaluated in the EIS.[13]

The CEQ regulations defining the "human environment" endorse the majority approach:

[E]conomic or social effects are not intended by themselves to require preparation of an environmental impact statement. When an environmental impact statement is prepared and economic or social and natural or physical environmental effects are interrelated, then the environmental impact statement will discuss all of these effects on the human environment.

40 C.F.R. §1508.14 (1992). Recent cases follow this approach and often cite the CEQ regulation.[14]

The Supreme Court addressed the need for agencies to consider

---

11. See *McDowell v. Schlesinger,* 404 F. Supp. 221 (W.D. Mo. 1975) (EIS required to evaluate social and economic impacts of transfer of Air Force unit); *Goose Hollow Foothills League v. Romney,* 334 F. Supp. 877 (D. Or. 1971) (EIS required to evaluate the impacts of a federally funded high-rise apartment construction project on the character of the neighborhood, population concentration, and neighbors' views).

12. See *City of Rochester v. United States Postal Service,* 541 F.2d 967 (2d Cir. 1976) (construction of suburban postal facility and transfer of 1400 urban employees to it required EIS where socio-economic effects such as urban flight would have impact on physical environment, including urban decay and increased traffic and air pollution).

13. See *Breckinridge v. Rumsfield,* 537 F.2d 864 (6th Cir. 1976), *cert. denied,* 429 U.S. 1061 (1977) (closing of army depot and elimination of 2630 civilian jobs did not require EIS); *Township of Dover v. United States Postal Serv.,* 429 F. Supp. 295 (D. N.J. 1977) (construction of new mail processing facility did not require EIS unless plaintiff employees could allege a primary impact on physical environment sufficient to trigger an EIS).

14. See *Como-Falcon Community Coalition v. United States Dept. of Labor,* 609 F.2d 342 (8th Cir. 1979), *cert. denied,* 446 U.S. 936 (1980); *Olmsted Citizens for a*

the psychological effects caused by the risk of environmental damage in *Metropolitan Edison Co. v. People Against Nuclear Energy*, 460 U.S. 766 (1983) *("PANE ")*. On March 28, 1979, Unit 2 of the Three Mile Island nuclear power plant in Harrisburg, Pennsylvania, suffered a serious accident that resulted in damage to the reactor. The accident caused panic in the surrounding area and Governor Thornburgh recommended evacuation of all children and pregnant women. The President's commission on the accident found that severe mental stress was the most serious health effect of the accident.[15] Unit 1 had been shut down for refueling at the time of the accident and the NRC ordered the reactor to remain inactive until it had an opportunity to determine whether the plant could operate safely. A group of area residents opposed to operation of either TMI reactor offered evidence to the NRC that restarting Unit 1 would cause severe psychological health damage to persons living in the area and argued that NEPA mandated its consideration. The NRC decided not to consider this evidence in determining whether the reactor should be restarted. Metropolitan Edison, operator of the reactor, intervened to argue that a supplemental EIS was unnecessary because no new environmental effects of operating the reactor had arisen since the original EIS had been prepared.

The Supreme Court decided that psychological health effects of the risk of another nuclear accident need not be considered by the NRC. Writing for a unanimous court, Justice Rehnquist stated that while NEPA seeks to advance human welfare, including psychological health, it seeks to do so by means of reducing adverse effects on the physical environment. "[A] *risk* of an accident is not an effect on the physical environment." 460 U.S. at 775.

Accordingly, while NEPA requires agencies to evaluate the risk that a proposed action will cause harm to the physical environment,

---

Better Community v. United States, 793 F.2d 201 (8th Cir. 1986). See also Note, *Como-Falcon v. Dept. of Labor: The Role of Public Hearings and Socio-Economic Impacts in Determining Whether NEPA Requires an EIS*, 6 Colum. J. Envtl. L. 165 (1980). The historical, cultural, and archeological aspects of significant effects on the physical environment have been held to mandate an EIS based on NEPA's text, the National Historic Preservation Act, and the Moss-Bennet Act. See *Morris County Trust for Historic Preservation v. Pierce*, 714 F.2d 271 (3d Cir. 1983) (EIS required for demolition of historic building). Although aesthetic values are also explicitly promoted under NEPA, the courts have been reluctant to mandate an EIS for such effects because ruling on such subjective matters may be arbitrary. See Note, Beyond the Eye of the Beholder: Aesthetics and Objectivity, 71 Mich. L. Rev. 1438 (1973).

15. See President's Commission on the Accident at Three Mile Island, The Need for Change: The Legacy of TMI 13, 35 (1979); Note, Rejection of Risk Under NEPA: Stress and People Against Nuclear Energy, 33 Am. U.L. Rev. 535, 537 n.19 (1984).

and the adverse effects on human welfare that will result from such environmental damage,[16] the psychological damage to humans caused by the perception of such risk is not a sufficient basis for requiring an EIS.

NOTES AND QUESTIONS

1. *Hanly II* doubted "whether psychological and sociological effects upon neighbors constitute the type of factors that may be considered" in determining whether an EIS is required because "they do not lend themselves to measurement." 471 F.2d at 833. The court did, however, find that the risk of crime must be considered. Is this latter conclusion good law after *PANE?*

2. Must an EIS be prepared on a high-rise public housing project because of "the fears of the neighbors of prospective public housing tenants"? See *Nucleus of Chicago Homeowners Assn. v. Lynn,* 524 F.2d 225, 231 (7th Cir. 1975).

d. Mitigation

If an agency's original proposed action would have significant environmental effects requiring preparation of an EIS, can the agency avoid the EIS requirement by amending its proposed action by introducing mitigation measures to reduce the environmental effects below the threshold level of "significant"? In *Cabinet Mountains Wilderness / Scotchman's Peak Grizzly Bears v. Peterson,* 685 F.2d 678 (D.C. Cir. 1982), the D.C. Circuit found that specific mitigation measures imposed by the Forest Service in its EA justified its approval of an exploratory mineral drilling project without preparation of an EIS, notwithstanding the agency's finding that the drilling program as originally proposed, without mitigation, would adversely impact the grizzly bear, an endangered species. The mitigation measures involved restricting drilling to an exploratory program, restricting the times of year when it could be carried out, reducing timber sales, and ordering seasonal road closures. The court rejected plaintiffs' reliance on CEQ's memorandum, *Forty Most Asked Questions [Concerning NEPA],* 46 Fed. Reg. 18,026 (1981), which stated that an agency could not rely on mitigation measures to avoid preparing an EIS unless they were required by statute or regulation or contained in the original proposal. The court held that it was

---

16. See Comment, Federal Regulation of the Biotechnology Industry: The Need to Prepare Environmental Impact Statements for Deliberate Release Experiments, 27 Santa Clara L. Rev. 567 (1987).

sufficient that the agency adopt "specific mitigation measures . . . prior to implementation" which it "convincingly establish[ed]" reduced environmental impacts "to a minimum." 685 F.2d at 682. Which is the better view, that of the court or that of CEQ?

Under the *Peterson* approach, must the mitigation measures adopted be legally binding on the agency? Compare *Foundation for North American Wild Sheep v. United States Department of Agriculture*, 681 F.2d 1172 (9th Cir. 1982), rejecting a Forest Service decision not to prepare an EIS in connection with its grant of a permit for the reconstruction and use of a road passing through the habitat of the Desert Bighorn Sheep, an environmentally "sensitive" species. The Forest Service stated that it would monitor possible impacts on the sheep and take corrective actions to close the road if necessary. The court stated that this amounted to "an agency decision to act now and deal with the environmental consequences later. Such conduct is plainly inconsistent with the broad mandate of NEPA." Id. at 1181. Hence, an EIS was required.

2.   WHEN IS THERE A "PROPOSAL" FOR AGENCY ACTION?

KLEPPE, SECRETARY OF THE INTERIOR V. SIERRA CLUB

427 U.S. 390, 394-415 (1976)

Mr. Justice POWELL delivered the opinion of the Court.

[The EIS requirement of NEPA §102(2)(C) applies to "proposals for legislation and other major Federal actions." This decision addresses the standard for determining whether a "proposal" exists, or, more precisely, whether there exists a broad proposal for a class of actions, meriting a "programmatic" impact statement to cover the whole class, or merely one or more discrete proposals for individual federal actions, each subject to a project-specific EIS.]

I

Respondents, several organizations concerned with the environment, brought this suit in July 1973 in the United States District Court for the District of Columbia. The defendants in the suit, petitioners here, were the officials of the Department and other federal agencies responsible for issuing coal leases, approving mining plans, granting rights-of-way, and taking the other actions necessary to enable private companies and public utilities to develop coal reserves on land owned or controlled by the Federal Government. Citing widespread interest in the reserves of a region identified as the "Northern Great Plains region," and an alleged threat from coal-related operations to their members' enjoyment of the region's environment, respondents claimed that the federal officials could not allow further development without preparing a "comprehensive environmental impact statement" under §102(2)(C) on the entire region. They sought declaratory and injunctive relief.

II

The Northern Great Plains region identified in respondents' complaint encompasses portions of four States — northeastern Wyoming, eastern Montana, western North Dakota, and western South Dakota. There is no dispute about its richness in coal, nor about the waxing interest in developing that coal, nor about the crucial role the federal petitioners will play due to the significant percentage of the coal to which they control access. The Department has initiated, in this decade, three studies in areas either inclusive of or included within this region. The North Central Power Study was addressed to the potential for coordinated development of electric power in an area encompassing all or part of 15 States in the North Central United States. It was aborted in 1972 for lack of interest on the part of electric utilities. The Montana-Wyoming Aqueducts Study, intended to recommend the best use of water resources for coal development in southeastern Montana and northeastern Wyoming, was suspended in 1972 with the initiation of the third study, the Northern Great Plains Resources Program (NGPRP).

While the record does not reveal the degree of concern with environmental matters in the first two studies, it is clear that the NGPRP was devoted entirely to the environment. It was carried out by an interagency, federal-state task force with public participation, and was designed to "assess the potential social, economic and environmental impacts" from resource development in five States — Montana, Wyoming, South Dakota, North Dakota, and Nebraska. Its primary objective was "to provide an analytical and informational framework for policy and planning decisions at all levels of government" by formulating several "scenarios" showing the probable consequences for the area's environment and culture from the various possible techniques and levels of resource development. The final interim report of the NGPRP was issued August 1, 1975, shortly after the decision of the Court of Appeals in this case.

In addition, since 1973 the Department has engaged in a complete review of its coal-leasing program for the entire Nation. On February 17 of that year the Secretary announced the review and announced also that during study a "short-term leasing policy" would prevail, under which new leasing would be restricted to narrowly defined circumstances and even then allowed only when an environmental impact statement had been prepared if required under NEPA. The purpose of the program review was to study the environmental impact of the Department's entire range of coal-related activities and to develop a planning system to guide the national leasing program. The impact statement, known as the "Coal Programmatic EIS," went through several drafts before issuing in final form on September 19, 1975 — shortly before the petitions for certiorari were filed in this case. The Coal Programmatic EIS proposed a new leasing program based on a complex planning system called the Energy Minerals Activity Recommendation System (EMARS), and assessed the prospective environmental impact of the new program as well as the alternatives to it. We have been informed by the parties to this litigation that the Secretary is in the process of implementing the new program. . . .

IV

A

The Court of Appeals, in reversing the District Court, did not find that there was a regional plan or program for development of the Northern Great Plains region. It accepted all of the District Court's findings of fact, but concluded nevertheless that the petitioners "contemplated" a regional plan or program. The court thought that the North Central Power Study, the Montana-Wyoming Aqueducts Study, and the NGPRP all constituted "attempts to control development" by individual companies on a regional scale. It also concluded that the interim report of the NGPRP, then expected to be released at any time, would provide the petitioners with the information needed to formulate the regional plan they had been "contemplating." The Court therefore remanded with instructions to the petitioners to inform the District Court of their role in the further development of the region within 30 days after the NGPRP interim report issued; if they decided to control that development, an impact statement would be required.

We conclude that the Court of Appeals erred in both its factual assumptions and its interpretation of NEPA. We think the court was mistaken in concluding, on the record before it, that the petitioners were "contemplating" a regional development plan or program. It considered the several studies undertaken by the petitioners to represent attempts to control development on a regional scale. This conclusion was based on a finding by the District Court that those studies, as well as the new national coal-leasing policy, were "attempts to control development by individual companies in a manner consistent with the policies and procedures of the National Environmental Policy Act of 1969." But in context, that finding meant only that the named studies were efforts to gain background environmental information for subsequent application in the decisionmaking with respect to individual coal-related projects. This is the sense in which the District Court spoke of controlling development consistently with NEPA. Indeed, in the same paragraph containing the language relied upon by the Court of Appeals, the District Court expressly found that the studies were not part of a plan or program to develop or encourage development. . . .

Moreover, at the time the Court of Appeals ruled there was no indication in the record that the NGPRP was aimed toward a regional plan or program, and subsequent events have shown that this was not its purpose. The interim report of the study, issued shortly after the Court of Appeals ruled, described the effects of several possible rates of coal development but stated in its preface that the alternatives "are for study and comparison only; they do not represent specific plans or proposals." All parties agreed in this Court that there still exists no proposal for a regional plan or program of development. . . .

Even had the record justified a finding that a regional program was contemplated by the petitioners, the legal conclusion drawn by the Court of Appeals cannot be squared with the Act. The court recognized that the mere "contemplation" of certain action is not sufficient to require an impact statement. But it believed the statute nevertheless empowers a court to require the preparation of an impact statement to begin at some point prior to the formal recommendation or report on a proposal. The Court of Appeals accordingly devised its own four-part "balancing" test for determining when, during the contemplation of a plan or other type of federal action, an agency must begin a statement. The factors to be considered were identified as the likelihood and imminence of the program's coming to fruition, the extent to which information is available on the effects of implementing the expected program and on alternatives thereto, the extent to which irretrievable commitments are being made and options precluded "as refinement of the proposal progresses," and the severity of the environmental effects should the action be implemented.

The Court of Appeals thought that as to two of these factors — the availability of information on the effects of any regional development program, and the severity of those effects — the time already was "ripe" for an impact statement. It deemed the record unclear, however, as to the likelihood of the petitioners' actually producing a plan to control the development, and surmised that irretrievable commitments were being avoided because petitioners had ceased approving most coal-related projects while the NGPRP study was underway. The court also thought that the imminent release of the NGPRP interim report would provide the officials with sufficient information to define their role in development of the region, and it believed that as soon as the NGPRP was completed the petitioners would begin approving individual projects in the region, thus permitting irrevocable commitments of resources. It was for this reason that the court in its remand required the petitioners to report to the District Court their decision on the federal role with respect to the Northern Great Plains as a region within 30 days after issuance of the NGPRP report.

The Court's reasoning and action find no support in the language or legislative history of NEPA. The statute clearly states when an impact statement is required, and mentions nothing about a balancing of factors. Rather, as we noted last Term, under the first sentence of §102(2)(C) the moment at which an agency must have a final statement ready "is the time at which it makes a recommendation or report on a *proposal* for federal action." *Aberdeen & Rockfish R. Co. v. SCRAP,* 422 U.S. 289, 320 (1975) *(SCRAP II)* (emphasis in original). The procedural duty imposed upon agencies by this section is quite precise, and the role of the courts in enforcing that duty is similarly precise. A court has no authority to depart from the statutory language and, by a balancing of court-devised factors, determine a point during the germination process of a potential proposal at which an impact statement *should be prepared.* Such an assertion of judicial authority would leave the agencies uncertain as to their procedural duties under NEPA, would invite judicial involvement in the day-to-day decisionmaking process of the agencies, and would invite litigation. As the contemplation of a project and the accompanying study thereof do not necessarily result in a proposal for major federal action, it may be assumed that the balancing process devised by the Court of Appeals also would result in the preparation of a good many unnecessary impact statements. . . .

[The remainder of Justice Powell's opinion, excerpted infra, p. 958 considered whether future coal-related federal actions in the region were so "related" as to require a programmatic EIS notwithstanding the absence of a programmatic proposal. He found that they were not. He concluded:]

[Since] there exists no proposal for regionwide action that could require a regional impact statement, the judgment of the Court of Appeals must be reversed, and the judgment of the District Court reinstated and affirmed. The case is remanded for proceedings consistent with this opinion.

[Justices MARSHALL and BRENNAN dissented in part.]

NOTES AND QUESTIONS

1. Is the Court's deference to the Department of Interior for determining the proper timing of the preparation of an EIS appropriate? Does NEPA preclude courts from determining when an EIS is required? In his separate opinion, Justice Marshall argued that the effect of the Court's decision is to prevent federal courts from addressing a violation of NEPA until it is too late to fashion a remedy. Do you agree? In view of this concern, is the four-part balancing test employed by the D.C. Circuit appropriate? Is it a persuasive interpretation of NEPA?

2. Compare with *Kleppe* the D.C. Circuit's decision in *Scientists' Inst. for Pub. Info., Inc. v. Atomic Energy Commn.*, 481 F.2d 1079 (D.C. Cir. 1973) *("SIPI")*. There, SIPI claimed that the AEC must file an EIS on its liquid metal fast breeder reactor research, development, and demonstration program. The AEC had conceded that it must file an EIS on each major test facility or demonstration plant that it operated, but argued that an EIS for the program as a whole was not required, or, alternatively, was not yet due, since practical implementation of fast breeder reactor technology was still a goal rather than a fixed plan. The court first held that a programmatic statement was required, quoting CEQ guidance then in force:

> Individual actions that are related either geographically or as logical parts in a chain of contemplated actions may be more appropriately evaluated in a single, program statement. Such a statement also appears appropriate in connection with . . . the development of a new program that contemplates a number of subsequent actions. . . . [T]he program statement has a number of advantages. It provides an occasion for a more exhaustive consideration of effects and alternatives than would be practicable in a statement on an individual action. It ensures consideration of cumulative impacts that might be slighted in a case-by-case analysis. And it avoids duplicative reconsideration of basic policy questions. . . .

Id. at 1087-1088, quoting CEQ, Memorandum to Federal Agencies on Procedures for Improving Environmental Impact Statements (May 16, 1972). The court added that NEPA applies to technological research and development activities by the federal government, regardless of government participation in later implementation:

> [T]here is "Federal action" within the meaning of the statute not only when an agency proposes to build a facility itself, but also whenever an agency makes a decision which permits action by other parties which will affect the quality of the environment. . . . The Commission does precisely [that] here by developing a technology which will permit utility

companies to take action affecting the environment by building LMFBR
power plants. . . .

Id. at 1088-1089. Furthermore, in light of federal expenditures on the
program of over $100 million per year, and future projected expendi-
tures of over $2 billion, the program was ripe for an EIS:

> [B]ecause of the long lead times necessary for development of new com-
> mercially feasible technologies for production of electrical energy, the
> decisions our society makes today as to the direction of research and
> development will determine what technologies are available 10, 20, or 30
> years hence when we must apply some new means of producing electrical
> energy or face the alternative of energy rationing, through higher prices
> or otherwise. The manner in which we divide our limited research and
> development dollars today among various promising technologies in ef-
> fect determines which technologies will be available, and what type and
> amount of environmental effects will have to be endured, in the future
> when we must apply some new technology to meet projected demand.

Id. at 1090. The court therefore required an EIS.

    Was there a *proposal* for federal action affecting the environment
in *SIPI*, as required by *Kleppe*, or should we take *SIPI* to be impliedly
overruled by *Kleppe*? Did the Court in *Kleppe* give sufficient weight to
the advantages of programmatic EISs, as identified in *SIPI*? Consider in
this regard the remainder of the *Kleppe* decision, excerpted infra, p.
958.

    3. When does a "proposal" crystallize? To what extent may an
agency take "interim" or "temporary" action without preparation of an
EIS? Review in this respect *Calvert Cliffs'* ruling, p. 905 supra, that the
AEC must prepare an EIS on projects for which construction permits
had been issued, and may not postpone the EIS process until the operating license stage. See also *Natural Resources Defense Council v. Nuclear
Regulatory Commission*, 539 F.2d 824 (2d Cir. 1976), *vacated and remanded
to consider question of mootness*, 434 U.S. 1030 (1978) (Nuclear Regulatory
Commission must prepare generic EIS before authorizing "interim" use
by nuclear plants of new forms of fuel); *Silentman v. Federal Power Commission*, 566 F.2d 237 (D.C. Cir. 1977) (pending completion of an EIS
on a coal gasification facility by the Interior Department as the "lead
agency," FPC may grant conditional license to the facility without an
EIS because the conditional license has no irreversible consequences);
Comment, Second Circuit, CEQ Clarify Permissibility of Interim Actions Prior to Completion of Program EIS, 6 Envtl. L. Rep. 10254 (Nov.
1976).

3.   WHAT IS A "FEDERAL" ACTION?

An EIS is required for "major *federal* action that significantly affects the quality of the human environment." This requirement is not restricted to projects undertaken entirely by the federal government, such as the GSA construction of a federal building in *Hanly,* but includes state and private actions that require a federal license, permit, or certification; see *Calvert Cliffs,* supra, p. 899, (AEC license of electrical company's construction of a nuclear power plant), and state and private actions that use federal funding.

How much federal involvement in a nonfederal project is necessary to "federalize" it, and at what point in time does a project become so federalized as to require an EIS? The CEQ regulations on the subject provide little guidance in the borderline cases.[17] Despite years of judicial interpretation, the precise delimitation of what is "federal," or the test for determining such, is far from clear.

The "federal" question is tricky precisely because it requires courts to evaluate the scope and role of federal government involvement in light of federalism principles and property rights. Federal regulations are already prevalent through the broad reach of the Commerce Clause, and federal funding of one type or another is evident in every state and industry. Yet, Congress believed that "federal" was a significant limitation on the reach of NEPA.

Some general principles have been settled. Direct federal appropriations for a specific project have been consistently held to federalize a project. Block grants to a state for a broad category of purposes, such as law enforcement, have been sufficient to federalize a project, see *Ely v. Velde,* 451 F.2d 1130 (4th Cir. 1971) (prison construction), but if the block grant is only used to create the plan of action, federal involvement is insufficient, see *Bradley v. United States Dept. of Hous. & Urban Dev.,* 658 F.2d 290 (5th Cir. 1981). General revenue-sharing grants have typically been found not to federalize a project, because they are intended to be free from the usual federal requirements. See *Carolina*

---

17. 40 C.F.R. §1508.18(b) (1992): Federal actions tend to fall into one of four categories:

(1)   the adoption of official policies, such as rules and regulations;
(2)   the adoption of "formal plans . . . which guide or prescribe alternative uses of federal resources, upon which future agency actions will be based";
(3)   the adoption of "programs, such as a group of concerted actions to implement a specific policy or plan" or "allocating agency resources to implement" a statutory program or executive directive;
(4)   the approval of specific projects such as "actions approved by permit or other regulatory decision as well as federal and federally assisted activities."

Action v. Simon, 389 F. Supp. 1244 (M.D.N.C.), *aff'd mem.,* 522 F.2d 295 (4th Cir. 1975).

There are, however, two types of federal funding cases that have presented much greater difficulty. One, involving the timing of federal funding, arises when a state or local project is initiated in the expectation of federal funding. By the time the federal funds are actually committed, the project may be so advanced that an EIS will be a largely meaningless exercise. For example, in *City of Boston v. Volpe,* 464 F.2d 254 (1st Cir. 1972), Boston sought to enjoin the Massachusetts Port Authority from expanding Logan Airport until it filed an EIS. The Port Authority requested funding for the expansion, and the FAA had made a "tentative allocation" of these funds. However, the court held that until the federal agency had made a "final decision" no EIS was required. As a result, the taxiway construction could go on without regard to NEPA. See Brown, Applying NEPA to Joint Federal and Non-Federal Projects, 4 Env. Affairs 135 (1975). The First Circuit took a different approach in *Silva v. Romney,* 473 F.2d 287 (1st Cir. 1973). A private developer sought a mortgage guarantee and interest grant from HUD for a housing project. The court of appeals enjoined the developer from cutting trees on his property prior to the filing of an EIS because there was a sufficiently close nexus between the developer's actions and the federal involvement.

A second type of problem arises when federal grants fund only a portion of a state project, such as a highway. For example, the federal agency and a state may allocate federal funds to the environmentally uncontroversial segment of a highway, seeking to avoid preparation of an EIS on the more environmentally significant segments, which are state-funded. These cases involve two sets of issues. First, do the various segments amount to a common action or project? If so, the federal grant to a portion of the project will serve to "federalize" the entire project, subjecting it to NEPA.[18] Second, what is the scope of the remedy that a federal court should grant for failure to prepare an EIS on the entire project? Should the remedy be an injunction against federal funding? May the injunction extend to the state-financed portions of

---

18. See, e.g., *Named Individual Members of the San Antonio Conservation Society v. Texas Highway Dept.,* 446 F.2d 1013 (5th Cir. 1971) (rejecting state's attempt to "defederalize" central, environmentally controversial portion of highway by foregoing federal funding as to that portion, where state and federal funding agency had initially viewed whole highway as a single project, and state would still receive federal funding for the rest of the highway), *cert. denied,* 406 U.S. 933 (1972). See also Ellis & Smith, The Limits of Federal Environmental Responsibility and Control Under the National Environmental Policy Act, 18 Envtl. L. Rep. 10055 (Feb. 1988).

the project? What if the state relinquishes any federal funding of the project or reallocates federal funds to other projects?[19]

What about federal failure to act? *State of Alaska v. Andrus*, 591 F.2d 537 (9th Cir. 1979), held that no EIS was required when the Secretary of Interior failed to exercise authority to prevent private bounty-hunters from shooting wolves on federal lands. What about agencies that simply carry on business as usual? The Federal Emergency Management Agency (FEMA) continues to grant, on a routine basis, flood insurance for homeowners on the Florida Keys, as provided by law. It does so under long-standing FEMA regulations recognizing the Florida Keys as a flood prone area. Under the regulations, any property owner that falls within the defined area and meets certain eligibility requirements is automatically entitled to flood insurance. Environmental groups claim that FEMA flood insurance encourages development of the Florida Keys, destroying the critical habitat of the Florida Key Deer, an endangered species. FEMA asserts that it is simply executing its congressional mandate and that it has no statutory discretion or authority to deny insurance to property owners within a defined flood area. Or suppose that the Bureau of Reclamation in the Interior Department continues to operate a federal dam, as it has done for 30 years, in order to accumulate water against a drought, even though the reduced flows needed to build up storage threaten fish populations downstream?

4. NEPA THRESHOLD PROBLEMS

PROBLEM 1: OUTREACH CENTER

Under a newly enacted federal welfare, work, and educational program, the Employment and Education Agency (EEA) of the U.S. Department of Education is authorized to establish Outreach Centers providing disadvantaged inner city youths basic education, vocational skills training, work experience, counseling, and opportunities to enjoy and learn about the natural environment. Outreach Centers are designed to provide a structured and well supervised environment for their participants.

In November 1987, the EEA proposed to establish an Outreach Center on the former campus of Heartland College in Brower, Massa-

---

19. Compare *Named Individual Members*, supra (enjoining both federal funding and state construction in respect of the whole highway), with *Thompson v. Fugate*, 347 F. Supp. 120 (E.D. Va. 1972) (enjoining both federal funding and state construction in respect of the controversial segment only), and *Sierra Club v. Volpe*, 351 F. Supp. 1002 (N.D. Cal. 1972) (preliminarily enjoining federal funding only of the controversial segment).

chusetts. The Heartland College campus, constructed in the 1920s in a largely rural area, features four dormitories (one of which has a cafeteria), a library, four classroom buildings, a gymnasium, sports playing fields, and an administration building. During the most successful years at Heartland College, the campus accommodated 640 residential students and 260 off-campus students.

The proposed Heartland Outreach Center would utilize the existing buildings and facilities on the Heartland campus; the EEA proposal does not contemplate the addition of any new buildings. The Center would be residential and co-educational with a maximum of 600 participants. The EEA has spent $5 million to acquire the site and plans to spend an additional $2.3 million to renovate the existing buildings and grounds. Operation and maintenance costs for the Center are expected to be approximately $4.8 million per year ($8000 per participant).

The Heartland campus is now bordered on the east and south by single family houses on half acre and one acre lots. To the west is farm land and to the north is a water reservoir and a state park. A major shopping area is located less than a mile away (to the southeast). Although the Governor of Massachusetts and the Mayors of Boston and Worcester (from where many participants will be chosen) have strongly supported the choice of Heartland College campus in Brower for the Outreach Center, residents of Brower have voiced opposition. At various town meetings since the purchase of the Heartland Campus by the EEA, Brower citizens have expressed concern about the impact of the proposed Center upon the level of criminal activity, the amount of traffic in the vicinity of the Heartland campus, the demands on community social services, and the alteration of the character of the neighborhoods surrounding the Heartland campus. Nearby residents of the Heartland campus have formed the Brower Community Preservation Association (BCPA), the main objective of which is to prevent the establishment of the Heartland Outreach Center.

In February 1988, the EEA decided to proceed with its proposal to establish the Heartland Outreach Center. In its public announcement, the EEA stated that the Center did not constitute "a major federal action significantly affecting the quality of the human environment" and therefore the EEA was not required to prepare an environmental impact statement.

The BCPA seeks your advice on this case. In developing your strategy, you might wish to consider the following questions:

1. Is the EEA required to hold a public hearing before it can decide not to produce an EIS for the Heartland Outreach Center?

2. What standard of review should be applied to the EEA's decision not to produce an EIS?

3. Is the EEA required to prepare an EIS for the Heartland Outreach Center?

PROBLEM 2: TRANSPORTATION OF RADIOACTIVE MATERIALS BY HIGHWAY

Pursuant to the Hazardous Materials Transportation Act, the U.S. Department of Transportation (DOT) began consideration of rules to govern the transportation of large-quantity shipments of radioactive materials via highways. The rules would govern routing, extra safety precautions, and other requirements for transporters of large shipments of radioactive materials. After publishing its proposed rules in the Federal Register, DOT conducted eight public hearings and received more than 1600 written comments on the proposed regulations. Most of the comments discussed the routing aspects of the proposed rules; a few comments recommended that the DOT consider other methods of transportation such as rail and barge. The rulemaking considered two alternatives for routing radioactive materials carried by truck: (1) the "avoid urban areas" alternative — routing all large-quantity shipments of radioactive materials around heavily populated areas; and (2) the "interstate" alternative — routing such shipments on interstate highways, including interstate highways through and around major cities. The Secretary is prepared to issue final rules adopting the interstate alternative.

You, as an attorney in the Office of the General Counsel, have been asked to provide an opinion on whether or not an EIS must be prepared prior to the promulgation of these regulations. As background material for this assignment, you have been given DOT's draft Environmental Assessment (EA). It divides the relevant health risks into "latent fatalities" (that is, cancer deaths due to radiation exposure that occur more than a year after exposure) and "early fatalities" (that is, cancer deaths due to radiation exposure that occur within a year of exposure). It addresses two distinct aspects of risk: (1) the overall effects of transporting radioactive materials on the level of background radiation; and (2) the risk that such transportation might result in accidents that would release radiation.

With regard to the background risk issue, DOT's study finds that Americans receive an average dose of background radiation of 40,000,000 rems. Of this total, transportation of radioactive material contributes 24,360 rems, or less than 0.1 percent. This component of the background dose can be expected to cause an average of 3.07 latent cancer fatalities per year. Relative to the current situation, the option to "avoid urban areas" would reduce background radiation by 15.1 rems per year (and thus reduce latent cancer fatalities by 0.002 per year). The "interstate" option would reduce background radiation by 10.7 rems per year (thereby reducing latent cancer fatalities by 0.0013 per year).

With regard to the accident-related risks, the draft EA first analyzes the overall risk of latent injuries attributable to all accidents. Latent cancer deaths associated with accidents under current transportation practices are at 0.017 per year. The "interstate" alternative would reduce this figure by .00062 per year, whereas the more circuitous "avoid urban areas" alternative would increase it by .00031 per year.

Next, the EA analyzes the risk of serious accidents that would cause one or more early fatalities. The current risk is 9.12×10^{-4} annually, or approximately one such accident every thousand years. The "interstate" alternative would reduce this risk by $.9 \times 10^{-4}$ whereas the "avoid urban areas" alternative would increase it by $.37 \times 10^{-4}$.

The draft EA also considers the consequences of a "worst case" accident. According to a study conducted for DOT by Sandia Laboratories, under the "interstate alternative" the most lethal credible release of radioactive materials would be a serious rupture of a vehicle carrying plutonium in New York City. Such an accident could result in 5 early fatalities and 1800 latent cancer fatalities. The cost of the most economically disastrous credible accident could be as high as $9 billion (taking into account reduced land values). The draft EA notes that the probability of such an accident is 3×10^{-9}, or approximately once every 300 million years (based on 1975 shipment figures). On this basis, the draft EA concludes that the final rules do not constitute "a major federal action significantly affecting the quality of the human environment."

The Secretary of DOT would like to issue the final rules as soon as possible. She would like your legal opinion on whether the draft EA adequately discharges DOT's NEPA obligations. She is particularly interested in your analysis of the following questions:

(1)   Is an EIS needed to assess the background radiation issue?
(2)   Is an EIS needed to assess the accident issues?
(3)   Are there any other factors that you think that the DOT should look into?

PROBLEM 3: RENEWAL OF LONG-TERM FEDERAL WATER CONTRACTS

More than 40 years ago, the federal government completed the construction of a massive water storage and diversion facility known as the Central Valley Project (CVP), located entirely within the state of California. Each year, the CVP delivers more than 7 million acre feet (MAF) of water to its customers — primarily state-created quasi-political entities known as irrigation districts, who in turn deliver water to agricultural users of the water. In exchange for the receipt of this water, the irrigation districts agree to pay the federal government a specific rate per acre foot of water delivered. The agreements between the federal government and the CVP customers are formalized in long-term water service contracts, generally spanning a term of 40 years.

You are an attorney for Sierra Streams, an environmental organization interested primarily in water quality and conservation issues in the western United States. The water resource specialists and economists employed by Sierra Streams recently published several studies concluding that substantial amounts of the CVP water currently used by irrigation farmers could be saved if the farmers would implement relatively simple and inexpensive conservation strategies. These studies also conclude that the continued diversion of enormous quantities of water from natural watercourses via the CVP facilities exacerbates agricultural drainage problems by leaching harmful metals and chemicals from the soil, impairs water quality, and threatens the natural habitats of many endangered species.

Moreover, Sierra Streams economists inform you that CVP customers are paying far less than the market price for the water they receive under contract; in some instances, CVP customers pay less than $10 per acre foot of water, whereas the market price that must be paid by municipal or industrial users is more than $200 per acre foot of water. The economists posit that the federal government's pricing policies are encouraging over-consumption of water by agricultural interests. In addition, the low price for water acts as a disincentive for the irrigators to invest in water conservation technology or to retire marginal lands from agricultural production.

Last month, the Apple Blossom Irrigation District petitioned the Department of Interior to renew its 40-year contract for CVP water, which is due to expire in the near future. The District contends that the Department is obligated to renew the contracts under essentially the same terms and conditions. To support this contention, the District points to a federal law passed in 1956 that expressly provides a right of renewal to a requesting party "under terms and conditions mutually agreeable to the parties." The legislative history indicates Congress' concern to provide security of supply to agricultural users, who have made substantial investments in the expectation of the continued availability of water from federal projects. Last week, the Solicitor General of the Department of the Interior issued a memorandum concluding as a matter of law that the 1956 Act deprives the Department of any discretion with respect to whether the contracts can be renewed. The Department has therefore proposed to renew the Apple Blossom Irrigation contract. Moreover, the DOI has decided to negotiate a single form contract for all CVP contracts (virtually all the contracts will expire within the next two years) and to enter into joint negotiations with irrigation contractors on a single Basis of Negotiation to expedite the renewal process.

Yesterday, the Environmental Protection Agency (EPA) referred this DOI proposal to the Council on Environmental Quality (CEQ) pursuant to section 309 of the Clear Air Act and the CEQ regulations implementing the NEPA. 40 C.F.R. §1504.1(b). The EPA believes that the DOI's act of renewing the Apple Blossom Irrigation District contract constitutes a "major federal action significantly affecting the quality of the human environment" and is thus subject to the requirements of NEPA. The DOI contends renewal will simply preserve the status quo; in any event, DOI argues that renewal would result in only modest changes in existing contracts and should be presumed to have no significant impact on the environment. Finally, the DOI points to the fact that the Apple Blossom Irrigation District receives only 370,000 acre feet of water annually under its contract; the diversion of such a small amount of water cannot be said to "significantly" affect the environment.

Sierra Streams opposes the renewal of the Apple Blossom Irrigation District contract and you have been asked to draft a motion for preliminary injunction, asking the court to enjoin the DOI from renewing the contract. Prior to preparing this motion, you should consider the following questions:

(1) Does renewal of the Apple Blossom Irrigation District contract constitute a major federal action significantly affecting the quality of the human environment?
(2) If so, should the designated agency be required to prepare an EIS under these circumstances?

C. EXEMPTIONS

1. LEGISLATIVE PROCESSES

ANDRUS v. SIERRA CLUB

442 U.S. 347, 348-365 (1979)

Mr. Justice BRENNAN delivered the opinion of the Court.

The question for decision is whether §102(2)(C) of the National Environmental Policy Act of 1969 (NEPA) requires federal agencies to prepare environmental impact statements (EIS's) to accompany appropriation requests. We hold that it does not.

I . . .

In 1974, respondents, three organizations with interests in the preservation of the environment, brought suit in Federal District Court for the District of Columbia alleging that §102(2)(C) requires federal agencies to prepare EIS's to accompany their appropriation requests. Respondents . . . alleged that proposed curtailments in the budget of the National Wildlife Refuge System (NWRS) would "cut back significantly the operations, maintenance, and staffing of units within the System." Complaint P. 17. The System is administered by the Fish and Wildlife Service of the Department of the Interior, and consists of more than 350 refuges encompassing more than 30 million acres in 49 states. . . . Respondents alleged that the proposed budget curtailments would significantly affect the quality of the human environment, and hence should have been accompanied by an EIS prepared by both the Fish and Wildlife Service and by OMB.

. . . [T]he Court of Appeals concluded that §102(2)(C) required the preparation of an EIS only when an appropriation request accompanies "a 'proposal' for taking new action which significantly changes the status quo," or when "the request for budget approval and appropriations is one that ushers in a considered programmatic course following a programmatic review." [581 F.2d 895, 903 (1978).]

II

NEPA requires EIS's to be included in recommendations or reports on both "proposals for legislation . . . significantly affecting the quality of the human environment" and "proposals for . . . major Federal actions significantly affecting the quality of the human environment." [§102(2)(C).] Petitioners argue, however, that the requirements of §102(2)(C) have no application to the budget process. The contrary holding of the Court of Appeals rests on two alternative interpretations of §102(2)(C). The first is that appropriation requests which are the result of "an agency's painstaking review of an ongoing program," are "proposals for legislation" within the meaning of §102(2)(C). The second is that appropriation requests which are the reflection of "new" agency initiatives constituting "major Federal actions" under NEPA, are themselves "proposals for . . . major Federal actions" for purposes of §102(2)(C).

A . . .

There is no direct evidence in the legislative history of NEPA that enlightens whether Congress intended the phrase "proposals for legislation" to include requests for appropriations. At the time of the Court of Appeals' decision, however, CEQ guidelines provided that §102(2)(C) applied to "[r]ecommendations or favorable reports relating to legislation including requests for appropriations." 40 CFR §1500.5(a)(1) (1977). At that time CEQ's guidelines were advisory in nature, and were for the purpose of assisting federal agencies in complying with NEPA. §1500.1(a).

In 1977, however, President Carter, in order to create a single set of uniform, mandatory regulations, ordered CEQ, "after consultation with affected agencies," to "[i]ssue regulations to Federal agencies for the implementation of the procedural provisions" of NEPA. Exec. Order No. 11991, 3 C.F.R. 124 (1978). The President ordered the heads of federal agencies to "comply with the regulations issued by the Council. . . ." Ibid. CEQ has since issued these regulations, 43 Fed. Reg. 55978-56007 (1978), and they reverse CEQ's prior interpretation of §102(2)(C). The regulations provide specifically that " '[l]egislation' includes a bill or legislative proposal to Congress . . . but does *not* include requests for appropriations." 43 Fed. Reg. 56004 (1978) (to be codified at 40 CFR §1508.17). (Emphasis supplied.) CEQ explained this reversal by noting that, on the basis of "traditional concepts relating to appropriations and the budget cycle, considerations of timing and confidentiality, and other factors, . . . the Council in its experience found that preparation of EISs is ill-suited to the budget process." 43 Fed. Reg., at 55989. . . .

CEQ's interpretation of the phrase "proposals for legislation" is consistent with the traditional distinction which Congress has drawn between "legislation" and "appropriation." The rules of both Houses "prohibit 'legislation' from being added to an appropriation bill." . . . The distinction is maintained "to assure that program and financial matters are considered independently of one another. This division of labor is intended to enable the Appropriations Committees to concentrate on financial issues and to prevent them from trespassing on substantive legislation." House Budget Committee, Congressional Control of Expenditures 19 (Comm. Print 1977). . . . Since appropriations therefore "have the limited and specific purpose of providing funds for authorized programs," *TVA v. Hill*, 437 U.S. [153,] 190 [(1978)], and since the "action-forcing" provisions of NEPA are directed precisely at the processes of "planning and . . . decisionmaking," 42 U.S.C. §4332(2)(A), which are associated with underlying legislation, we conclude that the distinction made by CEQ's regulations is correct and that "proposals for legislation" do not include appropriation requests.

B

The Court of Appeals' alternative interpretation of NEPA is that appropriation requests constitute "proposals for . . . major Federal actions." But this interpretation distorts the language of the Act, since appropriation requests do not "propose" federal actions at all; they instead fund actions already proposed. Section 102(2)(C) is thus best interpreted as applying to those recommendations or reports that actually propose programmatic actions, rather than to those which merely suggest how such actions may be funded. Any other result would create unnecessary redundancy. . . .

Even if changes in agency programs occur *because* of budgetary decisions, an EIS at the appropriation stage would only be repetitive. For example, respondents allege in their complaint that OMB required the Fish and Wildlife Service to decrease its appropriation request for the NWRS, and that this decrease would alter the operation of the NWRS in a manner that would significantly affect the quality of the human environment. But since the Fish and Wildlife Service could respond to OMB's budgetary curtailments in a variety of ways, it is impossible to predict whether or how any particular budget cut will in fact significantly affect the quality of the human environment. OMB's determination to cut the Service's budget is not a programmatic proposal, and therefore requiring OMB to include an EIS in its budgetary cuts would be premature. . . . And since an EIS must be prepared if any of the revisions the Fish and Wildlife Service proposes in its ongoing programs in response to OMB's budget cuts would significantly affect the quality of the human environment, requiring the Fish and Wildlife Service to include an EIS with its revised appropriation request would merely be redundant. . . .

C

We conclude therefore, for the reasons given above, that appropriation requests constitute neither "proposals for legislation" nor "proposals for . . . major Federal actions," and that therefore the procedural requirements of §102(2)(C) have no application to such re2-quests. The judgment of the Court of Appeals is reversed.

NOTES AND QUESTIONS

1. The Supreme Court showed the CEQ regulations "substantial deference," despite the fact that the new regulations reversed CEQ's practice over eight years of interpreting the statute to require EISs for appropriations, and were not even in effect at the time of the Court's decision. Do you suppose the Court would have deferred to the CEQ had the agency stuck to its initial view regarding appropriation requests? What is the relevance of *Chevron* in this respect? Should *Chevron*-type deference by courts apply at all in NEPA cases? If so, to whom should *Chevron* deference be accorded, the program agency or CEQ? See Note, NEPA After Andrus v. Sierra Club: The Doctrine of Substantial Deference to the Regulations of the Council on Environmental Quality, 66 Va. L. Rev. 843 (1980).

2. Does the blanket exemption of appropriation requests from the EIS process make better sense than the "functional" approach of the D.C. Circuit? Would an EIS at the budgetary stage be redundant in light of environmental analyses performed earlier in connection with authorizing legislation, or later in connection with specific agency projects? Consider that appropriations decisions about agency budgets often have more direct impact on what government actually does than authorization statutes. After appropriations decisions are made, agencies may have only limited effective discretion to reallocate priorities through decisions about particular projects or programs. Even if an EIS is prepared at this later decisional stage, will it come too late to have a real impact on overall policy?

3. A study team at the University of Colorado found EISs to be "generally inadequate, prepared as project justifications rather than decisionmaking instruments, and prepared at a stage at which it was difficult to modify or reverse plans." Cortner, A Case Analysis of Policy Implementation: The National Environmental Policy Act of 1969, 16 Nat. Resources J. 323, 324 (1976). Some commentators argue that an EIS must be prepared at the highest levels and at the earliest opportunity if NEPA is going to have a chance of meeting its goal of affecting policy decisions. Do these observations show that *Andrus v. Sierra Club* was wrongly decided?[20] What other implications do they have?

PUBLIC CITIZEN V. UNITED STATES TRADE REPRESENTATIVE

---

[20] For divergent assessments of *Andrus v. Sierra Club*, see Shortsleeve, Note, *Andrus v. Sierra Club: No Effective Environmental Review in the Federal Budget Process*, 9 B.C. Envtl. Aff. L. Rev. 205 (1980); CEQ General Counsel Outlines Development Involving New NEPA Rules, 10 Env. Rep. 557 (1979).

5 F.3d 549, 550-554 (D.C. Cir. 1993)

MIKVA, Chief Judge:

Appellees Public Citizen, Friends of the Earth, Inc., and the Sierra Club (collectively "Public Citizen") sued the Office of the United States Trade Representative, claiming that an environmental impact statement was required for the North American Free Trade Agreement ("NAFTA"). The district court granted Public Citizen's motion for summary judgment and ordered that an impact statement be prepared "forthwith." . . . . Because we conclude that NAFTA is not "final agency action" under the APA, we reverse the decision of the district court and express no view on the government's other contentions.

I. BACKGROUND

In 1990, the United States, Mexico, and Canada initiated negotiations on the North American Free Trade Agreement. NAFTA creates a "free trade zone" encompassing the three countries by eliminating or reducing tariffs and "non-tariff" barriers to trade on thousands of items of commerce. After two years of negotiation, the leaders of the three countries signed the agreement on December 17, 1992. NAFTA has not yet been transmitted to Congress.

Negotiations on behalf of the United States were conducted primarily by the Office of the United States Trade Representative ("OTR"). OTR, located "within the Executive Office of the President," 19 U.S.C. §2171(a) ("Trade Act of 1974" or "Trade Acts"), is the United States' chief negotiator for trade matters.

Under the Trade Acts and congressional rules, NAFTA is entitled to "fast-track" enactment procedures which provide that Congress must vote on the agreement, without amendment, within ninety legislative days after transmittal by the President. The current version of NAFTA, once submitted, will therefore be identical to the version on which Congress will vote. . . .

II. DISCUSSION

In drafting NEPA . . . Congress did not create a private right of action. Accordingly, Public Citizen must rest its claim for judicial review on the Administrative Procedure Act. 5 U.S.C. §702 . . . Section 704 [of the APA] allows review only of "final agency action." 5 U.S.C. §704 (emphasis added); see *Lujan v. National Wildlife Fed'n*, 497 U.S. 871, 882 . . . (1990). . . .

In support of its argument that NAFTA does not constitute "final agency action" within the meaning of the APA, the government relies heavily on *Franklin v. Massachusetts*, . . . 112 S. Ct. 2767 (1992). Franklin involved a challenge to the method used by the Secretary of Commerce to calculate the 1990 census. The Secretary acted pursuant to a reapportionment statute requiring that she report the "tabulation of total population by States . . . to the President." 13 U.S.C. §141(b). After receiving the Secretary's report, the President must transmit to Congress the number of Representatives to which each state is entitled under the method of equal proportions. 2 U.S.C. §2(a)(2). The Supreme Court held that APA review was unavailable because the final action under the reapportionment statute (transmittal of the apportionment to Congress) was that of the President, and the President is not an agency [for purposes of the APA]. *Franklin*, 112 S. Ct. at 2773; see *Armstrong v. Bush*, . . . 924 F.2d 282, 289 (D.C. Cir. 1991) (the President is not an "agency" within the meaning of the APA).

. . . The *Franklin* Court found that although the Secretary had completed her decisionmaking process, the action that would directly affect the plaintiffs was the President's calculation and transmittal of the apportionment to Congress, not the Secretary's report to the President. Id.

This logic applies with equal force to NAFTA. Even though the OTR has completed negotiations on NAFTA, the agreement will have no effect on Public Citizen's members unless and until the President submits it to Congress. Like the reapportionment statute in *Franklin*, the Trade Acts involve the President at the final stage of the process by providing for him to submit to Congress the final legal text of the agreement, a draft of the implementing legislation, and supporting information. 19 U.S.C. §2903(a)(1)(B). The President is not obligated to submit any agreement to Congress, and until he does there is no final action. If and . . . when the agreement is submitted to Congress, it will be the result of action by the President, action clearly not reviewable under the APA.

The district court attempts to distinguish *Franklin* by noting that unlike the census report (which the President was authorized to amend before submitting to Congress), NAFTA is no longer a "moving target" because the "final product . . . will not be changed before submission to Congress." . . . This distinction is unpersuasive. NAFTA is just as much a "moving target" as the census report in *Franklin* because in both cases the President has statutory discretion to exercise supervisory power over the agency's action. It is completely within the President's discretion, for example, to renegotiate portions of NAFTA before submitting it to Congress or to refuse to submit the agreement at all. . . . Although we acknowledge the stringency of *Franklin*'s "direct effect" requirement, we disagree that it represents the death knell of the legislative EIS. *Franklin* is limited to those cases in which the President has final constitutional or statutory responsibility for the final step necessary for the agency action directly to affect the parties.

. . . When the President's role is not essential to the integrity of the process, however, APA review of otherwise final agency actions may well be available.

The government advances many other arguments opposing the preparation of an EIS, including weighty constitutional positions on the separation of powers and Public Citizen's lack of standing, as well as the inapplicability of NEPA to agreements executed pursuant to the Trade Acts in general, and NAFTA in particular. It also suggests that the judicial branch should avoid any conflict with the President's power by exercising the "equitable discretion" given it by §702 of the APA. We need not and do not consider such arguments in light of the clear applicability of the *Franklin* precedent.

[The court reversed the district court's grant of summary judgment to Public Citizen.]

RANDOLPH, Circuit Judge, concurring:

[Judge Randolph took exception to the court's suggestion that an EIS might be required when legislation is submitted to Congress by a federal department or agency, rather than by the President.]

Franklin held not only that the President is outside the APA's definition of "agency," but also that "action" cannot be considered "final" under the APA unless it "will directly affect the parties." 112 S. Ct. at 2773. When the alleged "action" consists of a proposal for legislation, how can this condition for judicial review be satisfied? . . . In general . . . it is difficult to see how the act of proposing legislation could generate direct effects on parties, or anyone else for that matter. . . . [O]nly a Member of Congress may introduce a bill embodying [a] proposal, and even then no one will be affected, directly or otherwise, unless and until Congress passes the bill and the President signs it into law. If one takes *Franklin* at its word, a legislative proposal's lack of any direct effects would seem to mean that there can be no final action sufficient to permit judicial review under the APA. Of course, there is a big difference between saying that APA review is unavailable and saying that officials do not have to comply with NEPA when they suggest legislation. If Congress believed an agency had not lived up to its obligation to prepare an impact statement, it could always refuse to consider the agency's proposal. Or, if Congress wanted to evaluate environmental impacts before putting the measure to a vote, congressional committees could hold hearings on the subject. This is how a large proportion of legislative proposals already must be treated. NEPA's impact statement requirement applies only to federal agencies. Members of Congress, who alone introduce bills and offer amendments, are not covered. Neither are private individuals, corporations, labor unions, citizen groups or other organizations, all of which frequently avail themselves of their First Amendment right to petition the government.

I am therefore not prepared to say whether in NEPA cases, the act of proposing legislation constitutes final action under §704 of the APA, as *Franklin* has interpreted that provision. . . .

NOTES AND QUESTIONS

While the majority's reasoning limits the effect of *Public Citizen* to a relatively narrow range of cases where the President has the responsibility to submit proposals for legislation, Judge Randolph's concurring opinion suggests that a judicial remedy might not be able to enforce the EIS requirement with respect to any legislative proposal. Would this be a bad result? Consider that Congress can simply refuse to act on a proposal if it lacks an accompanying EIS. Why isn't Congress in the best position to enforce NEPA's requirements with respect to the legislative process? Is there any real need for an EIS on NAFTA, whose environmental implications have been exhaustively studied and debated throughout North America and will be the subject of a specific side agreement that must be implemented through congressional legislation?

2. APPLICATION OF NEPA OUTSIDE OF THE UNITED STATES

ENVIRONMENTAL DEFENSE FUND, INC. v. MASSEY

986 F.2d 528, 529-537 (D.C. Cir. 1993)

[The National Science Foundation (NSF) operates the McMurdo Station research facility in Antarctica. NSF for many years disposed of food wastes at the Station by burning them in an open landfill. It then planned to dispose of the wastes through use of an incinerator. EDF sued to require an EIS on the proposal, claiming that the incinerator would generate highly toxic pollutants. The district court dismissed the suit on the ground that NEPA does not apply to activities in Antarctica. The court of appeals reversed.]

MIKVA, Chief Judge:

I

As both parties readily acknowledge, Antarctica is not only a unique continent, but somewhat of an international anomaly. Antarctica is the only continent on earth which has never been, and is not now, subject to the sovereign rule of any nation. Since entry into force of the Antarctic Treaty in 1961, the United States and 39 other nations have agreed not to assert any territorial claims to the continent or to establish rights of sovereignty there. . . . Hence, Antarctica is generally considered to be a "global common" . . .

. . . Since the issuance of Executive Order 12114, . . . NSF has contended that proposed action affecting the environment in Antarctica is governed by the Executive Order, not NEPA. See Exec. Order 12114, 3 C.F.R. 356 (1980). . . .

Executive Order 12114 declares that federal agencies are required to prepare environmental analyses for "major Federal actions significantly affecting the environment of the global commons outside the jurisdiction of any nation (e.g., the oceans or Antarctica)." E.O. 12114 §2-3a. According to the Executive Order, major federal actions significantly affecting the environment of foreign countries may also require environmental analyses under certain circumstances. Id. Although the procedural requirements imposed by the Executive Order are analogous to those under NEPA, the Executive Order does not provide a cause of action to a plaintiff seeking agency compliance with the EIS requirement. The Executive Order explicitly states that the requirements contained therein are "solely for the purpose of establishing internal procedures for Federal agencies . . . and nothing in [the Order] shall be construed to create a cause of action." E.O. 12114 §3-1. . . .

A. THE PRESUMPTION AGAINST EXTRATERRITORIALITY

As the district court correctly noted, the Supreme Court recently reaffirmed the general presumption against the extraterritorial application of statutes in *Equal Employment Opportunity Commission v. Arabian American Oil Co.*, 111 S. Ct. 1227 (1991) ("Aramco"). Extraterritoriality is essentially, and in common sense, a jurisdictional concept concerning the authority of a nation to adjudicate the rights of particular parties and to establish the norms of conduct applicable to events or persons outside its borders. More specifically, the extraterritoriality principle provides that "[r]ules of the United States statutory law, whether prescribed by federal or state authority, apply only to conduct occurring within, or having effect within, the territory of the United States." Restatement (Second) of Foreign Relations Law of the United States §38 (1965). . . . As stated by the Supreme Court in *Aramco*, the primary purpose of this presumption against extraterritoriality is "to protect against the unintended clashes between our laws and those of other nations which could result in international discord." *Aramco*, 111 S. Ct. at 1230.

Most recently, in *Aramco*, the Supreme Court held that Title VII of the 1964 Civil Rights Act does not apply extraterritorially to regulate the employment practices of United States firms that employ American citizens abroad. *Aramco*, 111 S. Ct. at 1236. In that case, the discriminatory conduct that allegedly violated the Title VII occurred within the jurisdiction of another sovereign, although perpetrated by a U.S. firm. . . .

There are at least three general categories of cases for which the presumption against the extraterritorial application of statutes clearly does not apply. First, as made explicit in *Aramco*, the presumption will not apply where there is an "affirmative intention of the Congress clearly expressed" to extend the scope of the statute to conduct occurring within other sovereign nations. Id. at 1230. . . .

Second, the presumption is generally not applied where the failure to extend the scope of the statute to a foreign setting will result in adverse effects within the United States. Two prime examples of this exception are the Sherman Anti-Trust Act, 15 U.S.C. §§1-7 (1976), and the Lanham Trade-mark Act, 15 U.S.C. §1051 (1976), which have both been applied extraterritorially where the failure to extend the statute's reach would have negative economic consequences within the United States. . . .

Finally, the presumption against extraterritoriality is not applicable, when the conduct regulated by the government occurs within the United States. . . .

B. REGULATED CONDUCT UNDER NEPA

NEPA is designed to control the decisionmaking process of U.S. federal agencies, not the substance of agency decisions. By enacting NEPA, Congress exercised its statutory authority to determine the factors an agency must consider when exercising its discretion, and created a process whereby American officials, while acting within the United States, can reach enlightened policy decisions by taking into account environmental effects. In our view, such regulation of U.S. federal agencies and their decisionmaking processes . . . does not raise extraterritoriality concerns.

. . . Because the decisionmaking processes of federal agencies take place almost exclusively in this country and involve the workings of the United States government, they are uniquely domestic. . . .

NEPA, unlike many environmental statutes, does not dictate agency policy or determine the fate of contemplated action. . . . *Strycker's Bay Neighborhood Council, Inc. v. Karlen*, 444 U.S. 223, 227-228 (1980) (per curiam). . . .

. . . NEPA . . . creates no substantive environmental standards and simply prescribes by statute the factors an agency must consider when exercising its discretionary authority.

Moreover, NEPA would never require enforcement in a foreign forum or involve "choice of law" dilemmas. . . .

In sum, since NEPA is designed to regulate conduct occurring within the territory of the United States, and imposes no substantive requirements which could be interpreted to govern conduct abroad, the presumption against extraterritoriality does not apply to this case.

C. THE UNIQUE STATUS OF ANTARCTICA

Antarctica's unique status in the international arena further supports our conclusion that this case does not implicate the presumption against extraterritoriality.

. . . The United States controls all air transportation to Antarctica and conducts all search and rescue operations there. Moreover, the United States has exclusive legislative control over McMurdo Station and the other research installations established there by the United States Antarctica Program. This legislative control, taken together with the status of Antarctica as a sovereignless continent, compels the conclusion that the presumption against extraterritoriality is particularly inappropriate under the circumstances presented in this case. . . .

D. FOREIGN POLICY CONSIDERATIONS

. . . NSF argues that the EIS requirement will interfere with U.S. efforts to work cooperatively with other nations toward solutions to environmental problems in Antarctica. In NSF's view, joint research and cooperative environmental assessment would be "placed at risk of NEPA injunctions, making the U.S. a doubtful partner for future international cooperation in Antarctica." Appellee's Brief at 45.

. . . [W]e are not convinced that NSF's ability to cooperate with other nations in Antarctica in accordance with U.S. foreign policy will be hampered by NEPA injunctions. We made clear in *Natural [sic] Resources Defense Council v. Nuclear Regulatory Commission*, 647 F.2d 1345, 1366 (D.C. Cir. 1981) ("NRDC"), that where the EIS requirement proves to be incompatible with Section 102(2)(F), federal agencies will not be subject to injunctions forcing compliance with Section 102(2)(C).[21] Section 102(2)(F) specifically requires all federal agencies

---

21. [Ed. Note: This decision, discussed further below, involved an NRC grant of permits for export of nuclear materials and reactor technology to the Philippines.]

to

recognize the worldwide and long-range character of environmental problems and, where consistent with the foreign policy of the United States, lend appropriate support to initiatives, resolutions, and programs designed to maximize international cooperation. . . .

42 U.S.C. §4332(F).

. . . In *Committee for Nuclear Responsibility v. Seaborg*, 463 F.2d 796 (D.C. Cir. 1972) . . . we refused to issue an injunction under NEPA, despite the real potential for significant harm to the environment, because the government made "assertions of harm to national security and foreign policy." Id. at 798. In that case, conservation groups sought to enjoin an underground nuclear test on the grounds that the Atomic Energy Commission failed to comply fully with NEPA. Although there was reason to believe that the petitioners would succeed on the merits of their claim, we denied the requested injunction in light of the foreign policy concerns.

NRDC and *Seaborg* illustrate that the government may avoid the EIS requirement where U.S. foreign policy interests outweigh the benefits derived from preparing an EIS. . . .

E.   NEPA's Plain Language and Interpretation . . .

We also note, that prior to the issuance of Executive Order 12114, the Council on Environmental Quality ("CEQ") maintained that NEPA applies to the decisionmaking process of federal agencies regarding actions in Antarctica. CEQ is the agency created by Congress to oversee the implementation of NEPA, and its interpretation of that statute is generally entitled to "substantial deference." [Anyway, CEQ's view is] not only reasonable, but fully supported by the plain language of the statute.

CONCLUSION

. . . NSF has provided no support for its proposition that conduct occurring within the United States is rendered exempt from otherwise applicable statutes merely because the effects of its compliance would be felt in the global commons. . . .

We find it important to note, however, that we do not decide today how NEPA might apply to actions in a case involving an actual foreign sovereign or how other U.S. statutes might apply to Antarctica. . . .

Reversed and remanded.

NOTES AND QUESTIONS

1. Executive Order No. 12,114, 44 Fed. Reg. 1957 (1979), cited by Chief Judge Mikva, requires EISs for "major federal actions significantly affecting the environment of the global commons," §§2-3, 2-4(b)(i). With respect to environmental effects on "the environment of a foreign nation," it requires a less formal international environmental study or concise environmental review only for (i) actions prohibited or strictly regulated in the United States because of concerns over toxic or radioactive pollution, and (ii) international actions with transboundary effects on a non-participating foreign nation's environment. §§2-3(b), 2-3(c), 2-4(b)(ii), (iii), 3-5. Exemptions from these requirements are provided for "actions taken by the President," §2-5(a)(ii), emergency actions and actions implicating national security, §§2-5(a)(iii), 2-5(c), export licenses, and most "nuclear activities," §2-5(a)(v). Agencies are also given some scope to modify normal NEPA requirements respecting the "contents, timing and availability of documents." §2-5(b). As Chief Judge Mikva notes, the Order states that it does not create a cause of action in the courts. §3-1.[22] As you read the following notes, consider the extent to which judicial decisions have been, or should be, consistent with the policy expressed in the Order.

2. How persuasive is the court's argument that the presumption of extraterritoriality is inapplicable because the actual preparation of an EIS would take place in the United States? What about its contention that NEPA is purely procedural and therefore does not regulate activities outside the United States?

3. Chief Judge Mikva refers to *Natural Resources Defense Council, Inc. v. Nuclear Regulatory Commn.*, 647 F.2d 1345 (D.C. Cir. 1981). There, the D.C. Circuit held that NEPA did not "impose[] an . . . EIS requirement on nuclear export decisions with respect to impacts falling exclusively within foreign jurisdictions," id. at 1347-1348, and so allowed the NRC to grant permits for export to the Phillippines of a nuclear reactor and complementary nuclear materials without preparing an EIS. (The NRC had found that there would be no significant environmental impacts on United States territory or on the global commons such as might merit an EIS.) Judge Wilkey stated that he was "reluctan[t] to apply NEPA extraterritorially." Id. at 1366. Moreover, he inferred from the Atomic Energy Act and the Nuclear Non-Proliferation Act (NNPA) a congressional policy

---

22. See generally CEQ, Environmental Effects Abroad of Major Federal Actions, Executive Order 12114, Implementing and Explanatory Documents, Memorandum for Heads of Agencies with International Activities, 44 Fed. Reg. 18,722 (Mar. 21, 1979); Gaines, Environmental Effects Abroad of Major Federal Actions: An Executive Order Ordains a National Policy, 3 Harv. Envtl. L. Rev. 136 (1979); D. Mandelker, NEPA Law & Litigation §5:18 (1984 & Supp.).

to win fellow adherents to our philosophy of nonproliferation. NNPA promises cooperation, not confrontation, so long as the principle of peaceful exploitation of nuclear power is vindicated by the recipient nation. This understanding of the statute discourages inviting an administrative review likely to trench on foreign sensibilities. The foreigners' conviction that they themselves are competent to regulate their own environment is not to be lightly rejected.

Id. at 1361. He therefore held, applying NEPA §102(2)(F), that "unilateral EIS review," with the attendant potential for litigation and delay, would be inconsistent with U.S. foreign policy. Id. at 1366.

Are the courts qualified to judge the foreign relations and national security implications of requiring EISs on federal government actions where environmental effects will occur outside the U.S.? Did Congress intend them to?

4. In *Greenpeace USA v. Stone*, 748 F. Supp. 749 (D. Haw. 1990), *dismissed as moot*, 924 F.2d 175 (9th Cir. 1991), environmental groups sought a preliminary injunction to prevent the U.S. Army from shipping obsolescent nerve gas weapons, stockpiled by the U.S. in West Germany, to the Johnston Atoll, a U.S. territory in the Pacific, for incineration. The Army had published an EIS covering the effects of the handling and destruction of the nerve gas on the atoll, and a separate Global Commons Environmental Assessment under E.O. 12,114 covering the transport of the gas on the high seas, but had not issued any assessment of the potential impacts of transportation of the gas within Germany from U.S. military stockpiles to the North Sea. The district court stated: "NEPA *may* require a federal agency to prepare an EIS for action taken abroad, especially where United States agency's action abroad has direct environmental impacts within this country, or where there has clearly been a total lack of environmental assessment by the federal agency or foreign country involved." 748 F. Supp. at 761. However, it applied *NRDC v. NRC*, emphasizing that the removal of the nerve gas had been agreed upon by the President of the U.S. and the German Chancellor, and that the activities within Germany had been reviewed by the German courts and found compliant with German environmental laws.

3.   Other Exemptions

1. Where there is "clear and unavoidable conflict" between existing statutory requirements and NEPA, "NEPA must give way." *Flint Ridge Dev. Co. v. Scenic Rivers Assn.*, 426 U.S. 776, 788 (1976). *Flint Ridge* concerned provisions in the Interstate Land Sales Full Disclosure Act, which requires real estate developers to file a disclosure statement with

the Department of Housing and Urban Development (HUD). The statement automatically becomes effective within 30 days of filing, unless HUD determines that it is incomplete or inaccurate, in which case it becomes effective within 30 days after these deficiencies are corrected. HUD has no authority to evaluate the substance of the development. Plaintiffs, fearing adverse environmental effects from a local development, filed suit to require HUD to prepare an EIS on the developer's disclosure statement. While stating that HUD could require inclusion of environmental information in a disclosure statement, the Court held that an EIS was not required on a disclosure statement because it would be impossible to prepare an impact statement within 30 days, and because the Act gave HUD no authority to suspend the effectiveness of a disclosure statement pending preparation of an EIS. Query: Even if there were no 30-day provision for automatic effectiveness in the Act, should an EIS be required in connection with disclosure statements, given HUD's limited responsibilities?

CEQ has taken the position that the exemption recognized in *Flint Ridge* is a narrow one. CEQ regulations provide that agencies shall comply with NEPA "except where compliance would be inconsistent with other statutory requirements." 40 C.F.R. §1500.3 (1992). Case law supports this view. See, e.g., *Ely v. Velde*, 451 F.2d 1130 (4th Cir. 1971).

2. Express statutory exemption, or partial implied repeal of NEPA, is of course possible even in the absence of statutory imposition of a conflicting and incompatible requirement on the agency. However, the courts will not find a statutory exemption unless one is very clearly expressed. For example, the Second Circuit has held that the Postal Service is subject to the EIS requirement, notwithstanding §410(a) of the Postal Reorganization Act of 1970, 39 U.S.C. §410(a) (1988), which provides that "no Federal law dealing with public or Federal contracts, property, works, officers, employees, budgets, or funds . . . shall apply to the exercise of the powers of the Postal Service." See *Chelsea Neighborhood Assn. v. United States Postal Serv.*, 516 F.2d 378 (2d Cir. 1975).

3. Courts have, however, refused to require EPA to prepare EISs in connection with environmental regulatory decisions by EPA, reasoning that EPA rulemaking or adjudicatory proceedings will address all relevant environmental considerations and are the "functional equivalent" of an EIS. See, e.g., *Environmental Defense Fund, Inc. v. Environmental Protection Agency*, 489 F.2d 1247, 1256 (D.C. Cir. 1973) (EIS not required before cancelling registrations for use of DDT); *State of Wyoming v. Hathaway*, 525 F.2d 66 (10th Cir. 1975) (EIS not required before cancelling or suspending registration of three coyote poisons). Note that many of the cases seeking to require preparation of an EIS by EPA are brought by businesses contending that the agency has ignored other environmental aspects of its decision than the immediate regula-

tory objective. For example, it may be claimed that EPA has ignored the water-pollution side effects of air pollution control requirements. Should an EIS be required for EPA's decisions on how much and how to clean up a Superfund site? See Montrose, Comment, To Police the Police: Functional Equivalence to the EIS Requirement and EPA Remedial Actions Under Superfund, 33 Cath. U.L. Rev. 862 (1984). Why shouldn't other federal agencies, such as the Interior Department, also get the benefit of the "functionally equivalent" principle?

Congress has by statute specifically exempted certain EPA decisions from the EIS requirement. All actions taken under the Clean Air Act are statutorily deemed not to be "major Federal actions" requiring an EIS, 15 U.S.C. §793(c)(1) (1988), as are actions under the Clean Water Act other than financing of publicly owned treatment works and issuing of new source discharge permits. 33 U.S.C. §1371(c) (1988).

The EPA has exempted itself from preparing an EIS when issuing permits under the Resource Conservation and Recovery Act (RCRA). 40 C.F.R. §124.9(b)(6) (1991). Has the EPA exceeded its authority by exempting itself from NEPA requirements? See Hauenstein, Note, RCRA Immunity from NEPA: The EPA Has Exceeded the Scope of Its Authority, 24 San Diego L. Rev. 1249 (1987).

4. The CEQ has promulgated a regulation excusing agencies from preparing an EIS "[w]here emergency circumstances make it necessary to take an action with significant environmental impact without observing the provisions of these regulations. . . ." 40 C.F.R. §1506.11 (1992). In such circumstances, the agency "should consult with the Council about alternative arrangements." Id.; for examples, see CEQ, Environmental Quality: 23rd Annual Report of the Council on Environmental Quality — 1992 155 (1993). This provision has been used by HUD to grant Detroit a $60 million loan guarantee in order to help lure General Motors into building a new automobile manufacturing plant there. *Crosby v. Young,* 512 F. Supp. 1363 (E.D. Mich. 1981). For the argument that this is a dangerous expansion of the emergency exemption rule, see Orsi, Note, Emergency Exceptions from NEPA: Who Should Decide?, 14 B.C. Envtl. Aff. L. Rev. 481 (1987).

5. There is no "national security" exception in NEPA. Important military projects are potentially subject to the EIS requirement. See *Romer v. Carlucci,* 847 F.2d 445 (8th Cir. 1988) (MX missile program). There are instances, however, where national security interests in confidentiality may, as a practical matter, preclude judicial challenge to the military's failure to prepare an EIS. In *Weinberger v. Catholic Action of Hawaii/Peace Education Project,* 454 U.S. 139 (1981), the plaintiffs sought to require the Navy to prepare an EIS for the construction of a weapons storage facility at its base on Oahu, Hawaii, and to consider the risk presented by the storage of nuclear weapons at the facility. The Navy

had already concluded that an EIS was unnecessary, but, in accordance with its general policy regarding information on the location of nuclear weapons, would not confirm or deny whether nuclear weapons were stored at the facility. The Supreme Court held that information about nuclear weapons storage was exempt from disclosure under the Freedom of Information Act, and hence that plaintiffs' litigation must fail because of their inability to establish a fact — storage of nuclear weapons at the facility — essential to their claim that an EIS was required. For criticism of this opinion, see Debois, Comment, The United States Supreme Court Deals A Severe Blow to NEPA, 22 Nat. Resources J. 699 (1982), suggesting as an alternative to the outcome in *Catholic Action* that the Navy prepare an EIS for internal use. Id., at 705-706. The general counsel of the CEQ has warned, however, that secret EISs are worthless because they preclude oversight by private parties. See CEQ General Counsel Outlines Development Involving New NEPA Rules, 10 Envt. Rep. (BNA) 557 (July 6, 1979).

D. EIS PRACTICE IN THE FEDERAL GOVERNMENT

1. The preparation of environmental analysis in order to comply with NEPA has now become a routine part of federal administrative practice. The bureaucratic process normally comprises seven stages, outlined below. For a routine EIS, these typically take a total of six to nine months; however, an EIS on a large controversial project can take two years or more. If the EIS process is programmed as part of the overall project plan, the EIS should not in most cases result in significant delay unless it is successfully challenged in court and the project is enjoined pending preparation of another EIS, infra, pp. 1011-1016.

a. Once it has decided to prepare an EIS, an agency is required to publish a notice of intent in the Federal Register. 40 C.F.R. §§1501.7, 1508.22 (1992). This notice, in conjunction with required specific invitations to federal, state and local agencies, Indian tribes and other affected parties, 40 C.F.R. §1501.7(a)(1) (1992), opens up the EIS process for public involvement. It also begins the "scoping" process, an "open" process of consultation and planning among agencies and the public. The scoping process provisionally determines the issues to be addressed in the EIS and establishes an administrative plan and schedule for preparing it. 40 C.F.R. §1501.7 (1992).

b. The agency will assemble a team with a variety of specialties to prepare the draft of the EIS. See 40 C.F.R. §1502.6 (1992). Such assembly is handicapped by (a) Congress's failure to appropriate much money for NEPA activity and (b) the shortage of interdisciplinary experts with writing and editing skills. Sometimes it is also handicapped by (c) the low regard and little reward given within agencies for NEPA work. In many cases an EIS is prepared by outside consultants. Such consultants are concerned with obtaining future contracts with the agency and may thus be inclined to prepare statements favorable to the agency's proposed action. Moreover, the use of outside consultants tends to impede the integration of articulated environmental goals with the agency's process of decision. Also, supporting information and analyses may be prepared by state or local governments or private parties seeking federal funding or approval for projects they wish to undertake. See 40 C.F.R. §1506.5 (1992).

c. A draft version of the EIS is reviewed internally. "Ordinarily, a draft will be subject to at least six reviews involving up to 15 reviewers and as many as four rewrites before it is filed with CEQ." Task Force, A Review of Environmental Impact Statement Processes Within the Department of the Interior, III-3 (1974). In this process, there may be conflicts between those preparing the EIS, who often hold an environmental viewpoint, and the agency's line program officers.

d. The draft then goes to EPA, 42 U.S.C. §7609 (1988), and to any agencies participating in the project being assessed. If the EPA or other federal agencies find the draft unsatisfactory and cannot resolve their environmental concerns in consultation with the preparing agency, they may refer it for review to CEQ. 40 C.F.R. §1504 (1992).

e. The draft EIS is then issued for public comment, and a notice of its issuance is published in the Federal Register. 40 C.F.R. §1506.10(a) (1992). CEQ regulations require that the comments of other federal, state and local agencies, Indian tribes, and interested persons and organizations be sought. 40 C.F.R. §1503.1 (1992). The agency must generally allow a minimum of 45 days for comments on the draft EIS before proceeding to a final EIS, and, in any case, cannot make a final decision on the proposed action until 90 days have elapsed since the publication of notice of the draft EIS. 40 C.F.R. §1506.10(b)(1), (c), (d) (1992). Many federal agencies comment, as do citizens, and some states have set up clearinghouses to facilitate commenting. Sometimes an EIS on a crucial project will be a runaway popular item. Some have even had whole books of critical analysis directed at them.

f. Following this commenting on the draft, a second, similar preparation sequence follows for the final version of the EIS. The CEQ regulations prescribe a minimum 30-day period for commenting on the final EIS (absent "compelling reasons" to reduce that period). 40 C.F.R. §1506.10(b)(2), (d) (1992). Because courts judge the adequacy of an

EIS in part by whether it responds adequately to criticisms in the public comments of the project and the draft EIS, the final EIS typically contains extensive discussion of and rejoinder to public comments. CEQ regulations also require responses to comments. 40 C.F.R. §1503.4 (1992). On occasion, comments will reveal basic flaws in the agency's data and analysis, requiring major revisions or even the preparation of a revised or supplemental draft EIS, which must undergo a fresh round of public comment. The process is analagous to notice and comment rulemaking, see supra, pp. 855-857. In preparing the final EIS, the agency must often assess the risks of proceeding with a thoroughly criticized draft or starting over for a better version. In the case of the programmatic impact statement for the national coal leasing program, for example, the Interior Department was tied up for five months debating which way to proceed. It eventually chose to proceed with a weak draft and lost a subsequent court challenge. See *Natural Resources Defense Council v. Hughes*, 437 F. Supp. 981 (D.D.C. 1977).

g. The agency must prepare and make public a Record of Decision (ROD) when it makes a final decision adopting a proposal. The ROD must identify alternatives to the action taken, designating those deemed to be environmentally preferable. It must also state "whether all practicable means to avoid or minimize environmental harm from the alternative selected have been adopted and, if not, why they were not." 40 C.F.R. §1502.2 (1992).

The EIS process is subject not only to the CEQ regulations but also to NEPA regulations adopted by particular federal agencies such as the Corps of Engineers, the Department of Agriculture, and so on. These regulations are designed to tailor the EIS process to the agency's particular programs and organization. As permitted by CEQ regulations, 40 C.F.R. §1507.3(b)(2)(ii) (1992), agencies may by regulation adopt "categorical exclusions" defining categories of actions whose environmental effects are not sufficiently significant to warrant preparation of an EIS, thus simplifying the EA process. If an action falls within a categorical exclusion, no EA or EIS need be prepared. Of course, a litigant is free to challenge the categorical exclusion as unjustified.

2. Based on this summary, which of these proposals would have any effect on environmental planning within agencies? Which would have the most effect?

(a) Greater funding for EIS preparation.

(b) Greater substantive review by courts.

(c) Adoption of the EIS as the "decision-making document" for agency decisions. This role is presently occupied by various other, less environmental types of documents, such as Interior's Program Decision Option Document (PDOD). By con-

trast, the EIS is normally prepared after the basic agency
decisions have already been made, and often criticized by
environmentalists as an exercise in post-hoc rationalization.
What incentives could be provided for agencies to make the
EIS the decision-making document?

(d)   Facilitating (for instance, by funding grants or attorney fee
awards) challenges to EISs by environmental or other citizens' groups at either the agency level or the level of judicial
review.

NOTE ON THE "LEAD AGENCY" CONCEPT

The problem of who should prepare an EIS arises when there is
more than one federal agency involved in a project. It seemed a waste
to have more than one EIS done on a single project, so the "lead
agency" concept was developed — that one of the involved agencies
would be considered the leader, with the responsibility to prepare the
EIS. The other agencies, known as "cooperating agencies," use the leader's EIS for their own decisionmaking and, of course, to satisfy the
courts.

Unfortunately, the "lead agency" concept has run into both substantive and procedural problems. The substantive problems were
rather starkly revealed in *Upper Pecos Assn. v. Stans*, 452 F.2d 1233 (10th
Cir. 1971), *vacated*, 409 U.S. 1021 (1972). In *Upper Pecos* the federal
Economic Development Agency (EDA) provided 80 percent of the
funding for a local road that would require a U.S. Forest Service permit.
The EDA gave its grant without preparing an EIS for what was admittedly a major federal action significantly affecting the environment,
contending that the Forest Service would prepare the EIS since the
Service was the "lead agency." Both the district court and the majority
of the appellate panel accepted the argument. But as the Solicitor General found after certiorari was granted, the EDA had made its grant
before the Forest Service prepared an EIS, making a mockery of the
NEPA process. He asked the court to vacate the judgment below. Commentators suggest that *Upper Pecos* is not atypical, and that no agency
will scrutinize adequately another agency's document; arguably even
several EISs are demanded by NEPA. See Humphreys, NEPA and Multi-
Agency Actions — Is the Lead Agency Concept Valid?, 6 Nat. Res. L.

---

23. The CEQ regulations provide for the designation of a lead agency to
supervise the preparation of an EIS if multiple agencies are involved in a major
federal action. 40 C.F.R. §1501.5 (1991). If the agencies cannot reach
agreement on the lead agency, the CEQ regulations require that the following
factors be used (in descending order of importance) in designating a lead

257 (1973).

In other cases, there are sharp disputes between agencies over who should be the leader. In one situation, the Interior Department and the Federal Power Commission planned to do a joint EIS on a proposed natural gas pipeline in Alaska. But the company filing the proposal with the FPC, El Paso Natural Gas, refused to file with the Interior Department because Interior, unlike FPC, makes applicants pay the costs of EIS preparation on their proposals. Considerable confusion and disruption resulted as the applicant played off the two agencies. See Interior Issues Draft Statement on Arctic Gas Proposed Pipeline, 6 Envt. Rep. (BNA) 594 (Aug. 8, 1975).[23]

Problem: Refer back to the Federal Water Contracts Threshold Problem, supra, p. 934. Should CEQ accept the EPA referral in order to resolve this interagency disagreement? Should the DOI or the EPA be designated the lead agency in this matter?

E.   CONTENTS AND ADEQUACY OF AN EIS

Under NEPA, an EIS must be "a detailed statement" on:

(i)   the environmental impact of the proposed action,
(ii) any adverse environmental effects which cannot be avoided should the proposal be implemented,
(iii) alternatives to the proposed action,
(iv) the relationship between local short-term uses of man's environment and the maintenance and enhancement of long-term productivity, and
(v)   any irreversible and irretrievable commitments of resources which would be involved in the proposed action should it be implemented.

42 U.S.C. §4332(2)(C) (1988). This section will consider the aspects of these requirements that have given rise to the most litigation: (1) the extent to which other, related federal actions must be considered for an EIS on a particular action to be adequate; (2) the extent to which indirect effects of the proposed action must be addressed; (3) the requirement to consider alternatives; (4) how to address uncertainty and whether and when a "worst case analysis" may be required; and (5) the

---

agency: "(1) Magnitude of agency's involvement; (2) Project approval/disapproval authority; (3) Expertise concerning the action's environmental effects; (4) Duration of agency's involvement; [and] (5) Sequence of agency's involvement." 40 C.F.R. §1501.5(c) (1992).

circumstances under which a supplemental EIS will be required.

Some of the earliest EISs were quite short, and were judicially invalidated as inadequate. Agencies responded by preparing in many cases voluminous statements with mountains of detail that often obscured the basic issues at stake. CEQ regulations sought to address this problem by providing that agencies should "focus on significant environmental issues and alternatives and . . . reduce paperwork and the accumulation of extraneous background data. Statements shall be concise, clear, and to the point." 40 C.F.R. §1502.1 (1992). The regulations also provide that EISs "shall be analytic rather than encyclopedic," and "shall be written in plain language." 40 C.F.R. §§1502.2, 1502.8 (1992). "Agencies should employ writers of clear prose." 40 C.F.R. §1502.8 (1992). Needless to say, these objectives have been only very imperfectly realized. EISs are subject to a 150-page limit (300 pages for proposals of unusual scope or complexity). 40 C.F.R. §1502.7 (1992). However, technical and other appendices can run to many volumes.

EISs describe the impacts of proposed actions and alternatives on the physical environment and on economic and social activity. But they generally do not describe, at least in any systematic way, the values held by a relevant population on the proposed action and alternatives. Would it be helpful and appropriate to include information on the values held by the public and various organized interests to assist decisionmakers to choose the socially preferred course of action? How would such information be obtained? See Gregory, Kenney & von Winterfeldt, Adopting the Environmental Impact Statement to Inform Decisionmakers, 11 J. Policy Analysis & Mgmt. 58 (1992) (proposing a decision analytic process to elicit public values and incorporate them in EISs). What about using contingent value methodology surveys and other economic methodologies to determine the economic value that the public places on the natural resources in question? See pp. 1184-1200, infra.

1.   RELATED FEDERAL ACTIONS: "CONNECTED," "CUMULATIVE," AND "SIMILAR" ACTIONS

In reviewing this and the next subsection, which are concerned with the identification of those effects that can be attributed to a given federal action, note that the process of attributing effects to an action serves a dual purpose under NEPA: (1) it determines what effects should be included in an EIS and so goes to the adequacy of an EIS when one is prepared; and (2) it determines what effects should be included in an environmental assessment, and so goes to whether, given the particular facts of the case, an EIS will be required.

KLEPPE V. SIERRA CLUB

427 U.S. 390, 408-415 (1976)

Mr. Justice POWELL delivered the opinion of the Court.

[The main body of the opinion, finding that there was no actual federal proposal for a program to develop coal reserves on a regional basis, is reproduced at p. 922-926.]

V . . .

Respondents insist that, even without a comprehensive federal plan for the development of the Northern Great Plains, a "regional" impact statement nevertheless is required on all coal-related projects in the region because they are intimately related.

There are two ways to view this contention. First, it amounts to an attack on the sufficiency of the impact statements already prepared by the petitioners on the coal-related projects that they have approved or stand ready to approve. As such, we cannot consider it in this proceeding, for the case was not brought as a challenge to a particular impact statement and there is no impact statement in the record. It also is possible to view the respondents' argument as an attack upon the decision of the petitioners not to prepare one comprehensive impact statement on all proposed projects in the region. This contention properly is before us, for the petitioners have made it clear they do not intend to prepare such a statement.

We begin by stating our general agreement with respondents' basic premise that §102(2)(C) may require a comprehensive impact statement in certain situations where several proposed actions are pending at the same time. . . . Thus, when several proposals for coal-related actions that will have cumulative or synergistic environmental impact upon a region are pending concurrently before an agency, their environmental consequences must be considered together. Only through comprehensive consideration of pending proposals can the agency evaluate different courses of action.

Agreement to this extent with respondents' premise, however, does not require acceptance of their conclusion that all proposed coal-related actions in the Northern Great Plains region are so "related" as to require their analysis in a single comprehensive impact statement. Respondents informed us that the Secretary recently adopted an approach to impact statements on coal-related actions that provides: that a "regional EIS" will be prepared "if a series of proposed actions with interrelated impacts are involved. . . ." The Department's internal guidance document also provides that: "In such cases, the region covered will be determined by basin boundaries, drainage areas, areas of common reclamation problems, administrative boundaries, areas of economic interdependence, and other relevant factors." Thus, the Department has decided to prepare comprehensive impact statements of the type contemplated by §102(2)(C), although it has not deemed it appropriate to prepare such a statement on all proposed actions in the region identified by respondents.

Respondents conceded at oral argument that to prevail they must show that petitioners have acted arbitrarily in refusing to prepare one comprehensive statement on this entire region, and we agree. . . . The determination of the region, if any, with respect to which a comprehensive statement is necessary requires the weighing of a number of relevant factors, including the extent of the interrelationship among proposed actions and practical considerations of feasibility. Resolving these issues requires a high level of technical expertise and is properly left to the informed discretion of the responsible federal agencies. . . . Absent a showing of arbitrary action, we must assume that the agencies have exercised this discretion appropriately. Respondents have made no showing to the contrary.

Respondents' basic argument is that one comprehensive statement on the Northern Great Plains is required because all coal-related activity in that region is "programmatically," "geographically," and "environmentally" related. . . .

As for the alleged "environmental" relationship, respondents contend that the coal-related projects "will produce a wide variety of cumulative environmental impacts" throughout the Northern Great Plains region. They described them as follows: Diminished availability of water, air and water pollution, increases in population and industrial densities, and perhaps even climatic changes. Cumulative environmental impacts are, indeed, what require a comprehensive impact statement. But determination of the extent and effect of these factors, and particularly identification of the geographic area within which they may occur, is a task assigned to the special competency of the appropriate agencies. Petitioners dispute respondents' contentions that the interrelationship of environmental impacts is region-wide. [Interior's guidance document, quoted above, takes the position that the appropriate scope of comprehensive statements should be based on basins, drainage areas, and other factors.] . . . We cannot say that petitioners' choices are arbitrary. Even if environmental interrelationships could be shown conclusively to extend across basins and drainage areas, practical considerations of feasibility might well necessitate restricting the scope of comprehensive statements.

In sum, respondents' contention as to the relationships between all proposed coal-related projects in the Northern Great Plains region does not require that petitioners prepare one comprehensive impact statement covering all before proceeding to approve specific pending applications. As we already have determined that there exists no proposal for regionwide action that could require a regional impact statement, the judgment of the Court of Appeals must be reversed.

[Mr. Justice MARSHALL, joined by Mr. Justice BRENNAN, dissented in part.]

NOTES AND QUESTIONS

1. CEQ regulations recognize that there are several different bases on which the environmental effects of one federal action should be considered together with the effects of another federal action for NEPA purposes. In the terms of the CEQ regulations, the Sierra Club's claim that the coal-related projects in *Kleppe* were "environmentally" and "geographically" related can be read either as a claim that the actions were "cumulative," or that they were "similar":

> . . . (2) Cumulative actions, which when viewed with other proposed actions have cumulatively significant impacts . . . should . . . be discussed in the same impact statement.
>
> (3) Similar actions, which when viewed with other reasonably foreseeable or proposed agency actions, have similarities that provide a basis for evaluating their environmental consequences together, such as common timing or geography. An agency [should] analyze these actions in the same impact statement . . . when the best way to assess adequately the combined impacts of similar actions or reasonable alternatives to such actions is to treat them in a single impact statement.

40 C.F.R. §1508.25(a)(2), (3) (1992). Notwithstanding *Kleppe*, such claims have met with success in some subsequent cases. See, e.g., *LaFlamme v. Federal Energy Regulatory Commn.*, 852 F.2d 389, 401-402 (9th Cir. 1988) (finding inadequate an EA and FONSI on a hydroelectric plant, where FERC failed to study the potential cumulative impact of the project in conjunction with other actual or pending projects on the water system of the American River Basin as a whole).

The regulations also identify a third set of related actions that must be considered together in an EIS, "connected actions." "Similar" or "cumulative" actions are related in terms of their environmental effects. "Connected" actions are related in terms of their objectives:

> (1) . . . Actions are connected if they:
>   (i)   Automatically trigger other actions which may require environmental impact statements.
>   (ii) Cannot or will not proceed unless other actions are taken previously or simultaneously.
>   (iii) Are interdependent parts of a larger action and depend on the larger action for their justification.

40 C.F.R. §1508.25(a)(1) (1992). See, e.g., *Thomas v. Peterson,* 753 F.2d 754, 758 (9th Cir. 1985) (where Forest Service proposed to build a road which "would not be built but for the comtemplated timber sales," the road building and the timber sales were both "connected" and "cumulative" actions, and their combined environmental impact must be addressed).

Typical of the cases that fall within the "connected actions" provision are the "segmentation cases," where agencies attempt to avoid the preparation of an EIS for a large project with a single overall purpose by breaking it down to a number of smaller actions so that each segment does not rise to the level of "significant" and no EIS is required. In such cases, plaintiffs contend that the proper subject of analysis is the larger project, which is significant enough to require an EIS. In other cases agencies have attempted to segment out the portion of the project that significantly affects the environment and proposed it only after the remaining segments had been completed, foreclosing, as a practical matter, less environmentally risky alternatives.

Many of the segmentation cases involve highway projects[24] that were clearly part of an overall plan, but were treated as independent segments for purposes of environmental analysis. Courts have developed the following criteria to determine whether or not an overall EIS

---

24. For a compendium of the early highway cases, see D. Mandelker, NEPA Law and Litigation, §§9.12-9.14 (2d ed. 1992).

25. As discussed previously, supra, p. 930, analogous issues arise when federal and state governments fund different portions of a highway project.

26. See *Taxpayers Watchdog, Inc. v. Stanley,* 819 F.2d 294 (D.C. Cir. 1987) (four-mile subway in Los Angeles did not require overall EIS despite fact that it was first leg of a larger system because it met the four criteria).

27. See *Environmental Defense Fund v. Marsh,* 651 F.2d 983 (5th Cir. 1981) (Army Corps of Engineers need not evaluate effect of possible improvements for Black Warrier-Tombigbee Waterway in EIS for Tennessee-Tombigbee Waterway that serves as connecting link in a continuous waterway between Tennessee, Upper Mississippi, and Ohio Valleys to the Gulf of Mexico because the two projects were "historically distinct" and improvements had not yet been "proposed").

is required: (1) whether the segment is as long as practicable to permit consideration of environmental matters on a broad scope and has logical termini; (2) whether the segment has independent utility; (3) whether the segment length assures an adequate opportunity for the consideration of alternatives; and (4) whether the segment fulfills important state and local needs and does not irretrievably commit federal funds for closely related segments. See, e.g., *Adler v. Lewis,* 675 F.2d 1085 (9th Cir. 1982); *Daly v. Volpe,* 514 F.2d 1106, 1109-1111 (9th Cir. 1975).[25] The first three of these criteria have since been adopted by the Federal Highway Administration for use in determining when a project requires an EIS. 23 C.F.R. §771.111(f) (1992); *Coalition on Sensible Transp., Inc. v. Dole,* 826 F.2d 60 (D.C. Cir. 1987). Query: could an overall EIS also be required in highway cases on the ground that the actions are "cumulative"?

The courts have also applied segmentation analysis in cases involving a mass transit system,[26] a water project,[27] and the decommissioning of a radioactive milling facility by the NRC.[28] Similar concerns have also arisen in the context of Forest Service programs for oil and gas exploitation, in which the Forest Service has treated the leasing of land for exploration and subsequent authorization of exploitation as distinct actions, thus purporting to avoid any necessity for an EIS at the leasing stage. See, e.g., *Conner v. Burford,* 836 F.2d 1521, 1527-1532 (9th Cir. 1988); see also Comer, Note, NEPA Compliance in Oil and Gas Leasing: Leasehold Segmentation and the Decision to Forego an Environmental Impact Statement, 58 U. Colo. L. Rev. 677 (1988).

2. Recall Justice Marshall's argument in his separate opinion in *Kleppe,* discussed in the notes to the first *Kleppe* excerpt at p. 927. He protested that *Kleppe* allowed the agency too much scope to define the "proposal" that is the subject of NEPA review. The CEQ regulations and the segmentation cases can be viewed as an attempt to respond to this concern, by requiring that the agency's NEPA analysis encompass foreseeable federal actions which it ought to regard as part and parcel of the same proposal, whether or not it does so. Do they do so adequately, or is there still too much scope for agency avoidance of an adequately comprehensive EIS? What else, if anything, could the courts or the CEQ do to ensure that the broader picture is considered in agencies' NEPA analyses?

3. When a programmatic EIS is held to be necessary, will it also be

---

28. See *City of West Chicago, Ill. v. United States Nuclear Regulatory Commn.,* 701 F.2d 632 (7th Cir. 1983) (amendment to operator's license permitting the destruction of six buildings and receipt and on-site storage of contaminated material that had previously been removed from site for use as landfill was not improperly segmented because it did not prejudice selection of permanent disposal plan for which draft EIS already had isssued).

sufficient to excuse the preparation of further EISs on the various more specific federal actions which it encompasses? See the discussion of tiering, infra, p. 996.

4. *Problem:* Refer back to the Federal Water Contracts Threshold Problem, supra, p. 934. Should the lead agency be required to prepare a programmatic EIS? If so, what should be the scope of such an EIS?

2. INDIRECT EFFECTS

SIERRA CLUB v. MARSH

769 F.2d 868, 872-880 (1st Cir. 1985)

BREYER, Circuit Judge:
[Maine's Department of Transportation proposed to build a cargo port and a causeway at Sears Island, an undeveloped, 940-acre island in upper Penobscot Bay, at Searsport, Maine, a busy port.]

The most recent proposal for Sears Island consists of three parts: (1) a 1200-floor solid-fill causeway that would connect Sears Island to the mainland with a railroad line and a two-lane road; (2) a dry-cargo marine terminal designed principally for the shipping of lumber and agricultural products, containerized cargo, and, possibly at a later stage in the project, coal; and (3) an industrial park in an area adjacent to the cargo port. The precise nature of the industrial park is now uncertain, for the park's eventual shape depends on what businesses choose to locate there. The plans for the other two components, however, are definite. . . .

[The Federal Highway Administration and the Army Corps of Engineers decided to grant the necessary funding and permits for the causeway and port development, without preparing an EIS, having made findings of no significant impact. The Sierra Club sued to require preparation of an EIS.

Judge Breyer reviewed the potential environmental impacts of the port and causeway, but concluded that they were probably insufficient, without more, to require an EIS. He continued:]

The problems just noted become significant, however, when combined with a more serious omission by the Corps and the Federal Highway Administration — their failure to consider adequately the fact that building a port and causeway may lead to the further industrial development of Sears Island, and that further development will significantly affect the environment. The CEQ says that agencies must take account of such "indirect effects," which it defines as those that are

caused by the action and are later in time or farther removed in distance, but are still reasonably foreseeable. Indirect effects may include growth inducing effects and other effects related to induced changes in the pattern of land use, population density, or growth rate, and related effects on air and water and other natural systems, including ecosystems.

40 C.F.R. §1508.8 (emphasis added). Of course, agencies need not consider highly speculative or indefinite impacts. See, e.g., *Kleppe v. Sierra Club*, 427 U.S. 390 (1976). But, here the 'impacts' seem neither speculative nor indefinite.

Whether a particular set of impacts is definite enough to take into account, or too speculative to warrant consideration, reflects several different factors. With what confidence can one say that the impacts are likely to occur? Can one describe them "now" with sufficient specificity to make their consideration useful? If the decisionmaker does not take them into account "now," will the decisionmaker be able to take account of them before the agency is so firmly committed to the project that further environmental knowledge, as a practical matter, will prove irrelevant to the government's decision? . . .

In this case, the record contains clear answers to these questions. And those answers show that the agencies should have taken account of the "secondary impacts." First, the record makes it nearly impossible to doubt that building the causeway and port will lead to further development of Sears Island. Local planners have considered the port, causeway, and industrial park to be components of an integrated plan. . . . This theme is echoed in several of the EA's . . . Maine DOT . . . projected further industrial development after construction of the cargo port:

> *Development of the cargo terminal will. . . . act as the principal stimulus to further industrial development on the island itself. . . .* [Emphasis aded.]

Second, the plans for further development are precise enough for an EIS usefully to take them into account. The record contains, for example, a 35-page "Land Use Plan/Industrial Marketing Study" prepared for the owner of southern half of the island, and the town's 50-page "Municipal Response Plan for the Industrial Development of Sears Island." These documents provide detailed descriptions of likely further development, including a plot plan of the proposed industrial park . . . and locations for railroad and secondary road loops. . . .

Third, once Maine completes the causeway and port, pressure to develop the rest of the island could well prove irreversible. . . . [I]f the Sears Island terminal is built, there will probably not be another major port facility built in Maine for a long time, and whatever new shipping traffic and industrial development is created by the project will be funneled into the Searsport area. . . .

sonably foreseeable." 40 C.F.R. §1508.8(b) (1992). How should courts interpret this criterion? Is the foresight of environmental objectors indicative of what is "reasonably foreseeable"? Are common law precedents from torts cases relevant? Could CEQ have provided more helpful guidance?

2. Note the close factual association between "segmentation" and "indirect effects" issues. Once it is accepted that the setting aside of land for an industrial park is an "aspect of the [federally supported] project," it seems a relatively short step to the conclusion that effects of private industrial occupancy of that park can be attributed to the "project." Might the case have been decided differently if documents prepared by Maine DOT and the federal agencies had not identified private development as a major purpose of the project?

PROBLEM

The Bonneville Power Administration, a federal agency within the Department of Interior, is charged by statute with marketing and delivering power from hydroelectric plants on the Columbia River to public and private consumers. BPA has negotiated a draft contract with the Aluminum Company of America (ALCOA) for the supply of power to a new ALCOA plant. ALCOA has warned the BPA Administrator that delay in signing the contract on BPA's part could imperil its commercial viability and ALCOA's willingness to proceed. The draft contract has three principal provisions:

(1)   ALCOA undertakes to construct a new magnesium smelter in an agricultural area in Washington State, and to purchase power for that plant from BPA.
(2)   BPA undertakes to sell 124,000 kilowatts of interruptible power to the ALCOA plant. (Interruptible power is subject to availability and may be curtailed in whole or in part at BPA's discretion.)
(3)   BPA undertakes to construct 25 miles of new transmission lines, plus a new substation near the plant, to supply it.

The BPA Administrator hands you a file containing the following:
(i) a detailed environmental impact statement on ALCOA's plant, prepared by the Washington State Department of Ecology (WDE), as required by the state's environmental policy act (which is similar to NEPA in all material respects). This statement finds that the plant and associated ALCOA mining facilities will have a significant impact on the local environment, both in terms of air and water quality impacts and by creating local jobs that will cause a substantial population influx.

However, it finds that the impact is not excessive in light of the plant's benefits to the local economy and concludes that WDE should grant the state permits that are necessary for the plant's operation. BPA took no part in the preparation of this statement; and

(ii) comments submitted by the Sierra Club, which contends that the massive kilowattage promised to ALCOA by the draft contract would cause a major drain on the BPA power system, which may experience massive deficits during the next decade due to water scarcity that will reduce capacity from BPA's existing hydro facilities or construction delays on new BPA generating units. The Sierra Club points out that the kilowattage involved is equivalent to the municipal use requirements of a city of 250,000 people. It also notes that the BPA system provides approximately 80 percent of the Pacific Northwest's power transmission capacity, and that many utilities in the region are reliant on it for power. It contends that BPA's commitment to ALCOA may force those utilities to resort to more environmentally harmful thermal or nuclear power sources. It also claims that even if the BPA power system does not experience a deficit, the ALCOA contract would still be diverting energy resources away from possible use by utilities in the Southwest, which BPA could supply via an existing inter-tie transmission system.

The Administrator asks you to advise him as to how BPA should respond to the Sierra Club's comments. He also wants to know if preparation of an EIS can be avoided. If an EIS will be required, he seeks guidance regarding its scope. He also asks whether an EIS, if necessary, could be postponed until after the signing of the contract (but before BPA takes action to fulfill it).

3.   CONSIDERATION OF ALTERNATIVES

NATURAL RESOURCES DEFENSE COUNCIL, INC. V. MORTON

458 F.2d 827, 829-838 (D.C. Cir. 1972)

LEVENTHAL, Circuit Judge:

This appeal raises a question as to the scope of the requirement of the National Environmental Policy Act (NEPA) that environmental impact statements contain a discussion of alternatives. Before us is the Environmental Impact Statement filed October 28, 1971, by the Department of Interior with respect to its proposal, under §8 of the Outer Continental Shelf Lands Act, for the oil and gas general lease sale, of leases to some 80 tracts of submerged lands, primarily off eastern Louisiana. The proposal was finally structured so as to embrace almost

380,000 acres, about 10 percent of the offshore acreage presently under Federal lease. [Environmental groups challenged the adequacy of the Interior Department's EIS on the sale. The district court granted a preliminary injunction.]

Paragraph (iii) of §102(2)(C) [provides that an EIS must examine] "The alternative ways of accomplishing the objectives of the proposed action and the results of not accomplishing the proposed action."

NEED TO DISCUSS ENVIRONMENTAL
CONSEQUENCES OF ALTERNATIVES

We reject the implication of one of the Government's submissions which began by stating that while the Act requires a detailed statement of alternatives, it "does not require a discussion of the environmental consequences of the suggested alternative." A sound construction of NEPA . . . requires a presentation of the environmental risks incident to reasonable alternative courses of action. . . .

ALTERNATIVE AS TO OIL IMPORT QUOTAS

We think the [Interior Department's] Statement erred in stating that the alternative of elimination of oil import quotas was entirely outside its cognizance. Assuming, as the Statement puts it, that this alternative "involves complex factors and concepts, including national security, which are beyond the scope of this statement," it does not follow that the Statement should not present the environmental effects of that alternative. While the consideration of pertinent alternatives requires a weighing of numerous matters, such as economics, foreign relations, national security, the fact remains that, as to the ingredient of possible adverse environmental impact, it is the essence and thrust of NEPA that the pertinent Statement serve to gather in one place a discussion of the relative environmental impact of alternatives.

The Government also contends that the only "alternatives" required for discussion under NEPA are those which can be adopted and put into effect by the official or agency issuing the statement. . . .

While we agree with so much of the Government's presentation as rests on the assumption that the alternatives required for discussion are those reasonably available, we do not agree that this requires a limitation to measures the agency or official can adopt. This approach would be particularly inapposite for the lease sale of offshore oil lands

Supply of Energy and Clean Air, as part of an overall program of development to provide an accommodation of the energy requirements of our country. . . .

When the proposed action is an integral part of a coordinated plan to deal with a broad problem, the range of alternatives that must be evaluated is broadened. While the Department of the Interior does not have the authority to eliminate or reduce oil import quotas, such action is within the purview of both Congress and the President, to whom the impact statement goes. The impact statement is not only for the exposition of the thinking of the agency, but also for the guidance of these ultimate decision-makers, and must provide them with the environmental effects of both the proposal and the alternatives. . . .

The need for continuing review of environmental impact of alternatives under NEPA cannot be put to one side on the ground of past determinations by Congress or the President. We are aware that the 1953 Outer Continental Shelf Lands Act contains a finding of an urgent need for OCS development and authorization of leasing. Similarly we are aware that the oil import quota program was instituted by the President on a mandatory basis in 1959, following earlier voluntary programs, and that the President's authority, based on national security considerations, is contained in legislation derived from a 1955 enactment and subsequent amendments, 19 U.S.C. §1862. But these enactments are not dispositive. As to both programs Congress contemplated continuing review. . . .

. . . Nor is it appropriate, as Government counsel argues, to disregard alternatives merely because they do not offer a complete solution to the problem. If an alternative would result in supplying only part of the energy that the lease sale would yield, then its use might possibly reduce the scope of the lease sale program and thus alleviate a significant portion of the environmental harm attendant on offshore drilling.

OTHER "ALTERNATIVES"

The foregoing establishes that we cannot grant the Government's motion for summary reversal. We discuss other aspects of the case in anticipation that the Secretary may choose to supplement or modify the Statement. . . .

We think there is merit to the Government's position insofar as it contends that no additional discussion was requisite for such "alternatives" as the development of oil shale, desulfurization of coal, coal liquefaction and gasification, tar sands and geothermal resources.

The Statement sets forth . . . that while these possibilities hold great promise for the future, their impact on the energy supply will not

safeguards and technological developments. Since the Statement also sets forth that the agency's proposal was put forward to meet a near-term requirement, imposed by an energy shortfall projected for the mid-1970's, the possibility of the environmental impact of long-term solutions requires no additional discussion at this juncture. . . .

Furthermore, the requirement in NEPA of discussion as to reasonable alternatives does not require "crystal ball" inquiry. Mere administrative difficulty does not interpose such flexibility into the requirements of NEPA as to undercut the duty of compliance "to the fullest extent possible." But if this requirement is not rubber, neither is it iron. The statute must be construed in the light of reason if it is not to demand what is, fairly speaking, not meaningfully possible, given the obvious, that the resources of energy and research — and time — available to meet the Nation's needs are not infinite.

Still different considerations are presented by the "alternatives" of increasing nuclear energy development, listed in the Statement, and possibilities, identified by the District Court as a critical omission, of federal legislation or administrative action freeing current offshore and state-controlled off-shore production from state market demand prorationing, or changing the Federal Power Commission's natural gas pricing policies.

The mere fact that an alternative requires legislative implementation does not automatically establish it as beyond the domain of what is required for discussion, particularly since NEPA was intended to provide a basis for consideration and choice by the decision-makers in the legislative as well as the executive branch. But the need for an overhaul of basic legislation certainly bears on the requirements of the Act. We do not suppose Congress intended an agency to devote itself to extended discussion of the environmental impact of alternatives so remote from reality as to depend on, say, the repeal of the anti-trust laws.

In the last analysis, the requirement as to alternatives is subject to a construction of reasonableness. . . . Where the environmental aspects of alternatives are readily identifiable by the agency, it is reasonable to state them. . . .

There is reason for concluding that NEPA was not meant to require detailed discussion of the environmental effects of "alternatives" put forward in comments when these effects cannot be readily ascertained and the alternatives are deemed only remote and speculative possibilities, in view of basic changes required in statutes and policies of other agencies — making them available, if at all, only after protracted debate and litigation not meaningfully compatible with the time-frame of the needs to which the underlying proposal is addressed.

A final word. In this as in other areas, the functions of courts and agencies, rightly understood, are not in opposition but in collaboration, toward achievement of the end prescribed by Congress. So long as the officials and agencies have taken the "hard look" at environmental consequences mandated by Congress, the court does not seek to impose unreasonable extremes or to interject itself within the area of discretion of the executive as to the choice of the action to be taken.

VERMONT YANKEE NUCLEAR POWER CORP. V. NATURAL RESOURCES DEFENSE COUNCIL, INC.

435 U.S. 519, 550-554 (1978)

[This decision dealt with several consolidated cases. The controversy dealing with the AEC's issuance of a license to Vermont Yankee to construct a nuclear power plant without individualized consideration of the environmental consequences of the spent nuclear fuel that the plant would generate were examined in the portion the *Vermont Yankee* decision excerpted supra, p. 858. The portion of the opinion excerpted here deals with the opposition by a local group, Saginaw, to the NRC's issuance of a license to Consumers Power Co. to construct two nuclear generating units. After the NRC issued a draft EIS on the proposed license, Saginaw submitted 119 environmental contentions, including 17 contending that energy conservation would be an environmentally superior alternative to constructing the plants. Saginaw did not appear or submit evidence at subsequent licensing hearings or file additional comments in respect of the evidence developed at the hearings. The NRC stated that it had an obligation to consider energy conservation alternatives which were "reasonably available," would curtail electricity demand to the point where the proposed plants would not be needed, and were susceptible of a reasonable degree of proof. It found that Saginaw had failed to meet the threshold burden of identifying such alternatives and offering some showing that they deserved serious consideration. The final EIS did not discuss energy conservation alternatives. The NRC granted the license. In accordance with the judicial review provisions of the Atomic Energy Act, Saginaw sought review in the D.C. Circuit Court of Appeals, which set aside the NRC's action for failure to prepare an EIS. *Aeschliman v. NRC*, 547 F.2d 622 (D.C. Cir. 1976). The Supreme Court reversed in an opinion by Justice Rehnquist.]

The Court of Appeals ruled that the Commission's "threshold test" for the presentation of energy conservation contentions was inconsistent with NEPA's basic mandate to the Commission. . . . The Commission, the court reasoned, is something more than an umpire who sits back and resolves adversary contentions at the hearing stage. . . . And when an intervenor's comments "bring 'sufficient attention to the issue to stimulate the Commission's consideration of it,' " the Commission must "undertake its own preliminary investigation of the proffered alternative sufficient to reach a rational judgment whether it is worthy of detailed consideration in the EIS. Moreover, the Commission must explain the basis for each conclusion that further consideration of a suggested alternative is unwarranted."

While the court's rationale is not entirely unappealing as an abstract proposition, as applied to this case we think it basically misconceives not only the scope of the agency's statutory responsibility, but also the nature of the administrative process, the thrust of the agency's decision, and the type of issues the intervenors were trying to raise.

There is little doubt that under the Atomic Energy Act of 1954, state public utility commissions or similar bodies are empowered to make the initial decision regarding the need for power. 42 U.S.C. §2021(k). The Commission's prime area of concern in the licensing context, on the other hand, is national security, public health, and safety. §§2132, 2133, 2201. And it is clear that the need, as the term is conventionally used, for the power was thoroughly explored in the hearings. Even the Federal Power Commission, which regulates sales in interstate commerce, 16 U.S.C. §824 et seq. (1976 ed.), agreed with Consumers Power's analysis of projected need.

NEPA, of course, has altered slightly the statutory balance, requiring "a detailed statement by the responsible official on . . . alternatives to the proposed action." 42 U.S.C. §4332(C). But, as should be obvious even upon a moment's reflection, the term "alternatives" is not self-defining. To make an impact statement something more than an exercise in frivolous boilerplate the concept of alternatives must be bounded by some notion of feasibility. As the Court of Appeals for the District of Columbia Circuit has itself recognized:

> There is reason for concluding that NEPA was not meant to require detailed discussion of the environmental effects of "alternatives" put forward in comments when these effects cannot be readily ascertained and the alternatives are deemed only remote and speculative possibilities. . . .

Natural Resources Defense Council v. Morton, 458 F.2d 827, 837-838 (1972). . . . Common sense also teaches us that the "detailed statement of alternatives" cannot be found wanting simply because the agency failed to include every alternative device and thought conceivable by the mind of man. Time and resources are simply too limited to hold that an impact statement fails because the agency failed to ferret out every possible alternative, regardless of how uncommon or unknown that alternative may have been at the time the project was approved.

With these principles in mind we now turn to the notion of "energy conservation," an alternative the omission of which was thought by the Court of Appeals to have been "forcefully pointed out by Saginaw in its comments on the draft EIS." . . . Again, as the Commission pointed out, "the phrase 'energy conservation' has a deceptively simple ring in this context. Taken literally, the phrase suggests a virtually limitless range of possible actions and developments that might, in one way or another, ultimately reduce projected demands for electricity from a particular proposed plant." . . . Moreover, as a practical matter, it is hard to dispute the observation that it is largely the events of recent years that have emphasized not only the need but also a large variety of alternatives for energy conservation. Prior to the drastic oil shortages incurred by the United States in 1973, there was little serious thought in most Government circles of energy conservation alternatives. Indeed, the Council on Environmental Quality did not promulgate regulations which even remotely suggested the need to consider energy conservation in impact statements until August 1, 1973. See 40 C.F.R. §1500.8(a)(4) (1977); 38 Fed. Reg. 20554 (1973). And even then the guidelines were not made applicable to draft and final statements filed with the Council before January 28, 1974. Id. at 20557, 21265. . . . All this occurred over a year and a half after the draft environmental statement for Midland had been prepared, and over a year after the final environmental statement had been prepared and the hearings completed.

We think these facts amply demonstrate that the concept of "alternatives" is an evolving one, requiring the agency to explore more or fewer alternatives as they become better known and understood. This was well understood by the Commission, which, unlike the Court of Appeals, recognized that the Licensing Board's decision had to be judged by the information then available to it. And judged in that light we have little doubt the Board's actions were well within the proper bounds of its statutory authority. Not only did the record before the agency give every indication that the project was actually needed, but also there was nothing before the Board to indicate to the contrary.

We also think the court's criticism of the Commission's "threshold test" displays a lack of understanding of the historical setting within which the agency action took place and of the nature of the test itself. In the first place, while it is true that NEPA places upon an agency the obligation to consider every significant aspect of the environmental impact of a proposed action, it is still incumbent upon intervenors who wish to participate to structure their participation so that it is meaningful, so that it alerts the agency to the intervenors' position and contentions. This is especially true when the intervenors are requesting the agency to embark upon an exploration of uncharted territory, as was the question of energy conservation in the late 1960's and early 1970's.

[C]omments must be significant enough to step over a threshold requirement of materiality before any lack of agency response or consideration
becomes of concern. The comment cannot merely state that a particular
mistake was made . . . ; it must show why the mistake was of possible
significance in the results . . .

Portland Cement Assn. v. Ruckelshaus, 486 F.2d 375, 394 (1973), *cert. denied sub nom. Portland Cement Corp. v. Administrator, EPA,* 417 U.S. 921
(1974). Indeed, administrative proceedings should not be a game or a
forum to engage in unjustified obstructionism by making cryptic and
obscure reference to matters that "ought to be" considered and then,
after failing to do more to bring the matter to the agency's attention,
seeking to have that agency determination vacated on the ground that
the agency failed to consider matters "forcefully presented." In fact,
here the agency continually invited further clarification of Saginaw's
contentions. Even without such clarification it indicated a willingness
to receive evidence on the matters. But not only did Saginaw decline to
further focus its contentions, it virtually declined to participate, indicating that it had "no conventional findings of fact to set forth" and that
it had not "chosen to search the record and respond to this proceeding
by submitting citations of matter which we believe were proved or dis-
proved."

   We also think the court seriously mischaracterized the Commission's "threshold test" as placing "heavy substantive burdens . . . on
intervenors. . . ." On the contrary, the Commission explicitly stated:

   We do not equate this burden with the civil litigation concept of a
   prima facie case, an unduly heavy burden in this setting. But the showing
   should be sufficient to require reasonable minds to inquire further.

We think this sort of agency procedure well within the agency's discretion.

   In sum, to characterize the actions of the Commission as "arbitrary
or capricious" in light of the facts then available to it as described at
length above, is to deprive those words of any meaning.

NOTES AND QUESTIONS

   1. Does *Vermont Yankee* overrule that part of *Calvert Cliffs* that holds
that an agency (there, the AEC's Atomic Safety Licensing Board) has
an affirmative obligation in making licensing decisions to consider the
environmental issues raised in an EIS even though they have not been
put in issue by any party? Or does it just elicit better information from
commenters? Will environmental groups now have to make greater use
of scientists and economists, rather than relying primarily on lawyers?

2. Does *Vermont Yankee* overrule the rulings in *Calvert Cliffs* and *NRDC v. Morton* that a licensing agency must consider environmental effects and alternatives that are primarily the responsibility of other agencies? Does it overrule *Scenic Hudson I?*

In fact, *Vermont Yankee* has not been read to relieve agencies of the obligation to consider alternatives to a proposed action, including alternatives beyond their authority to implement. See 40 C.F.R. §§1502.14, 1502.16 (1992). The alternative of no action — simply not undertaking the proposed action — must always be considered, 40 C.F.R. §1502.14(d) (1992). What other alternatives must be considered?

In *California v. Block*, 690 F.2d 753 (9th Cir. 1982), the court reviewed the EIS developed by the Forest Service on its decision allocating roadless areas in national forests between its three land use planning categories: wilderness, nonwilderness, and further planning. The proposed action would allocate 59 percent of the relevant lands to nonwilderness, 23 percent to wilderness, and 18 percent to further planning. The EIS considered eight alternatives. The highest wilderness allocation of any of the alternatives was 33 percent. The court held that the EIS was deficient because it failed to include an alternative that would allocate significantly more than a third of the lands to wilderness. The Forest Service had failed to explain why it had not considered such an alternative. The Forest Service argued that it had not directly selected the percentage allocations in the different alternatives. Rather, they had been generated by giving different relative weights to a number of land use criteria that were applied to the lands in question. The court found that the specific weights given to the criteria were not adequately explained or justified.

Consider, by contrast, *Citizens Against Burlington, Inc. v. Busey*, 938 F.2d 190 (D.C. Cir.), *cert. denied*, 112 S. Ct. 616 (1991), involving the FAA's approval of an expansion of the Toledo, Ohio, airport in order to accommodate a plan by Burlington Air Express to move its air cargo operations to Toledo from Fort Wayne, Indiana. The FAA's EIS considered only two alternatives: expanding the runway at Toldeo or no action. It justified the expansion decision by reference to the need to facilitate air cargo hubs, and Burlington's selection of Toledo. A local Toledo group challenged the EIS for failure to consider the alternative of Burlington remaining in Fort Wayne. The court of appeals, in an opinion by (then) Judge Clarence Thomas, found the EIS adequate on the ground that it was primarily the responsibility of the agency to define the relevant objective of the proposed action. It found that in this case the objective was to facilitate Burlington's desire to build a new hub and Toledo's desire for economic development. Expansion of the Toledo airport was therefore the only plausible means of advancing the agency's objectives. Other alternatives (other than no action) need not be considered. Judge Buckley dissented, criticizing the FAA and the majority for uncritically acquiescing in claims by Burlington and Toledo that Toledo was the only suitable hub for Burlington's operations. See Kirsch & Rippy, Defining the Scope of Alternatives in an EIS After Citizens Against Burlington, 21 Envtl. L. Rep. 10701 (Dec. 1991).

4.   TREATMENT OF UNCERTAINTY

BALTIMORE GAS & ELECTRIC CO. V. NATURAL RESOURCES DEFENSE COUNCIL

462 U.S. 87, 89-106 (1983)

Justice O'CONNOR delivered the opinion of the Court.

. . . As part of its generic rulemaking proceedings to evaluate the environmental effects of the nuclear fuel cycle for nuclear powerplants, the Nuclear Regulatory Commission (Commission) decided that licensing boards should assume, for purposes of NEPA, that the permanent storage of certain nuclear wastes would have no significant environmental impact and thus should not affect the decision whether to license a particular nuclear powerplant. We conclude that the Commission complied with NEPA and that its decision is not arbitrary or capricious within the meaning of [§706] of the Administrative Procedure Act (APA). . . .

I

The environmental impact of operating a light-water nuclear powerplant includes the effects of offsite activities necessary to provide fuel for the plant ("front end" activities), and of offsite activities necessary to dispose of the highly toxic and long-lived nuclear wastes generated by the plant ("back end" activities). The dispute in these cases concerns the Commission's adoption of a series of generic rules to evaluate the environmental effects of a nuclear powerplant's fuel cycle. At the heart of each rule is Table S-3, a numerical compilation of the estimated resources used and effluents released by fuel cycle activities supporting a year's operation of a typical light-water reactor.[29] [The Court noted

---

29. For example, the tabulated impacts include the acres of land committed to fuel cycle activities, the amount of water discharged by such activities, fossil fuel consumption, and chemical and radiological effluents (measured in curies), all normalized to the annual fuel requirement for a model 1,000 megawatt light-water reactor. . . .

that the NRC had adopted the Table S-3 measures of the potential fuel cycle environmental impacts of an additional nuclear power plant through notice and comment rulemaking. The procedural adequacy of the rulemaking procedures had been challenged by NRDC and ultimately upheld by the Supreme Court in *Vermont Yankee*, supra, p. 858. Meanwhile, the NRC had reopened the rulemaking proceedings, but ultimately adhered to the conclusions (1) that high-level nuclear spent fuel wastes from nuclear power plants would be solidified and buried in deep salt-bed repositories developed and operated by the federal government; (2) that during the initial period of between 6 and 20 years when the repository remained open for the reception of wastes, all radioactive gasses in the spent fuel would escape; (3) that when the repository was closed, there would be no further release of radioactive material and no harm to the environment; (4) that the numeric determination of the back-end environmental hazards of spent nuclear fuel specified, through the rulemaking, in Table S-3 on the basis of these assumptions should not be re-examined in the context of any individual licensing proceeding to approve a particular plant. See 44 Fed. Reg. 45, 362 (1979).] [The NRC] acknowledged that its ["zero-release"] assumption was uncertain because of the remote possibility that water might enter the repository, dissolve the radioactive materials, and transport them to the biosphere. Nevertheless, the Commission predicted that a bedded-salt repository would maintain its integrity, and found the evidence "tentative but favorable" that an appropriate site would be found. The Commission ultimately determined that any undue optimism in the assumption of appropriate selection and perfect performance of the repository is offset by the cautious assumption, reflected in other parts of the Table, that *all* radioactive gases in the spent fuel would escape during the initial 6- to 20-year period that the repository remained open, . . . and thus did not significantly reduce the overall conservatism of Table S-3. . . .

The Commission rejected the option of expressing the uncertainties in Table S-3 or permitting licensing boards, in performing the NEPA analysis for individual nuclear plants, to consider those uncertainties. It saw no advantage in reassessing the significance of the uncertainties in individual licensing proceedings. . . .

The NRDC and respondent State of New York petitioned for review of the final rule. The Court of Appeals consolidated these petitions for all purposes with the pending challenges to the initial and interim rules. By a divided panel, the court concluded that the Table S-3 rules were arbitrary and capricious and inconsistent with NEPA because the Commission had not factored the consideration of uncertainties surrounding the zero-release assumption into the licensing process in such a manner that the uncertainties could potentially affect the outcome of any decision to license a particular plant. . . .

II

Congress in enacting NEPA . . . did not require agencies to elevate environmental concerns over other appropriate considerations. See *Stryckers' Bay Neighborhood Council v. Karlen,* 444 U.S. 223, 227 (1980) (*per curiam*). Rather, it required only that the agency take a "hard look" at the environmental consequences before taking a major action. See *Kleppe v. Sierra Club,* 427 U.S. 390, 410, n.21 (1976). The role of the courts is simply to ensure that the agency has adequately considered and disclosed the environmental impact of its actions and that its decision is not arbitrary or capricious. See generally *Citizens to Preserve Overton Park, Inc. v. Volpe,* 401 U.S. 402, 415-417 (1971).

In its Table S-3 rule here, the Commission has determined that the probabilities favor the zero-release assumption, because the Nation is likely to develop methods to store the wastes with no leakage to the environment. The NRDC did not challenge and the Court of Appeals did not decide the reasonableness of this determination, and no party seriously challenges it here. The Commission recognized, however, that the geological, chemical, physical, and other data it relied on in making this prediction were based, in part, on assumptions which involve substantial uncertainties. Again, no one suggests that the uncertainties are trivial or the potential effects insignificant if time proves the zero-release assumption to have been seriously wrong. After confronting the issue, though, the Commission has determined that the uncertainties concerning the development of nuclear waste storage facilities are not sufficient to affect the outcome of any individual licensing decision.

It is clear that the Commission, in making this determination, has made the careful consideration and disclosure required by NEPA. The sheer volume of proceedings before the Commission is impressive. Of far greater importance, the Commission's Statement of Consideration announcing the final Table S-3 rule shows that it has digested this mass of material and disclosed all substantial risks. 44 Fed. Reg. 45367-45369 (1979). The Statement summarizes the major uncertainty of long-term storage in bedded-salt repositories, which is that water could infiltrate the repository as a result of such diverse factors as geologic faulting, a meteor strike, or accidental or deliberate intrusion by man. The Commission noted that the probability of intrusion was small, and that the plasticity of salt would tend to heal some types of intrusions. The Commission also found the evidence "tentative but favorable" that an appropriate site could be found. Table S-3 refers interested persons to staff studies that discuss the uncertainties in greater detail. Given this record and the Commission's statement, it simply cannot be said that the Commission ignored or failed to disclose the uncertainties surrounding its zero-release assumption.

Congress did not enact NEPA, of course, so that an agency would contemplate the environmental impact of an action as an abstract exercise. Rather, Congress intended that the "hard look" be incorporated as part of the agency's process of deciding whether to pursue a particular federal action. It was on this ground that the Court of Appeals faulted the Commission's action, for failing to allow the uncertainties potentially to "tip the balance" in a particular licensing decision. As a general proposition, we can agree with the Court of Appeals' determination that an agency must allow all significant environmental risks to be factored into the decision whether to undertake a proposed action. We think, however, that the Court of Appeals erred in concluding that the Commission had not complied with this standard.

As *Vermont Yankee* made clear, NEPA does not require agencies to adopt any particular internal decisionmaking structure. Here, the agency has chosen to evaluate generically the environmental impact of the fuel cycle [through notice and comment rulemaking] and inform individual licensing boards, through the Table S-3 rule, of its evaluation. The generic method chosen by the agency is clearly an appropriate method of conducting the "hard look" required by NEPA. See *Vermont Yankee*, 435 U.S., at 535, n.13. The environmental effects of much of the fuel cycle are not plant specific, for any plant, regardless of its particular attributes, will create additional wastes that must be stored in a common long-term repository. Administrative efficiency and consistency of decision are both furthered by a generic determination of these effects without needless repetition of the litigation in individual proceedings, which are subject to review by the Commission in any event. . . .

The Commission's decision to affix a zero value to the environmental impact of long-term storage would violate NEPA only if the Commission acted arbitrarily and capriciously in deciding generically that the uncertainty was insufficient to affect any individual licensing decision. In assessing whether the Commission's decision is arbitrary and capricious, it is crucial to place the zero-release assumption in context. Three factors are particularly important. First is the Commission's repeated emphasis that the zero-release assumption — and, indeed, all of the Table S-3 rule — was made for a limited purpose. . . . [T]he purpose of the rule was not to evaluate or select the most effective long-term waste disposal technology or develop site selection criteria. A separate and comprehensive series of programs has been undertaken to serve these broader purposes.[30] . . .

---

30. In response to *Minnesota v. NRC*, 195 U.S. App. D.C. 234, 602 F.2d 412 (1979), the Commission has initiated a "waste confidence" proceeding to consider the most recent evidence regarding the likelihood that nuclear waste can be safely disposed of and when that, or some other offsite storage solution, can be accomplished. 44 Fed. Reg. 61372 et seq. (1979). See id., at 45363. The recently enacted Nuclear Waste Policy Act of 1982, Pub. L. 97-425, 96 Stat.

Second, the Commission emphasized that the zero-release assumption is but a single figure in an entire Table, which the Commission expressly designed as a risk-averse estimate of the environmental impact of the fuel cycle. It noted that Table S-3 assumed that the fuel storage canisters and the fuel rod cladding would be corroded before a repository is closed and that all volatile materials in the fuel would escape to the environment. Given that assumption, and the improbability that materials would escape after sealing, the Commission determined that the overall Table represented a conservative (i.e., inflated) statement of environmental impacts. It is not unreasonable for the Commission to counteract the uncertainties in postsealing releases by balancing them with an overestimate of presealing releases. A reviewing court should not magnify a single line item beyond its significance as only part of a larger Table.

Third, a reviewing court must remember that the Commission is making predictions, within its area of special expertise, at the frontiers of science. When examining this kind of scientific determination, as opposed to simple findings of fact, a reviewing court must generally be at its most deferential. See, e.g., *Industrial Union Dept. v. American Petroleum Institute,* 448 U.S. 607, 656 (1980) (plurality opinion); id., at 705-706 (Marshall, J., dissenting).

With these three guides in mind, we find the Commission's zero-release assumption to be within the bounds of reasoned decisionmaking required by the APA. . . .

We also find significant the separate views of Commissioners Bradford and Gilinsky. These Commissioners expressed dissatisfaction with the zero-release assumption and yet emphasized the limited purpose of the assumption and the overall conservatism of Table S-3. Commissioner Bradford characterized the bedded-salt repository as a responsible working assumption for NEPA purposes and concurred in the zero-release figure because it does not appear to affect Table S-3's overall conservatism. 44 Fed. Reg. 45372 (1979). Commissioner Gilinsky was more critical of the entire Table, stating that the Commission should confront directly whether it should license any nuclear reactors in light of the problems of waste disposal, rather than hide an affirmative conclusion to this issue behind a table of numbers. He emphasized that the "waste confidence proceeding," see n. 30 supra, should provide the Commission an appropriate vehicle for a thorough evaluation of the problems involved in the Government's commitment to a waste disposal solution. For the limited purpose of individual licensing pro-

---

2201, 42 U.S.C. §10101 et seq. (1982 ed.), has set up a schedule for identifying site locations and a funding mechanism for development of permanent waste repositories. The Environmental Protection Agency has also proposed standards for future waste repositories, 47 Fed. Reg. 58196 et seq. (1982).

ceedings, however, Commissioner Gilinsky found it "virtually inconceivable" that the Table should affect the decision whether to license, and characterized as "naive" the notion that the fuel cycle effluents could tip the balance in some cases and not in others. 44 Fed. Reg. 45374 (1979).

In sum, we think that the zero-release assumption — a policy judgment concerning one line in a conservative Table designed for the limited purpose of individual licensing decisions — is within the bounds of reasoned decisionmaking. It is not our task to determine what decision we, as Commissioners, would have reached. Our only task is to determine whether the Commission has considered the relevant factors and articulated a rational connection between the facts found and the choice made. . . . *Citizens to Preserve Overton Park, Inc. v. Volpe*, 401 U.S. 402 (1971). Under this standard, we think the Commission's zero-release assumption, within the context of Table S-3 as a whole, was not arbitrary and capricious.

[The Court noted that Table S-3 describes radioactive and other releases in terms of the amounts released, and did not determine the health or other social consequences of such releases. The Court agreed with the NRC that the rule did not preclude consideration of such consequences in individual licensing decisions, and that, so interpreted, the rule and the Commission's procedural arrangements were consistent with NEPA.]

NOTES AND QUESTIONS

1. The NRC prepared an EIS in connection with its adoption of the rule incorporating Table S-3 as a generic determination of the environmental consequences of the spent nuclear fuel generated by a typical new reactor. As a result, the EIS prepared by the Commission in licensing a particular new reactor will not independently examine the environmental consequences of the waste fuel from that reactor. Cf. 40 C.F.R. §1508.28 (1992). Can this arrangement be squared with the language of §102(2)(C) of the NEPA? Does *Baltimore Gas* overrule that portion of *Calvert Cliffs* that requires agencies to engage in a fine-tuned, case by case balancing of the environmental and other considerations associated with a particular plant? Note that *Calvert Cliffs* itself involved review of agency rulemaking.

2. A decade after the *Baltimore Gas* decision, the problem of disposing of high level radioactive waste from utility reactors is still far from solved. After a tortuous administrative and legislative process, Congress in 1987 adopted a rider to an appropriations bill designating Yucca Mountain, located on federal land in Nevada, as the sole site to be evaluated by DOE as a repository for such wastes. The suitability of

the site has been sharply questioned. DOE studies of Yucca Mountain's characteristics will continue for many years. Nevada has resisted through litigation and other legal maneuvers evaluation or use of the site. Meanwhile, storage space for spent fuel at utility reactors is approaching capacity. Construction of an interim above ground storage facility seems inevitable. Does this history show that *Baltimore Gas* was wrongly decided? That NEPA is not a suitable tool for resolving the nuclear waste problem? Consider that the waste to be generated by any new utility reactors would equal only a tiny fraction of the waste generated to date.

3. In preparing an EIS, agencies have an affirmative duty to gather available information and use available research methodologies to describe the environmental effects of the proposed action and alternatives. In doing so, an agency must acknowledge and characterize uncertainties that cannot be resolved on the basis of present knowledge, and set forth differences in scientific views about likely effects. The extent to which it must elaborate on uncertainties is, however, subject to a "rule of reason." See, e.g., *Scientists Inst. for Pub. Info., Inc. v. Atomic Energy Commn.*, 481 F.2d 1079, 1092 (D.C. Cir. 1973).

4. Are there circumstances in which an agency must postpone a decision pending development of additional information to resolve uncertainty? The CEQ regulations dealing with "Incomplete or unavailable information," 40 C.F.R. §1502.22 (1992), suggest that there may be:

> When an agency is evaluating reasonably foreseeable significant adverse effects on the human environment in an environmental impact statement and there is incomplete or unavailable information, the agency shall always make clear that such information is lacking.
>
> (a) If the incomplete information relevant to reasonably foreseeable significant adverse impacts is essential to a reasoned choice among alternatives and the overall costs of obtaining it are not exorbitant, the agency shall include the information in the environmental impact statement.

But at least one court has held that, while an agency must weigh the risks of proceeding without developing additional information, an agency may decide that such risks are outweighed by the benefits of proceeding promptly with a project; courts may not insist that the project be delayed pending the development of more information. *State of Alaska v. Andrus*, 580 F.2d 465, 473-474 (D.C. Cir.), *vacated in other respects sub nom. Western Oil & Gas Assn. v. Alaska*, 439 U.S. 922 (1978), *citing Kleppe v. Sierra Club*, 427 U.S. 390, 410 n.21 (1976). Is the CEQ regulation consistent with *Baltimore Gas & Electric*?

5. There has been considerable controversy as to how, in the face of substantial uncertainty, an agency should characterize the more seri-

ous potential adverse effects of its proposed action. As originally promulgated in 1978, 40 C.F.R. §1502.22 also provided that:

> (b) If (1) the information relevant to adverse impacts is essential to a reasoned choice among alternatives and is not known and the overall costs of obtaining it are exorbitant or (2) the information relevant to adverse impacts is important to the decision and the means to obtain it are not known (e.g., the means for obtaining it are beyond the state of the art) the agency shall weigh the need for the action against the risk and severity of possible adverse impacts were the action to proceed in the face of uncertainty. If the agency proceeds, it shall include a worst case analysis and an indication of the probability or improbability of its occurrence.

43 Fed. Reg. 55,997 (1978). What exactly is a "worst case" analysis? In *Sierra Club v. Sigler*, 695 F.2d 957 (5th Cir. 1983), Sierra Club challenged a Corps of Engineers decision to grant permits for a channel dredging project that would allow supertankers access to Galveston Bay, which serves as an important wildlife habitat. Sierra Club challenged the failure in the EIS to describe, as a "worst case," the effects of a total loss of oil cargo from a supertanker as a result of an accident. The district court held that such an analysis was not required because it could not be performed; available modelling techniques could only predict the pattern of oil dispersion for the first 24 hours following a spill. Moreover, the effects of any such spill would depend to a great extent on its exact location, tides and currents, weather, and the time of year. The district court concluded that the possible consequences of all these variables were too "remote" to make analysis of such consequences anything more than "guesswork" based on "uninformed speculation and conjecture."

The Court of Appeals reversed, finding the EIS deficient. It noted wide agreement that a total cargo loss could possibly occur. It found that the uncertainties involved in performing an analysis of the effects of such an event were not as great as the district court had thought. For example, the 24-hour dispersion model could be supplemented by available information on tides and current in the Bay. Moreover, it noted that CEQ's Forty Most Asked Questions Concerning CEQ's NEPA Regulations, 46 Fed. Reg. 18026, 18032 (1981), had interpreted §1502.22(b) as requiring "analysis of a low probability / catastrophic impact event" as well as "events of higher probability but less drastic impact." A total loss of cargo was precisely the sort of "catastrophic impact event" that should be the subject of worst case analysis. To refuse to perform such analysis because it might involve some uncertainties would contradict the regulations' endorsement of worst case analysis as an appropriate means of characterizing uncertainty.

Query: under the court's approach, must a worst case analysis be performed on a collision between two supertankers, both of whom lose all cargo?[31]

6. With *Sigler,* compare *San Luis Obispo Mothers for Peace v. National Regulatory Commn.,* 751 F.2d 1287 (D.C. Cir. 1984), *vacated in part,* 760 F.2d 1320 (D.C. Cir. 1985) (en banc), upholding the NRC's refusal to issue a supplemental EIS for the Diablo Canyon, California, nuclear plant to describe and consider the consequences of a severe class 9 nuclear accident resulting in breach of the reactor containment structures and release of large amounts of radioactive material to the general environment. The court upheld the NRC's conclusion that the probability of a class 9 accident was too low — one in a billion or less per year for a large reactor — to warrant inclusion in an EIS. The court said that: "There is a point at which the probability of an occurrence may be so low as to render it almost totally unworthy of consideration," quoting Carolina Study Group v. United States, 510 F.2d 796, 799 (D.C. Cir. 1975). It noted that the NRC's methodology in estimating probabilities had not been challenged, and further stated that "the accident at Three Mile Island" did not establish "that the probability of a class nine accident with significant environmental consequences is anything but very small."

7. How should uncertainty be dealt with in an EA? Does the existence of a very small probability of serious adverse impacts establish that the effects of a proposed action are significant, requiring preparation of an EIS, even if the much more likely consequences are not significant? What if it is unknown whether potentially serious effects might occur?

In *Foundation for N. Am. Wild Sheep v. United States Dept. of Agric.,* 681 F.2d 1172 (9th Cir. 1982), the Agriculture Department issued a FONSI on a decision to allow mining vehicles to use a Forest Service road in a remote area inhabited by Bighorn sheep. The EA did not contain information on the possible effects of the vehicle traffic on the sheeps' reproductive and other behavior. The court of appeals held that an EIS must be prepared, based on the Ninth Circuit rule that EISs must be prepared on actions that "may" significantly affect the environment, observing that the function of an EIS is to "obviate the need for . . . speculation by insuring that available data is gathered and analyzed prior to the implementation of the proposed action." Id. at 1179. Note that the Supreme Court's subsequent 1989 decision in *Marsh v. Oregon Natural Resources Council,* infra p. 989, apparently overruled the Ninth Circuit's requirement of an EIS for actions that "may"

---

31. Would the EIS in *Baltimore Gas & Electric* pass muster under §1502.22, as interpreted in *Sigler?* The regulation did not become effective until after the *Baltimore Gas & Electric* EIS had been completed.

significantly affect the environment. If so, is *North American Wild Sheep* still good law?

Compare *City of New York v. United States Dept. of Transp.*, 715 F.2d 732 (2d Cir. 1983), the basis for Threshold Problem II, supra p. 933, upholding DOT's decision not to prepare an EIS on rules it had adopted for the shipment by truck of nuclear fuel. The Second Circuit, following an interpretation of NEPA that requires an EIS only if the proposed action will — not "may" — significantly impact the environment, concluded that DOT's decision "cannot be said to be an abuse of discretion." Id. at 75. Judge Oakes entered a strong dissent with respect to the mass accident issue. He argued that in light of the severity of the catastrophic accidents projected in the studies:

> . . . [it] seems almost nonsense to talk of no "significant" impact. "Worst-case" accidents have a way of occurring — from Texas City to the Hyatt Regency at Kansas City, from the Tacoma Bridge to the Greenwich, Connecticut, I-95 bridge, from the Beverly Hills in Southgate, Kentucky, to the Cocoanut Grove in Boston, Massachusetts, and from the Titanic to the DC-10 at Chicago to the I-95 toll-booth crash and fire. . . . [I]t is the *potential* environmental effect that is important. In my opinion, the effect of the "worst-case" accident alone would be sufficiently substantial to justify an EIS, since the effect of [the DOT rule] is to permit the transportation of nuclear waste and other materials through the most densely populated city in the United States, when "credible" accidents may occur.

Id. at 753. Judge Oakes also questioned whether, given very limited experience, it could reasonably be concluded that the possibility of a catastrophic accident was as low as DOT claimed.

The majority, in an opinion by Judge Newman, responded to Judge Oakes as follows:

> Our dissenting colleague appears to take the view that the very existence of the "worst case" possibility would be sufficient to require preparation of an EIS, regardless of the infinitesimal probability that the "worst case" accident will happen. We do not doubt the general proposition that "worst cases" do occur. Planes crash, and the Titanic sank. What we reject is an automatic rule requiring preparation of an EIS for every action that has any possibility, however remote, of causing serious accidental injury. Such a rule would routinely require an EIS for federal actions, since it is hard to imagine any agency action involving people or equipment that is not subject to some estimatable risk of causing serious accidental injury. In this case, reasonable minds may differ as to whether or not the gravity of the "worst case" accident or other less serious accidents, discounted by their improbability, presents an overall risk of sufficient significance to warrant an EIS. So long as that choice falls within the range of reasonable dispute, an agency's informed decision not to require an EIS is neither arbitrary nor capricious.

Id. at 752.

8. In 1986, CEQ amended 40 C.F.R. §1502.22(b) to provide as follows:

> (b) If the information relevant to reasonably foreseeable significant adverse impacts cannot be obtained because the overall costs of obtaining it are exorbitant or the means to obtain it are not known, the agency shall include within the environmental impact statement:
>
> (1) A statement that such information is incomplete or unavailable; (2) a statement of the relevance of the incomplete or unavailable information to evaluating reasonably foreseeable significant adverse impacts on the human environment; (3) a summary of existing credible scientific evidence which is relevant to evaluating the reasonably foreseeable significant adverse impacts on the human environment, and (4) the agency's evaluation of such impacts based upon theoretical approaches or research methods generally accepted in the scientific community. For the purposes of this section, "reasonably foreseeable" includes impacts which have catastrophic consequences, even if their probability of occurrence is low, provided that the analysis of the impacts is supported by credible scientific evidence, is not based on pure conjecture, and is within the rule of reason.

ROBERTSON v. METHOW VALLEY CITIZENS COUNCIL

490 U.S. 332, 349-354 (1989)

[The plaintiffs challenged the Forest Service's issuance of special use permits for private development of the Early Winters Ski Resort on Sandy Butte in the Okanogan National Forest in Washington. The court of appeals found the Service's EIS inadequate for two reasons. First, the state game department had predicted a 50 percent loss in the mule deer herd. The EIS adopted a 15 percent estimate, but admitted that the off-site effects of allowing development of the resort were uncertain because they depended on the extent of private development. The court of appeals held that the EIS should have included a worst-case analysis of the potential adverse effects of unrestricted private development. Second, the EIS recommended and relied on a wide range of possible mitigation measures to reduce the impact, including locating runs, ski-lifts and roads so as to minimize interference with wildlife, restricting access to selected roads during the fawning season, various rezoning options, acquiring conservation easements and land tracts along the deer's migration path, and regulating driving speed to minimize road kills. However, those measures, many of which would require action by nonfederal agencies, had not been finally decided on, developed or tested. The court held that the EIS was inadequate because it did not contain a complete mitigation plan to protect wildlife, and also lacked a plan to protect air quality. The Supreme Court reversed in an opinion by Justice Stevens.]

Simply by focusing the agency's attention on the environmental consequences of a proposed project, NEPA ensures that important effects will not be overlooked or underestimated only to be discovered after resources have been committed or the die otherwise cast. Moreover, the strong precatory language of §101 of the Act and the requirement that agencies prepare detailed impact statements inevitably bring pressure to bear on agencies "to respond to the needs of environmental quality." 115 Cong. Rec. 40425 (1969) (remarks of Sen. Muskie).

Publication of an EIS, both in draft and final form, also serves a larger informational role. It gives the public the assurance that the agency "has indeed considered environmental concerns in its decision making process,". . . , and, perhaps more significantly, provides a springboard for public comments. . . .

. . . Although these procedures are almost certain to affect the agency's substantive decision, it is now well settled that NEPA itself does not mandate particular results, but simply prescribes the necessary process. . . .

If the adverse environmental effects of the proposed action are adequately identified and evaluated, the agency is not constrained by NEPA from deciding that other values outweigh the environmental costs. . . . In this case, for example, it would not have violated NEPA if the Forest Service, after complying with the Act's procedural prerequisites, had decided that the benefits to be derived from downhill skiing at Sandy Butte justified the issuance of a special use permit, notwithstanding the loss of 15 percent, 50 percent, or even 100 percent of the mule deer herd. Other statutes may impose substantive environmental obligations on federal agencies, but NEPA merely prohibits uninformed — rather than unwise — agency action.

To be sure, one important ingredient of an EIS is the discussion of steps that can be taken to mitigate adverse environmental consequences.[32] The requirement that an EIS contain a detailed discussion

---

32. CEQ regulations define "mitigation" to include:

"(a)   Avoiding the impact altogether by not taking a certain action or parts of an action.
"(b)   Minimizing impacts by limiting the degree or magnitude of the action and its implementation.
"(c)   Rectifying the impact by repairing, rehabilitating, or restoring the affected environment.
"(d)   Reducing or eliminating the impact over time by preservation and maintenance operations during the life of the action.
"(e)   Compensating for the impact by replacing or providing substitute resources or environments." 40 C.F.R. §1508.20 (1987).

of possible mitigation measures flows from both the language of the Act and, more expressly, from CEQ's implementing regulations. [Citing 40 C.F.R. §§1502.16(h), 1505.2(c), and 1508.25(b).]

There is a fundamental distinction, however, between a requirement that mitigation be discussed in sufficient detail to ensure that environmental consequences have been fairly evaluated, on the one hand, and a substantive requirement that a complete mitigation plan be actually formulated and adopted, on the other. In this case, the off-site effects on air quality and on the mule deer herd cannot be mitigated unless nonfederal government agencies take appropriate action. Since it is those state and local governmental bodies that have jurisdiction over the area in which the adverse effects need be addressed and since they have the authority to mitigate them, it would be incongruous to conclude that the Forest Service has no power to act until the local agencies have reached a final conclusion on what mitigating measures they consider necessary. Even more significantly, it would be inconsistent with NEPA's reliance on procedural mechanisms — as opposed to substantive, result-based standards — to demand the presence of a fully developed plan that will mitigate environmental harm before an agency can act. . . .

We thus conclude that the Court of Appeals erred, first, in assuming that "NEPA requires that 'action be taken to mitigate the adverse effects of major federal actions,' " and, second, in finding that this substantive requirement entails the further duty to include in every EIS "a detailed explanation of specific measures which *will* be employed to mitigate the adverse impacts of a proposed action," . . .

The Court of Appeals also concluded that the Forest Service had an obligation to make a "worst case analysis" if it could not make a reasoned assessment of the impact of the . . . project on the mule deer herd. . . .

[The Court summarized the original version of 40 C.F.R. §1502.22(b) as adopted in 1977, and the amendments made in 1986.]

The Court of Appeals recognized that the "worst case analysis" regulation has been superseded, yet held that "[t]his rescission . . . does not nullify the requirement . . . since the regulation was merely a codification of prior NEPA case law." This conclusion, however, is erroneous in a number of respects. Most notably, review of NEPA case law reveals that the regulation, in fact, was not a codification of prior judicial decisions. The cases cited by the Court of Appeals ultimately rely on the Fifth Circuit's decision in *Sierra Club v. Sigler*, 695 F.2d 957 (1983). *Sigler*, however, simply recognized that the "worst case analysis" regulation codified the "judicially created principl[e]" that an EIS must "consider the probabilities of the occurrence of any environmental effects it discusses." Id. at 970-971. As CEQ recognized at the time it superseded the regulation, case law prior to the adoption of the "worst case analysis" provision did require agencies to describe environmental impacts even in the face of substantial uncertainty, but did not require that this obligation necessarily be met through the mechanism of a "worst case analysis." CEQ's abandonment of the "worst case analysis" provision, therefore, is not inconsistent with any previously established judicial interpretation of the statute. . . . CEQ explained that by requiring that an EIS focus on reasonably foreseeable impacts, the new regulation "will generate information and discussion on those consequences of greatest concern to the public and of greatest relevance to the agency's decision, rather than distorting the decision making process by overemphasizing highly speculative harms." In light of this well-considered basis for the change, the new regulation is entitled to substantial deference.

QUESTIONS

1. What justifies CEQ's amendment of §1502.22(b): The difficulties in defining the "worst case?" The problems in analyzing worst-case consequences in the face of the almost inevitably large uncertainties of characterizing the consequences of very low-probability events? The chance that a worst case focus would mislead administrators and the public by overemphasizing very low probability events and distracting attention from the more likely range of less severe impacts?

2. Is the holding in *Sigler* still good law?

5.   WHEN IS A SUPPLEMENTAL EIS REQUIRED?

a.   New Information

MARSH V. OREGON NATURAL RESOURCES COUNCIL

490 U.S. 360, 378-385 (1989)

[In 1962, Congress authorized the Army Corps of Engineers to construct three dams in the Rogue River basin in southwest Oregon. The Rogue is one of the nation's premier trout streams. Two dams were built. In 1971, the Corps completed an EIS on the third dam, the Elk Creek Dam, and began acquiring 26,000 acres of land and relocating residents, a road, and utilities. In 1975, the Corps prepared a supplemental EIS, which it termed the Final Environmental Impact Statement Supplement, or FEISS, on the effects of the Elk Creek Dam on turbidity. Suspended or dissolved matter released as a result of the dam could make the water turbid — cloudy or opaque — reducing its value as a fish habitat and fishing ground. In 1982, the Corps decided to proceed with construction of the dam, subject to the necessary congressional appropriations; these were approved in 1985. In 1985, local environmental groups filed suit in district court to enjoin construction of the Elk Creek Dam on the ground, among others, that new information in two documents regarding the potential effects of the dam on water quality required a second supplemental EIS.

The Court described these documents as follows:]

The first of the documents is the so-called "Cramer memorandum," an intra-office memorandum prepared on February 21, 1985 by two scientists employed by ODFW. The Cramer Memorandum, in turn, relied on a draft ODFW study describing the effects of the Lost Creek Dam on fish production. The second document is actually a series of maps prepared in 1982 by SCS to illustrate the composition of soil near the Elk Creek shoreline. The information was provided to the Corps for use in managing the project. Although respondents contend that the maps contained data relevant to a prediction of the dam's impact on downstream turbidity, the maps do not purport to shed any light on that subject. Nor do they purport to discuss any conditions that had changed since the FEISS was completed in 1980.

[The district court concluded that the Corps' decision not to prepare a further supplemental EIS was "reasonable" because it was entitled to discount the significance of the concerns expressed in the documents, based on the judgment of the Corps and independent experts. A divided Ninth Circuit Court of Appeals reversed; the majority concluded that the two documents brought to light "significant new information" concerning turbidity, water temperature, and epizootic fish disease; that this information, although "not conclusive," is "probably accurate"; and that the Corps' experts failed to evaluate the new information with sufficient care. Judge Wallace, writing in dissent, held that it was reasonable for the Corps to have concluded, based on its own expert evaluation, that the information contained in the ODFW document was inaccurate and the information contained in the SCS document was insignificant.

By 1989, when the case reached the Supreme Court, construction of the dam was about one-third completed. The Supreme Court reversed the Ninth Circuit's decision, in an opinion by Justice Stevens.]

The subject of post-decision supplemental environmental impact statements is not expressly addressed in NEPA. Preparation of such statements, however, is at times necessary to satisfy the Act's "action-forcing" purpose. NEPA does not work by mandating that agencies achieve particular substantive environmental results. Rather NEPA [is designed to focus] government and public attention on the environmental effects of proposed agency action. . . . By so focusing agency attention, NEPA ensures that the agency will not act on incomplete information, only to regret its decision after it is too late to correct. . . . It would be incongruous with this approach to environmental protection, and with the Act's manifest concern with preventing uninformed action, for the blinders to adverse environmental effects, once unequivocally removed, to be restored prior to the completion of agency action simply because the relevant proposal has received initial approval. As we explained in *TVA v. Hill*, 437 U.S. 153, 188, n.34, "NEPA cases have generally required agencies to file environmental impact statements when the remaining governmental action would be environmentally 'significant.' "

This reading of the statute is supported by Council on Environmental Quality (CEQ) and Corps regulations, both of which make plain that at times supplementation is required. The CEQ regulations, which we have held are entitled to substantial deference, see . . . *Andrus v. Sierra Club*, 442 U.S. 347, 358, . . . impose a duty on all federal agencies to prepare supplements to either draft or final EIS's if there "are significant new circumstances or information relevant to environmental concerns and bearing on the proposed action or its impacts." [40 C.F.R. §1502(9)(c)(1)(ii).] Similarly, the Corps' own NEPA implementing regulations require the preparation of a supplemental EIS if "new significant impact information, criteria or circumstances relevant to environmental considerations impact on the recommended plan or proposed action."

The parties are in essential agreement concerning the standard that governs an agency's decision whether to prepare a supplemental EIS. They agree that an agency should apply a "rule of reason," and the cases they cite in support of this standard explicate this rule in the same basic terms. These cases make clear that an agency need not supplement an EIS every time new information comes to light after the EIS is finalized. To require otherwise would render agency decisionmaking intractable, always awaiting updated information only to find the new information outdated by the time a decision is made. On the other hand, and as the Government concedes, NEPA does require that agencies take a "hard look" at the environmental effects of their planned action, even after a proposal has received initial approval. . . . Application of the "rule of reason" thus turns on the value of the new information to the still pending decisionmaking process. . . . If there remains "major Federal actio[n]" to occur, and if the new information is sufficient to show that the remaining action will "affec[t] the quality of the human environment" in a significant manner or to a significant extent not already considered, a supplemental EIS must be prepared.

The parties disagree, however, on the standard that should be applied by a court that is asked to review the agency's decision. The Government argues that the reviewing court need only decide whether the agency decision was "arbitrary and capricious," whereas respondents argue that the reviewing court must make its own determination of reasonableness to ascertain whether the agency action complied with the law. In determining the proper standard of review, we look to §10(e) of the Administrative Procedure Act (APA), 5 U.S.C. §706, which empowers federal courts to "hold unlawful and set aside agency action, findings, and conclusions" if they fail to conform with any of six specified standards. We conclude that review of the narrow question before us of whether the Corps' determination that the FEISS need not be supplemented should be set aside is controlled by the "arbitrary and capricious" standard of §706(2)(A).

[The Court rejected Respondent environmental groups' contention that the question whether given effects are "significant" under NEPA is a question of law, and that accordingly the reviewing court should independently decide whether the Corps acted reasonably in concluding that information in the documents did not establish environmental effects that were "significant" and not previously considered.]

The question presented for review in this case is a classic example of a factual dispute the resolution of which implicates substantial agency expertise. Respondents' claim that the Corps' decision not to file a second supplemental EIS should be set aside primarily rests on the contentions that the new information undermines conclusions contained in the FEISS, that the conclusions contained in the ODFW memorandum and the SCS survey are accurate, and that the Corps' expert review of the new information was incomplete, inconclusive, or inaccurate. The dispute thus does not turn on the meaning of the term "significant" or on an application of this legal standard to settled facts. Rather, resolution of this dispute involves primarily issues of fact. Because analysis of the relevant documents "require a high level of technical expertise," we must defer to "the informed discretion of the responsible federal agencies." *Kleppe v. Sierra Club*, 427 U.S. 390, 412, ... Under these circumstances, we cannot accept respondents' supposition that review is of a legal question and that the Corps' decision "deserves no deference." Accordingly, as long as the Corps' decision not to supplement the FEISS was not "arbitrary or capricious," it should not be set aside.[33]

---

33. Respondents note that several Courts of Appeals, including the Court of Appeals for the Ninth Circuit as articulated in this and other cases, have adopted a "reasonableness" standard of review, and argue that we should not upset this well-settled doctrine. This standard, however, has not been adopted by all of the Circuits. Moreover, as some of these courts have recognized, the difference between the "arbitrary and capricious" and "reasonableness" standards is not of great pragmatic consequence. Accordingly, our decision today will not require a substantial reworking of long-established NEPA law.

As we observed in *Citizens to Preserve Overton Park, Inc. v. Volpe* . . . in making the factual inquiry concerning whether an agency decision was "arbitrary or capricious," the reviewing court "must consider whether the decision was based on a consideration of the relevant factors and whether there has been a clear error of judgment." This inquiry must "be searching and careful," but "the ultimate standard of review is a narrow one." Ibid. When specialists express conflicting views, an agency must have discretion to rely on the reasonable opinions of its own qualified experts even if, as an original matter, a court might find contrary views more persuasive. On the other hand, in the context of reviewing a decision not to supplement an EIS, courts should not automatically defer to the agency's express reliance on an interest in finality without carefully reviewing the record and satisfying themselves that the agency has made a reasoned decision based on its evaluation of the significance — or lack of significance — of the new information. . . .

The significance of the Cramer Memorandum and the SCS survey is subject to some doubt. Before respondents commenced this litigation in October 1985, no one had suggested that either document constituted the kind of new information that made it necessary or appropriate to supplement the FEISS. Indeed, the record indicates that the Corps was not provided with a copy of the Cramer Memorandum until after the lawsuit was filed. Since the probative value of that document depends largely on the expert qualification of its authors, the fact that they did not see fit to promptly apprise the Corps of their concern — or to persuade ODFW to do so — tends to discount the significance of those concerns. . . .

The Court of Appeals attached special significance to two concerns discussed in the Cramer Memorandum: the danger that an increase in water temperature downstream during fall and early winter will cause an early emergence and thus reduce survival of spring chinook fry and the danger that the dam will cause high fish mortality from an epizootic disease. Both concerns were based partly on fact and partly on speculation.

[In response to the plaintiffs' invocation of the two documents, the Corps prepared a Supplemental Information Request ("SIR") explaining why it did not credit the documents' concerns. The SIR's response to the Cramer Memorandum] acknowledged that the "biological reasoning is sound and has been recognized for some time," but then explained why the concern was exaggerated. The SIR stressed that because the model employed by ODFW had not been validated, its predictive capability was uncertain. Indeed, ODFW scientists subsequently recalculated the likely effect of a one degree centigrade increase in temperature, adjusting its estimate of a 60 to 80 percent loss downward to between 30 and 40 percent. Moreover, the SIR supplied a variable missing in the Cramer Memorandum, suggesting that the Elk

Creek Dam would, in most cases, either reduce or leave unchanged the temperature of the Rogue River. Discernible increases were only found in July, August, and December of the study year, and even during those months the maximum temperature increase was only 0.6 degrees centigrade. Ibid. Finally, the SIR observed that the Cramer Memorandum failed to take into account the dam's beneficial effects, including its ability to reduce peak downstream flow during periods of egg incubation and fry rearing and its ability to reduce outflow temperature through use of the multiport structure. Given those positive factors, the Corps concluded that any adverse effects of the 0.6 degree temperature increase can be offset.

With respect to the second concern emphasized by the Court of Appeals, the Cramer Memorandum reported the fact that "an unprecedented 76% of the fall chinook in 1979 and 32% in 1980 were estimated to have died before spawning" and then speculated that the Lost Creek Dam, which had been completed in 1977, was a contributing cause of this unusual mortality. The Corps responded to this by pointing out that the absence of similar epizootics after the closure of the Applegate Dam and the evidence of pre-spawning mortality in the Rogue River prior to the closing of the Lost Creek Dam were inconsistent with the hypothesis suggested in the Cramer Memorandum. In addition, the Corps noted that certain diseased organisms thought to have been the cause of the unusually high mortality rates were not found in the outflow from the Lost Creek Dam.

In thus concluding that the Cramer Memorandum did not present significant new information requiring supplementation of the FEISS, the Corps carefully scrutinized the proffered information. Moreover, in disputing the accuracy and significance of this information, the Corps did not simply rely on its own experts. Rather, two independent experts hired by the Corps to evaluate the ODFW study on which the Cramer Memorandum was premised found significant fault in the methodology and conclusions of the study. We also think it relevant that the Cramer Memorandum did not express the official position of ODFW. . . .

[The Court also concluded that the SCS survey did not require a supplemental EIS. The concerns raised by the survey — that soil composition at the Elk Creek Dam was different from that estimated in the FEISS, and that logging and construction in the Elk Creek Water Shed had resulted in higher turbidity than forecasted in the FEISS — were met by other data and analysis invoked by the Corps tending to show that any increases in turbidity due to such factors were insignificant or temporary.]

There is little doubt that if all of the information contained in the Cramer Memorandum and SCS survey was both new and accurate, the Corps would have been required to prepare a second supplemental

EIS. It is also clear that, regardless of its eventual assessment of the significance of this information, the Corps had a duty to take a hard look at the proffered evidence. However, having done so and having determined based on careful scientific analysis that the new information was of exaggerated importance, the Corps acted within the dictates of NEPA in concluding that supplementation was unnecessary. Even if another decisionmaker might have reached a contrary result, it was surely not "clear error of judgment" for the Corps to have found that the new and accurate information contained in the documents was not significant and that the significant information was not new and accurate. As the SIR demonstrates, the Corps conducted a reasoned evaluation of the relevant information, and reached a decision that, although perhaps disputable, was not "arbitrary or capricious."

NOTES AND QUESTIONS

1. Which is the more significant aspect of the Court's opinion? That it embraced the more deferential "arbitrary and capricious" standard for reviewing the Corps' decision that a supplemental EIS was required? Or the extent to which it engaged in a "searching and careful" review of the Cramer Memorandum and SCS study and the reasons given by the Corps for discounting their significance?[34]

2. Note that the Court frames the issue as whether "the new information is sufficient to show that the remaining action will affec[t] the quality of the human environment in a significant manner." Does this effectively overrule the prior Ninth Circuit rule, see supra, p. 916, requiring preparation of an EIS if a proposed action *may* have significant effects? While acknowledging the Supreme Court's correction of the standard of review from "reasonableness" to "arbitrary and capricious" as applicable to decisions not to prepare initial, as well as supplemental, EISs, subsequent Ninth Circuit cases have continued to frame the issue as whether the action "may" have significant effects. See, e.g., *Inland Empire Pub. Lands Council v. Schultz*, 992 F.2d 977, 980 (9th Cir. 1993) (if environmental plaintiffs have " 'alleged facts which, if true, show that the proposed project may significantly degrade some human environmental factor' . . . an EIS must be prepared")(quoting *Sierra Club v. United States Forest Service*, 843 F.2d 1190, 1193 (9th Cir. 1988)). The

---

34. For different evaluations of the decision, see Rossman, NEPA: Not So Well At Twenty, 20 Envtl. L. Rep. 10174 (May 1990); Mandelker, NEPA Alive and Well: The Supreme Court Takes Two, 19 Envtl. L. Rep. 10385 (Sept. 1989). The general issue of supplemental EISs is discussed in Blomquist, Supplemental Environmental Impacts Statements Under NEPA: A Conceptual Synthesis and Critique of Existing Legal Approaches to Environmental and Technological Changes, 8 Temple Envtl. L. & Tech. J. 1 (1989).

application of the standard may, however, be more significant than the framing of the issue: In *Inland Empire,* the court deferred to the Forest Service's "scientific methodology," since it was not arbitrary and capricious, notwithstanding that its plan would involve logging beyond the "threshold of concern" established in Forest Service models of potential adverse effects from deforestation, and the court's own statement that "[s]ignificant environmental effects certainly are possible" under the agency's plan. See id. at 980-982. See also *Greenpeace Action v. Franklin,* 982 F.2d 1342, 1352 n.11 (9th Cir. 1992) (while the existence of a "substantial dispute" may require preparation of an EIS, case law dictates only that the "existence of uncertainty" must be indicated in an EIS, if prepared, and not that uncertainty itself necessitates an EIS).

b.   Tiering

Agencies from time to time adopt programmatic EISs. Will a program EIS avoid the need for subsequent EISs on the specific projects that make up the program? This is known as the issue of "tiering." CEQ regulations provide that:

> "Tiering" refers to the coverage of general matters in broader environmental impact statements (such as national program or policy statements) with subsequent narrower statements or environmental analyses (such as regional or basinwide program statements or ultimately site-specific statements) incorporating by reference the general discussions and concentrating solely on the issues specific to the statement subsequently prepared. . . .

40 C.F.R. §1508.28 (1992). The subsequent EAs or EISs can, of course, rely on the initial programmatic EISs.

When is a second-tier, project-specific, EIS required? Since *Marsh v. Oregon NRC,* courts have held that the same "arbitrary and capricious" test resolves this question. For example, in *Headwaters, Inc. v. Bureau of Land Management,* 914 F.2d 1174 (1990), *reh'g denied,* 940 F.2d 435 (9th Cir. 1991), the Ninth Circuit upheld the BLM's refusal to prepare a site-specific EIS on a timber sale that was encompassed in a broader Timber Management Plan for which it had filed an EIS seven years earlier. Applying the "arbitrary and capricious" standard, the court found that, inter alia, new evidence that spotted owls inhabited the site did not constitute "significant new circumstances" such as would require a supplemental EIS under 40 C.F.R. §1502.9(c)(ii), since the original EIS had "specifically adverted to [that] possibility." Id. at 1178.

F.   THE SCOPE OF SUBSTANTIVE REVIEW

STRYCKER'S BAY NEIGHBORHOOD COUNCIL, INC. V. KARLEN

444 U.S. 223, 223-231 (1980)

Per Curiam

The protracted nature of this litigation is perhaps best illustrated by the identity of the original federal defendant, "George Romney, Secretary of the Department of Housing and Urban Development." At the center of this dispute is the site of a proposed low-income housing project to be constructed on Manhattan's Upper West Side. In 1962 the New York City Planning Commission (the Commission), acting in conjunction with the United States Department of Housing and Urban Development (HUD), began formulating a plan for the renewal of 20 square blocks known as the "West Side Urban Renewal Area" (WSURA) through a joint effort on the part of private parties and various government agencies. As originally written, the plan called for a mix of 70% middle-income housing and 30% low-income housing and designated the site at issue here as the location of one of the middle-income projects. In 1969, after substantial progress toward completion of the plan, local agencies in New York determined that the number of low-income units proposed for WSURA would be insufficient to satisfy an increased need for such units. In response to this shortage the Commission amended the plan to designate the site as the future location of a high-rise building containing 160 units of low-income housing. HUD approved this amendment in December 1972.

Meanwhile, in October 1971 the Trinity Episcopal School Corp. (Trinity), which had participated in the plan by building a combination school and middle-income housing development at a nearby location, sued in the United States District Court for the Southern District of New York to enjoin the Commission and HUD from constructing low-income housing on the site. The present respondents, Roland N. Karlen, Alvin C. Hudgins, and the Committee of Neighbors to Insure a Normal Urban Environment (CONTINUE), intervened as plaintiffs, while petitioner Strycker's Bay Neighborhood Council, Inc., intervened as a defendant.

The District Court entered judgment in favor of petitioners. See *Trinity Episcopal School Corp. v. Romney,* 387 F. Supp. 1044 (SDNY 1974). It concluded, inter alia, that petitioners had not violated the National Environmental Policy Act of 1969 (NEPA), 83 Stat. 852, 42 U.S.C. §4321 et seq.

On respondents' appeal, the Second Circuit affirmed all but the District Court's treatment of the NEPA claim. See *Trinity Episcopal School*

Corp. v. Romney, 523 F.2d 88 (CA2 1975). While the Court of Appeals agreed with the District Court that HUD was not required to prepare a full-scale environmental impact statement under §102(2)(C) of NEPA, . . . it held that HUD had not complied with §102(2)(F), which requires an agency to "study, develop, and describe appropriate alternatives to recommended courses of action in any proposal which involves unresolved conflicts concerning alternative uses of available resources." 42 U.S.C. §102(2)(E). . . . According to the Court of Appeals, any consideration by HUD of alternatives to placing low-income housing on the site "was either highly limited or non-existent." . . . Citing the "background of urban environmental factors" behind HUD's decision, the Court of Appeals remanded the case, requiring HUD to prepare "[a] statement of possible alternatives, the consequences thereof and the facts and reasons for and against. . . ." The statement was not to reflect "HUD's concept or the Housing Authority's views as to how these agencies would choose to resolve the city's low income group housing situation," but rather was to explain "how within the framework of the Plan its objective of economic integration can best be achieved with a minimum of adverse environmental impact."

On remand, HUD prepared a lengthy report entitled "Special Environmental Clearance." After marshaling the data, the report asserted that, "while the choice of site 30 for development as a 100 percent low-income project has raised valid questions about the potential social environmental impacts involved, the problems associated with the impact on social fabric and community structures are not considered so serious as to require that this component be rated as unacceptable." Special Environmental Clearance, at 42. The last portion of the report incorporated a study wherein the Commission evaluated nine alternative locations for the project and found none of them acceptable. While HUD's report conceded that this study may not have considered all possible alternatives, it credited the Commission's conclusion that any relocation of the units would entail an unacceptable delay of two years or more. According to HUD, "[m]easured against the environmental costs associated with the minimum two-year delay, the benefits seem insufficient to justify a mandated substitution of sites." Id., at 54.

After soliciting the parties' comments on HUD's report, the District Court again entered judgment in favor of petitioners. See *Trinity Episcopal School Corp v. Harris*, 145 F. Supp. 204 (S.D.N.Y. 1978). The court was "impressed with [HUD's analysis] as being thorough and exhaustive," 445 F. Supp. at 209-210, and found that "HUD's consideration of the alternatives was neither arbitrary nor capricious"; on the contrary, "[i]t was done in good faith and in full accordance with the law." Id., at 220.

On appeal, the Second Circuit vacated and remanded again. The appellate court focused upon that part of HUD's report where the agency considered and rejected alternative sites, and in particular upon HUD's reliance on the delay such a relocation would entail. The Court of Appeals purported to recognize that its role in reviewing HUD's decision was defined by the Administrative Procedure Act (APA), 5 U.S.C. §706(2)(A), which provides that agency actions should be set aside if found to be "arbitrary, capricious, an abuse of discretion or otherwise not in accordance with law. . . ." Ibid. Additionally, however, the Court of Appeals looked to "[t]he provisions of NEPA" for "the substantive standards necessary to review the merits of agency decisions. . . ." 590 F.2d, at 43. The Court of Appeals conceded that HUD had "given 'consideration' to alternatives" to redesignating the site. 590 F.2d, at 44. Nevertheless, the court believed that " 'consideration' is not an end in itself." . . . Concentrating on HUD's finding that development of an alternative location would entail an unacceptable delay, the appellate court held that such delay could not be "an overriding factor" in HUD's decision to proceed with the development. . . . According to the court, when HUD considers such projects, "environmental factors, such as crowding low-income housing into a concentrated area, should be given determinative weight." . . . The Court of Appeals therefore remanded the case to the District Court, instructing HUD to attack the shortage of low-income housing in a manner that would avoid the "concentration" of such housing on Site 30. . . .

In *Vermont Yankee Nuclear Power Corp. v. NRDC*, 435 U.S. 519, 558, we stated that NEPA, while establishing "significant substantive goals for the Nation," imposes upon agencies duties that are "essentially procedural." As we stressed in that case, NEPA was designed "to insure a fully-informed and well-considered decision," but not necessarily "a decision the judges of the Court of Appeals or of this Court would have reached had they been members of the decisionmaking unit of the agency." *Vermont Yankee* cuts sharply against the Court of Appeals' conclusion that an agency, in selecting a course of action, must elevate environmental concerns over other appropriate considerations. On the contrary, once an agency has made a decision subject to NEPA's procedural requirements, the only role for a court is to insure that the agency has considered the environmental consequences; it cannot "interject itself within the area of discretion of the executive as to the choice of the action to be taken." *Kleppe v. Sierra Club*, 427 U.S. 390, 410, n.21. . . .[35]

In the present case there is no doubt that HUD considered the

---

35. If we could agree with the dissent that the Court of Appeals held that HUD had acted "arbitrarily" in redesignating the site for low-income housing, we might also agree that plenary review is warranted. But the District Court expressly concluded that HUD had not acted arbitrarily or capriciously and our reading of the opinion of the Court of Appeals satisfies us that it did not overturn that finding. Instead, the appellate court required HUD to elevate

environmental consequences of its decision to redesignate the proposed site for low-income housing. NEPA requires no more. The judgment of the Court of Appeals is therefore
    Reversed.

    Mr. Justice MARSHALL, dissenting:
    The issue raised by these cases is far more difficult than the *per
curiam* opinion suggests. . . .
    In the present case, the Court of Appeals did not "substitute its
judgment for that of the agency as to the environmental consequences
of its actions," [quoting the majority opinion] for HUD in its Special
Environmental Clearance Report acknowledged the adverse environmental consequences of its proposed action: "the choice of Site 30 for
development as a 100 percent low-income project has raised valid questions about the potential social environmental impacts involved." These
valid questions arise from the fact that 68% of all public housing units
would be sited on only one crosstown axis in this area of New York City.
As the Court of Appeals observed, the resulting high concentration of
low-income housing would hardly further racial and economic integration. The environmental "impact on social fabric and community structures" was given a B rating in the Report, indicating that from this
perspective the project is "questionable" and ameliorative measures are
"mandated." The Report lists 10 ameliorative measures necessary to
make the project acceptable. The Report also discusses two alternatives,
Sites 9 and 41, both of which are the appropriate size for the project
and require "only minimal" amounts of relocation and clearance. Concerning Site 9 the Report explicitly concludes that "[f]rom the standpoint of social environmental impact, this location would be superior
to Site 30 for the development of low-rent public housing." The sole
reason for rejecting the environmentally superior site was the fact that
if the location were shifted to Site 9, there would be a projected delay
of two years in the construction of the housing.
    The issue before the Court of Appeals, therefore, was whether
HUD was free under NEPA to reject an alternative acknowledged to be
environmentally preferable solely on the ground that any change in
sites would cause delay. This was hardly a "peripheral issue" in the case.
Whether NEPA, which sets forth "significant substantive goals," *Vermont
Yankee Nuclear Power Corp. v. NRDC,* 435 U.S., at 558, permits a projected
two-year time difference to be controlling over environmental superiority is by no means clear. Resolution of the issue, however, is certainly
within the normal scope of review of agency action to determine if it is

---

environmental concerns over other, admittedly legitimate, considerations. Neither NEPA nor the APA provides any support for such a reordering of priorities
by a reviewing court.

arbitrary, capricious, or an abuse of discretion. The question whether HUD can make delay the paramount concern over environmental superiority is essentially a restatement of the question whether HUD in considering the environmental consequences of its proposed action gave those consequences a "hard look," which is exactly the proper question for the reviewing court to ask. *Kleppe v. Sierra Club*, 427 U.S., at 410, n.21. . . .

The issue of whether the Secretary's decision was arbitrary or capricious is sufficiently difficult and important to merit plenary consideration in this Court. Further, I do not subscribe to the Court's apparent suggestion that *Vermont Yankee* limits the reviewing court to the essentially mindless task of determining whether an agency "considered" environmental factors even if that agency may have effectively decided to ignore those factors in reaching its conclusion. Indeed, I cannot believe that the Court would adhere to that position in a different factual setting. Our cases establish that the arbitrary or capricious standard prescribes a "searching and careful" judicial inquiry designed to ensure that the agency has not exercised its discretion in an unreasonable manner. *Citizens To Preserve Overton Park, Inc. v. Volpe*, 401 U.S. 402, 416. . . . Believing that today's summary reversal represents a departure from that principle, I respectfully dissent.

It is apparent to me that this is not the type of case for a summary disposition. We should at least have a plenary hearing.

NOTES AND QUESTIONS

1. The essential holding of *Strycker's Bay* appears to be that NEPA does not impose any constraints on an agency's authority and discretion to choose among relevant alternative courses of action, other than requiring an agency to describe and discuss their environmental consequences and provide a reasoned response to comments and criticisms raised during the EIS process. In particular, it does not direct agencies to give any extra or preferred weight to environmental factors in choosing among alternatives. See fn. 35 to the Court's opinion, supra p. 999. Is this a sound interpretation of the statute? Inevitable? What about all of the provisions of NEPA other than §102(2)(C)? Does the legislative background of NEPA and the generality of its language, discussed supra pp. 907-908, support the Court's interpretation? Consider also *Calvert Cliffs* and its emphasis on the EIS provision in NEPA as the focus of judicial efforts to ensure its implementation. Did *Calvert Cliffs* start NEPA interpretation on a path that leads straight to *Strycker's Bay*? Is there a viable and appropriate "substantive" interpretation of NEPA? What about the notion, derived from "least restrictive alternative" analysis in the civil liberties area, that NEPA be interpreted to require selec-

tion of that alternative that is least environmentally damaging and still consistent with accomplishing the agency's basic statutory mission?

2. Is *Strycker's Bay* a result of defining the relevant "environment" too broadly to include social and economic factors in addition to effects on the ecosystem? See pp. 918-921, supra.

3. The Court's insistence in *Strycker's Bay* that NEPA does not constrain or control agencies' discretion or authority to choose among relevant alternatives was followed in subsequent Court decisions that we have already examined, including *Baltimore Gas* (NRC may conclude that environmental effects associated with nuclear waste generated by a given reactor are too minor to affect licensing decision) and *Methow Valley* (NEPA does not require agency to adopt measures to mitigate adverse environmental effects of proposed action).

4. Despite *Strycker's Bay* and subsequent Court decisions, it would be error to conclude that NEPA has no substantive implications at all. NEPA §102(1) provides that "to the fullest extent possible," the "policies, regulations, and public laws of the United States shall be interpreted and administered in accordance with" the policies set forth in NEPA. This provision authorizes agencies to take into account the full range of environmental considerations and consequences in making decisions, unless squarely precluded by the particular statute under which they operate. Recall that one of the reasons for adoption of NEPA were court decisions holding that the AEC was precluded from considering the effects of thermal discharges of cooling water by nuclear plants because the AEC's statutory responsibility was focused on radioactive hazards. See, e.g., *New Hampshire v. Atomic Energy Commn.*, 406 F.2d 170 (1st Cir.), *cert. denied*, 395 U.S. 962 (1969).

The precise extent to which NEPA expands agency statutory authority to include environmental considerations as a basis for decision is, however, unclear. In *Environmental Defense Fund v. Mathews*, 410 F. Supp. 336 (D.D.C. 1976), the court struck down an FDA regulation, 21 C.F.R. §6.1(a)(3) (1992), which provided that

> A determination of adverse environmental impact has no legal or regulatory effect and does not authorize the Commissioner to take or refrain from taking any action under the laws he administers. The Commission may take or refrain from taking action on the basis of a determination of an adverse environmental impact only to the extent that such action is independently authorized by the law he administers.

As the court observed, "the amending regulation limits the grounds on which the Commissioner of FDA can base any action to those expressly provided for in the Food, Drug and Cosmetic Act . . . or in other statutes which FDA administers." 410 F. Supp. at 338. The FDA contended that its statutes provide that it should act in accordance with specified criteria, and "to the extent that NEPA demands considerations of additional criteria, it is in direct conflict with those statutes." Id. The court, however, rejected the assertion of conflict. While the FDA's statutes listed certain factors that it should consider, it did not exclude other factors, or compel action if the listed factors were met. The court concluded:

> This is not to say that NEPA requires FDA's substantive decisions to favor environmental protection over other relevant factors. Rather, it means that NEPA requires FDA to *consider* environmental factors in its decision-making process and supplements its existing authority to permit it to act on those considerations. It permits FDA to base a decision upon environmental factors, when balanced with other relevant considerations. Since the contested regulation prohibits FDA from acting on the basis of such environmental considerations, it is directly contrary to the letter and spirit of NEPA.

Id.

While *EDF v. Mathews* arose in the abstract context of general FDA regulations, courts have held that NEPA authorizes agencies to take particular actions on environmental grounds notwithstanding the failure of the agency's organic statute to grant such authority. See *Grindstone Butte Project v. Kleppe*, 638 F.2d 100 (9th Cir. 1981) (Interior Department may impose terms and conditions to protect environment in irrigation rights of way grants despite failure of 1891 enabling act to grant such authority); *Public Serv. Co. of New Hampshire v. United States Nuclear Regulatory Commn.*, 582 F.2d 77 (1st Cir.), *cert. denied*, 439 U.S. 1046 (1978) (Nuclear Regulatory Commission must consider nonradiological environmental impacts in light of NEPA, and may condition nuclear power plant permits on environmentally sensitive routing of off-site transmission lines). But see *National Resources Defense Council v. Environmental Protection Agency*, 859 F.2d 156, 169-170 (D.C. Cir. 1988) (EPA may not impose environmental conditions unrelated to water quality in an NPDES permit for an exisiting source). See also 40 C.F.R. §1500.6 (1992).

5. Another potential substantive implication of NEPA follows from the fact that it directs agencies to consider the environmental consequences of their actions and in some cases, as just discussed, supplements agencies' statutory authority to authorize and require consideration of environmental factors that they would otherwise lack power to take into account. The APA, §706, authorizes courts to strike down agency actions as "arbitrary, capricious, an abuse of discretion, and otherwise not in accordance with law." Courts' application of this standard has generally taken the form of review to determine whether the agency has taken a "hard look" at relevant alternatives and decisional factors. The court determines whether the agency has taken the requisite "hard

look" by examining its decision, its explanation for the decision, its response to criticisms of the decision, and the underlying record. The Supreme Court has acknowledged that this "hard look" review is appropriate in APA review of agency decisions involving NEPA issues. See, e.g., *Baltimore Gas,* supra, p. 976. If the agency's decision fails to identify relevant environmental impacts, fails to identify and discuss alternatives, fails to respond adequately to criticisms, or is based on determinations not supported by the record, the decision may be deemed arbitrary and capricious in a "procedural" sense: The agency has failed to justify its choice on the basis of reasoned decisionmaking. The normal remedy in case of such a failure is to remand the matter to the agency for further proceedings. In NEPA cases, remand contemplates preparation of an EIS, where none has been prepared, or preparation of a modified EIS, when the one prepared is deficient. But, whether in NEPA cases or other APA cases, the agency on remand is free to reach the same result as before, so long as it provides a reasoned justification for its decision. Nonetheless, might a judicially monitored requirement of reasoned decision indirectly constrain the agency's choice of action?

In a small number of APA cases, arbitrary and capricious review may involve another, more directly substantive aspect. On occasion, reviewing courts hold that an agency's balancing of discretionary factors in choosing a given outcome was so arbitrary and irrational that it may not choose that outcome, regardless of the possible rationale advanced. In such cases, the court does not remand to the agency, but reverses the agency's decision outright. Such cases are quite rare, for they involve the court in substituting its judgment for that of the agency on discretionary considerations of policy. Nonetheless, courts occasionally do so. See S. Breyer & R. Stewart, Administrative Law and Regulatory Policy 361-362 (3d ed. 1992). Because NEPA requires agencies to include environmental factors among those it must weigh in exercising discretion, could it provide the basis for a court to conclude that an agency's failure to give any weight to environmental factors in reaching a given result was substantively arbitrary? This conclusion would not be based on an interpretation of NEPA as giving environmental values any special or preferred weight, but the court's overall judgment that the balance struck by the agency among relevant factors, including environmental factors made relevant by NEPA, was irrational. There is, however, no judicial decision to survive appellate review that has found an agency's disregard of environmental values recognized by NEPA to be substantively irrational in the sense described.

G.   SPECIAL ISSUES OF STANDING AND REMEDY IN NEPA CASES

1.   STANDING

Courts have held that NEPA is essentially a procedural statute, aimed at forcing preparation of EISs in order to ensure "full disclosure" to the public as well as government decisionmakers of the environmental effects of proposed government actions. Given this information-based interpretation of NEPA, can an individual or environmental organization obtain standing to bring suit against an agency's failure to prepare an EIS by alleging an interest in the information that would be generated by the EIS?

In *Scientists' Inst. for Pub. Infor., Inc. v. AEC*, 481 F.2d 1079 (D.C. Cir. 1973), discussed supra, p. 927, the court held that the AEC must prepare an EIS on the Liquid Metal Fast Breeder Reactor (LMFBR) program, designed to recycle plutonium from used nuclear reactor fuel. In a footnote, the court stated in dicta that SIPI had informational standing:

> With respect to appellant's standing to sue, we think appellant has alleged sufficient "injury in fact" to satisfy the standing test recently set out by the Supreme Court in *Sierra Club v. Morton*, 405 U.S. 727 (1972). . . .
>
> The activities of the plaintiff organization in this case, as described in a memorandum submitted to the District Court on the standing issue, include making available to the public scientific information relevant to important social issues and stimulating and informing public discussion of the scientific aspects of questions of public policy. The AEC's decision not to provide an impact statement on the overall LMFBR program has an adverse effect on these organizational activities by limiting appellant's ability to provide the public information on the LMFBR program. Appellant thus has alleged and shown more than the "mere 'interest in a problem'" held insufficient in *Sierra Club*. See 405 U.S. at 739. Any other approach to standing in the context of suits to ensure compliance with NEPA for long-range Government programs not yet resulting in injury to discrete economic, aesthetic or environmental interests would insulate administrative action from judicial review, prevent the public interest from being protected through the judicial process, and frustrate the policies Congress expressed in NEPA, a result clearly inconsistent with the Supreme Court's approach to standing. [Citing *Sierra Club*.]

481 F.2d at 1087 n.29. Subsequent decisions of the D.C. Circuit Court of Appeals seemed to acknowledge the principle of informational standing, but in those cases the plaintiffs had also established a substantive interest in the environmental consequences of the prepared action.

See, e.g., *National Wildlife Fed. v. Hodel*, 839 F.2d 694 (D.C. Cir. 1988) (federal delegation to state authorities of authority to approve strip mining plans).

In *Lujan v. National Wildlife Federation*, 497 U.S. 871 (1990), discussed supra, p. 832, plaintiffs had alleged, among other matters, that the Interior Department's land withdrawal review "program" had been carried out without preparation of an EIS, resulting in injury to the organization's ability "to provide adequate information and opportunity for public participation" with respect to the program. The Court ruled that, even assuming that this amounted to a cognizable "injury," plaintiffs could not prevail because the "program" was not a specific "agency action" for which review could be had under the Administrative Procedure Act. Id. at 890-894. The D.C. Circuit followed this reasoning in *Foundation on Economic Trends v. Lyng*, 943 F.2d 79 (D.C. Cir. 1991), upholding the dismissal of a group's NEPA action seeking to require preparation of an EIS in connection with the Agriculture Department's alleged "germplasm preservation program." The court read *Lujan v. NWF* to cast great doubt on the nature of "informational standing," but decided the case on the ground that plaintiffs had not identified specific agency action as the basis for review. See id. at 84-86. Judge Buckley, dissenting, found that the Department's issuance of a FONSI stating that its "activities in the area of germplasm collection, maintenance, evaluation, and distribution" did not involve significant environmental effects amounted to reviewable "agency action," and that plaintiffs' informational standing should be recognized. Id. at 88.

In NEPA and other cases, environmental groups and other plaintiffs have also claimed standing to challenge an agency's failure to follow required decisionmaking procedures. For example, in *City of Davis v. Coleman*, 521 F.2d 661 (9th Cir. 1975), the City challenged the federal Department of Transportation's failure to prepare an EIS on a nearby highway interchange. The court found that the City had standing by virtue of its claims that industrial development spurred by construction of the interchange might pollute the City's water supply and disrupt its "controlled growth" planning efforts. But it also found that the City had standing on the following basis:

> [If] a NEPA plaintiff's standing depends on "proof" that the challenged federal project *will* have particular environmental effects, we would in essence be requiring that the plaintiff conduct the same environmental investigation that he seeks in his suit to compel the agency to undertake. . . . It is the federal agency, not environmental action groups or local government, which is required by NEPA to produce an EIS.
>
> The procedural injury implicit in agency failure to prepare an

EIS — the creation of a risk that serious environmental impacts will be overlooked — is itself a sufficient "injury in fact" to support standing, provided this injury is alleged by a plaintiff having a sufficient geographical nexus to the site of the challenged project that he may be expected to suffer whatever environmental consequences the project may have.

Id. at 671.

In *Defenders of Wildlife v. Lujan*, 911 F.2d 117 (8th Cir. 1990), the court of appeals held that plaintiffs, an environmental organization and its members, had standing based on procedural injury because the Secretary of Interior had failed to adopt regulations holding the Endangered Species Act ("ESA") to apply to federal government actions outside the United States, with the result that federal agencies sponsoring development projects abroad did not consult with Interior's Fish and Wildlife Service (FWS) regarding the potential effects of such projects on endangered species. This theory of standing in the ESA context was, however, rejected by the Supreme Court on appeal, reversing the Eighth Circuit's decision:

LUJAN V. DEFENDERS OF WILDLIFE

112 S. Ct. 2130, 2142-2143 (1992)

Justice SCALIA delivered the opinion of the Court.

[The main body of the opinion, addressing other asserted bases for standing, appears supra, p. 828.]

The Court of Appeals found that respondents had standing for an additional reason: because they had suffered a "procedural injury." The so-called "citizen-suit" provision of the ESA provides, in pertinent part, that "any person may commence a civil suit on his own behalf . . . to enjoin any person, including the United States and any other governmental instrumentality or agency . . . who is alleged to be in violation of any provision of this chapter." 16 U.S.C. §1540(g). The court held that, because §7(a)(2) requires inter-agency consultation, the citizen-suit provision creates a "procedural righ[t]" to consultation in all "persons" — so that *anyone* can file suit in federal court to challenge the Secretary's (or presumably any other official's) failure. 911 F.2d, at 121-122. To understand the remarkable nature of this holding one must be clear about what it does *not* rest upon: This is not a case where plaintiffs are seeking to enforce a procedural requirement the disregard of which could impair a separate concrete interest of theirs (e.g., the procedural requirement for a hearing prior to denial of their license application or the procedural requirement for an environmental impact statement before a federal facility is constructed next door to them).[36] . . . Nor, finally, is it the unusual case in which Congress has created a concrete private interest in the outcome of a suit against a private party for the government's benefit, by providing a cash bounty for the victorious plaintiff. Rather, the court held that the injury-in-fact requirement had been satisfied by congressional conferral upon *all* persons of an abstract, self-contained, noninstrumental "right" to have the Executive observe the procedures required by law. We reject his view.[37]

We have consistently held that a plaintiff raising only a generally available grievance about government — claiming only harm to his and every citizen's interest in proper application of the Constitution and laws, and seeking relief that no more directly and tangibly benefits him than it does the public at large — does not state an Article III case or controversy. . . .

In *United States v. Richardson,* 418 U.S. 166 (1974), we dismissed for lack of standing a taxpayer suit challenging the Government's failure to disclose the expenditures of the Central Intelligence Agency, in alleged violation of the constitutional requirement, Art. I, §9, cl. 7, that "a regular Statement and Account of the Receipts and Expenditures of all public Money shall be published from time to time." We held that such a suit rested upon an impermissible "generalized grievance," and was inconsistent with "the framework of Article III" because "the impact on [plaintiff] is plainly undifferentiated and common to all members of the public." *Richardson,* supra, at 171, 176-177. And in *Schlesinger v. Reservists Committee to Stop the War,* 418 U.S. 208 (1974), we dismissed for the same reasons a citzen-taxpayer suit contending that it was a violation of the Incompatibility Clause, Art. I, §6, cl. 2, for Members of Congress to hold commissions in the military Reserves. We said that the

---

36. There is this much truth to the assertion that "procedural rights" are special: The person who has been accorded a procedural right to protect his concrete interests can assert that right without meeting all the normal standards for redressability and immediacy. Thus, under our case-law, one living adjacent to the site for proposed construction of a federally licensed dam has standing to challenge the licensing agency's failure to prepare an Environmental Impact Statement, even though he cannot establish with any certainty that the Statement will cause the license to be withheld or altered, and even though the dam will not be completed for many years. (That is why we do not rely, in the present case, upon the Government's argument that, *even if* the other agencies were obliged to consult with the Secretary, they might not have followed his advice.) What respondents' "procedural rights" argument seeks, however, is quite different from this: standing for persons who have no concrete interests affected — persons who live (and propose to live) at the other end of the country from the dam.

37. . . . We *do not* hold that an individual cannot enforce procedural rights; he assuredly can, so long as the procedures in question are designed to protect some threatened concrete interest of his that is the ultimate basis of his standing. . . .

challenged action, "standing alone, would adversely affect only the generalized interest of all citizens in constitutional governance. . . ."

To be sure, our generalized-grievance cases have typically involved Government violation of procedures assertedly ordained by the Constitution rather than the Congress. But there is absolutely no basis for making the Article III inquiry turn on the source of the asserted right. Whether the courts were to act on their own, or at the invitation of Congress, in ignoring the concrete injury requirement described in our cases, they would be discarding a principle fundamental to the separate and distinct constitutional role of the Third Branch — one of the essential elements that identifies those "Cases" and "Controversies" that are the business of the courts rather than of the political branches. "The province of the court," as Chief Justice Marshall said in *Marbury v. Madison,* 5. U.S. (1 Cranch) 137, 170, 2 L. Ed. 60 (1803) "is, solely, to decide on the rights of individuals." Vindicating the public interest (including the public interest in government observance of the Constitution and laws) is the function of Congress and the Chief Executive. The question presented here is whether the public interest in proper administration of the laws (specifically in agencies' observance of a particular, statutorily prescribed procedure) can be converted into an individual right by a statute that denominates it as such, and that permits all citizens (or, for that matter, a subclass of citizens who suffer no distinctive concrete harm) to sue. If the concrete injury requirement has the separation-of-powers significance we have always said, the answer must be obvious: To permit Congress to convert the undifferentiated public interest in executive officers' compliance with the law into an "individual right" vindicable in the courts is to permit Congress to transfer from the President to the courts the Chief Executive's most important constitutional duty, to "take Care that the Laws be faithfully executed," Art. II, §3. It would enable the courts, with the permission of Congress, "to assume a position of authority over the governmental acts of another and co-equal department," . . . and to become " 'virtually continuing monitors of the wisdom and soundness of Executive action.' ". . .

[Justice BLACKMUN, joined by Justice O'CONNOR, dissented, arguing that failure to follow the "action forcing" procedural requirements of statutes such as the ESA (consultation requirements) and NEPA (EIS requirement) was integrally related to disregard of the substantive environmental interests that the procedures were designed to protect. The dissent quoted the Court's assertion in *Robertson v. Methow Valley Citizens Council,* excerpted supra, p. 986, that NEPA's "procedures are almost certain to affect the agency's substantive decision." 112 S. Ct. at 2160 (quoting 490 U.S. at 2160). It also expressed concern that the Court's broad constitutional rationale would unduly constrain Congress' power to broaden standing by legislation.]

NOTES AND QUESTIONS

1. The Court asserts that only a person with a concrete stake in the substantive outcome of an agency decision has standing to challenge a procedural violation made by the agency in making that decision. Yet in note 36 to its opinion, the Court states that such a litigant need not show that correction of the procedural violation will increase the likelihood of a substantive outcome more favorable to the plaintiff. Is this rule consistent with the Court's denial of procedural standing to the plantiffs in *Lujan?* With its conclusion that they failed to establish a sufficiently concrete substantive stake in the challenged agency action? See Sunstein, What's Standing After Lujan? Of Citizen Suits, "Injuries," and Article III, 91 Mich. L. Rev. 163 (1992).

2. Is *Lujan v. Defenders* truly a constitutional decision, such as will limit standing under other statutes, such as NEPA, in the same way? Or is it specific to the ESA, or to a particular interpretation of the ESA, as Sunstein suggests? In *Fund for Animals, Inc. v. Espy,* 814 F. Supp. 142, 149 (D.D.C. 1993), the plaintiff environmental group claimed procedural standing under NEPA, seeking to distinguish *Defenders* by claiming that NEPA's "entire fabric is procedural," unlike the ESA, which focuses on the substantive goal of protecting endangered species. The court, however, read *Lujan's* rejection of purely procedural standing and its requirement of a "concrete interest" in the substantive outcome of a controversy as founded on Article III of the Constitution. It accordingly concluded that any differences between the statutes were irrelevant, and rejected plaintiff's procedural standing claim.

3. If the *Espy* interpretation of *Lujan v. Defenders* is correct, NEPA plaintiffs must show that they would suffer some *substantive* "injury in fact" as a result of the proposed action, as well as showing that their interest is "arguably within the zone of interests protected or regulated" by the NEPA. In many cases, including *Espy* itself, this will be easy to establish on the basis that the plaintiff or its members use or visit a resource. See, e.g., *Fund for Animals, Inc. v. Espy,* 814 F. Supp. at 149-150 (recognizing standing of plaintiffs who visited wild bison habitats to observe and study the bison to challenge NEPA violations in federal programs involving capture and killing of the bison). In a small but potentially important group of cases, however, it may be difficult to establish a sufficiently concrete nexus between a substantive interest of the plaintiff and the challenged government action, particularly given the Supreme Court's increasingly strict requirements regarding pleading and proof of "injury in fact." See *Lujan v. National Wildlife Foundation,* 497 U.S. at 882-889, discussed at p. 832, supra. For example, can an individual or environmental group plaintiff establish standing to challenge an agency's failure to discuss possible global warming effects from an energy development project or a proposed timber sale? Cf.

Foundation on Economic Trends v. Watkins, 794 F. Supp. 395 (D.D.C. 1992).

4. The cases on informational and procedural standing are reviewed and criticized in Gerschwer, Note, Informational Standing Under NEPA: Justiciability and the Environmental Decisionmaking Process, 93 Colum. L. Rev. 996 (1993). If courts were to recognize informational or procedural standing, would there be any practical limits on standing? There is scarcely any individual or group who cannot plausibly claim an interest in an agency's decisional process or the information that it would generate. This was precisely the concern expressed by the Supreme Court in *Sierra Club v. Morton,* supra, p. 812, when it rejected Sierra Club's effort to obtain standing based on its interest in environmental issues.

Also, consider whether wide-open standing would be good for the environment. Standing could be gained by businesses or other economic interests intent on blocking or delaying environmentally beneficial measures. Under current law, business or development-oriented plaintiffs are often denied standing to challenge government decisions protective of the environment, either because they fail to show injury in fact caused by the decision or because they fail to show that they are within the zone of interests arguably protected by NEPA and other environmental statutes. See, e.g., *Region 8 Forest Serv. Timber Purchasers Council v. Alcock,* 993 F.2d 800, 811 (11th Cir. 1993), denying claims by a timber industry association to informational and procedural standing in challenging a Forest Service plan to protect the red-cockaded woodpecker. Finally, is there something to Justice Scalia's argument that overly broad standing might ultimately undermine the authority of the courts and their ability to protect the interests of individuals — including environmental interests?

2.   REMEDY

Given the absence of any provisions for judicial review in NEPA, a plaintiff challenging a NEPA violation by an agency will generally have to base review on the APA. In most instances, the federal district courts will have jurisdiction under the general jurisdictional statutes, 28 U.S.C. §§1331 (federal question), 1361 (mandamus). In some cases, NEPA issues may be raised in connection with other issues under the review procedures provided by a specific statute. For example, the Atomic Energy Act provides that decisions by the NRC shall be reviewed in the Courts of Appeals. In *Vermont Yankee,* supra, pp. 858, 971, petitioners raised their NEPA challenges in review proceedings before the court of appeals.

While statutory review provisions contain specific time limits, generally requiring filing within 60 or 90 days after the agency's final decision, neither the APA nor the general jurisdictional statutes contain a limitation period. The government may nonetheless seek to challenge a NEPA plaintiff's delay in bringing suit by invoking the equitable doctrine of laches. See *Save Our Wetlands, Inc. v. United States Army Corps of Engineers*, 549 F.2d 1021 (5th Cir. 1977) (laches invoked where suit was delayed until after investment on highly visible, publicized project had begun). Such delays may be quite frequent in the case of local controversies when opposition to a project is diffuse and poorly organized.

The normal remedy sought by plaintiffs in NEPA litigation is a declaratory judgment and a permanent injunction against the challenged project. Plaintiffs will generally seek a preliminary injunction pending trial on the merits or, on appeal from an adverse decision, an injunction pending appeal. In deciding whether to grant interim relief, courts apply the usual balancing test, including a consideration of any irreparable harm that plaintiffs may suffer if the project goes forward, plaintiffs' likelihood of success on the merits, and consideration of the public interest. See *Alpine Lakes Protection Soc. v. Schlapfer*, 518 F.2d 1089 (9th Cir. 1975) (denying plaintiffs injunction pending appeal).

Plaintiffs' delay in bringing suit is an issue in decisions on preliminary or interim relief. In *Steubing v. Brinegar*, 511 F.2d 489 (2d Cir. 1975), plaintiffs had waited a year before suing to challenge a federally funded bridge project and the investment of substantial planning and preliminary construction efforts by defendants. The court of appeals nonetheless upheld the district court's grant of a preliminary injunction. It noted that the government did not claim that its failure to prepare an EIS was lawful and also that the construction had not proceeded to the point where any significant environmental damage had already been done, or where economic commitments were so overwhelming that an injunction would be unwarranted.

Is a NEPA plaintiff automatically entitled to a permanent injunction if he or she establishes that the government violated the statute? In *Weinberger v. Romero-Barcelo*, 456 U.S. 305 (1982), the Court held that courts are not required automatically to issue an injunction against conduct violating the Clean Water Act. But in a line of cases beginning with *Save Our Ecosystems v. Clark*, 747 F.2d 1240 (9th Cir. 1984), the Ninth Circuit embraced a rule that injunctions should automatically issue in cases of NEPA and other environmental statutory violations, except for rare instances where an injunction would cause more harm to the environment than its denial. In the following case, on appeal from a Ninth Circuit grant of a preliminary injunction, the Supreme Court evaluated this presumption in the context of the Alaska National Interest Lands Conservation Act (ANILCA).

AMOCO PRODUCTION CO. V. VILLAGE OF GAMBELL

480 U.S. 531, 540-545 (1987)

Justice WHITE delivered the opinion of the Court.

[The Secretary of the Interior granted oil and gas leases to oil companies in the Bering Sea under the Outer Continental Shelf Lands Act (OCSLA). In a suit brought by several Native villages, the Ninth Circuit directed the entry of a preliminary injunction against all activity in connection with the leases, based on probable violations of ANILCA §810, 16 U.S.C. §3120, requiring that Interior carefully consider the effects of leasing on subsistence uses or needs and minimized adverse effects on subsistence uses if leasing is deemed necessary. The district court had found that Interior had violated ANILCA and NEPA by failing to follow appropriate procedures and make appropriate findings regarding subsistence uses and the effects of leasing. The district court nevertheless] concluded that injunctive relief was not appropriate based on the following findings:

> (1)   That delay in the exploration of the OCS may cause irreparable harm to this nation's quest for new oil resources and energy independence. Expedited exploration as a policy is stated in OCSLA. . . ;
> (2)   That exploration will not significantly restrict subsistence resources; and
> (3)   That the Secretary continues to possess power to control and shape the off-shore leasing process. Therefore, if the ANILCA subsistence studies require alteration of the leasing conditions or configuration the Secretary will be able to remedy any harm caused by the violation.

Id., at 62a-63a. . . .

The Ninth Circuit reversed. *People of Gambell v. Hodel,* 774 F.2d 1414 (1985). . . . [It] stated: "'Irreparable damage is presumed when an agency fails to evaluate thoroughly the environmental impact of a proposed action.'" 774 F.2d, at 1423. It ruled that "injunctive relief is the appropriate remedy for a violation of an environmental statute absent rare or unusual circumstances." Ibid. "Unusual circumstances" are those in which an injunction would interfere with a long-term contractual relationship . . . or would result in irreparable harm *to the environment* . . . 774 F.2d, at 1423-1425. The court found no such circumstances in the instant case. The Ninth Circuit also concluded that the policy declared in OCSLA to expedite exploration of the OCS had been superseded by ANILCA's policy to preserve the subsistence culture of Alaska Natives. . . .

Petitioners assert that the Ninth Circuit erred in directing the grant of a preliminary injunction. We addressed a similar contention in *Weinberger v. Romero-Barcelo,* 456 U.S. 305 (1982). The District Court in that case found that the Navy had violated the [Clean Water Act] by discharging ordnance into the sea without a permit. 456 U.S., at 307-308. The court ordered the Navy to apply for a permit but refused to enjoin weapons-training operations during the application process because the Navy's "technical violations" were not causing any "appreciable harm" to the quality of the water and an injunction would cause grievous harm to the Navy's military preparedness and therefore to the Nation. Id., at 309-310. The First Circuit reversed and directed the District Court to enjoin all Navy activities until it obtained a permit, concluding that the traditional equitable balancing of competing interests was inappropriate where there was an absolute statutory duty to obtain a permit. Id., at 310-311. We reversed, acknowledging at the outset the fundamental principle that an injunction is an equitable remedy that does not issue as of course [and stating that the] "grant of jurisdiction to ensure compliance with a statute hardly suggests an absolute duty to do so under any and all circumstances. . . ." Id., at 313. Finally, we stated:

> Of course, Congress may intervene and guide or control the exercise of the courts' discretion, but we do not lightly assume that Congress has intended to depart from established principles. . . .

Ibid.

Applying these principles, we concluded that the purpose of the [Clean Water Act] — to restore and maintain the integrity of the Nation's waters — would not be undermined by allowing the statutory violation to continue during the permit application process because the ordnance was not polluting the water. 456 U.S., at 314-315. . . . An injunction against all discharges was not the only means of ensuring compliance with the Act[38] and we found nothing in the Act's language and structure or legislative history which suggested that Congress intended to deny courts their traditional equitable discretion.[39]

We see nothing which distinguishes *Romero-Barcelo* from the in-

---

38. We noted that, in addition to a court order to apply for a permit, the FWPCA could be enforced through fines and criminal penalties . . . 456 U.S., at 314. The Ninth Circuit believed that the absence of such enforcement provisions in ANILCA distinguished the FWPCA and *Romero-Barcelo*. 774 F.2d, at 1426, n.2. It stated that the injunctive relief it granted was the only means of insuring compliance under §810. The Court of Appeals was incorrect. Here, as in *Romero-Barcelo*, compliance could be obtained through the simple means of an order to the responsible federal official to comply. . . .

39. We distinguished *TVA v. Hill,* 437 U.S. 153 (1978), in which we had held that Congress, in the Endangered Species Act . . . had foreclosed the traditional discretion possessed by an equity court and had required the District Court to enjoin completion of the Tellico Dam in order to preserve the snail darter, an endangered species. That statute contains a flat ban on destruc-

stant case. The purpose of ANILCA §810 is to protect Alaskan subsistence resources from unnecessary destruction. Section 810 does not prohibit all federal land use actions which would adversely affect subsistence resources but sets forth a procedure through which such effects must be considered and provides that actions which would significantly restrict subsistence uses can only be undertaken if they are necessary and if the adverse effects are minimized. There is no clear indication in §810 that Congress intended to deny federal district courts their traditional equitable discretion. . . . The District Court's refusal to issue a preliminary injunction against all exploration activities did not undermine this policy. The District Court . . . expressly found that exploration activities would not significantly restrict subsistence uses . . . [and] that "the Secretary continues to possess power to control and shape the off-shore leasing process,". . . . The Court of Appeals did not dispute [those findings]. Instead, the court stated that "[i]rreparable damage is *presumed* when an agency fails to evaluate thoroughly the environmental impact of a proposed action." 774 F.2d, at 1423 (emphasis added). This presumption is contrary to traditional equitable principles and has no basis in ANILCA. Moreover, the environment can be fully protected without this presumption. Environmental injury, by its nature, can seldom be adequately remedied by money damages and is often permanent or at least of long duration, i.e., irreparable. If such injury is sufficiently likely, therefore, the balance of harms will usually favor the issuance of an injunction to protect the environment. Here, however, injury to subsistence resources from exploration was not at all probable. And on the other side of the balance of harms was the fact that the oil company petitioners had committed approximately $70 million to exploration . . . which they would have lost without chance of recovery had exploration been enjoined. Id., at 1430. . . .

[The Court reversed the Ninth Circuit and denied injunctive relief.]

NOTES AND QUESTIONS

1. How should the "irreparable injury" requirement for a preliminary injunction be assessed in NEPA cases? Consider Sunstein's argument, discussed at supra, p. 833, suggesting that an understanding

---

tion of critical habitats of endangered species and it was conceded that completion of the dam would destroy the critical habitat of the snail darter. We stated: "Refusal to enjoin the action would have ignored the 'explicit provisions of the Endangered Species Act.' 437 U.S., at 173. Congress, it appeared to us, had chosen the snail darter over the dam. The purpose and language of the statute [not the bare fact of a statutory violation] limited the remedies available to the District Court; only an injunction could vindicate the objectives of the Act." 456 U.S., at 314. . . . [T]his case is similarly distinguishable from *Hill.*

of NEPA's purpose as being to prevent a *risk* to the environment from uninformed decisionmaking, rather than to prevent ultimate environmental deterioration, should affect what counts as "injury in fact" for purposes of standing. Does *Village of Gambell* foreclose a similar argument about what counts as "irreparable injury" for purposes of the preliminary injunction test?

2. Several courts have interpreted the *Village of Gambell* decision narrowly in the NEPA context. See, e.g., *Sierra Club v. Marsh*, 872 F.2d 497, 504 (1st Cir. 1989) (emphasizing that "the risk implied by a violation of NEPA is that real environmental harm will occur through inadequate foresight and deliberation," and not merely harm to a "legalistic 'procedure' "). See also Comment, Injunctions for NEPA Violations: Balancing the Equities, 59 U. Chi. L. Rev. 1263 (1992) (arguing that a purposive interpretation of NEPA should lead to a more liberal grant of injunctive relief). Does it make any sense to argue that injunctions should be more readily granted in NEPA cases because NEPA does not impose enforceable substantive constraints on agency discretion?

H. ASSESSMENTS OF NEPA

SAX, THE (UNHAPPY) TRUTH ABOUT NEPA

26 Okla. L. Rev. 239, 240, 248 (1973)

[This article is a strongly negative assessment of NEPA by a distinguished environmental scholar and advocate. Sax views NEPA as premised on the view that decisions will be improved if administrators "articulate the standards and principles that govern their discretionary decisions in as much detail as possible" and provide "a framework for principled decision making" (quoting *Environmental Defense Fund, Inc. v. Ruckelshaus*, 439 F.2d 584, 589 (D.C. Cir. 1971)). He continues:]

I cannot imagine a more dubious example of wishful thinking. I know of no solid evidence to support the belief that requiring articulation, detailed findings or reasoned opinions enhances the integrity or propriety of the administrative decisions. I think the emphasis on the redemptive quality of procedural reform is about nine parts myth and one part coconut oil. . . .

[NEPA] arose out of a concern that many agencies had been insufficiently sensitive to the environmental costs of their programs; NEPA's obvious, if unstated, assumption was that by requiring the agencies to explore, consider, and publicly describe the adverse environmental effects of their programs, those programs would undergo revision in favor of less environmentally damaging activities.

How, exactly, was this to come about? Neither the statute nor its history makes this clear, but there are a number of likely hypotheses upon which it is fair to assume that the draftsmen of the law operated:

1. To the extent that agencies had simply not been alerted to environmental problems, NEPA might serve as a sort of road sign warning of dangers ahead.

2. Insofar as NEPA required a study and report, it would require new, environmentally knowledgeable staff and consultants; persons whose own professional perspectives might help revise traditional agency perspectives.

3. To the extent that NEPA statements would be made public, they would alert other interested persons or agencies who could bring their weight to bear in encouraging agencies to modify their actions.

4. Because NEPA articulates a congressional policy, it may induce the agency to shift its emphasis to accord with perceived new congressional goals.

5. Because the NEPA statement will reveal important data, the force of fact will itself induce modifications in traditional agency patterns of behavior.

[Professor Sax then seeks to test these hypotheses by an examination of NEPA's impact on airport expansion decisions, detailing a number of well recognized alternatives to airport expansion as a means of dealing with airport noise and congestion, including modification of landing fee structures and flight schedules, use of VTOL plans, ground transport, and installation of quieter aircraft. Professor Sax finds that although these alternatives are regularly discussed in EISs, they are never implemented by the Federal Aviation Administration (FAA) or local airport authorities because airport expansion is the solution preferred by the relevant organized interests — the FAA, the airlines, and local airport authorities — and Congress has regularly provided the funds for expansion.]

Is the situation hopeless? No. Conduct can be modified as long as we understand the forces that impel it. We must begin by rooting out legal sentimentality and revising our legal structure to reflect behavioral realities. Here are the five basic rules of the game as I see them.

1. Don't expect hired experts to undermine their employers.

2. Don't expect people to believe legislative declarations of policy. The practical working rule is that what the legislature will fund is what the legislature's policy is.

3. Don't expect agencies to abandon their traditional friends.

4. Expect agencies to back up their subordinates and professional colleagues.
5. Expect agencies to go for the least risky option (where risk means chance of failing to perform their mission).

These rules tell us that it is nearly certain that airport authorities will continue recommending and building new runways as the solution to their noise and congestion problems, whether or not there is a NEPA and whether or not courts require them to file elaborate, multi-volume impact statements.

If we want them to change their behavior, we must give them signals that will register. If, for example, we really want them to choose between new runways and flight consolidation, we must make it as easy for them to effectuate one solution as the other. If we want a choice to be made between investment in engine retrofit and new runways, we must make money as freely available for one purpose as the other.

If we want the interest of people who live near the airports to get as much consideration as the interests of contractors who build airports, we must assure each equivalent degrees of political and economic power. We can make these adjustments, for example, by direct money subsidies, by the grant of enforceable legal rights, or even by extensive public opinion campaigns.

If we want the fullest data to be presented, we must ensure that the data gatherers have no incentives that bind them regularly to any particular client group. Obviously NEPA is now producing exactly the opposite development.

Until we are ready to face these hard realities, we can expect laws like NEPA to produce little except fodder for law review writers and contracts for that newest of growth industries, environmental consulting.

FRIESEMA & CULHANE, SOCIAL IMPACTS, POLITICS, AND THE ENVIRONMENTAL IMPACT STATEMENT PROCESS

16 Nat. Res. J. 339, 339-340 (1976)

The effectiveness of the EIS requirement is open to a great deal of debate. While the EIS is mandated to be a multidisciplinary, scientific evaluation of agency proposals, a host of plaintiffs have alleged that particular EIS's were inadequate, and certain scholars have characterized the EIS process as less science than "proliferating paperwork." At least one environmental lawyer has charged environmental statements with "squandering massive amounts of time, talent, public and private moneys," and argued that EIS's "have little relationship to actual decision making on location, design, construction, and operation of the endeavor being studied. Often they are done after basic development decisions have been made."

Perceptions of the ineffectiveness of the EIS process appear to result in large part from associating unattainable norms with the EIS process. NEPA, the Guidelines of the Council on Environmental Quality (CEQ), and the normative expectations of agencies' critics anticipate EIS's which (a) are scientific and multidisciplinary, (b) take into account all relevant factors, (c) evaluate the unquantifiable, (d) produce policy which mitigates all damage, and (e) are coordinated with the policy of all other relevant governmental entities. For students of public administration these prescriptions have a familiar ring. The study of public administration in the first half of the twentieth century was dominated by the theory that the bureaucracy could be managed in a scientific manner.

During the 1960's scientific management took the form of planning-programming-budgeting systems (PPB), an attempt to determine program expenditures on the basis of cost-benefit evaluation of programs and program alternatives. The expectation that NEPA will cause federal agencies to produce scientific, wholistic, optimizing, evaluating, mitigating, and coordinating policy seems to be the latest manifestation of the rational decisionmaking perspective on bureaucratic behavior. In fact, some scholars would even have NEPA carry the burden of technology assessment, the evaluation of whole classes of applications of science and engineering.

Modern students of public administration have rejected the scientific management perspective on the bureaucracy because bureaucratic decisionmaking is not wholistic, but incremental; decisionmakers do not optimize, but make the minimum satisfactory decision; budgeting is not so much a process of rational analysis, as PPB advocates argue, as the crux of the political process; and administrative agencies' interactions with each other are not so much cooperative as competitive. In short, public administrative behavior is not scientific management; it is politics.

[I]f one evaluates EIS's in terms of the quality or even potential quality of the science which is brought to bear on environmental policy issues, the evaluation is discouraging. However, if one takes a more political perspective, NEPA seems to have created a new, complex political process which can be and has been used very effectively to improve the social and environmental sensitivity of government decisionmakers. . . .

TURNER, THE LEGAL EAGLES

Amicus J. 25, 30 (Winter 1988)

[This article first sets forth arguments in support of its claim that the *Vermont Yankee* decision has had a chilling effect on environmental litigation. It continues:]

Nevertheless, scores of places have been rescued from oil and gas drilling, from logging and roading, from strip mining and flooding by well-timed NEPA lawsuits that bought enough time for the legislative act that would finally spare them. A comprehensive list would take pages, but here are a few:

- Little Granite Creek, Wyoming, leased for oil and gas development, leasing blocked by a court, now secure in the Gros Ventre Wilderness;
- Deep Creek, Montana, leased for oil and gas, leases suspended by the court, currently on appeal;
- Mineral King Valley, California, leased for a ski development, now in Sequoia National Park;
- The Cross-Florida Barge Canal, one of the more dramatic examples: ten days after a preliminary injunction was issued, President Nixon withdrew the project; the coup de grace was administered in the early eighties;
- Admiralty Island, Alaska, contracts signed by Forest Service that would have seen entire island clear-cut, now mostly protected as a national monument;
- Redwood National Park, California, seriously threatened by erosion from logging upslope from park, lawsuit delayed logging until Congress could add critical areas to park;
- Blue Creek, California. Forest Service proposed to build a road and sell timber in remote primitive area important for wildlife and sacred to California Indians. Lawsuit stopped road on environmental grounds, Supreme Court now considering religious freedom arguments;
- Canaan Valley, West Virginia, proposed for flooding under pumped storage reservoir, Supreme Court just declined to review decision that spared the valley, which may become a national wildlife refuge;
- Misty Fjords National Monument, Alaska, lawsuit has kept at bay plans for the world's largest open pit mine (for molybdenum) in the heart of the monument. Eventual fate still unresolved;
- Gore Range Eagles Nest Primitive Area, Colorado, Forest Service proposed logging area without studying its potential as wilderness, area now protected as wilderness.

Another dramatic NEPA victory came in response to suits filed by Gus Speth, a former NRDC attorney and now head of the World Resources Institute, and by Tony Roisman. Speth had challenged the EIS for an experimental fastbreeder nuclear reactor the federal government planned to build at Clinch River, Tennessee. That suit, plus a later one by Roisman that successfully delayed a government plan to commence retrieving plutonium from spent light-water reactor fuel, according to Roisman, "gave [President] Carter the ammunition and the time he needed to kill the plutonium option. . . ."

L. CALDWELL, NEPA REVISITED: A CALL FOR A CONSTITUTIONAL AMENDMENT

The Environmental Forum (Nov./Dec. 1989) 18

Because only the explicit mandatory EIS procedure was clearly justiciable, the administrative history of NEPA to date has been largely one of litigation, adjudication, and regulation regarding process. Much of this time-consuming and costly activity could be avoided if the President, perhaps through the CEQ or OMB, would stop environmentally destructive proposals at their source in the federal agencies. For example, millions of dollars were spent on impact statements for the mobile MX missile system and the Two Forks Dam, two projects among many others, that should have been rejected at the outset as inconsistent with NEPA. There is precedent: Richard Nixon did cancel work on the Cross-Florida Barge Canal — a project actually in construction at the time.

Unfortunately, a provision intended to brake the free-wheeling of mission-narrow administrators became a bonanza for public-interest lawyers. Decisions on policy that should have been taken in the White House to hold agencies to NEPA principles were abandoned to trial-by-combat in the courts. The Executive Branch off-loaded its constitutional responsibilities onto the public who perforce turned to lawyers and litigation to stop action that the President could have stopped. As long as the courts decline to review most substantive provisions of NEPA, and the President and the Congress are unable or unwilling to resolve the issues in controversy, the litigation route seems the only recourse open to objectors. . . .

The substantive provisions of NEPA are enforceable through executive orders as well as through legislation such as the Federal Land Policy and Management Act, the National Forest Management Act, and statutes administered by EPA. The Reagan Administration used its executive authority over appointments, budgets, and permitting to weaken the force of environmental legislation. The same authorities could also be used to strengthen environmental administration. The EIS is not the only instrument for applying the goals of NEPA. Most notably, the provisions of Title II, §204 — which authorize CEQ to conduct research — have not been fully utilized. . . .

Yet, in honoring the EIS requirement, a risk remains in displacing purpose by process. The EIS alone cannot compel adherence to the principles of NEPA. The EIS is necessary but insufficient as an action-forcing procedure; it has prevented ill-conceived actions, but cannot advance positive measures.

A field of policy as fundamental in principle as the environment requires the undergirding of a constitutional provision. . . .

A constitutional basis for environmental policy could have a three-fold effect. First, clearly placing responsibility for environmental policy on the list of constitutional obligations would make it much more difficult for a president to evade or ignore. Second, the courts would be authorized, even required, to consider the merits of environmental disputes rather than deferring judgment to the bureaucracies. And third, a constitutional provision that clearly establishes the obligation of the United States to honor environmental principles . . . would enhance the credibility of our nation in participating in international environmental protection efforts, notably on global climate change, preservation of the ozone layer, and transboundary transport of pollutants.

NOTES AND QUESTIONS

1. The proposed constitutional amendment referred to by Professor Caldwell and adopted by the National Wildlife Federation would provide:

> Each person has the right to clean air, pure water, productive soils and to the conservation of the natural, scenic, historic, recreational, aesthetic and economic values of America's natural resources. There shall be no entitlement, public or private, competent to impair these rights. It is the responsibility of the United States and of the several States as public trustees to safeguard them for the present and for the benefit of posterity.

Would adoption of this proposal be desirable? What effect would it have? See Krier, The Environment, the Constitution, and the Coupling Fallacy, 32 Mich. L. Quadrangle Notes 35 (1988).

2. How effective would you suspect NEPA has been in inducing agencies to give greater weight to environmental values in cases where judicial review is neither instituted nor credibly threatened? The vast majority of NEPA-mandated decisions never become the subject of litigation: In 1991, for example, a total of 94 suits involving NEPA claims

were filed against federal agencies, which prepared a total of 456 EISs in 1991 and at least 45,000 EAs in 1992. See CEQ, Environmental Quality: 23rd Annual Report of the Council on Environmental Quality — 1992 153, 162, 169 (1993). In the late 1970s and early 1980s, an average of 124 NEPA cases were filed each year, and an average of 1000 EISs were prepared annually. Do their statistics show that enforcement of and compliance with NEPA are slipping? If so, what might be the cause(s)? Are there other explanations for the decline in NEPA litigation and EISs?

3. The adherents of NEPA supposed that the impact statement process would shape decisions by forcing agency decisionmakers to develop additional data and consider environmental impacts, by giving the agency bureaucracy a broader outlook through the infusion of environmentally trained personnel to prepare impact statements, and by stimulating public and congressional oversight. What would you suspect the magnitude of these impacts to be? Are there other ways in which NEPA might influence agency policies even if they are not eventually challenged in court? The NEPA impact statement process can be seen as designed to ease the burden on loosely organized, poorly financed environmental interests by forcing action by agencies to initiate an inquiry into environmental impacts. But can this objective ever be successful if the principal mechanism for enforcing NEPA is court litigation?

4. In cases where judicial review is obtained, can the court's use of NEPA temporarily to delay a project because of inadequacies in an impact statement be justified as a means of forcing agency "reconsideration" of a project? Compare in this regard the *Scenic Hudson* cases, p. 804, 807 supra. Can it be justified as a means of forcing congressional reevaluation? Can it be justified as a "holding action" to enable environmental groups to mobilize political forces?

5. Consider the story of the proposed Kennedy Library and Museum complex in Cambridge, Mass., as a case study in the uses and possible abuses of the current EIS process. The responsible federal agency, the General Services Administration (GSA) delegated the preparation of the EIS to consulting firms. The result was a massive two-volume statement with technical appendices running nearly a thousand pages. The EIS concluded that the impact of the complex on Harvard Square would be minimal because most of the visitors would come at off-peak times (primarily summers and Sundays). Crucial to this conclusion were a number of questionable assumptions about visitor projections, commercial impacts, and the unimportance of nonpeak effects, most of which were buried in the technical appendices and not adequately examined. The Harvard Square Task Force's Academic Advisory Committee, which included individuals expert in relevant disciplines, had monitored the preparation of the impact statement

closely and was keenly aware of its deficiencies. Local neighborhood associations were capable of financing a war chest to fight the project in the courts, and promised a protracted legal challenge if the project were pushed ahead. Faced with the prospect of lengthy administrative and court proceedings, a more or less fixed supply of funds for the project, and soaring costs, GSA and the Kennedy Library Corporation abandoned plans to build the complex in Cambridge, and instead built it on a somewhat remote site on Boston harbor.

Is this a "success" story?

6. On the whole, do you think NEPA is a helpful approach to the problem of forcing special purpose agencies to give greater weight to interests or values they might otherwise ignore or slight? If so, should the same technique be extended to other interests that might similarly be "undervalued"? Should we have a "Poverty Impact Statement" for federal actions? An executive order issued by President Reagan requires federal agencies to prepare a "Federalism Assessment," identifying federalism concerns, costs or burdens imposed on states, and inhibitions of state sovereignty that may result from federal policies with significant "federalism implications." Exec. Order 12,612, 52 Fed. Reg. 41,685 (Oct. 30, 1987). See Remarks to State and Local Republican Officials on Federalism and Aid to the Nicaraguan Democratic Resistance, 1988 Pub. Papers 363 (Mar. 22, 1988). Executive Order 12,612 is, however, apparently not enforceable in the courts. See Exec. Order No. 12,612; *Louisiana v. United States Department of Health & Human Services*, 905 F.2d 877, 882 (5th Cir. 1990). Chief Justice Burger has proposed a "court impact statement" detailing the impact on the federal courts' workload of new congressional legislation. Where do we stop?

7. If you believe that NEPA is not an appropriate response to the problem of inducing special purpose agencies to give due weight to environmental values, what alternatives would you propose? More explicit "substantive" review by the courts? An independent, executive-branch "policy review board" of experts to assess the data and analysis relied upon by agencies in reaching environmental resource decisions? See B. Ackerman et al., The Uncertain Search for Environmental Quality 156 (1974).

I. STATE ENVIRONMENTAL POLICY ACTS

Shortly after NEPA was enacted, numerous states followed suit. Building on a model drafted by Professor Joseph Sax, Michigan's Environmental Policy Act became effective on October 1, 1970. Among its innovations was to provide expressly for citizen suits to protect the environment from degradation by public or private entities. See Sax & Conner, Michigan's Environmental Protection Act of 1970: A Progress Report, 70 Mich. L. Rev. 1003 (1972). NEPA has since been emulated in approximately half of the states. See Renz, The Coming of Age of State Environmental Policy Acts, 5 Pub. Land L. Rev. 31 (1984). In most of these jurisdictions, litigation has, like NEPA, focused on an impact statement requirement. See *Wisconsin's Envtl. Decade, Inc. v. Public Serv. Commn.*, 79 Wis. 2d 409, 256 N.W.2d 149 (1977). A particularly notable decision is *Friends of Mammoth v. Board of Supervisors of Mono County*, 8 Cal. 3d 247, 104 Cal. Rptr. 761, 505 P.2d 1049 (1972), holding that California's Environmental Quality Act (CEQA), requiring preparation of an Environmental Impact Report, was not limited to state public works projects, but also applied to private developments, such as residential subdivisions or condominiums, requiring state or local governmental regulatory or zoning approval. These state acts have taken on added significance in light of the Supreme Court's narrowing interpretations of NEPA. As a result, many of the state acts are construed more broadly and applied more stringently than NEPA. See Renz, supra.

In addition, some state courts have required agencies to adhere to the substantive policies of their state environmental policy acts. See generally Renz, supra, at 49-52. For example, the Minnesota Supreme Court in *In re City of White Bear Lake*, 247 N.W.2d 901 (Minn. 1976), held that environmental considerations could require the Department of Natural Resources to deny a development permit even where economic considerations favor the issuance of the permit and the permit is limited to the least environmentally damaging alternative identified in the EIS. Cf. *Town of Henrietta v. Department of Envtl. Conservation*, 430 N.Y.S.2d 440, 447-449 (1980) (upholding a permit imposing numerous protective conditions upon a development); *Polygon Corp. v. City of Seattle*, 578 P.2d 1309, 1312 (Wash. 1978) (rejecting argument that state act is purely procedural); but see Cal. Pub. Res. Code §21004 (West 1986) (prohibiting state agencies from imposing mitigation conditions on projects without authorization from some legislation other than CEQA).

Does the substantive role of some state environmental policy acts suggest that substantive review under NEPA would be viable? Desirable?

9

Protection of Ecosystems and Natural Resources

Environmental law and policy extends well beyond the regulation of pollution to the vast body of law governing the protection of ecosystems and natural resources. This field — encompassing public land law, wildlife protection, oil and gas law, mining law, energy law, water law, fisheries regulation, land use, among others — is the subject of a variety of courses and hence is too voluminous to cover comprehensively in a survey course on environmental law and policy. Yet certain fundamental themes that run through this broad domain are essential for environmental lawyers and policy analysts. They include the normative bases for protecting ecosystems and natural resources, the choice of institutional regime for managing ecosystems and natural resources, the design of policy instruments for protecting ecosystems and natural resources, and the role of the judiciary in resolving the conflicts that arise in the use of natural resources.

This chapter highlights these essential themes through materials and case studies drawn from a variety of areas. Since the predominant mode of land ownership and management in the United States is private property, the chapter begins with a survey of the principal judicial doctrines governing the regulation of private property and the disposition of public resources: takings law and the public trust doctrine. The chapter then surveys the institutional structure of public land law, focusing upon the management of public forest resources. The next section explores the regulation of public and private lands under the Endangered Species Act. The final section returns to the role of courts as front-line agencies of environmental protection, analyzing the efficacy of natural resource damages as a means of protecting ecosystems.

A.   LEGAL LIMITATIONS ON THE REGULATION AND DISPOSITION OF RESOURCES

As highlighted in Chapter 2, private ownership of resources, in conjunction with a market system, will lead to an efficient allocation of resources in the absence of externalities. In addition, the institution of private property promotes important liberty interests. Our constitutional and legal tradition provides basic protections for private property. The Fifth Amendment to the U.S. Constitution states that private property shall not "be taken for public use, without just compensation."

Unconstrained use of private property, however, can result in serious conflicts among property owners and the public at large when activities on one parcel spill over onto another or adversely affect common resources. We saw this most directly in the pollution context where factory emissions pollute the air and effluents degrade the water. Unregulated use of private property can also result more generally in serious disruption of ecosystems. Clearing trees on one parcel of land can disturb the watershed affecting many parcels, altering aquatic and forest ecosystems. Decisions of property owners to fill wetlands for development projects can threaten the survival of migratory waterfowl. Through the web of ecological interconnections, these impacts will have ramifications throughout other ecosystems. Ecosystems and their constituent elements can also be usefully viewed as common resources. It is often infeasible to establish ownership rights in migrating species, interdependent communities of species, and entire ecosystems. Thus, just as in the case of air and water pollution, government intervention may be called for to protect these common resources.

Up until now, we have implicitly assumed that the government possesses broad legal authority to regulate polluting activities. As we move into the field of ecosystem protection, however, we approach the limits of these powers. Regulations to protect wetlands and coastal areas, for example, can bar substantially all economically viable uses of land. This section explores the rationale and doctrines for these limits on government regulation of private property. It also explores the public trust doctrine, which limits the government's ability to dispose of certain critical resources.

1. TAKINGS DOCTRINE: LIMITATIONS ON PUBLIC CONTROL OF PRIVATE PROPERTY

Since takings doctrine is commonly introduced in first year Property and Constitutional Law courses, we will not attempt to survey the entire subject.[1] Rather, we will highlight the key environmental issues through the juxtaposition of two prominent cases reflecting divergent modes of analysis. The first case, *Just v. Marinette County*, shows a highly deferential attitude toward government regulation of activities adversely affecting ecosystems. The second case, *Lucas v. South Carolina Coastal Council*, reflects the Supreme Court's more recent trend limiting the Government's power to regulate private property without just compensation. As you read through these cases, consider the model of the legislative/regulatory process underlying the analysis in each case, the proper role of the judiciary in allocating resources, and the broader implications of these decisions for ecosystem protection.

JUST V. MARINETTE COUNTY

56 Wis. 2d 7, 201 N.W.2d 761 (Wis. 1972)

[Pursuant to a state statute, Marinette County adopted a zoning ordinance designating swamps and marshes (as identified on U.S. Geological Survey maps) as "conservancy districts." The ordinance authorizes such land to be used for harvesting wild crops, sustained yield forestry, hunting, fishing, and certain other conservative uses. The ordinance requires the owner to obtain a special permit in order to make other uses, such as filling. The Justs filled an area of wetlands on their property without obtaining a special permit.]

The real issue is whether the conservancy district provisions and the wetlands-filling restrictions are unconstitutional because they amount to a constructive taking of the Justs' land without compensation. Marinette county and the state of Wisconsin argue the restrictions of the conservancy district and wetlands provisions constitute a proper exercise of the police power of the state and do not so severely limit the use or depreciate the value of the land as to constitute a taking without compensation.

To state the issue in more meaningful terms, it is a conflict between the public interest in stopping the despoilation of natural resources, which our citizens until recently have taken as inevitable and

---

1. For those students who have not covered this area, we suggest reviewing the takings materials in J. Dukeminier & J. Krier, Property (3d ed. 1993).

for granted, and an owner's asserted right to use his property as he wishes. The protection of public rights may be accomplished by the exercise of the police power unless the damage to the property owner is too great and amounts to a confiscation. The securing or taking of a benefit not presently enjoyed by the public for its use is obtained by the government through its power of eminent domain. The distinction between the exercise of the police power and condemnation has been said to be a matter of degree of damage to the property owner. In the valid exercise of the police power reasonably restricting the use of property, the damage suffered by the owner is said to be incidental. However, where the restriction is so great the landowner ought not to bear such a burden for the public good, the restriction has been held to be a constructive taking even though the actual use or forbidden use has not been transferred to the government so as to be a taking in the traditional sense. *Stefan Auto Body v. State Highway Comm.* (1963), 21 Wis. 2d 363, 124 N.W.2d 319; *Buhler v. Racine County* (1966), 33 Wis. 2d 137, 146 N.W.2d 403; . . . Whether a taking has occurred depends upon whether "the restriction practically or substantially renders the land useless for all reasonable purposes." *Buhler v. Racine County,* supra. The loss caused the individual must be weighed to determine if it is more than he should bear. As this court stated in *Stefan,* at pp. 369-370, 124 N.W.2d 319, p. 323, ". . . if the damage is such as to be suffered by many similarly situated and is in the nature of a restriction on the use to which land may be put and ought to be borne by the individual as a member of society for the good of the public safety, health or general welfare, it is said to be a reasonable exercise of the police power, but if the damage is so great to the individual that he ought not to bear it under contemporary standards, then courts are inclined to treat it as a 'taking' of the property or an unreasonable exercise of the police power." . . .

This case causes us to reexamine the concepts of public benefit in contrast to public harm and the scope of an owner's right to use of his property. In the instant case we have a restriction on the use of a citizen's property, not to secure a benefit for the public, but to prevent a harm from the change in the natural character of the citizens' property. We start with the premise that lakes and rivers in their natural state are unpolluted and the pollution which now exists is man made. The state of Wisconsin under the trust doctrine has a duty to eradicate the present pollution and to prevent further pollution in its navigable waters. This is not, in a legal sense, a gain or a securing of a benefit by the maintaining of the natural status quo of the environment. What makes this case different from most condemnation or police power zoning cases is the interrelationship of the wetlands, the swamps and the natural environment of shorelands to the purity of the water and to such natural resources as navigation, fishing, and scenic beauty. Swamps and

wetlands were once considered wasteland, undesirable, and not pictur-
esque. But as the people became more sophisticated, an appreciation
was acquired that swamps and wetlands serve a vital role in nature, are
part of the balance of nature and are essential to the purity of the water
in our lakes and streams. Swamps and wetlands are a necessary part of
the ecological creation and now, even to the uninitiated, possess their
own beauty in nature.

Is the ownership of a parcel of land so absolute that man can
change its nature to suit any of his purposes? The great forests of our
state were stripped on the theory man's ownership was unlimited. But
in forestry, the land at least was used naturally, only the natural fruit of
the land (the trees) were taken. The despoilage was in the failure to
look to the future and provide for the reforestation of the land. An
owner of land has no absolute and unlimited right to change the essential natural character of his land so as to use it for a purpose for which
it was unsuited in its natural state and which injures the rights of others.
The exercise of the police power in zoning must be reasonable and we
think it is not an unreasonable exercise of that power to prevent harm
to public rights by limiting the use of private property to its natural
uses.

This is not a case where an owner is prevented from using his land
for natural and indigenous uses. The uses consistent with the nature of
the land are allowed and other uses recognized and still others permitted by special permit. The shoreland zoning ordinance prevents to
some extent the changing of the natural character of the land within
1,000 feet of a navigable lake and 300 feet of a navigable river because
of such land's interrelation to the contiguous water. The changing of
wetlands and swamps to the damage of the general public by upsetting
the natural environment and the natural relationship is not a reasonable use of that land which is protected from police power regulation.
Changes and filling to some extent are permitted because the extent of
such changes and fillings does not cause harm. We realize no case in
Wisconsin has yet dealt with shoreland regulations and there are several
cases in other states which seem to hold such regulations unconstitutional; but nothing this court has said or held in prior cases indicates
that destroying the natural character of a swamp or a wetland so as to
make that location available for human habitation is a reasonable use
of that land when the new use, although of a more economical value to
the owner, causes a harm to the general public. . . .

The Justs rely on several cases from other jurisdictions which have
held zoning regulations involving flood plain districts, flood basins and
wetlands to be so confiscatory as to amount to a taking because the
owners of the land were prevented from improving such property for
residential or commercial purposes. While some of these cases may be
distinguished on their facts, it is doubtful whether these differences go

to the basic rationale which permeates the decision that an owner has a right to use his property in any way and for any purpose he sees fit.

[The court reviewed the cases relied on by the Justs.]

It seems to us that filling a swamp not otherwise commercially usable is not in and of itself an existing use, which is prevented, but rather is the preparation for some future use which is not indigenous to a swamp. Too much stress is laid on the right of an owner to change commercially valueless land when that change does damage to the rights of the public. It is observed that a use of special permits is a means of control and accomplishing the purpose of the zoning ordinance as distinguished from the old concept of providing for variances. The special permit technique is now common practice and has met with judicial approval, and we think it is of some significance in considering whether or not a particular zoning ordinance is reasonable. . . .

The Justs argue their property has been severely depreciated in value. But this depreciation of value is not based on the use of the land in its natural state but on what the land would be worth if it could be filled and used for the location of a dwelling. While loss of value is to be considered in determining whether a restriction is a constructive taking, value based upon changing the character of the land at the expense of harm to public rights is not an essential factor or controlling.

We are not unmindful of the warning in *Pennsylvania Coal Co. v. Mahon* (1922), 260 U.S. 393, 416, 43 S. Ct. 158, 160, 67 L. Ed. 322:

> We are in danger of forgetting that a strong public desire to improve the public condition is not enough to warrant achieving the desire by a shorter cut than the constitutional way of paying for the change.

This observation refers to the improvement of the public condition, the securing of a benefit not presently enjoyed and to which the public is not entitled. The shoreland zoning ordinance preserves nature, the environment, and natural resources as they were created and to which the people have a present right. The ordinance does not create or improve the public condition but only preserves nature from the despoilage and harm resulting from the unrestricted activities of humans.

LUCAS v. SOUTH CAROLINA COASTAL COUNCIL

112 S. Ct. 2886 (1992)

Justice SCALIA delivered the opinion of the Court.

In 1986, petitioner David H. Lucas paid $975,000 for two residential lots on the Isle of Palms in Charleston County, South Carolina, on which he intended to build single family homes. In 1988, however, the South Carolina Legislature enacted the Beachfront Management Act, S.C. Code §48-39-250 et seq. (Supp. 1990) (Act), which had the direct effect of barring petitioner from erecting any permanent habitable structures on his two parcels. See §48-39290(A). A state trial court found that this prohibition rendered Lucas's parcels "valueless." This case requires us to decide whether the Act's dramatic effect on the economic value of Lucas's lots accomplished a taking of private property under the Fifth and Fourteenth Amendments requiring the payment of "just compensation."

I

A

South Carolina's expressed interest in intensively managing development activities in the so-called "coastal zone" dates from 1977 when, in the aftermath of Congress's passage of the federal Coastal Zone Management Act of 1972, 86 Stat. 1280, as amended, 16 U.S.C. §1451 et seq., one Management Act of 1972, 86 SAct of 1972, 86 Stat. 1280, as amended, 16 U.S.C. §1451 et seq., the legislature enacted a Coastal Zone Management Act of its own. See S. C. Code §48-39-10 et seq. (1987). In its original form, the South Carolina Act required owners of coastal zone land that qualified as a "critical area" (defined in the legislation to include beaches and immediately adjacent sand dunes, §48-39-10(J)) to obtain a permit from the newly created South Carolina Coastal Council (respondent here) prior to committing the land to a "use other than the use the critical area was devoted to on [September 28, 1977]." §48-39-130(A).

In the late 1970's, Lucas and others began extensive residential development of the Isle of Palms, a barrier island situated eastward of the City of Charleston. Toward the close of the development cycle for one residential subdivision known as "Beachwood East," Lucas in 1986 purchased the two lots at issue in this litigation for his own account. No portion of the lots, which were located approximately 300 feet from the beach, qualified as a "critical area" under the 1977 Act; accordingly, at the time Lucas acquired these parcels, he was not legally obliged to obtain a permit from the Council in advance of any development activity. His intention with respect to the lots was to do what the owners of the immediately adjacent parcels had already done: erect single-family residences. He commissioned architectural drawings for this purpose.

The Beachfront Management Act brought Lucas's plans to an abrupt end. Under that 1988 legislation, the Council was directed to establish a "baseline" connecting the landward-most "point[s] of erosion . . . during the past forty years" in the region of the Isle of Palms that includes Lucas's lots. §48-39-280(A)(2) (Supp. 1988). In action not challenged here, the Council fixed this baseline landward of Lucas's parcels. That was significant, for under the Act construction of occupable improvements[2] was flatly prohibited seaward of a line drawn 20 feet landward of, and parallel to, the baseline, §48-39-290(A) (Supp. 1988). The Act provided no exceptions.

B

Lucas promptly filed suit in the South Carolina Court of Common Pleas, contending that the Beachfront Management Act's construction bar effected a taking of his property without just compensation. Lucas did not take issue with the validity of the Act as a lawful exercise of South Carolina's police power, but contended that the Act's complete extinguishment of his property's value entitled him to compensation regardless of whether the legislature had acted in furtherance of legitimate police power objectives. Following a bench trial, the court agreed. Among its factual determinations was the finding that "at the time Lucas purchased the two lots, both were zoned for single-family residential construction and . . . there were no restrictions imposed upon such use of the property by either the State of South Carolina, the County of Charleston, or the Town of the Isle of Palms." The trial court further found that the Beachfront Management Act decreed a permanent ban on construction insofar as Lucas's lots were concerned, and that this prohibition "deprive[d] Lucas of any reasonable economic use of the lots, . . . eliminated the unrestricted right of use, and render[ed] them valueless." Id., at 37. The court thus concluded that Lucas's properties had been "taken" by operation of the Act, and it ordered respondent to pay "just compensation" in the amount of $1,232,387.50. Id., at 40.

The Supreme Court of South Carolina reversed. It found dispositive what it described as Lucas's concession "that the Beachfront Management Act [was] properly and validly designed to preserve . . . South Carolina's beaches." 304 S. C. 376, 379, 404 S.E.2d 895, 896 (1991). Failing an attack on the validity of the statute as such, the court believed itself bound to accept the "uncontested . . . findings" of the South Carolina legislature that new construction in the coastal zone — such as petitioner intended — threatened this public resource. Id., at 383,

---

2. The Act did allow the construction of certain nonhabitable improvements, e.g., "wooden walkways no larger in width than six feet," and "small wooden decks no larger than one hundred forty-four square feet." §§48-39-290(A)(1) and (2) (Supp. 1988).

404 S.E.2d, at 898. The Court ruled that when a regulation respecting the use of property is designed "to prevent serious public harm," id., at 383, 404 S.E.2d, at 899 (citing, inter alia, *Mugler v. Kansas*, 123 U.S. 623 (1887)), no compensation is owing under the Takings Clause regardless of the regulation's effect on the property's value. . . .

II

[The majority dismissed the argument that this case is inappropriate for plenary review on ripeness grounds. After briefing and argument but prior to the issuance of the South Carolina Supreme Court's decision, South Carolina amended the Beachfront Management Act to authorize the Council, in certain circumstances, to issue "special permits" for the construction or reconstruction of habitable structures seaward of the baseline. Despite the fact that Lucas may be able to obtain such a permit, the majority concluded that the case is ripe because the South Carolina Supreme Court did not rest its decision on ripeness grounds, thereby precluding Lucas from any remedy for his alleged deprivation up to the time of the 1990 amendment. See *First English Evangelical Lutheran Church of Glendale v. County of Los Angeles*, 482 U.S. 304 (1987) (holding that temporary deprivations of use are compensable under the Takings Clause).]

III

A

Prior to Justice Holmes' exposition in *Pennsylvania Coal Co. v. Mahon*, 260 U.S. 393 (1922), it was generally thought that the Takings Clause reached only a "direct appropriation" of property, *Legal Tender Cases*, 12 Wall. 457, 551 (1871), or the functional equivalent of a "practical ouster of [the owner's] possession." *Transportation Co. v. Chicago*, 99 U.S. 635, 642 (1879). See also *Gibson v. United States*, 166 U.S. 269, 275-276 (1897). Justice Holmes recognized in *Mahon*, however, that if the protection against physical appropriations of private property was to be meaningfully enforced, the government's power to redefine the range of interests included in the ownership of property was necessarily constrained by constitutional limits. 260 U.S., at 414-415. If, instead, the uses of private property were subject to unbridled, uncompensated qualification under the police power, "the natural tendency of human nature [would be] to extend the qualification more and more until at last private property disappear[ed]." Id., at 415. These considerations gave birth in that case to the oft-cited maxim that, "while property may be regulated to a certain extent, if regulation goes too far it will be recognized as a taking." Ibid.

Nevertheless, our decision in *Mahon* offered little insight into when, and under what circumstances, a given regulation would be seen as going "too far" for purposes of the Fifth Amendment. In 70-odd years of succeeding "regulatory takings" jurisprudence, we have generally eschewed any " 'set formula' " for determining how far is too far, preferring to "engag[e] in . . . essentially ad hoc, factual inquiries," *Penn Central Transportation Co. v. New York City*, 438 U.S. 104, 124 (1978) (quoting *Goldblatt v. Hempstead*, 369 U.S. 590, 594 (1962)). See Epstein, Takings: Descent and Resurrection, 1987 Sup. Ct. Rev. 1, 4. We have, however, described at least two discrete categories of regulatory action as compensable without case-specific inquiry into the public interest advanced in support of the restraint. The first encompasses regulations that compel the property owner to suffer a physical "invasion" of his property. In general (at least with regard to permanent invasions), no matter how minute the intrusion, and no matter how weighty the public purpose behind it, we have required compensation. For example, in *Loretto v. Teleprompter Manhattan CATV Corp.*, 458 U.S. 419 (1982), we determined that New York's law requiring landlords to allow television cable companies to emplace cable facilities in their apartment buildings constituted a taking, id., at 435-440, even though the facilities occupied at most only 1 1/2 cubic feet of the landlords' property, see id., at 438, n.16. See also *United States v. Causby*, 328 U.S. 256, 265, and n.10 (1946) (physical invasions of airspace); cf. *Kaiser Aetna v. United States*, 444 U.S. 164 (1979) (imposition of navigational servitude upon private marina).

The second situation in which we have found categorical treatment appropriate is where regulation denies all economically beneficial or productive use of land. See *Agins*, 447 U.S., at 260; see also *Nollan v. California Coastal Comm'n*, 483 U.S. 825, 834 (1987); *Keystone Bituminous Coal Assn. v. DeBenedictis*, 480 U.S. 470, 495 (1987); *Hodel v. Virginia Surface Mining & Reclamation Assn., Inc.*, 452 U.S. 264, 295-296 (1981). As we have said on numerous occasions, the Fifth Amendment is violated when land-use regulation "does not substantially advance legitimate state interests *or denies an owner economically viable use of his land.*" *Agins,* supra, at 260 (citations omitted) (emphasis added).[3]

---

3. Regrettably, the rhetorical force of our "deprivation of all economically feasible use" rule is greater than its precision, since the rule does not make clear the "property interest" against which the loss of value is to be measured. When, for example, a regulation requires a developer to leave 90% of a rural tract in its natural state, it is unclear whether we would analyze the situation as one in which the owner has been deprived of all economically beneficial use of the burdened portion of the tract, or as one in which the owner has

We have never set forth the justification for this rule. Perhaps it is simply, as Justice Brennan suggested, that total deprivation of beneficial use is, from the landowner's point of view, the equivalent of a physical appropriation. See *San Diego Gas & Electric Co. v. San Diego*, 450 U.S., at 652 (Brennan, J., dissenting). "[F]or what is the land but the profits thereof [?]" 1 E. Coke, Institutes ch. 1, §1 (1st Am. ed. 1812). Surely, at least, in the extraordinary circumstance when no productive or economically beneficial use of land is permitted, it is less realistic to indulge our usual assumption that the legislature is simply "adjusting the benefits and burdens of economic life," *Penn Central Transportation Co.*, 438 U.S., at 124, in a manner that secures an "average reciprocity of advantage" to everyone concerned. *Pennsylvania Coal Co. v. Mahon*, 260 U.S., at 415. And the functional basis for permitting the government, by regulation, to affect property values without compensation — that "Government hardly could go on if to some extent values incident to property could not be diminished without paying for every such change in the general law," id., at 413 — does not apply to the relatively rare situations where the government has deprived a landowner of all economically beneficial uses.

On the other side of the balance, affirmatively supporting a compensation requirement, is the fact that regulations that leave the owner of land without economically beneficial or productive options for its use — typically, as here, by requiring land to be left substantially in its natural state — carry with them a heightened risk that private property

---

suffered a mere diminution in value of the tract as a whole. (For an extreme—and, we think, unsupportable—view of the relevant calculus, see *Penn Central Transportation Co. v. New York City*, 42 N.Y.2d 324, 333-334, 366 N.E.2d 1271, 1276-1277 (1977), *aff'd*, 438 U.S. 104 (1978), where the state court examined the diminution in a particular parcel's value produced by a municipal ordinance in light of total value of the taking claimant's other holdings in the vicinity.) Unsurprisingly, this uncertainty regarding the composition of the denominator in our "deprivation" fraction has produced inconsistent pronouncements by the Court. Compare *Pennsylvania Coal Co. v. Mahon*, 260 U.S. 393, 414 (1922) (law restricting subsurface extraction of coal held to effect a taking), with *Keystone Bituminous Coal Assn. v. DeBenedictis*, 480 U.S. 470, 497-502 (1987) (nearly identical law held not to effect a taking); see also id., at 515-520 (Rehnquist, C.J., dissenting); Rose, Mahon Reconstructed: Why the Takings Issue is Still a Muddle, 57 S. Cal. L. Rev. 561, 566-569 (1984). The answer to this difficult question may lie in how the owner's reasonable expectations have been shaped by the State's law of property — i.e., whether and to what degree the State's law has accorded legal recognition and protection to the particular interest in land with respect to which the takings claimant alleges a diminution in (or elimination of) value. In any event, we avoid this difficulty in the present case, since the "interest in land" that Lucas has pleaded (a fee simple interest) is an estate with a rich tradition of protection at common law, and since the South Carolina Court of Common Pleas found that the Beachfront Management Act left each of Lucas's beachfront lots without economic value.

is being pressed into some form of public service under the guise of mitigating serious public harm. See, e.g., *Annicelli v. South Kingstown,* 463 A.2d 133, 140-141 (R.I. 1983) (prohibition on construction adjacent to beach justified on twin grounds of safety and "conservation of open space"); *Morris County Land Improvement Co. v. Parsippany-Troy Hills Township,* 40 N.J. 539, 552-553, 193 A.2d 232, 240 (1963) (prohibition on filling marshlands imposed in order to preserve region as water detention basin and create wildlife refuge). As Justice Brennan explained: "From the government's point of view, the benefits flowing to the public from preservation of open space through regulation may be equally great as from creating a wildlife refuge through formal condemnation or increasing electricity production through a dam project that floods private property." *San Diego Gas & Elec. Co.,* supra, at 652 (Brennan, J., dissenting). The many statutes on the books, both state and federal, that provide for the use of eminent domain to impose servitudes on private scenic lands preventing developmental uses, or to acquire such lands altogether, suggest the practical equivalence in this setting of negative regulation and appropriation. See, e.g., 16 U.S.C. §410ff-1(a) (authorizing acquisition of "lands, waters, or interests [within Channel Islands National Park] (including but not limited to scenic easements)"); §460aa-2(a) (authorizing acquisition of "any lands, or lesser interests therein, including mineral interests and scenic easements" within Sawtooth National Recreation Area); §§3921-3923 (authorizing acquisition of wetlands); N. C. Gen. Stat. §113A-38 (1990) (authorizing acquisition of, inter alia, " 'scenic easements' " within the North Carolina natural and scenic rivers system); Tenn. Code Ann. §§1115-101-11-15-108 (1987) (authorizing acquisition of "protective easements" and other rights in real property adjacent to State's historic, architectural, archaeological, or cultural resources).

We think, in short, that there are good reasons for our frequently expressed belief that when the owner of real property has been called upon to sacrifice all economically beneficial uses in the name of the common good, that is, to leave his property economically idle, he has suffered a taking.[4]

---

4. Justice Stevens criticizes the "deprivation of all economically beneficial use" rule as "wholly arbitrary", in that "[the] landowner whose property is diminished in value 95% recovers nothing," while the landowner who suffers a complete elimination of value "recovers the land's full value." This analysis errs in its assumption that the landowner whose deprivation is one step short of complete is not entitled to compensation. Such an owner might not be able to claim the benefit of our categorical formulation, but, as we have acknowledged time and again, "[t]he economic impact of the regulation on the claimant and . . . the extent to which the regulation has interfered with distinct investment-backed expectations" are keenly relevant to takings analysis generally. *Penn Central Transportation Co. v. New York City,* 438 U.S. 104, 124 (1978).

B

The trial court found Lucas's two beachfront lots to have been rendered valueless by respondent's enforcement of the coastal zone construction ban. Under Lucas's theory of the case, which rested upon our "no economically viable use" statements, that finding entitled him to compensation. Lucas believed it unnecessary to take issue with either the purposes behind the Beachfront Management Act, or the means chosen by the South Carolina Legislature to effectuate those purposes. The South Carolina Supreme Court, however, thought otherwise. In its view, the Beachfront Management Act was no ordinary enactment, but involved an exercise of South Carolina's "police powers" to mitigate the harm to the public interest that petitioner's use of his land might occasion. 304 S.C., at 384, 404 S.E.2d, at 899. By neglecting to dispute the findings enumerated in the Act[5] or otherwise to challenge the legislature's purposes, petitioner "concede[d] that the beach/dune area of

---

It is true that in at least some cases the landowner with 95% loss will get nothing, while the landowner with total loss will recover in full. But that occasional result is no more strange than the gross disparity between the landowner whose premises are taken for a highway (who recovers in full) and the landowner whose property is reduced to 5% of its former value by the highway (who recovers nothing). Takings law is full of these "all-or-nothing" situations. Justice Stevens similarly misinterprets our focus on "developmental" uses of property (the uses proscribed by the Beachfront Management Act) as betraying an "assumption that the only uses of property cognizable under the Constitution are developmental uses." We make no such assumption. Though our prior takings cases evince an abiding concern for the productive use of, and economic investment in, land, there are plainly a number of noneconomic interests in land whose impairment will invite exceedingly close scrutiny under the Takings Clause. See, e.g., *Loretto v. Teleprompter Manhattan CATV Corp.*, 458 U.S. 419, 436 (1982) (interest in excluding strangers from one's land).

5. The legislature's express findings include the following:

The General Assembly finds that: (1) The beach/dune system along the coast of South Carolina is extremely important to the people of this State and serves the following functions: (a) protects life and property by serving as a storm barrier which dissipates wave energy and contributes to shoreline stability in an economical and effective manner; (b) provides the basis for a tourism industry that generates approximately two-thirds of South Carolina's annual tourism industry revenue which constitutes a significant portion of the state's economy. The tourists who come to the South Carolina coast to enjoy the ocean and dry sand beach contribute significantly to state and local tax revenues; (c) provides habitat for numerous species of plants and animals, several of which are threatened or endangered. Waters adjacent to the beach/dune system also provide habitat for many other marine species; (d) provides a natural healthy environment for the citizens of South Carolina to spend leisure time which serves their physical and mental well-being. (2) Beach/dune system vegetation is unique and extremely important to the vitality and pres-

South Carolina's shores is an extremely valuable public resource; that the erection of new construction, inter alia, contributes to the erosion and destruction of this public resource; and that discouraging new construction in close proximity to the beach/dune area is necessary to prevent a great public harm." Id., at 382-383, 404 S.E.2d, at 898. In the court's view, these concessions brought petitioner's challenge within a long line of this Court's cases sustaining against Due Process and Takings Clause challenges the State's use of its "police powers" to enjoin a property owner from activities akin to public nuisances. See *Mugler v. Kansas,* 123 U.S. 623 (1887) (law prohibiting manufacture of alcoholic beverages); *Hadacheck v. Sebastian,* 239 U.S. 394 (1915) (law barring operation of brick mill in residential area); *Miller v. Schoene,* 276 U.S. 272 (1928) (order to destroy diseased cedar trees to prevent infection of nearby orchards); *Goldblatt v. Hempstead,* 369 U.S. 590 (1962) (law effectively preventing continued operation of quarry in residential area).

It is correct that many of our prior opinions have suggested that "harmful or noxious uses" of property may be proscribed by government regulation without the requirement of compensation. For a number of reasons, however, we think the South Carolina Supreme Court was too quick to conclude that that principle decides the present case. The "harmful or noxious uses" principle was the Court's early attempt

---

ervation of the system. (3) Many miles of South Carolina's beaches have been identified as critically eroding. (4) . . . [D]evelopment unwisely has been sited too close to the [beach/dune] system. This type of development has jeopardized the stability of the beach/dune system, accelerated erosion, and endangered adjacent property. It is in both the public and private interests to protect the system from this unwise development. (5) The use of armoring in the form of hard erosion control devices such as seawalls, bulkheads, and rip-rap to protect erosion-threatened structures adjacent to the beach has not proven effective. These armoring devices have given a false sense of security to beachfront property owners. In reality, these hard structures, in many instances, have increased the vulnerability of beachfront property to damage from wind and waves while contributing to the deterioration and loss of the dry sand beach which is so important to the tourism industry. (6) Erosion is a natural process which becomes a significant problem for man only when structures are erected in close proximity to the beach/dune system. It is in both the public and private interests to afford the beach/dune system space to accrete and erode in its natural cycle. This space can be provided only by discouraging new construction in close proximity to the beach/dune system and encouraging those who have erected structures too close to the system to retreat from it. . . . (8) It is in the state's best interest to protect and to promote increased public access to South Carolina's beaches for out-of-state tourists and South Carolina residents alike.

S. C. Code §48-39-250 (Supp. 1991).

to describe in theoretical terms why government may, consistent with the Takings Clause, affect property values by regulation without incurring an obligation to compensate — a reality we nowadays acknowledge explicitly with respect to the full scope of the State's police power. See, e.g., *Penn Central Transportation Co.*, 438 U.S., at 125 (where State "reasonably conclude[s] that 'the health, safety, morals, or general welfare' would be promoted by prohibiting particular contemplated uses of land," compensation need not accompany prohibition); see also *Nollan v. California Coastal Commission*, 483 U.S., at 834-835 ("Our cases have not elaborated on the standards for determining what constitutes a 'legitimate state interest[,]' [but] [t]hey have made clear . . . that a broad range of governmental purposes and regulations satisfy these requirements"). We made this very point in *Penn Central Transportation Co.*, where, in the course of sustaining New York City's landmarks preservation program against a takings challenge, we rejected the petitioner's suggestion that *Mugler* and the cases following it were premised on, and thus limited by, some objective conception of "noxiousness":

> [T]he uses in issue in *Hadacheck, Miller,* and *Goldblatt* were perfectly lawful in themselves. They involved no "blameworthiness, . . . moral wrongdoing or conscious act of dangerous risk-taking which induce[d society] to shift the cost to a pa[rt]icular individual." Sax, Takings and the Police Power, 74 Yale L.J. 36, 50 (1964). These cases are better understood as resting not on any supposed "noxious" quality of the prohibited uses but rather on the ground that the restrictions were reasonably related to the implementation of a policy — not unlike historic preservation — expected to produce a widespread public benefit and applicable to all similarly situated property." 438 U.S., at 133-134, n. 30. "Harmful or noxious use" analysis was, in other words, simply the progenitor of our more contemporary statements that "land-use regulation does not effect a taking if it 'substantially advance[s] legitimate state interests'. . . ."

Nollan, supra, at 834 (quoting *Agins v. Tiburon,* 447 U.S., at 260); see also *Penn Central Transportation Co.,* supra, at 127; *Euclid v. Ambler Realty Co.,* 272 U.S. 365, 387-388 (1926).

The transition from our early focus on control of "noxious" uses to our contemporary understanding of the broad realm within which government may regulate without compensation was an easy one, since the distinction between "harm-preventing" and "benefit-conferring" regulation is often in the eye of the beholder. It is quite possible, for example, to describe in either fashion the ecological, economic, and aesthetic concerns that inspired the South Carolina legislature in the present case. One could say that imposing a servitude on Lucas's land is necessary in order to prevent his use of it from "harming" South Carolina's ecological resources; or, instead, in order to achieve the "benefits" of an ecological preserve.[6] Compare, e.g., *Claridge v. New Hampshire Wetlands Board,* 125 N.H. 745, 752, 485 A.2d 287, 292 (1984) (owner may, without compensation, be barred from filling wetlands because landfilling would deprive adjacent coastal habitats and marine fisheries of ecological support), with, e.g., *Bartlett v. Zoning Comm'n of Old Lyme,* 161 Conn. 24, 30, 282 A.2d 907, 910 (1971) (owner barred from filling tidal marshland must be compensated, despite municipality's "laudable" goal of "preserv[ing] marshlands from encroachment or destruction"). Whether one or the other of the competing characterizations will come to one's lips in a particular case depends primarily upon one's evaluation of the worth of competing uses of real estate. See Restatement (Second) of Torts §822, Comment g, p. 112 (1979) ("[p]ractically all human activities unless carried on in a wilderness interfere to some extent with others or involve some risk of interference"). A given restraint will be seen as mitigating "harm" to the adjacent parcels or securing a "benefit" for them, depending upon the observer's evaluation of the relative importance of the use that the restraint favors. See Sax, Takings and the Police Power, 74 Yale L.J. 36, 49 (1964) ("[T]he problem [in this area] is not one of noxiousness or harm-creating activity at all; rather it is a problem of inconsistency between perfectly innocent and independently desirable uses"). Whether Lucas's construction of single-family residences on his parcels should be described as bringing "harm" to South Carolina's adjacent ecological resources thus depends principally upon whether the describer believes that the State's use interest in nurturing those resources is so important that any competing adjacent use must yield.

When it is understood that "prevention of harmful use" was merely our early formulation of the police power justification necessary to sustain (without compensation) any regulatory diminution in value; and that the distinction between regulation that "prevents harmful use" and that which "confers benefits" is difficult, if not impossible, to discern on an objective, value-free basis; it becomes self-evident that noxious-use logic cannot serve as a touchstone to distinguish regulatory

---

6. In the present case, in fact, some of the "[South Carolina] legislature's 'findings' " to which the South Carolina Supreme Court purported to defer in characterizing the purpose of the Act as "harmpreventing," 304 S.C. 376, 385, 404 S.E.2d 895, 900 (1991), seem to us phrased in "benefit-conferring" language instead. For example, they describe the importance of a construction ban in enhancing "South Carolina's annual tourism industry revenue," S.C. Code §48-39250(1)(b) (Supp. 1991), in "provid[ing] habitat for numerous species of plants and animals, several of which are threatened or endangered," §48-39-250(1)(c), and in "provid[ing] a natural healthy environment for the citizens of South Carolina to spend leisure time which serves their physical and mental well-being." §48-39-250(1)(d). It would be pointless to make the outcome of this case hang upon this terminology, since the same interests could readily be described in "harm-preventing" fashion. . . .

"takings" — which require compensation — from regulatory deprivations that do not require compensation. A fortiori the legislature's reci-
tation of a noxious-use justification cannot be the basis for departing
from our categorical rule that total regulatory takings must be compensated. If it were, departure would virtually always be allowed. The South
Carolina Supreme Court's approach would essentially nullify *Mahon*'s
affirmation of limits to the noncompensable exercise of the police
power. Our cases provide no support for this: None of them that employed the logic of "harmful use" prevention to sustain a regulation
involved an allegation that the regulation wholly eliminated the value
of the claimant's land. See *Keystone Bituminous Coal Assn.*, 480 U.S., at
513-514 (Rehnquist, C.J., dissenting).[7]

Where the State seeks to sustain regulation that deprives land of
all economically beneficial use, we think it may resist compensation
only if the logically antecedent inquiry into the nature of the owner's
estate shows that the proscribed use interests were not part of his title
to begin with. This accords, we think, with our "takings" jurisprudence,
which has traditionally been guided by the understandings of our citizens regarding the content of, and the State's power over, the "bundle
of rights" that they acquire when they obtain title to property. It seems
to us that the property owner necessarily expects the uses of his property to be restricted, from time to time, by various measures newly enacted by the State in legitimate exercise of its police powers; "[a]s long
recognized, some values are enjoyed under an implied limitation and
must yield to the police power." *Pennsylvania Coal Co. v. Mahon*, 260
U.S., at 413. And in the case of personal property, by reason of the
State's traditionally high degree of control over commercial dealings,
he ought to be aware of the possibility that new regulation might even
render his property economically worthless (at least if the property's
only economically productive use is sale or manufacture for sale), see
Andrus v. Allard, 444 U.S. 51, 66-67 (1979) (prohibition on sale of eagle
feathers). In the case of land, however, we think the notion pressed by
the Council that title is somehow held subject to the "implied limitation" that the State may subsequently eliminate all economically valuable use is inconsistent with the historical compact recorded in the
Takings Clause that has become part of our constitutional culture.

---

7. E.g., *Mugler v. Kansas*, 123 U.S. 623 (1887) (prohibition upon use of a
building as a brewery; other uses permitted); *Plymouth Coal Co. v. Pennsylvania*,
232 U.S. 531 (1914) (requirement that "pillar" of coal be left in ground to
safeguard mine workers; mineral rights could otherwise be exploited); *Reinman
v. Little Rock*, 237 U.S. 171 (1915) (declaration that livery stable constituted a
public nuisance; other uses of the property permitted); *Hadacheck v. Sebastian*,
239 U.S. 394 (1915) (prohibition of brick manufacturing in residential area;
other uses permitted); *Goldblatt v. Hempstead*, 369 U.S. 590 (1962) (prohibition
on excavation; other uses permitted).

Where "permanent physical occupation" of land is concerned, we have refused to allow the government to decree it anew (without compensation), no matter how weighty the asserted "public interests" involved, *Loretto v. Teleprompter Manhattan CATV Corp.*, 458 U.S., at 426 — though we assuredly would permit the government to assert a permanent easement that was a pre-existing limitation upon the landowner's title. Compare *Scranton v. Wheeler*, 179 U.S. 141, 163 (1900) (interests of "riparian owner in the submerged lands . . . bordering on a public navigable water" held subject to Government's navigational servitude), with *Kaiser Aetna v. United States,* 444 U.S., at 178-180 (imposition of navigational servitude on marina created and rendered navigable at private expense held to constitute a taking). We believe similar treatment must be accorded confiscatory regulations, i.e., regulations that prohibit all economically beneficial use of land: Any limitation so severe cannot be newly legislated or decreed (without compensation), but must inhere in the title itself, in the restrictions that background principles of the State's law of property and nuisance already place upon land ownership. A law or decree with such an effect must, in other words, do no more than duplicate the result that could have been achieved in the courts by adjacent landowners (or other uniquely affected persons) under the State's law of private nuisance, or by the State under its complementary power to abate nuisances that affect the public generally, or otherwise. On this analysis, the owner of a lake bed, for example, would not be entitled to compensation when he is denied the requisite permit to engage in a landfilling operation that would have the effect of flooding others' land. Nor the corporate owner of a nuclear generating plant, when it is directed to remove all improvements from its land upon discovery that the plant sits astride an earthquake fault. Such regulatory action may well have the effect of eliminating the land's only economically productive use, but it does not proscribe a productive use that was previously permissible under relevant property and nuisance principles. The use of these properties for what are now expressly prohibited purposes was always unlawful, and (subject to other constitutional limitations) it was open to the State at any point to make the implication of those background principles of nuisance and property law explicit. See Michelman, Property, Utility, and Fairness, Comments on the Ethical Foundations of "Just Compensation" Law, 80 Harv. L. Rev. 1165, 1239-1241 (1967). In light of our traditional resort to "existing rules or understandings that stem from an independent source such as state law" to define the range of interests that qualify for protection as "property" under the Fifth (and Fourteenth) amendments, *Board of Regents of State Colleges v. Roth,* 408 U.S. 564, 577 (1972); see, e.g., *Ruckelshaus v. Monsanto Co.,* 467 U.S. 986, 1011-1012 (1984); *Hughes v. Washington,* 389 U.S. 290, 295 (1967) (Stewart, J., concurring), this recognition that the Takings Clause does not require compensation when an owner is barred from putting land to a use that is proscribed by those "existing rules or understandings" is surely unexceptional. When, however, a regulation that declares "off-limits" all economically productive or beneficial uses of land goes beyond what the relevant background principles would dictate, compensation must be paid to sustain it.

The "total taking" inquiry we require today will ordinarily entail (as the application of state nuisance law ordinarily entails) analysis of, among other things, the degree of harm to public lands and resources, or adjacent private property, posed by the claimant's proposed activities, see, e.g., Restatement (Second) of Torts §§826, 827, the social value of the claimant's activities and their suitability to the locality in question, see, e.g., id., §§828(a) and (b), 831, and the relative ease with which the alleged harm can be avoided through measures taken by the claimant and the government (or adjacent private landowners) alike, see, e.g., id., §§827(e), 828(c), 830. The fact that a particular use has long been engaged in by similarly situated owners ordinarily imports a lack of any common-law prohibition (though changed circumstances or new knowledge may make what was previously permissible no longer so, see Restatement (Second) of Torts, supra, §827, comment g. So also does the fact that other landowners, similarly situated, are permitted to continue the use denied to the claimant.

It seems unlikely that common-law principles would have prevented the erection of any habitable or productive improvements on petitioner's land; they rarely support prohibition of the "essential use" of land, *Curtin v. Benson*, 222 U.S. 78, 86 (1911). The question, however, is one of state law to be dealt with on remand. We emphasize that to win its case South Carolina must do more than proffer the legislature's declaration that the uses Lucas desires are inconsistent with the public interest, or the conclusory assertion that they violate a common-law maxim such as *sic utere tuo ut alienum non laedas*. As we have said, a "State, by *ipse dixit*, may not transform private property into public property without compensation. . . ." *Webb's Fabulous Pharmacies, Inc. v. Beckwith*, 449 U.S. 155, 164 (1980). Instead, as it would be required to do if it sought to restrain Lucas in a common-law action for public nuisance, South Carolina must identify background principles of nuisance and property law that prohibit the uses he now intends in the circumstances in which the property is presently found. Only on this showing can the State fairly claim that, in proscribing all such beneficial uses, the Beachfront Management Act is taking nothing. . . .

The judgment is reversed and the case remanded for proceedings not inconsistent with this opinion.

So ordered.

[Justice Kennedy concurred in the judgment, but would not have applied such a narrow view of property owner's "reasonable, investment-backed expectations." In his view, such expectations "must be understood in light of the whole of our legal tradition," not merely nuisance law. Justice Blackmun dissented, arguing that Takings Clause precedent allows the State to prohibit land uses that are injurious to public health, safety, or welfare without compensation "no matter how adverse the financial effect on the owner." Justice Stevens also dissented, arguing that the Court's categorical rule is without foundation in Supreme Court jurisprudence, prone to abuse, and would "freeze the common law." Justice Souter would dismiss the writ of certiorari as having been improvidently granted on the ground that the trial court's determination that the state regulation had deprived the owner of his entire economic interest in the subject property is highly questionable.]

NOTES AND QUESTIONS

1. What are the holdings of these cases? With respect to *Marinette County,* are there no limits to the reach of the government's police power to protect ecosystems? With respect to *Lucas,* must the government pay compensation only when a regulation that goes beyond background nuisance principles eliminates the entire remaining economic value of a parcel of land?

2. What model of the legislative/regulatory process underlies the analysis of each case? Does this different view of the governmental decisionmaking process explain the difference in approach and results? What institutional structures do the two cases establish for protecting ecosystems via governmental regulation? What is the role of the judiciary and the legislature in each of these structures? Do these roles accord with their institutional advantages and disadvantages?

3. Which approach to the Takings Clause is most likely to yield an efficient allocation of resources? Which interepretation is most fair?

4. The Takings Clause jurisprudence was quite muddled prior to the *Lucas* case. Does the majority opinion clarify the law in a way that will make it easier to predict the validity of government regulations? How would the following problems be resolved following *Lucas?*

- A developer, fearing a zoning change that would limit development to single-family dwellings in an area, purchases the right to build a multi-family home on a particular lot. The City later rezones the area as single-family housing.
- Recent scientific studies have shown an alarming loss of wetlands throughout the United States. This loss threatens the survival of waterfowl and other important levels of the ecological pyramid. Based upon these studies, the Wisconsin legislature enacts the "No Net Loss of Wetlands Act." The law does not preclude the development of any particular plot of land. Rather

it requires that any land developer who wishes to fill a wetland to acquire and donate to the Wisconsin Department of Natural Resources for preservation an equivalent amount of wetland elsewhere in the state. For example, a developer could purchase a converted, diked wetland and reconvert it to its natural state by opening the dikes to permit tidal flow over the land.

- Notwithstanding the *Lucas* decision, South Carolina remains intent on protecting coastal areas from the erosive forces of the ocean. It enacts the "Critical Coastal Area Construction Code Upgrade Act" which requires that all new buildings constructed in inlet areas along the coast be stabilized by heavily reinforced jetties, terminal groins, or other structures, and by heavily reinforced foundations. The cost of meeting these new code requirements will make the development of many parcels economically infeasible, although the code is carefully tailored to ensure that it would be technologically feasible to develop all coastal properties. In addition, all existing structures must be upgraded to code requirements as a condition of any sales contract. Moreover, all owners of structures in critical areas are subject to a special annual assessment of 3 percent of the assessed value of improvements to their property. This supplemental property tax will be used by the South Carolina Coastal Council to stabilize the coastal ecosystem.

5. The majority opinion determines the extent of the state's power to eliminate substantially all economic value by reference to background principles of nuisance law. Justice Kennedy would expand this reference point to include "all reasonable expectations," which would include "new regulatory initiatives in response to changing conditions." In light of the cases in Chapter 3 and the adoption of CERCLA, which approach do you find more appropriate? What problems would you foresee in applying the two approaches?

6. What are the broader implications of the *Lucas* opinion? Justice Stevens warns that the majority's approach will "greatly hamper the efforts of local officials and planners who must deal with increasingly complex problems in land-use and environmental regulation." Justice Scalia, however, is careful to point out that the majority's approach will not significantly affect the government's ability to "go on" because of "the relatively rare situations where the government has deprived a landowner of all economically beneficial uses." Is Justice Scalia's assurance convincing? What are the implications of *Lucas* for the protection of ecosystems and natural resources?

7. Professor Sax interprets *Lucas* as conveying the message that "[s]tates may not regulate land use solely by requiring landowners to maintain their property in a natural state as part of a functioning eco-

system, even though those natural functions may be important to the ecosystem." Property Rights and the Economy of Nature: Understanding *Lucas v. South Carolina Coastal Council,* 45 Stan. L. Rev. 1433, 1438 (1993). He welcomes the Court's recognition of the emerging view of land as a part of an ecosystem, as opposed to merely private property, but criticizes the Court's effort to limit the legal foundation for an ecosystem conception. Professor Sax offers an alternative definition of property, designed to accommodate both economic considerations and the needs of nature's economy. He suggests that it would have the following features:

1. Less focus on individual dominion, and the abandonment of the traditional "island" and "castle-and-moat" images of ownership.
2. More public decisions, because use would be determined ecosystemically, rather than tract by tract; or more decisions made on a broad, system-wide scale.
3. Increased ecological planning, because different kinds of lands have different roles.
4. Affirmative obligations by owners to protect natural services, with owners functioning as custodians as well as self-benefitting entreprenuers.

45 Stan. L. Rev. at 1451. Is the Takings Clause's definition of "property" sufficiently capacious to embrace this definition? How would it work in practice? Would the *Lucas* case come out differently? How would the problems in note 4 be decided under Sax's approach? What would be the effect of Sax's approach upon the pattern of land development?

2.   THE PUBLIC TRUST DOCTRINE: LIMITATIONS ON PUBLIC DISPOSITION AND PRIVATE USE OF CRITICAL RESOURCES

ILLINOIS CENTRAL R.R. CO. V. ILLINOIS

146 U.S. 387 (1892)

Justice FIELD delivered the opinion of the court.
    [In 1869 the Illinois legislature made a substantial grant of submerged lands — a mile strip along the shores of Lake Michigan extending one mile out from the shoreline — to the Illinois Central Railroad in fee simple. In 1873, the legislature changed its mind and repealed the 1869 grant. The State of Illinois sued to quiet title.]
    The question, therefore, to be considered is whether the legisla-

ture was competent to thus deprive the State of its ownership of the submerged lands in the harbor of Chicago, and of the consequent control of its waters; or, in other words, whether the railroad corporation can hold the lands and control the waters by the grant, against any future exercise of power over them by the State.

That the State holds the title to the lands under the navigable waters of Lake Michigan, within its limits, in the same manner that the State holds title to soils under tide water, by the common law, we have already shown, and that title necessarily carries with it control over the waters above them whenever the lands are subjected to use. But it is a title different in character from that which the State holds in lands intended for sale. It is different from the title which the United States hold in the public lands which are open to preemption and sale. It is a title held in trust for the people of the State that they may enjoy the navigation of the waters, carry on commerce over them, and have liberty of fishing therein freed from the obstruction or interference of private parties. The interest of the people in the navigation of the waters and in commerce over them may be improved in many instances by the erection of wharves, docks and piers therein, for which purpose the State may grant parcels of the submerged lands; and, so long as their disposition is made for such purpose, no valid objections can be made to the grants. It is grants of parcels of lands under navigable waters, that may afford foundation for wharves, piers, docks and other structures in aid of commerce, and grants of parcels which, being occupied, do not substantially impair the public interest in the lands and waters remaining, that are chiefly considered and sustained in the adjudged cases as a valid exercise of legislative power consistently with the trust to the public upon which such lands are held by the State. But that is a very different doctrine from the one which would sanction the abdication of the general control of the State over lands under the navigable waters of an entire harbor or bay, or of a sea or lake. Such abdication is not consistent with the exercise of that trust which requires the government of the State to preserve such waters for the use of the public. The trust devolving upon the State for the public, and which can only be discharged by the management and control of property in which the public has an interest, cannot be relinquished by a transfer of the property. The control of the State for the purposes of the trust can never be lost, except as to such parcels as are used in promoting the interests of the public therein, or can be disposed of without any substantial impairment of the public interest in the lands and waters remaining. It is only by observing the distinction between a grant of such parcels for the improvement of the public interest, or which when occupied do not substantially impair the public interest in the lands and waters remaining and a grant of the whole property in which the public is interested, that the language of the adjudged cases can be reconciled. General language sometimes found in opinions of the courts, expressive of absolute ownership and control by the State of lands under navigable waters, irrespective of any trust as to their use and disposition, must be read and construed with reference to the special facts of the particular cases. A grant of all the lands under the navigable waters of a State has never been adjudged to be within the legislative power; and any attempted grant of the kind would be held, if not absolutely void on its face, as subject to revocation. The State can no more abdicate its trust over property in which the whole people are interested, like navigable waters and soils under them, so as to leave them entirely under the use and control of private parties, except in the instance of parcels mentioned for the improvement of the navigation and use of the waters, or when parcels can be disposed of without impairment of the public interest in what remains, than it can abdicate its police powers in the administration of government and the preservation of the peace. In the administration of government the use of such powers may for a limited period be delegated to a municipality or other body, but there always remains with the State the right to revoke those powers and exercise them in a more direct manner, and one more conformable to its wishes. So with trusts connected with public property, or property of a special character, like lands under navigable waters, they cannot be placed entirely beyond the direction and control of the State.

The harbor of Chicago is of immense value to the people of the State of Illinois in the facilities it affords to its vast and constantly increasing commerce; and the idea that its legislature can deprive the State of control over its bed and waters and place the same in the lands of a private corporation created for a different purpose, one limited to transportation of passengers and freight between distant points and the city, is a proposition that cannot be defended. . . .

It is hardly conceivable that the legislature can divest the State of the control and management of this harbor and vest it absolutely in a private corporation. Surely an act of the legislature transferring the title to its submerged lands and the power claimed by the railroad company, to a foreign State or nation would be repudiated, without hesitation, as a gross perversion of the trust over the property under which it is held. So would a similar transfer to a corporation of another State. It would not be listened to that the control and management of the harbor of that great city — a subject of concern to the whole people of the State — should thus be placed elsewhere than in the State itself. All the objections which can be urged to such attempted transfer may be urged to a transfer to a private corporation like the railroad company in this case.

Any grant of the kind is necessarily revocable, and the exercise of the trust by which the property has held by the State can be resumed at any time. Undoubtedly there may be expenses incurred in improvements made under which a grant which the State ought to pay; but, be that as it may, the power to resume the trust whenever the State judges best is, we think, incontrovertible. The position advanced by the railroad company in support of its claim to the ownership of the submerged lands and the right to the erection of wharves, piers and docks at its pleasure, or for its business in the harbor of Chicago, would place every harbor in the country at the mercy of a majority of the legislature of the State in which the harbor is situated.

QUESTIONS

Does the Illinois Central Railroad have a valid takings claim? If not, could South Carolina have asserted a public trust interest in the *Lucas* case?

SAX, THE PUBLIC TRUST DOCTRINE IN NATURAL RESOURCE LAW: EFFECTIVE JUDICIAL INTERVENTION

68 Mich. L. Rev. 471, 474, 556-557, 565-566 (1970)

Of all the concepts known to American law, only the public trust doctrine seems to have the breadth and substantive content which might make it useful as a tool of general application for citizens seeking to develop a comprehensive legal approach to resource management problems. If that doctrine is to provide a satisfactory tool, it must meet three criteria. It must contain some concept of a legal right in the general public; it must be enforceable against the government; and it must be capable of an interpretation consistent with contemporary concerns for environmental quality. . . .

It is clear that the historical scope of public trust law is quite narrow. Its coverage includes, with some variation among the states, that aspect of the public domain below the low-water mark on the margin of the sea and the great lakes, the waters over those lands, and the waters within rivers and streams of any consequence. Sometimes the coverage of the trust depends on a judicial definition of navigability, but that is a rather vague concept which may be so broad as to include all waters which are suitable for public recreation. Traditional public trust law also embraces parklands, especially if they have been donated to the public for specific purposes; and, as a minimum, it operates to require that such lands not be used for nonpark purposes. But except for a few cases like *Gould v. Greylock Reservation Commission,* it is uncommon to find decisions that constrain public authorities in the specific uses to which they may put parklands, unless the lands are reallocated to a very different use, such as a highway.

If any of the analysis in this Article makes sense, it is clear that the judicial techniques developed in public trust cases need not be limited either to these few conventional interests or to questions of disposition of public properties. Public trust problems are found whenever governmental regulation comes into question, and they occur in a wide range of situations in which diffuse public interests need protection against tightly organized groups with clear and immediate goals. Thus, it seems that the delicate mixture of procedural and substantive protections which the courts have applied in conventional public trust cases would be equally applicable and equally appropriate in controversies involving air pollution, the dissemination of pesticides, the location of rights of way for utilities, and strip mining or wetland filling on private lands in a state where governmental permits are required.

Certainly the principle of the public trust is broader than its traditional application indicates. It may eventually be necessary to confront the question whether certain restrictions, imposed either by courts or by other governmental agencies, constitute a taking of private property, but a great deal of needed protection for the public can be provided long before that question is reached. Thus, for example, a private action seeking more effective governmental action on pesticide use or more extensive enforcement of air pollution laws would rarely be likely to reach constitutional limits. In any event, the courts can limit their intervention to regulation which stops short of a compensable taking. . . .

NATIONAL AUDUBON SOCIETY v. THE SUPERIOR COURT OF ALPINE COUNTY AND DEPARTMENT OF WATER AND POWER OF THE CITY OF LOS ANGELES

33 Cal. 3d 419, 658 P.2d 709 (1983), cert. denied, 464 U.S. 977 (1983)

BROUSSARD, Justice.

Mono Lake, the second largest lake in California, sits at the base of the Sierra Nevada escarpment near the eastern entrance to Yosemite National Park. The lake is saline; it contains no fish but supports a large population of brine shrimp which feed vast numbers of nesting and migratory birds. Islands in the lake protect a large breeding colony of California gulls, and the lake itself serves as a haven on the migration route for thousands of Northern Phalarope, Wilson's Phalarope, and Eared Greve. Towers and spires of tufa on the north and south shores are matters of geological interest and a tourist attraction.

Although Mono Lake receives some water from rain and snow on the lake surface, historically most of its supply came from snowmelt in the Sierra Nevada. Five freshwater streams — Mill, Lee Vining, Walker, Parker and Rush Creeks — arise near the crest of the range and carry the annual runoff to the west shore of the lake. In 1940, however, the Division of Water Resources, the predecessor to the present California Water Resources Board, granted the Department of Water and Power of the City of Los Angeles (hereafter DWP) a permit to appropriate virtually the entire flow of four of the five streams flowing into the lake. DWP promptly constructed facilities to divert about half the flow of these streams into DWP's Owens Valley aqueduct. In 1970 DWP completed a second diversion tunnel, and since that time has taken virtually the entire flow of these streams.

As a result of these diversions, the level of the lake has dropped: the surface area has diminished by one-third; one of the two principal islands in the lake has become a peninsula, exposing the gull rookery there to coyotes and other predators and causing the gulls to abandon the former island. The ultimate effect of continued diversions is a matter of intense dispute, but there seems little doubt that both the scenic beauty and the ecological values of Mono Lake are imperiled.

Plaintiffs filed suit in superior court to enjoin the DWP diversions on the theory that the shores, bed and waters of Mono Lake are protected by a public trust. . . .

This case brings together for the first time two systems of legal thought: the appropriative water rights system which since the days of the gold rush has dominated California water law, and the public trust doctrine which, after evolving as a shield for the protection of tidelands, now extends its protective scope to navigable lakes. Ever since we first recognized that the public trust protects environmental and recreational values (*Marks v. Whitney* (1971) 6 Cal. 3d 251, 98 Cal. Rptr. 790, 491 P.2d 374), the two systems of legal thought have been on a collision course. (Johnson, Public Trust Protection for Stream Flows and Lake Levels (1980) 14 U.C. Davis L. Rev. 233.) They meet in a unique and dramatic setting which highlights the clash of values. Mono Lake is a scenic and ecological treasure of national significance, imperiled by continued diversions of water; yet, the need of Los Angeles for water is apparent, its reliance on rights granted by the board evident, the cost of curtailing divisions substantial. . . .

1.   BACKGROUND AND HISTORY OF THE MONO
LAKE LITIGATION

DWP supplies water to the City of Los Angeles. Early in this century, it became clear that the city's anticipated needs would exceed the
water available from local sources, and so in 1913 the city constructed
an aqueduct to carry water from the Owens River 233 miles over the
Antelope-Mojave plateau into the coastal plain and thirsty city.

The city's attempt to acquire rights to water needed by local farm-
ers met with fierce, and at times violent, opposition. (See generally
County of Inyo v. Public Utilities Com. (1980) 26 Cal. 3d 154, 156-157, 161
Cal. Rptr. 172, 604 P.2d 566; Kahrl, Water and Power: The Conflict
Over Los Angeles' Water Supply in the Owens Valley (1982).) But when
the "Owens Valley War" was over, virtually all the waters of the Owens
River and its tributaries flowed south to Los Angeles. Owens Lake was
transformed into an alkali flat.

The city's rapid expansion soon strained this new supply, too, and
prompted a search for water from other regions. The Mono Basin was
a predictable object of this extension, since it lay within 50 miles of the
natural origin of Owens River, and thus could easily be integrated into
the existing aqueduct system.

After purchasing the riparian rights incident to Lee Vining,
Walker, Parker and Rush Creeks, as well as the riparian rights pertaining to Mono Lake, the city applied to the Water Board in 1940 for
permits to appropriate the waters of the four tributaries. At hearings
before the board, various interested individuals protested that the city's
proposed appropriations would lower the surface level of Mono Lake
and thereby impair its commercial, recreational and scenic uses.

The board's primary authority to reject that application lay in a
1921 amendment to the Water Commission Act of 1913, which authorized the board to reject an application "when in its judgment the proposed appropriation would not best conserve the public interest."
(Stats. 1921, ch. 329, §1, p. 443, now codified as Wat. Code, §1255.) The
1921 enactment, however, also "declared to be the established policy of
this state that the use of water for domestic purposes is the highest use
of water" (id., now codified as Wat. Code, §1254), and directed the
Water Board to be guided by this declaration of policy. Since DWP
sought water for domestic use, the board concluded that it had to grant
the application notwithstanding the harm to public trust uses of Mono
Lake.

The board's decision states that "[i]t is indeed unfortunate that
the City's proposed development will result in decreasing the aesthetic
advantages of Mono Basin but there is apparently nothing that this
office can do to prevent it. The use of which the City proposes to put
the water under its Application . . . is defined by the Water Commis-

sion Act as the highest to which water may be applied and to make available unappropriated water for this use the City has, by the condemnation proceedings described above, acquired the littoral and riparian rights on Mono Lake and its tributaries south of Mill Creek. This office therefore has no alternative but to dismiss all protests based upon the possible lowering of the water level in Mono Lake and the effect that the diversion of water from these streams may have upon the aesthetic and recreational value of the Basin." (Div. Wat. Resources Dec. 7053, 7055, 8042 & 8043 (Apr. 11, 1940), at p. 26, italics added.) . . .

2. THE PUBLIC TRUST DOCTRINE IN CALIFORNIA

"By the law of nature these things are common to mankind — the air, running water, the sea and consequently the shores of the sea." (Institutes of Justinian 2.1.1.) From this origin in Roman law, the English common law evolved the concept of the public trust, under which the sovereign owns "all of its navigable waterways and the lands lying beneath them 'as trustee of a public trust for the benefit of the people.' " (*Colberg, Inc. v. State of California ex rel. Dept. Pub. Works* (1967) 67 Cal. 2d 408, 416, 62 Cal. Rptr. 401, 432 P.2d 3.) The State of California acquired title as trustee to such lands and waterways upon its admission to the union (*City of Berkeley v. Superior Court* (1980) 26 Cal. 3d 515, 521, 162 Cal. Rptr. 327, 606 P.2d 362 and cases there cited); from the earliest days (see *Eldridge v. Cowell* (1854) 4 Cal. 80, 87) its judicial decisions have recognized and enforced the trust obligation.

Three aspects of the public trust doctrine require consideration in this opinion: the purpose of the trust; the scope of the trust, particularly as it applies to the nonnavigable tributaries of a navigable lake; and the powers and duties of the state as trustee of the public trust. We discuss these questions in the order listed.

(a) THE PURPOSE OF THE PUBLIC TRUST

The objective of the public trust has evolved in tandem with the changing public perception of the values and uses of waterways. As we observed in *Marks v. Whitney*, supra, 6 Cal. 3d 251, 98 Cal. Rptr. 790, 491 P.2d 374, "[p]ublic trust easements [were] traditionally defined in terms of navigation, commerce and fisheries. They have been held to include the right to fish, hunt, bathe, swim, to use for boating and general recreation purposes the navigable waters of the state, and to use the bottom of the navigable waters for anchoring, standing, or other purposes." (P. 259, 98 Cal. Rptr. 790, 491 P.2d 374.) We went on, however, to hold that the traditional triad of uses — navigation, commerce and fishing — did not limit the public interest in the trust areas. In language of special importance to the present setting, we stated that "[t]he public uses to which tidelands are subject are sufficiently flexible to encompass changing public needs. In administering the trust the state is not burdened with an outmoded classification favoring one mode of utilization over another. [Citation.] There is a growing public recognition that one of the most important public uses of the tidelands — a use encompassed within the tidelands trust — is the preservation of those lands in their natural state, so that they may serve as ecological units for scientific study, as open space, and as environments which provide food and habitat for birds and marine life, and which favorably affect the scenery and climate of the area." (Pp. 259-260, 98 Cal. Rptr. 790, 491 P.2d 374.)

Mono Lake is a navigable waterway. (*City of Los Angeles v. Aitken*, supra, 10 Cal. App. 2d 460, 466, 52 P.2d 585.) It supports a small local industry which harvests brine shrimp for sale as fish food, which endeavor probably qualifies the lake as a "fishery" under the traditional public trust cases. The principal values plaintiffs seek to protect, however, are recreational and ecological — the scenic views of the lake and its shore, the purity of the air, and the use of the lake for nesting and feeding by birds. Under *Marks v. Whitney, supra,* 6 Cal. 3d 251, 98 Cal. Rptr. 790, 491 P.2d 374, it is clear that protection of these values is among the purposes of the public trust.

(b)   THE SCOPE OF THE PUBLIC TRUST

Early English decisions generally assumed the public trust was limited to tidal waters and the lands exposed and covered by the daily tides (see Stevens, op. cit. supra, 14 U.C. Davis L. Rev. 195, 201 and authorities there cited); many American decisions, including the leading California cases, also concern tidelands. (See, e.g., *City of Berkeley v. Superior Court* (1980) 26 Cal. 3d 515, 162 Cal. Rptr. 327, 606 P.2d 362; *Marks v. Whitney,* supra, 6 Cal. 3d 251, 98 Cal. Rptr. 790, 491 P.2d 374; *People v. California Fish Co.* (1913) 166 Cal. 576, 138 P. 79.) It is, however, well settled in the United States generally and in California that the public trust is not limited by the reach of the tides, but encompasses all navigable lakes and streams. (See *Illinois Central Railroad Co. v. Illinois* (1892) 146 U.S. 387, 13 S. Ct. 110, 36 L. Ed. 1018 (Lake Michigan); *State of California v. Superior Court* (Lyon) (1981) 29 Cal. 3d 210, 172 Cal. Rptr. 696, 625 P.2d 239 (Clear Lake); *State of California v. Superior Court* (Fogerty) (1981) 29 Cal. 3d 240, 172 Cal. Rptr. 713, 625 P.2d 256 (Lake Tahoe); *People v. Gold Run D.&M. Co.* (1884) 66 Cal. 138, 4 P. 1152

(Sacramento River); *Hitchings v. Del Rio Woods Recreation & Park Dist.* (1976) 55 Cal. App. 3d 560, 127 Cal. Rptr. 830 (Russian River).)

Mono Lake is, as we have said, a navigable waterway. The beds, shores and waters of the lake are without question protected by the public trust. The streams diverted by DWP, however, are not themselves navigable. Accordingly, we must address in this case a question not discussed in any recent public trust case — whether the public trust limits conduct affecting nonnavigable tributaries to navigable waterways.

This question was considered in two venerable California decisions. The first, *People v. Gold Run D.&M. Co.* (1884) 66 Cal. 138, 4 P. 1152, is one of the epochal decisions of California history, a signpost which marked the transition from a mining economy to one predominantly commercial and agricultural. The Gold Run Ditch and Mining Company and other mining operators used huge water cannons to wash gold-bearing gravel from hillsides; in the process they dumped 600,000 cubic yards of sand and gravel annually into the north fork of the American River. The debris, washed downstream, raised the beds of the American and Sacramento Rivers, impairing navigation, polluting the waters, and creating the danger that in time of flood the rivers would turn from their channels and inundate nearby lands.

Although recognizing that its decision might destroy the remains of the state's gold mining industry, the court affirmed an injunction barring the dumping. The opinion stressed the harm to the navigability of the Sacramento River, "a great public highway, in which the people of the State have paramount and controlling rights." (P. 146, 4 P. 1152) Defendant's dumping, the court said, was "an unauthorized invasion of the rights of the public to its navigation." (P. 147, 4 P. 1152) Rejecting the argument that dumping was sanctioned by custom and legislative acquiescence, the opinion asserted that "the rights of the people in the navigable rivers of the State are paramount and controlling. The State holds the absolute right to all navigable waters and the soils under them. . . . The soil she holds as trustee of a public trust for the benefit of the people; and she may, by her legislature, grant it to an individual; but she cannot grant the rights of the people to the use of the navigable waters flowing over it. . . ." (Pp. 151-152, 4 P. 1152.)

In the second decision, *People v. Russ* (1901) 132 Cal. 102, 64 P. 111, the defendant erected dams on sloughs which adjoined a navigable river. Finding the sloughs nonnavigable, the trial court gave judgment for defendant. We reversed, directing the trial court to make a finding as to the effect of the dams on the navigability of the river. "Directly diverting waters in material quantities from a navigable stream may be enjoined as a public nuisance. Neither may the waters of a navigable stream be diverted in substantial quantities by drawing from its tributaries. . . . If the dams upon these sloughs result in the obstruction of Salt River as a navigable stream, they constitute a public nuisance." (P. 106, 64 P. 111.)

DWP points out that the *Gold Run* decision did not involve diversion of water, and that in *Russ* there had been no finding of impairment to navigation. But the principles recognized by those decisions apply fully to a case in which diversions from a nonnavigable tributary impair the public trust in a downstream river or lake. "If the public trust doctrine applies to constrain *fills* which destroy navigation and other public trust uses in navigable waters, it should equally apply to constrain the extraction of water that destroys navigation and other public interests. Both actions result in the same damage to the public interest." (Johnson, Public Trust Protection for Stream Flows and Lake Levels (1980) 14 U.C. Davis L. Rev. 233, 257-258; see Dunning, The Significance of California's Public Trust Easement for California Water Rights Law (1980) 14 U.C. Davis L. Rev. 357, 359-360.)

We conclude that the public trust doctrine, as recognized and developed in California decisions, protects navigable waters from harm caused by diversion of nonnavigable tributaries.

(c)   DUTIES AND POWERS OF THE STATE AS TRUSTEE

In the following review of the authority and obligations of the state as administrator of the public trust, the dominant theme is the state's sovereign power and duty to exercise continued supervision over the trust. One consequence, of importance to this and many other cases, is that parties acquiring rights in trust property generally hold those rights subject to the trust, and can assert no vested right to use those rights in a manner harmful to the trust.

As we noted recently in *City of Berkeley v. Superior Court,* supra, 26 Cal. 3d 515, 162 Cal. Rptr. 327, 606 P.2d 362, the decision of the United States Supreme Court in *Illinois Central Railroad Company v. Illinois,* supra, 146 U.S. 387, 13 S. Ct. 110, 36 L. Ed. 1018, "remains the primary authority even today, almost nine decades after it was decided."

[The court summarized the *Illinois Central* case and reviewed subsequent California cases.]

Finally, in our recent decision in *City of Berkeley v. Superior Court,* supra, 26 Cal. 3d 515, 162 Cal. Rptr. 327, 606 P.2d 362, we considered whether deeds executed by the Board of Tidelands Commissioners pursuant to an 1870 act conferred title free of the trust. Applying the principles of earlier decisions, we held that the grantees' title was subject to the trust, both because the Legislature had not made clear its intention to authorize a conveyance free of the trust and because the 1870 act and the conveyances under it were not intended to further trust purposes.

Once again we rejected the claim that establishment of the public trust constituted a taking of property for which compensation was required: "We do not divest anyone of title to property; the consequence of our decision will be only that some landowners whose predecessors in interest acquired property under the 1870 act will, like the grantees in *California Fish,* hold it subject to the public trust." (P. 532, 162 Cal. Rptr. 327, 606 P.2d 362.)

In summary, the foregoing cases amply demonstrate the continuing power of the state as administrator of the public trust, a power which extends to the revocation of previously granted rights or to the enforcement of the trust against lands long thought free of the trust (see *City of Berkeley v. Superior Court,* supra, 26 Cal. 3d 515, 162 Cal. Rptr. 327, 606 P.2d 362). Except for those rare instances in which a grantee may acquire a right to use former trust property free of trust restrictions, the grantee holds subject to the trust, and while he may assert a vested right to the servient estate (the right of use subject to the trust) and to any improvements he erects, he can claim no vested right to bar recognition of the trust or state action to carry out its purposes.

Since the public trust doctrine does not prevent the state from choosing between trust uses (*Colberg, Inc. v. State of California,* supra, 67 Cal. 2d 408, 419, 62 Cal. Rptr. 401, 432 P.2d 3; *County of Orange v. Heim* (1973) 30 Cal. App. 3d 694, 707, 106 Cal. Rptr. 825), the Attorney General of California, seeking to maximize state power under the trust, argues for a broad concept of trust uses. In his view, "trust uses" encompass all public uses, so that in practical effect the doctrine would impose no restrictions on the state's ability to allocate trust property. We know of no authority which supports this view of the public trust, except perhaps the dissenting opinion in *Illinois Central R. Co. v. Illinois,* supra, 146 U.S. 387, 13 S. Ct. 110, 36 L. Ed. 1018. Most decisions and commentators assume that "trust uses" relate to uses and activities in the vicinity of the lake, stream, or tidal reach at issue (see, e.g., *City of Los Angeles v. Aitken,* supra, 10 Cal. App. 2d 460, 468-469; *State of Cal. ex rel. State Lands Comm. v. County of Orange,* supra, 134 Cal. App. 3d 20, 184 Cal. Rptr. 423; Sax, op. cit. supra, 68 Mich. L. Rev. 471, 542). The tideland cases make this point clear; after *City of Berkeley v. Superior Court,* supra, 26 Cal. 3d 515, 162 Cal. Rptr. 327, 606 P.2d 362, no one could contend that the state could grant tidelands free of the trust merely because the grant served some public purpose, such as increasing tax revenues, or because the grantee might put the property to a commercial use.

Thus, the public trust is more than an affirmation of state power to use public property for public purposes. It is an affirmation of the duty of the state to protect the people's common heritage of streams, lakes, marshlands and tidelands, surrendering that right of protection only in rare cases when the abandonment of that right is consistent with the purposes of the trust.

3.   THE CALIFORNIA WATER RIGHTS
SYSTEM . . .

Thus, the function of the Water Board has steadily evolved from the narrow role of deciding priorities between competing appropriators to the charge of comprehensive planning and allocation of waters. This change necessarily affects the board's responsibility with respect to the public trust. The board of limited powers of 1913 had neither the power nor duty to consider interests protected by the public trust; the present board, in undertaking planning and allocation of water resources, is required by statute to take those interests into account.

4.   THE RELATIONSHIP BETWEEN THE PUBLIC
TRUST DOCTRINE AND THE CALIFORNIA WATER
RIGHTS SYSTEM

As we have seen, the public trust doctrine and the appropriative water rights system administered by the Water Board developed independently of each other. Each developed comprehensive rules and principles which, if applied to the full extent of their scope, would occupy the field of allocation of stream waters to the exclusion of any competing system of legal thought. Plaintiffs, for example, argue that the public trust is antecedent to and thus limits all appropriative water rights, an argument which implies that most appropriative water rights in California were acquired and are presently being used unlawfully. Defendant DWP, on the other hand, argues that the public trust doctrine as to stream waters has been "subsumed" into the appropriative water rights system and, absorbed by that body of law, quietly disappeared; according to DWP, the recipient of a board license enjoys a vested right in perpetuity to take water without concern for the consequences to the trust.

We are unable to accept either position. In our opinion, both the public trust doctrine and the water rights system embody important precepts which make the law more responsive to the diverse needs and interests involved in the planning and allocation of water resources. To embrace one system of thought and reject the other would lead to an unbalanced structure, one which would either decry as a breach of trust appropriations essential to the economic development of this state, or deny any duty to protect or even consider the values promoted by the public trust. Therefore, seeking an accommodation which will make use of the pertinent principles of both the public trust doctrine and the appropriative water rights system, and drawing upon the history of the public trust and the water rights system, the body of judicial precedent, and the views of expert commentators, we reach the following conclusions:

a. The state as sovereign retains continuing supervisory control over its navigable waters and the lands beneath those waters. This principle, fundamental to the concept of the public trust, applies to rights in flowing waters as well as to rights in tidelands and lakeshores; it prevents any party from acquiring a vested right to appropriate water in a manner harmful to the interests protected by the public trust.

b. As a matter of current and historical necessity, the Legislature, acting directly or through an authorized agency such as the Water Board, has the power to grant usufructuary licenses that will permit an appropriator to take water from flowing streams and use that water in a distant part of the state, even though this taking does not promote, and may unavoidably harm, the trust uses at the source stream. The population and economy of this state depend upon the appropriation of vast quantities of water for uses unrelated to in-stream trust values. California's Constitution (see art. X, §2), its statutes (see Wat. Code, §§100, 104), decisions (see, e.g., *Waterford I. Dist. v. Turlock I. Dist.* (1920) 50 Cal. App. 213, 220, 194 P. 757), and commentators (e.g., Hutchins, The Cal. Law of Water Rights, op. cit. supra, p. 11) all emphasize the need to make efficient use of California's limited water resources: all recognize, at least implicitly, that efficient use requires diverting water from in-stream uses. Now that the economy and population centers of this state have developed in reliance upon appropriative water, it would be disingenuous to hold that such appropriations are and have always been improper to the extent that they harm public trust uses, and can be justified only upon theories of reliance or estoppel.

c. The state has an affirmative duty to take the public trust into account in the planning and allocation of water resources, and to protect public trust uses whenever feasible. Just as the history of this state shows that appropriation may be necessary for efficient use of water despite unavoidable harm to public trust values, it demonstrates that an appropriative water rights system administered without consideration of the public trust may cause unnecessary and unjustified harm to trust interests. (See Johnson, op. cit. supra, 14 U.C. Davis L. Rev. 233, 256-257; Robie, Some Reflections on Environmental Considerations in Water Rights Administration (1972), 2 Ecology L.Q. 695, 710-711; Comment, op. cit. supra, 33 Hastings L.J. 653, 654.) As a matter of practical necessity the state may have to approve appropriations despite foreseeable harm to public trust uses. In so doing, however, the state must bear in mind its duty as trustee to consider the effect of the taking on the public trust (see *United Plainsmen v. N.D. State Water Con. Commission* (N.D. 1976) 247 N.W.2d 457, 462-463), and to preserve, so far as consistent with the public interest, the uses protected by the trust.

Once the state has approved an appropriation, the public trust imposes a duty of continuing supervision over the taking and use of the appropriated water. In exercising its sovereign power to allocate water

resources in the public interest, the state is not confined by past allocation decisions which may be incorrect in light of current knowledge or
inconsistent with current needs.

The state accordingly has the power to reconsider allocation decisions even though those decisions were made after the consideration of
their effect on the public trust. The case for reconsidering a particular
decision, however, is even stronger when that decision failed to weigh
and consider public trust uses. In the case before us, the salient fact is
that no responsible body has ever determined the impact of diverting
the entire flow of the Mono Lake tributaries into the Los Angeles Ac-
queduct. This is not a case in which the Legislature, the Water Board,
or any judicial body has determined that the needs of Los Angeles outweigh the needs of the Mono Basin, that the benefit gained is worth
the price. Neither has any responsible body determined whether some
lesser taking would better balance the diverse interests. Instead, DWP
acquired rights to the entire flow in 1940 from a water board which
believed it lacked both the power and the duty to protect the Mono
Lake environment, and continues to exercise those rights in apparent
disregard for the resulting damage to the scenery, ecology, and human
uses of Mono Lake.

It is clear that some responsible body ought to reconsider the allocation of the waters of the Mono Basin. No vested rights bar such reconsideration. We recognize the substantial concerns voiced by Los
Angeles — the city's need for water, its reliance upon the 1940 board
decision, the cost both in terms of money and environmental impact of
obtaining water elsewhere. Such concerns must enter into any allocation decision. We hold only that they do not preclude a reconsideration
and reallocation which also takes into account the impact of water diversion on the Mono Lake environment.

NOTES AND QUESTIONS

1. If the state, after reconsideration of water allocation decisions
in light of the public trust, were to affirm its earlier decisions, would
the court have authority to alter the allocation of water resources under
the public trust doctrine? Or is the holding essentially procedural, in
much the same way as NEPA?

2. Does this case persuade you that the public trust doctrine can
be a valuable check on governmental allocation of resources? Should
the court have gone further in requiring substantive changes in order
to protect the public trust?

Huffman, Trusting the Public Interest to Judges: A Comment on the Public Trust Writings of Professors Sax, Wilkinson, Dunning, and Johnson

63 Denver Univ. L. Rev. 565 (1986)

After several decades of chugging along far more slowly than the Illinois Central Railroad, the public trust doctrine has taken flight during the last decade. Courts from Massachusetts to California have increasingly relied upon the public trust doctrine to justify an assortment of decisions that have the purpose of protecting natural resources from degradation or destruction. Proponents of the public trust doctrine urge that it is time to realize that the continent has been conquered and that something must be done to save it from those who would unknowingly or selfishly destroy it. Because legislators and administrators have been parties to rampant environmental destruction, proponents argue that we must look to the courts for our salvation and offer the public trust doctrine as an ideal remedy for the courts to prescribe. Unfortunately, the doctrine is a bit limited in its historic application, but that should be no problem for the creative judge. A good hard look will surely reveal that something needs to be done.

The rebirth and dramatic growth of the public trust doctrine is in no small part the product of a classic article on the subject by Joseph Sax. Those who are troubled by the new public trust doctrine must therefore pay close attention to Sax's writing. Other legal scholars have come to Sax's aid in shouldering the burden of justifying and explaining the public trust doctrine. Their writings therefore also deserve attention. In this article, I will comment on the writings of Professor Joseph Sax, Charles Wilkinson, Ralph Johnson, and Harrison Dunning. . . .

This discussion of the works of four distinguished scholars leads to a few broad conclusions about the public trust doctrine. First, the doctrine is clearly part of a trend which Sax argues has resulted in "property rights . . . being fundamentally redefined to the disadvantage of property owners." I think this trend is an unfortunate one in terms of the management and allocation of increasingly scarce natural resources. Garrett Hardin and other writers have reminded us of the tragedy of the commons. The solution of the commons tragedy is not a management committee or dictator, it is private property. The trend represented by the public trust doctrine is simply a return to the commons. The only difference is that the commons is totally closed to some interests, while the permitted development interests must jump through an assortment of legislative, administrative, and judicial hoops.

Having to jump through hoops may slow the process of exploitation, thereby postponing the tragedy, but the combination of increasing demand and diminishing supply will assure that the resources are exhausted, particularly where the effect of governmental action is to redistribute wealth. Therefore, society should give some consideration to private alternatives to the commons.

Second, assuming that Sax's democracy theory is the central justification for the doctrine, that it is just another form of the hard look doctrine as Rodgers suggests, I am at a loss for why we should be enamored with the democratic allocation of resources. I do not doubt that democracy is the best form of government, but I do not think that leads to the conclusion that the best way to make any or every resource allocation decision is democratically. To the contrary, the fact that the best form of government is democracy argues for making as few decisions as possible through government. The democratic process, when employed to allocate resources, is simply a more or less civilized scramble for the distributional benefits of particular allocations of resources. Because ours is often a less than civilized society, many members of which value the roar of motorized transport over the calm of a mountain wilderness and the comforts of a high-energy life style over the fish runs of the Columbia River, the public trust doctrine permits the more civilized members of our society to appeal to the courts to force the democracy to reconsider its decisions and come to a wiser choice.

Surely we are not deceived by this bit of legal fast shoe. If we believe in democracy, we should certainly live with its consequences. The public trust doctrine and its relations are tools for political losers or for those seeking to avoid the costs of becoming political winners. It forces the proponents of legislative action to justify a particular decision in isolation from the give-and-take of the legislative process. It is frequently argued that if the legislature does not like what the courts do, they can change it. Legislative action, however, does not come easily in the modern state legislature. Controversial issues, even where there is a clear majority position, are easily overlooked in the interests of other legislative agendas. Some will assert that a legislature's failure to act is an act in and of itself. However, the logic of that proposition is lost in the legislative context where the potential agenda always consists of more issues than can be considered meaningfully.

Third, the contention that the public trust doctrine is just another form of the "hard look" doctrine should not persuade us to be comfortable with the public trust approach. Instead, it should lead us to be skeptical of the "hard look" doctrine. Rodgers is right in linking the two because both are concepts used to justify judicial intervention in legislative and executive actions. The "hard look" doctrine tries hard to appear purely procedural and outcome neutral, but the public trust version of that doctrine reveals its substance. How hard a court looks does not depend exclusively upon the adequacy of the legislative and executive procedure, it also depends upon the substantive action that was taken. If we have learned nothing else from the legal realists, we should have come to understand the impact of values on judicial decisions.

Although I do not wish to defend democracy as a resource allocator, neither do I wish to defend the resource allocation efforts of legislators and administrators. Thus, the real issue in all of this is what institutional mechanisms should we employ to allocate resources. The public trust doctrine is part of a widespread presumption in favor of public allocation, although it is really a remedy for the perceived failure of public allocation. Thus, it parallels our approach to environmental law, which has been to regulate the regulators with at least as much vigor as they regulate private actions. If public resource allocations are perceived to be a problem, we should look at the possibility of improving the private rights system before resorting to reliance on an arcane doctrine that probably never meant what its proponents claim it means and that ignores the fact that the foundation of our resource allocation system is private property rights. Thus, state courts should take a "hard look" at the shortcomings of public trust theory before jumping into Mono Lake with the California Supreme Court.

NOTES AND QUESTIONS

1. What assumptions about the political process and institutions underlie Professor Sax's approach to the public trust doctrine? Do you find Professor Huffman's critique persuasive? What assumptions about the political process and institutions underlie his perspective?

2. Recall the *Reserve Mining* and *Boomer* cases discussed earlier. They highlighted courts' institutional limitations in addressing complex, modern environmental problems. The *Boomer* court, in fact, called for a legislative solution to the problem of air pollution. Do these cases suggest caution in expanding the public trust doctrine to address modern, complex environmental problems?

3. At the time Professor Sax wrote his seminal article about the public trust doctrine, there was widespread concern that the state and federal legislatures were not adequately addressing substantially all environmental problems. Moreover, NEPA was just coming into law and administrative law doctrines severely limited citizens' abilities to challenge government action. Shortly thereafter, the federal government and more recently state legislatures dramatically increased environmental regulation and protection of natural resources and expanded avenues for judicial review of administrative action. Do these developments suggest a lesser role for the public trust doctrine? Or does the

continuing dysfunction of the environmental protection efforts despite extensive statutory protections indicate that the courts can and should play a larger and more substantive role in protecting natural resources?

B.   THE PUBLIC LANDS

1.   NORMATIVE PERSPECTIVES

At this juncture, it is worthwhile to review the philosophical materials in Chapters 1 and 2. These readings — especially Leopold, Baxter, Taylor, and Devall — provide a variety of perspectives on the role for public ownership and management of lands. The following excerpt, emphasizing recreation policy, highlights the promise and tensions of public lands policy.

SAX, MOUNTAINS WITHOUT HANDRAILS: RECREATION POLICY FOR THE FEDERAL LANDS

23 Law Quadrangle Notes, Univ. Mich. L. School 14-17 (No. 1 Fall 1978)

Recreation has been a federal concern since 1864, when Congress entrusted Yosemite Valley and the Mariposa Grove to California "for public use, resort and recreation." Yet the question of why we made it a public task to give people opportunities to encounter nature is one that neither the Congress nor the public land management agencies has ever probed very deeply.

Engagement with nature is a permanent theme in American literature, from Cooper and Melville to Faulkner and Hemingway. The nature writers — Muir, Thoreau, Burroughs, Leopold, Abbey — have always attracted a substantial and devoted readership. The idea that nature is profoundly important to us is deeply implanted in the American consciousness. Nonetheless, one searches out public land policies in vain for any specific notion of how its promise is to be fulfilled.

To look at the public recreation lands in operation is inevitably to wonder what goals are being sought. At some major national parks — Yosemite, Yellowstone, and the south rim of the Grand Canyon — thousands of people visit on a single summer day, with traffic jams, long lines at restaurants and shops, noise, congestion, and litter — banal, standardized tourism. The style and rhythm of urban life have been imposed on a series of highly scenic backdrops.

On the California desert, or in the snow-covered north country, recreational vehicles import the noise, intensity, and high-speed free-way style to the public lands.

Nightclub entertainment in the parks, a golf course on the desert at Death Valley, and motorized trips down the timeless Colorado River in Grand Canyon, all defended on the grounds that they are necessary to meet tight vacation schedules, complete a picture of incongruity. Of course there is nothing new in this. Even the gentle John Muir, in a letter to a friend, remarked on "the blank, fleshy apathy" of most of those who come to Yosemite in the early days. "They climb sprawlingly to their saddles like overgrown frogs," he said, "ride up the valley with about as much emotion as the horses they ride upon and, comfortable when they have 'done it all' long for the safety and flatness of their proper homes."

The familiar comment that the parks have been the victims of their own success turns out to be a cliche with more bite than is usually recognized. The problem is not simply that the parks' physical capacity to meet demand is being strained; rather, their popularity is largely built upon uses quite at odds with the idea that underlies their very existence.

Our reluctance to recognize that something incongruous is happening rests on a tension between two very different public philosophies. A prescriptive tradition, illustrated by the writings of figures such as John Muir, Frederick Law Olmsted, and Theodore Roosevelt, holds that nature is important to use and that it is the task of government to provide encouragement and opportunity of engagement with nature as a democratic ideal. Echoing what Olmsted had said nearly 40 years earlier in his brilliant Yosemite Report, Roosevelt remarked, on laying the Yellowstone cornerstone in 1903:

> I cannot too often repeat that the essential feature in the present management of the Yellowstone Park, as in all similar places, is its essential democracy — it is the preservation of the scenery, of the forests, of the wilderness life and the wilderness game for the people as a whole, instead of leaving the enjoyment thereof to be confined to the very rich who can control private reserves.

But like Olmsted, Roosevelt believed the lands should be reserved as settings in which the American people could test and affirm fundamental social values — not merely as amenities, but as necessities for a nation of free, independent people.

This prescriptive view is in tension with a libertarian, neutralist tradition, far more familiar to us, that rests upon a deep suspicion of government's attempts to make people good, and on an even deeper distrust of the notion that public servants know what is good for people.

Much of what we see as the fashioning of public policy for recreation lands is an effort to reconcile these two conflicting traditions without admitting that any real conflict of political philosophies need be faced. We continue to be captivated by the idea that our parklands should be managed to promote encounters with nature as something fundamentally important to the citizens of an urban, industrial society; and we resist their assimilation into the model of industrial tourism, however great and popular the pressures in that direction may be. At the same time we resist diligently the proposition that some "we" — the government or the National Park Service — knows better than the visitor how he or she ought to experience the lands.

The dilemma has created some strange anomalies. The first and most common of these is the assumption that we don't really have to make recreation policy at all. Rather, it is thought, we need only "manage the resource" by scientific principles. The seemingly neutral value of scientific land management appears to avoid the painful necessity of having to choose among various visitor preferences. Of course any intelligent policy must prevent abuses that destroy the land; and of course it is appropriate to have a preservation policy — to maintain species, to promote scientific study or to reserve options for the future. While such policies are to some extent necessary for, and consistent with a recreation policy, they are not themselves a recreation policy; and it is disingenuous to treat them as if they were.

Every human use affects the resource to some extent, and no scientific principle can tell us whether 500 or 5000 or 15,000 people should be allowed to boat down the Colorado River in the Grand Canyon; whether a ski lift should be installed in an alpine valley or a highway be permitted to cross a park. Land-management knowledge may tell us how severe and how long lasting the impacts of such decisions will be. But recreation policy necessarily asks a different question: How do we find a balance between impact on the land and the sustenance of some kind of level of human experience? These are questions of policy, not of science.

Nor can recreation-policy choices be avoided by referring to something called public demand. Demand is simply a measure of how people are willing to spend their time and money. There is no doubt that if we were to build gambling casinos, elegant restaurants, race tracks, and carnivals in the parks, they would attract a large clientele. There is public demand — perfectly legitimate, it may be assumed — for all these activities. But to meet such demand would put government in the position of a mere landlord and would abdicate the public policy question altogether.

Neither is it sufficient to claim that public recreation lands ought to be reserved for those uses that cannot, or will not, be served by private entrepreneurs. No entrepreneur can offer the opportunity to visit Yosemite Valley or the Colorado River in Grand Canyon, whose attraction lies in their uniqueness. The question remains, which of the various and conflicting demands to use those resources should be favored?

Nor, finally, can we avoid the difficulty of choice by asserting that we will simply hold the resources available and permit the users themselves to decide how to enjoy them. Management decisions must perforce be made, and those decisions themselves imprint an agenda on the landscape. When the government decides to build hotels, supermarkets, restaurants and shops in Yosemite Valley, the valley necessarily provides a different kind of experience than if it had been left undeveloped, and it will attract different numbers and a different mix of visitors. Demand is not some ethereal presence; it is generated in significant part by management decisions. A park with an elegant hotel generates a demand for certain kinds of supportive services, just as a park filled with roads generates a demand for a number of service stations, and as a park managed to serve many thousands of visitors requires measures for crowd control.

The fact is that demand exists, in its most important form, simply as an enormous quantity of leisure time that Americans have to spend. The public lands have the capacity to provide space to fill as much or as little of that time as we wish to make available. They could be managed to absorb more of that time, and one can imagine a range of choices, from the present situation to something like a Disneyworld Complex. No principle of science or economics tells us where on that spectrum we must alight. Certainly no catch-phrase like "meeting the recreation needs of the American people" tells us anything decisive.

Ultimately, we have to decide what ends we want our public recreation lands to serve. Beneath the prescriptive and neutralist traditions, behind our efforts to find compromising principles, lies a conflict between the parks as institutions serving popular demands and the parks as a vehicle to promote our aspirations to become better than we are. In either case they could meet the standard for a free society; that government must give us what we want rather than what some official thinks we ought to want. The dilemma is that we want both things in some degree — service of current preferences as well as opportunities to probe our ideal aspirations — and we can't have all of everything simultaneously.

The key to understanding the problem of public recreation is an appreciation that the issue is not, at its heart, a conflict between some elite minority and a popular majority, but a conflict within us all — one in which current gratification of perfectly legitimate desires set against the chance to explore a more ideal version of what we would like to be. That is the secret of the continuing appeal of a figure like John Muir.

The precise balance to be drawn between these competing desires is not a matter I can explore in these few pages. I do want to suggest here that the prescriptive tradition is more than just self-indulgent escapism or the preference of some discrete minority of climbers, backpackers, and misanthropes. It rests upon an idea of culture values that are not only appropriate to, but important for a free and democratic society. Therefore, the choices in park management must be made on a basis far more profound than the notion that some official thinks he knows how to make us good, or that some vocal elite thinks it is entitled to a disproportionate share of tax supported public resources.

I began with the observation that there is something about the idea of an encounter with nature that has a powerful hold on the American imagination — an idea of independence, of self-reliance, self-sufficiency, and autonomy. These are ideas that lie very close to the core of the culture values we prize most, and that seem peculiarly to be threatened by the style of modern, urban, industrial society. The opportunity for an encounter with nature — of which the parks are a physical symbol — can be seen as an act of resistance against the threat. Rather than being a symbol of escape from the harsh facts of the real world, the parklands can be seen as a culture-bearing medium, a setting in which deeply held values can be renewed, reaffirmed and realized as a source of strength and confidence against the pressures continually being exerted in the workaday world.

Perhaps such a view sees the parks as an artifact of secular religion, and I am prepared to accept this as an apt description. The encounter with nature, in these terms, is very much like a sabbatical experience; a venture out of the everyday world, not as an act of rejection but as an experience of renewal and reaffirmation. It is significant, I think, that John Muir entitled one of his most celebrated articles "The Gospel for July," and in it he invited those who were "business-tangled and . . . burdened to duty" to take time out for an experience of renewal.

In the same vein, in what is perhaps the greatest of all American nature stories, Hemingway's "The Big Two-Hearted River," Nick undertakes his fishing venture as a means to restore contact with authentic values, knowing full well that he soon must and will return to the conventional and brutal world. So he uses the experience to renew values that come from what Thoreau called, in Walden, the art of living deliberately. There has probably never been in literature a more beautiful description of deliberateness than that in "The Big Two-Hearted River" — the camping, the cooking, the preparation for the fishing ritual. And with it, the powerful feeling of self-renewal: "Now things were done. . . . He had made his camp. He was settled. Nothing could touch him . . . He was there, in the good place. He was in his home, where he had made it."

Aldo Leopold, in his essay "Wildlife in American Culture," has described this experience in another form. "There is value," he said, "in any experience that reminds us of our distinctive national origins and evolution . . . that stimulates awareness of history. . . . On [these experiences] is based a distinctively American tradition of self-reliance, hardihood, woodcraft and marksmanship. These are intangibles, but they are not abstractions. Theodore Roosevelt was a great sportsman, not because he hung up many trophies, but because he expressed this intangible American tradition in words any schoolboy could understand. It is not far amiss to say that such men created cultural value by being aware of it, and by creating a pattern for its growth."

These observations suggest a content for an authentic idea of the encounter with nature, drawing upon culture values that have both contemporary vitality and practical (rather than merely escapist) relevance. It is an idea of personal engagement with basic values through a ritual of self-discovery and reaffirmation. It rests upon a conscious detachment from the values, expectations, and preconceptions we carry around from our daily experience, for the purpose of finding a gauge against which to test our goals, our behavior, and our institutions.

Like literature and art, the encounter with nature is a means of self-discovery, unburdened by conventional expectations; though, notably, it is more accessible to the general population than the bulk of high culture. Discovery may take any of a number of forms. It may unfold as challenge — finding out what we can do, measured against standards we set for ourselves. It may express itself as discovery of what interests us, abstracted from conventional ideas of what ought to be interesting. It may involve a means to provoke understanding, looking at the world and seeing it whole: as complexity, as ambiguity, as struggle, serenity, continuity, repose, or change.

Encounters with nature offer the opportunity for freshness of perception, for individualization and for intensity of experience. Engagement with nature — at its best — is distinctive to the extent that it offers what art offers: a fresh vision of the world, independent of customary moral and aesthetic views, demanding effort and a creative response from an audience. Such encounters are everything that differs from the packaged, familiar, standardized recreation, offering only what is accepted, predictable, and unproblematic, its end implicit in its beginning.

Perhaps I can give some concrete content to these reflections by describing what I have called an authentic encounter with nature. Hiking with a pack on one's back appears superficially to be a strangely unappealing activity. The hiker, vulnerable to insects and bad weather, carries a heavy load over rough terrain, only to end up in the most primitive sort of shelter, where he or she eats basic foods prepared in the simplest fashion. Certainly there are often attractive rewards, such as a beautiful alpine lake with especially good fishing. But these are not sufficient explanations for such extraordinary exertions, for there are few places indeed that could not be easily made more accessible, and by much more comfortable means.

To the uninitiated backpacker a day in the woods can be, and often is, an experience of unrelieved misery. The pack is overloaded; tender feet stumble and are blistered. It is alternatively too hot or too cold. The backpacker has the wrong gear for the weather or has packed it in the wrong place; the tent attracts every gust of wind and rivulet of water. The fire won't start, or the stove fails just when it's needed. And the turns that seemed so clear on the map have now become utterly confusing.

Such experiences, familiar in one form or another to all beginners, are truly unforgiving and when things go wrong, they do so in cascading fashion. Yet others camping nearby suffer no such miseries. Though their packs are lighter, they have an endless supply of exactly the things that are needed. Their tents go up quickly; they have solved the mystery of wet wood, and they sit under a deceptively simple rain shelter, eating their dinner in serene comfort. What is more, they are having a good time. The woods, for the beginning and endless succession of indistinguishable trees apparently designed to bewilder the hapless walker, conceal a patch of berries or an edible mushroom; nearby, but unseen, are beautiful grazing deer, or overhead, a soaring eagle.

With time, patience, and effort one recognizes that these things are available to everyone; that one can get in control of the experience. The pack lightens as tricks are learned; how to substitute and how to improvise quickly, out of available materials, the things previously lugged. Everything put in the head lessens what has to be carried on the shoulders. The sense of frustration falls away, and with it, the fear that things will break down. One knows how to adapt. The pleasure of adaptation is considerable in itself because it is liberating; one is able to take advantage of conveniences, but is not a captive of them.

It isn't only a lifting of burdens. The backpacker discovers that the positive quality of the voyage is directly related to one's own knowledge and resources. There is often a dramatic revelation that the woods are full of things to see — for those who know how to see them.

The kind of encounter that routinely takes place in the modern motorized vehicle, or in the managed, prepackaged resort, is calculated to diminish these opportunities. Rather than exposing us, it insulates us from immediacy of experience and makes it unnecessary to see and feel the details of our surroundings with clarity. Nothing distinctive about us as individuals is crucial. The margin of error permitted is great enough to neutralize the importance of what we know. If we roar off in the wrong direction, we can easily roar back again, for none of our energy is expended. It isn't important to pay close attention to the weather; we are insulated from it. We need not notice a small spring;

we are not at the margin where water counts. The opportunity for intensity of experience is drained away.

It is not that the motorized tourist or the visitor at a highly developed site must necessarily lose intensity or deliberateness; or that he is compelled to experience his surroundings at a remove, just as it is not inevitable that backpacking or fly-fishing will produce these responses. Rather it is that the circumstances we impose on ourselves have the power to shape our experience. The automobile visitor, as Edward Abbey noted, is routinely drawn into "tedious traffic jams, the awful food of park cafeterias and roadside eateries, the nocturnal search for a place to sleep or camp, the dreary routine of One-Stop Service. . . ." And for this reason, the questions he asks change: as Abbey puts it, with his usual sharpness of tongue, the three things the motorized tourist most often wants to know are: [1] Where's the john? [2] How long does it take to see this place? and [3] Where's the Coke machine?

The challenge for public land recreation, then, is this: If the great promise of the lands is to be kept, the experience they distinctively offer should be uncommon and must demand a good deal from the visitor. For the encounter with nature essentially means an opportunity to engage the world freshly and on one's own. Nothing in public-land management should suggest that the familiar, predictable, comforting facilities, and activities many visitors expect are improper or unenjoyable. Rather, the visitor can be told that in these places he is offered something out of the ordinary, the whole purpose of which is to present a contract to what has become familiar and predictable.

This does not by any means suggest that our recreation lands should be managed only for experienced backcountry hikers or those who are prepared to go ski-touring in the wilderness. Perhaps the most important management task is dealing with those who are new to encounters with nature; they should be encouraged. As novices, they are often understandably hesitant and fearful, for the woods are dark and deep. The danger is that in seeking to make the lands accessible we make them familiar — and that visitors who come to a park (often hesitant, often without clear expectations) to find out what John Muir was talking about, find themselves confronted by a full panoply of urban facilities and services designed (with every good intention, to be sure) to put their fearfulness at rest but with the result that they find themselves in a version of the protected urban environment to which the public land can be a contrast.

In the case of such visitors the task is to offer more provocative and unfamiliar settings — a desert where one is made aware of the heat, the geological and biological complexity and the sparseness of life rather than a place where one can go from air conditioned room to roadside scenic overlooks to an irrigated golf course; a valley where the predominant sounds are of birds and water, rather than of motors; a place where — if dangerous wildlife lives — it is the visitors who must accommodate; mountains without handrails.

Nearly 40 years ago, the Forest Service published a book entitled Forest Outings, in which it captures precisely the task of mediation that faces public management officials, spelling out policy objectives that steer the middle course between making the lands familiar and unchallenging to the novice and ignoring his needs altogether. The goal, it said, was "to provide graded steps through which the individual may progressively educate himself from enjoyment of mass forms of forest recreation toward the capacity to enjoy those demanding greater skills, more self-reliance, and a true love of the wild. Most men or women previously unacquainted with the forest in its natural state would experience discomfort and fear. . . . But if progressively they may experience the urbanized forest park, the large forest campground, the small camping group, the overnight or week-end hike, and so gain a sense of confidence in their own resourcefulness and lose the fear of wild country, then the final step is simple and natural."

Converting this illustrative suggestion into a coherent set of management decisions is the central task for a public land recreation policy.

PROBLEM

The beauty of Professor Sax's imagery inspires much promise for publicly owned and managed lands. Is this vision achievable within our political institutions? Return to the Grand Canyon problem posed in Chapter 1, supra, p. 22. Does Professor Sax provide a useful framework for approaching the issues presented?

2.   OVERVIEW OF THE FEDERAL LAND SYSTEM

THE PUBLIC LANDS OF THE UNITED STATES, IN E. MOSS (ED.), LAND USE CONTROLS IN THE UNITED STATES

(1977)

Approximately one-third of the land in the United States is owned by the federal government and managed by federal agencies. Most of these public lands are located in the eleven western states and in Alaska, where the federal government still owns vast acreages, but there are also important holdings in the eastern states as well. . . .

THE PUBLIC LANDS

The public lands of the United States are remarkably diverse in character. They range from the northern tip of Alaska to the southern end of Florida, encompassing all types of climates, terrains, and vegetation. The highest point in North America, Mount McKinley, lies on public land, and so does the lowest point in the United States, Death Valley. Mountains, valleys, tundra, river deltas, swamps, and seashores all are represented in the vast federal holdings, as are a broad range of actual or potential resources, including timber, minerals, forage, watersheds, sites for the expansion of towns and cities, and settings for recreation and associated activities.

During the nineteenth century a basic policy of the United States government was to encourage westward expansion and settlement through the disposal of public lands. Homestead grants made land available to settlers, land grants to the new states encouraged education and other supportive uses, and grants such as those for railroad construction stimulated the construction of public facilities. Beginning with the establishment of Yellowstone Park in 1872, however, the federal government began to reserve certain portions of its land for special purposes and permanent federal ownership. During the ensuing years, millions of acres of federal lands were withdrawn from entry under the disposal laws, often to protect natural resources from private exploitations, as well as to serve emerging national needs. In addition, the federal government began to purchase or repurchase selected tracts of land for particular purposes.

Today the public lands include both (1) the so-called "public domain" lands which have never left federal ownership since they were ceded to the federal government by the original states or were acquired from other countries; and (2) lands which have been acquired by the federal government for specific purposes.

In 1964, when it established the Public Land Law Review Commission, Congress stated that:

> It is hereby declared to be the policy of Congress that the public lands of the United States shall be (a) retained and managed or (b) disposed of, all in a manner to provide the maximum benefit for the general public. [43 U.S.C. §1391.]

The Public Land Law Review Commission itself, in its recommendations which were released in 1970, urged that future disposal of public lands be made only when such action would provide the maximum benefit for the general public. Regarding the lands retained in federal ownership, the commission stressed that their "values must be preserved so that they may be used and enjoyed by all Americans."

MANAGING AGENCIES

The following four agencies manage most of the public lands of the United States:

1. The Forest Service of the U.S. Department of Agriculture.
2. The Bureau of Land Management (BLM) of the U.S. Department of the Interior.
3. The Fish and Wildlife Service of the U.S. Department of the Interior.
4. The National Park Service of the U.S. Department of the Interior.

1. THE FOREST SERVICE

The Forest Service is responsible for the national forests, which comprise about one-fourth of all public lands or around 187 million acres. The vast bulk of these national forests (over 160 million acres) is located in the western states, including Alaska. In all, there are 155 different national forests in 40 states.

The Forest Service manages the national forests under two principal acts, the Organic Act of 1897, [16 U.S.C. §475] which was the first comprehensive act governing the management of the national forests, and the Multiple Use-Sustained Yield Act of 1960. [16 U.S.C. §§528-31.] Under the Organic Act national forests were to be established to provide favorable conditions of water flow and to furnish a continuous supply of timber for the use of American citizens. These purposes were enlarged by the Multiple Use-Sustained Yield Act to include outdoor recreation, range, timber, watershed, and fish and wildlife purposes. Renewable resources are to be managed on a sustained yield basis, which means "the achievement and maintenance in perpetuity of a high-level annual or regular periodic output of the various renewable resources of the national forests without impairment of the productivity of the land." In making its management decisions, the Forest Service must give due consideration to the relative values of the various resources in particular areas. Finally, the main goal of the multiple-use law is to produce "management of all the various renewable surface resources of the national forests so that they are utilized in the combination that will best meet the needs of the American people. . . ."

Under the terms of the Multiple Use-Sustained Yield Act, the Forest Service draws up multiple use plans for the national forests on a forest-by-forest basis. These plans then govern management decisions on matters such as the sale of timber, methods of timber harvest, and

regarding whether these decisions have in fact served the broad purposes of the act and some have argued that the terms of the act itself
are so discretionary that they impose virtually no congressional standards on the Forest Service.

The Forest and Rangeland Renewable Resources Planning Act of
1974 [16 U.S.C. §1601 et seq.] requires the Forest Service to carry out
long-term planning for the national forests in accordance with principles set forth in the Multiple Use-Sustained Yield Act and the National
Environmental Policy Act (NEPA). Under the [ ] 1974 act, the Forest
Service must prepare a renewable resource program first for the four-
year period from 1976 through 1980 and subsequently for each decade.
These programs must include an inventory of specific needs and opportunities for public and private program investments in the national forests, along with an analysis of anticipated costs and benefits, priorities,
and personnel requirements. [Forest resource planning was substantially expanded by the National Forest Management Act of 1976
(NFMA) and a variety of other more specialized forest management
acts. Part C will explore the NFMA.]

2.   The Bureau of Land Management (BLM)

The BLM is responsible for the administration of some 470 million acres or over 60 percent of all federal lands. Most of this acreage
is comprised of public domain lands which have not been reserved for
particular uses. Almost two-thirds of the BLM lands are in Alaska, and
the remainder are almost entirely in the eleven western states. Essentially, these are lands which are not suitable for agriculture and have
not been included in the national forests or national parks systems.

The BLM also plays the lead role, along with the Geological Survey
of the Department of Interior, in the supervision of the resource development of the submerged lands of the Outer Continental Shelf. The
accelerated program of offshore oil leasing which has followed in the
wake of the energy crisis has greatly increased the significance of this
responsibility.

[Until 1976, there was] no comprehensive, organic act regulating
the vast holdings of the federal government which fall within the jurisdiction of the BLM. [The Federal Land Policy and Management Act
of 1976 (FLPMA), 43 U.S.C. §§1701-84, established a comprehensive
planning process for BLM lands and authorized BLM to manage its
holdings on the basis of multiple-use and sustained yield principles. In
addition, many] of the old laws governing private use or disposal of
public domain lands (the Homestead Laws, for example) are still on
the statute books, but only a limited number have relevance and importance today. Among these are the Mineral Leasing Act of 1920 [30

U.S.C. §181 et seq.], an antiquated law which governs the leasing of mineral rights for coal, oil, gas, and oil shale, and the Taylor Grazing Act of 1934 [43 U.S.C. §315 et seq.], which established a permit and fee system for livestock grazing on public domain lands. . . .

3.   THE FISH AND WILDLIFE SERVICE

The agency administers the National Wildlife Refuge System, which includes over 340 national wildlife refuges and game ranges, comprising over 30 million acres, and about a hundred small fish hatcheries. By statute, the components of this system are those areas under the jurisdiction of the Department of the Interior which are administered "as wildlife refuges, areas for the protection and conservation of fish and wildlife that are threatened with extinction, wildlife ranges, game ranges, wildlife management areas, or waterfowl production areas." [16 U.S.C. §668dd(a).]

4.   THE NATIONAL PARK SERVICE

This agency administers the National Park System, which includes over 23 million acres of land. The National Park Service Act of 1916 established that all national parks are to be managed:

> To conserve the scenery and the natural and historic objects and the wildlife therein and to provide for the enjoyment of the same in such manner and by such means as will leave them unimpaired for the enjoyment of future generations. [16 U.S.C. §1.]

The individual components of the system are governed by particular statutes which generally aim to maintain the land in its natural state, but differ in the details of management.

The individual components include not only the national parks, but other types of areas as well. For administrative purposes, the National Park Service has grouped its lands into the following three categories: natural areas, historical areas, and recreation areas. The natural areas include the national parks and national monuments of scientific significance. The historical areas include those lands which have historical or archaeological significance. The recreation areas include those areas which were established primarily for recreational purposes, notably national recreation areas, seashores, lakeshores, scenic parkways, and wild and scenic rivers.

C.   FOREST RESOURCES: PROBLEMS IN IMPLEMENTING THE CONCEPT OF MULTIPLE USE

1.   HISTORICAL BACKGROUND TO FORESTRY POLICY

R. O'TOOLE, REFORMING THE FOREST SERVICE

20-24 (1988)

The national forests were first conceived in 1891, when a law was passed allowing the president to designate public lands as "forest reserves." The 1897 Organic Administration Act allowed timber sales and other management activities in these reserves and specified that the goals of the reserves were to "improve and protect the forests . . . , securing favorable conditions of water flows, and to furnish a continuous supply of timber."

The Forest Service itself did not come into existence until 1905, when the forest reserves were transferred from the Department of the Interior to the Bureau of Forestry in the Department of Agriculture. That bureau was headed by the charismatic Gifford Pinchot, who changed its name to Forest Service and gave himself the title of chief forester. Although nominally under the authority of the secretary of agriculture, Pinchot in fact reported directly to President Theodore Roosevelt and was considered a member of Roosevelt's "kitchen cabinet." . . .

By 1891, when the act authorizing creation of forest reserves was passed, few lands remained in federal ownership in the eastern United States. A law passed in 1911 authorized the Forest Service to purchase forested or cut-over lands in the East for "the regulation of the flow of navigable streams or for the production of timber." Under this law, national forests are now scattered throughout the South, Midwest, and Northeast, but most are still concentrated in the West.

With plenty of timber still available on private lands, the demand for national forest timber was low through the early 1940s. National forest management up to that time was largely custodial in nature, oriented toward forest protection, research, and administration of grazing, recreation, and other forest uses.

The concept of designating an area as "wilderness," withdrawing it from timber or other developments, was first conceived by a Forest Service landscape architect named Arthur Carhart. The idea was strongly promoted by two other Forest Service employees, Aldo Leopold and Robert Marshall. Leopold went on to found the wildlife management profession, and together with Marshall, cofounded the

Wilderness Society. Marshall became the Forest Service's director of recreation and convinced the agency to classify over 5 million acres of land as wilderness or primitive areas.

The post-World War II housing boom, combined with the depletion of private timber supplies in many parts of the country, increased demand for national forest timber. To gain access to this timber, the Forest Service embarked on a large-scale road construction program. The volume of timber national forest managements were allowed to sell increased from 5.6 billion board feet in 1950 to 12.8 billion by 1968.

In many cases, agency managers found that some of the best stands of timber were within the boundaries of classified wilderness areas. Since wilderness was an administrative, rather than legal, classification, the Forest Service could simply change the boundaries and build roads into the former wilderness areas. This led to increasing controversy, and in 1956 the Wilderness Society and other conservation groups began to ask Congress for legal protection of wilderness areas.

Such protection was not immediately forthcoming, largely due to opposition from the Forest Service. Instead, the agency offered its own new legislation, the Multiple-Use Sustained-Yield (MUSY) Act. Passed in 1960, this law required the Forest Service to manage the national forests for "outdoor recreation, range, timber, watershed, and wildlife and fish purposes." Wilderness supporters in Congress added a statement to the Forest Service's proposed language, which said that wilderness was "consistent with the purposes and provisions of this Act."

2.   FOREST RESOURCES PLANNING: THE CONCEPT OF MULTIPLE USE IN THEORY AND PRACTICE

Section 1 of the Multiple-Use Sustained-Yield Act proclaims that "[i]t is the policy of the Congress that the national forests are established and shall be administered for outdoor recreation, range, timber, watershed, and wildlife and fish purposes." Section 2 directs the Secretary of Agriculture "to develop and administer the renewable surface resources of the national forests for multiple use and sustained yield of the several products and services obtained therefrom." Section 4 of the Act, 16 U.S.C. §531, defines the terms "multiple use" and "sustained yield" as follows:

   (a) "Multiple Use" means: The management of all the various renewable surface resources of the national forests so that they are utilized in the combination that will best meet the needs of the American people; making the most judicious use of the land for some or all of these resources or related services over large areas enough to provide sufficient latitude for periodic adjustments in use to conform to changing needs and conditions; that some land will be used for less than all of the resources; and harmonious and coordinated management of the various resources, each with the other, without the impairment of the productivity of the land, with consideration being given to the relative values of the various resources, and not necessarily the combination of the uses that will give the greatest dollar return or the greatest unit output.

(b) "Sustained yield of the several products and services" means the achievement and maintenance in perpetuity of a high-level annual or regular periodic output of the various renewable resources of the national forests without impairment of the productivity of the land.

CLAWSON, THE CONCEPT OF MULTIPLE USE FORESTRY

8 Envtl. L. 281, 282-284, 286-287, 290-293 (1978)

Though the basic theory of multiple use of forests is apparently simple, perhaps deceptively so, its application often grows complicated. . . .

Optimum multiple use management of a forest requires consideration of at least three basic factors:

(1) Inputs of various productive factors such as labor, capital, and the output of the forest under its natural conditions of climate and soil;

(2) Trade-offs between one kind of output and another for such level of inputs; and

(3) Margins of total output value over total input for all combinations of inputs and outputs. This assumes that maximization of value of all outputs, subject to whether constraints may exist, is the goal of the forest owner or manager.

It is the measurement of the costs and values and the specific application of simple principles which present the difficult and often controversial problems. Application of the general idea of multiple use management requires consideration of at least the following problems.

(a) Production functions, or the relationship of inputs of productive factors to the volume and kind of output, for each of the various outputs of the forest. If the forest owner/manager spends money to plant tree seedlings, by how much is the output of wood increased? Similar questions arise for every other forest practice and for every forest output.

(b) Trade-off functions, or the relationships of the volume (and sometimes the quality) of one kind of output to the volume of other kinds of forest outputs, with any specified mix of inputs (including land). If one increases wood production by some management plan, what is the effect on stream flow? Such trade-off questions require trade-off functions for every pair of forest outputs, over the whole conceivable range of outputs of each. Trade-offs between outputs may vary according to the scale of the inputs or according to the mix of outputs.

(c) Measurement of the value of all forest outputs. Sometimes this can be done adequately by market prices, although such prices are not invariably an accurate measure of value. However, for many forest outputs there is no market price, even though there is obviously a value to the output.

(d) Measurement of the cost of all inputs, including capital as well as labor input. The inputs must be those necessary for the most economical production of the package of outputs. In forestry, as in many other economically productive activities, many costs are "overhead" in the sense they are incurred irrespective of volume of outputs and of kind of outputs. In many instances, what are called overhead costs do vary to some degree with the kind of management practiced and the kinds of outputs produced, and hence to some extent at least are attributable to particular kinds and amounts of outputs. But in most forestry, there will remain some costs which cannot reasonably be allocated to any kind or amount of output.

(e) Since the timing of inputs or costs and the timing of outputs or products is typically somewhat different, some means must be devised for bringing the various inputs and outputs to a common moment in time. The usual solution to this latter problem is "discounting," or the calculation of that present sum which, with interest, will yield the amount of the future cost or income which is anticipated. While simple in concept, this idea involves many complications in practice, including making several rather arbitrary choices or decisions which will be considered in more detail later. . . .

TRADE-OFF FUNCTIONS

Although every forest produces more than one kind of output — some highly valued, others less so — the proportions among outputs can be varied considerably in most cases. At least seven major forest outputs and the general relationships among them can be described in generalities (Table 1 on pages 1084-1085) and often measured in quantitative terms. The three rival outputs which are the least compatible with one another are wood, wilderness, and active recreation. Wilderness is the least tolerant of the three because logging or intensive recreation could seriously damage the wilderness character of an area. However, there is limited compatibility between recreation and forests managed for wood production, since some wood can be produced and harvested on many intensive recreation areas. The other four forest uses listed in the Table — attractive environment, wildlife, water, and general conservation — are to a large extent compatible with each of the three less tolerant uses.

MEASURING THE VALUE OF OUTPUTS

The various outputs from multiple use management of a forest can be measured in different terms: cubic or board feet for timber, acre feet for water, user days for recreation and wilderness, number of important wildlife species, and the like. Before comparing the values or benefits from one forest management program with those from another program, the various outputs must be converted to a common unit of comparison. The only such common unit yet invented is money, and the various kinds of outputs from the forest must be assigned a monetary value.

A major difficulty with this type of evaluation is that monetary values are ordinarily not placed on many forest outputs, and some "shadow price" or other estimate must be substituted. Many noneconomists, faced with the characteristics of some outputs and their consumption patterns, argue that it is impossible to estimate such monetary values. "You cannot place a value on a beautiful sunset, any more than you can on a mother's love."

The valuation problem is inescapable, and in fact values are placed on forest outputs all the time. Even the most vocal opponent of monetary valuation, when offered a limited sum for development of the forest output he is most interested in, will choose some program or projects and reject others, deciding that the latter are "not worth it" when the total funds available are inadequate to do everything he would desire. He has placed a higher, though non-quantitative, value on one output than on the other. If a forest manager takes the view that it is impossible to evaluate the scenic quality of a particular forest program and ignores that value, he is in effect placing a value of zero upon this output. If he took the view that evaluation was impossible and that the scenic value must be preserved at all costs, then he is placing an infinite value on this forest output. Either way, he has made a valuation — and almost surely a bad one. . . .

TABLE 1
Degree of Compatibility Among Various Forest Uses

PRIMARY USE	SECONDARY USE						
	Maintain attractive environment	Provide recreation opportunity	Wilderness	Wildlife	Natural watershed	General conservation	Wood production and harvest
Maintain attractive environment	✕	Moderately compatible: may limit intensity of use	Not inimical to wilderness but does not insure	Compatible to most wildlife, less so to a few	Fully compatible	Fully compatible	Limited compatibility: often affects amount of harvest
Provide recreation opportunity	Moderately compatible unless use intensity excessive	✕	Incompatible: would destroy wilderness character	Incompatible for some kinds; others can tolerate	Moderately compatible: depends on intensity of recreation use	Moderately compatible: incompatible if use too heavy	Limited compatibility depends on harvest timing and intensity: roads provide access
Wilderness	Fully compatible	Completely incompatible, can't tolerate heavy use	✕	Highly compatible to much wildlife, less so to others	Fully compatible	Fully compatible	Completely incompatible, precludes all harvest

Wildlife	Generally compatible	Limited compatibility: use intensity must be limited	Mostly compatible though some wildlife require vegetative manipulation	✕	Generally fully compatible	Generally fully compatible	Generally limits volume or conditions of harvest
Natural watershed	Fully compatible	Moderate compatibility: may require limitation on intensity	Not inimical to wilderness but does not insure	Generally compatible	✕	Fully compatible	Moderate compatibility: restricts harvest methods but does not prevent timber harvest
General conservation	Fully compatible	Moderately compatible if use not excessive	Not inimical to wilderness but does not insure	Generally compatible	Fully compatible	✕	Compatible but requires modifications in methods of timber harvest
Wood production and harvest	Compatible if harvest methods strictly controlled	Moderately compatible	Completely incompatible: would destroy wilderness	Compatible if harvest methods fully controlled	Compatible if harvest methods fully controlled	Compatible if harvest methods fully controlled	✕

QUESTIONS

1. Does the MUSYA provide coherent guidance about how the Forest Service should set forestry policy? Consider the following forests. How should they be managed? What uses should be given highest priority? Lowest? How should conflicts among uses be resolved?

- The Tongass National Forest, encompassing 16 million acres along the Gulf of Alaska, is the largest national forest in the United States. It contains vast stands of western hemlock and Sitka spruce, which are considered pulpwood species. The pulp industry has become established in this area, although the inaccessibility of this region and the variability of timber markets have made commercial timber production in this area unprofitable for much of the past decade. As a result, the federal government has provided large subsidies for road building and surveying the forest to bolster the local economy. Despite extensive logging activity, the Tongass National Forest contains vast areas of uncharted and unexplored forest. The forest provides habitat for numerous wildlife species, including the threatened bald eagle, trumpeter swan, Alaskan brown bear, black bear, moose, and Sitka black-tailed deer. The Tongass National Forest offers camping, hiking, hunting, fishing, and kayaking opportunities, although recreational use of the forest is relatively low due to its inaccessibility.

- The Delta National Forest, containing 59,000 acres in west-central Mississippi, is part of the Southern Forest which produces 70 percent of U.S. pulpwood. The climate and forest conditions assure rapid growth of the southern pines. Commercial mills are nearby and transportation systems to move products to market are excellent. Labor costs in this region are low. The heat and humidity of the region as well as the proliferation of snakes discourage most recreational uses of the forest. Water activities and hunting attract some users.

- The Siskiyou National Forest, spanning 1 million acres in southwestern Oregon and northern California, is part of the West Coast Forest. It contains vast areas of old growth forest, which exhibit trees of remarkable size and beauty. Much of this forest land is critical habitat for the threatened northern spotted owl. These birds rely upon the features of old growth forests and therefore are particularly vulnerable to all but the most sensitive timber production methods. The enormous size of the timber as well as the ruggedness of this region, however, make selective harvesting impractical. The Siskiyou National Forest has been referred to as a "botanist's paradise." It offers excellent camping, hunting, fishing, and nature study opportunities.

- The Pike National Forest, containing 1.1 million acres west of Colorado Springs, is part of the Western Interior Forest. It contains mountainous terrain and is most well-known for Pikes Peak and a variety of scenic areas. Its high altitude, rugged terrain, and slow growing rate make timber production less practical. Timber from this region cannot compete with the western and southern forests; consequently, timber production is principally of local importance. Pike National Forest contains beautiful scenery and offers excellent camping, hiking, fishing, and winter sports activities.
- The Santa Fe National Forest, containing more than 1.5 million acres in northern New Mexico, is part of the southern Western Interior Forest. The high altitude and rugged features of this forest make timber production unprofitable. Many areas within the forest are sacred to native peoples. The forest contains thousands of cultural sites, including impressive ruins of ancient villages. The Santa Fe National Forest contains some of the finest scenery in New Mexico. Recreation in New Mexico is anticipated to grow significantly in the coming years.

2. How would the following types of persons give content to the concept of multiple use: a natural resource economist, a recreationist (for instance, a hiker, fisher, or hunter), a preservationist, a deep ecologist, a professional forester for the Forest Service, a timber industry executive? How would you like to see the national forests described above managed?

SIERRA CLUB V. HARDIN

325 F. Supp. 99 (1971)

[In 1968, the Forest Service entered into a contract to sell more than 8.7 billion board feet of North Tongass National Forest timber over a 50-year period. Conservationists brought suit to enjoin the sale, the largest in history, on a variety of grounds including violation of the MUSYA.]

XI.   THE MULTIPLE USE — SUBSTANTIAL YIELD ACT

The Tongass National Forest constitutes the bulk of the land area of Southeastern Alaska. There are 16,016,000 acres in the Tongass National Forest of which approximately 4,555,000 are commercial forest lands. As of February 6, 1958, only 6/10ths of 1% of these commercial forest lands were reserved from logging. The Multiple Use Management Guide for the Alaska Region, April 1964, ¶213.1 states:

About 95% of the commercial forest land of Southeastern Alaska is occupied by overmature[8] stands of hemlock, spruce and cedar. Silviculturally, these decadent stands should be removed by clear-cutting methods as soon as possible to make way for new stands of fast growing second growth timber.

As part of the policy of liquidation of the old-growth forests in Southeastern Alaska, the Juneau Unit Sale was made.

The Multiple Use-Sustained Yield Act, 16 U.S.C. §§528-531 (Supp. 1970) provides five basic purposes for which the national forests are to be administered, to-wit: (1) outdoor recreation, (2) range, (3) timber, (4) watershed, (5) wildlife and fish purposes. The definitions of "multiple use" and "sustained yield" are set forth in §531. . . .

Plaintiffs introduced substantial testimony as well as documentary evidence, much of it in the form of offers of proof, to show that the Tongass National Forest is being administered predominantly for timber production. While the material undoubtedly shows the overwhelming commitment of the Tongass National Forest to timber harvest objectives in preference to other multiple use values, Congress has given no indication as to the weight to be assigned each value and it must be assumed that the decision as to the proper mix of uses within any particular area is left to the sound discretion and expertise of the Forest Service. Accordingly, evidence was admitted only for the purpose of showing that the Forest Service failed to give consideration[9] to any of the competing uses or that it took into consideration irrelevant matters

---

8. Maturity is defined as follows: "For a given species or stand, the approximate age beyond which growth falls off or decay begins to increase at a rate likely to assume economic importance."

9. The Act requires that the Forest Service give "due" consideration to the various competing uses. Plaintiffs argue that "due" could only mean "equal." This interpretation would seem to be precluded by the language of §531, which clearly contemplates that some areas may be unsuited to utilization of all resources. "Due" is impossible to define and merely indicates that Congress intended the Forest Service to apply their expertise to the problem after consideration of all relevant values. In the absence of a more satisfactory or objective standard the court considered that evidence in the record of "some" consideration was sufficient to satisfy the Act absent a showing that no *actual* consideration was given to other uses.

Professor Reich comments on the breadth of the Multiple Use-Sustained Yield Act of 1960 in a paper entitled "Bureaucracy and the Forests" (copyright The Fund for the Republic, Inc., Center for the Study of Democratic Institutions at Santa Barbara, California), as follows:

The standards Congress has used to delegate authority over the forests are general, so sweeping, and so vague as to represent a turnover of virtually all responsibility. 'Multiple use' does establish that the forests cannot be used exclusively for one purpose, but beyond this it is little more than a phrase expressing the hope that all competing interests can somehow be satisfied and leaving the real decisions to others.

which it should not have considered. Plaintiffs' parade of expert witnesses might have swayed the decision of the Forest Service or influenced the result in this case had it been properly presented at an administrative proceeding. Introduced as non-record evidence in this proceeding, however, it utterly fails to impeach the record provided by the Forest Service by showing that the administrative decision makers either lacked actual knowledge or failed to consider the myriad reports and studies available to them. The court must presume, therefore, that the Forest Service did give due consideration to the various values specified in the Multiple Use Sustained Yield Act. Having investigated the framework in which the decision was made, the court is forbidden to go further and substitute its decision in a discretionary matter for that of the Secretary.[10] . . .

NOTES AND QUESTIONS

1. As interpreted by the court in *Sierra Club v. Hardin,* does the MUSYA provide substantive constraints upon the Forest Service in deciding policy? On what facts would the court rein in the Forest Service? Could the Forest Service decide that every tree in the Tongass National Forest be cut and still be acting within its authority under the Act?

On appeal, the Ninth Circuit, in an unpublished (and hence not precedential) opinion, remanded the case to the District Court to consider a newly discovered expert report concluding that the cutting plan did not provide adequate protection for ecological values of the forest. The court cautioned that " 'due consideration' . . . requires that the values in question be informedly and rationally taken into balance. The requirement can hardly be satisfied by a showing of knowledge of the consequences and a decision to ignore them." *Sierra Club v. Butz,* 3 E.L.R. 20292 (9th Cir. 1973). Does this warning provide an enforceable substantive standard for Forest Service decisionmaking? Or is it more in the nature of NEPA's procedural standards?

2. The MUSYA was supposed to usher in a new era of greater concern for a broad range of forest values beyond timber production. If MUSYA does not provide much constraint on Forest Service decisionmaking, what does? What factors influence the implementation of the MUSYA by the Forest Service?

---

10. The Forest Service had at its disposal a number of highly technical studies covering a broad range of possible use alternatives. A great deal of expertise went into the composition of Multiple Use Plan for the Chatham Ranger District, which was referred to in drawing up the timber sale contract. The contract itself contains a number of provisions relating to environmental safeguards, including a provision allowing the Forest Service to exempt up to 800,000 acres within the sale area from cutting.

3.   THE CLEARCUTTING CONTROVERSY AND REFORM OF FORESTRY POLICY

The rapid rise in timber demand following World War II — generated by the dramatic increase in new home construction for returning veterans flush with accumulated wartime savings and veterans' benefits — shifted the focus of the Forest Service from a custodial agency to an active promoter of timber resources. The housing boom opened up new markets for timber in remote places, such as the national forests in the Rocky Mountains. It also spurred the Forest Service to make expanded use of intensive harvesting methods such as clearcutting to increase the short-term output of timber commodities.

These shifts in the Forest Service's mission and forestry methods brought forest policy to center stage by the early 1970s. We introduce this discussion with a brief summary of forest science highlighting the use and effects of clearcutting. The following excerpt discusses the critical events leading up to the major reforms of forestry policy that took place in the mid 1970s.

a.   An Overview of Silviculture

Derived from the latin term *silva* meaning forest, silviculture is the cultivation of forests. Just as agriculture seeks to increase the yield of fields, silviculture aims to increase the productivity of forestlands. Building upon forest ecology — the study of how the constituents of forest ecosystems interact — and economic considerations, silviculture is the applied science of manipulating forests in order to satisfy human demands for forest products.

Forests are typically classified by their composition and age-class. A *pure* stand is composed of predominantly the same species of trees; a *mixed* stand features a variety of tree species. An *even-aged* forest consists of trees of the same maturity; an *uneven-aged* forest has stands of different age classes.

All four types of forest occur naturally in the United States. Even-aged stands are typically the result of a fire or other natural disturbance that eliminates the entire overstory of trees. Over time, however, understories of shrubs and tree seedlings develop, gradually giving way to uneven-aged stands. Similarly, pure stands can develop following extensive fires or other natural catastrophes such as floods. They also form where an aggressive species takes hold and crowds out competitors. In addition, pure stands exist in severe climatic conditions in which only a few tree species can survive, such as the upper timberline and the arctic. Within the United States, natural pure stands are most common in the West.

Economic considerations typically favor pure stands, whereas ecological considerations tend to favor mixed stands. With pure stands, foresters can devote the entire area to the most valuable species compatible with the site conditions. Management of the stand and eventual harvesting are relatively simple and inexpensive. Mixed stands, however, have important ecological advantages, including utilization of the soil, wind resistance (when shallow and deep-rooted species are mixed), mineral cycling, and resistance to disease and insects. Some of these ecological advantages produce economic benefit, such as reduction of soil maintenance costs. In addition, mixed stands are often more aesthetically pleasing, offer greater recreational opportunities, and often have a greater carrying capacity for wildlife.

There are four principal methods for harvesting trees. *Clearcutting* is the harvesting of the entire stand at the same time. It results in an even-aged stand. Regeneration of the stand occurs naturally from seeds left on the ground or blown from the surrounding area or through planting. The *seed tree system* is similar to clearcutting, except that a few large-crowned trees are left in order to regenerate the cleared area. The *selection system* consists of periodic light partial cuts of a stand. It is suitable for tree species that naturally reproduce and grow in small openings of the canopy. The *shelterwood method* is intermediate to clearcutting and the selection system, using a significant partial cut to spur the regeneration process by providing growing space and cover. Once the new stand is established, the remaining mature growth is harvested.

Economic considerations tend to favor even-aged management and the use of clearcutting (or the seed tree system), while ecological and aesthetic considerations often favor the other harvesting methods. Even-aged management is relatively simple and produces higher volumes of timber per hectare. Moreover, the resulting timber is relatively uniform and therefore easier to handle and use. Clearcutting dramatically reduces the direct costs of harvesting since trees need not be marked, fewer roads need to be built and maintained, and effort need not be devoted to protecting the residual stand. Clearcutting may offer some modest ecological benefits compared to selective harvesting since fewer roads need to be constructed, thereby reducing soil erosion. In addition, areas of open sunlight created by clearcutting may enhance the habitat of some animal species such as deer and black bear. Even-aged management and clearcutting, however, can have significant environmental drawbacks including adverse effects on soil conditions, soil erosion on sloped areas, increased susceptibility of the pure stand to disease and insect infestation, and loss of habitat for species of wildlife that live in old trees. In addition, most people consider clearcut areas to be aesthetically unattractive. These drawbacks can be reduced by prudent application of clearcutting and the use of protective measures such as cutting patterns that harmonize with the landscape.

A few additional comments should be made. First, this overview of silviculture has focused on a few principal elements — forest composition, age characteristics, and harvesting methods. Silviculture encompasses a broad range of activities, including site preparation, stand maintenance, genetic selection, herbicide, fertilizer, and pesticide treatments, and fire control. Application of the broad range of silviculture practices can increase the productivity of U.S. forests up to 300 percent within 50 years. See Spurr, Silviculture, 240 Sci. Am. 76 (1979). Second, in view of the long life cycle of forests and the relative youth of forest sciences, silviculture is far from an exact science. Many important effects of forestry, particularly those relating to forest ecology, are only incompletely understood.

NOTES AND QUESTIONS

1. Should forestlands be managed according to the principles of silviculture? What values are served by this approach? What values are overlooked? If the principles of silviculture are not the appropriate standard for managing forestland, does that imply that the principles of agriculture are not appropriate for the management of farmland? What might distinguish these contexts?

2. Is clearcutting that is applied in a silviculturally sound manner nonetheless objectionable in some circumstances? What are they? How would an ecologist answer these questions? a professional forester? an economist?

3. In Switzerland, forest management has shifted from the conventional approach discussed above — that is, pure even-aged stands and intensive management — toward a more naturalistic approach. Selective cutting is used in such a way as to maximize the economic return from a mixed, uneven-aged stand. The site remains ecologically stable as new growth is naturally established and the mix of species and age classes reduces the forest's susceptibility to disease and insect infestation. Silvicultural costs are kept low, although yield and cutting costs are also reduced. What might explain these international differences?

Should the national forests in the United States be managed in this way? Or should they be operated as tree farms? On what does your analysis depend? How might your analysis of these questions dovetail with your views on designation of wilderness areas?

SPURR, CLEARCUTTING ON NATIONAL FORESTS

21 Natural Resources J. 223 (1981)

THE NATIONAL FORESTS IN 1970

. . . In 1970, according to the U.S. Forest Service, national forests contained 18 percent of the commercial forest land in the United States. This acreage, however, held 51 percent of the softwood sawtimber growing stock, or slightly more than one-half of a principal raw material upon which housing and other wood-using industries were dependent.

Harvest of softwood sawtimber on national forests had more than doubled from 1952 to 1970. . . . Over this period, the proportion of the nation's total production of softwood lumber and plywood from these public lands increased from 15 to 27 percent. In 1970, softwood trees of sawtimber size were being cut faster than they were being grown on national forests. . . .

This was also a period of great activity by conservation groups, particularly the Sierra Club, Friends of the Earth, and the Wilderness Society. With the successful passage of the act creating the National Wilderness system in 1964, these and other similar organizations were actively promoting the setting aside of additional large roadless tracts in the national forests as wilderness areas. At the same time, these groups were becoming increasingly concerned about widespread clearcutting on national forest lands.

Thus the stage was set for a confrontation between industry and conservationists regarding management practices in the national forests. The specific issue to emerge was the practice of clearcutting.

BITTERROOT NATIONAL FOREST

The case of the Bitterroot National Forest in Montana raised the curtain on the debate. In 1969, Senator Lee Metcalf of Montana wrote to Dean Arnold Bolle of the University of Montana School of Forestry:

> Enclosed are copies of letters I have received recently from constituents in the Bitterroot Valley.
>
> I am especially concerned, as are my constituents, over the long-range effects of clear-cutting, and the dominant role of timber production in Forest Service policy, to the detriment of other uses of these national resources.

The object of concern was a large-area clearcut that had been terraced by bulldozers in an effort to obtain better survival and growth for planted seedlings. This and other clearcuts were highly visible scars on the mountainside above the well-settled Bitterroot River valley. In 1968, the Ravalli County Resource Conservation and Development Committee [a local citizens' organization that had enlisted retired Forest Service officers and other knowledgeable individuals and interest groups] objected to these forestry practices. In response the Regional Forester appointed an internal task force which first reported in April, 1970.

In its report, the task force admitted that the Forest Service had placed timber production ahead of multiple use management, that communications with the public had been inadequate, and that in several cases land management had been substandard. Regarding silvicultural systems, the task force recommended that the selection system or shelterwood methods be used for ponderosa pine. For other timber types, clearcutting could be used only where it was the only feasible method. Where clearcutting is done, the task force recommended that patches should be small enough and shaped in such a manner as to stimulate natural openings.

A concurrent study by Bolle and other faculty members of the University of Montana was published by Congress in 1970. The Bolle report was less critical of clearcutting as a silvicultural tool but highly critical of the economic justification of clearcutting and terracing as practiced on the forest, concluding that it was the abuse, not the use of clearcutting that was objectionable. In subsequent years, clearcuts on the forest have been made much smaller and less frequent.

The Bolle report emphasized that the rather intensive management practices of the Forest Service were not economically justified on many sites and that timber production was unduly weighted compared to other legally-mandated uses of the forest. Although clearcutting was not evaluated in terms of its silvicultural justification for timber production, the report was seized by environmentalists as a professional study that condemned the general use of clearcutting.

MONONGAHELA NATIONAL FOREST

Across the country, in West Virginia, the Monongahela National Forest changed its management plan in 1964 from one based on all-age management (selection system) to even-aged (clearcutting). This change was made because partial or selective cuttings removed the more valuable trees and left lower value trees to take over the site, thus deteriorating the forest by "high-grading." In contrast, clearcutting created an even-aged stand of young hardwoods, mostly sprouts from the stumps of the cut trees, that could be managed from the beginning for the production of quality timber. The forest management, however, placed little emphasis on the fact that many of the "worthless" old trees were valuable nest and food trees for raccoons, squirrels, and other animals. In particular, one large clearcut on the side of a mountain which was highly visible from the valley concerned and antagonized many people and visitors from nearby Washington, D.C. . . .

[T]he Chief of the Forest Service in 1970 established a Special Review Committee. Its report defended even-aged management by clearcutting, but was critical of the manner in which the system had been applied. In short, the Forest Service planned to continue to clearcut but to do it better. . . .

THE NADER STUDY

The clearcutting controversy became so prominent in the public arena that a Ralph Nader Study Group was organized to investigate the management of national forests. This investigation spawned a 1974 report, a chapter of which detailed the history of the clearcutting controversy from an environmentalist's point of view.[11] Claiming that clearcutting causes significant deterioration of national forests, the report argued that adequate scientific information on the effects of clearcutting was not available and that the Forest Service courted disaster by continuing the present level of clearcutting. Favorably impressed with the competence and attitudes of Forest Service personnel, the Nader group recommended Congressional guidance, favoring true multiple use management, better funding, and increased public involvement in its activities.

THE MONONGAHELA AND TONGASS COURT
DECISIONS

In early 1973, the clearcutting controversy stood at dead center. In Congress, environmentalist pressure had scuttled the proposed National Timber Supply Act, but industry counterpressures had stifled thoughts of putting the Church Committee guidelines [significantly restricting the use of clearcutting on public lands] into law. In the executive branch, the attempt of the Council of Environmental Quality to have the President issue an Executive Order putting clearcutting structures into effect had been stopped by industry, while environmentalist concerns had stymied efforts to increase the allowable cut on the national forests. The Forest Service had the Resources Planning Act to back its effort to fund the management of public forests on a true multi-

---

11. See D. Barney, The Last Stand (1974).

ple use basis, but the Office of Management and Budget or Congress showed little interest in providing such funding.

At this juncture, enter the courts. In May, 1973, a number of conservation organizations filed suit in federal district court against the Secretary of Agriculture, alleging that clearcutting was violative of the Organic Act of 1897. That act provides for the management of the national forests and limits the cutting of trees to those that are "dead, matured or large growth" and that are "marked and designated." This case, entitled *Izaak Walton League v. Butz,* was decided in favor of the conservationists, and affirmed on appeal to the Circuit Court in Richmond, Virginia in 1975.[12]

. . . The Fourth Circuit Court of Appeals found that the restrictions of the 1897 Organic Act applied literally and that the government was legally restricted to cutting only trees that were "dead, matured or large growth" and that were "marked and designated." The court based its decision on a reading of an authoritative dictionary (the Terminology of Forest Science, Technology, Practice and Products published by the Society of American Foresters), the record of Congress in considering the original legislation, and the regulations published by the Forest Service over the years. It concluded that the congressional language was unambiguous and must be obeyed:

> We are not insensitive to the fact that our reading of the Organic Act will have serious and far-reaching consequences, and it may well be that this legislation enacted over seventy-five years ago is an anachronism which no longer serves the public interest. However, the appropriate forum to resolve this complex and controversial issue is not the courts but the Congress.

As a result of this decision, the Forest Service was forced to close down most timber sales in the four states within the jurisdiction of the Fourth Circuit Court.

A similar line of reasoning was followed by the U.S. District Court in *Zieske v. Butz,*[13] which involved logging on the Tongass National Forest in Alaska. "The issue is one purely of statutory interpretation," said the court, and found that the language of the Organic Act of 1897 must be literally interpreted, "although it may not coincide with the concept of the Forest Service as to sound timber management." . . .

With these two decisions, it became obvious that virtually any timber sale on national forests could be curtailed by an injunction issued by any federal district court. . . .

---

12. *West Virginia Div. of the Izaak Walton League of America v. Butz,* 367 F. Supp. 422 (N.D. W. Va. 1973), *aff'd,* 522 F.2d 945 (4th Cir. 1975).
13. 406 F. Supp. 258 (D. Alaska 1976).

QUESTIONS

1. Did the MUSYA and the underlying institutional dynamics of forest policy foster the excessive use of clearcutting? In what ways?

2. Was the strong reaction to clearcutting based on valid forest management and ecological concerns, or was it an overreaction based principally on aesthetic judgments?

3. Should the courts in the Monongahela and Tongass court decisions have interpreted a 78-year old statute literally? How else might a court have approached this question of statutory interpretation? What interpretation seems most sensible today? What about *Chevron?*

b.   Reform of Forestry Policy

MORRISON, THE NATIONAL FOREST MANAGEMENT ACT AND BELOW COST TIMBER SALES: DETERMINING THE ECONOMIC SUITABILITY OF LAND FOR TIMBER PRODUCTION

17 Envtl. L. 507 (1987)

B.   THE FOREST AND RANGELAND RENEWABLE RESOURCES PLANNING ACT

Congressional concern with the continuing controversy surrounding the management of the National Forest System resulted in the Forest and Rangeland Renewable Resources Planning Act of 1974 (RPA). The planning process mandated by the RPA attempts to rectify the MUSYA's failure to specify a method of determining the combination of resource use that best meets the needs of the American people.

The RPA requires the Forest Service to make a periodic national assessment of the current and expected demand for forest and rangeland resources and the nation's potential to meet those demands. The assessment provides the basis for the development of a national program to guide the management of the National Forest System. Each program must include an inventory of investment opportunities on both public and private lands, a discussion of the priorities of those investment opportunities, and an analysis of Forest Service personnel requirements. In addition, each program is to specify Forest Service investments and expected outputs, or production goals, in a manner that facilitates a comparison of anticipated costs and total benefits, including direct and indirect returns to the federal government.

As part of the RPA planning process, the Act requires the Forest

Service to develop management plans for individual national forests. In developing these management plans the Forest Service must use a systematic and integrated interdisciplinary approach. The RPA did not provide any detailed guidelines on the development of these unit plans and emphasized the national program as the dominant process for guiding the management of the national forests. Thus, the RPA represents "top-down" planning, where national goals and opportunities dictate the management priorities for the sub-units of the National Forest System. . . .

C.   THE NATIONAL FOREST MANAGEMENT ACT

Congress extensively amended the RPA when it passed the National Forest Management Act (NFMA) in 1976. The immediate impetus for the NFMA was a decision of the Fourth Circuit Court of Appeals upholding a permanent injunction against clearcutting of the Monongahela National Forest in West Virginia. Yet Congress, in enacting the NFMA, went beyond the issue of even-aged timber management and attempted a comprehensive resolution of persistent controversies in national forest management. The NFMA refined the RPA process for determining the combination of management activities and objectives that best serve the national interest by expanding the procedural guidelines for the development of management plans for individual national forests and incorporating into the forest planning process many substantive standards that limit Forest Service discretion.

1.   GENERAL PLANNING PROVISIONS

Section 6 of the NFMA, the principal statutory source of procedural guidelines for the development of forests plans, reaffirms and strengthens the MUSYA by expanding upon the RPA requirement of a systematic and integrated interdisciplinary approach to forest planning. The central theme of section 6 is that the planning process must be based on the integrated consideration of the multiple uses defined in the MUSYA. Each forest plan must "include coordination of outdoor recreation, range, timber, watershed, wildlife and fish, and wilderness." Forest management systems and procedures, including harvest levels, must be determined "in the light of all" those multiple uses, "and upon the availability of lands and their suitability for resource management." Section 6 further promotes a balanced consideration of each of the multiple uses by requiring that the Forest Service provide for and foster public participation in the planning process.

Section 6 also requires that the Forest Service promulgate regulations that prescribe the planning process. The regulations are required to specify guidelines that (1) identify the suitability of lands for resource management, (2) consider the economic and environmental aspects of resource management, (3) provide for diversity of plant and animal communities, and (4) prevent substantial impairment of the productivity of the land. In addition, the regulations are to ensure that timber harvesting will occur only where soil and watershed conditions will not be irreversibly damaged; that water resources, including fish, will be protected from serious damage; that the harvested area can be adequately restocked with trees within five years; that the harvesting system cannot be selected primarily because it will produce the greatest dollar return or greatest timber output; and that even aged harvesting systems, such as clearcutting, are to be applied only where other multiple use and aesthetic resources are protected.

2.   SECTION 6(K)

Section 6(k) of the NFMA requires each forest plan to identify lands not suitable for timber production "considering physical, economic, and other pertinent factors to the extent feasible, as determined by the Secretary of Agriculture." Timber harvesting is prohibited on these lands except for salvage sales and sales required to protect other multiple use values. The legislative history of section 6(k) demonstrates that the congressional concern with the economics of timber production is significantly different from the congressional intent expressed in the RPA that forest planning consider the overall long-term costs and benefits of all Forest Service management activities.

Section 6(k) originated in an amendment to the Senate bill commonly referred to as the "marginal lands provision." This provision required the application of a strict economic test to determine the suitability of land for timber production. The provision prohibited timber harvesting on lands where the "estimated cost of production will exceed estimated economic return." The Senate bill defined the "estimated cost of production" to include "only direct timber production costs," not costs associated with "access, protection, revegetation and administration for multiple-use purposes."

This strict economic test contained in the marginal lands provision caused considerable debate in the Senate. The debate focused on two issues: (1) the allocation of costs between timber and other multiple uses and (2) the effect of the provision on harvest levels and local employment in the more arid region of the west. Regarding the allocation of costs, the Senate Agriculture Committee Report stated that only "direct timber production costs and returns should be evaluated. Costs and benefits attributable to other resource values should be excluded because of the lack of certainty involved in assigning values to other benefits derived." In addressing the issue of harvest levels and local employment, the Committee stated that it expected the Secretary of Agriculture "to assure that precipitous action is not taken which may have drastic and widespread economic impacts in the Inter-Mountain West or other areas which seem to have low productivity areas."

The Senate debates did not conclusively resolve the issues surrounding the provision. Nevertheless, the general intent of the provision — that timber production not be a management goal on lands where it will not recover its costs — was made clear. Despite a proposed amendment to delete the marginal lands provision, the Senate retained the provision and anticipated that the conference committee would resolve those issues.

The House Agriculture Committee considered and rejected an amendment to the House bill that was substantially similar to the Senate's marginal lands provision. The issues debated in the House regarding the amendment were generally the same as those in the Senate: the difficulty of allocating costs between the various multiple uses and the desire to defer the resolution of the issues surrounding the provision to the conference committee.

Unfortunately, the conference committee ambiguously modified the Senate's marginal lands provision without confronting the concerns addressed in both the House and the Senate. The conference report merely states that section 6(k) modifies the marginal lands provision of the Senate bill to require that the Forest Service consider "to the extent feasible physical, economic, and other pertinent factors" in determining the suitability of lands for timber production. Furthermore, different Senators and Representatives expressed different interpretations of the conference report language regarding economic suitability during consideration of the conference report.[14]

Although the conference report deleted the Senate language requiring a strict economic test, it is clear that Congress intended that

---

14. Representative Symms, a conferee, stated that the conference committee "agreed that it would be unwise to impose rigid and inflexible economic or other constraints to be applied to all national forest lands in all parts of the country," and that "[i]t was noted during the conference that the Forest Service . . . will take into account the impact on local dependent economies in their implementation of the language." 122 Cong. Rec. 34,228 (1976). Senator Randolph, who was not a conferee, remarked that the conference bill rendered the Senate's marginal lands provision "virtually meaningless." Id., at 33,838. However, Representative Baucus declared that section 6(k) limits the use of "commercially unproductive land for timber." Id. at 34,231. Senator Nelson declared that "the conference report retains the Senate's prohibition on managing an area for timber production on marginal lands if the cost of management exceeds the sale price of the timber that is proposed to be harvested." Id. at 33,958. . . .

the Forest Service consider the profitability of timber production in determining the suitability of land for timber production. However, Congress left the problems of cost allocation and potential impacts on local employment to the discretion of the Forest Service. . . .

CITIZENS FOR ENVIRONMENTAL QUALITY V. UNITED STATES

731 F. Supp. 970 (D. Colo. 1989)

SHERMAN G. FINESILVER, Chief Judge.

III.   NATURE OF THE LITIGATION

The parties have filed cross motions for summary judgment pursuant to Fed. R. Civ. P. 56. Plaintiff Citizens for Environmental Quality and Plaintiff-Intervenors ("Intervenors") seek judicial review of an administrative decision by Defendants to issue a comprehensive Land Resource Management Plan ("LRMP" or "the Plan") for the Rio Grande National Forest.[15] . . .

The present litigation centers on the issue of whether the National Forests should be used or preserved and reflects the need for balancing the nation's legitimate economic needs with its limited natural resources. Congress addressed this problem in 1976 by passing the National Forest Management Act which directed the Secretary to develop, maintain, and revise LRMP's for units of the National Forest System ("NFS"). The task of satisfying the nation's need for timber and other forest products while preserving forest lands for the use of future generations is a complex one. Nonetheless, the NFMA contemplates that through careful planning and management both economic and aesthetic need will be met.

The potential impact of the NFMA planning process on the nation poses important environmental and economic issues. Of the 191 million acres included in the National Forest System, 108.1 million acres have been developed for recreation, logging and other uses: 32.5 million are protected as official wilderness and an additional 50.4 million acres remain roadless with 5.5 million of them recommended for classification as wilderness.

In 1985, cash receipts from NFS activities amounted to $1.1 billion

---

15. The area covered by the Plan, the Rio Grande National Forest, is located in South Central Colorado and contains 1,851,792 acres of National Forest System lands.

dollars in revenue, $225 million of which was returned to county governments for support of schools and roads. In the same year, recreational use amounted to 225 million visitor-days with an estimated assigned monetary value of about $2.2 billion. Forest plans average about $2.5 million each to develop.

Pursuant to NFMA mandate, the U.S. Forest Service is in the final stages of developing LRMP's for all national forests. Because of the financial value of the resources at stake and the cost of producing plans, sixty-two final plans have been the subject of formal administrative appeals within the Forest Service. These appeals have reflected an intense concern that the plans resolve resource use issues, meet requirements of the NFMA, are financially feasible, and are politically supported by the people most affected. This case is among the first requesting broad judicial review of Forest Service decisions regarding forest land management plans. Additional litigation is anticipated as more of these plans reach the implementation stage.

IV. STATUTORY AND REGULATORY
BACKGROUND

By enacting the National Forest Management Act as an amendment to the Forest and Rangeland Resources Planning Act ("RPA"), Congress directed the Secretary of Agriculture ("Secretary") to develop, maintain and revise LRMPs for units of the National Forest System. 16 U.S.C. §1604(a). LRMPs must provide for the multiple use and sustained yield of the products and services obtained from the Forest in accordance with the Multiple-Use Sustained-Yield Act of 1960. ("MUSY"), 16 U.S.C. §§528-531. See also 16 U.S.C. §§1604(b), (d), and (e).

The general procedure, content and process requirements for forest planning are set forth in regulations promulgated in 36 C.F.R. §219. See 16 U.S.C. §1604(h). Under the regulations, the purpose of the LRMP is to provide for multiple use and sustained yield of goods and services from the National Forest System in a way that maximizes long term net public benefits in an environmentally sound manner. 36 C.F.R. §219.1(a). The essential planning tool in implementing the multiple use / sustained yield mandate is a cost-benefit analysis, where both costs and benefits to which a monetary value can be assigned, and those to which no quantitative value can be assigned, are considered. 36 C.F.R. §219.3 (Definition of "net public benefits").

Under the NFMA regulations, planning begins with the formal identification of purpose and need (§219.12(b)), the establishment of planning criteria (§219.12(c)), and the collection of data. §219.12(d). Planning then proceeds through the formulation of a range of alternative management scenarios (§219.12(f)), the evaluation of those alternatives (§219.12(h)), and the formal recommendation and adoption of an alternative as the Plan, §219.12(i) & (j). The regulations also provide for on-going monitoring and evaluation of the Plan. §219.12(k). . . .

The decisions of the Regional Forester in approving a LRMP may be categorized as:

1. Establishment of forest-wide multiple-use goals and objectives (36 C.F.R. §219.11(b));
2. Establishment of forest-wide management requirements (standards and guidelines) to fulfill the requirements of the NFMA relating to future activities (resource integration requirements of 36 C.F.R. §§219.13 to 219.27);
3. Establishment of management area direction (management area prescriptions) applying to future management activities in that management area (36 C.F.R. §219.11);
4. Designation of land suitable for timber production and the establishment of allowable timber sale quality (36 C.F.R. §§219.14 and 219.16);
5. Nonwilderness multiple-use allocations for those roadless areas that were reviewed under 36 C.F.R. §219.17 and not recommended for wilderness designation;
6. Monitoring and evaluation requirements (36 C.F.R. §219.11(d)).

Of primary concern in this case is the designation of land suitable for timber production.

Section 219.14 sets forth a series of criteria for making the identification of lands suitable for timber production, together known as Stage 1. Under Stage 1, land is considered unsuitable for timber production if: (1) it currently and historically has less than 10% tree cover; (2) technology is not available to insure that timber production will not cause irreversible damage to soil or watersheds; (3) it cannot be restocked within 5 years; and (4) it has been administratively withdrawn from timber production.

Land which passes the Stage 1 criteria is considered tentatively suitable for timber production, and may be assigned production management prescriptions. The remaining criteria include two economic analyses. The first analysis requires an economic evaluation of management prescriptions as applied to particular analysis areas. This evaluation is referred to as Stage 2 analysis. The purpose of Stage 2 analysis is to determine the financial costs and measurable economic benefits of each management prescription. In essence, it is designed to provide information on the financial attractiveness of the various proposed alternatives.

Stage 3 of the suitability determination process provides in part that lands are not suitable for timber production if they are not "cost-efficient" in meeting the objectives of the alternative. 36 C.F.R. §219.14(c). The consideration of cost-efficiency applies to the alternative as a whole, and not to timber production on a particular analysis area. Stage 3 is not a strict formulaic analysis that directly considers the financial costs and revenues associated with timber production on individual acres or analysis areas. Rather, it is a flexible analysis which must estimate the indeterminate values of non-economic benefits such as esthetics and recreation. The result of the Stage 3 analysis is the somewhat conclusory statement that all acres assigned to timber production in an alternative are suitable for timber production, and all areas which are not assigned to timber production are unsuitable. . . .

VIII.   STANDARD OF REVIEW

Judicial review of LRMPs is unlike the review of typical agency decisions. We must consider the technical complexity of the issues involved, and the possibility that years of costly research and planning may be undone in the event of a remand to the agency. It is generally accepted that federal agencies are entitled to a presumption of good faith and regularity in arriving at their decisions. *Sierra Club v. Costle,* 657 F.2d 298, 334 (D.C. Cir. 1981). Nonetheless, we must resist the temptation to "rubber stamp" agency decisions in the face of complex issues, and act to ensure that Forest Service decisions meet the required standards of regularity and rationality.

In reviewing the Forest Service's procedural decisions, we have considered whether the action was reasonable. *Portela v. Pierce,* 650 F.2d 210, 213 (9th Cir. 1981). In the instant case, the reasonableness of the procedural decisions is dependent upon whether the Forest Service complied with the requirements and regulations of the National Forest Management Act, the National Environmental Policy Act, and the Endangered Species Act. . . .

IX.   THE NFMA CLAIMS

Plaintiff asserts that the Rio Grande Forest Plan violates the NFMA because Defendants improperly applied the computer model FORPLAN 1[16] for the following reasons.

---

16. [FORPLAN 1 is a computer analysis model used by the Forest Service to compare and evaluate alternative LRMPs. Through linear programming, FORPLAN 1 analyzes and describes how a forest may be expected to respond to anticipated management. Plaintiff's original first claim, which alleged that

1.   UNSTABLE SOILS

Plaintiff alleges that the Forest Service misapplied FORPLAN by failing to remove lands with unstable soils from timber production as required by §§6(k) and 6(g)(3). Defendants contend that they have complied with these sections by promulgating appropriate regulations in 36 C.F.R. §219.14. Specifically, Defendants defend their suitability determination on the basis of compliance with the technology exception of §219.14(a)(2). Plaintiff attacks the implementing regulations both facially and as applied.

A review of the statutory and regulatory framework is necessary to an analysis of this issue. Section 6(k) provides that, when developing LRMPs, the Forest Service

> shall identify lands within the management area which are not suited for timber production, considering physical [, economic, and other pertinent] factors . . . and shall assure that . . . no timber harvesting shall occur on such lands for a period of 10 years.

16 U.S.C. §1604(k). Section 6(g)(3) requires the Secretary to promulgate regulations which

> shall include, but not be limited to . . . (3) specifying guidelines for land management plans developed to achieve the goals of the Program which —
> (E) insure that timber will be harvested from National Forest System lands only where —
> (i)   soil, slope or watershed conditions will not be irreversibly damaged.

16 U.S.C. §1604(g)(3)(E)(i).

The applicable implementing regulation reads as follows:

> During the forest planning process, lands which are not suited for timber production shall be identified in accordance with the criteria in paragraphs (a) through (d) of this section.
> (a) During the analysis of the management situation, data on all National Forest System lands within the planning area shall be reviewed, and those lands within any one of the categories described in paragraphs (a)(l) through (4) of this section shall be identified as not suited for timber production —
> (2) Technology is not available to ensure timber production

---

FORPLAN 1 was a fundamentally flawed tool to use in the planning process and the preparation of the RIO GRANDE Forest Plan, was dismissed at oral hearing by stipulation of the parties.] [Taken from 731 F. Supp. at 980 n.12.]

> from the land without irreversible resource damage to soils produc-
> tivity, or watershed conditions.

36 C.F.R. §219.14(a)(2).

The Forest Service applied this regulation in its Analysis of the
Management Situation (AMS), where it set forth its determination of
the availability, capability and suitability of lands for timber production.
AMS, Ch. VII. The Forest Service stated:

> Two physical suitability tests are required in the process to determine if
> land is suitable for timber production.
>
> 1.   The first test is whether technology is available that will en-
> sure that timber production activities, including harvesting, can occur
> on the land without irreversible resource damage to soil productivity
> or watershed condition. Availability of technology is judged on
> whether technology is currently developed and available for use. *This
> is not an economic test, and the technology does not have to be available in the
> local area.* It has been determined that the technology is available to
> harvest timber from all areas of the Forest while adequately protecting
> the soil and water resources.

AMS, Ch. VII (emphasis added in AMS).

Plaintiff submits that 36 C.F.R. §219.14(a)(2) and the Forest Service's reliance thereon do not conform to Congress' intent as expressed
in §§6(g) and 6(k). Plaintiff argues that the primary intent of §6(g) is
to remove lands from timber production which are "physically unsuitable." We disagree. The intent of §6(g)(3) is to insure against irreversible damage to soil, slope and watershed conditions. The section does
not require the prevention of any and all damage to the above conditions as a result of timber harvesting.

In our view, Section 6(g)(3) contemplates that timber harvesting
may be carried out even though such harvesting may cause temporary
or short-term damage to soil and watershed conditions. Section 6(g)(3)
goes no farther than to charge the Secretary with the duty of promulgating regulations to insure that soil, slope and watershed conditions
will not be irreversibly damaged as a result of timber harvesting. The
Secretary's regulation provides adequate guidelines for insuring against
such irreversible damage. 36 C.F.R. §219.14. This regulation is consistent with the language and intent of §§6(g) and 6(k). . . .

Defendants rely on the technology exception of 36 C.F.R.
§219.14(a)(2) as justification for the Plan's suitability determination.
AMS Ch. VII. We interpret §219.14(a)(2) as follows. If there exists technology which is capable of adequately repairing short-term damage due
to timber harvesting within a reasonable time, and provisions are made
for the use of that technology, then timber production may be carried

out despite whatever short-term damage may be caused. However, where timber harvesting is contemplated on potentially unsuitable lands, then the technology to be used in preventing irreversible damage must be identified and provisions made for its implementation.

In our view, the Forest Service erred by its failure to adequately identify the technology which would allow it to proceed with timber harvesting under §219.14(a)(2). The EIS stated that there were no forested areas which were technologically unsuitable for timber production. EIS III-54. However, the EIS did not specifically identify the technology which would be employed to protect these resources. Likewise, the Forest Service's conclusory statement in its AMS that such technology exists is arbitrary and does not comply with this section. AMS Ch. VII.

Defendants are directed to review the Planning documents and identify the technology upon which they rely for the §219.14(a)(2) exception, and outline the provisions for its implementation.

4. TIMBER PRODUCTION GOALS / COST-EFFICIENT TIMBER BASE

Intervenors join Plaintiff in alleging that Defendants improperly relied upon timber production goals in determining the suitable timber base for timber production in the Rio Grande Forest. Plaintiff and Intervenors claim that allowing predetermined production goals to weight the timber suitability analysis violates the intent of Section 6(k).

Defendants reply that timber production goals are a relevant factor in determining the suitability of lands for timber production. Defendants rely on the provisions of §6(k) earlier outlined and the following implementing regulation:

> Lands shall be tentatively identified as not appropriate for timber production to meet objectives of the alternative being considered if —
> > (3) The lands are not cost efficient, over the planning horizon, in meeting forest objectives, which include timber production.

36 C.F.R. §219.14(c)(3).

We disagree with Plaintiff's contention that production goals may not be used in determining the suitability of lands. Section 6(k) provides the Forest Service with ample discretion to consider both economic and other pertinent factors in identifying land suitable for timber production. Section 219.14(c)(3) provides for the consideration of production goals as part of this discretion. In general an agency's contemporaneous construction of its responsibilities under its enabling statute is entitled to deference. *ALCOA v. Central People's Utility District,*

467 U.S. 380, 390, 104 S. Ct. 2472, 81 L. Ed. 2d 301 (1984). There is no reason to depart from the general rule.

However, we find that if production goals are to be given greater weight in the suitability analysis, then adequate reasons must be set forth for so doing. Defendants must provide justification for allowing production goals, or any other factor required by §6(k) and the regulations, to weigh more heavily than other factors. In the instant case, no such justification has been set forth.

Plaintiff argues alternatively that even if the above regulations are held to be valid, the suitable timber base proposed by the Plan violates those regulations because it is not cost-efficient[17] as required by §219.14(c)(3). Lands which are tentatively identified as not appropriate for timber production under this subsection are to be designated as not suited for timber production in the preferred alternative. 36 C.F.R. §219.14(d). . . .

Defendant are DIRECTED to review the planning documents and set forth the justification for allowing production goals to weight the analysis. In all other particulars, the contentions of Plaintiff and Intervenors are rejected.

5. BROAD RANGE OF REASONABLE ALTERNATIVES

We agree with Plaintiff and Intervenors that the Rio Grande Forest Plan failed to formulate a broad range of alternatives in violation of Forest Service regulation 36 C.F.R. §219.12(f). That section provides:

> The interdisciplinary team shall formulate a broad range of reasonable alternatives according to NEPA procedures. The primary goal in formulating alternatives, besides complying with NEPA procedures, is to provide an adequate basis for identifying the alternative that comes nearest to maximizing net public benefits. . . .

This section requires that the Forest Service take a "hard look" at alternatives which not only emphasize differing factors, but lead to differing results. Consideration of alternatives which lead to similar results is not sufficient under NEPA and this section. *State of California v. Block,* 690 F.2d 753 (9th Cir. 1982).

---

17. "Cost efficiency" is defined as follows:

Cost efficiency: The usefulness of specified inputs (costs) to produce specified outputs (benefits). In measuring cost efficiency, some outputs, including environmental, economic, or social impacts, are not assigned monetary values but are achieved at specified levels in the least cost manner. Cost efficiency is usually measured using present net value, although use of benefit-cost ratios and rates-of-return may be appropriate. 36 C.F.R. §219.3.

The Forest Planners considered nine alternatives in arriving at the LRMP for the Rio Grande National Forest. Among the alternatives were a "no action alternative", a "market output" alternative, a "non-market" alternative, and a "reduced budget" alternative. Two of the alternatives (Alternatives E and I) provide for a reduction in timber production from current levels. Intervenors claim that Defendant's use of harvest level constraints in its FORPLAN model skewed the formulation of alternatives analysis so that no alternative which harvested timber at an overall profitable level could be considered. Intervenors allege that this failure prevented the agency from considering a broad range of alternatives as required by 36 C.F.R. §219.12(f).

From the record, it appears that the Forest Service first established production goals, and then formulated alternatives which would reach those goals through employing data constraints. The remaining lands were then declared to be unsuitable for timber production after the production goals had been satisfied. We have earlier held that production goals may be used in determining the suitable timber base for timber harvesting. However, we also ruled that such goals may not control the suitability analysis absent adequate explanation. Similarly, Defendants provide no adequate justification for allowing production goals to control the formulation of alternatives.

We find that this result-biased decision making process prevented the Forest Service from establishing a legitimately broad range of reasonable alternatives as required by the statutory and regulatory scheme. The intent behind §219.12(f) is clear — to establish a legitimately balanced range of proposed actions which reflect a wide range of goals. Defendants' range of alternatives cannot be said to reflect a wide range of goals since the proposed alternatives each contemplate timber production at a highly unprofitable level. A broad range of alternatives must also include an alternative which contemplates timber harvesting at a profitable level even if that level requires reducing current timber production levels.

We do not hold that an alternative which provides for profitable timber production must be selected. We merely hold that it must be considered in the same way as other alternatives. Defendants are DIRECTED to review an alternative which is based on a profitable timber production program and set forth reasons for its selection or rejection.

We are not persuaded that Defendants adequately considered each of the alternatives which were developed during the planning process. In its Evaluation of Alternatives, the Forest Service "readily dismissed" Alternatives E and I stating:

> Alternatives E, F and I [do not] provide commercial timber yields or make available forage and grazing lands in amounts necessary to satisfy pressing public needs. There are both local and nation (sic) needs for

these materials and resources, but local needs for them are genuinely pressing and urgent.

(Evaluation of Alternatives, p. 31). No data is cited in support of the proposition that there are "pressing public needs" for an increase in timber production.

From its evaluation, it is clear that the Forest Service gave a "hard look" only to those alternatives which increased timber production. Alternatives which reduced timber production were "readily dismissed." The Forest Service thus considered only alternatives which led to a similar result — increased timber production. This does not constitute a consideration of a broad range of alternatives as contemplated by §219.12(f). While nothing prevents the Forest Service from adopting an alternative which increases timber production, this does not permit the Forest Service to seriously consider only those alternatives which provide for increased timber production, to the exclusion of alternatives which do not have the same end result. *State of California v. Block,* 690 F.2d at 768. . . .

7.   TIMBER SALES

Plaintiff alleges that Defendants failed to conduct an economic feasibility analysis on each timber sale offered by the Rio Grande National Forest in violation of 16 U.S.C. §1604(g)(3)(F)(ii). That section requires that regulations be promulgated which:

> (F)   Insure that clearcutting, seed tree cutting, shelterwood cutting, and other cuts designed to regenerate an even-aged stand of timber will be used as a cutting method on National Forest System lands only where —
> (ii)   the interdisciplinary review as determined by the Secretary has been completed and the potential environmental, biological, esthetic, engineering, and economic impacts on each advertised sale area have been assessed, as well as the consistency of the sale with the multiple use of the general area.

Plaintiff asserts that this section mandates an economic feasibility analysis on each timber sale. We disagree.

Section 1604(g)(3)(F)(ii) requires only that regulations be promulgated which insure that economic impacts on sale areas be carried out. The Secretary has complied by promulgating 36 C.F.R. §219.27(A)(7):

> (A)   Resource Protection. All management prescriptions shall —
> (7)   Be assessed prior to project implementation for potential

physical, biological, aesthetic, cultural, engineering, and economic
impacts and for consistency with multiple uses planned for the general area.

Nothing in the enabling statute nor the implementing regulations requires that an economic feasibility analysis be carried out in the LRMP.
The economic impact analysis may be performed any time prior to the
implementation of the project. Plaintiff's claim on this point is therefore DISMISSED. . . .

NOTES AND QUESTIONS

1. Upon introducing the NFMA, Senator Humphrey proclaimed
that: "The days have ended when the forests may be viewed only as trees
and trees viewed only as timber. The soil and the water, the grasses and
the shrubs, the fish and the wildlife, and the beauty that is the forest
must become integral parts of resource managers' thinking and actions." 122 Cong. Rec. 5619 (1976). Does the NFMA as enacted effectuate these reforms? What aspects of the NFMA seem to support
Humphrey's assertion? Detract from it?

2. Do you agree with the court that C.F.R. §219.14(a)(2) for determining the suitability of forest lands for timber harvesting comports
with the NFMA? What could be meant by the "availability" of technology? Does the court's analysis of this regulation place significant constraints on the Forest Service's discretion in designating lands as
suitable for timber production?

3. Do you agree with the court's construction of NFMA §6(k) regarding economic suitability? Consider the legislative history of this
provision, discussed supra, pp. 1099-1101 (Morrison article). Did the
court eviscerate the NFMA by not interpreting the Act as placing
greater constraints on the agency in making below-cost timber sales?
Did Congress doom the NFMA by not including a strict economic test?
When is it ever appropriate to lose money in timber sales?

A similar concern is raised by NFMA §6(g)(3)(E)(ii), requiring
the Forest Service insure that lands "can be adequately restocked within
five years after harvest." Agency planners have interpreted this language as requiring only that lands be restocked within five years of
"final" harvest, implying that reforestation need not occur so long as
some trees are standing. C. F. Wilkinson & H. Anderson, Land and
Resource Planning in the National Forests 190 (1987). Suppose that
clearcutting were applied on national forest land with but a few seed
trees left remaining. Would this satisfy the restocking requirement?
What if regeneration by this method was not expected to occur for
decades? Is such an outcome consistent with the NFMA?

4. With regard to harvesting methods, Congress directed the Forest Service to:

> insure that clearcutting, seed tree cutting, and shelterwood cutting, and other cuts designed to regenerate an evenaged stand of timber will be used . . . only where —
>
> (i)   for clearcutting, it is determined to be the optimum method, and for other cuts it is determined to be appropriate, to meet the objectives and requirements of the relevant land management plan;
>
> (ii) . . . potential environmental, biological, esthetic, engineering, and economic impacts on each advertised sales area have been assessed . . . ;
>
> (iii) cut blocks, patches, or strips are shaped and blended to the extent practicable with the natural terrain;
>
> (iv) there are established . . . maximum size limits for areas to be cut in one harvest operation . . . ; and
>
> (v) such cuts are carried out in a manner consistent with the protection of soil, watershed, fish, wildlife, recreation, and esthetic resources, and the regeneration of the timber resource.

NFMA §6(g)(3)(F).

Do these provisions significantly constrain the Forest Service?

In view of the clearcutting controversy that led to the enactment of the NFMA, the Forest Service was sensitive to public concerns in promulgating clearcutting regulations. Although the regulations governing the choice of harvesting method require that economics be one of the factors considered, they state that economics cannot be the primary basis for deciding. On the other hand, the method chosen must be "practical" from an economic perspective. 36 C.F.R. §219.17(b).

5. Has the NFMA overcome the problems of the MUSYA? Does it create serious substantive standards and significantly alter the incentive structure driving forest planners, or does it simply erect more procedural and semantic hoops for forest managers seeking to promote the interests of the forest industry and local communities? Does the RPA top-down planning approach, especially the development of timber production goals, get forest planning backwards? Wouldn't a bottom-up approach and greater reliance upon decentralized planning be more conducive to multiple-use goals? Does the decentralized planning approach of the NFMA counteract the biases of the RPA system or does it introduce other distortions?

4.   THE CURRENT CONTROVERSY: BELOW-COST
     TIMBER SALES

PROJECT '88 — ROUND II INCENTIVES FOR
ACTION: DESIGNING MARKET-BASED
ENVIRONMENTAL STRATEGIES

*(sponsored by Senators Timothy Wirth and John Heinz,
Robert N. Stavins, Project Director, May 1991)*

THE PROBLEM OF BELOW-COST TIMBER SALES

In the 1960's and 1970's, Congress passed laws establishing the
Forest Service's policies of pursuing sustained yields and multiple-use
management, the latter referring to the use of National Forests for timber, recreation, wildlife habitat, and watershed purposes. Further, the
National Forest Management Act of 1976 explicitly directed the Forest
Service to consider economic factors in identifying lands not suitable
for timber production.

Despite these intentions, neither the Forest Service nor the Bureau of Land Management (the two principal agencies managing forests on public lands) are under legal or regulatory requirements to sell
the public's timber at a price that will recover the government's costs
of growing and marketing that timber, and in fact, a substantial amount
of publicly-owned timber is sold "below cost." That is, under current
Federal policy, the commercial activity of moving timber from public
lands into the marketplace frequently costs Federal taxpayers significantly more than they get in return.

The Forest Service's disregard of timber-production costs has led
to extensive road-building and excessive logging in unproductive National Forests. In 1989, 102 of 120 National Forest units operated below-
cost timber programs, costing Federal taxpayers approximately $365
million. Below-cost timber sales are pervasive in the National Forests
throughout the Rocky Mountains and in the arid West, Alaska, and the
eastern United States. Indeed, only one management unit outside of
California, Oregon, and Washington — the Allegheny National Forest
in Pennsylvania — made a positive contribution to the Treasury. Forty-
eight forests returned less than 10 cents to Federal taxpayers for every
dollar Congress appropriated to the timber program.

Perhaps the most frequently stated justification for below-cost timber sales is that they foster community stability. In many parts of the
West, Federal timber sales are crucial to local timber industries; these
sales provide jobs and related economic benefits. In addition, revenues
from sales are shared with local governments, and in many instances

are an important component of local road and school budgets. But, as every recession has demonstrated, the availability of Federal timber alone — even below-cost timber — is no guarantee of community stability. It is inevitable that the domestic timber industry will continue to experience substantial shifts in employment, resulting from broad economic factors (such as changing interest rates, exchange rates, and business cycles), from labor-saving technological changes in logging, milling and transporting, and from the gradual migration of the timber industry to regions of higher productivity. Federal below-cost timber sales cannot overcome these pervasive forces, but they do impede the necessary process of adjustment.

CURRENT AND PROPOSED FEDERAL POLICIES

The existing Federal Timber sale program plays an important role in the national timber market. In 1989, the government sold 13 billion board feet of timber, accounting for about 15% of all domestic logging. In a typical year, the Forest Service and Bureau of Land Management offer a total of 250,000 to 300,000 individual timber sales, ranging in value from a few hundred dollars to several million dollars. For a given tract, an agency's advertised price — the minimum acceptable bid — is established by a prior appraisal of the timber. Once the timber is appraised and advertised, bids are accepted, and the sale is awarded to the highest bidder. The advertised price does not, even in principle, reflect the Federal government's cost of providing timber to the market.

While the Forest Service is directed to undertake timber appraisals and to earn "fair market value," it is under no legal or regulatory obligation to sell the public's timber at a price that will recover the government's costs of growing and marketing the timber. Typically, the timber is priced as if it were already physically accessible, but frequently it is not, and the Forest Service ultimately has to pay to build the roads to access the timber which it sells. The high cost of building the roads is not reflected in the advertised price, and frequently is greater than the bid for the timber itself. Indeed, if the Forest Service were a private firm, the value of its assets would place it among the top five of the *Fortune* 500 list of largest corporations, while in net income terms it would be classified as bankrupt.[18] . . .

18. See R. O'Toole, Reforming the Forest Service, Washington, D.C.: Island Press, 1988.

NOTES AND QUESTIONS

1. The issue of below-cost timber sales is complicated by the difficulty of matching costs with benefits in forest management. How should the cost of a road that serves both timber harvesting and recreation be allocated? How are the benefits of recreation measured? Partly as a result of these complexities, the existence of below-cost timber sales did not surface until the late 1970s and early 1980s with the release of two studies by the Natural Resources Defense Council. Even then, debates over how to assess the economic viability of timber sales delayed recognition of a problem. The lack of an adequate accounting system still plagues Forest Service accountability and congressional oversight.

2. Are below-cost timber sales the problem or a symptom of the problem? In what ways does the answer to this question depend upon your perspective? Consider below-cost timber sales from the perspective of a resource economist, a recreationist, a preservationist, a professional forester, a forest industry worker, and the forestry industry.

3. Under what circumstances might below-cost timber sales be justified? The Project '88 report suggests that community stability concerns are a driving force behind below-cost timber sales. Should community stability be an objective of national forestry policy? What might justify providing economic assistance to towns located near national forests and not those located in other areas? Do community stability concerns reflect market failure or public choice problems? Does the NFMA planning process — with its decentralized planning structure and extensive public comment opportunities — elevate community stability above environmental objectives?

Assuming that community stability was a legitimate objective of forestry policy, how should it be factored into national forest planning? Is community stability a workable concept? How should "community" be defined? What is meant by "stability"? Maintaining the status quo? Something else? Should management of the national forests compensate for changes in harvest levels on neighboring private lands? Variations in market prices for forest products? What about changes in harvesting, forest maintenance, and forest product production technologies that reduce the labor/output ratio?

Are harvest levels the appropriate policy instrument for addressing community stability concerns? What other policy instruments might be better tailored to addressing the problem?

4. The problem of below-cost use of public lands is by no means limited to timber harvesting policies. Similar problems have arisen with regard to leasing of national range resources. Grazing fees are often significantly below the cost of maintaining the range and only about one-fifth the price of using comparable private land. See Schneider, Senate Blocks Rise in Grazing Fees, N.Y. Times, at A10 (Sept. 15, 1993).

Moreover, excessive grazing on these lands can result in severe environmental damage to important watershed and other sensitive areas.

5. How should the problem of below-cost timber sales be addressed? Would this problem have arisen had the original Senate version of the marginal lands provision, discussed supra, p. 1099 (Morrison article), been included in the NFMA? What drawbacks might this provision have had? Congress has considered attacking below-cost timber sales through riders on Forest Service appropriations. What are the advantages and disadvantages of this approach? How else might the problem of below-cost timber sales be addressed? Consider the following proposals.

Alternative Institutional Structures for Forest Management

STROUP & BADEN, NATURAL RESOURCES: BUREAUCRATIC MYTHS AND ENVIRONMENTAL MANAGEMENT

(1983)

It is a common misconception that every citizen benefits from his share of the public lands and the resources found thereon. Public ownership of many natural resources lies at the root of resource control conflicts. With public ownership resources are held in common; that is, they are owned by everyone and, therefore, can be used by everyone. But public ownership by no means guarantees public benefits. Individuals make decisions regarding resource use, not large groups or societies. Yet, with government control, it is not the owners who make decisions, but politicians and bureaucrats. The citizen as beneficiary is often a fiction. . . .

THE FRAMEWORK OF ANALYSIS

The appropriate focus in analyzing public sector behavior is the individual decision maker. It is the individual bureaucrat, the professional public servant, who makes most of the decisions about governmental operations. The average citizen plays little part in this process. Though altruism may sometimes guide bureaucratic behavior, self-interest generally influences the bureaucrat's decision no less than other individuals. Salary, position in the bureaucracy, amount of discretionary budget control, workplace amenities, and office perquisites all contribute to the bureaucrat's well-being. If an agency is expanding its budget and authority, these components of the bureaucrat's welfare improve also. On the other hand, a decrease in the agency's size and budget are generally accompanied by fewer benefits to the bureaucrat. Thus, bureaucrats face strong incentives to increase their agencies' authority and areas of responsibility.

Unconstrained by the need to generate profits, bureaucrats may ignore or exaggerate the economic efficiency of the projects they administer. The bureaucratic entrepreneur must only arouse sufficient support from a specific clientele that will benefit from the proposed activity. That support, translated into political influence, can result in the necessary congressional appropriation of tax money to finance the action. For the bureaucrat, the tax base is essentially a common pool resource ripe for exploitation.

Few checks exist to shackle bureaucratic discretion and its abuse because voters cannot monitor or influence bureaucratic decision making. Voters are rationally ignorant, not out of apathy, but because acquiring the necessary information to analyze bureaucratic decisions is costly relative to the impact such knowledge provides the individual. . . .

GOOD INTENTIONS, POOR RESULTS

The following review illustrates the dramatic negative externalities that can result from public sector resource control. Each example helps to explode the widespread belief that negative externalities are absent in bureaucratic resource management.

UNECONOMIC FOREST HARVESTS

The Forest Service administers vast areas of timberland in the western United States. Some of this timberland, notably in northern California and western Oregon and Washington, is extremely productive — the forest equivalent of Iowa cornland. In contrast, the land in the Rocky Mountain states is more productive for recreational and aesthetic uses than for growing trees as a crop. Silvicultural treatments, such as clear-cutting, on many of these high, dry, and ecologically fragile sites often destroy other forest values. In essence, there are trade-offs between timber management and management for other valued uses. In the less productive regions, much of this timber has a *negative value* as commercial timber. The resources used to harvest the timber are often worth more than the timber harvested, even when discounting to zero the value of other uses foregone. It is only because

this process is so heavily subsidized that massive ecological disturbances
are undertaken. . . .

PLANNING VERSUS MARKET COORDINATION

When well-trained economists look at the planning process, they
see many problems in the way values are assigned, in the way criteria
are set, and in the lack of distinction between the two. These problems
can be easily explained. They are caused by the lack of good data inherent in a failure to price outputs as well as inputs, in a failure to recognize the opportunity cost of capital, and to the pressures that must
come to bear when decision makers are held accountable only through
the political system. The wonder is that the national forests have been
managed as well as they have.

Privatizing the national forests should end many of the obstacles
to good management. Not only would decision makers be given larger
amounts of validated and continuously updated information, but political obstacles to efficient management would largely disappear. Perhaps
just as important, environmentalists, timber producers, miners, recre-
ationists, and others who make demands on the Forest Service would
quickly move away from their carping and faultfinding toward positive
and constructive accommodation.

Whenever someone owns a piece of land, everyone with a potential interest in it begins to act *as if* they cared about everyone else. Each
party's goals can best be reached by close, constructive, and even imaginative cooperation with all other parties. This results whenever trade
occurs by the rule of willing consent, for such trade must be mutually
beneficial. This process contrasts sharply with debates over public land,
where the name of the game is discrediting the other side's views and
rejecting compromises unless defeat appears imminent. When the
price is zero, each side naturally wants it all.

PRIVATIZING THE NATIONAL FORESTS: A MODEST
PROPOSAL

. . . We believe that it does not matter very much who owns a
resource when it comes to determining how that resource will be used.
Any owner, whatever his goals, will find those goals frequently met
more fully by cooperation with others through trade. Since dollars, additional wilderness lands, buffer zones for existing wilderness, and
other items attainable through trade are desired by any potential
owner, it follows that even a zealot who owns the land can gain by
listening carefully and discussing constructively the alternatives pro-

posed by nonowners who desire wilderness, mineral, or other values from the landowner. Until all rights are (for the moment) optimally allocated among competing and compatible uses and users, further trade can make all parties to the trade better off in the pursuit of their various goals. . . .

Clearly, the sale of commercial timberlands from the national forests should be gradual. Early sales would provide solid evidence of both potential revenues and the degree of potential improvement in management. Since the values of timber, minerals, and amenity sheds all fluctuate with time and the economy, bids on any portion of the forest system would fluctuate as well. Like a conservative investor constructing a stock portfolio, the averaging process brought about by gradual sales would reduce the element of chance in the production of revenue. In addition, gradual sales would ensure that prices would not be artificially driven down by large and temporary gluts on the market.

The size of plots to be sold is another important consideration. It is vital that the plots be large enough to allow private planning, especially where amenities are involved. When large investors, clubs, partnerships, and corporations can purchase tracts large enough to incorporate what otherwise would be external effects, then the externalities are internalized. The purchasing firm is able to use restrictive covenants where necessary to maximize the value of the total land package and then sell off in smaller pieces whatever is not necessary to its own plans. This is commonly done in setting up large resorts. The integrity of the land use plan is preserved. This is simply the "planned unit development" concept applied in a forested setting.

The point is that if a mining company bought an entire forest, it would have every incentive to maximize the value of the 98 percent that it didn't really want by carefully considering the amenity effects of its exploration and mining operations. Similarly, if the Audubon Society submitted the high bid on ecologically critical portions of all the resold part of the forest, it would carefully consider its information and preferences. Demanding more only increases the required bid. The major reason we expect improvement in forest management is that a market system holds every private owner accountable to the rest of society by having to outbid everyone else — or reject others' bids — for every alternative forgone (or destroyed) on the land.

It is easy to see how the private ownership system fosters cooperation. Each party wants to get or meet its own desires at *minimum cost* to itself and thus must think in terms of what others want. But what about the individual who does not want to buy a part of the national forest but still wants access? Consider what people from Montana do when they want to use facilities in New York City but do not want to purchase real estate there. Just as some of the living space in New York is rented by the day or by the month, some of the private land in our country is leased by the hour, the week, or the year. Some people will pay a higher price for vacations filled with amenities, and many owners of the world's resources are happy to accommodate such vacationers. Access to a unique ecological site may be compared with access to a Rembrandt painting. In both cases, the admission fee can make it worthwhile for the owner to share the asset and, indeed, take elaborate precautions against its depreciation.

A key feature of our proposal is that the immense forest wealth of our nation would be more broadly shared among all citizens. Instead of a few favored firms and individuals enjoying the benefits of the forest, everyone would benefit from the revenues. Those revenues would capture the high bidder's estimate of the present capitalized value of all future benefits that could be derived from the land.

How large would the revenues from the sale of the national forests be? No one really knows. But it is not the *average* person's value that would determine the sale price of any tract. It is, rather, the most optimistic view, shared by the minimum number of people necessary to win the auction for a piece of land. Indeed, the winning bid would reflect a composite of the most optimistic bids, since interests in each large tract would tend to be subdivided, with relevant precautions taken by means of protective covenants in order to enhance each parcel's value. In short, the value of the land, as of all other private land, would be held down only by the limits to the imagination of the most optimistic bidders.

Marion Clawson estimated that the national forests were worth $42 billion in 1976. Since then there have been large increases in timber prices, in the value of strategic minerals, and in the value of oil and gas potential. In addition, the demand for recreation opportunities and amenity values continues to increase. With reduced opportunities for "free" forest services, we would expect prices to rise significantly. Note, however, that this does *not* mean that the average citizen, or even the forest user, is necessarily disadvantaged. Currently, every citizen is a member of one of the most expensive clubs in the world: the U.S. Forest Service. Our club dues are measured in tax dollars paid and in productivity values forgone. With the constructive attitudes and imaginative entrepreneurship unleashed by implementation of our proposal, the national forests could be sold for several hundred billion dollars. . . .

NOTES AND QUESTIONS

1. In order to understand the effects of institutional structures, it is necessary to have some model of decisionmaking. Is it appropriate to model federal forest officials as motivated solely or even significantly

by self-interest? One recent study of agency decisionmaking portrays government officials in a better light. See S. Kelman, Making Public Policy: A Hopeful View of American Government (1987). On the other hand, is it appropriate to model public officials as omniscient scientific managers, concerned solely with carrying out congressional intent? What is the proper perspective? The limitations of both systems are discussed in Menell, Institutional Fantasylands: From Scientific Management to Free Market Environmentalism, 15 Harv. J. L. & Pub. Pol. 489 (1992).

2. What resource problems might a system of unregulated private ownership of forestlands produce? Are there any externalities associated with timber production and harvesting? How might the problems of private ownership be alleviated through regulation? How far could such regulation go without running afoul of the U.S. Constitution? Would a government ban on clearcutting on all private land constitute a taking?

Would the allocation of resources within a private property system be worse than the distortions resulting from public ownership and management? What else is lost by the disposition of national forests?

3. Given Baden and Stroup's views about bureaucrats' motives in managing the national forests, what makes them so confident that these same people can be relied upon to sell the forests in a disinterested way? American history is replete with examples of land giveaways. Would corruption in the disposition of federal lands be worse than the continuation of below-cost timber sales?

4. In at least one sense, Baden and Stroup's analysis proved all too prescient. Soon after the notion of privatizing significant parcels of the public lands was floated by Reagan Administration officials in early 1982, the numerous beneficiaries of federal land subsidies — ranchers who received below-cost grazing fees, local communities that received federal lands for "public purposes" and federal payments for services, and hunters, fishers, and other recreational users of public lands who enjoyed free access — rebelled. Moreover, all of the interest groups that had learned to work within the complex political structure associated with federal ownership and management realized that their investments would be lost. The political fallout from the privatization proposal precipitated a hasty retreat. The story of privatization's demise is chronicled in Nelson, The Subsidized Sagebrush: Why the Privatization Movement Failed, Regulation 20 (July/August 1984).

The constraining influences of the political economy of natural resource policy emerged again following the election of President Bill Clinton. In one of its first environmental initiatives, the Clinton Administration announced a plan to roll back more than a century of government policies that have promoted the development of the West at government expense. See Egan, Sweeping Reversal of U.S. Land Policy

Sought by Clinton, N.Y. Times, Feb. 24, 1993, at A1. The proposed plan would charge market rates for commercial use of public resources. Despite strong support among environmentalists and budget analysts, the proposal was hastily withdrawn weeks later after a coalition of western Congress members vowed to derail the Administration's overall budget plan.

The Clinton Administration has vowed to pursue its proposal through administrative changes. On April 29, 1993, the Forest Service announced that it would end low-price logging on 62 of the 156 national forests. See Schneider, U.S. Would End Cutting of Trees in Many Forests, N.Y. Times, Apr. 30, 1993, at A1. This plan was scuttled in July, when a Senate panel voted to continue money-losing timber sales in national forests but trimmed $46 million from the program by increasing minimum bids and cutting administrative expenses. See Forests: Senate Panel OKs Continuation of Below-Cost Sales, Greenwire (Jul. 28, 1993); see also Schneider, Senate Blocks Rise in Grazing Fees, N.Y. Times, Sept. 15, 1993, at A10 (rebuffing Interior Secretary Babbitt's effort to raise grazing fees on public rangelands). Nonetheless, there is some backing among Eastern lawmakers to eliminate below-cost timber sales. See, e.g., S. 1550 "The Federal Spending and Deficit Act of 1993," Cong. Rec. S13555 (Oct. 15, 1993) (proposing a five-year phase out of below-cost timber sales estimated to save $.2 billion) (introduced by Senator Joseph Lieberman (D-Conn.)).

SAX, THE CLAIM FOR RETENTION OF THE PUBLIC LANDS

In S. Brubaker (ed.), Rethinking the Federal Lands 125,
125-126, 128-129, 131, 144-147 (1984)

There are sufficient practical and political reasons to make it unlikely that any large-scale sale of federal lands is in the offing. But the issue is a perennial in American political discourse because some profound issues of public policy are raised by substantial public land ownership and management in a nation deeply committed to private proprietorship of major resources and industries. . . .

Despite some of the flamboyant journalistic accounts of the issue, there is nothing in any plan put forward by the Reagan administration to suggest that the national parks might be put on the auction block or that the administration plans to dispose of designated wilderness areas. Whether there is some secret and nefarious agenda behind the public words is beyond my knowledge, but the fact is that, to date, discussion has been limited to unspectacular lands largely used for commodity purposes (such as grazing) held by the Bureau of Land Management

(BLM) and the Forest Service. However obvious it may be to many people that the United States should own and control Yellowstone National Park or the Lincoln Memorial, it is far from self-evident why the United States should also own and control hundreds of millions of acres of rather ordinary land.

I do not assert that such lands should be sold, but I think the question is one that deserves serious consideration. It should be noted here that federal ownership is not based on any long tradition or constitutional principle. For many years it was everywhere assumed that the United States would dispose of its landholdings, and it did dispose of much of what it owned until the mid-1930s. As late as the 1890s it was still considered a serious constitutional question whether the United States could acquire land for the purpose of establishing a memorial to the Civil War. But it was not until 1976 that the Congress, in the Federal Land Policy and Management Act (FLPMA), declared its general intention to retain in permanent federal ownership the remaining public lands, which then constituted about three-quarters of a billion acres. . . .

Ownership, although it is the focus of the current debate over the future of the federal lands, is, in fact, a poor measure of the real relationship that exists between government control and private market decision making on the public lands. For example, nothing in the fact of government ownership itself prevents the government from managing its lands precisely as a private entrepreneur would do. Following the same model of behavior that the proprietor of an office building uses in leasing space in a skyscraper, the federal government could lease lands for mineral or timber production to maximize economic efficiency. . . .

The real issue that divides advocates of sale (or "marketeers") from those who seek retention (or "regulators") is found in the unstated assumption that underlies discussion of "preferences." The marketeers assume that the only real or legitimate preferences are those that are expressed by individuals behaving atomistically. Thus, if an outcome differs from that which would have occurred through the expression of individual preference (the sort that occurs in market transactions), ipso facto it must be wrong (except in those relatively rare instances where the market does not reveal true preferences). The regulators believe that individuals have more than one kind of preference, and that because individual behavior in the market reveals only one species of preference, it therefore is incomplete. There is, they say, a kind of preference that people hold solely in their capacity as members of collectivities, and for which only collectivities speak. One such collectivity is the political community, or the government. When the government regulates, or controls use as owner, it is expressing a collective preference. . . .

What possible distinctive interest could the national political community have in the hundreds of million acres of publicly owned land, mostly in the western United States, and largely valuable primarily for commodity production, that would induce it to maintain ownership? . . .

I think the answer to the question of the political community's possible interest in the public domain lies in a much more general relationship between public values and the use of land. Without hoping to be exhaustive, let me sketch briefly the transition I see taking place in that relationship, of which the debate over the public domain is only one modest element.

I must begin with the trite observation that there is always some link between the rights that individuals are permitted to obtain in property and some public notion of the public interest. Perhaps the point is most easily illustrated by a very old issue, the right of inheritance. At the outset it is always the political community that decides what interests people may, and may not, obtain in property. To permit individuals to acquire the right to transmit their property to their heirs through inheritance demonstrates a social value. Laws that prohibit or impair the transmission of wealth through inheritance embody quite different collective values. Every rule of property, including rules about what rights of use, or sale, or inheritance, are adopted, begins with some social value.

Of course the conventional rules about property in America are socially based too, though these original social values are now so deeply embedded in traditional thinking that we tend to accept them as inevitable. Our tradition, made explicit by writers like Blackstone, views it as desirable that private rights be given out very extensively, and that private owners should be permitted to do as they wish with their property, conditioned only by the constraint that they should not cause affirmative harm to others (such as creating a nuisance).

That is a view of private ownership perfectly consistent with a production-oriented, developing, and industrializing world. For the kind of uses owners would generally make of their property when left largely free were the sort of productive, developmental uses that the society viewed as progress. So that, generally, what was good for the owner in producing profit and personal benefit was also perceived as being good for the society in producing economic growth. One might make the same point about property and the "cowboy" society of the American West in earlier years. Both the settlement and taming of the West, and the development of its mineral and other natural resources, were in harmony with American political policy for the West.

Thus, traditional views of the rights that property owners had, and should have, were not "made in heaven," but were compatible with, and grew out of, the dominant collective values of the time.

Today we are in a state of transition away from some of those values. I do not wish to be understood as overstating the point. I do not assert that conventional ideas of progress and economic growth are dead; far from it, I assert only that those ideas are less dominant and unanimous than they once were and that there is much more controversy about those traditional values than there once was. The so-called environmental movement, to take but a single example, is one instance of a growing (though perhaps still a minority) view that growth is not so good, or at least not unquestioningly good, or unlimitedly good.

As traditional values feel the stress of change, the institutions that grew out of those values will be reexamined, as, indeed, they have been. One might also expect significant changes regarding a shifting relationship between the rights of owners and the scope of public regulation. And we have seen — particularly in recent decades — some very dramatic changes.

To put the matter simply, we have seen increasing regulation constraining traditional ownership — regulation that implements skepticism about the desirability of largely untrammeled economic growth. The most obvious examples, of course, are conventional air and water pollution laws, constraints on hazardous substances like pesticides, and controls over the management and disposition of wastes. All these laws are, as industrialists are fond of pointing out, limitations on economic development. So they are. It might be said that these laws are simply modern examples of the sort of control over harmful externalities that can be traced back centuries to the law of nuisance. So they can, though the balance of interests has certainly shifted away from the traditional encouragement of industrialization that made nuisance a quite limited legal remedy.

But there is also a wide range of controls on property that have no obvious antecedents and which underline sharply the growing idea that nonuse, or preservation, rather than development and exploitation, may well be the highest and best use of property. One example is the recent growth of historic preservation laws, which are remarkable when considered from a traditional perspective. Owners who have done nothing "wrong," who cannot in any ordinary way be said to be imposing harm on others, are nonetheless often required to leave their property as it is, because it is believed that retention of historical structures is a more valuable use of the property than any developmental changes would be. Suburban growth-control ordinances are another example of the same phenomenon; however controversial such laws may be, they are revealing of a sharply changed notion. Communities that traditionally encouraged development, and measured their success by how rapidly they were growing, now often seek to slow or even end growth, because they view maintenance of their rural character, or their quietude, as of the highest importance. Open-space ordinances in towns, and wilderness designation in the country, illustrate a similar principle: Doing nothing is viewed as the highest and best use of the land. . . .

From the perspective I have just identified, the controversy over the public lands begins to come into focus. There is resistance to sale, because public ownership is seen as a means (and perhaps the most effective means) of control. Control is seen as necessary — more necessary than ever — because public values are more than ever divergent from the interests of private owners. Private uses are still thought appropriate, of course, and they may and often will still dominate the public lands. But those uses are increasingly constrained, just as urban uses are constrained, by zoning, growth control, environmental legislation, historic preservation, architectural controls, open-space regulation, and a host of other elements of the "new idea of progress." Retention of the public lands is really just another version of what occurs by regulation elsewhere. . . .

NOTES AND QUESTIONS

1. As discussed in Chapter 2 and in many other places in this book — the evolution of the Clean Air Act, the difficulties of statutory interpretation — the public choice literature raises serious questions about the ability of our political system to reflect the will of the people. The incentives of legislators and the actions of interest groups often produce skewed legislation and delegation of decisionmaking authority to agencies prone to capture. In view of the multiplicity of interest groups concerned with public lands policy and the biased nature of our political institutions, can we be sure that collective preferences will emerge in the political process? Or are "collective preferences" simply whatever comes out of the legislative process?

2. Professor Sax offers a strong argument, based on the proliferation of environmental laws in the 1970s and 1980s, that the American public places great value upon the protection of federal lands. Yet the reality of federal ownership and management of forests during the past two decades has been exploitation of our forestlands at taxpayers' expense. It is unlikely that private ownership of these same forests would have led to the extent of harvesting brought about with federal subsidization. If public ownership of federal lands is a reflection of collective preferences, are we to conclude that forestry policy, including below-cost timber sales, also reflects these preferences? What might explain this apparent anomaly? Assuming that public ownership does reflect collective preferences for environmental protection and that below-cost timber sales do not, how might forestry policy better effectuate these collective values?

3. Does Professor Sax's argument persuade you that selective privatization would be worse than the present system?

PROJECT '88 — ROUND II INCENTIVES FOR ACTION: DESIGNING MARKET-BASED ENVIRONMENTAL STRATEGIES

(sponsored by Senators Timothy Wirth and John Heinz, Robert N. Stavins, Project Director, May 1991)

OVERVIEW OF APPROACHES TO ELIMINATING BELOW-COST TIMBER SALES

Federal timber sales link road building, land management services, and annual payments to state and local governments to the activity of logging. These links create budgetary and political incentives for continued (and expanded) timber operations, even on money-losing sites. These incentives are of great significance because they are the most important forces that block efforts to solve the below-cost timber sale problem.

Since 1905, when Congress transferred the forest reserves to the Department of Agriculture and created the Forest Service, a driving objective has been to achieve an even distribution of timber stands among different age classes — as rapidly as possible. To achieve this objective, deposits from timber buyers are retained by the Forest Service for reforestation and brush disposal, 10% of gross timber receipts are earmarked for constructing and maintaining roads and trails, and credits are given against timber payments for purchaser-built roads. Such earmarked funds based on the number of acres logged and gross timber receipts make up a substantial portion of the Forest Service's budget. As such, they encourage the agency's managers to use timber sales to perpetuate development of the forest. Even timber sales which are net losses for taxpayers contribute to a manager's budget.

This system has fostered vested bureaucratic and political interests for continuing high timber-harvest levels, both within and outside of the Forest Service. Forest industry firms, workers, and local communities have all become dependent on National Forest timber harvests, creating a set of strong constituencies for more logging. It is important to modify the existing system so that public-land managers and others face incentives which reflect the full social value of forests. At a bare minimum, this would mean making forest management decisions according to sound financial criteria. At private firms, sales which fail to cover their costs simply are not tolerated. Yet a principal justification for Federal ownership of forests is that the government can exercise better stewardship over the environmental amenities that private firms have trouble incorporating. Therefore, incentives should go beyond the purely financial criteria of comparing revenues with outlays where high-value environmental (non-financial) uses are sacrificed through logging. As noted earlier, such uses would include, but not be limited to habitat protection, watershed values, and biological diversity. What is needed is a set of self-enforcing inducements to protect and enhance the *full social values* of individual forests. . . .

(1) DECENTRALIZED MANAGEMENT OF SELF-FINANCED NATIONAL FORESTS

A major step toward improving the incentive structure facing the Forest Service would be to decouple forest management decisions from centrally-determined production targets and appropriations by funding activities on each forest — to the extent possible — from net receipts earned on that forest.[19] This approach would eliminate many of the perverse incentives that reward forest managers for losing money on timber sales and for ignoring some production costs in their decision making. This system could be structured around specific management objectives for different classes of forest lands. The system should begin by separating out lands unsuitable for timber production. While such a provision is already a part of the National Forest Management Act of 1976, its implementation has not been satisfactory. Forests designated as suitable for timber harvesting would be run in an efficient and business-like manner, charging market prices and paying market costs. The Forest Service would not set timber targets for each forest; rather, each forest manager would take actions intended to maximize net revenues from the specific forest-resource asset base.

Critical to the success of such a system is allowing forest managers to capture revenues from timber *and* non-timber uses of the forest. The current system is fundamentally flawed in its near absolute dependence on timber sales for revenue. By some estimates, timber may represent only 25% of the value of forests, but timber sales generate more than 80% of revenues. On the other hand, recreation represents 41% of gross forest value[20] and is thus the single most valuable use, but it generates only 3% of forest revenues. Other potential activities from which

---

19. For an analysis of how to implement such an approach to forest management on public lands in the U.S., see: O'Toole, Randal. "Testing New Incentives on Selected National Forests." C.H.E.C. Oak Grove, Oregon, 1990.

20. This estimate of recreational value is from studies by the U.S. Forest Service of total willingness-to-pay by visitors to National Forests. It is based

a forest manager could generate revenues would be grazing rights, oil and gas, and mineral resources.

In addition to efficiency arguments, there are also strong equity arguments for making each use pay for itself. Timber consumption is not a public good; all benefits are purely private. Hence, Federal law states that timber buyers should pay fair market value. The same should be expected for other private forest uses. Recreation benefits, for example, arguably accrue to those who can afford to pay for them. Yet recreation users received a $90 million subsidy in 1985. There is certainly substantial precedent for the notion of users of publicly owned natural resources paying for benefits they derive.[21]

Many environmental benefits are hard to translate into cash receipts through conventional market mechanisms. Likewise, many citizens value the existence of wilderness who may never visit the forests. For both sets of benefits, it is difficult to implement any form of direct charge. Therefore, an important Federal role would be to provide funding to individual forests for protecting these amenities. Such funds could come from a portion of aggregate net receipts earmarked for the purpose.

NOTES AND QUESTIONS

1. Does this proposal adequately address the problems of national forest management? What is there to ensure that forest managers will make the best use of their forests? Doesn't this system bias forest managers toward those uses that have market values to the detriment of those that do not? Is such a approach better or worse than the present system? Consider these questions from the perspective of a resource economist, a recreationist, a preservationist, a member of the Forest Service, and the timber industry.

2. Is it appropriate to charge the "fair price" for recreation? How is this price to be determined? What if the most profitable recreational pricing structure leads to access for only the wealthy? Is such a policy equitable? What other values are served by encouraging access to the public lands? What pricing/access system is most appropriate for the public lands?

---

upon contingent-valuation and other standard methods of estimating the economic benefits of recreational opportunities.

21. For example, the Pittman Robertson Federal Aid in Wildlife Restoration Act of 1937 levies an 11% manufacturers excise tax on sporting rifles, shotguns, ammunition, handguns and archery equipment. Similarly, the 1951 Dingell-Johnson Federal Aid in Sport Fishing Restoration Act levies a 10% manufacturers excise tax on sport fishing equipment.

3. What alternative institutional approaches might be worth considering for managing the national forests?

D.   PROTECTION OF BIOLOGICAL
DIVERSITY

Over the past two decades, the protection of biological diversity has emerged as one of the most significant and controversial areas of environmental law and policy. Biological diversity comprises three related concepts: genetic diversity, species diversity, and ecosystem diversity. Genetic diversity refers to the range of heritable characteristics possessed by the organisms on the Earth. Species diversity concerns the range of distinct organisms. Ecosystem diversity describes the range of coherent biological communities of organisms.

By any of these measures, biological diversity has been dramatically affected by human activity. The rates at which species are becoming extinct and ecosystems lost vastly exceed natural rates of change and are accelerating. A recent government report estimates that 20 percent of all species could become extinct within the next 30 years. The human activities most responsible for loss of biological diversity are the vast expansion of human settlements, alteration of lands for agriculture and timber production, modification of water systems, overharvesting of animal and plant species, introduction of non-native species, fragmentation of ecosystems by transportation systems, and environmental pollution.

The legal regime that has evolved for protecting biological diversity reflects a fascinating interaction of philosophy, science, economics, politics, and legal institutions. This section begins with an exploration of the normative underpinnings of biological conservation. The second section presents a case study of the celebrated controversy surrounding the snail darter as a means of surveying the evolution of the Endangered Species Act (ESA). The final section focuses upon the most salient biological diversity controversy today, involving the northern spotted owl and the ancient forests of the Northwest, to highlight the critical issues involved in applying the ESA.

1.   NORMATIVE UNDERPINNINGS OF THE CONCERN
     FOR BIOLOGICAL CONSERVATION

SMITH, THE ENDANGERED SPECIES ACT AND
BIOLOGICAL CONSERVATION
———————————————————————————
57 U.S.C. L. Rev. 361 (1984)

II.   JUSTIFICATIONS FOR BIOLOGICAL
         CONSERVATION

A.   BASIC SCIENCE AND BIOLOGICAL CONSERVATION

Charles Darwin's well-known study of the finches of the Galapagos Islands influenced his theory of the origin of species. The profusion of closely related finch species led Darwin to conclude that "one might really fancy that from an original paucity of birds in this archipelago, one species had been taken and modified for different ends." He later wrote that "species occasionally arriving after long intervals of time in the new and isolated district, and having to compete with new associates, would be eminently liable to modification and would often produce groups of modified descendants."

Other groups of species exhibit evolutionary diversification patterns even more striking than those of Darwin's finches. The Hawaiian honeycreepers, birds of the family *Drepanididae* which are endemic to the islands, are the most striking example of adaptative radiation from a single ancestor of any bird family in the world. This process of species formation, or speciation, exhibited by the honeycreeper is referred to as adaptive radiation when the species evolves from a common ancestral population. A valuable opportunity to understand the speciation process is presented by adaptive radiations of the honeycreeper species.

The human destruction of biological diversity through modification of natural ecosystems is eliminating opportunities to observe and study evolutionary processes such as speciation. Consider the plight of one species of the honeycreeper, the palila *(Psittirostra bailleui)*. The palila is specially adapted to feed on the seeds of trees endemic to the island of Hawaii. Seeds of the mamane tree *(Sophora chrysophylla)*, found with the naio tree *(Myoporum santalinum)* in forests at altitudes above 4000 feet, are the primary food for the palila. As a result of the combined effects of human intervention in the island's ecosystem, mamane-naio forests are now found only on the slopes of Mauna Kea between 6500 feet and the tree line; bulldozing and the grazing of feral sheep and goats have destroyed other areas of mamane-naio forests. One of the few remaining honeycreepers having a finchlike bill, the palila is in serious danger of extinction, and is listed as endangered under the ESA. The plight of the species caused wildlife groups to bring suit in order to force the State of Hawaii to alter its wildlife habitat management policies to protect the palila. Unless the palila and other *Drepandididae* species can be protected, a valuable evolutionary phenomenon will be lost before scientists can fully study it.

The conservation and study of wild primates may also shed light on the persistent mystery that has motivated generations of scientists concerning the origin of the human species, *Homo sapiens*. The inference that mankind evolved from lower species fueled much of the firestorm of controversy surrounding early discussions of Darwin's theories. Although acceptance of the concept of *Homo sapiens* as the product of evolution from lower species has become commonplace, research into the behavior of anthropoid species that share common paleonthological ancestry with *Homo sapiens* may offer an opportunity to understand certain aspects of human culture and behavior. Moreover, such research may allow comparison that will test the treasured ideology of the uniqueness of the human species. . . .

B.   INSTRUMENTAL USES OF BIOLOGICAL DIVERSITY

Beyond discoveries through basic research, biologically diverse ecosystems provide resources and services. Two recently published volumes outline the pragmatic necessity of preserving the diversity of species and ecosystems. Those arguments are impressive. Most of the human race relies primarily on domesticated plant species for food. Yet of all the potential crop species available, fewer than twenty provide the vast majority of the harvest. By maintaining the genetic variability necessary for these harvested species to survive the constant onslaught of new parasites and diseases, the wild progenitors of these crop species provide a critical resource for the protection of the world's food supplied. Furthermore, many wild plant species could become direct food sources or, through hybridization, could contribute to harvests of new crops. If we continue to allow wild plant species to be extinguished without evaluating their value as genetic reserves and potential new crops, we may lose precisely those resources that could make it possible to support the expanding world population.

Another impressive pragmatic argument for preserving variety in species lies in the potential for the discovery of new medicines from the study of seemingly obscure and unimportant species. While the possibility for medical advancement through the study of any particular exotic species may be limited, recent scholarship indicates that vast potential exists in hundreds of plants and animals thought to have no value to mankind. In fact, in passing the ESA, Congress specifically noted that the discovery of the chemical properties of a previously unstudied and otherwise useless plant made oral contraceptives possible. Unfortunately, tropical deforestation may well be destroying hundreds of species before they can even be named and classified, let alone studied for biomedical potential.

C.   THE ETHICAL ARGUMENTS

Additional considerations beyond basic research and preservation of exploitable resources support biological conservation efforts. Unlike the scientific and instrumental arguments, which are necessarily human-centered in light of the threats posed to our existence by the loss of biological diversity, several arguments for species conservation attempt to add elements not captured by a focus on contemporary human interests. These arguments are termed "ethical" because, unlike the pragmatic considerations previously offered, they de-emphasize anthropocentric goals identified by shortrun utilitarian analysis and look instead to the welfare of the species and the biological community of which the species is a part.

The first ethical argument, which does contain traditional anthropocentric elements, assumes that there is moral force to support the protection of the interests of future generations. If there is such a moral force, then an appropriate theory of justice would preserve future generations' opportunities to use natural resources. This moral obligation would in turn support the conservation of biological diversity. Cost-benefit analyses of natural resource exploitation strategies frequently fail to consider the difficulty in properly considering the opportunity cost of the total destruction of a species. . . .

It can be argued that the destruction of species results in an inadequate appreciation of the value of life and a callous insensitivity to the causing of pain in other living entities. Legal sanctions against cruelty to animals are quite familiar; they may reflect a determination that such behavior is immoral. Just as we are shocked when the dramatist introduces a character who systematically pokes out the eyes of horses, we should be appalled at the lonely death of the last passenger pigeon in the Cincinnati Zoological Garden after the extermination of hundreds of millions of its kind.

This particular ethical argument has serious limitations when relied on to support biological conservation. First, the purported immorality is most immediately identified when human beings directly kill or injure animals; outrage comes easily against the perpetrators of the slaughter of dolphins at Iki, Japan. Rarely, however, are the causes of the loss of biological diversity in the contemporary world connected with the direct exploitation of the lost species. Rather, they are related to the destruction of the species' habitat by activities conducted in total ignorance of the effect on the species — occasionally in ignorance even of the existence of the species. Moral judgments about the actors who participate in such habitat destruction are much more difficult, particularly when those actors may be filling critical human survival needs.

Second, this cruelty-based argument may have different force for different species. Observers may have drastically different responses to mass killings of dolphins than they would have to mass killings of rattlesnakes. Indeed, it is possible that the human loathing of reptiles is a reflection of our evolutionary make-up. In short, our ability to respond morally to the mass destruction of a species may be connected to our ability to identify in some way with that species. Therefore, while this cruelty-based moral argument has force with regard to some species, it cannot provide a consistent basis for a general theory that would support biological conservation. Protection of ecological communities would require us to protect all species, even those we may find aesthetically unappealing.

A third moral argument is based on a conception of human membership in a broad biological community. Traditionally, our conception of the human community has been intrinsically linked to the ability to communicate. Recent work with a number of species has raised the possibility that *Homo sapiens* may not be the only species with the power to participate in rudimentary dialogue. In fact, the limitation upon the potential for interspecies communication may rest more in human inability to comprehend messages from other species than in the species' inability to communicate in a sophisticated manner. If it is true that other species have the potential to participate in an intelligible dialogue, then one could forcefully contend that it is immoral to jeopardize the continued existence of those species. While such a contention could challenge our established conception of humanity, it would nonetheless force us to acknowledge the value and right of other species.

Although the biological community argument also appears to be biased in favor of certain species, namely, species potentially capable of communication, a broader conception of communication could avoid some of that bias. After all, when we are attracted by the songs of birds, the beauty of butterflies, and the sophisticated organization of bee colonies, *something* has been communicated. That we find such communication only in species we consider "intelligent" or aesthetically pleasing may be only a reflection of the limits of our concepts of intelligence and beauty. Perhaps it is in the expansion of those concepts that the value of our membership in the broader biological community can be best understood. . . .

NOTES AND QUESTIONS

1. Which basis or bases for biological conservation do you find most compelling? Consider the following problems. How would they be resolved under the various normative frameworks?

- The snail darter is a three-inch fish thought to reside solely in the Little Tennessee River. This river is due to be inundated upon the closing of the floodgates of the Tellico Dam, a $100 million federal project that would provide electricity to thousands of homes, shoreline development opportunities, flatwater recreation, and flood control. The snail darter has no known (nor contemplated) unique human uses.

- The red wolf, once in abundance in the southeastern United States, became officially extinct in the wild in 1975. The few remaining red wolves are now in captivity. As part of its efforts to restore biological diversity, the U.S. Fish and Wildlife Service has drawn up plans to reintroduce the red wolf into its native habitat. Recent analysis of DNA from the red wolf, however, suggest that it is not a distinct species; rather it is a hybrid of the coyote and the gray wolf. In light of this finding, should the reintroduction plan be pursued? Does saving the red wolf enhance biological diversity? Are other purposes served by pursuing the plan? Given the limitedness of resources for biological restoration efforts, should the funding for the project, $600,000 for the first year alone, be redirected to saving genetically distinct species?

- Small pox is an acute, infectious viral disease. It is characterized by vomiting and an eruption of pustules on the skin. Advances in medicine are capable of eradicating this disease.

- Salmon lead an adventurous life. Hatched in fresh water riverbeds and lakes, they are flushed by river currents into the ocean where they live and grow for a few years. When mature, salmon swim upstream to their birthplace, where they spawn and die. The Columbia River currently supports approximately 200 distinct runs of salmon. Over the years, the development of hydroelectric power plants on the rivers of the northwest has impeded the life cycle of the salmon. Even with the construction of fish ladders which enable the mature salmon to circumvent the dams, an estimated 220 salmon runs on the Columbia River have died out since the turn of the century and many of the remaining runs have been declining. The low cost power from these hydroelectric facilities has fueled the region's economic development. In addition, vast diversions of water from the northwest's river system have transformed deserts into productive farmland. On the other hand, the valuable salmon fisheries of the northwest are jeopardized by the continued loss of salmon runs. Environmentalists, Native Americans, sport fishers, and commercial salmon fishers seek to protect the remaining runs of salmon, some arguing that each run of salmon, because of its unique homing ability, is a distinct species.

• The northern spotted owl lives predominantly within the ancient forests of the Pacific Northwest. As a nocturnal bird, it is rarely encountered by humans. The ancient forests of the Pacific Northwest, however, are a unique and sublime ecosystem, offering a variety of recreational opportunities. The home range of the typical northern spotted owl pair is quite large, about 5000 acres. Approximately 3000 pairs remain, although their numbers are dwindling. Most spotted owl habitat on private land has been obliterated by development and clearcutting. Their remaining habitat on federal lands is being gradually eroded by clearcutting. Alteration of harvesting methods or reduction of harvesting levels, however, would likely result in the loss of thousands of timber industry and related service jobs. Many of the communities that would be affected by harvesting restrictions already have high unemployment. Moreover, these rural areas have few nontimber industries.

2. The goal of preserving a particular species can conflict with the protection of a unique ecosystem. Consider the case of the Everglades ecosystem and the endangered snail kite. Florida water management policies have reduced water flow in the Everglades, threatening its ecological integrity. A federal plan to divert water to the Everglades, however, would alter the habitat of one of the few remaining populations of snail kites. Which interest is more important? This example raises the more general question of whether protection of biological diversity should focus on the preservation of species (and their habitats) or the protection of representative ecosystems. In what ways do the various philosophical bases for biological conservation resolve this question? How might policy differ under these approaches to biological conservation?

3. How far should society be willing to go to preserve species or ecosystems? Is the objective of fostering biological conservation subject to a utilitarian calculus? If not, on what basis should decisions regarding the protection of biological diversity be made? How could this approach be defended against Professor Baxter's utilitarian critique, supra, pp. 19-21?

4. Review the Endangered Species Act, especially the Congressional Findings and Declarations of Purposes and Policy, ESA §2. What

normative basis or bases underlie the Act? Are Congress' purposes anthropocentric? Utilitarian? Ecological? Does the Act recognize any intrinsic value for species? Is the Act concerned principally with
preservation of species or protection of ecosystems?

2. THE EVOLUTION OF THE ENDANGERED SPECIES ACT

The Endangered Species Preservation Act of 1966 established the
first federal program to conserve, protect, and restore selected species
of native fish and wildlife. Largely hortatory, the 1966 Act directed the
Departments of Agriculture, Interior, and Defense, "insofar as is practicable and consistent with their primary purposes," to preserve the habitats of endangered species on federal lands within their manadate. The
Act authorized these agencies to acquire lands that would serve this
purpose. The Endangered Species Conservation Act of 1969 retained
the general approach of the 1966 Act while expanding the list of protected species to include invertebrates and reptiles, prohibiting importation of listed species, and providing money for land acquisition.

These protections, however, did little to stem the loss of biological
diversity. Rising public concern for the environment in the early 1970s
led to the passage of the Endangered Species Act of 1973, which put
into place an aggressive federal policy for the protection of all species.
The limits of this regime were tested in the following case.

TENNESSEE VALLEY AUTHORITY V. HILL

437 U.S. 153 (1978)

Mr. Chief Justice BURGER delivered the opinion of the Court.

The questions presented in this case are (a) whether the Endangered Species Act of 1973 requires a court to enjoin the operation of a
virtually completed federal dam — which had been authorized prior to
1973 — when, pursuant to authority vested in him by Congress, the
Secretary of the Interior has determined that operation of the dam
would eradicate an endangered species; and (b) whether continued
congressional appropriations for the dam after 1973 constituted an implied repeal of the Endangered Species Act, at least as to the particular
dam.

The Little Tennessee River originates in the mountains of northern Georgia and flows through the national forest lands of North Carolina into Tennessee, where it converges with the Big Tennessee River

near Knoxville. The lower 33 miles of the Little Tennessee takes the river's clear, free-flowing waters through an area of great natural beauty. . . .

In this area of the Little Tennessee River the Tennessee Valley Authority, a wholly owned public corporation of the United States, began constructing the Tellico Dam and Reservoir Project in 1967, shortly after Congress appropriated initial funds for its development. Tellico is a multipurpose regional development project designed principally to stimulate shoreline development, generate sufficient electric current to heat 20,000 homes, and provide flatwater recreation and flood control, as well as improved economic conditions in [the area]. . . . When fully operational, the dam would impound water covering some 16,500 acres — much of which represents valuable and productive farmland — thereby converting the river's shallow, fast-flowing waters into a deep reservoir over 30 miles in length.

The Tellico Dam has never opened, however, despite the fact that construction has been virtually completed and the dam is essentially ready for operation. Although Congress has appropriated monies for Tellico every year since 1967, progress was delayed, and ultimately stopped, by a tangle of lawsuits and administrative proceedings. . . . [Local citizens and national conservation groups were initially successful in halting the project in 1972 for failure to comply with the Natural Environmental Policy Act. The courts subsequently upheld the adequacy of TVA's Environmental Impact Statement.]

A few months prior to the District Court's [1973] decision dissolving the NEPA injunction, a discovery was made in the waters of the Little Tennessee which would profoundly affect the Tellico Project. Exploring the area around Coytee Springs, which is about seven miles from the mouth of the river, a University of Tennessee ichthyologist, Dr. David A. Etnier, found a previously unknown species of perch, the snail darter, or Percina *(Imostoma)* tanasi. This three-inch, tannish-colored fish, whose number are estimated to be in the range of 10,000 to 15,000 would soon engage the attention of environmentalists, the TVA, the Department of the Interior, the Congress of the United States, and ultimately the federal courts, as a new and additional basis to halt construction of the dam.

Until recently the finding of a new species of animal life would hardly generate a cause celebre. This is particularly so in the case of darters, of which there are approximately 130 known species, 8 to 10 of these having been identified only in the last five years. The moving force behind the snail darter's sudden fame came some four months after its discovery, when the Congress passed the Endangered Species Act of 1973 (Act), 87 Stat. 884, 16 U.S.C. §1531 et seq. (1976 ed.) This legislation, among other things, authorizes the Secretary of the Interior to declare species of animal life "endangered" and to identify the "critical habitat" of these creatures. When a species or its habitat is so listed, the following portion of the Act — relevant here — becomes effective:

> The Secretary [of the Interior] shall review other programs administrated by him and utilize such programs in furtherance of the purposes of this chapter. All other Federal departments and agencies shall, in consultation with and with the assistance of the Secretary, utilize their authorities in furtherance of the purposes of this chapter by carrying out programs from the conservation of endangered species and threatened species listed pursuant to section 1533 of this title and *by taking such action necessary to insure that actions authorized, funded, or carried out by them do not jeopardize the continued existence of such endangered species and threatened species or result in the destruction or modification of habitat of such species* which is determined by the Secretary, after consultation as appropriate with the affected States, to be critical.

16 U.S.C. §1536 (1976 ed.) (emphasis added).

In January 1975, the respondents in this case and others petitioned the Secretary of the Interior to list the snail darter as an endangered species. After receiving comments from various interested parties, including TVA and the State of Tennessee, the Secretary formally listed the snail darter as an endangered species on October 8, 1975. . . . In so acting, it was noted that "the snail darter is a living entity which is genetically distinct and reproductively isolated from other fishes." . . . More important for the purposes of this case, the Secretary determined that the snail darter apparently lives only in that portion of the Little Tennessee River which would be completely inundated by the reservoir created as a consequence of the Tellico Dam's completion. . . .

[The Secretary found that impoundment of the waters behind the Tellico Dam would result in total destruction of the snail darter's "critical habitat," and that the provisions of §1536 were therefore applicable to the dam.

The dam had been authorized and funded by Congress and 50% completed before the Endangered Species Act was enacted, and was 70-80% completed by the time Interior listed the snail darter as endangered. Following congressional hearings, at which TVA argued that the Act did not apply to a substantially completed project and advocated completion of the dam despite the destruction of the snail darter, Congress approved TVA's general budget, which authorized funds for completion of the dam.

Pursuant to §11(g) of the Act, which authorizes "any person" to bring suit to enjoin violation of the Act, plaintiffs brought suit to enjoin completion of the dam. The district court refused to grant an injunction, on the ground that the project was substantially complete and that it would not be in the public interest to abandon it. Thereafter, Congress appropriated funds for completion of the dam. The court of appeals then reversed the district court, holding that since a violation of the Act was shown, issuance of an injunction was mandatory.

Congress then appropriated monies to finance TVA's efforts to relocate the snail darter; relevant committee reports expressed the view that the Act did not apply to substantially completed projects.]

We begin with the premise that operation of the Tellico Dam will either eradicate the known population of snail darters or destroy their critical habitat. Petitioner does not now seriously dispute this fact. . . .

It may seem curious to some that the survival of a relatively small number of three-inch fish among all the countless millions of species extant would require the permanent halting of a virtually completed dam for which Congress has expended more than $100 million. The paradox is not minimized by the fact that Congress continued to appropriate large sums of public money for the project, even after congressional Appropriations Committees were apprised of its apparent impact upon the survival of the snail darter. . . . We conclude, however, that the explicit provisions of the Endangered Species Act require precisely that result.

One would be hard pressed to find a statutory provision whose terms were any plainer than those in §7 of the Endangered Species Act. Its very words affirmatively command all federal agencies "to *insure* that actions *authorized, funded,* or *carried out* by them do not *jeopardize* the continued existence" of an endangered species or "*result* in the destruction or modification of habitat of such species. . . ." 16 U.S.C. §1536 (1976 ed.) (Emphasis added.) This language admits of no exception. Nonetheless, petitioner urges, as do the dissenters, that the Act cannot reasonably be interpreted as applying to a federal project which was well under way when Congress passed the Endangered Species Act of 1973. To sustain that position, however, we would be forced to ignore the ordinary meaning of plain language. . . .

Concededly, this view of the Act will produce results requiring the sacrifice of the anticipated benefits of the project and of many millions of dollars in public funds. But examination of the language, history, and structure of the legislation under review here indicates beyond doubt that Congress intended endangered species to be afforded the highest of priorities. . . .

The legislative proceedings in 1973 are, in fact, replete with expression of concern over the risk that might lie in the loss of *any* endangered species. Typifying these sentiments is the Report of the House Committee on Merchant Marine and Fisheries on H.R. 37, a bill which contained the essential features of the subsequently enacted Act of 1973; in explaining the need for the legislation, the Report stated:

As we homogenize the habitats in which these plants and animals evolved, and as we increase the pressure for products that they are in a position to supply (usually unwillingly) we threaten their — and our own — genetic heritage.

The value of this genetic heritage is, quite literally, incalculable. . . .

From the most narrow possible point of view, *it is in the best interests of mankind to minimize the losses of genetic variations.* The reason is simple: they are potential resources. They are keys to puzzles which we cannot solve, and may provide answers to questions which we have not yet learned to ask.

To take a homely, but apt, example: one of the critical chemicals in the regulation of ovulations in humans was found in a common plant. Once discovered, and analyzed, humans could duplicate it synthetically, but had it never existed — or had it been driven out of existence before we knew its potentialities — we would never have tried to synthesize it in the first place.

Who knows, or can say, what potential cures for cancer or other scourges, present or future, may lie locked up in the structures of plants which may yet be undiscovered, much less analyzed? . . . Sheer self-interest impels us to be cautious.

The institutionalization of that caution lies at the heart of H.R. 37. . . . H.R. Rep. No. 93-412, pp. 4-5 (1973). (Emphasis added.) . . .

[The Court discusses additional elements of the legislative history, including the elimination of proposed qualifications in the protection which the proposed Act could afford.]

It is against this legislative background that we must measure TVA's claim that the Act was not intended to stop operation of a project which, like Tellico Dam, was near completion when an endangered species was discovered in its path. While there is no discussion in the legislative history of precisely this problem, the totality of congressional action makes it abundantly clear that the result we reach today is wholly in accord with both the words of the statute and the intent of Congress. The plain intent of Congress in enacting this statute was to halt and reverse the trend toward species extinction, whatever the cost. . . .

It is not for us to speculate, much less act, on whether Congress would have altered its stance had the specific events of this case been anticipated. . . .

[The Court considered the argument that Congress never contemplated that the Act would halt a project that would burden] the public through the loss of millions of unrecoverable dollars [that] would greatly outweigh the loss of the snail darter. But neither the Endangered Species Act nor Art. III of the Constitution provides federal courts with authority to make such fine utilitarian calculations. On the contrary, the plain language of the Act, buttressed by its legislative history, shows clearly that Congress viewed the value of endangered species as "incalculable." Quite obviously, it would be difficult for a court to balance the loss of a sum certain — even $100 million — against a congressionally declared "incalculable" value, even assuming we had the power to engage in such a weighing process, which we emphatically do not.]

Notwithstanding Congress' expression of intent in 1973, we are urged to find that the continuing appropriations for Tellico Dam constitute an implied repeal of the 1973 Act, at least insofar as it applies to the Tellico Project. . . .

[The Court rejected this argument. It then considered whether equitable considerations showed led the courts to refuse an injunction even though completion of the dam would violate the Act.]

Here we are urged to view the Endangered Species Act "reasonably," and hence shape a remedy "that accords with some modicum of common sense and the public weal." . . . But is that our function? We have no expert knowledge on the subject of endangered species, much less do we have a mandate for the people to strike a balance of equities on the side of the Tellico Dam. Congress has spoken in the plainest of words, making it abundantly clear that the balance has been struck in favor of affording endangered species the highest of priorities, thereby adopting a policy which it described as "institutionalized caution."

Our individual appraisal of the wisdom or unwisdom of a particular course consciously selected by the Congress is to be put aside in the process of interpreting a statute. Once the meaning of an enactment is discerned and its constitutionality determined, the judicial process comes to an end. We do not sit as a committee of review, nor are we vested with the power of veto. The lines ascribed to Sir Thomas More by Robert Bolt are not without relevance here:

> The law, Roper, the law. I know what's legal, not what's right. And I'll stick to what's legal . . . I'm *not* God. The currents and eddies of right and wrong, which you find such plain-sailing, I can't navigate, I'm no voyager. But in the thickets of the law, oh there I'm a forester . . . What would you do? Cut a great road through the law to get after the Devil? . . . And when the last law was down, and the Devil turned round on you — where would you hide, Roper, the laws all being flat? . . . This country's planted thick with laws from coast to coast — Man's laws, not God's — and if you cut them down . . . d'you really think you could stand upright in the winds that would blow then? . . . Yes, I'd give the Devil benefit of law, for my own safety's sake.

R. Bolt, A Man for All Seasons, Act I, p. 147 (Three Plays, Heinemann ed. 1967).

We agree with the Court of Appeals that in our constitutional system the commitment to the separation of powers is too fundamental for us to pre-empt congressional action by judicially decreeing what accords with "common sense and the public weal." Our Constitution vests such responsibilities in the political branches.

Affirmed.

Mr. Justice POWELL, with whom Mr. Justice BLACKMUN joins, dissenting.

The Court today holds that §7 of the Endangered Species Act requires a federal court, for the purpose of protecting an endangered species or its habitat, to enjoin permanently the operation of any federal project, whether completed or substantially completed. This decision casts a long shadow over the operation of even the most important projects, serving vital needs of society and national defense, whenever it is determined that continued operation would threaten extinction of an endangered species or its habitat. . . .

In my view §7 cannot reasonably be interpreted as applying to a project that is completed or substantially completed when its threat to an endangered species is discovered. Nor can I believe that Congress could have intended this Act to produce the "absurd result" — in the words of the District Court — of this case. . . .

[Justice Powell undertook an extensive analysis of the Act's history.]

I have little doubt that Congress will amend the Endangered Species Act to prevent the grave consequences made possible by today's decision. Few, if any, Members of that body will wish to defend an interpretation of the Act that requires the waste of at least $53 million . . . and denies the people of the Tennessee Valley area the benefits of the reservoir that Congress intended to confer. There will be little sentiment to leave this dam standing before an empty reservoir, serving no purpose other than a conversation piece for incredulous tourists.

[Justice REHNQUIST also filed a dissenting opinion, arguing that the Act did not foreclose the traditional equitable discretion of courts in issuing injunctions, and that in the circumstances of this case an injunction should not issue.]

QUESTIONS

1. What approach to environmental protection is manifest in the Endangered Species Act of 1973? How does this compare to the other environmental statutes that we have seen? Why did Congress adopt such an absolute regime with respect to species preservation, yet rely on more flexible approaches — such as balancing, discretion — elsewhere?

2. Was this litigation strategically well-advised for environmental-ists to undertake? Think about this question as you read the epilogue.

Epilogue

The subsequent history of the Tellico Dam is full of rich ironies. Following *TVA v. Hill,* Congress in 1978 amended the Endangered Species Act to provide an exemption procedure for government projects that would otherwise violate the Act. See ESA §7(e)-(h). The process would require approval by five out of seven members of an Endangered Species Committee after investigation by a three-member review board. The Committee is composed of various high government officials from agencies with different constituencies. It has come to be known as the "God Squad" because of its power to decide the fate of specific species. The provision was regarded as something of a victory for environmentalists, who believed that the process would ward off hasty congressional exemption of particular projects by ad hoc legislation, and that few exemptions would be granted by the Committee.

A Committee exemption was sought for Tellico Dam by Senator Howard Baker of Tennessee. The effort failed, in part as a result of studies questioning whether the economic benefits of Tellico would exceed even the incremental costs of completing it. Environmentalists had opposed the Dam as an uneconomic "pork barrel" project that would destroy a beautiful free-flowing river; the snail darters conveniently provided a legal claim against the Dam. Another study indicated that a "river development" alternative could provide net benefits nearly as great as those provided by completion of the dam and reservoir, without endangering the fish.

Senator Baker then succeeded in tacking a rider onto a general authorization bill, exempting the Tellico Dam from the Endangered Species Act and mandating its completion. This precedent has made environmentalists reluctant to employ the Act in litigation to stop federal projects for fear that Congress will mandate approval of such projects on an ad hoc basis (possibly cutting off other legal claims in the process) or amend the Act to weaken it.

In November 1979, the floodgates to the dam were closed after several hundred snail darters were moved to another location. In 1980, quite by chance, an apparently indigenous group of snail darters was found in another stream, twenty-five miles from the Tellico Dam. Other populations were subsequently discovered, eventually leading to the removal of the snail darter from the endangered species list.

3.   TESTING THE LIMITS OF THE ENDANGERED
SPECIES ACT: THE NORTHERN SPOTTED OWL

a.   The Listing Decision

NORTHERN SPOTTED OWL V. HODEL

716 F. Supp. 479 (W.D. Wash. 1988)

ZILLY, District Judge. . . .

Since the 1970s the northern spotted owl has received much scientific attention, beginning with comprehensive studies of its natural history by Dr. Eric Forsmann, whose most significant discovery was the close association between spotted owl and old-growth forests. This discovery raised concerns because the majority of remaining old-growth owl habitat is on public land available for harvest.

In January 1987, plaintiff Greenworld, pursuant to Sec. 4(b)(3) of the ESA, 16 U.S.C. §1533(b)(3), petitioned the Service to list the northern spotted owl as endangered. . . .

The ESA directs the Secretary of the Interior to determine whether any species have become endangered or threatened[22] due to habitat destruction, overutilization, disease or predation, or other natural or manmade factors. 16 U.S.C. §1533(a)(1).[23] The Act was amended in 1982 to ensure that the decision whether to list a species as endangered or threatened was based solely on an evaluation of the biological risks faced by the species, to the exclusion of all other factors. See Conf. Report 97-835, 97th Cong., 2d Sess. (Sept. 17, 1982) at 19, reprinted in 1982 U.S. Code Cong. & Admin. News 2807, 2860. . . .

In July 1987, the Service announced that it would initiate a status

---

22. The ESA defines an "endangered species" as "any species which is in danger of extinction throughout all or a significant portion of its range. . . ." 16 U.S.C. §1532(6). A "threatened species" is "any species which is likely to become an endangered species within the foreseeable future throughout all or a significant portion of its range." 16 U.S.C. §1532 (20).

23. Section 4(a)(1), codified at 16 U.S.C. §1533(a)(1), provides that:

The Secretary (of Interior in the case of terrestrial species) shall . . . determine whether any species is an endangered species or a threatened species because of any of the following factors:

(A)   the present or threatened destruction, modification, or curtailment of its habitat or range;
(B)   overutilization for commercial, recreational, scientific, or educational purposes;
(C)   disease or predation;
(D)   the inadequacy of existing regulatory mechanisms; or
(E)   other natural or manmade factors affecting its continued existence.

review of the spotted owl and requested public comment. 52 Fed. Reg. 34396 (Sept. 11, 1987). The Service assembled a group of Service biologists, including Dr. Mark Shaffer, its staff expert on population viability, to conduct the review. The Service charged Dr. Shaffer with analyzing current scientific information on the owl. Dr. Shaffer concluded that:

> the most reasonable interpretation of current data and knowledge indicate continued old growth harvesting is likely to lead to the extinction of the subspecies in the foreseeable future which argues strongly for listing the subspecies as threatened or endangered at this time.

M. Shaffer, letter of November 11, 1987, to Jay Gore, U.S. Fish and Wildlife Service, Region 1, Endangered Species, attached to Final Assessment of Population Viability Projections for the Northern Spotted Owl [Administrative Record at III.A.1].

The Service invited a peer review of Dr. Shaffer's analysis by a number of U.S. experts on population viability, all of whom agreed with Dr. Shaffer's prognosis for the owl, although each had some criticisms of his work.

The Service's decision is contained in its 1987 Status Review of the owl ("Status Review") [Administrative Record at 11.C] and summarized in its Finding on Greenworld's petition ("Finding") [Administrative Record at I.D.1.]. The Status Review was completed on December 14, 1987, and on December 17 the Service announced that listing the owl as endangered under the Act was not warranted at that time.[24] 52 Fed. Reg. 48552, 48554 (Dec. 23, 1987). This suit followed. Both sides now move for summary judgment on the administrative record before the Court.

This Court reviews the Service's action under the "arbitrary and capricious" standard of the Administrative Procedure Act ("APA"), 5 U.S.C. §706(2)(A). *Friends of Endangered Species v. Jantzen,* 760 F.2d 976, 980-81 (9th Cir. 1985). This standard is narrow and presumes the agency action is valid, *Ethyl Corp. v. EPA.* 541 F.2d 1, 34 (D.C. Cir.), *cert. denied,* 426 U.S. 941, 96 S. Ct. 2662, 49 L. Ed. 2d 394 (1976), but it does not shield agency action from a "thorough, probing, in-depth review,"

---

24. The Service's Finding provides as follows:

> A finding is made that a proposed listing of the northern spotted owl is not warranted at this time. Due to the need for population trend information and other biological data, priority given by the Service to this species for further research and monitoring will continue to be high. Interagency agreements and Service initiatives support continued conservation efforts. This finding will be published in the Federal Register and the petitioner will be notified.

Findings at 5 [Administrative Record at I.D.1.].

Citizens to Preserve Overton Park v. Volpe, 401 U.S. 402, 415, 91 S. Ct. 814, 823, 28 L. Ed. 2d 136 (1971). . . .

The Status Review and the Finding to the listing petition offer little insight into how the Service found that the owl currently has a viable population. Although the Status Review cites extensive empirical data and lists various conclusions, it fails to provide any analysis. The Service asserts that it is entitled to make its own decision, yet it provides no explanation for its findings. An agency must set forth clearly the grounds on which it acted. *Atchison T. & S.F. Ry v. Wichita Bd. of Trade*, 412 U.S. 800, 807, 93 S. Ct. 2367, 2374-75, 37 L. Ed. 2d 350 (1973). Judicial deference to agency expertise is proper, but the Court will not do so blindly. The Court finds that the Service has not set forth the grounds for its decision against listing the owl.

The Service's documents also lack any expert analysis supporting its conclusion. Rather, the expert opinion is entirely to the contrary. . . .

The Court will reject conclusory assertions of agency "expertise" where the agency spurns unrebutted expert opinions without itself offering a credible alternative explanation. See, e.g. *Americans Tunabout Ass'n v. Baldrige*, 738 F.2d 1013, 1016 (9th Cir. 1984). Here, the Service disregarded all the expert opinion on population viability, including that of its own expert, that the owl is facing extinction, and instead merely asserted its expertise in support of its conclusions.

The Service has failed to provide its own or other expert analysis supporting its conclusions. Such analysis is necessary to establish a rational connection between the evidence presented and the Service's decision. Accordingly, the United States Fish and Wildlife Service's decision not to list at this time the northern spotted owl as endangered or threatened under the Endangered Species Act was arbitrary and capricious and contrary to law. . . .

QUESTIONS

1. How does the extent of deference shown by the court to the responsible administrative agency in this case compare to that in other environmental cases we have seen, such as application of the MUSYA *(Sierra Club v. Hardin)*, supra p. 1087? Is the court's level of scrutiny appropriate? What factors favor this level of scrutiny? Detract from it?

2. Is the lack of adequate data a legitimate basis for not listing a species? Should it be?

FISH AND WILDLIFE SERVICE, DEPT. OF
INTERIOR, DETERMINATION OF THREATENED
STATUS FOR THE NORTHERN SPOTTED OWL

55 Fed. Reg. 26114 (June 26, 1990)

BACKGROUND

The spotted owl *(Strix occidentalis)*, consisting of three subspecies (northern, California, and Mexican), is a medium-sized owl with dark eyes, dark-to-chestnut brown coloring, with whitish spots on the head and neck and white mottling on the abdomen and breast . . . .

Although a secretive and mostly nocturnal bird, the northern spotted owl is relatively unafraid of human beings. The adult spotted owl maintains a territory year-round; however, individuals may shift their home ranges between the breeding and nonbreeding season. Monogamous and long-lived, spotted owls tend to mate for life, although it is not known if pair-bonding or site fidelity is the determining factor.

Spotted owls are perch-and-dive predators and over 50 percent of their prey items are arboreal or semiarboreal species. Spotted owls subsist on a variety of mammals, birds, reptiles, and insects, with small mammals such as flying squirrels, red tree voles and dusky-footed woodrats making up the bulk of the food items throughout the range of the species. . . .

Northern spotted owls are distinguished from the other subspecies by their darker brown color and smaller white spots and markings. . . .

Secific [sic] spotted owl pairs usually do not nest every year nor are nesting pairs successful every year. Nesting behavior begins in February to March with nesting occurring from March to June; however, the timing of nesting and fledgling varies with latitude and elevation. The modal clutch size is 2 eggs, with a range of 1 to 4. . . .

The current range of the northern spotted owl is from southwestern British Columbia, through western Washington, western Oregon, and northern California south to San Francisco Bay. . . .

Spotted owls have been observed over a wide range of elevation, although they seem to avoid higher elevation, subalpine forests. . . .

The age of forests is not as important a factor in determining habitat suitability as are vegetational and structural components. Suitable owl habitat has moderate to high canopy closure (60 to 80 percent); a multi-layered, multi-species canopy dominated by large (> 30 inches in diameter at breast height [dbb]) overstory trees; a high incidence of large trees with various deformities (e.g. large cavities, broken tops, dwarf-mistletoe infections, and other evidence of decadence); numerous large snags; large accumulations of fallen trees and other woody debris on the ground; and sufficient open space below the canopy for owls to fly. Usually the features characteristics of owl habitat are most commonly associated with old-growth forests or mixed stands of old-growth and mature trees, which do not assimilate these attributes until from 150 to 200 years of age. The Interagency Scientific Committee reports that its members have seen sites used by owls throughout the range of the owl where the attributes of suitable owl habitat are present in relatively young forests (60 + years). Attributes of owl habitat are sometimes found in younger forests, especially those with significant remnants of earlier stands that were influenced by fire, wind storms, inefficient logging, or highgrading (removal of the most economically valuable trees). However, nests and major most sites were located, in almost all instances, in the portions of the stand containing the oldest components. . . .

Forsman et al. (1977) computed an index to density of spotted owls based on response rates to simulated calls in Oregon, and estimated that spotted owl pairs were 5 to 12 times more abundant in old growth than in young-growth forests. Of 1,502 owl sites, Forsman et al. (1987) found that 1,282 were in old growth, 22 in mature forest, 131 in old-growth/mature forest, and 67 in stands less than 100 years age, demonstrating that the spotted owl is dramatically and disproportionately found in association with old growth.

Northern spotted owls have relatively large home ranges. . . . Median annual pair home ranges were estimated to be 9,930 acres for the Olympic Peninsula (n = 10), 6,308 acres for the Washington Cascades (n = 13) 2,955 for the Oregon Cascades (n = 11), 4,766 acres for the Oregon Coast Range (n = 22), and 3,340 acres for the Klamath Province (n = 36). Home range size varied from 1,035 acres in the Klamath Province to a high of 30,961 acres in the Washington Cascades. . . . These data strongly suggest that paired northern spotted owls require large tracts of land containing significant acreage of old forest to meet their biological needs (e.g. foraging and breeding). . . .

There are no estimates of the historical population size and distribution of the northern spotted owl within preferred habitat, although spotted owls are believed to have inhabited most old-growth forests throughout the Pacific Northwest prior to modern settlement (mid 1800s), including northwestern California. Spotted owls are still found within their historical range in most areas where preferred and suitable habitat exist, although most of the owls are restricted within this range to mature and old-growth forests managed by the Federal government. Approximately 90 percent of the roughly 2000 known breeding pairs of spotted owls have been located on federally managed lands, 1.4 percent on State lands, and 6.2 percent on private lands. . . .

The provisions of section 4 of the Act and regulations promulgated to implement the Act (50 C.F.R. part 424) were followed. A species may be determined to be an endangered or threatened species due to one or more of the five factors described in section 4(a)(1). These factors and their application to the northern spotted owl *(Strix occidentalis courina)* are as follows:

A.   *The Present or Threatened Destruction, Modification, or Curtailment of Its Habitat or Range. . . .*

Habitat for northern spotted owls has been declining since the arrival of European settlers. Although the extent of suitable habitat before the 1800s is difficult to quantify, estimates of 17.5 million acres in 1800 and 7.1 million acres today suggest a reduction of about 60 percent in the past 190 years. Other estimates suggest that the reported decline in historical habitat, in fact, may have been as high as 83 to 88 percent. Habitat reduction has not been uniform throughout the range of the spotted owl, but has been concentrated at lower elevations and the Coast Ranges. Reduction of old growth is largely attributable to timber harvesting and land conversion practices, although natural perturbations, such as forest fires, have caused losses as well.

Current surveys and inventories have shown that while northern spotted owls are not found in all old-growth forests, nor exclusively in old-growth forests, they are overwhelmingly associated with forests of this age and structure. It is well established that northern spotted owls tend to be associated with forest stands in which many of the trees are more than 80 years old ("older forest"). . . .

Approximately 90 percent of suitable habitat for northern spotted owls now occurs on public land. . . . Historically, non-Federal lands probably contained a significant amount of owl habitat and may still offer the opportunity to provide vital linkages between islands of federally managed habitat in many areas. However, current logging practices, such as clearcutting, even-aged management, and short logging rotations, preclude development of future mature and old-growth conditions from most existing young forest stands.

The Forest Service manages 79 percent of the habitat on federal land, the Bureau of Land Management manages 14 percent, and the National Park Service manages 7 percent. Of the 6.8 million acres of northern spotted owl habitat in government ownership, 60 percent is classified as timber production land, 28 percent is withdrawn from timber harvest [principally land in Wilderness Areas and National Parks], and 12 percent is classified as unsuitable for timber production.

The amount of northern spotted owl habitat on land suitable for timber production has decreased rapidly since 1960 . . . for Forest Service Land in Washington and Oregon. While future events are difficult to predict, past trends strongly suggest that much of the remaining unprotected spotted owl habitat could disappear within 20 to 30 years, and on some forests, the unprotected habitat could disappear within 10 years. . . .

At present, a substantial amount of land on Forest Service and Bureau of Land Management land has been dedicated to spotted owl management areas. This system, however, has been called into question by Thomas et al. (1990), who consider it inefficient and unlikely to succeed in preserving northern spotted owls. They have urged that this approach be abandoned and have proposed a new system.

Under current management plans, the distribution of spotted owl habitat remaining in the near future will closely coincide with National Parks, reserved areas on federally managed forests, or other lands that are not considered suitable or available for timber harvest for other reasons (e.g. lands too steep or rocky for timber production, lands needed for hydrologic protection, scenic areas, etc.). These areas will contribute to maintaining spotted owl populations only to the extent that they contain suitable habitat of adequate size and quality for the birds. By then, most remaining suitable habitat will no longer be continuous, but will exist as islands of varying size, spacing, and suitability spread over the range of the subspecies. . . .

Many of the current Wilderness Areas and parks are largely high-elevation lands above timberline and it is unlikely that northern spotted owl populations would be viable if their habitat were restricted to these areas. These protected areas are concentrated within only about one-third of the current range. Furthermore, abundance and reproductive success of northern spotted owls in these areas is much lower than in good habitat outside the protected areas. The low productivity is especially significant because it suggests strongly that reproductive success in these areas would be too low to balance mortality due to natural causes. . . .

The effect of timber harvest on northern spotted owls depends on whether even-aged, or mixed-aged techniques are used. . . . More than 90 percent of the timber harvest throughout the range of the northern spotted owl is accomplished using clearcutting or other methods that produce even-aged stands. . . .

Several studies have concluded that northern spotted owls are seldom found in even-aged stands younger than currently planned rotation ages. . . .

Northern spotted owls appear to use at least some land that has been managed to produce uneven-aged stands, but this silvicultural approach is generally rare throughout the range. Land managed to produce uneven-aged stands includes small patches of older forest along streams and in areas unsuitable for timber harvest, but such lands generally comprise 20 percent or less of the areas. In these areas northern spotted owls are rare and have low reproductive success. . . . It is difficult to predict whether these lands will support owl populations in the future because current harvest methods favor even-age stands and trees younger and smaller than many of the trees that were present in these studies. . . .

As a result of past and present harvest patterns, potential isolation of several subpopulations of northern spotted owls is also of considerable concern. . . . The smaller a population or subpopulation and the greater its isolation from other populations, the greater the risk of its elimination as a result of chance demographic and environmental events or genetic effects. . . .

A recent assessment of the effects of forest fragmentation suggests that in areas of highly fragmented and isolated habitats in northwestern California, there may be lower reproductive fitness among owls relative to birds in nearby, more contiguous habitat. . . .

Fragmentation of habitat also may adversely affect spotted owls by: (1) Directly eliminating key roosting, nesting, or foraging stands; (2) indirectly reducing the survival of dispersing juvenile owls; (3) perhaps increasing competition or predation, and (4) reducing population densities and interaction between individuals. These factors may interact to decrease habitat quality, suitability, or effectiveness for supporting a well-distributed population of spotted owls over time.

Fragmentation can also have harmful genetic consequences through its effect on the effective population size. . . .

The patchwork pattern of even-aged, dispersed, clearcut timber harvest systems has imposed a checkerboard pattern on present old-growth and mature forests, fragmenting remaining habitat throughout the owl's range and reducing the total amount of suitable spotted owl habitat. . . .

Although the actual numbers of owl sites and pairs on all lands is not precisely known, recent surveys (1985-1989) indicate that there are about 2,000 known pairs of northern spotted owls within the present range of the subspecies, although 3,000-4,000 pairs are suspected. Of these, approximately 90 percent are found on federally managed lands. . . .

According to the Service's results [on population trends], the resident population of owls on [two large study] areas was declining sharply and significantly in both areas but was sustained each year by owls from surrounding areas. . . . Hence, the Service maintains that these areas are population sinks where mortality exceeds recruitment. Because there has been a dramatic loss of suitable habitat throughout the range of the northern spotted owl, it seems likely that the population of owls has declined substantially throughout its range. . . .

It is unknown whether the amount and distribution of spotted owl habitat remaining at the end of commercial harvest of old-growth forests on public lands will be adequate to support a viable population of the northern spotted owl. Attempts to answer this question by using the concepts and tools of population viability assessments have been undertaken by the Forest Service, Lands, and Doak. Although subject to criticism on a number of grounds, the population viability assessments indicate that implementation of the Forest Service's preferred alternative for managing the spotted owl in Oregon and Washington (Alternative F) will not provide a high probability of persistence for the spotted owl over the next 50 to 100 years, at least not in significant portions of its range. . . .

The dependence of northern spotted owls on older forest, the low probability that significant amounts of suitable habitat will persist outside of preserved areas, and the inability of the protected areas to support a viable population of northern spotted owls, all indicate that the northern spotted owl is likely to become endangered within the foreseeable future throughout all or a significant portion of its range.

B. Overutilization for Commercial, Recreational, Scientific, or Educational Purposes

Considerable research by Federal, State, and private groups is being conducted on this subspecies. This work is providing valuable information and is not having a negative impact on the subspecies. The spotted owl is not a game bird, nor is there any known commercial or sporting use.

C. Disease or Predation

Predation by great horned owls has been identified as a major source of juvenile mortality in spotted owls. Concern has been expressed that increasing habitat fragmentation may be subjecting spotted owls to greater risks of predation as they move into or across more open terrain, or come into more frequent contact with forest edges where horned owls may be more numerous. . . .

In a recent study, the incidence of hematozoa in spotted owls was found to be one of the highest of any avian species yet examined. Recent research indicates there may be both long-and-short-term ecological effects of hematozoa on birds such as the possibility of adversely influencing their energetics.

D.   The Inadequacy of Existing Regulatory Mechanisms

Although there are numerous State and federal laws and regulations that, if enforced, may protect spotted owls and, to a lesser extent, spotted owl habitat, the implementation and effectiveness of these laws to date has been variable. The precarious status of the northern spotted owl has been recognized in Washington, where it is listed as endangered, in Oregon, where it is considered threatened, and in California, where it is classified as a sensitive species. . . .

Based on present State regulations and policy, clearly no State legislates adequate protection for spotted owls. Private and State-owned forest lands in Washington, Oregon, and northern California total over 21 million acres. Less than 1 percent, mostly in State parks in northern California, provides long-term protection to the northern spotted owl. Although approximately 4 percent of known reproductive pairs occur on private lands, particularly in northern California, current regulatory mechanisms neither account for their presence, nor protect them. . . .

The cumulative impact of timber-cutting practices by land managing agencies increases and exacerbates the fragmentation of existing owl habitat. The proposed spotted owl management plans of the Forest Service and Bureau of Land Management are untested. Recent legal actions aside, there is no indication from the land management agencies that the current rate of change from old growth to young even aged forest management will diminish. Further, as agencies concentrate their clearcutting activities outside designated spotted owls habitat management options will be lost if currently planned habitat networks prove later to be deficient. Existing regulatory mechanisms are insufficient to protect either the northern spotted owl or its habitat.

E.   Other Natural or Man Made Factors Affecting Its Continued Existence

The barred owl has undergone rapid range expansion over the past 20 years into the range of the spotted owl in the northwestern United States. . . .

The barred owl's adaptability and aggressive nature appear to allow it to take advantage of habitat perturbations, such as those that result from habitat fragmentation, and to expand its range where it may compete with the spotted owl for available resources. The long term impact to the spotted owl is unknown but of considerable concern. . . .

There are numerous examples of extrinsic factors such as fires, wind damage, and volcanic action affecting forest habitat including known spotted owl habitat. . . .

Several instances of malicious taking of spotted owls have been reported. In one case, a mutilated spotted owl was found hanging from a Forest Service kiosk. . . .

Under the [Endangered Species] Act's definition, to be considered for endangered classification, the spotted owl would have to be currently in danger of extinction throughout all or a significant portion of its range. While the available data indicate a gradual, rangewide decline in the species commensurate with habitat loss, they do not suggest that extinction is an imminent possibility. The Service recognizes that the situation is most serious in the California Coast Range (especially Marin and Sonoma Counties), the Shasta/Modoc area in California, the Oregon Coast Ranges (beginning with Coos Bay Bureau of Land Management lands north to the Columbia River), and from the Olympic Peninsula south to the Columbia River. However, when the status of the entire subspecies is analyzed rangewide, it is the Service's conclusion that the likelihood of extinction of the subpopulations of the owls in these areas is not so immediate as to justify a rangewide endangered classification at this time. . . .

NOTES AND QUESTIONS

1. Should the Northern Spotted Owl have been listed as an endangered rather than a threatened species? Applying the statutory definitions and the above description of the context, how would you argue for the stronger finding? What factors weigh against this finding? In what ways does endangered status provide greater protection than threatened status?

2. Reconsider the red wolf, small pox, and salmon examples above, supra, pp. 1135-1136. Must they be listed under the ESA?

b. The Critical Habitat Determination

NORTHERN SPOTTED OWL v. LUJAN

758 F. Supp. 621 (W.D. Wash. 1991)

ZILLY, District Judge. . . .
On June 23, 1989, the [U.S. Fish and Wildlife] Service proposed

to list the northern spotted owl as a "threatened" species under the Endangered Species Act. See 54 Fed. Reg. 26,666 (1989). On June 26, 1990, the Service published its final rule confirming that listing decision. See 55 Fed. Reg. 26,114 (1990). In both the proposed and final listing rules, the Service expressly deferred designation of critical habitat for the spotted owl on grounds that it was not "determinable."

Plaintiffs move this Court to order the federal defendants to designate "critical habitat" for the northern spotted owl. As defined under the ESA, "critical habitat" refers to geographic areas which are essential to the conservation of the spotted owl and which may require special management considerations or protection. 16 U.S.C. §1532(5)(A)(i). . . .

Section 4(a)(3) of the Endangered Species Act requires the Secretary of the Interior "to the maximum extent prudent and determinable," to designate critical habitat *concurrently* with the decision to list a species as endangered or threatened under the Act. 16 U.S.C. §1533(a)(3).[25]

The language employed in Section 4(a)(3) and its place in the overall statutory scheme evidence a clear design by Congress that designations of critical habitat coincide with the species listing determination. The linkage of these issues was not the product of chance; rather, it reflects the studied and deliberate judgment of Congress that destruction of habitat was the most significant cause of species endangerment. See H.R. Rep. No. 1625, 95th Cong. 2d Sess. 5 reprinted in 1978 U.S. Code Cong. & Admin. News 9453, 9455 ("The loss of habitat for many species is universally cited as the major cause for the extinction of species worldwide."). S. Rep. No. 307, 93d Cong. 1st Sess. 1-2 reprinted in 1973 U.S. Code Cong. & Admin. News 2989, 2990.

As originally enacted, the ESA admitted no exceptions to the requirement that the critical habitat designation occur concurrently with the listing determination. . . .

In 1978, Congress clarified that the Secretary was required, "to the maximum extent prudent," to specify critical habitat "[a]t the time [the

---

25. Section 4(a)(3) codified at 16 U.S.C. §1533 (a)(3) provides that:

(3) The Secretary [of the Interior] by regulation promulgated in accordance with subsection (b) of this section and to *the maximum extent prudent and determinable* —
   (a) shall, *concurrently* with making a determination under paragraphs (1) that a species is an endangered species or a threatened species, designate any habitat of such species which is then considered to be critical habitat and
   (b) may, from time to time thereafter as appropriate, revise such designation.

16 U.S.C. §1533 (a)(3) (emphasis added).

species] is proposed [for listing]." 16 U.S.C. §1533(a)(1) (current version at 16 U.S.C. §1533(a)(3); see also 16 U.S.C. §1533(c)(1) (requiring Secretary to specify critical habitat within range of endangered or threatened species). By its 1978 amendments, Congress expressly linked the timing of the critical habitat designation to the decision to list the species. A single exception to this duty was recognized when the habitat designation was not "prudent." The Secretary's discretion to decline to make a designation on this basis was intended to be circumspect:

> The Committee intends that in most situations the Secretary will . . . designate critical habitat at the same time that a species is listed as either endangered or threatened. It is only in rare circumstances where the specification of critical habitat concurrently with the listing would not be beneficial to the species.

H.R. Rep. No. 1625, 95th Cong. 2d Sess. 17, reprinted in 1978 U.S. Code Cong. & Admin. News 9453, 9467. Under current regulations, a critical habitat designation is not "prudent" only if it is not in the best interest of the species.[26]

In 1982, Congress expressed frustration at the slow pace of implementing the Endangered Species Act. Particular concern focused on the Secretary's critical habitat responsibilities as a source of delay. . . .

The solution adopted by Congress permits the Secretary to defer the habitat designation upon finding that critical habitat is not "determinable" at the time the Secretary proposes to list the species under the ESA or at the time of his final listing decision. 16 U.S.C. §1533(b)(6)(C). In no event may the Secretary delay the designation of critical habitat for more than twelve months after publication of the final listing rule. In crafting this solution, Congress expressly reaffirmed its earlier judgment that the critical habitat designation is to occur *concurrently* with the listing decision, except in the limited circumstances when critical habitat is not "determinable" or when it is not "prudent" to do so. . . .

This Court rejects as incongruous the federal defendants' arguments that Section 4(b)(6)(C) authorizes an automatic extension of

---

26. The regulations of the Fish and Wildlife Service define only two situations when designation of critical habitat is not "prudent" within the meaning of 16 U.S.C. §1533(a)(3):

> (i) The species is threatened by taking or other human activity, and identification of critical habitat can be expected to increase the degree of such threat to the species, or
> (ii) Such designation of critical habitat would not be beneficial to the species.

50 C.F.R. §424.12(a)(1).

time merely upon a finding that critical habitat is not presently "determinable," even where no effort has been made to secure the information necessary to make the designation. To relieve the Secretary of any affirmative information gathering responsibilities would effectively nullify Congress' charge that the species listing and habitat designation occur concurrently, "to the maximum extent . . . determinable." 16 U.S.C. §1533(a)(3).

Turning to the record presented, this Court is unable to find any support for the federal defendants' claim that critical habitat for the northern spotted owl was not determinable in June 1989 when the Service proposed to list the species, or when the Service issued its final rule one year later. Critical habitat received only brief discussion in both published rules. The Service offered the following explanation to justify its decision not to propose critical habitat in its June 1989 rule:

> The extensive range of the northern spotted owl, from British Columbia to San Francisco Bay, involves over 7 million acres of its preferred old-growth and mature forest habitat and an undetermined amount of other forest types that may also be of significance to the survival and recovery of the subspecies. Much of this habitat has been fragmented by logging, and many stands are isolated from each other or of such small size as not to support viable populations of spotted owls. The specific size, spatial configuration, and juxtaposition of these essential habitats as well as vital connecting linkages between areas necessary for ensuring the conservation of the subspecies throughout its range have not been determined at this time, nor have analyses been conducted on the impacts of a designation.

54 Fed. Reg. at 26,675. The Service also solicited input on critical habitat from the public and concerned governmental agencies.

When the Service published its final listing rule one year later, the agency again deferred designation of critical habitat on grounds that it was not then "determinable." The explanation offered by the Service was virtually a verbatim repetition of its 1989 finding, quoted above. . . .

More is required under the ESA and the Service's own regulations than the mere conclusion that more work needs to be done. See 50 C.F.R. §424.12(a)(2).[27] It cannot be established upon the record pre-

---

27. The regulations of the Fish and Wildlife Service define two situations when critical habitat is not "determinable":

> (i) Information sufficient to perform required analyses of the impacts of the designation is lacking, or
> (ii) The biological needs of the species are not sufficiently well known to permit identification of an area as critical habitat.

50 C.F.R. §424.12(a)(2).

sented that the Service "considered the relevant factors" or that it "articulated a rational connection between the facts found and the choice made." *Pyramid Lake Paiute Tribe,* 898 F.2d at 1414. Accordingly, this Court must find the Service abused its discretion when it declined to designate critical habitat for the northern spotted owl.

The Service's actions in June 1990 merit special mention. In its final rule the Service stated that the northern spotted owl is "overwhelmingly associated" with mature and old-growth forests. 55 Fed. Reg. 26-175. The Service further stated that, at present rates of timber harvesting, much of the remaining spotted owl habitat will be gone within 20 to 30 years. 55 Fed. Reg. 26,182. Despite such dire assessments, the Service declined to designate critical habitat in its final rule, citing the same reasons it gave one year earlier. Whatever the precise contours of the Service's obligations under the ESA, clearly the law does not approve such conduct. Indeed, the Thomas Committee, which included Service personnel, warned that "delay in implementing a conservation strategy [for the spotted owl] cannot be justified on the basis of inadequate knowledge." A Conservation Strategy for the Northern Spotted Owl, at 1.

The federal defendants have attempted to supplement the administrative record by submitting two declarations from Marvin Plenert, regional director for the Fish and Wildlife Service. While this Court's review is properly limited to the administrative record, see *Camp.,* 411 U.S. at 142, 93 S. Ct. at 1244, 36 L. Ed. 2d at 111, the proffered materials further reinforce the conclusion that the Service's actions were unexcused under the ESA and governing regulations. Much of the information provided relates to the very substantial efforts by the Service to complete the listing of the northern spotted owl and to consult with affected federal agencies. In his only statement pertinent to the decision to defer designation of critical habitat, director Plenert explained:

> Because of the funding and workload required to complete the rulemaking process for the listing decision, the need to allocate many of the [Service's] knowledgeable biologists to conferences on Federal projects affecting the owl, and the fact that the Thomas Committee final report was not released until the month before the listing decision was due, the Service was not able at the time of listing to determine whether the areas outlined by the Thomas Committee (or other areas) met the ESA definition of "critical habitat" . . . These same funding, workload, and time constraints prevented the Service from analyzing and considering the economic and other relevant impacts of designating particular areas as critical habitat as required by section 4(b)(2) of the ESA.

Plenert (First) Decl., at 4-5.

That the Thomas Committee was working to develop conservation strategies for the spotted owl did not relieve the Service of its obligation under the ESA to designate critical habitat to the maximum extent determinable. . . .

This Court is mindful of the prodigious resources dedicated by the Service to the spotted owl. The listing process required a truly remarkable effort by the Service given the volume of comments received and the complexity of the issues raised. The inter-agency consultations have consumed additional manpower and financial resources. Pursuant to Section 7 of the ESA, the Service must consult with other federal agencies whose programs may jeopardize an endangered or threatened species, or "result in the destruction or adverse modification of [the critical] habitat of such species. . . ." 16 U.S.C. §1536(a)(2).

In any event, such efforts, which the Court assumes have been on going since prior to June 1989, do not relieve the Service of its statutory obligation to designate critical habitat concurrently with the species listing, or to provide a rational and articulated basis for concluding that critical habitat is not determinable. Cf. *Natural Resources Defense Council, Inc. v. Train,* 510 F.2d 692, 712 (D.C. Cir. 1975) (delay may be excused for impossibility); *Sierra Club v. Gorsuch,* 551 F. Supp. 785, 788-89 (N.D. Cal. 1982) (agency bears heavy burden of demonstrating impossibility). The simultaneous tasks assigned to the Service under the ESA are not insubstantial as the present case amply demonstrates. Nevertheless, designation of critical habitat is a central component of the legal scheme developed by Congress to prevent the permanent loss of species. Only under limited circumstances not demonstrated here may the Service properly defer its habitat designation responsibilities.

Upon the record presented, this Court finds the Service has failed to discharge its obligations under the Endangered Species Act and its own administrative regulations. Specifically, the Service acting on behalf of the Secretary of the Interior, abused its discretion when it determined not to designate critical habitat concurrently with the listing of the northern spotted owl, or to explain any basis for concluding that the critical habitat was not determinable. These actions were arbitrary and capricious, and contrary to law. 5 U.S.C. §706.

Common sense dictates that the spotted owl would be poorly served by a hastily crafted or uninformed habitat plan. Congress expressly provided for periodic revisions to critical habitat plans to avoid this result. See 16 U.S.C. §1533(a)(3)(B). Accordingly, the Service is ordered to submit to the Court by March 15, 1991 a written plan for completing its review of critical habitat for the northern spotted owl. The Service is further ordered to publish its proposed critical habitat plan no later than forty-five days thereafter. The final rule is to be published at the earliest possible time under the appropriate circumstances. . . .

NOTES AND QUESTIONS

1. What role does the critical habitat designation play in the ESA system of protections? Must a critical habitat be designated in order for substantive protections of the Act to be in force? What are the advantages of critical habitat designation? Disadvantages?

2. In view of the enormity of the designation task — complicated by numerous biological uncertainties surrounding the northern spotted owl, the vast range of the owl, and the pervasive economic implications of protecting the owl — was Judge Zilly's conclusion sound? Was his order dictated by the statute?

3. The standard for designating critical habitat is contained in ESA §4(b)(2). Suppose that the FWS were to determine that economic factors weigh in favor of excluding all areas that are suitable for timber production from the designation of critical habitat for the northern spotted owl. On what basis, consistent with the ESA, might the agency seek to justify such exclusions? Would such a justification be consistent with the studies presented in the FWS's listing determination?

4. In fact, in response to the court's order the Fish and Wildlife Service reached a very different conclusion regarding the economic considerations of critical habitat designation. Attributing the principal economic consequences of spotted owl protection to federal land agencies' previously announced protective measures, the FWS concluded that critical habitat designation would have little incremental economic cost. Therefore, the FWS's critical habitat designation excluded few federal areas on the basis of economic considerations. Was the FWS's economic analysis consistent with the statute? What is the institutional mission of the FWS? On the other hand, the FWS did conclude that the costs of designating critical habitat on private lands did outweigh the benefits.

5. While the law theoretically makes it very difficult for the Fish and Wildlife Service *not* to designate critical habitat at the time of listing, in practice relatively few threatened and endangered species receive designated critical habitats. As of 1988, only 22 percent of listed species had designated critical habitats. A variety of factors explain this pattern:

- Fear of encouraging takings partially explain some of the cases. Endangered cacti, for example, carry an enormous price on the black market. Designation of their critical habitats, therefore, complete with maps in the Code of Federal Regulations, would undoubtedly contribute to their extinction. This concern, however, is significant in relatively few cases.
- A second factor, reflected in the northern spotted owl case, is the tight budget of the Fish and Wildlife Service. In particular,

the requirement that the economic implications of critical habitat designations be evaluated adds an enormous burden to the already complex biological assessment. Empirical evidence suggests that the burden of designating critical habitat at the same time that listing decisions are made may delay listing decisions.

● A third factor, and perhaps the most important, appears to be the concern that communities in designated critical habitats will protest. As one Fish and Wildlife Service veteran has expressed it, "As soon as you draw a line on the map, [local people] see it as the first step toward the feds condemning the land. 'Critical habitat today, wildlife refuge tomorrow and we're out of business.' "

Which of these factors are legitimate bases for not designating critical habitat? In view of the (mis)perceptions of communities about the effect of critical habitat designations, might the standard for designating critical habitat undermine the effort to protect biological diversity?

c.   Scope of ESA Protection

As a means of examining the ESA's substantive protections, evaluate the following management strategies for the federal lands in the northern spotted owl's habitat:

(1)   *Forest Service Spotted Owl Conservation Guidelines.* The Forest Service manages approximately 70 percent of the remaining northern spotted owl habitat, containing approximately 68 percent of known owl pairs. These lands are generally managed for multiple use, with 63 percent of the spotted owl habitat subject to timber harvest. On the basis of a comprehensive study of planning alternatives for spotted owl management, the Forest Service on December 8, 1988, adopted conservation guidelines (Alternative F) that provide for a network of approximately 650 owl sites (Spotted Owl Habitat Areas or SOHAs) containing 1000 to 3000 acres of suitable habitat. In combination with existing wilderness areas and areas allocated to uses other than timber production, these guidelines would protect approximately 48 percent of remaining spotted owl habitat on national forests in Oregon and Washington and 66 percent of remaining owl habitat on national forests in California. SOHAs are intended to protect the habitat needs of between one and three spotted owl pairs. In total, it is estimated that 880 pairs are contained on SOHAs. Between 60 to 70 percent of the SOHAs would be

surrounded by timber harvesting areas. Approximately 1 percent of remaining spotted owl habitat would be logged annually.

(2) *Interagency Scientific Committee Conservation Strategy.* In 1988, the Forest Service, the Bureau of Land Management, and the National Park Service, and the Fish and Wildlife Service entered into an agreement to cooperatively manage northern spotted owl habitat.[28] The Interagency Scientific Committee (ISC) was formed to develop a conservation strategy to protect the spotted owl. On April 4, 1990, the ISC issued its report which recommended that the federal land management agencies set aside a network of approximately 190 blocks of spotted owl habitat for preservation, referred to as habitat conservation areas (HCAs). The optimum HCA would be 50,000 to 60,000 acres and could support at least 20 pairs of owls. Because of constraints, proposed HCAs range from 50 acres on one site in northern California to 676,000 acres on Washington's Olympic Peninsula. It is estimated that proposed HCAs provide habitat for 1465 pairs on federal lands and that this network could eventually sustain 2000 pairs.

Sections 7 and 9 of the ESA as well as the following case provide guidance in evaluating these management plans.

SIERRA CLUB V. LYNG

694 F. Supp. 1260 (E.D. Tex. 1988)

ROBERT M. PARKER, District Judge.

BACKGROUND

Picoides borealis, commonly known as the red-cockaded woodpecker, is a small undistinguished woodpecker indigenous to the southern United States. The evolutionary niche it has carved out places it at odds with modern man and man's industrialized society. The red-cockaded woodpecker is not well adapted to the real world as it exists today in the Texas national forests. The fact that its survival depends on a very specialized habitat bodes ill for the future of this bird. The

---

28. The agreement contains no means for implementation and allows any agency to cancel the plan after 30 days' notice.

voluminous evidence, both written and oral, introduced in the trial of this case leaves this Court with the firm persuasion that we are presiding over the last rites of this cohabitant of the blue planet.

This woodpecker makes no great or even necessary contribution to ecological balance, his song is unremarkable, and his plumage causes no heads to turn. However, these apparent shortcomings do not enter into the equation of the task assigned to this Court. The red-cockaded woodpecker's chief claim to fame is the fact that it succeeded in having its name inscribed on the endangered species list.

The red-cockaded woodpecker is a small bird that lives almost exclusively in pine forests throughout the southern regions of the United States. The woodpecker prefers to nest in old growth pine trees, where it forages on insects, and occasionally small fruits and seeds. The birds do not feed on the ground and usually forage in trees thirty years or older, preferring those sixty years or more. The woodpecker's foraging range may include an area up to one mile across.

The red-cockadeds are susceptible to various predators including snakes, owls and other birds. The structure of their nests (more properly described as cavities) within living trees is such that sap oozes out around the actual cavity hole, thereby lessening the chances that predators will get to the young. The red-cockadeds also must fend off larger competing woodpeckers that attempt to "take over" their cavities and enlarge the nests. Individual cavity trees are referred to as colonies and on the average contain several birds. The last remaining populations of these birds are concentrated in the national forests, primarily because the old growth pines on private lands have largely been eliminated.

The national forests of Texas are managed under a multiple use system where the Forest Service is charged with the duty to provide recreation and protect wildlife, while simultaneously producing timber for industry. The proceeds of timber harvested inure to the Forest Service itself in the form of various discretionary funds, and to localities surrounding the national forest. Unfortunately for the woodpeckers, the current system of harvesting on a rotation system where trees are allowed to grow to only 60 to 80 years of age before they are harvested is in many respects, incompatible with their shelter, feeding, and reproduction requirements. . . .

FINDINGS OF FACT

I

The red-cockaded woodpecker population in the Sabine National Forest has declined seventy-six percent (76%) between the years 1978 through 1987.

II

The red-cockaded woodpecker population in the Davy Crockett National Forest has declined forty-one percent (41%) during the years 1983 through 1987.

III

The red-cockaded woodpecker population in the Angelina National Forest has declined forty-two percent (42%) during the years 1983 through 1987.

IV

The entire population of red-cockaded woodpeckers in the Texas national forests will be extinct by 1995 if no changes are made in the present practices of the Forest Service.

V

The causes of the rapid decline in the red-cockaded woodpecker population over the past ten years in the Texas national forests include the following:

A. Fragmentation of habitat by clear-cutting practices which has resulted in separation of nesting and foraging areas.

B. Clear-cutting within foraging areas thereby reducing foraging habitat available to birds within their effective range.

C. Clear-cutting within 200 feet of actual colony sites and, in some instances, even up to cavity trees.

D. Failure to control hardwood mid-story encroachment around cavity trees in colony sites, around potential cavity trees in sites adjacent to colonies, and in foraging areas.

E. Failure to employ regular prescribed fire in colony and foraging areas to control hardwood and young pine encroachment.

F. Failure to provide an appropriate basal area in colony and potential recruitment stand sites.

G. The lack of availability of cavity trees of sufficient age — 100 plus years — due to silvicultural practices employed over the past twenty (20) years by the Forest Service.

H. Disruption of colony area by permitting the establishment of logging roads and the utilization of regularly traveled off-pavement roadways through site areas.

I. Damage to colony site and foraging area habitat trees by logging trucks and logging equipment.

J. The failure to identify and preserve mature trees containing redheart in habitat areas.[29]

VI

The forest supervisor for the national forest and grasslands in Texas, William Lannan, recognized that the Forest Service mandate regarding endangered species takes precedence over the Forest Service activities and made budget requests sufficient to comply with the requirements and suggestions contained in the Forest Service's red-cockaded woodpecker handbook. However, the budget submitted by the Administration and approved by the Congress for the past eight years has provided approximately ten percent (10%) of the funds necessary to comply with the Forest Service's red-cockaded handbook. Moreover, no funds have been provided for mid-story removal as prescribed by the red-cockaded handbook for the past eight years.

VII

Funds received from the sale of the timber on clear-cut tracts are available as discretionary funds for use in the management of the red-cockaded woodpecker. However, no such funds have been committed to red-cockaded habitat preservation.

VIII

The red-cockaded woodpecker handbook, prepared in 1973, has never been fully implemented in the Texas national forests as it relates to habitat preservation or improvement.

IX

The Forest Service in Texas has not implemented a program to control hardwood mid-story, which is essential to the maintenance of red-cockaded woodpecker colonies.[30]

---

29. Redheart disease is a naturally occurring infection that softens portions of the heartwood of pine trees, thereby making it easier for woodpeckers to excavate cavities. . . .

30. Hardwood mid-story is the growth of vegetation of the hardwood trees that surrounds pine trees containing the woodpeckers' cavities. Hard-

X

Areas clear-cut are not suitable for foraging by red-cockaded woodpeckers for a period of at least thirty (30) years from the date of reforestation, resulting in fragmentation and isolation of colonies and shunning of clear-cut areas for thirty (30) years by red-cockaded woodpeckers.

XI

Old trees — 100 years or more — containing redheart are essential for bird survival and establishment of new or replacement colony trees. Any program that provides for harvesting these old trees mitigates [sic] against survival of the species in the Texas national forests.

XII

Sixty (60) square foot basal area is the optimum density taking into consideration the requirements of the red-cockaded woodpecker and factors relating to control of the southern pine beetle.[31]

XIII

Any rotation period of cutting by even-aged management methods (clear-cutting) that is economically advantageous to the Forest Service is incompatible with the survival of the red-cockaded woodpecker within colony and foraging habitat areas.

XIV

An analysis of clear-cutting versus selection management methods persuades the Court of the following facts:

---

wood mid-story encroachment reduces available foraging habitat and makes woodpecker cavities more accessible to predators such as owls and snakes.

31. The basal area, simply stated, is the measurement of the density of trees in a given area. The Wildlife Management Handbook of the Forest Service recommends a basal area of sixty (60) to ninety (90) square feet per acre for woodpecker foraging habitat. Obviously, clear-cutting reduces the basal area of the forest to zero. Seed-tree cutting (prior to the time the seed-trees are removed) averages about twenty (20) square feet per acre basal area, while shelterwood cutting leaves about forty (40) square feet of basal area.

1. Selection management has an initial twenty to twenty-five percent (20-25%) economic advantage over clear-cutting as a result of the necessity of artificially seeding clear-cut areas.

2. Uneven age or selection management produces more wood per dollar spent and is more economically efficient over the productive life of a tract of timber.

3. Uniformity is best served by even-aged management.

4. Even-aged stands are more susceptible to southern pine beetle infestation.

5. The Forest Service contention that at rotation age there is little difference economically between clear-cutting and selection management is not persuasive to the Court. The Court is persuaded that selection management does have economic advantages resulting from the avoidance of the high cost of regenerating clear-cut areas and the costs associated with the care required by highly vulnerable young stands. Selection management provides a good return during the entire lifetime of the period in question. Taking into consideration the value of money coupled with the high initial expense of even-age management, economic factors mitigate [sic] in favor of selection management. In addition to excellent economic returns, a well managed selection forest provides excellent habitat for deer and other wildlife, for recreational uses, and is pleasing to the eye of even city dwellers.

6. The sole reason for the Forest Service's adoption of even-age or clear-cutting as the management method of choice is the fact that it is preferred by the timber companies. The Forest Service is an agency that has experienced a high degree of the "revolving door" phenomenon between governmental and private interests. That is to say that the greatest market for government employees in private industry is with the large timber companies. This fact provides an incentive for agency personnel to accommodate industry desires — thus, that explains the high level of influence the timber companies have over policies and practices of the Forest Service.

XV

The initial Connor-Rudolph report introduced as Plaintiffs' Exhibit 27 is, as a whole, the best evaluation and study of the crisis facing the bird and the management practices that are essential, if survival is possible.

The Court finds that the following practices, at a minimum, must be adopted and implemented without delay if extirpation is to be avoided:

A. All initial red-cockaded management should be focused on active woodpecker colonies. Only after active colonies have received appropriate management should management be directed at inactive colonies as future recruitment stands.

B. When thinning cuts are made within colony buffer areas, the basal area should be reduced in the entire colony area. Relict pine and other mature pines should be left standing and not cut as has been the case in the past.

C. The implementation of an aggressive removal program of existing hardwood mid-story is needed. The few large mast producing hardwoods that are found in colonies may be left standing within colony areas if they are not directly encroaching on cavity trees. All smaller hardwoods should be eliminated.

D. An aggressive prescribed burning program within woodpecker colonies and in colony home ranges is necessary. Fire should be used at least every two years on longleaf sites and every three to four years on loblolly sites or as soon as those sites will support a burn.

E. Stands within 1,200 meters of active woodpecker colonies should be thinned to a basal area of sixty (60) square feet per acre. Clear-cutting within 1,200 meters of active colonies must be eliminated and replaced with selection management. Old growth trees within 1,200 meters should not be harvested at all. A plan must be implemented providing more foraging habitat for the woodpecker than that which is contained in the current recovery plan, since anticipated required cuts to control the southern pine beetle will reduce woodpecker foraging habitat below minimum supply levels.

F. Within colony sites, logging roads or other off-pavement roadways should be eliminated and alternate routes utilized. In colony sites and within 1,200 meters of colony sites, extreme care should be taken when logging equipment is utilized for thinning or mid-story control activities.

DISCUSSION

1) ENDANGERED SPECIES ACT CLAIMS

The taking claim is the primary issue currently before the Court. In short, the Plaintiffs argue that the Forest Service's silvicultural practices and methods of managing the national forests of Texas have resulted in a taking of the red-cockaded woodpecker within the meaning of Section 9 of the Endangered Species Act (ESA). . . . Section 7 of the Endangered Species Act, and the regulations promulgated thereunder, also imposes a duty on the Defendants to refrain from activities that jeopardize endangered species. The regulations also require the

Defendants to re-initiate consultation with the United States Fish and Wildlife Service upon the receipt of new information that may affect endangered species. . . .

The Endangered Species Act, through its various provisions, imposes a continuing duty on federal agencies. First, Section 7 of the ESA states that the various federal agencies must:

> . . . *insure* that any action authorized, funded, or carried out by such agency . . . is not likely to jeopardize the continued existence of any endangered species or threatened species. . . .

16 U.S.C.A. §1536(a)(2) (emphasis added). . . .

Section 9 of the ESA provides that "it is unlawful for any person subject to the jurisdiction of the United States to . . . take any such species within the United States or the territorial sea of the United States. . . ." 16 U.S.C.A. §1538(a)(1)(B) (West 1985). It is undisputed that the red-cockaded woodpecker is an endangered species. 50 C.F.R. 17.11 (1987). In fact, it was one of the earliest species placed on the endangered list, since it was so designated on October 13, 1970. 37 Fed. Reg. 16047 (1970). It is also clear that the Defendants fall within the meaning of a "person" for the purposes of the Act since the definition includes ". . . any officer, employee, agent, department, or instrumentality of the Federal Government. . . ." 16 U.S.C.A. §1532(13) (West 1985); *Tennessee Valley Authority v. Hill,* 437 U.S. at 184-85, 98 S. Ct. at 2297.

The term "take" applicable to the above cited provision means, "to harass, harm, pursue, hunt, shoot, wound, kill, trap, capture, or collect, or to attempt to engage in any such conduct." 16 U.S.C.A. §1532(19) (West 1985). The relevant element of the "take" definition that is of concern in the case sub judice is the prohibition against "harming" an endangered species. The definition of harm is described in the Forest Service Regulations at 50 C.F.R. §17.3 (1987), as follows:

> "Harm" in the definition of "take" in the Act means an act which actually kills or injures wildlife. *Such an act may include significant habitat modification* or degradation where it actually kills or injures wildlife by significantly impairing essential behavioral patterns, including breeding, feeding or sheltering.

50 C.F.R. §17.3 (1987) (emphasis added). It is uncontested that a severe decline in the population of woodpeckers has occurred in the past ten years. "Harm" does not necessarily require the proof of the death of specific or individual members of the species. See, *Palila v. Hawaii Dept. of Land and Natural Resources,* 471 F. Supp. 985 (D. Hawaii 1979), *aff'd.,* 639 F.2d 495, 498 (9th Cir. 1981) *(Palila I), Palila v. Hawaii Dept. of Land*

and Natural Resources, 649 F. Supp. 1070, 1076-77 (D. Hawaii 1986), *appeal docketed,* No. 87-2188 (9th Cir. June 10, 1987) *(Palila II),* but as the numbers show themselves, large percentages of the few remaining birds have died. . . .

The Forest Service contends that its continuing conduct does not fall within the definition of "take" described above. The Forest Service even prepared a document, referred to in the record as the "Strategy," that was presented to the Court on the eve of trial, setting forth a series of practices that the Forest Service was willing to implement to remedy past management decisions that have impacted upon the woodpecker. Nonetheless, based upon the findings of this Court, one cannot escape the conclusion that the Forest Service's practices have harmed the birds within the meaning of the regulations, in a number of different ways, evidenced by the precipitous decline in the woodpecker population in recent years. [Citations omitted.]

The practice of even-aged management has resulted in significant habitat modification in varied ways described in the findings of fact. This is not merely a situation where the recovery of the species is impaired by the agency's practices, *Palila,* 649 F. Supp. at 1075, but rather the agency's practices themselves have caused and accelerated the decline in the species. For example, in the Sabine National Forest, the population as estimated in 1987 was seven (7) red-cockaded woodpecker colonies, which represented only thirteen (13) birds. It may prove to be too late to save this population, however the remaining birds in the other forests may be saved from extinction if current forest management practices are modified. The entire remaining population of red-cockaded woodpeckers in the three national forests surveyed in the several Conner reports was only 113 birds as of 1987.

It is apparent that all four factors cited in the regulations defining "harm" are implicated by the current management practices employed by the Forest Service. First, essential behavioral patterns of the woodpeckers have been impaired by isolation of woodpecker colonies from one another by creating "islands" of older growth stands surrounded by clear-cuts. Even-aged management within 1,200 meters of woodpecker colonies alters the customary habits of the birds to survive and produce young. For example, maintaining high basal areas to maximize lumber return makes the forests generally, and the woodpecker colonies particularly susceptible to outbreaks of southern pine beetles. Failure to employ mid-story removal of hardwoods also contributes to woodpecker abandonment of cavity areas. Second, isolation of particular colonies interferes with breeding practices, since males cannot find females to breed with, thereby contributing to the population decline. Isolation also causes the gene pool to be reduced with fewer birds in a given area, causing genetic problems and abnormalities in the subsequent generations.

Third, with clear-cutting in close proximity to woodpecker colonies, foraging areas are limited, making it difficult for the birds to find nourishment since they do not feed on the ground. This forces the birds to expend more energy in searching for any remaining trees with food than they can derive from the nourishment they eventually find. Obviously, the "law of diminishing returns" comes into play, decreasing the chances for the birds' survival, not to mention the possibility for recovery. Furthermore, with the harvesting of older pine trees, the birds have more difficulty finding insects to eat on the remaining younger pines with smooth bark and less surface area. The older pines with rough bark crevices and cracks where insects can live, thereby providing the birds with an available food source.

Fourth, even-aged management has eliminated the older stands of pines needed by the birds for excavation of cavities to use as nests. In addition, cutting of trees which serve as windbreaks around the cavity trees subjects the cavity trees to increased chances of blow-downs or windthrow. This is especially true since the cavity trees are already somewhat weakened by redheart and the excavation of the woodpecker nest. Since it takes a red-cockaded woodpecker anywhere from one to four years to excavate a cavity, the loss of the cavity tree is a significant loss for the bird who must expend lots of energy to excavate another cavity. Certainly, other practices and policies of the Defendants described in the findings of fact, when taken as a whole, detrimentally impact upon the woodpecker and are largely responsible for the rapid decline of the remaining birds in Texas.

The Court has also further concluded that the actions described above, relevant to the taking issue, similarly implicate Section 7 of the ESA because they also "jeopardize" the species within the meaning of the Act. 16 U.S.C.A. §1536(a)(2) (West 1985); *Tennessee Valley Authority v. Hill*, 437 U.S. at 181-87 S. Ct. at 2295-98. The federal regulations, 50 C.F.R. §402.02 (1987), define "jeopardize," as used in the ESA to mean:

> . . . To engage in an action that reasonably would be expected, directly or indirectly, to reduce appreciably the likelihood of both the survival and recovery of a listed species in the wild by reducing the reproduction, numbers or distribution of that species.

50 C.F.R. §402.02 (1987). The management practices employed, that have lead this Court to conclude that a taking has occurred, necessarily includes a finding that such conduct also jeopardizes the species. Accordingly, the Court concludes that the Plaintiffs have carried their burden of proof in showing that the Defendants have failed to take the "actions necessary to insure" that their current management practices do not jeopardize the continued existence of the woodpecker or will not destroy or modify habitat essential for its survival. *National Wildlife*

Federation v. Coleman, 529 F.2d 359, 372 (5th Cir. 1976), *cert. denied,* 429 U.S. 979, 97 S. Ct. 489, 50 L. Ed. 2d 587 (1976).

REMEDIAL MEASURES TO BE IMPLEMENTED BY
THE DEFENDANTS

Based upon the above findings of fact and conclusions of law, the Court hereby issues a permanent injunction enjoining the Defendants from failing to implement the following practices and procedures within 1,200 meters of identified active and inactive red-cockaded woodpecker colony sites in the national forests of Texas:

(1) Conversion of forest harvesting techniques from even-aged management to a program of selection or uneven-aged management that preserves "old growth" pines from cutting, within 1,200 meters of any colony site.

(2) Establishment of a basal area of sixty (60) square feet per acre, within 1,200 meters of any colony site.

(3) Establishment of a program of mid-story removal of hardwoods in and adjacent to colony sites.

(4) Discontinue the use of existing logging roads or other non-paved roads within colony sites and restrict the use of such roadways to the essential minimum within 1,200 meters of any colony site.

Additionally, the Court grants the Defendants sixty (60) days to produce and compile a "Comprehensive Plan" to address all aspects of future management techniques, consistent with the findings and conclusions of the Court, designed to maximize the probability of survival of the red-cockaded woodpeckers in the national forests of Texas. . . .

NOTES AND QUESTIONS

1. In view of the dire situation faced by the red-cockaded woodpecker, is the court's remedy likely to save this species from extinction? If not, is the remedy inconsistent with the ESA? Should the ESA's prohibitions apply even when the endangered species is apparently beyond rescue?

2. Are courts capable of making the complex biological determinations needed to evaluate and choose remedies to protect threatened and endangered species?

3. Returning to the spotted owl controversy, suppose that the Forest Service continues to implement Alternative F, which would include

continued, albeit somewhat reduced and restricted, clearcutting of northern spotted owl habitat. Using the description of the northern spotted owl contained in the Fish and Wildlife Service's listing decision, apply the substantive standards in §§7 and 9 of the Act (as interpreted in *Lyng*). Would the Forest Service's guidelines pass judicial muster? Would the ISC proposal satisfy the requirement of the ESA?

4. The ISC proposal received mixed reactions within the federal government. The Forest Service favored its adoption, while the Department of Interior, the Bureau of Land Management, and the Bush Administration opposed the recommendations as too costly.

5. Is aggressive enforcement of the ESA protections in the northern spotted owl case a sound strategy for environmentalists?

d. Political Escape Valves

The economic effects of protecting the northern spotted owl could be devastating, especially for many highly timber-dependent communities in Oregon. The Northwest Forest Resource Council, a lobbying group for the timber industry, predicts that habitat protection measures could eliminate 130,000 industry and related service jobs as well as cost the federal government $1.6 billion and local governments over $450 million in lost timber revenues per year. A study produced by researchers at the University of Washington, Oregon State University, and the University of California concludes that the ISC conservation plan would most likely reduce employment by 48,000 direct and indirect jobs. Environmentalists challenge these job loss and economic estimates, noting that automation of production mills and declining harvests (independent of spotted owl protections) would displace many of the jobs that the timber industry attributes to spotted owl protection. The Forest Service estimated that Alternative F would result in the loss of 1,683 to 3,367 direct and indirect jobs in Washington and Oregon. The Forest Service's most protective option (Alternative L) — in which all suitable habitat and habitat capable of becoming suitable in 100 years is preserved — would result in the loss of 16,890 to 33,781 jobs in Washington and Oregon.

Regardless of which estimates are believed, the stage is set for a full-scale political battle between environmentalists and the timber industry to override the ESA's requirements. On July 2, 1992, Judge William L. Dwyer issued an injunction blocking most timber sales in the spotted owl range of western Oregon and Washington and northern California. *Seattle Audubon Society v. Moseley*, 798 F. Supp. 1484 (W.D. Wash. 1992). The epilogue to the snail darter case illustrates the two principal means of overriding the ESA: intervention by the Endangered Species Committee and legislative reversal of ESA determinations. Both of these possibilities have been raised in the northern spotted owl controversy. Timber interests lobbied the Bush Adminstration aggressively for intervention by the Endangered Species Committee and Congress for legislation to resolve this controversy through the political process.

PROBLEM: THE ENDANGERED SPECIES COMMITTEE

Review the procedural and substantive provisions governing the Endangered Species Committee contained in §7 of the ESA. Is it likely that the God Squad would exempt the Forest Service or the Bureau of Land Management from the ESA's requirements with regard to spotted owl habitat management? If so, what mitigation and enhancement measures would be advisable?

PROBLEM: PROPOSED LEGISLATION TO OVERRIDE THE ESA PROCESS

Since the listing of the northern spotted owl, numerous bills have been introduced in Congress to protect the northern spotted owl and the ancient forests as well as the economic stability of timber-dependent communities in the Pacific Northwest. H.R. 2807 (102d Cong., 1st Sess.), which is typical of the bills offered, would:

(1) *Establish a congressionally determined "ecologically significant old growth forest reserve system."* This reserve would be smaller than the northern spotted owl's critical habitat (as designated by the Fish and Wildlife Service, see supra, pp. 1148-1155). Timber harvesting upon these federal lands would be banned except for forest protection purposes.

(2) *Provide for the revision of the forest reserve system.* The secretaries of departments responsible for federal lands in the regions covered would be required, after receipt of National Academy of Sciences reports, to recommend to the Congress recommendations for boundary adjustments on the basis of social, economic, and environmental impacts.

(3) *Restrict the management of other federal lands.* The bill would restrict the timber harvesting methods used upon those other federal lands designated as critical habitat for the northern spotted owl in the following ways: (a) by banning the harvesting of trees older than 400 years of age; (2) requiring the maintenance of sufficient trees for a stand to qualify as old growth forest upon the regeneration of the

understory; and (3) requiring the use of management prescriptions that encourage biodiversity.

(4) *Provide economic adjustment assistance* for communities and
wood products and timber employees dependent on old
growth forests in the Pacific Northwest.

QUESTIONS

1. Does H.R. 2807 strike you as a good approach for accommodating the range of interests involved? Is it better or worse than relying
upon the ESA?

2. Isn't Congress the appropriate body for addressing these large
public policy issues? Our biological conservation regime can be
thought of as a two-tier system. The ESA provides a set of requirements
and prohibitions for handling the less controversial cases, but Congress
can and should step in to handle the cases involving major impact. How
does this arrangement comport with the normative questions discussed
at the outset of this set of materials? Does it reflect the lack of a coherent set or hierarchy of values and approaches to address the problems
of biological conservation within a democratic system?

3. It seems somewhat incongruous for a society to place preservation of non-human species above all else, regardless of connection to
human needs. On the other hand, the absolutist prohibitions in the
ESA can be viewed as a counterbalance that reflects our uncertainty
about the benefits of little studied species and the human propensity
for overdevelopment, which can only be overturned by the God Squad
or Congress. Might there, however, be a better approach, one that attempts to prioritize efforts to preserve biological diversity? What factors
affect your analysis of this question? What changes in the ESA might
better prioritize the various concerns? What considerations weigh
against such an effort?

4. Some conservative lawmakers have developed a new tact on
reforming the ESA. Representative Billy Tauzin (D-Louisiana) has proposed that the government pay compensation to landowners whose
economic use of property is restricted as a result of endangered species
protections. See Stevens, Battle Looms on Plans for Endangered Species, N.Y. Times, Nov. 11, 1993, at B5. Does the ESA in its present form
potentially raise constitutional takings issues in light of the recent Supreme Court decision in *Lucas,* supra, p. 1032? Even if it does not, does
the ESA allocate the burden of species preservation fairly within our
society? Consider the case of two landowners who purchased adjoining
tracts at the same time many years ago. One landowner rapidly developed her tract into a shopping mall. The other landowner maintained

the tract in a natural state. How would the ESA affect these two land-owners if their tracts were found to be part of the habitat for an endangered species? Does this mode of analysis address the full range of issues raised here? Should property be viewed apart from its connection to an ecosystem? Consider Sax's ecosystem-oriented framework for defining property, supra, pp. 1047-1048.

5. What does the interaction between law and politics evident in the ESA process say about environmentalists' strategies in conserving biological diversity? When should they push for the strictest application of the ESA? When are other approaches more likely to achieve their objectives?

EPILOGUE: THE NORTHERN SPOTTED OWL

On May 15, 1992, the Endangered Species Committee approved an exemption for the Bureau of Land Management for 13 of 44 timber sales, only the second exemption ever granted. Environmental groups challenged the decision alleging improper ex parte contacts between the White House and members of the Committee tainted the decision-making process. The Ninth Circuit held that the Committee's proceedings are subject to the APA's prohibition on ex parte communications, including those with the President. *Portland Audubon Society v. Endangered Species Committee*, 23 Envtl. L. Rep. 20561 (Feb. 10, 1993, amended Apr. 1, 1993). The court denied the environmental groups' motion for discovery but ordered that the case be remanded for an evidentiary hearing before an administrative law judge.

Following up on a campaign promise, President Clinton announced a compromise plan on July 1, 1993 entitled "The Forest Plan for a Sustainable Economy and a Sustainable Environment." The plan:

- allows for logging of about 12 billion board feet of timber over 10 years, or about 1.2 billion annually on Federal lands in the Northwest that produced more than 5 billion in the 1980s;
- establishes reserves for the northern spotted owl in which logging would be limited to dead and dying trees and thinning of some live ones, but only where that poses no threat to the owl;
- sets up 10 special management areas where experimental harvesting techniques would be used;
- establishes no-logging buffer zones around sensitive streams and protects entire watersheds to try to avoid endangering salmon and other wildlife;
- asks Congress to spend $1.2 billion over five years, including $270 million in the fiscal year 1994, to assist the region's econ-

omy through economic development grants, small business
loans, job training, and funds to have loggers restore rivers damaged by excessive logging;
  • asks Congress to encourage more domestic milling by eliminat-
    ing a tax subsidy for timber companies that export raw logs.

Egan, Upheaval in the Forests: Clinton Plan Shifts Emphasis from Logging But Does Not Create Off-Limits Wilderness, N.Y. Times, Jul. 2,
1993, at A1. Both environmentalists and logging interests found the
plan wanting. See BNA Daily Report, Clinton Announces Forest Plan;
Disappoints Both Sides of Debate (Jul. 2, 1993). The Administration
must prepare an EIS and present the plan to Judge Dwyer, who will
decide whether to lift the injunction banning timber sales. Following
a "Forest Summit" among affected interests in the Pacific Northwest
convened by President Clinton, several environmental groups and the
Administration announced an agreement that would allow modest logging in some Northwest forests subject to Judge Dwyer's May 1992 injunction. BNA Daily Reports, Environment: Forestry Ban Would Be
Partially Lifted Under Agreement With Environmentalists (Oct. 8,
1993). The proposal must be approved by Judge Dwyer.

CONCLUDING NOTES AND QUESTIONS

1. In addition to economic disruption, significant restrictions on
clearcutting in the Pacific Northwest poses another dilemma. The bark
of the Pacific yew, a tree found only in old growth forests of the Pacific
Northwest, is the source of taxol, the only effective drug for treating
many cases of ovarian cancer, breast cancer, and lung cancer, which
collectively kill over 150,000 Americans per year. The current harvesting rate for yews produces enough taxol to treat fewer than 1000 patients per year. The yew is slow-growing and quite rare. Only trees that
are 100 years old contain a sufficiently high concentration of taxol in
their bark. Six such trees are required to treat one patient. As a result,
many foresters believe that the only effective means of harvesting the
tree in sufficient quantities is by clearcutting. Should this urgent need
for taxol outweigh the interests of protecting the northern spotted owl
and the ancient forests? Or does this example demonstrate an even
stronger basis for the protection of biological diversity in general and
the ancient forests in particular?
2. Many endangered species cases seem more concerned with
stopping federal projects or protecting larger ecosystems than with actually saving the target species. Chief Justice Burger's opinion in *TVA
v. Hill* strongly suggests that the plaintiffs were more concerned with
stopping the Tellico Dam than with protecting one of 130 known spe-

cies of darter. Many assert that the effort to save the northern spotted owl is similarly instrumental. Consider the following statement by Andy Stahl of the Sierra Club Legal Defense Fund: "The northern spotted owl is the wildlife species of choice to act as a surrogate for old-growth protection, and I've often thought that thank goodness the spotted owl evolved in the Northwest, for if it hadn't, we'd have to genetically engineer it. It's a perfect species for use as a surrogate." Is this a constructive way of approaching ecosystem protection issues?

3. Wouldn't it be more honest (and perhaps administratively sensible) to recognize that there are tradeoffs involved in conserving biological diversity and to develop methodologies and standards for making such tradeoffs? Alternatively, wouldn't it be better to recognize that development is inevitable in some places and therefore to establish significant habitat preserves (where there will not be competition with development and the need for co-existence)?

4. In one of his first policy initiatives, Interior Secretary Bruce Babbitt has proposed a pro-active, preventative ecosystem-wide approach to species conservation. See Stevens, Interior Secretary Is Pushing a New Way to Save Species, N.Y. Times, Feb. 17, 1993, at A1. Among the elements of this approach are improved scientific understanding of the interactions within ecosystems (including the development of a National Biological Survey akin to the U.S. Geological Survey), greater inter-agency coordination, and negotiated settlements that plan the future of entire ecosystems before individual species are endangered. This approach has been tried with reasonable success by the Nature Conservancy. In the hill country outside Austin, Texas, for example, the Conservancy brokered a plan to protect ecologically healthy areas while allowing development to proceed around them. Although development will destroy some habitat, the most important areas will be protected. Can this approach succeed under existing law? What changes would foster this approach?

5. The northern spotted owl controversy, although unique in many respects, has relevance to other endangered species contexts. Consider the following case. Efforts have recently gotten underway to save the gnatcatcher, a small, seemingly ordinary bird native to Orange County, a densely populated community in Southern California. It is estimated that as many as 100 - 200,000 jobs would lost in the short term if construction were halted during a study of the bird's habitat. See Reinhold, Tiny Songbird Poses Big Test for U.S. Environment Policy, N.Y. Times, Mar. 16, 1993, at A1. Does this strike you as a good case for the application of the ESA? How would Secretary Babbitt's pro-active approach work?

E. NATURAL RESOURCE DAMAGES

1. INTRODUCTION

Damage liability for injury to public natural resources represents an emerging "third wave" of environmental liability, in addition to CERCLA liability for cleanup of hazardous wastes and "toxic tort" liability under state law for injuries to individuals or private property from pollution or hazardous wastes. Liability for natural resource damages has been created by two federal statutes, CERCLA and the Oil Pollution Act, and by counterpart state statutes.[32]

CERCLA. Sections 107(a)(4)(C) and (f)(1) authorize the federal and state governments and Indian tribes to recover damages for "injury to, destruction of, or loss of natural resources resulting from" a release of a hazardous substance. "Natural resources" are statutorily defined as "land, fish, wildlife, biota, air, water, drinking water supplies, and other such resources belonging to, managed by, held in trust by, appertaining to, or otherwise controlled by" a government or an Indian tribe. §101(16).[33] As this definition suggests, a government need not own the injured resources in order to recover damages under CERCLA. "Rather, a substantial degree of government regulation, management, or other form of control" is sufficient. *State of Ohio v. DOI,* 880 F.2d 432, 460 (D.C. Cir. 1989). Courts have held, for example, that governments can bring damage actions for injury to aquifers underlying private property, or for injury to wildlife and sport fish. *Artesian Water Co. v. New Castle County,* 851 F.2d 643, 650 (3d Cir. 1988); *State of Idaho v. Southern Refrigerated Transp., Inc.,* 1991 U.S. Dist. LEXIS 1869 (D. Idaho, Jan. 24, 1991).

CERCLA provides the same basic principles of liability for natural resource damages as it imposes for cleanup. Strict liability, subject only to very limited defenses, is imposed on present or former owners and operators of hazardous waste sites and on generators or transporters. There are, however, some distinctive provisions that apply only to natural resource damage claims.

The causation requirement for natural resource damages, which are based on injury to resources "resulting from . . . a release," CERCLA §107(a)(4)(C), is more robust than the causation requirement for response costs, see supra, pp. 628-630. CERCLA also provides a special

---

32. Other federal statutes authorize natural resource damage actions in specific, limited circumstances. These statutes include the Deepwater Port Act of 1974, the Outer Continental Shelf Lands Act, and the Trans-Alaska Pipeline Act. Over half of the states have enacted statutes providing for some form of natural resource damages.

33. The statute does not authorize a damage remedy for private owners of natural resources.

limitations period for natural resource damages claims, §113(g)(1), and provides a defense to liability for releases authorized by a federal permit, §107(f)(1). Also, no natural resource damages are recoverable when "such damages and the release of a hazardous substance from which such damages resulted have occurred wholly before enactment of this Act [December 11, 1980.]" §107(f)(1). While this provision appears to offer relief from retroactive liability, the relief may be largely illusory. Even if the waste was generated and deposited before 1980, the government will contend that any post-1980 migration of the wastes is a "release" and that in any event the presence of the contaminants in soil or groundwater is causing continuing "damage."

Damage actions must be brought by federal or state officials or agencies who are designated as "trustees" for the injured resource by the President or the governor of a state, or by trustees designated by Indian tribes. The principal federal trustees are the Department of Interior, the Department of Agriculture, and the National Oceanic and Atmospheric Administration (NOAA) in the Department of Commerce. Interior and Agriculture manage vast tracts of public lands. Interior, through the Fish and Wildlife Service, asserts regulatory and management authority over fish and migratory birds, while NOAA is responsible for marine mammals and marine and coastal environments.

A trustee must first assess the natural resource damages resulting from a hazardous substance release and then, if warranted, bring a damage action against those responsible. CERCLA authorizes the Department of Interior (DOI) to promulgate regulations to guide trustees in assessing natural resource damages. §301(c). Trustee findings made pursuant to these regulations have "the force and effect of a rebuttable presumption on behalf of the trustee." §107(f)(2)(C). DOI has issued such regulations; they are discussed further below.

Federal or state trustees must use any damages recovered "to restore, replace, or acquire the equivalent of" the injured resource. CERCLA §107(f)(1). Damages also include the "reasonable costs" incurred by trustees in assessing injury and damages.[34] Federal trustees may expend damage recoveries for restoration without further authorization or appropriation by Congress, freeing trustee agencies from the constraints of the regular budget process. The federal Superfund cannot be used to pay either the costs of assessing injury to natural resources or restoring or replacing such resources.

Oil Spill Liability. The 1977 Amendments to the Clean Water Act

---

34. The Interior Department's natural resource damage assessment regulations provide that the costs of a damage assessment are reasonable if they do not exceed the expected damage recovery. Is this a reasonable definition of "reasonable costs"?

adopted a scheme of liability for injury to natural resources caused by oil spills from vessels or onshore or offshore facilities. These provisions were amended and extended by the 1990 Oil Pollution Act (OPA). As under Superfund, liability is strict and defenses are limited. Actions must be brought by state, federal, or tribal trustees for the affected resources. OPA §§1002, 1006, 33 U.S.C. §§2702, 2706. Damages are limited to the costs of restoring or replacing the damaged or destroyed natural resources, and do not include interim or continuing injuries. Trustees must spend recoveries for such restoration or replacement; federal trustees may do so without further authorization or appropriation by Congress. The OPA created an Oil Spill Liability Trust Fund, financed by assessments on oil production and transportation. $50 million is available from the fund to federal trustees annually to finance damage assessments and restoration plans. OPA §1012. The OPA directs NOAA to promulgate natural resource damage assessment regulations for oil spills similar to the DOI regulations authorized under CERCLA. OPA §1006(e).

Like CERCLA, the OPA creates a system of divided responsibility for cleanup and restoration. The Coast Guard is responsible for undertaking or supervising cleanup of offshore spills and initiating actions to recover cleanup costs. In the case of onshore spills, EPA has these responsibilities. But federal and state trustees are responsible for restoration and natural resource damage assessment.

Implementation. After a slow start, dozens of federal and state natural resource claims have been asserted, although only two cases have as yet been tried.[35] There are at least four dozen federal consent decrees or proposed consent decrees providing for natural resource damage payments under CERCLA or the OPA. Federal and state authorities now regularly assert natural resource damage claims in connection with Superfund cleanup actions and oil spills. To date, the most significant natural resource damage case is the $900 million settlement of claims by the United States and Alaska against Exxon for natural resource damages caused by the Exxon Valdez spill in Prince William Sound.[36] Government recoveries in the tens of millions of dollars have also been obtained for oil spills in San Francisco Bay and New York Harbor and for hazardous substances contamination in New Bedford Harbor, Seattle Harbor, and at Kennecott's copper smelter in Utah. The United States is seeking over a billion dollars in damages from Shell for toxic contamination at the Rocky Mountain Arsenal in Colorado. Natural

---

35. *In re Natural Gypsum Co.,* Blc. No. 390-37213-SAF-11 (Bankr. N.D. Tex., June 24, 1992); *Idaho v. Southern Refrigerated Transp., Inc.,* 1991 U.S. Dist. LEXIS 1869 (D. Idaho, Jan. 24, 1991).

36. In addition, the plea agreement that settled the federal government's criminal case against Exxon provided $100 million in restitution, which may be spent for restoration of damaged natural resources, and a $25 million criminal fine.

resource damage claims are becoming an important and widely used part of government's armory of environmental remedies.

Major natural resource damage cases are, however, extraordinarily complex and costly. As explained further below, there are great difficulties and significant uncertainties in determining the extent of injury to natural resources, establishing causation, selecting appropriate remedial action, and measuring damages. These complexities are rendered more difficult by the issue of jury trial. There is no jury trial for OPA claims for oil spills in navigable waters, which fall under the admiralty jurisdiction. Nor is there jury trial under CERCLA when the government seeks to recover the costs of clean-up; courts have held that such a remedy is equitable in character. While the government has argued that natural resource damage claims under CERCLA are also equitable and restitutionary in character because they aim at restoration of the injured resource, all three federal courts that have considered the issue have held that there is a right to jury trial, reasoning that natural resource damage actions are akin to common law tort actions.[37] Jury trial of injury, causation, remedy, and natural resource damage valuation will further increase the cost, complexity, and delay in resolving claims. Query: Is a tort action for damages the best way to deal with oil spills and releases of hazardous chemicals that threaten public natural resources? What alternative institutional approaches should be considered?

Coordination Problems. Significant problems arise in coordinating cleanup of oil spills or hazardous releases and restoration of damaged natural resources. Under CERCLA, EPA performs or supervises cleanup of a waste site, which is designed to remove or contain existing contamination and prevent future releases. The trustees are supposed to restore injured natural resources. There is inevitably an overlap between these two activities, which proceed under the direction of different federal agencies pursuant to different statutory provisions and administrative regulations. Problems of coordination are further compounded when, as is frequently the case, state authorities assert a role in cleanup and also assert natural resource damage claims. The statute provides no guidance about how these conflicts are to be resolved or about what should be done when more than one trustee, state or federal, asserts responsibility over an injured resource. Responsible parties are sometimes caught in the middle, facing separate liabilities to two different categories of government plaintiffs whose remedial activities may conflict with or duplicate each other.

---

37. *United States v. City of Seattle,* No. C90-395WD (W.D. Wash. Nov. 28 1990); *Acushnet River and New Bedford Harbor: Proceedings re Alleged PCB Contamination,* 712 F. Supp. 994, 1000 (D. Mass. 1989); *United States v. Allied Chemical Co.,* No. C-83-5898 (N.D. Calif.) (Bench ruling). In all three cases jury trial was demanded by the defendants.

Under both CERCLA and OPA, a number of federal and state trustee agencies may assert an interest in natural resources injured by a release or spill. In addition, state authorities often assert authority with respect to cleanup. The statutes fail to provide any clear guidance as to how conflicts among these several authorities are to be resolved. Divided authority creates serious administrative and legal problems in coordinating both the physical processes of cleanup and restoration and the legal process for imposing cleanup and damage liability on responsible parties.

2.   THE MEASURE OF DAMAGES: STATE OF OHIO v. DOI

STATE OF OHIO v. DEPARTMENT OF INTERIOR

880 F.2d 432 (D.C. Cir. 1989)

[Various environmental groups, states, and industry groups sought judicial review of the natural resource damage assessment regulations promulgated by the Interior Department (DOI), challenging different parts of the regulations. The portions of the opinion excerpted below deal with issues relating to the valuation of damages. Part III of the opinion was written by Judge WALD, Parts VI and VII were written by Judge MIKVA, and Part XIII by Judge ROBINSON.]

III.   THE "LESSER-OF" RULE

The most significant issue in this case concerns the validity of the regulation providing that damages for despoilment of natural resources shall be "the *lesser of:* restoration or replacement costs; or diminution of use values." 43 C.F.R. §11.35(b)(2)(1987) (emphasis added).

State and Environmental Petitioners challenge Interior's "lesser of" rule, insisting that CERCLA requires damages to be at least sufficient to pay the cost in every case of restoring, replacing or acquiring the equivalent of the damaged resource (hereinafter referred to short-handedly as "restoration"). Because in some — probably a majority of — cases lost-use-value will be lower than the cost of restoration, Interior's rule will result in damages awards too small to pay for the costs or restoration.

. . . A hypothetical example will illustrate the point: imagine a hazardous substance spill that kills a rookery of fur seals and destroys a habitat for seabirds at a sealife reserve. The lost use value of the seals and seabird habitat would be measured by the market value of the fur seals' pelts (which would be approximately $15 each) plus the selling price per acre of land comparable in value to that on which the spoiled bird habitat was located. Even if, as likely, that use value turns out to be far less than the cost of restoring the rookery and seabird habitat, it would nonetheless be the only measure of damages eligible for the presumption of recoverability under the Interior rule.

After examining the language and purpose of CERCLA, as well as its legislative history, we conclude that Interior's "lessor of" rule is directly contrary to the expressed intent of Congress. The precise question here is . . . whether DOI is entitled to treat use value and restoration cost as having equal presumptive legitimacy as a measure of damages.

Interior's "lesser of" rule operates on the premise that, as the cost of a restoration project goes up relative to the value of the injured resource, at some point it becomes wasteful to require responsible parties to pay the full cost of restoration. . . . The logic behind the rule is the same logic that prevents an individual from paying $8,000 to repair a collision-damaged car that was worth only $5,000 before the collision. . . . What is significant about Interior's rule is the point at which it deems restoration "inefficient." Interior chose to draw the line not at the point where restoration becomes practically impossible, nor at the point where the cost of restoration becomes grossly disproportionate to the use value of the resource, but rather at the point where restoration cost exceeds — by any amount, however small — the use value of the resource. . . .

Interior's "lesser of" rule squarely rejects the concept of any clearly expressed congressional preference for recovering the full cost of restoration from responsible parties. The challenged regulation treats the two alternative measures of damages, restoration cost and use value, as though the choice between them were a matter of complete indifference from the statutory point of view: thus, in any given case, the rule makes damages turn solely on whichever is less expensive.

The strongest linguistic evidence of Congress' intent to establish a distinct preference for restoration costs as the measure of damages is contained in §107(f)(1) of CERCLA. That section states that natural resource damages recovered by a government trustee are "for use only to restore, replace, or acquire the equivalent of such natural resources." . . . It goes on to state: "The measure of damages in any action under [§107(a)(C)] shall not be limited by the sums which can be used to restore or replace such resources."

By mandating the use of all damages to restore the injured resources, Congress underscored in §107(f)(1) its paramount restorative purpose for imposing damages. . . .

Interior justifies the "lesser of" rule as being economically efficient. Under DOI's economic efficiency view, making restoration cost the measure of damages would be a waste of money whenever restoration would cost more than the use value of the resource.

The fatal flaw of Interior's approach, however, is that is assumes that natural resources are fungible goods, just like any other, and that the value to society generated by a particular resource can be accurately measured in every case — assumptions that Congress apparently rejected. As the foregoing examination of CERCLA's text, structure and legislative history illustrates, Congress saw restoration as the presumptively correct remedy for injury to natural resources. To say that Congress placed a thumb on the scales in favor of restoration is not to say that it forswore the goal of efficiency. "Efficiency," standing alone, simply means that the chosen policy will dictate the result that achieves the greatest value to society. Whether a particular choice is efficient depends on *how the various alternatives are valued.*

Our reading of CERCLA does not attribute to Congress an irrational dislike of "efficiency"; rather, it suggests that Congress was skeptical of the ability of human beings to measure the true "value" of a natural resource. Indeed, even the common law recognizes that restoration is the proper remedy for injury to property where measurement of damages by some other method will fail to compensate fully for the injury.[38] Congress' refusal to view use value and restoration cost as having equal presumptive legitimacy merely recognizes that natural resources have value that is not readily measured by traditional means.

Our reading of the complex of relevant provisions concerning damages under CERCLA convinces us that Congress established a distinct preference for restoration cost as the measure of recovery in natural resource damage cases. This is not to say that DOI may not establish some class of cases where other considerations — i.e., infeasibility of restoration or grossly disproportionate cost to use value — warrant a different standard. We hold the "lesser of" rule based on comparing costs alone, however, to be an invalid determinant of whether or not to deviate from Congress' preference.

VI.   THE HIERARCHY OF ASSESSMENT METHODS

The regulations establish a rigid hierarchy of permissible methods for determining "use values," limiting recovery to the price commanded by the resource on the open market, unless the trustee finds that "the market for the resource is not reasonably competitive." . . . If the trustee makes such a finding, it may "appraise" that market value in accordance with the relevant sections of the "Uniform Appraisal Standards for Federal Land Acquisition," . . . Only when neither the

---

38. See, e.g., *Trinity Church v. John Hancock Mut. Life Ins. Co.,* 399 Mass. 43, 502, N.E.2d 532, 536 (1987) (restoration cost is proper measure where diminution in market value is unsatisfactory or unavailable as a measure of damages, as in the case of structural damage to a church). . . .

market value nor the appraisal method is "appropriate" can other methods of determining use value be employed. . . .

Environmental petitioners maintain that Interior's emphasis on market value is an unreasonable interpretation of the statute, under the so-called "second prong" of *Chevron U.S.A., Inc. v. Natural Resources Defense Council, Inc.,* 467 U.S. 837, 845 . . . (1984), and we agree. While it is not irrational to look to market price as *one* factor in determining that use value of a resource, it is unreasonable to view market price as the exclusive factor, or even the predominant one. From the bald eagle to the blue whale and snail darter, natural resources have values that are not fully captured by the market system. . . .

As we have previously noted in the context of the "lesser of" rule, see supra . . . , market prices are not acceptable as primary measures of the use values of natural resources. . . . We find that DOI erred by establishing "a strong presumption in favor of market price and appraisal methodologies." 51 Fed. Reg. 27,720 (1986).

We are not satisfied that the problem is solved by the provision in section 11.83(c)(1) [of the regulations] permitting nonmarket methodologies to be used when the market for the resource is not "reasonably competitive." There are many resources whose components may be traded in "reasonably competitive markets, but whose total use values are not fully reflected in the prices they command in those markets. Interior itself provides ample proof of the inadequacy of the "reasonably competitive market" caveat. For example, DOI has noted that "the hierarchy established in the type B regulation" would dictate a use value for fur seals of $15 per seal, corresponding to the market price for the seal's pelt. . . . Another example of DOI's erroneous equation of market price with use value is its insistence that the sum of the fees charged by the government for the use of a resource, say, for admission to a national park, constitutes "the value to the public of recreational or other public uses of the resource." . . . [b]ecause "these fees are what the government has determined to represent the value of the natural resource and represent an offer by a willing seller," . . . This is quite obviously and totally fallacious; there is no necessary connection between the total value to the public of a park and the fees charged as admission, which typically are set not to maximize profits but rather to encourage the public to visit the park, see 16 U.S.C. §§460-k-3, 460l-6a. In fact, the decision to set entrance fees far below what the traffic would bear is evidence of Congress's strong conviction that parks are priceless national treasures and that access to them ought to be as wide as possible, and not, as DOI would have it, a sign that parks are really not so valuable after all.

Neither the statute nor its legislative history evinces any congressional intent to limit use values to market prices. On the contrary, Congress intended the damage assessment Regulations to capture fully all aspects of loss. CERCLA section 301(c)(2) commands Interior to "identify the best available procedures to determine [natural resource] damages, including both direct and indirect injury, destruction or loss." . . .

On remand, DOI should consider a rule that would permit trustees to derive use values for natural resources by summing up all reliably calculated use values, however measured, so long as the trustee does not double count. Market valuation can of course serve as one factor to be considered, but by itself it will necessarily be incomplete. In this vein, we instruct DOI that its decision to limit the role of non-consumptive values, such as option and existence values, in the calculation of use values rests on an erroneous construction of the statute. The regulations provide that "[e]stimation of option and existence values shall be used only if the authorized official determines that no use values can be determined," . . .

DOI has erroneously construed the statute. First, section 301(c)(2) requires Interior to "take into consideration factors including, *but not limited to* . . . use value." . . . The statute's command is expressly not limited to use value; if anything, the language implies that DOI is to include in its regulations other factors in addition to use value. Second, even under its reading of section 301(c), DOI has failed to explain why option and existence values should be excluded from the category of recognized use values. . . . Option and existence values may represent "passive" use, but they nonetheless reflect utility derived by humans from a resource, and thus, prima facie, ought to be included in a damage assessment. See Cross, Natural Resource Damage Valuation, 42 Vand. L. Rev. 269, 285-89 (1989) (noting that surveys reveal that the option and existence value of national parks may be quite large). DOI is entitled to rank methodologies according to its view of their reliability, but it cannot base its complete exclusion of option and existence values on an incorrect reading of the statute.

We hold that the hierarchy of use values is not a reasonable interpretation of statute.

[Part VII of the opinion upheld DOI's use of a 10 percent discount rate, based on an OMB circular, to discount future year costs and benefits in determining damages and making decisions about restoration plans. Environmentalists had challenged the 10 percent figure as unduly high, resulting in undervaluation of the long-range benefits of resource restoration.]

XIII. CONTINGENT VALUATION

A. THE REGULATORY BACKGROUND

DOI's natural resource damage assessment regulations define "use value" as:

the value to the public of recreational or other public uses of the re-source, as measured by changes in consumer surplus, any fees or other payments collectable by the government or Indian tribe for a private par-ty's use of the natural resource, and any economic rent accruing to a private party because the government or Indian tribe does not charge a fee or price for the use of the resource.

    The regulations provide several approaches to use valuation. When the injured resource is traded in a market, the lost use value is the diminution in market price. When that is not precisely the case, but similar resources are traded in a market, an appraisal technique may be utilized to determine damages. When, however, neither of these two situations obtains, non-marketed resource methodologies are available. One of these is "contingent valuation" (CV), the subject of controversy here.

    The CV process "includes all techniques that set up hypothetical markets to elicit an individual's economic valuation of a natural re-source." CV involves a series of interviews with individuals for the pur-pose of ascertaining the values they respectively attach to particular changes in particular resources. Among the several formats available to an interviewer in developing the hypothetical scenario embodied in a CV survey are direct questioning, by which the interviewer learns how much the interviewee is willing to pay for the resource; bidding formats, for example, the interviewee is asked whether he or she would pay a given amount for a resource and, depending upon the response, the bid is set higher or lower until a final price is derived; and a "take or leave it" format, in which the interviewee decides whether or not he or she is willing to pay a designated amount of money for the resource. CV methodology thus enables ascertainment of individually-expressed values for different levels of quality of resources, and dollar values of individuals' changes in well-being. The regulations also sanction resort to CV methodology in determining "option"[39] and "existence"[40] values.

    Industry Petitioners' complaint is limited to DOI's inclusion of

---

    39. Option value is the dollar amount an individual is willing to pay al-though he or she is not currently using a resource but wishes to reserve the option to use that resource in a certain state of being in the future. Final Rule, supra note 70, 51 Fed. Reg. at 27,692, 27,721. For example, an individual who does not plan to use a beach or visit the Grand Canyon may nevertheless place some value on preservation of the resource in its natural state for personal enjoyment in the event of a later change of mind.

    40. Existence value is the dollar amount an individual is willing to pay although he or she does not plan to use the resource, either at present or in the future. The payment is not the knowledge that the resource will continue to exist in a given state of being. Final Rule, supra note 70, 51 Fed. Reg. at 27,692, 27,721. Though lacking any interest in personally enjoying the re-source, an individual may attach some value to it because he or she may wish to have the resource available for others to enjoy.

CV in its assessment methodology. They claim fatal departures from CERCLA on grounds that CV methodology is inharmonious with common law damage assessment principles, and is considerably less than a "best available procedure." These petitioners further charge the DOI's extension of CERCLA's rebuttable presumption to CV assessments is arbitrary and capricious, and violative of the due process rights of a potentially responsible party. We find none of these challenges persuasive.

B. Consistency with CERCLA

Industry Petitioners point out that at common law there can be no recovery for speculative injuries, and they contend that CV methodology is at odds with that principle. CV methodology, they say, is rife with speculation, amounting to no more than ordinary public opinion polling.

We have already noted our disagreement with the proposition that the strictures of the common law apply to CERCLA. . . . CERCLA does, however, require utilization of the "best available procedures" for determinations of damages flowing from destruction of or injury to natural resources, and Industry Petitioners insist that CV methodology is too flawed to qualify as such. In their eyes, the CV process is imprecise, is untested, and has a built-in bias and a propensity to produce overestimation.

It cannot be gainsaid that DOI's decision to adopt CV was made intelligently and cautiously. DOI scrutinized a vast array of position papers and discussions addressing the use of CV. It recognized and acknowledged that CV needs to be "properly structured and professionally applied." . . . We find DOI's promulgation of CV methodology reasonable and consistent with congressional intent, and therefore worthy of deference.

The primary argument of Industry Petitioners is that the possibility of bias is inherent in CV methodology, and disqualifies it as a "best available procedure." In evaluating the utility of CV methodology in assessing damages for impairment of natural resources, DOI surveyed a number of studies which analyzed the methodology, addressed the shortcomings of various questionnaires, and recommended steps needed to fashion reliable CV assessments. For example, an early study by the Water Resources Council advised that questions in CV surveys be "carefully designed and pretested," . . .

Industry Petitioners urge, however, that even assuming that questions are artfully drafted and carefully circumscribed, there is such a high degree of variation in size of the groups surveyed, and such a concomitant fluctuation in aggregations of damages, that CV methodology cannot be considered a "best available procedure."[41] We think this attack on CV methodology is insufficient in a facial challenge to invalidate CV as an available assessment technique. The extent of damage to natural resources from releases of oil and hazardous substances varies greatly, and though the impact may be widespread and severe, it is in the mission of CERCLA to assess the public loss.[42] . . . The argument of Industry Petitioners strikes at CERCLA, not CV's implementation, and can appropriately be considered only by Congress.

Similarly, we find wanting Industry Petitioners' protest that CV does not rise to the status of a "best available procedure" because willingness-to-pay — a factor prominent in CV methodology — can lead to overestimates by survey respondents. The premise of this argument is that respondents do not actually pay money, and likely will overstate their willingness-to-pay. One study relied upon by Industry Petitioners hypothesizes that respondents may "respond in ways that are more indicative of what they would like to see done than how they would behave in an actual market," . . . The simple and obvious safeguard against overstatement, however, is more sophisticated questioning. Even as matters now stand, the risk of overestimation has not been shown to produce such egregious results as to justify judicial over-ruling of DOI's careful estimate of the caliber and worth of CV methodology.

We sustain DOI in its conclusion that CV methodology is a "best available procedure." As such, its conclusion in the Natural Resource Damage Assessment regulations was entirely proper.

NOTES AND QUESTIONS

1. In order to understand the court's condemnation of DOI's "lesser of" rule, one must first examine the hierarchy of resource valuation methodologies adopted in the regulations, which provided as follows:

---

41. Industry Petitioners cite a study estimating the combined option and existence values to Texas residents of whooping cranes at $109,000,000 (13.9 million Texas residents x $7.13). The estimate rested upon responses to a survey eliciting the amount an individual would pay for a permit to visit the National Wildlife Refuge where the whooping crane winters. Had the survey been nationwide in scope, the estimate would have been $1.58 billion. Brief for Industry Petitioners at 14 n.24 (referring to J. Stoll & L. Johnson, Concepts of Value, Non-market Valuation, and the Case of the Whooping Crane (Natural Resources Working Paper Series, National Resource Workgroup, Dep't of Agricultural Economics, Texas A & M Univ.) (1984) at 23-24, J.A. 2828-2829).

42. Thus, in the whooping crane scenario referred to by Industry Petitioners, see note 86 supra, the intent of CERCLA would be realized, not contravened, by a more expansive survey and a correspondingly higher assessment of damages if people beyond the borders of Texas were affected.

(a) A resource should be valued by its market price, if a market for the resource exists and is reasonably competitive. The entrance fee charged by the government for visiting national parks is taken as the equivalent of a market price for this purpose.

(b) In the absence of a competitive market price, the resource is to be measured by its use value: the aggregate amount that individuals would be willing to pay to use or visit the resource.

But how does one determine that amount in the absence of a market? Economists have devised three techniques for doing so, see supra, pp. 86-87; each has limitations.

One is travel cost methodology: empirical studies are conducted to determine how much more money individuals actually spent to travel to and visit, say, a wilderness area in Alaska than they would have spent to visit some other outdoor area in, say, Wyoming. Some studies also add an amount equal to the wages that the individual could have earned while travelling. Travel cost understates individuals' use value, which is presumably greater than the cost of visiting the site.

A second use valuation methodology is hedonic pricing. The analyst first determines the attributes of the public resource being valued: pure air, scenic vistas, sparkling water, etc. She then examines the premiums that people pay for properties with comparable attractive attributes in the private sector, and imputes this premium to the public resource. But some exceptionally scenic public resources such as the national parks have no close private sector counterparts.

A third approach consists of contingent valuation methodology (CVM) surveys that ask a sample of a relevant population how much they would be willing to pay to use the resource. The values given are added up, and the total is then multiplied by the ratio between the total relevant population and the sample to obtain the aggregate willingness to pay of the relevant population. Among the problems in designing CVM studies is selecting the relevant population and adequately describing the resource to persons not familiar with it. A more fundamental difficulty is that the individuals surveyed do not actually have to pay any money. By contrast, travel cost and hedonic pricing are based on individuals' revealed preferences: amounts actually spent to use or acquire a resource.

(c) If neither market prices or use values are available, non-use values such as option and existence values should be used to value the resource.[43] Non-use value consists of the amount that people would be willing to pay to preserve a resource, independent of any present use that they might make of it. Non-use value may include existence value (the satisfaction that a person derives in having a resource preserved),

---

43. While the court and DOI's regulations refer to these values as "'passive' use values," the term "non-use" value is commonly used today and is also more accurate.

option value (the value to a person of having the resource preserved in order to have the option of using it in the future), and bequest value (the value of preserving the resource for future generations).

There is no market-type measure of non-use values. Markets exist only for those resources that have the property of excludability. A loaf of bread or a visit to the theater have the property of excludability; the owner of the bread or the theater can make it available to those who will pay for using it, and denied to those who will not. The satisfaction that people derive from knowing that a beautiful, pristine resource is being preserved does not have the quality of excludability. The resource owner has no way of limiting such satisfaction to those who will pay him for preserving it, and denying such satisfaction to those who do not pay. For similar reasons, travel cost methodology and hedonic pricing cannot be used to measure such value.

Non-use values are nonetheless real, as evidenced by public support for government expenditures to acquire and maintain pristine, scenic, or ecologically valuable resources and by contributions to support efforts by environmental groups to preserve resources that the contributors do not visit or otherwise use. The only method presently available to measure non-use values are CVM surveys. Surveys describe the resource in question to respondents, who are asked how much they would pay to preserve it unspoiled or to restore it after it has suffered damage.[44] Some surveys are conducted by mail or telephone, others at public locations such as shopping malls. CVM surveys of non-use values

---

44. An alternative measure of value is the amount that people would be willing to accept (WTA) to see the resource destroyed or damaged. Some CVM surveys have used both willingness to pay (WTP) and WTA questions. The values elicited for WTA were much higher than for WTP — often three to four times greater on average. Cf. supra pp. 65-66. Such a disparity is inexplicable on standard economic theory. Under WTA, the respondent implicitly has an entitlement to preserve the resource; she is being asked how much she would accept to relinquish it. Under WTP, the entitlement implicitly belongs to someone else, and she is asked how much she would pay to acquire it. Under WTA, the respondent implicitly has somewhat greater total wealth or income than under WTP; in addition to all her other assets, she has a resource preservation entitlement. Because her total wealth is somewhat greater, she may be expected to place a somewhat higher economic value on any given resource, including the preservation of the resource described in the survey. But this "income effect" would not, on standard economic assumptions, be great enough to explain the enormous disparities between WTP and WTA obtained in some CVM surveys.

What else might explain such disparities? Are respondents simply offended at the suggestion that they would accept money to allow the Grand Canyon to be despoiled? Today, most CVM surveys use the WTP measure on the ground that it is a lower and therefore conservative measure of value. But criticisms of CVM contend that the disparity between the WTA and WTP surveys shows that both responses are inconsistent with standard economic behavior, and therefore that neither can be accepted as a reliable measure of economic value.

are expensive; a well-designed, state-of-the-art study costs hundreds of thousands of dollars.

2. The difficulties with CVM studies, noted above, are especially severe in the case of non-use values. The basic concept of non-use value is unfamiliar to most people. Since there are no markets for non-use values, respondents may have difficulty in putting a price tag on them. Also, it is not easy to devise a survey instrument that will concisely and accurately describe the non-use aspect of a given resource and its impairment in terms intelligible to survey respondents. Survey results show that the values elicited vary quite widely depending on the precise formulation. Another difficulty is how to define the relevant population for purposes of a non-use CVM survey. Should it be limited to those in the locality of the resource? Should it include everyone in the United States? The world? Should it be limited to those that were familiar with the resource prior to injury? Should it also include those who became familiar with the resource as a result of post-injury publicity? As a result of the survey? Consider that survey questions may lead the latter category of respondents previously unaware of a resource to impute a value for preserving the resource that they would never have held if they had not been told about the resource in a survey and asked to value it.

CVM survey results are often inconsistent with economic behavior. Normally, people will pay more for a larger quantity of a commodity, absent satiation. But CVM non-use surveys often report a marked lack of sensitivity by respondents to the quantity of the non-use resource that they are asked to value.[45] For example, in one study respondents stated that they would pay no more to save 2 million birds than they would pay to save 20,000 birds. It is also normally expected under economic theory that persons will pay about the same for a particular commodity, such as a loaf of bread, whether they are valuing it alone or "embedded" as a part of a larger bundle of commodities, such as a dozen grocery items. But CVM respondents' expressed non-use values for a given resource vary dramatically depending on the level of embedding.[46] For example, if asked how much they would pay to preserve an endangered species, such as northern spotted owls, respondents may state that they would pay $75 or $100. But if respondents are asked how

---

45. E.g., J. Kahneman & J. Knetsch, Valuing Public Goods: The Purchase of Moral Satisfaction, 22 J. Envtl. Econ. & Mgmt. 57 (1992); W. Desvousges, F. Johnson, R. Dunford, K. Wilson, H. Banzaf & K. Stettler, Using CV to Measure Non-Use Damages: An Assessment of Validity and Reliability (Research Triangle Institute 1992); P. Diamond, Submission to NOAA Panel Addressing Nonuse Damage Assessments (1992).

46. E.g., Kahneman & Knetsch, supra, note 45; M. Kemp and C. Maxwell, Exploring a Budget Concept for Contingent Valuation Estimates, in Contingent Valuation: A Critical Assessment (J. Hausman ed., 1993). See also R. Cummings & G. Harrison, Identifying and Measuring Nonuse Values for Natural and Environmental Resources: A Critical Review of the State of the Art (1992).

much they would pay to preserve the owls and are asked at the same time how much they would pay to preserve ten or twenty other species or scenic resources, the stated willingness to pay to preserve the owls drops dramatically to $5 or so.[47] The large disparities between the amounts given by respondents who are asked how much they would be willing to pay to preserve a resource and how much they would be willing to accept to allow its degradation, see note 44, supra, are also inconsistent with economic behavior.

These response patterns may reflect the fact that respondents have a relatively fixed budget for environmental preservation generally; if so, the survey should in some fashion ask them to consider all possible resources that they would like to see preserved and then ask them how much they would allocate to the particular resource in question versus all other resources. This may be a very difficult task to accomplish within the constraints of a standardized survey questionnaire. On the other hand, these response patterns have led some psychologists to conclude that they do not reflect the economic value that respondents place on a specific resource but generalized attitudes and feelings about the environment and the moral satisfaction of expressing support for a "good cause."[48]

Finally, there remains the fundamental problem that respondents do not actually have to spend any of their own money to back up their responses. When CVM surveys are used to measure use values, the response can be compared with the results of travel cost and hedonic pricing studies, which are based on amounts that people actually expend. In the case of non-use values, no similar means of validating and calibrating CVM survey responses is available.[49] The aggregate willing-

---

47. When respondents are asked how much they would pay to preserve a series of resources, they tend to place a higher value on whichever resource comes first in a sequence.

48. See, e.g., D. Schkade & J. Payne, Where Do the Numbers Come From? How People Respond to Contingent Valuation Questions, in Contingent Valuation, A Critical Assessment (J. Hausman ed. 1993); J. Payne, Comments on the Use of the Contingent Valuation Method to Calculate Nonuse Values in Natural Resource Damage Assessments (Submission to NOAA, July, 1992); D. Kahneman, supra, note 45.

49. Recent studies of non-use values indicate the values reported in CVM non-use surveys are much higher than the amounts that the same survey respondents will actually pay to join an environmental organization; see K. Seip & J. Strand, Willingness to Pay for Environmental Goods in Norway: A Contingent Valuation Study with Real Payment (SAF Center for Applied Research, University of Oslo Department of Economics, 1991), or to preserve instream flows to support fish life, see J. Duffield and D. Patterson, Field Testing Existence Value: An Instream Flow Trust Fund for Montana Rivers (1992). This disparity might, however, be explained by free-rider problems. People may contribute less to securing a collective good such as a clean environment than the value that they place on the environment because they hope or expect that they can free ride on others' contributions.

ness-to-pay values reported in many studies are so high as to be implausible and incredible. For example, one study reported that Americans would pay $32 billion annually to save the whooping crane.[50]

3. Not surprisingly, there is enormous controversy over the use of CVM surveys to measure non-use values. The *Ohio* court rejected industry's challenge to DOI's endorsement of CVM surveys in its regulation, although the court cautioned that resource values must be "reliably calculated." 880 F.2d at 464. DOI's endorsement of CVM to measure non-use values must, however, be understood in the context of its valuation methodology hierarchy, under which non-use values would be measured only if there was neither a market price nor a use value for the resource in question. Such instances would be quite rare. Under the court's approach, non-use values must presumably be determined in every case where they are significant. Also, most of the CVM studies in the rulemaking record, including those cited by the court in approving DOI's endorsement of CVM, dealt with use values rather than non-use values. See 880 F.2d at 476-477 n.82 As noted above, CVM use valuations can be corroborated by travel cost and hedonic pricing studies; CVM non-use valuations can not.

Since the *Ohio* decision, more non-use CVM surveys have been conducted. The economic literature on the subject has burgeoned.[51] Many economists are highly critical of such surveys, citing the difficulties described; some contend that CVM methodology is inherently incapable of producing valid, reliable results because there is no way of corroborating survey responses by reference to the revealed preferences of "consumers."[52] Defenders of CVM acknowledge the difficulties but insist that they can be overcome by refining and improving the methodology.[53] This controversy may be one reason why DOI has yet to issue final regulations to replace the damage valuation provisions in

---

50. See J. Mead, Review and Analysis of Recent State-of-the-Art Contingent Valuation Studies, in Contingent Valuation: A Critical Assessment (J. Hausman ed., 1993). By contrast, annual giving to all environmental causes in the United States in 1991 amounted to $2.5 billion.

51. For an overview, see Raymond Kopp & V. Kerry Smith, Valuing Natural Assets (1993).

52. See, e.g., Contingent Valuation: A Critical Assessment (Jerry Hausman ed., 1993).

53. See R. Mitchell & R. Carson, Using Surveys to Value Public Goods: The Contingent Valuation Method (1989).

The existing legal literature on natural resource damages tends to support the use of CVM surveys to measure non-use values, reasoning that such values are significant and that no other means of measuring them is available. See, e.g., Anderson, Natural Resource Damages, Superfund, and the Courts, 16 Envtl. Affairs 405 (1989); Cross, Natural Resource Damage Valuation, 42 Vand. L. Rev. 270 (1989); Woodard & Hope, Natural Resource Damage Litigation under the Comprehensive Environmental Response, Compensation, and Liability Act, 14 Harv. Envtl. L. Rev. 189 (1990).

its original rule that were set aside and remanded by the *Ohio* court in 1989.

In connection with its development of natural resource damage regulations for oil spills under the OPA, NOAA convened a distinguished panel of economists chaired by Economics Nobel Laureates Kenneth Arrow and Robert Solow. The panel's report, 58 Fed. Reg. 4601 (1993), acknowledged the difficulties in using CVM surveys to measure non-use values, suggested criteria that could be used to improve such surveys, and concluded that properly designed surveys could provide "useful information" that can provide a "starting point" for damage determination by judges and juries. 58 Fed. Reg. at 4610. The panel acknowledged that the CVM surveys tend to produce overstated non-use valuations, but suggested that judges and juries could cure this problem by scaling back the reported willingness-to-pay amounts. Query: What yardstick are judges and juries to use in scaling survey results?

There is only one case in which the issue of using CVM surveys to measure non-use values in connection with natural resource damage has been brought to trial. The court disallowed the use of a CVM study to measure non-use existence values of fish in a river on the ground that the study was "not persuasive" and it would have been "conjecture and speculation" to allow natural resource damages based its results. *Idaho v. Southern Refrigerated Transport Company,* 1991 WP 22479 (D. Idaho 1991).[54]

4. Does it make any sense to conduct a public opinion survey and have the experts conducting the survey testify before a judge or jury about how valuable the public believes a natural resource to be? Consider that in private tort actions, the principal elements of damages consist of economic losses as measured by the market: property damage, lost wages and medical expenses in the case of personal injury. But in personal injury cases, plaintiffs can also recover for pain and suffering. There is no market for the intangible value of pain and suffering; we simply rely on the jury or (in a case tried without a jury) the judge to place a dollar value on pain and suffering, relying on their general experience and values.[55] Why not follow the same approach to value the non-use elements of natural resource damages? Are there any other means of valuing natural resources? Must we use CVM surveys, despite

---

54. Cf. *Mercado v. Ahmed,* 756 F. Supp. 1097, 1103 (N.D. Ill. 1991), *aff'd,* 974 F.2d 863 (7th Cir. 1992) (economist wanted to testify as to value of a plaintiff's lost pleasure of life based on an amalgam of CVM willingness-to-pay studies; court excluded testimony because of the variability and lack of economic consensus as to the validity and reliability of this application of CVM).

55. At least one court in a personal injury case has rejected the admission into evidence of expert testimony about the value that respondents in a CVM survey placed on pain and suffering for a given injury. See supra, note 54.

apparently serious problems with their reliability, because the only alternative is ignoring non-use values altogether?

5. As should be evident from the foregoing, it becomes progressively much more difficult and much more costly to measure the economic value of a resource as one moves from market prices to use values to non-use values. Does this fact explain and justify DOI's hierarchy of valuation methodologies?

On the other hand, if non-use values are excluded, damage recoveries would fail to capture some of the most significant elements of the value of public natural resources. Consider why it is that national parks, wildlife refuges, and wilderness areas are publicly rather than privately owned. Would a system of private ownership and market transactions adequately protect the non-use values associated with such resources? The non-use values? In this connection consider the *Ohio* court's observation that the government allows access to national parks and other public lands at prices far lower than those that a private owner/entrepreneur would charge. Does this practice help explain why such resources are publicly owned, even though they have the property of excludability? Does the practice represent a subsidy of use values at the expense of non-use values? Recall the controversy over the pricing of timber taken from National Forests, supra, pp. 1113-1130.

6. Now consider the *Ohio* court's rejection of DOI's rule that damages should equal the lesser of the costs of "restoration or replacement" or the diminution in the value of the resource as a result of the injury. *If* the value of the resource is primarily defined by its market value, as was the case under DOI's valuation methodology hierarchy, the court's argument is quite powerful, isn't it? But what if value is determined, as the court later requires, not only on the basis of market prices but also, to the extent that they can be reliably measured, use and non-use values as well? Why should one pay more to restore a resource than it is worth, if all relevant values are counted in determining its worth?

7. What does it mean to "restore" an injured resource? In a strict sense, one can never restore a resource to the exact same physical and biological condition that existed prior to the injury. Recall Heraclitus: "One can never step in the same river twice," and the discussion in Chapter 1 about scientific and philosophical difficulties in defining a "natural state." But should the presumptive goal be to approximate the pre-injury condition as closely as possible? Consider that neither CERCLA nor the OPA mandates that an injured resource must be restored to its pre-injury condition. CERCLA, for example, provides that sums recovered by a government trustee may be used "only to restore, replace, or acquire the equivalent of" the injured resources. §107(f)(1).[56]

---

56. OPA §1006(d)(1)(A) provides that the measure of natural resource damages includes "the cost of restoring, rehabilitating, replacing, or acquiring the equivalent of, the damaged natural resources."

This seems to give the trustee an unrestricted option of replacing or acquiring the equivalent of an injured resource rather than restoring it. The *Ohio* court insisted that CERCLA makes "restoration" the presumptive remedy, but in doing so defined "restoration" as including "restoring, replacing, or acquiring the equivalent of the injured resource."

This analysis provokes a further question: How does one determine what replacement or acquisition of the equivalent of an injured resource would amount to? The approach taken by the proposed but not yet adopted DOI regulations on remand from *Ohio* is to define a resource in terms of the services that it provides. These include both use services, such as fishing or hiking, and non-use services, such as the satisfaction of knowing that a pristine ecosystem is preserved. Under this approach, the first step in remedying natural resource injury would be to determine the "baseline" services provided by a resource prior to injury. Next one would determine the various alternatives for restoring services. For example, in the case of a wetland damaged by an oil spill or release of a hazardous substance, one might remove the contamination and hope for natural restoration; replace the damaged marsh grass with new plantings; or acquire and preserve an adjacent wetland that would otherwise be destroyed by development. Is the alternative of leaving a contaminated wetland in its contaminated state and acquiring an adjacent wetland of the same size and quality the equivalent of decontaminating the injured wetland? What if decontaminating costs two or three times as much as acquisition? Must the trustee choose the cheaper alternative, in accordance with the common law doctrine that plaintiffs must take reasonable steps to minimize their damages?

How does one determine whether an alternative to restoring a resource to its pre-injury condition is equivalent? Suppose that the groundwater which feeds a spring in a rock that hikers use for drinking water becomes contaminated. Rather than decontaminating the groundwater, may a trustee pipe in water to a drinking fountain on the same spot? Pipe drinking water into the rock so that it gushes forth in the same fashion as the spring? Must the trustee choose these alternatives if they are cheaper than decontamination? If a resource is defined in terms of services, are the services limited to those provided to humans? What about the services that a resource provides to other resources, such as the habitat that a wetland provides to migratory birds or the habitat that groundwater provides for soil organisms?

8. While insisting that resource restoration (including the options of replacement or acquisition of equivalent resources) is the presumptive remedy under CERCLA, the court observed that if the costs of restoration become "grossly disproportionate" to the value of the resource it would be "wasteful" to require the responsible parties to pay the full costs of restoration. What is the standard for determining whether the costs of restoration, replacement, or acquisition become "grossly dis-

proportionate" to the value of the resource? Are trustee agencies required to follow the "grossly disproportionate" limitation?

9. In addition to recovering (in the normal case) the costs of restoring the injured resource, the trustee can presumably recover damages for the interim reduction in the value of the resource in the interim between injury and restoration.[57] In addition, if full restoration is not feasible, the trustee can also presumably recover damages for permanent impairment of its value. These two items of damages would have to be based on the various elements of resource value already discussed. Note that these recoveries must also be spent to "restore, replace, or acquire the equivalent" of the injured resource. CERCLA §107(f)(1).

In cases where only damages for interim injury are in issue, the resource will already have been fully restored. Why shouldn't recoveries for interim damages be paid into the Treasury? Why shouldn't all recoveries be paid into the Treasury, leaving it to Congress to authorize and appropriate monies for such restoration activities as it judges appropriate? Because trustee agencies may spend natural resource damage recoveries without being subject to the discipline of the budget process, is there a danger that recoveries will be used to aggrandize the bureaucracy rather than protect the environment? A recent GAO report on the Exxon Valdez case found that most of the $240 million recovered thus far under the settlement agreement had been used to cover federal and state personnel expenses, and that little or nothing had been done in the way of restoration efforts. See "Abuses" Cited in Exxon Valdez Spending; Salmon Fishermen End Blockade of Alaska Port, BNA Envtl. Rptr. Current Develops. 781 (Aug. 22, 1993).

10. Do the natural resource damage provisions of CERCLA and the OPA represent a conceptually sound and workable approach to dealing with the problem of injury to public natural resources? Is the private tort model an appropriate one for public resources? Are there any plausible alternatives?

NATURAL RESOURCE DAMAGE VALUATION PROBLEM

Western Copper Company has operated a large copper smelter in a rural area of Utah for many decades. Residues of sulfur and some heavy metals from its smelting operation have contaminated the

---

57. This remedy is explicit in the OPA, which provides that the measure of natural resource damages includes not only the costs of restoration but also "the diminution in value of [the injured] natural resources pending restoration." §1006(d)(1)(B). In addition, both the OPA and CERCLA provide that trustees may recovery the "reasonable cost" of assessing damages. OPA §1006(d)(1)(C); CERCLA §107(a)(4)(C).

groundwater in the area. The sulfur contamination has extended to the groundwater in an aquifer underlying adjacent farms and ranches. As a result the groundwater cannot be used for drinking water for humans or cattle, although it can still be used for irrigation and other purposes. The State of Utah sued Western for natural resource damages under CERCLA. Western claimed that sulfur is not a "hazardous substance" for purposes of CERCLA. It noted that a substantial number of groundwater aquifers throughout the West are contaminated by naturally occurring sources of sulfur. It also pointed to evidence that the groundwater contaminated by its operation had already been contaminated to some degree by minerals that occur naturally in adjacent mountains which were leached by rainwater and washed into adjacent valleys. In some parts of the area, this natural contamination had already made the groundwater only marginally suitable for use as drinking water.

Western and Utah settled the case. The settlement provides that Western will pay the state $12 million, which the parties determined was the market price of purchasing a permanent supply of pure drinking quality in an annual amount equal to the annual maximum safe yield of the contaminated aquifer.[58] In accordance with the provisions of CERCLA, Western and the State submit the agreement to the federal district court for review and approval. The local water district and the local chapter of the Sierra Club file objections to the settlement, arguing that it must be disapproved because it does not provide any recovery for impairment of non-use values. How should the court rule?

3.   THE EXXON VALDEZ OIL SPILL[59]

Late on the night of March 23, 1989, the Exxon Valdez, a massive supertanker loaded with over 1,280,000 barrels of North Slope crude oil, departed from the port of Valdez, Alaska, heading out through the narrows at the mouth of the port into Prince William Sound. The Exxon Valdez was owned and operated by Exxon Shipping Co., wholly owned subsidiary of Exxon Corp. The Sound is a beautiful and pristine area, ringed by mountains and glaciers on three sides and by the ocean on the fourth, and dotted by islands. It extends roughly 35 miles by 40 miles. Beyond the narrows there are two shipping lanes, monitored by Coast Guard radar at Valdez Traffic Control, for outbound and in-

---

58. Annual maximum safe yield is an amount, determined by the State Water Engineer, to be the maximum that can be withdrawn by pumping from the aquifer in a year without unduly depleting the permanent supply.

59. Richard Stewart served as Assistant Attorney General of the Environment Division of the U.S. Department of Justice during the prosecution of the Exxon Valdez case.

bound travel through the Sound. On the night of March 23, drifting icebergs from the Columbia Glacier partially blocked the outbound lane. Instead of slowing to maneuver around the ice, the Exxon Valdez requested permission from the Coast Guard to change lanes. While this was against regulations, apparently it was a relatively common practice. The Coast Guard approved the request and the Valdez changed course, turning to its left into the inbound lane, which was free of ice.

The Valdez had charted a course in which it would turn right, back into the outbound lane when the ice cleared. Beyond the left side of the inbound lane was Bligh Reef, a well marked and known hazard. At some time after leaving the outbound lane, Captain Hazelwood left the bridge in charge of Third Mate Gregory Cousins, with Able Bodied Seaman Robert Kagan at the helm. For reasons that are still not entirely clear, the countermaneuver was not executed at the right time. The Valdez continued on its diagonal path across the inbound lane and hit Bligh Reef and grounded just past midnight on March 24. Immediately oil began to spill out of the holds. Captain Hazelwood returned to the bridge, and radioed the Coast Guard that he was grounded and losing oil. He took steps to secure the boat on the rocks, a wise maneuver because the ship was in danger of capsizing and losing its entire cargo. Later, when he was charged with operating the tanker while intoxicated, these actions became an important part of his defense.

The next day divers found that 50 percent of the tanker's bottom had been damaged. It was now balanced near its midpoint on an outcrop of rock. Ultimately, 240,000 barrels of oil or about a fifth of its cargo spilled into the Sound. Many factors contributed to the spill. Crew fatigue combined with cutbacks by Exxon Shipping in the size of the crew could have played a role. According to several reports they had not had the required amount of rest before the Valdez departed. In addition, the pilots who were required to guide the tankers out of the port and through the narrows were dropped off before the tankers had cleared Bligh Reef. Exxon Shipping and other oil shipping companies, facing declining oil prices, had taken this step in order to save money and time. Kagan was not regarded as adequately competent. After being twice refused promotion, he was finally promoted to Able Bodied Seaman, and thus eligible to man the helm, because of strong pressure from the seamen's union. This also was part of an effort by Exxon to save time and money. Hazelwood had a history of drinking problems. He had taken leave to undergo a rehabilitation program. But since that time he had two convictions for driving a car while intoxicated. He failed to report these convictions to Exxon Shipping, although there was scuttlebutt in the organization about Hazelwood and "his first mate, Jack Daniels." Witnesses reported seeing Hazelwood drinking in a Valdez bar shortly before the Exxon Valdez left port. Finally, there had been lax enforcement of government regulations regarding shipping in Port Valdez. Budget cuts had reduced the size and technical resources of the Coast Guard station.[60]

No one was adequately prepared to handle a spill of 240,000 barrels of oil. When Congress approved the Trans-Alaska Pipeline, which runs from the North Slope oil fields to Valdez, it required that Alyeska, the consortium of oil companies that was to build and manage the pipeline, create a contingency plan to respond to spills. The plan was to be highly specific, setting out a timetable for the response, what equipment would be on-hand and used, which contractors would be employed. Alyeska claimed that it could handle major spills, but it failed to live up to the plan. As the oil companies began to cut costs, preparation for spills was scaled down. After the spill, the Commissioner of the Alaska Department of Environmental Conservation called Alyeska's contingency plan "the greatest work of maritime fiction since Moby Dick," but he had approved it.[61] The Department did not have adequate staff or funds for monitoring the contingency plan and Alyeska's preparedness.

Exxon was left with lead responsibility for cleanup operations, under the overall supervision of the Coast Guard. Luckily, the weather was calm for three days after the spill; most of the spilled oil floated on the surface of the Sound in the vicinity of the ship. Exxon wanted to collect some of the oil using skimmers, burn some of it under controlled conditions, and use chemical dispersants to break up the rest of the slick. The skimming operations were hampered by a lack of proper equipment. The burning and dispersant plans were slowed both by a lack of equipment and delays in receiving approval from federal and state administrative authorities, some of whom feared that these measures would exacerbate the adverse effects of the spill. One commenter concluded that the "[r]esponse to the spill was becoming paralyzed by indecision, a struggle over authority, and vastly different and conflicting expectations as to which measures would work."[62]

By the third day after the spill, only 3,000 barrels of oil had been recovered by Exxon. The company finally received permission for dispersant use and controlled burning. However, there was not enough dispersant on hand to break up the oil slick. That night the weather changed and a large storm hit Prince William Sound. The high waves spread the slick, broke it apart, and churned oil and water together. Burning and dispersants were no longer effective. The storm drove the oil onto the islands and beaches within the Sound and out into the Gulf

---

60. See J. Keeble, Out of the Channel: The Exxon Valdez Oil Spill in Prince William Sound (1991).

61. A. Davidson, In the Wake of the Valdez: The Devastating Impact of the Alaska Oil Spill 79-80 (Sierra Club 1990).

62. A. Davidson, supra, note 61, at 45.

of Alaska, carrying it as far as Kodiak Island some 300 miles away. The oil coated and killed hundreds of thousands of fish, tens of thousands of birds and thousands of otters and other marine mammals. For example, the local bald eagle population was badly hit by the spill. The oil covering their feathers prevented them from flying properly, causing many to crash into trees or rocks. Others either starved because they could not hunt, or ate oily carrion. The oil matted sea otters' fur, destroying their ability to stay warm. It also burned their eyes and lungs, and damaged their buoyancy regulation that allowed them to both float and dive in the water. The plight of these animals was dramatized daily by the television networks.[63]

Exxon and federal and state officials now faced the task of deciding what to do about the oil-coated rocky beaches and islands. Exxon initially hired hundreds of people to remove oil from the rocks with rags. Eventually a massive cleaning operation began. Exxon hired hundreds of boats and crews. The boats were equipped with large boilers to heat water, which was sprayed on the rocks; the runoff of oil into the water was collected by skimming. This process succeeded in removing large amounts of oil, although considerable amounts of oil remained lodged in the soil beneath the rocks. On the other hand, the heated water killed almost every organism it hit, stripping the beaches and islands of plant and animal life. Some scientific studies conducted later concluded that it would have been better for the environment not to use heated water and instead rely on waves to eventually clean the beaches. The cleanup continued during the summers of 1989 and 1990; it was suspended during the rest of the year, when severe storms precluded clean up operations. Exxon eventually spent over $2 billion to collect and remove the spilled oil. The removal effort created an economic bonanza for local boat owners and workers; one local newspaper suggested that Captain Hazelwood be elected Governor in recognition of what he had done to boost the Alaska economy.

Almost immediately after the spill, the lawsuits started. The first were filed on March 28, five days after the accident. Several class actions for damages were filed, both in state and federal court. The plaintiffs were divided into five classes: commercial fishermen; seafood processors and distributors; area businesses; persons claiming that their use and enjoyment of the environment had been injured; and Native Alas-

---

63. Exxon hired people to catch birds and mammals and clean them, but logistical problems remained. There were few available facilities to wash and keep the animals. Once they were cleaned, no one knew what to do with them. If they were kept in captivity, there was a large risk that infectious disease could kill them all. However, if they were released they would probably return to the beach where they were first oiled. Eventually, it was decided to release the survivors. Private volunteer efforts to save otters were banned by the U.S. Fish and Wildlife Service.

kans. Some towns and villages also filed suit. Many damage claims stemmed from the State of Alaska's decision to ban the sale of salmon and other fish caught in the areas affected by the spill. While many fish caught were apparently uncontaminated, the State feared that consumers, influenced by television, would believe that the fish were tainted, doing permanent damage to the reputation of Alaskan salmon and other fish. As new complaints were filed, and others amended, the list of defendants expanded to include Exxon, Exxon Shipping, Captain Hazelwood, the pipeline liability fund established pursuant to the Trans-Alaska Pipeline Act, and Alyeska and the six oil companies who owned it.[64]

Exxon quickly opened claims offices. Payments were made to fishers and others who could establish economic loss as a result of the spill. Exxon made the payments without demanding a release from liability in exchange. Its apparent strategy was to pay a large enough portion of a claimant's loss to make litigation for the remainder an uneconomic proposition for plaintiffs' attorneys. Exxon also paid millions of dollars directly to towns and villages to help their cleanup operations.

By August, approximately 150 suits, including both class and individual actions, had been filed in state and federal court. Alaska Superior Court Judge Shortell and Chief United States District Judge Holland consolidated their cases for pretrial hearings and discovery. However, they made separate legal rulings. In October 1990, Judge Shortell ruled that Exxon and Exxon Shipping were strictly liable for all damages proximately caused by the oil spill. In December 1990 Judge Holland ordered all of the claimants in the federal court actions to seek initial relief from the pipeline liability fund, and refused to certify any class actions.[65]

In August 1989, The National Wildlife Federation, the Wildlife Federation of Alaska, and the Natural Resources Defense Council filed suit in state court against Exxon and other oil company defendants claiming impairment of their rights to use and enjoy the environment and pass it on undamaged to future generations. The Sierra Club and

---

64. The federal court claims were based on theories of strict liability and negligence under the Trans-Alaska Pipeline Authorization Act, unseaworthiness, maritime negligence, and violations of the Alaska National Interest Lands Conservation Act. The state cases were based on the Alaska Environmental Conservation Act, strict liability for abnormally dangerous activity, negligence, negligent misrepresentation, fraud, public nuisance, private nuisance, and common law trespass.

65. In October 1991, Exxon brought suit against Sperry Marine, claiming that the navigation system of the Exxon Valdez, which Sperry had manufactured, had malfunctioned, causing the grounding of the tanker. The parties settled out of court on undisclosed terms in October 1992.

other environmental groups also filed a complaint in the federal court based on the citizen suit provisions of the Clean Water Act and the Resource Conservation and Recovery Act. The plaintiffs sought the imposition of civil penalties and an order for a complete cleanup of the Prince William Sound area.[66]

Several hours after the spill, a blood sample was taken from Captain Hazelwood; it had an alcohol content of 0.06 percent. Medical experts estimated that if he had not drunk alcohol after but only before the grounding (a fact never established) his level would have been about 0.2 percent at the time of grounding. The legal limit for ship masters is .04 percent. The State of Alaska indicted him on a felony charge of criminal mischief and misdemeanor charges of reckless endangerment, negligent discharge of oil and operating a vessel while intoxicated. At the trial, Hazelwood claimed that he had drunk only after the accident, asserted irregularities in the handling of the crew's blood samples, and invoked a provision of the Clean Water Act which (prior to its amendment by the 1990 Oil Pollution Act) granted use immunity from anyone who reported an oil spill to the authorities. The jury convicted Hazelwood of negligent discharge of oil, but acquitted him of the other counts. He was sentenced to perform 1,000 hours of spill clean up work and pay a fine. The Alaska Court of Appeals later reversed the conviction, upholding the immunity defense. The state's appeal from this ruling is pending before the Alaska Supreme Court.[67]

In August 1989, Alaska filed civil claims in state court against Exxon, Alyeska, and the consortium's owners, seeking damages for injury to natural resources pursuant to the provisions of the Clean Water Act (later superseded by the OPA) and an injunction to continue the cleanup of Prince William Sound. The United States had decided to press criminal charges against Exxon before seeking civil relief. The United States and Alaska encountered difficult problems in coordinating their legal strategies and claims, particularly their claims for natural resource damages. Both governments had strong claims to jurisdiction over the resources affected by the spill; the Clean Water Act provided no guidance as to how to resolve these potentially competing claims, which gave Exxon the opportunity to play one government off against the other. For example, if one government settled with Exxon and the other government then sought natural resource damages, Exxon might defend on the ground that it had already discharged its obligations. Litigation between the United States and Alaska as to which govern-

---

66. See Tolbert, The Public as Plaintiff: Public Nuisance and Federal Citizen Suits in the Exxon Valdez Litigation, 14 Harv. Envtl. L. Rev. 511 (1990).

67. A Coast Guard Administrative Law Judge also suspended his license for nine months as part of a bargain in which the Coast Guard dropped its intoxication charge and Hazelwood admitted to two lesser charges.

ment had jurisdiction over the salmon or the sea otters would only redound to Exxon's benefit.

Coordination problems also existed within as well as between the governments. In the case of the United States, for example, Interior, Agriculture, and NOAA all claimed trustee responsibility over the injured resources. President Bush had charged EPA Administrator Reilly with responsibility for supervising restoration of the Sound, although EPA had no statutory authority in the matter. The Coast Guard, located in the Transportation Department, supervised the efforts to remove the spilled oil, but also faced potentially large damage liabilities as a result of the conduct of its employees at Valdez Traffic Control. Similar competition and conflict existed among branches of the Alaska government. The two governments were, however, able to devise a joint plan for studying the effects of the spill and spent about $60 million on such studies in the two years after the spill.

A federal grand jury issued a ten-count indictment against Exxon and Exxon Shipping in February 1990. The companies were charged with felony violations of the Ports and Waterways Safety Act and the Dangerous Cargoes Act, and misdemeanor violations of the Clean Water Act (negligent discharge of oil without a permit), the Refuse Act (release of oil without a permit, a strict liability offense), and the Migratory Bird Treaty Act (killing migratory birds, also a strict liability offense). The federal government asserted a novel agency theory to hold Exxon criminally liable for the acts of its wholly owned subsidiary, Exxon Shipping. See Raucher, Raising the Stakes for Environmental Polluters: The Exxon Valdez Criminal Prosecution, 19 Ecology L.Q. 147 (1992). Judge Holland denied Exxon's motion to dismiss the indictment against it. The ruling was important in setting the stage for an eventual settlement by allowing the government to reach Exxon's assets; Exxon Shipping's net assets amounted to several hundred millions of dollars. On the other hand, the maximum possible fines that could be imposed under the statutes forming the basis for the ten counts in the indictment would total only about $3 million.

The federal government, however, also relied on the "Alternative Fines" provision of 18 U.S.C. §3623(c)(1), which gives a sentencing judge discretion to impose a fine equal to twice the pecuniary loss or gain resulting from a violation. At the time of the indictment, Exxon had paid over $350 million to reimburse private claimants for losses and the state and federal governments for expenses incurred in responding to the spill. The United States argued that Judge Holland therefore had authority to impose a fine in excess of $700 million. Exxon argued that the Act was intended to deal only with financial crimes, not environmental violations. It also argued that imposing a fine based on its payments to others would be counterproductive because it would discourage future violators from making any voluntary payments that could later provide the basis for large criminal fines. Judge Holland took the issue under advisement.

In March 1990, Alaska, the United States, Exxon, and Exxon Shipping announced that they had agreed to a settlement of the federal criminal charges, and all civil claims of Alaska and the United States. The agreement called for Exxon to pay $100 million in criminal fines and $900 million in civil damages to reimburse the governments for cleanup and damage assessment activities and fund restoration activities. The civil recoveries were to be paid over ten years; after reimbursement of the governments' expenses, the recoveries would be paid into a restoration fund to be managed jointly by Alaska and the United States. There was a provision for a civil liability reopener that would require Exxon to pay an additional $100 million if future studies showed injury to the Sound of a sort that was not known or anticipated at the time of the settlement. Several groups of Native Alaskans immediately disputed the settlement on the ground that it made no provision for recovery by them of damages for injury to ability to use the affected resources for subsistence; they filed suit in federal district court in Washington to block it. Judge Sporkin issued a temporary stay in order to examine the agreement.

The settlement also required approval by Judge Holland in Anchorage, who retained jurisdiction over the federal criminal case. In April, he rejected the agreement, holding that the $100 million criminal fine was inadequate. Judge Holland was apparently incensed by a statement to the press by Exxon's Chairman, Lawrence Rawl, that Exxon had established reserves to pay for the settlement, and that it would have no material impact on Exxon's financial position. A few weeks later the civil settlement collapsed as well. The Alaska House of Representatives denied approval of the agreement; Exxon then exercised its right under the settlement agreement to terminate the deal.

In September 1990, the parties again reached an accord. The provisions governing the civil recoveries were unchanged. But the criminal fine was raised to $125 million; $100 million was remitted on the condition that it be paid as restitution to Alaska and the United States. Some claimed that the $125 million figure was too low, given the effects of the spill and Exxon's enormous income and assets. Yet, the fine was nearly twenty times larger than the biggest fine ever previously imposed for an environmental violation. Agreements were also reached with the Native Alaskans; the settlement contained an explicit provision that it in no way affected their rights to litigate their own claims for natural resource damages. Finally, Exxon Chairman Rawl appeared before Judge Holland and apologized for the spill. In early October 1990, Judge Holland approved the agreement. Alaska and the United States later settled their suits against Alyeska for failing to respond quickly enough to the spill for $32 million.

As of the fall of 1993, the damage claims filed by private parties and local governments and the lawsuits filed by environmental groups were still pending in federal and state court, awaiting trial.

NOTES AND QUESTIONS ON NATURAL RESOURCE DAMAGE ASSESSMENT

Suppose that you are an official with one of the federal trustee agencies, charged with responsibility for overseeing the assessment of the natural resource damages resulting from the Exxon Valdez spill. How would you deal with the following questions:

1. How would you go about determining the baseline ecological condition of Prince William Sound prior to spill? There are good data on some parameters, such as commercial fish catches, but data on others, including the population abundance of various species of birds and aquatic life and the condition of the bethnic areas at the bottom of the Sound are fragmentary or nonexistent.

Another complicating factor is the issue of causation. A recent study by a geochemist working for the U.S. Geological Survey has discovered that many of the oil residues on the shores of Prince William Sound emanated from an unnoticed 1964 spill. See Salpukas, A New Slant on Exxon Valdez Spill, N.Y. Times, Dec. 1, 1993, at C1.

2. How do you go about determining the extent of resource injury?

(a) Can you do so without good baseline data?

(b) Does the death of individual animals amount to injury to a natural resource? In a short time the spill killed tens of thousands of birds and hundreds of otters and other marine mammals as a result of oiling; the federal government collected and preserved (in refrigerated trucks) the carcasses of those that were washed ashore for use as evidence in criminal and civil litigation against Exxon. Consider that biological mechanisms tend to stabilize a population despite individual losses. When an appreciable number of individuals are lost, whether as a result of natural causes or human activities such as fishing or an oil spill, competition among those that remain for available resources, including habitat and food, is diminished. As a result, the remaining individuals mature faster, reproduce earlier, and have a better chance of survival, increasing the population to the point where limited resources constrain further growth. Is the relevant test injury to individuals or the local population of a species? Even if the loss of individuals counts as natural resource damage, is the damage mitigated by the fact that within a generation or two (a short period of time for many species) they will be replaced?

Consider also that at some point the proportion of a population killed may be so large that the population's ability to recover may be crippled, and it may even be driven to extinction. How does one determine when this point is reached for a given population in a given area, other than by waiting for a period of years to see what happens? Some populations of birds on small islands in and beyond the Sound were wiped out because the spill killed so many birds that they were unable successfully to reproduce and defend their young against predators. A few other populations were significantly depleted, but their long run status is still unclear.

(c) Even if post-spill populations are reduced, how does one determine whether the reduction is the result of the spill and permanent, or whether it is a reflection of natural fluctuations or other ecosystem changes? See Stevens, Balance of Nature: What Balance is That? N.Y. Times, Oct. 22, 1991, at p. C4. The year after the Exxon Valdez spill, pink salmon catches in the Sound were much reduced. But the following year's catches set a record high.[68]

(d) How does one term the potential longer-term effects of the oil that remains at the bottom of the Sound and in the soil below the rocky beaches on the Sound's ecosystem and the species that are part of it? Both the data and the science needed to answer such questions are patchy at best. On the one hand, the oil may have caused subclinical changes in organisms and ecosystems that will not become manifest for years. On the other hand, damaged ecosystems have significant ability to cleanse themselves and recover naturally. A number of studies of large oil spills in temperate areas have found no indications of significant damage ten years later, although a few studies have raised questions about possible continuing, long term effects on some parts of the local ecosystem. Can the results of these studies be extrapolated to Prince William Sound, which is a large body of water but one that is less open than the ocean, and located in a cold environment?

In two years, the federal and Alaska trustee agencies spent $60 million to study the impacts of the spill. Most of these expenditures represented the salaries of scientists and others already on their payrolls. These studies identified many uncertainties but produced few answers.

3. What restoration measures would you consider? Attempting to remove the oil that remains below the rocks of the beaches and on the bottom of the Sound would be extraordinarily costly and probably

---

68. Another problem, not presented in the Exxon Valdez case, is that of untangling responsibility when a resource may have been injured by more than one human activity. For example, portions of Seattle harbor have been contaminated by hazardous substances released from a number of different sites. Or how does one determine the damage caused by an oil spill in New York Harbor when the harbor is already polluted by other oil spills and discharges of other pollutants from facilities on the shore?

counterproductive from an environmental viewpoint. Fish stocking facilities can be established to stock young fish. Restocking is probably not feasible for most other species, including the bird populations that were wiped out on some of the small islands. Coastal habitat can be protected by acquiring buffer zones around the edge of the Sound to protect fish spawning streams and the habitat of terrestrial mammals such as bears, although such mammals do not appear to have been much affected by the spill. The Alaskan native corporations own much of the timber on the mountains that adjoin the Sound. In order to obtain needed revenues, the corporations propose to clearcut and sell the timber. Many have proposed that the damages recovered from Exxon be used to buy up the corporations' timber rights. Environmental groups have proposed the creation of a foundation to finance ongoing research on the effects of the spill and the Sound's ecosystem. Does the law allow damage recoveries to be used for such purposes?[69]

(4) How would you go about assessing the damages resulting from the spill?

(a) How would you go about assessing the costs of restoring, replacing, or acquiring the equivalent of the injured resources? For reasons noted above, there are tremendous uncertainties in determining the extent of ecological damage caused by the spill; some of those uncertainties will not be resolved for years, and many will never be resolved. Nature's natural restorative capacities must be taken into account, but their extent is highly uncertain. The activities that humans can feasibly undertake to restore the Sound and its inhabitants to their pre-spill condition are limited.

(b) How would you go about determining the impairment of the use value of the natural resources affected by the spill?

The primary market measure of value is the commercial fish catch. As noted, fish populations have fluctuated; there is no clear evidence of marked overall decline in the abundance of commercially important fish in the area, although uncertainties remain. The value of the catch is a function of a variety of commercial factors, including the price of competitive substitutes as well as local abundance. When the pink salmon run two years after the spill reached record highs, the price per pound of salmon plummeted to record lows.

How would you go about estimating those use values affected by the spill that are not directly reflected in market prices? Ironically, because of the publicity generated by the spill, more tourists and other visitors visited the Sound in the year following the spill than ever before in history.

---

69. Do these difficulties help explain why federal agencies have to date spent so little of the recoveries from Exxon on restoration, and spent most of it to reimburse themselves?

(c) How would you go about assessing the non-use values affected by the spill? Such assessment would require that a CVM survey be designed and conducted. How would the spill and its consequences be described? How would the survey questions deal with the tremendous uncertainty regarding the effects of the spill? How would it deal with the fact that most people only became aware of the existence of Prince William Sound because of the tremendous television publicity created by the spill? What is the relevant population?

Because the function of natural resource damages is compensation, not retribution, the damage valuation should not be based on the moral outrage that many expressed against Exxon. In theory, the non-use value placed on preservation or restoration of a resource should be exactly the same, regardless of whether the resource injury was caused by Exxon's spill or a natural release of oil from the bed of the Sound. But the injury to the Sound is inextricably linked in most people's mind with outrage against Exxon. How should a CVM survey deal with this problem? Should it describe a hypothetical Sound that is not Prince William Sound but quite similar, and describe a hypothetical mechanism of injury that is not an oil spill? How realistic is such a hypothetical? Will respondents nonetheless identify the hypothetical with Prince William Sound and with Exxon?

How should the survey design deal with the other difficulties with CVM surveys of non-use values, discussed above? Where will the monies to fund the survey be found?[70]

5. One of the Alaskan native villages has asked for your assistance in preparing their claims for damages, which are based largely on the impairment of their subsistence economy caused by oil contamination of the shellfish that are a principal part of the natives' diet. The traditional subsistence economy was also undermined by the infusion of cash by Exxon, who hired many native villages and their boats to help clean up the spilled oil. This cash infusion led many to switch from hunting and gathering to purchases of canned or prepared foods as well as such items as motorcycles and boomboxes, to the detriment of traditional village culture and ways. How should the village's damage claims be formulated?

In light of the above questions, do you believe that the settlement negotiated by the government in the Exxon Valdez case was adequate? Should the government set its negotiating priorities on obtaining higher criminal fines, and lower natural resource damage recoveries?

---

70. A pilot CVM study conducted by the federal government asked for respondents' willingness to pay to prevent a spill like the one that occurred in Prince William Sound. When the answers were multiplied by the entire population of the United States, the aggregate willingness to pay was a minimum of $2.5 billion. How much reliance could you place on such a study in litigation? Would it be admitted into evidence by the judge? What weight would a jury give it?

Does the enormous size of Exxon's earnings and assets make the settlement inadequate?

CONCLUDING QUESTIONS ON NATURAL RESOURCE DAMAGES

1. Environmental groups are lobbying to add natural resource damage liability provisions to the Clean Water Act and other federal environmental regulatory statutes. They also favor amendments to the citizen suit provisions of these statutes to allow private plaintiffs to sue for damages to public natural resources resulting from regulatory violations. The damages would be used for restoration of the damaged resources. Are these desirable innovations?

2. Is the enthusiasm of environmental groups for natural resource damages consistent with their rejection of cost-benefit analysis in the regulatory and resource management contexts? Is valuing public natural resources on the basis of CVM surveys of individuals' willingness appropriate? Environmentalists generally assert that environmental protection is not a matter of economics or private welfare, but rather reflects public values that should be determined through open dialogue and deliberation. By embracing natural resource damages, are environmental groups in danger of selling their birthrights for a mess of pottage?

3. How would you evaluate the following two alternatives to the current system of natural resource damages:

(a) Ships transporting petroleum and petroleum products and generators of hazardous wastes would pay a fee based on the amount of petroleum carried and the amount and toxicity of the waste created. The payments would go into a fund that would be used by the government to restore, replace, or acquire the equivalent of injured natural resources.

(b) Persons spilling oil or releasing hazardous substances would automatically pay a civil penalty based on the amount spilled or released and its toxicity. The amount of the penalty would be calculated in accordance with a schedule adopted by legislation or administrative regulation. The schedule might vary the amount of the penalty based on the character of the environment where the spill or release occurred. For example, the schedule might divide environments into five categories, ranging from the pristine (such as Prince William Sound) to the polluted (such as New York Harbor). The more pristine the environment, the greater the amount of the penalty. Civil penalties paid under the scheme would go into a fund that would be used by the government to restore, replace, or acquire the equivalent of injured natural resources.

Table of Cases

Index

1223